KONRAD ADENAUER

KONRAD ADENAUER

*A German Politician and Statesman
in a Period of War, Revolution and Reconstruction*

Volume I
From the German Empire to the Federal Republic, 1876–1952

Hans-Peter Schwarz

Berghahn Books
Providence • Oxford

Published by
Berghahn Books

Editorial offices:
165, Taber Avenue, Providence, RI 02906, USA
Bush House, Merewood Avenue, Oxford, OX3 8EF, UK

© German edition 1986 Deutsche Verlags-Anstalt.
Originally published as Adenauer: Der Aufstieg: 1876–1952
© English-language edition 1995
Berghahn Books Ltd.
Translated from the German by Louise Willmot

Library of Congress Cataloging-in-Publication Data
Schwarz, Hans-Peter, 1934-
    Konrad Adenauer : a German politician and statesman in a period of
war, revolution, and reconstruction / by Hans-Peter Schwarz ;
[translated from the German by Loulse Willmot].
        p. cm.
    Includes bibliographical references and index.
    Contents: v. 1. From the German Empire to the Federal Republic, 1876-
1952.
    ISBN 1-57181-870-7 (v. 1 : alk. paper)
    1. Adenauer, Konrad, 1876-1967. 2. Heads of state--Germany
(West)--Biography. 3. Germany--Politics and government--1871-1933.
4. Germany--Politics and government--1933-1945. 5. Germany (West)--
Politics and government. 6. Mayors--Germany--Cologne--Biography.
    I. Title.
DD259.7.A3S3313 1995
943.08'092--dc20   95-37776
[B]   CIP

British Library Cataloguing in Publication Data
A catalogue record for this book is available
from the British Library.

Printed in the USA on acid-free paper.

CONTENTS

APPENDIX

For my wife Annemie

17 August 1986

Konrad Adenauer's grandparents
August and Maria Scharfenberg

PROLOGUE: COLOGNE

I ascended the tower, and beneath a dull grey sky, somewhat in harmony with my thoughts, contemplated this marvellous city.

Cologne on the Rhine is built like Rouen on the Seine and Antwerp on the Scheldt, that is, like all cities seated on broad and rapid rivers, in the form of a strung bow, of which the river is the cord.

The roofs are slated, and crowded together, and packed like cards doubled together: the streets are narrow, the gables carved and ornamented. A red boundary of city walls, rising on all sides above the roofs, hems in the town, buckling it as in a belt to the river. From the tower of Türmchen, to the superb Bayenturm, among the battlements of which stands the marble statue of a bishop bestowing his benediction on the Rhine – from Türmchen to Bayenturm, the city exhibits, to the length of a league, a façade of fronts and windows. Midway, a long bridge of boats, gracefully curving with the current, crosses the river, connecting that multifarious mass of gloomy architecture, Cologne, with Deutz, which consists of a small cluster of white houses.

From the centre of Cologne, and round the peaked roofs, turrets, and flower-decked attics, arise the varying steeples of twenty-seven churches. Apart from the Cathedral, four of these are majestic Roman edifices, each of a different design, and worthy of the title of cathedral. To the north is St Martin; to the west, St Gereon; the church of the Holy Apostles to the south; and St Marie-in-Capitol to the east – forming a forest of towers, steeples, and domes.

Considered in detail, this city is all life and animation, the bridge being crowded with passengers and carriages, the river with sails, and the banks with masts. The streets swarm – the windows chatter – the roofs sing in the sunshine. Here and there groves of trees refresh the gloomy-looking houses; while the old edifices of the fifteenth century, with their long friezes of fruits and flowers, afford a refuge to the pigeons and doves who sit cooing there to their hearts' content.

Around this vast community – rich from industry, military from necessity, maritime from site – an extensive and fertile plain extends in all directions, depressed towards Holland, most part of which is watered by the Rhine. Towards the north-east it is bounded by that nest of romantic legends called the Seven Mountains.

This was Victor Hugo's description of Cologne – 'a city of trade and of dreams' – in 1840.[1] The city had changed little when Konrad Adenauer was born on 5 January 1876, a third of a century later. The picturesque drawbridge, which was raised for an hour each morning and evening to let sailing boats and steamers pass through, and had to be removed completely during floods and ice-drifts, was still there. Next to the cathedral a squat lattice-bridge now connected the two banks of the Rhine. This bridge was open to pedestrians, and for many years the people of Cologne paid a toll of two pfennigs for their Sunday stroll from the main station through the fortified neo-Gothic portals to Deutz on the right bank of the Rhine. The lattice-bridge was the first fixed bridge in Cologne. More importantly, it was a vital part of the Cologne-Minden railway which connected the city with the Ruhr and the heartland of the Prussian provinces as far as Berlin. Its squat steel construction reflected the technological age which was being welcomed with such enthusiasm in the city. Karl Marx, then editor-in-chief of the *Rheinische Zeitung* – though many people did not care to remember this after the 1848 Revolution – once called the railway the true revolutionary force of the nineteenth century. It is a claim which is particularly true of the city in which Adenauer grew up. The transformation of Cologne into a great railway junction was largely the work of Gustav Mevissen, a man who can justly be compared with the American railroad barons and who, during the course of the 1860s, turned Cologne into the great turn-table of western German railway traffic and the junction of the region's two biggest railway companies. In peacetime these railways carried coal, ore and industrial products; in wartime, troops, munitions and forage.

Cologne was the biggest trading centre in western Germany and was to remain so for decades to come. The city had links with Brussels, Antwerp and London on one side, and with the industrial heartland of Westphalia as far as Berlin on the other. Much of its economy continued to be based on the activity of its merchants and small craftsmen, who generally prospered despite occasional bad times and helped their city to flourish. Nevertheless, it was railway construction which was pushing Cologne into the industrial age.

Looking out from city hall over Cologne and the outlying districts in 1876, the year of Adenauer's birth, an observer would have seen huge new factories and forests of chimneys belching out clouds of unfiltered smoke. Within the city itself, sugar refineries, including world-famous companies such as Gebrüder Stollwerk, had become established. The Stollwerk factory in Annostraße, a five-storied Gothic 'castle' with a chimney in the courtyard, was more like a fairy-tale building than a creation of the industrial age. However, the biggest plants were sited outside the city walls – up the Rhine in Bayenthal and in Zollstock or further down the river in Nippes and Ehrenfeld: cotton and hemp spinning mills and factories making rubber goods; timber plants; the famous Rhenish glassworks; a growing number of metal-processing plants. Subsequently, from the early

1880s, the company Helios AG launched a short-lived technology of the future venture in Ehrenfeld, where the company established itself as western Germany's leading manufacturer of lighting equipment, steam-lighting machines, alternating-current machinery and transformers. The biggest concentration of industrial plants could be found on the opposite bank of the Rhine, in Deutz and Mülheim, Kalk and Vingst. This region would become the industrial heartland of Cologne, built up by entrepreneurs, craftsmen and skilled workers with roots in the Bergisches Land. In Kalk, the Humboldt machine construction company was employing over 1,400 workers on its rolling mill trains and steam hammers in 1876. In Deut, the gas engine company of the same name was thriving; its founder Nicholaus August Otto had invented the four-cylinder engine in Cologne before the company was taken over by Gottlieb Daimler in 1872. Five years later production began on 'Otto's new engines', which could generate up to one hundred horsepower. Both the Deutz and Humboldt companies were eventually bought by Peter Klöckner to form KHD and create one of the most powerful companies in Cologne. A former director of this company, Günter Henle, was later to be a highly influential figure in the industrial wing of Adenauer's CDU after the Second World War.

During Adenauer's youth, the Carlswerk of Felten & Guilleaume, a manufacturer of rope products based in Mülheim, was the leading company in the region. The company had been founded in 1824 by Johann Theodor Felten and his son-in-law Franz Karl Guilleaume before being transformed by the founder's grandson, Franz Karl Guilleaume, into an international concern specialising in the manufacture of telegraph and wire cables. In wartime the company also manufactured barbed-wire as a by-product.

Factory buildings, offices, railway lines, warehouses and workers' housing began to appear all round Cologne. Despite occasional downturns in the business cycle, industrial growth was occurring at an explosive pace. It was obvious that the future prosperity of the city lay in the hands of the engineers and managers in its factories. Nevertheless, Cologne continued to be a 'city of dreams' with a glorious and sometimes troubled past. This mood was typified by the desire of Friedrich Wilhelm IV of Prussia for a suspension bridge to be built towards the cathedral chancel, thus allowing railway travellers to see a glorious view of a symbol of Gothic art and 'the spirit of the Middle Ages'. At the foot of the bridge an equestrian statue of Friedrich Wilhelm would remind future travellers of the links between the city and Cologne's greatest friend among the Prussian kings. In the area round the cathedral, however, the Romantics were defeated by an alliance of hard-nosed bankers, insurance salesmen, and industrial and commercial strategists and forced to accept the construction of the main railway station in wedding-cake-style on the site of the beautiful botanical gardens.

The industry and trade of Cologne depended on the activity of numerous large, medium-sized and small businesses – there were 2,000 metal-processing firms alone before the First World War. Nevertheless, the modernisation of the city was based on a number of recognisable centres where important decisions were made and the fate of many businesses was sealed. These centres could be found in the city's financial district. It was here that the Schaafhausen Bank was established before being taken over by Gustav Mevissen in 1848 to play a leading part in managing the industrial growth of the Rhineland. Baron Eduard von Oppenheim, a member of the great financial dynasty, also had his headquarters in the city here. Nearby were the banking houses of Deichmann, J.H. Stein, A. Levy and I.D. Herstatt, some of which had been involved in wholesaling, transport and the wine trade before concentrating on the financing – and sometimes the management – of industry in the Rhineland and Westphalia. In the later nineteenth century these institutions were involved in many areas where the investment of risk capital offered the prospect of high returns: in the railways, mechanical engineering and mining, as well as in the expanding chemical industry in Kalk, Raderberg and further down the Rhine in Leverkusen.

Cologne's bankers quickly extended their activities beyond the Rhineland and Westphalia to establish links with the country's financial centre in Berlin, though their own existence was sometimes threatened by the great Berlin joint-stock companies. Some of these Cologne banks and their directors were to play an important role in the life of Konrad Adenauer. Here it will suffice to name three of them. Louis Hagen, who supported Adenauer during his rise to power and came to be regarded by many as a virtual second mayor of the city during the 1920s, was a grandson of Abraham Loeb (later Levy). For ten years before the First World War, Robert Pferdmenges worked for the Disconto-Gesellschaft in London and Antwerp before becoming director of the Schaaffhausen Bank in Cologne in 1919. Baron Kurt von Schröder, who was to play a dubious historical role in January 1933 by establishing contact between Hitler and von Papen, was another close acquaintance of Adenauer, a partner in the J.H.Stein banking house with close links to London banks including the Bank of England.

The industrialists and bankers had propelled Cologne into the modern age in the quarter of a century before Adenauer was born. Nevertheless, they were working in a city which still had a mediaeval city wall in 1876 and had no control over the outlying regions where the vital industries of the future had been established. The massive city wall, the biggest medieval fortification in Germany, stretched for 4,400 metres in a vast semi-circle around the city. Once the source of pride, the wall was increasingly seen as a burden. As every schoolchild knew, the construction of the wall and its vast gates had been approved in 1180 by the Emperor Frederick Barbarossa himself, and it had never been scaled by an enemy force. There was great civic pride in the story of the inhabitants' battle against the followers of a deposed archbishop at Ulre Gate in 1268, thus securing the freedom of the city until 1794, when French revolutionary troops had entered the city without a fight. It was this incident to which Adenauer was referring when, in the 1960s, he informed sceptical American television journalists that Germany had a democratic tradition which was centuries old. The modest house in which Adenauer was born stood barely a hundred metres from the wall, in Balduinstrasse, and close to the Hahnentor, the gate through which the Holy Roman Emperors had passed on their way to coronation in Aachen.

Several times during its history the city had suffered brutal attacks – by Huns, Franks and Normans (and on 31 May 1942 it was to be devastated by British bombs in the 'thousand bomber raid'). Yet the city had not been destroyed during the seven-hundred years in which it had been protected by the wall. The fortifications – eventually reinforced by earthworks and advance forts – evoked memories of Cologne's history as a Free Imperial City at a time when the Hohenzollern kings had been no more than local noblemen or margraves in Nuremberg and Brandenburg.

After the Rhineland fell into Prussian hands in 1815, the military authorities protected the old stone wall despite the fact that advances in modern artillery required the construction of earthworks and forts along its length. Every plan to re-direct city roads or widen the gates had to be examined and approved by the military commandant to ensure that the security of fortress Cologne was unimpaired. Even in 1910 the military authorities objected to the city's plans to build a tramway to a suburb on the right bank of the Rhine, on the grounds that it would enable enemies to advance and besiege the city more easily. However, on this occasion the building plan was finally accepted when the city fathers reluctantly agreed to pay one million gold marks for additional defensive measures.

Since 1864 the business community and the citizens of Cologne had begun to call for radical measures and, like the inhabitants of other central European cities – Vienna, Basle, Mainz, Koblenz – to demand the removal of the troublesome city wall. The inner city was appallingly overcrowded. Although sanitary conditions had improved since the 1820s and 1830s, when the rubbish occasionally stood metres high along the passageways, the wall continued to prevent the circulation of fresh air along the stuffy and dusty streets. Most important of all, the wall prevented the necessary extension of transport routes; all traffic had to pass through gates which were only 3.5 metres wide and had been built with twists and curves for added security. Without removing the wall it was impossible to construct roads to the growing industrial suburbs and residential areas outside the wall. Wide streets were also essential to ease the congested traffic from north to south, as well as the passage from the west of the city to the Rhine port and the bridge.

Decisions which appear inevitable with hindsight could have been long delayed had it not been for speculation by private capital in the building industry. Investors were vociferous in their demands for the partial or total removal of the wall and the expansion of the city borders. In 1869 the Elzbacher finance house offered to pay the treasury 4.3 million thalers (old German coinage) for the entire fortified grounds; during the 1870s the Prussian government negotiated with several Belgian companies which saw the potential for substantial profits on the property. However, the fact that Cologne had to remain a fortified city made a satisfactory solution difficult to achieve. In the end the military authorities agreed only to move the forts outward by some 500-600 metres. They also insisted that the railway lines, which would be needed to supply the forts with munitions and other supplies in the event of siege, must remain within the fortified band.

The way was thus prepared for the follies which did so much to define the appearance of the modern city. The city itself eventually purchased the fortified area – some 120.85 hectares – from the state of Prussia for 11,749,000 marks, in the hope of selling parts of it at a profit. However, their actions led to the replacement of the picturesque stone belt from the Middle Ages by a modern wall, noisy and bleak, around the new part of the city: the embankments of the railway bypass with their goods stations and sidings. Very few voices were raised in protest at a time of general enthusiasm for expansion, even though they included the conservative Centre Party politician August Reichensperger. Then the debate focused largely on a successful bid to force the Prussian government to retain a number of beautiful old gate-houses.

The demolition of the old wall finally began on 11 June 1881. The event turned into something of a festival with all groups having something to celebrate: the business community, which had finally achieved its objective; the building firms, which expected a major boom in contracts; and the building workers themselves, who anticipated secure employment for years to come. The mayor responsible for inaugurating the project was Hermann Becker, known as 'red Becker' after his five-year gaol sentence following the trials of Communists in the city in 1852. Becker, who had long since made his peace with bourgeois society, made a speech which reflected the new approach: 'Six hundred years ago our ancestors built a wall around the city which helped it to become what it was … What they built to make Cologne great, we must tear down to prevent Cologne becoming small.'

Several decades later it was generally thought to have been an appalling mistake for the city to adopt such a radical and destructive approach to the solution of its traffic problems, particularly as the continued existence of the fortifications brought no permanent relief. Yet it is reasonable to ask how else Cologne could have entered the industrial age. This, at any rate, was the view of the majority of its inhabitants and of Konrad Adenauer himself. His later decisions were to demonstrate an acute understanding of the importance of modernisation, although he was eager to combine support for industrialisation and transport with cautious conservation of monuments. The Cologne of Adenauer's youth resembled a gigantic building site, with the widening of roads in the old city and the laying of sewage pipes to serve the expanding population. Cologne's 'new town' was created in the region between the belt of fortifications and the old city, and splendid ring-roads were constructed on the site of the razed city wall.

Much of the new face of the city was shaped by Joseph Stübben. Appointed to Cologne after a period as architect in Aachen, Stübben was given a task unique in Germany – to plan an entire district according to the latest principles of urban architecture. Today he would be regarded as a fanatical technocrat, an architect in the style of Haussmann, the moderniser of old Paris under Napoleon III. Yet despite subsequent criticism of Stübben's relentless modernism, his work in Cologne during the 1880s and 1890s demonstrates a profound creative energy.

The guiding principles of the project appeared simultaneously revolutionary and reasonable. Of paramount importance was the need to deal efficiently with the flow of traffic. Since there were no plans for a wide north-south passage through Cologne in the near future, the city ring road would serve as the main traffic artery, making both the old and new towns accessible to horseback riders, coaches and – eventually – cars. In contrast to the narrow streets of the old city which deprived its inhabitants of fresh air, the elegant new apartments on the ring roads would have the full benefit of light and air. The wide streets, ranging in width from 32 to 114 metres, allowed for the construction of dual carriageways and the planting of two or three rows of trees along the centre.

Nevertheless, transport had not yet become an end in itself. The city ring, adorned by magnificent apartment houses, consisted of ten separate sections of roads of various widths, each containing squares with planted areas and monuments. The whole project took two decades to complete. During the last phase of construction, towards the end of the century, churches and a synagogue, the opera house and the Hohenstaufen baths were added. The affluent bourgeoisie of Cologne now had a magnificent boulevard along which, in the evening, a parade of coaches could carry them to the opera house in Rudolf Square. These privileged sections of society were encouraged to believe that their city had achieved the sophistication of the great metropolitan centres of Europe – Paris, Vienna, Berlin and Brussels. The remaining medieval gatehouses were little more than scenic backdrops to the impressive new buildings and architectural modernism of the city.

The expansion of the city was combined with a carefully planned policy of incorporating outlying towns. In common with the administrators of other large cities in the German Reich, the city fathers recognised the need to establish control over the industrial plants, workers' housing and transport routes on the outskirts of Cologne. The city would profit from the trade tax levied on such companies, while the firms themselves wanted improved transport routes to the inner city. Over-populated Cologne would benefit from more living space, but also needed land for new industrial plants, public utilities and – it was quickly realised – public parks, recreation areas and sports facilities.

The city's expansion into the outlying region, later taken to a climax and temporary conclusion by Adenauer, was thus inevitable. The suburbs on the left bank of the Rhine were incorporated in the 1880s; in the first decade of the twentieth century Cologne took control of the industrial areas along the right bank; and on the eve of the First World War Mülheim and Merheim were incorporated. Cologne had thereby swallowed up all the regions in its immediate orbit.

The population increased from 129,000 in 1871 to 635,000 in 1914. Though its income and economic prospects had multiplied, the city also faced growing problems. There was a need for co-ordinated planning of industrial development and building; large amounts of money had to be found for the infrastructure of the city; public transport systems and recreational facilities had to be constructed. Alongside these administrative and financial burdens were political problems arising from the inevitable clash of interests between the different districts of the city and the various classes who lived within them. Cologne was spared major political crises before 1914. This relative calm enabled the city to evolve within fifty to sixty years from an interesting, but stagnant and narrow community into the second largest industrial centre in Prussia. This process possessed its own internal logic, producing efficiency and positive results while also encouraging a faith in progress – irrespective of social background – among the city's leaders and the population as a whole. Later, this faith was to be profoundly shaken by catastrophes of the twentieth century. During the years of Adenauer's childhood in Cologne, however, a spirit of optimism prevailed – a belief in progress, a fascination with technology, a faith in modernisation and the power of industrial development. Significantly, there was also an awareness that the process of transformation which had begun must be planned and controlled. As a young man Konrad Adenauer was influenced by this spirit, which may have encouraged his restless activity and experimentation in later life, both as mayor of Cologne and Chancellor of West Germany. One of the lessons he had learned during his youth in Imperial Germany was that the changes and problems of modernity could not be avoided, but must be faced and mastered in a dynamic spirit.

The Cologne of his youth was a large city moving into the industrial age. It was also – and had been since 1815 – a Prussian city. An equestrian statue of Friedrich Wilhelm III, designed by Alexander Callandrelli and Gustav Bläser in Berlin and costing 850,000 marks, stood in the centre of the busy haymarket to remind the inhabitants of the unification of the Rhineland with Prussia. Other statues, of Friedrich Wilhelm IV and Wilhelm I, also cast in bronze, were placed on the Rhine bridge. The last of these has survived all the calamities of the twentieth century to look down upon a modern city which the Emperor himself would scarcely have recognised. The city also boasted statues of Bismarck, the creator of German unity, and Moltke, the architect of military victory over France in 1870. The greatest monument to the Hohenzollern dynasty was Cologne cathedral, which was finally completed in 1880. The cathedral, a dream which became a stone monument, and at 156 metres was the tallest building in the world for a short time, symbolised the importance of Cologne to the dynasty and reflected the technical and architectural virtuosity of the nineteenth century. Yet it was also the product of a combination of political and religious forces. Before the resumption of construction in 1842 the cathedral had already captured the public imagination throughout Germany. Sulpiz Boisserée, with the cautious encouragement of Goethe and in accordance with the views of large numbers of pious Catholics, wanted the cathedral to recreate the universal spirit of medieval religiosity. For Joseph Görres and the German national movement, on the other hand, the resumption of construction was 'a symbol of the new Reich we wish to build'.[2] The proud and patriotic grand bourgeoisie, obsessed with the legacy of the Middle Ages, saw the construction of the cathedral as a monument not only to Germany, but also to themselves.

These mixed and sometimes contradictory impulses were channelled by the Prussian monarchy and its desire – especially in the person of Friedrich Wilhelm IV – to demonstrate its attachment to the Rhineland. The Hohenzollern faith in the unity and greatness of Germany, expressed with growing zeal after the 'war of unification' in 1870/71, was now to be proclaimed from the steps of the cathedral itself. The dynasty provided indispensable financial backing for the project and used the great festivals of construction in order to glorify their own role. The process reached its apogee during the celebrations held to commemorate the completion of the cathedral, on 15 and 16 October 1880, which were blatantly orchestrated by the monarchy for political effect. Surrounded by his family, senior military figures, numerous German rulers and the wealthy and obsequious bourgeoisie of Cologne, Wilhelm I used the opportunity to celebrate the unity and greatness of Germany and the birthday of his brother Friedrich Wilhelm IV. The spectacle was the most ambitious and effective display of German unity and strength since the Imperial proclamation at Versailles after the Franco-Prussian War. Until well into the twentieth century the cathedral was not simply the greatest religious monument in Cologne, but also the symbol of German self-assertion on the Rhine.

In the following years the German emperors continued to visit the city on numerous occasions, either with large entourages or smaller groups. The last official visit took place shortly before the First World War, when Adenauer was already First Councillor, and involved the arrival of Wilhelm II, the Empress Augusta Victoria and the Princess Victoria Louise for the ceremonial opening of the Hohenzollern bridge. The Imperial Age drew to a close amid great jubilation and with a spectacular firework display. During these decades the Prussian presence in Cologne was by no means purely symbolic. In order to travel to the city on foot or by carriage, it was necessary to cross a well-fortified belt. In the early 1880s twelve large forts with communication trenches, artillery posts and embrasures surrounded the city on the left bank of the Rhine; another four were positioned on the opposite side in Deutz. Strict regulations forbade any building or planting on a strip of land one-hundred metres wide in order that the defenders of the city would have a clear field of fire. When the new town became too crowded, the city administration conducted secret negotiations with the War Ministry in Berlin to push the fortifications as far out into the countryside as possible. These negotiations eventually bore fruit: in 1908 the city purchased a broad area inside the border of the fortified grounds. The new 'detached forts' were placed some five kilometres from the city centre, while some of the abandoned forts were converted into attractive parks. Yet Cologne remained a fortified city despite fears that it would be unable to withstand a sustained attack. Until the end of the First World War the districts on the left bank of the Rhine were surrounded by eight forts, fourteen intermediate defences and 119 military bases along a length of forty-two kilometres.

During Adenauer's school-days the city was host to seven infantry, artillery and cavalry regiments – a total of 12,000 troops in a total population of 150,000. Most of these soldiers were accommodated in the city centre, sometimes in converted cloisters. The barracks, often resembling prisons, were connected to bakeries, storage depots, mess halls and military prisons. During this period the military was part and parcel of the everyday life of the city, even becoming an important social factor; while lieutenants courted the 'respectable' young women of the city, the non-commissioned officers and men married their maids and workers in industry. There were no signs of animosity or anti-military sentiment among the population. The barracks were as much a part of life as the schools, the churches, the public houses, the craftsmen's shops and the factories. At the administrative level the city was part of the Rhine Province. However, the Oberpräsident and the military command were based in Koblenz rather than Cologne, while the provincial assembly met in Düsseldorf. The only official institutions to be found in Cologne were the Court of Appeal, the district tax office and the provincial midwifery institute. Locals suspected that the absence of administrative bodies reflected the antipathy of the Prussian government towards their Catholic city on the Rhine. A more likely explanation, however, was a simple shortage of suitable administrative buildings in 1815, when the Rhineland came into Prussian hands.

Cologne enjoyed a high degree of local autonomy. Thanks to the municipal statute of 1856 it had extensive powers to administer its own affairs. Eligible voters elected an assembly of city councillors; this city council voted at its own discretion for a mayor who was then appointed by the king of Prussia (also German emperor after 1870). Ultimate authority naturally rested with the Regierungspräsident appointed by the king, while the status of fortress Cologne inevitably brought further restrictions with the need for the approval of the military governor in many cases. Nevertheless, the city's administrative bodies had jurisdiction over wide areas: shipyard and port installations, bridges, markets, urban utilities and transport companies, building and housing, health services, schools and technical colleges, social welfare, music, museums, theatres and libraries. In many of these fields the city worked harmoniously with the state despite occasional conflicts between them. The measures of the Prussian reformers Hardenberg and Stein in the early nineteenth century enabled the city to develop its own political style, and pride in its achievements, initiative and creativity. There was no need for the imposition from above of the orderly and disciplined spirit of Prussian administration, because it had already been freely adopted in Cologne. As mayors the city councillors usually elected well-known individuals, men who had made a reputation in other city administrations or had worked in the city's legal community. Occasionally, however, they would select a Prussian Oberpräsident such as Max Wallraf, Adenauer's predecessor – though he was also a member of the 'Kölner Klüngel' (the Cologne Clique), as the ruling elite of businessmen, politicians, clergy etc., are known.

On the surface, then, the administration of Cologne was successfully integrated into the Prussian state. However, it has been argued that this was a largely deceptive impression and that there was a latent opposition to the 'Prussians', particularly in the form of Berlin and its bureaucracy. Equally, it has been suggested that the Rhenish brand of Catholicism generally obstructed attempts at integration into Protestant-dominated Prussia. These are important questions, particularly as they affect Adenauer, who was to play a significant role with respect to the Rhineland Movement in 1918-1919 and again in 1923. His attitude towards Prussia, and indeed to the Germany created by Bismarck as a whole, has been controversial ever since.

Historians of the Rhineland continue to devote much attention to the relationship between the Rhineland and Prussia. However, in contrast to earlier historians in the tradition of national liberalism, national conservatism, and social democratic interpretation of history, or of historians in the tradition of the Centre Party, they no longer believe in polarisation between the two.

To understand the complex psychological and political relationship between the Rhineland and Prussia it is essential to look beyond clichés. One illuminating example is provided by the story of Alexander Bachem, who was mentioned in *The City of Köln in the First Century of Prussian Rule, 1815-1915*, a three-volume work published by the city in 1916. Bachem was a native of Cologne who spent a number of years in the court of appeal and was mayor of the city between 1863 and 1875. To judge from the city chronicle, he was efficient, self-confident and pugnacious; the city council, it reported, 'felt the force of his independence and high-handedness though he never entered into obligations himself. No "mayor from the east" – according to the myths which were current in Cologne – could have done more. He conducted proceedings with great strictness and made them even more rigid than before, so that some members complained that "they did not want to be treated like schoolchildren".'[3] 'The east' implied harsh, ruthless and autocratic behaviour – but it was a quality that could just as easily appear in a native of Cologne as in a 'genuine' Prussian.

Adenauer himself would have no qualms about exploiting these clichés. In 1924, for example, he gave a speech to commemorate his great predecessor Wilhelm von Becker, mayor of the city between 1886 and 1907.[4] His expressions of respect included the remark that Becker's political views 'were basically closer to the east than the west'. Becker had come from Tangermünde and was the son of a Protestant superintendent; for Adenauer he was the perfect example of those virtues which could be defined as 'Prussian': 'energy', 'complete commitment' to his position, 'independence and self-discipline', 'a high sense of duty, seriousness, firm belief in God, endless diligence and incredible tenacity in the pursuit of his goals'.

Interpreted in a positive light, this cliché of the 'east' reflected the strict, functional virtues of Prussian state authority. It represented qualities similar to those celebrated by the historian Heinrich von Treitschke in his *German History in the Nineteenth Century*: 'a new north German tribe hard and weather-proof, made strong by hard work on barren land and through continual struggles in border regions, clever and independent in the way of colonisers, accustomed to look down with the pride of masters on their Slav neighbours, as curt and spirited as the good-natured coarseness of the Low Germans will allow.'[5]

From the more critical stand-point of the Rhineland, however, the eastern, Prussian outlook appeared domineering, provincial and inflexible, authoritarian and undemocratic, even intolerant – especially of Catholicism with its universalist approach and its focus beyond the Alps. The citizens of Cologne were aware of the social conditions which had shaped the 'eastern' view of the state. Prussia was dominated by traditional feudal values rooted in the static social relations of its heartland; it was these which had generated the bureaucracy, the officer corps and the traditional forms of Prussian economic management.

Attitudes towards Prussia in the Rhineland and Cologne were therefore ambivalent. Yet it should not be forgotten that a similar ambivalence was perceptible even in the Prussian heartlands themselves. Since the era of German idealism and Prussian reformism, the region had benefited from the blend of liberalism, cosmopolitanism, classical education and an awareness of the unique characteristics of individual regions. At the opposite pole stood Cologne and the 'west'. In the view of many of its citizens, this represented a dynamic economic and social modernity, open-mindedness, flexibility combined with shrewdness, love of life, individualism, a degree of pluralism and, not least, a more or less liberal Catholicism. 'West' also meant pride in Cologne as an old imperial city and a jealous defence of the administrative privileges granted by Stein and Hardenberg. Rhinelanders tended to regard themselves as more civilized than the inhabitants of the Prussian heartlands ('you're all Lithuanians', Görres had told them), but were impressed by Prussian military efficiency and administrative competence as revealed by the Napoleonic wars of liberation and Franco-Prussian wars.

Cologne was part of Prussia for more than one-hundred years. During that period the city witnessed a complex process of cultural exchange and integration in which the dominant role was played by the latter. The Hohenzollerns made every effort to win the favour of the Rhineland and Cologne in particular. In turn, the political claims of the 'eastern upstarts' were enhanced by their control of the cultural treasures of the Rhineland and the Romantic movement with which it was closely associated. After a period of reserve during the early decades of Prussian rule, the city began to accept the 'Prussians'. The synthesis of Rhenish and Prussian culture gathered pace; at the same time, the regions of the German Customs Union fused into a vibrant economic zone. Eventually the state of Prussia received credit for having promoted economic development in the west despite initial misgivings in the Rhineland. As the inhabitants of Cologne recognised these achievements, relations between the Prussian state and the Rhineland improved.

The building of the railways enabled businessmen and parliamentary deputies from Cologne to reach Berlin by night train. During the second half of the century their links with Berlin increased and capital markets were integrated. Following the 1848 revolution, liberal Cologne bankers, industrialists and businessmen discovered many common interests with conservative circles in Prussia. Berlin was no longer the distant centre of bureaucracy, but a city increasingly familiar to Rhinelanders with business interests or political and administrative ambitions. Informal co-operation improved as inhabitants of Cologne established contacts in the Imperial administration and in the companies and banks of Berlin; some of these contacts were natives of Cologne, while others were Prussians who had served in the Rhineland as district presidents or local administrators and had come to appreciate a more pleasant lifestyle than was to be found in Old Prussia. Later, as mayor, Adenauer himself would make use of these political connections.

Despite occasional conflicts of interest in economic matters, the process of integration was largely successful. Cologne needed the Prussian crown and the Prussian military as protection against French encroachment. Public attitudes towards France were determined by several factors: the occupation of the Napoleonic period, which had also caused nationalist resentment in Cologne, the euphoria of the Wars of Liberation, the outburst of anti-French sentiment in 1840, and the patriotism engendered by the Franco-Prussian War which preceded German unification. Bernhard von Bülow, Chancellor of Germany between 1900 and 1909, later recalled the scenes at Cologne's railway station following the French declaration of war on Prussia in July 1870.[6] The city was gripped by an enthusiasm which reached fever-pitch with the arrival of Wilhelm I on his way to the army: 'It sounds almost incredible, but for three-quarters of an hour the cheering never stopped for a second, "Wacht am Rhein" could be heard all around the cathedral.'[7]

These scenes had a profound psychological effect on those who witnessed them. The inhabitants of Cologne were also aware that the city and its cathedral had become the symbol of Prussian and German self-assertion on the Rhine – especially against France – since 1840. The writer Nikolaus Becker, who as a young man was a clerk at a court in the Rhineland, had written a poem which reflected these sentiments and continued to arouse deep emotions well into the twentieth century: 'Sie sollen ihn nicht haben, den freien deutschen Rhein' (they shall not have her, the free German Rhine).

Yet, in Cologne and the Rhineland at least, German chauvinism was frequently leavened by a mockery of Prussian militarism which found its subtlest expression at carnival time. Businessmen in Cologne, moreover, knew that they depended on the economic markets of western Europe as much as on the domestic market. In the beer halls of the city there continued to be grumbles about the dominance of Old Prussian civil servants, usually Protestants, in the regional administration, but this was due as much to the relative shortage of university-educated Catholics as to the policy of the Prussian minister of the interior. Nevertheless, during the Wilhelmine era the educated and propertied middle classes in Cologne and throughout Germany became increasingly fascinated by Prussian feudal values. The phenomenon was encouraged by the student corps, by military service and by the *Burschenschaften* (student fraternities).

Among those most favourably disposed towards Prussia were the rich Jews of Cologne, who had long admired the Prussian state as a force for equal rights, the protection of minorities and emancipation.

Though serious tensions did arise as a result of the different traditions of the Rhineland and Prussia, strengthened by the explosive pace of modernisation, there was no movement for political autonomy in Cologne before 1918. Critics of Prussia sought to reform the Prussian state in the spirit of liberal constitutionalism rather than to leave it; they hoped for increased self-administration, the protection of minorities and greater representation of middle-class interests. It was the internal structure of Prussia that was at issue rather than allegiance to the Prussian crown.

Nevertheless, it was impossible to overlook the friction between the government in Berlin and the Catholics, which had first emerged in the 1830s and intensified in the *Kulturkampf* (cultural struggle) of the 1870s. It created a deep and lasting mistrust which was always liable to recur at critical moments. Liberals, National Conservatives and Social Democrats were all prepared to exploit anti-Catholic sentiment by resorting to slanders about 'ultramontane' and 'black' parties and 'enemies of the Reich'. The *Kulturkampf* also persuaded Treitschke to describe the Catholic Rhineland as the 'region of the crosier' and to portray the inhabitants of Cologne as perpetually tempted by 'ultramontane' forces under the control of Rome and associated with France. Such views were to reappear after the First World War in the election propaganda of the German National People's Party, the National Liberals and the Social Democrats, before being adopted in extreme form by Hitler's National Socialists. Even today they continue to influence some historians.

In order to defend itself during the *Kulturkampf*, the Centre Party in turn had resorted to attacks on 'Berlin' and the Prussian state power. These, too, were repeated in later years. Adenauer's great speeches as Chairman of the CDU in the British Zone after the Second World War still contained classic examples of Centre Party rhetoric in the form of attacks on the Prussian-style 'overmighty state'.

On 31 March 1874 Archbishop Paulus Melcher was arrested by Friedrich Leopold Devens, chief of police in Cologne. His arrest, seven-month detention in Klingelpütz prison and subsequent flight to Holland remained fresh in the memory of the Catholic population. Although the Prussian government eventually adopted a more reasonable stance, the celebrations surrounding the completion of the cathedral took place without the archbishop and were greeted with reserve by the clergy and laity, who had been asked by August Reichensperger to show 'dignified restraint'. Nevertheless, the affair did not prevent Johann Conrad Adenauer, a retired lieutenant in the Prussian army and a loyal Catholic, from pointing out the Kaiser to his four-year-old son. From the balcony in the home of family friends, the young Konrad Adenauer watched the emperor ride by in an open carriage. It was a scene he was never to forget. Even as a eighty-nine year old man, in 1961, he referred to this highlight of his early years.

Influential figures in Cologne also realised that the real driving forces behind the *Kulturkampf* were the Liberals in alliance with the Old Catholics. The city council's Liberal majority – not the government in Berlin – voted in 1875 to cut financial aid for the Corpus Christi procession on the grounds that it was taking decisive action against 'ultramontane' anti-German and anti-Reich elements in the Centre Party. One of these Liberals was Johann Hamspohn, a convert to Old Catholicism who, fifty years later, was a member of the board of AEG and an important friend to the young mayor Adenauer.

In another petty dispute the Cologne Liberals attempted to prevent the scattering of leaves, which had long been a Palm Sunday tradition in Catholic Cologne, by claiming that they caused traffic problems. On this occasion the government refused this request, thereby appearing more tolerant than the Liberals of the city. Much greater bitterness was caused by the issue of education – whether elementary schools should be supervised by non-denominational bodies and whether denominational schools should be replaced by inter-denominational ones. Once again it was the Prussian authorities, this time in the shape of the Ministry of Culture, Education and Church Affairs, which showed the greater foresight and enforced tolerance. At regional level, however, education continued to play an important part in political debates between the Centre Party and the Liberals. The tone remained acrimonious for many years, particularly in the party press. Before elections in the prelude to the First World War, the liberal *Kölner Stadtanzeiger* would periodically condemn the 'inconsiderate' and 'spiteful' language of the Centre Party press, especially the *Kölnische Volkszeitung*, which was quick to respond in kind.

The *Kulturkampf* aroused resentment among the Catholic churchgoers of Cologne – against Bismarck, against the Prussian government and against the dominant Protestant political culture of the Prussian state. The Centre Party in Cologne therefore began to adopt a defensive and suspicious attitude towards the state and liberal Protestants. Yet there was no 'break away from Prussia movement', and the Centre Party was to become one of the pillars of the conservative government in the Reichstag only a few years after the *Kulturkampf*. The Centre Party in Cologne eventually contained what Peter Reichensperger, referring to the party throughout Germany, called 'damned heterogeneous elements'. With Catholics in Cologne and throughout Germany cast in the role of underdogs, they went out of their way to express their loyalty to the Reich and the nation. It was a tendency that continued to be apparent well into the twentieth century. If Catholics hoped for any significant change at all, then it was to reform the internal structure of the state in their own interests. Prussia and the Reich were never subjected to serious attack.

The prelates of Cologne, too, were loyal to Prussia. Though they resisted attacks on Church privileges and autonomy whenever necessary, they also searched for a mutually satisfactory *modus vivendi* with the government in Berlin. After the turn of the century the national government was careful to make very sparing use of its rights in the election of bishops in Cologne; it was rewarded by the appointment of two strongly conservative and patriotic bishops, von Hartmann and Schulte, during the First World War. These two provided firm support for the national and Prussian governments during the crises of the war and the post-war period.

The idea that the Catholicism of the Rhineland and Cologne was anti-Prussian is therefore a myth. The truth is much more complex. As the Centre Party had discovered during the *Kulturkampf* and afterwards, the Hohenzollern dynasty and its senior civil servants were less of a danger than intolerant Liberals and intolerant and atheist Social Democrats. In turn, the Prussians grew to appreciate the fundamental conservatism of the Catholics and their organisations. The minority status of German Catholics – including those of Cologne – led them to fear that the eventual introduction of universal suffrage in Prussia would hand control to anti-clerical Social Democrats and Liberals. In this sense the Prussian throne was an ally, though the fact was not admitted openly.

Cologne Catholicism was by no means politically homogeneous. Not all politically active Catholics supported the Centre Party: many were Liberals, while others, including Adenauer's predecessor as mayor, remained independent of the parties. Wallraf did not join any party until after the 1918 Revolution, and then joined the German National People's Party (DNVP) rather than the Centre Party. It would be incorrect to claim that 'Cologne' equalled 'Catholic' equalled 'Centre Party', quite apart from the fact that some twenty per cent of its inhabitants were Protestants and another two per cent were Jewish. There were also serious disagreements within the Centre Party itself, and between the Centre and the Archbishop, especially as regards the role of the Christian trade unions.

Sociologists thus face great difficulties in their attempts to evaluate the shifting attitudes of Cologne and its Catholics towards Prussia and the Prussian-dominated German Reich. In fact, such changes in attitude were often the result of fluctuations in the immediate political situation and the policies pursued by various influential figures at any given time.

During Adenauer's childhood and youth the city was in the process of modernisation in which it became Prussian but retained its own individual character. Unlike Berlin or other dynastic centres, Cologne was dominated by the middle classes. In Germany, the term 'bourgeoisie' covered a wide social spectrum which tended to obscure its diversity. Even so, it was easier to detect the dividing line between this class and 'non-bourgeois' groups than in later decades.

By the late nineteenth century the grand bourgeoisie had developed a lifestyle modelled on that of the nobility. Yet although some of its representatives sought to acquire titles of nobility along with their wealth, the aristocracy and the bourgeoisie continued to inhabit separate worlds. The two classes themselves were aware of this fact, as one celebrated incident involving Madame Neven du Mont makes clear. During the line up at a reception given by the emperor, when the lord chamberlain made the announcement, 'Your Majesty, the nobility ends here', Madame Neven du Mont retorted equally loudly: 'But here, your Majesty, is where the money begins'.[8]

Not all of Cologne's grand bourgeoisie was as eager to join the ranks of the nobility as the Oppenheim, Guilleaume, Deichmann and Schnitzler families. Even without a patent of nobility they knew that they stood at the top of the social pyramid. Not until the turn of the century did 'blood' and 'money' form closer links. Initially these ties were on equal terms – but, in Cologne at least, people knew that the future belonged to money.

Class divisions at the bottom of the social pyramid were considerably more pronounced. Until the reform of the electoral system in 1918 the Prussian Three-Class Franchise marked the division between the bourgeoisie and non-bourgeois groups, since only home owners or those with an annual income of at least 400 thaler had the right to vote. In 1891, when Adenauer was still at school, only 16,683 inhabitants of Cologne were entitled to vote in a city of 286,000 people. In terms of social class, the franchise was less restrictive than may appear at first sight, since women were completely disenfranchised whatever their personal wealth. In this period of large families, the number of men of voting age probably hovered between 60,000 and 70,000, which means that some 75-80 per cent of the male population was disenfranchised and thus – by extension – did not belong to the bourgeoisie. The figure includes all manual workers, a sizeable number of day-labourers who travelled in from the country, domestic servants and commercial employees, handicraft apprentices and those dependent on charity.

At the same time, the Three-Class Franchise revealed that the bourgeoisie was by no means a homogeneous social class. In 1891 only 567 citizens of Cologne – bankers, industrialists, businessmen, successful lawyers, senior civil servants and gentlemen of leisure – belonged to the first class, which occupied a third of the seats in the city council. The second class, also occupying a third of the seats, was reserved for representatives of the 2,858 males of the well-off middle classes, who included businessmen, merchants, lawyers, doctors, high-ranking clergy, and journalists. The 13,258 voters in the third class can be defined as petty bourgeois; they included small and medium-scale merchants, low and middle-level civil servants and employees, and, during the reign of Wilhelm II, some successful skilled workers. As a result of greater prosperity a few thousand of the lower classes eventually rose into the ranks of the petty bourgeoisie, while there was also increased mobility between the petty bourgeoisie and the well-off middle classes. Good careers were available in trade and commerce, as well as in all those professions which required a higher education and a university degree. Young men such as Konrad Adenauer, who managed to advance into the ranks of the educated middle class and the administrative élite at local and national level, were often the sons of middle and low-ranking civil servants without academic training.

Differences in social status between the various middle-class groups were more pronounced than in later times. The 'cream' of society tended to live in pretentious and luxurious town houses with large stairwells and vast salons for winter dinner parties. In summer the grand bourgeoisie would move to their country houses, preferable converted castles or neo-Gothic mansions. Here the trend was set by the Oppenheims with their homes near Bonn and in Schlenderhahn and Bassenheim, and the Guilleaumes at Malgersdorf Castle. Louis Hagen, who had reached the summit of Cologne's grand bourgeoisie, held court at Birlinghoven Castle. In his case as in others, the spartan simplicity of his office made an effective contrast to the splendour of his home.

Although the lifestyle of Cologne's wealthy capitalists was not typical of the entire well-to-do bourgeoisie, it did much to set the tone. Members of the well-off middle class followed the spirit of the times by building new houses in the old city or buying luxurious houses on the city ring, where they would rent out the more modest apartments to well-off tenants in order to cover the mortgage. The new and still relatively rural suburbs, such as Marienburg to the south of the city and Lindenthal in the west, were also increasingly popular. A large domestic staff was typical of the bourgeois lifestyle, with two or three maids frequently employed to assist the lady of the house in the running of the household and the care of the children. This pattern of life was to continue into the 1930s. Konrad Adenauer, who employed three maids in his home during his period as mayor, was doing no more than was customary for a man in his position.

Wealthy individuals – of whom there were relatively few before the turn of the century – would build holiday or retirement homes in Rolandseck or Bad Godesberg. After 1900 it also became popular for the wealthy to travel and to take rest cures. Those who could not afford to visit Bad Gastein, Bad Mergentheim or the Bühlerhöhe every year could at least aspire to a honeymoon trip to the Italian Riviera, Florence or Venice and to visit Switzerland, the Black Forest or the North Sea for their annual holidays. It was a pattern Adenauer was to follow in his own life.

Much of the socialising for which Cologne was famous took place in the home. However, clubhouses and theatres were increasingly popular as venues for social gatherings. For the grand bourgeoisie, the most magnificent of these was the Gürzenich concert hall, renovated in grand style by the urban architect Raschdorff in the middle of the nineteenth century. British cultural influence had been particularly strong at the time, and the interior of the hall was decorated much like a Westminster or Hampton Court on the Rhine. In nearby Augustinerplatz was the meeting-place of the 'Recreation Society' where the guests could walk in the indoor garden and play skittles, and the Wolkenburg theatre, which was famous for staging its comedies in the local dialect and was also home to the city's famous choral society. The Freemasons, too, had their local Lodges such as Minerva Rhenana. Other locals would attend meetings of the Book Club or the clubhouse for Catholic journeymen founded by Adolf Kolping. In short, there was something for everyone, from the upper classes to the craftsmen. These were the years when Cologne carnival, re-established with all its old rituals in 1823, became famous throughout Germany. The most enthusiastic participants were the prosperous middle classes. The wide popular appeal of the carnival was a fact of life which had to be recognised and accommodated by all holders of political office, even those such as Adenauer who were personally unimpressed by the festivities.

When the native inhabitants of Cologne felt threatened by the influx from abroad they turned to the popular sketches of local life performed in dialect, and to traditional puppet theatres and entertainments. It was in these years that official Cologne founded the 'Native Society of Old Cologne', that Tünnes and Schäl jokes gained popularity outside the city, and that the songs of Willi Ostermann became widely known. These developments reflected both the strength of regional culture and a desire for organised social life. Beyond that, they revealed the extent of bourgeois complacency, a middle class at ease with itself and the world. This was the class that greeted the tensions of the industrial age with the old saying, 'Things always turn out for the best'.

During Adenauer's youth the various elements within the bourgeoisie began to intermingle, not only within the various clubs and societies, but also through marriage. Adenauer, for example, was related through marriage to the families Berghaus, Weyer, Wallraf, Wahlen and Cardauns. The traditional professions of the members of these families were highly typical of bourgeois Cologne: for example, Johann Peter Weyer had been a famous urban architect, but the clan also included a clergyman, a mother superior, a Privatdozent and many members of the legal profession.

The family clans were important economic and social factors in the city. Where outsiders simply saw the 'Cologne clique', insiders were aware of the intrigues and mistrust between the families despite their common bonds. Nevertheless, citizens who were born or married into these clans were thoroughly socialised by them unless they embarked on the career of an artist or an intellectual – thus risking the fate of being regarded as an outsider. Even outsiders performed a significant social function, providing endless topics for conversation at baptisms, marriages, birthdays and funerals. More important, every assiduous and conventional family member would know that other clan members would help them in their career whenever possible. Bourgeois families expanded along with society at large and drew new blood from the outlying regions of the Ruhr and the Rhineland. On the whole, however, they continued to recruit mainly from Cologne and its immediate vicinity.

These extended families continued to be a significant factor beyond the wealthier sections of society, in the lower-middle and working classes. Their family trees, however, were rarely recorded in handbooks and had to be carefully researched and compiled – as was the case with the Adenauer family. When upwardly mobile families from the lower-middle class moved to Cologne from the towns and villages near Bonn, Cologne and the Bergisches Land, they brought with them an emotional attachment to these regions which often lasted for generations. To an inhabitant of the city at the turn of the century, Cologne was not an alienated or faceless society of uprooted workers but a widespread and tight-knit network of families with ties to the land which continued to provide emotional support.

The changing city was held together not only by its family clans, societies and professional bodies, but also by the church. In late nineteenth-century Cologne this meant the Catholic Church, which was a powerful institution in the history and everyday life of the city. Some of its great churches were built on the foundations of early Roman basilicas and heathen temples. According to legend, during Roman times 11,000 virgins under the leadership of Ursula, the daughter of a British king, had been martyred in the vicinity of St Ursula's. St Gereon church had a history dating back to the century of Constantine the Great. The church of St Cunibert had been the site of a seventh-century church dedicated to St Clemens, patron saint of sailors. The churches of St Pantaleon and St Andreas were foundations of the Ottonian kings. The men of the Middle Ages had built on top of the original structures, renovating them and adding new pearls of Christian architecture: the cathedral, St Cecilia, St Apostle, St George and St Severin. All such places contained treasures in the form of masonry, wood carvings, altar pieces, paintings and stained-glass windows. The modern age had added, painted over, made general 'improvements': Cologne always fluctuated between traditional piety and the desire to adapt church buildings and decorations to meet current fashions. Though much was lost during the French occupation, no other German city contained such a rich heritage of art and architecture.

Following the Napoleonic era and the wars of revolution, religious fervour increased as a result of the restoration and the integralist movement. The nineteenth century witnessed passionate debate between different religious tendencies, but in Cologne the ultramontane strand, with its emphasis on veneration of saints, missionary work, strict worship and family morality, was dominant. The church of Adenauer's childhood was predominantly anti-modern and anti-liberal. Nevertheless, it proved able and willing to mobilise its members using the modern weapons of mass psychology.

Since the 1840s Cologne had become an important centre for Catholic organisations. Adolf Kolping, the 'father of journeymen' and founder of several social welfare programmes and populist newspapers, was born in nearby Kerpen. Kolping was a tireless vicar of the cathedral and rector of the Minorite church. Instead of Marxist revolution he demanded that religious faith be reformed, proposing that workers who had been uprooted from their surroundings should be integrated into a close community based on family, church services and – the new element – dynamic Catholic organisations in which laymen would play an important role. Kolping and like-minded individuals made Cologne into a bulwark of social Catholicism. Since the 1870s the city also had become a political stronghold of the Centre Party and, in the 1880s, Johann Peter Oberdoerffer, the priest of St Martin, organised the Catholic workers' movement in the city. In 1887 the Catholic workers' associations in Cologne had some 3,500 members.

By the end of the 1890s the time was ripe for the establishment of Christian trade unions. These were controversial from the start, attacked from one side by the Social Democratic unions and regarded with suspicion from the other side by the middle-class wing of the Centre Party and by conservative members of the episcopacy with reservations about their non-confessional stance. Cardinal Kopp of Breslau, the leading conservative among the German bishops, thus dismissed them as a 'contamination from the west'. Nevertheless, Catholic workers were organised on an impressive scale in the two decades before the outbreak of the First World War. Local membership was to reach 11,000 in 1913. The progressive Cologne-Mönchen-Gladbach faction, which advocated social and political reform, had many adherents in Cologne and was also supported by the archbishops.

Every year Catholic Cologne celebrated its faith and strength at the Corpus Christi procession. Bernhard Falk, the Jewish leader of the National Liberals on the city council, provided an account of this procession in his memoirs. Falk was well informed about Cologne Catholicism although it never ceased to be strange to him: 'The festive procession in "holy" Cologne was unmatched in all Germany. Marching in the procession were societies and clubs representing Catholic students, civil servants, businessmen, journeymen, workers, academics, social groups, young people, mothers and young ladies and – at least before the war – even Poles with banners and standards.'[9] A further impressive display of the power and worldwide influence of the Catholic Church was provided by the Eucharistic Congress which met in Cologne in 1909 and attracted priests, cardinals and archbishops from a wide area.

The Catholic Church in Cologne thus organised, disciplined, led and integrated a wide spectrum of the faithful in Cologne. Naturally there were conflicts within it, such as the schism of the Old Catholics in the 1870s, the dispute within the church and the Centre Party over Christian trade unions, and a public controversy over theological modernism in the Bonn Theological Faculty. On the whole, however, Catholicism in Cologne, whether of reformist or conservative stamp, was a force for stability and an important corrective to the dynamism of the capitalist era. Many of the evils and excesses of capitalism were both criticised and softened as a result of the spiritual values rooted in the Catholic community of Cologne.

However, one should remember that the bourgeoisie of Cologne, though materialistic, were also capable of great generosity. The city's culture would never have blossomed in Imperial Germany without the enthusiasm of bourgeois sponsors. Whether the motives of these patrons of the arts were unselfish or designed to improve their own reputations, their contributions were of major significance. A remarkably large number of wealthy citizens thus devoted a proportion of their wealth to endowments. The Gustav-von-Mevissen Foundation was the basis for the college of commerce which, in 1919, was developed into the University of Cologne. Johann Heinrich Richartz, who had made his fortune in the South American hide trade, donated 900,000 marks over the years to help fund the museum which eventually bore his name. These decades witnessed a constant flow of contributions large and small for museums and music, for charitable work and education, for the cathedral-building association and the restoration of old churches, for the theatre, monuments and the zoo. Wealthy patrons enhanced the reputation and success of their city by contributing to a wide range of cultural and charitable organisations. Throughout Germany, wealthy families in the cities of Cologne, Leipzig, Frankfurt, Hamburg, Bremen, Nuremberg and Danzig competed with the dynastic rulers who were making endowments to their own capitals of Berlin, Dresden, Munich, Stuttgart, Karlsruhe, Darmstadt and Weimar. These classes took great pride in their endeavours. In return, however, they took pains to insist on their continued over-representation in municipal politics under the Three-Class Franchise.

In the second half of the nineteenth century Cologne developed into a major German centre for fine art. The cathedral capitular Alexander Schnütgen, *grand gourmand* and great connoisseur, for example, amassed an important collection of Christian art from the Rhineland and Westphalia for which he was granted the freedom of the city in 1910. His collection was housed in the museum which bore his name. Another great collector was Professor Adolf Fischer, creator of the city museum devoted to Far-Eastern culture.

Above all, the nineteenth century was the great era of German music. In Imperial Germany Cologne became a centre of music and music appreciation following the inauguration of the Gürzenich concerts and the Lower Rhine music festivals at the beginning of the century. The conductor Ferdinand Hiller had made the conservatory into one of the best in the world and attracted the most famous of European composers to the city: Verdi conducted his *Requiem* in Cologne in 1873; Charles Gounod attended; Brahms conducted the 'Song of Triumph' in the Gürzenich Hall in 1874 and returned five years later with the Second Symphony. The young Arthur Rubinstein – pursued as ever by a horde of enthusiastic women fans – gave electrifying piano recitals in the city.

During the decades of Richard Wagner's greatest influence, Cologne like other German cities was divided into admirers and opponents of his work. Hiller, who had no sympathy for the anti-Semite from Bayreuth, attempted to exclude Wagner's music from Gürzenich and was supported by local music critics at a time when Cologne was regarded as the bastion of conservative opposition to Wagnerian music. Yet it was difficult to swim against the tide. Adenauer himself was to be a lifelong lover of Wagnerian opera. During his youth Wagner enthusiasts would meet in the city theatre to listen to *Meistersinger*. However, the *Ring of the Nibelungen* was never presented in its entirety because sections of the audience protested. Finally, in the 1890s, with Franz Wüllner established as Hiller's successor, Wagner's music became part of the opera programme in Cologne. Audiences in the city nevertheless remained conservative in their tastes despite the presence of Richard Strauss on the programme (even this was not without incident: two women, unaccustomed to the unusual sounds, fainted during the rehearsal of 'Death and Transfiguration' and had to be carried unconscious from the hall). During this great period in the musical life of the city, Cologne maintained an orchestra of international stature.

The city possessed a lively cultural scene. Some sections of the community were enthusiastic about traditional forms of culture, while others debated modern art with a passion which would be unthinkable today. Shortly before the outbreak of the First World War the 'Sonderbund' exhibition created a furore in Cologne; bitter debates accompanied the exhibition of paintings by Matisse, Vlaminck, Picasso, Mondrian and the German Expressionist schools Der Blaue Reiter (Blue Rider) and Die Brücke (The Bridge). Some perceptive observers sensed that more was at stake than a revolution in the arts alone: 'God save us', said Munch, 'we're heading for difficult times'. The old world was coming to an end in Cologne as elsewhere; the bourgeois age would soon give way to the age of wars and revolutions.

Yet it would be incorrect to claim that the Cologne of Adenauer's youth was entirely dominated by the bourgeois spirit. The city revealed many different facets, often depending on the social background of the observer. Nor did the dominance of the bourgeoisie go unchallenged. With hindsight, from the standpoint of 1914, 1918, 1923, 1933 and 1945, it is easy to detect tensions in society and to define them as portents of catastrophe. Yet the capacity of German society prior to the First World War, to synthesize, compromise and evolve should not be underestimated despite the tensions of the modern world.

Many of the social problems of the industrial age remained unresolved, in Cologne as elsewhere in Germany and Europe. Cologne society in Imperial Germany was a class society. While Gustav Mevissen was promoting the modernisation of the city in the spirit and with the methods of liberal capitalism, the socialist leader August Bebel, son of an NCO in the Prussian army, was born in Deutz. At the same time as old and new money was assuming its place as the cream of society, Adolf Kolping was working for the unemployed and exploited of Cologne and attempting to prevent the ill-housed and ill-paid journeymen from resorting to drink, violence and vice. The efficient Prussian civil service did not consist solely of successful officials, judges and public prosecutors, but also contained clerks from modest backgrounds such as Adenauer's father, who had to provide for his family from his meagre salary as a clerk at the court of appeal, as well as support his sons in their efforts to find a career. Nevertheless, as a civil servant Adenauer's father was in a more enviable position than the workers in Rhenish industries affected by periodic economic depression. Even geographically the city was divided, with the wide boulevards and elegant houses of the bourgeoisie in the wealthy districts making a stark contrast to the cramped back-to-back dwellings of the workers in Mülheim, Kalk, Poll, Nippes and Ehrenfeld. Throughout the city the class barriers and wide disparities in income were obvious. Major problems had to be faced in the fields of politics and social welfare, transport, housing and education.

The municipal administration thus faced a series of major challenges. These were accompanied by rancorous debates of the type characteristic of local politics in all free societies. Until the end of the 1880s the Three-Class Franchise produced a Liberal majority in the city council. Despite a degree of internal pluralism in the party, Liberal members responded to the challenge posed of their main adversary, the Centre Party, by closing ranks. With the first tax category dominated by the Liberals and the third by the Centre Party, the major contest was for control of the second category. In the three decades before the revolution of November 1918, however, the Centre generally had a majority.

Even after their return to the political scene during the Wilhelmine era, the Social Democrats did not play a decisive role at municipal level. One major reason was the structure of the Three-Class Franchise, which largely excluded workers; another was the strength of the Centre Party with its strong social wing in Cologne. The voting patterns of the city's Catholics reflected religious convictions rather than socio-economic factors. Although workers were increasingly organised into trade unions, they were unable to exert their full political weight in local politics before 1914, partly because the big industrial areas on the right bank of the Rhine were not incorporated until that year. The Liberals and members of the Centre Party therefore dominated the city council and were able to carry on their ideological disputes undisturbed by the Social Democrats. At the same time, they were responsible along with the mayor, for the welfare and prosperity of the city.

There were a number of areas in which differences between the parties were especially marked. One of these was education, where Liberals attempted to roll back the influence of the Catholic church in schools against the bitter opposition of the Centre. Yet the basic divide between the parties was also revealed by less obvious issues, such as the decision over whether to accept a huge bequest of one million marks from Rothschild, a councillor in the Land Supreme Court, for the building of a crematorium. This controversy was to continue into Adenauer's period in office, with Liberals and Social Democrats supporting cremation and the Centre adopting the hostile stance of the Catholic Church.

Material interests frequently placed the two parties on opposite sides of the political divide, particularly on issues affecting the crucial second tax category. Here the potential clients of the Liberals tended to be owners of capital opposed to the imposition of higher income taxes, while the Centre Party was anxious to relieve the tax burden on small home owners. Equally, political issues involving the interests of craftsmen would be certain to obtain the support of the Centre; the Liberals, on the other hand, were inclined to support the demands of the Chamber of Commerce. The Centre Party was also sympathetic to calls for an extension of the franchise – though only to limited changes that would keep the Social Democrats out of city hall.

Some of the most intense disputes involved the allocation of jobs in the municipal administration and the education system. The Liberals were frequently enraged and frustrated by the skill of the Centre in placing their own supporters. Falk later recalled: 'The leaders of the Centre were usually so accommodating and obliging but were ruthless when it came to appointments involving one of their own. The Liberal faction maintained that posts were settled in their party offices, and that the old-boys' register of Catholic fraternities was just as important in this process as the Almanac de Gotha was for diplomats and senior administrative civil servants.'[10]

Political confrontations, then, were always possible. Yet apart from the *Kulturkampf* of the 1870s, party differences in Cologne remained surprisingly moderate during the seventy years between the revolutions of 1848 and 1918. Much of the credit must go to a series of perceptive and competent mayors who were able to win the support of reluctant majorities for their modernisation plans. Cologne had possessed a so-called Bürgermeistereiverfassung (mayoral constitution) since the middle of the nineteenth century, when the Rhenish municipal statutes of 1856 gave the parishes the right to choose between the dual system of a municipal constitution or a mayoral constitution. Cologne had chosen the latter. Its constitution was similar to the French *maire* system which had been imposed during the years of its affiliation with France. This structure established a relationship between mayor and city council – the latter elected under the Three-Class Franchise – which resembled that between a constitutional monarch and parliament. The mayor, elected for a twelve-year term, was the sole leader of the city administration. There was no legal requirement for him to delegate specific tasks to the full-time deputies, though this regulation proved untenable in practice. The mayor was the sole representative of the administration in his dealings with the city council, and he alone was responsible for implementing its decisions. Moreover, his influence was further increased by the fact that he was himself at the head of the council which was to control the administration.

Over the years, the mayors increasingly assumed the role of business manager of Cologne. As the city took on more entrepreneurial functions, the duties and responsibilities of its mayor in the economic sphere increased. He was responsible for the establishment of the city's public utilities, which, starting from 1873, eventually included the gasworks, power supply, waterworks and sewage system; the transport system demanded his close attention and gradually came under his control; the harbour and shipyard installations required constant modernisation and the planning and construction of new bridges. In 1889 the city took control of all the horse-drawn trams previously run by the Société Anonyme des Tramways de Cologne. These were converted to electricity and an expansion programme to the suburbs was authorised. In addition to his traditional duties the mayor supervised a growing number of municipal responsibilities including transport planning, housing, hospitals and hygiene, welfare, the arts, schools and education.

The mayor also represented his city to the outside world in the manner of a constitutional monarch. He was in constant contact with the various Prussian ministries and state secretaries within the Imperial government, with the governor of the Rhine Province, and with the administrators of the neighbouring districts. As the representative of an important city, the mayor of Cologne also sat in the Prussian upper chamber and in the provincial Landtag in Düsseldorf. Furthermore, he was spokesman for his city in all the major associations representing municipal interests.

Thanks to his growing entrepreneurial role the mayor had numerous contacts with firms and associations in Cologne and the outlying districts, with banks and insurance companies, with private transport companies, building societies, energy companies and other firms which might have a role to play in a major city. In theory he was subject to controls from two sides as he undertook these tasks: on the one side from the supervisory authorities of the state, and on the other side from the city council. However, an experienced city leader had every chance of retaining a significant degree of personal influence and control.

Though the supervisory authorities frequently intervened to establish rules and offer encouragement or objections, they were basically content for an efficient and far-sighted agency to take responsibility for the management of a range of complex tasks. The city councillors were not lacking in power and prerogatives, but in view of the growing complexity of the decisions confronting them they were prepared to leave much of the initiative, planning and implementation to the municipal administration. Moreover, the mayor held office for twelve years while they were elected only for six. It was extremely difficult for councillors to work against a mayor who sat like a spider in the web of administration, had a wealth of information at his disposal, and could pit the various political factions against each other. Given a reasonable degree of skill a mayor could also hope to win over the press. Despite several attempts by the councillors to curb the power of the mayor, they had little success against the determined and powerful Wilhelm Becker in the 1880s.

The quasi-monarchical position of the mayor, then, was by no means an invention of Adenauer. Becker was the first to make a great success of the role between 1886 and 1907. When he took office there was some doubt about whether the dynamic energies unleashed in the middle decades of the century could be productively channelled; the city wall had been demolished, but the twin problems of expansion and modernisation had yet to be solved.

In a long letter to his friend Konrad Adenauer in 1956, the Belgian-American businessman Dannie N. Heineman recalled the city of Cologne at the turn of the century: 'I visited Cologne for the first time at the beginning of the nineties; I thought it a provincial city then, not a metropolis, despite the archbishop, the university in Bonn, the Gürzenich, the carnival, the Rhine and its shipping, a great railway junction, Charlotte Huhn and Emil Goetze with the silvery Lohengrin armament. I don't forget the industry in Deutz, etc. I knew the Hotel Ernst with its iron stove in every room, and every guest having to fill his own stove with coal. What has Cologne become? Your foresight and your courage made its development possible.'[11]

In reality Cologne had already become the second most important Prussian city under the leadership of Becker. If Adenauer had not achieved international stature after 1949, local historians would have ranked him alongside Becker as one of the city's most influential mayors of the nineteenth and twentieth centuries. Wilhelm Becker, one of the great urban managers of Imperial Germany, was fifty-one years old when he was appointed mayor. A trained municipal civil servant, he had previously spent ten years as mayor of Düsseldorf. His two great achievements in Cologne were to initiate expansion into the surrounding districts on both sides of the Rhine, and to transform Cologne into a modern city able to meet the challenges of the twentieth century. Both developments were possible only because, beginning with his term of office, the city administration became an important force for progress. In 1813 Cologne had employed no more than fifty-nine workers. The city administration expanded particularly rapidly under Becker, and by 1924 Adenauer was in command of a small army of municipal civil servants, white-collar workers and manual workers – some 4,902 men and women.

The planned expansion into the surrounding area was continued and concluded by Wallraf and Adenauer, but it was Becker who had initiated the project. In 1888 the incorporation of a number of suburbs on the left bank, together with Deutz and Poll on the right bank, had increased the urban area elevenfold. Becker was also responsible for moves to incorporate the previously independent industrial belt of Mülheim and Merheim, which extended the urban area from 11,106 to 19,674 hectares.

Mayor Becker frequently had difficulty in persuading the city council to take ambitious action. Incorporating the outlying towns, councillors were well aware, meant 'marrying into a very poor family'; the integration of these areas would undoubtedly cost large sums of money for a city which was already facing the massive expense of modernisation. The decision to proceed with incorporation and modernisation not only increased the population of the city from 143,000 inhabitants in 1882 to 436,000 in 1907, but also led to a profound change in the quality of life. Alongside the expansion of the transport system, of sanitary and health services, of schools, education and culture, the city administration also needed to plan recreation areas to satisfy the needs of a growing population. It was these considerations which gave rise to the plans for the largest city park – the Stadtwald.

This concept was inspired and, in terms of municipal politics at the time, revolutionary. In a number of important speeches Becker emphasised that the open countryside was only accessible to ordinary people by train. In order to help working class families and low-paid white collar workers to recover from the pressures of work, even for a short time on Sundays, it was essential to create an accessible city park which could be reached on foot. This park should have large open spaces and woods; it should have paths for carts, horseback riders and pedestrians, ponds and playgrounds. Becker stressed that such parks were not a luxury but a social necessity: woods in particular had a soothing effect which would help ordinary citizens cope with the stresses and strains of everyday life. The alternative, it was feared, would be increasing drunkenness.

In later life Adenauer recalled how controversial these 'explosive' plans had been. Despite widespread dismay at the enormous projected costs, Becker had pushed through his plans with an iron will. In so doing he had changed the face of modern Cologne and improved the lives of its citizens.

Growing municipal responsibilities required an efficient municipal administration, and Becker had built the apparatus from which his more famous successor was to benefit. A new city-finance policy was equally essential. The parties on the city council, the most conservative element in the modernisation process, were naturally eager to hold down the tax burdens of their own supporters. Becker frequently urged the councillors to adopt a long-term perspective of development and to accept the need for short-term debts in order to achieve long-term growth. He reminded his critics that Cologne and the other Rhenish cities were not part of the 'impoverished east' and could afford to repay their debts. Becker was proved correct: his shrewd successor, Max Wallraf, presided over a phase of financial consolidation.

Becker's second successor, Konrad Adenauer, applied the same theory of accepting short-term debt in the expectation of long-term benefit. During his school and university career, then later as a lawyer and the youngest full-time deputy in the last year of Becker's tenure, he had observed Becker's ability to overcome obstacles and persuade his city to adopt a daring and visionary course. Adenauer was determined to emulate the achievements of this predecessor.

In the event Adenauer was forty years old before he had the opportunity to realise his own vision. During the intervening period his personal development was influenced not only by his parents, but also by the vibrant city in which he grew to manhood. Although there are few accounts of his early years, it is certain that his home city – beautiful, diverse and modern – provides an important key to understanding the complex man who was to become its mayor and, in 1949, Chancellor of his shattered country.

I

THE YOUNG MASTER ADENAUER 1876-1906

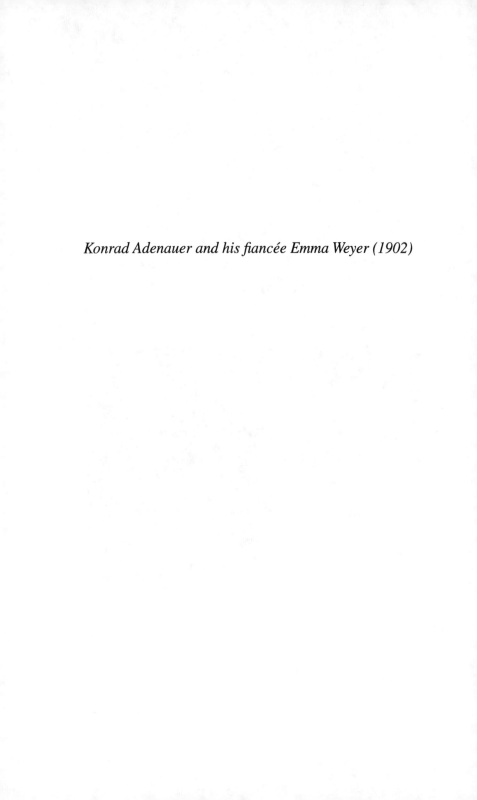

Konrad Adenauer and his fiancée Emma Weyer (1902)

Early Beginnings

Adenauer's birth certificate was written in the elaborate language of the nineteenth century. However, it records all the relevant information so precisely that it deserves to be quoted in full: 'No. 90. Cologne, 6 January 1876. The Court of Appeal secretary and retired Lieutenant Johann Conrad Adenauer, resident in Cologne, Balduinstraße 6, of the Catholic religion, appeared today before the undersigned registrar, to whom he is known, to declare that Maria Christiana Helena Adenauer née Scharfenberg, his wife, of the Catholic religion, resident with him in Cologne, gave birth to a male child at seven thirty in the morning of fifth January in the year eighteen hundred and seventy six. The child was given the Christian names Conrad Hermann Joseph. Read out, approved and signed Joh.Conr.Adenauer (signature of the registrar).'[1]

Adenauer thus was officially registered as a native of Cologne. However, his father was a newcomer to the Rhenish capital and his mother's family had been resident there for no more than a generation. The expansion of the service sector in the industrial age had enabled Adenauer's father to find work as a civil servant in the city, while his mother's father was a bank clerk.

The family tree had deep roots not only in the countryside but also in Bonn, a town with a rich tradition and an unsuspected political future. Like millions of other German families drawn to the big city, the Adenauers did not have a purely urban mentality, since many uncles and aunts, nephews and cousins, continued to live outside Cologne in the villages around Bonn. The family continued to hold regular gatherings and were in no sense uprooted. The traditional virtues of generations of farmers and craftsmen – hard work, dependability, faith, frugality, patience – helped them to endure the strains of urban life. No further discoveries by genealogists and local historians are likely to cast significant new light on this facet of Adenauer's background.

Konrad Adenauer's father was from a baker's family in Bonn on his father's side. His great-grandfather, Jacob Adenauer, had settled there in

1789, the year of the French Revolution. Previously, like generations of his family before him, Jacob had been a farmer in Flerzheim, a village in the flatlands of the Erft near Bonn. In Remagen, Münstereifel and other villages of the region, the name Adenauer can be traced back to the seventeenth and early eighteenth centuries. The name can also be found in Bonn from the beginnings of the modern age, from 1500. At some unknown date all these various clans had their origins in the simple village of Adenauer not far from the Nürburgring, one of the most famous racing-car circuits in Germany in the twentieth century.

At the age of twenty-six Adenauer's great-grandfather decided to try his luck in Bonn, and set up home not far from the electoral barracks near the city wall at An den Kasernen 375. After being renovated and rebuilt several times over the years, the house finally fell victim to the town traffic planning regulations in 1957. Today, anyone who takes the two-lane Oxfordstraße to the Kennedy Bridge can tell themselves that they are driving over the site of the ancestral home of the Adenauer family.

In 1835 Konrad Adenauer's grandfather Franz Adenauer, born in 1810, ran a bakery at the house. These biographical details were unearthed by Herbert Weffer, who discovered that a bakery had survived there until after the Second World War, claiming to be the region's 'first and oldest bakery specialising in rye bread'. We will be reminded of this origin by Adenauer's attempts to produce 'Cologne bread' during the privations and shortages of the First World War.

Adenauer's paternal grandfather eventually gave up this bakery, left his many relatives in Bonn and set up a new bakery in the nearby town of Messdorf. Elderly townspeople still claim to have seen the large bread oven in the cellar of his home. Modern visitors to the town, which is now a suburb of Bonn, will find a community full of new housing, with only a few traces of the nineteenth century in the shape of half-timbered houses, a stone cross, a small statue of Mary and a neo-Gothic church. During this period Messdorf was one of the many local villages whose farmers grew grain and potatoes and supplied the market in Bonn with apples.

Franz Adenauer (the 1833 town register still records his name as 'Adeneuer') married at the age of twenty-one, relatively early for the time, a woman six years his senior. The couple had three children, including Adenauer's father Johann Konrad, born in 1833. However, in 1837 Franz Adenauer's wife died shortly after the death of one of her children. Early deaths and subsequent re-marriages – perhaps even two or three times – were by no means unusual, and two months after the death of his first wife Franz Adenauer was married again, this time to a bricklayer's widow. In 1840 Franz Adenauer himself died, at barely thirty years of age, after a fall from an orchard tree. His two young children were now looked after by his second wife, Eva.

The young Johann Konrad Adenauer was first sent to work in a brick-works before obtaining employment in the Messdorfer Burg as servant to one Peter Josef Ostler. The links between Ostler and his former servant were maintained in later years. According to town legend the two men were to serve in the same unit during the Franco-Prussian War, and the next generation of the two families certainly kept in touch. Over the years Johann Konrad's four children would often return from Cologne to Mess-dorf for summer and autumn holidays. Konrad Adenauer's sister Lilli became a close friend of Margaretha Ostler and the young Konrad him-self was said to find her irresistible; there were even unconfirmed rumours of an engagement.

Johann Konrad now faced the prospect of a decline in his social status as a member of the commercial petty bourgeoisie to the rank of farmer, which his grandfather had left by moving to the town. He therefore decided to become a career soldier after completing his military service. It is not clear whether he had joined the army 'with the Prussians' with the aim of spending his life as a career soldier, or whether he intended to become a civil servant after serving for twelve years and achieving the highest rank open to him as a private soldier.

Johann Konrad's military papers have survived to allow a reconstruc-tion of his military career. On 1 October 1851, at the age of eighteen, he enlisted as a three-year volunteer in 4th Company of the Second Rhenish Infantry Regiment 28. In 1858 he transferred to the Third Westphalian Regiment 16, then to 9th Company of the Seventh Westphalian Regiment 56. This Regiment had first been established in Paderborn in 1860,[2] and was later named after its regimental commander, Vogel von Falckenstein.

Johann Konrad was promoted to sergeant in 1860 and to staff-sergeant in the following year. His regiment did not see action during the Prusso-Danish War. Its regimental history was recorded in 1910 by Colonel Karl Wehmann: in 1864 'our regiment received the pleasant news that, in accordance with an order of 12 November 1864, our regiment was being transferred to Cologne'. He reported in great detail how the officer corps had survived the 'temptations' of the city and had been stimulated by the 'high culture' of Cologne. The officer corps, Wehmann wrote, 'was on good terms with the people of the city but without being too convivial with the native families'.[3]

The NCOs were probably less reserved. It seems likely that the attrac-tive Johann Konrad Adenauer met his future wife during his time in the garrison at Cologne. A photograph that has survived shows him as a well-built soldier, proudly wearing a handlebar moustache. Helene Scharfen-berg was the daughter of a bank clerk and, sixteen years younger than Johann Konrad Adenauer, would have been fifteen or sixteen years old when he was stationed in the city. Her father August Scharfenberg, born in Bad Sachsa near Erfurt in 1818, had come to Cologne as a regimental musician and decided to make his home there. His ancestors had been traditional craftsmen – carpenters, smiths, a miller. Adenauer's maternal grandfather was from Thuringia, but his wife, Anna Maria Schell, was a native of Bonn where her parents owned a general store. Her ancestral roots, like those of the Adenauers, can be traced back to the farming communities of the Erft region.

Adenauer's grandfather had not only come from central Germany, but was also a Protestant who had married according to Protestant ritual. However, Anna Maria Schell's children were raised as good Catholics, while she herself appears to have been particularly devout. Nevertheless, in later years Konrad Adenauer kept silent about the fact that his mother was the offspring of a 'mixed marriage', which was relatively rare at the time.

The genealogical evidence is clear: Konrad Adenauer was not a genuine man of Cologne and, in many ways, had greater links with Bonn. Furthermore, he had no exclusive links with the Rhineland, nor an exclusively Catholic family background.

Before he settled down in Cologne in 1871 to begin the first generation of Adenauers in the city, Johann Konrad survived the War of 1866 with Austria and the Franco-Prussian War of 1870-1871. Many years later, Konrad Adenauer mentioned to his biographer, Paul Weymar, a story which was current in his family and told how his badly wounded father had been found under a pile of bodies at the battle of Königgrätz, clutching a captured Austrian flag in his hand.[4] As soon as the biography appeared the accuracy of the anecdote was questioned. Having been asked about the incident, Adenauer's eldest son (also called Konrad) wrote a letter to his father, to which Adenauer sent the following detailed reply on 2 April 1962:

> I do not know what Weymar said about my father's heroic deeds in the War of 1866. Very probably I have never read it, and if I had read it I would not have remembered it. I will tell you what my father, once and once only, told me. He mentioned it while we were on holiday visiting my brother Hans in Fritzdorf. Actually he told me about it as we were sitting next to each other, resting, during a walk. I can recall the entire scene and everything he said. He told me about his injuries in the battle of Königgrätz, about the very inadequate provision for the wounded who, himself included, were left starving. He went on to say that he had been promoted to Second Lieutenant in 1866 for 'bravery in the face of the enemy'. Only two other NCOs had been promoted to officer then. However, he had decided not to pursue a career as an officer because he had become engaged to our mother. They wanted to marry but were not in the position to pay the security required for the marriage licence. He said nothing about any particular achievement in the War of 1866. My father was very reticent and cautious when he spoke of himself. Boasting was most unlike him. He never mentioned these details again. He did not like to talk about it. – I cannot tell you anything else. I remain fully convinced that my father told me the absolute truth – without embellishment or self-glorification.[5]

The actual events of the battle can be reconstructed not only from the regimental history and Theodor Fontane's description of the battle of

Königgrätz, but also from the discharge papers of Johann Konrad Adenauer. In the heat of the battle, the Seventh Westphalian Infantry Regiment 56 was deployed in the storming of a strategic position on the heights near the village of Problus. Following a twelve-hour march the 28th Brigade, of which Regiment 56 was part, scaled a muddy 1,500 metre slope from Popowitz to Problus with flags and fifes, 'resolute and truly stoic'.[6] From above, where the 3rd Saxon Infantry brigade was waiting in ambush, they were greeted with volleys of infantry fire along the flanks. This attack, followed by a close-quarters battle in the fortified town, was one of the bloodiest of the war. Within minutes five officers and eighty-seven NCOs had been killed; the captain of Adenauer's company was hit in the head and both flag-bearers fell.[7] Further heavy casualties were sustained in warding off an Austrian counter-offensive.

It seems, then, that a flag did indeed play a role in the battle – but it was their own flag, the battalion flag of the Westphalian 56. It is possible that Adenauer had been the last to pick it up, and that this was the origin of the tale involving a captured Austrian flag. Certainly such incidents were the stuff of legend – and school text-books – at the time. A similar event, for example, occurred during the Franco-Prussian War at the battle of Dijon in January 1871. It was commemorated for a generation of Prussian children in a poem by Julius Wolff, 'The Flag of the Sixty-Eighters'.[8]

At any rate, Adenauer's name was recorded in the regimental history. He was one of the eighty-six NCOs and men to receive the Military medal second class for his endeavours. In addition, the regimental history noted: 'Mention is made of the fact that on 10 August 1867 Staff-Sergeant Adenauer, who was seriously wounded at Problus, was awarded the rank of Second Lieutenant.' Though there was no reference to a captured flag, promotion from staff sergeant to second lieutenant was sufficiently unusual to be recorded in the regimental history.

These events are important in revealing that Konrad Adenauer was raised in a family with respect for military virtues. Yet Johann Konrad was also prepared to tell his children about the darker side of military glories. Konrad Adenauer was to see its effects for himself in 1914 when his young relative, Hans Scharfenberg, volunteered for military service during his last year at school and Adenauer helped him enlist as an officer cadet. Scharfenberg realised his ambition to become officer, but was physically and mentally destroyed by his war experiences. Over the following years Konrad Adenauer wrote many letters in an attempt to find adequate care for him.[9]

The life of Johann Konrad after he left the army is not well documented. His discharge papers are dated 1 July 1867, before his promotion to Second Lieutenant, and report that he was discharged in the city of Cologne 'as a full invalid temporarily incapable of fulfilling an occupation'. He was to receive a monthly service pension of ten thalers, plus the following monthly bonuses: two thalers for his injuries, five thalers for disability, and an additional three thalers for not making use of the public health care certificate until October 1869.[10]

At first sight it is difficult to reconcile these events with Johann Konrad's alleged desire to leave the service owing to lack of funds for a marriage licence. However, the apparent contradiction is explained by the fact that, following his recovery, he was reactivated as a Second Lieutenant and saw service in the Franco-Prussian War. On this occasion Johann Konrad did not see combat but worked as an 'economy officer' behind the lines. A document found among Adenauer's papers, dated April 1873 and signed by General von Goeben, commanding General of Eighth Army Corps, certifies that 'Konrad Adenauer, retired Second Lieutenant and Economy Officer of the Craftsmen Detachment of the Reserve Battalion, Second Rhenish Infantry Regiment 28', had been awarded the war service medal in steel. The text, embellished with its stout figures of Germania, has precious little artistic value but provides information about the military career of Johann Konrad Adenauer. It bears the battle honours of the Eighth Corps in which he served: Woerth, Vionville, Gravelotte, Beaumont, Sedan, Strasbourg, Metz, Amiens, Orleans, Le Mans, Montbéliard, St Quentin, Paris, Pontarlier.[11]

The document also provides support for the story that Adenauer and Ostler served together in the Franco-Prussian War. The regiment took part in the bitter forest battles near Gravelotte on 18 August 1870 and laid siege to Metz before marching into northern France. The battlefields of the First World War – Amiens, Bapaume, St Quentin – had already played a part in the life of Adenauer's father.

After the Franco-Prussian War, the thirty-eight year old reserve officer had apparently seen enough of war. It seems likely that he was given the option of serving in the regular infantry but refused because of his impending marriage. In later years Johann Konrad had little taste for discussion of his military exploits; he mentioned them only when he wished to instruct his sons in civic virtues. When a major fire lured his son August from his studies, for example, the father gave way to one of his periodic fits of rage: 'Even if cannons are fired right next to you, you must remain at your work!'[12]

Johann Konrad Adenauer had served the king of Prussia as soldier for seventeen years. Then, until his death in 1906, thirty years later, he was to work as a middle-ranking civil servant in the administration of justice – a routine job conscientiously fulfilled. His career, although slow, was steady, and in the end he attained the highest position possible for a man without higher education. In 1873 he was appointed secretary to the Court of Appeals, placing him at the *Königliches Landgericht* (Royal District Court). When he began his career this was the highest court in Cologne and was based in a beautiful neo-classical building built in the

1820s to a design by the architect Johann Peter Weyer. Weyer's grand-daughter, Emma Weyer, was to marry Konrad Adenauer in 1904. Later Johann Konrad worked in the neo-Gothic Palace of Justice built between 1888 and 1893; it was here that two of his sons, including the young Konrad, were to complete their legal training.

In 1883, ten years after beginning his work in the legal administration and despite the fact that he had received no more than an elementary school education, the fifty-year old Johann Konrad Adenauer was appointed *Kanzleirat* (Chancellery Councillor). He was to hold this position until his death. On 18 January 1891, the twentieth anniversary of German unification, he was awarded the coveted Order of the Red Eagle fourth class. Later Johann Konrad was described by Councillor of Justice Bernhard Falk, who had many dealings with him: 'He was a stern man, not particularly likeable but highly responsible and conscientious.' It was a description very much in line with Konrad Adenauer's own memories of his father. Falk too, had been told that Johann Konrad, 'who had worked his way to the top of his profession', had been promoted to officer rank as a reward for his courage at the battle of Königgrätz; it was, reported Falk, 'a very rare case of the highest recognition'. His military exploits continued to arouse more interest than his punctilious work as a civil servant.[13]

As a young man, Konrad Adenauer had great respect for his father. Johann Konrad was always correctly dressed, his beard well groomed, his appearance dignified and stern. He was punctual, modest and orderly – the very model of a Prussian civil servant. Moreover, it was probably his encouragement which persuaded two of his sons, August and Konrad, to enter the legal profession. Though himself in contact with the profession only at the lower levels, he was anxious for his eldest son, at least, to enjoy the opportunities he had been denied.

For information about Konrad Adenauer's mother we must rely solely on the stories recounted by Adenauer himself and his older children. She appears to have been an energetic and indefatigable woman who became the driving force of the family. Adenauer described her as a Rhinelander 'of incredible vitality', which for him was the highest form of praise. He recalled that she was very devout, though prone to occasional outbursts of temper. Adenauer, whose own outbursts were to become legendary, once told his biographer that he had inherited his volatile temperament from his parents.[14] Father and son, however, had both learned a greater degree of restraint.

Johann Konrad was content for his wife to take most of the responsibility for running the home and raising the children. It was a pattern which his son Konrad was later to copy. During his years as mayor of Cologne and leader of the Christian Democratic Union his patriarchal style was famous; it is easy to recognise it as a style modelled on his own experiences within the parental home, and characterised by strict control, modesty and order, competitiveness, religious devotion and strong family ties.

Konrad Adenauer's intimates were impressed by his filial devotion. He continued to visit his parents on his way home from work even after he had established his own family, and he moved his mother and sister into the first floor of his home following the death of his father. In later years he was to hang portrait photographs of his parents in his bedroom in Rhöndorf: his father bearded and in his stiff collar, and his mother kindly and resilient in her Sunday best clothes.

Johann Konrad Adenauer and Christiana Helena Scharfenberg were married in Cologne on 8 August 1871. Their first son, born only nine months later, was christened Franz Johann Ludwig *August*. The names of the children and the order in which they were given were determined according to custom: Franz (the baker from Bonn) was the paternal grandfather, Johann the maternal grandfather (he died in 1906, the same year as Adenauer's father, at the age of eighty-eight).

The second son, Johannes Franz Richard, called *Hans,* was born eighteen months later, followed by *Konrad* Hermann Joseph. The first daughter, Emilie Helene Marie Louise Adenauer, called *Lilli*, was born in the spring of 1879. A fifth child, also a girl, was born in 1882 but survived for only four months.

Konrad Adenauer was thus surrounded by siblings very close to his own age. He was never alone, but could always rely on a supportive family which would help him through difficult times. Little new information has emerged about the development and temperament of these four children from a middle-class home in Cologne; the only reliable sources remain the reports of subsequent generations.

The Adenauer children were brought up to be competitive but also to support one another. The strong bonds forged between them were to last a lifetime. All three brothers completed their *Abitur,* the school leaving certificate, in the same school, the Apostelngymnasium in the city. The eldest boy, August, went on to study law and became a respected lawyer. Konrad Adenauer later claimed that his own decision to study law, rather than join a bank as his father had planned, had been influenced by his classmates. However, the example of his brother must also have been influential: August completed his *Abitur* three years before his brother and had finished his legal studies by the time Konrad chose his own career.

August Adenauer, the eldest son, was as ambitious and hard-working as his more famous brother and appears to have been the more gifted lawyer. He not only completed his studies in the shortest possible time, but also quickly repaid his father for the cost of his training and helped to finance Adenauer's own studies. On three occasions during his life, August Adenauer established a flourishing legal practice. The first, set up before the First World War, was disrupted by his war service as a reserve officer in the Bonn Hussars. When he returned August began again, quickly gaining a reputation as one of the outstanding lawyers in Cologne and being awarded an honorary professorship at the university. After 1933 he was shunned because of his links with his brother; despite losing almost all his clients August survived this period by specialising in international civil law and building up a new practice. During the war he was bombed out, but started up once more in his weekend home in Gelsdorf after 1945. In May 1952 Konrad Adenauer was to leave a vital cabinet meeting in order to celebrate his brother's eightieth birthday.

By then the worst times were behind them. The bond between the brothers proved its durability during the critical years between 1933 and 1937, when August provided his brother's most important legal defence, helping him to dismiss criminal charges relating to his period as mayor and to win a more acceptable settlement in his legal dispute with the city of Cologne.

Adenauer's brother Hans also provided important support during bad times. In a staunch Catholic family it was expected that one of the sons would enter the priesthood, and it was Hans who followed this tradition. Unlike his two brothers, Hans had an affectionate and open temperament. In a note, written on New Year's Eve 1917, his brother Konrad described him as 'a man with a kind heart and almost too sensitive a disposition'.[15] Following his ordination, Hans lived in Fritzdorf, a town south-west of Bonn famous for its fruit-growing which Adenauer and his family enjoyed visiting on holiday. After the death of his first wife, Emma, Konrad Adenauer was to experience one of the worst periods of depression of his life. Every Sunday afternoon his brother would travel to see him from his new parish of Rath near Düsseldorf. Adenauer's oldest daughter Ria was then five years old; later she was to recall the long talks between her lonely father and her uncle at the Adenauer home on Max-Bruch-Straße. The relationship between the two brothers was further strengthened by her uncle's prolonged visit to St Blasien, where Konrad Adenauer was spending a three-month convalescence after a serious car accident.[16] In 1922 Hans Adenauer was appointed a cathedral capitulary in Cologne, though it is not clear whether his brother played a role in the decision. He died in 1937.

Of all his siblings, Adenauer's sister Lilli played the most important role in his life – largely because of her marriage to Willi Suth, a lawyer who began his career with the Aachen District Court between 1909 and 1915. In October 1915 Suth was appointed legal assistant to the Cologne administration where, as Adenauer's direct subordinate, he was responsible for food supply. He was elected deputy of the city of Cologne early in 1920. It seems clear that Suth was regarded as highly competent since charges of nepotism played no part in the election and even the Social Democrats voted for him. Between 1920 and his fall from office in 1933, Adenauer entrusted Suth with the key department of finance within the

administration. During these years he was one of the mayor's most efficient and loyal subordinates.

However, as Adenauer became an increasingly controversial figure in
the late 1920s, charges of nepotism were finally made in relation to Suth.
The head of the SPD group, Görlinger, therefore suggested that it would
be better for Suth to accept the post of treasurer in Frankfurt-am-Main.
He declined, and was later removed from office at the same time as
Adenauer. After the Second World War Suth returned to favour even
before his brother-in-law, being appointed temporary mayor of Cologne
by the Americans. Subsequently, from 1946 until his retirement, he held
the position of *Oberstadtdirektor* in the city.

Throughout these years Adenauer had the fullest confidence in Suth in
matters both big and small. It was his brother-in-law who organised car
transport for him in 1946 when he was chairman of the fledgling CDU;
it was also Suth who borrowed some silverware from the city of Cologne
in 1950 when the infant Federal Republic had no suitable tableware with
which to entertain the French foreign minister, Robert Schuman.

The four Adenauer children grew to adulthood in the decades following German unification. They were raised in a modest, but harmonious
household, surviving on the relatively meagre salary of Johann Konrad
Adenauer. Following his appointment as secretary to the Court of Appeal
on 13 April 1873, Johann Konrad had an annual income of some seven-
hundred thalers. The family cupboards were frequently bare during Konrad Adenauer's childhood: the family went without meat on two Sundays
each December in order to afford a Christmas tree; in winter only the
kitchen and one other room were heated. Their mother supplemented the
family income by sewing oilcloth aprons, and when the sons were old
enough to offer private lessons they too made a contribution.

The Adenauers also took in lodgers. One of these was Konrad Tonger,
who became godfather to the future German Chancellor. Tonger
remained on very good terms with the family and later bequeathed his
godchild 30,000 marks, an incredible sum for the time. However, Johann
Konrad – like his son in years to come – was unfortunate with his investments; most of the inheritance was lost in the crash which followed the
economic boom of the 1870s. Adenauer remembered his godfather with
affection. He carefully preserved a gold watch Tonger had given him and
later had his grave moved from Cologne to the cemetery in Rhöndorf.

For the rest of his life Adenauer's attitude towards money was affected
by the frugal years of his childhood. His thrift – bordering on stinginess
– was to become legendary. Even as the well-paid mayor of Cologne,
Adenauer insisted on being reimbursed for all the expenses he incurred
on his official business. For example: '3 October 1932: in the interests of
the city of Cologne I have laid out 1.75 marks. This amount to be repaid
to me.'[17] As Federal Chancellor he once paid the Allied High Commis-

sioners the rare honour of an invitation to his home in Rhöndorf, where he served the less than sumptuous repast of sandwiches and wine. At home he took great pride in wearing an old jacket made for him by his tailor in Cologne before the war, and his daughters always had great difficulty persuading him to extend his limited wardrobe. He was notorious among local handymen for being difficult to please.

Of course Adenauer was also capable of generosity and undemonstrative support for good causes. In 1959, as Chancellor, he donated a half-ton bronze bell to his baptismal church of St Mauritius in Cologne and made contributions to his parish church in Rhöndorf, where a place of honour was reserved for him after he became Chancellor. Adenauer was also a regular contributor to children's charities. Good works and charitable giving, however, belong to a rather different category. It remains true that his everyday expenditures were dictated by those iron rules of thrift which became second nature to him in his first twenty-five years, both at home and university. These procilivities in him were reinforced by his father in particular. Once, when Adenauer and his friend Schlüter had made a six-week tour of northern Italy during their student days, on money saved from his monthly allowance of ninety marks, his father made a furious scene. In adulthood Adenauer kept detailed accounts of all his expenditures which were found in his desk in Rhöndorf after his death.

Thrift, however, was considered a virtue in all classes of society, not only at the time but well into the twentieth century. Adenauer was aware that wealthier men than himself were notoriously careful with money. In his later correspondence with Dannie N. Heineman he would now and then mention the example of the wealthy magnate August Thyssen: 'I know', he wrote, 'that he never used porters, never travelled first class and would get out of his car at the Ruhr bridge and walk across on foot in order to avoid the expensive toll.'[18]

For the Adenauers thrift was both a virtue and a necessity. Their two-storey house in the Balduinstraße was dark and narrow, with the first floor and half the ground floor rented out to lodgers. In later life Adenauer recalled sharing a bed with one of his brothers until he had turned seventeen and being forced to wear their old clothes. Surviving family photographs, of course, show all the children in their Sunday best.

Behind the house the Adenauers had a small garden with two vines, typical of many German city houses, plus a vegetable patch and a lawn which was used for bleaching linen. Later the family moved to a nearby apartment without a garden – a deprivation which seems to have encouraged Adenauer's love of nature and gardening in later life.

Holidays in the country must have seemed like paradise to the children. Then the family would visit a friend in Lessenich near Messdorf, a sexton who also ran a guest-house. There the young Konrad helped at hay-making and harvest and discovered an eagle-owl nesting in the church loft. Throughout his adult life Adenauer had a great love of the outdoors and, as a young lawyer, often dreamed of starting up as a notary on the outskirts of Cologne. Later, following his dismissal as mayor of Cologne, Adenauer chose to retire to the idyllic village of Rhöndorf. Most of his holidays were spent in the countryside or unspoiled areas of natural beauty. This love of nature was characteristic of millions of other Germans who, like Adenauer, had no deep roots in the city.

The Cologne of Adenauer's adulthood was no longer the romantic city of his youth. He was born in the last years of the medieval city wall and had played near its great ramparts. In 1878 the artist Jacob Scheiner had painted a romantic winter scene of the Hahnentor with horses pulling a sledge to the gates;[19] Balduinstraße, where Adenauer was born, lay close by. Although living conditions were relatively congested and unhealthy, the wall provided a wonderful children's playground. Adenauer's secretary, Anneliese Poppinga, recalled many years later how the eighty-eight year old Chancellor had spoken of his childhood: 'Horse-drawn carriages and buses frequented the streets. Everything was peaceful and leisurely, not so hectic and rushed as life today.'[20]

The city's modern era can be said to have begun when Adenauer was at school, with the demolition of the city wall and its transformation into a vast building site. It was a dramatic break with Cologne's past. Despite the tendency for childhood memories to be more rosy than the reality, Adenauer's recollections generally tally with historical records and surviving accounts. At this time, the most important values in his life were self-discipline, thrift, filial obedience, family, security and love of nature.

An important part was also played by religious observance: family prayers in the morning and evening; morning mass at the church of St Apostle on Sundays; silent prayers on Sunday afternoons. Johann Konrad was said to have knelt in front of a Black Madonna in a nearby street every day on his return home from work. Religious belief also permeated several family scenes which left a profound impression on the young Adenauer. Three-quarters of a century later Konrad Adenauer vividly recalled his father kneeling to pray with his wife and children when he discovered that his infant daughter had contracted meningitis, and asking God to take her to Him rather than leave her mentally retarded. Not until later did the young Adenauer fully understand that his father had been praying for her death.

Both children's upbringing and their adult lives were deeply influenced by religion. Adenauer attended church every Sunday until the end of his life. When on his trips abroad, he would try to attend Mass; foreign correspondents reported that he knelt in prayer during his visits to Paris, Washington, Rome and Moscow. Until his death he was the most famous Catholic dignitary in the Corpus Christi procession from Honnef to the island of Grafenwerth. Grace was always said in the Adenauer home and, both as mayor of Cologne and Chancellor of West Germany, Konrad

Adenauer would conscientiously fast during Lent. He was to bring up his own children with the same religious awareness of human fallibility and sinfulness in which he had himself been raised. References to hell-fire and purgatory were a frequent part of his parental discipline. His children were convinced that their father retained a literal faith in these terrors for many years. Fear of God and God's wrath were a cardinal element of his religious beliefs, and it was only in later years that he began to question the truth of at least some of these dogmas.

Adenauer's deep religious faith had two aspects – fear of, but also complete trust in, a personal God. It was a faith to which he referred only in times of great crisis, for example when his sons came to visit him in autumn 1944 following his imprisonment by the Nazis: 'We are in the hands of God', he told them.[21] To non-believers in a less religious age, Adenauer's faith may seem striking and even embarrassing. Nevertheless, it is impossible to understand his complex personality without taking into account both the religious aspect of his upbringing and his life-long faith.

Sunday was naturally the day when religious observance in the Adenauer household was at its height. During Adenauer's years as mayor, his acquaintances reported that Sundays were boring and austere: other children were not allowed into the house and his own children were not allowed out. Sunday was kept sacred, with strict attendance at Mass and regular confession. Neither snow nor rain was permitted to keep the children away from school Mass during weekdays or family Mass on Sunday.

Like many religious people Adenauer took a serious approach to sexual morality. He demanded to know the details of his children's reading and forbade all literature he considered pernicious, as his own father had done before him. Once, as mayor of Cologne, he even returned as unsuitable a gift from an industrialist in the city – the memoirs of Casanova.[22] He also appears to have observed the church's strict ban on premarital and extramarital sexual relationships, though in this respect biographer are bound to restrain their judgement.

These were the virtues which Konrad Adenauer was taught to respect as a child and which he demonstrated later as Chancellor. All were rooted in his family background: hard-working, diligent, lower middle class and devoutly Catholic. However hard biographers may seek new and more sensational information, none has been discovered as yet.

Signs of Adenauer's distinct personality are hard to detect during a childhood spent within a close-knit family and an extended circle of relations in Cologne, Bonn, Messdorf and Lessenich. There is simply not enough information, and much of what exists is subjective. Adenauer's own memory was excellent even in old age; his recollections have been verified in those cases where they can be compared with other sources. Yet he talked only of events he had witnessed personally, and remained silent on many others.

Aside from his own memories there are few anecdotes about his childhood. One of these, from his former classmate Hubert Lohmer, who was to become a health officer in Cologne, tells of the young Adenauer pestering and cajoling his mother into giving him money for a book on botany.[23] At a pinch this could be seen as providing early evidence of a lifelong stubbornness and tenacity – a refusal to abandon plans he had formed. Adenauer was also observed to behave like a dutiful boy in his mother's presence for as long as she lived. In this, too, he was by no means unusual. Between the ages of nine and fourteen he was an avid reader of adventure stories by such authors as Karl May, Sophie Wörishofer and Jules Verne – a common habit in an age without television. Some tales also survive of Adenauer's capacity for school pranks. On one occasion, for example, he persuaded his sick teacher Herr Brüggemann to tell him the topics that would appear in the *Abitur* examination, and then the class wrote out in advance the German essay and the Latin translation.

More significant are the stories of Adenauer's physical ailments as a child. For example, 'for six weeks he had to lie in plaster and later walk around with steel braces up to his hips'.[24] His family also knew that he had survived tuberculosis, an illness which was common at the time and not necessarily linked with malnutrition. Following his student days he suffered a recurrence of the illness and, even after his recovery, his lungs remained susceptible to infection for the rest of his life.

Frequent illness in children can encourage both stoicism and a certain introversion. Though we cannot be certain to what extent this was the case with Adenauer, his classmate Lohmer later recalled that he 'seemed to be a rather eccentric boy'. In old age Adenauer himself remembered 'that he had been very shy as a child and even as a young man. When people spoke to him his face always went red.'[25] Someone, who as a girl attended the same dance class as Adenauer, recalled him as clumsy and far from polished.'[26]

Adenauer's occasional awkward behaviour as a Gymnasium pupil, especially in the presence of girls, was due in part to his unpretentious background. These handicaps help to explain why Adenauer took so long to mature and realise his potential in early manhood. His legendary self-discipline may well have been the product of both his physical weakness and his humble social origins.

Too little is known about his early years to draw general conclusions from these observations. Adenauer seems to have remained free from serious illness at the Gymnasium, though he had been a sickly child at elementary school and was to suffer again after university. Reports of his isolation from fellow pupils tend to contradict other stories of mischief-making with his friends. In any case, it is clear that the young Konrad was neither a genius nor a born leader with fixed objectives. The two features which do stand out in his childhood, as in his later life, were religious conviction and a capacity for hard work.

At home the Adenauer children were taught to believe that work was the only route to success in life. School had to be taken seriously; Adenauer's father had spent many evenings at home teaching his children to read and write and enabling them to skip the first year of elementary school. For Johannn Konrad the great hurdle was surely the acceptance of his sons into the grammar school, the Apostelngymnasium. Entry into this establishment meant that they had reached the top of the educational pyramid: at a time when the Adenauer children were successfully completing the *Abitur*, ninety-two per cent of German children were receiving only an elementary-school education. Of the remaining eight per cent only a fraction attended a classical Gymnasium.

Education at a Gymnasium offered the key to social entry to the university. Furthermore, pupils from élite schools such as the Protestant Royal Friedrich-Wilhelm Gymnasium or the Catholic Aposteln, Marzellén-Gymnasium had reached the tip of the social pyramid in a highly stratified society. They wore caps, blazers, ties and collars which set them apart from their elementary-school peers.

The Apostelngymnasium, founded in 1860, was situated in an imposing neo-romanesque building designed by the famous Cologne architect, Raschdorff. Each of its eight classrooms could hold fifty pupils and – a sign of modernity – it had modern physics equipment. However, there were also two rooms for the incarceration of badly behaved pupils. The school's headmaster and domestic staff had apartments on the premises.[27] By the time Adenauer arrived the school was in its twenty-sixth year and no longer seemed fresh and modern, at least to its pupils. Even in old age Adenauer was able to recite a favourite piece of doggerel about his school as a 'shop of horrors' where little boys were tortured.[28]

The school lay in a busy part of the city, near the market in Apostles Square and a local fire station. By the front of the building were points and a station for horse-drawn trams. The sounds of the city being modernised echoed through the corridors during lessons.

Most of the funds for building the school were provided by an endowment from a Catholic foundation. Originally the school bore the name of 'Catholic Gymnasium at the Apostles Church', but the state gradually provided more of the funds and finally took full control of the school. In 1876, the year of Adenauer's birth, it changed its name to 'Royal Catholic Gymnasium at the Apostles Church'. Perhaps the new name reflected the desire of the school board and the teaching faculty for a synthesis of Christian humanism and Prusso-German patriotism in the curriculum. Its headmaster, August Waldeyer, who remained throughout Adenauer's years at the school, emphasised this new direction in his inaugural speech.

Though the school had always been open to pupils of all religious denominations, its Catholic character was unmistakable. Mass was held every morning until restricted to Thursdays and Sundays by a change of policy in the 1870s. Another tradition ended by the *Kulturkampf* was for students to take part in the annual Corpus Christi procession carrying two large flags. The Mass *pro fundatoribus*, however, was held each year on 3 November. Until 1929, pupils in the lower classes would go to the school with their parents after their first communion in order to receive the congratulations of the head. The school also encouraged patriotism among its students: the Kaiser's birthday was celebrated every year with a special assembly, with choir-singing and speeches and the awarding of prizes to outstanding pupils.

Appropriately enough, the most vociferous patriot was the veteran choir-master, Hermann Knipper, who also composed for a local male-voice choir and worked as a concert critic. He was a man for whom Adenauer had no great affection. In the early 1890s Knipper staged a performance of his own works, with titles which speak for themselves: 'Prince Heinrich of Prussia's Travels Round the World' (1890) with prologue, main section, epilogue and trumpet fanfare, and 'For the Fatherland' (1892). In 1893 Adenauer and his friends were treated to a performance of 'From School to War', recounting the adventures of three pupils who had taken part in the Franco-Prussian War of 1870.

Adenauer was thus exposed to a heavy dose of patriotic and Teutonic rhetoric during his nine years at school. His political contemporaries, like later observers, were curious to know how much he had been affected by these sentiments. What is clear is that his schooling, with its symbiosis of Catholic and Prusso-German sentiment, betrayed no sign of that latent antipathy towards Prussia which was thought to be characteristic of the Cologne middle classes. Nor was there any hint at the Apostelngymnasium of any ultramontane Catholic disregard for German unity and the empire.

Yet patriotic and religious celebrations played only a minor part in the everyday life of the school. In its core curriculum the school was a classical Gymnasium like hundreds of others throughout Germany, with the ancient languages at the centre. Though in 1892 a decree was issued ordering more hours to be devoted to German, physics and gymnastics at the expense of Latin and Greek, teaching continued to be dominated by the classics. The lion's share of the thirty-six hours of lessons each week was taken by the major *Abitur* courses of religion, German, Latin, Greek, French history, geography, mathematics, physics, gymnastics and singing. Latin and Greek continued to account for fourteen hours of study even in 1893.

Adenauer adapted to his schooling in the same way as generations both before and since. There is no doubt that he was a diligent pupil. In later years he was generous in his praise of the classical Gymnasium, though not without a characteristic note of irony. He visited his old school three times in later years, as Chancellor and after his retirement, to extol its Christian spirit and liberality of outlook. Yet he was not excessively fulsome: 'Ladies and Gentlemen', he told his audience on one occasion, 'I do not intend to go down memory lane. All of us who have been at school are in the know; we don't have to fool ourselves.'[29]

Other former pupils had similar memories. One of them, Rudolf Amelunxen, first minister-president of the new Land of North Rhine Westphalia after the Second World War, attended the school from 1900 and recalled it as an 'illustrious institution'.[30] Adenauer himself would probably have been less bombastic. Bernhard Falk, who had been at the school ten years before the young Adenauer, also had praise for its agreeable classical education. According to Falk, the Protestant teacher of religious instruction had been the only non-Catholic member of staff; over three-quarters of the students had also been Catholics, usually from particularly devout families. Falk himself came from an Orthodox Jewish home, but claimed that the school had demonstrated the most sincere religious tolerance he had ever encountered.[31]

Naturally the school had its darker side. Amelunxen, for example, recalled several 'vicious teachers', including one 'who tormented us by boxing our ears, six to eight blows each side … He was only withdrawn after he had damaged the eardrums of one of my classmates'.[32] In addition, the school was a crammer which placed great emphasis on learning by rote. Adenauer consequently belonged to a generation of students who, even in old age, could recite by heart long passages from Virgil, Horace and Homer.

The actual influence of a classical education is difficult to gauge. Most classical Gymnasia at that time concentrated on text comprehension and translation above all else. The comment on Adenauer's *Abitur* report reflects this emphasis: 'He combines good knowledge of grammar with skill in the interpretation and translation of the school texts.'[33] His abilities in Latin and Greek were assessed as 'good'. It is not clear, however, whether Adenauer's encounter with classical literature, philosophy and history provided him with lasting intellectual stimulation in line with the original aims of the classical Gymnasium. In later life, though he made positive references to the value of the Graeco-Roman heritage, his statements were relatively general and superficial.

Adenauer apparently showed a genuine interest in one specific area of classical studies. One of his teachers, Professor Ernst Petit, was an acquaintance of Heinrich Schliemann, the discoverer of Troy, and in 1879 he published *A Journey to Athens and Argos* to awaken interest in Greek art. Every Sunday Petit would invite Adenauer and a number of his friends to his home to show them photographs of the latest archaeological digs and encourage their interest in Greek culture. Many years later, Adenauer was to claim that it had been Petit who had inspired his life-long interest in art. He had, according to Adenauer, invested his meagre savings in paintings and sculptures as well as subscribing to a monthly art magazine with high quality reproductions.[34]

Adenauer's aesthetic interests were eventually shifted from the ancient world towards Dutch paintings and late-Gothic art. He was never a collector of antiques, although he kept in his study a statue presented to him during a state visit to Athens. The only painting with a classical theme in his collection was an oil-painting of a Greek temple, which was given pride of place behind the desk in his office in the Bonn Bundesrat. In this case, however, it was the artist and not the subject which was important: the painting was a gift from Winston Churchill. In any case, it was due to the Apostelngymnasium that Adenauer developed a hobby that provided him with great satisfaction; this was the ability to appreciate fine pieces of art.

During his nine years at the Apostelngymnasium the young Adenauer developed other hobbies and interests. Though in practical matters a profoundly unsentimental man, he had a lasting love of German poetry. As Chancellor he was said to read a poem every night before settling down to sleep.[35] During his incarceration in a concentration camp in 1944 he found solace in Eichendorff's poem 'Aus dem Leben eines Taugenichts' (From the Life of a Good-for-Nothing),[36] and was comforted in his subsequent imprisonment by his ability to recite numerous poems he had learned by heart at school.

His secretary Anneliese Poppinga recalls that Adenauer tended to prefer melancholy and serious poetry. To celebrate his ninety-first birthday she asked the publishers Deutsche Verlags-Anstalt to produce a special edition of his favourite poems, mostly works he had memorised at school. Poetry anthologies during his childhood – especially those in use at schools – were extensive, often stretching to five hundred pages, and tended to concentrate on hymns to nature, patriotic songs, and contemplative and didactic poetry. The most popular poets were Ernst Moritz Arndt, Chamisso, Joseph von Eichendorff, Goethe, Heine, Nikolaus Lenau, Eduard Mörike, August Graf von Platen, Friedrich Rückert, Schiller, Theodor Storm and Ludwig Uhland. These were also the poets of which Adenauer was most fond. The collection published in his honour included many nature poems as well as contemplative poetry such as Schiller's 'Hoffnung' and Goethe's 'Gesang der Geister über dem Wasser', and tragic ballads such as Heine's 'Die Wallfahrt nach Kevelaer'. It is noticeable that Adenauer did not include patriotic poetry among his personal favourites. Had he turned away from patriotic verses, overfed by zealous teachers? Or had he always shied away from national and heroic phrases from the very beginning? Probably not the latter. A cursory glance at the public speeches he gave as mayor of Cologne between 1916 and 1918 is sufficient to reveal that he was no less susceptible to such sentiments than most of his contemporaries. Other poems in the collection, by

Friedrich Nietzsche, Richard Dehmel, Josef Weinheber and Hermann Hesse, were not included in the standard school anthologies.

Throughout his life Adenauer loved to memorise, recite and read poetry – and in youth even to write his own. His tastes in this sphere remained constant. He had little sympathy for the Expressionist poets, nor for the neo-Romantic Hugo von Hofmannsthal. Nor was there a single line by great twentieth-century authors such as Bertolt Brecht, Gottfried Benn, Karl Krolow and Paul Celan. Quite obviously, Adenauer's preferences were profoundly influenced by the education he had received at school.

Adenauer first began to enjoy the performing arts – opera, drama, comedy – when he was a student in Munich. His experience of these art forms during his school-days was very limited, primarily because he could not afford to pay for tickets.

For his *Abitur* examination Adenauer had to answer one of three questions. He and his twenty classmates had discovered the topics beforehand:

1. Why is a German right to be proud of his Rhine?
2. Tasso and the two female characters in Goethe's play.
3. Misfortune itself has little value; but it has three good children: strength, experience, pity.

Much to the regret of historians and journalists, Adenauer chose not to answer the first topic, which perhaps would have provided valuable grist to the mills of open or veiled nationalists critical of his Rhineland policy between 1918 and 1924. He also avoided the third question, being too inexperienced at eighteen to have anything useful to say (although at seventy he would not have been at a loss for an answer). His essay on Tasso and the female characters in Goethe's play was not particularly good, being a typically stilted *Abitur* essay containing the usual platitudes: 'Of all the characters Countess Leonore is the least noble, although she does not deserve to be described as plain bad. Beautiful, clever, charming, she has both feet on the ground and knows how to influence people, but she is scheming and vain ...'

Adenauer's description of Tasso reveals rather more of his own ideas: 'Tasso possesses the two main qualities of a gifted poet: a sensitive temperament and a creative imagination. But these valuable gifts make him very introspective and isolate him from other people. He turns his back on the realities of life and becomes lost in solitude. In consequence his character, which can "only be shaped in the current of life", remains untried and untested. Imagination works at the expense of will and energy; there is no powerful striving and struggling for clear goals which makes a man into a real man.'

Given the development of the writer over the following decades, this last sentence has a real resonance. At the time of his *Abitur* Adenauer was still an immature boy, as revealed in the concluding lines of his essay: 'So the man Tasso was ruined; he threw his happiness away for ever. Only one thing is left to him: he can sing his song to the world in sweet melody; poetry remains as a solace to him, which provides us with a consoling view of his future.'

The essay was below Adenauer's usual standard in German. His overall *Abitur* grade in German was 'good', and the report took pains to stress where his strengths lay: 'He has developed the ability to deal logically with themes he is set and to write about them correctly and fluently. He has shown the same skill in oral presentation. His knowledge of leading German writers and their main works is thoroughly satisfactory. The examination essay was merely satisfactory.'

Even in old age Adenauer could still be amused by a similar assessment made by his German teacher at elementary school: 'The essays are short but are well and clearly organised. Adenauer, organisation is your strength!'[37] The truth of these remarks was to be amply confirmed in later life by the outlines of his numerous speeches and memoranda, carefully planned and structured with roman and arabic numbers and written in his sweeping hand. A talent for organisation was something that the young Adenauer learned at school.

His schooling also gave him knowledge which was of little use in his professional career but appealed to his inventive brain and encouraged a lasting interest. In physics he obtained the grade of 'good' and the following remarks: 'Through his enthusiastic participation in lessons he has gained a satisfactory knowledge of physics.' In the 1890s this science had been given greater emphasis in the German school curriculum. Adenauer himself was so fascinated by it that, after 1904, he began to work on his own inventions in his spare time. Eventually he began a correspondence with the Imperial Patent Office and with the Cologne patent lawyer Dr Rülf.

Between 1904 and 1908 Adenauer devoted much attention to his scientific projects, including 'The Elimination of Dust Generated by Automobiles', 'Reactive Steam Engines', 'Improved Cylinders for Vehicles Powered by Steam etc.'. During his enforced retirement between 1935 and 1943 he was to return to a hobby which probably had its origins in physics lessons at school. As always Adenauer took his efforts very seriously and exhibited the commitment of the auto-didact; on several occasions the engineers at the Patent Office had to return his work on 'Reactive Steam Engines' with details of basic flaws in his logic. Without doubt Adenauer had developed an extended basic knowledge of physics and of general scientific laws. It is this most advanced branch of higher education that captured his imagination.

Adenauer's school reports provide little information about his work in history, the field in which biographers have the greatest interest. In his *Abitur* report he was awarded the grade 'good' for both history and geography: 'He has a satisfactory knowledge of the most important events in world history, particularly German and Prussian history, with their dates, locations and historical causes. In geography he has also fully satisfied the necessary requirements.'

No significant conclusions can be drawn from comments as vague as these. His own later comments, in conversations and when working on his memoirs in old age, must be treated with some caution. They do not relate to history lessons as such, but to the political attitudes of the pupils and one of his teachers. When Adenauer wanted to convince American listeners that Germany had an honourable democratic tradition, he occasionally told the story of a teacher, an ardent republican who had made a deep impression on his pupils at the Gymnasium.[38] Adenauer did not say whether he himself had any republican sympathies during these early years. In fact, idealistic republicanism was by no means unusual among teachers at the time: most educated Germans knew of Theodor Mommsen's enthusiastic description of republican Rome, and Cologne remained proud of its part in the 1848 Revolution. Yet these sentiments did not prevent many former students, following their entry into the state administration, from accepting constitutional monarchy as the most natural form of government for modern Germany. Even Bismarck, in his memoirs which appeared in 1898, claimed to have left school convinced 'that the republic was the most sensible form of government'.

In fact the Gymnasium students did take some part in political activity at school. In 1888 the senior boys took sides in the local elections, engaged in disputes among themselves, sometimes beating each other up and working to get the voters to the polls (at a time when votes were cast publicly). Seventy years later Adenauer recalled that his father had been an admirer of Bismarck, but that he and his brothers had been critical of the old man's domestic policies, especially the anti-Socialist laws and the *Kulturkampf* against the Catholics. Since the young Konrad was only fourteen when Bismarck stepped down, either his brothers had done most of the talking or the conversations must have taken place after Bismarck's retirement, when he had continued to intervene in politics from his estate at Friedrichsruh.

Adenauer had no reservations about calling Bismarck a 'very great and far-sighted man' in the realm of foreign affairs. In August 1957, as Chancellor, he was to describe Bismarck as 'a great international statesman but a very bad domestic politician', a comment which must be taken to include the facts of German unification themselves. His only specific criticisms were of Bismarck's domestic policies, and his reasons were entirely conventional: the anti-Socialist legislation had been a mistake because domestic affairs would have developed 'much more healthily' without it. Even more significant was Adenauer's retrospective criticism of the *Kulturkampf* as preventing the establishment of a strong German Liberal Party on the fertile ground of the German west. Instead, the

Catholics, feeling isolated and under attack, had joined the Centre Party; religious differences, far from being diminished, had been intensified.

Adenauer had no such criticism of Bismarck's foreign policy: 'Germany was a great power on the international scene and that was indisputably the achievement of Bismarck. But by his domestic policy Bismarck prevented this immense power being given a solid foundation.'[39]

What was Adenauer's attitude towards Prussia? Though this was a controversial question in later years, there is little evidence available on this stage of his life. One of the most important accounts of the mood among Adenauer's fellow pupils in Cologne was provided by Professor Heinrich Lehmann. Born like Adenauer in 1876, Lehmann also attended the Apostelngymnasium although a year behind the young Konrad. The two men forged an acquaintance and a mutual respect that was to last for life. Before his appointment to the new University of Cologne in 1921/22 as its second rector, Lehmann was an expert in economic law at the University of Strasbourg.

The Lehmann family had moved to Cologne in 1891 following the father's appointment as prosecutor to the District Court. Lehmann's observations on entering the upper school are of particular interest: 'At the Gymnasium I had a circle of friends who, for the most part, came from staunch Catholic families which had – at the very least – a critical approach towards Bismarck and the Prussianisation of Germany. After history lessons pupils would engage in debates in which the idealisation of Frederick the Great was criticised, with reference to Onno Klopp and other historians, and Bismarck's cultural policy was vehemently condemned.'[40] These observations tally with Adenauer's own reports. Lehmann continued:

> I did not detect any real sympathy for Prussia among my Cologne-born fellow pupils from Catholic families and this, for the first time, made me aware of the differences among the German tribes. I can still vividly remember the day one of my school friends told me: 'We Rhinelanders are the true Germans. The Prussians are Obotrites, Wends, Slavs and the like who have put together their state by theft and violence.'

However, Lehmann then added an important rider:

> This anti-Prussianism in the Rhineland declined over the years as the memories of the *Kulturkampf* faded, the Centre Party attained significant influence in the legislative bodies, and the advantages of belonging to the Imperial state forged by Bismarck became perceptible. Nevertheless, many Rhinelander never completely lost their suspicions of Prussia's rather anti-Catholic cultural policy.

There is some evidence that Adenauer himself belonged to this circle of friends 'from staunch Catholic families'. If so, Lehmann's description is probably an accurate portrayal of the young Adenauer's attitudes at the time. The school took some time to complete its synthesis of Catholicism and Prussianism – and Adenauer was never wholly to lose his feeling of cultural superiority towards Prussia. Yet there is no evidence to suggest that, as a schoolboy, he was critical of German unification by Prussia. Nor are there any signs of criticism of 'Little Germany' typical of those contemporaries who wanted a 'Greater Germany' including Austria or who after 1866, mainly for religious reasons, deplored the exclusion of this great Catholic country.

It is reasonable to assume that the young student had some cultural misgivings and that he shared the standard reservations about Prussian cultural-religious policy and the anti-Socialist laws. Yet the evidence is not sufficient to justify upholding the myths about his intrinsic hostility towards Prussia and disloyalty towards the Reich. It is more likely that Johann Konrad – the veteran of Königgrätz – and his family were as proud and enthusiastic about the creation of a powerful and unified Germany as most other Germans. Such sentiments could easily exist alongside a desire for the Rhineland Germans to have more political clout within the Reich.

One vital and under-estimated aspect of Adenauer's life as a school-boy was the fact that he and his fellow pupils belonged to an 'interim generation'. The passions unleashed by the Revolution of 1848 had sub-sided and a united Germany had been established almost twenty years before. Outside small circles of initiates the name of Nietzsche was almost unknown, and the diverse and frenetic cultural life of late-Wil-helminian society, which included the Wandervogel youth movement, lay some distance in the future. The Apostelngymnasium was a thor-oughly conventional institution. It did not produce young intellectuals with an awareness of the dangers and problems of late-nineteenth-cen-tury society. Instead its young students read the popular German authors of the day in addition to writers such as Rudyard Kipling and Joseph Conrad (who was still considered an adventure writer at the time).

Adenauer's education is also significant for what it did *not* contain. Although there were fourteen hours of Latin and Greek in the curriculum and the *Abitur* required the ability to translate from German into Latin, the young Adenauer did not learn French conversation or study English at all. He was never to study or live abroad for any length of time during his pro-fessional career. Adenauer's inability to master a foreign language was to be a lifelong handicap. It was one he shared with other German politicians of his generation: Stresemann, for example, spoke French just as badly. Nevertheless, Adenauer was always troubled by his need for an interpreter when speaking to foreign dignitaries, and he always stressed to his chil-dren the value of foreign study. As an old man he even asked his secretary, Anneliese Poppinga, to practise English conversation with him so that he would at least be able to utter a few phrases during a state visit to London.

In later years Adenauer was to recall having wanderlust as a child. By the age of seventeen he had read many books on South America, particularly Brazil with its 'large German colonies ... in which the conductors spoke German on the trains'. For a period he hoped to visit Brazil, and he continued to take a positive view of colonialism for many years. As an old man Adenauer was to give two reasons for his youthful idea of emigration to Brazil – to start a new life, and to escape the social barriers that held back hard-working men and women in Germany.

Adenauer went to school when Cologne was still a relatively relaxed city in which coaches and horse-drawn trams represented the only forms of transportation. His school years were tranquil. Bismarck's comments about his own education – 'I left school as a normal product of our state-run classrooms' – could also apply to Adenauer. When he completed his schooling on 6 March 1894, his school report described him as a good student and awarded grade 2 in every category except singing (grade 1). As regards 'conduct and diligence', his teachers Velten and Müller observed: 'His conduct was always orderly and beyond reproach. He gave his full attention and diligence to classroom activities.' It was signed by the headmaster, Waldeyer.

Since Adenauer's two older brothers were already students and the funds from the Tonger inheritance were exhausted, plans were made for the young Konrad to train in banking at the Seligmann bank. However, this career was abandoned after no more than a few weeks when, as Adenauer recalled, his father decided to continue saving in order to finance his youngest son's legal studies.[41] Konrad had wanted to study law for several years and, even though the question of finance had still to be resolved, the *Abitur* commission had been convinced that he was leaving school 'in order to devote himself to the study of law'.

Student Years
in Freiburg, Munich and Bonn

Why did Adenauer begin his law studies first in Freiburg in Breisgau, and then move to Munich? The answer is quite simple: the 'herd mentality' prevailing among Cologne students. One of his contemporaries was Heinrich Lehmann who finished school one year later than Adenauer and migrated in the same direction. He wrote in his memoirs: 'In April 1895 I went to the beautiful town of Freiburg with a group of friends, including old boys of other Cologne Gymnasia. It was normal for many Rhinelanders to spend their first term there. Young law students in particular went in droves, causing lectures in the first term to be overcrowded although in subsequent terms only the people from Baden attended them.'[1]

Since Adenauer never provided detailed information about his university years, it is sensible to examine the comments of Lehmann, whose student career was very similar. The general idea was that during the early Wilhelmine era Freiburg offered something of a holiday term for young men who were preparing for a career as judges, lawyers, academics and administrative civil servants: 'Naturally the number of students who enrolled for lectures was much higher than the number who actually attended. The temptations of Freiburg and its beautiful surroundings – the nearby Black Forest, Höllental and Feldberg – were too great to assure regular attendance.'

Just as important as the lectures – and for some of these young men more important – were the student associations, which made every effort to recruit 'even vaguely suitable students'. Like Adenauer the previous year, Lehmann therefore joined Brisgovia: 'Since my best friends had decided to join the Catholic student association Brisgovia I followed their example, particularly because I had no taste for wearing student colours and adopting rigid codes of conduct. Brisgovia drinking sessions were kept within acceptable limits and the corporation, which sometimes had Protestant guests, laid its main emphasis on informal gatherings and hikes. Because the association had accepted so many 'foxes' (freshmen), around thirty or forty, smaller groups of like-minded students soon got together for outings or spent the evenings together in their rooms, in pubs, or at Dattlers on the Schlossberg with its spectacular view. My Cologne friends and I thus remained in a tight-knit group augmented only by a few fellow members or guests of the association.'

This picture of a first term at Freiburg is completed by the accounts given by other association members to Paul Weymar, Adenauer's biographer, in the 1950s.[2] The social environment of Brisgovia was well suited to Adenauer, consisting mainly of the sons of civil servants or small businessmen. One of Adenauer's closest friends, Raimund Schlüter, was from a Westphalian farming family. Other social groups congregated in other student fraternities: the *jeunesse dorée* in the Corps, and the Protestant middle class in the traditional corporations, the *Burschenschaften.*

During his studies in Freiburg Adenauer apparently remained hardworking and thrifty, combining study and leisure activities without undue effort. Long walks in the Black Forest would be followed by evening visits to an inn on the Feldberg; Sunday walks to Sankt Blasien and Titisee were accompanied by return hikes through the Höllental – but Adenauer always appeared punctually for lectures at eight o'clock on Monday morning. Ten years later, in February 1904, he was to return to Freiburg on honeymoon with his first wife Emma, drawn by the peaceful and lovely town and its cathedral.[3]

The Baden area of the Black Forest became one of Adenauer's favourite holiday resorts and he was to return to the Schweigmatt in the early 1920s. In later years he also discovered the northern Black Forest. In October 1935, in the difficult weeks after his expulsion by the Nazis from the administrative district of Cologne, he retired to the spa hotel of St Elisabeth in Freudenstadt, and returned the following year. On both occasions the weather was appalling, as he wrote to friends: 'We are stuck here in bad weather. If you know Freudenstadt then you know what that means.'[4] As Federal Chancellor in the 1950s he occasionally held meetings on the Bühlerhöhe; during one of these breaks, on 30 August 1954, he was to receive the unwelcome news of the French National Assembly's rejection of the European Defence Community (EDC).

In the summer of 1894 – or as in retrospect, it was to appear to Adenauer and many of his contemporaries – Imperial Germany was experiencing a golden age. Very few among this generation of students were able to detect the warning signals of a more dangerous and uncertain future, though Lehmann was later to recall a lecture on Nietzsche 'who had appeared on the scene like a blazing comet'. It is very unlikely, however, that Adenauer was touched by the spiritual and intellectual turmoil of the *fin de siècle*.

Konrad Adenauer was still only eighteen years old. Photographs of him at this time, often bearing his nickname 'Toni', show an adolescent with a wide oval face, moustache, dreamy eyes and sensitive hands. Physical signs of his strong will and self-discipline – which were eventually to dominate his features – only began to appear five years later, during his training for the higher civil service. At eighteen he still had the appearance of a well-behaved and malleable youth. A student acquaintance of the young Konrad was later to recall, in the 1950s: 'He always gave the impression of living separate from others behind an insulating wall.'[5] At this stage he had yet to develop his own identity. Moreover, his freedom continued to be restricted by shortage of money: Adenauer was still dependent on a monthly allowance of ninety marks from his father and a foundation in Cologne. His first university books were carried in an oil-cloth bag made for him by his mother; he kept it all his life and, in 1964, in response to questions about his student days in Freiburg, was able to produce it from a cabinet in his study.[6]

The family home in Cologne continued to be a main focus of Adenauer's life. He took part in the 41st German Katholikentag (Convention of Catholics) in the city in August 1894, before moving for two terms to study in Munich. In choosing this location he was again following the usual pattern adopted by the rising lawyers of Cologne, as Lehmann indicates: 'For the second and third terms I went to Munich, again following my friends from Cologne ...'[7] In Munich as in Freiburg Adenauer remained a conscientious student, attending the obligatory lectures, but he was now able to combine his studies with visits to the opera, concert hall and art galleries as well as continuing with his walks.

Most intelligent students, including Lehmann, adopted the same course. Lehmann recalled that this was a vibrant time for the performing arts in Munich: the directors von Possart and Levi had introduced the revolving stage to the Residenz theatre; Richard Strauss came to play the harpsichord with his left hand while conducting the orchestra with his right; the operas *Don Giovanni, Figaro* and *Rigoletto* were in almost constant performance, and belcanto opera could be heard at the State Opera. In addition, enthusiasm for Wagner was at its height. Tickets were inexpensive: a student would pay as little as 80 pfennigs for a place in the standing section.

Like Lehmann, who came to Munich a year later, Adenauer retained fond memories of these performances. Though he had seen his first opera, Lortzing's *Zar und Zimmermann,* in Cologne,[8] it was in Munich that he developed a genuine love of music. When he became mayor of Cologne he was to visit the opera and concert house on many occasions; much later, as Chancellor, he would spend his evenings listening to recordings of his favourite composers at home. His taste in music – Haydn, Mozart, Schubert, Beethoven – was as conservative as his taste in poetry.

It was also in Munich that Adenauer deepened his interest in the visual arts. He later recalled visiting the Alte Pinakothek at least three or four times each week in order to study the paintings which made a lasting impression on him. This seems to have been no exaggeration, since Lehmann had similar experiences: 'If we had no lectures, we spent the whole morning in the art museum, especially the Pinakothek. Apart from lectures we did no other work and simply lived, though in a cultural sense. We did not waste our youthful energy on degrading drinking or sexual excesses, but enjoyed seeing the greatest products of humanity.'

Life in Munich was still relatively cheap. As long as Adenauer managed his money sensibly, he could enjoy a good life on his monthly allowance of 90 marks. Lehmann kept a record of his own expenses which is helpful in reconstructing Adenauer's own lifestyle: a room with breakfast cost 27 marks per month; regular lunch at his local restaurant (soup, two courses and dessert) was 85 pfennigs, or one mark with a half litre of beer (11 pfennigs) and a small tip. For the first time in his life, then, Adenauer was able to save small sums for excursions and holidays. Later he remembered visits to the Bavarian lakes and holidays with his friend Raimund Schlüter in Bohemia, Switzerland and Italy.[9] On these occasions they would travel fourth class, often resort to walking and, if necessary, sleep in the waiting rooms of railway stations. Adenauer's friends in Freiburg all recalled him as an enthusiastic hiker.

Occasionally, when the money ran out, the two friends went hungry. Adenauer later enjoyed telling the story of his adventures at the Achensee in Northern Tyrol. He and Schlüter had reached the end of their tour of

Italy, had run out of money, and were considering whether to borrow some from a priest. As they walked along the side of the lake they saw two large, fresh fish that had been tossed onto the shore by a storm during the night. They climbed down to fetch the fish and took them gratefully to a local inn to be fried.

It seems that the main function of Adenauer's year in Munich was to widen his horizons even though, as a diligent student, he continued to attend lectures, for example by the economist Lujo Brentano. In later life he was often to return to the places he discovered during this year: to the Black Forest and Switzerland, and – in the late 1920s – to Bohemia with his second wife. Towards the end of his life, moreover, northern Italy became almost a second home.

Adenauer seems to have visited Italy twice during his student days in Munich. Among his papers were found a number of photographs of Venice, Innsbruck and the Eisack valley, with the insciption 'Whitsun Holidays Munich-Venice, S.S.Munich 1895'. One of these photographs – the bell tower of San Marco – bore the pencilled inscription 'Adenauer fecit' on the back.

In old age Adenauer also mentioned a six-week tour of Italy, again in the company of Schlüter, 'my only real friend'. This holiday was devoted to culture and took him to Venice, Ravenna, Assisi and Florence. On this occasion, however, there was an unhappy aftermath, with Adenauer's father furiously accusing him of wasting his time in Munich. The young Konrad not only had to provide a humiliating account of his expenses,[10] but was also forced to transfer his studies closer to home where he could be supervised by his family. In any case, he was required to complete his final terms at a Prussian university. Adenauer promised to devote his energies to work and to complete his studies in six terms, the shortest possible time.

Adenauer therefore spent an extended period in Bonn for the first time in his life. For a short while he lodged with his relatives in the bakery at Kasernenstraße 40, the old family home. He also joined a Catholic student association, the Bonn Arminia; Max Wallraf, his predecessor as mayor of Cologne, who had been an active member of the association eighteen years previously, later recalled that it had some sixty members, primarily from the Rhineland and Westphalia, reflecting many different academic disciplines.[11] Members included various politicians and senior civil servants, the most important of whom was Reich Chancellor Wilhelm Marx, who had been a member ten years before Adenauer joined. Ten years later the association was also to accept Robert Schuman, the son of a Lorraine customs officer who was to achieve prominence as a French and European statesman in the 1950s. Many of the most successful members of Arminia remained in contact in Cologne, where they helped younger associates to obtain influential posts in the city administration, the district court, and the education system.

Bonn, like Freiburg, was a stronghold of fraternity life. Though the scene was dominated by the élitist Corps, the Catholic organisations were also popular and lively; the members of Arminia, for example, visited restaurants in Bad Godesberg and enjoyed trips to the Schaumburger Hof, the Drachenfels, and Rolandsbogen. Later Adenauer enjoyed telling stories about his iron discipline and hard work as a student, about the times when he revised through the night with his feet in a tub of cold water to stop himself from falling asleep. Though his achievement of the grade 'good' in his civil service examination after the minimum six terms of study is testimony to his self-discipline, he also found time for hikes with his friends around Messdorf, the region he had known since childhood. Later, as mayor, he would talk of retiring to Honnef or Rhöndorf at the foot of the Breiberg.[12]

Adenauer, like most students, had greatly enjoyed his early student days, but subsequently turned his attention towards a career. The most famous teacher in the law faculty in Bonn was Professor Ernst Zitelmann; others included Hermann Seuffert, who taught criminal and trial law, and Konrad Cosack, who specialised in commercial law. Another, Julius Baron, was reputed to have prepared Herbert Bismarck for his examinations in Berlin, and – despite his Jewish origins – to have been rewarded with a professorship in Bonn over the opposition of the faculty. He was also the author of a brief and popular digest which prepared students for the civil service examination.[13]

Little is known of Adenauer's likes and dislikes in the subject, nor whether he followed the common pattern of employing a tutor to help him prepare for the examination. There is no indication that he was influenced by any specific teacher or school of thought. His approach seems rather to have been pragmatic. Much later, as Chancellor, whenever he was particularly irritated by Ludwig Erhard, Adenauer would observe that two terms of economics under Lujo Brentano had taught him more than enough. Yet his studies had been too short for him to acquire anything more than a superficial knowledge of academic trends and controversies.

Justitia Coloniensis

Adenauer was a young man of twenty-one when he began his four-and-a-half years of training for the higher civil service. He was still unpaid, and therefore remained financially dependent on his father. His application included a statement of his father's responsibility for his keep: 'For the five years of his legal training I commit myself to grant my son Konrad Adenauer the means of subsistence appropriate to his standing.

Notes for this section begin on page 704.

Cologne, 24 May 1897. Adenauer, Kanzleirat.'[1] Though we have no precise details of Johann Konrad's income, a man in a similar position is known to have received 3,600 marks a year plus a stipend of 297 marks for rent. It seems likely therefore, that Adenauer's father earned something in the region of 325 marks per month. Although Adenauer could live on less than the 90 marks he had received during his student days, he obviously remained a real financial burden for his father. At least his older brothers had now completed their own training: Hans Adenauer was accepted into the priesthood on 10 August 1897.

Psychologically, Adenauer faced a difficult relationship with his parents. As a student he had been more or less his own master, but was now forced to readjust to their standards and – even more difficult – show due gratitude. His continuing financial dependence on his family may have been a burden to him. Socially, too, his life as a student had been easier, since he had been accepted by his fellow students in Freiburg, Munich and Bonn, even those from more respected and wealthy families. Now, however, he was again a young man from a modest background, the poor son of a low-ranking civil servant. He was unable to meet on equal terms with other legal trainees of his own age, many of whom came from upper middle-class or academic homes.

A lifetime later, when Adenauer was world famous, he frankly admitted that he had felt socially inferior during this period. Even after he had passed his legal examinations and become a paid civil servant, he was not made welcome by many of the Cologne families who received his wealthier student colleagues. He was aware of his family's lack of social status and understood the restrictions associated with it.[2] However, 'young Mr Adenauer', as he was called to distinguish him from his father, could hardly have been indifferent to these problems.

Once Adenauer himself achieved high office after ten years in subordinate posts, he was often regarded as possessing 'the arrogance of the upstart'. Given the humiliations he had endured as a trainee and a junior civil servant, this reaction is not entirely surprising. Whenever his superiors assessed his performance during these years, they praised such attributes as his 'great diligence', 'enthusiasm', 'prudence', 'modesty', 'punctuality' and 'flexibility'. The element of condescension, even if unintentional, was unmistakable. These are virtues which are essential in any profession, but from a young man with Adenauer's humble background they were *de rigueur.*

His career postings were recorded in his file at the Royal District Court in Cologne, which contained 190 handwritten pages covering almost every day of his training and included the assessments of his superiors, his applications for leave, his absences due to illness, and his references.

On 28 May 1897, six days after receiving the grade 'good' in his legal examination, Adenauer took the oath of office at a public meeting of the

1st Civil Court: 'I Konrad Adenauer swear by Almighty God that I will be submissive, loyal and obedient to his Royal majesty, King of Prussia, my most gracious lord, will carry out to the best of my ability and conscience the duties of my office, and will conscientiously observe the constitution, so help me God.'

Traditionally the first posting for a legal trainee in Cologne was the District Court in Bensberg. Adenauer served there for nine months, learning the 'responsibilities of a judge and a clerk of the court', and demonstrated 'solid knowledge, a quick mind and practical skills. His performance was thoroughly satisfactory.'[3] This was followed by twelve months preparatory service at the Cologne District Court. For the first six weeks Adenauer was responsible for taking the minutes for the investigative committee, then spent one month in the 4th Criminal Court, five months in the 2nd Civil Court, two months in the 4th Civil Court and two months in the 1st Chamber for Commercial Affairs. On days when no proceedings were held he spent his afternoons working as a clerk of the court. Adenauer subsequently spent four months in the office of the state prosecutor, six months with *Justizrat* Schniewind, from whom he obtained a glowing reference, and the same with the Royal Notary, *Justizrat* Schäfer III. (Adenauer himself had to sign himself 'Adenauer II' throughout his legal traineeship in order to avoid confusion with his father.) On 3 January 1900 he was sent for a further six months 'preparatory service' to Cologne Lower District Court before spending October and November of that year working for Schniewind, who clearly admired his abilities. In December he returned to the Upper District Court. On 30 May 1901 Adenauer 'obediently' asked the President of the Royal District Court in Cologne 'to approve my admission to the final state examination'.

His assessments, which were exemplary, were dispatched to the Prussian Ministry of Justice in Berlin. He received a provisional assessment of each stage of his training on 12 September 1900, with a summary which ran as follows: 'His previous preparatory service can be described as "good". The conduct of the candidate both at work and in private was entirely appropriate.'

As always, such assessments contained additional information for those who knew where to look. The only doubtful comment, handwritten by the President of the District Court on 31 May 1901, appeared on the letter proposing Adenauer for the final state examination and accompanying the required documents. It noted: 'The candidate has been referred to the Home Reserve and has not served.' Not having served was unlikely to recommend him to the Prussian administration, a fact of which Adenauer must have been aware. It is surprising that, a conformist in every other respect, he had not fulfilled expectations on this issue. His conduct was certainly out of line with family tradition; in addition to his father's career, his brother August was an officer in the reserve.

Later in life, when asked why he had not served, Adenauer cited his ill health. The documents inform us that Adenauer (no. 130 on conscription list BIII in the city of Cologne) was transferred for service with the Home Reserve on 27 June 1898. A year before, on 8 July, he had asked for leave between 15 July and 1 September and then for eight more days 'with reference to an enclosed medical certificate'. This was granted and calculated as part of his preparatory service. Dr Keller, a specialist in illnesses of the ear, nose and throat, certified that 'the man in question has recently suffered from a bronchial catarrh which can best be cured by a holiday of at least six weeks in a particularly quiet rural area'. According to family legend, spots on Adenauer's lungs had been discovered shortly after he completed his studies, hinting at a recurrence of his tuberculosis. The certificate, however, made no such reference.

In the following year Adenauer produced a certificate from another doctor, also stating that he had chronic bronchial catarrh and required at least a month to convalesce. He was granted permission to take leave between 13 June and 10 July 1898, and again between 15 August and 11 September 1898. This incident appears to have ended his bout of ill-health, since thereafter he took only the leave to which he was entitled. Though the one-month leave at the end of his training in June 1899 was recorded as sickness leave, this seems to have been an administrative error.

It thus seems likely that Adenauer, who remained a keen hiker, remained susceptible to bronchitis during this period and was therefore exempted from military service. We cannot be sure how the Law Examination Commission in Berlin reacted to the comment in Adenauer's papers.

Rather surprisingly, since his previous grades had always been 'good', he received nothing better than 'satisfactory' for his *Assessor* examination (the second civil service examination) in October 1901. The reason for this unimpressive performance remains unknown, but the results were nearly catastrophic since he needed a better grade in order to obtain a position in the Upper District Court. At least Adenauer was now fully qualified and employed, although still without pay. He received his license to practice on 19 October 1901. The Ministry of Justice in Berlin instructed the President of the Upper District Court to find Adenauer an unpaid post in the Lower District Court. However, Adenauer instead requested a position in the State Prosecutor's Office. This was approved and, in January 1902, Adenauer obtained a position as temporary replacement for a sick prosecutor named Bacmeister. For the first time in his life, at the age of twenty-six, Adenauer received a modest salary.

Once again Adenauer tackled his work with diligence; one of his superiors soon noted that 'Herr *Assessor* Adenauer is excellently suited for the State Prosecutor's Office'. In an assessment of 24 March 1902 his work was described as 'very good' and on 6 May he was licensed as a full prosecutor by the Senior Prosecutor – though with the proviso that his license could be revoked.

Adenauer's career had begun. One year later, however, he was still working as assistant to the prosecutor on a monthly salary of 200 marks. When asked about this work later, he replied that it had not been particularly enjoyable. At 200 marks per month, and with little prospect of a successful career, this bleak assessment was hardly surprising. Nevertheless, sixty years later he was to remember his experiences there in a more positive light. During the 'Spiegel' affair, Chancellor Adenauer angrily ordered his Minister of Justice, Stammberger, to arrest General Reinhard Gehlen on charges of espionage. When told that this was impossible without a judicial warrant, Adenauer retorted that 'things were a lot easier at the Cologne Prosecutor's Office'.

In the autumn of 1903 Adenauer left the administration of justice. He was granted a year's leave of absence from October to enable him to act as temporary replacement for the ailing *Justizrat* Hermann Kausen. This assignment also opened up the prospect of the most prestigious lawyer's jobs at the Upper District Court. Though he could not know it at the time, Adenauer had taken the first step on a career path that would lead remarkably swiftly to the upper ranks of the city administration. After the first year, his leave of absence was extended for another twelve months, enabling him to serve two full years as a lawyer.

When his work as a replacement ended on 10 October 1905, Adenauer took four weeks of leave. He then submitted a medical certificate confirming that he had diabetes and prescribing another period of leave – between four and six weeks – in which to recover his strength. It remains uncertain whether this illness – for which there was no generally effective treatment – was first detected at this time, but it was to trouble Adenauer for the next fifteen years. As First Deputy he was forced by the illness to observe strict discipline in his consumption of food and drink. Later Adenauer was to admit to Anneliese Poppinga that he had not always been able to keep to his diet: 'He would then eat heartily and afterwards drank a glass of warm water and stuck his finger down his throat.'[4]

The sick leave was granted. From the point of view of the President of the District Court, however, it quickly became clear that Adenauer wanted to move on. On 6 October 1905 Adenauer showed him an application for a job as a notary in Kempten and asked for a reference. From 1 December 1905 he was asked to act as temporary replacement for one Dr Johnen as councillor to the Cologne District Court. He thus spent his last four months in the Prussian legal service as an assistant judge before finally obtaining a salaried post as a deputy in Cologne on 1 April 1906.

Adenauer had spent over four arduous years training for the higher civil service at Cologne's Royal District Court, and the same period again in trainee positions as an *Assessor*. When he finally obtained his post in the city administration his reputation was complete – he was the man who was to strike terror into all idlers at the town hall. He had become a pedantic administrative lawyer, obsessed by detail and always conscious of the correct procedures and division of responsibilities. Adenauer worked long hours and expected those around him to do the same. In short, he was the very model of a senior Prussian civil servant.

His future conduct both as mayor of Cologne and Chancellor of West Germany is easier to understand in the light of his background as a lawyer, since the profession played an important part in shaping his personality. Adenauer had learned to analyse, test and present each case on its merits before resolving it according to standard legal norms and procedures. He had learned to use precise and subtle arguments and to present his own ideas with conviction. Most of all, he had come to realise that contentious issues were the norm, rather than the exception, in both private and public life.

Adenauer was also learning to use his skills of observation and intuition on other people: his superiors and colleagues with their personal eccentricities; private individuals who came into contact with the law; law-breakers of various kinds. He developed a sixth sense for separating lies from truth and, as he later described it, discovered that there were three forms of truth: the truth, the pure truth and the untarnished truth. Conflicts and problem-solving, he came to believe, were in the nature of a lawsuit: they needed to be handled with foresight and with sufficient imagination to understand likely developments several years on. Most of the qualities for which he was later admired – caution, firmness combined with subtlety, prudence, cleverness, flexibility – were developed by his legal training and experience.

'A Talent Takes Shape in Stillness'

Over nine years Adenauer made slow and unspectacular progress in the administration of justice in Cologne and appeared destined for a relatively modest future. Our understanding of his personal life during these years is incomplete, because most of his correspondence was seized by the Gestapo in August 1944 and never recovered. However, the surviving material does reveal an Adenauer rather different from his later image, first in Cologne and then the world outside, as a dynamic, authoritative politician with a good sense of irony. In order to understand his development over these years one has to examine not only his surviving letters and papers, but also some books which he claimed had influenced his thinking.

Notes for this section begin on page 705.

His family possesses two items which are of greater interest than these meagre sources and the thick folder which documents his scientific experiments.[1] The first is a volume of poems written by Adenauer, probably between August 1899 and June 1900, and showing a man capable of personal and religious feeling. Following his unofficial engagement to Emma Weyer, Adenauer had written out a fair copy of the poems and dedicated them to his future wife on 10 September 1902. The second item was written not by Adenauer but by Emma Weyer, and takes the form of a 120-page diary written on their three week honeymoon in Switzerland, the south of France and Italy. Artistic and gifted, she embellished the diary with picture postcards and short poems of her own.

Clearly it is the public Adenauer who is of greatest interest to historians, and particularly his progression from the Prussian administration to the responsibilities of re-structuring first his city and then, after the Second World War, his country. Yet the private man is also worthy of attention during this period if we wish to understand the hidden forces which motivated him and fired his ambition and will.

Following his return to Cologne in 1897, Adenauer faced the problem of re-adjusting to the religious tone of life in his family. Though his faith was not broken, he did pass through a period of reappraisal and reflection. In later life, in conversation with his biographer Weymar, he made casual reference to a religious crisis after his examinations.[2] Adenauer was to claim that the work of Carl Hilty had helped him to reach his own personal position.

Hilty was a man of some significance in the intellectual history of Switzerland. Born in 1833 in the picturesque town in Werdenberg in the canton of St Gallen, he had been a professor of national and international law in Berne from 1874 and gained an international reputation through his works on Swiss national law, Swiss studies and neutrality policy. Hilty played an active part in public life, becoming a member of the National Council in 1890, chief auditor of the army and – towards the end of his life – was named his country's first representative at the new International Court of Arbitration at The Hague. However, his fame in the German-speaking world rests chiefly on his authorship of a number of works outlining a practical philosophy of life. These include his observations on *Happiness*, which appeared between 1891 and 1899 and had sold 100,000 copies by 1910.

Two of Hilty's works, *Happiness* and *What is Faith*, had a place on a shelf in Adenauer's bedroom until the end of his life. Certain passages were underlined in pencil, as was Adenauer's custom when he found something significant and wanted to understand it fully. Since Hilty's writings were apparently important to him and we have very little information about this stage of Adenauer's life, their contents deserve closer scrutiny.

The commemorative plaque in Hilty's birthplace describes him as a 'conscientious critic of culture, moral writer and Christian lay preacher'.

He was a Protestant who nevertheless drew his inspiration from all Christian sources and combined his faith with a profound sympathy for the teachings of the Stoics. Having studied in Paris and London, he was also a man of wide experience who combined strongly conservative views with sound common sense.

Hilty's three-volume work on *Happiness* opens with praise of the 'art of work': 'The art of work is the most important of all arts. One should not "enjoy" life as such but should wish to organise it productively.' This insight is combined with practical rules of conduct: work should be begun promptly and 'a certain carefully measured amount of time' be devoted to it each day; no time should be spent 'on purposeless activity', either in clubs or in politics. The chapter concludes with Hilty's own cyclical model of the rise and fall of élites. Unlike the Italian economist and sociologist Vilfredo Pareto, who believed that this rise and fall was determined by cunning and forcefulness, Hilty regarded personal diligence as the decisive factor: 'As things stand in the world today, it seems reasonable to expect that another social revolution will elevate the workers of today into the ruling class, just as the revolution at the beginning of the nineteenth century elevated the productive citizen above the idle aristocrats and clerics. Wherever that citizen has since become an idler, simply living off his unearned income, i.e., off the work of others, he too must disappear. Now and always the future belongs to work and it deserves to rule.'

The following chapter, entitled 'Epiktet', contains Stoic rules of life with a Christian commentary. The rules are tailor-made for an aspiring young man of Adenauer's religious and social background: '1) Visualise a character, an ideal person, whom you would wish to emulate both in private and in public life. 2) Keep silent most of the time, or say only what is essential, and that with few words ... 8) Physical things such as food, drink, clothing, accommodation, servants should be used only to the extent that is essential. Avoid entirely anything that can be regarded as luxury. 9) Abstain from sexual intercourse as much as possible; otherwise indulge in it in the legal way ... 13) If you wish to enter into conversation with someone, particularly a person of distinction, imagine how Socrates or Zeno would have behaved in this situation ...,i.e., without being obsequious, without unseemly arrogance either, with dignified respect for their rank ... If you do something in the certain conviction that it must be done, then do not hesitate to do so openly, even if the masses (the public) take a different view ...'

Though Hilty attempts to make careful distinctions between the Christian and the Stoic way of life, he concludes that they produce the same result: 'Today Stoic morality comes more easily than religious faith to many people'; as a result, Stoicism can be a necessary transitional stage 'in order to prevent people from sinking into a purely materialistic existence.'

It is highly doubtful whether Adenauer was permanently influenced by Hilty's ideas about 'how it is possible to pass through life without intrigue but in constant struggle against evil'. However, he did underline the claim that 'a certain tendency towards isolation is absolutely necessary for a calm spiritual development'.

The following passages contain key ideas and terms on which Adenauer later drew while attempting to define his own personal philosophy: 'Fearlessness ... Most of what we will encounter in life can be endured ... Courage, it is certain, is one of the most important human attributes for the achievement of happiness ... One should only hate things, not people ... However, one should not allow oneself to be duped by others, or even give the appearance of being deceived, but should always let clever people see that we have read their thoughts ... It is wise to appear cool in front of people who wish to impress us ... Particularly in front of distinguished people, the rich and "ladies", three kinds of people who are always inclined to misinterpret the love shown them ... Every form of self-education begins with the crucial decision to pursue a significant goal in life and to turn away from anything contrary to it.' Last but not least, readers were advised that 'misfortune is a necessary part of human life'.

Like the Christian lay preacher he was, Hilty moves from laying down rules for living to more metaphysical speculations, which are summarised in a final chapter. Its title must have appeared bizarre even at the time: 'What is man, where does he come from, where is he going, who dwells above the golden stars?' According to Hilty, 'God cannot be and should not be explained or proven, but rather must first be believed in and then experienced on a personal level'. Adenauer added his own note in the margin: 'Explanations and proofs are not the same. The explanations are inadequate.' Heavily underlined was the assertion that 'no greater certainty has yet been found than that offered by Christianity in the great questions of life and the life to come, while the individual and sometimes uncertain results of "natural science" cannot suffice in themselves'.

Hilty was inclined to an optimistic philosophy of history, though without offering a justification for his view: 'The fact that mankind is constantly progressing to a better world is the best proof of God's existence.' He viewed liberalism combined with Christian moral law as the best guarantee for moral – and thus historical – progress: 'The world must attain perfection through freedom, not through force and violence of any kind. The aim and goal of world history is the obedience of each individual and eventually of all nations to the great moral world order. But the sole true progress of mankind occurs historically, through life, and not philosophically through mere contemplation.'

It is always difficult to be certain whether books read at an impressionable age can exert a lasting, rather than a temporary influence. Nevertheless, the evidence indicates that Adenauer took the book to heart;

certainly he used similar terms and concepts later in life. There is no doubt that many of his principles were compatible with those of Hilty, whose practical and matter-of-fact style also appealed to a man with little taste for abstract philosophy and theology. Adenauer's career left little time for this kind of reading. In these circumstances, Hilty's writings may well have provided a systematic summary of Adenauer's own beliefs and practices offered reassurance regarding the validity of an undogmatic Christian faith. In 1933, after his secure life had collapsed, Adenauer made reference to Hilty's wisdom in a letter. It was at this time that he bought another book, *For Sleepless Nights*; it bears the inscription 'Adenauer, Maria Laach 1933'.

Adenauer continued to hold fast to the forms of his religion. He attended Mass regularly, fasted at the prescribed times and lived a suitably austere life. As a man with a brother in the priesthood he was no blind believer in the wisdom of priests, but the Christian community in Cologne was nevertheless correct to regard him as a conscientious Catholic.

His faith was reflected in the poetry he had written at the turn of the century, for example in a marriage hymn in free verse written for his brother August, in February 1900. It combined advice and exhortations in the customary fashion:

> Be the protector of your loved ones, their adviser,
> As a man and a Christian be the protector of the good,
> Be just, wise, the enemy of evil!

These standard Christian themes were linked with – somewhat prematurely – good wishes for the couple in their declining years:

> When your life eventually draws to its close,
> It will pass away calmly, as the tired
> Sun in late autumn; you will fall asleep
> So that you may awake
> To eternal Spring in eternal life.

The quality of the poetry is irrelevant here; the verses resemble many other marriage verses of the time. Yet they are striking for their powerful religious sentiment and for the naive optimism which allowed Adenauer – at the beginning of the twentieth century – to envisage the couple facing the future under the safe protection of God:

> The splendid future lies before you, like the
> Wide sunlit ocean, and seaworthy also
> Is your little ship of life, its sails
> Filled a following wind, Love has its sure hand on the tiller. Hail!
> Happy will be your journey.

Adenauer's family has in its possession further poems which remain unpublished, including a number in the style of hymns. They reflect a deep and sincere religious conviction and appear to have been written during the period of religious contemplation leading up to Easter. In them Adenauer expressed his own sense of temptation and awareness of sin. However, at the same time he also wrote non-religious verses in a much more cheerful vein, mostly nature poetry modelled on the styles of Heine, Eichendorff and Uhland, but including a rollicking drinking song.

During Adenauer's youth it was acceptable and even fashionable for young people to turn their hands to verse, usually in a style modelled on the Romantic poets. By the early twentieth century, though the *avant-garde* had rejected sentimental poetry or, like the neo-Romantics, at least sought new modes of expression, most of the middle class maintained its attachment to the traditional forms. Some even published their own volumes of poetry: Max Wallraf, Adenauer's predecessor as mayor of Cologne, thus included a number of his own verses at the end of his memoirs in 1926.

Adenauer was apparently more self-critical. He may have abandoned his own efforts when his wife Emma Weyer revealed much greater mastery of the genre, or may have regarded them as providing sufficient proof that he was more than the dry and colourless lawyer he might appear. In later years, Adenauer presented only the harsh and unrelenting aspect of his personality to public view. That there was a more sensitive side is revealed both in his own poetry, and in his life-long affection for the verses of others.

When he was guaranteed a modest but secure income, Adenauer could take a more active part in social life. Several photographs dating from the early years of the century show him standing in a group of young men and women, casually holding a tennis racket over his shoulder. In these photographs, and in others of him as a lawyer, his appearance has changed for the better: his face looks stronger and more mature, his eyes commanding, and he sports an impressive moustache. Frequently he cuts a more impressive figure than his friends, and dominates the photographs even on the relatively rare occasions when he is not at the centre of them. His youthful poetry reveals that much of this new self-confidence was superficial, but it seems reasonable to assume that Adenauer was beginning to develop his characteristic combination of austerity at work and and relative sensitivity in private life.

Cologne's first clay tennis court had been built in Klettenberg in 1892. At this stage the game was played in highly ceremonial fashion: the men would arrive in jacket and tie, which they removed before playing, while the women wore long skirts and frilled blouses. Socialising was more important than fitness, as was reflected in the fact that rackets were jokingly called 'engagement paddles'. One of the early tennis clubs termed itself the 'wet throughs' because of the members' determination to play three times every week whatever the weather. Non-members, however, knew it as the 'Black Custodis Club', probably because most of the participants came from the deeply religious Catholic Custodis clan.[3] It was significant that Adenauer chose to join this club; even during his leisure activities he gravitated towards friends from his own Catholic background.

One club member was 'Ella' Wahlen, who was to remain on good terms with the Adenauer family into the 1950s. The daughter of a wealthy brickworks owner in the city, 'Ella' was to marry Dr Benedikt Schmittmann, later the Professor of Social Policy at the University of Cologne. Schmittmann was both a pacifist and an anti-Prussian federalist; later, his opposition to the National Socialists was to result in his brutal death in a concentration camp at the beginning of the Second World War. In 1901, however, these events were in the distant future. In this year Hitler was still at school in Braunau, Austria; Himmler was no more than a baby; and Heydrich had yet to be born.

Emma Weyer, a cousin of 'Ella' Schmittmann, was another member of the group. Then twenty years old, she came from a 'good' family and was the daughter of a director of a Cologne re-insurance company. Her father had joined the company at the age of twenty-four after two years spent working in a Paris insurance company. Weyer played a major part in the re-organisation of the company and can justly be regarded as a founding father of the city's insurance industry before his death in a hiking accident in 1884, at the early age of forty-eight.[4]

In the early 1890s the name of Weyer was already famous in Cologne through the person of Emma Weyer's grandfather Johann Peter Weyer. The son of a businessman in the city, Weyer had studied architecture at the École des Beaux Arts in Paris at the end of the Napoleonic era. He was recalled by the city council at the age of twenty-one and appointed *Beigeordneter* (deputy to the city architect). One year later the councillors elected him to the post of city architect. Though the government delayed the appointment for five years, between 1822 and 1843 Johann Peter Weyer was in charge of public building works in Cologne.

Under Weyer's stewardship the city began to revive after the miseries of the Napoleonic Wars. Part of his legacy was the restoration of a number of historic churches – St Apostles, St Gereon, St Mary-in-the-Capitol, St Martin's, and St Mauritius where Adenauer was later baptised. This work encouraged Weyer's lasting fascination with medieval and early modern religious art. He also built, or at least provided the plans, for many of the new secular buildings which gave the city a new face, including the Court of Appeal and the city hospital as well as a number of new schools. In addition, the stock exchange was renovated along with a number of beautiful but derelict assembly houses.[5] It was also Weyer's idea to built a large shopping avenue in the heart of the city, following the model he had seen in Paris. During Adenauer's youth, the shops in this 'Pasaasch', as the inhabitants called it, were the most elegant in the city.

In 1843 Weyer left government service to join the railway industry, where he became an entrepreneur on a grand scale whose speculative investments made him a controversial figure. Nevertheless, his love of the Old Masters continued. Near his grand villa at Rothgerberplatz and Perlengraben, built in the classical style, he established the city's one and only private art gallery, the Gemäldegalerie J.P.Weyer. A catalogue dating from 1852 records 364 paintings, including Byzantine and Italian altarpieces, paintings of the Upper German school, Cologne and Belgian schools, and Italian and Dutch Masters from the seventeenth and eighteenth centuries.[6] An auction catalogue, this time from 1862, mentions 586 paintings, including works by Cranach, Dürer, Holbein, Lochner, Memling, van Dyck, Rembrandt and Rubens. The masterpiece was Rubens' *The Holy Family with Elizabeth and John the Baptist*, which now hangs in the city's Wallraf-Richartz museum.

Weyer's enterprises and his gallery were ill-fated. His speculations eventually cost him a large part of his fortune and forced him to auction off many of his paintings for the meagre sum of 65,076 thalers. Only a few works of art remained in the hands of the family; Emma Weyer was to bring several – mainly Dutch Masters – to her marriage.

Weyer's background before his death in 1864 helps us to understand the thinking of Adenauer, since after his marriage in 1904 he absorbed much of the family tradition. Whether consciously or not, he strove to emulate his wife's grandfather. As mayor of the city, Adenauer was gripped by the same urge to modernise and to plan on a grand scale, whilst also seeking to preserve what was valuable from the past. He also developed a similar love of the Old Masters, his previous tastes being intensified by the family connection. When he began to earn enough money, Adenauer established his own comparatively modest collection and, as Chancellor, retired each evening to his own climatically-controlled gallery (which was always kept at exactly twenty degrees centigrade) in order to contemplate his carefully illuminated paintings.

Emma Weyer's mother also came from a prominent family. Her great-grandfather was Franz Xaver Joseph Heinrich Berghaus, a high-ranking civil servant in the legal service. Prior to 1815, when Cologne was a French city, Berghaus had already been a lawyer at the Court of Appeal, an institution which was to be closely connected with Adenauer's family history. In 1840 he was appointed Royal Prussian Procurator General. However, six years later, at the age of sixty-three, he became politically controversial and retired. During the unrest in Cologne in 1846 he had released the city's prisoners in order to prevent a bloody uprising, a reaction which was condemned as being too lenient. Berghaus, a deeply religious man, subsequently dedicated himself to charitable causes. In a city where poverty and misery were always present, he remained president of the city administration of poor relief until shortly before his death in 1868.[7]

This branch of Emma Weyer's family was notable for its involvement in the legal profession and for its religious devotion. Emma's mother became even more religious after the sudden and early death of her husband. According to Emma's brother – later director of the District Court in Aachen – their mother had retreated into an 'isolated convent-like atmosphere' and suffered prolonged depressions, before her death in 1911. Her death notice accurately recalled the spirit of the household: 'Great devotion to duty, deep piety and quiet goodness determined her life and will secure her place in the memory of those who remain. We commend her dear soul to the oblations of the priests and the pious prayers of the faithful so that she may rest in eternal peace.'

It was scarcely surprising that the young woman longed to flee this house of mourning. Exuberant, cheerful and musical, Emma Weyer was a typical product of a 'good' family and of an education designed for 'young ladies'. She and Adenauer quickly became romantically involved. Adenauer's old restraint and ironic detachment in his dealings with women, surely a sign of insecurity, now began to change. Some of Adenauer's critics have argued that he calculated this marriage on the grounds that it would improve his social standing – and indeed, he cannot have failed to see that this would be the case. Nevertheless, all the indications are that, for both partners, it was a love match. The young couple became engaged during a lawyers' summer outing to the Rolandsbogen, overlooking the Rhine near Rolandswerth. Emma's brother Max, who was part of the group, recalled how Emma – wearing a large hat decorated with cherries – ran up to tell him: 'Max, I've just got engaged to Konrad Adenauer. Adenauer followed some distance behind. It struck me how self-controlled he was. I observed that even when he spoke to Emma he had that light ironic tone which he often used when talking to women.'[8]

On the following Sunday a traditional nineteenth-century scene was played out at the Weyer family home: Emma Weyer's mother, with great formality, received Adenauer in the family drawing-room, where the young lawyer in his special high collar asked for her daughter's hand in marriage. When asked how he would support Emma, he replied that he hoped to take over a notary's office and could expect to earn 6,000 marks a year.

Adenauer's poor results in the *Assessor* examinations that autumn destroyed this plan and placed him in a difficult position: he could hardly afford to marry on a salary of 200 marks per month from the prosecutor's office. Nevertheless, the engagement was announced early in 1902; the family had confidence in Adenauer's ability to make a successful career, while any gap in social standing between the two families was overcome by their common religious faith. Emma's mother also possessed sufficient means to support the couple in the difficult early years.

Adenauer now began to search for a permanent position. In April he showed an interest in the position of deputy in the municipal administration at Gelsenkirchen; a letter to that effect was found in his papers after his death.[9] However, he was then given the opportunity temporarily to stand in for the ailing *Justizrat* Kausen, a renowned lawyer and chairman of the Centre Party group in the Cologne city council.

Here he appears to have found his natural home. These early years not only trained him in political debate, but also introduced him to those members of the Cologne legal circles whose opinions could be vital for his future. Adenauer had the priceless ability to sift quickly through a mass of detail and find the crucial point, as well as to argue a position from several different points of view. One of his colleagues recalled later: 'Though he was not a lawyer who could make brilliant oratorical speeches, he had an incredibly effective way of convincing people by means of sober and factual argument. His eloquence worked on the judges like a gentle and persistent country rain that washes away all opposing arguments.'[10]

The young couple was now able to marry. Adenauer was almost exactly twenty-eight years old when he married Emma Weyer on 26 January 1904. The newlyweds then took an extended honeymoon tour, as befitting a middle-class couple of the time. Their first stop was Bonn, foggy and bleak in the depths of winter. On the morning after their arrival the couple walked to the Alter Zoll: 'A fine mist lies over the Rhine. The sky is not entirely cloudless, but we can clearly see the Seven Hills. Gulls fly restlessly above the river ... Not for a long time have we looked into the future in such a happy and carefree manner.' Konrad and Emma Adenauer wandered back through the market place, pausing at the old churches on the way.

Their next stop was Montreux and Chillon Castle. Here the weather was already springlike: 'A pale blue sky above the wide endless plain ... Flocks of white gulls hovering on the gusts of wind ...' They climbed the snow-covered heights of Les Avants:

> We sledged down the slope over a snow-covered path and joyfully passed the white pine forests, which looked ghostly enough to be concealing a fairy-tale in their dark depths, above us the blue sky, around us the mountains, below us the wide expanse of Lake Geneva. Can you imagine anything more wonderful! How our sledge raced and our cheeks reddened! What fun! Playful as children we enjoyed sledging over the snowy ground, happy as children we gazed at the unending beauty.

In the hotel the Adenauers observed with compassion and a certain horror the faces of the many visitors with tuberculosis.

> These poor people, they hope for a cure but many of them already have the mark of death upon them ... The majority are middle aged, young people are less common. But the guests in general make a good impression, not like the international idlers whom one often sees in winter health resorts. In any case we have stumbled upon a unique world here.

The honeymoon tour moved on to Geneva, where the Adenauers admired the beauty of the lake and engaged in some window shopping. Then they travelled through the Rhône valley towards Marseilles:

> The train races through the wide stretches of Provence. The rain still comes down in fine strands, but the countryside is already covered by a tinge of warmer beauty. The minnesingers, who once made this region the special focus of their poetry, appear before us singing songs in praise of southern ardour and beauty ... The entire region could justifiably be called the white land since everything is covered by a gentle bright ray of light which seems to emanate from the ground. But the light is darkened by the solemnity of the cypress trees which appear almost to shield the land. The towns, whose houses have white roofs, lie scattered peacefully among the hills ... Vegetation is sparse, and further south one can find a few olive trees, but it is winter now.

In Marseilles the scene was very different:

> Yesterday the grey, dreary winter landscape – today a mild spring air that has tempted us onto the main street of Marseilles in late evening. In the Rue de Cannebière a whole new picture unfolds. We have entered another country, and the important thing is to take in the new impressions. Figs, dates, bananas, oranges, tangerines, all are sold in incredible quantities on the open street ... Even if one didn't know the language, one would be able to understand the lively mime and inviting hand movements of the vendors. We could not have walked through here so proudly and with such resistance had it not been for the fact that our evening meal was so generous. Visitors to the cafés put their chairs on the open street and postcard sellers walk among them, little brown boys and girls who reveal considerable agility and eloquence. 'Une douzaine pour dix', that is not dear, but not much can be expected. Girls in native costume sit at the stands selling violets, a little bit dirty but exotic and unusual looking. One horse-drawn vehicle after another passes by, mixed with the loud and monotonous shouts of the drivers, the jingling of an organ, the haggling of the vendors. All is life and movement.

Though this has a certain interest as a piece of cultural history – a young German honeymoon couple touring the south of France during the calm before the First World War – its chief significance is the fact that the groom was Konrad Adenauer. He was making his first visit to France as a tourist, free of any political calculation. His second brief visit to the country was to take place on 6 June 1919 when he visited the German peace delegation at Versailles and stopped for a matter of hours in Paris. By that time Adenauer was mayor of Cologne, and the world he and his contemporaries had known lay in ruins. His third visit was to take place in April 1951, forty-seven years after the first, when he was Chancellor of the Federal Republic of Germany.

The journey also shows how Adenauer was drawn to the landscape and life-style of the south which he observed in Provence and northern Italy. It was a sentiment he was to re-discover in old age following his discovery of Cadenabbia.

The honeymoon tour then took the Adenauers to Monte Carlo, where they made the traditional visit to the casino. Here they walked through the crowds and observed the wealthy guests before placing a few small bets. Emma Adenauer won a small sum and lost it again before her husband – ever the austere Prussian civil servant – quietly led her away from the table.

After Monte Carlo the couple travelled to the Italian Riviera, where they indulged in Adenauer's lifelong pastime of taking long walks. In addition to Bordighera, Santa Margherita and Portofino, they also visited Genoa, San Remo and Rapallo, which were to become famous after 1918 as post-war European governments tried to reconstruct the shattered 'world of yesterday'. The journey took them from Genoa and Milan – with a brief stop to admire Leonardo's *Last Supper* – through Switzerland (Lugano and Lucerne) to Freiburg and reminders of Adenauer's student days. Following their return to Cologne the couple moved into a well-furnished apartment at Klosterstrasse 71. The house was situated at the edge of a new housing area and faced a meadow, a market-garden and a few detached houses.

This was another side of Adenauer, one that is easily forgotten given his rapid rise from modest beginnings. Although he was generally regarded as obsessed by work, the young Adenauer also enjoyed domestic tranquillity and a happy marriage. His later claim that he had wanted to become a country notary is entirely credible.[11] His brother-in-law remembered that Adenauer had previously written an application for the post of notary in the north Rhenish town of Rheinberg and, in October 1905, six months before he began his job in the city administration, he again sought a post, in Kempten on the left bank of the Rhine. However, he abandoned these plans after closer examination of the inadequate pay and conditions he could expect.

During these years Adenauer enjoyed his holidays. In July 1904, not long after the honeymoon tour, the couple spent two weeks with his brother Hans in Fritzdorf, and in January 1905 they returned to Les Avants for four weeks. Of course, it is also possible that he was forced to take longer vacations than he would have wished, as a result of his health problems; a life insurance company refused him cover on the eve of his marriage because of his poor health, and in 1905 his diabetes went on the record.

As his hobbies reveal, Adenauer was not wholly obsessed by the law despite his desire for a successful career. At this stage he revealed no sign of great interest in politics, nor of any social commitment. As soon as he had moved into his own house he began mulling over various patents, entering into serious correspondence with the Imperial Patent Office and with a patent lawyer. He conducted his disputes with the patent office with an acute knowledge of the procedural possibilities and the determination to use the legal skills he had acquired in his years of training.

All the signs are that this was a young man who was still finding his way and remained uncertain of his future; a wrong decision at this stage could have ended his ambitions. Under other circumstances, the happy marriage to Emma Weyer might have made him dull and smug, instead of increasing his motivation and his desire to succeed. He could easily have decided to devote himself to a modest career in the law and to his scientific hobbies.

During the first twenty-nine years of his life, Adenauer's career was decent but relatively mediocre – and might easily have led him to a notary's office in some small Rhenish town. He was a man who had encountered problems which he was able to solve only with difficulty: his simple background, perhaps allied with religious constraints, prevented the early development of self-assurance and confidence. Adenauer seems not to have realised his own potential until he had served as temporary replacement for Kausen, and even then he contemplated taking a rural notary's job. Moreover, he apparently remained relatively unpolitical, especially in comparison with those of his contemporaries who also entered political life. Gustav Stresemann, two years younger than Adenauer, was also from the lower middle class, his father owning a *Weissbier* store in a working class district of Berlin. Like Adenauer, he could not join an old student corporation and had to settle for a reform fraternity. Nevertheless, while still a student he had published a number of political essays and taken an active part in political life. As early as 1902, he founded the Association of Saxon Industrialists within the Bund der Industriellen (League of Industrialists). He achieved financial independence through his marriage in 1903.

Another politician born in the same decade as Adenauer, Julius Bachem, was leader of the Rhenish Centre Party and had been a city councillor in Cologne by the age of thirty. Karl Trimborn, also from Cologne and one of the most influential members of the Rhenish Centre Party, had become politically active as soon as he completed his legal studies. The future President of West Germany, Theodor Heuss – eight years Adenauer's junior – had become involved in political and journalistic debates during his student years in Munich. In 1905 Heuss was already deputy editor of Friedrich Naumann's journal *Die Hilfe* at a time when Adenauer was still working at the Cologne District Court. Significantly, however, these last three were all sons of well-to-do middle-class families that could help them on their way, and they were blessed with better health than the young Adenauer. Nevertheless, it remains true to say that in comparison with many of his peers, Adenauer discovered his own political inclinations relatively late.

There have been many attempts by historians to portray Adenauer as an ambitious careerist, but all have failed on closer examination. He made life difficult for himself in his youth, revealed uncertainty about the career he ought to follow, and became determined not to abandon the choices he had made. Though he was universally acknowledged to be diligent, dependable and efficient, he had yet to reveal the talent which he would exhibit as mayor and, later, as a Federal Chancellor of international stature.

One of Adenauer's most obvious characteristics – and one which was to assist his career – was loyalty to his peers and seniors from the familiar Catholic background. Though his contacts were to be helpful to him they were in no sense the result of a Machiavellian plan, but a response to a personal need. It was in these groups that Adenauer met his first wife.

Adenauer was able to achieve success despite his unpromising background by emphasising just those skills such as his sense of duty, tireless diligence, piety and dependability which he had learned as a child. He became successful, in fact, by remaining true to himself. Yet it is also true to say that he finally achieved real stature in his elevated posts by developing unsuspected talents: a creative will, imagination, acute political instinct, enjoyment of power, independence and pride. In the words of Tasso, and the subject of his school essay: 'A talent takes shape in stillness, a character is formed in the current of life'.

In these early years Adenauer's personality, like his career, was nothing out of the ordinary. As a politician he was later to be compared to the first Chancellor of the united Germany, Bismarck – and in many ways Adenauer emerges well from the comparison. Yet there is no doubt that the Prussian aristocrat had infinitely more vitality than Adenauer, the dutiful son of a middle-ranking civil servant in Cologne – as he demonstrated in his tempestuous student days in Göttingen, and his passionate pursuit of an Englishwoman with whom he had fallen in love. Any biographer of Bismarck is inevitably struck by his gargantuan appetites, tremendous drive, and a political instinct which led him into the United Assembly of Prussia at the age of thirty-two. In addition, his letters to his fiancé and speeches in parliament revealed a genuine literary talent.

Adenauer was the opposite in almost every way: career-oriented studies quickly completed; no idleness in his student days; no signs of wanting to become a drifter; a willingness to accept the lower middle-class lifestyle of his parents; a strict diet without excess in food or drink; the lack of love affairs; some minor versifying which does not compare with Bismarck's powerful language; and, most of all, the apparent lack of political passion.

This focus on the solid and orderly first thirty years of Adenauer's life does not in any way diminish his subsequent achievements. On the contrary, it was remarkable that this insecure and apparently mediocre young man, with only ten years experience in the municipal administration of Cologne, was transformed into a leader of such originality after the crises of 1918. Even after discovering his calling Adenauer was unaware of the political demon within him. At this stage his main ambition was to guarantee a solid bourgeois existence for himself and his wife.

II

THE FIRST RAPID RISE
1906–1917

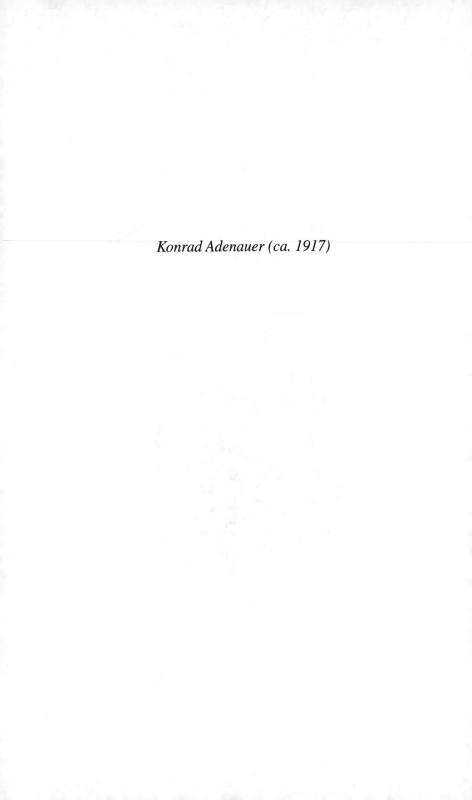

Konrad Adenauer (ca. 1917)

Adenauer's Lucky Streak – Rise in the Cologne Municipal Administration

The year of his thirtieth birthday, 1906, was a significant one for Adenauer. He found a job and lost his father in the same month, and in the course of the year his first child was born.

Even in old age Adenauer had vivid memories of his appointment as a deputy for the city of Cologne: 'It was more by chance than anything else. I wanted to be a notary, and in the countryside if possible.'[1] The post of deputy had become vacant unexpectedly owing to the early retirement of the director of civil engineering. Initially it appeared that Adenauer was not in line for the post, because the head of the Centre Party group, Kausen, wanted to appoint a County Court judge named Schmitz. When Adenauer heard of this he went to see his old boss: 'Why don't you take me, Herr *Justizrat*? I'm certainly as good as the other man.'[2] Kausen then spoke to Johannes Rings, who controlled the Cologne Party machine in his capacity as head of the personnel department, and apparently told him: 'That young man, Adenauer, he wants to enter politics. Tell me if he's got potential and if we can make something out of him.'[3]

When the two candidates presented themselves to the *Verfassungs-kommission* (Constitutional Commission), Kausen mobilised his group behind Adenauer and obtained the consent of Mayor Becker. Apparently it was recognised as the Centre Party's turn, since the city council gave its unanimous approval with only two invalid votes. Adenauer thus became the youngest of the city's twelve deputies on 7 March 1906. His work was to include responsibility for the taxation department, while the former deputy in charge of taxation was moved to civil engineering. Adenauer received the salary of 6,000 marks per year, a considerable sum for the time and 2,000 marks more than his father had earned after a lifetime of work.

Even the last of Johann Konrad's sons now seemed to have a secure future. His father congratulated Konrad and encouraged him to maintain his ambition: 'Konrad, now you must aim to become the mayor of Cologne.'[4] Although he had been a relatively humble civil servant from a modest background, Johann Konrad had clearly bequeathed to his children a quiet but strong determination to succeed, as well as a devotion to duty. Three days after this conversation Adenauer was called from a court appointment – he still had three weeks to serve as assistant judge – to discover that his father had died of a stroke at the age of seventy-three.

Adenauer never discussed his feelings about his father's death at the time when his own career was forging ahead. On 15 March 1967, four weeks before his own death, he spoke with the art dealer Heinz Kisters in Rhöndorf and asked him to wait while he went to his bedroom. Adenauer returned with a photograph which he presented to his guest. It showed a dignified old man lying on his death bed, eyes closed and hands clasped. 'It's my father', Adenauer said quietly.[5]

The inscription on his father's gravestone reflected the dignity and strength of Johann Konrad's life: 'Here rests in peace Royal *Kanzleirat* Konrad Adenauer, chief secretary of Cologne Upper District Court, retired Lieutenant, Knight of the Royal Crown Order Third Class and the Order of the Red Eagle Fourth Class.' The inscription closed with the lines from Sirach 45.1: 'Blessed be his memory.'[6]

Adenauer and Emma's first son, born that same year, was named after his grandfather. Despite the joy of the birth, his wife's health now began to deteriorate. She had returned from the honeymoon in high spirits and had noted in her diary: 'May we always be as happy as on this evening when we move into our new home.' However, her recovery from childbirth was painfully slow. When the cause of her ailments could not be detected, Adenauer consulted various specialists and took his wife to a sanatorium for observation. There it was discovered that a curvature of the spine was preventing the kidneys from functioning normally; rest and a strict diet were recommended. It was at this time that Adenauer's mother and his sister, Lilli, moved into the first floor of his new home in the suburb of Lindenthal, an expanding middle-class residential area.

In 1910 the couple's second son, Max, was born without complications. However, Adenauer was not optimistic: his doctors had told him that his wife was more or less terminally ill. He kept the information to himself until the end, not wishing to distress his wife, and did not reveal until many years later that he had been aware of her condition from the start.

Childbirth was apparently too much for his wife's frail constitution. Her suffering intensified after the birth of the third child – their daughter Maria ('Ria') in 1912. She was now a virtual invalid, unable to leave the house. Adenauer's own health was also poor. In order to keep his diabetes under control he was forced to observe strict discipline in the intake of food and drink. At public functions, where alcohol was served freely, he would take only a small sip to observe the formalities, and occasionally had his glass filled with water instead. Though some regarded him as a puritanical figure unable to appreciate the pleasures of life, he was in fact acting to preserve his health. During this period, as later, Adenauer also suffered from chronic headaches. These helped to decide the routine of taking long holidays in the Black Forest or the Swiss mountains each year, since the mountain air brought temporary relief from a pain that was otherwise constant.

None of these difficulties persuaded Adenauer to abandon his habits of diligence, strict attention to detail, an organised daily routine, and stoical acceptance of physical suffering. Nevertheless, his inclination to be pessimistic – often observed later on – probably increased during these years of coping with his wife's steady decline and his own ill-health. His reluctance to socialise and entertain more than was absolutely essential also reflected the family circumstances. Adenauer's conservative upbringing and his precarious health prevented him from engaging in the frivolities of these last golden years before the First World War, and distinguished him from other members of the Cologne middle class.

It would be wrong to imagine – and Adenauer's children have denied it – that the family home resembled a house of mourning. Despite their physical ailments, the relationship of Konrad and Emma Adenauer was warm and affectionate. As Adenauer became preoccupied by his career, his wife acted as the focus of the family. Emma Adenauer was a cultivated woman with a wide social network of friends, cousins and aunts. She remained somewhat in awe of her husband and ran the family in the manner characteristic of the solid middle classes, with two maids to relieve her of many of the burdens of housework. Not a trace of Adenauer's modest origins remained; his financial position had been secured by his appointment as First Deputy in 1909.

On closer analysis, Adenauer's rapid rise to the top of the municipal hierarchy was not completely untroubled. Though he had learned a great deal about people and institutions during his stint in the prosecutor's office and in court, he had now entered an entirely new environment. It was by no means unknown for an industrious young man in his early thirties to be appointed a deputy, but until 1912 Adenauer was the youngest of the twelve deputies in an environment where the principle of seniority remained extremely important. Most of his colleagues had considerably more experience. Moreover, within the committee of deputies there was a degree of tension between the majority of qualified lawyers and the technical specialists, who were able to obtain higher salaries on the basis of skills which were also attractive to business.

There was also a political context to be taken into account. Most of the deputies neither wished, nor were able to avoid the issue of their political affiliations. It was common knowledge that the Centre Party had engaged in an aggressive personnel policy for decades. We do not know exactly when Adenauer joined the Centre Party, but he must have done so at a relatively early stage; in 1919, at the first post-war conference of the Rhenish Centre Party, Karl Trimborn was to refer to him as 'an old and faithful member of our party'. In any case, he was always regarded as a Centre Party man, for example by Bernhard Falk, a Liberal city council-lor from 1908 to 1930 and head of the Liberal group after 1915.

The Liberals were careful to ensure a correct balance of forces at the town hall. In autumn 1906, after Adenauer had been a deputy for six months, the Upper Administrative Court in Berlin declared that the 1905 city council elections for the Second Class had been invalid. This was unfortunate for the Centre Party, which lost its slim majority to the Lib-erals in the new election.

Despite this change, the Liberals sensibly assumed that their majority in the city council would not last. The mayor of the city, Wilhelm Becker – now seventy-one years old – was persuaded to retire two years before his term expired, in order to increase the chances of electing a Liberal candidate to replace him. The Centre Party's candidate for the post was Wilhelm Farwick. Just before losing its majority, the Centre brought Far-wick from his post as deputy mayor of Münster and appointed him First Deputy in Cologne, obviously with the aim of establishing him as the successor to Becker. However, it was now the Liberals who were in the strongest position. Their candidate was Wilhelm Spiritus, who was mayor of Bonn but who had also served four years as a deputy in Cologne. The builder of the city ring, Hermann Josef Stübben, was also a candidate, along with the independent, Max Wallraf. A Prussian civil servant now serving as district president in Cologne, Wallraf had previ-ously been Landrat of Malmedy and St Goar, later the police president in Aachen and was now Oberpräsident in Koblenz.

Wallraf had three vital advantages: he was a native son of Cologne from the Wallraf clan; he was a Catholic; and his father-in-law, the land-owner Joseph Pauli, was a member of the Liberal group in the city coun-cil. Pauli now declared that, after two Protestants, it was high time for the city to elect a Catholic mayor. Since the Liberals had a majority of one vote, his proposal could not safely be ignored. Wallraf thus became the compromise candidate, acceptable to the Liberals because he was not a member of the Centre Party, and to the Centre because he was a Catholic.

Along with the retirement of several municipal deputies, this game of musical chairs inevitably affected Adenauer as a member of the Centre Party which was no longer the largest party in the city council. Becker was forced to respect the new political balance. Shortly before his retire-ment he presented the council with a new plan for the division of duties, which would have moved Adenauer from the tax department to a much less important role. However, Adenauer was apparently able to call on his party colleague Farwick for assistance. In his capacity as First Deputy,

Farwick postponed the implementation of the new plan until Wallraf became mayor, and it was then discreetly dropped 'for the moment'.

Becker's plan would, in all probability, have brought Adenauer's career in the municipal administration to a premature end. He was not likely to have been satisfied with the new duties envisaged for him – flood control and road building – for any length of time. The abandonment of the plan also had a historical dimension, since the deputy who would have been given responsibility for the tax department was Karl Jarres, who was close to the Liberal group. Jarres made a brief appearance in Cologne before moving to Duisburg to advance his career. In 1921 their paths crossed again over the chairmanship of the Prussian State Council. Then, at the height of the Ruhr crisis in 1923, Adenauer again clashed with Jarres, who was by then Minister of the Interior, in the cabinet of Gustav Stresemann.

It has frequently been maintained that Max Wallraf's success facilitated Adenauer's own rise to the position of mayor: Wallraf was Emma Weyer's uncle, the younger brother of her mother Emilie Wallraf. Yet the charge of nepotism appears to be ill-founded. Wallraf – the Adenauers called him 'notre cher oncle' in the presence of their children – valued Adenauer primarily as a subordinate whom he could use effectively. He also appreciated Adenauer's ability to deal with Kausen, the suspicious head of the Centre Party's caucus on the city council. From his point of view it was advantageous to have working for him a diligent young man who, as a relative, would not cause political trouble and could also act as a bridge to the Centre Party.

Adenauer's relations with Wallraf were not always harmonious, partly because of the attitude of Wallraf's wife, who was a member of the Pauli family, and from a branch of farmers which had prospered as the city expanded and incorporated old agricultural areas. From the outset she had adopted a distant and haughty tone in her dealings with Adenauer.

Wallraf's strategy and tactical approach to his time as mayor is difficult to assess. His uninformative memoirs reveal a man of little more than average abilities, certainly not an instinctive or talented politician, despite the fact that he became Minister of the Interior for several months in 1917-1918 and President of the Reichstag in 1924 at the end of his career. He was popular in Cologne and had certain obvious advantages: an elegant appearance, a convincing speaking style, impressive administrative experience and good connections. In general Wallraf was typical of the complacent and self-satisfied Wilhelmine era, which was so soon to be eclipsed. However, he was also a regional patriot who hung traditional Cologne flags from the Gürzenich and adorned the town hall with historic relics. An enthusiastic hunter, Wallraf ran the municipal administration on the principle that hard-working subordinates should be given a free hand, in order to give them plenty of time to enjoy the good life – which in his case included dabbling in poetry.

Under his stewardship the communities on the right bank of the Rhine were finally incorporated. Since he was neither a member of one of the large parties nor affiliated with them, he based his twelve-year tenure on the principle of compromise, which enabled him to survive without major political challenges at the local level. The press also gave him reasonable treatment, except on one occasion when *Kladderadatsch,* the satirical paper produced in Berlin, claimed that, in preparation for the Kaiser's visit, he had installed a toilet made of pure marble in the town hall. There was no truth in the story, but it shows the suspicions which the flexible and extrovert Wallraf could arouse.[7]

Leaders such as Wallraf need diligent lieutenants to keep the administration running smoothly. By a combination of circumstances, Konrad Adenauer became Wallraf's right-hand man only three years after entering the municipal administration. At the outset he was responsible for the administration report and electoral matters, for supervising the covered markets and the municipal statistical office, and – most important of all – for the tax department, where he tried various strategies for raising extra revenue in order to balance the budget and eliminate the deficit.

Adenauer's own tax policy is difficult to assess. However, the surviving documents reveal certain features which were more likely to find popularity from a public interested in economic efficiency than from lower-ranking civil servants, many of whom came to regard him as a difficult boss. For example, he demanded that his subordinates produce a list recording every item of business that had taken more than two weeks to process, and announced that 'I will take direct action against civil servants who take an excessive time to complete their work'.[8]

This declaration of war on inefficiency, aimed at the bureaucratic sloppiness of Cologne, could scarcely have been more Prussian in spirit. By the time it was made Adenauer was already First Deputy, the post having become vacant following the appointment of Wilhelm Farwick to the board of the Schaaffhausen Bank in the spring of 1909. Farwick had been the representative of political Catholicism at the top of the administration; Adenauer appears to have been so highly regarded by the Centre Party caucus that it proposed him as Farwick's successor. Since the Centre again had a majority of seats on the city council, the result was virtually a foregone conclusion.

Adenauer's nomination was undoubtedly a reward for his commitment and competence, but was also linked to his political orientation. There was some opposition to him from leading Liberals such as Councillor of Commerce Neven Du-Mont and the chemist Theodor Kyll, who were eager to counter the Centre; although Adenauer's abilities were not in question, they wanted the post to be given to a longer-serving deputy associated with the Liberals. However, at a meeting of the Liberal caucus, Adenauer's candidacy was defended by a lawyer colleague, Emil Schmitz, who asserted that he had known Adenauer for some time and that he was 'tolerant and not the worst type of ultramontane Catholic'.[9] Mayor Wallraf refused to take sides, declaring that both Adenauer and an older deputy, Bruno Matzerath, were qualified for the job.

After long debate, the Centre Party asserted its position as the majority party. Wallraf, on the grounds of his family ties with Adenauer, abstained from voting. The leader of the defeated Liberal group, the famous hygienist Professor Edouard Lent, stressed that his party did not doubt Adenauer's skills and qualifications, but felt that the decision could not be 'justified by the needs arising from the interests of the city'.[10] In plain language, the Liberals believed that the appointment was politically motivated. Adenauer realised that in future he would be treated as and perhaps suspected of being purely a party man unless his work was transparently objective and competent.

Until 1912 Adenauer was the city's youngest deputy. The resentment of his colleagues on the Advisory Council was understandable, since the post of First Deputy offered the ideal springboard for the job of mayor, in Cologne and other cities. It also carried the high salary of 15,000 marks per year, which was increased by another 3,000 marks once the controversy surrounding his appointment had subsided. Adenauer was now so well paid that he could afford to buy land and build a magnificent house near the city park in Max-Bruch-Straße, one of the most exclusive districts of Cologne. At the age of thirty-three Adenauer was the mayor's senior representative and the second most powerful man in the municipal administration. In addition to his responsibility for the tax department, he also supervised financial affairs and personnel matters relating to civil servants and white-collar workers. However, Wallraf took care to keep Adenauer under his control; in the most important issues of financial administration he was appointed simply as Wallraf's Permanent Representative. Nevertheless, Adenauer now had the opportunity to learn all ramifications of the municipal administration, and to test his skills in dealing with a vast administrative apparatus.

It is difficult to say whether the city's fiscal policy was the work of Wallraf or of Adenauer. When Wallraf took office Cologne had an income of some 96 million marks and a budget deficit of 1.5 million marks. Tax increases thus seemed necessary, along with a tight fiscal policy and the creation of savings accounts and government bonds. Both as director of the tax department, and subsequently as First Deputy, Adenauer was the key figure in the implementation of this programme of consolidation. The administration was fortunate because an economic recovery began in 1909; a balanced budget was presented in the following year. The city then began to establish a financial cushion which helped it through the hard years of the First World War.

Increasing tax revenue also enabled the city authorities to plan long-term projects: a city loan bank, a second fixed bridge over the Rhine to

Deutz, the purchase of Rhein-Braun shares and shares in local transport companies, the expansion of utility companies. In 1911 the First Deputy urged the city council to issue a loan of 79 million marks, double the sum his predecessor had requested. Adenauer was able to convince the city council that productive investments would yield higher returns. In fact, city councils in Cologne had been familiar with these arguments ever since Becker's term in office, and were to hear them repeated many times over the following years. The loan was not completed for some time, with the last instalment being issued only in 1918. By that time, however, Adenauer was already mayor of Cologne and Germany was in its fourth and final year of war.

The First World War

By the beginning of the First World War Adenauer's personality was fully developed. Yet he never ceased to learn, because life in a rapidly changing world had taught him that the problems of the modern era could be mastered only by creative action. At this stage he did not doubt that the world in which he had found his niche was basically rational. Only after the war and the revolution did he discover that modern civilisation, which he had thought so secure, had been built on sand.

Adenauer belonged to a generation which was not directly responsible for the coming catastrophe. The great errors had been made by the older generation, since political power in the German Empire had rested in the hands of men who were more than fifty years old. Wilhelm II, born in 1859, was one of the youngest among its leaders; the Imperial Chancellor von Bülow – for many years the dominant figure of Wilhelmine Germany – was born in 1849, as was Admiral von Tirpitz; Bülow's successor Bethmann Hollweg was born in 1856. Even the most daring thinkers and intellectual provocateurs had been born in the 1860s: in 1914 Max Weber was 50, Friedrich Naumann was 54, Walther Rathenau was 47 and Maximilian Harden was 53.

Adenauer's immediate contemporaries were the young lions of the 1870s who were to determine the fate of the Weimar Republic before returning to prominence in the early years of the Federal Republic after 1945. By 1914 they had reached only the second rank in politics, although very close to the top. Friedrich Ebert, born in 1871, thus became chairman of the Social Democratic Party in 1914. Gustav Stresemann, born in 1878 and legal adviser to the Association of Saxon Textile Industrialists, was a National Liberal member of the Reichstag with growing influence after

Notes for this section begin on page 705.

1907. Matthias Erzberger, only a few months older than Adenauer, was already a leading figure in the Centre Party by 1914. The unfortunate Chancellor of 1922/23, Wilhelm Cuno, born the same year as Adenauer, had an important position in the Reich Ministry of Finance. Joseph Wirth, born in 1879, Cuno's predecessor as Chancellor, was a Gymnasium teacher in Baden, still far from the levers of power in 1914. The later Chancellor Hans Luther, born in 1878, was – like Adenauer – advancing his career at local level. Another Chancellor of the Weimar Republic, Franz von Papen – born in 1879 – was preparing for a future of controversy and political intrigue by working as German military attaché in Mexico.

The men of the 1880s – Heinrich Brüning (1885), Kurt von Schleicher (1882), Carl Goerdeler (1884), Theodor Heuss (1884) were at the beginning of their careers in 1914 and would not reach the centres of power for another ten or fifteen years.

Seen with the benefit of hindsight, the members of these age groups appear to have shared many common ideas despite their different origins and political outlook. None of them doubted the greatness, power, unity and right to existence of the German Reich. Apart from the Social Democrats, who had deep reservations about the nature of bourgeois society – though they too were becoming more pragmatic – all of them supported the existing order despite accepting the need for some reform.

Almost more important than the actual experiences of these men were the experiences they did not have. None of the members of this political generation was influenced by the German Youth Movement. The ideas of the Movement – its romanticism, its impulse to reform, its critique of civilisation, its tendency to support the very diverse and sometimes extreme political factions – were largely alien to them. Their careers were already under way, even those of the men who were later to become prominent in the Federal Republic. Though they were affected by the crises of the First World War and the post-war period, the men of the 1870s and 1880s did not feel the need for radical political change and were not assailed by the doubts and disillusion felt by the front-line generation of the First World War.

The generation born in the 1890s and at the turn of the century – the men who would eventually destroy the old world in 1933 – developed their political outlook in very different conditions to those faced by Adenauer and his contemporaries. They were the war generation who had either marched enthusiastically to the front in 1914 or had still been at school. In 1914 Hermann Göring, with whom Adenauer was to clash in 1933, was only twenty-one; the future Gauleiter of Cologne, Josef Grohé, was a twelve-year old schoolboy; and Josef Goebbels was a Gymnasium pupil.

These names need to be mentioned in order to place Adenauer in the appropriate generational perspective. He was old enough to be profoundly influenced by the Bismarck and Wilhelmine era, but by 1914 he was already too old to be drafted into the army and was needed in political life at home. Unlike Brüning, he never witnessed the transforming effect of years, or even months, of service on the western front on an entire political generation. Adenauer lived through the crisis of the Wilhelmine era on the home front, which undoubtedly broadened his horizons, but he never saw service at the front, which led some to support radical militarism, some to radical pacifism, others to reject established class-based society, and still others to embrace the previously unknown concept of a *Volksgemeinschaft*. Many members of the older generation had some understanding of the sentiments underlying the vague slogans of mass society, nihilism, the collapse of values and the crisis of civilisation. Nevertheless, most of them retained faith in a system of stable values which, however questionable, were yet based on reason.

Adenauer was a realist. Though he did not lack imagination, he had nothing in common with the longings and despair of the generation which came of age in the later Imperial era. This was to remain the case throughout his career. He was immune to the intellectual chaos which had begun to affect Europe even before the war – a chaos which, despite its creative aspects, was primarily destructive. Adenauer was not affected by the rationalism of the technological age, nor was he a politically unstable romantic. He did not question the values of bourgeois society; he had no sense of the stimulus of explosive ideas and late-night discussions, and no sympathy for excessive emotion in personal or political life.

Instead, Adenauer placed his faith in bourgeois common-sense, bourgeois order, bourgeois and Christian morals and values, bourgeois diligence and intelligence. His temperament, career and responsibilities made him a natural enemy of disorder, inefficiency, irrationality and political immorality. In the last years of his life he once said that he would have liked to add to the Catholic Index of Banned Books Goethe's *Faust*[1] which, along with Nietzsche's *Zarathustra* and Hölderlin's *Hyperion*, was the book carried in the knapsacks of the members of the Youth Movement as they went to volunteer for the war. Adenauer was a solid middle-class citizen who would always mistrust – and even loathe – the German tendency towards extremes. He was a man without direct experience of front-line service or the Youth Movement; a local politician who had no hand in framing Wilhelmine foreign policy and therefore felt free to criticise it; an upwardly mobile member of the middle classes with some awareness of the social needs of his time; and a man who was old enough to be convinced that violence, revolution and radical Utopianism would only intensify current crises.

There are no surviving records of Adenauer's views regarding the war, nor of his attitude towards the pre-war foreign policy of Imperial Germany. Nevertheless, from observations he made as Chancellor over forty years later, we can tell that certain events made a powerful impression upon him. Like many other Germans of his generation, he was haunted by the trauma of "encirclement". Even in the 1960s he could still recall how the French fleet had visited the Russian port of Kronstadt in 1891 in the prelude to the Franco-Russian military convention. There is no doubt that co-operation between France and Russia against Germany was one of his most deep-rooted foreign-policy fears. Adenauer's later view of Russia – and the Soviet Union – as a world power appears to have been influenced by the attitudes of the German middle classes in the last two decades of the nineteenth century – when it was regarded as an autocratic empire, an expansionist colossus, which could only be prevented from aggression by means of superior strength and a superior alliance policy.

When Adenauer did make private criticisms of Germany's pre-war foreign policy, he drew particular attention to its lack of plain common sense. Adenauer, who loved historical digressions, once told John Foster Dulles that the decline of Britain had only been concealed because the German leadership had been so foolish as to rally an entire army of opponents against Germany in both 1914 and 1939.[2] Such statements reveal that, at least in regard to 1914, his interpretation of events was unaffected by notions of guilt and fate. The tragedy, or so he thought later, had been the result of a lack of political wisdom: '1914-1918 was a war which was brought about by the stupidity of everyone.'

One of the certainties of Adenauer's youth was his belief in the superiority of European civilisation and technology. At the second party conference of the CDU in the British Zone, held at Recklinghausen in August 1948, he gave voice to this belief: 'If you think back more than forty-five years and realise what Europe was when France and Italy were great powers, when England was the greatest naval power with a fleet bigger than the two next biggest fleets combined, when the United States was still a debtor nation, when Austria-Hungary and the Balkan states were still connected to western Europe, when Russia was not ruled by its Asiatic sector alone but the west-Russian sector still had influence – and when you look at Europe today, you recognise its shocking decline.'[3] This sense of pride in the powerful role of Germany and the concert of leading European nations was expressed at a time when these great powers had been overtaken by catastrophe. In all likelihood Adenauer had been influenced by the enormous self-confidence of the European great powers in the pre-war period – and had not suspected its potentially catastrophic consequences.

Adenauer's attitude towards colonialism was also typical of his generation. As late as 1927, in response to a questionnaire, he answered: 'The German Reich must strive to acquire colonies at all costs ... We must have more room for our people, and therefore colonies.' He believed that the best solution would be for Germany to have its own colonies as in the period before 1914; as a step in this direction, a colonial mandate should be sought. In the early 1930s he had no misgivings about being elected deputy president of the German Colonial Society for a short time. This decision was almost certainly the result of his links with Cologne banking circles, which had been involved in colonial business before 1914, and was probably suggested by Robert Pferdmenges. However, Adenauer did not take up this honorary post, for reasons which remain unclear; his name does not appear on the list of board members between 1931 and 1934 and his few remarks on the colonial question are generally uninformative.[4] Yet the fact that he retained an interest in the topic in the late 1920s gives a strong indication of his earlier attitudes.

As Chancellor in the 1950s, his private comments on the subject of decolonisation reveal misgivings about the retreat of the colonial powers, partly for geo-political reasons but also because he doubted the ability of the underdeveloped countries to take responsibility for their future. He told Ben Gurion that Albert Schweitzer had said to him that the Africans were still incapable of ruling themselves. Ben Gurion, whose government was adopting a progressive policy towards Africa, had little sympathy for this view, but Adenauer shared Schweitzer's opinion.[5] In 1960 he drew the attention of Couve de Murville to the fact that the developing countries would soon have the majority of seats in the UN, adding that the policy was absurd and would lead to the self-destruction of the white race.[6]

Although Adenauer called for liberal solutions to the conflict in Algeria, which preoccupied him greatly at the end of the 1950s and in the early 1960s, his attitude towards the demand of colonial peoples for independence remained fundamentally paternalistic. Traces of the imperialist spirit of Wilhelmine Germany continued to influence his thinking.

It is thus possible to recognise Adenauer's response to certain events that he witnessed as an observer – and not a participant – before 1914. However, we have no documents which might shed light on his attitude in the war years themselves. For that reason we can only suspect that he too was swept along by the wave of patriotic emotion which overwhelmed the peoples of Europe in August 1914. The Cologne-based regiments left for the front amid scenes of great jubilation. The oldest Adenauer son, Konrad, was to remember his mother standing with other women on Dürener Straße near their home, handing glasses of raspberry juice to the passing soldiers.[7] Adenauer was not drafted. After 1898, owing to his poor health, he had been found fit only for the first reserve of the home guard,[8] though he had to make an appearance before the Army Reserve Office from time to time during the war. There, however, the officials took the view that he could best serve his country by remaining in his key job within the municipal administration rather than by joining the home guard as a private.

At the beginning of the war Adenauer was fully occupied by the new tasks confronting the municipal administration. Just as Cologne had been a dynamic force behind the economic and cultural boom in pre-war Germany, it was now an important contributor to the war effort. However, complete mobilisation of civilian life for the war effort occurred only gradually and step by step.

The emergency measures of summer 1914 reflected the widespread popular expectation of a rapid victory followed by a peace settlement favourable to Germany. Only in the 1920s was Ernst Jünger to coin the phrase 'total mobilisation' to describe the progress of events. However, at the top of the municipal administration in Cologne it was clear that the city was facing new responsibilities. Cologne was now a genuine fortress city. It was also a railway junction serving the front in Belgium and northern France; during the mobilisation a train full of soldiers passed over the Hohenzollern bridge every ten minutes. Industry too was converted to armaments production. Instead of art enthusiasts, the city was now crowded with soldiers on leave. As young men were drafted into the armed forces, women took work in the factories and offices for the first time. Over the next four years, the cultural life of the city was devoted primarily to the maintenance of morale. Moreover, the city authorities now faced the same basic problems as any other fortress: food supplies had to be procured and distributed; the wounded and civilians had to be cared for; important raw materials had to be obtained, which included the melting down of the cathedral's five-ton Imperial bell.

Even before war was declared, conferences were held between officials at the town hall, the district president and the regional government to discuss ways of supplying fortress Cologne with food. Adenauer, who became the key figure in the procurement of foodstuffs for the city, was already at the centre of events. The military authorities, which wanted to ensure that the city was well supplied in case of siege, demanded the establishment of large warehouses to supply the garrison of some 60,000 men. On 5 August 1914 a decree was issued preventing food from being removed from the fortified area. At the same time, the city authorities launched an ambitious programme of buying whatever non-perishable goods were available. Mountains of flour, lentils, rice, fat and peas were collected in the great warehouses at Rheinau dock.

At the outset Adenauer was involved mainly in financing these purchases. On 2 August 1914 the city council passed a six million mark credit for advance provisioning, four millions of which was spent after three weeks. Cologne now had sufficient supplies for two-and-a-half months, but the military authorities were pressing for the building up of stocks which would last for five months. This decision paid off in the winter of 1918/19, when Cologne was occupied by the British but was still suffering the effects of the blockade.

From the first weeks of the war until his serious accident in early 1917, Adenauer, in addition to his other duties for the city's Foodstuffs

Office, was responsible for supplying Cologne with wood, coal and petroleum. Since no central procurement authority had been established, his Procurement Commission purchased whatever it could find: dairy cows and meat from Holland, powdered milk from Kleve, sauerkraut from Neuss. One thousand calves were herded into the festival hall where the Werkbund exhibition had recently been held, and were permitted to graze in the city parks. The city authorities signed contracts with the surrounding regions and with individual farmers for the delivery of food supplies. Pastures in Oldenburg, Gummersbach and Waldbröl were leased and successful attempts made to deep-freeze meat. However, Adenauer's independent activities in this area came to an end in the spring of 1916 after the national government established its own 'Reich Meat Office'. The consequences of this expansion of bureaucracy were easy to foresee: several months later meat rationing had to be imposed in Cologne, which had previously been relatively well supplied.

Savings were the order of the day everywhere. Initially Adenauer had a good reputation with the public for his energetic efforts to provide supplies. Gradually, however, he came to bear the brunt of popular criticism as the war dragged on, food shortages became widespread and the quality of the available foodstuffs deteriorated. Nevertheless, as the descendant of a Bonn baking family, Adenauer was proud of his work with the brothers Jean and Josef Oebel of the Rhenish Bread Factory in the development of 'Cologne bread'.[9] This bread, made of corn, barley and ground rice, was available without bread coupons until Romania entered the war in 1916. It was very far from being a delicacy, particularly after Adenauer, in an attempt to restrain people's appetite, ordered bakeries only to sell bread that had been stored for two days. Bread, milk and meat all became scarce and deteriorated in quality. The longer the war lasted, the greater was the recourse to foodstuffs which had not been intended for human consumption: a vegetable substitute instead of potatoes, ersatz coffee made of barley and chicory, horse meat, turnips which were normally fed to cattle. Thenceforth the head of the city food supply authorities was given the uncomplimentary nickname 'Graupenauer' (Pot-Barley Adenauer).

Nevertheless, it was clear to informed observers, aware of the complexities of politics and administration, that Adenauer's achievements in supplying the city with food were considerable. Admittedly he made enemies of certain vested interests, such as the city's bakers, most of whom would have preferred to sell higher priced goods to their wealthy clients despite the restrictions on the consumption of flour. Adenauer, who realised the dangers of acute shortages, insisted on partial rationing and a single form of bread. Though he sympathised with the commercial middle class which had always been close to the Centre Party, he was convinced that the public authorities must take decisive action. If the bakeries would not produce what was necessary, the city would have to bake bread in factories and turn the bakeries into mere bread outlets.

Germany's comfortable old order was thus eclipsed within three years of the onset of war. In addition to the municipal food-supply sales outlets, giant kitchens were established in working-class districts to mince and press an almost tasteless paste which could supply 200,000 rations per day. Though the city was proud to show these institutions to foreign observers, local consumers were conspicuous by their absence.

At this stage Adenauer also began to voice those criticisms of distant, over-bureaucratic central authorities for which he was to be well known as mayor. He complained that the city was being forced to pay the price for wrong decisions taken in far-away Berlin; although a high degree of automony in the procurement of supplies would be best for Cologne, events were moving in the opposite direction. For the *Kölnische Zeitung* Adenauer wrote a number of articles on the subject which were published in 1915 by the Berlin publishing house Concordia under the title *New Regulations for Our Food Supply Economy*. His arguments, however, evoked little response.

Adenauer was tireless in his efforts to organise and experiment, devoting particular attention to the need for appropriate regulations to control the situation. At the same time – like many middle-class civil servants and politicians in those years – he discovered the importance of the workers and the trade unions. 'War socialism' and its theoretical justifications did not leave him untouched.

He had never been indifferent or unsympathetic to the ordinary people. Awareness of the social problems and requirements of the time had been encouraged not only by his personal development, but also by his background and associations in the Centre Party. Already, in 1902, when he was applying for a legal position in Gelsenkirchen, he had noted in a letter – never sent – that the advantage of working at municipal level was that 'one could become socially active'.[10] This might have been a tactical approach, since the socially active wing of the Centre Party, the Mönchengladbach school, was influential in Gelsenkirchen. However, in 1906, after Becker had congratulated Adenauer on his election to Deputy, Adenauer gave a short speech in which he again mentioned the social aspect of municipal activity in addition to the standard assertions about its ethical and cultural values.[11]

On the other hand, his previous activities as First Deputy tend to indicate that Adenauer's main interests were efficiency, rationalisation and budget cutting. His own rise into the ranks of Cologne's prosperous middle classes may well have blunted some of his social awareness. Nevertheless, during the war he was confronted each day with evidence of the needs of ordinary people, and in particular of manual workers and their families. Adenauer was also distressed by the rampant greed of the black-marketeers and other war profiteers. He quickly realised that he would need close contact with the Social Democrats, the unions and consumer groups. Moreover, the unions and the majority Social Democrats were already working in the commissions responsible for the distribution of goods. According to the SPD newspaper in Cologne, it was there that he discovered that 'Cologne's poorest sons were her most loyal'.[12]

The liveliest of Cologne's Social Democrats was Wilhelm Sollmann. Born in Thuringia in 1881 and thus almost a contemporary of Adenauer, Sollmann had been devoted to his adopted city ever since beginning a commercial apprenticeship there. After 1903 he had also become a committed and occasionally aggressive Social Democrat. Lean and intellectual, Sollmann was self-educated after leaving his Gymnasium early; he was also a strict tee-totaller who had met his wife at a meeting of the Good Templars. He was associated with the *Rheinische Zeitung* as the local editor and made his name during the Cologne 'baksheesh trial' of 1914 in which corrupt police officers were brought to justice; Sollmann had managed to get the city's police president dismissed.

Along with his friend Johann Meerfeld, Sollmann quickly became the dominant figure in the city's SPD. At the outbreak of war he remained a convinced Marxist in the ranks of the majority Socialists, the party which initially tried to outdo all others with its patriotism. Unable to serve in the army because of a heart condition, Sollmann worked in the party and through the *Rheinische Zeitung* in order to persuade his comrades to continue their support for the war. At the same time, he attempted to pressurise the obdurate bourgeoisie into extensive and overdue domestic reforms: elimination of the Three-Class suffrage, votes for women, the eight-hour work-day, and the nationalisation of the means of production.

Sollmann made a deep and favourable impression on many of those with whom he came into contact. He was described by Arnold Brecht, an undersecretary in the Reich Ministry of the Interior, as 'one of the most splendid men I have ever met, manly, courageous and direct'.[13] Wilhelm Marx, Centre Party member and Chancellor between 1923 and 1925, offered similar praise: 'He was somewhat passionate, but an idealistic and very decent man.'[14]

After 1914 Sollmann moved increasingly to the right. During the war he came to embody that element of the SPD which was to support the Weimar coalition after the November Revolution despite continuing ideological differences with the Centre Party and the Liberals. In early postwar Cologne Sollmann became one of Adenauer's most important partners and opponents at a time when Adenauer was evolving from an administrator into a political figure.

Even before his election as mayor, Adenauer agreed with Sollmann that in 1918 three Social Democrats would at last be included in the *city council*, which had previously been controlled by the Liberals and Centre Party alone. Later the SPD was to acknowledge this decision openly: an article in the *Rheinische Zeitung* on 28 December 1920 asserted that 'during the war it was he who, when his predecessor had not even begun to reconsider, had sought and found the way to an understanding with the socialist workers and to achievable goals.'[15]

Sollmann watched Adenauer's development with interest. Following Adenauer's election as mayor, Sollmann published an editorial on 19 September 1917 which provides the best portrait of Adenauer during this period.[16] Though Adenauer was known to be a 'pious, church-going Catholic', there had been no known occasion when 'he could be suspected of adopting a party – political position in favour of any denomination'. The rise of such a relatively young man had certainly been facilitated by the support of the Centre Party in the town hall, but 'competence and extraordinary diligence had also played a part'. He had not failed in any of his duties.

Sollmann described Adenauer as a 'sober, almost boring person. He is no dazzler.' And he conceded: 'it is certain that during the war he has shown the valuable ability to learn. The Mayor Adenauer of 1917 is a different person from the First Deputy of 1914. We are certain of one thing: he has social feeling and social understanding. His origins in the broad classes of the people will perhaps make this easier for him. After all, the father of the city's new leader was a minor official in the legal service whose family had worries of its own, and being aware of them can be very useful to a high public official.'

Over the following years the two men were to clash on many occasions. All in all, Adenauer's attitude to Sollmann was marked by cautious detachment combined with genuine respect. In 1945, when Adenauer swiftly began to restore the links that had been broken in 1933, one of his longest – and uncharacteristically warm – letters was written to Sollmann, who had emigrated to the United States and was living and teaching at the Quaker College of Pendle Hills: 'I always liked to remember you even if we were sometimes of different opinions. Intellectual disagreements are a part of life and are necessary for any progress. The intellectual disagreements with you were always a pleasure to me.'[17] Sollmann took a similar view. After visiting the Chancellor in 1949 he wrote to Fritz Heine of the SPD executive: 'Adenauer has been my opponent and my personal friend since 1915. Between 1916 and 1933 we discussed and did many things which demanded the closest mutual trust and honest mutual information. In those years Adenauer never disappointed me.'[18]

This was more than the desire to see the past in the best possible light. The two men were referring to an important political bond which both – for good reasons – had little wish to make public; it had been created during the increasingly difficult war years between 1914 and 1918 and subsequently withstood all further strains until Sollmann's death in 1951.

During the war, the Social Democrats in Cologne remained a latent rather than a dominant political force. Only the Centre Party and the Liberals were represented on the city council, the former with thirty-six seats and the latter with twenty-four. Nothing could be done without, or against the wishes of, the leading figures on the wartime council, who would continue to set the tone during the sixteen years of Adenauer's tenure as mayor.

Since Karl Trimborn had left Cologne's Centre Party caucus for a high-profile position in the Reichstag and the Prussian Landtag, the local party had been dominated by Hugo Mönnig and Johannes Rings. Dr Mönnig, a *Justizrat* who represented the middle-class wing of the Centre Party, was elected to the city council in 1902 and, at the age of fifty, was in the prime of his life when war broke out in 1914. For the next two decades, until the political catastrophe of spring 1933, he was at the heart of Centre Party politics in Cologne and the Rhineland. In 1921 he was appointed chairman of the caucus in the city council, was involved with the party press, supervised the organisation and financing of election campaigns, and negotiated with the parties in the town hall and with the city administration. In short, he was a power broker in the American style, a self-confident man whose relations with Adenauer remained relatively distant. In 1945 Mönnig was one of the veteran Centre Party leaders who supported the creation of a Christian Democratic Union. He even lived to see, at the age of eighty-six, the election of Adenauer as Chancellor.

The working-class wing of the party was represented by Johannes Baptist Rings, a former printer's supervisor who was forty-four years old when he was elected to the council in 1900. He was later to recall how the fine gentlemen of the bourgeois Centre Party had refused to shake hands with this 'Centre proletarian' after his election. However, this situation quickly changed as the white-haired and bearded Rings became chief editor of the *Kölner Lokalanzeiger*. Between 1919 and 1933 he was party chairman in Cologne, where he kept firm control of the lower middle-class and working-class membership. Rings was a decent and unselfish individual. Despite occasional differences of opinion between himself and Adenauer, their relationship was marked by a mutual respect based on recognition of shared qualities of conscientiousness, diligence and sound political sense.[19]

If the Centre Party was generally a tight-knit and unified organisation, the Liberals in Cologne were more diverse and contained a larger proportion of headstrong proprietors and professional men. After the election of 1909 their most glamorous figure was Louis Hagen. His grandfather, Abraham Loeb – a man of relatively modest means – had worked his way up from being a messenger at the Sal. Oppenheim Jr. & Cie Bank to the position of banker. Successful speculation on the stock market and a good marriage assisted the rise of Loeb's son and, in the next generation, Louis Heymann Levy followed in his father's footsteps. Born in 1855, Hagen was a man of great vitality, charm, organisational skills and business acumen. At the age of thirty-three he married Emma Hagen, the daughter of a Christian industrialist, converted to the Catholic faith (it was rumoured, mysteriously, that he had been baptized twice), and took the name Louis Hagen. One Cologne anecdote about his baptismal instruction deserves to be quoted because it reveals how the man thought and how others thought of him. When the priest asked if he knew any good works, Hagen answered 'Harpen, Gelsenkirchen, Phoenix'. The startled priest said he had meant Christian works, to which Hagen was said to have replied 'Siemens'.[20]

Hagen did indeed have a sixth sense for this type of good work. He reached the top of the Rhenish 'money aristocracy' not only through successful speculation and social glamour, but also through his sound judgement in organising industrial takeovers. From an early stage he was active in the financial markets of Berlin and Cologne. In the Wilhelmine era Hagen was regarded as a very successful 'marriage broker' between industrial firms and trading houses, and also between Cologne banks and Berlin banking houses, including Eugen Gutmann's Dresdner Bank and the Disconto-Gesellschaft. Whatever the outcome of the mergers, Hagen himself made a profit from his activities. Before war broke out he was on the boards of thirty-nine companies; in the 1920s he held the German record for being on the most boards; towards the end of his life he was reputed to have been on the boards of ninety companies.

Increasingly Hagen was also appointed to honorary economic posts. From 1915 until the year of his death in 1932, he was president of Cologne's Chamber of Commerce as well as on the boards of various national and international chambers. He also tried to emulate the glamorous lifestyle of the Oppenheimers. In the 1890s he was considered to be something of a playboy – though he always attempted to be discreet. One of Hagen's many attractive female companions was Jenny Gross, the Berlin actress and socialite; another was an attractive Hungarian artist. His daughters married into the German aristocracy – one to the German tennis star Gottfried von Cramm.

Invitations to the Hagen home were sought by everyone who wanted to be part of Cologne society. Though the Hagens had been shunned at the turn of the century, this period of social exclusion was now past. Like other members of the city's upper classes, Hagen was a generous patron of his city: the beneficiaries ranged from the University to the zoo. Large numbers of men in the business community had some form of obligation to him, but his philosophy was to use his power in a manner that would not cause resentment or offence. One of the men whose career he assisted – again without causing the recipient any humiliation – was Konrad Adenauer. None of the other Liberal members of the *Stadtrat* could rival Hagen's influence or reputation, not even Gustav von Mallinckrodt, Josef Neven DuMont, or Emil von Rath of the sugar dynasty.

During this period the chairman of the Liberals, *Justizrat* Bernhard Falk, a lawyer in the Court of Appeal, was one of the most politically influential members of the caucus. A practising member of the Jewish community, Falk was an open-minded man and a patriot, proud of having served Prussia and Germany as a reserve officer. He began his career as a reforming Liberal in the Naumann style, while his wife was the driving force of the womens' associations in Cologne. Falk was on good terms with Adenauer, and it was he who provided one of the most detailed accounts of Adenauer's early days as mayor.

The Youngest Mayor in Prussia

The complicated manoeuvres for the office of mayor began in February 1916. Chief among the protagonists were the Centre Party members Hugo Mönnig and Johannes Rings, the Liberals Louis Hagen and Bernhard Falk, and the mayor himself, Max Wallraf. That month – Adenauer had just celebrated his fortieth birthday – saw the death of the mayor of Aachen, Philipp Veltmann. The Centre was the majority party in the city, and Adenauer was quickly informed that its members had agreed to support his candidacy for mayor.

In this instance the manoeuvres of the First Deputy deserve close scrutiny. They reveal more about Adenauer and the circumstances of his election as mayor of Cologne than the relatively smooth negotiations of the following year. In theory Adenauer should have been delighted by the offer from Aachen, a city with a population of some 160,000 where he would have been the dominant figure. If he stayed in Cologne he would remain second in command, since Wallraf's term was not due to expire until 1919. It was doubtful that the sixty-year-old mayor either would or could run for re-election, especially without the direct backing of any of the parties. On the other hand, it was also probable that the Three-Class Electoral Law would be abolished at the end of the war, which might easily damage the Liberals and produce a strong Social Democratic presence. Wallraf's relations with the Social Democrats were not particularly good, and the Centre Party had reservations about such an openly independent mayor. Why did Adenauer not accept the flattering offer from Aachen and wait to see how the situation developed in Cologne? He might very well have been able to return home after three years in Aachen. Financially, too, the prospects were excellent: the salary in Aachen would be 40,000 marks, twice his salary in Cologne.

Notes for this section begin on page 706.

Part of the reason for Adenauer's decision not to take the post involved the associated political uncertainties. In addition, there was a rival waiting in the wings, a man with whom he was on friendly terms – Wilhelm Farwick of the Schaaffhausen Bank. If Adenauer were to leave Cologne, the Centre could well regard Farwick as a viable alternative when the time came to elect a new mayor.

Adenauer first spoke privately with Wallraf. The mayor, who had no wish to see his hard-working First Deputy leave Cologne, advised him to stay on. Wallraf knew and liked Aachen, having served there as president of police between 1900 and 1903, but he warned that 'the unique Aachen milieu' might not suit Adenauer and his wife Emma.[1] He then remarked, significantly, that he had no plans to grow old in Cologne.[2]

Wallraf's exact meaning is not clear. He may have wanted to hint that he either could not, or did not wish to, be nominated for another term as mayor in 1919. However, as a former senior Prussian civil servant he was known to have good connections in Berlin and had been a member of the Prussian Upper Chamber since 1907. Was there perhaps an important government post in the offing? Several months later, the mayor of Düsseldorf heard rumours to that effect.[3]

Subsequently Adenauer held talks with Hugo Mönnig, leader of the Centre Party, and with members of the Liberal caucus, though the subject of the talks remains a mystery. It is possible that Adenauer wanted to discover whether he might have the chance to return from Aachen to Cologne in 1919. Or was he merely hoping to obtain declarations of goodwill to enable him to push up his price for moving to Aachen? In any case, the Liberals in the city council discussed the problem at the end of February, and the Centre even earlier. Mönnig told Adenauer that if the election were held now, the Centre would support him, and the Liberals let it be known that they would regard Adenauer as an acceptable candidate.

These proceedings, though understandable, were nevertheless unusual. Understandable in that the city councillors wanted to persuade Adenauer of their esteem in order to convince him to stay in Cologne; and unusual because they were meeting behind closed doors and talking directly with the First Deputy about the succession to a mayor who had not shown any signs of retirement.

Initially Adenauer appears to have handled matters somewhat hesitantly. However, the situation became more complicated after Wallraf had an accident in early May 1916 and had to rest for three weeks in a sanatorium. He then decided to round off his rest cure by going hunting – whereupon the butt of his rifle bounced into his face and injured his eye.[4] Adenauer could no longer concentrate on negotiating his departure from Cologne, since his first priority was to stand in for his injured boss. On the other hand, during Wallraf's prolonged absence he had the perfect opportunity to show that he could do the job well.

This temporary arrangement was not only a chance to make a good impression. It was also at this stage that Adenauer made his first recorded comments on international relations, at a dinner for foreign delegates. He gave his opinion as follows: 'Alliances between nations are not a matter of sentiment, they must be built on a foundation of common political and economic interests and goals. That is the first condition for their durability. If to these equal interests is added common ground in thought and sentiment and mutual understanding, then a second bond will be wrapped around peoples that are already firmly associated.'

It might be tempting to detect in these words a hint of Adenauer's later support for an 'organic integration' of the German economy with the economies of the western European nations. Yet this particular declaration was not directed to the west: the delegates were from Bulgaria, the only one of the smaller Balkan countries to be allied with the Central Powers.[5]

The pressure from Aachen continued to mount. At the beginning of July 1916 Adenauer discovered that the position would now be advertised in the regular fashion, but that if he were to apply, he would be guaranteed a unanimous vote anyway. Once again he discussed the situation with Mönnig, who was now somewhat more precise. His Centre Party colleague pointed out something which Adenauer must already have realised: it was unlikely that the Centre Party would be able to retain its majority on the city council in 1919. Adenauer then mentioned Wallraf's remark about not intending to grow old in Cologne, and asked if the election might not be held much earlier than expected. Mönnig, however, told him that he could make no guarantees for the period after 1917.

The issue appears to have involved more than Adenauer's own future plans. In all probability the Centre was gripped by the same mood that had seized the Liberals in 1907 over the future of Wilhelm Becker. Did the Centre Party want to hasten Wallraf's departure and put their own man in place while they still had a majority? In any event Adenauer was in a difficult position. It seemed that he would have to accept the post in Aachen, unless Wallraf was prepared to give him more details about his own plans. Yet how could Adenauer ask the mayor, who was still convalescing, without arousing Wallraf's suspicion that his deputy was gaining the support of the parties in the town hall and trying to push him out of office?

Drafts of letters written to Wallraf in Freiburg were found among Adenauer's unpublished documents after his death. These reveal how Adenauer hedged, and the care he devoted to the contents and style of the letter.[6] Nevertheless, he made mistakes. At first he told Wallraf that he had turned down the offer from Aachen and that Mönnig had assured him of the goodwill of the Centre Party in future. Wallraf answered with a friendly letter on 9 July 1916, telling Adenauer that he had made 'a good decision'.[7]

Five days later Adenauer felt the need to write again in order to explain his problem in detail. He had concluded that 'I can only turn down

Aachen, which I can certainly have, if I can be certain to succeed in Cologne'. There was much to be said for taking the job in Aachen, he wrote. It would mean a less complicated political landscape in the foreseeable future; there would no risk of getting stuck in a subordinate post in Cologne; and there was the financial aspect. On the other hand, he had no wish to leave Cologne in the difficult situation it faced. Finally he came to the point: 'Will the Centre be placed in a position where it has to elect a new mayor by the end of 1917? An answer of yes to this question would mean me turning down Aachen.'[8] The question was raised in such a way, involving the Centre Party caucus, that it could be seen as a hidden threat.

That was not all. Adenauer again approached the Liberals, encouraging them to state their position on his political future in Cologne. In February the Liberals had politely declined to give a blank cheque for the distant future, but now thought it advisable to send a delegation to Freiburg to ask the convalescent Wallraf exactly what was happening. By now the mayor had replied to Adenauer's express letter with a relatively brusque rejection. Should Adenauer go to Aachen, he wrote, 'I would find that regrettable for the city at the present moment. But I cannot give you my word that I will definitely step down from my post within a year in order to allow you to turn down Aachen. If you now decide on Aachen, then please notify me as soon as possible so that I can give my doctor notice that I will break off my treatment.'[9] Though the letter was couched in formal terms, it could hardly have expressed his displeasure more clearly.

Wallraf's convalescence in Freiburg was scarcely improved by the information from his Liberal visitors that Adenauer had asked the caucus to consider the matter. For their part, the Liberals were astonished to discover that Adenauer had failed to notify the mayor. The caucus therefore decided to send Adenauer packing, maintaining that they had never confirmed him as their choice as Wallraf's successor. Adenauer was now forced to grit his teeth and write again to his 'dear Uncle Max'. He had, he wrote, been under considerable strain at work when he wrote the letter of 16 July, and he tried to interpret the affair as a misunderstanding (which it was not). In any case, the result was that 'I will not go to Aachen'.[10] Adenauer had after all decided not to take the easy prize, but to wait for his opportunity in Cologne.

This interlude did him no lasting harm. By 1917 it seemed to have been forgotten, perhaps even by Wallraf – although his memoirs conspicuously fail to mention his successor. In November 1916 Wilhelm Farwick was appointed mayor of Aachen, effectively putting him out of the running when the question of the succession to Wallraf was raised again in the summer of 1917.

The year 1916 was a bad one for Adenauer. His wife Emma died only three months after this damaging episode. Her kidney disease had confined her to bed for long periods, and even prolonged stays in spa resorts had been unable to effect a cure. Adenauer's brother-in-law reported that his behaviour during this long illness had been exemplary. When he came home from work at night he had cared for his wife – who no longer wished to see other people – and continued to do his best to comfort and entertain her. Her death occured when Adenauer was on a business trip to Berlin in October. The family ate a meal of spoiled mushrooms. All of them became ill, but Frau Adenauer died of kidney failure.

In those days, death had not yet been pushed aside to hospitals and funeral parlours. Emma Adenauer lay, until her funeral, at the family home in Max-Bruch-Straße. Their eldest son Konrad later recalled that her bed had been covered with roses. Adenauer himself led the funeral procession – women were not allowed to take part – to the Melaten cemetery. The tombstone was carved from a square piece of sandstone, and the relief, which was created for Adenauer by Professor Theodor Georgii, showed Christ rising from the dead. Following the death of his second wife in 1948, Adenauer had the tombstone and the remains of his first wife moved to the wooded cemetery in Rhöndorf which was eventually to become his own last resting place.

Adenauer found his loss difficult to bear. His children later reported that he had been inconsolable for months after Emma's death. His family continued to wear mourning until Christmas 1917, over a year later. Adenauer's mother, who lived in the family home, did her best to take over the running of the household, but there were disputes with maids and incidents of theft in the motherless household. Adenauer's brother Hans, now a priest in Rath near Düsseldorf, visited frequently to offer what comfort he could.

At weekends Adenauer made an effort to fulfill his obligations to his young family. On Sundays in the winter he and his oldest boy, ten-year-old Konrad, took their sledge and caught the Frankfurt train, getting off in Königswinter to go sledging in the Siebengebirge. Usually they would stop at the Löwenburg inn to eat sandwiches and a thin soup before sledging down the hill together.

In March 1917 Adenauer's troubles were compounded by a serious accident. The chauffeur of his limousine fell asleep at the wheel and the car crashed into a tram. Adenauer was thrown through the glass partition, suffering serious cuts to his face and lip and breaking his nose and jaw. Despite further injuries to his knees, hands and feet, he crawled out of the wreckage and walked straight to the hospital, where he had to be stitched without anaesthetic because of the amount of blood he had lost. His sight was still impaired some weeks later and, indeed, the problem never completely left him: from then on he tended to see double when he walked downstairs whilst looking at the floor. The headaches he had suffered since he was twenty-three got even worse.[11] Adenauer remained in hospital for three weeks, followed by three months of convalescence in St Blasien.

Adenauer recorded his feelings after the accident in a note written on 31 December 1917: 'Despite physical suffering I had a feeling of spiritual liberation, the feeling that I was now released from my entire spiritual suffering, and although I hovered between life and death, the first days after my accident were full of spiritual quiet and spiritual peace such as I had not known since summer 1913, since my wife became seriously ill.'[12] As well as demonstrating his stoicism, the accident also gave Adenauer his characteristic facial features. Sharp tongues claimed that he had 'the head of a mongol', while more generous souls compared his face to that of an Indian chief.

These circumstances did nothing to lift Adenauer's depression. At the end of 1917 he began writing a diary – which, unfortunately for his biographers, he abandoned after less than five pages. Nevertheless, his comments on New Year's Eve 1917 provide a rare insight into his inner life:

> 1917 was difficult, very difficult for me, full of physical and spiritual torture and anguish. The whole year was filled with pain and suffering and longing for my dear wife. My concern for the upbringing of my beloved children, to whom I could not devote sufficient attention, also weighed heavily on me; motherless children – that is something endlessly sad. The first months of the year brought me excessive amounts of work; for me the work was a drug to alleviate my suffering. Ever since I was appointed to a high position while still young I have been much envied, but I am wretched, terribly wretched![13]

At the time this account was written Adenauer was a successful civil servant who had reached the pinnacle of his career some three months earlier, on 18 September 1917. At the age of forty-one he had become mayor of his home city and the youngest mayor in Prussia.

Wallraf had finally been called to Berlin in August 1917. There is no reason to doubt the claim in his memoirs that he had been surprised by the offer of the post of State Secretary at the Ministry of the Interior; his earlier comment about not wanting to grow old in Cologne was probably nothing more than a cryptic reference to possible retirement in 1919. The ministerial post was vacant because of the decision of Chancellor Bethmann Hollweg to step down on 13 July 1917 and the appointment as his successor of the devout Georg Michaelis, former under secretary and head of the *Reichsgetreidestelle* (Imperial Grain Bureau). It was Michaelis who offered Wallraf, a man he knew well, the Ministry of the Interior, now shorn of some of its responsibilities by the creation of the *Reichswirtschaftsamt* (Reich Economics Department). Wallraf, unaware of how short-lived this adventure would be, left Cologne at extremely short notice: the appointment was announced on 8 August and he held a farewell celebration in the Gürzenich hall the following day.

Adenauer finally faced the situation he had been waiting for ever since turning down the post in Aachen. However, he was still recuperating in the Black Forest and had just written to say that he planned to extend his stay until the middle of December.[14] There was an immediate exchange of letters between Cologne and St Blasien, which enable us to reconstruct Adenauer's election in some detail.

The Centre Party remained in control of events. Its leaders were well aware of the main – and potentially serious – obstacle to the appointment of Adenauer. The question was whether he had suffered any permanent injuries – perhaps even brain damage – in his accident. Mönnig and Rings came to visit him, consulting with his doctor before holding a long conversation with Adenauer. They also had to get used to his 'new' face. At the end of their talk Adenauer told them: 'Gentlemen, I'm only abnormal on the outside!'[15] Once their minds had been set at rest, Mönnig and Rings could talk about the elections and return to Cologne with reassuring news.

Shortly before this visit, Louis Hagen of the Liberals had written to tell Adenauer about the situation in the town hall. Subsequently, in a letter dated 25 August, he informed Adenauer that 'I was genuinely happy to receive the very good reports brought by the gentlemen Mönnig and Rings concerning the state of your health. Now the last trace left by that dreadful accident has disappeared. Your appearance, your memory, everything was flawless – thank God!'[16]

However, the decision-making process among the Liberals was less smooth than in the Centre Party. Here the role of kingmaker was played by Louis Hagen. The support given to Adenauer by this representative of Cologne's capitalist community was striking. The candidate must have been impressed by Hagen's detailed reports – often handwritten – from his office in Cologne or from Birlinghoven Castle. Part of Hagen's reasoning may have been tactical: he was aware that Adenauer would soon be in control and knew the important of ties of mutual respect. Yet Hagen's support may also have been the result of his observation of the rising star and his conclusion that Adenauer was the best man for the city and Hagen's own business interests. Whatever the reasons, Hagen's friendly support for Adenauer during these weeks was recognised by political insiders. Over the following years the older and the younger man established a close alliance. Despite occasional disagreements their relationship was characterised by mutual respect and the knowledge that each could rely on the other.

To a certain extent, the Liberals would have to ignore their principles in order to support Adenauer. However, they were also aware that there could have been worse Centre Party candidates. The leader of the Liberal group, Bernhard Falk, wrote later that the majority party in the town hall had wanted 'a dyed-in-the-wool Centre-Party man', but he added: 'From the beginning of our acquaintance until today I have regarded Adenauer as a tolerant, candid and progressive man with strong democratic and social convictions.'[17] In an important conversation between the two men, Adenauer told Falk that 'if you do not want me, you will get Mr Whatshisname, mayor of some medium-sized city on the Rhine, who might have made a name for himself at municipal level but who will also have been a particularly active servant of the Centre Party'. Falk had no need to be persuaded.

This assessment of Adenauer, which is taken from Falk's memoirs, was widely shared, as the press reports of the time confirm: 'a first class administrator', 'a tireless worker', 'a knowledgeable municipal politician', 'an excellent speaker'. In retrospect he was credited with both 'unyielding energy' and initiative; moreover – and this was the constant factor – he knew the local administration 'inside out'. There were certain doubts, which Adenauer eventually removed, concerning his ability to represent the city in style. It was generally thought that here Wallraf had set standards which could not be matched.

Nevertheless, in the eyes of some local Liberal councillors Adenauer remained an 'inveterate party man'.[18] One of the most critical voices came from the editor of the city's Liberal *Stadtanzeiger*, who argued that the post should be advertised officially because 'even the most hardworking deputy could only too often fail completely as mayor'.[19] Johannes Rings of the Centre Party dismissed this approach as 'outrageous slander.[20] It was followed by a somewhat half-hearted campaign for the introduction of a municipal constitution in place of a mayoral constitution for the city.

Louis Hagen and Bernhard Falk persuaded the Liberal caucus to support Adenauer, though only on condition that the party was allowed to nominate a First Deputy of its choice. After long debate they selected Bruno Matzerath, the man Adenauer had already bypassed in 1909.

The only outstanding issue was the salary of the new mayor. Adenauer again proved to be a tough negotiator when it came to financial matters. He drew up a list recording the income levels of other mayors, but was discouraged to discover that only in Berlin did the mayor earn the handsome sum of 40,000 marks that was under discussion. Eventually a pensionable figure of 42,000 marks was agreed, with Adenauer also receiving an additional 10,000 marks as a member of the board of Fortuna (Rheinische Braunkohlen AG). Adenauer was now a wealthy man.

In the election of 18 September 1917 Adenauer obtained 52 of the 54 votes cast, with two abstentions. The election was approved by the Prussian Interior Ministry on 6 October, and shortly afterwards Adenauer's appointment was announced. On 18 October he was sworn in as mayor by the Regierungspräsident (district president). The fine Renaissance city hall was beautifully decorated for the occasion. The front of the building showed three reliefs: Daniel in the lion's den, Samson's battle with the lion, and – in the centre – Cologne's mayor Gryn fighting a third lion. They were meant to remind the mayor of the predicaments he might face. The two oldest councillors, Emil vom Rath (a member since 1875) and Ferdinand Thönissen, led Adenauer and the district president into the

ceremony and the official speeches.[21] During these, the district president
Karl von Starck proclaimed that the 'dawn of a new age' would follow
the horrors of war, while Hugo Mönnig reminded the audience that
100,000 citizens of Cologne were in the armed forces and emphasised
that the city was facing grave social problems. Bernhard Falk called out:
'What are the life and happiness of an individual worth if the life and
freedom of the nation are threatened by enemies. Vivere non necesse est.
But being German is necessary.' Falk would live to see 'Crystal Night' in
1938, when a mob of SA men destroyed the picture of his son, an air
force officer who had been killed in action during the First World War.[22]

Adenauer joined the patriotic chorus, though in a more muted tone.
'You can rest assured', he stated at the outset, 'that the city of Cologne, the
metropolis of the Rhineland which is indissolubly linked with the German
Reich, will always feel itself to be a member of the great German fatherland.' This assertion of solidarity with Germany was linked to his belief in
an active and creative life: 'The finest content of human life is to be active
with the entire force of the mind and soul, with the whole personality.'
More prosaically, he listed three main goals for the future: 'healthy
finances', 'maintaining Cologne's proud position in German and international economic life', and 'our social obligations' of which the war had
made them aware. His final remarks praised the heroic courage of the German people in war and battle, in endurance and suffering: 'We on the Rhine
consider this with particular gratitude, since the enemy's onslaught and
thirst for conquest is directed above all against the Rhine and its metropolis. There can be no better way to honour this decisive hour for Cologne
than to make a passionate declaration of loyalty to Kaiser and Reich.'

A little more than a year after the cheers for king and emperor had
subsided, the Kaiser had packed his bags and fled to Holland. Shortly
afterwards, British armoured cars rolled to a halt in front of the city hall.
Adenauer was to discover the twilight world in which he would be forced
to operate if he wished to remain loyal to his country while also steering
his city through difficult times.

III

THE MAYOR
1917-1933

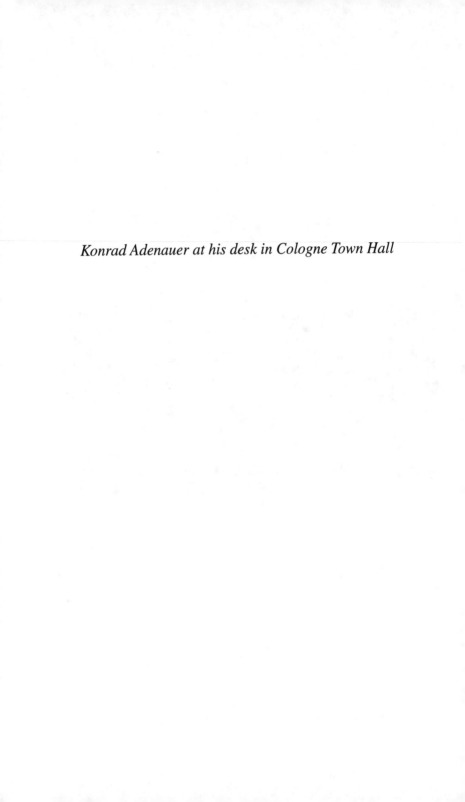

Konrad Adenauer at his desk in Cologne Town Hall

Revolution and Occupation

It is not clear when Adenauer recognised that the war was irretrievably lost. Like the rest of the German élite, he was probably torn between scepticism and hope. One of his rare public comments on more general issues concerned the wretched supply situation, when he looked back at the previous year on 10 January 1918: 'It was pure luck that 1917 … brought us a record harvest, but Germany's fate cannot be allowed to depend on that in the coming year.'[1] His solution to these problems was to place food supply into the hands of self-regulating communal associations, an experiment that had been successful in the city between 1914 and 1916. He failed to mention the fact that the wealthier communes would be the first to benefit from this approach. The decision clearly reflected Adenauer's sceptical attitude towards large and centralised bureaucracies, whose workings he knew from his visits to Berlin and the hundreds of decrees they issued.

If these comments are examined in the light of later controversy about Adenauer's attitude to Berlin and the east of Germany, then it is difficult to detect any trace of anti-Prussian sentiment. He might have been critical of the conduct of some senior civil servants from east of the Elbe river, but did not express these views openly. Another motive, then and later, appears to have been decisive: the confident bourgeois insistence that the rights of local administrations be respected. 'Never', he commented, 'since the existence of self-administration have they been burdened with such great and difficult tasks as in this war.' Though he admitted that this development might well have been inevitable, he considered that the desire of central bureaucracies to interfere had grown at a disproportionate rate. In future, he demanded, 'the citizens in its organs of self-administration should be given that freedom of action to which it had a justified claim'. Such comments do not suggest a Rhinelander's hostility to Berlin, but the opposition of a confident city-dweller in the liberal age to the interference of large bureaucracies which, deriving their

Notes for this section begin on page 707.

power from the economic and social requirements of war, also sought to expand their spheres of influence.

Nevertheless, Adenauer's views in January 1918 were marked by a hopeful note. The year, he thought, 'ends with the most favourable situation for us since the beginning of the war, with the prospect of a good, honourable peace'. Though he did not give his reasons for this optimism, they were obvious: Russia had collapsed; unrestricted submarine warfare still seemed to hold out the possibility of success; and the Army High Command was preparing a mighty spring offensive in the west after the relief of troops at the eastern front.

Later comments, however, reveal the disquiet of Adenauer and other more reflective observers at the collapse of Imperial Russia, despite the respite this offered Germany. For the second time since 1905, the European aristocracy and middle classes had witnessed the emergence of explosive new forces. Perceptive observers were aware of the same elements seething under the surface in Cologne: workers near starvation in bleak suburbs; radical agitators in flight from the authorities; war-weary soldiers, especially in the rear areas; and resentful masses grumbling about 'profiteers' and 'capitalists' who were living off the misery of others.

The situation in Germany was not yet comparable to that of Russia. In Germany the workers continued to follow the course laid down by the leaders among the majority Socialists and the trade unions. Adenauer had known these leaders – Social Democrats like Wilhelm Sollmann, Johann Meerfeld and August Haas – for several years and had come to respect their outlook and, especially, their patriotism. But how long would the leadership be able to retain control if mass misery intensified and if the government of the ruling classes presided over military and political failure?

Adenauer knew that the problems facing both Germany and Europe were of a long-term nature. Even peace, whether on favourable terms or not, could not bring about dramatic improvement. 'After the war', he told the city council at the beginning of March 1918, 'things will never be as they were before. The war will transform the relations between states, as well as political, economic and social conditions within states, in a total and lasting way'.[2] It was obvious that social tensions had spread and intensified. Though social issues involving 'wage earners' – the term 'working class' was avoided – had been recognised before the war, politicians would also face other problems. While 'a few' had seen their position dramatically improved by the war, broad 'classes' had suffered an 'abrupt fall'. Other issues which would have to be considered were 'the woman question which is one part of the social question', and 'the great interdependencies in all economic sectors'.

Adenauer's ideas for solving these problems were couched in very general terms. He was convinced that stability could be restored only after a long and complicated process of adaptation, which he saw as a 'harmonisation of social differences and conflicting interests'. In order to achieve this objective, the modern social sciences must be used to examine and analyse in an objective and undogmatic way the causes, extent and internal logic of social issues. In the spring of 1918 Adenauer called for the establishment of an Institute for Social Research, which had already been proposed by Professor Christian Eckert of the College of Commerce in Cologne. This was already being considered as a step towards the creation of a fully-fledged university for the city. Of more immediate interest, however, is Adenauer's expectation of future developments. He seems to have had few illusions, leading Wilhelm Sollmann to note: 'It is certainly a sign of the times when the mayor of a great Prussian city feels himself so much affected by the powerful social upheavals of the war years.'[3] Equally worthy of note, however, is Adenauer's confident belief that difficulties could be subjected to scientific and rational analysis and then mastered by balanced and well-judged policies.

He quickly developed the ability to locate the problems of Cologne in a wider national perspective. Even before the collapse of the Imperial order, his position had given him access to the German élites and had helped him to establish links with individuals in the world of politics, state administration and the economy. As mayor of the second largest Prussian city he had several official positions: a seat in the Rhenish *Provinziallandtag* (Provincial Assembly) and then in the *Provinzialausschuß*, and – from 1918 – in the Prussian *Herrenhaus* (Upper Chamber).

Adenauer's position brought him into close contact with a number of leading businessmen. Among them, as we have seen, was Louis Hagen, who became a close associate of the mayor and switched from the Liberals to the Centre Party in 1919. Leading figures in Ruhr industry also began to take an interest in Adenauer following his emergence as a powerful force in the Rhineland in 1918-1919. He was thus sent detailed handwritten notes by August Thyssen, accompanied by a typed transcript from the industrialist's office since his writing was almost illegible as the result of an eye complaint. Adenauer also had contacts with Hugo Stinnes and Albert Vögler. Paul Silverberg, a colleague of Adenauer's at the Court of Appeals in 1903, returned from military service in 1917 and resumed control at Rheinbraun. These contacts enabled Johann Hamspohn of AEG in Berlin, a close acquaintance of Adenauer and a man with intimate knowledge of both the German and international economies, to write in 1920 that the mayor not only had outstanding administrative skills which made him suitable for the most senior positions, but was also 'very well versed' in economic issues.[4]

Hamspohn, who was born in Cologne in 1840, was more than thirty years older than Adenauer. The affectionate relationship between the two men dated back to 1907, when Hamspohn was already one of the leading figures at AEG. He had worked for a time in the city council and been a member of the Reichstag between 1881 and 1887. He had made his career at AEG. From 1902 to 1910 he was head of the Union Elektricitäts-Gesellschaft AG and was a member of the AEG executive board, before joining the supervisory board in 1910 and serving until his death in 1926. From the outset he had close ties with western European countries such as France, Belgium and Britain. AEG was a company which exported a large percentage of its products and was a leading investor in foreign markets. It represented a branch of German industry interested in close international cooperation. During the war and the post-war period, its managers concentrated on maintaining the good connections they had established in the years before 1914. From 1917 onwards Adenauer and Hamspohn conducted a regular correspondence which reveals that their association was not based purely on the economic interests of Cologne and the AEG, but also reflected genuine and lasting affection.

Hamspohn, whose daughter was married to Professor Karl Cramer of Cologne, was fond of the dynamic young mayor and was prepared to use his varied international connections to support him. During the war the two men met regularly when Adenauer travelled to Berlin. When strikes prevented him from taking his usual room at the Hotel Kaiserhof – and in the turbulent early years of the Weimar Republic this was not an infrequent occurrence – Adenauer would stay in Hamspohn's villa in Wannsee. The mayor repaid Hamspohn for his 'many services'[5] to himself and his city; during the British occupation he arranged papers which allowed Hamspohn to visit Cologne, and in 1921 he encouraged the University to offer him an honorary doctorate – which Hamspohn modestly declined to accept.[6]

The two men also engaged in detailed discussions of Germany's future after the war. Hamspohn had a wealth of knowledge about the the web of economic and personal links in western Europe which he shared with Adenauer, who was always eager to acquire new information. Adenauer was aware that it was these complex relationships which would do much to decide the future of Cologne. It was in their wartime correspondence that the name of Dannie N. Heineman, a man who was to play an important role in Adenauer's life until 1962, was mentioned for the first time.

Heineman was an American, born in Charlotte, South Carolina, in 1872. He studied electrical engineering in Brunswick before working for the Union Elektricitäts-Gesellschaft for six years, including a year in Koblenz, where he established the electricity works in Schützenhof and electrified the tramways. Here, too, he met an army officer named Paul von Hindenburg, then a colonel and the chief of staff of 8th Corps. It was at the Union Elektricitäts-Gesellschaft that he became acquainted with Hamspohn.

Heineman was a creative, independent and restlessly active man who had worked all over Europe and the United States, in New York, Cologne,

Bonn, Rome, Naples, Berlin, Paris, Brussels and London. His list of personal contacts was impressive: the father of Henry Morgenthau, who had gone to the United States from Mannheim and never lost his German accent; Woodrow Wilson's adviser, Colonel House; the British Foreign Secretary Joseph A. Chamberlain; the French Prime Minister Paul-Prudent Painlevé; the French President Alexandre Millerand; the Belgian King Leopold III; the physicist Heinrich Hertz; the businessmen August Thyssen and Walther Rathenau; the painter Henri de Toulouse-Lautrec; the writer Gerhart Hauptmann; the composer Richard Strauss.

Heineman, who was an engineering fanatic, joined the Brussels Société Internationale et Financière (SOFINA) in 1905, when it had only three employees. By the time Heineman retired fifty years later, the company employed 40,000 people. Bankers feared him because he understood the natural sciences as well as money and had little respect for them. He was described by the banker Hans Fürstenberg as a highly cultivated man 'of great versatility, a social conscience and a passion for art which is expressed in the collecting of magnificent pictures'. Yet Fürstenberg added that Heineman was not an easy man to deal with: 'He was a sadist in his dealings with bankers since his technically trained mind regarded them more or less as good-for-nothings. And as they ran after him it was easy for him to take this view.'[7]

His insatiable urge to expand into the sphere of municipal transport, the railways, petrochemicals, and the construction of power stations brought him into contact with politicians. His opinion of them was as low as his view of the bankers: Heineman thought that the economy was productive and that politicians created disorder. His faith in progress was limitless, and until his death Heineman continued to believe that if no obstacles were placed in the way of the technologies of the future and flows of capital, then technology and the natural sciences could solve most of the world's problems. He summarised his lifelong convictions in 1960: 'As always everything depends on the economy, and the economy to a large degree on science. And politics decides.'[8]

In the first decade of the twentieth century Heineman had laid the foundations for his rapidly growing business empire. In 1907 he was formally introduced by Hamspohn to the thirty-one year old Adenauer, about whom he had heard from the board of AEG.[9] They remained in touch, either directly or through Hamspohn. Heineman was convinced that Germany would be the leading economic power in Europe in the twentieth century owing to its ability to add technical creativity to its artistic pre-eminence in music and literature. He did profitable business with the British and French and was aware of their strengths, but regarded them as declining powers by the beginning of the century: they underestimated technology and were less capable of modernisation than the Germans.

Heineman and Adenauer were also on good terms because of their mutual business interests. As Heineman increased his involvement with municipal public utilities throughout Germany, Adenauer was quick to sense the possibilities for Cologne. Their contacts were not interrupted by the First World War; Heineman remained in Brussels, though he was careful to keep his distance from the German occupiers.

Belgium had been important to the economy of Cologne ever since its foundation in 1830, and its significance increased during the war years. The opportunity seemed to be opening up for the whole of western Germany, but especially Cologne, to extend its influence westward to the Channel and to establish links with the port of Antwerp. It was largely for these reasons that the industrialists of the Rhine and Ruhr provided sustained support for annexationist German war aims. Even within the Rhenish Centre Party, a majority of the leadership supported the incorporation of Belgium, especially its Channel ports, into the German sphere of influence. What remained controversial, however, was the form and extent of the intervention. There was also some dispute about when these war aims should be declared openly. Some supported a comparatively liberal notion of hegemony whereby Belgium would remain in existence as a German satellite state, while others advocated personal union with the Hohenzollern monarchy and still others wanted outright annexation. Debates about the correct policy sometimes spilled over into the public domain. Julius Bachem, for instance, was known to have left the *Kölnische Volkszeitung*, the leading Centre Party newspaper, because it was taking a harsh annexationist line under Karl Bachem. On the other hand, Pope Benedict XV's call for the restoration of Belgian independence had made many loyal Catholics take a more considered approach.

We do not know Adenauer's own views on this issue. It seems likely that he supported a more reasonable policy towards Belgium, based on encouraging its people – not least the Catholic Church there – to co-operate with Germany. In this context it is worth quoting from a letter he wrote to Hamspohn on 11 December 1917, reporting a meeting with Heineman. Adenauer had been mayor of Cologne for three months: 'Director Heineman came to visit me yesterday from Brussels. We spoke for about an hour and a half about all sorts of things, and I had the impression that he had come out of his shell. He fully approved of the idea of making Cologne the centre of attempts to revive cultural and economic ties with neighbouring countries after the war. He promised me that he would make contact with some leading Belgians immediately on his return and would write to tell me the result of his efforts.'[10]

We have no information about the plans they discussed, and Heineman's promised report to Adenauer has not survived. Nevertheless, the basic thinking behind the project is clear: Cologne as the axis for German interests in western Europe. We cannot know whether Adenauer, who had a tendency to be pessimistic, already expected Germany to lose the war; he may still have hoped for a brokered peace, or even for a reasonable 'peace of victory'. Soon after the war, at any rate, the mayor quickly discovered that defeat itself had given the city and its mayor the opportunity to make further progress.

In the autumn and winter of 1918, however, the Rhineland was convulsed by the Revolution and the military collapse. In July 1918, when Ludendorff's third offensive came to a halt before Reims, the result was a rapid deterioration in public order and war morale, in Cologne as elsewhere. In the winter of 1917-1918 criminality had already increased alarmingly, with a spate of robberies and thefts from factories, especially of drive-belts. In the spring of 1918 there were an estimated 16,000 to 18,000 deserters in the Cologne district. *Justizrat* Mönnig claimed in September that a citizens' militia would have to be created if the situation continued to deteriorate.[11] The city was hit by an influenza epidemic in October, with 324 deaths between 14 and 23 October alone. The schools were closed for fourteen days, and the city administration and factories were crippled by sickness.

Bad news from the front, the negotiations for an armistice and the Austro-Hungarian surrender all signalled that collapse was imminent. Once the news of the revolutionary events in Kiel reached Cologne, Adenauer remained almost permanently at his desk. He understood that the role of two men – the governor, Lieutenant-General von Kruge, and Wilhelm Sollmann of the majority Social Democrats – would be crucial. Like Ebert and Scheidemann in Berlin, Sollmann and his colleagues among the moderate Social Democrats in Cologne, worked to prevent the SPD and the unions from losing control over the workers.

Mass demonstrations in the city were planned for Saturday 9 November on the theme of 'The Needs of the Moment'. On 6 November the revolution spread from Kiel to Hamburg and Hanover. Sollmann now persuaded a popular assembly in the SPD stronghold of Cologne-Mülheim to accept a resolution summarising the demands of the hour: immediate release of all political prisoners; immediate abdication of the Hohenzollern dynasty; rapid summoning of a National Assembly elected by all adult men and women; creation of a 'greater German socialist republic'. At the same time, everything must be done to ensure that 'in the Cologne area the unstoppable revolutionary movement proceeded without bloodshed and in an orderly fashion'.[12] A proposal to storm the prisons was rejected.

On the following morning urgent discussions began at the town hall. Adenauer's policy, to which he remained committed, was to work with the leaders of the political parties in deciding the course to be adopted. In this way all the groups would be kept under control and none would be able to strike out on its own. The representatives discussed whether to summon a militia and issue a proclamation to the inhabitants of the city. The representatives of the Christian trade unions – one of them Jakob Kaiser, a determined patriot even then – called for a decisive show of force against any sign of political unrest. Sollmann warned against resorting to arms, believing that, in an emergency, civil order could only be maintained by Social Democratic spokesmen.

Mayor Adenauer then went to the governor's offices to discuss matters with Lieutenant-General von Kruge, whom he found to be in an alarmingly apathetic state. Kruge informed him that sailors from Kiel were on their way to Cologne with the aim of releasing the inmates of the military prisons. Adenauer advised Kruge, as the commander of 60,000 soldiers in fortress Cologne, not to let the train carrying the mutineers reach Cologne station, but rather to arrest them before they reached it. If the sailors arrived at the station, Adenauer warned, the people could not be held back. Kruge could not bring himself to take decisive action, stating only that men who got off the train wearing red rosettes would not be allowed through the barrier. Later, a company with machine guns was sent to the station, only to be called back – partly at the urging of the moderate Social Democrats, who continued to oppose the use of force. This was one of the incidents which formed Adenauer's rather less than respectful view of generals.

To keep Sollmann on his side, Adenauer agreed to the sending of a telegram to the Social Democrat Philipp Scheidemann, who since October had been state secretary in the government of Prince Max of Baden, in Berlin. The telegram recommended a legal amnesty for all military prisoners. At the main station, crowds had gathered to listen to excited speeches by majority Socialists, representatives of the USPD (anti-war Independent Socialists) and sailors. In the streets of Cologne – Neumarkt and Hohe Straße – the familiar scenes of twentieth-century revolution were acted out by trucks of armed men and shouting crowds. During the night three prisons were stormed without resistance from the guards, and military prisoners and common criminals released indiscriminately. (Among them were twenty-eight mentally ill gangsters who caused major problems over the following days).[13]

Next morning the city continued to be in turmoil. The military governor was advised by Sollmann and his comrades to clear the Neumarkt, which had been blockaded by the troops. Adenauer pointed out that there was a battery of armed artillerymen, armed and ready for action, at the Apostelngymnasium. The governor refused to act. When, in the future, people spoke to him of Prussian conduct, Adenauer liked to recall what the captain of this battery had told him a few weeks later. When the battery commander asked whether he should open fire, his commander had answered: 'A Prussian officer in such a situation must himself know what he has to do.'[14] As quickly as possible, the governor acquired a permit and a vehicle from the new authorities and disappeared.

The various barracks within fortress Cologne rapidly joined the mutiny and military discipline collapsed. Troops wearing red cockades gathered at the major transport crossings and in the squares, where they confiscated weapons and tore the epaulettes from the shoulders of army officers. These were scenes that were repeated throughout Germany. At the same time, liberated military prisoners were roaming the streets in their striped uniforms and clogs. The crowds which had gathered at Cologne's Neumarkt 'elected' five leading majority Socialists, including Sollmann, and five representatives of the Independent Socialists (USPD) from the crowd to a workers' and soldiers' council. An additional five soldiers were 'elected' in the Gürzenich hall and in the Bürgergesellschaft (citizens' association). A few days later the trade unionist August Haas, one of the three SPD Councillors and subsequently the president of Hessen-Nassau, told Bernhard Falk that he would not have believed it to be so easy to stage a revolution.[15]

Sollmann now came to Adenauer with some confidence to discuss the situation. After the meeting he delivered the following verdict on the mayor: 'He was the first representative of the authorities in Cologne to face the new realities without hesitating.'[16]

What concrete decisions were reached? Adenauer allowed the workers' and soldiers' council to meet in two large rooms in the town hall. The council, which met at 3 pm on that same day, 8 November, now had a central headquarters with access to typewriters and a telephone switchboard. On the other hand, Adenauer was able to prevent them from raising the red flag over the town hall.

One of the first documents produced by the workers' and soldiers' council illustrates its mixture of revolutionary fervour and the desire to ensure an orderly transition. It states: 'The bearer of this document is the representative of the workers' and soldiers' council for the maintenance of quiet and order. Everyone, whoever he is, must obey his commands. Cologne, 8 November 1918. workers' and soldiers' council.' The document bears the signature of two members of the council, Fuchsius and Runge, and carried two stamps: 'Social Democratic Association. Cologne City and Land', alongside the seal of the city of Cologne with the coat of arms of the King of Prussia. It is not clear whether this document was produced for Adenauer himself or for the two chairmen of the Commission for Public Safety.

Adenauer's decision shows that, despite his oath of loyalty to the King of Prussia, he had quickly decided to work with the moderate – but still revolutionary – Social Democrats. Moreover, he had reached his decision the day before the declaration of the republic in Berlin, when the fate of the old order was still in the balance. Later, when Adenauer was Chancellor, commentators often – and not always accurately – remarked on his tendency to make 'lonely decisions'. The decision of 8 November was not actually reached in isolation, but only after a series of meetings and telephone conversations. Nevertheless, it was lonely to the extent that Adenauer was at the centre of a power vacuum and was compelled to act on his own. He accepted the challenge without hesitation. Adenauer's ability to adapt quickly to radically changed conditions, which was to become one of the most marked features of his political life, was revealed for the first time in November 1918.

Among the first of Adenauer's measures was an order that the various schools must serve meals to hungry military personnel, more or less irrespective of whether these were revolutionaries, deserters or freed prisoners. The main objective was to prevent the men from looting. Looting is a negative aspect of every revolution, and one which Cologne could not escape in November 1918 despite these efforts. Falk, who was with Adenauer at the town hall, gave his own account of the scene some twenty years later: 'From the windows of his office we saw a wretched pack of men and women looting a depot in the Old Market near the town hall. For years I remained furious about this shameful act, which I was powerless to prevent.'[17]

The workers' and soldiers' council needed a functioning administration if it wanted to govern. The council, led by majority Social Democrats and still uneasy with its new powers, was easily convinced that the first priority was to re-establish order. This was Adenauer's opportunity. Over the following weeks he filled the power vacuum from his office in the town hall, taking charge of events in the city of Cologne.

Falk was later to praise his efforts: 'Adenauer was intuitively aware of the need to create the *Wohlfahrtsausschuß* (welfare committee) of the city of Cologne, in which we bourgeois leaders met the Social Democrats and Independents every day in room 29 of the town hall.' Under the chairmanship of Adenauer, it included leading councillors of every political colour, representatives of the state authorities, local industry, representatives of the Christian trade unions and members of the workers' and soldiers' council. 'The decisions were made here, not in the workers' and soldiers' council or anywhere else: the payment of the garrison troops, their demobilisation, the transporting of Polish workers back home, the release of Cologne men from army service, the transportation of unemployed people from outside, emigrants, delousing problems, the closure of the brothels, the milk supply, Rhine shipping, employment certificates, the curfew, controls on food supplies, the conduct of the citizens during the occupation.'[18]

The welfare committee also set up a militia under the command of Professor Christian Eckert of the College of Commerce, then close to Adenauer, who was later to be the first rector of the University. The militia – made up of discharged soldiers, older men and youths – received a daily wage of 15 marks in return for their duties, which included patrolling the streets and preventing the looting of the supply depots established by the city and the garrison.

The councillors, including the Social Democrats, were accustomed to the calm authority of the mayor. Over the following weeks, by contrast, the government in Berlin and the Army High Command sent a plethora of confused and confusing signals. It was in this situation that the revolutionary forces accepted Adenauer (wearing the armband of the workers' and soldiers' council) as the virtual master of Cologne. Naturally he was careful to keep both the workers' and soldiers' council and the welfare committee involved in his decisions and deliberations, and not to flaunt his own authority and prerogatives. A letter of 20 November 1918 written by Josef Thedieck, a local lawyer, gives us an accurate account of the scene. It was found by chance in the city archives: 'Fortunately the conditions did not last long: order was soon restored through the diplomatic skill of Mayor Adenauer, who had always treated his pair of Social Democratic councillors well. The Bolsheviks have been repelled for now, the authorities are working under the supervision of the soldiers' council, we have as controller a lawyer whom we notice little. The prisoners are being gradually rounded up again, though they have done enough damage in the meantime.'[19]

During these first weeks of cooperation, the workers' and soldiers' council was well satisfied with the conduct of the mayor. Its chairman, Heinrich Schäfer – who was also Adenauer's 'adviser' – made his position clear before the city council on 21 November, when he took the opportunity 'to express to the mayor the gratitude of the workers' and soldiers' council for staying resolutely at his post in the critical days that lie behind us, and for making every effort to re-establish law and order in our home city in association with the workers' and soldiers' council'.[20] This comment reveals that Adenauer also had reason to be satisfied with the behaviour of the Cologne revolutionaries.

The chaos nevertheless continued for some weeks. There were demonstrations by hungry crowds in the suburbs and in front of the town hall, because the Entente blockade was still in force and food supplies from the east had failed to arrive. At night the peace of the city was disturbed by looting and violence; car thefts were particularly common. The city was full of discharged and returning soldiers. All this was occurring even before Cologne was hit by a drastic fall in economic production and a rapid increase in unemployment.

Adenauer, who remained a fanatic for order all of his life, saw the chaos as the first great challenge of his career as mayor. He was an impressive figure; even his critics would later concede that he came into his own during moments of crisis. It was a quality which was revealed for the first time during the weeks of revolution and upheaval in 1918. In the later summer of 1917 he had been elected mayor because of his reputation as a talented administrator, but he was now able to demonstrate that he had a cool head, powerful political intuition and a genuine talent for leadership. Throughout Germany, the old Wilhelmine authorities were losing power, but Cologne possessed a mayor who supervised the affairs of the city like a republican monarch and utilised both old and new forms of leadership. On the one hand, there was the old authoritarian and bureaucratic style of Imperial times, which most people recognised and many would have been glad to do away with, if they had known with what to replace it. On the other hand, there was a new, republican brand of leadership based on the attempt to achieve a balance between the various political forces – the parties, trade unions, businesses and the established and revolutionary centres of power. Reasoned argument, compromise, intelligent and sometimes legalistic operations – these were the new styles of leadership which entered the political life of post-Imperial Cologne.

Adenauer's self-assurance, which was so obvious to observers in the years to come, appears to have developed as a result of these experiences. During the upheaval, both the public and Adenauer himself came to recognise his leadership qualities. Subsequently his sense of superiority was marked; his cool and pitiless observation of human beings in action convinced him that, in times of crisis, most people were either foolish, emotional or doctrinaire – or a combination of the three.

Revolutionary fervour in Cologne quickly subsided, to be replaced by a very different political spirit. Once the Entente armistice conditions became known there was an outburst of almost uncontrollable patriotic fervour. These emotions were intensified by the return of the German army in its field-grey uniform, marching through the city and across the Rhine bridges into the interior. Cologne in particular was badly hit by the armistice conditions. The occupied territories and the whole region on the left bank of the Rhine were to be evacuated within three weeks, prior to the entry of the British occupying forces. Under these conditions the political parties quickly discovered common ground. The relentless timetable also imposed enormous demands of organisation. Two armies -the 6th and 7th – with more than 500,000 men and 300,000 horses were to pass day and night through the needle's eye of the Rhine bridges or face captivity.

As the first units arrived in the city, the church bells were rung. It was the moving image of August 1914 in reverse. The city was a sea of flags – the black, white and red of Imperial Germany, here and there the republican black, red and gold and the red flag of the revolution. There were long discussions in the welfare committee regarding which flags were to be flown over official buildings before a typical Cologne compromise was reached: the Imperial flag, the flag of the republic and the city flag hung peacefully side by side.

Adenauer instructed the city council to give a hearty welcome to the 'hundreds of thousands of courageous warriors'. He was never at a loss for patriotic words: 'Our brothers in field grey are coming home. They are coming home after four years of defending house and home with their bodies, with the greatest heroism world history has even seen, in the most terrible battle the human mind could ever imagine; they are coming home to us, not defeated and not beaten; they are coming home to us, though not as we all thought and dreamed they would ...' He promised 'from the bottom of my heart and soul ... that we will never forget them, what they have done for Germany, what they have done for the Rhineland'.[21]

The people of the city came out in force on 27 November to greet the return of the 65th Division, which had been stationed in Cologne before the war. In an emotional speech Adenauer thanked the returning soldiers on behalf of the city. The front-line divisions which were now returning to Cologne included units whose commanders were eager to do away with the 'red nightmare'. Adenauer, who knew that the orderly withdrawal would be endangered by a sudden coup against the now tame workers' and soldiers' council, was forced to use all of his diplomatic skills to prevent such a rash move. He was supported by a captain on the General Staff, Otto Schwink, who had been sent to the Cologne bridgehead to replace the incompetent Governor General, and organise the troop withdrawal and handover. The two men developed great respect for each other's efficiency and devotion to duty during these weeks.

The city had to organise quarters and rations for the vast numbers of soldiers, as well as preparing assembly camps for those who were to be discharged. The stores in the fortress posed a particular problem; these had to be sold, secured and transported away as quickly as possible, in order to prevent them from falling into the hands of looters or the British. Stocks of alcohol – always inflammatory in revolutionary times – were destroyed, with 725,000 litres of spirits and 1,400 demijohns of French cognac being pumped into the Rhine.

Schwink described the melodramatic conclusion to the withdrawal operation in an account written some time later: 'On 3 December the last German regiment left Cologne. At the foot of the proud cathedral stood the small group of fighters drawn up in a square. A charming children's choir sang, no louder than the December rain that splashed down, a cry of hurrah for our Germany was again heard around the cathedral, and the last German troops paraded at brisk pace before the history of Cologne. "Auf Wiedersehn!" cried the children. The adults, who could scarcely believe what was happening, watched with aching hearts.'[22] Patriotic sentiments were mixed with sorrow, and fear of the future. The last vestiges of the old Imperial order were departing; the new order had yet to be secured. Above all there was the fear of occupation, and of temporary separation from unoccupied Germany.

The armistice terms envisaged an occupation of the area on the left bank of the Rhine by Entente troops, with three large bridgeheads on the right bank opposite Cologne, Koblenz and Mainz. The north Rhine area was to be occupied by the Belgians; Cologne, Bonn, Aachen and their outlying districts were to be in the hands of the British; the U.S. zone would extend from this region as far as Koblenz and Trier (after the U.S. withdrawal the region was taken over by the French); French troops entered the Rhineland Palatinate and the Saar. The local authorities were to continue their administration under the supervision of the occupying powers. No-one could know whether these provisional measures marked the beginning of a permanent separation of this area from the rest of Germany. In the event, the British stayed in the Cologne region for seven years, from December 1918 until January 1926.

After the departure of the last German troops public order once more threatened to collapse with the recurrence of looting and robberies. Adenauer began almost to long for the arrival of British troops. He tried to persuade the advance party to parade cavalry and tanks through the city streets in order to make a show of authority and deter further disorder.

British officers appeared in front of the town hall in six armoured cars on the afternoon of 6 December 1918. Forty years later, the old Chancellor was still able to recall the scene. He had the greatest respect for the leader of the advance party, General Lawson, who appears to have behaved impeccably. Their first meeting and a series of subsequent discussions are well documented, as Adenauer instructed the interpreters to take precise minutes.[23] These give an indication of why the mayor came to have a measure of sympathy for the British, and regarded their occupation as the least of the evils that could have befallen his city, as well as revealing Adenauer's own dignified and self-assured manner.

Nevertheless, this was still an occupation. During the early months in particular, the administrative and economic burdens were as difficult to bear as they had been in the first weeks after Germany's collapse. No fewer than 55,000 British troops were stationed in Cologne until 1920, when the number was cut approximately by half. By 1925, the year before the final withdrawal, there were no more than 9,160 British troops in the city. Until then the various units – the Inniskilling Dragoons, the Northumberland Fusiliers, the Cameron Highlanders, the King's Rifle Corps, the Black Watch Regiment, the Canadians, the Gurkhas – were quartered in 88 schools, 52 hotels, more than 2,000 private homes and a number of factories which had been shut down.[24]

Discipline on the streets was good and there were comparatively few violent incidents. During the entire period of occupation the official statistics reveal 18 cases of murder and manslaughter, 81 deaths through careless driving, 977 muggings, cases of grievous bodily harm and rape and approximately 4,000 cases of damage to property. Most of these incidents occurred during the early weeks, when soldiers who had escaped death on the battlefield reacted by getting very drunk, with predictable consequences.

More burdensome were the strict security measures which were gradually relaxed after long discussions with the Military Governor. The curfew – from 7 pm until 5 am – was quickly lifted. However, the occupation authorities overturned a centuries' old tradition of Cologne, whereby the city's inhabitants were permitted to live without identity papers or having to report to the police; now anyone wanting to travel to the unoccupied territory required a special permit. Particular tension was produced by an order bearing the signature of Field Marshal Haig which obliged all adult inhabitants of the city to salute British officers. The mayor had already opposed this measure during his first meeting with the British, and it was abandoned after several further discussions. Adenauer, who was a proud man, was never to forget this presumption.

Most devastating of all was the initial decision to seal off the Cologne Zone from the unoccupied Rhineland. The economy, which was integrated with that of the Ruhr, was in danger of collapse. Unemployment quickly became a major problem, exacerbated by the return of the soldiers and the release of workers from the armaments industry. By December 1918 25,000 inhabitants of Cologne were unemployed and the figure was rising weekly. The city administration quickly launched an emergency work programme.[25] Some 4,000 men were set to work in the city woods, and what began as a temporary emergency measure eventually continued until the mid-1920s. The future of the food supply continued to be alarmingly uncertain: with the blockade still in effect, deliveries from overseas could not get through and supplies in the city dwindled fast.

At the beginning of January 1919 Adenauer gave his first foreign interview to the French correspondent Lucien Chassaigne. An incomplete version has survived in the form of translator's notes, which have been translated back from the French.[26] The reporter was very impressed: 'Monsieur Adenauer, tall, sturdy, extraordinarily cool and prudent took upon himself, without the slightest hesitation, the heavy responsibility currently involved in the administration of a big German city.' The mayor painted a dismal picture of the situation. He showed Chassaigne a parcel containing one person's weekly ration: 3.5 kilograms potatoes, 2 kilograms war bread, 200g meat or sausage, 50g fat, 200g marmalade, 75g flour, 150g sugar, 75g coffee substitute. Even the supplies for these rations would only last for five weeks.

When the Frenchman reminded Adenauer that the blockade was designed to force the Germans to accept the forthcoming peace treaty, Adenauer replied as follows: 'There is no longer any German army.' When the German troops marched through Cologne the truth was apparent: the soldiers were poorly dressed, poorly shod, emaciated and poorly armed. The barracks no longer had any importance: 'The German army had reached the end of its tether!' There was also the psychological shock: 'This army, which had fought with courage despite the strain, had been dealt a final terrible blow which had finished it completely – the inexplicable, shameful, disastrous flight of its supreme leader, Kaiser Wilhelm. What should be done after such a flight in the heat of battle? That means the end of all resistance!' Even the officers had left their units. It was over, said Adenauer, all over. The strength of the Reich was broken, but hunger and unemployment would push the country into the arms of the Bolsheviks: 'Every day does more to ruin us than a month of war. Just think what favourable ground the revolution is finding to spread itself. If it spreads here, then it will not take long before it reaches you!'

Adenauer gave a similar warning to the British governor, General Fergusson, in a discussion on 30 December 1918:[27] 'In conclusion the mayor referred with some urgency to the dangers of the Bolshevik threat, which could also affect British and French subjects.' Louis Hagen, who attended the discussion as president of the Chamber of Commerce, also warned of the dangers: there was no money to pay the workers their wages, and the present calm was deceptive because the workers were no longer controlled by their leaders. Yet again Adenauer urged the British to be on their guard and advised the withdrawal of British troops from private homes.

The homes that had been sequestered, of course, were hardly in working-class districts. The British Governor General, for example, had his 250 bodyguards accommodated in the luxury villas of the city ring. Though it is possible that Adenauer only mentioned the threat of revolutionary sentiment among the occupying forces in order to persuade the British to end the use of private homes, the impression remains that he genuinely feared a revival of crisis conditions over the weeks to come. The situation in Berlin was still unsettled, the news from the Ruhr was alarming, and the events of November and the rapid spread of revolutionary events from Kiel remained fresh in the memory. Adenauer's experience of the collapse of the Imperial order had apparently produced a finely tuned sense of political danger which he was never to lose. In future, Bolshevism for him would be not merely an abstract ideology, but also a memory of the months of instability during the winter of 1918/19.

During these months, with the future of Cologne and Germany still uncertain, Adenauer was remarkably successful in consolidating his own power base in Cologne. The British Military Governor made no secret of his desire to deal directly with the mayor on all important issues, including police matters theoretically outside of his competence. Adenauer was satisfied with his first meeting with General Fergusson on 12 December, after which he made the following note: 'The Governor decided at the end that they wanted to deal with me alone, as I alone bear the responsibility for the obeying of all regulations. It will therefore be necessary to inform the Regierungspräsident and the Police President of this decision by the Governor and to ask these gentlemen to notify me of important matters.'[28] Cautious person that he was, however, he requested, after a while, to be given the binding minutes of the meeting by the British and eventually received the hoped-for information: 'The Governor would prefer to deal directly with the Burgomaster.'[29]

The British also helped to ease the pressure on Adenauer from the workers' and soldiers' council. The mayor noted that during the revolution the councils had assumed rights to which they were not entitled, but conceded that their conduct had been 'on average good'. The workers' and soldiers' council did not pose a threat to the peace of the city.[30] Sollmann and his comrades were present at this discussion and could not claim that Adenauer had pushed the council aside with the help of the British. However, Adenauer did mention in passing that the workers' and soldiers' council 'consists of about one-hundred armed persons and the leaders are well known to the police'; in so doing, he may have been hinting that the security-conscious occupying forces would be wise to take vigorous action. A British major ordered their immediate arrest, though this was not carried out.[31] Politically, however, the council – which was removed from the town hall even before the arrival of the British – no longer had a role to play.

Within two short months Adenauer had become the key figure in occupied Cologne. The British regarded him as the legimate head of the Germans, respected him and valued his advice. The Centre Party was eager to recognise him as a leader in his own right even though he was not at the head of the local party. The future of the Liberals remained uncertain, but Adenauer was able to work with Falk, of whose respect and support he was assured. The Social Democrats, moreover, were as dependent on Adenauer as he was on them. Their future strength in Cologne had yet to be seen, but the revolution had greatly increased their influence, especially as the Social Democrats were still in control in Berlin. Even the city's business community was dependent on political decisions and could be expected to do the mayor's bidding. During these weeks neither Sollmann nor Hagen strayed far from Adenauer's side.

Adenauer realised the need for careful manoeuvring between the various political factions. His goal during this period was to reach agreement with all the parties by establishing a network of contacts with every individual who was either important at the time or might be influential in the future. Adenauer was also careful to cover himself by engaging in constant discussions with the leaders of the parties in the town hall, and the British, the Prussian and national governments, and by writing minutes and reports, and bringing in witnesses during delicate negotiations. He quickly mastered the art of saying enough to achieve the desired effect, but not enough to commit himself to any specific course of action.

At the same time he became the master of nuance, able to combine a direct approach with procedural flexibility. It was a successful initiation into the hard world of politics. Although he made mistakes – and would continue to do so – Adenauer never stopped learning from experience. In retrospect, it would be fair to say that this transition from revolutionary turmoil to the relative calm of the mid-1920s was the time when Adenauer finally developed to the full his natural political talents.

The Rhineland Movement 1918-1919

November 1918 was the month of revolution, military collapse and the birth of the republic. It also saw the beginnings of the Rhineland movement, which was highly controversial from the outset and has been a source of dispute among historians ever since. Despite a wide range of sources and academic literature on the subject, it is impossible to reconstruct many of the ideas, motives and objectives of the principal protagonists with any degree of certainty.

Between the armistice on 11 November 1918, the signing of the Versailles Treaty on 28 June 1919 and the introduction of the new constitution in July of that year, there was profound uncertainty and political confusion. Attitudes towards the Rhineland question were also changing continuously, which makes the conduct of the participants very difficult to understand. There were nevertheless some important points at stake. Should the 'Rhenish republic', as envisaged by the Rhineland movement, remain part of the Reich or should it become a buffer state, a second Luxembourg? Should this republic include only the regions on the left bank of the Rhine or should it incorporate Hessen-Nassau, Westphalia and perhaps even Oldenburg? How should the objective be achieved: by strictly legal means and with the full agreement of the Prussian and national governments, or by the independent action of political forces in the Rhineland, or even with the support of France and Britain?

The vagueness of these goals and attitudes reflected the uncertainty of the political situation. The Rhineland movement came into being at a time when three major and closely interlinked issues had yet to be settled: the outcome of the revolution, the territorial reorganisation of Germany, and the policy of the victorious powers with regard to the future of the lands on the left bank of the Rhine. Uncertainty regarding the first issue – the outcome of the revolution – was removed with the suppression of the Spartacists in Berlin and the election of the National Assembly on 19 January 1919. Subsequently there was every chance that the November revolution would lead to the establishment of a democratic and constitutional state. At least in the short term, observers in the Rhineland no

Notes for this section begin on page 707.

longer had reason to expect the victory of anti-democratic elements or the outbreak of civil war.

As regards the second issue – the reorganisation of the Reich and the possible division of Prussia – clear legal conditions were established in February and March 1919 although no final decisions were taken. On 10 February 1919 a law was passed which laid down that an internal reorganisation could only be undertaken by the National Assembly at Weimar. On 13 March 1919 the National Assembly unanimously endorsed the declaration of Reich Minister-President Scheidemann to the effect 'that any constitutional restructuring before the conclusion of peace is liable to threaten the unity of our fatherland'. The 'regulation of the relationship of the Rhenish lands to the Reich' was also described as a 'purely internal German affair'. From then on it was clear, at least in theory, that the division of Prussia – if it happened at all – could only be decided by the constituent assembly at Weimar.

The third issue – the policy of the Entente powers towards the Rhineland – was the last to be clarified. The terms of the Versailles Treaty, which were delivered to the Germans on 7 May 1919, made it clear that there was no intention to annex the Rhineland. The Entente governments were prepared to make do with a fifteen-year occupation of the bridgeheads of Cologne and Mainz and the permanent demilitarisation of the Rhineland. Prospects for revision of the treaty in Germany's favour were uncertain, but appeared poor. In May and early June 1919 it was not clear whether the Germans would accept or reject the treaty; if the latter approach was adopted, then the situation facing the Rhineland would be even worse. Even in the event of an occupation lasting fifteen years, there was surely a danger that the French would manage to separate the Rhineland from the rest of Germany.

The signing of the Versailles Treaty on 28 June 1918 at least clarified certain points. Most importantly, there was no longer any sensible reason for the Germans to advocate a 'Rhenish republic' on foreign-policy grounds in the hope of improving the peace terms. Adenauer's own Rhineland policy must, therefore, be judged in this specific chronological context.

The idea of a 'Rhenish republic' originated among the owners and editors of the *Kölnische Volkszeitung*, the main newspaper of the Centre Party. 'The father of the idea', according to Fritz Brüggemann, a liberal but well-informed opponent, was Dr Josef Froberger, an Alsatian living in Bonn. Until 1911 Froberger had been the head of an international order, founded in 1868 and entitled 'The Missionaries of Our Dear Lady of Africa or the White Fathers of Cardinal Lavigerie', which was based in Algiers and active mainly in the Mahgreb. Froberger was a specialist in Oriental studies, had detailed knowledge of Spain and close contacts with France. Since 1911 he had been working at the editorial desk of the

Kölnische Volkszeitung, whose editor-in-chief Dr Karl Hoeber was another influential supporter of the Rhenish movement.

From the outset, opponents of the two journalists accused them of being stalking-horses for the French, but without offering any convincing evidence.[1] Some fifty-five years later new material was discovered when a researcher from Berlin, Henning Köhler, unearthed documents in the French Foreign Ministry which, he claimed, proved that the French had bought the newspaper six months before the defeat of Germany. The entire story sounds like a tale from Somerset Maugham's *Ashenden*, with mention of Dutch middlemen, a purchase price of one million marks including 400,000 marks paid when the transaction was completed in June 1918. Of this money some 15,000 marks was earmarked for the intermediary. The action was taken by the Deuxième Bureau in the hope of steering this previously annexationist paper on a course more acceptable to the French. Köhler claimed that the transaction was approved by the French Minister of War, Clemenceau, and that it explained the paper's new editorial stance after the armistice.[2]

Köhler's conclusions were questioned as soon as his account was published. There was no mention of either of the Bachem brothers, nor of any of the influential members of the editorial board. A visiting card in the name of Bachem was the only written evidence of the legitimacy of the negotiator, but the forenames are not those of either brother. Moreover, the deal was supposedly made at a time when German victory on the western front appeared within reach. It seems most unlikely that a newspaper such as the *Kölnische Volkszeitung*, known as a strong supporter of the High Command and annexationist heavy industry, could have changed its policy so dramatically without arousing suspicion. Even if some member of the Bachem family had been prepared to commit high treason for money, for which there is no convincing evidence, it must be doubtful whether that person would really have agreed to risk his reputation and, in the event of discovery, even his life, for a few hundred thousand marks.

In 1980, in *Revue d'histoire moderne et contemporaine*, Köhler's arguments were demolished by an article by Jean-Claude Montant.[3] The French historian made a careful examination of the sources, paying particular attention to the elements which made it highly unlikely that the owners of the *Kölnische Volkszeitung* would have allowed themselves to be bribed by Paris. In fact the Deuxième Bureau had abandoned the project in November 1918 because the paper continued to exhort the population to hold firm. Montant could find no evidence that the paper's support for a Rhenish republic after the armistice was influenced by the French secret service.

The affair remains mysterious. Perhaps the Deuxième Bureau had fallen into a trap set by the German secret service, although its motives cannot be proved. Montant believes that such an operation by the Germans might have been carried out with the knowledge of the Bachem publishing house or at least some of its members, since there were known to be several different strands of opinion within the firm.

If this interpretation is correct, then the paper's support for the policy of separation from Prussia after the armistice, can at least be seen as an understandable attempt to avoid reprisals by the French. Yet even this hypothesis is far-fetched. It remains conceivable that some of the editorial staff of the *Kölnische Volkszeitung*, particularly Froberger himself, had fallen under the influence of the French, although no evidence of such influence has been found. The call for a 'Rhenish republic' did not in fact tally with the policy being developed in Paris in the weeks following the German collapse. To the extent that the French took any notice of events in British-occupied Cologne, they saw them as a largely tactical manoeuvre, designed to make capital out of the political failure of the Prusso-German Reich, combined with a stubborn provincialism.

Whatever the background and the reasons, the *Kölnische Volkszeitung* did initiate, and provide sustained support for, the idea of a 'Rhenish republic'. The journalists who supported it claimed to have important secret information from Paris (and here Froberger's account is credible), according to which the French would demand – and might be granted in the peace treaty – the Rhine as the border between the two countries. The *Kölnische Volkszeitung*, however, argued that the establishment of a 'Rhenish republic', based on the concept of national self-determination so dear to the heart of President Woodrow Wilson, would be able to 'stave off' the French bid for annexation. It remained an open question as to how far the separation of the Rhineland from Prussia would also mean leaving the German Reich.

In the midst of the political chaos, the small but active and hard-working group at the *Kölnische Volkszeitung* managed to gain the support of larger numbers of people for their ideas, and to obtain publicity for them. Their cause was helped by the fact that Prussia and Germany now both had governments made up of the majority Socialists and the radical USPD. Though the future remained uncertain, it was clear that the Prussian government was liable to pursue a more secular policy. These produced fears of a new *Kulturkampf* against the Catholics and persuaded large parts of the Rhenish Centre Party to unite against the 'Berlin Bolsheviks'. Even the grand old man of the Rhenish Centre, Karl Trimborn, was won over by the slogan 'away from Berlin'. Trimborn, a native of Cologne, was chairman of the Rhenish Centre Party, leader of the Centre Party caucus in the Reichstag in 1917-1918, State Secretary in the Reich Office of the Interior under the chancellorship of Prince Max of Baden, and first chairman of the Catholic organisation 'Volksverein für das katholische Deutschland'.

On 4 December 1918, two days before the British arrived in Cologne, the supporters of a 'Rhenish republic' held a rally in the *Bürgerverein* in Cologne. Trimborn's speech included the following remarks: 'We support the maintenance of Reich unity, the strengthening of the national idea. With the fall of the Hohenzollern dynasty we no longer have any serious obligation to hold firm to Prussia. For us there is no longer any obligation of loyalty to old Prussia. We must wait and see how the great German Reich is carved into great federal states. This must be decided by the people and all the parties with their organisations.'[4] The highly respected Centre Party leader had thus outlined with relative clarity, despite his caution about the procedure to be adopted, the programme of a 'Rhenish republic'.

The reasons why Trimborn and other genuinely patriotic Germans supported the Rhineland movement had more to do with domestic than foreign affairs. In these circumstances it was easy for opponents of the Centre to argue that they were preparing to create a Centre Party state – a 'coal-black' western German republic. In the event, a 'Rhenish republic' was called into being at the rally, but without effect.

Even within the Centre Party these vague plans remained controversial. At the same meeting of 4 December Wilhelm Marx, himself a native of Cologne, claimed to be the best judge of the city's character: 'The Cologners have all got bats in the belfry to some degree. But I never thought they would become quite so crazy in my absence! Do they really think that, having started on the alphabet of separation and said the letter "A", they will be allowed to make a deal over the rest of the alphabet under the eyes of the Entente? Don't they see that, once they have said "A", the Entente will deal with all the rest?'[5] It was an argument which was often to be used during the Rhineland debate. Though some supporters of the Rhineland movement saw it as a means of escaping the control of the Bolsheviks in Berlin and warding off annexation by France, Marx had perceived the dangers in this approach. Between a republic as a federal state of the German Reich and an autonomous state such as Luxembourg and perhaps, sooner or later, annexation by the French there was only a small degree of difference. Cardinal von Hartmann, a committed patriot, also raised his voice against the plan.

Although support for the idea was not restricted to members of the Centre Party, it nevertheless became an object of dispute between the parties. As early as 6 December the Social Democrats called a large protest meeting which also involved the chairman of the Liberals. At the same time, the *Rat der Volksbeauftragten* (Council of People's Representatives) under Friedrich Ebert had begun to oppose the plans. Nevertheless, vague calls for a 'Rhenish republic' – or whatever name the new entity was to be called -continued to capture the imagination of influential Rhinelanders for several months.

Further support was provided by some members of the landed aristocracy, who feared property reform whilst also recognising that rural society had remained untouched by the revolutionary events in the cities. It was also clear that the idea was giving rise to wild speculation in Cologne's business community. In particular, several bankers banded together and began to establish contact with interested parties. Rumour had it that some of the gentlemen in the banking quarter of 'Unter Sachsenhausen' – Consul Heinrich von Stein, or perhaps *Kommerzienrat* Albert Ahn – were afraid that as German citizens they would lose their positions on the board of the International Bank of Luxembourg. In fact, the French did insist on the removal of the Germans at the end of April 1919.

It is no longer possible to determine the exact approach taken by Louis Hagen, the powerful president of the Chamber of Commerce in Cologne. On 1 March 1919 he and Heinrich von Stein sent a twenty-five page memorandum to the Foreign Ministry,[6] which suggests that at this stage at least, he was opposed to the creation of a buffer state on the left bank of the Rhine or in the Rhineland for both economic and political reasons. He pointed to the close integration of the economy on both sides of the Rhine as well as arguing that the Rhenish industry was crucial to the economic well-being of Germany as a whole. Political considerations also made the idea of a buffer state unattractive: if the Entente powers accepted it, they would want to dominate it both economically and politically. As things stood, a solution along the lines of the Luxembourg model of pre-war days, in which political independence went hand in hand with extensive economic integration with Germany, was impossible. The Entente powers intended 'to turn the attention of the Rhineland from the east to the west ...'. Hagen concluded: '... as for the Reich, so also for the Rhineland – whether the buffer state being contemplated included the left bank of the Rhine or the whole of the Rhineland – separation from the Reich and isolation in a buffer state would be completely intolerable.'

These were unequivocal statements. Hagen was a perceptive businessman, much of whose life's work had been devoted to the integration of the Rhenish banking system and industry with those of the Ruhr and Berlin, and his rejection of the buffer state idea appears to have been based on these experiences. However, he was not necessarily hostile to the idea of a 'Rhenish republic' within the framework of continued German unity. In fact, he appears to have been increasingly receptive to arguments calling for separation from Prussia. All of these plans and discussions continued to be shrouded in a dense fog -partly because the situation in Germany as a whole was unresolved, and especially because the policy of the Entente had yet to be clarified. It was even possible that Germany's enemies might resume hostilities if the Germans refused to accept the peace terms.

Everything was in flux. In the eyes of the Prussian and national governments, the political opponents of the Centre Party, and the enemies of
Cologne's powerful capitalists and conservative landowners, the hectic
activities of the various groups within the 'Rhineland movement' must have
been deeply unsettling. The crisis intensified in the spring of 1919, when Dr
Adam Dorten, one of the leading exponents of the movement in the French
Zone, was increasingly revealed as being a puppet of the French.

What was Adenauer's own position in the middle of these confused
and sometimes dubious dealings? His emergence as a key figure in the
Rhineland ensured that his support was sought from all sides and, as he
felt personally responsible for the fate of his city, he was also eager to
maintain contact with all the major protagonists.

On 9 November, with the revolutionary events still in full spate,
Adenauer wrote a detailed account describing how he was visited at the
town hall by:

> gentlemen from several Centre Party circles, including city councillor Mönnig,
> city councillor Rings, city councillor Maus, city councillor Bollig, the priest
> Kastert, editor-in-chief Dr Hoeber and Dr Froberger of the *Kölnische Volks-
> zeitung*, a man then unknown to me. Dr Froberger declared that according to
> his information the Entente would award the Rhine Province to France. Ger-
> mandom on the Rhine could only be saved by separation from Prussia and the
> creation of a special state. The gentlemen asked me if I would put them in
> touch with the other parties so that they could discuss these questions jointly.
> As I thought the whole thing was absurd, I refused to take such a step. Over the
> following days I became doubtful that I alone should bear responsibility for
> such a refusal. I therefore informed Herr Meerfeld and Herr Sollmann of the
> Social Democratic Party and Herr Falk of the Liberal parties of what had hap-
> pened and also, so that they could form their own opinion, put the gentlemen
> in personal contact with Dr Froberger. In several joint discussions and deliber-
> ations we became convinced that the responsibility of separating the Rhineland
> from Prussia was so great that it could only be taken if it were certain that there
> was no other way of protecting the Rhineland from being incorporated into
> France ... In these discussions it was decided without contradiction that a
> Western German Republic would only have sufficient powers of resistance
> against France if it remained within the Reich and was anchored as far as pos-
> sible on the right bank of the Rhine. It was considered desirable that, if it were
> created at all, it must include the Rhine Province, Rhine-Hessen, the Rhineland
> Palatinate and large parts of Hessen-Nassau, Westphalia and parts of Olden-
> burg. Such a large territory would, in the unanimous conviction of all those per-
> sons with whom I spoke on the matter, provide the mixture of religious faiths
> and parties so necessary for the success of the whole.[7]

Adenauer's version of these events is credible. Politicians such as
Sollmann and Falk, who were to be passionate opponents of a 'Rhenish
republic', never at any time accused the mayor of handling the matter
either carelessly or with separatist intent.

The main features of the approach he was later to develop more fully
were already apparent: separation from Prussia, if the international situa-

tion made it seem necessary; federal integration of this new territory into the German Reich; the 'Rhenish republic' should include territory on both the left and right banks of the Rhine; it was not to be a Centre Party republic, as he argued shortly afterwards: 'I would prefer the socialist republic to a new state structure ruled by the pastor and the sexton.'[8] What is also striking is his determination to clarify this intensely political question by involving all the parties in detailed discussion. As the opposition of the Social Democrats and Liberals to all plans for a buffer state was well known, he could use it to keep waverers in the Centre Party in line.

Later Adenauer was often accused of sympathising with the plans for a 'Rhenish republic' because of a deep-seated hostility to Berlin and Prussia. In the period in question, however, there is no convincing evidence of any emotional rejection of the national capital. Apart from Cologne, Berlin was the city to which Adenauer travelled most often and in which – according to the surviving evidence – he felt at home. During his time as mayor, with the exception of his holidays, Adenauer would regularly spend between two and five days per month in Berlin. He would generally take the night train and stay in his 'usual rooms' in the Hotel Kaiserhof: a quiet bedroom and a smaller study, where discussions would generally begin over breakfast. This would be followed by various committees, his regular visits to the various ministries and, usually, in the evening, dinners, political and social obligations or theatre trips. At least in the period before 1934, none of the supposed 'anti-Berlin' sentiments are perceptible.

Adenauer also took a balanced view of Prussia. He realised that the Prussian state had many facets, some of which were unpleasant or difficult for a Rhinelander to accept, but never showed any profound hostility during his whole period as mayor. Even in those days Adenauer was not a man to hide his opinions. Berhard Falk, himself a devout Prussophile among the Rhinelanders, expressed doubt in his memoirs that Adenauer 'has ever been a good Prussian'.[9] There may indeed have been, in his demeanour, some element of the cultural superiority of the quick-witted Rhinelander over the stiff Prussians. As yet, however, there is no evidence for the view that Adenauer's Rhineland policy sprang from deep-rooted anti-Prussian sentiments. Falk went on: 'But his opponents did him a great injustice when they denied his German patriotism and loyalty to the German fatherland, which grew out of his love for the soil of Cologne and for his Rhenish homeland.'

It seems certain that Adenauer's willingness to see the advantages of a 'Rhenish republic' in the crisis years of 1918/19 and 1923 were a direct response to the enormous problems and uncertainties which confronted him as mayor. Here his anxiety about French policy probably weighed even more heavily than his fear of a Bolshevik victory in Berlin, which had receded – at least for the time being – by the end of January 1919.

In the latter part of December 1918 Adenauer was very pessimistic about the situation in the Rhineland, especially the long-term danger of occupation by the victorious powers. His views emerge clearly from the minutes of a conversation drawn up by a Captain Loog, probably a representative of the High Command, after a visit to Adenauer on 22 December. These found their way to the Foreign Ministry.[10] In the conversation the mayor appealed to Berlin for help. Economic separation from the rest of Germany was creating impossible conditions: unemployment, hunger, disorder. The discipline of the occupying troops left much to be desired; the Scots in particular had been responsible for much looting. But behind it all, he thought, was a deliberate policy. Governor General Fergusson had told the Regierungspräsident that 'to the West everything lay open to the people of Cologne ... Both the overall picture and the sum of the little incidents clearly reveal a far-sighted Entente plan to alienate the Rhineland from the Reich and orient it economically towards the West.'

How should the national government respond? Adenauer warned that Berlin must not encourage these tendencies 'by isolating itself and holding back'. The Reichsbank, for example, was no longer redeeming the coupons from war loans. Furthermore, the government in Berlin must press for the lifting of the blockade and a rapid signing of the peace treaty. Only this could 'save' them.

During the following years Adenauer was frequently to complain that the national government, though constantly reassuring the Rhineland Germans of its concern, was doing almost nothing to help them. Yet many of his apparent reservations about Prussia were simply a response to his sense of powerlessness as the representative of an occupied territory who felt that he was being left to cope almost alone.

Adenauer feared that a long occupation, undertaken with the intention of turning the Rhineland towards the West, would sooner or later break the will to resist of the Rhenish population. He had little faith in his fellow citizens: 'Today the Cologners support the unity of the Reich, but as time passes their hopeless dilemma and the threat of ruin will induce them to take the hand that the West hold out to them. Once these ties to the West have been established, and given the hostility towards Berlin which has become fear of Berlin as a result of conditions there, then the result of any possible referendum on whether to remain in the Reich seems very uncertain.'

The report contains much of interest. Adenauer regarded 'orientation towards the West' as a danger for the Rhineland and the deliberate long-term aim of British and French policy. At this stage he did not recognise that Britain would oppose French plans. The key words were 'hopeless dilemma'. Captain Loog reported: 'The seriousness with which he viewed the situation is revealed by the comment: if we just become a buffer state, then at least we still have the prospect of coming back to

Germany.' It appears that Adenauer at this stage feared annexation, possibly legalised by a referendum, the outcome of which might be decided by the desire of voters to escape from their misery.

A man who took such a pessimistic view – and there was much to support it – was also liable to grasp at straws. He believed that the best approach would be for the national government to negotiate the lifting of the blockade and end the economic separation of the Rhineland from the unoccupied territory. But according to the cirumstances – though he did not say this to Loog – it might be necessary to improve the situation by a reorganisation of the Reich. And if the Entente did insist on separation, then the establishment of a buffer state would be better than outright annexation.

A note from General Groener played a role in Adenauer's pessimistic assessment. This was written on 9 December and brought to Adenauer by emissaries, and stated that the Rhineland was in great danger of being annexed by France. Adenauer sent a telegram to Reichspräsident Fehrenbach to request the immediate convening of the Reichstag.[11] In the meantime news had leaked out that on 28 November Marshal Foch had sent a memorandum to the French premier Georges Clemenceau demanding a border on the Rhine; since then Foch had been agitating for the creation of various buffer states which would lie strategically and economically within the French sphere of influence. At the end of March 1919 the French government also adopted this approach. Thus there was every reason for concern.

Those who regard Adenauer as an opportunist have referred to three apparently incriminating facts from this period. First, he continued to talk to unpatriotic autonomists associated with the *Kölnische Volkszeitung*, even though he must have been aware of their objectives. Second, he often attended meetings and discussions dominated by individuals and groups whose conduct was dubious at best. Third, and most important, until March 1919 he had a number of conversations with Dr Dorten, which obviously aroused suspicion and led to misinterpretations by outsiders.

In response to these accusations, Adenauer always argued that it was his duty to gather information from all sides and to keep control of events as far as possible. The party leaders, with whom he was continually in discussion, made no criticism of him on this score. This leaves only his relations with Dorten to be assessed. Like Froberger, Dorten had pushed for a meeting by claiming that his aunt had met Adenauer during a summer holiday in 1900. We know of three visits by Dorten to the town hall in Cologne, all of which occurred before the separatist had begun his open collaboration with the French. In Mainz and Wiesbaden, where he was very active as an advocate of autonomy for the Rhineland, he appears to have boasted of his close contacts with the mayor of Cologne.

In 1937, from his home on the Riviera, Dorten wrote his memoirs under the melodramatic title *Mein Verrat* (My Treason), an edited version of which was published in France in 1945. Even more so than in most memoirs, the book was a colourful mixture of self-justification and half-truth, particularly in the passages in which Dorten attempted to explain to a French audience exactly why his plans had failed. His great *bête noire* was Adenauer, whom he described as 'a born opportunist and intriguer, but accustomed to operating with caution and, whenever possible, to taking the credit for the work of others ...'[12]

According to Dorten, until the end of January 1919 Adenauer was prepared to create a 'Western German Free State', either from territories in the British Zone or from the occupied territory as a whole, including the French Zone. Dorten himself had promised to discover as much as he could about French intentions through his contacts in the French headquarters in Mainz, and to encourage the mayors of the towns in the south of the Rhine Province to make contact with Adenauer regarding the 'Western German Republic'.

Adenauer for his part mentioned two discussions with 'the public prosecutor Dr Dorten', whom he had never met before. At their first meeting Dorten had made a reasonable impression apart from appearing somewhat rash. During their second encounter, however, Dorten's conduct gave Adenauer cause for concern.[13] For the rest of his political career he was to suffer for his failure to keep sufficient distance from Dorten, despite the fact that he subsequently asked Professor Eckert to make enquiries in Mainz and Wiesbaden and became considerably more cautious on receiving Eckert's report.

Even Bernhard Falk – a man well-disposed towards Adenauer – had doubts about Adenauer's judgement of people: 'Though he regarded people he did not know with a healthy degree of mistrust, his judgement was formed too quickly. Quite a few people were able to impress him and use this to achieve important positions. But rapid rise was very often followed by abrupt fall. He went through a lot of people in a short period ...'[14] During the course of his long life, mistrust and scepticism became increasingly marked features of Adenauer's personality. In the case of Dorten, however, his sense of danger was not yet developed. The revelation that Dorten had become a traitor was to damage Adenauer's reputation for the rest of his life.

Adenauer had another character trait which is obvious to anyone who studies the records of his conversations with small groups of his political contacts. Naturally enough, he became skilled at concealing his true intentions and developed the art of remaining silent, listening rather than speaking, and misleading his audience as to his own views. On the other hand, Adenauer would sometimes say a surprising amount at such meetings: broad analyses of the situation, which permitted ill-intentioned listeners to draw strange conclusions, cutting assessments of individuals and pessimistic comments about the course of events. He was a man who decided his course of action after holding detailed talks which allowed him to test and modify his own ideas and gain a better understanding of those of others. Yet once he relaxed, his genuine enjoyment of conversation occasionally led him into a startling and sometimes unwise loquacity.

This process of decision-making has many advantages, chief among them being the production of a wealth of information. There is, however, one major drawback – that the other participants may leap to premature conclusions about what is said. Comments made with reservations, the airing and testing of ideas, can appear as definitive statements; judgements about third parties do not always remain confidential.

Adenauer was soon to win a deserved reputation as a masterly and cautious tactician. But he sometimes failed to consider what he was saying, to whom, and what the consequences might be. People whose ideas were already fixed when they met him were naturally inclined to ignore the 'ifs and buts' in Adenauer's discourse and to seize upon the elements that seemed to tally with their own ideas.

Dorten's account of the Rhineland movement contains many proven inconsistencies which undermine the credibility of his case against Adenauer. The exact content of their conversations is impossible to reconstruct. Critics of Adenauer, those who see his activities as evidence of sinister or dubious intentions, may be prepared to believe the claims of an intriguer rather than Adenauer's own account, even though there is no objective basis for doing so. Politically, Adenauer was to pay dearly for his short discussions with the state prosecutor from Wiesbaden.

By the end of January 1919 Adenauer's period of observation, discussion and evaluation had come to an end. On the one hand, he was fully convinced that a West German Republic within the German Reich would play an important part in the defence against French Rhineland policy. On the other hand, the elections to the National Assembly had made it clear that there was only one way to achieve this project – by influencing the constitutional talks which were due to begin in Weimar on 6 February. Therefore, after contacting the parties, on 28 January Adenauer called a meeting at the town hall in Cologne, to be held on 1 February. To this meeting he invited all the delegates elected to the National Assembly from the occupied Rhine Province, plus the chairman of the *Provinzialausschuß* of Rhine Province and the mayors of Aachen, Bonn, Trier, Krefeld, Mönchen-Gladbach, Neuß, Rheydt, Saarbrücken, Trier and Koblenz. The decision to invite the mayors was influenced by the Prussian draft constitution, which envisaged that the representatives of communities of a certain size should have the right to call a referendum on the subject of leaving the former federal state. His intention was clear: to influence the Rhenish delegates to the Constituent Assembly and thus the Assembly itself, with the aim of advancing the plan for a Western German federal state.

In retrospect it was argued – for example, by Dorten – that Adenauer called this meeting with the aim of proclaiming a 'Rhenish Republic' there and then, but was prevented from doing so by the opposition of the Social Democrats and the German Democratic Party. Indeed, on the morning of 1 February the *Rheinische Volkszeitung* asserted that the Rhineland was at a 'historical crossroads' and urged the Rhineland delegates to move so far towards the creation of a Rhenish Free State, even before the first meeting of the National Assembly, that it would be an 'irrevocable fact'. Yet close examination of Adenauer's speech to this meeting[15] reveals that it was not simply the result of improvisation or a tactical desire to avoid risky plans for autonomy. Instead he offered a considered and logical plea for a 'Western German federal state within the framework of the German Reich', if possible incorporating territory on both the left and right banks of the Rhine, to be established using the appropriate legal channels.

At this stage, significantly, Adenauer's motives were not based on federal ideas for their own sake. As he pointed out: 'It is not possible that the German Reich will now become a unitary state, that the federal states will disappear. For myself I would welcome it if developments were to move in that direction.' However, neither the south German states nor the Entente powers would permit it. Why did he go on record in support of a unitary state? Was it to eliminate the power of the Prussian state, which – as he maintained shortly afterwards[16] – 'completely' dominated the Reich? In any event, his main motive was not a desire to reorganise Germany in a more balanced way by amputating parts of Prussia. The current mood within Germany favoured the reinforcement of federalism, which may have been seen as a desirable side-effect. His main motives, however, were based on his analysis of the international situation and his own calculations.

In France, Adenauer argued, there were two competing schools of thought. The first was chauvinistic and hoped to turn the Rhine into the French political border, while the second school wanted to establish a buffer state in the Rhineland. How could they be stopped? 'Germany is completely powerless. The Americans have no love for us' and would do little to help. That left the British. Even at this early stage Adenauer was aware that the interests of the French and British would quickly begin to conflict after their military victory. France, strengthened by 'Alsace-Lorraine whose industry we developed', would become a serious rival for the British, especially as French hegemony was now established on the continent. Taking colonial rivalries and Britain's need for peace into account, the future was relatively clear: 'Following its traditional policy, England will take the side of the weaker continental power, Germany, against a France which has become too strong.' This gave some reason for the hope that Britain would oppose French plans for the Rhineland – which it was in fact to do in April 1919.

Nevertheless, all of Germany's opponents – not just the French – regarded 'Prussia as Europe's evil spirit, in their eyes Prussia is the bulwark of uncivilized, aggressive militarism.' If there was any chance of persuading the British to obstruct French plans for the Rhineland, it could only be achieved by the division of Prussia and the creation of a Western German federal state: 'By virtue of its size and economic significance this Western German Republic would play an important role in the new German Reich and would accordingly be able to influence Germany's foreign policy in its peace-loving spirit.'

The speech was thus addressed to two parties: first, to the delegates to the future Weimar Constituent Assembly, and secondly to the British government, to which Adenauer hoped to present his ideas through General Sidney Clive, the deputy to Governor Fergusson.

The assembly was impressed and accepted the concept as its platform. Unanimously -with only Mayor Farwick of Aachen expressing reservations – a resolution was passed, opposing all plans to separate the Rhineland from Germany and adopting the following position regarding a Western German Republic: 'Since the division of Prussia is being given serious consideration, the committee elected by us is empowered to produce plans for the establishment of a Western German Republic within the framework of the German Reich and on the basis of the Reich constitution to be created by the German National Assembly.' This committee, chaired by Adenauer, contained representatives of all the major parties.

Essentially, the autonomists had been out-manoeuvred. However questionable the accuracy of many passages in Dorten's memoirs, his anger over Adenauer's 'treachery' was genuine. In future the French, probably influenced by Dorten, were to regard Adenauer as one of the strongest opponents of their Rhineland policy; Clemenceau's memoirs contained bitter words about the mayor of Cologne.[17]

In Cologne at least, the chapter on the Rhineland movement was more or less closed. Those groups which continued to urge an independent approach for the Rhineland were marginalised, largely because from April 1919 British policy began to take shape as Adenauer had hoped. He himself did whatever he could to influence British representatives on the spot in the desired direction.

At the negotiations over the peace treaty with Germany, the French met with determined resistance from London as well as from President Wilson. The British and Americans rejected not only plans for annexation, but also attempts to establish pseudo-autonomous French satellite states on the left bank of the Rhine. This struggle between the victorious powers ended in a compromise which was presented to the German peace delegation in Versailles on 7 May 1919: the Prussian Rhineland, with the exception of the Saar, was to remain within the Reich; however, the territory on the left bank and the bridgeheads on the right bank were to be occupied for fifteen years and then, along with a fifty-kilometre strip on the right bank, permanently demilitarised.

Adenauer was far from happy with these proposals from the victors. His fear that the Rhineland would be separated from the Reich by means of a fifteen-year occupation grew even greater. After the terms of the peace treaty became known, he spent a month feverishly trying to discover whether the solution he had proposed in his speech of 1 February might lead to a softening of the Entente plans for the Rhineland. His most important contact on the British side was General Clive, who made several remarks which gave Adenauer cause for hope.

Adenauer also attempted to influence the headquarters of Marshal Foch. At the end of May he met the leader of a small group of French officers based in Cologne, the Commission Interalliée de Navigation de Campagne, to explain his view of the general usefulness of a Western German federal state. This, he argued, would be more democratic than Prussia in the east, and could channel Germany's foreign and domestic policy in a peaceful direction. The precondition, however, was continued attachment to Germany and more lenient peace terms. He told the French, as he had already told the British, that such a proposal must come from the victors themselves in order to create the desired effect within Germany. Furthermore, the public could not support these ideas as long as French policy towards the Rhineland was compromised by individuals such as Dorten.[18] Though the report on this discussion was passed to higher authorities, Adenauer's proposals had no effect on French policy. After all, he was nothing more than a provincial German mayor, whose opinions carried little weight in the tense weeks before the signing of the Treaty of Versailles.

The future of the idea now depended on the national government and the majority in the National Assembly. Here too Adenauer's proposals were regarded with disfavour. Adenauer referred to the positive remarks made by General Clive in his unsuccessful attempts to gain the support of Chancellor Scheidemann and persuade him that the German government should incorporate the proposal for a Western German Republic in its response to the draft Versailles Treaty. He warned Scheidemann that if the treaty 'were signed as it is proposed and the Entente thus acquired the right ... to keep the Rhineland occupied for fifteen years or for an unspecified time beyond it, with authority to interfere in the administration, then it is my firm conviction that the Rhineland would be lost for Germany'.[19]

Scheidemann was not convinced. He believed that the information from Clive was a bluff and did not think that there would be any important modifications to the peace treaty. Heinrich Albert, the under secretary of state, believed that the Rhine Province was lost whatever happened, and that if parts of the right bank were added to a Rhenish Republic then Germany would lose an even larger area.

On 30 May 1919, for the first and only time, Adenauer called a meeting of the Western German political committee created on 1 February. There the participants discussed information – some of it from questionable sources – indicating that General Mangin, the Commander in Chief in the French Zone, had also shown signs of a willingness to compromise. Adenauer was – or at least claimed to be – reluctant to act as chairman of the committee. He accepted that he was not an elected representative of the people, thought that the Rhineland would probably be lost 'at least for the foreseeable future', and had no desire to continue bearing the responsibility. He implored the delegates to make the government in Berlin aware of the dangers. It was his view that the national government was too preoccupied with the fate of Silesia and Danzig and had insufficient feeling 'for what is at stake for us here'.[20]

His pessimism was increased by a sense that all the available alternatives were equally dangerous. If the peace treaty were signed, then force of circumstances – and deliberate French policy – would bring about separation from Germany. But if the German government refused to sign, there was a real danger that France would cause its supporters in the French Zone to declare a 'Rhenish Republic'. With a resumpion of hostilities likely at the same time, the result would be the end of the German Rhineland.

Finally the committee agreed to inform Foreign Minister Count Brockdorff-Rantzau and the German peace delegation in Versailles of the various comments suggesting that the establishment of a 'Western German federal state' might lead to a significant improvement in the peace terms. The minister himself should decide whether to take the matter further. As Adenauer argued constantly, 'if a Rhenish Republic within the framework of the German Reich is founded, if' (as he inserted into the protocol in his own hand) 'at the same time the occupation envisaged in the peace treaty and the economic separation from Germany are dropped, then in my opinion it is impossible for the Entente gradually to separate such a state from Germany by granting it special economic advantages'.[21]

Events now moved quickly. On Sunday 1 June 1919, supported by the French Commander in Chief Mangin, Dorten and his followers attempted to proclaim a 'Rhenish Republic' in the French and Belgian Zones. In fact the coup in Wiesbaden thoroughly discredited this section of the Rhineland movement. It was glaringly obvious that the French were behind the endeavours to proclaim a 'comic-opera' republic in the parliament at Wiesbaden. The move not only put an end to the idea of an autonomous 'Rhenish Republic', but also cast grave doubt on proposals for a 'Rhenish Republic' within the framework of the Reich. Since it was not clear whether Dorten's coup would incite further unrest, the British were quick to assert control in their Zone. Adenauer advised General Clive to take firm counter-measures. Clive, on the other hand, favoured a cool approach; on the day of the coup he summoned the editors of the

Cologne newspapers to tell them what had happened and ordered them to report events in Wiesbaden without banner headlines or comment. The matter was deliberately played down. Adenauer later explained that at Clive's request he had dictated the text of a proclamation to a British officer, stating that any change to the form of the state was forbidden.[22]

Whatever the effect of the developments on 1 June, it is certain that Adenauer had taken a clear and effective stand against the autonomy movement represented by Dorten. On 6 June 1919 Count Brockdorff-Rantzau held another discussion with a Rhenish delegation in Versailles. This was Adenauer's second visit to France, lasting for only one day, but including a short stop in Paris where he bought some balloons for his children. He was accompanied by the Regierungspräsident of Cologne, Karl von Starck, who was appointed Reich Commissioner for the occupied territories three weeks later, Louis Hagen, the Centre Party politicians Ludwig Kaas of Trier and Friedrich Loenartz of Koblenz, and the Cologne Social Democrat Wilhelm Sollmann. Count Brockdorff-Rantzau was just as sceptical as the politicians in Berlin before him had been. He dismissed the argument that the treaty would be improved if a Rhenish Republic were created within Germany as nothing more than 'bait from the Entente'. The minutes noted that 'The Rhenish gentlemen did not refute these arguments'.[23]

Brockdorff-Rantzau thought it advisable to impose further constraints on the representatives and decided to accompany the delegation on the night train back to Cologne. Next morning he paid a visit to the Catholic archbishop, Cardinal von Hartmann, who assured him that there was no question of any separatist movement in favour of France; on the contrary, there was a bitter hatred of the French. The clergy were fully under control. Count Brockdorff-Rantzau gained the impression that people in the Rhineland expected – and even wanted – the treaty to be signed.

Despite the negative approach of the national government, Adenauer did not abandon his efforts. As long as the peace treaty was unsigned, he was haunted by the nightmare of separation from Germany during a long occupation. This fear induced him to adopt a risky course by making contact with the French through the mediation of *Reichsrat* Franz von Buhl in Deidesheim and – as with the British before them – trying to persuade them to accept his own solution at the eleventh hour. On 16 June he sent Buhl a note authorising him to act: 'You yourself will be in a position to assess what is suitable to be passed on.'[24]

'France', he continued, 'wants recovery and security for the future'. The French believed that they could obtain this by inflicting the greatest possible economic and political damage on Germany. But a ruined Germany would not be able to pay the large sums in reparations which France expected: 'The position of Germany resembles that of a businessman facing bankruptcy. If the creditors (the Entente) give him no prospect of being able to lead a decent existence again after the bankruptcy proceedings are settled, and if they fail to secure the debtor's cooperation in settling the case, then they will suffer most because only a few per cent of the estate will be salvaged ...' The French 'policy of destruction' could not have the desired effect: 'It is impossible to destroy such a populous and strong people as the Germans on a permanent basis.' The greater the pressure, the greater the reaction would be: 'A war of revenge by a revived Germany against France would then be quite inevitable.'

This was the point stressed by Adenauer:

A change in the internal structure must satisfy France as offering protection for the future, and can indeed do so. Here the establishment of a Rhenish republic within the German Reich would play a significant role. The creation of a Rhenish republic as a federal state of Germany will bring about the division of Prussia. The outcome will be a complete change in the political character of the German Reich. Henceforth the votes of this Rhenish federal state will make a strong impact in the future *Staatenausschuß*, and the Rhenish state will also be able to exert its mediating influence on foreign policy towards the west.

There followed an astonishing piece of information which contradicted Brockdorff-Rantzau's report of the meeting in Versailles:

For domestic and foreign policy reasons, the peace delegation in Versailles takes the view that such a Rhenish republic should be established. A communiqué written in our presence, appearing in the *Kölnische Zeitung* on the seventh of this month, was designed to make foreign countries aware of this question and of the attitude adopted by the peace delegation and the government. However, such an approach is only feasible if the peace treaty is softened at the same time, thus enabling Germany to fulfil it and entertain the hope of freeing itself from its burdens by paying them off within a foreseeable period. In my view, lasting peace between Germany and its neighbours is only possible if the terms of the peace treaty are moderated and a Rhenish republic is established at the same time.

The relevant item in the *Kölnische Zeitung* claimed that the Rhenish population was 'firmly attached to the Reich without distinction of party political inclination, rank, and religion.' The dramatic proclamation of Herr Dorten and his clique should not be taken seriously. The report continued: 'From discussions with the peace delegation, the Rhineland representatives have gained the impression that the national government fully understands the desire for unity and resulting wishes, and is prepared to settle the Rhenish question together with the Rhenish delegates for the benefit of Germany.' If this was a signal to Paris, it was not a very clear one. The French did not shift their stance.

On 28 June the Treaty of Versailles was finally signed. Despite a letter to Adenauer from Franz von Buhl on 9 July 1919, informing him of some interest on the part of his French contact, [25] the affair had run its course. In the event, Adenauer's pessimism was unfounded. Despite the burdens of occupation during the following period, it quickly became clear that British-occupied Cologne was in an advantageous position owing to its ability to function as a bridge between the German economy in the occupied Reich territory and the British and Belgian economies. When French and Belgian troops occupied the Ruhr in January 1923, the British Zone in the Cologne sector actually came to be regarded as Insel der Seligen (Elysian fields).

Adenauer himself recognised that the situation, however precarious, offered unique advantages for Cologne. As he demonstrated in his great projects for the modernisation of the city, he was determined to exploit every opportunity. Ideas for a West German Republic were dropped, especially after the abandonment of various plans for the division of Prussia which had arisen during the constitutional talks at Weimar.

Furthermore, since the beginning of 1919 Prussia had been pursuing a policy strongly sympathetic to Cologne. The government in Berlin had proved ready to accede to many of the requests made by officials in the city. There were undoubtedly good reasons for this generosity; in particular, the Prussian government took the view that Cologne's precarious position called for extra efforts to maintain its close links with Prussia and the rest of Germany.

Adenauer's appointment as chairman of the *Provinzialausschuß* of the Rhine Province in December 1920, and his election as President of the Preussischer Staatsrat, the second chamber of Prussia, in May 1921, were achieved partly because of the key role of the Centre Party of which he was a prominent member. However, his rise also provided highly public evidence – not least to Adenauer himself – that the most senior official in Cologne could also be appointed to the highest posts in Prussia itself. Adenauer's election as President of the Prussian State Council also gave him the personal satisfaction of outstripping Karl Jarres, the mayor of Duisburg.

Adenauer's great projects to make Cologne one of the most modern cities in the whole of Germany included the green belt, the new university, and the harbour project. None of these would have progressed as quickly without the co-operation of the Prussian government. Indeed, Adenauer could not have achieved more for Cologne in a West German Republic than he was able to do within Prussia itself. The abortive schemes for a Rhine state had helped to persuade the government in Berlin to accommodate many of the plans put forward by the mayor of Cologne.

In the summer and autumn of 1923, Adenauer returned for a short time to the old plans for a Rhenish state. During these months, when Germany was in crisis owing to rampant inflation, the occupation of the Ruhr and the collapse of passive resistance there, the Rhineland again lay exposed and vulnerable on Germany's western flank. As before, the plans for a West German Republic were the product of economic and political misery, and were revived in an attempt to prevent complete economic collapse. They were again abandoned when circumstances unexpectedly improved.

In the light of these circumstances, the claim that Adenauer was always committed to the idea of a West German Republic is not convincing. In all likelihood, the plan was a temporary expedient to which he resorted only when his city and its people faced acute distress. Nor should much weight be given to his occasional assertions that a West German Republic could play an important 'peace-loving' role within the German federation. This argument was directed mainly towards the Western Powers. In reality, Adenauer was well aware that Germany's annexationist policy during the First World War had been very popular in the Rhineland and the Ruhr; he cannot have taken the idea of the 'peace-loving' Rhinelanders too seriously. The assertion was designed to pander to the anti-Prussian prejudices which currently dominated the thinking of the Western Powers and were preventing the development of more reasonable policies towards Germany as a whole.

From the outset Adenauer had worked for a policy of reconciliation between Germany and its western neighbours. However, the abortive plan for a West German Republic was never at the heart of this policy. Much more important – in the long, as well as the short term – was an approach which was influenced by his early beliefs, and which involved the attempt to encourage mutual, supranational ties to assist in the solution of political disputes.

Pater Familias

While he worked to avert the threat of political chaos, Adenauer was making important changes in his personal life. On 25 August 1919 he married Gussie Zinsser, the daughter of the dermatologist Ferdinand Zinsser, a professor at the University of Cologne. The wedding ceremony was conducted by Adenauer's brother, Hans. Owing to the uncertain political situation in the city, the newly-weds spent their honeymoon in nearby Rolandseck. During this period, Adenauer's young wife became well aware of what her future would hold; later she would jokingly warn her stepdaughter, Ria Adenauer, 'Never marry a mayor!'. In fact, the wedding was the start of twenty-nine years of happy marriage. Almost without exception, their acquaintances were convinced that this complex man, frequently beset by serious emotional and political problems, had found the ideal wife.

There were a number of obstacles to the union which had to be overcome. The age gap between them, of nineteen years, was considerable, while Adenauer's children from his first marriage were only thirteen, nine and seven years old. Furthermore, the Zinssers were Protestant, which created another potential obstacle to the marriage; Adenauer insisted that Gussie must convert to Catholicism. However, the situation was eased by the fact that the two families had known each other for some time. The Zinssers lived next door to Adenauer's house on Max-Bruch-Straße. Good relations had already been established between the families during Emma Adenauer's lifetime, when the Adenauer children were welcome visitors to the Zinsser home. These ties of friendship were deepened by music evenings of the kind Adenauer loved, containing pieces for piano, violin, and cello, as well as two-part folk-songs.

The enduring popular image of the private Adenauer is as a gardener and rose-grower. However, in addition to this life-long interest, which he shared with his new wife, the two were brought together by a love of music. Although Adenauer played no instrument, all of his family made music – good bourgeois music at home – of the kind that was common in Germany throughout the nineteenth century and well into the twentieth.

Gussie Adenauer was an attractive young woman from a hospitable and happy family. She re-introduced her husband to the social life he had neglected, encouraged him to attend concerts and the theatre, and was an admirable partner at official events. Even more importantly, she shared Adenauer's view of the central importance of Christian family life. In 1922, at Munich, Adenauer had made a keynote speech to the Katholiken-tag convention regarding the need to overcome materialism: 'As for ourselves, we intend to make a start, each person for himself and his family. That is our first duty. Not until we ourselves live as Christians, and Christian life rules in our own families, will we have the right to argue for the validity of these principles in public life.'[1] After their marriage the couple attempted to organise their own family life according to these principles.

Gussie Adenauer, an unselfish and accommodating woman, seemed to adjust without difficulty to her new religious affiliation. She soon established a close and loving relationship with the children of the first marriage. Their education continued to be strict, owing largely to the patriarchal attitudes of Adenauer himself: the children's reading matter was strictly controlled, their acquaintances were closely supervised, and the whole family regularly attended nine o'clock Mass on Sunday mornings. The requirement to fast was strictly observed, and special religious holidays and saints' days were observed with care.

For a short time at the beginning of the marriage, it seemed that the tragedy of Emma Adenauer's illness and death would be repeated. During her first pregnancy in 1921, Gussie fell ill with a kidney disease, and the baby lived only four days. Fortunately the illness was short-lived. The Adenauers' family life thereafter developed happily: Paul Adenauer – later to be a priest – was born in 1923, Lotte in 1925, her sister Libet in 1928, and the baby of the family, Georg, in 1931.

Each year, for anything from four to six weeks, Adenauer took his growing family for an annual holiday to a quiet resort. When political circumstances and currency problems made it impossible to travel abroad, these holidays were taken in the Black Forest. In 1921 and 1922, for example, the family went to the health resort of Friedenweiler, near Neustadt in the Höllental district; in 1923 they went to Schweigmatt on the southern slopes of the Hohe Möhr, with its views beyond the Wiesental and the Rhine valley into Switzerland – and on clear days as far as the Alps. From 1924, however, the family travelled to Switzerland, to the Grand Hotel at Chandolin in the Valais. Adenauer had discovered the resort before the war, and had first gone there with his friend Johannes Horion (later head of the Rhine Province), a member of the same student fraternity.

Adenauer was apparently concerned that he was unable to spend much time with his children during the regular school year. In consequence, he was eager to use the family holidays – from which only the most urgent work was allowed to disturb him – to enjoy their company, and to apply himself to extending their education. In 1923, for example, he wrote to the educational authorities to ask for his sons to be released from school a few days early:'As a result of the enormous demands of my business affairs, I can only dedicate myself to the education of my sons Konrad and Max – the first in his eighth year at secondary school and the latter in his fourth – during my vacation.'[2]

His approach to their education was typically systematic, extending even to the regimented walks he organised for them in Chandolin, which lay in the mountainous Valais region 2,000 metres above sea level. Not surprisingly, many of the children later remembered these holidays with rather less pleasure than their father, who went there at least a dozen times.

Even by the standards of the day, the health resorts and hotels chosen by Adenauer were thoroughly bourgeois and simple. Nevertheless, Chandolin was popular with public figures in search of absolute peace and quiet: the names in the visitors book included the airship constructor Graf Ferdinand von Zeppelin, Grand Admiral Alfred von Tirpitz, the pilot and deep-sea diver Auguste Piccard, the composer Paul Hindemith, the Dutch industrialist A.F. Philips, the Swiss businessman and patron of the arts Werner Reinhart, who had enabled Rilke to stay in the Valais château of Muzot, and even the Italian socialist leader Giacomo Matteotti before his murder by Italian fascists in 1924.

The rest and fresh air of Chandolin temporarily cured Adenauer of his constant headaches. The climb to the resort evoked memories of travel in Switzerland a century before, since there were no train or bus connections for the last steep climb from the valley station of Les Pontis. This last trek had to be made on foot, with twelve mules to carry the family's baggage. Conditions in the hotel itself were equally simple. The rooms on the first floor had no running water, while the guest lounge was plain and simply furnished. However, the beauty of the countryside and the peace and quiet were more than adequate compensation for Adenauer. He also found the hotel owner, Pierre Pont, a congenial host who shared his interest in naturopathy.

During these years Adenauer continued to be troubled by ill-health, so much so that his older children feared he would not live to reach fifty. His diet was generally so restricted that outsiders regarded him as something of a crank. In Chandolin he usually drank milk and rose-leaf tea, only occasionally sipping from a glass of wine. Though this was sometimes interpreted as a ruse to draw out his companions at table, in reality it was a habit developed during the fifteen years he had suffered from diabetes. When Adenauer was forty, a talented specialist, Dr. Funke, had cured him of the illness even before the discovery of insulin.[3] By then, however, moderation in eating and drinking had become second nature to him.

This insistence on moderation in all pleasures, plus a daily routine organised down to the last detail, were the principles by which Adenauer ordered his life. In Cologne, after taking breakfast with his wife, he would leave the house just after eight o'clock to take his sheepdog for a fifteen-minute walk in the Cologne woods. Adenauer was a dog-lover, but disliked cats. After being told that sheepdogs were supposed to be decadent, he bought a Rottweiler when his own dog died.

Punctually, at a quarter to nine he was driven in his official car to the city hall. At 1.45 pm he returned to Max-Bruch-Straße for lunch, which he and Gussie ate with their three older children while the three younger ones sat with the nanny at a separate table. Lunch was followed by Adenauer's famous midday nap. In good and bad weather alike, he would spend half an hour or more asleep on a couch in the fresh air on his covered terrace, with a black blindfold over his eyes and plugs in his ears. Occasionally, he slept in his bed instead. He would then return to the city hall, from which he generally returned late. The couple frequently went out in the evenings but were almost always back home by half-past ten.

Despite his carefully regulated day, Adenauer was prone to rapid changes of mood, perhaps owing to the headaches with which he was afflicted in the unhealthy climate of the Cologne region. He also had a volcanic temper which sometimes overcame his customary self-discipline. Within the family circle he could be inconsistent; though often understanding, helpful, benevolent, humorous and even boisterous, he was also susceptible to occasional bouts of irritability and moodiness. As a rule however, his behavior was authoritarian and pedantic. It was never clear whether these mood swings were the result of his worries at work or were the product of his delicate health. At any rate, he was handled with great care during his brief free time and his annual leave. Until 1933, his working life was dedicated to the major project of making Cologne into the most modern city in the west of Germany. Everything else – personal comfort (though this was of little interest to him anyway), private inclinations, political friendships, even his family – was subordinated to that end.

Modern Cologne

According to his brother-in-law, Willi Suth, Adenauer told him shortly after Germany's collapse in 1918 that: 'Times of political catastrophe are especially suitable for building something new!'[1] Even if these were not his exact words, the sentiment is singularly appropriate. All the great projects which made Adenauer famous, first in Cologne and then throughout Germany, have their roots in the period immediately following the First World War.

For a politician with ideas and the strength to carry them through, these critical years offered many opportunities for effective work. Without any action from within Cologne itself, a number of conditions had changed for the better. By order of the Entente Powers, the city fortifications – which had been an enormous problem for every mayor for many years – had to be demolished, thus opening up new opportunities for city planning. The Treaty of Versailles also forbade Germany from continuing to subsidise railway freight rates to the Hanseatic cities of Hamburg and Bremen. If Cologne was able to build a functioning inland port quickly enough, part of this traffic could be directed through the city; it would then be possible to exploit the opportunities for freight traffic on the Rhine, and to forge a link with the Rhine-Schelde canal.

Shortly after the end of the war, it became clear that Germany's western neighbours – the Dutch, Belgians, British and even, hesitantly, the French – were aware of the need for renewed economic exchange with Germany. The British bridgehead in Cologne offered an ideal trading centre during this process, as well as a base for profitable investments.

At the same time, the benefits of incorporation were beginning to be seen. Before 1914, a number of areas on the right bank of the Rhine had been incorporated into the city, the last of these shortly before the outbreak of war. The outbreak of war had deprived officials in Cologne of the opportunity to use these incorporations for city development and ambitious industrial settlement projects. Now, however, Adenauer could reap the benefits of the policy initiated by his predecessor, Wallraf.

The economic climate was also conducive to large-scale development projects. In the early post-war years there was strong demand for both consumer goods and capital goods, thus creating a strong trend towards growth. Moreover, the 'lax' currency policy of the Reich government initially produced financial conditions favourable to this process. Though the inflation period was soon to follow, for a time there was sufficient money available for major projects to be begun on credit.

During these years the senior officials of Cologne were also able to realise their dream of founding a university in the city. Following the loss of Strasbourg to France, Bonn was the seat of the only remaining German university on the left bank of the Rhine. There was thus a very strong argument, in the interests of German cultural self-assertion, for establishing another academic centre in the occupied territory.

Opportunities existed in many fields for those with the will to see them through. The starting-point for urban planning inevitably centred on the fate of the Cologne fortifications. Adenauer, it appeared, had been waiting for just this moment. On 2 December 1918, exactly a day before the last German regiment disappeared into the mist across the Hohenzollern bridge to the east, he chaired a meeting of the administration conference. The minutes of the meeting contained a highly significant entry regarding the issue of 'the compulsory purchase of the belt of countryside to the left and right of the Rhine: following the presentation by the mayor, the conference unanimously agreed to present for discussion by the City Council the request to the appropriate state authorities for compulsory purchase rights for the land to the left (circa 700 marks per square meter) and right (circa 300 marks per square meter) of the Rhine.'[2] To avoid alerting land speculators at an early stage, the proceedings were kept secret.

The fortifications, in the shape of two broad belts, enclosed the entire city area to the left and right of the Rhine. The outer layer – between 800 and 1,000 metres wide – contained the outer forts, demilunes, earthworks, and depots for the fortifications. Here there was a complete ban on building, which guaranteed a free field of fire. Within the outer layer of fortifications was sited a vast inner belt, which had been partly acquired by the city before the First World War; according to a development plan dating from that period, this had been envisaged as a major residential zone. With the conditions applying to the outer belt no longer applicable, it was now also logical to draw up new plans for the development of the inner layer.

The issue of the fortifications was linked with other problems for which a satisfactory solution now appeared possible. If the opportunity was lost, however, it would not come again. Owing to the near-exhaustion of the more distant lignite deposits to the west of Cologne, mining was beginning to encroach upon the city itself, with serious negative implications in the form of dust, fumes and the destruction of the landscape. At the same time, the location of the belt enclosing Cologne provided the temptation to use some of the newly-obtained land to the west for industrial settlements. Owing to the prevailing west-east winds, however, such a decision would be a major planning error.

In order to avoid such a mistake, a major planning project was required. The future industrial area would have to be pushed along the belt almost as far as the Rhine itself, in order to provide a vast new working area in the north and link it with a new port on the Rhine. Since the existing territory of the city was not large enough for the building of the required residential area for the workers' families, it would also be necessary to incorporate into the city the municipality of Worringen to the north of Cologne. This process was successfully completed in 1922.

The planning and implementation of this enormous task was undertaken in several stages between 1919 and 1923. Its leading figure was Professor Fritz Schumacher, an urban planner of genuine vision, who agreed to come from Hamburg to Cologne for three vital years between 1920 and 1923. However, Adenauer was the driving-force behind the project, and Schumacher's overall plan was produced only after constant discussions with the mayor. Schumacher's book, *Köln: Entwicklungsfragen einer Großstadt* (Cologne: Questions of the Development of a City), published in 1923, described their ambitious – and for its time revolutionary – concept of modern city and country planning.

When Schumacher first arrived in Cologne in 1919, he was informed of the urgent problems which complicated the tasks of city development: military occupation, unemployment, the danger of economic separation from unoccupied Germany, inflation and the falling real income of large groups. There were widespread doubts about the wisdom of Adenauer's ambitious plans. 'If I came', Schumacher was told, 'I would see the things I was supposed to work on burst like soap bubbles.'[3] He was probably correct to believe that the city's problems were insurmountable under normal conditions and could only be solved in abnormal ones: 'All decisive changes in cultural policy are possible only in stirring times which, for a few short moments, make pliable things that are normally rigid. It is a tragedy if there is nobody with the courage to grasp that pliable mass and give it form.'

Adenauer was such a man, and his charisma is described in Schumacher's memoirs. In 1935, when his book appeared, the National Socialists were firmly in control; it was to Schumacher's credit that he was prepared to acknowledge the virtues of a man who had been politically ostracised by the regime:

'Adenauer was a man with qualities of inspiration which could only develop to the full outside of normal conditions, when he could capitalise on possibilities that were beyond the capacity of average virtues. Then the imagination of the tactician and the passion of the great chess-player were aroused in him. I have often thought that the most powerful part of his personality might have lain fallow under the well-regulated constraints faced by the mayors of German cities in ordered conditions. If he had lived in earlier centuries he would have been a great church dignitary, one of those men with two great two qualities: the craft to pursue their objectives as resolute politicians in the cut-and-thrust of German politics, and the strength to translate their boundless will into deeds.'[4]

Creating an overall concept was only part of the task. Adenauer and Schumacher also needed the freedom of manoeuvre to implement the best possible solution. This required several separate measures. Thus the government and the National Assembly in Berlin had to create the necessary legal basis for the changes. Within Cologne itself, the new city plan had to be accepted in municipal politics. Running parallel to this process, the success of the project would also depend on the course of negotiations with the neighbouring municipalities and the provincial administration. Finally, the British and the Inter-Allied Rhineland Commission in Koblenz would also be required to give their consent to the planned restructuring of the belt of fortifications. Beyond these legal and overtly political conditions, the plans for the national railway would have to be amended and the support of industry and commerce obtained for the project. Finally, but of vital importance for the viability of the whole project, the plans had to be financed. The process of reshaping modern Cologne generated mountains of documents which clearly reveal the leading role of Adenauer – not only his complete confidence in the plans, but his willingness to employ every technique of persuasion and relentless pressure to push them through.

Adenauer's favourite project was the green belt, the foundation for all the other developments. Until the end of his life, he regarded it as one of his greatest achievements. The idea had its roots in his own history as a city boy who grew up without a garden. From the perspective of the late twentieth century, his ideas appear to anticipate modern ecological programmes, but they were also a response to the sentiments and programmes of a larger public even before the First World War. Other expressions of these ideas included the Wandervogel youth movement, the allotment movement, land-reform programmes and the demand for the building of suburban single-family homes. The sentiments evoked a response well beyond narrow intellectual circles, for example, in contemporary popular songs.

Adenauer was always sympathetic to these ideas. Emma Weyer's honeymoon diary began with a vivid description of the view from the first house inhabited by the couple – colourful gardens, trees, a summer-house and distant meadows. Her own deep love of nature had been shared by her husband, who never forgot his boyhood memories of Fritzdorf with its vast fruit plantations and the harvest visits to Messdorf. After the war, from a position of power in local politics, Adenauer attempted to realise his own youthful dreams on behalf of his community. Furthermore, the project was in keeping with some of the older traditions of urban planning in Cologne, particularly under the stewardship of Mayor Wilhelm Becker. Adenauer's detailed plans were probably also influenced by a visit to Düsseldorf and his admiration for its Hofgarten.

At the outset, his project was obstructed by the bureaucracy of the occupation authorities. The military representatives of the Inter-Allied

Rhineland Commission favoured the simplest solution to the problem of the Cologne fortifications – which was to blow them up without worrying about what would happen to the ruins. Adenauer's first task was to prevent this wholesale destruction, since the city did not have the resources to deal constructively with the desert of rubble that would be the result.

The British authorities *in situ* were receptive to the arguments of Adenauer and Schumacher. However, the French – who had their headquarters in Koblenz – also had to be persuaded. Adenauer worked to convince them by means of numerous letters and discussions arranged through his friend Johann Hamspohn in Berlin. The old gentleman had connections dating from the pre-war era, helping Adenauer to establish contacts within the French embassy, which his old friend Dannie N. Heineman helped to establish. In November 1920, Hamspohn arranged contacts between Adenauer and the French ambassador, Charles Laurent. Formerly an Inspector of Finances, Laurent had close ties with the banking world and was anxious 'to take part as best he could in the reconstruction of economic relations between the two countries.'[5] After a long conversation, Laurent recognised Adenauer's sincerity as a rapprochement politician, and gladly offered to help undermine the resistance of the military authorities to the civilian use of the former fortifications.

In Berlin too, there was much opposition to be overcome. 'The muddleheadedness in our Reich authorities is terrible', Hamspohn wrote to Adenauer in July 1921.[6] Even in Cologne itself there was often little understanding or sympathy for the project. Two Reich laws of 1919 and 1920 had given the city administration the opportunity for large-scale transfers and compulsory purchases. Neither of the major plans – the great development project in the inner section and the creation of the green belt – could be implemented without significant encroachment on private property. As a result, approximately a thousand aggrieved property owners, some of them farmers, were up in arms against the city's plans.

Adenauer launched a press campaign to try and persuade the population. On 8 June 1920, his article for the *Kölner Stadtanzeiger* was published under the headline 'A Vital Issue for Cologne – Woods, Fields and Meadows from Rhine to Rhine'. Adenauer argued that the 'lex Cologne' of April 1920 involved the 'entire future' of the city. Cologne was at a crossroads: it must decide whether it would 'become a giant desert of stones, or a city whose inhabitants can lead an existence fit for human beings.'[7]

The mayor also made a concerted effort to win over the city's burgeoning cycling associations, and indeed all of its sports enthusiasts. Like many people who were themselves unable to participate in sports, Adenauer compensated by providing vigorous support for sporting issues. During these years, intelligent mayors throughout Germany began to recognise the indirect political potential of these associations. In the case of Cologne, they might also be mobilised in any emergency caused by the temporarily threatening violence of separatist groups.

At the heart of the green-belt scheme lay the Müngersdorfer stadium, which was completed with remarkable speed. Like many of Adenauer's projects during this period, it rapidly assumed an enormous scale, at least by the standards of the time. In their size, levels of equipment and modernity, Cologne's sporting facilities soon compared favourably with those of any city in the country. His long-term objective was to make Cologne into an Olympic city, although his bid for the 1936 Olympics failed: the prize was awarded to Berlin.[8]

In 1919 a major building programme was begun in the outer section and throughout the city. All of this took place against the background of political uncertainty and galloping inflation. Fritz Schumacher recalled later: 'The more things seemed to be falling apart, the greater was the energy with which Adenauer pushed the work forward.'[9]

City development in the early 1920s thus advanced dramatically. Paradoxically, Adenauer was helped by the fact that Cologne was occupied by the British. He used every available means – including Hamspohn in the early days – to encourage British commercial interests and industrial companies to become involved in his city. In the long-term, however, the great success of his industrial relocation policy was the establishment of the Ford works at the new port area of Cologne-Niehl on the Rhine; Henry Ford I personally attended the ceremony to lay the foundation stone in 1930. In 1927, the French firm Citroën was also persuaded to move to Cologne, but this project proved to be unsuccessful.

At this stage, the Luxembourgian investors began to show a lasting interest in Cologne. During the period of inflation, when conditions for foreign buyers were exceptionally favourable, the Luxembourg company ARBED established an interest in the Carlswerk company. The link with Luxembourg became a useful bridge to the west. In 1926 a modern synthetic-fibre factory was established in Cologne; half of the capital for the Glanzstoff-Courtaulds GmbH was provided by Dutch shareholders and the other half by British.

As a matter of deliberate policy, Adenauer was renewing and encouraging the process of integration between the national economies of the western nations. A quarter of a century later, when taking responsibility for the course of West Germany's politics after the collapse in 1945, he was again to encourage an 'organic integration of the French, the Belgian and the German economies in order to secure a lasting peace.'[10] His sympathy then for the concept of organic integration of German and foreign industry had its roots in a much earlier period, the early 1920s. This plan, much more than the plan for a 'West German Republic', should be seen as his genuine attempt to resolve the enormous problems of German relations with the Entente states. The idea of economic integration was always more than a purely theoretical programme for the mayor of Cologne; in his city it was a living reality, and had been so for decades prior to the upheavals of 1918/19.

Cologne's role as a bridge to the western economy and as a transport centre was determined by geography and by the structure of local industry. These factors were strengthened by unique foreign-policy conditions after the First World War. Nevertheless, developments would have been much less dramatic without Adenauer's far-sighted policy of modernisation. His great contribution was to reconcile the interests of industrial and transport policy in the city with the foreign-policy requirements of Germany. Though German public opinion was not fully aware of it, his work in Cologne helped to develop the model of a system that was established at the national level after the Second World War.

These years saw the development of the green belt and the inner ring, the construction of a port and exhibition grounds, and the industrial settlement policy. Furthermore, Adenauer was determined to make Cologne into the unrivalled cultural centre of western Germany. Existing institutions and strengths were expanded, for instance by the establishment of a music academy to improve the provision of music teaching of the city. Most important, however, was the foundation of Cologne University.

The creation of a city university preoccupied Adenauer throughout his long tenure of office. He was convinced that an academic institution ought to provide its host city with practical benefits. He was influenced in this view by the successful example of the first German college of commerce, which had been founded in 1901, following a donation from Gustav von Mevissen. The Institute for Social Policy, which had already been established during Adenauer's period of office, also reflected his belief that academic work should be of practical use.

Throughout the 1920s Adenauer was eager to involve the city's leading academics in research which would benefit Cologne. One example of this tendency was an investigation by Bruno Kuske into 'The City of Cologne as an Economic and Social Entity'. This study was undertaken at the mayor's instigation and finished within a few months, since it had to be completed for the start of the 'Pressa' exhibition in 1928.

Adenauer was convinced that, as the dynamic centre of western Germany, Cologne urgently required a university that was in touch with the current state of the economy, administration, and medical developments. Nevertheless, he was wise enough to recognise that a purely practical university would be unable to win a significant reputation among existing German academic institutions. Moreover, thanks to his interest in history and art history, he also had some sympathy for the study of the humanities as an end in itself. He was aware that, in the current ideological climate, the university could act as a force for stability and an intellectual focus. It was this combination of factors that attracted distinguished scholars, including the philosopher Max Scheler and the political economist and sociologist Leopold von Wiese, to Cologne.

The new institution was frequently criticised by its rivals on the grounds that the Centre Party exerted an excessive influence on the ideological outlook of its teaching staff. In reality, to the extent that he had any influence over appointments, Adenauer was reasonably concerned to encourage a certain pluralism of opinion. Among the predominantly conservative German universities of the Weimar Republic, Cologne can be regarded as relatively liberal and loyal to the republic.

The precarious early days of the university occurred during the revolutionary period. It seems highly probable that the Prussian government's support for the scheme was based partly on a belief that the new university could provide a source of opposition to separatist tendencies in the Rhineland. Politicians and administrators in Cologne, with Adenauer at their head, were happy to respond by stressing the national function of the new university. The argument was made explicitly in the memorandum of 21 December 1918, and again in Adenauer's speech of 17 January 1919 to academics from the Cologne colleges and the Academy of Medicine: 'Though the plan was previously encouraged more from motives of local patriotism, the armistice and associated events quickly revealed that Germandom on the Rhine will have a hard struggle against the advance of western culture associated with the victory of France.'[11] One of the objectives, therefore, was to establish a centre of German intellectual life on the Rhine.

Adenauer was certainly capable, both then and later, of emphasising patriotic objectives of this kind. However, his speech at the university foundation ceremony in Gürzenich Hall on 12 June 1919 indicates that he could also look beyond motives of narrow patriotism. He noted that of course the university had a duty 'to co-operate in the work of the recovery of our people', specifically in overcoming the spirit of discord and revolt exemplified by the Spartacists and Bolsheviks at home. At the same time, however, the university had a European task extending beyond narrow German self-assertion: '

> Whatever the shape of the peace treaty, over the coming decades German culture and the cultures of the western democracies will meet here on the Rhine, the old thoroughfare of the nations. If there is no reconciliation, if the European peoples fail to recognise and value the elements common to all European cultures as well as demanding the justified protection of their own unique identity, if they fail to re-unite the peoples through cultural rapprochement, and if they fail to avoid another European war, then Europe's pre-eminence in the world will be lost for ever. It is the special task of the University of Cologne to promote the noble work of lasting international reconciliation and international community for the welfare of Europe ... Above all ... it should show the relationship of all European culture; it should show that there is much more that unites the European peoples than divides them. Its holy vocation is to serve the real league of nations, the progress of the peoples to a higher stage of development!'[12]

In mid-June 1919, in the emotional atmosphere that preceded the signing of the Treaty of Versailles, this speech transcended university politics; it can be regarded as an affirmation of a distinct set of foreign-policy values. In the 1920s, key words such as 'reconciliation', 'rapprochement', 'international community', 'league of nations' were a constant theme of Adenauer's major speeches. He did not lack pride in German culture, but recognised that it was made attractive not by arrogance or sterile isolation, but by the capacity for exchange. To a sympathetic observer, his advocacy of national cultures growing and thriving in the ancient soil of common European culture bears some similarities to the concept of a 'Europe of the nations' which was outlined by de Gaulle forty years later.

Political Recognition at National Level

Only fragmentary information is available to illuminate the development of Adenauer's political ideas during the 1920s. Of these, his domestic political views are the easiest to discern. He accepted the republic from the outset. Though he was prepared for dialogue with monarchists such as his friend from secondary school, Ildefons Herwegen, now abbot of Maria Laach, he never ignored the genuine differences between them.[1] This conviction led him into a dispute with Munich's Cardinal Archbishop Michael von Faulhaber, who was an open advocate of a restoration of the House of Wittelsbach in Bavaria. Thirty years later, Dannie N. Heineman vividly recalled a furious argument between the two men at the Katholikentag in Munich during August 1922.[2]

Adenauer was gravely concerned at the course of political developments within Germany. Following the murder of Walther Rathenau, the Foreign Minister, he wrote to Hamspohn regretting this unexpected confirmation of his view that 'we are internally much more torn by conflict than was the case three years ago.'[3] He made no attempt to conceal his pessimism about the course of events.[4] Society in general, as he told a large audience at the Katholikentag, seemed in danger of collapse:

> First for several years the burden and hunger of the war! We bore it all in the hope that the burden would be lifted in the end. The war came to a close, but there was no end to suffering and no peace. We continued to starve, we sank into misery which lasted for four more years. Thousands upon thousands die silently, soundlessly. Our children are withering, and how will they be able to take up the struggle with life ... And our old people! With a terrible certainty, they see the time approaching when their hard-earned savings have lost all value and they will be left to starve to death. The glittering facade we have inherited from a better past, behind which we seek to hide our poverty and

need, cannot disguise this appalling tragedy. There is no hope of improvement, no prospect of a change for the better! Is it any surprise that people are worn down and defeated by this desperate daily struggle? Can we wonder that they begin to think only of material things or seek oblivion and stupor? Our people are being tormented physically and psychologically, providing a breeding ground for materialism and love of Mammon; the awareness of what is spiritual and religious will disappear, and immorality and lack of authority are bound to prosper. Materialism, immorality, lack of authority – these are the sicknesses to which our people have utterly succumbed.

These passages contain virtually all the elements of Adenauer's critique of the age. They were, of course, views held by large numbers of Centre Party members. Decades later, in the difficult years after the Second World War, Adenauer made many remarks which echoed the sentiments he had expressed in 1922, but he was rarely so open about his sense of hopelessness. In his diagnosis, the ills of society could not be attributed to the war alone. Other factors included the influence of non-Christian principles for more than fifty years, and the dominance of materialism over the preceding decades. Technological advances and the vast fortunes they had produced had undermined 'the awareness, the understanding of tradition, of the spiritual, the supernatural ...'

Adenauer argued that, in this respect, city life was a great evil. Experience showed that 'the spiritual sickness of the people' developed first in the cities before spreading 'with tremendous rapidity' to the countryside. 'The real malaise of the city is the rootlessness of its people. Unlike the inhabitants of the smaller towns and the countryside, they lack the calming balance, the relaxation and regeneration that is constantly provided by attachment to the soil, to nature, and they lack the support given by the fact of belonging to a smaller community ... The German people cannot cope with the fact that several generations have been born and brought up in the big cities, however much we legislate to improve conditions.'

These were astonishing remarks from the mayor of a great city and a man evidently committed to progress and modernisation. Indeed, they have led some people to regard Adenauer as having a deeply divided personality: an urban man constantly trying to return to nature; a dynamic municipal leader who really doubted that his problems could ever be solved; a man who believed in progress but was also convinced that it would bring ruin to the people. In this sense, the Cologne green-belt project can be viewed as Adenauer's attempt to reconcile the irreconcilable.

He continued his speech by arguing that universal materialism was also destroying international relations: 'The seed sowed by materialism has borne terrible fruit. Its last and most important one is war: this is produced by the desire for dominance among the peoples that is inseparable from the materialistic view of the world. Nobody who has followed the history of the last decades can have been surprised that the entire development ended in an appalling catastrophe ...'

Against this background of an age in chaos, Adenauer appealed to his Catholic audience. In particular, he called for the adoption of a number of key policies: the nurture of Christian life in the family; strong and united representation of Catholics; an attempt to enlighten the public about the 'works and services' of the Catholic faith; a search for 'allies' among non-Catholics; the re-designing of the cities; and re-organisation of international relations according to the principles of right and justice.

Of these, only his proposals for reform of the cities were described in more detail. Adenauer outlined the Utopia which had inspired his own plans for Cologne: 'The big city of today must be remodelled, through gradual and far-sighted work, into an organism that consists of a business centre and self-contained small-town or even village communities. Such a city will provide its inhabitants with an attachment to soil and nature, and also with the feeling of support that comes from belonging to a small community.'

Adenauer's call for the reshaping of Germany according to the Christian spirit was brave and sincere, even if his portrayal of a lost age was more vivid. These were the ideas that dominated his thinking when, at the age of forty-five, he was first approached with a view to putting his name forward as a potential Reichskanzler. Key members of the business community had been contemplating an Adenauer candidacy for some time. In February 1920, he discovered that Louis Hagen had told *Geheimrat* Deutsch that Adenauer would be the most suitable successor to Finance Minister Matthias Erzberger, who had recently resigned. Hamspohn, who gave him the information, added: 'I confirmed this view, but remarked that I did not believe you would abandon your important position in Cologne in order to accept the difficult office of Reich Treasury Minister.'[5] In fact, this was the main obstacle to emerge whenever it seemed likely that Adenauer would have the opportunity to serve in the national government.

During this period, Chancellors and Reich Ministers were in office for a very short time only. In autumn 1923 Gustav Stresemann was Chancellor for a mere three months, while even the more durable Chancellors such as Wilhelm Marx and Heinrich Brüning lasted, along with their cabinets, for less than three years. Nevertheless, Adenauer knew that in the Weimar Republic, Germany's mayors had always been regarded as potential leaders at national level. The National Assembly of 1919/20 had contained nine mayors among its 421 delegates.

As political conditions stabilised, it became clear that the mayors of German cities would be forced to come to a decision about their political futures. Not many could take on the burdens of work as a Reichstag deputy in addition to their mayoral tasks. On the other hand, membership of the Prussian State Council was much more compatible with the office of mayor, as well as allowing the mayors to arrange their business in Berlin to coincide with meetings of the Council.

Former mayors played an important role in the Reichstag caucuses and the cabinets. During the years 1920-1926, there were frequently as many as three former mayors in the Reich cabinets. During the Weimar era as a whole, a total of 102 ministers held 300 cabinet posts; though only eight of them were current or former mayors, these eight held forty-four cabinet posts over the years. The undisputed star among them was Hans Luther, former mayor of Essen, who held nine different cabinet posts, including the office of Reichskanzler on two separate occasions. Otto Gessler, who transferred to national politics from the town hall in Nuremberg, occupied no fewer than fifteen ministerial posts over the years. His colleagues Erich Koch-Weser from Kassel, Karl Jarres of Duisburg and the former mayor of Constance, Hermann Dietrich, each held five cabinet posts. However, all of them were, at some stage, forced to choose between their roles in municipal government and their ambitions at national level. For many the choice was actually made by the voters who, by removing them from the mayoral office, encouraged their move into national politics.

Adenauer was first confronted with the prospect of becoming chancellor in May 1921. The question recurred on two further occasions shortly afterwards, though no details of the later occasions have survived. In May 1921 Germany faced another foreign policy crisis. The Entente governments had just sent an ultimatum to Berlin: Germany was to agree to pay 132 milliard gold marks in reparations, to finally pay off its outstanding reparations debts, and convict its war criminals – otherwise the Ruhr would be occupied forthwith. Furthermore, Germany's second mining region, Upper Silesia, was threatened by an uprising led by the former Polish deputy in the German Reichstag, Wojciech Korfanty, with the encouragement of the Polish government. Faced with this situation the Fehrenbach government had resigned.

In terms of foreign as well as domestic policy, then, a decision to accept the office of chancellor appeared little more than a suicidal gamble. It was impossible to predict whether another purely bourgeois government would be formed, or whether the Centre Party and the other middle-class parliamentary parties would be forced to form a coalition with the Social Democrats. Various possible candidates for the chancellorship were being discussed. Some of them – for example Adam Stegerwald, Prussian minister-president for a short period in 1921 – had already declined. On the evening of 9 May, the Centre Party delegation held a meeting to discuss the issue. The Minister of Labour, Heinrich Brauns, a Centre politician from Cologne and a representative of the party's left wing, had proposed Adenauer as a suitable candidate – apparently on the grounds that he would also be acceptable to the Social Democrats. By coincidence Adenauer was already in Berlin. Late that evening, in the restaurant of the Prussian Landtag, he held discussions with Adam Stegerwald, Heinrich Brauns, Ludwig Kaas of Trier and

Rudolf ten Hompel. Though the details of the conversation are not known, Adenauer ended by saying that he wanted to think things over during the night, and would meet the executive committee of the parliamentary party the following morning.

Next day the crisis intensified. In a conversation with President Ebert, the Centre Party chairman, Karl Trimborn, had reported that the SPD was not prepared to participate in the government. Ebert was furious. He sent word to his own party and the Centre demanding 'the decision of the parties by 13.00 in order to be able to build the cabinet, [since] he refused to make a fool of himself in front of all Europe and would resign his office if it proved necessary.'[6]

Afterwards Adenauer declared that in principle he was willing to accept the office of chancellor. However, he laid down a series of conditions that were totally unacceptable to the Social Democrats: a change of fiscal policy with greater emphasis on indirect taxes; the renunciation of nationalisation 'in the near future'; the re-introduction of the nine-hour work-day; and the chancellor's right to choose the cabinet at his own discretion and to change it as he saw fit.[7] In effect, he was demanding the slaughter of a number of sacred cows close to the hearts not only of the Social Democrats and the trade unions, but also the left wing of the Centre Party associated with Joseph Wirth, who had become Erzberger's successor as Finance Minister in 1920. Adenauer insisted that his terms amounted to more than a convoluted refusal to become chancellor. Yet he was no longer a political novice, and must have known that the only conceivable coalition to support this programme would be with the bourgeois parties – and even then there would be protests from the left of the Centre Party. Was he also trying to indicate that, in different circumstances, he might later be prepared to lead such a coalition?

Shortly afterwards, Adenauer denied that his conduct had been purely tactical. In decisions of such importance, he maintained, it was essential to speak honestly and without reserve as he had done. Whatever his reasons, the deputy Peter Spahn observed that the Centre Party must now turn to Wirth, and thus accept a centre-left coalition headed by a representative of the Party's left wing. Trimborn was also aware that the SPD could not be expected to accept Adenauer's programme.

At a subsequent meeting of the Centre Party delegation, in which Adenauer did not take part, minister-president Stegerwald reported: If a lasting cabinet is to be built, Adenauer is the right man for chancellor, otherwise Dr Wirth.[8] Though various Centre Party delegates were still strongly in favour of Adenauer, it was now known that the SPD was demanding to propose the chancellor itself and was refusing to make common cause with Stresemann's German People's Party (DVP).

Deliberately or not, it appeared that Adenauer had participated in the game being played by a majority on the Centre Party executive committee. Under current conditions, these men believed that co-operation with the SPD under Wirth was the correct option; before making that decision, however, they wanted to demonstrate that a solution involving the right was unworkable. Protracted negotiations with the SPD were inconceivable given the pressure of the Entente ultimatum. Adenauer certainly suspected that he would have sacrificed his position at Cologne needlessly if he accepted the chancellorship. He therefore set out conditions which, although he personally was serious about them, were quite unacceptable to all socially progressive groups.

News of the affair soon got into the press. When Adenauer's demand for the abolition of the eight-hour day became known, the Cologne Social Democrats and the unions joined forces to attack the mayor. At a meeting of the city tramwaymen's shop stewards, he was described as being on the 'most reactionary side of the Centre Party'; the proposal itself was regarded as 'a declaration of war on the entire German proletariat'. The SPD delegation in the city council demanded an explanation.

Adenauer protested indignantly at the tone of the attack by municipal workers against their 'highest superior'. Why had they not come to him to discuss the matter openly? However, he also attempted to explain his conduct, claiming that the abandonment of the eight-hour day was only a temporary solution, and one of a number of measures to raise reparations for the Entente. Yet he would not back down: 'The German workforce has a greater interest in the continued existence of Germany – also for them as a working class – than achieving a temporary change in the eight-hour day to intervene'. What was more, he argued, municipal workers in Cologne had better working conditions than those in virtually any city in Germany. Nobody could be in any doubt about his progressive social attitudes.[9]

Although other problems quickly pushed these disputes into the background, the Cologne Social Democrats and trade unionists never forgot Adenauer's attitude towards the eight-hour day. Still, they were also aware that in the past he had made some concessions to the political demands and ideas of the SPD. The first election to the city council after the abolition of the Three-Class Franchise in October 1919 had produced a very different distribution of seats. The Centre had obtained 49 seats; the majority Socialists 43; the Independent Socialists (USPD) won 7 seats; the Liberal Working Group of the German Democratic Party (DDP) and the German People's Party (DVP) had 13 city councillors between them; two more went to the German National People's Party (DNVP).

With one eye on the election result, Adenauer proposed three Social Democrats as his deputies. He had chosen three men who, in his view, had proved their worth by their reasonable conduct during the First World War and the revolutionary period. August Haas came from the metalworkers' union, had been a city councillor since 1917 and a member of the workers' and soldiers' council during the critical weeks at the end of 1918. Heinrich Schäfer, an unskilled worker, had temporarily been appointed 'supervisor' of the mayor by the workers' and soldiers' council. Adenauer respected both men, and in Haas he gained a deputy who was also able to promote the interests of Cologne in his capacity as a Landtag deputy. This was also true of Johann Meerfeld, a skilled leather worker and veteran journalist. In the winter of 1918/19 he had already served his city well during negotiations with the Prussian government over the foundation of the University of Cologne. Though Meerfeld was not much liked by the bourgeois parties, Adenauer had a great deal of respect for him. The mayor was well aware of the value of the pragmatic Social Democrats in Cologne, particularly since his relations with the Prussian SPD government and the long-standing SPD majority in the Landtag were not always smooth.

Notwithstanding his contacts with the socialists, Adenauer's efforts to forge links with industry were more vigorous and striking during the early years of the Weimar Republic. In many ways the comprehensive nature of his modernisation plans made this approach inevitable. Louis Hagen had also played an important role in Adenauer's rise to power; close links between the two men continued throughout the period, especially after Hagen became a member of the Centre Party caucus from 1919. Adenauer also had links with other industrialists, of whom August Thyssen has already been mentioned. Another was Florian Klöckner, who had strongly advocated an Adenauer chancellorship in 1921 within the Centre Party caucus in the Reichstag. At that time Adenauer enjoyed the trust of Christian trade unions as well as the industrial wing of his party. Until 1933, moreover, the Klöckner firm had provided generous assistance on occasions when the Centre Party found itself in financial difficulties. Adenauer also had links with privy councillor Carl Duisberg, a representative of the dye-stuff manufacturer Bayer. Moreover, it was at this stage that he was developing his relationship with Hugo Stinnes, then the most powerful man in the western German mining industry.

Only fragmentary information about these and other links has survived. Almost all the significant contacts took the form of confidential conversations – in the Kaiserhof in Berlin, in the town hall in Cologne, and occasionally during visits by Adenauer to the homes of industrial magnates on the Rhine and Ruhr. Nevertheless, the public did note that Adenauer was gradually shifting his political emphasis. When he complained to Wilhelm Sollmann that the *Kölnische Volkszeitung* had described him as the 'favourite of heavy industry' for the office chancellor, Sollmann wrote back: 'Of course I would not have described you as the candidate of heavy industry. However, I would probably have indicated that you have presumably retreated somewhat from your very democratic and far-reaching social views of years ago. Would I be mistaken? I would be glad.'[10]

Adenauer's relations with Stinnes gave the Social Democrats particular cause for concern. After a brief flirtation with the trade unions during the collapse of 1918, Stinnes was increasingly set on a course of confrontation with the demands of organised labour. In May 1920, the extension of the eight-hour day was the main issue in his secret conversations with representatives of French heavy industry. The connection between his demands then, and Adenauer's programme for a possible chancellorship, was surely no accident.

His connection with Stinnes probably gave Adenauer greater understanding of the possibilities for economic integration between Germany and its western neighbours – Belgium, Luxembourg and France. During the years before the First World War, the Stinnes company had expanded its interests into Lorraine and Luxembourg. Largely as a result of this development, Stinnes had been among the most ruthless advocates of a German annexationist policy during the war, especially at the expense of Belgium.

He and his leading associates responded to Germany's defeat in an apparently inconsistent manner. On the one hand, as might have been expected given his views and his links with the DVP, he made a number of strongly patriotic statements. For example, at the reparations conference in Spa, in July 1920, he made a furious attack on the 'madness of the victors' and expressed his determination to 'look the enemy delegates in the eye'. Though this gladdened the hearts of German nationalists, it also aroused suspicion and hostility among the Allied delegations. With his huge head, ill-kempt black beard and piercing eyes, Stinnes looked more like an Assyrian king than one of the smooth economic managers of the late Wilhelmine era and the Weimar Republic.

Yet there was also another side to his views. Leading French and Belgian industrialists were aware that Stinnes was negotiating with high-ranking representatives of the French steel industry in an attempt to bring about agreements which satisfied the interests of both sides. The issues involved the price of reparations coal, increased supplies of coal for France to relieve its coal crisis, and a resumption of the coal-ore exchange between Lorraine and the Ruhr. In effect, Stinnes was working for the re-establishment of the central European economic network between Lorraine, Luxembourg and the Ruhr which had been torn apart at the end of 1918. He knew that powerful forces in French political and economic life wanted to satisfy French coal requirements through the forcible seizure of Ruhr coal – either by means of deliveries forced by treaties, or by military occupation. Stinnes was determined to resist any use of force. At the same time, however, he continually strove to reach agreement with the more forthcoming representatives of French industry, who believed that a reasonable balance of interests would bring better results than brutal hegemonic politics. In the view of Stinnes, competition from Britain and the United States necessitated an agreement between continental European cartels and the recreation of the earlier networks; this appeared to him to hold out better long-term prospects of success than a sterile policy of confrontation.

Adenauer thus received first-hand information about the progress of Franco-German economic negotiations in 1920 and 1922. In autumn 1922, it seemed that the negotiations between Hugo Stinnes and the Marquis de Lubersac might even lead to a comprehensive agreement. Lubersac, the Président de la Conféderation générale des Coopératives de Réconstruction des regions dévastées, had received assurances from Stinnes that extensive building materials would be delivered to assist the devastated regions of northern France. In the following weeks, during further discussions, proposals emerged for an enormous Franco-German trust which Belgian and Luxembourg firms would have been forced to join. However, the French premier Raymond Poincaré decided on the occupation of the Ruhr instead.

Even before the crisis developed, Adenauer was thus aware that various schools of thought were vying for influence in both France and Germany. His contacts with Stinnes and other industrialists such as Paul Silverberg of Rheinbraun and Albert Vögler of Vereinigte Stahlwerke were made to help him protect the interests of Cologne, to keep him informed of the course of events in the interests of conciliation between Germany and the West and, if possible, to enable him to influence them in that direction.

He was as frank as Stinnes had been at Spa in his attack on French intransigence. Adenauer's speech in the presence of foreign guests at the Munich Katholikentag was extremely forceful: 'In the European history of the Middle Ages and the modern era, there is no document that so defies all human, all Christian principles as the Diktat of Versailles. Its authors have taken a dreadful guilt on themselves, the responsibility for material and moral misery … I turn especially to the French Catholics: France makes martyrs of us, France torments us, even us, your brothers in faith!' He went on to urge an understanding between the two countries: 'For the honour of France, we believe that France is behaving in this way because it thinks it must so do. Believe us, France is mistaken. There are other ways for France to achieve what is due to it.'[11]

1923 – Year of Crisis

On 11 January 1923 French and Belgian divisions began the occupation of the Ruhr. The justification given for the invasion was that Germany had fallen behind with reparations deliveries. In reality, the French government under Poincaré had resolved on a trial of strength with Germany. There were a number of reasons for this. One of these was the fear that France might be unable to obtain more reparations from Germany in the years to come, particularly as inflation was destroying the prospect of significant cash payments. This made 'productive deposits', especially coal deliveries, appear even more important.

In addition, the French had failed to effect any decisive weakening of Germany. By the end of 1922, Germany was producing as much steel as it had done within its borders of 1913. French hopes of building up a significant heavy industrial counterweight to Germany had not been fulfilled, even though Lorraine had been restored to France and French capital was now in control of large sections of the steel industries of Luxembourg and the Saar. In the months before the occupation of the Ruhr, the entire output of French iron-ore mines was only forty-eight per cent of production in 1913. The refusal of German smelting works to process material from Lorraine or Luxembourg was partly responsible for this state of affairs.

However, French readiness for a 'showdown' was also a result of the Quai d'Orsay's analysis of the development of international relations: the Entente with Britain had become much looser; London was pressing for a reasonable treatment of Germany; finally, the German-Soviet agreement at Rapallo had aroused the fear of an alliance between the two 'losers' of the war, thereby endangering the French alliance system in central Europe.

The occupation of the Ruhr led to a form of cold war between France and Germany. A fresh wave of nationalism swept Germany, including the occupied Rhineland. The German government proclaimed 'passive resistance' (or 'social defence', as peace researchers were to name it fifty years later). Workers in the mining industry went on strike, while white-collar workers, managers and engineers refused to co-operate with the occupation authorities. At the same time, the German government finally ruined the value of the currency by making extensive payments in order to maintain passive resistance. The occupying powers reacted by installing their own transport administration and drawing up a demarcation line between the occupied territories and the unoccupied area. As in the first six months of 1919, the French military representatives on the spot, particularly the president of the Inter-Allied Rhineland Commission, Paul Tirard, began to support separatist groups in the territory occupied by France and Belgium.

The Cologne Zone continued under British occupation. Even here, however, there were problems. Food supplies were threatened as they had been in 1918; it was only after enormous efforts that the President of the Chamber of Commerce, Hagen, managed to bring vegetable and fruit imports in on the waterways from The Netherlands and the Palatinate. Inflation and unemployment increased dramatically, in Cologne as elsewhere.

For Adenauer, this was the situation he had feared in the spring of 1919 if Germany failed to sign the Treaty of Versailles: France and Belgium were acting together against Germany, which was too weak to offer effective resistance. He feared that the trial of strength would end with the subjugation of Germany, and the risk of a permanent – or at least long-term – separation of the Rhineland.

Britain was his last and only hope, as it had been since the first months of the occupation in 1919. For the moment, every effort must therefore be made to encourage the British to remain in their zone. Unrest among the population, and armed intervention by separatist groups, must be prevented at all costs. If the region erupted in the chaos of civil war, the government in London might well withdraw from its zone. That might mean French troops in Cologne and thus, almost certainly, the end of the German Rhineland.

The presence of British troops was not the only issue. London – and perhaps Washington as well – had to be persuaded to oppose the one-sided policy of force being pursued by the French. Adenauer was convinced that the only sensible solution lay in the adoption of the ideas to which he had long been committed: voluntary and equal economic cooperation and – if all else failed – a return to the concept of a 'Rhenish Republic', hopefully within the framework of the Reich.

Adenauer continued to forge ahead with his building projects. Fritz Schumacher recalled later: 'Though it seemed that the disruption of all money relations would force building to be stopped, and at a time when people throughout Germany were giving up, he carried on at an increased tempo without seeking any additional grants, even with the enormous luxury buildings of the exhibition grounds.'[1] From an economic point of view, therefore, conditions in British-occupied Cologne were much better than in the Ruhr, where the French and Belgians were systematically attempting to destroy 'passive resistance'. Nevertheless, it was clear that sooner or later Cologne would be drawn into the crisis.

Visitors to Adenauer at the city hall were given very pessimistic assessments of the likely outcome. Shortly after the invasion, General Henry T. Allen, the U.S. high commander in the Rhineland and one of the chairmen of the Inter-Allied Rhineland Commission, was sent a report from a British member of the Commission who had spoken with Adenauer. It concluded that Adenauer 'foresees the destruction of Germany by France and Europe's return to Napoleonic conditions; England, France and Russia would remain as the main states. His pessimism leads him so far as to believe that England will fall if it does not reach agreement with Russia ...'[2] The Polish Consul General received a similar message.[3]

Was this pessimism deliberate, the attempt to elicit a desired response? Adenauer was aware that the Quai d'Orsay would hear of his opinion that this 'tearing apart of Germany would be a source of persistent wars for all

Europe'. Perhaps people there or in Warsaw would remember that revolutionary Russia was still a European Great Power. Any Power that caused chaos in Germany was preparing the way for Bolshevik revolution. For the Germans themselves, however, this would be no consolation. A general European war, he concluded with resignation, would be fought out on German soil with Germany no more than its helpless object. But who in western Europe or in Poland would benefit? Was it really statesmanship for the French to destroy the country from which they wanted to obtain reparations?

In the early summer of 1923, levels of inflation and confrontation intensified. The British liaison officers then informed London that Adenauer was reviving his old schemes for an internal re-organisation of Germany, in the hope of freeing the Rhineland from the catastrophic pressure of the French occupation. Colonel Rupert S. Ryan, deputy to the British High Commissioner, discussed these plans with the mayor at the end of May. Adenauer made it clear that he would have had nothing to do with such notions if Germany had been in a strong position. As things stood, however, they were the lesser evil. The Reich was threatening to fall apart into two or three states, which would pose the greatest danger to European peace. Of course France could not broach the subject of re-organisation, since everyone in Germany would then reject it outright. Nor could the German government be expected to raise the matter; if it did so it would be brought down and probably replaced by the Social Democrats, who were more hostile to the idea than all of the other parties. The British government alone could propose a solution of this kind, although only with the greatest caution.

Adenauer was certainly aware of the risks involved. As we now know, comparable plans were being hammered out at Tirard's headquarters in Koblenz; he and his colleagues were contemplating the possibility of coming closer to their own more radical ideas by reviving the federal state solution advocated by the Rhineland movement in 1918/19. This might be linked with a plan to station allied troops, possibly under the auspices of the League of Nations. The British approach to Adenauer, through Ryan, had actually occurred on the basis of previous contacts with Tirard and his colleagues. However, Tirard knew that the Germans would only contemplate an internal reorganisation if the country's position had become desperate. In the summer of 1923, moreover, Poincaré had not yet given the green light to the plans for a Rhenish state. The British too were temporizing. Adenauer was rightly regarded in Koblenz as the shrewd exponent of a policy designed to counteract the separatism encouraged by Tirard. The mayor's approach was to advocate a constitutional solution which did not endanger the unity of Germany.

The soundings from the mayor's office throughout 1923 must be seen in the context of the enduring collapse of official communications between the German and French governments. Berlin had withdrawn its ambassador from Paris after the occupation of the Ruhr. For his part, Poincaré was unwilling to discuss the prospects for a re-organisation before the abandonment of 'passive resistance' – in effect, until he was acknowledged as the clear victor. He was more interested in achieving a new Inter-Allied diktat, comparable to the Treaty of Versailles, rather than a bilateral dialogue between Germany and France. In these circumstances, influential German representatives in the Rhineland would have two main goals in their contacts with representatives of the Entente: first, discussions should be held on the spot in order to reduce the actual hardships of occupation and inflation; secondly, the German side must work out the possible outlines of an overall solution on which Berlin would eventually have to negotiate.

In the autumn of 1923 the crisis rapidly came to a head. Stresemann had become Chancellor on 13 August as head of a cabinet that included the Cologne Social Democrat Wilhelm Sollmann as Minister of the Interior. From the end of July, the exchange rate for one dollar exceeded a million marks, and notes to the value of 44,000 milliard marks were in circulation. The German currency had ceased to function. Moreover, the budgets of the regional authorities were completely out of control. The middle classes were ruined. Worse still, after a period in which it had survived by exporting or by selling equipment for foreign currency, industry was also facing the abyss. Saxony and Thuringia were ruled by radical leftist governments, while right-wing extremists were in the ascendancy in Bavaria.

By the beginning of September the cost of passive resistance had reached 40 million gold marks per day. Reich Finance Minister Luther, the former mayor of Essen, decided to give absolute priority to currency reform through the introduction of a Rentenmark, insisting that it must not be endangered by further payments to the occupied areas. Stresemann, at the head of a cabinet of Grand Coalition, responded by calling a halt to passive resistance on 26 September. The German authorities in the Rhineland thus faced an appalling dilemma. In the prevailing conditions only one solution appeared feasible: whatever the possible consequences for a separate political development, the issuing of a Rhineland currency seemed unavoidable.

The Rhineland thus seemed to be at the mercy of Franco. However, Poincaré's chosen course of action would depend on his judgement and on the international situation. Stresemann therefore clung to the hope that France could be isolated through the intervention of the British and Americans. In the short term, however, he had no idea how the hardships of the occupied areas could be alleviated.

Karl Jarres, *Oberbürgermeister* of Duisburg in the occupied zone and an influential politician in Stresemann's DVP, was now advocating vague ideas for an 'ultimative solution', according to which Germany should declare the Treaty of Versailles invalid. This would mean that sole responsibility for affairs in the occupied areas, including economic matters, would rest with the occupying powers. The heads of the municipalities, preferably associated in a form of federal committee, would then have the task of representing the interests of the German people in discussions with the occupying powers. Similar ideas were circulated in Cologne by Professor Moldenhauer, a Reichstag delegate from the DVP. Though not advocating any 'thunderbolt' in foreign policy, Moldenhauer saw no alternative to the creation of some form of 'self-administration body' (*Selbstverwaltungskörper*) in the occupied areas to negotiate directly with the occupiers.

All of these proposals were the products of desperation, although they remained less absurd than the solutions being proposed by radicals on the right and left. From the extreme right, Hitler was calling for resistance until death and evoking the vision of the Ruhr in flames. (In fact, it was to be over twenty years before he was able to realise these fantasies in February 1945.) On the left, the Communists were urging the unification of right-wing and Communist nationalism in the struggle against 'Entente capital'. These were the demands of the extremists – but in the autumn of 1923 no solution seemed beyond the bounds of possibility.

What was Adenauer's policy during these dramatic weeks? Yet again he was afraid that public order would collapse in Cologne and throughout the occupied region. A second November 1918 seemed to be imminent, accompanied by hunger riots, looting and an increase in support for Bolshevism. In his view, the primary objective had to be the restoration of the solvency of the municipalities and private companies, since only this basic prerequisite of stability would maintain calm among the population. The Reich government would have to step into the breach. If it were not prepared to do so, the only solution would be to establish a Rhenish currency. To this end the political and economic representatives of the region would be forced to negotiate with the occupying powers on the one hand, and with the German government on the other. Louis Hagen, a kind of 'second king' of Cologne alongside Adenauer during these months, advocated this step as an immediate solution, although he remained anxious to reach agreement with the Reich government.

Alarmingly for the future of Germany, large numbers of representatives now entered into despairing and uncoordinated negotiations with the occupiers, thus laying themselves open to manipulation by the French. One of these committees was the Wirtschaftsausschuß für die besetzten Gebiete (Economic Committee for the Occupied Territories), which was founded in 1921 and included Adenauer among its members. Elsewhere, Stinnes again sought private contacts in France, Belgium and Luxembourg. Individual industrialists and economic associations attempted to negotiate a *modus vivendi*, culminating in the so-called

MICUM agreement in November, which allowed work to be resumed in the factories at the cost of deliveries of material to the Entente. Mayors, private individuals and provincial notables presented their ideas for a solution to the various occupation authorities. Alongside them operated the leaders of semi-criminal separatist groups, who were being encouraged by Tirard to exert pressure through illegal occupations of town halls and administrative buildings. In these circumstances, Adenauer's main aim was to establish a legal committee with authorisation from the national government to conduct negotiations. On such a committee, he hoped, he might be able to exert a decisive influence.

Adenauer was increasingly doubtful that a purely federal solution was still practicable. Nevertheless, he continued to regard a Rhine-Ruhr state within the framework of the Reich – though with particular status – as the best of all conceivable possibilities. This was linked with his concept of an 'organic integration' of the mining companies in the Rhine-Ruhr with those of Luxembourg, Belgium and France. In this respect, he saw Stinnes as one of his most important allies.

On 14 September Tirard was at last ready for his first discussions with Adenauer in a meeting arranged by the British colonel, Ryan. On 7 September – even before passive resistance was halted – Stresemann had given authority for Adenauer to hold the talks. The subject concerned advance payments in paper marks for the occupation and the issue of Rhenish banknotes. There was enormous – and justified – mistrust on both sides. The French suspected that the 'bilious and tough' Adenauer had been one of the driving forces behind passive resistance. For his part, Adenauer was aware that Tirard, a confidant of Marshal Foch, had been encouraging Rhenish separatist forces from his headquarters in Koblenz ever since 1919. However, unless Tirard showed an interest in the concept of a constitutional solution, there was little chance of persuading the French government. Though it remained an open question as to who would outwit whom during the course of these talks, it was clear that the Germans had the weaker hand.

The French saw Adenauer as Britain's man. To the extent that he was trying to maintain British involvement in order to frustrate French policy towards the Rhineland, the charge is accurate. However, as he was to do again between 1945 and 1963, Adenauer was also making a cautious attempt to exploit Franco-British rivalry in order to achieve his own objectives. He therefore suggested to French contacts, such as Ambassador Laurent, that he was by no means as naïvely pro-British and anti-French as he was portrayed in the French press. In fact, he was well aware that the British wanted to prevent a French resurgence and would therefore try to stop agreement and co-operation between Germany and France.

The first conversation between Adenauer and Tirard was no more than tentative. Nevertheless, Tirard did tempt Adenauer with talk of a possible constitutional solution. Adenauer was anxious to make it clear that support for separatist groups was making the French position utterly unacceptable to all 'decent Germans'. For Tirard, the conversation was only one of many contacts between French representatives and representatives of the occupied areas. For his part, Adenauer saw it as a chance to put out feelers with the knowledge and toleration of the Reich government, and also as an opportunity to make contact with a leading French representative.

In the following weeks the situation deteriorated even further. The Stresemann government was forced to retreat step by step, leaving the representatives of Ruhr industry free to agree to deliveries with French representatives. Paris had thus achieved its objective of making the Ruhr a 'productive deposit'. On 20 and 24 October, at the suggestion of Finance Minister Luther, the German government decided that it would stop sending payments to the Rhine and Ruhr in the near future. With Luther pressing for the shortest of deadlines, Stresemann told his cabinet that 'We could no longer finance the struggle. The aim must be to part in love, not hatred.'[4]

In order to reach a *modus vivendi* with the occupying powers, the Reich Chancellor now agreed to the establishment of a Direktorium to conduct negotiations with the occupiers, although this would naturally be in close consultation with the national government. In these circumstances, it seemed inadvisable to define the authority of such a controversial ad hoc committee more precisely. Moreover, Stresemann had no wish to advertise the fact that, with the tacit consent of Berlin, a group of representatives of the occupied areas was negotiating on matters which were actually the responsibility of the Reich or Prussia.

This decision was reached by the German government on the eve of a conference in Hagen that was due to decide the course to be adopted after joint consultations between the Reich government and representatives from the Rhineland and the Ruhr. On 24 October, leading political and economic representatives from these areas had already met in unoccupied Elberfeld-Barmen for a preliminary exchange of views. Chancellor Stresemann arrived on 25 October.

It is no longer possible to establish the exact course of the negotiations at the pre-conference meeting in Elberfeld-Barmen, since the memoranda and memoirs do not provide a conclusive picture. It seems that Adenauer again advocated the creation of a Rhenish state. The preconditions for such a development: a solution to the reparations problem, the removal of the Rhineland Commission and the withdrawal of the occupying forces. The detachment of the Rhineland from the Reich might also be necessary, but then this would have to be accompanied by improvements in the peace treaty for Germany. Jarres noted that: 'Adenauer clearly wants the establishment of a new state. We will not escape the fate of constitutional changes either *de facto* or *de iure*.'[5] As in the winter and spring of 1919, many of the participants refused to accept Adenauer's argument. In particular, there was scepticism regarding his claim that the adoption of this constitutional solution could lead to an alleviation of the burdens of occupation. Instead, his opponents argued, France would only use the concession as a springboard for even greater demands (a method later known as 'salami tactics').

On the following day, the Hagen conference was held in equally confused circumstances. The uncertainty extended to the status of the Rhineland-Westphalian representatives and the policy discussion itself. As at the Elberfeld pre-conference, all the participants were anxious to avoid making unconditional commitments; their statements – including those of Adenauer – remained hypothetical. When Jarres summarised the previous day's discussions in the presence of the Chancellor, he made a deliberate attempt to reduce their significance by commenting that 'everything that was suggested was of an exploratory nature'.[6]

At the beginning of the gathering, Jarres made a brief survey of several approaches, including Adenauer's arguments from the previous day. The most precise account of Adenauer's remarks on that occasion, taking into account his own precisions in the following discussion, appears to have been provided by Anton Erkelenz, a member of the Reichstag. According to Erkelenz, Adenauer had argued on the day before that if the Reich government adopted Professor Moldenhauer's proposal and gave representatives of the occupied areas the authority to reach decisions and to negotiate on central issues (currency, budget, taxation) in the place of the Reich or Prussia, this would be tantamount to sanctioning anarchy. Then sovereignty would be held neither by the Reich, nor by Prussia, nor even by the Rhineland:

> In this way the occupied territory would become something like a French colony. There must therefore be negotiations with France in order to establish a new legal structure for the occupied territory. The most moderate solution would be separation from Prussia alone whilst remaining within the Reich. But that was probably no longer possible, it was too late. In the worst case, separation from the Reich must also be considered. This would relieve the Reich of the burdens of the peace treaty. The remainder of Germany would no longer be occupied. Then the elimination of the Rhineland Commission must be achieved so that the occupied territory could administer itself. But we can only achieve all this if all parties keep together.[7]

Later, when third parties provided their own versions of these ideas, Adenauer again summarised his basic conditions for all negotiations with the occupation authorities. Negotiations, if necessary, must be undertaken only with the agreement of the Reich government and the Prussian government, and must grant pride of place to the interests of Germany as a whole.

However, Adenauer's clash with Stresemann in Hagen was of greater interest than his disputed comments of the previous day. As the Chancellor had brought a secretary with him, a transcript of this discussion is available. During a long discussion of his position, Stresemann made what was virtually a declaration of bankruptcy.[8] He began with the grandiloquent assertion 'that, as Chancellor of the German Reich, I reject as a matter of course any discussion of separation of parts of the German Reich from the existing Reich. That is completely impossible for me.' This statement, however, was followed by gloomy comments about the financial position of Germany and the observation that, 'it is your task to draw conclusions from this situation.'

Germany, he argued, was at the end of its tether. Of course, 'so long as there are no political changes and it remains economically possible to do so, the occupied territories will also receive the payments of such contributions as are granted in the German national territory.' Prime examples of such payments were unemployment benefit and payment of civil-service salaries. However, it was impossible to predict how long the Reich would be able to do so. 'The rupture with France', continued the Chancellor, 'appears to me unavoidable'. However, it would have to be prepared with great care diplomatically, so that the whole world would see France as the wrongdoer. There was no hope of a dialogue between the national government and France, even on economic questions.

Stresemann then described Germany's desperate internal condition before launching an unprovoked attack – although he did not name him – on Adenauer, who had not even spoken:

> Gentlemen, it is such a Utopia to believe – I beg you not to take this amiss – that a decision to establish a Rhenish state would solve the Rhine question. Even if the whole territory no longer belonged to us politically, harassments and sanctions from France would not cease … If you believe that they will treat a Rhenish state especially well out of a joy that a Rhenish state is being established, I believe that you are misreading the entire situation, which is actually based on the desire to defend France on the Rhine against a re-emergent Germany, and thus on the desire to keep France's main forces here permanently … If a Rhenish state is considered, you will keep the occupation to the end, because they will mistrust it just as they mistrust us in the rest of Germany … Nor do I see any prospect that the Rhine state will suddenly be relieved of the obligation to deliver coal taxes, reparations and coal.

After this sudden dismissal of Adenauer's favoured idea, Stresemann finally revealed the direction of his thinking: 'Whether, in view of the inability of the government – I mean the inability that the conduct of France has forced on the government – to conduct negotiations with France and Belgium, there is a need for your side to elect committees to conduct these negotiations so as to prevent things being left to separatist elements such as Dorten, Smeets, Matthes etc., that is a matter which lies in your hands. The more all parties make common cause, the better it will be.'

The ambiguous attitude of the Reich government could not have been more clearly expressed. At the outset there was vigorous rejection of any separation of the Rhineland, followed by a declaration of bankruptcy in domestic and foreign policy, interspersed with a sudden attack on Adenauer's ideas for a solution. Finally, Stresemann had attempted to absolve the national government from responsibility and leave everything for the Rhinelanders to sort out.

Adenauer answered courteously.[9] First of all, he noted that he was speaking in the name of the Centre Party and at the request of the Association of Cities for the occupied territories. He noted understandingly that, as Chancellor, Stresemann was obliged to reject any separation of the Rhineland from Germany; this would be welcomed by all those on the Rhine and Ruhr who were loyal to Germany. But what was the position in the occupied territory? In Cologne alone, where things were relatively easy, there were 140,000 unemployed, in addition to a shortage of money and anxiety over the food supply. Public opinion in the Rhineland had opposed the first attempted putsch by the separatists, but it was no exaggeration to say 'that the second putsch attempt will find the population in a much worse mental and physical condition than at the time of the first'. There would soon be 'very great unrest as a result of the bad social situation …' He concluded the first part of his response by arguing that: 'We see these conditions coming with absolute certainty. We are convinced that the Reich and the Länder cannot help us despite their best intentions.' Should the Rhinelanders simply let this happen, or try to prevent it?

Next he paid for Stresemann back for his attack. The Chancellor – 'if I have understood you correctly' – would not object

> if the parties elected a committee to conduct negotiations with the French, in order to ensure that they, and not men such as Dorten and Smeets, deal with the French. Herr Reich Chancellor, that is the beginning of a course of action whose end cannot be seen. In my opinion, such negotiations would end with the Rhine and Ruhr no longer belonging to Prussia, and in the foreseeable future perhaps not even to the Reich. It is my view that if such negotiations begin at all, they will undoubtedly lead the parties and the negotiators to a point where separation will come about, whether from Prussia or from the Reich … At least for myself – for I have not been able to discuss this with my friends – I can only regard this middle course as something uncommonly dangerous. One must be clear that this is what might happen and must not attempt to avoid a decision whether one should do this or that by saying: we want to try this here.

After a brief break in the meeting, Adenauer continued to speak, rubbing salt into the Chancellor's wounds. On behalf of his party colleagues, he pressed Stresemann with a number of critical questions. They all had one aim: to make it crystal clear that the Chancellor had come to Hagen empty-handed, and was leaving the occupied territories to their own devices without offering any clear directions.

The interpretation of these events is open to dispute. After all, must one not assume that Adenauer himself was equally convinced of the need for negotiations with France? Had he not pointed out only the day before that, in the worst case, such negotiations might even lead to the establishment of a new state? Was he trying to safeguard his own position and lay the blame on Stresemann? Or had he simply been infuriated by Stresemann's apparent deviousness?

Adenauer had no doubt that the Reich government was playing a dangerous political game. With a grand gesture Stresemann had rejected the federal state solution, even a temporary separation, but at the same time he had agreed to the establishment of a Rhineland negotiating committee without any comment on the possible consequences. The Chancellor had openly declared that he could see no solution in the current circumstances, but added with a degree of cynicism that the Rhinelanders must draw their own conclusions. Though he dismissed as Utopian the hopes associated with a Rhenish state, he had refrained from spiking the guns of those Rhenish politicians and economists who saw some form of negotiation with the French as the only possible solution. The Chancellor was probably convinced that, in the short-term, priority had to be given to the survival of the unoccupied Reich, and that the Rhinelanders would have to look after their own interests as best they could. However, if their negotiations produced results that were unacceptable to unoccupied Germany, Berlin would be able to argue that the Rhinelanders had been negotiating alone and had displayed a regrettable lack of loyalty to the Reich.

In Stresemann's view, Adenauer was equally hypocritical. His own reports demonstrated that he had tried to use the Constitutional solution in dealing with the British and, through them, with the French. Indeed, he seemed to have regarded it almost as a miracle weapon. Now, however, he was arguing that any negotiations for a federal solution within the framework of the Reich might end with an autonomous Rhenish state on the Luxembourg model. But people had been telling him this for years! Worse still, Adenauer had surely worked deliberately towards the creation of a negotiating committee; now he was telling his Chancellor – who had been forced to agree to it – that the entire enterprise was highly dubious! Was Adenauer not satisfied that Stresemann had at least given the occupied territories permission to negotiate with the enemy? Was it necessary for him to be so rude?

In essence, this was a clash between two men with very different responsibilities. It did not reflect differences between Prussia and the Rhineland, nor was there any conflict between loyalty to the Reich and particularism. Instead, it was a dispute between a Chancellor who was responsible for the whole of Germany, and a Rhineland representative whose first duty was to rescue the occupied territories, and not least his native city, without betraying the national interest.

Some observers have wondered whether the future relationship between the two men might have been different if they could have reached a private agreement beforehand instead of clashing publicly. In all probability there would have been little change: each was behaving quite rationally from his own point of view. However, it is not surprising that relations between Adenauer and Stresemann remained cool after this argument, which had so agitated Stresemann that after the meeting in Hagen he suffered a collapse. Following discussions in an atmosphere of great confusion, the conference ended with the establishment of a committee of fifteen party representatives. This committee was to be empowered to negotiate – although it was still not clear what about.

As we now know, Premier Poincaré had decided that same day to give Tirard the green light for unlimited support of the separatist groups, and thus to accelerate the creation of an autonomous Rhenish state.

At the beginning of November 1923 Cologne itself was threatened by separatist groups. Though disaster was averted by the British garrison and the German police, Adenauer's alarm increased as the weeks passed. In a letter to Hamspohn on 2 November, Adenauer urged his friend to mobilise his contacts in London and Paris: 'The population is starting to become demoralised.' The only hope of salvation lay in the internationalisation of the Rhineland question: 'If it remains simply a question involving Germany, France, Belgium and the Rhinelands, we are lost.' He himself was unwell: 'As a convalescent I have been too much caught in a maelstrom which exhausts body and soul.'[10]

On 13 November Adenauer and Stresemann clashed again, this time in Berlin. By now the situation in the occupied areas was desperate, with two million unemployed, separatist terror, lack of money for public services, and the collapse of the paper currency. During November and December alone, for example, the city of Cologne issued between seventeen and eighteen trillions of marks in emergency money. Businesses were virtually insolvent. The Rhineland authorities had begun to press for permission for the establishment of a Rhenish issuing bank. The new Rhenish currency should be based on gold. The scheme provided for a foreign capital stake of forty-five per cent of shares, and thirty per cent of them would have to be held by French banks.

In Berlin the will to resist had collapsed. Sollmann, the Cologne Social Democrat who was one of the last advocates of unselfish support for the occupied territories, left the cabinet on 15 November. His successor as Reich Minister of the Interior was the former mayor of Duisburg Karl Jarres, who had proposed the so-called 'Versackungstheorie', i.e., he proposed dramatic action, including the renunciation of the Treaty of Versailles, thereby saddling the occupying powers with full responsibility for the occupied territories. It was common knowledge that the establishment of a Rhenish state separated from Germany would be the almost inevitable result of such a desperate move. Stegerwald's predecessor and successor as minister-president of Prussia was Otto Braun. Adenauer asked him how, 'as Prussian minister-president, you can take responsibility for surrendering two Prussian provinces to the French?'[11] Braun's only response was a shrug of resignation.

The surviving minutes do not cover the most dramatic stages of the disputes of 13 November between the cabinet members under Stresemann's leadership and a delegation from the Rhineland headed by Adenauer. In the early 1950s, Adenauer told his biographer Paul Weymar that he had vigorously opposed the abandonment of the occupied territories. His assertion is confirmed by records of later meetings that same day.

The events of the day were marked by feverish discussions at various levels. Adenauer's deputy, Meerfeld, went to Reichspräsident Friedrich Ebert, a fellow Social Democrat, to oppose the cabinet decision. 'Poor Germany',[12] said Ebert, but he could not offer any alternative. Particularly bitter was the clash between Adenauer and Finance Minister Luther, the driving force behind the decision not to allow the new currency to be wasted on endless payments to the occupied territories. Adenauer argued that 'the Rhineland must be worth more than one or two or even three new currencies. But if the Reich Finance Minister wants to save the new currency, his ulterior motive is to abandon the Rhineland in order to be rid of reparations.'[13] Luther vigorously denied the allegation. During the heated exchanges, Stresemann suffered a chest pains and had to be led outside by two of his aides.

A press declaration by the Reich government had been set for 6 pm on 13 November to announce that payments to the occupied areas were being stopped. As a result of the events of the day, its publication was postponed. Yet government policy remained firmly clear: within a short time a halt to payments would become inevitable. As far as representatives of the occupied territories were concerned, therefore, if anything was to be achieved in negotiations with the French, an attempt had to be made before the cessation of payments. In the face of opposition from the Länder representatives, the committee of fifteen recorded it in the minutes that it would negotiate with Tirard for a change of the burdens of occupation.

The drama now switched to Koblenz, where Adenauer and the negotiating committee met Tirard the following day for discussions which had been arranged by various leading figures in Cologne, including Cardinal Archbishop Karl Joseph Schulte. Tirard had thought it right to show reluctance. By now he had been informed that Adenauer was receptive to plans for the establishment of a Rhenish state. The initial discussions produced little, but Tirard finally recognised that French policy had been greatly discredited by French support for separatist groups. Tirard apparently ruled out any annexation of the Rhineland by France. However, he was still hoping for the creation of three largely autonomous states in the region. Though Tirard refused to define his own ideas about the constitutional forms of a possible reorganisation with any precision, the concept of self-determination for the Rhinelanders was mentioned.

This meeting was followed by further discussions in Berlin. Confusion continued to reign, with parallel negotiations being conducted at various levels without any knowledge of where these might lead. Adenauer was only one of a number of figures involved in this complex game. For his part, Stresemann continued to cling to the hope that the British and Americans would bring pressure to bear on France. Elsewhere, a number of individuals were attempting to establish contact with the French, to entice or deter them, to widen the available room for manoeuvre; they included the German chargé d'affaires in Paris, Leopold von Hoesch, as well as Louis Hagen, Hugo Stinnes, and Albert Vögler. All of them, however, knew that the terms of the solution would ultimately be dictated by France.

On 23 November Stresemann resigned. He had been brought down by the Social Democrats, who were angered by the harsh response of the government to the Communist uprising in Saxony, in contrast to the restraint shown in the face of right-wing insurrection in Bavaria. A new Reich government was formed under Wilhelm Marx, this time with Stresemann as Foreign Minister. Marx, a Centre Party politician, had been born in Cologne in 1863 (thirteen years before Adenauer), the son of a local headmaster. He had made his career in the administration of justice in the Rhineland, particularly in Düsseldorf, ending as Landgerichtspräsident in Limburg. Marx also held a number of honorary posts in German Catholic associations. Cardinal Faulhaber occasionally called him 'the Bonifatius of the Catholic school'. He had been a member of the Prussian chamber of deputies from 1899, and of the Reichstag since 1910, and was widely admired for his well-balanced judicial temperament. Now this thoroughly reliable, ordinary, reasonable but utterly uncharismatic man had been appointed Chancellor in the depths of the national crisis.

The appointment of Marx brought some relief in the Rhineland, since the new Chancellor was genuinely aware of the region's problems. In December 1918, when many members of the Rhineland Centre Party had been drawn to the idea of a 'Rhenish Republic', Marx had been careful to keep his distance from their efforts. Six months later, in June 1919, his sober acceptance of the inevitable had led him to advocate the signing of the Treaty of Versailles. Like Adenauer, he had been an early supporter of a policy of reconciliation in international relations, but French intervention on the Rhine had seen him take a leading role in supporting passive resistance. In August 1923, he had responded to the severe financial difficulties this involved by ordering that the Reich government should be empowered to seize all uncoined gold, diamonds and pearls in private hands.

Marx's accession to office considerably strengthened the political influence of Adenauer in Berlin. The two men had known and respected each other for many years, partly because of their common background.

Adenauer was well aware that Marx had little sympathy for his idea of a Rhenish federal state, which Marx tellingly considered to be 'theoretically very good, not workable in practice'.[14] The crucial factor, however, was the mutual trust between them. Adenauer perceived that he would finally be able to pursue his own ideas for a solution, with the knowledge of the Chancellor but – for the time being – without the knowledge of Stresemann.

On 29 November, even before Marx was appointed, Adenauer and Tirard met once again. The latter finally handed over a document sketching his own view of the principles behind a Rhine state solution. This left Adenauer in no doubt that his own concept of an overall solution was very different from the objectives of France. He noted on the draft: 'Declared to be impossible'.[15] Tirard stipulated that an autonomous confederation of several states should be created in the Rhineland, with sovereign parliaments, their own currency, and their own foreign representation; the population would then be able to retain its German nationality. It was envisaged that each state in this confederation would be represented in the Reichstag, but there was no mention of delegates in the Reichstag.

Adenauer's hopes that the creation of a Rhenish state would be rewarded with a softening of the burdens of occupation or reparations were specifically rejected. The railways would also remain under Allied control. Only a few vague references were made to possible alleviations. There was no mention of any re-organisation of relations between France and Germany, particularly with relation to the reparations question which Adenauer continued to present as the main objective of his plans.

Even after this setback Adenauer did not abandon his efforts, which speaks volumes for his tenacity. After promising to offer his own point of view, he set to work establishing direct links with Paris, over Tirard's head. Hamspohn had not been idle since Adenauer's appeal in early November. At his suggestion, a French engineer named Arnaud visited Adenauer at city hall in Cologne on 4 December. Arnaud, who had been a chief engineer of the French roads and bridges administration, was a friend of Ambassador Laurent in Berlin. During the meeting, he claimed that Poincaré had been told about his visit to Adenauer, and had welcomed it. On his return to Paris Arnaud intended to report immediately to his head of government.

The two men quickly agreed that Tirard's ideas were completely impossible. Adenauer then explained his own ideas and described his connection with Stinnes, who was eager for a twenty-five per cent exchange of the shares in his own company for a corresponding number of Lorraine shares. Adenauer also spoke of his intention to travel to Berlin that evening for discussions with the Reich Chancellor. Details of Marx's position, along with a document from Stinnes, would immediately be sent to Arnaud, who also took a memorandum from Adenauer which he promised to hand to Poincaré.

Next day in Berlin, Adenauer reported the failure of his negotiations in Koblenz. The response was as expected. Officials in Berlin believed that the mayor and his contacts were already too closely involved, and that negotiations should now be conducted by Berlin. Nevertheless, on the following day Adenauer succeeded in bolstering his own position by giving details of his indirect contact with Poincaré. Marx remained characteristically sceptical, but finally authorised Adenauer to continue with his private soundings. Curious to discover what the French would offer through Tirard, their official representative, the Chancellor also told Adenauer to continue negotiations with him. Adenauer was thus able to inform Tirard that he was speaking with the agreement of the German government, though not on its behalf.

Adenauer provided Tirard with an extended version of the ideas that he had given Arnaud for Poincaré. This contained a broad explanation of the benefits of a federal state solution. The idea of a 'buffer state' would have to be dropped once and for all: 'A lasting peace between France and Germany can only be based on the way I envisage, by strengthening the influence of western Germany within the Reich and creating common economic interests between western Germany and France.' It would thus be counter-productive to give such a federal entity a separate status. Agreement to a reorganisation of the Reich could be achieved only by the simultaneous solution of the reparations problem, the occupation question, and the issue of the Rhineland Commission: 'Only if this federal state were free of occupation and free of the Rhineland Commission would it be able to exert its full influence on German policy on behalf of lasting, peaceful co-operation with France.'[16]

As a result of his close relationship with the Chancellor, Adenauer had become a more desirable partner in discussions than previously. In his report on the discussion, which he delivered to Poincaré on 15 December, Tirard noted Adenauer's conviction that any federal state solution must involve a Rhenish-Westphalian state of 12 million inhabitants, including the south of Rhine Province. But he, Tirard, had indicated that this could not be exchanged for the security guarantees France had obtained from the peace treaty. Adenauer had only just returned to Cologne when he received an over-optimistic letter from Arnaud. He and Laurent had spoken with Poincaré for half an hour: 'He put forward several criticisms and objections, all very reasonable and cautious.'[17] Tirard did not need to know of this visit.

However, Arnaud sent a long report to Hamspohn on 14 December [18] which revealed that Poincaré was far from ready to accept Adenauer's ideas. With some justification, the French premier had pointed out that the Westphalian population tended to look 'towards the east'. He was well aware that the people there had responded very coolly to the plans for a Rhenish state – a serious weakness in Adenauer's scheme from the outset. Furthermore, would the Palatinate really be willing to be absorbed into a Rhenish state? This was followed by Poincaré's main point – that neither side should be under any illusions. Even after five years, France had not received a single billion in reparations. Instead of paying, Germany had chosen to ruin itself by printing paper money in what was the biggest swindle that mankind had ever seen! The occupation would last for a suitable period. An international police force, as proposed by Adenauer, was not an adequate substitute. Words alone were not enough, not even when they related to the constitution of a new federal state or to new treaties. Agreement might be reached with a new federal state, to the effect that the occupation would not damage its development or its relations with the rest of Germany. Apart from that – as ever – France demanded reparations and security. In spite of Arnaud's attempts to sweeten this bitter pill, the French premier's response actually amounted to a polite rejection of Adenauer's ideas.

Despite this setback, Adenauer persevered with a persistence that is surprising even in retrospect. This was a feature of his personality which can be observed throughout his political career. Instead of accepting that his efforts had failed, he asked Hamspohn to write to Arnaud again, this time in Nice, urging him to make contact with Stinnes. Furthermore, as Tirard lacked the necessary qualifications to bring the negotiations to a satisfactory conclusion, could Arnaud make himself available for further discussions?

Adenauer's low opinion of Tirard did not prevent him from seeking out the Frenchman again, this time on 27 December. As he later reported to Marx and Stresemann, Tirard now adopted a very different approach. He showed himself much more amenable to the idea of a federal state, did not raise any objection to the size of this federal state, and did not return to his old demand for several smaller states.

At the beginning of January 1924, Adenauer believed that his ideas were gradually gaining acceptance. It even appeared that an overall solution was within reach. Stinnes and Vögler, he thought, could conduct parallel negotiations with the French experts on the reparations question. If a breakthrough was imminent in this field, objections to the internal restructuring of the Reich could also be overcome. Negotiations for the establishment of a Rhenish emergency issuing bank, associated with Louis Hagen, could also proceed.

Meanwhile, the Reich government continued to adopt delaying tactics. Adenauer nevertheless hoped that Chancellor Marx would eventually side with him to overcome the palpable mistrust of Stresemann. The Chancellor had followed Adenauer's efforts closely and had ensured that Stresemann was not involved at the outset. On New Years's Day 1924,

Marx discussed the issue with Hamspohm and examined the correspondence to date. However, he still would not come to a decision.

At the beginning of January, Adenauer and Stinnes urged the Chancellor to adopt a joint and strictly confidential deadline for discussions. On 9 January 1924, along with Vögler and Silverberg, the two came to the Reich Chancellery for discussions with Marx, Foreign Minister Stresemann and Finance Minister Luther. Also present were Jarres, the Minister of the Interior, and the influential Minister of Labour, Brauns, another representative of the Centre Party in Cologne.[19] Adenauer again presented a vigorous case for an overall solution to the problems of reparations, the occupation, the Rhineland Commission, and the scheme for a Western German federal state. He also provided a detailed report of his contacts with Poincaré and the discussions with Tirard. Adenauer did not fail to describe the idea of a Western German federal state as 'actually undesirable', and expressed grave doubts about the honourable intentions of the French. However, he argued that immediate action was necessary to avert the possibility of the disintegration of Germany and the establishment of a Rhenish buffer state. The most important thing now was to let the Stinnes group, in discussions with representatives of French industry, discover whether a comprehensive overall solution was possible.

Stinnes and Vögler then presented their proposals for promoting mutual participations among French and German mining companies as a way of avoiding the bottleneck of the reparations question. Such a solution would offer one great advantage for Germany: instead of the intolerable demand for reparations in cash, paid from the national budget, French needs could be met by deliveries in kind. Naturally, the Reich would have to compensate the German businesses involved. In this case, public and private economic interests would be inseparably entwined.

The brief minutes of this discussion of strategy reveal that the German government – including Chancellor Marx – viewed these ideas with great scepticism. 'France', he pointed out, 'will take control of the beginnings and thereafter decide for itself. [I] am dubious about its success.' Five years previously, on 4 December 1918, he had expressed similar reservations about the plan for a Rhenish Republic when speaking to the civic meeting in Cologne. Jarres made no attempt to conceal his own view that Adenauer's plans were 'disastrous'. He adhered to his well-known position.

Most interesting of all was the negative view taken by Stresemann. He pointed out that the tide had already begun to turn against Poincaré during the past weeks. Not only had the value of the French franc begun to fall dramatically, but Poincaré's policy was vigorously opposed within France itself. Elections to the French National Assembly were due to be held on 5 April, when it seemed likely that the 'Bloc National' under Poincaré would lose. If the German government were to declare its agreement to the idea of a Rhenish federal state, it might strengthen Poincaré's shaky position. The best thing to do was to play for time as events in France unfolded.

It is not clear how much Stresemann already knew about plans for a different solution to the reparations issue, which were emerging as a result of decisions taken by the British and Americans. (These were to lead, in August 1924, to the Dawes Plan.) In any case, the Foreign Minister was aware that the President of the Reichsbank, Hjalmar Schacht, had been in London at the turn of the year, where Montagu Norman, the Governor of the Bank of England, had offered massive support for the Rentenmark. Schacht later maintained that the project of a Rhenish issuing bank had also been discussed, and that the French had anticipated significant British investments in it. Now British banking circles were drawing back, and French banks were facing a franc crisis. The central element of a Rhenish state, for the French – a Rhenish bank of issue – was thus condemned to failure owing to a shortage of capital.

From a German point of view, there was much to recommend a cautious policy of wait-and-see. Adenauer and Stinnes did obtain permission to continue with their private contacts, though naturally on the condition that they kept the German government closely informed. Nevertheless, it was becoming clear that times were changing; the catastrophic conditions that had forced the Rhinelanders into diplomatic activity were coming to an end. In future, Franco-German questions must be dealt with by the authorities that were actually responsible for them, that is by the French and German governments themselves. Even Poincaré was reaching the same conclusion.

However, the saga had not yet run its course. The president of SOFINA, Dannie N. Heineman, arrived in Berlin from Brussels that same day (9 January), probably at the instigation of Hamspohn or Adenauer. He introduced the mayor to a previously unknown French industrialist, apparently a confidant of State President Millerand, who wanted Adenauer to tell him whether Stinnes and Vögler had been authorised by the cabinet to conduct preliminary negotiations. Adenauer confirmed this, but was informed immediately afterwards that Stresemann had refused to accept Stinnes and Vögler as negotiators. When Adenauer met Stinnes that evening on the sleeper to Cologne, the industrialist still expected to travel on to Paris and even showed Adenauer his ticket. Adenauer told him that Stresemann had vetoed the plan. He could give back the ticket.[20]

Since the discussion on 9 January, Stresemann had been aware of Adenauer's diligent efforts to negotiate behind his back. He now refused to sign the secret protocol of the meeting of 9 January. A few days later, *Justizrat* Mönnig, who had also been present, noticed the absence of the Foreign Minister's signature on the protocol signed by Marx and Jarres; he therefore notified Chancellor Marx, on behalf of the other Rhenish representatives. This gave Stresemann another opportunity to oppose a policy which he now regarded as politically inappropriate.

Stresemann's long letter was sent to the Chancellor on 16 January 1924. In it, the Foreign Minister once again summarised his objections to Adenauer's plans.[21] In his view, the French demand for additional securities over and above the stipulations of the Treaty of Versailles was unjustified. It was highly regrettable that Adenauer had told some French contacts that this claim was 'objectively justified'. Adenauer's prediction that Germany might collapse within two months was also mistaken: 'The political conditions in Germany are considerably calmer.' Talk of this kind damaged German interests and might endanger the negotiations regarding foreign support for the proposed gold bank of issue.

Moreover, in his capacity as Foreign Minister, Stresemann felt obliged to refuse to inform the gentlemen about the nature of the continuing negotiations of the Foreign Ministry. Government authorisation of private negotiators was an absurdity which could only cause confusion. This was particularly true in the case of Stinnes and his group: 'We would be asked on the basis of what mandate from German industry we had given the Stinnes' concern the right to conduct negotiations with France on behalf of German industry.' Furthermore, the Prussian minister-president had not even been informed about the discussions which involved the future existence of his Land. The German People's Party (DVP), of whose parliamentary delegation he was a member, was very critical of all the plans for a Rhenish federal state. New ministerial discussion was therefore needed.

This was the final blow to Adenauer's plans from the German side. The *coup-de-grâce* from the French came on 19 January, in a last meeting with Tirard. Adenauer was informed that the French would only agree to discussions on reparations with Stinnes and Vögler if they had been introduced as official negotiators by the German ambassador, von Hoesch. Poincaré feared that if such negotiations took place without official authorisation, the German government might later claim that these had merely been discussions of private individuals.

Adenauer was finally forced to accept that circumstances had changed. On 23 January 1924 he wrote to the Chancellor to inform him, on behalf of all the Rhenish participants, that they would refrain from any further activity.

What insights into Adenauer's personality and politics do these events provide? First, it is clear that separatist inclinations played no part in his conduct. His reports on the discussions, stretching over months, were constantly fed back to the German government at various levels. The negotiations were necessary partly because of the desperate situation in the occupied territories, and partly because of the long refusal of France to conduct negotiations at government level on all the issues involved.

During the discussions Adenauer was a key representative of western Germany, but he was not the only one. Louis Hagen, Hugo Stinnes and leading politicians in other parties in the Rhineland also took part in the talks, which were protracted and sometimes exceptionally complex. Contemporary and later references to Adenauer as the 'King of the Rhineland', pulling the strings from city hall in Cologne, are exaggerated. It may well have suited Adenauer's temperament to operate behind the scenes, and he was certainly convinced that his ideas were correct. Yet his role was mainly one of reacting to events and conditions that changed from day to day: to the ideas that were developing in Berlin; to British and French signals; and, not least, to various political and economic crises in the Rhineland and Westphalia. It would be wrong to assume that he was pursuing a single grand design. Despite his detailed involvement and important role, he was not the main operator, and he acted only when the problems became acute.

Adenauer's close co-operation with certain high-ranking figures in finance and industry remains a remarkable feature of this period. Though necessary in the circumstances, these contacts also involved Adenauer in connections whose full implications he could not foresee, and in which he was forced to place his trust in the competence and judgement of economic leaders. He used, and was in turn used by, men such as Hagen, Stinnes, Vögler and Silverberg. Yet this did not make him a puppet either of high finance or of the Stinnes concern. His own individualistic approach, and the specific interests of Cologne, were much too strong for that. From his point of view, questions of international economic integration were particularly intricate and important. Here he also relied on the advice of an older friend, Hamspohn, in whose unselfishness and integrity he had great faith. Nevertheless, considering Adenauer's ignorance of high finance and the politics of large companies, the boldness with which he entered this jungle – armed only with a few relatively simple convictions about the usefulness of 'organic integration' – is striking.

Equally notable was his willingness to make use of private contacts in parallel to official channels. Adenauer certainly took the view that desperate situations justified unorthodox methods. Nevertheless, the image of a Prussian mayor making contact with the French premier via an almost unknown intermediary remains remarkable. It also tells us something about Adenauer's personality. In later years, too, he was frequently to display a penchant for backstairs manoeuvres in foreign policy.

A willingness to take risks and a tenacious adherence to the course he deemed right were features of Adenauer's first excursion into foreign policy. Also significant was the profound pessimism that underpinned his approach. Even in January 1924, when Germany and the Rhineland had already withstood their greatest crisis, he continued to fear the imminent disintegration of Germany and the psychological collapse of the will to resist in the occupied territory. It is inappropriate to regard this attitude as mere calculated pessimism, or to see it as a cloak for more sinister separatist purposes. In years to come he often revealed the same tendency to expect catastrophe. Paradoxically, this did not prevent – and may even have encouraged – his efforts to take control of the situation and stave off disaster. However, it does explain his willingness to engage in dangerous temporary measures even when a calmer approach might have been more appropriate.

Once the crisis had passed, allegations and recriminations were not slow in coming. The leading politicians involved in the drama tended to recall those scenes and incidents which reflected them in the best possible light as national figures, and to be critical of the words and deeds of their political opponents.

Early in 1925, when Karl Jarres was seeking the Reich presidency, Adenauer became involved in a public controversy over the events. None of the protagonists would now admit to having accepted the possibility of losing the Rhineland, even as a temporary expedient. Eventually – and with some difficulty – agreement was reached at the home of Louis Hagen on 5 April 1925, to the effect that events would no longer be mentioned publicly. All sides now tried to take the credit for the positive outcome. The Centre Party thus praised the former Chancellor, Wilhelm Marx, as the saviour of the occupied territory. The Social Democrats, the German Democratic Party (DDP) and the German Peoples' Party (DVP) also sought to take the credit for themselves and to call attention to the failures of others.

Adenauer himself later frequently claimed that he had prevented the abandonment of the occupied territories by his conduct in Berlin on 13 November 1923. Alongside Luther, he portrayed Stresemann as his real opponent. Other versions were equally one-sided. When Henry Bernhard published a selection of Stresemann's papers in 1932, he was careful to omit all references to Stresemann's doubts that the Rhineland could be saved. However, he retained a diary entry about Adenauer, dated 16 May 1925: 'On a personal level, Adenauer is undoubtedly brilliant for Cologne, but it is probably doubtful whether he is already acting in the national interest.'[22]

When the National Socialists began their witch-hunt against Adenauer at the beginning of the 1930s, they played up allegations of separatism to the utmost. Even in 1932, the Berlin publisher Walter Bacmeister had begun to criticise Adenauer's role in events. In 1933 the vocabulary of separatism was finally used to discredit the entire Rhenish Centre Party.

Ideally the NSDAP would have liked to have put Adenauer on trial on a charge of high treason. The documents were meticulously examined to that end, while a state prosecutor was dispatched from Cologne to Nice to gather incriminating material from Dorten. However, no evidence to justify charges was found.

Nevertheless, Adenauer and even Wilhelm Marx were accused of separatism in various publications – in October 1933 in the *Süddeutsche*

Monatshefte, and in 1934 in a pathetic piece by a retired major, Walther Ilges, entitled *Hochverrat des Zentrums am Rhein* (High Treason by the Centre Party on the Rhine). The work had an undeservedly long life: even in the 1950s and early 1960s it was still being used by Communist authors in the GDR in an attempt to discredit Adenauer.

Both Adenauer and Marx were disturbed by the appearance of these allegations and were determined to refute them. On behalf of Adenauer and himself, Marx wrote to State Secretary Lammers in the Reich Chancellery, asking to be released from the obligation to official secrecy to enable him to answer the attacks.[23] The application was passed on to the Propaganda Ministry under Goebbels and there neglected.

To protect himself, Adenauer then made contact with Julian Piggott, who from 1920 to 1925 had been responsible for political connections in the British staff at Cologne and was now working for the British Steel Export Association. Like General Sidney Clive, now a Marshal of the Diplomatic Corps in London, Piggott wrote to exonerate the mayor from the charge of separatism and to confirm that he had always been a bitter opponent of the separatist movement.[24]

In defending himself against these attacks, Adenauer grew increasingly inclined to portray his initiative as a largely tactical manoeuvre to counteract French policy towards the Rhineland and to gain control over separatist tendencies. Only after 1945 did he think it advisable to refer to the progressive core of his concept. There had been two main elements: first, the aim of satisfying French security needs by means of industrial integration; and second, instead of the buffer state desired by France, the creation of a West German Land within the Reich, which would be inclined towards peaceful co-operation with western Europe by virtue of its economic and cultural interests. He was not alone in suppressing the recollection of the full extent of his part during the worst of the Ruhr crisis. Under the terrible pressure of events he, like Stresemann and other members of the German government, had in fact had visions of the worst case that the occupied areas might be temporarily separated from the rest of Germany and that they might have been forced to collaborate in this solution.

'The Mayors of Contemporary Germany Are the Kings of Today'

Stability in foreign policy was restored remarkably quickly. From 1924, politicians who favoured a policy of reconciliation with Germany held power in the major European capitals: Ramsay MacDonald, who in 1914 had opposed his country's entry into the war, in London; Edouard Herriot and Aristide Briand, both sympathetic to pacifist ideals, in Paris; Wilhelm Marx and Gustav Stresemann in Berlin. The Rentenmark rapidly established itself as a stable currency. In August 1924 the London reparations conference made a vital breakthrough: although Germany had to commit itself to pay yearly reparations of 2.5 billion gold marks; the commitment was matched by the Allies with a binding plan for the evacuation of the occupied territories. The Ruhr was to be evacuated within a year, the Cologne Zone by 31 January 1926. Moreover, the reparations agreement gave Germany access to the U.S. capital market; American investors thenceforth began to invest in Germany some of their profits from the boom of the 1920s – not least in the form of short-term loans to the German municipalities.

There was great relief in Cologne at the normalisation of the economic situation. Unemployment, of course, continued to be high, since manufacturing industry took some years to recover. In 1923 the city had 50,000 unemployed, in 1924 54,000, and in 1925 21,000 were still without work. Relief schemes for the unemployed thus had to be maintained and continued to burden the city budget. Nevertheless, there were justified grounds for optimism. It was now that Adenauer's wide-ranging measures to improve infrastructure began to take effect. The new Rhine port took an increasing volume of shipping; coal lighters from the Rhine fleets of Stinnes and Haniel revived the river and demonstrated the returning strength of the economy; new industries were set up; the use of motorised transport increased, thereby making transport cheaper and generating jobs, though also creating apparently insoluble traffic problems in the narrow inner city.

The city's future began to take shape, as factory chimneys and highrise buildings eclipsed the churches which had previously dominated the skyline. Nevertheless, visitors returning to Cologne after a prolonged absence maintained that the city was not only smarter than before and equally as lively, but also offered a better quality of life. Its historic buildings were once again well tended; the left and right banks of the Rhine had grown into an organic whole; the exhibition grounds were a striking modernist development. Above all, as the German and foreign press reported, the green belt was an outstanding success. The photographs by August Sander provide a vivid impression of Adenauer's remarkable city, both the economic hub of western Germany and the traditional centre with museums and churches that continued to attract thousands of visitors every year.

In the middle and later twentieth century, Cologne was also a focus for contemporary culture and science. After the disaster of the Nazi years, former students and professors from the 1920s were able to recognise the extent of the intellectual achievements of the new university. The liberal political scientist John Herz, who had since settled at Columbia University in New York, remembered lectures by such diverse figures as Carl Schmitt and Hans Kelsen, Eugen Schmalenbach and Max Scheler.[1] The Germanist Friedrich von der Leyen believed that the new Philosophy Faculty had been the best in Germany.[2] Hans Mayer, whose shift to the left continued after the end of the 1920s, testified that not even critics of capitalism had been bored there.[3] Success brought its own problems, however. Even in the winter semester of 1922/23, Cologne was the second largest university in Prussia; a new building, which proved exceptionally difficult to finance during the world economic crisis, soon became essential.

Within two short years it had been forgotten – or, at least, the memory was suppressed – that even the national government had recently despaired of keeping the Rhineland within Germany. The British occupation now retreated discreetly into the background, much as the Western Allies were to do before the return of sovereignty between 1952 and 1955. Cologne's role within the German Reich was again emphasised. Thus, on 11 May 1924, President Friedrich Ebert attended the opening of the exhibition grounds on the bank of the Rhine. The reflected glory of this visit also fell on Adenauer, his host. Typically, however, the mayor followed the visit by presenting his administration with a detailed list of all the mishaps that had occurred in the presence of the head of state.[4] He was as anxious to cut as fine a figure as his predecessor, Wallraf, had done.

Barely a year later Adenauer was giving the obituary speech for Ebert. It took the form of a vigorous declaration of faith in the republic and in a Social Democrat who had been attacked from many sides: 'He gave the office dignity and prestige within and without, he won the trust of the Wehrmacht. By the exemplary manner in which he occupied office, he contributed immeasurably to the establishment of internal calm and consolidation, to the re-establishment and maintenance of the concept of authority that is indispensable for the welfare of the individual and the whole people.'[5]

The opening of the exhibition grounds in the presence of the Reichspräsident was only the first in a series of outstanding promotions for modern Cologne – and, at the same time, for its mayor. In summer 1925 the great Thousand Year Exhibition of the Rhineland, a huge display of Rhenish history in all its ramifications, was mounted. In 1926 a new climax was reached with the withdrawal of the British occupying forces. Rudolf Amelunxen, later minister-president of North Rhine-Westphalia during 1946/47 when he opposed Adenauer because of his own loyalty to the old Centre Party, was present on this occasion. He described his impressions as follows:

> In late afternoon of the last day in January the Tommies left the cathedral city. Six hours later, as the clock struck twelve, the midnight festival of liberation began in front of the cathedral. The people of Cologne filled the cathedral

area, the adjacent streets and squares. A hundred marks changed hands to secure a place at the window. The twelfth chime had not died away when Konrad Adenauer, the mayor of the city, spoke from the broad steps outside the deep portals of the sacred cathedral: 'Hear me! Cologne is free!' He spoke briefly and boldly, from the step where the eighty-three year old Kaiser Wilhelm I had stood on in October 1880, when he read his famous cathedral speech in front of the newly completed building after a cantata by Emil Rittershaus...At the end of the hour of celebration there rang out over Cologne the muffled tones of the new, five hundred-weight bell of St Peter, the most powerful bell in Germany. It had been cast in May three years before to replace the Kaiser bell that had been given to the war effort.[6]

This reference to the Kaiser may not have been entirely coincidental: by now, many observers in Cologne had begun to regard Adenauer as a kind of king. The Liberal Dr Johann Kaiser, one of Adenauer's most bitter critics, was particularly critical of this development. Three years later, in the city council, he claimed: 'It is popularly said, if I may be humorous, that in Cologne you have more say than ever the King of Prussia or the German Kaiser did.'[7]

Adenauer, who had celebrated his fiftieth birthday on 5 January 1926, regarded the midnight festival of liberation at the cathedral as the highpoint of his life. However, the celebrations were not yet finished. In March, a great liberation banquet was held in Gürzenich Hall, with the new Reich President Paul von Hindenburg as guest of honour. At the side of the former Field Marshal, Amelunxen noted pointedly, sat Prussia's Social Democratic minister-president Otto Braun, the son of a barracks attendant. Adenauer had sent out the invitations on hand-made cards; by each of the six hundred place-settings was a bottle of eau de cologne, contributed by its manufacturer Johann Maria Farina, and five special cigars from the Feinhals cigar house with Adenauer's head on the band.[8]

Adenauer, always conscious of history and tradition, had achieved his heart's desire. Here, in Gürzenich Hall, his predecessors had entertained the potentates of the Reich over the centuries: in the fifteenth century the Habsburg Emperor Friedrich III, then Kaiser Maximilian and Karl V; in 1848, at the six hundredth anniversary of the laying of the cathedral foundation stone, Prussia's King Friedrich Wilhelm IV and the Reichsverweser Archduke Johann of Austria. A few days later Adenauer wrote one of his last letters to Johann Hamspohn, who died shortly afterwards at the age of eighty-six: 'About our festival of liberation you will have read a great deal in the newspaper; it was a truly overwhelming rally. The bearing of the population was impeccable.'[9]

Adenauer himself was unwell again and had found it hard to keep going. When the celebrations were finished, he withdrew to the Godesberger Hof for eight days with some detective novels sent to him by *Geheimrat* Deutsch of AEG: 'I intend to use the excellent spring weather to relax for a few days.'[10]

At this stage of his life, however, his enjoyment was limited. His diabetes continued to force him to adopt the most rigorous of diets. Nevertheless, the many photographs taken during these successful years show a much-changed man. In the crises of the early 1920s, Adenauer had looked ascetic and unhealthy, almost as though he was suffering from a wasting disease. By 1926, however, his smooth-shaven face was well-fed and almost chubby. And whenever the face under the homburg was photographed with a smile of satisfaction, it was reminiscent of the caricatures of bourgeois types by George Grosz.

Adenauer had by now been awarded several honorary doctorates, including four from the University of Cologne between 1919 and 1923. He took the honour seriously, and in the future was always known as Dr Konrad Adenauer.

Meanwhile, the celebrations continued. In 1926, Adenauer opened Cologne airport circling it on a special flight from which he returned to firm ground with some relief to . In 1928 tens of thousands of gymnasts came to the city for the German Gymnastics Festival. That same year the mayor officially launched the cruiser *Köln*. More important, however, this was the year of the 'Pressa' exhibition.

Today, large cities stage major cultural activities almost as a matter of course. In 1928, however, the International Press Exhibition, containing detailed information about all aspects of the press and mounted at considerable expense, drew attention from all over Europe. Numerous foreign guests came to see it, including Soviet functionaries, whose appearance led to right-wing attacks on Adenauer, and Edouard Herriot, then the French Minister of Education.

Adenauer was now strongly in favour of reconciliation with France. His speech at the dinner in honour of Herriot accurately reflected his attitude during these years:

> I am no diplomat and not a representative of the government. I am a free man and citizen and can therefore speak openly...We have lived through terrible things, we have seen the fate that threatens humanity if the methods of an advanced technology, the human multitudes of our age, and our age's capacity for organisation are used for purposes of destruction. The old Europe lies in ruins – we are standing at the threshold of a new age, a new epoch of humanity. The new age can and must be a better one, if well-meaning people in all countries want it and work for it; want and work in all seriousness, with perseverance, with devotion, without being discouraged by mockery and failures, in the secure conviction that the idea of peace and reconciliation must succeed if Europe is not to go under. The ideas of outlawing war, of disarmament, of rapprochement, of the peaceful settlement of all disputes, the gathering of all peoples into a society whose members enjoy equal rights – these ideas are marching, they are marching, albeit slowly. Many people in Germany – I was one of them myself – initially regarded these ideas with great doubt and caution, but we have been convinced. The way is long, and the goal is high. It will be reached stage by stage, and there will be setbacks. There will

be heights to be scaled and depths to be crossed. But only in this way can the goal, the rapprochement of peoples, the equality of all peoples, the welfare of all peoples, be achieved.[11]

In addition to Adenauer and Herriot, the dinner was attended by several men who were to play an important role in the coming decades. For example, the keynote address was given by the former Reich Minister of the Interior and later mayor of Dresden, Wilhelm Külz of the German Democratic Party. In 1945 Külz, who was born in 1873, became chairman of the Liberal-Demokratische Partei (LDPD) in Berlin and the Soviet zone and pursued a course in foreign policy similar to Jakob Kaiser's CDU. His death in 1948 saved him from further compromising himself by co-operating with the Communists.

After his return to France, Herriot wrote to thank Adenauer for 'each of your actions and gestures' and the 'genuine cordiality' of the encounter: 'Sincerely devoted as I am to the cause of peace, convinced of the great role that two nations such as Germany and France can play in the development of culture, my conviction has been further strengthened during these memorable days'.[12] As Federal Chancellor in the early 1950s, Adenauer renewed the acquaintance by visiting Herriot, now President of the Chamber, in Paris. Despite his sufferings during the war, Herriot greeted Adenauer warmly, although he waged a bitter struggle against the European Defence Community (EDC) which was then an integral element of Adenauer's entire Western policy.

Adenauer had begun to make both official and private visits to other European countries. The first of these, in spring 1929, took him to London, where his son Konrad was a student. Dannie N. Heineman, who had contacts throughout the European transport system from his base in Brussels, arranged for his friend to be treated like royalty on the railways and boats.[13] Adenauer had been planning to visit Britain for a number of years, but had regarded it inappropriate as long as the British were occupying Cologne.

In autumn of the same year he made an official visit to the city of Amsterdam. Documents in the Cologne archives clearly reveal the interest and intellectual curiosity he brought to his travels: a three-page memorandum summarises his impressions of the housing construction and housing estates in Holland.[14] In 1930 he made an official visit to Antwerp, where another Catholic local politician, Frans van Cauwelaert, a supporter of Coudenhove's pan-European ideas, was mayor.[15] Vivid local memories of the recent German occupation ensured that the visit had to be handled with tact. Moreover, Adenauer was aware that many Flemings had been sympathetic to the Germans during the First World War (as some were to be during the Second), which made a cautious approach even more essential. Adenauer chose to travel by car 'because on a car trip through villages and towns a municipal official will always see all kinds of things that interest him'.[16] Other journeys, to the United States[17] and to Rome, were planned but did not come about.

In 1929 and 1930 Adenauer also made two private visits to Bohemia, in order to stay at a health resort in Karlsbad and visit museums in Vienna. The family continued to take its annual holiday in Switzerland, four or five weeks in Chandolin usually followed by a couple of days at Thunersee. Adenauer felt comfortable among the Swiss, especially when the Swiss Consul-General in Cologne, Franz-Rudolph von Weiss, ordered that he be treated almost like a visiting head of state, with special clearance at customs and a reserved compartment on Swiss trains. Adenauer's office in Cologne also arranged for preferential treatment at the German customs. These details demonstrate that there was some truth in Stresemann's observation that 'in reality, the mayors of contemporary Germany are, alongside big industrialists, the kings of today.'[18]

No major conclusions can be drawn from Adenauer's trips to the West. He genuinely enjoyed travelling and took every opportunity to see the world, while the 'Pressa' exhibition in particular gave him the chance to make numerous contacts. Of course, his links with western-European politicians of reconciliation also fitted in with his European and internationalist outlook. Like many representatives of centrist parties in the Weimar Republic, he was receptive to the pan-European idea, though he had reservations about its chief propagandist, Count Coudenhove-Kalergi.[19] Among his many honorary positions, Adenauer was a member of the German Committee of the Pan-European Union. At the time of the Locarno Pact of 1925, the Thoiry discussions between Briand and Stresemann in 1926 and the Kellogg-Briand Pact of 1928, he also believed that the international community of European politicians and economists working for reconcilation would come together to overcome sterile nationalism.

In late autumn 1930, when the September elections had already swept 107 National Socialists into the German Reichstag, Adenauer asked Dannie N. Heineman to give a lecture in Cologne and sought to publicise his ideas through the Görreshaus printing company. There was also a business context to Heineman's visit: Adenauer was currently engaged in a desperate search for foreign loans for his debt-ridden city, and wanted to encourage Heineman's interest in the Cologne transport services and public utilities. Against the background of the deteriorating international climate and in the light of Adenauer's subsequent policy of integration, the ideas of this optimistic and imaginative American are worthy of note. Despite mounting problems, there was still interest in Briand's European initiative; the idea of peaceful international co-operation had not yet failed entirely.

By chance, an account of Heineman's lecture given in the Hanse room of city hall has survived. Written by a French visitor from Alsace, Jean de Pange, it shows the effect of the surroundings on visitors from abroad:

I look at this magnificent Hanse hall, one of the purest artistic monuments of the fourteenth century, with its ridged wooden arch, the walls adorned with the coats of arms of patrician families such as the Overstolz, the Hardefust and the Quattermarkt, and its statues of the kings on their pedestals behind the speaker. The allied Rhenish states sent their emissaries here to Cologne. This league had courts of arbitration for the conciliation of disputes. It had been founded in the thirteenth century 'in order to guard the preservation of holy peace'. Here in this hall were gathered the representatives of the famed Hanseatic League, who ruled all the seaways from Spain to Nizhni-Novgorod and were strong enough to declare war on states. What an example! Will those powerful corporative organisations arise again to protect the élite and halt the advance of the totalitarian state? What a response Mr Heineman's appeal to create Europe finds here![20]

Heineman had entitled his seventy-five minute lecture 'Outline of a new Europe'.[21] He used it to examine the idea of a European federation from the standpoint of an engineer. According to his panorama of the industrial age, a combination of applied science and capital had altered the world beyond recognition over the past fifty years. Heineman argued that the earth was now 'a great living entity in which the lines of communication – railways, steamships, telegraphs and aircraft – form a kind of arterial system. And the heart of this giant organism consists of two chambers, one lying in Europe (between London, Paris and Berlin), and the other in the United States (between New York and Chicago).'

In Heineman's view, the technologically advanced parts of the United States and Europe were already an organic unity. However, this technically and economically interdependent organism remained politically divided. Regardless of size, each nation demanded its autonomy: 'This produces the disorder and disquiet of contemporary Europe. The disequilibrium between politics and economy is the great sickness of contemporary Europe.' How could it be cured, and by whom? In future, politics and economics must be adjusted to take account of each other. '...I would gladly see Europe organised by statesmen who use technical means to achieve the economic goal with the co-operation of industrialists and businessmen.' In the first instance these would be statesmen who had recognised that the welfare of their own people depended on that of all the others.

Heineman warned against the naive belief that all of Europe's ills could be cured by the creation of a federal state on the model of the United States. Such an attitude ignored the lessons of U.S. history. The Union had broken asunder in the American Civil War because the internal economic balance had been disturbed. However, three factors had allowed the United States to grow together again in its current form: the great transcontinental railways provided the technological form of organisation; the Interstate Commerce Commission provided the administrative form; and the Federal Reserve System provided the financial organisation. The U.S. federation now rested on this threefold basis.

If Europe wished to learn the appropriate lessons from the U.S. example, it must develop along similar lines. The financial, administrative and technical preconditions must be established first, followed by a solid constitution. The banking system could be based on the gold standard and customs barriers must disappear; a permanent form of administrative co-operation – of the kind proposed by the French Foreign Minister, Briand – could lead in this direction. The Bank for the International Settlement of Payments would play a similar role to the Federal Reserve System. Furthermore, it was indispensable to develop the largely pre-industrial eastern-central and eastern areas of Europe through an ambitious programme of electrification and the extension of the road network. These measures alone could create the great market of 140 million people, only these would establish the indispensable balance between industry and agriculture. Would a united Europe be a danger to the United States? Not at all, according to Heineman. Far-sighted Americans would prefer to deal with a large, united European continent rather than with twenty-four separate political units.

'The crisis', Heineman concluded, 'is growing worse. In order to control it, businessmen, high-ranking civil servants, big industrialists, leaders of the workers' and peasants' associations – all those with some leverage on the economic world of Europe – must unite in order to re-establish the shattered economic balance of the old continent. The European confederation will arise, because it is necessary.' Thirty years later, on 28 November 1961, Heineman wrote to Adenauer: 'When I read of the Common Market... and I re-read my lecture in Cologne of 1930, I am astonished at my foresight.'[22]

However, before the emergence of an economically united Europe, history was to take a bloody detour: the 1930s saw the rise of Hitler, Mussolini and Stalin come to power. Adenauer, one of the European figures to whom Heineman appealed in November 1930, had urged him to make this speech. After the lecture he wrote to Heineman: 'I believe you would do great service if you were to continue on the path you have taken, since your position in economic life and your nationality will ensure that your remarks are particularly appreciated.'[23]

During these years, however, Adenauer did not himself intend to become a national political leader to promote the ideas of European co-operation. Though it was obvious that he would not end his days in a rural notary's office, the evidence indicates that he was content with his role as mayor of Cologne, both during the good years of the Weimar Republic and in the disastrous crisis that followed.

In 1926 he had one last opportunity to transfer from city hall to the Reich Chancellery. However, the prospects for an Adenauer chancellorship were diminished not only by the balance of forces in the Reichstag, but also by his own doubts about whether it would be the right course to take.

When Chancellor Hans Luther resigned in May 1926, the various *Reichstag* delegations again considered the possible combinations for a coalition government. Certain elements in the Centre Party were hopeful of creating a grand coalition stretching from the Social Democrats to the DVP, and it was these groups who again sought to involve the mayor of Cologne. Adenauer was unenthusiastic. Nevertheless, following a telephone conversation with the deputy chairman of the Centre Party *Reichstag* caucus, Adam Stegerwald, he agreed to come to Berlin for discussions.

Adenauer's prestige was then high, even with President Hindenburg. Once in Berlin, he discussed the prospects at the Hotel Kaiserhof with Adam Stegerwald and Theodor von Guérard, who was also deputy chairman of the Centre Party caucus. He still had doubts. The recent fall of Chancellor Luther, who had also been a former mayor, was one factor militating against his acceptance. Furthermore, any decision to leave Cologne would be final. The fate of his predecessor Wallraf was another permanent warning. Accepting the Reich Chancellorship, which was constantly at the mercy of 'the hatred and favour of the parties', would have meant an irrevocable decision to concentrate on national politics with the prospect, sooner or later, of failure, followed by a move to a lucrative job in industry.

Adenauer spent long hours discussing the issues with his wife, who had travelled with him. Gussie advised him to accept, as did Heineman, but Adenauer was not convinced.[24] 'I believe that your acceptance of the chancellorship could have changed much in the world', Heineman suggested later. 'You would have been a different chancellor from all the others.'[25]

By now Adenauer was familiar with the problems associated with an outsider candidacy. The candidate had only a few hours in which to explore or improve his chances through discussions with the leading politicians of other parliamentary parties. Much depended on the opinion of the presidiums of the various executive committees on which the candidate could exert no direct influence. This was true even of his own Centre Party.

The discussions quickly revealed that there were two stumbling-blocks that could not be overcome. First, it was clear that a grand coalition was out of the question and that at best there would be another minority cabinet. Differences between the Social Democrats and the German People's Party (DVP) proved insurmountable; equally, the German National People's Party was hostile both to Stresemann and to the Centre Party. The second stumbling-block was Stresemann himself, who had no desire to work in a cabinet led by Adenauer. Wolfgang Stresemann recalled his father's satisfied comment after the meeting of the DVP caucus: 'Today we stopped Adenauer becoming chancellor.'[26]

Adenauer wrote a memorandum on his talks, containing comments on Stresemann's foreign policy which later became well-known:

> The gentlemen are aware of my position on Locarno. Since the conclusion of Locarno I have faced up to the facts completely, including inwardly, in order

to get the best out of it for Germany, but I still disapprove of this inconsistancy and fluctuation in German foreign policy, the *way* this policy was made. In my view Germany, as a completely disarmed nation, should seek to keep out of the conflicts of others as much as possible, until she is needed. It is also my view that the negotiations in Locarno were badly conducted from the German side. Further developments in Geneva could easily lead to a defeat for Germany, which would naturally be blamed on the new government. I could not, therefore, regard the foreign policy that has been pursued until now as a happy one.'

There was no way forward without Stresemann, but with Stresemann in the cabinet difficulties would arise 'in the event that I did not reach agreement with him'.[27]

Adenauer's disquiet over the 'inconsistancy and fluctuation' in German foreign policy has led some observers to conclude that Adenauer – in the 1950s a resolute opponent of a see-saw policy between East and West – was referring to Stresemann's refusal to support League of Nations sanctions, which could only have been directed against Bolshevik Russia. According to this retrospective interpretation, he had reproached Stresemann for not providing unconditional support to the Western powers against the Soviet Union. In fact the Foreign Minister had just signed the German-Soviet friendship treaty of 24 April 1926. However, the memorandum does not in fact support such a broad interpretation. First and foremost, Adenauer was critical of the style of Stresemann's foreign policy. Adenauer also disliked the result of Locarno itself, but without giving details of his reasons. He doubted whether Germany would be granted a seat in the League of Nations, as Stresemann expected, after the conclusion of the Locarno treaties. On the other hand, Adenauer was not announcing any intention to make common cause with the two Western Great Powers. His observation that Germany should wait until it was needed reveals that he advocated a cautious approach.

Nevertheless, it is clear that Adenauer had reservations about Stresemann, even if he indicated that he did not rule out the possibility of an agreement between them. In fact, the two never came together. Much later, in 1958, Adenauer was asked by a journalist for his opinion of Stresemann. His answer was revealing: 'I do not like to answer such personal questions. I believe Stresemann meant well, but he did not have the necessary prestige in Germany, and in the last years of his life he was too much weakened and handicapped by illness to battle against the opposition.'[28]

In 1926 Adenauer was content to stay in Cologne. Still, he was gratified by Georg Bernhard's comments in the *Vossische Zeitung*: 'It is a pity that attempts to build an Adenauer cabinet were unsuccessful. The mayor of Cologne is admittedly a difficult personality, but he is one.'[29] Had the admiration that he was shown in Berlin gone to his head? In the following period, his treatment of the Cologne city council appears to have been even more authoritarian than before.

The dispute over the Mülheim bridge, which was built between 1927 and 1929, is particularly notorious. A majority on both the jury and the city council had decided on the construction of a comparatively old-fashioned lattice bridge with columns set in the river. Adenauer, however, preferred a beautiful but more expensive suspension bridge, mainly – as he said – for aesthetic reasons, although other factors also played an important part. For example, in a letter to Adenauer, Director General Georg Zapf of Felten & Guilleaume, which was to manufacture large parts of the bridge, noted that the mayor's support for the suspension bridge had been influenced by the desire 'to guarantee work for the industry of Cologne'.[30]

Johannes Albers, who was to be active in the *Sozialausschüsse* (Social Issues Committees) of the CDU during the late 1940s and 1950s, was working in the Christian trade union movement. At the height of the dispute he informed Adenauer that, 'in response to representations from the works' councils of Carlswerk and the Pohlig firm, I have committed myself to ensuring that the work for this project is kept in Cologne as far as possible, so that Cologne workers gain employment.'[31] Rumour had it that Adenauer had won the votes of the Communist city councillors in the decisive ballot because he had praised the beauty of the Leningrad suspension bridge. In fact, the KPD delegates were much more impressed by the arguments of the works' council at Felten & Guilleaume.

At any rate, this *cause célèbre* in Cologne local politics reveals the toughness, skill and resolution of Adenauer in carrying forward projects he had begun. But as he was also to discover as Federal Chancellor, there was a price to be paid: parliamentarians who have been humiliated or defeated in a crucial vote frequently bear a lasting grudge.

His relations with the Social Democratic caucus on the city council had long since cooled, partly because of ill-feeling between Adenauer and its chairman, Robert Görlinger. On the other hand, the support of the Cologne Social Democrats was no longer so essential to Adenauer's majority in the city council, thus removing another reason for him having to take their views into account.[32]

Since 1924 the Centre Party had had 30 city councillors (1919:49), compared with 11 for the SPD (Majority Socialists in 1919: 43), 16 for the Communists (Independent Socialists in 1919: 7), 11 for the Liberals (1919: 13), 5 for the German National People's Party (1919: 2), 15 seats for small middle-class parties and a mere 2 for the Völkisch-Sozialer Block. In comparison with the city council elected in 1919, there had thus been a shift to the centre-right. Since the Social Democrats and Communists virtually cancelled each other out, Adenauer was assured of a comparatively comfortable majority if he could obtain the support of the Centre Party, the bourgeois groups to the right of centre and the Social Democrats for his projects.

Adenauer's public image was not helped by the major dispute over the Mülheim bridge. In the prelude to the municipal election of 1929, the political atmosphere was deteriorating on all sides. Even in the good years, the image of the 'golden twenties' was an inaccurate reflection of the economic difficulties faced by the city. Early in 1928, when *Justizrat* Mönnig recalled his twenty-five years on the city council in a speech replying to Adenauer's praise of his achievements, he noted that: 'We were elected in a very different time from today, in comparison to today perhaps in a golden age.'[33] This was in 1928, widely seen as the Weimar Republic's best economic and political year!

At the end of 1927 Adenauer received a bitter letter from Robert Görlinger of the SPD caucus. Görlinger complained about the 'impression of aimless activity which, in the long term, was intolerable to our *Fraktion*'; this, he argued had been the result of 'the excessive haste with which a number of projects were pushed through'. The construction of public amenities in the suburbs had not been a success; in addition, a 'transport catastrophe' was developing.[34] With its exhibition policy and its promotions, the city was simply attempting to do too much. The mayor's relationship with the city council and the deputies' college left a great deal to be desired: Adenauer was restricting his own deputies to their specialist areas and had no responsible advisers to provide an overall view. Last but not least, the city finances were in an alarming condition.

Even the loyal Johannes Baptist Rings of the Centre Party was beginning to complain. Though Adenauer attempted to brush his protests aside with a typically detailed and vigorous letter, this time Rings refused to back down. He informed Adenauer in writing that, despite his personal esteem for the mayor, he could no longer accept his policies. For a number of years he, Rings, had been warning about the massive expenditure of the city. The figures spoke for themselves: 1924 – 180 million marks, 1925 – 233.7 million, 1926 – 262 million, 1927 – 280 million, 1928 – 321.6 million. In five years expenditure had increased by 141 million marks! The situation could not be allowed to continue: 'What would happen if a stop is not put to this development!'[35]

Whenever he was subjected to open criticism, Adenauer responded aggressively. In a letter to the Centre Party *Fraktion,* he complained that it had failed to discuss its differences with him; he had 'merely' received a letter from Herr Rings (who, it is fair to point out, was actually its chairman) 'which contains a series of completely false figures and bases its comments on this false picture.' The Centre Party had made an agreement with the Liberal Working Group and 'heedlessly voted down my bills'. He was 'very offended'.[36]

Once again these disputes involved money, the Achilles heel of Adenauer's municipal policy. Without hesitation, and with much good fortune, he had been able to push through some of his major projects during the period of inflation. The devaluation of the mark until the end of 1923 had offered a two-fold advantage during these years. First, like all other regional administrative bodies in the Reich, Cologne was freed from a considerable part of its debts. Second, the remaining investments of the years 1919-1923 had been financed partly with inflationary money. After the beginning of 1924, however, this ceased to be possible; from then on there was an annual income deficit in the city budget. Each year there were bitter budget debates in the city council, incorporating all the arguments and possible solutions which have marked the development of municipal financial policy in the welfare state ever since.

Adenauer consistently argued that most of the blame for Cologne's financial misfortune lay with the 'tremendous craving for concentration' in Berlin.[37] The capital had saddled the municipalities with endless welfare burdens and had issued compulsory regulations for the payment of municipal officials. On the other hand, it had also limited the opportunities for municipalities to resort to the capital market in order to meet their needs.

What was to be done? In Adenauer's view, the answer was obvious: a raising of the state contributions, combined with rigorous cut-backs of social expenditures. In fact, the first of these proposals was almost impossible to achieve, since Cologne was regarded as a wealthy city. The second, however, aroused strong hostility from the political parties of the left. Adenauer advocated a solution to which he was to return as Federal Chancellor when the burdens of the welfare state appeared to be becoming excessive: restriction of social expenditure to the genuinely needy, combined with drastic reductions in unnecessary and peripheral spending. In the 1920s, his plea for a 'complete and ruthless' elimination of payments to those not in need led not only to a direct clash with the parties of the left, but also to disquiet within the Centre Party itself. Such unrest was intensified when the city administration proposed to increase charges, for example for gas and electricity, in order to cover costs.

From the vantage point of the supervisory authorities in Berlin, Cologne's budget problems appeared quite different. There seemed to be good reasons to criticise the dynamic mayor for having burdened his city with an excessive number of modernisation projects, though it was accepted that some of them had been necessary to remove the backlog that had accumulated during the War. The luxury buildings of the exhibition grounds aroused particular criticism. It was even argued that Adenauer's display of municipal extravagance might have negative repercussions on the reparations question, since the Reich government had based its arguments on Germany's inability to pay. In a letter to Jarres on 24 November 1927, Stresemann asked how reparations could possibly be reduced when 'Adenauer builds a wonderful exhibition hall and boasts that he has installed the greatest organ in the world..., when, if the reports are true, a new Rhenish museum is to be built in Cologne...'[38]

Since the mid-1920s, Cologne had come to be regarded as representing the classic example of a brilliant, creative, but extravagant municipal policy. Adenauer, as everyone was aware, had been the driving force behind it. Thanks to his powerful position in the Rheinischer Provinzialausschuß, the Deutscher Städtetag and the Prussian Council of State, he had many allies who were able to overrule most opposition to his plans. Occasionally he failed to achieve his objectives – for example, his scheme to take over the Cologne Rural District as part of the city's expansion into the surrounding area. More often, however, Adenauer got what he wanted in Berlin.

In dealing with Berlin and with the city councillors of Cologne, Adenauer employed the same combination of persuasion, accusation, *faits accomplis* and pressure. If the council protested against his plans, its members were subjected to long and detailed speeches pointing out that they had agreed to all the schemes he had submitted to them, and that between 1925 and 1928 they had refused to vote for essential tax increases and price rises. At the same time he continued to propose expensive new projects – the Mülheim bridge, the new building for Cologne University, the 'Pressa' exhibition, the establishment of a Rhenish museum in the old cuirassier barracks on the Rhine. The entertainment expenses for the 'Pressa' alone ran to 799,748.36 marks.[39]

The obvious and perhaps inevitable solution was to incur either short-term or long-term debts. Like other municipalities, Cologne benefited from the golden rain of U.S. dollar loans to Germany between 1925 and 1929. These loans helped to create a sham boom, which was finally destroyed by the onset of the world economic crisis in autumn 1929. Hjalmar Schacht, the president of the Reichsbank, had issued a number of warnings about the likely course of developments and was one of Adenauer's fiercest critics in Berlin. The ambitious building plans of Cologne – like many other projects in Germany – had been financed on credit which depended on strong economic growth; a severe recession would bring the whole house of cards down. In these conditions, future investment in transport, exhibitions, and trade provided no immediate profits, and were actually a serious burden because of interest payments. Tax revenues declined drastically at the same time that payments to the unemployed increased. Extravagant expenditures, originally undertaken in the optimistic circumstances of a modest economic upturn, now appeared as the product of reprehensible recklessness. In this sense, the light and shadow of Adenauer's great projects were almost inseparable.

Even before the crisis began in autumn 1929, Adenauer realised that public opinion in Cologne was turning against him. He sought to defend himself in a wide-ranging speech to Centre Party colleagues, which at least succeeded in keeping his own party behind him. In 1929 Adenauer was due to face re-election. He could not expect any votes from the Communists; the Social Democrats were becoming increasingly hostile – Sollmann's *Rheinische Zeitung* had denounced the 'enormous unscrupulousness of the Renaissance man' Adenauer;[40] even the Liberals were turning against the mayor on the grounds that his financial policy would eventually raise the tax burden to intolerable levels. The liberal publishing house Neven DuMont, which produced the national *Kölnische Zeitung*, was also less well-disposed towards Adenauer than before. Even the business community appeared to be moving away from him.

Adenauer nevertheless survived the election. He was fortunate that it took place on 17 November 1929, at the beginning of the crisis. The Centre Party obtained 35 seats, 5 more than in 1924; the Social Democrats improved their position to 21; Communist representation fell to 13; the German Democratic Party won 10 seats and the left-wing Liberal Democrats 3, thus giving the Liberals the same result as in 1919; 2 seats went to smaller right-wing groups and 4 to the NSDAP; finally, 8 seats (instead of the previous 15) were won by representatives of middle-class splinter parties.

Adenauer was re-elected as mayor on 17 December 1929 by the smallest of margins. To win at all, he had been forced to make a number of concessions, agreeing to hand over to the city the 9,200 marks he was paid for his work as a board member of the Rheinisch-Westfälische Elektrizitätswerke, and the 10,700 marks he had received as a member of the board of the Deutsche Bank. This latter honorarium had been particularly unpopular with the public.

Though no serious candidate was standing against him, Adenauer's candidacy was supported only by the Centre Party, the German People's Party (DVP) and the Democrats, along with the deputy Matzerath as the statutory representative of the administration. This gave him a total of 49 votes. There were 47 votes against him, including the SPD. Moreover, in voting for Adenauer, the German Peoples' Party and the Democrats had actually broken their election promise to oppose him. The result bore some resemblance to his first election as Federal Chancellor in 1949: Adenauer was elected with the barest of majorities, and was supported by a coalition of parties from the middle and moderate right of the political spectrum. The Social Democrats, as well as the extremists of the right and left, opposed him.

Thus, his second term of office had a somewhat inauspicious start. Furthermore, it quickly developed into one of the most unpleasant periods of his life.

In the Maelstrom
of the World Economic Crisis

For some time, one of the main propaganda weapons used against Adenauer by the Communists and National Socialists had been the allegation that he was drawing a princely salary while welfare recipients went hungry. As the economic crisis intensified, the attacks on his salary, entertainment expenses and lifestyle became increasingly vicious.

Gradually, however, information began to leak out to the effect that Adenauer himself had become a victim of the stock market crash. Though the financial crisis facing Cologne was plain to see, Adenauer was managing to limit the consequences of his own disastrous financial misjudgements. Nevertheless, these were a serious handicap to him, politically as well as psychologically.

The threat of bankruptcy was the greatest problem confronting the city. Head of his financial department was his brother-in-law Willi Suth. Adenauer and Suth worked tirelessly to keep the city functioning. However, at the same time, the personal situation of the major had become desperate.

Until 1928, Adenauer had looked after his considerable wealth as cautiously and responsibly as might have been expected. At the end of 1927, in addition to the house in Max-Bruch-Straße, he possessed assets of approximately one million marks.[1] His fortune was administered by the Cologne branch of the Deutsche Bank, which had invested the money in a portfolio of gilt-edged shares and bonds. Dr Anton Paul Brüning, the director of the branch, another member of the 'black', or Catholic, establishment and a close friend of Adenauer, had recently taken personal charge of Adenauer's private account. Adenauer's confidence in the professional competence of Cologne bankers was unbroken until the end of the 1920s. For example, in July 1924, from his base in Chandolin, he had authorised the banker Ahn to make some – cautious – changes of the limits for buying certain shares on his own initiative.

Until 1928 Adenauer's stock exchange manoeuvres were limited in volume. Moreover, he had retained shares of which he had a degree of personal knowledge: 'Machine and crane building, Elberfeld dyes, Cologne gas and Düsseldorf machines.'[2] By 1928, however, the value of U.S. shares was reaching dizzy heights. For months, conversation among the wealthy bourgeoisie had been dominated by the topic of how to exploit the vast potential of the U.S. market and thereby make enormous profits within a short space of time. Bankers were among Adenauer's regular contacts, privately as well as in public affairs; he was repeatedly given details of successful speculations. In these circumstances, it is hardly surprising that he was tempted to participate.

Notes for this section begin on page 710.

His financial nemesis appeared early in February 1928 in the shape of Dr Fritz Blüthgen, director general of the Vereinigte Glanzstoffwerke (United Rayon). During a banquet at the exhibition hall, Blüthgen took the opportunity to describe the profits Adenauer could expect to make from the purchase of shares in American Bemberg and American Glanzstoff, both of which were subsidiaries of the German Glanzstoffwerke. Adenauer, caught fire and began to scribble figures on a menu card, discovering that he had apparently been foolish to content himself with the modest, though safe, returns from his securities portfolio at the Deutsche Bank. Blüthgen recommended the American shares as excellent and secure investments; shortly afterwards he backed up his claims in a letter referring to circulars from the Tixeira de Mattos bank. The shares were currently being offered at twenty per cent below their face value. In the medium term they could be expected to produce a dividend of some ten U.S. dollars per share, in addition to the profit from the inevitable rise in value.

Adenauer had never before indulged in large-scale speculation. Nevertheless, he now asked Director Brüning whether he could safely invest his wealth in such shares. Brüning gave a positive answer, on the grounds that he had been provided with admirably precise and safe information. Adenauer thus launched himself into the venture. Within a few months, through the Deutsche Bank, he had sold his existing shares and used the proceeds to buy shares in two unknown American firms. When the value of these shares began to fall in May 1928, he refused to abandon them even when Brüning advised him to sell the shares at a profit and, if necessary, to buy them back again later at a lower price. Adenauer, who was no stock market expert and did not study the share prices every day, refused to take this advice, choosing to maintain his risky policy of a long-term investment in speculative stocks. He was only too glad to let Blüthgen convince him to keep all the stocks. In October 1928, Blüthgen advised him by telegraph from New York to exchange Bemberg and American Glanzstoff shares. In this transaction new shares would be issued and the old shares offered subscription rights; however, a significant cash deposit was necessary for the purchase of new shares.

By now Adenauer had begun to grow uneasy. Once again he turned to Brüning at the Deutsche Bank to ask whether an increase in his bank debt would be dangerous. Brüning assured him that the transaction was safe, since the share account was available as security. The Deutsche Bank therefore advanced the money for new shares, in part charging the old shares and in part Adenauer's remaining German holdings. Shortly afterwards the Vereinigte Glanzstoffwerke established another company in the United States, the Associated Rayon Corporation, to which it transferred all its holdings in American Bemberg shares and American Glanzstoff shares. Any prospect of obtaining an accurate overall view of what was going on between the German company and its U.S. subsidiaries had by now disappeared.

Thenceforth the price fell all the time. Adenauer now realised that he had behaved extremely foolishly. In letters and in person, he asked Blüthgen whether he should sell everything in order to save at least some of his money and cover his bank debts. Blüthgen continued to reassure him, persuading Adenauer to let things take their course. Though these events had begun considerably before 'Black Friday' in October 1929, the crash accelerated the downward trend of these shares. Within a short time, Adenauer's bank debt was considerably greater than the market value of his shares. By summer 1930 Adenauer was in debt to the Deutsche Bank to the tune of 1.4 million marks.

Insiders soon heard of these developments. During that summer, Louis Hagen discussed the matter with Adenauer at some length. Adenauer complained to the Deutsche Bank for not giving him sufficient warning, and even threatened the institution with a claim for damages. The affair was utterly disastrous for him. While negotiating with the Deutsche Bank to avert personal bankruptcy, he also faced critical negotiations with the institution in his capacity as mayor of Cologne over the issue of short-term loans. Furthermore, political allegations against him were intensifying in the run-up to the mayoral election of December 1929. In 1927 Adenauer had joined the supervisory board of the Deutsche Bank, of which Blüthgen was also a member. The payments he received for this role made him vulnerable to attack by demagogues of the right and left, even though at the end of 1929 he promised to hand them over to the city. But what if news of his private financial affairs were to become public knowledge?

The exact details of Adenauer's rescue from financial disaster are somewhat obscure. Yet it is certain that the Deutsche Bank was unwilling to allow the insolvency of their supervisory board member to become public knowledge. Robert Pferdmenges, who was already a confidant of Adenauer's and was involved in the merger of the Disconto-Gesellschaft and the Deutsche Bank in 1929, apparently joined Louis Hagen to play an important role in the rescue. Most of the evidence – business, political, personal – points in that direction. As a result, Adenauer's disastrous excursion into the realms of international share speculation was settled with tolerable discretion.

Pferdmenges suggested to the main administration of the Deutsche Bank that Berlin should assume control of the section of the Cologne account that had been involved in the disastrous affair. Some of Adenauer's shares remained in Cologne. At the same time, the Berlin branch would take responsibility for most of the debit account and transfer a considerable sum to Adenauer's account in Cologne. Nevertheless, he had lost his personal wealth. Early in the autumn of 1930, moreover, the nature of any final settlement remained uncertain.

This unsuccessful speculation was not without repercussions in Adenauer's political life. On two occasions, indiscretions by the bank meant that some details of the affair became public knowledge. In the heated political atmosphere of 1930, these details provided welcome ammunition to the DNVP and National Socialists. They were able to depict this model representative of the Weimar 'system' as a man whose speculation had made him dependent on the big banks – the same banks that might be called on to assist the indebted city of Cologne. Adenauer was obviously vulnerable to political attack: he was still a member of the supervisory board of the Deutsche Bank and was receiving an allowance for his services at a time when his own financial affairs were in crisis.

Behind the scenes, Adenauer was also involved in difficult negotiations on behalf of his city relating to the repayment of a short-term loan of 12 million marks, which had been financed by the Deutsche Bank on an interim basis after the withdrawal of foreign money. The Prussian government, through its Finance Minister Höpker-Aschoff and its Minister of Welfare Heinrich Hirtsiefer, a party colleague of Adenauer, reached a precarious settlement – and one which verged on illegality – with the city of Cologne and the Deutsche Bank. The Deutsche Bank in Cologne, again with the involvement of Director Brüning, guaranteed the city the desired loan, but on a short-term basis. As a form of security it received a discountable bill of exchange to the value of 12 million marks from the Preussenkasse (the Prussian Central Co-operative Fund). Consequently, legal ties existed only between the Preussenkasse and the Deutsche Bank.

This transaction had one legal snag: according to statute, the Preussenkasse was not actually permitted to grant any municipal credit at all. From a strictly legal point of view, however, it was open to debate as to whether a loan had been given. None of the participants was happy with the transaction, but the Prussian government felt obliged to offer some support to the virtually bankrupt city.

This complicated credit transaction threatened to turn sour when the loan was due to be prolonged in mid-1931. The directors of the Deutsche Bank now feared that the bank was in danger of being cheated by the government; the cautious financial bureaucrats and the chastened ministers were tempted to extricate themselves from the affair by using formal legal arguments. The Deutsche Bank therefore turned to the city of Cologne. The bank itself would be prepared to repay the 12 million marks to the Preussenkasse only when the city of Cologne had repaid its own debt.[3] By this stage, however, the city was virtually insolvent.

During this affair, which troubled him until his removal from office, Adenauer was forced to conduct difficult negotiations between the Prussian government, the Preussenkasse and the Deutsche Bank. It was no surprise when, after the seizure of power, the National Socialists tried to exploit the affair to destroy not only Adenauer but also the Finance Minister Otto Klepper. However, the intensive investigation failed to produce any evidence that justified criminal charges against Adenauer. Klepper, who had been a member of the German Democratic Party, chose emigration to avoid further persecution.

With hindsight, there is no evidence that Adenauer's personal indebtedness at the Deutsche Bank had any detrimental effect on the city's finances. The indirect loan from the Preussenkasse was recalled because of the desperate financial position of Cologne and the Land of Prussia. The mayor had managed, at least temporarily, to transfer his own financial distress and that of his city to the Deutsche Bank. Nevertheless, the entanglement remained unfortunate, even though only parts of it were actually made public. It provided the backdrop against which Adenauer made attempts to put his own finances in order.

At the end of 1931 the German National councillors, supported by the National Socialists, raised the issue in the city council. Adenauer's opponents demanded details of his personal relationship with the Deutsche Bank. The insinuation was that a mayor who was himself deeply in debt to this institution could no longer properly represent the interests of the city in negotiations with it. Shortly before the issue was raised, Adenauer had come to his arrangement with the Deutsche Bank in Berlin; on behalf of his institution, its board member Oscar Schlitter declared himself prepared to expunge Adenauer's debt in return for the takeover of the block of shares and a significant deposit of Aku shares. At the end of the negotiations, Schlitter argued that the bank was not doing this for Adenauer's sake, but for its own, since it was still possible that the shares might be worth something one day. Moreover, the bank was concerned that Adenauer might claim compensation if he were driven into a corner.

At a stormy meeting in Cologne town hall on 26 February 1931, Adenauer had the unpleasant task of declaring a question by a spokesman of the German National People's Party regarding his personal financial relationships as inadmissable. However, he was at least able to state truthfully that 'the interests of the city of Cologne are completely separate. I am not dependent upon anyone either financially or in any other way. I have no debit account at all.' He had been authorised to make this statement by a letter from the board of the Deutsche Bank dated 7 February 1931.

The episode demonstrates that Adenauer had a well-concealed gambler's instinct which occasionally overcame the sober and sensible side of his nature. His speculation had occurred at the most inappropriate moment possible. Now he was forced to withstand the most gruelling period of his mayoralty in personally weakened circumstances. Moreover, when he was driven from office in February 1933 he had no financial reserves on which to fall back.

Adenauer's personal distress was only one individual tragedy in a worldwide recession, which now struck Cologne with full force. By the end of 1930 there were already 60,300 registered unemployed in the city; some 500 firms had gone bankrupt. Public services began to suffer under the emergency measures taken by Chancellor Heinrich Brüning. Drastic reductions in tax revenues and simultaneous increases in welfare spending eliminated any freedom of manoeuvre in financial affairs. The city was threatened with the deadline of autumn 1932, when 40 million marks of short-term loans would fall due for repayment. In June 1931 unemployment in the city reached 66,715; a year later it stood at 99,293.

In these circumstances there could be no more talk of a long-term municipal policy. Financially, Cologne resembled a damaged ship, with more leaks being located as soon as one was repaired. Adenauer was reduced to moving as a petitioner from one authority to another. There were endless negotiations in the Prussian Finance Ministry, with the Rheinische Provinzialbank, and with private banks over the deferment of payments, bridging loans, and debt conversions. Foreign loans were no longer available.

From Brussels, Dannie N. Heineman considered for a time whether to take a stake in the city's transport and public utilities and bring them under his control. Adenauer was hopeful of progress, though he was alarmed to realise that SOFINA would only participate if it could gain the majority interest.[4] Eventually the negotiations broke down and Heineman transferred his interest to BEWAG in Berlin. He wrote to Adenauer afterwards: 'We talked about the electricity works of Cologne. Perhaps you would have done a bad deal, since the bankers' demands were limitless. In any case I stood aside from any group and would not have wanted to negotiate with you anyway. You are too close to me. Cologne did not sell the electricity works and is content. I would have been very uneasy about negotiating with you, since you might have been dissatisfied with the outcome, or both of us might.'[5]

The municipalities had lost any capacity to help themselves. Adenauer therefore concentrated his efforts on an attempt to persuade the national and Prussian governments to help them and to change the policy of deflation. This put him on a collision course with Chancellor Brüning. Earlier, however, he had welcomed the appointment of his party colleague as Chancellor. He told the chairman of the Centre Party, Ludwig Kaas, that the two men had held long discussions shortly after Brüning took office. Thereafter Adenauer took a positive attitude: 'He is taking a very serious path which requires great courage. The speech he made here in Cologne a short time ago was quite excellent.'[6]

This sympathetic judgement did not last. However, the clash between the two was a product less of Brüning's basic policy than of the different interests of the national government and the city of Cologne. In July 1930, Adenauer sent Brüning a long personal letter pointing out the distress of the municipalities. He predicted that, in autumn and winter 1930, rising unemployment would render their financial situation catastrophic: 'They will not be in a position to pay benefits any more and this will certainly lead to serious unrest'.[7]

The prospect of 'serious unrest' was the nightmare that had haunted Adenauer since the days of November 1918. He followed the observation by warning that intimates of the Reichsbank President Luther reckoned that the cabinet would fall if this situation occurred. What was at stake was not merely the interests of the cities, but the very survival of the government. He therefore asked Brüning to intervene in the matter: at the moment, the Reichstag would 'swallow' further tax laws to help the cities, but by the autumn it might no longer be prepared to do so. Adenauer's appeal was in vain. Like many politicians in Berlin, Brüning believed that the municipalities – especially Cologne – were largely responsible for their own misfortunes. He did not answer the letter.

The first clash between the two men occurred in December 1930. Part of the Chancellor's long-term plan to stabilise the economy involved the restriction of municipal expenditure and the passing of legislation to permit the reduction of real taxes. To that end, the Prussian government fixed a series of compulsory budgets for specific municipalities. In his memoirs, which appeared in 1970, Brüning argued that Adenauer's response had been little short of insolent. In opposition to national government policy, 'and despite his position as the President of the State Council, he raised real taxes for his municipality against the spirit of the emergency decree, only a short time before the closure on 20 December. That was open defiance of state authority.'[8]

Relations between the two men were permanently damaged, despite a letter of explanation from Adenauer. In it he argued that the city of Cologne would have become insolvent during the following fifteen months if he had failed to raise taxes. Its losses would then have been much greater. Moreover, even the Social Democrats had agreed to the tax increase. He asked Brüning to persuade the Finance Ministry to give its approval.[9] Once again, Brüning did not reply, though Hermann Pünder, the State Secretary in the Reich Chancellery, did his best to maintain some semblance of good relations between the two.

In September 1931 Adenauer made a new request. At this stage, he was attempting to consolidate municipal debts by encouraging the interest of the Reichs-Elektro-Gesellschaft in the city's public utility works. The support of the Reichsbank would be required for such a venture. Would the Chancellor at least be prepared to offer his advice in this matter? Adenauer accompanied this request for support with a rare admission of his own mistakes: 'Nevertheless, I believe I can demonstrate that although the city of Cologne has over-extended itself in one case or another, in general this indebtedness has not been brought about by wasteful expenditures.'[10]

In these circumstances, it was obvious that Adenauer was not a good choice to join Hirtsiefer, the Prussian minister of welfare, in convincing the Chancellor of the need for an ambitious work-creation programme. When Brüning fell, Adenauer was able to claim that he had long predicted the disastrous failure of the rigid deflationary policy.

During the last months of the Weimar Republic, Adenauer was sympathetic to the right wing of the Centre Party. This brought him close to Ludwig Kaas. Between November 1929 and April 1930, Adenauer made a series of efforts to bring the chairman of the Centre Party, who was still prelate in Trier, to Cologne as dean of the cathedral. The move would have been accepted by Archbishop Schulte – 'not fickle, just weak', in Adenauer's merciless description – but the cathedral chapter would not accept it. Like Kaas himself, Adenauer was deeply critical of 'the muddle-headedness of the Reichstag, the utter inner inconsistency of the Social Democratic Party and the German People's Party'.[11] Did these criticisms mean that Adenauer was willing to condone a fundamental departure from the principle of a national government responsible to parliament, in favour of a presidential government resting on Article 48 of the constitution? We have no contemporary record of Adenauer's reaction to this vital constitutional dispute. During this period, his opinions were largely restricted to his own field of municipal politics, where he kept up a barrage of criticism against the prevailing tendency towards centralisation.

The attitude of large parts of the Centre Party towards the National Socialist mass movement remained uncertain during these years. Adenauer's attitude towards it, as towards important constitutional issues, remains equally unclear. Though the results of the election of September 1930 were less shattering in Cologne than in the rest of Germany, the NSDAP still managed to increase its support to 17.6 per cent, up from a derisory 4.6 per cent in the local election of 17 November 1929. In the national election of 31 July 1932, the National Socialists again increased their vote to 24.5 per cent, though the Centre Party had also strengthened its position to 28.2 per cent.

Three days after the 'electoral catastrophe' of 14 September 1930, Adenauer wrote a reassuring letter to Dannie N. Heineman: 'In many respects I do not think the result of our election is quite as bad as it appears on the outside. It is just very regrettable that there are such large numbers of completely radical and desperate people in Germany. Here I include the Communists and the National Socialists. It is to be hoped that the economic situation improves in the foreseeable future. That is the best, and indeed the only, means of regaining control over the dangers inherent in the entire situation.'[12]

These remarks may have been deliberately optimistic, since Adenauer was hoping to persuade Heineman to loan between 25 and 30 million marks to the city of Cologne. In such circumstances, it would be counter-productive to do or say anything that might increase the fears of foreign investors. However, Heineman drew his own conclusions from the election and refused to become involved. Adenauer's subsequent comments reveal that he regarded economic desperation as the main cause of Hitler's success. Still, by 1932 at the latest, he was also aware that the NSDAP had won many votes from middle-class Germans who were not yet impoverished.[13] They had to be won back – but how?

Adenauer was enough of a politician to distinguish between the events of municipal politics and decisions taken at national level. Since 1929, the NSDAP in Cologne had campaigned with the slogan 'Away with Adenauer!' and attacked him as the incarnation of 'black' Cologne. The Nazi newspaper *Westdeutscher Beobachter* joined the small group of National Socialists in the city council in a ruthless agitation against the mayor. The main points of attack were: his anti-social austerity policy; his obsession with status and excessive expenditure on entertainment; the scandalously high salaries paid to Adenauer and the deputies; and a complex and unacceptable mingling of private interests with city concerns.

Even the fact that Adenauer took his modest holidays in Switzerland, and had once travelled in a specially provided car, offered material for agitation against him. Similar attacks had been made upon him in the early 1920s, when the Communists and left-wing Socialists had been the agitators. There had been rowdy scenes in council meetings ever since the November revolution in 1918. Adenauer's professional approach and ironic manner had always enabled him to keep a measure of control. (Indeed, this education was to be of great help to him after 1947, when the time came for him to handle debates in the parliamentary bodies of Western Germany).

The agitation by the far right from 1930 onwards, however, was much more effective than that of the extreme left. Between 1930 and 1933 Adenauer became the great bogeyman of all the radicals in Cologne, and his image suffered accordingly. In spring 1933, the inhabitants of the city accepted his dismissal with a composure that was surely influenced to some extent by the constant attacks to which he had been subjected.

For Gauleiter Ley, then for Gauleiter Grohé and their supporters, Adenauer's open sympathy for the Jews was a main point of attack. Leading anti-Semites in the NSDAP were even convinced that Adenauer himself was Jewish. Johann von Leers's scandalous publication *Juden sehen Dich an* contained a section on 'Blood Jews', with photographs and inflammatory captions referring to leading figures. These included Karl Marx, Rosa Luxemburg, Karl Liebknecht, Münzenberg, Bela Kun (Kohn), Leviné-Nissen, Schlesinger, Grzesinski, Gumbel, Oskar Cohn, Kurt Rosenfeld, Trotsky (Leiba Braunstein), Erzberger, and Adenauer himself. The mayor was described as 'the great show-off of Cologne, [who] ruined Cologne through extravagance etc.'[14] It was well known that, since his employment as first deputy, Adenauer had maintained close links with the Jewish community. This was now used to attack him, along with the fact that, like any civilised citizen, Adenauer had many links with Jews in the economy, culture and academic life. Even those National Socialists who did not believe him to be a 'blood Jew' regarded him as a sympathiser with the Zionist movement.

In fact, Zionism had some of its strongest roots in Cologne. After 1891, when the corporate lawyer Max Bodenheimer began to encourage discussions of political Zionism, the Cologne section of the Zionist movement became one of the most important in Germany. In 1927 Adenauer became a member of the German 'Pro Palästina' society, having been proposed by Ludwig Kaas and another party colleague, the former Chancellor Joseph Wirth.[15] Though this committee did not advocate an exclusively Jewish state in Palestine, it supported the idea that Jews who wished to emigrate there should be guaranteed a homeland.

In addition to this catalogue of sins, the Cologne Nazis also attacked Adenauer's national and patriotic credentials by accusing him, either openly or by innuendo, of separatism. Equally, his sympathy for pan-European ideas was regarded as evidence of an 'un-German' attitude. In the eyes of the radical right, not even Adenauer's opposition to the Young Plan with Hans Luther and Carl Duisberg (as usual, he was opposing the policies of Stresemann) could free him from this charge.

National Socialist demagogy and lies quickly became familiar to Adenauer. His response was cool and flexible, as it had been against the far-left on previous occasions. He stopped all open attacks and attempted to keep a measure of control by insisting on the order of business in the city council. On the other hand, he was not persuaded by the argument that 'organisations hostile to the state' should be excluded from city halls and seats, even when the Prussian Minister of the Interior ordered such a move. This was probably not an attempt to keep his options open. It should be regarded instead as an insistence on his own independence as head of the administration, and an indication of reluctance to 'outlaw' organisations such as the NSDAP and KPD. With 17.6 per cent and 17.0 per cent of the vote respectively in the fifth national election in 1930, and 27.1 per cent and 14.7 per cent in the 6th election in 1932, the two anti-democratic parties had won more than a third, and then almost half, of the votes of the Cologne electorate.

Only when it was too late did Adenauer realise that it was naive to insist on the democratic rules of the game when dealing with the opponents of democracy. As a result of his experiences in the Third Reich, after 1945 he was to be among the strongest advocates of preventive defensive measures provided by a 'wehrhafte Demokratie' (combative democracy). As yet, very little information has emerged regarding the details of Adenauer's attitudes towards the National Socialist mass move-

ment at the time. On the other hand, he made many comments on the subject afterwards, when the catastrophe had run its course. These show an
inclination to explain the mentality of the National Socialist leaders by
reference to their social situation. In Adenauer's view, they were 'almost
all uprooted individuals...or people who had taken examinations, e.g.
Goebbels, but had no position...; Hitler had no position, Goebbels had no
position, Göring had no position.' All of them had 'pretensions.., but they
had no means, no position and were more or less rootless'.[16]

He gave a similar explanation for the rise of Hitler's movement. Consequently, his comments on the issue combine almost all of the elements
of the traditional interpretation: the crisis of authority after the collapse
of Imperial Germany; the 'unwise' policy pursued by the Allies after the
First World War; inflation, which had struck particularly hard at the 'middle classes'", always 'the most dominant and from the point of view of
the state possibly the best element'. National Socialism had been 'able to
take root because the German people were thrown into such disorder by
the lost war, by the removal of authority, by the creation of new authorities which did not have the influence and the reputation, and by the
removal of these bourgeois classes'. In this situation, 'all these unre-
strained and unbridled individuals rose to the top'. The truly shocking
experience had been the 'sudden confusion' of the people.

Hitler and Adenauer never met, though Adenauer had heard the
Führer's speeches on the radio from time to time. Adenauer detested him.
His impression: 'I never regarded Hitler as particularly clever, but as a
man who was evidently able to fascinate the masses and who, whether on
his own or through advisors very close to him, particularly Goebbels
who played a big part in it, presented himself as a man of will, of character, a great leader etc.! I did not have the impression that this had come
from within him; but I believe he was putting on an act his whole life; I
may be wrong.' Göring too 'was an actor [who] liked to appear magnificent and to have the greatest possible splendour around him. As a man I
thought Himmler worse than Göring.'

After the collapse of the Third Reich, Adenauer made several important speeches in which he attempted to give systematic form to these
insights. One of these was given at Cologne University on 24 March
1946. He frankly admitted that the temporary mass enthusiasm for
Hitler's total state was partly explained by lasting distortions in the relationship between the state and the individual in Germany. In his view,
'the exaggerated and excessive Prussian view of the state' had a distorting effect on German attitudes, not only among the élites. In the Third
Reich this attitude had been taken to extremes. In addition, spiritual
bonds had been inadequate. Even before 1914, he thought, Germany had
been 'one of the most irreligious and un-Christian peoples of Europe'. It
was no wonder that anti-Christian parties had been popular, nor that the

NSDAP had been most successful in regions where the ground had been prepared by the materialistic socialism of Karl Marx.[17] In addition, the political élites had been weak: 'When National Socialism was growing and bidding for power, in my view it could never have succeeded if the people in control had made use of their power. But they failed, and that too is worthy of blame.'[18]

Adenauer viewed the coming political catastrophe with much the same fatalism as many of his political and business contacts. At the end of September 1931, Dannie N. Heineman wrote to tell him of a meeting he had held with Louis Hagen: 'He too is unable to make head or tail of the current situation. The events are too massive to be grasped by the human mind.'[19] Adenauer replied: 'I am afraid that things in the world will get even worse before any effective remedy is possible.'[20] His prediction was correct, though in autumn 1931 he could not know just how bad things would become.

Another letter, this time to Heineman in January 1932, reveals that he did not know how to respond. He was attempting to console himself with Friedell's *Kulturgeschichte*, which described similar economic and cultural dislocation following the Thirty Years War in Europe. However, he added sceptically: 'Since 1918 I have never seen a political and economic situation so bungled as the current one. How Germany will come out of it, and how Europe will come out of it, is a complete mystery to me at present.'[21]

Heineman, writing from Brussels, Italy and the United States, remained generally optimistic. He wrote that he had recently met the Belgian king and queen, before adding: 'The politicians will swing to and fro a great deal before agreement is reached, but I believe that the stormy sea of unreason will gradually grow calm, since the economic obstructions will gradually disappear. Agreement would have been reached long ago if the various neighbours had got to know each other better, if trust were not lacking and people could understand the situation better.'[22] Adenauer remained sceptical: 'Unfortunately I am afraid that the politics and psychology of the peoples will continue to triumph over all economic insight for some time to come.'[23]

Heineman disagreed: 'I do not believe what you wrote about the politics and pyschology of the peoples, only individual people are responsible for this and not the great mass. If the leaders in the various countries, in so far as these exist, would reach an understanding among themselves for quiet work, the masses would follow without further ado. The masses believe very easily, think of the Rentenmark...People will cling to absolutely anything in order to escape from chaos, but I fear that not much will happen.'[24] In an earlier letter, he had expressed the widespread hope for strong men to take the lead: 'The current crisis can only be ended if some strong leading people are willing to be unpopular for a number of years. History has always shown this.'[25]

Heineman was not thinking so much of dictators as leaders like Brüning. He soon came to see Roosevelt as the right man for the United
States. In Germany, democracy had already been swept away when he
wrote to Adenauer on 9 March 1933: 'I believe that America will play a
great role in the reconstruction despite the current situation, since the new
President Roosevelt has the necessary courage and energy and enjoys the
confidence of the people.'[26] Heineman did not mention Hitler.

In this correspondence, Adenauer made no reference to the need for
strong leaders to overcome the crisis. Nevertheless, he was suspected in
some quarters of being prepared to seek an authoritarian way out of Germany's difficulties. Some of his opponents maintained that he was sympathetic to Mussolini and Fascism. Conclusive evidence on this subject,
however, is lacking.

Harold Nicholson, who was attached to the British embassy in Berlin
between 1927 and 1929, visited the mayor of Cologne on 14 March
1929, before the onset of the great crisis. He described his visit in a letter to his wife, Vita Sackville-West (in the knowledge that she appreciated literary virtuosity):

> 'After writing to you yesterday I went to see the Oberbürgermeister. His
> name is Adenauer and he is a rather remarkable figure in modern Germany.
> There are some who say that if Parliamentarianism really breaks down in
> Berlin they will summon Adenauer to establish some form of fascismo. For
> the moment he rules Cologne with an iron hand...There was some sort of fuss
> going on around his room when I got there, private secretaries dashing about,
> people opening doors, squinting in, then shutting them again rapidly. I was
> asked to sit down while bells buzzed and people hurried in and whispered to
> each other, and then hurried out again. I am to this moment unaware what
> had happened, but the contrast between the scurrying and whispering out-
> side, and the sudden peace of his own large study, was most effective, and
> this strange Mongol, sitting there with shifty eyes in a yellow face, sitting
> with his back to the window, talking very slowly and gently, pressing bells
> very slowly – 'Would you ask Dr Pietri to come here?' – snapping with icy
> politeness at the terrified Dr Pietri when he arrived – possessed all the man-
> ner of a Dictator. It is not a manner which I should like, but it is a manner
> which once seen is never forgotten. I feel I could adopt it at once. I shall try
> to do so. One of the main stunts is to create an atmosphere of rush and flurry
> around one and to be oneself as calm as the hollow in the centre of a typhoon.
> Another stunt is to talk to one's subordinates in a very gently voice but with
> a sudden flash of a shifty eye.'[27]

The letter provides a vivid picture of Adenauer in action. However, it
is not evidence of any inclination towards fascism on his part, any more
than his telegram of congratulations Mussolini and to Nuncio Pacelli
after the conclusion of the Lateran Treaties.[28]

In truth, though Adenauer can easily be imagined as chancellor of an
authoritarian presidential cabinet, it is extremely difficult to see him
being in sympathy with a populist mass movement of the kind repre-

sented by Italian Fascism. As in the revolutionary period of 1918, he seems to have fluctuated between support for two possibilities: first, the use of force against the Hitler movement; and second, if no men could be found to implement this policy, the attempt to tame the revolutionary forces by giving them a limited degree of responsibility.

A few oral reports have survived to hint that he might have been prepared for a temporary 'dictatorship of the democrats'. Adenauer was among the speakers at a confidential meeting of Centre Party leaders in Frankfurt am Main in the spring of 1932. The meeting had been called to discuss a propaganda campaign against Hitler, and Adenauer had claimed not to know who of them had lost their minds, himself or the previous speakers. It was madness to believe that Hitler could be stopped by propaganda, since the man understood only one language, that of powder and shot: 'And if we do not speak it to him, then in a year's time he will speak it to us.'[29]

After the Second World War, Otto Klepper reported that, before the Reich government's 'coup' against the Social Democrat government in Prussia in July 1932, he and some of his cabinet colleagues had joined with the southern German minister-presidents to discuss meeting von Papen's illegal action with force. The discussion involved the arrest of the national government and the NSDAP leadership clique, the declaration of a state of emergency and the imposition of a directorate comprising the minister-presidents of the five biggest Länder.[30] Discussions with Adenauer had also been held. At a later date, these bare facts were filled in by the Centre Party politician Carl Spiecker, who explained that the plan would have involved the transfer of the seat of the Prussian government and the state finances to Cologne. Adenauer had apparently agreed to the scheme.[31]

Whatever the facts, Adenauer was later harsh in his judgement of the spineless abdication by the Weimar democrats whom he considered to be primarily responsible. He was most critical of Heinrich Brüning, Otto Braun, and Carl Severing. Adenauer was least critical of the Reich President, Hindenburg, on the grounds that he was 'not exactly a political luminary'.[32] His view of Franz von Papen was less sympathetic, since Adenauer thought him 'extremely ambitious' and unprincipled. Here, too, there were some extenuating circumstances: 'I have always conceded mitigating circumstances in my judgement of him owing to his abnormally limited intelligence. Unfortunately many people allowed themselves to be deceived by his obliging manner and his pious talk.'[33]

This was one aspect of Adenauer's approach, revealing some willingness to be part of a temporary dictatorship of the democrats. Later, however, he was silent about a very different role played by himself and the Centre Party during this period. Some of the leaders of his party had become preoccupied by the idea of 'taming' Hitler; Adenauer himself had some sympathy with the approach. Once the 'coup' in Prussia in July

1932 had been accepted without resistance by the Social Democrats and trade unions, Adenauer came to believe that the inclusion of the National Socialists in the Prussian government was unavoidable.

His attitudes at this stage were influenced partly, but not exclusively, by the conservative wing of the Centre Party. The Cologne banking establishment also exerted a dubious influence on his thinking. Adenauer's close personal circle then included Kurt Freiherr von Schröder, who had risen through marriage to become a partner in the von Stein private bank. Through his cousin Bruno von Schroeder, Schröder had links with the international banking community: with J. Henley Schroeder & Company in London, a private bank which was associated with Montagu Norman, Governor of the Bank of England, and with the J. Henley Schroeder Banking Corporation in New York. Kurt von Schröder was initially a dyed-in-the-wool nationalist rather than a National Socialist, but he was among the many businessmen who planned to be ready if the NSDAP were ever included in the government.

Among these groups, a mixture of motives can be detected: business calculation, conviction, and attempts to safeguard their position whatever the outcome. Through Wilhelm Keppler, and later Walther Funk, Kurt von Schröder had been in contact with Hitler since the summer of 1931. He also knew Franz von Papen. Moreover, Schröder's wife was becoming a committed Nazi, which soon began to damage their relationship with friends such as the Pferdmenges and Adenauer families.

On 2 August 1932, Centre Party politicians held discussions at the Schröder home to decide on their course of action in Prussia. In April of that year the NSDAP had won 325 seats in the Prussian Landtag elections, only one short of an overall majority in Germany's most important state. The Prussian government of Otto Braun was then opposed by a broad majority of the NSDAP and KPD. Though it had remained in office, government activity was crippled. In this situation, Chancellor von Papen had 'forced into line' the government of Prussia on 20 July 1932 and became Reich Commissioner for Prussia in his own right.

A hand-written minute by Adenauer, on Schröder's own headed paper, gives details of the meeting on 2 August 1932. This stated that if a government of National Socialists and DNVP were to be formed with Hitler as Chancellor, the Centre Party would be prepared 'to tolerate it and to judge it wholly without bias by its deeds alone'.[34]

After the fall of Brüning, Adenauer seems to have believed that the Centre Party was wrong to concentrate on attacking Papen. He did not participate in the negotiations between the Centre Party and Hitler, because he had left for Chandolin. However, von Papen tried to exert some influence on Adenauer during his stay in Switzerland through the mediation of the former president of the German peace delegation in Versailles, Kurt Freiherr von Lersner, who was also maintaining links between von Papen and Schröder. At this stage, the Chancellor was seeking to prevent a Hitler government; he apparently received an assurance from Adenauer, as chairman of the Prussian State Council, that he would delay the election of a new Prussian government. It is obvious that Adenauer's own tactical position was frequently changing to take account of overall developments.

A memorandum from Lersner, dated 20 August 1932, reveals the main points of Adenauer's current line. This had been set out during a secret seven-hour discussion in Vissoie:

1. The Reich government should present itself to the Reichstag. In the event of a vote of no confidence, dissolution of the Reichstag and postponement of new elections until the spring.
2. The national government should take control of the Prussian police by emergency decree in order to remove the police from party conflict and intervention.
3. He does not want the police to be handed over to Hitler under any circumstances.[35]

Adenauer now apparently hoped that von Papen's presidential cabinet would keep the Hitler movement out of government; he no longer expected the NSDAP to be included. Moreover, he believed that it would be best to keep the Prussian police under the control of von Papen. Shortly afterwards, the negotiations between the NSDAP and the Centre Party collapsed. The Reichstag was dissolved and new elections called without a solution to the Prussian problem having been found.

Subsequently, Adenauer returned to the notion of taming the Nazis. In contrast to his earlier ideas, he was now keen to make use of the situation in Prussia. Following the appointment of Kurt von Schleicher as Chancellor, Adenauer wrote to Ludwig Kaas on 12 December 1932 and referred to a discussion in the Centre Party executive on 8 December. At this meeting, two alternatives had been discussed: first, the postponement of the formation of a government including the National Socialists in Prussia 'until the question of the entry of the National Socialists into the national government is resolved in a positive sense'; and second, the formation of a government in Prussia as quickly as possible, to facilitate the withdrawal of the Reich Commissioner. The second alternative appeared not to be acute at the moment, since von Schleicher was not prepared to withdraw the Reich Commissioner if Hermann Göring was elected as Prussian minister-president.

However, Adenauer also noted the urgent need to restore order in Prussia. All responsible individuals had the duty 'to ensure that, as soon as the political situation permits, a government including the National Socialists is formed in Prussia, which would have the withdrawal of the Reich Commissioner as its consequence...Subsequent negotiations with the National Socialists regarding their participation in the national government would not be damaged in my view, and might even be promoted, by the procedure in Prussia. I also think it correct for the National Socialists in Prussia, as the less dangerous place, to show whether they are really in a position to cope with such high offices.'[36]

In the event, a Hitler government was formed in Germany on 30 January 1930, but supported by a different coalition. The change was negotiated in Kurt von Schröder's house, where Hitler and Papen met on 4 January. Schröder thereafter satisfied his ambitions, serving from 1933 until 1945 as Gau Economic Leader and President of the Chamber of Commerce and Industry in Cologne.

In the last six months of the Weimar Republic, therefore, Adenauer was equally as short-sighted as most of his colleagues in the Centre Party. He had personal experience of the infamy of Nazi propaganda in Cologne, and had well-grounded fears regarding the leadership clique of the NSDAP. Nevertheless, like many others he believed that the Centre should no longer refuse to become involved. Like his colleagues, he clung to the hope that, if Hitler was forced to accept responsibility, he could be controlled or at least made to behave more reasonably.

This was an enormous error. Clearly, it was ludicrous to imagine that a Göring government in Prussia would be preferable to the Reich Commissioner, the authoritarian – but not totalitarian – Chancellor Schleicher! There are few more revealing examples of the blindness of the Weimar party establishment than Adenauer's letter of 12 December. If its contents had become public knowledge during his lifetime, it would certainly have damaged his career after 1945. Clearly, he knew that his own judgement of the danger posed by Hitler and his clique had been seriously flawed.

Sure, it must be remembered that conditions in Cologne were chaotic. Though Adenauer's political judgement had faltered after the *coup d'état* in Prussia, it had done so against a background of acute political and economic misery. In autumn 1932, the city of Cologne had become insolvent. The city budget for 1932 was eventually passed on 27 June 1932 with a deficit of 25 million marks. Moreover, tax revenues were in constant decline; by 30 September 1932, the deficit for the current budget year had reached an estimated 34 million marks. In winter 1932/33, a meeting of creditors was called, to advise how the city might pay its debts.

There were now 87,000 unemployed people in the city. In Cologne as elsewhere, running battles were being conducted on the streets by members of the SA, the Red Front and the police. The weeks before and after the Nazi seizure of power, when the dead and seriously injured were celebrated as 'blood witnesses' by the various camps, were especially alarming. Whenever the city council met there were scenes reminiscent of the revolutionary period and of 1923; the meetings were accompanied by 'hunger demonstrations' in the square in front of city hall, organised by one or other of the radical parties.

While the extremists terrorised the streets, the Centre Party's remaining powers of resistance were exhausted by the bankruptcy of Görreshaus, the largest Catholic printing house in the Rhineland and the publisher of the *Kölnische Volkszeitung*. The crisis had been gathering since spring 1930.[37] During the boom of the 1920s, the management had made too many investments; none of the attempts to rehabilitate the firm – often involving Chancellor Brüning – had been successful. From a political point of view, the involvement of some members of the Centre Party leadership, including *Justizrat* Mönnig, Prelate Ludwig Kaas and the publisher Julius Stocky, was disastrous. Moreover, the owners had not even been informed about the desperate situation until it was far too late. In February 1933 the three managing partners were arrested, along with Bank Director Brüning, who was also partly responsible for Adenauer's own financial problems.

Like the other members of the Catholic élite in Cologne, Adenauer was appalled by the Brüning affair, as he told Dora Pferdemenges: 'He carried out his swindles under the cover of religion in the most reprehensible fashion. Apparently he even swindled me over a sum that I now most painfully need, and under particularly unpleasant circumstances! I was suspicious of him for months, even of his religious belief for certain reasons, and for that reason I asked your husband to be careful, but I was not prepared for anything like this. For a long time I regarded him as irresponsible and slipshod and insincere, but not as a cold-blooded criminal.'[38]

By the time he wrote these lines it was already 4 May 1933. Hitler was firmly in control, while Adenauer had been forced from his post as mayor and was hiding in the monastery of Maria Laach.

IV

IN THE THIRD REICH
1933-1945

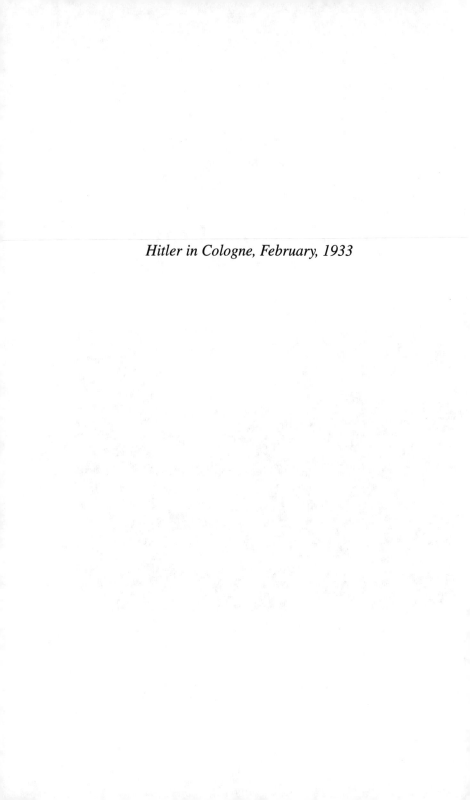

Hitler in Cologne, February, 1933

Fall from Power

In the hectic weeks between the Nazi seizure of power on 30 January 1933 and his banishment from office on 13 March, Adenauer revealed an impressive strength of character. Though predisposed by his nature to seek a way out of difficult situations by means of constant tactical manoeuvres, he also knew that in some situations the only thing to do was to take a stand – and go down fighting.

The last six weeks of his mayoralty were played out on two battle-fields, in Berlin and Cologne. After the dissolution of the Reichstag on 1 February 1933, the Hitler government hoped to call new elections in Prussia as well. Already, in April 1932, the Nazis had only just been short of an overall majority in the Prussian Landtag; it thus seemed almost inevitable that new Prussian elections in the wake of the national elections of 5 March would produce a majority for the NSDAP.

However, the decision to dissolve the Prussian Landtag had to be taken by a three-man committee consisting of the president of the Land-tag, the president of the Prussian State Council, and the minister-president. As long as Otto Braun had been in office, he and Adenauer together would have been able to block any attempt to dissolve the Landtag. After the dismissal of Braun on 20 July 1932, a dissolution could theoretically have been pushed through against the will of the chairman of the State Council, Adenauer: Hans Kerrl of the NSDAP was now the Landtag president, while Franz von Papen took over the function of minister-president in his capacity as Reich Commissioner in Prussia. The constitutional dispute before the Supreme Court, which brought Adenauer into conflict with Carl Schmitt as von Papen's representative, was won by the Reich government. However, during the summer and autumn of 1932, neither Papen nor his successor General von Schleicher had wanted to see the NSDAP in the Prussian government.

This situation was transformed by the seizure of power on 30 January 1933. The required majority in the three-man committee was then ensured by the National Socialist president of the Landtag, Kerrl, and Vice-Chancellor von Papen as Reich Commissioner for Prussia, with Adenauer in a minority as the last remaining representative of the 'system'. In negotiations on 6 February 1933, Adenauer continued to withhold his agreement to the dissolution of the Landtag.[1] Though his primary objection was constitutional, he also argued that even in its current composition the Landtag would be able to choose a government which did not damage the 'homogeneity' of the Reich. In fact, the course of the discussion gives rise to the conjecture that Adenauer wanted to discover whether a government including the Centre Party might be formed in Prussia.

Adenauer ended the conversation by observing that, in his opinion, Reich Commissioner von Papen was not justified in taking part in the dissolution of the Landtag according to Article 14 of the Prussian Constitution. He therefore felt obliged not to participate in the decision, which was not lawful. Once he had left the room, Papen and Kerrl ordered the dissolution of the Prussian Landtag for 4 March 1933.

Adenauer was equally unwilling to give way in other areas. On 25 February, in the presence of Papen, he tried to persuade Göring to repeal the 'shooting decree' to the Prussian police, which had been used to legalise numerous attacks. However, he was well aware that his protests and legal admonitions were futile, no more effective than the placing of a few sandbags against flood waters. The new government might take note, bide its time and make placatory noises – but it intended to gain a massive election victory, to legalise the 'national revolution', and to force the Centre Party into adopting a cautious policy of toleration as long as it was still needed.

In Cologne itself, the battleground consisted almost exclusively of Adenauer's defence against the government election campaign. The Prussian elections had been fixed one week after the national election, in tandem with the election for the city council. During the campaign Adenauer worked shoulder to shoulder with his Centre Party colleagues, as a party politician rather than a mayor, in the role he was to adopt after 1945. At the launch of the election campaign on 7 February, he was a keynote speaker at a large Centre Party rally in Cologne. In its time of greatest crisis, the party returned to its old traditions: Adenauer affirmed the values of the party slogan 'For truth, freedom and justice' and rejected opposing, disastrous, views 'with regard to what justice and constitution are'. His defiant words were greeted with storms of applause. In spring 1933, however, calls for moderation and justice were heard by few. Moreover, it seemed that the party in Cologne had still not recognised where the greatest danger lay: perhaps because of fear, the strongest attacks were directed at the German National Peoples's Party and not against the NSDAP.

On 17 February Hitler attended a mass rally in the city. Since the Reich Chancellor was flying in on a party-political mission only, Adenauer refused to greet him at the airport. In an attempt to soften the affront, he sent his deputy Heinrich Billstein, whose duties included the security of the airport surroundings. At the rally, the Nazis were forbidden to decorate municipal buildings with flags, and the Rhine was not illuminated in Hitler's honour. When two swastika flags appeared overnight on the pillars of the Rhine bridge – on city property – Adenauer ordered city workers to take them down. Swastikas could be raised only in front of the exhibition halls where Hitler appeared, and even then the local fire brigade had to be mobilised to fetch flagpoles. Farce was still not a capital offence in the spring of 1933. Nevertheless, the *Westdeutscher Beobachter* noted ominously that these incidents revealed Adenauer's 'deepest aversion' towards National Socialism. It added: 'Herr Adenauer might like to know that such challenges will be avenged in future.'[2]

Tickets for Hitler's campaign appearance in the exhibition halls fetched as much as 100 marks on the black market. His speech was purely and simply a declaration of war on the Cologne Centre Party. By this stage, no election could be genuinely free: the Social Democratic *Rheinische Zeitung* was banned for three days on 6 February; the *Kölnische Volkszeitung* of the Centre Party from 11 to 13 March; the Cologne Communists had been outlawed since the Reichstag fire at the end of February; life in the streets was again marred by political murders, marches and street battles; the SA continued to disrupt the election meetings of other parties. Electoral freedom was further endangered by the presence at the polling stations of uniformed auxiliary policemen from the SA and SS, as Adenauer complained to Vice-Chancellor von Papen on 1 March 1933 in his last letter as President of the Prussian State Council.[3] By now however, he knew that these complaints could have no practical effect.

In the Reichstag elections, the NSDAP obtained one-third of the vote in Cologne. Thereafter, all restraint was abandoned. In the week leading up to the municipal election on 12 March, no opponent of the NSDAP was safe. On 9 March, Wilhelm Sollmann was taken by SA men to the 'Brown House' in Mozartstraße and brutalised. Other Social Democrats were taken into 'protective custody'.

The NSDAP objective in the municipal election was: 'Away with Adenauer! End the corrupt black-red majority! Down with enormous salaries! National Socialists into Cologne city hall!'[4] Adenauer was now forced to fly the party's flags on municipal buildings. Regierungspräsident Hans Elfgen of the Centre Party informed him by telephone that the police would not be available to prevent the raising of swastikas on official buildings.[5] Meanwhile Adenauer was inundated with threats made on his private telephone at home. His eldest son Konrad saw a collection box being passed round the centre of the city to gather money for 'a bullet for Adenauer'. A troop of SA 'auxiliary police', stationed in Max-Bruch-Straße as a 'protective guard', amused themselves by taking baths in the family home.[6] It was a very Rhenish seizure of power.

Adenauer decided to make a detailed speech in defence of his fifteen years of work as mayor, and to deliver it at a final Centre Party rally in the Cologne exhibition halls. The draft of the speech has survived.[7] It is a remarkable document – the response of a mayor claiming to have been patriotic and anxious to maintain order and efficiency. His achievements in the weeks and months after Germany's collapse in 1918 were sketched in outline; he, Adenauer, had not fled as others had done. Then he listed his achievements in municipal policy – the creation of the green belt, modernisation, industrial settlement, cultural development. He blamed the city's debt problems on the general economic crisis.

His work over the previous years was described in a mixture of broad outline and extensive detail, reminiscent of many of his speeches to the city council. Finally, he defended himself vigorously against the accusation of separatism, which obviously caused him great distress. For the first time, he described the dramatic scene in the Reich Chancellery on 13 November 1923, when he had clashed with Stresemann over government policy. Adenauer had planned to conclude with two quotes from President Hindenburg's speech in Cologne in 1926, in which he had praised the Rhinelanders for their exemplary solidarity and patriotism.

His speech was never given. The meeting was banned at short notice on the grounds of a possible danger to public order. However, Adenauer did ensure that his defence was made public through leaflets. His arguments show both the strengths and the limitations of the man during this period of political upheaval. Though it is strongly marked by sentiments of injured innocence, the basis of his argument was defensive. The planned speech was the response of a mayor whose honour had been impugned, not the battle cry of a politician calling for a last battle against the enemy within the gates. His arguments were limited to Cologne and to the issues of recent municipal history. All provocation was carefully avoided.

In historical terms, this was Adenauer's farewell to his role as mayor. He had moulded the office and extended its powers on all sides, but had avoided making the transition to national politics. If his career had continued as planned, he could have been mayor of Cologne until 1941, when he would have been able to retire with his place in local politics secure. Mayor Adenauer would thus have played an important role in the history of Cologne, but would have been no more than a footnote in the history of Germany.

In the event, his work was destroyed by the disaster that overtook his country in economic, domestic and foreign policy. Before 1933 Adenauer had been powerful because he confined himself to his city, but this concentration had also made him ineffective at national level. He finally achieved national significance without seeking it only after the Weimar Republic – and the entire establishment of which he was a member – had been brought down.

Without the seizure of power by Hitler, and the catastrophe of the National Socialist regime, there would have been no Chancellor Adenauer. It was his experiences at the hands of the Nazis that forced him to consider how to reconstruct Germany and re-establish its position in the world. But for his dismissal as mayor, he would have continued the course he had chosen and remained subject to the vagaries of national politics. In this limited sense the catastrophe of March 1933 was a hidden opportunity for him. Furthermore, it provided conclusive evidence that order could not be restored by decisions taken at local level, but only by achieving national political influence.

In the spring of 1933, however, Adenauer had no time for such contemplation. Indeed, his very survival was in question. Instead of the Centre Party rally on the exhibition grounds, a mass rally was held at night by the NSDAP, with the election slogan 'Down with Adenauer!' The star speaker was the Kaiser's fourth son, Prince August Wilhelm of Prussia, now an SA leader and known derisively as 'Auwi', who claimed that the famous Reichsfreiherr vom Stein would have been appalled by the corruption and mismanagement of the black-red city halls.

Adenauer continued to work on his documents at city hall until 10 March, when he heard that the SA intended to haul him to the Neumarkt that night in order to parade him before the people. There was now a danger that he would suffer the same fate that had befallen Wilhelm Sollmann the previous day. Adenauer was well aware what sort of treatment fallen politicians could expect in the new Germany. Many of his acquaintances had begun to avoid him – and his wife – on the street. He was fast becoming a political outlaw.

In the company of Peter Josef Schaeven, the secretary of the Centre Party in Cologne, Adenauer left the city that evening and took refuge with friends in Bonn. When he returned home, he took his leave of Schaeven with the remark that he had decided never to greet anyone again, since he no longer knew whether his greeting would be welcome. Nevertheless, he intended, as he told Schaeven, to go down bravely and with loyalty to his friends. As a precautionary measure, the children were taken to the Caritas hospital in Hohenlind, the first of several occasions on which the institution offered sanctuary to his family. Frau Adenauer also left the family home.

On Sunday 12 March the municipal elections took place. Adenauer received advice from various sources that he should disappear, and the Regierungspräsident suggested that he should take two weeks leave. Adenauer, however, was determined to see things through to the bitter end. His last public appearance in Cologne was a memorial ceremony for the dead of the First World War, which took place in Gürzenich Hall on the morning of 12 March. He was treated like a leper. His deputy Eberhard Bönner, who had maintained good relations with his chief despite his switch of allegiance to the NSDAP, warned him that violence was being planned for the following Monday morning.

When Adenauer asked the police president for protection for city hall, it was refused. He therefore returned to his office to make his farewells, before closing its doors behind him forever. Though Adenauer kept the key, which was found in his desk at Rhöndorf after his death, he never set foot in the city hall again: it burned down during a British air raid.

At these elections the NSDAP finally made its breakthrough in Cologne, partly because many voters had been too frightened to come to the polls. Instead of its previous four councillors, the NSDAP now had 39. Five seats were won by its allies, the Black-White-Red Front made up of the DNVP and the Stahlhelm ex-Servicemen's association. The sole successful candidate from the German People's Party promptly went over to the National Socialists, along with one Social Democrat, giving the 'national revolution' a total of 46 seats. The Centre Party still had 27 seats, the Social Democrats 13, and the officially outlawed Communists 10. Since this would have kept the NSDAP and their allies in a minority, the Communist seats were declared 'dormant'. Adenauer thus had a majority against him. He would either have to resign or be removed against his will – whether by legal means or by force.

On the evening of 12 March, the latter course of action seemed more likely. Adenauer nevertheless remained president of the Prussian State Council. He therefore decided to go to Berlin to complain to Göring, the Prussian Minister of the Interior, about conditions in Cologne. In order to deceive the SA guard on his home, he ordered the official car to come for him at nine o'clock on Monday morning, but slipped out at seven to meet his friend Pferdmenges, who took him to catch the train to Berlin. Adenauer stayed in the official rooms of the President of the Prussian State Council; here, in the government quarter, two doors away from Göring, the police ensured that quiet and order were maintained.

At the same time, Nazi formations conducted a mass march past Cologne city hall. The building was occupied by Gauleiter Josef Grohé , who ordered the Regierungsprasident to declare Adenauer suspended until further notice. From the balcony, Grohé declared that Adenauer had been dismissed, along with the Social Democratic deputies Fresdorf and Meerfeld, who had been taken into 'protective custody'. In Adenauer's place he presented Günter Riesen as temporary mayor – stressing that he was prepared to do the job on an honorary basis, without a high salary.

A few days later, Adenauer was granted a meeting with Göring. However, he was greeted by a demand for information regarding five million marks he had taken from the Cologne finance department, an accusation that Adenauer refuted with indignation. He then made his own complaints about the illegal events in Cologne, about which he had heard on the radio; he was particularly incensed by the inaction of the Regierungspräsident and of the police president, both of whom had refused to put the city hall under police protection. Göring then criticised Adenauer's removal of the swastika flags during Hitler's visit. When Adenauer defended himself, Göring ended the discussion by observing that he had ordered a former State Secretary, Carl Christian Schmid, to begin an investigation.[8]

It was now clear that the new government intended to justify the removal of Adenauer from office on strictly legal grounds. Adenauer resolved to use all of the legal means still at his disposal in order to defend himself against the accusations. In a letter to Riesen, he demanded a hearing concerning the accusations made against him. The temporary mayor answered with a three-page letter of startling vulgarity.[9] Adenauer kept it, noting 'criminal letter' on the envelope.

Riesen concluded his diatribe with the following sentences:

> You are a criminal, Herr Adenauer, a criminal against the people entrusted to your care, whom you have brought into terrible distress by your guilt, a criminal against our religion, whose exponent you were, a criminal against the city you have ruined, a criminal against your subordinates, whose human dignity you took away and many of whom – honourable men away from your influence – have now been seriously incriminated. You are a criminal against your family and your wife, and I am deeply sorry for them in their ignorance. You are a criminal against our Lord God and against all the people who have come into contact with you. You are the accused, I am your accuser, and the people are your judge. That is the situation between us.

Adenauer's wife, who came to stay with him in Berlin during this period, told him that Riesen had paid her a visit to offer her his protection. Adenauer regarded this as a particular insult.[10] In 1948, when Riesen had the effrontery to ask Adenauer to exonerate him politically,[11] he informed the denazification officials that the 'criminal letter' had been dictated to him by the Nazi Gau leadership.

In spring 1933, Adenauer was in more danger from the remorseless attention of the state administration than from Riesen's letter. On 4 April, the Regierungspräsident sent a letter to Adenauer, announcing the introduction of an official disciplinary action to remove him from public office. For the time being, he was suspended from service with immediate effect; his salary would be cut by half from 1 May 1933.

Ten points were made to justify this action, all of which had played a part in local political agitation in recent years. The complaints against Adenauer were as follows: the affair of the twelve-million mark loan from the Preussenkasse; serious abuses in the administration of the municipal waste-disposal plant; allegations that he had favoured certain individuals in real estate matters; the use of special advantages in regu-

lating his 'public salary' and public dwelling; excessive expenditure during the 'Pressa' exhibition in 1928; unreasonable finance policy; nepotism; 'undertaking personal speculative transactions in securities and
covering the losses sustained'; disregard of a savings decree of 1931;
arbitrary additional payments to himself and the city deputies in 1932.

Adenauer refuted these allegations point by point in a very precise
eighteen-page document – the first of many such efforts in the years that
followed. He was deeply disappointed that the Centre Party's councillors in Cologne failed to defend him against the allegations of the
Regierungspräsident; this, he thought, had been a 'shabby act'.

One man who did remain loyal was Adenauer's friend, Cardinal
Schulte. However, when he contacted Vice Chancellor von Papen on Adenauer's behalf, he received only an embarrassed shrug of the shoulders in
reply. Another loyal friend was the former State Secretary in the Reich
Chancellery, Hermann Pünder, who was still Regierungspräsident in Münster. Pünder wrote to him: 'I have followed with fury and bitterness the
treatment meted out to you from the balcony of your venerable city hall.'
The representatives of the state authority – meaning Regierungspräsident
Elfgen – should have prevented it: 'People who are not up to such tasks
should at least accept the consequences. But people are in a bad way if they
slowly let their backbones bend without even noticing. Especially in times
of revolution, which we are facing once again, the local representatives of
the state must do their utmost to ensure the stabilisation of state authority.'[12]

Adenauer thanked him by return of post, though he was as reticent as
ever in expressing his innermost feelings: 'I have had to bite my lips during these days. – By the way, you have hit the nail on the head with your
assertion; the public authorities failed, they expressly refused me the help
I asked for …'[13]

The city of Cologne stopped all payments to him for the time being,
and the Deutsche Bank also decided to freeze his account (Director Brüning had been arrested shortly before). Adenauer therefore found himself
virtually penniless in his rooms on Wilhelmstraße, while the rest of
Berlin indulged in an orgy of celebration of the 'national awakening'.

He had very few visitors. Robert Pferdmenges and Dannie N. Heineman were honourable exceptions. Two days before his dismissal, after a
gap of several months, Adenauer had received another long letter from
the industrialist. Heineman told him that he would be in Berlin during the
week of 20 March and asked if the two of them could meet there. He
made no mention at all of Hitler and the seizure of power, devoting a sentence to economic matters only: 'You in Germany are in the very happy
situation of having already gone through the worst of the sickness, and
you are accordingly able to take the measures to avoid any relapse.'[14]

Adenauer had replied to this letter on 11 March; since then his circumstances had changed. Originally he had planned to spend two or three

days in Berlin on or around 20 March, to deal with official business. Now, though he was still officially president of the Prussian State Council, he was a virtual refugee in his official apartments. Heineman had been forced to change his plans, inducing Adenauer to write to him again on 11 April. Like the rest of the correspondence between Adenauer and Heineman, this letter escaped the extensive burning of files at SOFINA as German troops advanced on Brussels in May 1940. It offers an authentic record of Adenauer's mood in the first weeks after his fall:

> You will find it difficult to obtain a picture of the changes that have taken place in Germany since our last exchange of letters. Owing to great agitation and vituperation against me, I have been forced to leave Cologne and seek refuge here in Berlin, where I am not known. Since 13 March I have been in the house that is mine as president of the State Council – where I will remain until 25 April; then I will have to leave here too. Where I will go thereafter I still do not know; presumably I will not be able to return to Cologne, since the people who were so devoted to me until a short time ago have been too indoctrinated. My wife is with me, my children are in Cologne. This is the outcome of sixteen years' work as mayor and the rescue of the city from the 1918 revolution and protecting the Rhineland from the danger of being separated from Germany! It is dreadful to contemplate. I will not be able to return to my office, at best I may receive a small pension. In this situation, without work and without significant or any adequate income, which is doubly difficult for me with my seven children, I turn to you with the heartfelt request that you examine whether you might be able to help me so that I can obtain income and work that can at least partly fulfil me. Perhaps, despite the difficult economic situation, it may somehow be possible for you to help me. I ask you to understand why I keep this as brief as possible and say only that my position, inwardly and outwardly, is frankly desperate.[15] Even more alarming were two lines he wrote the next day: 'I am here as a refugee. Currently living at Wilhelmstr.64. I prefer not to meet you at the Kaiserhof, I am too well-known there.'[16]

Heineman did not let him down. When the two met at Wilhelmstraße 64, a scene took place which Adenauer never forgot: 'I had never had much cash in the house. I saw the critical moment approaching when I would have to sell valuables in order to support my family. In this situation, my good friend Dannie Heineman from Greenwich, Connecticut came to me. Heineman was Jewish. Without my saying a word about my financial worries, he said that he imagined I must be in a serious position financially. He had brought me the sum of 10,000 marks so that I would not get into difficulties.'[17] Adenauer described the scene in the second volume of his memoirs, in connection with the signing of the restitution agreement with Israel in Luxembourg on 10 September 1952. He had remembered the scene as he sat across from the Israeli Foreign Minister, Moshe Sharett.

At the same time, he recalled another incident which took place the following year. In 1934, he received a visit from Professor Kraus, the father of the Social Democratic town clerk of Cologne, Dr Herta Kraus, who had already emigrated to the United States. The professor enquired about Adenauer's circumstances and was informed that his family was not currently in financial difficulties thanks to the generous assistance of Heineman. Kraus, who was about to emigrate, then offered his own savings to Adenauer. Adenauer was deeply touched, but refused the offer with expressions of his gratitude. Thirty years later he wrote about these incidents: 'As mayor of Cologne I had many friends. Heineman and Professor Kraus were the only ones to offer me their help after my dismissal. Their behaviour towards me reminded me that "Thou shalt love thy neighbour as thyself" comes from the Old Testament.'[18]

Heineman offered his help on more than one occasion and told Adenauer to let him know if he needed more assistance. Despite his pride, Adenauer was forced to rely on his friend for three long years.

He could not remain in Berlin. After the Reichstag had passed the Enabling Act, Adenauer sent a telegram to *Justizrat* Mönnig informing him that he would not again be prepared to stand for election to the Prussian State Council. The new State Council was to meet on 26 April. The practical consequence was that he had to leave the official rooms where he had taken sanctuary during the weeks that decided the fate of Germany.

From now on, apart from a few friends like Heineman and Pferdmenges, Adenauer could rely only on his family and his church. On 17 April Adenauer asked his old schoolfriend Ildefons Herwegen, the abbot of Maria Laach, for sanctuary in his monastery for one or two months: 'There I would have the tranquillity, and particularly the spiritual atmosphere, that I urgently need for my physical and mental recovery. I have no special requirements, only the one wish for tranquillity and rest. For that reason I would also like to take meals in my room. In a hotel I would not find the necessary rest and seclusion. Of course it is important to me that I do not cause you any costs and, of course, that I am not a burden to you. I would be grateful to you with all my heart if I could come, and you would be doing me a good deed.'[19]

Herwegen was then following a very different political approach. In the spring of 1933, the abbot, who had achieved some renown as a restorer of the Gregorian liturgy and was a convinced royalist, believed that the restoration of the monarchy was within reach. The 'Day of Potsdam' had taken place only four weeks before. Yet in some ways his host's relative support for the 'national revolution' would actually offer Adenauer extra security. Herwegen did not hesitate: 'It is a sincere pleasure for me to offer you our hospitality, and I cordially invite you to spend some time with us in order to collect yourself and calm yourself in tranquillity. You can come at any time. Your loyal Herwegen.'[20]

Struggle for Survival

Four years passed between Adenauer's dismissal on 13 March 1933 and his final settlement with the city of Cologne in August 1937. This was the most depressing period of Adenauer's whole life. Though he never found it easy to express his feelings, he told his few remaining friends that there were weeks when he was almost at the end of his tether: 'I will not waste many words on my state of mind, contenting myself by saying one thing: without my family and my religious principles, I would have ended my life long ago, it is so little worth living.'[1]

Adenauer was in poor health and without a permanent home. Moreover, for over a year after his dismissal he feared that his political opponents were determined to use legal proceedings to ruin him entirely. His desperate attempts to find himself a new profession ended in failure. However, his greatest worries were about money, more serious than any he had known since he was a student. At least in his student days he had been without dependents, whereas now he was the head of a family of nine.

Owing to his fear of SA attacks, Adenauer did not dare return to his home in Cologne, though his family continued to live in the Caritas Hohenlind institution in the city. Accompanied by his wife, he moved to the Benedictine monastery of Maria Laach in the last week of April. The guest rooms where he stayed reflected the character of the old Benedictine abbey, dignified but far from luxurious. Adenauer had a large room panelled with dark wood, with a high window, a carpet, and a simple writing desk with a lamp. Photographs of the room show a crucifix on the desk and a *prie-dieu* by the wall.

The monastery church, founded by Pfalzgraf Henry II in 1093, is a magnificent example of late Romanesque architecture. It lies by a lake, close to meadows and deciduous forest, though remaining easy to reach by car and bus. As a guest, Adenauer was not involved in the fixed rhythms of monastery life – the choir, prayers, work in the garden, pottery, painting and academic study – and was, in theory, free to walk in the woods or along the lake. However, he had been warned not to appear outside more than was necessary. As a result, he often attended religious services, watching from the organ-loft where he would not come face-to-face with visitors. When he wished to go into the wood, he left through a small gateway in the monastery wall.

His stay in Maria Laach was far from idyllic. Nevertheless, rather like the period after the death of his first wife, it was a time when Adenauer was forced to reflect deeply upon his life and attitudes. After that earlier catastrophe, however, he had at least been busy with official business, leaving only Sundays for unhappy reflection. The situation in 1933 was very different.

Our picture of Adenauer's thoughts and activities during these months is provided partly by reports from his acquaintances, but also by a correspondence he kept up with his wife and with a few friends throughout the years of dictatorship and war. These letters give an insight into the inner feelings of a man who was otherwise concise and very reserved. During 1933 and 1934 in particular, he wrote often and with feeling to Dannie Heineman, mainly on the subject of his economic prospects and distress. His letters to Dora Pferdmenges in Cologne are even more important during this early period. In these he felt free to mention his views on many different subjects: the National Socialist revolution and foreign policy in the spring and summer of 1933; his own struggle for survival; the family; the atmosphere in the monastery; his reading material; memories of visits to the opera; the countryside round Maria Laach; trees and plants.

The Adenauer and Pferdmenges families had already become acquainted during the last years of the Weimar Republic. Adenauer and Dora Pferdmenges had two mutual interests, the Cologne theatre and their love of gardening, which drew them together. Furthermore, in 1933 the Pferdmenges couple were among the few friends in Cologne who had taken the trouble to help Adenauer and his wife. It was Robert Pferdmenges who had assisted his efforts to evade the SA guard and get away to Berlin. Frau Pferdmenges visited Adenauer in Maria Laach in May 1933, gave him courage through her letters, and maintained contact with his isolated family in Cologne. Adenauer, who trusted her completely, told her frankly of his opinions. In addition, he may well have hoped to influence the thinking of her husband, who was forced to be exceptionally careful in these months owing to his links with Jewish banks, and therefore had to limit his direct contacts with Adenauer.

These personal accounts can be filled out by reports from others, particularly from the family circle. Gussie Adenauer visited him regularly, sometimes alone, sometimes with one of her older sons. Adenauer's letters to Dora Pferdmenges leave no doubt that his wife's visits, and his contact with his sons, helped to ease his loneliness and keep him emotionally stable: 'It is good, as a father, when one can talk with one's grown sons about our time.'[2] In the summer holidays of 1933 his son Paul, who was then ten years old, was able to live in the monastery for a few days. At Christmas 1933, the whole family travelled by train and post bus to Maria Laach to celebrate the season together; they attended midnight mass and listened to Gregorian chants in the candle-lit basilica before enjoying the simplicity of a traditional family Christmas. Despite his difficulties, he wrote to Heineman a few days later, '... Christmas in these surroundings has a magic of its own.'[3]

The protection offered by the abbey ensured it a special and lasting place in the affections of the family. Some of the younger children married there. For a time, Paul Adenauer contemplated whether to enter the Benedictine order, but finally decided to become a theology student after 1945, since this allowed him to remain near to his parents, particularly his sick mother. Adenauer himself, though sometimes driven almost to distraction by the monastic tranquillity, was later to regard it as an oasis of peace in his life. During the efforts to form a government in 1949, he wrote to Father Vollmar: 'In the confusion which surrounds me, I sometimes think back with longing to Maria Laach.'[4] When he became Chancellor, he donated a window above the west chancel, and monks from Maria Laach arrived at his home in Rhöndorf each year to bring carp from the lake.

In the hectic months of the 'national awakening', however, not even Maria Laach was cut off from contemporary events. In spring 1933, Abbot Ildefons Herwegen was himself temporarily infected by the prevailing spirit. In Cologne on 30 May 1933, according to a complacent report in the *Westdeutscher Beobachter*, Herwegen had declared that the people and state had been united 'in the great Führer, Adolf Hitler', the 'father of the nation'.[5] Between 21 and 23 July 1923, the third sociological meeting of the Catholic Academic Association took place in Maria Laach. At this meeting, which was attended by Vice Chancellor von Papen, Hitler's new state was welcomed with enthusiasm. Adenauer mentioned the meeting in a letter at the end of July, but noted that he would prefer to reserve discussion of it and the Concordat until a personal meeting.[6]

In Maria Laach he felt 'banished', and once referred to 'my exile' in a letter.[7] Adenauer followed political events closely, and was disturbed both by the fate of Germany and its implications for his own future. Until the summer of 1933, he was unsure about the future of the Hitler government.

'The movement is composed of heterogeneous elements', he wrote to Frau Pferdmenges on 4 May 1933, 'and carries the germs of such different kinds of development within it, that it is impossible at this stage to find a specific attitude ...'. In reply to a comment from Frau Pferdmenges that has not survived, he noted that people who had been 'compelled by external forces' to take part should do so 'in an appropriate manner'; others, however, 'should wait until it is clear where the journey is going.'[8]

Personally, he saw every indication of a coming conflict with the churches. In a letter of 6 May 1933, he commented that he was observing 'the renewal of the Prot. church' and had a 'lively interest' in its fate. (The Pferdmenges were themselves Protestant.) He continued: 'Though the accompanying phenomena are not pleasant, they show that luckily the right man has been chosen'. The exact meaning of this can only be guessed at, since the letters from Dora Pferdmenges have not survived, but he may have been referring to the Königsberg pastor Ludwig Müller, who had been appointed by Hitler on 25 April as Plenipotentiary for the Affairs of the Protestant Churches. During these weeks, many in the Protestant camp -wrongly, as it turned out – regarded him as relatively trustworthy. Adenauer continued: 'I fear that in the foreseeable future we will see a clash between the political authorities and the two churches, the Protestant and the Catholic; if these remain consistent, it cannot be avoided. It is a pity that I cannot explain myself in person on this subject, like much else in this deeply shaken time.'[9]

Adenauer returned to the fate of the Protestant church in subsequent letters. By the end of June the NSDAP had clashed with *Reichsbischof* Friedrich von Bodelschwingh, whom Hitler refused to accept, and differences had also arisen over the appointment of a Church Commissioner in Prussia. Adenauer observed: 'The events in the Protestant church fill me with real sorrow. When will the Catholic church get into difficulty?'[10] A week later, on 5 July, he sent Frau Pferdmenges a number of newspaper cuttings – as he had done before – and noted: 'Certainly you and your husband will be interested in the events in the Protestant church. How will it all end! I hope for the best and for new life. But it is still very sad to see how much pain and agonies of conscience are hidden behind it all.'[11]

These letters reveal that he was establishing his own view of developments by detailed reading of the *Frankfurter Zeitung*, the *Neue Zürcher Zeitung* and French newspapers. He made no direct comments about the negotiations between the Vatican and the Reich government which ended in the Concordat of 20 July, but did offer several sharp observations about events in the Centre Party, for example on 29 June: 'I weep no tears for the Centre Party; it has failed; in the past years it was not filled with new spirit at the right time ...'[12] He continued in this vein on 5 July: '

> The Centre will probably have ceased to exist by the time I write this. I view this with mixed feelings. On the one hand, a burden falls from my soul. I have always regarded a denominational party as a necessary evil, or rather the lesser good, and as you know I have been unhappy with the Centre Party leadership for a number of years; on the other hand, one is bound to leave with heavy heart a party to which one has belonged for one's whole life, and furthermore, what will the future be? Today the Catholic priest of the nearby village has been taken into protective custody, the pastors of the Trier diocese are more militant than their fellows in Cologne.'[13]

In his view, foreign affairs were as impenetrable as the domestic political situation. In this early phase of the seizure of power, however, the Hitler government was anxious to convince the world of its peaceful intentions. In the letters he wrote in 1933, therefore, Adenauer expressed no anxiety about a possible foreign policy adventurism on the part of the German government. In these early months of the Third Reich, he was much more concerned with Germany's weak position in foreign trade. Referring to the world economic conference which met in London in June 1933, he noted:

I do not believe we will achieve significant success. Political confidence is lacking in the world – see Geneva – we gain nothing from the fixing of the dollar and the pound unless we go along with it, then everything will be as before, our goods will only be allowed in if we take the others' products, we have not been paying war debts for some time and now we have no other foreign debts either, which should be particularly good for us! Eventually the London Conference will try to blame the Geneva Conference for its failure, and vice versa. And in Germany! Everything is going more slowly than one thinks, for good or ill, until suddenly things occur that have been been developing gradually and have gone almost unnoticed. More than ever I believe what I told you: people will either have to change or they will soon be ruined by bad management.[14]

Behind these gloomy thoughts there was an element of calculation. Adenauer thought it likely that the realities of international politics would either bring the Hitler government to reason, or force the Nazi leader to his knees. On 16 May – a day before Hitler's major 'peace speech' in the Reichstag – he made another sober assessment of foreign policy: 'The foreign policy perspective is certainly depressing, nor do I know whether tomorrow's Reichstag meeting will have a powerful effect in foreign policy, yet I cannot believe that no way out of the situation can be found; if it is not found, though, we can expect very bad developments.'[15]

His attitude towards the disarmament plan of the British Prime Minister, MacDonald, which was currently being discussed in Geneva, revealed the same wavering between hope and scepticism. At any rate, he was convinced that a fundamental realignment in the international system was taking place: 'I have the feeling that the biggest shifts in the position of the states towards one another have been taking place for months; the active policy of Russia is also a part of it, and it is as though the world had been turned completely upside down.'[16] In the early days of the Third Reich he did not suspect that Hitler would, within a short time, overthrow the entire European order.

The revolutionary character of events in Germany itself was much more obvious to him. At the end of June, Alfred Hugenberg, who had been Minister of Economic Affairs and Food in Hitler's government, resigned and his German National People's Party disbanded itself. Adenauer made a sarcastic comment in a letter of 29 June: 'What will happen now? Hugenberg gone, shares rising, rents falling; now comes the battle against "interest slavery". German National Party gone, Centre's days numbered! By the way, Hugenberg will go down in history as the man who destroyed parliamentarianism in Germany.'

A few pages later – after a description of his own difficult position and some references to books and flowers – he returned to his theme: 'May I talk politics yet again? Every revolution destroys, it must destroy. The only question is what and how much. If it destroys so much, and so quickly, and so fundamentally that reconstruction becomes impossible or almost impossible, if the revolutionary period fails to give way to a period of new tranquillity and new building in time, then catastrophe comes. We are waiting now, but it is high time for the time of stabilisation and building to begin.'

How could this be achieved? He had made a brief observation on this subject earlier in the letter: 'In my view our only salvation is a monarch, a Hohenzollern or in my opinion even Hitler, first as president for life, then comes the next stage. In that way the movement would reach calmer waters.' And he added: 'A heartfelt request at the conclusion of the political part: do not discuss things with a Nazi, you would only harm yourself.'[17]

Perhaps the idea of a Hohenzollern restoration was a response to the ideas of Adenauer's protector Herwegen during these months. It will not be welcomed by historians who are anxious to detect signs of his anti-Prussian attitudes at every turn; others will be disconcerted to find him prey to an illusion shared by many at the time – that Hitler was one of the more moderate elements within a radical movement. The general confusion of the public in spring and summer 1933 was also shared by Adenauer, and by many others whose anti-Nazi credentials are not in doubt. Yet he had never been – and never would be – committed to a rigid policy without allowing himself to contemplate alternatives.

These letters from 1933 reveal that Adenauer remained deeply preoccupied with politics. He was too dynamic and committed to be reconciled so quickly to a purely private existence. Nevertheless, his months in the monastery also led him to think, to contemplate his religious belief, and to take a more reflective view of life than he had done during his twenty-five years of public service.

He did not always find his isolation easy to bear. 'I have been here for almost a week', he wrote to Heineman on 2 May, 'the tranquillity and solitude were oppressive at first but one gets used to them. I am working and studying to some degree and observing developments with some anxiety, in Europe and America too.'[18] Even after long months spent adjusting to the calmer rhythms of monastery life, he always found it difficult to return after a visit outside. On 4 March 1934 – he had just returned from a longer stay in Berlin – he observed: 'here it is deep winter, high snow and much fog, the house is dominated by the austere atmosphere of Lent, e.g. apart from Sundays the organ is not played from Ash Wednesday until Easter, the text and melody of the songs are very austere. After an absence of seven weeks it was very difficult for me to cope for a few days. Christmas is much easier; things are tolerable now, to some extent.'[19]

Yet he was ready to adapt to his unusual environment: 'You have judged me correctly', he wrote to Frau Pferdmenges in his first letter from Maria Laach, 'the tranquillity and solitude here, the whole spiritual atmosphere – an atmosphere of religiosity and piety, nature, art and science – is doing me a great deal of good; I feel it clearly. I also love the solitude and the tranquillity for its own sake. Except for the separation from loved ones, and concern for the future, one might be content. I am sincerely trying to master the time and my inner self. Hilty, whom you admire too, writes in one of his books of the "levels of life". I will attempt to climb to another level.'[20]

In these weeks he found most solace in nature: 'the plums and pears have stopped flowering, the apples trees that are so plentiful by the lake are beginning to blossom, the entire beech wood has turned green overnight. I have never seen such beautiful forget-me-nots as here in the woods. Whole places are blue. The white wood flowers, too, which last year blossomed so beautifully ... in Baden-Baden, are there already ...'[21] Two days later, Adenauer lost his normal reserve and became almost lyrical:

> I have never been able to watch all of nature in springtime in the way I can here, where I am living in the midst of nature; I am quite moved and shaken by the enormous force nature has presented in these six weeks, revealing a completely different picture almost every day; so much is achieved at this time. In fourteen days it will be the solstice again – winter solstice is so much more significant – then nature already begins to care for the next spring; if only our own times were as constant as well as so serious, we could do it too. I am afraid that as things stand, all we can do is be patient ... Of course there are backward steps, but there are also advances; one is never too old to learn. Anyhow I am much better spiritually than physically. Nerviness is not dangerous, but unpleasant.[22]

Though he was constantly aware of the need to fight for his economic survival, his resolution was occasionally impaired by the contemplative mood: 'As far as my personal affairs are concerned, I am almost afraid that I will be too forgetful of them. I often have to tell myself that an ugly struggle awaits me still and I shrink from the struggle for which I do not feel sufficiently strong.'[23]

Periods of inner reflection were followed by days of dejection and sometimes despair. 'For some days I have been really depressed', he acknowledged in mid-May 1933;

> the foreign policy situation, my family's future, my future work, the separation, the humiliation of my current situation etc. Your letter, which arrived on Sunday, came just in time to be doubly comforting. If you are convinced that I am in control of things, then I will be convinced of it too and not disappoint this conviction. You are right to say that every sin is avenged on this earth, there is no exception to the sentence, so I agree with you that the future holds much ill-fortune for our country. All we can do is to make ourselves inwardly as strong as possible, and then we will have the strength to overcome. I believe these times can only be borne if one becomes accustomed to seeing the bigger picture, by striving to regard earthly existence as only a part of human life, and by firmly believing that there is a God who, though he shows himself in visible things *as well*, also stands *above* them and is independent of them. Do not smile at 'monastic' observations, though the atmosphere here certainly encourages such observations they are no less important for that.'[24]

As in all of these volatile letters, he switched rapidly from his 'monastic observations' back to politics and then to descriptions of the countryside: 'This morning I was in the beech wood, where we went together eight days ago, it was wonderful. For the first time for days, blue sky and *white* clouds, then the sun, the wonderful bay, the lake and the view into the far distance to the north. Your father would have enjoyed the walk, I saw eight deer in an hour.' He finished with another assessment of his own condition: 'I am somewhat better, but the sleeplessness and the tendency to tire easily are reluctant to go.- I ask you cordially, as calmly as possible – as I am trying to do – to face current events, otherwise one cannot get through them, and there are harder times ahead.'[25]

At the end of June 1933 he had no illusions, writing that a campaign to ruin him was under way. 'I thank you for your optimistic opinion regarding my future', he told Dora Pferdmenges, 'unfortunately I cannot share it. For a week my nerves have been under general attack. I have been deeply affected by the request on the basis of paragraph 4 of the civil service law. And then there are the other humiliations, the whole humiliation of my current situation, my stay in short, I am currently very far from a state of perfection and calm endurance; I really do not know how it will all end, or what will become of my family'[26]

As this letter reveals, his father-in-law, Professor Zinsser, had twice come from Tübingen to Cologne to be 'received' by Gauleiter Grohé – 'and to hear precisely why I am being persecuted and despised in this way'. For a short time, it appeared that a settlement was within reach after a discussion between Zinsser and Grohé at the end of June, probably over the granting of a pension to Adenauer.[27] By the beginning of July he had accepted that his dismissal would soon be made official.

However, these hopes were dashed when Adenauer visited Berlin in July and reported 'a complete change for the worse'.[28] On 24 July, moreover, he received the final order for his dismissal with the question of his pension still unresolved. Equally damaging, a significant part of his income had consisted of money paid as compensation for the fact that he did not use an official residence. He had used this money to pay the high mortgage on his beautiful house in Max-Bruch-Straße. After his dismissal this money also disappeared, along with the director's allowances for executive positions he had taken on in his official capacity.

His future now depended upon the development of the disciplinary action against him. Documents relating to Adenauer's mayoralty had been under examination for some time, first in Cologne, then by the consultant in charge of the Prussian Ministry of the Interior, and finally by a commission of the Ministry. At the end of July Adenauer concluded that, whatever the final settlement might be, his comfortable lifestyle was over forever.

His initial reaction to this blow was revealed in a letter to his confidante during these months, Dora Pferdmenges:

You have heard from my wife over the telephone that they brought me the order of dismissal yesterday; my son had read it out to me over the telephone the day before. I went to the hill where we went in spring, which gives such a beautiful view over the lake and the far countryside. There I sat down and drew up a balance-sheet of my work, and I was content with it. It was not that I had made no mistakes, everyone makes those, but I am convinced that my view of the work facing me was correct and that I gave it my full strength; nor will the work have been in vain, of that I am certain. I have also worked for my homeland and for Germany to the best of my ability. Some years ago I was already aware that the verdict of posterity is more important and correct than what one's contemporaries say. That was always my belief and will remain so. I must make one criticism of myself: because of my obsession with my work I neglected my family, and that gives me pain on my family's behalf. But thank God my family is thoroughly courageous, and if my body continues to endure it, as my old family doctor confirms with astonishment, then something will turn up – It is remarkable how things go in life. Since my early adulthood I have worried and worried about the distant future, and now the Lord God shows me the heavy and difficult truth that one should rely less on oneself, and put one's trust in Him. I am almost cheerful despite everything, though there are gloomy hours and days – In 'Cavour', who interests me greatly, I will write to you about it later, I have read that it is a sign of a passive nature to surrender without any struggle, and I am not passive – but I am getting over it well. You know, 'lost dignity cannot be regained', and none of my enemies will be able to say that I lost my dignity. I had already slowly detached myself from my work ... Now pardon me if I have written too much of this event: it is better to talk about it than to write.'[29]

The idea of 'lost dignity' had obviously struck a chord with him. In an earlier letter he had noted the discovery of a 'very good saying' during his recent reading: 'Lost power may be regained, but not so lost dignity'.[30]

This long and remarkable letter of 27 July then dealt with issues of 'job creation and monetary policy' and the personal position of his own family and the Pferdmenges, before turning to plants, always a favourite theme of this correspondence:

Phlox and Helenium; I can imagine your garden so well; I had proposed the same arrangement for my own garden, if I still have it next year. You must not smile at my enthusiasm for plants, to me every plant is like a living being, but so quiet and helpless; I can very well understand the Greek notion that there was a Dryad living in every tree, I would almost like to believe it myself. To prevent myself appearing too superstitious, I must also say that I am cross about the Trier pilgrimages; of course the robe is not genuine, I think there are eighteen holy robes in existence, and I do not think that the church should encourage anything of that kind even though many pilgrims are deeply affected.[31]

To some extent, this comment can be seen as an indication that Adenauer was attempting to retain his sense of ironic detachment from the world. However, it was directly followed by a return to politics, in the form of remarks about the Concordat and the meeting attended by Franz von Papen in Maria Laach. After another reference to flowers, Adenauer added a postscript: 'Because of your interest in the natural sciences – I have never seen living cuttlefish – I will send you an issue of *Kosmos* to look at; I can greatly recommend the -cheap – subscription.'[32]

This was the letter in which Adenauer acknowledged that he had finally been removed from power and ruined by his enemies in Cologne and Berlin. He refused to give way to hatred. A month later he wrote: 'I do not know whether you have read the reports about the International Meeting of Social Democracy in Paris. The socialist movement, so far as it is led by Social Democrats, seems also to be flagging at international level. I found the speech given by the chairman of the former German Social Democrats, Wels, very weak; "Revenge" – he spoke of it – I think and believe it is unworthy, here I agree with you, however difficult the renunciation of it may be.'[33] He was continually trying to be positive: 'How long I stay here cannot be guessed even approximately; it is truly a severe test of patience; in addition, for a man whose entire previous life has seemed to be secure, it is a great problem to see the future so completely clouded. In the truest sense of the word one must put oneself wholly in *God's hands*, and that *demands great faith* and *great trust*.'[34]

Adenauer's correspondence with Heineman at the same time was much more prosaic, owing to the fact that he had been in financial difficulties since the spring of 1933. As the year progressed, his situation became increasingly precarious. In 1930 his overall annual income had been 108,250 marks. After his removal from office, though he had received no salary for several months, the mortgage payments on his house in Cologne still had to be made. From 1 November 1933, it was finally agreed that the city of Cologne would pay him a monthly pension of 1,013.80 marks, at least for the time being, though even this was not paid in full. The housing subsidy due to him, from which his mortgage payments and land taxes were paid, was removed. By the beginning of 1935, Adenauer was so much in arrears with the payments for the property that a trustee was appointed to administer it for a time.

His financial future depended on the further course of the disciplinary action against him. Until June 1934, the outcome was uncertain. As his legal adviser, Adenauer managed to obtain a well-known trial lawyer from Essen, Professor Friedrich Grimm. A talented legal practitioner, Grimm was also an ardent nationalist, which made him popular with the new rulers and persuaded him to join the NSDAP. However, Grimm was also a decent man with a clear grasp of a basic reality of twentieth-century politics: though systems changed, every new system used the law against its opponents, and these would require good defence counsel. Grimm had made a name for himself in the Ruhr in 1923 as the defender of champions of 'passive resistance', and had subsequently defended some *Fememörder*, i.e., assassins motivated by nationalism. After the National Socialist seizure of power, however, he was asked to defend very different victims of political 'justice': in Essen he spoke up for the rights of Jewish lawyers, and in Cologne he assisted *Justizrat* Mönnig during the Görreshaus trial. Now the former mayor of Cologne was one of his clients. Grimm came to Maria Laach for a week with his briefs in order to prepare the defence. Every evening Ildefons Herwegen, 'the splendid abbot of the monastery', invited Adenauer and Grimm to share a bottle of wine with him.[35]

It was obvious that the proceedings had nothing to do with justice and were entirely political. The unfortunate business of Adenauer's share speculation was a vital point to be clarified. Grimm noted later: 'It was astonishing how maladroit this man had been in private things, though in public he had been so skilful as mayor of the great city of Cologne.'[36] In political terms, however, it was the allegations of separatism that were especially dangerous. Grimm himself was an authority on the subject, and he took great care to interrogate Adenauer on the subject. He noted in his memoirs that he had never fully understood all the details of Adenauer's approach, but he did not believe that Adenauer had ever held treasonable attitudes. Moreover, it is safe to assume that Grimm told his Nazi comrades of this view.

Oddly enough, it seems that Hitler himself had been rather impressed by Adenauer. During this period, two architects, Albert Speer and Herbert Giesler, were rivals for the Führer's favour. After 1945, Speer was chastened by his experience of the Third Reich, while Giesler remained unrepentant, but the two men were agreed that Hitler had admired the mayor. 'Adenauer', Hitler thought, according to these witnesses,

> 'was a separatist and was an opponent of the party because of his militant Catholicism, and was therefore intolerable to us as mayor. Yet Adenauer was a mayor of great calibre, and he proved it. He was conscious of the historical and regional significance of this city. He promoted it with all the means at his disposal. He was also clearly aware of the city of Cologne as an organism and therefore ordered and took responsibility for the essential measures of urban development. Of course that cost money and the debts caused his economic downfall. But the city of Cologne will pay off these debts and the citizens of Cologne will recognise that Adenauer's achievements deserve recognition and not the withdrawal of his pension ...'[37]

This grudging praise from the tyrant does nothing to enhance Adenauer's reputation and would probably have been unwelcome to him if he had ever come to hear of it. However, in the first years after the seizure of power, Hitler's positive judgement could only strengthen his position, particularly when it was expressed to visitors from Cologne. Hitler's view of Adenauer as reported is for the year 1936, but it may have had a beneficial effect on the outcome of the disciplinary action beforehand.

Adenauer had also managed to mobilise former British occupation officials to refute the allegations of separatism. The regime was currently eager for good relations with the British, and there was thus a possibility that the German government would take notice of these declarations.

Adenauer had kept in touch with Julian Piggott, the long-serving British member of the Inter-Allied Rhineland Commission, even after Piggott had left Cologne. Piggott, now working with the British Steel Export Association, was informed about the situation when he visited Cologne in February 1934. On 3 April 1934 he wrote to confirm that Adenauer, whom he had observed at first hand from November 1920 until February 1925, had not shown the slightest sympathy for the separatist movement; instead he had done everything in his power to maintain the constitutional link between the Rhineland and Prussia.[38]

Even more important for Adenauer was support from the former Governor of Cologne, General Clive. After his stint in Cologne between December 1918 and November 1919, Clive had held a number of senior diplomatic posts before taking the job of Marshal of the Diplomatic Corps – a liaison role between the Court and the Foreign Office in London – in autumn 1934. Clive met Adenauer in Berlin at the turn of 1934/35 and, after his return to London, made representations on his behalf to Leopold von Hoesch, the German ambassador.[39] Hoesch then wrote a detailed report to Berlin, in which he stressed Clive's well-known sympathy for Germany and his high rank. The Foreign Minister, Konstantin von Neurath, informed the Reich and Prussian Minister of the Interior, Wilhelm Frick, and Reich Minister Rudolf Hess, the Führer's deputy. Though the disciplinary action against Adenauer already was being wound down by this stage, the initiative may have ensured that the allegation of separatism was never revived.

On 4 June 1934, disciplinary proceedings were halted – albeit on tortuous grounds – by the disciplinary chamber of the government in Cologne.[40] However, the dispute between the city of Cologne and Adenauer lasted another three years. Adenauer employed various lawyers to represent him in this dispute – his brother August Adenauer, the Cologne barrister Friedrich Manstetten, and his deputy Ernst Schwering, who had also been dismissed in 1933. All of them worked tenaciously for an out-of-court settlement.

The abandonment of the disciplinary action did not in itself alter Adenauer's financial position. When his situation became especially critical, Adenauer sold a couple of his pictures, part of his garden in Max-Bruch-Straße, and his remaining shares. Insurance money received by Frau Adenauer after the theft of her jewellery also helped them to survive. Until spring 1936, via a covering address, Dannie N. Heineman also sent several contributions of a thousand marks.

Immediately after his dismissal, Adenauer had been hopeful of making a career in the business world. In summer and autumn 1933, he engaged in a protracted correspondence with Heineman over a job with SOFINA. Ingenious as ever, he had written from Maria Laach to describe an idea which would involve Heineman, Pferdmenges, Vögler and Flick.

Robert Pferdmenges was a partner in the Oppenheim and Levy banking houses, which had been forced to re-organise after the Nazi seizure of power because of their Jewish links. According to a letter from Adenauer in June 1933, Pferdmenges had persuaded Albert Vögler and Friedrich Flick to take shares in the banks. Adenauer provided excellent references for all three. Pferdmenges: 'An excellent character and a strikingly gifted banker of the old school, particularly solid and careful, who is not involved in speculation but has a very good nose for business possibilities and an extraordinary skill in dealing with people.' He had high praise for Vögler: 'Above all he is also a very decent person.' Finally Flick: 'He comes from Siegen, now lives in Berlin. He has worked his way up by his own efforts, is a very big iron and steel industrialist – Maxhütte, Charlottenhütte – and probably one of the richest men in Germany today. As I know from my own experience, he is very pleasant in social relations and, as his friend Pferdmenges has always told me, he is decent and honourable as a person and as a businessman.'[41]

What role was Adenauer intending for himself in this connection? He told Heineman that the moratorium on capital transfers would last for some years, at least. It might therefore be sensible for Heineman to consider investing the capital that could not be transferred into this new undertaking. The most important thing would be for Heineman to make available his own experiences and connections, 'and – here comes the catch, you will be thinking – appoint me in some form as the guardian of your interests. The catch is not as big as it may seem at first glance. Of course I do not have the knowledge to be a partner or something like it in such an undertaking, but I believe that I have so much knowledge of business matters that I could do something, and if Pferdmenges proceeds with this conversion with the other men I have named, I am convinced that the new undertaking will certainly do well.' He added a request for discretion: Pferdmenges himself was still unaware of his plan.

Adenauer appeared very taken with this idea when he committed the proposal to paper on 18 June 1933. As always, when he made plans he was able to forget his problems: 'I am still in M.L., and intend to remain there. I work and study all kinds of things, so that at least the time does not drag. I think that I have got over my fall fairly well, though of course the separation from my family and thinking about their future weigh on my mind.'

A month later he had lost much of this composure. Heineman had not been in touch, but he had heard from the Prussian Minister of the Interior:

Yesterday I was dismissed from the service of the city of Cologne by the Prussian Minister of the Interior on the basis of Article 4 of a law called the Law for the Restoration of the Professional Civil Service. This Article 4 runs as follows: 'Civil servants whose previous political activity makes it impossible for them to guarantee that they will unreservedly support the national state at all times may be dismissed from the service.' – In addition my pension, already insufficient, is reduced by three-quarters, and according to another clause in the same law I must repay part of the salary I received in 1932 – 8,000 marks. My position has been damaged even more because the temporary mayor has frustrated my friends' plans to retain me in a private capacity on the supervisory board of Rheinbraun, by categorically refusing to accept it – the city of Cologne has shares in Rheinbraun. Even if I can avoid getting into difficulties over the next months because of your help, my future still seems extraordinarily gloomy as regards employment and earnings for myself.

He asked cautiously whether anything had become of the plans Heineman had been considering when they talked in April. Furthermore, what did Heineman think of his plan for the Levy bank? 'You would not believe how much I need a certain hope in my current state of mind.'[42] In fact, Heineman was unable to support Adenauer's ideas. It was a principle of SOFINA business policy, he told Adenauer, not to become involved in banking. He promised to speak with Pferdmenges on the subject: 'However, the present plan seems to me to be very difficult to carry out.'[43] He would not be able to come to Germany before mid-September. For the first time Heineman had hand-written the greeting 'Dear friend' above this letter, after Adenauer had used it in his own letter of 31 May.

In one respect this was still the Adenauer of old days, in that he never gave up when he encountered resistance. In his next letter to Heineman, he reported that he had told Pferdmenges about the correspondence and asked him to run 'appropriate combinations of possibilities through his mind'. Adenauer himself had been unwell. However: 'My wife is courageous, my children are working hard and are undaunted about the future, which is a real comfort to me.'[44]

Heineman maintained his offer of rapid extra help, but he did not shirk the unpleasant task of being honest with his friend: 'At the risk of disappointing you I must tell you that it is extraordinarily difficult to find an occupation that could be agreeable to you.'[45] Adenauer still continued to hope for a positive result from discussions between Pferdmenges and Heineman, and from personal talks with Heineman when he came from Brioni to the Rhineland in mid-September.

At the same time, he sent Heineman a detailed description of his desperate economic situation.[46] Until 31 December 1933, he had 8,350 marks in cash and anticipated income; during the same period, he would incur expenditure of 13,750 marks for mortgage-interest payments, taxes, and lawyers' fees alone. In addition, the city might demand 8,700 marks back from him. He himself had claims outstanding against the city of Cologne to the tune of 21,700 marks, but: 'The city does not pay, and for psychological and other reasons there is no purpose in complaining about it.'

He set out his income and expenditure for 1934 in a similar manner, reaching a deficit of 21,000 marks. Owing to his obligations for the house in Max-Bruch-Straße and costs for his family, he could not reduce his expenditure below 2,000 marks per month. He still had some assets but, with the exception of some securities held by Frau Adenauer, almost all of it was invested in the Cologne house. The danger was that the city, as the direct or indirect mortgage provider, might use its claim for 103,000 marks to deprive him of the entire property. Finally, Adenauer still had outstanding claims against the Deutsche Bank and Diskontogesellschaft totalling 20,000 marks and 120,000 marks respectively, though these were being disputed.

Under the heading 'intentions for the future', Adenauer attempted to explore his prospects for escaping from his financial predicament. These involved, first, the rapid sale or rent of the house in Max-Bruch-Straße, which was now like a millstone around his neck. If it was rented out, the rent must at least cover his expenses. If he sold it, he was not prepared to realise anything less than 200,000 marks. Even then he would lose 150,000 marks and, after paying off the mortgage, would be left with only 100,000. In the current situation, however, it seemed very doubtful that he could either sell or rent.

Meanwhile, he had decided that it was

almost impossible that I will manage to obtain a position which wholly fulfils me and also secures my position financially. I have some friends in Germany who were ready to make such an attempt, but they were not permitted to do so. Years might pass before conditions in Germany allow efforts of this kind to succeed. I cannot wait until then, but must look for various ways to create work and earnings. Here too, despite their best intentions, my German friends can do nothing for the reasons described above, so that you are the only person to whom I can turn.

Again he asked Heineman to examine the following possibilities for helping him:

a) Could you not give a significant assignment through me the Kabelwerk Rheydt? So that I could achieve a commission from Rheydt Cable Works? The Rheydt Cable Works is probably known to you, it is not very big, but is technically and economically very efficient. Herr Pferdmenges is chairman of the supervisory board or at any rate is very influential on it. That would enable the commission from the Rheydt Cable Works to be given to me in the most discreet way.
b) Would it not be possible for you to help me get on to the supervisory board or corresponding body of foreign subsidiaries of your concern?
c) If it is impossible for me to get onto the supervisory board because of the situation in Germany, would it not be possible for me to provide expert opinions or an arbitration for German subsidiaries?

Adenauer then returned to his plan for Heineman's participation in the Cologne banking house and referred to his discussion with Pferdmenges. The bank, he thought, should be organised as a joint-stock company, which would allow him to be appointed to the supervisory board and entrusted with specific tasks. In addition, Heineman might take over the mortgage payments for the house on Max-Bruch-Straße. He regarded both as completely safe investments. Of course, all of this was based on the assumption that Heineman had non-transferable capital in Germany. Finally, could he not consult Dr Solmssen of the Deutsche Bank and persuade the bank to recognise his just claims? 'The recognition of these demands', he added ominously, 'would be a very considerable relief for me, particularly with regard to the fate of my family after my death.'

In making this request, Adenauer was forced to tell Heineman all the details of his share speculations. The fact that he decided to do so can be regarded as a sign that he did not expect his plans for appointment to supervisory boards to be successful. He can hardly have expected that a hard-headed businessman like Heineman would be able with good conscience to appoint a man whose administration of his own finances had been so maladroit.

Against Director Brüning of the Cologne branch of the Deutsche Bank, Adenauer had made two allegations. Firstly, he reported that he had handed over 20,000 marks to Brüning to secure a share of the bank's interest in the Rheinische Spritzgußwerke in Cologne-Ehrenfeld. When Brüning was arrested in May 1933, Adenauer had reported this transaction to the Cologne branch and asked for its opinion. The answer had been that the Deutsche Bank had never had an interest in this concern and had no knowledge of what Brüning had done with the 20,000 marks. Adenauer was convinced that the bank was liable for the 20,000 marks lost as a result of the illegal conduct of its director, since he had carried out the swindle in his capacity as director of the Cologne branch.

Adenauer also described his speculation with the American shares. In February 1931 he had reached an agreement with the board of the Deutsche Bank in Berlin, according to which neither party would make a claim against the other. He had left a block of Rheinbraun syndicate shares with the nominal value of 60,000 marks with the bank. For two years after the agreement, dividends had been paid to him on these shares. In December 1932, however, the bank had also placed a blocking-order against these shares on the grounds that when it made the agreement it had not taken into account the shares being administered by another department, 'but that it was in line with the meaning of the agreement made then, that the bank should keep everything that it had in its hands.'

In Adenauer's view, reasons of justice and equity alike supported his claims for the Rheinbraun shares, which had a market value of about 120,000 marks. If the bank had advised him carefully when he bought the American shares, he would not have lost all of his capital assets. The explanation of his claims against the bank covered ten pages. He ended by noting: 'In the spare time that I now have, I have studied the entire affair very thoroughly, and I have no doubt at all that I have a claim against the bank for full compensation.' He wanted to avoid legal proceedings and would much prefer an amicable settlement, but this required a mediator: Dannie N. Heineman. In addition, the Deutsche Bank should help him with the investigation of Director General Blüthgen of Glanzstoff AG. Of course, he knew that he was asking a great deal of Heineman, 'but compelling circumstances, driving me almost to despair, are forcing me to do so, and I can add in self-justification that I have always supported my friends too.'

In the circumstances, it would have been understandable if Heineman had chosen to avoid further discussion. The planned meeting at Maria Laach in September did not in fact take place. Adenauer was now completely at a loss. Once before when his mood was critical – in 1917, after the death of his wife Emma – he had begun a diary. Now, exactly six months after 13 March, he started another. It contains only seventeen lines, recording his feelings after his dismissal: 'I thought I would be home again within a short time.' Instead the worst six months of his life, 'and the most decisive for my innermost soul', had just passed. The future was entirely black: 'How things will look in Germany in six months, where I may be, where my family, I do not know. Everything is uncertain, everything is undecided.'

He had come to see Heineman as the only man who could help him. When the busy industrialist sent only brief replies because his plans were constantly changing, Adenauer urged him to come as soon as possible. Normally a man of enormous pride and reserve, he had begun to complain about his fate:

> I cannot ... describe in detail all the insults and injury done to me over the past seven months. I have lived this entire period separated from my family, in an uncertainty about my family and my future and in an inactivity which has become almost intolerable to me. My condition can best be revealed by telling you that since 13 March I have not been able to sleep without sleeping tablets, and even with sleeping tablets only for a few hours. I have almost reached the end of my powers of resistance. My poor wife is in a similar condition, she remains brave but she too is almost finished. Since I would be taken immediately into protective custody in Cologne, we must go to Bonn or Godesberg as soon as possible, without selling or renting the house in Cologne, to enable the family to come through this time together ...[47]

This frank description of his situation was the prelude to another request for help from Heineman, especially in the form of mediation with the board of the Deutsche Bank. Adenauer had now discovered that Director Brüning, who was increasingly the villain of the piece in his eyes, had damaged him in the settlement of 1931 to the tune of another 111,000 marks in favour of the bank.

Heineman recognised that Adenauer was at the end of his tether and made firm plans to come to Maria Laach. However, after a date had been fixed, Adenauer had to leave the monastery for Berlin to deal with aspects of the disciplinary action.[48] He had intended to be away for a week, but was forced to remain in the capital for a month. He stayed at the Maria

Victoria hospital in the Karlstraße, a fact with symbolic significance: bourgeois society had largely turned its back on him, and only the church and its many institutions could be trusted. Adenauer's meeting with Heineman finally took place on 15 December. His hope of employment in the business world was revived. Adenauer still thought he had something to offer SOFINA, 'on the basis of my whole connections and experience'.[49] He hoped to obtain work with GASFUREL, a company associated with SOFINA, apparently in the form of a trial employment for three years.[50]

In January 1934, he saw 'the first ray of light for me in ten months'.[51] Friedrich Spennrath, who had been a deputy in Cologne for four years and a member of the AEG board in Berlin since 1931, offered Adenauer's eldest son Konrad a training position upon completion for his studies at the bar. Together with *Geheimrat* Hermann Bücher of AEG, Spennrath was one of the few to help Adenauer during these years of oppression. Adenauer never forgot people who had stood by him: later, as Federal Chancellor, he often discussed issues with Spennrath and took account of his advice in all matters relating to Berlin.

Not even Bücher and Heineman could find a solution to Adenauer's economic difficulties.[52] The reason was a simple one, though deeply depressing for Adenauer: any company – especially a foreign one – that offered a leading position to a political outlaw would damage its own position in Germany.

From 1934 onwards, Adenauer spent only part of his time in Maria Laach, partly because Herwegen had been told officially that Adenauer's stay was damaging the monastery. During the first months of 1934 he stayed mainly in Berlin, in the Franciscan hospital in the Burggrafenstraße.[53] Once again, the reason for his visit was the disciplinary action. At the end of February, however, he noted with relief that the matter was going well.[54]

Meanwhile, Abbot Herwegen had understood the real meaning of Hitler's state. Adenauer noted sardonically that 'during my absence a true Götterdämmerung – openly admitted – had taken place.' However, this very fact had served to make his sanctuary even less safe than before.[55] Furthermore, he was now desperate to gather together his family. Since a return to Cologne was impossible, he debated whether to settle in Berlin or in Bonn. In a letter from Maria Laach on 4 March, he asked the advice of Dora Pferdmenges and weighed the advantages and disadvantages of living in Berlin and Bonn: 'Certainly Berlin has many advantages over Bonn, the local air is perhaps more irritating to the nerves, but on the other hand I fear that the ties that bind me to the Rhineland might be loosened by the great distance.'[56] At the time of writing he was about to leave for Berlin, and noted ironically: 'The anniversary of my "exodus from Cologne", 13 March, I will celebrate in Berlin.'

Adenauer initially decided to rent a house in Neubabelsberg, 'between Berlin and Potsdam behind Wannsee', and to move there with the family at the beginning of May.[57] The owners of the house, who had just emigrated, were glad to have tenants who were unconnected with the NSDAP. Moreover, Berlin seemed to offer more opportunities as he searched for work.

Before he left Maria Laach, Adenauer was visited by an emissary from Heineman with the aim of clarifying the issue of the Glanzstoff shares.[58] In fact, the visit helped to convince Adenauer that he would be lucky to save anything from the wreckage of his affairs; Blüthgen had been ruined as well as Adenauer.[59]

Upon his departure from Maria Laach, Adenauer expressed his gratitude with generous gifts, including a gramophone for Father Johannes.[60] For their part, the fathers in Maria Laach bade Adenauer farewell with great affection: 'You had almost become one of us.'[61] The reunion with his wife and children quickly lifted Adenauer's spirits. Moreover, some aspects of his position appeared to be improving: on 6 June 1934, the disciplinary action was officially brought to an end.

However, this period of relative calm was short-lived. Throughout the years between 1933 and 1945, Adenauer was on various Nazi black-lists. When the Röhm affair gave the regime the opportunity to pursue more of its opponents in 1934, Adenauer was among those arrested. Throughout 30 June, Berlin was swept by rumours of arrests and political murders. The former Chancellor, General Kurt von Schleicher, was shot dead along with his wife not far from the Adenauers' new home. Adenauer also discovered Erich Klausener, the leader of Catholic Action and a confidant of Vice Chancellor von Papen, had been murdered. In order to overcome his fear, he decided to take the advice of Candide: 'We must cultivate our garden!' This he did literally as well as metaphorically, since his work in the garden helped him to escape a sense of impotence and idleness during the years when he was forbidden to work. In his view, a man who was growing flowers, weeding and trimming shrubs was still doing something productive, and he was watering his flowers when the Gestapo arrested him. After the news of the last few hours, he must have feared the worst.

Fortunately Adenauer did not share the fate of many other opponents of the regime. Though he was fearful for his life during the journey and his interrogation, his only punishment was preventive detention along with twenty-nine others in Potsdam. Adenauer was probably saved by Hitler's order of 2 July for the immediate release of all those arrested. However, the incident did serve to shatter any remaining illusions about his safety under National Socialism. Until the Nazi seizure of power, he had never been able to take the movement and its eccentric Austrian Führer entirely seriously, but he had since discovered at first hand that the National Socialists were willing to ride roughshod over justice and the law. He now began to doubt his previous belief that all revolutions, sooner or later, give way to periods of normality such as had occurred in 1918/19. Even before the Röhm affair, he had been horrified at the brutality with which the Nazis subordinated state and society to their will. However, the events of 30 June 1934 made a greater impact on him than anything that had gone before. He now knew beyond doubt that the government of Germany had fallen into the hands of cold-blooded killers and that the regime was capable of any crime. For the next eleven years, he lived with the knowledge that his own life had little value.

His short detention – from the evening of 30 June until the evening of 2 July – also demonstrated another fact of life. Among his fellow-detainees were a number of generals. In captivity, these men were pathetic figures, as unimpressive as the governor of *Festung* Cologne during the revolution of November 1918. Later, when attempts were made to draw him into opposition groups on the grounds that opposition was growing in the Wehrmacht, Adenauer's experiences in prison provided a powerful argument against participation.[62]

He had no confidence that his position was safe. Shortly afterwards, probably in August 1934, Herwegen sent him a warning to this effect. Adenauer therefore decided to disappear from Berlin. At the beginning of September 1934 he went to the Black Forest, to the guest-house 'Zum Sternen' in Kappel, not far from Lenzkirch.[63] When he returned to Neubabelsberg in mid-September,[64] his financial position was probably even worse than before.

In the first weeks after the Röhm Murders, during his search for a hiding place, Adenauer held a discussion with his party colleague, Rudolf Amelunxen. Another native of Cologne, Amelunxen had forged a career in the Prussian administration during the Weimar Republic before being dismissed by the Nazis. The two men discussed the situation during a stroll through the woods, and Adenauer asked Amelunxen how long he thought the Nazis would stay in control. Amelunxen replied pessimistically: 'It could be another two years!' Assassins could not get near enough to 'these criminals'; the Reichswehr had accepted the Nazis; the professors had forgotten the need for courage; big businessmen were making piles of money; the church leaders were jockeying for positions; and Hindenburg was isolated in Gut Neudeck 'in the smallest concentration camp in Germany'. Adenauer was appalled: 'Two years! For God's sake! I'll be too old to get back in again! You are still young and will be able to take part in the essential work of reconstruction! But you must be sure to crack down hard.'[65] Thirteen years later, in fact, both of them 'got back in again', Amelunxen as the first minister-president of North Rhine-Westphalia and Adenauer as chairman of the opposition CDU caucus. The incident is informative: though Adenauer was now well aware of the deadly danger of National Socialism, he apparently hoped for a rapid change in the political situation even after the Röhm affair.

Following Adenauer's narrow escape, the rest of the year passed more calmly, but was not without incident. Bank director Brüning – formerly one of Adenauer's friends – was put on trial in Cologne for embezzlement. He sought to save his own skin by claiming that Adenauer had participated in his share speculations and received 55,000 marks of the profits. That was not true – and even if it had been true it would not have been illegal, since there was no law forbidding a mayor from dealing in shares in association with his bank. However, the plan was obviously to accuse Adenauer of an improper mixing of official and business matters. Adenauer was not called to give evidence in the main public proceedings, which gives rise to the suspicion that the court was bowing to the wishes of the Gau leadership, and preventing the former mayor from appearing in public in the city. Was the objective to interrogate him away from the public gaze and use this testimony to bring charges against him?

August Adenauer, himself a lawyer, reached an agreement with the chairman of the court to the effect that a provisional interrogation would be carried out in the home of cathedral prelate Hans Adenauer. The scene that followed was not short of melodrama (though melodramas have a habit of ending with the downfall of the hero). The meeting was held in a room overlooking the west doors of the cathedral. The judge and the State Prosecutor were followed into the room by Brüning, two legal constables and his defence counsel. Brüning's testimony amounted to an allegation of passive corruption on the part of Adenauer: he claimed that Adenauer had received the amount in question, ostensibly the profits of share speculation, and supposedly to cover a mortgage. In reality, however, the two had agreed that the payment was a reward for especially favourable treatment of the Deutsche Bank during the financial transactions involving the city of Cologne. This, of course, was exactly what Nazi agitators had been alleging for years.

At this critical time, Adenauer had two advantages. First, he had used the months in Maria Laach to collect his bank statements and examine the details of his dealings with the Deutsche Bank. Second, his experience as a lawyer had taught him how to harry an untruthful witness until he broke down and admitted the truth. The interrogation of Brüning lasted six hours. The climax came when Adenauer pointed to the crucifix on the wall and demanded solemnly that Brüning tell the truth, 'by all that you hold most holy'.[66] Brüning broke down and admitted that Adenauer was right. When counsel for the prosecution warned him that this was the crux of the entire proceedings and that he could only damage himself, Brüning insisted on withdrawing his accusation against Adenauer. The attempt by the prosecution to re-open the allegation of corruption against Adenauer had failed. He was able to return to Berlin with an easier mind.

At the beginning of 1935, Germany was more firmly under Nazi control than ever. Though Adenauer had always enjoyed his stays in Berlin, the city was becoming unattractive to him owing to the mass displays of enthusiasm for the Third Reich. In addition, he now recognised the futility of his hopes of starting afresh in private business. The family was homesick for the Rhineland and, with his rental agreement ending in April, Adenauer began to search for a new home. Though Cologne continued to be out of the question, Adenauer was inclined to look to other parts of the Rhine, to the Siebengebirge or to the left bank of the Rhine between Bad Godesberg to Rolandseck.

Since Godesberg was out of the question because of its excessive enthusiasm for National Socialism, Adenauer thought it more sensible to choose a home on the right bank of the Rhine, where he thought people were more reasonable. Houses there were also considerably cheaper, which was a vital factor for Adenauer in the straitened circumstances of spring 1935. The Cologne garden director Josef Giesen, one of Adenauer's few remaining loyal friends, helped in the search. Finally his son Max, the third lawyer in the family, found a house in Rhöndorf. It lay at the entry to the little valley, a couple of hundred metres from the forest cemetery where Adenauer was to be buried thirty-two years later.

The family did not suspect that they had at last found their second home. However, Adenauer wrote two cards to Dora Pferdmenges on 17 April 1935 – a few days before the move – during a visit to the German spring flower show in Berlin. As usual, the spectacle of the flower-beds in bloom left him 'completely overwhelmed by this beauty'. He told her that the move would begin on 25 April. Gussie was travelling to Cologne to settle matters there, though he would stay overnight in the Leonhardus Home in Godesberg before the move on 29/30 April: 'What will happen there, heaven knows. I have little courage left, the strength to resist is lacking. For that reason I do not feel well … The hour here amid the flowers was something like a sigh of relief.'[67]

Adenauer was delighted with the new house at 76 Löwenburger Strasse, and particularly its setting. Even before the move he sent a description to Heineman: 'Our future home is very small and modest, but it has a wonderful position. We hope that the beauties of nature will give rich consolation for everything we have been forced to give up.'[68] On 5 May he wrote enthusiastically to Dora Pferdmenges from 'climate health resort Rhöndorf': 'The wonderful spring compensates us all for the past weeks. We are fairly well installed, there is much in the house we must get used to, but we are rooted in nature and that is frankly enchanting.'[69]

There were enough rooms in the house to accommodate the large family, while the rent of 110 marks per month corresponded to the family's financial difficulties; Adenauer was still very short of money. However, it was soon apparent that the house was far from ideal despite the beauty of the setting. It lay close to Rhöndorf's brook, and was run down, shady and damp; before long, the ill-health of the smaller children was an additional source of worry.[70] Nevertheless, the local people were friendly, and it began to appear that the family might at last find peace.

Less than three months after the move, however, a new problem arose. Though the occasion itself was risible, its consequences were potentially highly damaging. When Adenauer went to Rhöndorf, the Gestapo in Potsdam had handed him over for further discreet observation to the Gestapo of the Cologne administrative area. However, it was the Gau leadership rather than the local Gestapo that moved into action against him at the end of July. The letter from the National Socialist Kreisleiter of Siegburg to the head of the Siegburg district was a classic example of petty-minded tyranny, and deserves to be quoted, at least in part:

> The Honnef local group informs me that a short time ago the following incident took place in Rhöndorf: on the occasion of the feast-day, the *Junggesellen-Schützen-Verein* [marksmen's association] serenaded the former mayor, Adenauer, who had been living in Rhöndorf for a short time. In honour of Adenauer these Junggesellen performed a flag ceremony and the fire brigade band played too. For a finale this band played the Badenweiler march. As the *Ortsgruppe* discovered, Adenauer contributed a cash payment of 80 marks and 100 bottles of wine to the occasion. The marksmen's association is composed almost exclusively of people who are hostile to National Socialism. The same is the case with the fire-brigade band, this can hardly ever be obtained for National Socialist gatherings. Yesterday I informed the Gauleiter and the Regierungspräsident of this case. The Gauleiter requests the disbanding of this association. I therefore request you to arrange that immediately.'[71]

The situation was farcical, but an investigation by the local police sergeant, a sensible man by the name of Butt, quickly revealed the truth. The flag ceremony was a local custom among the better-off citizens, and the marksmen's association had asked beforehand whether it was acceptable. Adenauer had hesitated and pointed out that he was living in seclusion. In the end he had agreed for his children's sake, on the grounds that they ought to be allowed a little amusement. With due – but, as it turned out, insufficient – caution, he had listed himself as 'N.N.' in the records. The smallest contribution was five marks; he had paid eight and had offered a couple of glasses of wine.[72]

Another inquiry produced the same result:[73] There had been no political demonstration; the fire-brigade band had only played the Führer's favourite Badenweiler march because it could perform this piece without music; there had been no excessive expense (an allegation which was preposterous anyway, given the combination of Adenauer's legendary parsimony and straitened circumstances). Though the head of the district accepted the findings, the Gauleiter applied to the Regierungspräsident for the expulsion of Adenauer from the administrative area of Cologne. This was accomplished by decree of 10 August.[74]

Adenauer then indirectly contacted the Regierungspräsident of Cologne, Rudolf Diels, to tell him about the affair.[75] Diels had built up the Gestapo for Göring, thereby helping to secure the regime's hold on power during the first decisive months, but he had also attempted to curb the worst excesses of the SA. Despite his own high nominal SS rank, he had been defeated in the power struggle with the SS, and shunted off to Cologne. Diels was a playboy, a cynic of the first water and an opportunist, but he was no fool. When he heard the full story from Adenauer's brother, he promptly offered him a lecture on wise political conduct under a totalitarian dictatorship. He indicated that, even though the matter had been cleared up, the Gauleiter wanted a victim and Berlin would support the Gauleiter. He, Diels, would be laughed at if he tried to stop it. In fact, it might not be possible to help Adenauer anyway. After all, he had moved to the part of the district which contained two Leader Training Schools housing 'the wildest men in the party'.

In the opinion of Diels, Adenauer should have told the party what he was doing and given some assurances of his good behaviour. He followed this with some good advice on the Clive affair: it would be best if Adenauer obtained an official letter from the Foreign Ministry to help ensure that British wishes were respected and he was not harmed. It would be even better if this went through Ribbentrop. When August Adenauer argued that his brother should be allowed his rights, Diels was derisive. His advice was to wait, let tempers cool, then perhaps send an application to the Gauleiter. His expulsion from the district would only be temporary. The whole incident, in fact, was a fairly typical example of life in the Third Reich during the summer of 1935.

Adenauer was again separated from his family. Once more he sought sanctuary in Maria Laach, this time for a month, before moving to the Kurhaus St Elisabeth in the Black Forest resort of Neustadt. Finally, he spent ten long months in the Pax rest home for Catholic priests in Unkel, eight kilometres from Rhöndorf. Without the church and its monasteries, rest homes and hospitals, he would have had nowhere to go. Though Diels had regarded the expulsion with cynical detachment, knowing that it would be withdrawn after a few months, it brought Adenauer to the brink of despair. However, his family visited him frequently – his son Paul cycled to Unkel every day. He was still depressed by the isolation. At fifty-nine, Adenauer was no longer young. His nerves had been shattered by the tension of the last eighteen months, and he was constantly troubled by insomnia. Moreover, his financial worries had not been solved. By autumn 1935 it appeared that the new masters of Germany had succeeded in breaking this opponent, even without legal proceedings, by means of a series of petty persecutions.

Thirty years later, Adenauer could still recall the hopelessness he had felt in the autumn of 1935. Nevertheless, even during these months he never gave up or seriously contemplated suicide. One consolation was the work of Joseph Conrad. The figure of the Captain in the novel

Typhoon helped him to keep up his courage.[76] Even more important, almost before putting down roots in his temporary home in Löwenburg-erstrasse, he returned to the inventions that he had abandoned in 1908 when his official duties had become pressing. From May 1935, Adenauer carried on a lively correspondence on the subject with his few remaining friends. Fritz Spennrath of AEG in Berlin was bombarded with letters and telegrams and eventually lured to Rhöndorf to examine the industrial practicability of Adenauer's schemes. Adenauer tried to revive his old project of a reaction steam machine; his loyalty to it was to prove remarkably resistant to sceptical scientific analysis.

For three years, Adenauer devoted his attention to his 'Procedure and Installation for the Prevention of the Pollution of the Air by Emissions, Soot etc. from Fireplaces'. Aiming at the 'Removal of the Fog from the Big Cities', he proposed to 'close the chimneys overhead, connecting them to the sewage system below'.[77] In September 1935, he corresponded with the Schlitter Company of Cologne on the technical aspects of his idea. Moreover, no lesser a man than the founder and president of the Berlin Hochschule für Politik, Ernst Jäckh, who had left Germany for the New Commonwealth Institute in London, tried to help him with the patents in Britain. In earlier years, Adenauer had been impressed by his impeccable treatment at the hands of the Royal Patent Office in London. At the height of the First World War – on 26 June 1918 – it had issued patent number 131,402, entitled 'Improvements in the Composition and Manufacture of Sausage Meat and the Like', in his name. Jäckh, who had met the mayor during his involvement with the great Cologne Werkbund exhibition on 'The New Era', admired Adenauer greatly. It was with some distress that he informed him, on 1 May 1937, that he had received the following polite rejection from the Welsh mining company he had contacted: 'I am afraid his method is somewhat revolutionary and might cause very great inconvenience.'[78] To console Adenauer, Jäckh sent warm greetings from Sir Sidney Clive, who asked after Adenauer whenever they met.

Adenauer worked with even more dedication on another of his ideas, which was connected with his love of gardens. He loathed all plant-eating beetles and bugs, and became fascinated by the idea of destroying them, their larvae and insect eggs by using electric current. His basic idea was as follows: 'The effect of the electric current on the animal organism is different to the effect on the organism of plants. The method is based on this difference in the effect. The electric current would kill the animal organism without inflicting appreciable damage to that of the plant.'[79] This, he thought, could be achieved by a live brush.

He followed up this idea by using his customary methods. First, he contacted specialists – Josef Giesen in Cologne and Fritz Spennrath in Berlin, who mobilised AEG experts on his behalf. Next, Dr Rülf, who had worked for Adenauer between 1905 and 1908, was recalled to ser-

vice. Rülf was already under threat from the regime because, like another
of Adenauer's former patent agents, Julius Ephraim, he was Jewish. Nevertheless – and it was now 19 September 1935 – he refused to believe that
problems might arise if he made a patent application. Nor did Rülf understand why Adenauer wanted to apply for the patent in the name of his son
Max: after all, Konrad Adenauer was the inventor![80]

Adenauer used the help of these experts to define his ideas more precisely. He prepared practical trials, placed orders for appropriate equipment, and searched for a trustworthy physics student to carry out the
experiments on the insects. He was dismissive of objections from the specialists when Spennrath passed these on to him, especially those who
pointed out that significantly greater electric shocks were necessary to
kill small insects than to kill larger ones: 'In my view the formula constructed by Herr Dozler is incorrect. If the formula were right, then, for
example, a four to five times higher voltage would have to be applied to
kill an infant than to kill a grown person.'[81] Gradually he did begin to
wonder whether the profitability of this invention could be proved. If not,
industry – he was thinking of AEG – would never be persuaded of its
merits. The invention proved technically difficult and the Reichspatentamt was sceptical. Nevertheless, Adenauer continued to work on it until
almost the end of the war; the correspondence only petered out in 1945.

His relatives were secretly amused by this zeal for invention, which
they dismissed as a form of occupational therapy. Adenauer himself,
however, was deadly serious, as he was with all his projects. He may also
have hoped that a successful patent would earn him money. His active
brain was always producing new schemes. Once, when travelling at night
with Josef Giesen on some business connected with his electric brush, he
was disturbed by the constant dazzle of oncoming headlights; this immediately set him thinking of ways to instal a device 'for protection of dri-
vers, esp. of motor cars, against the dazzle of the headlights of oncoming
vehicles without impairment of the view of their own lane'.[82] The idea
kept him busy until the outbreak of war.

Occasionally Adenauer was willing to question his own abilities,
especially in technical matters and the natural sciences. On 10 July
1936, he wrote to Dr Vieth of E. Leyboldt's Nachfolger A.G., which
manufactured technical equipment, conceding that 'for a layman such as
myself it is very difficult to find one's way around in this area ...'[83]
However, in February 1938 he wrote to Dr Thiess of Aachen, with
whom he had been brought into contact by his son-in-law Reiners and
who was to help him in the future: 'Today I would like to bother you
with the so-called locomotive affair. I have deliberately kept it to myself
for a time. But the result of my abstinence is a renewed strength of conviction, and I believe that I can also refute your objections, which I have
now fully understood.'[84]

This description of Adenauer's scientific schemes has two main purposes. First, it helps to explain exactly how Adenauer spent his time in the Third Reich: he was in contact with other inventors and took part in entirely unpolitical activities. The suspicion that this was done as camouflage can be dismissed. In truth, practical tasks fascinated him. When he was prevented from carrying on his career in municipal government, he returned to old schemes that had fascinated him even before he became a great mayor.

Secondly, these incidents reveal that, even at the lowest point in his life, Adenauer continued to be resolute, inventive and tenacious. If there were objections to his ideas, he sought to refute them. Whenever they could no longer be ignored, he adjusted his schemes, tried to find solutions, made modifications. If legal remedies were available, he used them -for example by making repeated requests for extensions of the time-limit to the Reichspatentamt. To the experienced technicians in this office, Adenauer was an example of a common type: an eccentric inventor who regarded bureaucrats as his natural opponents and was almost deaf to their objections. This was indeed a part of Adenauer's personality and came to light on many other occasions. Yet whatever the actual quality of these inventions, the work certainly helped him to survive the difficult years between 1935 and 1937.

During this period, he was also visited by a few old acquaintances from Cologne, Bonn and Bad Godesberg. These loyal friends spent time with him and took him on car trips, which was especially important between 1933 and 1944 since Adenauer did not drive. One of these men was Paul Franken, who was to become director of the Bundeszentrale für Politische Bildung (Federal Centre for Political Education) after the war. On Adenauer's sixtieth birthday on 5 January 1936, of which Franken was unaware, Adenauer, his wife, and his daughter Ria planned a car journey through Niederlahnstein and the Mosel Valley to Cochem, where he had reserved a table for four in a restaurant. The party then drove to see Abbot Herwegen in Maria Laach; by now Herwegen himself had been on the Nazi black-list for some time, and had even spent some months in hiding. Adenauer mused on whether he, Adenauer, would live to celebrate his seventieth or even seventy-fifth birthday (nobody even considered an eightieth or a ninetieth).[85]

On the surface, the year 1936 was relatively quiet for Adenauer. In February he spent two weeks in Berlin, where Professor von Bergmann conducted a series of tests in the Franciscan hospital before concluding that the alarming symptoms he had detected were caused by a nervous complaint.[86] At the beginning of August 1936, his banishment from the Cologne administrative area was lifted and the family were able to travel to stay with the Zinssers in Tübingen. Another ray of hope lay in the fact that the children were now approaching the completion of their education: the eldest son was working for the AEG in Oslo; Max Adenauer was preparing for his second state examinations; his daughter Ria, who had also spent some time abroad, was preparing to take her examinations as an interpreter.[87] Clearly, the family was working on the principle that all the children should be able to make their way abroad if necessary.

In the meantime, Adenauer had continued his negotiations with the city of Cologne. At last Gauleiter Grohé signalled his willingness to reach an agreement as mayor Riesen left the city. Riesen's successor was a young lawyer aged thirty-two, Dr Karl Georg Schmidt, a representative of the NSDAP's economic wing and a relatively decent individual. Schmidt had previously served as the general manager of the Cologne Chamber of Commerce and Industry, the president of which, Kurt von Schröder, was to claim after 1945 that he had been able to plead Adenauer's case.

By the summer of 1937, the worst was over for Adenauer and the settlement with the city was finally arranged. He still suffered substantial damages, as the city took over the house in Max-Bruch-Straße at a knock-down price. However, the city was also prepared to repay the earnings that had been unlawfully withheld: in October 1937 Adenauer received the sum of 153,886.63 marks.

At a personal, as well as an official level, some gestures of accommodation were made. The final negotiations were carried out in person between Adenauer and the National Socialist mayor, Schmidt, on the relatively neutral territory of the town hall in Bonn. Once the negotiations were completed, the two men fell into conversation. Adenauer, whose whole concern in these years was for the future of his family, did not hide his anxiety that his sons in particular might suffer because they bore his name. Schmidt, who was young enough to have been Adenauer's son himself, assured him that if ever problems arose on that score, he would deal with them in person. (In fact, he died only four years later. By the time Adenauer's son Max became *Oberstadtdirektor* of Cologne in 1953, the family no longer needed the toleration or personal protection of Nazi leaders.)

Following the settlement of 1937, Adenauer's future was relatively secure. Even before it was finalised, he had managed to purchase the land on which the Rhöndorf house was built. He then became determined to improve it and make it a healthy place to live, a task which called on his creative imagination and his planning skills for several months. The plans for the property were designed by his brother-in-law, Ernst Zinsser, a young engineering graduate. The house was ready for occupation shortly before Christmas 1937. Thirty years later it had become a place of pilgrimage for hundreds of thousands of visitors, almost a German Mount Vernon. Adenauer had been far from certain that the regime would allow him to live there quietly. At first, however, this seemed likely to be his fate: history had apparently forgotten him.

A Pensioner in Rhöndorf

On the surface, the last years of peace and the war years up until 1944 formed one of the quietest periods in Adenauer's busy life. In Rhöndorf, he was largely isolated from events. As always, his day was carefully organised, because he could not have survived without a fixed schedule. Since he continued to have difficulty sleeping, he was in the habit of rising early to go into the garden, returning to take breakfast with the family before the children left for school. After their departure he would read the papers and work in the garden until lunch. In the afternoons he would rest before spending time with the children, walking in the Siebengebirge hills, and working on his inventions. In the evenings he liked to listen to music on the wireless and to read.

In effect, he was living the life of a pensioner like many thousands of others. On 20 November 1941 he described the course of a typical day in one of his regular letters to his son Paul, who had been doing Labour Service on the island of Sylt since October:

> This evening the pouring rain has made the ground very wet again. I have had the apple tree on the hill cut down, it was taking away too much sun and not providing anything. Its removal has altered the whole upper part of the rock garden. It has become very beautiful, it now has a more planned look, before it looked more like a conglomeration of beds. There is much more space for plants than previously, but I have enough plants because everything has grown too thick. Yesterday the fruit trees arrived from Dahs as well. Tomorrow or on Monday the roses etc. will come from Boehm and I will have to plant them by myself, but that can be done. This week I have a great deal to do, because by Saturday I have to get my technical ideas onto paper in some detail, with diagrams, there will probably be thirty-five typewritten pages. On Saturday young Thiess is coming from Aachen to talk the matter through with me to clarify everything. Then he will take my designs to his father in Aachen for him to examine them as well. I will probably have to write until late in the evening, it is not easy. Despite the two short periods of frost we had, there are still many flowers in the garden, some roses, chrysanthemums, violets, pansies and especially the lovely Christmas roses. You are often in my mind when I am in the garden. I hope that we will soon spend a beautiful and peaceful time together again ...

Photographs dating from this period show a tanned and resilient man who looks younger than his years. Adenauer appeared very different from the man who had been persecuted between 1933 and 1937 and especially during his stay in Maria Laach, when he had looked emaciated and drawn.

Suffering can destroy and degrade, but it can also ennoble, as a photograph taken in Neubabelsberg reveals. This shows Adenauer wearing his hat and winter coat, his expression serious and distant, with no trace of the waggishness and amusement of his successful years in the 1920s.

Notes for this section begin on page 714.

As Chancellor, Adenauer was noted for the preoccupied and thoughtful appearance that comes through for the first time in photographs dating from this period. Once he was settled in Rhöndorf, his air of confidence and his dignity increased. One photograph from this period shows him in conversation with the building supervisor in his half-finished house, with the Rhöndorf tower in the background. With the house under construction and the garden to be planned and completed, Adenauer was a man of substance again – even if only a pensioned mayor. As always, he was restored and rejuvenated as soon as he had work to do.

His most important concern was now his family. For the first and only time in a life that lasted over ninety years, Adenauer had time to spare for his wife and children, his sons and daughters-in-law, and eventually his grandchildren. The children from his first marriage had left the parental home. His oldest son Konrad worked for AEG in Norway for a time; at the beginning of 1937 Max Adenauer obtained a scholarship at Georgetown University in Washington; Ria had passed her translator's exam in Heidelberg and married soon afterwards. Adenauer was now able to practise his pedagogic skills on the four children from his marriage to Gussie, without interference from business affairs. The unity and solidarity of the family continued to be impressive: in particular, during the war, when the bombings began, its members sought shelter and support in the house at Rhöndorf. Though Adenauer was the *pater familias* he had always been, he began to relax once the problems of the early 1930s were behind him.

Outside of the family network, he had little social contact with Cologne and its people. Adenauer was disillusioned to discover that the majority of his old friends continued to avoid him even after his affairs had been settled. Most of those who came to see him were people who were hostile to the new regime or, like Ella and Benedikt Schmittmann, were also among its victims.

The Adenauers built up a new circle of friends and acquaintances in the Bonn area, many of them from the university. Most were families whose Catholic faith led them to reject National Socialism, and whose fears had been confirmed by the policies of the regime. There was little need for words to describe their sentiments; though they would share the latest jokes about Göring, they avoided constant discussions of politics and preferred to concentrate on whatever areas of cultural life remained relatively free of Nazi influence. For example, the art historian Josef Busley and his family were welcome visitors, and in 1937 the families travelled together to see works of art in southern Germany.

During these years, Adenauer was also close to Joseph Vollmar, a dentist in Bonn with whom he had become acquainted via Vollmar's brother in Maria Laach. In 1938 the Vollmars and Adenauers holidayed together in Chandolin. Later, in September 1944, when Adenauer fled from Hohenlind hospital to escape the Gestapo, he spent the night at Vollmar's house. His disparate circle of friends in Bonn also included the legal adviser to the Trade Corporation, Fritz Schliebusch. Some friendships also developed with inhabitants of Rhöndorf itself, as with the Schlüter family after 1941.

This new network of human contacts helped Adenauer to withstand his years of political isolation. In some cases, they developed a significance that outlasted the Third Reich; the writer Maria Schlüter-Hermkes, for example, had some influence on Adenauer's thoughts for a programme for the new CDU in autumn 1945. However, these contacts had no political significance at the time. As a rule, everyday life under the swastika, even among those who were hostile to the regime, was extremely cautious and tentative. For many, it never took a more radical form than conversations in small circles of like-minded individuals, cautious non-conformism, the retreat to as yet unpoliticised niches of the totalitarian state.

Nevertheless, Adenauer's attitude towards genuine resistance groups is clearly of political significance. Resistance means more than an inward hostility to the regime, and is not identical to the persecution and insults to which Adenauer himself had been subjected. Under the National Socialists, resistance could take many forms: the systematic discussion of political, economic and social plans for reconstruction after the fall of the Third Reich; the building of cells within the state apparatus; organised support of the persecuted, especially Jews; the development of a conspiratorial network with the aim of mounting a coup against Hitler; the attempt to make contacts abroad; actual agitation using home-produced leaflets and newspapers smuggled in from abroad. One kind of pre-resistance activity took the form of maintaining links with like-minded friends who had been dismissed, and often temporarily imprisoned, in 1933.

In the early days of the Nazi era, Adenauer was in contact with Catholic opponents of Hitler. At this stage the police apparatus of the Third Reich was not yet fully operational, and large numbers of people were convinced that Hitler's regime would soon be brought down by its own incompetence. A significant group of former members of the Centre Party therefore began to meet in Bonn. The most respected of these was the former Reich Chancellor, Wilhelm Marx, who was then (according to a slightly malicious comment by Rudolf Amelunxen) 'engaged on the careful styling of his memoirs ...though these unfortunately proved unfit for later publication.'[1]

Another significant individual was Andreas Hermes, who had been Reich Minister of Nutrition and Reich Finance Minister during the 1920s. Hermes was now living in Bad Godesberg and making plans for a People's Party which would include large sections of the political left. His circle included Professor Albert Lauscher, former chairman of the Prussian Centre Party, and – until his emigration in 1934 – the journalist

Waldemar Gurian, who later became a respected political scientist at Notre Dame University in the United States. One of the meeting places of this group was the home of Rudolf Amelunxen in Plittersdorf. Professor Benedikt Schmittmann and his wife Ella, long-standing friends of Adenauer, were also in contact with the group. Like Adenauer, they had been harshly treated by the Nazis: an SA gang had attacked them in their home on 1 May 1933 and taken them into 'protective custody' on an open truck for the entertainment of the Cologne mob. Though Schmittmann was released after six weeks, he had lost his professorship, and his pro-federalist journal *Heimat und Volk* was banned.

The Bonn-Bad Godesberg circle also included Wilhelm Farwick of Aachen and Johannes Gronowski, former Oberpräsident of Westphalia. Adenauer was in contact with the group in its early stages; for example, after the Röhm putsch he had found a temporary hiding place with Amelunxen. However, most members of the circle were quickly placed under observation by the Gestapo. As the regime strengthened its grip on power, greater caution became essential. Once Adenauer made Rhöndorf his permanent home in 1935, he took great care to avoid any activity that could have been interpreted as conspiratorial. The affair of the flag ceremony had proved that one could not be too careful.

Nevertheless, from time to time Adenauer was in touch, either directly or indirectly, with the Catholic 'resistance'. His intermediary was a young man of thirty-three named Paul Franken, who was the leader of the KV – the Kartellverband der Katholischen Studentenvereine in Deutschland (Confederation of Catholic Student Associations of Germany) until it was forcibly disbanded in 1936. Ideologically, Franken was close to the Christian-socialist wing of the Centre Party associated with Joseph Joos, Bernhard Letterhaus and Heinrich Körner. After the Nazi seizure of power, in the Rhineland and beyond, he had attempted to organise a network of contacts between opposition Centre circles. Franken also helped to write opposition documents and was taken into 'protective custody' from 1937 until 1939. After his release, like the later co-founder and chairman of the CSU, Josef Müller, Franken found sanctuary with the *Abwehr* (the military intelligence) run by Admiral Canaris. He was sent to Rome in its service, where he had dealings with the Vatican and also established discreet contacts with British and U.S. diplomats. When the Gestapo discovered his activities, Franken managed to go into hiding and survived the war.

Franken took the trouble to look after Adenauer at a time when many old acquaintances had turned away. Among other services, he offered to take Adenauer on various excursions in his car. In 1935 and 1936 in particular, Franken also tried to bring Adenauer into contact with a number of leading figures in the emerging Catholic resistance. However, Adenauer remained generally cautious and was only willing to receive information from Franken. From time to time he was prepared to go further. On one occasion, he agreed to a public rendezvous with Joseph Joos, Bernhard Letterhaus and Professor Alois Dempf, who agreed to meet for Sunday morning coffee at Haus Ernich. (Later, as Federal Chancellor he was often the guest of the French ambassador there.) This meeting, probably in 1935, served only to remind him of the need for extreme caution. On this particular Sunday, a small party of women from the old Centre Party in the Reichstag, including the later Bundestag deputy Helene Wessel, had also decided to meet there. Since the place was packed with disaffected Catholic politicians, there was great relief when the coffee party came to an end.

In the summer of 1936, Franken arranged a meeting between Adenauer and Jakob Kaiser. It was an event which was also to influence the course of developments after 1945, when the two men pursued very different policies within the CDU. Adenauer regarded Kaiser as a third-rate figure. They had become acquainted during the Weimar Republic, when Kaiser had spent nine years as regional manager of the Christian trade unions in western Germany. After the seizure of power he had reached an agreement with the National Socialist Deutsche Arbeitsfront (German Labour Front) to represent the interests of the Christian unions within it. Kaiser was thus forced to play a part in the *Gleichschaltung* (synchronisation) of his old association. However, he also used the opportunity to travel throughout the country on a legal basis and to make contact with his old colleagues in order to bring together a resistance network. In 1936, following mediation by the former mayor of Düsseldorf, Robert Lehr, the group associated with Kaiser and Heinrich Körner made contact with two senior members of the German armed forces. These officers, Colonel-General Kurt von Hammerstein-Equord and Colonel-General Werner von Fritsch, were increasingly alarmed at the risky foreign policy being pursued by Hitler, and in particular the re-militarisation of the Rhineland and German intervention in the Spanish Civil War. Though this contact itself remained without concrete results, it formed the background to the meeting between Kaiser and Adenauer.

In the summer of 1936, Franken, Kaiser and Körner came on foot to Rhöndorf, to which Adenauer had recently returned after his temporary exile. While Franken and Körner were given wine by Frau Adenauer, Adenauer and Kaiser withdrew for a discussion lasting three hours. Its exact details have never been made public. From later reports by Frau Kaiser-Nebgen and Paul Franken, however, we know that Kaiser gave Adenauer a survey of the resistance network in Germany and mentioned the newly-established links with the generals. Kaiser was convinced that change could only be effected with the help of the military leadership. Decades later he remembered Adenauer's reaction: 'Have you ever seen a general with an intelligent face?'[2] Adenauer did not believe that the Wehrmacht would bring Hitler down, though both he and Kaiser realised that Hitler's policy was leading to a world war and would end in catastrophe.

Kaiser did not succeed in gaining Adenauer's agreement to work with him and his colleagues. When the three visitors returned to Oberdollendorf, Kaiser would offer only a brief summary of his conversation with Adenauer: 'He cannot be counted on.'[3] In 1943/44, Kaiser again attempted to approach Adenauer through Franken, but Adenauer refused to meet him. We do not know whether Adenauer's refusal was influenced by Kaiser's strong nationalism and his admiration for things Prussian. According to Franken, Kaiser the Franconian Catholic, was 'of all the Bavarians I have known, the one who had become most Prussian'.

Equally unfruitful was a meeting that Franken arranged between Adenauer and Adam Stegerwald. Furthermore, when Andreas Hermes attempted to establish links with Adenauer in 1939, through the old Centre Party leader Wilhelm Elfes, Adenauer turned him away almost rudely.[4] Still, he did not entirely avoid semi-conspiratorial contacts. George N. Shuster, who was to become the U.S. commissioner in Bavaria after the war, recalled a visit to Adenauer's home in 1938 in the company of two members of a Cologne resistance group, when he had been forced to creep through the bushes to the house. He and Adenauer had held secret talks in the middle of the night. Though these talks centered mostly on the many-facetted aspects of Rhenish separatism, Shuster believed that – albeit with the utmost caution – Adenauer was somehow involved with the resistance.[5]

When it became clear that the Third Reich could no longer be brought down from within, Adenauer, in common with many German opponents of Hitler, began to look to the outside world for salvation. He was therefore dismayed by the appeasement policy of the Western Powers. Though no contemporary sources are available, his later references to Hitler's re-militarisation of the Rhineland in spring 1936 were unequivocal: 'At that time I had been expelled from my place of residence, from the Cologne administrative area, and was in Unkel. Until five o'clock in the afternoon I waited and waited for the French army to march in as a response. When nothing had happened by five o'clock, I said to myself that Europe was lost!'[6] Instead of opposing Hitler, the statesmen and diplomats of the Western democracies had decided to pay tribute to him at the Berlin Olympics. As Federal Chancellor, whenever he was lectured by foreign visitors about the collective responsibility of the Germans, Adenauer was quick to point out the responsibility of their own governments for Hitler's success.

Franken and Körner did not abandon their efforts. At the end of December 1942, in separate discussions, they again sought to win Adenauer's support for their plans. However, he strongly advised against them and refused to become involved. By now it was obvious to the initiated that the leading figure in the conservative resistance was Carl Goerdeler, the former mayor of Leipzig. Adenauer, who knew of

Goerdeler, regarded his notorious talkativeness as a very great danger; in autumn 1943 he threatened not to speak to Franken again if Franken met Goerdeler and Kaiser in Cologne. On the other hand, Adenauer never severed his links with Franken and Körner, meeting both in autumn 1943 and Körner alone in 1944. These meetings took place in conspiratorial circumstances at the surgery of Josef Vollmar in Bonn. According to Adenauer's own brief description, Körner had approached him on behalf of Kaiser, but 'I refused. I wanted nothing to do with it.'[7]

The picture is clear. Adenauer did have some contact with the resistance through a small number of individuals whose discretion he trusted. However, he regarded the activities of Goerdeler and the officers' conspiracy as exceptionally dangerous. Owing to the pivotal position occupied by his former colleague in Leipzig, Adenauer was absolutely unwilling to become involved. He was appalled by the fact that Goerdeler and Kaiser had discussed their plans to overthrow Hitler with more than one hundred people, thus ensuring that it could not possibly remain secret. This appeared to him to be almost criminal carelessness. Moreover, in 1943 he told Franz Thedieck, who was to become state secretary for All-German Affairs after 1945, that German generals could only command and obey; they had neither the will nor the talent for a putsch.[8]

In reality, Adenauer was given no freedom of manoeuvre that would have allowed him to take a significant part in resistance activities. He knew that he was being watched. Unlike many of the conspirators, he had no official position, nor even a private profession to give him a measure of independence. In his situation, conspiracies would be unproductive and could only bring him into personal danger. For his family's sake he felt to have a duty to be extremely cautious about secret discussions or activities, especially since he was not convinced that they would ever bear fruit. The most he could have done would have been to agree to the inclusion of his name on some lists drawn up by the conspirators for the government of Germany after a successful coup. Even this seemed unwise: if the conspiracy failed, as was likely, it would have meant certain death; if, on the other hand, the coup had succeeded, Adenauer knew that he would be needed whether he was on the list or not. In these circumstances it seemed wiser to keep out of it altogether.

Conditions convinced him that only a complete catastrophe would bring the criminal regime down, probably as a result of the war. He had great respect for the courage of the resistance members, but rather less for their wisdom. It could be argued that his cold realism was justified by the tragic history of the resistance in 1944. If Adenauer's name had been found on any of the lists that fell into the hands of the Gestapo after the 20 July, he would probably have been executed. Though Adenauer was obviously persecuted by the regime, his circumspection confined him only to the periphery of the resistance against Nazism.

The theme of 'Adenauer and the German resistance' played no role in the political debate after 1945. There were two main reasons for this. First, Adenauer did not wish to publicise his grave doubts about the activities of Goerdeler and the military resistance. Many of these men had sacrificed their lives in the struggle against Nazism, and some of the survivors – Jakob Kaiser, Andreas Hermes, Eugen Gerstenmaier, Theodor Steltzer, Otto Lenz – had become his party colleagues. Second, these former members of the conservative resistance had no desire to call public attention to the critical nature of Adenauer's support. After the 20 July and the trials that followed, they had been forced to admit that Adenauer had been right to doubt both their chances of success and the conspiratorial abilities of Goerdeler. Adenauer was already convinced that only his great caution had enabled him to avoid imprisonment, and possibly even death, even at the beginning of the war. He was heard to say that it had been 'a miracle of God' that he had survived at all.[9]

Though the years of retirement in Rhöndorf were far from idyllic, Adenauer did enjoy periods of relative relaxation. At the beginning of 1938, for example, he made a short trip to Brussels, where he met Dannie Heineman. Later, at exactly the time of greatest international tension, in 1938 and in 1939, he made two journeys to Switzerland. The first – from 8 July until the end of August 1938 – took him, with his wife, to Chandolin. The Swiss consul-general in Cologne, Franz-Rudolph von Weiss, one of his few remaining friends from better days, had arranged the journey for him. Adenauer was delighted: 'Chandolin is wonderful and fantastic, as ever. Everything here is filled with memories for us.'[10] They also travelled to Lake Geneva to meet Dannie N. Heineman and spent a 'lovely carefree day' with him.[11] When the world crisis reached its climax, however, Adenauer was already back in Rhöndorf.

This was not the case in 1939, when the storm broke in the middle of his holiday. Before he left, he had advised his friends Ella and Benedikt Schmittmann to go abroad as quickly as possible if war came.[12] He was convinced that there would be a spate of arrests if war broke out; it would therefore be better for those known to be hostile to the regime to be out of reach for a few days. The Adenauers left for Switzerland on 8 July and did not return, via Braganza, until 7 September 1939, the seventh day of war. Their children in Rhöndorf, who did not know where their parents were staying, had been deeply concerned for their safety. In fact the couple had started their holiday in Chandolin, but had been unable to meet Dannie N. Heineman there because of his determination to monitor the crisis from his base in Brussels.[13] Instead, he sent Adenauer 500 Swiss francs to enable him to extend his stay.[14] When war broke out, the Adenauers were in the Kurhaus Schinznach near Olten. Even if they had wished to do so, they could not have returned home immediately; the Swiss federal railway was reserved almost exclusively for domestic troop transports for eight days. When Adenauer finally got back to Rhöndorf, he discovered that Benedikt Schmittmann had been arrested, as he had predicted, on 1 September. Shortly afterwards, he heard that Schmittman had been killed in Oranienburg concentration camp. It appeared that Adenauer, however, had been removed from the regime's blacklist.

The family in Rhöndorf now began to share the wartime experience of millions of Germans. Their sons were conscripted one by one: Max took part in the campaign in France and was wounded. According to accounts from his contacts in those days, Adenauer was already certain – even in the weeks of euphoria after the defeat of France in June 1940 – that the war would end in catastrophe.

Towards the end of the 1950s, Adenauer recounted what he regarded as a typical tale of the 'Nazi mania' that had gripped his country during these years. At the beginning of 1939 he had met General Hans von Kluge, one of the cleverest men in the army leadership, at a reception in Düsseldorf. He had told von Kluge that the coming war would bring the downfall of Germany. Kluge had apparently responded by saying that the mistakes of the First World War would not be repeated, and that instead Germany would overrun its enemies one by one. When he heard this, Adenauer had asked whether von Kluge really believed that these nations would stand aside until all the others had been defeated. He then pointed out the enormous levels of industrial production in the United States, one of Germany's potential enemies. Kluge replied that he too had always been afraid of this, but that the Führer had entrusted Krupp with the task of constructing a cross-country vehicle. Krupp needed two years before it could put such a model into mass production. The Americans would not be able to achieve the same results in less time, and by then the war would be over.[15]

From the outset, Adenauer was deeply sceptical about the course of the war. He had seen the consequences of an intense and excessive war effort once before, and his son in the United States had given him reports of the prevailing public mood there. Hitler, he knew, could not win the war in the long term: 'I simply said to myself that if the whole world stands against one, then the one will lose!' On 11 December 1941 he wrote with resignation to his son Paul, then stationed on Sylt: 'Now Japan and the U.S. are in the war too, so it will last longer. Poor world!'

A letter of 6 June 1940 also brings out the contrast he felt between the tranquillity of home and the distant war: 'Our nights are only disturbed at a distance. The poor people of Bonn, however, have already had two unquiet nights this week. The port of Neuss has been hit with great accuracy, also the Werhahn company. We have still heard nothing from Max, you can imagine how much that is on our minds. Mother has still got her hayfever, the weather is very warm and dry, there are not many cherries because it was too dry, the strawberries are beginning, Jan has already got the first from the garden, the roses are flowering, in short, summer has arrived in the country with giant strides. In fourteen days it will be the longest day, by September England must be occupied or it will not be possible at all before the spring. Today a card came from Wim in Amsterdam, with praise for the German administration, their factories are still working.'[16]

On 15 January 1941 he celebrated his sixty-fifth birthday. Even his closest friends saw only a brief glimpse of his feelings. The time of relatively frank letters was past: 'I spent the day in the close family circle, without looking backwards or forwards, as far as was possible. I find that the older one becomes, the more baffling are the world and its people. Though I will not go so far as Leonardo da Vinci did, according to the last page of Foerster's book, by saying that I am no longer an active participant but a contemplative observer, it is nevertheless all very strange.'

Another remark in this birthday letter reveals that he was preoccupied by thoughts of death: 'I know the book *Das wahre Gesicht der Heiligen*. It is a great comfort to see the miracle of transfiguration when taking leave of the dead. I have experienced it twice, one never forgets it.' This was followed by a brief comment on the death of Schmidt, the mayor of Cologne, to whom he had cause to be grateful: 'Poor Cologne, unlucky with its mayors – Yet a city stands for a long time.' There followed some suitably ambiguous remarks: 'One longs for the spring and for work in the garden, but this is probably foolish; the spring will probably bring such unrest as to make one yearn for the calm of winter. Yet behind this unrest lies peace, let us trust in it.'[17]

This letter, ostensibly written on a happy occasion, is marked by an unmistakeable air of resignation. It took no prophetic gift to anticipate an unquiet year in 1941. Though peace no longer seemed so distant, it was possible that it would be a peace that would leave Hitler as master of Europe. No wonder that the world and his fellow men were increasingly baffling to Adenauer.

When Hitler attacked the Soviet Union and declared war on the United States, Adenauer, though still careful, allowed himself some flashes of sarcasm in his letters. On 3 January 1942, with the eastern front in danger of collapse, he wrote to his son Paul: 'You will probably not be sent so far forward; they cannot need you there at the moment. The army reports tell us that there is hard fighting there and that we are falling back as planned!' Usually he regarded developments with mixed emotions, like many other anti-Nazis whose hearts were with the front-line soldiers. With some pride, he informed Paul that the fighter pilot Werner Mölders, who had been shot down and killed, was a veteran of the Catholic youth movement: 'Do you know that Mölders was an enthusiastic member of Neudeutschland, actually a leader in it? I am sending you a picture of his lying in state, the picture is from the *Völkischer*

Beobachter, you can see the crucifix at his head ...' He also wrote about the army in the east near Moscow: 'Those brave people surely have to withstand an extraordinary amount of fighting and hardship ... They are indeed brave men, our troops!'[18] As the war dragged on, the atmosphere darkened even in peaceful Rhöndorf, owing to the intensification of the air raids, fear for the safety of their sons, and the general political situation. As a result of the bombing of German cities, Adenauer brought his extended family to the sanctuary of Rhöndorf: first his daughters-in-law and their children, and then his daughter Ria with her two children.

Towards the end of the war, Adenauer stopped working on his inventions. Between 1940 and 1943, he had concentrated on designing an improved spray nozzle for a watering can and persuaded his son-in-law, Reiners, to produce a model in order to apply for a patent. As the German army advanced to the Volga and almost to the Suez Canal, and then as its soldiers began to retreat, Adenauer maintained his dogged correspondence with the Reichspatentamt about his 'spray nozzle' and his 'insect exterminator'.

He was particularly eager for an extension to the deadline on his patent. 'The production of the desired model requires more time under current conditions', he protested on 29 March 1943.[19] The extension was approved. Subsequently, on 16 August 1943 Mussolini had been overthrown, southern Italy conquered by the Allies, and the war in the air was continuing to rage – he asked for another extension because of the 'conditions currently prevailing in the west'. The final application for an extension also marked the end of a correspondence that had lasted for some forty years, first with the Imperial Patent Office and then with its successor. Adenauer's parting shot was entirely characteristic. He noted on 6 November 1943: 'The craftsman who had taken over the production of the model referred to in the letter of 24.2.1943 has been conscripted. I have to locate another craftsman and therefore request an extension until 18 January 1944.' He received no answer, and in the post-war years was to find more important claims on his time.

In Rhöndorf, as throughout Germany, conditions were deteriorating. Adenauer was concerned about the fate of his family and friends, and about the increasing difficulties in obtaining food and fuel. In addition, he was alarmed by the political climate in the schools: even some of his daughters' teachers in Nonnenwerth, a Gymnasium run by Catholic nuns, had fallen prey to the prevailing spiritual confusion. More generally, Adenauer was anxious about the fate of Germany. Since the Adenauers lived alone, they were able to listen to foreign broadcasts – the BBC, the Soldatensender Calais, Radio Beromünster. Adenauer was well-informed, and therefore had good grounds for his forebodings.

Though Adenauer's immediate reaction to the destruction of the old city of Cologne on 31 May 1942 is unknown, he certainly believed that it could never be rebuilt. In autumn 1943, when the German literature

Professor von der Leyen visited him, Adeneuer's mood was one of sorrow. He had recently visited the city: 'Just think, I did not even recognise it, and I had trouble finding my way about – and Cologne was my life's work. Now that has been destroyed.'[20]

'It Is a Miracle of God That I Have Survived'

In the aftermath of 20 July 1944, it became clear that Adenauer's name was, after all, still on a blacklist. His situation soon became perilous. A first move by the Gestapo against him was set in motion after the arrest in Urfeld of the landscape gardener Giesen, who had supplied the family with foodstuffs. Adenauer was told by telephone on 21 July 1944 that he had been arrested for demoralisation of the troops. A letter to his son, containing an unguarded observation about the bombing of the refinery in Wesseling, had fallen into the hands of the censors. Adenauer, who expected the Gestapo to come for him at any time, waited calmly in Rhöndorf. The women of the house, on the other hand, engaged in feverish activity: supplies were hidden, letters burned, the radio tuned to the Reich radio service, and subversive books removed.

The Gestapo appeared at his door on 24 July. The event was described by Adenauer himself in a letter three days later to his daughter Ria, who was then in Mönchen-Gladbach. He wanted to warn her that she too might be investigated; with the help of his wife, Adenauer phrased the letter to pass on essential information in a manner that would not incur disapproval if the Gestapo read it:

> I had finally finished my previous week's letter on Sunday, after some interruptions, and it lay sealed on my desk when, at 1.15 – we were having our midday meal – seven officials from the Gestapo and SD in Bonn came and said they had to undertake a search of the house. I had to open the letter to you at once and they asked whether they could take it with them, to which I naturally said yes. The house search lasted until 4.30 on Sunday, then my room was sealed and the house search was continued from 10 o'clock until about 5.30 on Monday with a break at midday. The search for food produced nothing incriminating, but they were very interested in every paper in my room, and that was a lot, because since 1933 I have kept virtually my entire correspondence, disciplinary records, bank records etc. Only the correspondence actually aroused interest, and some of it was taken because there was no more time to examine it with me here in the house. But I was told that before anything was done against me on the basis of my correspondence, which would be unpleasant to them, they would seek information which might possibly resolve the matter. The gentlemen were very polite and correct. However, the whole thing was so time-consuming and such a strain on the nerves, of course,

that I told them I would not keep anything in future, which would save me from these investigations and them from extra work, which they thought reasonable. In truth we ought not to keep everything, it is never read afterwards anyway. Apart from that, all the Wassermann books and also the Undset were taken; we will not get them back.[1]

The search of his house was only the beginning. By this stage the German lines in Normandy had been broken, and British and U.S. armoured divisions were moving towards Paris. For an entire week the German western front virtually ceased to exist. In the east, the Army Group Centre was facing its catastrophic fate; Soviet troops were advancing on Warsaw. Within Germany, Operation 'Gitter' was launched on 23 August 1944. On the basis of ancient lists, including the names of many individuals who had since died or even become prominent party members, the decision was made to arrest large numbers of former members of the Centre Party, the SPD and other democratic parties, and the churches. Adenauer was taken to SD headquarters in Bonn, where he was held with two hundred other detainees, before being moved along the Rhine to an internment camp on the exhibition grounds in Cologne. Here he joined an army of political prisoners, convicts and Russian prisoners of war. On 23 August, the Swiss consul-general reported to Berne that 'a marked mood of terror' was perceptible in the Rhineland.[2]

Even in his misfortune, Adenauer had a stroke of luck. His camp senior was the Communist Eugen Zander, a long-term detainee who had spent nine years in Siegburg prison but had earlier been a municipal worker in Cologne. He even knew Adenauer personally, since he had worked in the garden at Max-Bruch-Straße from time to time. Zander now tried to protect his former boss who, though stoical, was now sixty-eight, tormented by insomnia, and unwell; he spent his days sitting quietly or pacing inside the barbed wire fence. At first, Adenauer was moved to the clothing section, which – like the camp as a whole – was infested with lice. When Zander discovered that Adenauer's card in the index of prisoners had been marked 'return not wanted', he knew that his former boss would be taken to a concentration camp. He therefore advised Adenauer to pretend to be ill. Two doctors certified that he had a 'pernicious anaemia' and he was transferred to the Hohenlind hospital in Cologne, where his family had found sanctuary in 1933. In theory Adenauer's imprisonment was now at an end, since he had been released on the advice of the camp doctor as 'unfit for camp and imprisonment'. However, Adenauer was not confident that his reprieve would last: 'intentions on the subject could change, after all.'[3]

In summer and autumn 1944 it seemed that the war would end that year. On 23 July 1944, Adenauer had already written, in one of the letters seized by the Gestapo, that he hoped the war would end that year – though, with sensible caution, he had added 'thanks to our new weapons'.[4]

The Americans were already in Liège, Maastricht, and Luxembourg. Nobody could know that Eisenhower's hesitation would prolong the war in the west for another six months. On 11 September, a patrol from the 85th American Reconnaissance Squadron crossed the Our at Stolzenburg to reach the bunkers of the West Wall. The American Secret Service had reported on 2 September 1944: 'The German army is no longer a coherent fighting force, but only a series of fleeing, disordered and demoralised combat groups without adequate arms and other equipment.'[5]

After his experiences in the wave of arrests following 20 July, which he had been fortunate to survive, Adenauer therefore decided to go into hiding for the remaining weeks of the war. In view of the strategic situation, his flight from Hohenlind hospital, which he undertook on 20 September with the help of his friend Major Hans Schliebusch of the Luftwaffe, was less rash than it may appear in retrospect. Schliebusch presented the female director of Hohenlind with a forged order from Wehrmacht High Command to take Adenauer to Berlin for interrogation. Instead, he travelled by a private car, first to Wesseling, then to Bonn to the home of his friend Vollmar. During the journey, Adenauer and Schliebusch heard the distant thunder of the guns at the front, which Schliebusch described as 'drums of freedom'. In April 1945, however, Schliebusch and his son lost their lives as a result of this incident. During the journey, and then with Vollmar in Bonn, the men discussed the war: Adenauer and Schliebusch thought that the Americans would advance very quickly, but Vollmar was doubtful. After spending the night in Vollmar's house, Adenauer travelled to the Nister Mühle, a hotel in Hachenburg in the Westerwald. Its owner, Josef Rödig, knew Adenauer, but allowed him to sign the register as 'Dr Weber' and took care that as few people as possible saw his face.

However, the disaster that threatened Adenauer was now visited upon his family. After his arrest, Frau Adenauer and his daughters had used all the means still at their disposal to force his release. Consul-general von Weiss, who had taken temporary residence in Rhöndorf after the Swiss consulate in Cologne was burned out, placed his contacts and car at their disposal. Adenauer's son-in-law Walter Reiners also offered his assistance. Gussie Adenauer went with Reiners to see Baron Kurt von Schröder, their friend from the years before 1933, in Rolandseck. Schröder, who was still president of the Chamber of Commerce in Cologne, refused to help. His wife, a particularly fanatical National Socialist, failed even to put in an appearance to offer words of consolation.[6] Nevertheless, the family managed to visit Adenauer in the camp in Cologne and in Hohenlind, and Gussie Adenauer was involved in the flight from the hospital.

When the Gestapo discovered that Adenauer had left Hohenlind, they arrested his wife. Gussie Adenauer was placed under enormous pressure during her interrogation, first in Honnef, then in Gestapo headquarters in Cologne, and finally in Brauweiler prison. Eventually, in order to save her daughters of nineteen and sixteen from being arrested, she told them where her husband was. Ignorant of the fate of her husband and daughters, and tortured by a sense of guilt, she subsequently attempted suicide by taking an overdose of sleeping pills and opening the artery in her left arm. Though she was found in time, the physical damage was permanent: probably as the belated consequence of the overdose, she contracted a serious illness that led to her early death.

Adenauer was arrested again and taken, like his wife, to Brauweiler prison. The two spent their silver wedding anniversary in separate cells in the same prison. Shortly before her release after ten days in prison, Gussie Adenauer was permitted to see her husband. Still deeply depressed, and with her arm bandaged and splinted, she was then allowed home to Rhöndorf. For Adenauer, however, the situation was critical.

The battle for Aachen had been raging since 2 October. When Adenauer was taken to Brauweiler, the Gestapo commissioner spoke to him: 'Please, don't commit suicide. It would cause me there greatest trouble. You are sixty-eight years old now and your life is over anyway'.[7] Adenauer knew only too well that the life of a detainee had no value. Fifteen years later he could still describe the scene to a U.S. reporter:

> In the Gestapo prison where I was, there were sixty-seven people at the time. Of these twenty-seven were hanged and one was shot, all Germans; that was still a large percentage. There were even children of sixteen hanged. But before they were hanged they had to take off their Hitler Youth jackets; I saw it with my own eyes. My cell was directly above the room in which people were tortured. It was a concrete construction and I could hear everything, and for nights on end I lay on my straw mattress covered with sweat because of the mental torture of hearing it all. You see, it became more clear to me than ever before that there is a devil, that evil has real power.[8]

The trauma was deep. On his death bed many years later, he became delirious as he faced the barred window of his bedroom in Rhöndorf: 'Now they are locking an old man in prison ...'

Yet again the family came through this time of trial, on this occasion due largely to the intervention of his second son. Max Adenauer had been a lieutenant in the *Abwehr* since 1943. On 4 October he received a telegram from his sister Libet: 'Urgently and sincerely request the address of Lieutenant Max Adenauer and to tell him that his return to Rhöndorf is urgently necessary as both parents missing'.[9] His wife explained the situation in person to Lieutenant-Colonel Reile, his commanding officer. Reile, who was well aware of what Gestapo detention might mean, granted Max Adenauer four weeks leave on 24 October. Two days later, Max visited his father in Brauweiler to discuss the details of a personal visit to the Gestapo in Berlin. There Max was joined by his brother, Paul, who was stationed in Mark Brandenburg. Adenauer's two sons discussed the affair with friends from the business community, including Friedrich Spennrath of the AEG; none of them, however, had any direct influence on the most senior ranks of the Gestapo.

Finally, Max Adenauer himself went to see the Gestapo officials in the Gestapo headquarters on Meineckestraße. Here it emerged that the only evidence against Adenauer was his escape from Hohenlind. The Gestapo officials did not react when Max described the flight as an act of panic, they knew that it was not unreasonable for a man in Adenauer's circumstances to run. In November 1944, one argument still had power to persuade them, and Max Adenauer did not hesitate to use it: 'Gentlemen, what effect do you think it has on a soldier at the front when he discovers that his relatives at home have been arrested and put in prison for no reason?'[10] He also discovered that the Adenauer documents had been taken to a cellar during an air raid, and since ignored. The Gestapo men promised to send the material to the Reichssicherheitshauptamt (Reich Security Main Office) immediately. Thereafter, Paul Adenauer and Robert Pferdmenges continued to deal with the affair.

Meanwhile, Aachen had fallen on 21 October and the Germans were retreating towards Cologne. On 19 November, the 9th and 1st US Armies launched a major offensive in the Hürtgenwald. It was not difficult to imagine the likely fate of the detainees when the Americans broke through: either transport to a concentration camp in the interior, or immediate execution. As late as March 1945, shortly before the Americans occupied Cologne, ninety political prisoners were hanged in Klingelpütz prison.

To Adenauer, his release on 26 November – his name-day – seemed almost providential. Though he often recounted the story later, the most authentic version was given on 29 November 1944 in a three-page letter to his son Max. The letter also reveals that his spirits had been restored with remarkable speed:

Dear Max, With luck you will have received the telegram informing you of my return. On Sunday 26 November, during an alarm in the air-raid cellar, I asked the official who was there about my case, and I received the answer: 'If you wish, you can go today, I have received the order for your release, but don't you want to stay till tomorrow?' He also said that, even before the order for my release arrived, an inquiry had come by telex from Berlin asking why my release had not yet been announced. Although my belongings – money, wallet, braces, tie – could not be handed over on the Sunday, I offered many thanks for the friendly offer, signed a declaration that I was given to sign, and was then released with a hearty handshake and without any kind of instruction or place of residence, announcement or anything of that kind. You can imagine my elation as I trotted to Sinn in Weiden. He received me with extraordinary warmth and sincerity and 'organised' a small delivery van for me, which took me at 18.30 from Weiden via Frechen, Brühl, Bonn. In Königswinter we found terrible floods and had to go via Margaretenhof, Löwenburg, Honnef; we arrived at 9.45 pm. I had sent a telephone message from Königswinter. It was a wonderful end, it was like a dream to me to be home again, and it often seems like a dream still. Once again I thank you for your efforts and your skill, without your help I would probably still be in Brauweiler – where, apart from everything else, the approach of the front is making things very unpleasant; it was high time that I got away. There is much air activity here, but of course it is very much less than in Brauweiler. I lost 11-12 pounds in weight there, and my heart was somewhat affected, but I think all will be well, especially if we do not become a battle zone, which I think unlikely. All the best, dear Max, and from the bottom of my heart many, many greetings! Your father ...'[11]

Adenauer thought that the police had probably ceased to worry about him. Only much later did he discover that he had escaped liquidation only by a hair's breadth during the last weeks of the war. In 1960, Robert Pferdmenges told him that the Gestapo had drawn up another list of people who were to be eliminated before its withdrawal from Cologne in 1945. This list was the subject of a dispute between Gauleiter Grohé and Gauleiter Terboven, the Oberpräsident of Rhine Province, with Terboven over-riding Grohé's argument that Adenauer should be left alive. He had been saved only by the rapid withdrawal of the Gestapo from Cologne.[12]

For the remainder of the war, Adenauer's sole interest was the survival of his extended family of fourteen in Rhöndorf: his wife, his daughters, his daughter-in-law and his grandchildren. The youngest member of the family arrived in January 1945:

'Lola was very brave, she worked until the last day. In the night of Thursday 9.1 she woke us at four in the morning. Gussie and I tramped with her through the deep snow to Honnef hospital, while the thunder of the guns from the front rumbled overhead. Lola already had strong pains, so we had to stop every five minutes. The child arrived at 11 ... The transport and the supply situations have become very difficult here, the railway has virtually stopped altogether, along with part of the electric rail. During recent days the sky has been relatively quiet because of the prevailing fog, especially at night ...'[13]

By now Adenauer was reacting as most ordinary Germans, without any thoughts of a political future. In 1962, as Federal Chancellor, he was interviewed by an obtuse U.S. reporter for CBS radio, who asked him how he had envisaged his future during the war years. Adenauer's answer was probably an honest one: 'There was no purpose in having any kind of ideas, one had to wait and see ... I made no plans. I had only one wish and one hope – that the world would be delivered from National Socialism. That was the be-all and end-all, and it was impossible to predict what might come afterwards.'[14]

He was, however, urgently interested in the immediate future, and particularly in the strategic plans of the U.S. and the British. Like most Germans in those years, Adenauer became something of an amateur strategist. He correctly recognised the two main axes of the Western attack on Germany: the first from the ports and plains of Belgium to the

Ruhr and the north German lowlands, the other through Mainz to the area around Frankfurt. In the middle Rhine, difficulties of terrain made major battles unlikely. It therefore seemed that Rhöndorf might remain relatively protected from severe fighting. However, the situation was altered at a stroke with the capture of the railway bridge at Remagen by the Americans on 7 March. On the morning of 8 March, Adenauer's sister Lilli Suth called with some relief from Unkel to tell them that '... the Americans are here ...'[15] For a number of days, it seemed that the great breakthrough into the interior of Germany would be achieved with a push down the Rhine with the pivot at Erpel. If that was the case, the Drachenfels would provide a natural fortress in the way of the Allies. For anyone with knowledge of the cautious strategy pursued by the Americans, it was easy to predict the fate of the buildings in Rhöndorf in the event of a breakthrough battle on both sides of the Siebengebirge hills: the town would offer an easy target for carpet bombing.

In the event, a number of factors combined to ensure that the fighting in the area was limited. The most important of these was Eisenhower's determination to advance steadily and securely, without making significant alterations to his overall strategic plans. When the surprise attack at Remagen succeeded, he did order the bridgehead to be enlarged to permit the Allies to force the Rhine line in March instead of May. However, the bridgehead was extended only gradually after Model threw his last reserves into the battle to prevent the breakthrough to the Cologne-Frankfurt autobahn. The main force of the Western Allies continued to be massed on the Lower Rhine and along the West Wall in the Palatinate. It was here that the decisive Rhine crossings and breakthroughs took place: Montgomery's crossing of the Rhine at Wesel on 23/24 March, at the head of approximately one million men, and the conquest of the Palatinate, which was crowned on 22 March by the Rhine crossing at Oppenheim. On the other hand, the bridgehead at Remagen served mainly to force the Germans to sacrifice their last strong battle formations on the middle Rhine. The limited strategic objective was the autobahn, which would bypass the Siebengebirge in the south.

Adenauer was probably pleased when the Rhine was crossed quickly at Honnef. If the front had stabilised on the Rhine for several weeks, as planned, hardly anything would have been left of the towns and villages on the eastern bank of the Rhine.

However, there was some protracted fighting in the area. After the first Americans had entered Honnef, German trenches still ran along the wood behind the Adenauer house. Though the opposite bank of the Rhine was already in U.S. hands, Rhöndorf continued to be held by the Wehrmacht. Adenauer therefore shepherded his family into the small air-raid shelter at the rear of the house, where they remained for eight days. Occasionally he would creep through the house and garden to study developments, impressing the family with his calm and composure. As always he was at his best in a crisis. Not even the sudden appearance of five escaped French prisoners-of-war troubled him; the family simply made room for them in the bunker. Nevertheless, and particularly because the shelter had no steel door to offer protection, there could still have been a tragedy. Numerous shells landed on the property, the house received two direct hits, and Adenauer himself had a lucky escape when three shells were fired at him – he actually believed he had seen the vortex of air as one passed by.

Rhöndorf was also protected by the presence of military hospitals in the village itself and in nearby Königswinter, which persuaded the German troops in the area to avoid too fanatical a defence. The Swiss Consul-General, von Weiss, who was active on the western bank of the Rhine in Bad Godesberg, also informed the Americans that there were large numbers of wounded in the area. At the height of 'the battle for Rhöndorf', von Weiss crossed the Rhine in a boat with a Swiss flag to mediate between the two sides. He managed to convince the Germans to withdraw after evacuating their wounded, and assured the Americans that they would also be able to occupy the region south of the Drachenfels without heavy casualties. Fifty German defenders therefore pulled back further into the interior, accompanied by thirty battle-hungry officer cadets on the Drachenfels.[16] In consequence, Rhöndorf, Honnef and Königswinter were damaged but not destroyed. The future Chancellor of the Federal Republic of Germany and his family survived the Third Reich unharmed, with the exception of the illness sustained by Gussie Adenauer.

One day before the surprise attack on the bridge at Remagen, the last pockets of resistance had been elimintaed in the ruins of Cologne. The city was then inhabited only by around forty thousand people.

However, the occupation did not bring an immediate end to the conflict. In the Rhineland, liberation also resulted in a wave of lootings, rapes and thefts, sometimes committed by combat soldiers, sometimes by liberated Russian and Polish prisoners or forced labourers. Rhöndorf saw its share of incidents. Adenauer's skeptical attitude toward the Americans during the first weeks of the occupation were, to a large extent, due to the attacks that had been reported to him. Conditions returned to normal only slowly. The horrors of war were over, but the misery of occupation had begun.

V

THE PARTY LEADER
1945-1949

Adenauer as chairman of the CDU in the British Zone

Attempts at Reorientation
amongst the Ruins

Konrad Adenauer was now sixty-nine years old and had already lived a full and dramatic life. And yet, his greatest adventure was about to begin. Two decades later, when he was regarded by many – and, increasingly, by himself – as a figure of historic significance, he was asked how he would divide the various phases of his long life. He answered: 'I would not distinguish up to 1917 and then from 1917 to 1933, but I would say: until 1933, until the Nazis came, then the Nazi era, and then the era after the collapse.'[1]

'Until 1933' – this was the period when Adenauer had made a major impact on the history of Cologne. For anyone from outside of his city, however, the first fifty-seven years of his life are of interest largely for sociological reasons, for the light they shed on the different conditions in Imperial Germany, the years of war and revolution, and the Weimar Republic. Yet the chief importance of this long phase of his life lay in the fact that it shaped the personality of the man who later, and quite unexpectedly, became a statesman of European significance.

In the second phase of his life, in the Third Reich, Adenauer was virtually a nobody. Political influence was denied him; like the majority of his countrymen, he was little more than the plaything of a history that was made by others. Nevertheless, there were a number of features in his story which transcended time and place: between 1933 and 1945 Adenauer's fate was typical of an entire group of influential individuals, across many generations, who have been subjected to abuse and threatened with death after a political upheaval. Despite changing historical circumstances, the ruthlessness of rulers and the fear and suffering of the persecuted are common elements – in the days of the Greek *polis*, during the English civil war of the seventeenth century, in the French Revolution, and during the ruthless change from democracy to dictatorship in Europe in the first half of the twentieth century, and in parts of Latin America today.

Notes for this section begin on page 715.

Like many victims of political persecution both before and after him, Adenauer was hurt and humiliated by his experiences. Yet, also like many before him, he gained in depth, and developed an absolute and uncompromising commitment to the struggle against tyranny.

In the spring of 1945 Adenauer was fully aware of the nature of totalitarian dictatorship, the extent and horror of which he had never suspected in 1933. He had seen at first hand the worst face of humanity – its vulnerability to temptation and its weakness. However, he had also recognised the factors that provided support and created order. In his view they included family, friends, the church, the institutions of the constitutional state, and also – in the hands of the resolute leaders of liberal democracies – military strength used in the defence of freedom. In this respect his experiences were like those of millions of other Europeans and Germans. It was this common experience which, in the following years, enabled him to perceive and understand both the wishes of the majority and the vital issues of the day.

In the first and second phases of his life, Adenauer's fate and insight thus had a genuine representative quality. However, they became significant in historical terms only because of his emergence from persecution to become the head of the new West German state in 1949. Since he had suffered personally under the totalitarian dictatorship, he was able to give voice to the profound anti-totalitarian sentiments that characterised much of public opinion in West Germany from 1945 until well into the 1960s.

Adenauer's own view of democracy was based on a powerful desire and demand for freedom. It was this experience that led him to reject the pacifist attitudes which were articulated with passionate enthusiasm by many other Europeans, especially those of the war generation. Of course, he assured the U.S. officers who sought him out on 16 March 1945, he wanted above all to educate the German people in peace from top to bottom.[2] Yet he quickly recognised that this was a concern shared by many, and that the defeated Germans had also lost all taste for war in the second half of the twentieth century. Adenauer himself had also suffered more from the terror of totalitarian dictatorship than from the horrors of war, which must have made it psychologically easier for him to advocate an assertive military stance by the free democracies, and to condemn pacifism as short-sighted and misguided.

In March 1945 Adenauer was still officially a nobody. Though all sorts of people began to contact him in the hope of connecting their careers to his, or in an attempt to clear themselves of charges of association with the Nazis, his political potential remained latent. It was still impossible to predict whether, and how, his political career would be revived. Nevertheless, he was already of interest to Americans and Germans alike, especially to the OSS (Office of Strategic Services) and CIC intelligence units attached to the US First Army task forces occupying

Cologne and the Bonn region. It was well known that these intelligence units possessed 'blacklists' of Nazi functionaries who were to be taken into custody. However, they had also brought 'white-lists' of those Germans who were known opponents of Hitler and were being considered for leading posts in the administration. On the white-list for Cologne, Adenauer was described as follows: 'Adenauer, Konrad: Bad Honnef, former mayor of Honef. Worth contacting by Allies for co-operation according to anti-Nazi P/W (May be identical with Adenauer, Konrad, *Oberbürgermeister* of Köln 1919-1933).'[3]

Adenauer soon learned that he was number one on the white-list for Germany. On 13 May, he wrote in English to the military police in Königswinter-Honnef, who had just arrested his daughter Lotte for breaking the curfew: 'I have been appointed by the Governor of the Reg.Bezirk of Cologne as *Oberbürgermeister* of this city, and I rank as Number One on the White List of Germany according to confidential informations of the CIC'.[4] He had discovered this information in a letter from Lieutenant-Colonel Patterson dated 8 May.

Adenauer was quick to inform others of his new status. At the beginning of July, he wrote to Hans Rörig, a former correspondent of the *Kölnische Zeitung* then in Berne, to explain that he would be well qualified as an adviser on German issues: 'Perhaps in this context it is important to tell you that I was in first place on the White List for Germany that was drawn up in Washington'.[5]

The influential occupation officers of the Rhine Province, including the CIC, undoubtedly regarded Adenauer as one of the leading figures in the region. Officers from Eisenhower's headquarters were sent to see him at intervals in order to discover his views. We cannot be certain whether the news of his position on the white-list encouraged him to seek greater influence from the very beginning. In any event, his first conversations with U.S. intelligence officers showed him that his judgement was valued – though he could not know how much, for how long, or for what purpose.

In March 1945 Adenauer was well aware that future developments were totally dependent on the decisions and thinking of the occupying powers. Gradually and cautiously, however, Germans who had not been compromised by their conduct in the Third Reich began to hold detailed discussions about the re-establishment of political life. By this stage Adenauer was already a figure of tangible political stature owing to his appointment as mayor of Cologne by the Americans. After a period when he had been used as their 'adviser', he took over his duties on an official basis on 4 May 1945. The attitude of the occupation authorities was also the decisive factor in the development of plans for a new German party system. Adenauer had accepted one of the most senior posts in the occupied territory before the official process of founding new parties and creating new administrative structures had begun.

He seems to have returned to the office of mayor with great pleasure. This was undoubtedly intensified by his sense of duty, a creative instinct that had been forcibly suppressed for over a decade, and the conviction that he was the man best equipped for the task. In 1965, while working on his memoirs, he told his secretary Anneliese Poppinga that 'it was my dream to become mayor of Cologne again'.[6] Nevertheless, as an experienced administrator, he was also aware that in prevailing conditions it would be impossible to meet the desperate needs of the city. The events of the next six months served to confirm this view.

Adenauer accepted the office of mayor only on condition that he was permitted to resign at any time, and at his own discretion. Various letters dating from July 1945 indicate that he did consider stepping down. On 6 July 1945, for example, he wrote to Dannie N. Heineman: 'After initial resistance I eventually allowed myself to be persuaded'.[7] Furthermore, his letter to Hans Rörig makes it clear that he was already thinking on a much larger scale than the administration of his shattered native city. In the letter, he explained that the British had taken responsibility for Cologne on 21 June. Rörig, he thought, might be able to help him ensure that sensible and substantial people from the British press, government and industry came to study the problems facing Germany on the spot. In this case, he would be able to act as a good adviser: 'My judgement, I hope, is quite unclouded by ambition. I intend to become and be nothing other than the mayor of the city of Cologne, and even that for a limited period only, until I have secured the reconstruction of the city at least in its early stages.'[8]

The fact that the Americans had located him immediately was, in Adenauer's view, good evidence of their organisational skills. Rhöndorf had been occupied for less than a day when a jeep arrived outside the Adenauer home in Zennigsweg. It contained the U.S. officers Lieutenant-Colonel Tuhus and Captain Emerson as representatives of the Governor of Cologne. They were accompanied by the mayor of Honnef and the art historian Werner Bornheim, who was to provide the most detailed accounts of the events of these first weeks. Adenauer received the U.S. officers stiffly and with formality – remembering, in all likelihood, a similar scene that had taken place at city hall in Cologne twenty-seven years previously. Then, however, he had been only forty-two years old; now he was an old man who had suffered considerably over the last twelve years.

On behalf of the Governor and the population of Cologne, the Americans asked Adenauer to accept the office of mayor. If Adenauer had ever allowed himself to daydream during the Third Reich, it had been of this moment: that one day, when the brown tide had receded, he would be able to return to his old job. That moment had arrived, even though he was being asked to take charge of a city in ruins.

Nevertheless, he expressed genuine reluctance, for the very good reason that his sons were still with the Wehrmacht. To ensure that no reprisals were carried out against them, he could not accept anything more than an advisory and background role. He was not yet prepared to do more, despite pressure from the Americans, who would have preferred to take him with them there and then.

Consul-General von Weiss, as dapper and cheerful as ever and with his reputation enhanced by his assistance in limiting the extent of hostilities near Rhöndorf, now joined the discussions between Adenauer and the Americans. As a long-standing admirer of Adenauer, he encouraged the Americans in their determination to appoint his friend as mayor of Cologne. Finally, after von Weiss had offered to take Adenauer to the city within a matter of days, the Americans withdrew.

That same day, Adenauer had also received a visit from Archbishop Frings. The archbishop, who had been bombed out in Cologne on no less than four occasions, had moved his residence to Rhöndorf some time previously. Some of the clergy in Cologne, like Adenauer himself, had lost much of their respect for him as a result. However, Frings now told Adenauer that he intended to return to the city as soon as possible. His visitor had only just left when the Americans made their appearance. These incidents had a revitalising effect on Adenauer, whose younger children were astonished to discover that their father was, after all, very much in demand.

Three days later, the Americans sent another emissary to Adenauer. On this occasion, they chose well: Captain Schweizer, an adjutant to the Governor of Cologne, was a man of forty-five who in civilian life had been a professor of architecture and urban planning in New York. He persuaded Adenauer to spend a few days in Cologne, where he and his wife would be accommodated in the Caritas St Elisabeth hospital in Hohenlind, which had been requisitioned for use by the Americans.

For Adenauer, the journey to Cologne through the spring sunshine was like a dream. Between Honnef and Rolandseck the entourage travelled over a pontoon bridge; the Rhine was partially covered by a smoke-screen, and the road to Mehlem was screened off from the other side by giant cloths. On all sides there was evidence of that vast array of modern war material and equipment which made such a profound impression on the defeated Germans during the spring of 1945. In Bonn, military transport provided the only sign of life; the autobahn to Cologne, planned by Adenauer and opened by Hitler, was completely empty. Signs of appalling devastation were everywhere. Adenauer thus returned to Cologne, almost twelve years to the day since he had been driven out.

During his first conversation with the City Commandant Hiles, a scene entirely characteristic of Adenauer took place. When the Lieutenant-Colonel left his visitor standing, Adenauer motioned Bornheim to fetch him a chair and sat down with a loud 'Well!'

Adenauer, who had always been a master tactician, now faced a challenge. Though he had resolved not to accept the office of mayor as long as it might endanger his sons in the Wehrmacht, he knew that the Americans were anxious for a solution and would appoint somebody else if they could not have him. If he refused, they would turn to his son-in-law Willi Suth, who had been at the head of the administration since 16 March. In order to prevent the post being given to another man, Adenauer discouraged the Americans from making such an appointment. He declared that he was willing to function as an adviser for the time being. In this capacity, he spent most of his weekdays in Cologne before returning to Rhöndorf for the weekends.

Experience had taught the Americans to have some sympathy for such caution. Only days after Adenauer's first discussions in Cologne, Franz Oppenhoff, the mayor of Aachen, was murdered by a Nazi squad flown in secretly for the purpose. The war was still being waged with great ferocity; some units of Model's army continued to occupy their positions on the east bank of the Rhine.

During those first days, Adenauer was constantly reminded of the past. He was driven to Gestapo headquarters on Appellhoffolatz, where all the doors and windows had been flung open and papers and files lay scattered on the floor. A photograph of Reinhard Heydrich still hung on the wall; Adenauer ordered it to be taken down and broke it over the edge of the table with his own hands. From the desk of a senior Gestapo official he took as a souvenir a bronze table lamp, installing it in his home in Rhöndorf.

There were other reminders of his past. The villa at Lindenallee 70 in Marienburg, which had been requisitioned to serve as the residence of the Military Governor, Lieutenant-Colonel Patterson, had once been occupied by Bank Director Brüning. Adenauer's old home on Max-Bruch-Straße had been destroyed, although the graves of his parents and Emma Adenauer in Melaten cemetery were undisturbed. The entire inner city was a ruin. Adenauer's doubts that it could ever be properly re-built were strengthened. Sometimes, in the evenings, he made tours of the individual districts of the city in an attempt to gain an idea of conditions there. He visited the damaged cathedral and suggested the establishment of a soup kitchen there to attract workers for essential repairs. In the company of his wife, Adenauer also went back to Brauweiler prison; Gussie Adenauer recalled that whenever there had been an air raid, she had always been the last person to be allowed into the safety of the shelter.

Occasionally Adenauer would try to describe conditions in the city to his acquaintances abroad. In April 1946, there was still utter desolation:

> Most of Cologne has been destroyed. Admittedly, there are 500,000 inhabitants again now. But roughly a third of them are living in cellars or buildings which have been destroyed to varying degrees. I have seen many German cities recently, but have not found any large city that has been destroyed as

much as Cologne. The cathedral is still standing, but large parts of the roof are missing. Most of the arches have collapsed. Nevertheless, it can be restored. Of the city hall there is almost nothing left. The porch is still there and part of the tower, otherwise nothing. As regards Gürzenich, the four surrounding walls are still standing.[9]

Adenauer was aware that this was no time for self-pity or self-indulgent memories of the past. Though the problems he faced appeared almost insoluble, an attempt had to be made to deal with them. During the hot days of May, for example, the worst-damaged areas were pervaded by the penetrating odour of rotting flesh.

Between the end of March and early May, Adenauer worked behind the scenes as shadow mayor of a city which had only 32,000 inhabitants when the occupation began. The nominal mayor was his son-in-law, Willi Suth. Of all German cities, at least in terms of personnel, Cologne offered the best example of a return to pre-Nazi days.

When hostilities finally came to an end throughout Germany, Adenauer had to decide whether to accept the role of mayor on a permanent basis. Governor Patterson, whose respect for Adenauer had increased steadily, urged him to take the job. In facing the appalling problems of administration in the shattered city, the Americans were glad to have a German of unimpeachable political reputation who could be expected to offer effective cooperation. He therefore accepted the post, on the condition that the Americans accepted his right to step down whenever he saw fit.

For a number of reasons, Adenauer now had relatively little enthusiasm for the task. His weeks as adviser had made clear the enormity of the task facing him as mayor. His attitude towards the U.S. occupying power was generally sceptical, though at the end of May he heard that the British were likely to take over responsibility for most of north-western Germany, including Cologne. At the same time, the outlines of a potentially much bigger role for him were beginning to take shape. An officer at Eisenhower's headquarters informed him of plans for a 'four-man committee' to administer the Rhine-Main area and the Ruhr. Adenauer had been asked for his co-operation, but had cautiously replied that he would wait and see how the situation developed.

On 3 May, Adenauer and the Governor, Lieutenant-Colonel Patterson, had a vital conversation which ended with Adenauer declaring his willingness to accept the office of mayor on an official basis. At the same time, he again asked about the larger project. On 25 May he told von Weiss that the Americans had wanted him for a senior post, but that he had not the slightest desire to make himself available owing the obstinate and unsatisfactory attitude of the U.S. army.

It is possible to argue that Adenauer was already beginning to feel that Cologne was too small a stage for him. A more extreme view has been taken by some observers, who have seen his actions solely as the products of ambition and the determination to climb to power. In reality, he was a complex man whose objectives and conduct are not susceptible to simplistic explanations. Nevertheless, there was growing evidence that his position in Cologne offered him little opportunity to get to grips with the major work of reconstruction.

Adenauer's decision to return to his old office on a temporary basis was made easier because the two men appointed to head the German administration had been known to him before 1933. The new president of the Rhine Province was Hans Fuchs. Born in 1874, Fuchs was a contemporary of Adenauer, also a member of the old Centre Party, and had occupied the same post between 1922 and 1933. Until the arrival of the British he had been based in Bonn, and was then transferred to Düsseldorf.

The British had previously offered this post to Adenauer himself, who regarded Fuchs as a 'little man,' as he told von Weiss, he had actually given Fuchs the presidency in 1922. Though most of the links between the two men had been broken between 1933 and 1945, Adenauer assumed that they would be able to achieve a satisfactory working relationship when Fuchs came to Hohenlind on 29 April to explain that he had been restored to his old post. In this he was mistaken. Fuchs quickly became ambitious on his own behalf and tried to set himself up as a virtual minister-president. He and Adenauer failed to work together. When Fuchs was dismissed by the British in early October, Adenauer had no regrets. He was also critical of the conduct of his former colleague in failing to act decisively against former members of the NSDAP in the presidium.

The third member of this group from the Weimar era to be restored to influence was *Geheimrat* Clemens Busch. Like Adenauer, he had grown up in Imperial Germany and, at sixty-six, would already have retired under normal conditions. Between 1913 and 1919 he had been district administrator in Altenkirchen, and from 1922 to 1936 he served as a judge at the Reich Fiscal Court in Munich. At Adenauer's suggestion, the Americans now appointed Busch as district president in Cologne. After a long period of impotence, Adenauer was at last once again able to exert a measure of personal and political influence.

In the Rhineland as elsewhere, members of the old guard were returning to senior positions. The reasons for the restoration of this élite, most of whom had gone to school during the era of Bismarck, were obvious: 'There are very few capable people. The two wars have torn great gaps, and the young talent is not there owing to the disastrous influence of the NSDAP'.[10]

As yet it is impossible to establish a precise picture of the first six months of the U.S. and British occupation. Adenauer's surviving correspondence gives only fleeting insights into his own thoughts and feelings. Moreover, the incidents that he chose to mention in his memoirs are significant mainly for the atmosphere and detail they convey. The real basis of his thinking during this period is scarcely perceptible.

Of the available sources, the richest consist of the detailed reports by Adenauer's friend, the Swiss consul-general, von Weiss. In the summer of 1943, when the Swiss consulate in Cologne was fire-bombed, he and his office had moved to Rhöndorf and Bad Godesberg, returning to Cologne only in 1946. During Adenauer's arrest in late summer and autumn 1944, the Swiss diplomat had been able to offer the family some assistance. From 1945 until the time of the Parliamentary Council, the two families were in very close contact. In particular, during 1945 and 1946 Adenauer and von Weiss met regularly for coffee at the weekends, using the opportunity to exchange information and ideas. Von Weiss regularly reported the political elements of these conversations to Berne. His vivid and informative reports reveal the broad outlines of Adenauer's views during the first months of occupation: his criticisms, his anxieties, and his attempts to find political solutions either through discussion or by making various contacts. Nevertheless, it is impossible to be certain how far the reports record Adenauer's exact opinions, and how far they are coloured by the personal judgements and objectives of von Weiss, at a time when the diplomat had firm views of his own. In fact, some time later von Weiss was rebuked by his minister in Berne. He had apparently allowed himself to be used by French occupation officials in nearby Bad Ems to pass details of Gaullist policy towards Germany into the British Zone.

A further source, published only at the beginning of the 1980s, was the account of the Mainz art historian Werner Bornheim. At the end of the war Bornheim lived in Honnef and was in regular contact with Adenauer. During the first weeks of Adenauer's work in Cologne, Bornheim frequently attended discussions as Adenauer's personal representative, and was later entrusted with a number of cultural tasks in the city administration of Cologne.

The accounts of Bornheim and von Weiss in many cases expand and confirm each other, thus making it possible for Adenauer's thinking during the first months of occupation to be defined with relative clarity. The main impression is of great despair – of chaos and uncertainty in every respect. In the early weeks, Adenauer was particularly appalled by the attacks perpetrated by U.S. soldiers. Von Weiss noted on 24 March: 'According to the reports of Herr Dr Adenauer, the American troops in Honnef and Rhöndorf appear to have been just as wild as in Godesberg etc., looting all the requisitioned dwellings and smashing everything to bits. It is very regrettable that large numbers of women have been raped by members of the American forces, especially by negroes'.[11] The situation, in Cologne as elsewhere, seemed almost reminiscent of the Thirty Years' War. Even after the soldiers had been brought under control, the rural areas of the region continued to be troubled until the summer by attacks on the part of DPs, the Displaced Persons in Germany. Adenauer complained about the conduct of the Americans to Lieutenant-Colonel

Patterson, the well-intentioned and civilised Governor of Cologne. Patterson's answer was to argue that U.S. troops would not have been prepared to fight in Europe at all unless they had been incited by anti-German propaganda. He also made a point of asking Adenauer how the Germans had behaved during the occupation of Czechoslovakia. In other words, the conversation between the two men degenerated into a typical session of mutual recrimination for past horrors.

Adenauer received equally little satisfaction when he raised the question of the food supply. When he pointed out that the daily ration of 1,150 calories was roughly equal to the rations he had received a couple of months before in a Gestapo concentration camp, Patterson responded with the information that the Germans had allowed the Dutch only 900 calories during the occupation of the Netherlands. Adenauer replied heatedly: 'Are you a Nazi?'[12]

Consul-General von Weiss met his friend again on 9 April. Adenauer had returned from Cologne some days before,

> having held three days of important conversations and discussions in the interests of his native city. He told me in strict confidence that, on the basis of the behaviour of the Americans, he saw the future as very black for Germany. Though the Governor of Cologne has the fullest confidence in him and he could do everything he proposes in the interests of the city, he also told the Governor bluntly that the behaviour of the American soldiers had aroused the greatest indignation among the population everywhere. At first they had genuinely welcomed the arrival of the Americans as a liberation and regarded their presence as a deliverance from tyranny. But since their arrival the American troops have made themselves so unpopular by their looting, stealing, and by their arrogant, unworthy conduct that their approach, if it does not change, will breed a new National Socialism, if not Bolshevism ...[13]

Adenauer was especially alarmed by conditions in the prison camps of Sinzig, Remagen and Kripp, which were arousing revulsion and horror in the Rhineland. In these camps, 300,000 prisoners-of-war, including women anti-aircraft auxiliaries, were being held in the open air without any shelter.[14] Most had to lie in the mud day and night, even in the pouring rain. Von Weiss, who took note of these details, had heard that between sixty and one hundred people were dying there every day.[15]

Adenauer had justifiably greeted the arrival of the Americans in March with a sense of liberation. However, this mood had very quickly disappeared. He now saw himself as a spokesman for a defeated people. It was a role he was to occupy for the next ten years. On the basis of his own unimpeachable political reputation, he was ready and willing to speak out against the occupation authorities on behalf of his fellow-countrymen.

At the outset, Adenauer was determined that all Nazi leaders should be punished. When discussing the issue with the U.S. Governor of Cologne, he made it clear that this punishment should also include the National Socialists in the armed forces. At this early stage he was also deeply hostile to the Nazi followers. In April, when the dean of Cologne, Grosche, was preparing to take a stand in the name of the clergy against the indiscriminate punishment of nominal party members, Adenauer tried to dissuade him. He argued that such a stand would be pointless, given the attitude of the Americans; besides, all party members were worthy of blame because of their cowardice. Grosche disagreed and claimed that distinctions must be made, on the grounds that many people had gone along with the regime to prevent worse things from happening. (This defence was to be extremely common over the following years.) Moreover, despite Adenauer's own views, Grosche was convinced that indiscriminate punishment would not be condoned by the population.[16]

In the event, Adenauer soon began to change his mind. By May 1945 he even felt that the CIC was in danger of taking the place of the Gestapo. NSDAP members in these first months of occupation now faced treatment which, in its bureaucratic precision, seemed to resemble the persecution meted out to Adenauer in the Third Reich. Occupied Germany was again a land of camps (now called internment camps rather than concentration camps), of extorted confessions, of political denunciation and spying. When the British took control in Cologne, they wasted little time before tapping Adenauer's telephone at the post office in Rhöndorf. Though the head postmaster did not dare tell Adenauer himself, he sent his wife to confession to tell the priest. Subsequently, the priest visited Adenauer and told him to 'be careful – your phone is being tapped'.

Practical considerations played an important part in persuading Adenauer to oppose the indiscriminate dismissal of all NSDAP members from the public service and economic posts. Early in April 1945, he told von Weiss that it was stupid to dismiss all party members from the city administration: for example, of twenty-one specialist workers in the city waterworks, all but three had been in the party. The efficiency of the administration would be virtually destroyed if ninety or ninety-five per cent of civil servants and white-collar workers were dismissed because of membership of the NSDAP. Equally important, such action would have political consequences, since a shortage of manpower would lead to the appointment of Communists in many cases. Moreover, indiscriminate punishment would probably encourage sympathy for a 'Werewolf' mentality and the growth of neo-Nazism. Even the health service would be shattered by the vigorous implementation of the original plans for denazification; in Bonn, for example, 102 out of 112 doctors had been party members.

In the middle of April, Adenauer warned the U.S. authorities against dismissing every single petty National Socialist. By June, he found conditions so intolerable that at the end of the period of U.S. occupation he sent a memorandum to Eisenhower, the Supreme Commander, asking for a revision of the indiscriminate jobs ban. On this issue Adenauer had quickly reached a position that he was to maintain over the following years. It contained a number of elements: strict punishment of the guilty; the removal of very active National Socialists from important positions; the inclusion of non-party members in the denazification process, especially industrialists who had donated large sums of money to the NSDAP; but the release of 'little' party members. It was essential, he thought, for individual cases to be examined by German courts.

In this context, it is necessary to distinguish between Adenauer's moral or emotional comments and his practical politics. In spring 1945, in the immediate aftermath of the Third Reich, he could be heard to argue that it was wrong to condemn all of the 'old fighters', those who had been involved with the NSDAP between 1930 and 1933, since these had included a number of deluded idealists. Instead, it was more important to punish those people who had joined the party after 1939, since by that time even an idiot could see what was happening.

However, his approach became increasingly political the longer he considered the issue. To enable the German people to build a lasting democracy, it was essential to concentrate punishment only on genuine wrongdoers and activists, and to let the millions of "followers", the so-called Mitläufer, go free. Where once he had complained about their cowardice, he now took a more objective view: human nature was weak, especially in a police state: 'Heroism is not an everyday occurrence.'[17]

On the other hand, in the spring and summer of 1945 Adenauer was still afraid of the great mass of irreconcilable Nazi supporters. At the end of June, he told von Weiss of his belief that these were concentrated in central and northern Germany. Measures of re-education were urgently necessary – but the occupation authorities were doing nothing. Adenauer feared that there might be a wave of political murders of the kind that had marred politics after the First World War. Even before the war was over, he had urged that reliable German prisoners-of-war should be armed and set to work as policemen.[18]

Adenauer's view of the psychological situation in Germany emerges from an account written by Stephen Spender after a long conversation with the mayor. This was published in autumn 1946, long before Adenauer's rise to fame. Adenauer told his British visitor that the Nazis had flattened German culture like 'the ruins on the Rhine and Ruhr'. Germany was a spiritual wasteland. Satisfying the hunger and thirst for spiritual values was just as important a task as material reconstruction. In this respect, the lead must be taken by a city with the cultural traditions of Cologne. To that end, it needed the 'best educational system, the best books, the best newspapers, the best music'.

At particular risk were the young, those between the ages of fourteen and twenty-five, who must be returned to the hands of reliable teachers as soon as possible. Vocational training was equally important. Adenauer ended the conversation with an emphatic remark: 'The people must be given new ideas!' Despite the fact that he was now seventy years old, the 'prominent Rhenish Catholic' made a significant impact on Spender: 'He gives an impression of energy, though at the same time the effect is somewhat unprepossessing: long, scrawny and oval face, almost no hair, narrow, lively eyes, a little nose and reddish skin colouring. He looks remarkably young and had the calmly confident manner of a successful and prudent younger man.' Spender recalled an incident during the exchange of greetings, when Adenauer told him that the name was familiar to him; after the First World War he had been interviewed by a member of an earlier generation of the Spenders.[19] At this stage, he was still relatively nostalgic for the British occupation of 1918-1926.

Despite Adenauer's reservations, the U.S. officers with whom he had dealings in Cologne were generally well-intentioned and diligent. He developed a good relationship with the military governor, Colonel Patterson, similar to that which he had enjoyed with General Clive and Julian Piggott during the British occupation of the 1920s. When Patterson left Cologne to take a command in Bavaria, he ignored the ban on fraternisation and spent the night with the Adenauers in Rhöndorf. The two men continued to correspond. On becoming Federal Chancellor, Adenauer replied to Patterson's letter from California with the cordial 'mit herzlichen Grüssen' – always a significant gesture from a man as punctilious as Adenauer – and invited him to Bonn.[20] Another American acquaintance from this period, Captain Schweizer, also received a warm letter in February 1948: 'When everything is in flower here on the Rhine, you must come with your wife. The Rhine is at its loveliest then.'[21]

The personal qualities of these officers were apparently superior to the bureaucracy in which they were working. Most of Adenauer's comments in 1945 reveal dismay at the incompetence of the U.S. administration in the early months of the occupation: 'The Americans have not the slightest idea of the German mentality and are the purest children in administrative matters. Not only in Cologne, but everywhere, a confusion reigns that is quite indescribable'.[22] He gave half a dozen examples to support his case, including that of an U.S. captain who had arbitrarily raised the wages of handicrafts workers by thirty-five per cent despite the pay freeze. Early in May, Adenauer talked about his experiences with a visitor from Bonn, Otto Schumacher-Hellmold, who was later to become the FDP mayor of that city. Schumacher-Hellmold, whose brother had emigrated to the United States, defended the Americans by saying that they were just big children. 'Yes', replied Adenauer, 'big, bad children.'[23]

Administrative structures were in a state of complete flux, both in the military administration and in terms of plans for the establishment of a German administration. In Adenauer's view, even the senior occupation officers in Cologne lacked sufficient knowledge and experience to master the problems confronting them. On every issue, whether it involved the restoration of the transport network or the food supply, the school system or the encouragement of the most basic economic activity, Adenauer was increasingly certain that reorganisation and recovery could only begin with action taken far above the level of the municipal administration.

In these conditions, it was no wonder that he became increasingly resigned. Nevertheless, he attempted to prevent the most nonsensical decisions, such as the obligation on all inhabitants of Cologne between the ages of sixteen and sixty-six to participate in forced labour for the reconstruction of the city. However, his role was inevitably limited to improvisation and to sporadic attempts to lay the foundation for the future work of reconstruction. Occasionally, he managed to secure additional administrative responsibilities, or to revive old projects such as the incorporation of Cologne-Land, Bergisch-Gladbach and Bensberg. As always, when he had set his heart on something, he was able to convince himself that it was essential. Cologne, he argued, had been so shattered that the only option was to rebuild it from the periphery – and that would require the use of the outlying rural district. This also gave him the opportunity to work on another pet project: the removal from the city centre, away from the cathedral and the Hohernzollern bridge, of the main railway station.

However, Adenauer was forced to recognise that this was not the time for rational planning. It was pointless to compare the occupation administration with normal administrative techniques, since these pre-supposed a functioning legal system, well-established political conditions and clearly defined areas of responsibility. The constant reorganisations of the early months, combined with frequent changes in personnel, made it seem pointless to engage in those complex struggles for position at which he was usually so adept.

At one point, Adenauer was told of plans to establish a presidium in Bonn to cover the entire Rhine Province, including Rhine-Hessen and the Palatinate. The U.S. Colonel Johnston, who was based at Tönnisstein in the Brohltal, apparently wanted to build it up into a huge ministry and to appoint its departmental leaders as ministers. Adenauer was in despair over the most basic elements of the plan – who, for example, would pay the wages of these senior officials? He therefore wrote a long memorandum to explain the workings of the previous administration to the Americans.[24] In fact, the scheme came to nothing. On 21 June 1945 the British assumed responsibility for the administrative regions of Cologne, Düsseldorf and Aachen. The southern Rhine Province was placed under French occupation administration.

Adenauer was not sorry to see the departure of the Americans. However, it was not long before his mood changed. At the end of July, von Weiss reported to Berne after a weekend meeting with Adenauer: 'This time he appeared to be extraordinarily despondent, since he had imagined that working with the English would be very different.'[25] On 5 October,

Adenauer wrote ruefully to Captain Schweizer, who was now working in Berlin: 'I can only repeat that I have now got to know two crosses. The old cross was decidedly better.'[26] His relatively positive experiences with the British between 1918 and 1926 were not repeated. However, it must be remembered that during these early months of the occupation Adenauer had little precise information regarding conditions in the other Zones. He was therefore assuming, not always correctly, that the situation was better elsewhere.

Remarkably, at the end of the war his attitude towards the Soviet Union was relatively positive. His approach had been influenced by his contacts with Soviet prisoners-of-war during his imprisonment in the concentration camp in Cologne. Early in April, he told an OSS officer that his encounter with these Russians had increased his respect for the achievements of that country. In particular, he admired the enormous strides that had been made in raising educational standards among the Russian masses; this, he thought, had been an important distinction from the Nazis.[27]

An even more surprising opinion was recorded by Otto Schumacher-Hellmold in his diary after a long conversation with Adenauer on 5 May. The mayor had told him that 'Stalin was a friend of Germany';[28] the Russians, he claimed, had behaved better than the Americans in enforcing the occupation. This remark about Stalin, because of its timing, cannot have been a reaction to the Soviet leader's propaganda speech of 9 May 1945, when he proclaimed that the Soviet Union did not plan 'to dismember or destroy Germany'. Instead, it reflected the knowledge of informed Germans that Stalin secretly admired Germany. Moreover, it was in striking contrast to the view expressed by Adenauer at the same time to the effect that Churchill was a 'hater of Germans'. At the very least, Adenauer was initially convinced that the Soviets were well-prepared for their task in Germany while the Americans were completely unprepared.

His imprisonment had also affected Adenauer's view of the German Communists. He told the same OSS officer that, even though their support had increased, it would be possible to work with the Communists on the condition that they pursued a policy independent of the Soviet Union.[29] It is open to question whether Adenauer was simply saying what the CIC wanted to hear, or whether his encounter with men like Zander had caused him to re-examine his opinions. Whatever the truth of the matter, immediately after the armistice he sent a large coach to Buchenwald to bring Zander and other Cologne prisoners home.

By the end of July, however, this positive attitude had completely disappeared. Adenauer was now aware of how the Soviets had behaved during the invasion and occupation of Germany. From this date, the views of the private citizen Adenauer were those with which the public was shortly to become familiar. He told von Weiss, for example, that 'in the Russian-occupied territory the number of rapes of women reached frightening proportions …'[30] Early in July, he complained to von Weiss about 'the methodical, complete plundering of Berlin by the Russians, with machines from heavy industry being transported off to Russia with their skilled workers and engineers.'[31]

Adenauer knew that Berlin had housed seventy per cent of the German low-voltage electricity industry and eighty per cent of the high-voltage, and he was well aware what the loss of these works might mean for Germany. As a result, he thought it inevitable that the big banks and industries of Berlin would have to relocate to the territory that was not occupied by the Soviets. He had a clear idea of the likely course of future developments. The Soviets, he thought, would continue their separate policy; the 'central commission' would not function; and the Zones would be divided. Adenauer was far from certain that unity would be maintained even within the existing Zones. He had heard that part or all of Schleswig-Holstein would be handed over to Denmark, there were rumours that the Americans wanted to annex Bremen as an import harbour, and serious attempts were being made to establish a city state in Hamburg: 'More and more one is convinced that the part of Germany not occupied by the Russians will be broken up into small pieces.'

Furthermore, Germany faced a serious debt problem. Adenauer believed that it had been estimated by experts at 1,000 billion marks. In the months before the Potsdam Conference he was profoundly pessimistic, and feared that the rapid growth of economic misery would lead to a rise in support for the Communists.

During the U.S. occupation, Adenauer had discovered that the occupation authorities did not dare oppose the Communists, who were in many cases being encouraged. He regarded the Germans as desperate and full of dull hatred towards the Western occupation. The atmosphere was likely to deteriorate still further with the onset of winter which, he believed, was likely to bring famine conditions. Even now tuberculosis was rife, and the danger of epidemics would increase during the cold months.

'Conditions are extraordinarily serious, and the future lies very black before us', he wrote to Dannie N. Heineman on 6 July 1945.[32] A letter to Hans Rörig in Berne was equally pessimistic:

> I watch developments in Germany with growing anxiety. Russia is bringing down an iron curtain. I do not believe that the administration of that half of Germany which has been handed over to them will be influenced in any way by the Central Control Commission. The more far-sighted English and American officers probably share this view, for they have no hope of obtaining supplies of foodstuffs from this part of Germany. As regards the administration of the British, the American and the coming French Zones, a disastrous confusion reigns. I believe that most of the military authorities now concerned with the administration of these territories are not motivated by ill-will, but they are completely lacking in knowledge of Germany, administrative experience, and above all any understanding of what even the remainder of Germany means

for Europe, especially for central Europe, thus also for Britain and France and ultimately for America too. In economic terms they have not gone beyond the most meagre of beginnings. You will be interested to know that production in the industrial area is ten per cent of normal and that, of this ten per cent, seven per cent goes to France. I do not need to point out that the remaining three per cent is not enough to boost the economy or the railway system, that no domestic fuel will be available. I fear that millions of people will die of hunger and cold in Germany this winter. Famine oedema as a cause of death is already far from rare ...[33]

Adenauer's reflections on the internal structure of Germany, which he was developing in a tentative fashion during these months, must be examined against this background of pessimism. In his view, the decisive factor was the need for an amalgamation of the largest possible administrative units, at least at Zone level. At his own request, he presented these ideas to the OSS officer Just Lunning on 28 March 1945. Adenauer was contemplating the development of a federal state consisting of Austria, the remainder of Prussia, western Germany (Westphalia and the Rhineland), and southern Germany. Introducing a note of self-criticism, he commented that he often wondered whether he had been wrong to oppose Stresemann in 1923 over the creation of a separate state. There were indeed two Germanies: one in the west, dominated by Roman culture, and one in the east under Prussian influence. However, if Prussia were to be only one of these four new federal states he had proposed, it would be possible to neutralise the non-German Prussian influence. If the decision were taken not to implement this idea, then the Rhineland would have to be recognised as an independent state. However, he added vehemently, the Rhineland must not be placed under the control of France, which would destroy it completely. British and American hegemony, on the other hand, would be tolerable. Frau Adenauer, who was also present, claimed that France would destroy the Rhineland and its culture if it had the opportunity.[34]

Brief and unauthorised memoranda of this kind must, of course, be treated with caution. It is open to doubt whether an American from the Office of Strategic Services was in a position to provide an accurate written summary of the complexities of Adenauer's position. Nevertheless, it is certainly true that during 1945 Adenauer said and thought a great deal that is not easily reconciled with the policy he adopted both earlier and later. In fact, during this period the situation often changed from week to week; no German could accurately judge the likely course of events.

Bornheim also recalled the same conversation, but gave it a rather different emphasis: 'Adenauer warns against crass dismemberment of Germany as the germ of an Irredenta. Tentatively proposes a form of federal states: Rhineland-Westphalia, central and northern Germany, Baden-Bavaria, eventually joined by Austria since it cannot exist alone. Patterson asks what Adenauer would think if the Rhineland, the wider Main territory and the Ruhr were allowed a separate status, for instance for the reconstruction, in the distribution of food-vouchers and so forth. Adenauer replies: 'I would reject it.' On the journey back I ask Adenauer why he had opposed this chance. The answer: 'So that the Rhineland cannot be accused later of separating itself from Germany in an emergency.'[35]

On the whole, Bornheim's report is the more precise of the two. Both sources agree that Adenauer's thinking was based on ideas for a federal state. As regards the possible separate development of the Rhineland, however, the two contradict each other totally.

During these months, Adenauer's deeply critical attitude towards Prussia was a striking element in his thinking. Perhaps it was connected with the fact that the Soviets were now in control there, although it was during these weeks that he seemed to have some confidence in them. Or was it the experiences of the Third Reich that made him take such a negative view of Prussia? Did he share the belief of many of his countrymen in post-war Germany that there was a profound cultural difference between 'colonial Germany' in the east and western, Roman Germany?

Adenauer made a similar comment to Noel G. Annan, a young British officer on the staff of General Templer, during Annan's visit to Rhöndorf in December 1945. Annan was one of a small number of officers with political influence behind the scenes. An historian by profession, he told Adenauer that after demobilisation he hoped to return to Cambridge to teach and write history. 'Then you will be able to tell me', said Adenauer, 'what was the greatest mistake that the English ever made in their relations with Germany?' Annan, not wishing to spoil the story, asked his host to answer the question himself. Adenauer replied: 'It was at the Congress of Vienna, when you so foolishly put Prussia on the Rhine as a safeguard against France and another Napoleon.'[36]

It is wise not to draw too many conclusions from the remark. Nevertheless, this comment and others like it reveal that Adenauer was now more critical of Prussia than he had been before, or ever would be again. One main reason for his attitude was his mistrust of the Soviet Union, linked with a suspicion that the British and Americans might prove incapable of dealing with Soviet manoeuvres in Germany. It may be, therefore, that Adenauer was deliberately trying to stir up the existing anti-Prussian phobias of the British and Americans in order to strengthen their resolve to oppose Soviet influence based in Berlin and the Prussian heartlands. However, in this year zero of modern German history, these tactical considerations were accompanied by a willingness to examine and re-evaluate the course of German history since the beginning of the nineteenth century.

The most important factor in his attitude, nevertheless, was the alarming knowledge that the Soviet Union was now established in the heart of Germany and might penetrate even further to the west. From June 1945, all of Adenauer's constitutional ideas developed in the light of his recognition that Soviet and Western policies had begun to diverge. He was convinced that the Soviet leaders were more single-minded in the pursuit of their objectives, while the Western Powers appeared short-sighted and inconsistent by comparison.

Early in July, Adenauer gave another outline of his ideas on the structure of Germany, on this occasion to a reporter from United Press. He was now arguing in favour of several developments: 1. Stabilisation of the currency without a devaluation of the mark; 2. 'For the German people to be informed which areas would remain German'; 3. 'For the creation of a form of German central administration to rule Germany together with the allied military government.' Most interesting of all was the fourth point. Adenauer proposed to 'establish a German federal state, consisting of three free states that largely coincide with the three large occupied zones of east, west and south Germany. The three free states should have the same currency and the same laws and have no customs barriers between them, but each would be permitted to have a regional government that is responsible to the federal government.'[37]

This outline of his ideas was made public shortly before the Potsdam Conference. It anticipated the concept of the Control Council – but without any mention of France. Adenauer made no reference to the historic Länder of Germany, assuming that, realistically, the occupation zones were likely to become the vital political units. He had heard from various sources that the occupation was likely to last between twenty and twenty-five years. Von Weiss reported to Berne that Adenauer was eager to turn the Rhineland zone as far as Hanover into a viable state structure.[38] He may have thought that this offered the only route to economic survival. Equally, he may have feared that the French would partition the Rhineland unless it was firmly attached to the east.

The situation became even more complicated once France established its position as the fourth occupying power. Until September 1945, Adenauer thought it possible that Cologne and Aachen would be added to the French Zone; Consul-General von Weiss had been informed that this was a possibility by General Billotte and officers on his staff in Bad Ems.

Adenauer, other senior officials, responded without hesitation to the bait. There are a number of possible reasons for his willingness to engage in discussions with the French. These included disappointment with the British, the desire to make early contact with potential new masters as a precautionary measure, and simple curiosity. All these factors probably played a part. At any rate, at the suggestion of the Swiss diplomat, he declared his willingness to meet Billotte, the Gaullist general. In the event, Billotte proved more cautious than Adenauer. Perhaps the French were concerned about the effect of such meetings on relations with the British, or perhaps there were important duties which led to the recall of Billotte to Paris. Despite plans for a personal meeting between Adenauer, von Weiss and Billotte on 4 August in Bad Godesberg, and arrangements for a further meeting on 25 August when the Swiss diplomat travelled with Adenauer to Bad Ems, Billotte was not present on either occasion. The French side preferred to use staff officers to conduct these highly delicate discussions with a mayor in the British Zone.

As far as we know, Adenauer met French officers on half a dozen occasions between August and early October 1945. The first of these occurred on 4 August, when he talked with Lieutenant-Colonel Mahieu, Billotte's chief-of-staff, at Villa Ringsdorff in Bad Godesberg, where von Weiss was holding a private dinner. Others took place on 25 August in Bad Ems, when Adenauer and von Weiss met an officer on Billotte's staff; on 1 September, again in the company of von Weiss, when Adenauer held talks with a Captain Goussault; and on 6 October, with von Weiss present, when the French were represented by Lieutenant-Colonel Gouraud, the 'Délégué Supérieur pour le Gouvernement Militaire de Rhénanie-Hesse-Nassau'. Adenauer also gave von Weiss details of two additional meetings he had held on consecutive days in September, with a captain from the staff of General Koenig, the Military Governor in the French Zone. If von Weiss is correct, these meetings took place on 12 and 13 September 1945.

After some delay, von Weiss sent a report on the discussions to the Department for Foreign Affairs in Berne. In his communication of 9 September 1945, he included the text of a page-long memorandum written by Adenauer on Sunday 2 September after his conversation with Goussault the preceding day. Adenauer had asked that the memorandum be handed to Captain Goussault or General Billotte in Bad Ems on 3 September.

In another report, dated 22 September 1945, von Weiss included the text of a second memorandum. This, he stated, had been given to him by Adenauer on 17 September with the request that he give it to Billotte's representative. Von Weiss suspected that this second memorandum also contained ideas from the president of the Rhine Province, Dr Fuchs, who had been with Adenauer on Sunday 16 September. The second memorandum was also dispatched to Bad Ems, where the French recipients promised to take it to General Billotte. The texts of both documents can be found in Adenauer's personal papers.[39]

The motives of the French in seeking these contacts, and their implications, have been difficult to investigate. However, the French government finally released two documents, previously marked *très secret*, in 1986. The most interesting is the first, dated 13 September and written by Captain Goussault about his meeting with Adenauer on 1 September in Bad Godesberg. The second document is a note by Lieutenant-Colonel Gouraud, Délégué Supérieur for Rhineland-Hesse-Nassau, covering a meeting on the evening of 6 October, when Adenauer's short term as mayor came to an end. The reports generally confirm the evidence provided by von Weiss, but do not permit any final conclusions about the significance of the affair.[40]

His discussions with the French reveal that, some time before his dismissal, Adenauer was preoccupied with much broader issues than the administration of his city. The motives of the French are relatively clear. Billotte and his staff wanted to win support for de Gaulle's Rhine plans in the British-occupied Rhineland. In September, in interviews and during a visit to the French Zone, de Gaulle had advocated a Franco-German rapprochement and had treated with respect the notables who came to meet him. He had thereby pursued his objective of turning the western regions of Germany towards France in political, economic and cultural affairs. Though raising the issue of close western European cooperation, de Gaulle was careful not to reveal that his main motive was the establishment of French hegemony.

Von Weiss had acted throughout the whole affair without instruction from his headquarters. He was apparently fascinated by the idea of being involved in developments of historical significance, and was undoubtedly influenced by the desire to help Adenauer, whom he regarded as an outstanding political figure. What of Adenauer himself? There is no doubt that he recalled his advocacy of Franco-German rapprochement in the 1920s, when Herriot and Briand had attended the 'Pressa' exhibition in the company of Laval. In the midst of the desperate situation of 1945, he may well have been attracted by the idea of conducting private talks with General Billotte, who was reputed to be a close confidant of the French premier, de Gaulle.

Billotte had told von Weiss of his conviction that the constant conflicts between France and Germany must be ended. De Gaulle, he claimed, took the same view, and for that reason, the French supported a policy of economic rapprochement with the Rhineland. At the first meeting, which was also attended by Gussie Adenauer, Adenauer expressed sympathy for de Gaulle's ideas and claimed 'that he agreed with economic cooperation between France and Germany on every point, naturally on certain conditions'.[41] He responded with enthusiasm to the summary given by Lieutenant-Colonel Mahieu, Billotte's chief-of-staff, claiming that he had never heard any Frenchman adopt such a clear and genuine position on the serious problem of Franco-German relations. The fact was that French ideas could indeed be reconciled with Adenauer's old schemes, though only 'on certain conditions'.

As proof of their good intentions, Adenauer's French contacts promised to return to Cologne the university library consisting of around 900,000 volumes, along with most of the valuable paintings from the Wallraf-Richartz Museum. The university rector, Kroll, was to travel to Bad Ems to negotiate the matter.

The first contact had been established. Though the return of the missing treasures to Cologne was a welcome extra benefit, it also offered a useful cover for discussions which would not have been welcomed by the British occupation authorities.

When he visited Bad Ems on 25 August, Adenauer again failed to meet Billotte. However, the possessions of the University of Cologne were made available to him. When it was discovered that a number of crates had been broken into, the building was placed under guard.

The second genuinely political discussion between Adenauer and the French took place on 1 September.[42] Captain Goussault reported that, through von Weiss, Adenauer had made several requests for a meeting with General Billotte. However, he was conscious of the need for discretion owing to his position in the British Zone. Goussault was impressed by his visitor:

> Herr Adenauer stands out among his countrymen and appears to be a man of great qualities. He is more than just a politician. His political experience, despite our legitimate reservations about it, and the sufferings he endured in the Nazi era, have turned him into a real personality, undoubtedly the most important personality in western Germany. He is sixty-nine years old, physically very well preserved and gives lively evidence of his intelligence and subtle thinking. This is combined with a distinctly human aura. One gets the impression that, as a result of a life with its share of suffering, he had achieved a state of 'wisdom'. At least that is the impression he creates ...

It is fair to assume that Goussault's positive view was also influenced by the information he had received from von Weiss. In particular, this information was probably responsible for his opinion that Adenauer – on 1 September 1945 – was the most important political personality in western Germany.

Adenauer gave Goussault a description of his struggle against the opportunism of the Centre Party, which had turned it into a force for centralisation and a servant of the policy of 'Prussianisation'. He was not associated with the errors of his former political friends. Adenauer continued by saying that he had been persecuted in the Third Reich but, unlike many of his colleagues, he had not 'fled' abroad. Now, towards the end of his life, he was prepared to come down from the high level to which life had taken him and to bear with his guilty countrymen a burden that was not his own. He wanted to help the Rhinelanders to escape from chaos and find their way towards the restoration of human dignity, freedom and democracy.

He then turned to more practical matters. The situation in Cologne was bad; in his view the British were not greatly concerned with the needs of the population and the coming winter was a fearful prospect. When Goussault observed that there was no shortage of coal in the British Zone, Adenauer replied that the British were preventing coal mining and were trying to destroy the whole of industry. On the other hand, he believed that the policy of France was different; he would be pleased to see a large part of the Rhineland under French control.

After revealing his opinion so clearly, Adenauer was asked by Goussault how he had reached this view. Adenauer replied: 'I believe that in the Rhineland France finds an economy that is complementary to its own, and that the integration of the Rhenish economy into the French economy is in the interests of France, while the attempt to undertake such a policy with Britain would be regarded by British industry as being against its interests.' British policy, he thought, was always selfish.

Compared with the mistrust of France he had expressed to Lunning in March 1945, this was a complete *volte face*. There are two possible reasons for it. First, Adenauer seems to have thought that the French were about to assume responsibility for the North Rhine Province, and was trying to establish himself as an important factor in the new situation that would follow. Second, he may have been so dissatisfied with British policy that he wanted to encourage the ambitions of the French. It is likely that both sentiments played a part in his conduct.

In any event, he was careful to compliment Goussault on the wisdom of French occupation policy. In fact, French policy towards the Rhineland during the inter-war years had been disappointing: though extensive in its political claims, it had been weak and incoherent in practice and had failed to ensure military security. The classic example of French failure during these years had been Hitler's remilitarisation of the Rhineland in March 1936.

Though Goussault made some attempt to defend his British allies, Adenauer's assessment remained negative. The British in 1945, he claimed, lacked the discretion, education and knowledge of their predecessors in 1918.

Adenauer then turned to his own constitutional ideas. According to Goussault's report, he explained his concept of a federalism 'of small German states' (*de petits états allemands*). What was necessary, he thought, was a Rhineland that included the North Rhine, the Ruhr, the Siegerland and the rural areas around Münster. Such a state would focus its economic and cultural activities on France.

Nevertheless, Adenauer expressed some fear that France would turn Communist. Goussault assured him that the French Communists were good patriots and that, in any case, the world situation needed to be changed. By contrast, Adenauer was critical of German Communism, which continued to alarm him. He ended with the assurance that if France were to pursue a durable and stable policy towards the Rhineland, he could prove that the leading figures of the North Rhine Province were sincere in their hopes for an independent Rhineland closely associated with France.

This conversation was echoed in the memorandum which von Weiss included in his report of 2 September 1945. These passages reiterated Adenauer's old ideas, including his aim of establishing 'through economic cooperation and integration, a lasting, very close rapprochement in cultural and eventually also political matters'. Of course, the fruits of this cooperation would benefit France in the first instance. Nevertheless, 'for psychological reasons they should, from the outset, not be withheld from the Rhineland'. This was his way of pointing out that the Germans would like to have the use of at least some of their own coal: 'From the start the Rhineland must be given the well-founded hope that it will not simply be a colony, but that its economy can and will develop in integration with the French to make its work worthwhile for the Rhinelanders themselves.' During his conversation with Goussault the previous day, Adenauer had used more picturesque language: 'If you want to milk a cow you must give it something to eat. And I will go further: once this precondition is fulfilled, then it is essential that you treat it well.'

Adenauer then returned to the ideas that he had first mentioned in the Cologne city hall twenty-seven years previously. The Rhineland, he insisted, must not be dismembered: 'It would not be good if the northern part of the Rhineland were not included in this territory.' Though he did not describe the preferred constitutional structure of the region, Adenauer did outline its size: 'The best prospect for full realisation of the goal would be the creation of a territory that included the whole of the Rhineland plus the entire industrial area belonging to it, if possible including Münster and the Siegerland.' In essence, this was the map of the future Land of North Rhine-Westphalia.

Adenauer went on: 'An international statute for the industrial area must be limited to its economic supervision, but should not otherwise affect its affiliation to this territory. France must have a decisive voice in this supervision, as France has by far the greatest interest. It must be left to the future to decide whether the economic rapprochement of the Franco-German economy to the Luxembourgian, Belgian and Dutch economies is possible ...' However, he was careful to list his conditions once again: the psychological factor – and it was clear that he was referring to the *German* psyche – would have to be taken into account from the outset: 'It would therefore be excellent if the French troops, like the Americans and English, were no longer fed off the land in future. Equally, more or less unregulated requisitions must be completely halted in future and restitution be made according to a fixed plan that also take account of the vital needs of the Rhinelanders. The aim is the *lasting gain*, not the domination, of the Rhineland.'

This memorandum was typical of Adenauer. It was designed to awaken interest in specific solutions, though the unpleasant details were still to be worked out. It signalled to his interlocutors that Adenauer could be a significant factor in their discussions so long as their aim was a policy of rapprochement. Lastly, it demonstrated to the astonished French that the mayor had little concern for the British occupation authorities.

In reality, Adenauer already suspected that his relations with the French – like the Americans and British before them – would bring their own share of problems. A few days later, he told von Weiss that there had been complaints from Baden because the small town of Oppenheim was being forced to cater for an occupying force of 7,000 French soldiers. But when de Gaulle's ideas were published in an interview of 11 September, Adenauer regarded the situation in Germany as catastrophic. These plans were 'at best a guarantee that what can still be saved from Germany will be saved'.[43]

No clear picture of Adenauer's flirtation with the Gaullist officers is yet possible. In discussions of 12 and 13 September 1945 with an Alsatian captain from Baden-Baden representing General Koenig, and in a further conversation on 6 October, he apparently thought it possible that a Rhine-Ruhr state, strongly influenced by France, might be created, along with two further west German states. Adenauer's main concern at this stage was with Soviet policy. The Soviets, he believed, were pursuing an increasingly independent line in the Eastern zone, and were also attempting to create a new Reich under Soviet influence based in Berlin.[44]

The reports of Consul-General von Weiss, previously the most important source of Adenauer's contacts with French emissaries from Bad Ems and Baden-Baden, reveal that he and Adenauer did not agree on every issue. On 26 September, the Swiss diplomat sent an eighteen-page memorandum to Berne outlining his own grandiose schemes for the re-organisation of Germany. Von Weiss was contemplating the establishment of a great Land, which he called the 'Rhine-state', to include the regions that subsequently became Lower Saxony, North Rhine-Westphalia, Hesse, and North Baden. The eastern border of France, he thought, should be moved to the other side of the Black Forest ridge, particularly since Alsace and Baden were populated by the same 'Allemans'. As the Soviet-occupied territory would have to be written off, Germany would thus consist of three loosely connected states: the Rhine-state, Württemberg, and Bavaria.[45]

These speculations were the product of a hectic period when the Balkanisation of Germany appeared to be imminent. It is likely that Adenauer was aware only of parts of this memorandum, whether written by von Weiss or someone else. His Rhöndorf papers contain only one passage from it. This concerns structural issues and begins with the sentence: 'A complete constitutional separation of the territory in question from the remaining parts of Germany would not be right, it would sow the seeds of future complications …' Assuming that the areas occupied by the Soviet Union, 'almost half of the old German territory', would take a separate path, two further smaller states were possible in the west alongside a 'Rhine-state'.

Von Weiss continued:

> With regard to the emerging imperialist tendencies of Russia, it is highly probable that Russia would maintain the fiction that this was the old Germany,

and that the three new states, especially the Rhine-state, would strive for reunification with this Germany. The face of the Rhine-state would be turned not to the west but to the east. To achieve the desired goals: 'elimination of the possibility of Germany preparing a new war, strengthening of the economic and political power of France as the leading power in western Europe', it is quite sufficient and actually better, for the reasons mentioned above, if the Rhine-state is left in a loose constitutional association with the other parts of Germany. In general terms their own rights to pass legislation, their own foreign policy representation, perhaps an international gendarmerie consisting of members of neutral states.

This passage, apparently produced by Adenauer, ended – unlike the full memorandum to the Swiss Foreign ministry – with the words 'consisting of'. In his own hand, Adenauer added 'Britain, Americans a[nd] neutral states (Sweden, Switzerland, Denmark)'.[46]

Four days before the dispatch of this memorandum, von Weiss sent to Berne a report dated 22 September 1945.[47] This dealt with Adenauer's discussions with General Koenig's envoy on 12 and 13 September. Though von Weiss had not taken part, he wrote that Adenauer had handed him a memorandum for transmission to General Billotte, which he had done.

The most controversial passage in this memorandum, which was attributed to Adenauer, was as follows:

Of course the issue will be raised of the fate of the remaining parts of Germany if a Ruhr-state, or rather Rhine-state, is established. On this subject it should be said: it seems that the territory occupied by Russia cannot be included in these deliberations for the foreseeable future. The appointment by the Russians of a shadow government for one zone, against the Potsdam resolutions, clearly proves that Russia has decided to go its own way. On the construction of a Rhine-state, two further states could probably be established from the remaining parts. These three states could then become a loose structure under international law, corresponding to the Commonwealth. All three states would have to pursue a foreign policy independent of the others, and each in particular would have its own foreign representation.

The second part of this memorandum was less explosive. It objected that, as a result of the 'de-industrialisation' of Germany, 'the industry of the Rhine-state would no longer be able to compete with American and English industry'. This fact would 'greatly endanger the aim pursued by the establishment of a Rhine-state – the strengthening of the economic power of France by means of integration with an efficient Rhenish industry. In addition, as a result of the great economic distress suffered by the inhabitants of the Rhine-state, this French sphere of influence would become a focus of sickness which would endanger the bordering states and the process of psychological and political rapprochement.'

On 5 October 1945, von Weiss was sternly rebuked by the Political Department in Berne for his highly political contacts with French officers and his reports.[48] He was informed that his actions were incompatible with the duties of a Swiss consul abroad:

It would have been your duty not to do anything which might have created the appearance that you had received instructions from Berne in this matter. However, we have established that you are already very exposed, and have even been active in support of separatist tendencies. We do not approve of your initiative in this matter and specifically and urgently request you to cease not only your active attempts to influence both parties but also all mediation in the issue.

After such a rebuke from his own minister, it seemed likely that von Weiss would defend himself by claiming that he had mainly been repeating Adenauer's own ideas, particularly since he was not sure 'what consequences there might be from my actions, apart from the judgement of my higher authorities'. However, this was not the appoach von Weiss adopted in his five-page letter of justification on 27 October. In it, the consul-general admitted that he had written the memorandum of 22 September, though he had previously claimed that it came from Adenauer:

In my report of 22.9.1945, political questions were broached for the first time. I stress that, on p.3 of this report, I expressly state that the three states to be created from the part of Germany not occupied by the Russians 'must become a loose structure under international law, corresponding to the Commonwealth'. There was no reference to a buffer state, on the contrary I believe that a constitutional link between these three states is necessary. I have expressly chosen the term 'Commonwealth' because this expression contains various nuances regarding the constitutional link, and of course I did not intend to go further than general ideas. Nor can I be reproached for my idea of giving these states the right to have their own foreign representation. The possible Ruhr-state would certainly be subject to a special economic arrangement. That would create the need for its own foreign representation; this could not then be withheld from the other two states. Otherwise, may I refer to the fact that various states of the Soviet Union and the members of the British Empire have the right to their own foreign representation.

The entire defence contained no reference at all to Adenauer as the author of the memorandum. In referring to it, and to his report of 8 September 1945, von Weiss wrote only:

In my report pp. 2,3 I have described in detail the earlier initiative taken by the mayor Dr Konrad Adenauer in these areas, in order to demonstrate that these discussions were only a continuation of this earlier policy, which was never about the creation of a buffer state. I also add that during the discussions with the French officers I described, Dr Adenauer specifically and vigorously repudiated separatist efforts. To the agreement of the French officers, he described separatism as the least suitable means of bringing about lasting peace in western Europe.[49]

It is obviously advisable to treat this part of the diplomat's reports with considerable caution. Even if the memoranda in question were located in the French archives, they might be filed as Adenauer memoranda which had been sent on by Consul-General von Weiss. In that case the situation would remain unclear. Despite the speculation, there is little prospect of the matter being fully explained.

Nevertheless, it is clear that Adenauer had begun a form of flirtation with Gaullist officers. Bearing in mind that the British already distrusted him, this must be regarded as an extremely foolish step, since discussions with the representatives of another occupying power were certainly not permitted. The conversations also reveal a certain consistency in Adenauer's views on Europe. These dated from the period immediately after the First World War, had continued through the late 1920s, and were eventually to find their most tangible expression in the Schuman Plan. His thinking on the subject of a reorganisation in the west was also influenced by his belief that the Soviets, with their stronghold in Berlin, were attempting to draw the Western Zones into their sphere of influence.

In contrast to the current French approach, Adenauer believed that the establishment of a great Rhine-Ruhr state was indispensable. De Gaulle, however, was inclined to favour the idea of setting up a number of smaller states, with only minimal links between them, on France's western border. Adenauer's insistence on the links between the Ruhr and the neighbouring regions, and his demand for the abandonment of the policy of de-industrialisation, also differed from the plans of the French.

Adenauer was fortunate that the French were discreet. Over the following years, there were many rumours about his secret contacts with the French, including a claim that he had met de Gaulle in Maria Laach. However, nothing precise was discovered. In mid-September General Billotte was transferred to Paris. The anticipated northwards extension of the French Zone did not take place. Early in October, Adenauer discovered that the British, whom he had not taken into account in his vague plans for the future of Western Europe, were not prepared to place their part of the Rhineland and Ruhr at disposal.

The views expressed during Adenauer's discussions with the French are also reflected in comments he made in a famous interview with representatives of the *News Chronicle* and the Associated Press on 5 October, and shortly afterwards in a long memorandum to the mayor of Duisburg, Heinrich Weitz.

The interview contains a number of the arguments that were included in the document Adenauer sent to Weitz. At the same time, he did not disguise his criticisms of the British occupation. Adenauer thus claimed that it was reprehensible not to give the Germans any coal for cooking; death, sickness and epidemics would be the result. De Gaulle had said in Saarbrücken that it was essential to remember that they were West Europeans, and he wished that a British statesman had also spoken of the Germans as West Europeans.

Adenauer argued that any Rhine-Ruhr state must be linked with the other parts of Germany not occupied by the Soviets. If these other areas were separated from each other, the Soviet Union would declare the Soviet Zone as the real German Reich, and the other parts would automatically strive for reunification with it. If three western states were created, they must remain constitutionally associated, eventually in a federal state. To that end it was necessary to integrate the economy of the remaining parts, especially that of the Rhine-Ruhr state, with France and Belgium, in order to promote the development of common economic interests. When the journalists finally asked whether it would therefore be sensible for France to occupy Cologne, Adenauer answered that this was not necessary and was an issue of secondary importance. If there was no other way, it would have to be accepted for the sake of the higher goal.[50]

This interview at Rhöndorf of 5 October 1945 was Adenauer's last as mayor of Cologne. The next day he was dismissed.

Adenauer expanded these ideas in a letter to Heinrich Weitz on 31 October. From now on, they provided the theoretical basis of his future foreign policy. Concepts that had previously been mentioned only in conversation or in private letters were now clearly set out: 'Russia has in its hands the eastern half of Germany, Poland, the Balkans, apparently Hungary, part of Austria. Russia is increasingly withdrawing from cooperation with the other great powers and is acting entirely as it thinks fit in the territories under its control. The lands it controls are already ruled by different economic and political principles to those in the rest of Germany. Division into Eastern Europe, the Russian territory, and Western Europe is therefore a fact.'[51] This was the post-war map on which his whole future foreign policy would have to be based. Six months later he made the point with even greater urgency: 'The danger is great. Asia stands at the Elbe.'[52]

His letter to Weitz continued: 'The part of Germany not occupied by the Russians is an integral part of Western Europe. If it remains sick, that would have the most serious consequences for the whole of Western Europe, including Britain and France. It is in the interests not only of the non-Russian-occupied part of Germany, but also of Britain and France, to combine Western Europe under their leadership, to bring political and economic health to that part of Germany that is not occupied by the Russians.' There should be no separation of the Rhineland and Westphalia, however, but the 'economic integration of Western Germany, France, Belgium, Luxembourg, Holland … If Britian also decided to take part in this economic integration, the desirable initial goal of a "union of the West European states" would be much closer.' As regards the constitutional form of Germany, he noted: 'A reasonable constitutional structure does not exist at the moment, it must be restored.'[53] A federal relationship must be established instead of a centralised state.

Almost exactly six months after the final defeat of Germany on 7 May, Adenauer's phase of tentative reflection and exploration had reached its end. Though the details of his assessment changed in many respects thereafter, its basic principles were firmly established. Moreover, Ade-

nauer was convinced that his concept was capable of dealing satisfactorily with transformed political conditions. In essence, the concept was his
old idea of the economic and political integration of Western Europe. The
basic factor underlying his assessment was the Cold War between the
West and the Soviet Union; the leitmotif of his foreign policy was the
concept of Europe.

Adenauer had already moved far beyond his restricted role in
Cologne. For some time he had devoted much of his intellectual energy
to the wider national and international scene. Nothing of significance
could be done from within his shattered city; effective action was only
possible at the highest political level. Nevertheless, it was far from certain
that he would have been the man to shape the future of Germany if the
British had not done him the greatest service they could have rendered in
the circumstances: they dismissed him.

Dismissal by the Liberators

Few events in Adenauer's life have been the subject of so much speculation as his dismissal by the British. In fact, the British themselves later felt
that Adenauer's personal resentment might have been the cause of many
of their later difficulties with the old man, especially at the end of the
1950s. On a number of occasions in later years, Adenauer took care to
remind them of the incident, either directly or through third parties. At the
beginning of the 1960s, Robert Pferdmenges – who knew him better than
most – claimed that Adenauer never overcame his resentment at his humiliating ejection from office. (Of course, even here there is a possibility that
Pferdmenges was deliberately being used to prick British consciences.)

In fact, the numerous clashes which marked Adenauer's relations with
Britain after 1946 can plausibly be explained by other reasons. It is not
necessary to believe that he was bent on revenge for past slights. Moreover, closer observation reveals that, until the 1950s at least, Adenauer
believed that European cooperation would require Britain as much as
France. In addition, his attitude towards Paris was equally touchy; anyone
who investigates his comments during this period will find as many
excessive remarks about the French as about the British.

With hindsight, Adenauer even recognised that the officer who dis-
missed him had done him a service. In 1962, during an interview with the
U.S. television network CBS, he was asked whether he would have become
Chancellor if he had not been dismissed. He replied: 'Quite certainly not ...

Then they would have had to look for someone else, perhaps someone better, perhaps someone worse; there were candidates.'[1] Only weeks after his dismissal he wrote philosophically to Heinrich Weitz: 'Whether it was a good thing that happened to me or a bad one, who can say?'[2]

The event itself was often described by Adenauer. Though Brigadier Barraclough has denied that there was ungentlemanly conduct on his part, in 1980 Adenauer's story was confirmed in all of its details by Colin Lawson, then deputy city-commandant and later a foreign correspondent.[3]

Trouble was clearly brewing between Adenauer and the representative of the Military Government for the city of Cologne, Major J. Alan Prior, when the British appointed a city council to reflect a wide range of views within the city. When this assembly convened on 1 October, Prior did not mince his words:

> Every day I hear the following complaints about the city administration:
> a) it is a purely party organisation and not the representation and the expression of actual public opinion ...;
> b) former National Socialists are being appointed again, while members of anti-fascist parties are still without responsible posts ....
> For the coming winter, the following emergency measures must be planned and implemented without delay: the building of homes and emergency repairs of houses; mass feeding and provision of fuel; health care.[4]

Prior's coldness was probably influenced by his knowledge that there was much dissatisfaction with the mayor in high places. In any event, he offered no word of recognition for the mayor's efforts over the past six months.

Adenauer did not comment on this fact in his reply. Nor, at the same time, did he give any sign of a sense of obligation towards the occupying power. Certainly he condemned the 'execrable people' who had brought about the misery. As so often in the spring of 1945, he alluded to Hitler's orders for the destruction of Germany; these orders had been particularly wicked, he argued, because they sought to increase the misery of the German people, thereby encouraging new thoughts of revenge and retaliation against the enemy. However, his remarks contained no trace of a sense of collective guilt or collective shame. Adenauer told his audience that 'We, you and I, are not to blame for this misery.'

Adenauer's description of the situation in Cologne also contained a hidden anti-British message:

> Standing on the right bank of the Rhine, in the midst of the ruins, among hundreds of people who are returning daily and who are pale, tired, careworn, hauling with them the few belongings they still possess, seeing the ghostly ruins of our once-beautiful bridges in the river, and there, on the left bank of the Rhine, an endless sea of shattered houses in which happy people once lived, of buildings and churches that stood for almost a thousand years, and seeing the cathedral above in lonely splendour, our cathedral, also desecrated and partly destroyed – then whose heart does not almost stop beating?

Cologne cathedral – 'desecrated and partly destroyed', in Adenauer's words. Was he not also asking his listeners to remember who had destroyed it?

The speech ended with a piece of defiant self-assertion: '... the towers that our cathedral stretched towards heaven are still pointing unbroken to heaven. So we will go to work together. Bowed, deeply bowed, but – ladies and gentlemen – not broken.'[5]

Shortly before this exchange of words there had been another clash between Adenauer and the British, who had threatened to cut down the trees in his beloved green belt in order to obtain firewood for the winter. Adenauer refused outright, demanding that the seized coal supplies should be released for the purpose instead, and that sufficient building materials should be made available.[6]

The military commander of North Rhine Province, Brigadier-General Sir John Barraclough, appeared in Cologne three days before Adenauer's dismissal to demand a greater effort: 'Cologne is the worst-cleared city in the British Zone.' The Corps Commander had been breathing down his neck as a result. Yet the mayor, according to Barraclough, was devoting his energies to political intrigue, and to insolence.[7]

Alan Prior, the city commandant, was a capable and reasonable man who, despite his business background, possessed sound political instincts. However, he was in London when the storm broke. Three days after Barraclough's visit, his deputy, Lawson, received a telegram from Düsseldorf instructing him to take Adenauer to headquarters in the Ringstraße. Adenauer was located in Bonn on a sad mission, attending the funeral of his friend Major Schliebusch. One year previously, Schliebusch had attempted to save him from the Gestapo. He was escorted back to Cologne to meet Barraclough, who had arrived from Düsseldorf. There followed a scene reminiscent of the movies. Barraclough remained seated at his desk; to his right stood the red-haired Major Lawson, who was stony-faced throughout and who had warned his chief against the measure; to his left were Colonel Charrington, a member of the famous brewing family, and a woman interpreter.

Adenauer, who did not appreciate being left standing, looked round for a chair. Barraclough barked out a peremptory 'Remain standing!' before reading out the order for his dismissal. It contained twelve points, including complaints that he had neglected the work of restoring buildings, clearing the ruins, and preparing for the winter. Barraclough maintained that the situation was grave: '... in my view you have not fulfilled your duty towards the population of Cologne'. As a result he was dismissed, banned from the city, and was under strict instructions to refrain from all political activity, either directly or indirectly. If he contravened these instructions, Barraclough informed him, 'you will be taken before the military court'. Adenauer was to confirm receipt of the order in writing. The temporary mayor was to be Willi Suth, of whose family ties with Adenauer the brigadier was apparently unaware.

Adenauer stood motionless, his hands locked together, his face completely immobile. When Barraclough pushed the order for his dismissal towards him across the desk, Adenauer reached into his breast pocket for his pen and signed. Asked if he had anything to say, he said simply 'No', and left the room.[8]

From the outset, Adenauer suspected that there had been political intrigue against him. On the evening of his dismissal, he told Lieutenant-Colonel Gouraud that the British Socialists were desperate to prevent the rise of his party, the CDU. He was suspicious of one individual, whom he did not name, within the German SPD: 'I must add that I owe this dismissal mostly to the intrigues of a German who is now in the pay of the British after earlier putting himself at the service of the SD.'[9]

The fact of the matter was that his old Social Democrat adversary, Robert Görlinger, had handed a document to the British in July. This stated that the social democratic and communist workers 'were most deeply incensed by the policy being pursued by Adenauer, Suth and Schwering, backed up by the Catholic clergy in Cologne'. The old Centre Party clique was reviving the confessional schools. Furthermore, on 28 June Adenauer had sent the U.S. military government a memorandum for General Eisenhower, asking whether the strict regulations against the Nazis could be relaxed.

Adenauer was convinced that this letter had contributed to his dismissal and therefore included extracts from it in his memoirs. As the British files show, William Strang, who was responsible for political issues relating to the occupation administration, had incorporated Görlinger's comments in one of his reports.[10]

In Britain the Labour Party had been in power since early August 1945. The new government, along with some circles in British headquarters, was aware that immediately after the occupation began, often on the recommendation of the conservative clergy, some appointments had been made that did not reflect the new political landscape. Labour delegates made frequent visits to the Control Council in Berlin and to Minden, headquarters of the Military Governor of the British Zone, in order to urge officers and their political advisers to make room for 'progressive' forces.

In mid-September, the mayor of Düsseldorf, Wilhelm Füllenbach, was replaced by the Social Democrat Walter Kolb, who later became mayor of Frankfurt. President Fuchs was dismissed on 2 October. A rumour rapidly spread that the British intended to fill every senior post with a Social Democrat. However, this soon proved to be unfounded. For example, as successor to Fuchs the British appointed Adenauer's old rival from Düsseldorf, Robert Lehr, a former member of the conservative-national DNVP who had also been an opponent of the Nazis.

The political climate in British headquarters was not particularly favourable to Catholic politicians, who were regarded by Labour as reactionaries. Nevertheless, it appears that Barraclough, though aware of opinion at headquarters, had acted on his own initiative; no evidence has yet emerged of any control from afar. This view is also supported by the fact that no successor was at hand. However, it should also be noted that four documents of the 'Germany' file in the Bevin Papers, dating from early October 1945, are closed up to the year 2049. Not until November did the British appoint Hermann Pünder as the new mayor of Cologne. He too was a former member of the Centre Party and a man with many ties to Adenauer.

In retrospect, it seems clear that Adenauer's time as mayor did not satisfy him. In the circumstances a major row, followed by his departure – either voluntarily or after his dismissal – appeared almost inevitable. Moreover, in August he had decided to link his future with the Christian Democratic Party, which was then being established throughout the country and had a strong regional base in Cologne. His contemporary correspondence and his contacts with Gaullist officers indicate that a desire to shape developments was taking him beyond his city even before he was ejected from office. Consul-General von Weiss, whom he met immediately afterwards for another exchange of views with French officers from Bad Ems, reported to his government on 13 October: 'Though this measure affects Herr Adenauer deeply, including in a personal sense ... I have seldom seen him in such a good mood as on the day in question, he was well aware of the Herculean task that awaited him in the coming winter.'[11]

This was confirmed by the report of Lieutenant-Colonel Gouraud. It quoted Adenauer as follows: 'My dismissal as mayor did not disturb me in the least. But what I find infuriating, I must admit, is the stipulation that bans me from any kind of political activity. Apart from me personally, this ban affects the entire Christian Democratic Party whose spokesman I am ...!'

Despite these assertions, he had been greatly hurt by his abrupt ejection from office. Adenauer was a proud man; his entire nature rebelled against the humiliating treatment meted out to him. The fact that his dismissal had been on grounds of incompetence was especially galling, and he knew that it might damage his political prospects. The event was also an unpleasant reminder of his experiences in March 1933: yet again, there was no-one to bid him farewell when he was forced out of Cologne.

Only one of his receptionists was roused to anger on his behalf, writing Barraclough a touching letter in which she described Adenauer's tireless efforts on behalf of his city. The British on the spot regarded her as an excellent translator, but this did not prevent Barraclough from giving her the sack.[12] However, Adenauer did receive a number of sympathetic letters. Robert Pferdmenges, for example, wrote of the '... sorrow and affliction! One continues to do one's duty, but one's heart is no longer in it ... Yet despite everything, I believe in Britain's fairness and I am convinced that one day you – you above all – will receive justice.'[13]

Adenauer was hit particularly hard by his ban from the city. Since her imprisonment in Brauweiler, Gussie Adenauer had suffered from a bone marrow disease which prevented the creation of more blood corpuscles and reduced the body's resistance to infection. When her husband was dismissed, she was being treated by a specialist, Professor Uhlenbruck, at Hohenlind. Prior and Lawson therefore intervened to circumvent the ban by granting Adenauer permission to visit his wife.

Potentially, his future career was most seriously jeopardised by the ban on all political activity. Only two days after his dismissal, he sought clarification on this point from the Military Government. He was careful to give an impression of righteous innocence by making precautionary reference to a number of political and journalistic contacts he had made. Adenauer was well aware that his famous interview of 5 October had probably displeased the British; if news of his various contacts with French officers were to leak out, his position would be even worse. It seemed that the best course of action was to behave as though his conduct had been entirely natural and normal: 'Since the start of the occupation, in both Rhöndorf and Cologne, I have often been visited by British, American and French journalists and politicians wanting my opinion on various questions, including the future shape of Germany. I request information on whether in future I may not hold such conversations on the grounds that they fall under category of political activity which is forbidden to me.'[14] He received no reply.

However, the affair now caused a disagreement among the British in the form of a furious row between Prior, Lawson and the Brigadier. Prior hastened back from London to Cologne. Lawson explained that in his last report he had noted that, of all the politicians he had met, Adenauer was the only one with the qualities required by a first post-war Chancellor. Prior, who was clearly a perceptive and astute observer, now went with Lawson to the Villa Hügel in Essen, where Barraclough was holding a reception. Here Prior angrily attacked his commander over his treatment of one of the most important politicians of pre-Hitler Germany. He ended his outburst with the comment: 'You are unfit for your job.'[15] Shortly afterwards Prior relinquished his command and his promotion was deferred. For a time he was threatened with court martial, but the threat was not carried out largely because Barraclough had realised that General Templer regarded his hasty action as a mistake.

At home in Rhöndorf, Adenauer received another interesting visitor in the form of a young British officer named Michael Thomas. He had been born Ulrich Hollaender, the son of a Viennese mother and a father who was a well-known writer, a theatre critic and the director of the Reinhardt theatre in Berlin. As a victim of the anti-Semitic Nuremberg Laws, Thomas, had left Berlin in 1938 for France and then for Britain. In the British Army he had been assigned to a Polish division, with which he served during the final months of the war, and had then been attached to the staff of General Templer. Well-informed emigrés such as Thomas proved very useful in keeping the British informed about German opinion in the immediate aftermath of the war. On 10 October he arrived in Rhöndorf, where Paul Adenauer was shocked at the sight of his uniform, to hear Adenauer's account of his fall. By now, the old man had recovered his good spirits. As he told Thomas, 'Particular intelligence has not been a characteristic of our parachute generals either'. He was interested to discover whether the Foreign Office had ordered his dismissal on suspicion that he had held a secret meeting with de Gaulle. If so, he told Thomas, it was not true.

These indications of an uneasy conscience were followed by protestations of his affection for Britain and of regret at the apparent decline in the idea of the British gentleman. 'Look', he continued, 'I am an old man. I no longer have any political ambition ...' According to Thomas, he replied: 'Herr Adenauer, I just don't buy that!'[16]

Cordial relations were quickly established between Adenauer and the Berliner in British uniform. Thomas liked Adenauer and enjoyed a number of conversations with him; he also wrote private letters when he felt it necessary to bypass the official channels. Later, the relationship was also encouraged by Herbert Blankenhorn, soon to become a confidant of Adenauer. Since Adenauer was ignorant of the English language and of the inner workings of the military administration as well, such contacts helped him considerably during the years of his rise to the office of Federal Chancellor. Emigrés such as Thomas had an excellent knowledge of both sides; conversations with them were often more informative than a whole series of official discussions, all of which had to be translated.

Adenauer's relationship with the British had begun to improve. Lieutenant-Colonel Noel G. Annan, a young man of twenty-seven, who had been briefed by Thomas, was another Englishman to visit him in Rhöndorf. A few years after his return to civilian life, as a don at Cambridge, Annan witnessed Adenauer's visit as Federal Chancellor, and later became Vice-Chancellor of the University of London. In October 1945 Annan was working as an intelligence officer with Christopher Steel in the Political Department of the Control Commission. 'Kit' Steel, a son-in-law of Lord Clive,[17] became Deputy High Commissioner in 1949 and was to serve as British ambassador in Bonn from 1957 until 1963. In autumn 1945, Annan and Steel were among a growing number of Britons who were convinced that the Berlin Control Council was little more than a charade. Though they were willing to work with the Soviets, a rupture seemed highly likely; in the event of such a break, they were eager to find German politicians who would prove reliable.

Annan, well-mannered and witty, was very much Adenauer's idea of an English gentleman. He also knew the details of Adenauer's fall. When Annan asked him for a political discussion, Adenauer offered his regrets and proposed that the two should travel to the border of the French Zone in Unkel; he could speak openly there, but not in Rhöndorf, since he was banned from all political activity in the British Zone on pain of court martial.[18] Whatever his inner amusement, Annan affected astonishment at this disclosure. The two men then held a mutually enlightening conversation. Adenauer was interested to hear that the British were apparently considering whether to allow him to take up a political role. Annan also told him that he had been regarded as anti-British, largely on the basis of information about the years of occupation of the Rhineland after the First World War. Adenauer vigorously denied the allegation, though he admitted that the course of modern history made it difficult for him to regard Britain as a European country. He then made the observation that British policy had been in error in allowing Prussia to mount 'the watch on the Rhine' in 1815.

These remarks can be interpreted in several ways. They can be regarded as a mere intellectual game; as a disguised criticism of British policy in the Control Council; as a reflection of his growing scepticism towards developments in modern German history; or as another example of his Prussophobia. In any case, it is obvious that Adenauer, in 1945, was deliberately exploiting the anti-Prussian notions of U.S., French, or British interlocutors in an attempt to intensify their mistrust of the Russians in the political heartland of Prussia. It would be wrong to exaggerate the significance of such remarks. In his talks with foreign observers, Adenauer had developed a habit of talking too much and, on occasion, contradicting himself.

Nevertheless, Annan was impressed by Adenauer. He and 'Kit' Steel intervened to lift the ban on his political activity – though not in the Cologne administrative district itself, on the grounds that it seemed unwise openly to disavow the actions of a British provincial governor, even if these had been mistaken.

This favourable turn of events enabled Adenauer to play a part in developments during the critical weeks when decisions were being taken about senior posts in the CDU in the British Zone. Carefully and discreetly, Adenauer began to establish contacts from his base in Rhöndorf. Singly or in small groups, German politicians began to make their way to the 'Obersalzberg on the Rhine', to use the mocking words of Walther Hensel, later CDU town clerk of Düsseldorf.[19]

In mid-December, the ban on Adenauer's political activity was lifted completely. He was invited to Düsseldorf on 7 December 1945, where Lieutenant-Colonel Annan was due to speak to prominent political leaders of the North Rhine Province. The signal was clear: the British wanted to demonstrate that Adenauer was back in favour. Barraclough was forced to accept this turn of events. Eight days later he summoned Adenauer to Düsseldorf and informed him 'in the most polite manner' that all bans, conditions and restrictions had been officially lifted.

The decision came just in time for Adenauer, since moves to establish the CDU were reaching a crucial stage. Between 14 and 16 December, a first CDU *Reichstagung* was scheduled to take place at Bad Godesberg, and Annan was eager for Adenauer to take part. News of his rehabilitation was passed to the CDU representatives from the three Western zones by the chairman of the meeting. At the same time, the executives of the important CDU local organisations were engaged in discussions over appointments to the top posts in the Rhenish CDU, and the establishment of a CDU committee in the British Zone. Consul-General von Weiss, who had been severely rebuked by his minister for his intervention in the Adenauer affair, wrote almost triumphantly to Berne on 28 December: 'It is assumed that Adenauer will be entrusted with the leadership of the Christian Democratic Union in the entire British Zone ... Dr Adenauer, though still without office at the moment, has become the dominant personality far beyond this narrow area.'[20]

Only a month later, on 22 and 23 January 1946 in Herford, Adenauer was elected temporary chairman of the CDU executive committee in the British Zone. On 5 February he was also elected chairman of the Land executive of the Rhenish CDU. His leading role in the Zone committee was confirmed on 1 March. From now on, the public was presented with a new Adenauer – the party leader.

'Adenauer's Seizure of Power'

It was as Federal Chancellor that Adenauer made his impression on German public consciousness – in such a profound and lasting manner that for decades he was virtually *the* Chancellor. His successors found it extremely difficult to emerge from his shadow. Before 1933, however, he had not been a significant figure outside of the Rhineland. In the rest of Germany, only the politically-aware public had heard of him, and then merely as a remarkable mayor.

Immediately after 1945 the situation was similar. In the years between March 1946 and the meeting of the Parliamentary Council in September 1948, Adenauer was chairman of the CDU in the British Zone; as such, he was one of two or three dozen leading personalities in German politics, along with the other party leaders, the minister-presidents, and the heads of the central administration. Yet the future shape of Germany was still unknown, as was the fate of the infant political groups of 1945, under the names Christian Democratic Union, Christian Democratic Party or Christian Social Union. Would these groups, originally autonomous, be able to form a coherent and united party? Which political approaches and regional centres would make a lasting impact? In 1945, and even in 1946 and 1947, these questions had still to be answered. Until the Bundestag election of 1949, no German or foreign observer could be certain of the role the 'Union parties' would play in the newly founded Federal Republic of Germany – the leading role, as one party in a coalition, or an opposition party making attacks on a government in which it played no part. Even in the days of the Parliamentary Council, perceptive observers of the Bonn scene regarded it as unlikely that the CDU would provide the new Chancellor and become an Adenauer party. Although he was now becoming familiar to journalists at home and abroad, in 1949 Adenauer was still relatively unknown among the general public.

In the British Zone he was definitely a man to be reckoned with since 1946, at least among CDU activists and sympathisers who admired his tough campaigning style. Naturally enough, after that date all Germany's leading politicians regarded him as an important factor in future political calculations. The majority of Germans, however, were taken by surprise by his election as Chancellor. Thereafter, there was much astonishment and wonder at the mixture of dynamism and good fortune that had marked his rise between 1945 and 1949. Over the years, there have been several interpretations of his success. Some observers maintain that Adenauer had been the driving-force in the CDU from the outset, even during the foundation of the Christian Democratic Party in Cologne. However, his less successful rivals and their journalistic contacts have painted a less flattering picture, of a coldly Machiavellian politician who waited for the right moment to remove his rivals within the party.

With the papers of almost all the participants now available, the period has been the subject of intensive research. It is now possible to provide a reliable account of Adenauer's journey to the chancellorship and to assess his significance for the success of the CDU.

Adenauer's first comments on political reconstruction after the war were made to the OSS officer Just Lunning on 28 March 1945. At that stage the fighting in the Ruhr was continuing, Hitler was directing the defence of Berlin from the Reich Chancellery, and fanatics had been mounting stiff resistance for months in the face of inevitable defeat. When asked about his ideas for political life in post-war Germany, Adenauer was therefore extremely cautious, arguing that there could be no political life in Germany for a long time. He also recommended that the military government should suppress all political activity for the time

being. Before political life could begin again, it was essential to re-edu-
cate all those Germans whose minds had been poisoned by the Nazis.
Later, political life might begin with the old parties, but it would be better if mergers produced a smaller number of them. Adenauer would not
be drawn into discussion on the future of the Centre Party. The number of
Communist voters, he thought, had probably increased considerably.[1]

During the following weeks, Adenauer was favourably placed to
observe, and to influence, the revival of political life in the Rhineland and
Westphalia. Large numbers of visitors came to see him, by day in the
temporary accommodation occupied by the city administration, and at
night at Hohenlind, where he was staying. He also made frequent trips to
Bonn and Bad Godesberg, where political activity was also under way.
For the time being, although such activity was not officially allowed, it
was tolerated by the Americans and later the British. At first Adenauer
was the only senior office-holder in the Cologne area. Though the Americans appointed an Oberpräsident and a Regierungspräsident at the beginning of May, it was generally known that Adenauer had been more
important than either during the 1920s and early 1930s. The situation
seemed unlikely to have changed. Almost inevitably, therefore, the various groups interested in the establishment of new parties made contact
with Adenauer at an early stage with the aim of winning his support.

Adenauer was quick to recognise that, in the defeated and apathetic
Rhineland, there were three potential political centres alongside the Social
Democrats and the Communists. First, there were the Catholic and Protestant groups which, in the words of the provisional programme of the
Cologne CDU in June 1945, wanted to build a party combining both
denominations and based on 'Christian and Western values'. Second, and
often hostile to the first movement, was a group which intended to pick up
the standard of the old Centre Party; in essence, its members wanted to
revive a party which, for all practical purposes, had been the political organisation of church-minded Catholics. Third, there were a number of liberal
groups which, in the first months after the defeat, were also convinced of
the need to break down barriers between the religious denominations.

The first discussions leading to the eventual foundation of the Christian Democratic Party began in Königswinter, not far from Adenauer's
home. A major part in these talks was played by Leo Schwering. Born in
1883 – and therefore almost as old as Adenauer – Schwering was a doctor of philology and a secondary-school teacher by profession. His whole
life outside the education system had been devoted to the Centre Party
and to Catholic organisations: in 1912 he had become leader of the
Cologne branch of the Volksverein für das Katholische Deutschland;
between 1921 and 1932 he had been a Centre Party delegate to the Prussian Landtag. The NSDAP had dismissed him from his post in 1934, and
a decade later he was sent to a concentration camp. As a result of these

experiences, Schwering was later to claim that the CDU had risen from the catacombs. Members of the founding generation of the CDU liked to compare themselves to the early Christians, who had survived persecution and saw the sacrifice of their martyrs as the legitimation of their political claims. Despite the exaggeration, there was some truth in the claim: the early CDU commemorated an impressive list of martyrs murdered by the Nazis, mainly members of the Catholic workers' movement.

The second most important man in the Königswinter nucleus of the CDU was Wilhelm Warsch, a lawyer who had been dismissed by the Nazis in 1933. Following discussions with like-minded individuals in April 1945, Schwering and Warsch concluded that the Centre Party in its old form had no future. The experience of the Weimar Republic had shown that the existence of a Catholic party would inevitably split the non-socialist vote. That same discovery had actually been made by the Cologne Centre Party shortly after the First World War, but its attempt to create a 'Christian People's Party' had proved unsuccessful owing to the strength of denominational traditions. Analysis of the disastrous events of spring 1933 also supported the conclusion that it would be inadvisable to revive the Centre Party. It would be easy for the Social Democrats and Communists to argue that the new Centre Party was no better than the old, which had voted for the Enabling Act of 23 March 1933.

Early in April 1945, Schwering went to see Adenauer in Rhöndorf to gain his support for the establishment of a non-denominational party. Adenauer's manner was discouraging. He did not shake Schwering's hand or make him welcome, and his prognoses for the future were gloomy. He showed no sign of willingness to offer political assistance. One reason for Adenauer's caution later became apparent: he regarded Schwering, a former back-bencher in the Prussian Landtag, as a political lightweight. In such circumstances, he wanted to stop Schwering from using the more influential name of the former mayor Konrad Adenauer to boost his plans.

Schwering did not really know where he stood with Adenauer. He noted in his diary: 'He cannot understand my idea for a possible and necessary party reform which does not stop at the Centre Party, and thinks the moment for it has not yet come. Besides, the Allies forbid any party-political activity. I explain that I believe the matter to be urgent and would keep it in mind. He wishes me luck, but again stresses that the matter is premature and unresolved. Possibly he also regards my ideas as Utopian ...'[2]

In the middle of May, Schwering returned to Cologne to launch several weeks of discussions in which a prominent role was played by representatives of the *Windthorstbund,* the Centre Party's youth organisation, and the Catholic workers' movement. The first meeting took place on 17 June in Cologne's Kolpinghaus and involved eighteen former members of the Centre Party. Here a number of preliminary decisions were taken and general approval given for the slogan 'Away with the Centre Party'. It was agreed that a new Christian party should be created to include Protestants as well as former members of the Centre Party. The first requirement was to locate these Protestants and convince them of the merits of the idea. Since British permission was needed before a new party could be established, the process must be accelerated to ensure a *fait accompli* before the old Centre Party had time to revive. The new organisation was to be called the Christian Democratic Party. A party programme was to be discussed with the help of the Dominicans in Walberberg.

As a result of this last decision, the Dominicans gained a strong but short-lived influence over the programme discussions. The head of the order, Laurentius Siemer, invited representatives to a first meeting in his monastery, fifteen kilometres from Cologne, on 23 August. The gathering included a number of Protestants and was also attended by Johannes Albers, who was later to build up the *Sozialausschüsse* (social issues committees) of the CDU.

Siemer was an impressive figure. Head of the German Dominicans since 1932, after the seizure of power he had adopted a course of confrontation with the National Socialists. He had eventually been imprisoned in Oldenburg after the 'foreign exchange' trials, but was released in January 1936 by one of Germany's remaining independent judges. From 1941 Siemer was in contact with resistance groups in Berlin; he was pursued by the Gestapo after 20 July 1944, but managed to hide until the arrival of the British. Along with Father Eberhard Welty, he put forward his own ideas for a programme for the new party.

The 'white cardinal' wanted to move post-war German politics decisively to the left. It was his term, 'Christian Socialism', that ran through all the programme discussions until 1947. Finally, during the second meeting to discuss the programme, Siemer passionately supported a proposal to give the new party the name 'Christian Socialist Union'. Most of the participants opposed the move, though many did so for tactical reasons alone. Siemer thereupon left the programme commission and told it that his monastery would no longer be available for talks.[3] Later it transpired that his activities had not been restricted to the Christian Democratic Party. Kurt Schumacher, Adolf Grimme and Robert Görlinger of the SPD, together with the socialist-minded Carl Spiecker of the Centre Party, also visited Walberberg, and Siemer made several unsuccessful efforts to remove the main obstacles standing in the way of co-operation between left-wing Christians and Social Democrats. The great stumbling-block was the issue of religious schools, which finally brought the whole project to a halt.

Adenauer watched these developments from a distance. He was convinced that two vital decisions were being taken during these months. The first would determine the political programme of a new Christian party in Germany; the second would establish whether a broad democratic-socialist front, stretching from the socialists associated with Schumacher to the Christian Democratic or a newly founded Centre Party, would be created within the post-war German party system.

After clarifying some of the issues, the founder-members returned to Adenauer at the end of July 1945 to seek his support for the new party. At a discussion on the premises of Allianz-Lebensversicherung, where the Cologne city administration was being housed on a temporary basis, it became clear that Adenauer shared the view that the name 'Centre Party' was no longer suitable. However, he continued to adopt a cautious approach, despite his promise to canvass opinion among Protestants during a trip he was planning to the eastern section of the British Zone. He did not like the party name 'Christian Democratic' and preferred 'Christian Social'.[4]

It later emerged that Adenauer's reservations concerned the founder-members of the party rather than the idea itself. He regarded these individuals as men of the second or third rank, and as such, probably incapable of achieving success. Adenauer was also annoyed that they wanted to keep their distance from Wilhelm Hamacher, a teacher and veteran general secretary of the Rhenish Centre Party who had become the leading protagonist of efforts to revive the old Centre Party. Adenauer foresaw the danger that two Christian parties – the Centre and the Christian Democrats – might end up fighting for the same voters and for support from the clergy.

Adenauer also disliked the word 'socialism' and its implications. He pointed out that even the National Socialists had pretended to be socialist. Moreover, he had no sympathy for programmes of nationalisation in a bureaucratised economy. Now of all times, in his view, Germany needed determined entrepreneurs to get the economy moving again. His greatest worry was that a Christian party (or even two) would adopt a position so far to the left that it would inevitably be dragged into the slipstream of the Social Democrats, who had, in any case, made the word socialism their own property. He did not believe that any socialist party existing alongside the SPD would be able to gain an electoral majority. A year later, he summed up this view in concise terms: 'With the word "socialism" we will win over five people and twenty will run away.'[5]

On this issue, the approach adopted by the bishops proved crucial. In the first months after the end of the war, Adenauer was in almost daily contact with the senior clergy in Cologne.[6] In the absence of the archbishop, he held long conversations about important issues affecting the new organisation with the dean of the city, Grosche. Adenauer urged the clergy to take an activist approach on the grounds that humanity would sink into dreadful barbarism if Christianity failed to offer help. He thought it proper for the clergy to accept some responsibility for re-shaping the world.[7] By this stage, in fact, Grosche was already receptive to the idea of an inter-denominational party.

When Archbishop Frings returned to the seat of his diocese he, like Adenauer, initially took up residence in Hohenlind. The two men met frequently to exchange views, though the contact was not always comfortable for Frings. After the first Corpus Christi procession in the city on 2 May 1945, for example, the two took lunch together and Frings expressed satisfaction that 20,000 of the 70,000 inhabitants of the city had taken part. Adenauer then asked Bornheim to tell the 'reverend gentleman' the latest joke circulating in the city about the two comic characters in traditional Cologne folklore: Schäl met Tünnes and told him off for not taking part in the procession. Tünnes replied: 'I'd no need to – I wasn't in the [Nazi] party!'[8] Though the warmth of their relations is open to doubt, Adenauer and Frings nevertheless remained in constant touch. As far as the new party was concerned, Adenauer quickly grasped the course favoured by the archbishop. This would consist of opposition to parties with a materialist conception of the world – the KPD and SPD – and support for a strong Christian party. It was not yet clear whether the old Centre Party or the new Christian Democrat group would provide the nucleus for such a party. Wisely, the Church was eager to build bridges between the two camps. Any group hoping to win the support of the Catholic Church, however, would have to accept the principle of religious schools. At the first conference of the West German Catholic bishops in Werl early in June 1945, a resolution was passed opposing those forces which supported the concept of class war and elevated their party programmes into an ideology or a substitute religion.

Adenauer was thus aware that the clergy would offer support in the struggle against atheistic parties of the left. As regards the vexed choice between the Centre Party and Christian Democracy, he thought it sensible to take the views of the Catholic Church into account by searching long and hard for an agreement between them. However, the bishops clearly had no desire to see the revival of the Centre Party in its old form.

Adenauer's sound instinct for politically important personalities led him to devote particular attention to Wilhelm Hamacher. As the situation developed, Hamacher found himself confronted by a double dilemma. On one hand, he realised that the foundation of a Christian Democratic Party was already under way, with – by and large – the approval of most of the clergy in the Rhineland. If an agreement were ever to be made with this group, now was the time to achieve it. On the other hand, he was also under pressure from Carl Spiecker, a leading protagonist of efforts to revive the Centre Party. Spiecker, who had been a Prussian civil servant before 1933 and had lived abroad between 1933 and 1945, was attracted by the ideals of the Labour Party in Britain and hoped to set up a similar organisation in Germany under the old Centre Party name. To make the party appeal to workers with no religious affiliation, he wanted to drop the demand for religious schools, and opposed the inclusion of the word 'Christian' in the party name. Though Hamacher and other opponents of the idea regarded this as quibbling over semantics, Spiecker was powerful enough to frustrate schemes for the fusion of the two groups. The internal dispute within the Centre Party ultimately weakened it and helped the Christian Democrats. However, Hamacher's need to take Spiecker into account also frustrated hopes of an agreement between himself and Adenauer.

While the old Centre Party politicians were debating the alternatives before them, Adenauer was also in contact with the third grouping outside the KPD and SPD – the liberals. In the nearby district of Gummersbach, an association calling itself the German Democratic Movement was established in spring 1945. Its founder was the young Catholic journalist Otto Schumacher-Hellmold. During the Third Reich Schumacher-Hellmold had been involved in opposition circles in Bonn, and his activities had thereafter been monitored with benevolent interest by the Americans. Early in May, Schumacher-Hellmold met Adenauer in the hope of gaining his support for the middle-class movement. Adenauer liked the younger man, whose Catholic background was in many ways similar to his own, and conceded that he thought it would be 'very inadvisable and inappropriate' to re-establish the Centre Party. 'Your movement', he told Schumacher-Hellmold, 'should be the correct solution. I will gladly be of assistance to you. However, I do feel the lack of the word 'Christian'.[9] As during his subsequent negotiations with the founders of the Free Democrats, and despite his determination to free the party from any clerical associations, Adenauer was not prepared to drop the word 'Christian' from the party name.[10]

The German Democratic Movement was only one among many groups then being established throughout the British Zone by middle-class liberals. However, following action against it by the British in October 1945, the group largely disbanded. Schumacher-Hellmold eventually joined the FDP. In the years to come he often met Adenauer in order to assist in the discreet resolution of differences between the FDP and CDU. During the summer of 1945, however, the liberal groups were still in a state of flux. Whereas Schumacher-Hellmold eventually joined the FDP, another of the liberals with whom Adenauer was in touch, August Dresbach, moved over to the CDU.

The vital issue facing the new Christian Democratic Party was its relationship with German Protestantism. Would it be possible to overcome the traditional inclination of the Protestants to support national-conservative or liberal parties and to include them in a non-denominational Christian party? In later years, when Adenauer reviewed the early history of the CDU, he claimed that the creation of the Centre Party after the

Kulturkampf with Bismarck, had been one of the biggest mistakes in the history of German party politics. Though Bismarck had been a master of foreign policy, his persecution of the Catholics at home had 'prevented the emergence of a great liberal party in Germany'.[11] Subsequently, the many differences between the two great religious denominations had become associated with party-political disputes. At the same time, thought Adenauer, this development had prevented members of the two churches from offering strong and purposeful opposition to the Marxists on the left of the political spectrum and the nationalists on the right. The political centre – Christian, liberal, moderate, bourgeois or whatever one chose to call it – had thus been fatally weakened before 1933 by mistakes made over sixty years previously.

Even in the favourable conditions of 1945, the attempt to include the Protestants in a non-denominational party was fraught with difficulty. In Adenauer's view, it could only succeed if the Catholic side forebore from any doctrinaire assertion of the Christian character of its policy. The pro-gramme must be flexible enough not to alienate conservative and liberal Protestants. On the other hand, however, there must be an open avowal of Christian principles, especially in the party name. Otherwise, the bound-aries separating the party from secular socialism and secular liberalism would become blurred, thereby making the new Christian party unac-ceptable to loyal Catholics and the clergy.

Several other factors also had to be taken into account. For instance, it was generally recognised that the Protestant section of the population had proved less resistant to the appeal of National Socialist doctrines than the Catholics. In future, National Socialist "followers" and the indoctrinated younger generation must be won over to responsible Chris-tian politics. Though it was not mentioned openly, it was recognised that only those parties which could tap the votes of millions of former National Socialists and those who went along with the regime *(Mitläufer)* would be able to win parliamentary majorities in future. The attempt would be bound to fail unless the group which had proved to be politi-cally the most vulnerable – the Protestants – was persuaded to support a responsible Christian party. The Christian Democrats must be made elec-table in the eyes of Protestants; any attempt to create a new German democracy would otherwise end in National Socialism or, Adenauer believed, in rule by the 'totalitarian-minded' Social Democrats and the Communists.[12] This entire issue was linked with fundamental questions of the economic order and social policy. Undoubtedly, the liberal and conservative Protestant middle class would be a reliable ally against the parties of the left, which – Adenauer thought – would all too gladly replace the 'omnipotent Nazi state' with a Marxist one. Yet he was con-vinced that these Protestant groups could never be won over if the Chris-tian Democrats presented themselves as a party of 'Christian Socialism'.

In that case, the Protestant bourgeoisie, along with many middle-class Catholics, would prefer to vote for a secular liberal or conservative party.

From Adenauer's point of view, victory in the struggle against the Christian Socialists, who were supported by the old Catholic workers' movement and by left-wing Catholic intellectuals, was an essential precondition for lasting success. In 1945, a stark choice seemed unavoidable: either a Christian Democratic party would make a breakthrough, or the old divisions would be repeated. In the latter case, he believed, the radical left would probably triumph.

Given the presence of a strongly pro-socialist wing in the Cologne founding group, in the Christian Democratic Union in Berlin, and among the Christian Democrats in Hesse, resistance to Adenauer's views was inevitable. His approach to the issue is reflected in his writings and speeches and in his political activities. First, he hoped that the left-leaning Catholic element could be brought to reason by bourgeois Protestants and middle-class representatives in the economy and administration; second, the middle-class right must be tamed by socially responsible Catholics in the party. In effect, a political balancing-act had to be performed.

Within these pages there is space for no more than a brief description of Adenauer's basic convictions, which inevitably makes them appear more abstract and concise than they appeared in political practice. But during these years he conducted an extensive correspondence, made a number of major speeches, and outlined his plans for a political programme. All of these serve to make his point of view apparent.

At this point Robert Pferdmenges began to play a crucial role in the development of the early CDU. As a Protestant and a successul businessman Pferdmenges combined, in an almost ideal form, the two elements that Adenauer regarded as essential in the new Christian Democratic Party. The two men had first come into contact as a result of Pferdmenges' strong Protestant convictions. After several years spent working in banking institutions in London and Antwerp, the young Pferdmenges had joined the Schaaffhausen banking group and moved to Cologne. On one occasion he became very annoyed when a soccer match was played near his home on Good Friday – the highest Protestant holiday -and he complained to the city's mayor. In his reply, Adenauer agreed that the situation was intolerable, and promptly banned soccer matches on municipal pitches on Good Friday. According to Pferdmenges' son, this was the start of their friendship.[13]

During the 1920s and 1930s Pferdmenges was one of the most influential bankers in Cologne, and indeed the whole of western Germany. The two men thus had links at various levels. Moreover, their families also developed a close relationship that withstood the test of the Third Reich. Pferdmenges played an honourable role in the Confessing Church (founded by Protestants critical of Nazism) and helped the Oppenheim family bank to survive the Third Reich. He was arrested after the events of 20 July 1944 and detained on his estate in Mark Brandenburg before returning to Cologne after the end of the war.

Even before his return, Adenauer had helped to ensure the political rehabilitation of Pferdmenges in the eyes of the Americans.[14] In Cologne, Pferdmenges became the leader of the city's Chamber of Industry and Commerce. The mutual support between the two men continued when Pferdmenges began to extol the political merits of his friend, for example in the Protestant founding-group of the Wuppertal CDU associated with Otto Schmidt. Pferdmenges' son later recalled a remark his father had made near Magdeburg in February 1945, even before the war had ended: 'If you come to the Rhineland, trace Adenauer. He is the only one who can get us out of this mess.'[15] Now, in autumn 1945, Pferdmenges regarded Adenauer as the best man to take over the leadership of the new party. He therefore mustered all of his influence to help his old friend. Adenauer was also able to make use of Pferdmenges' business contacts in order to add people with knowledge of the economy to the trade-union secretaries, journalists, teachers and municipal employees who were dominating the party committees.

Developments gradually began to take shape in the spring and summer of 1945. The group associated with Schwering, Schaeven, Scharmitzel and Warsch now pressed for formalisation. On 19 August the Cologne CDP was officially founded. The creation of separate Land associations for the Rhineland and Westphalia was imminent, and could only be prevented by a last-minute attempt to achieve a single organisation for both provinces. Adenauer knew that, as things stood, the rapid establishment of a Rhenish Land association would mean Schwering as chairman – and, in Adenauer's view, he was not up to the job. Adenauer therefore tried to delay the process, though by August at the latest he had recognised that the Christian Democrats rather than the Centre Party offered the best prospects for a successful Christian party. He knew that local Christian Democrat groups had been, or were about to be, established throughout Germany, including Berlin.

In Adenauer's view, the crucial requirement was for the founding members to avoid insoluble personal and political arguments. Even before he was willing to accept the leadership of the Rhenish CDP, he wrote a detailed letter on the subject to the mayor of Munich, Scharnagl.[16] Its main points were that the name of the Centre Party, and its organisation, must be dropped. 'The fundamental principles of the new party are as follows: 1. Leadership of the state on a Christian foundation, i.e. according to the principles that have been developed over centuries in Europe on the basis of Christianity. 2. Democracy. 3. Strongly progressive social reform and social work, not socialism.' On both the Catholic and the Protestant sides, activities were under way above regional level to ensure the support of both churches for the new organisation.

As Adenauer understood it, the direction of the new party was clear in both domestic and foreign policy. In party politics, its task was to oppose the Communists and Social Democrats who, at least in the Rhineland, had already formed a political working-group. In foreign policy, the new party was determined to resist Soviet influence: 'Union in such a party alone could make it the representative of the Christian principle against a-Christian parties, and I believe that our people can only recover if they are ruled by the Christian principle once more. I also believe that this is the only way to mount strong resistance against the form of state and world of ideas of the east – Russia – and to provide a conceptual and cultural link, and hence also a link in foreign policy, with Western Europe.'

This letter also revealed his differences with the Berlin CDU. Adenauer argued that, in the party programme, an attempt should be made 'to win over as many good and well-known personalities as possible from all parts of Germany not occupied by the Russians'. Furthermore, only the union of Christian and democratic forces could 'protect us from the dangers threatening from the east'. The letter left no doubt as to his belief that the new party ought to present itself to the public as the party of the Western Zones not occupied by the Soviet Union. Though Adenauer did not completely dismiss the Christian Democratic Union which had been founded in Berlin in June, he clearly wanted it to be sidelined. The party programme itself, he argued, must be restricted to a few fundamental ideas: 'Otherwise there is a danger that carefully-formulated sentences and demands might have to be jettisoned within a few months.' He expressed his views more bluntly to Otto Schmidt a few months later: '… I do not tie myself down unnecessarily … since anything might happen tomorrow!'[17] He suggested in his letter that Scharnagl might proceed in similar fashion in Bavaria, showing particular concern for unity. An emissary would be sent from Cologne.

Adenauer also attempted to win over the mayor of Hamburg, Rudolf H. Petersen, a former member of the German Democratic Party who was already moving towards the FDP. Adenauer told him that the establishment of the new party was an 'absolute necessity'. There were many arguments both for and against the name 'Christian Democratic': 'I believe that one should not spend too long on it. But we definitely think that the name "Union", chosen by the gentlemen in Berlin, should not be adopted for the following reason: it is impossible to know what path the Christian Democratic Union will take under pressure from the Russians. This might eventually provide valuable material for hostile agitation …'[18]

At this stage, the Schwering group was attempting to consolidate its position in the Rhineland and to obtain posts on the executive committee. Adenauer, however, considered it more important to establish the party across the Zones from the outset; this would allow for the creation of a unified party, although for the Western Zones only. His letter to Petersen demonstrates that even at this stage, six weeks before his dismissal by the British, Adenauer was not satisfied with his limited role in Cologne. In addition, it is evidence that he judged the whole of domestic politics from the perspective of the East-West conflict.

Developments among the founders of the revived Centre Party also made a cautious approach seem wise. Hamacher, albeit for transparent motives, swore that there would be no hasty action on their part. Each side still hoped to persuade the other of the merits of its case.

Adenauer coolly refused Schwering's request for his participation in the founding meeting of the Rhenish CDP on 2 September 1945. He calculated that Schwering's supporters would dominate the executive and use it to pursue their narrow, Cologne-based policies. He therefore informed Schwering: 'I need Sundays so urgently to deal with my private affairs in Rhöndorf that I must deny myself the pleasure of taking part in the foundation. I accept the election to the executive with many thanks.'[19]

When he wrote this letter he had already received a proposal from the former mayor of Düsseldorf, his old rival Robert Lehr, and from Baron von Gumppenberg, asking him if he would accept the post of first chairman in the Rhineland Land association.[20] Any resulting strain on Adenauer could be eased by the appointment of an executive general secretary (and Gumppenberg probably had himself in mind for this post). He had also received visitors from Düsseldorf, with Karl Arnold among those, who attempted to persuade him to accept the post. In fact, this group apparently feared that Adenauer might choose to join the Centre Party instead. Adenauer, who could see that the situation currently favoured Leo Schwering, politely declined.

The founding assembly in Cologne's Kolpinghaus was attended by two hundred representatives. A 'Council of Chairmen' with seven members was elected, along with a executive of twenty-three. Leo Schwering, as head of the Council of Chairmen, was the leading figure. This committee also included Adenauer, Johannes Albers, the headmistress Anne Franken, the farmer Deselaers from Pont-Geldern, Robert Lehr and Robert Pferdmenges. A dispute quickly developed over whether the Council of Chairmen was intended as a temporary body or as the definitive leadership committee.

Though the events of these weeks present a less than edifying spectacle, the stakes were high. With the misery and distress of the population increasing and winter approaching, small numbers of representatives of the old Weimar parties continued to jockey for positions in the new party system. The future was to show that their determined pursuit of their objectives had not been misplaced: in the months between summer 1945 and spring 1946, many vital decisions for the development of political parties throughout Germany were made.

Party organisations and structures inevitably remained in a state of flux at this time. However, the extended Council of Chairmen met quickly, the first and only time that Adenauer was to be active in this role. The conflicts over 'Christian Socialism' were already beginning. Though a draft programme was available in the form of the 'Cologne basic principles', the Düsseldorf and Wuppertal groups insisted on a completely new version. At this meeting, Johannes Albers advocated 'extensive nationalisation', thereby giving voice to ideas that were already to be found in the 'Cologne basic principles'. The minutes frequently contain the phrase 'Adenauer and Pferdmenges disagree'. Albers, as he was frequently to do in the future, was willing to give way on some points.[21]

For a time, this meeting ended Adenauer's official activity with the Rhenish Christian Democrats since his dismissal by the British prevented him from taking any further part. The response of the Cologne executive was characteristic. Schwering's letter,[22] in which he expressed his 'sincere regret' at the dismissal and praised Adenauer's work, had something of the tone of a funeral oration. The Land manager, Schreiber, expressed his own views more frankly to his Westphalian colleague, Kannengiesser: 'Now that we are rid of the ballast of Adenauer and the traditional and world-famous Cologne clique, we'll fare even better.'[23]

By 16 October, however, Adenauer was able to tell Schwering that, according to information from the British military government, he had no need to give up his membership of the executive of the Rhenish party 'although at least for the time being I may not take part in meetings in Cologne'.[24] They were not rid of him, after all.

At home in Rhöndorf, during the short period when he was free of the pressures of a demanding job, Adenauer wrote his own programme for the Rhenish Christian Democratic Party. When Michael Thomas visited him shortly after his dismissal, Adenauer read out to him the text of what was virtually a 'Rhöndorf programme'. On hearing it, Thomas advised him to omit the 'frequent bows to the occupying power'. Adenauer accepted the advice: 'You're actually quite right.'[25]

Adenauer may well have intended to demonstrate to Thomas, as an emissary from the British, that Barraclough had dismissed one of the leading brains of the new party. Whatever his motives, he had used the time to work on a new programme. Two conclusions can be drawn from this. First, it is clear that Adenauer was far from feeling resigned politically. Second, it is equally apparent that his basic ideas differed on certain important points from those held by the influential groups in the Rhenish CDP. The ideas that he wrote down after his discussions with Frau Schlüter-Hermkes were more than a modification of the 'Cologne basic principles'; they offered an alternative plan.

Historians have emphasised the very different assessments of the economy and society embodied in these two draft programmes. At one level, the drafts did indeed offer divergent assessments of what was necessary in the catastrophic circumstances of 1945. At a more fundamental level, however, they also reflected two very different versions of Catholic social teaching, although it is open to doubt whether Adenauer was fully aware of the theoretical roots of his ideas.

In 1945, there were at least two different approaches to modern Catholic social teaching. The first, to which the Dominicans in Walberberg were committed, went back to Thomas Aquinas and placed the community above the individual. Its theoreticians were convinced that relatively precise instructions for dealing with issues of constitutional order could be deduced from socio-philosophical principles relating to the common good. These ideas stood in contrast to the second, more liberal school of thought, whose ideas were reflected in the papal Encyclical Quadragesimo Anno of· 1931. Adherents of this school doubted whether the principles of society could be anything more than a broad regulatory framework, within which politicians maintained considerable room to manoeuvre. This more personal and individualistic understanding of state and society was supported above all by the Jesuits at this time; Adenauer too can be placed within this second grouping.

Though Adenauer's theoretical approach was not based on any deep philosophical knowledge, it was rooted in his own experience. Like every other Christian Democratic programme of 1945, his draft was also influenced by horror at the totalitarian state that had just collapsed. This revulsion ensured that the primacy of basic rights would constitute the first principle for the reconstruction of state and society. Adenauer wrote Part I of his draft by hand and did not make any major alterations at a later stage.

I. Individual and State

1. The principles of Christian ethics and culture, of true democracy must carry and pervade the life of the state. The power of the state is limited by the dignity and inalienable rights of the individual.
2. Right to political and religious freedom.
3. Right, equal justice and security of justice for all.
4. Recognition of the fundamental significance of the family for people and state.
5. Recognition and protection of the woman in her activity in the home and family. Participation of the woman in professional and public life.
6. The majority has no arbitrary and unlimited right over the minority. The minority, too, has rights and duties.[26]

State and society were thus judged from the standpoint of the individual. This was a doctrine of Christian personalism rather than liberal individualism, since in Adenauer's view the individual was firmly bound to the family and, like the people and state, came under the control of Christian moral law.

Unlike the socialists in the founding circle of Christian Democrats, Adenauer did not believe that the danger of totalitarianism had passed with the collapse of the Hitler movement. In his view, the total state and total society were also a threat in another ideological guise – in the form of Socialism and Communism. This fact would need to be taken into account during the reconstruction of the economic order. 'Satisfying needs' and 'fair sharing' were certainly important goals, but the crucial factor was that the new order must not endanger personal freedom. Though Adenauer repeated the 'Cologne basic principles' in calling for the economy to 'satisfy needs', he restricted the significance of this demand by adding that it must serve 'above all, the liberation and development of the working people'. There was not a word about 'Christian Socialism' nor about nationalisation.

Adenauer's own preferred emphasis was obvious. It was also apparent that his tightly-structured and disciplined programme had greater clarity than the inevitable compromise product which had emerged from the discussions of the founding circles in Cologne and Düsseldorf.

Adenauer now had his own programme ready. However, as long as his political activities were restricted by the British, he could not expect the powerful groups in the developing party to proclaim the dawn of an Adenauer era. In fact, he was probably fortunate that the group associated with Leo Schwering was given the first opportunity to demonstrate his own mettle.

After a short period, Schwering's limitations were clear to see. He knew relatively few people outside of the Rhine Province and Westphalia, and nobody outside that region had ever heard of him. Moreover, he had little knowledge of the economy, the administration, or foreign policy. Schwering's approach to party-political conflicts lacked any sophistication. All his energies were concentrated on outmanoeuvring the Centre Party, but otherwise he tended to share the view of the SPD's Carl Severing that the reconstruction of Germany was an 'above-party matter'.[27] As a result, Schwering saw no need to build up a powerful counterweight to the strong SPD organisation. In addition – and probably even more important at this stage – the CDP organisations in the Rhineland and Westphalia were struggling for influence, since at the end of the year it emerged that the British wanted the existing parties to establish their organisations at the Zonal level. The Soviets were much more advanced in this respect, leading London to fear that an under-developed party system would cause the Germans in the British Zone to be less successful at shaping opinion across the Zones.

Here the Rhenish and Westphalian Christian Democrats faced a number of serious questions. Could they present a leading personality who could command respect in Lower Saxony, Schleswig-Holstein and the Hanseatic cities, where Christian Democratic organisations were being established? Who would lead the new party in the Advisory Council for the British Zone, which the British had established to provide a first representation of the Germans? Who should be general secretary of the party? In all these questions, it seemed clear that, for all his qualities, Leo Schwering was not the right man for the task.

However, the choice of a leader remained difficult. Among the leading figures in the Rhenish party were Karl Arnold and Robert Lehr. Though Lehr certainly had the stature for a role extending beyond the Rhineland, he was out of the race for a number of reasons. The British had just appointed him as president of Rhine Province, which meant that he could not take on a party-political role. Besides, Lehr was a Protestant from the right-wing DNVP of the Weimar days. This would not in itself weigh decisively against him, since he had won much respect among the Catholic resistance during the Third Reich. However, the CDU still faced the task of either absorbing or breaking the revived Centre Party, and for this a Catholic party leader was probably necessary. Moreover, the Catholics from the former Centre Party were numerically stronger, and the party urgently needed the support of the Catholic clergy. All of these factors worked against the choice of Lehr, as they also did against Hans Schlange-Schöningen, a former Pomeranian landowner and minister in Brüning's cabinet, who had been building up the CDU in Schleswig-Holstein during these months.

If Karl Arnold had had another two years, he would certainly have taken the leadership himself. But now, in the late autumn and winter of 1945, he felt that he was not yet ready for the chairmanship. Arnold, born in the Swabian town of Biberach, had trained as a cobbler. For twelve years, during the Weimar republic, he had occupied a number of posts within the Christian trade unions in Düsseldorf. During the Third Reich he and a colleague had successfully run a company, Halbig and Arnold, and he had also been in contact with the Rhenish resistance. Like Adenauer he had been arrested during Operation 'Gitter' in August 1944, but had quickly been released. All of these factors qualified him for a career in post-war Germany. A mere nine months after the end of the war, however, his record was not yet strong enough to hold a major post in party politics.

After the Third Reich had collapsed, it was clear that the Rhineland had been almost laid bare of political leaders. Heinrich Brüning, the former Chancellor, was still in the United States, and made his interventions in the opinion-forming process only by letter. Wilhelm Marx, another former Chancellor, was now eighty-two years old and no longer capable of leadership. The same was true of most of the old Centre Party leaders who had been prominent during Adenauer's period as mayor. Occasionally Adenauer ran through the list of potential rivals:

> Herr Rings is still alive, he will be ninety years old this summer. His house in Cologne was totally destroyed. He fled to Brandenburg Province. He managed to get back across the border of the Russian Zone only a few months ago. The strains he had to bear were such that afterwards he collapsed altogether and we feared the worst. However, he seems to be recovering. Herr Mönnig too is still alive. He is now eighty-two years old, completely blind, but mentally still alert. Herr Falk died in Brussels in December 1944. Falk had been in hiding in Brussels during the entire occupation.[28]

Nevertheless, a few men had survived the Third Reich unscathed. One of these was Hermann Pünder. After the dismissal of Adenauer in October 1945, he spent three years as mayor of Cologne, than as *Oberdirektor* of the Bi-zone. However, in autumn 1945 his arrival on the scene was too late.

In addition, a number of former mayors had a political future after 1945. Among them was Hermann Weitz, who had been dismissed as mayor of Trier in 1933 and was now mayor of Duisburg. Only three days after Adenauer's dismissal, the Düsseldorf group proposed Weitz as his successor to the executive. Robert Lehr and Wilhelm Rombach of Aachen were two more members of this old guard.

At the same time, two natives of the Rhineland were making their political careers in Berlin. In winter 1945, Andreas Hermes seemed likely to be the great future leader of the CDU. Hermes, a man with extensive knowledge of the world outside Germany, had been a member of several cabinets in the Weimar Republic and had led the agrarian 'Green Front' during its last years. After a period of incarceration in 1933 he had travelled to Colombia, became associated with Beck and Goerdeler during the war, was condemned to death after the events of 20 of July 1944, was liberated by the Soviets and had spent a short time as deputy mayor of Berlin. In June 1945 he was one of the leading figures in the founding of the Berlin CDU. Hermes had originally established good relations with the Soviets. Since September 1945, however, he faced an issue of conscience: whether to accept the land reform which his experience as an agronomist led him to regard as foolish, or whether to risk a conflict with the Soviets. Hermes and Adenauer, who were completely different characters, never established a close working relationship.

His deputy was Jakob Kaiser, another active member of the resistance who had been fortunate enough to survive the aftermath of the 20 July plot. Neither Hermes nor Kaiser had forgotten that their roots lay in the Rhineland; both attempted to forge links with like-minded groups there, and to win support for the claims of Berlin to leadership of the new party.

Closer examination, however, reveals that Adenauer's claims to leadership could not be ignored. He had been regarded as a potential leader of his country even before 1933. By 1945, the death or ageing of so many potential rivals made his stature even more apparent. Adenauer had emerged from the Third Reich with an unimpeachable political reputation and, apparently, with his old dynamism intact. Some serious rivals did remain: Hermes; possibly Pünder, though he lacked any power base; Schlange-Schöningen had to be taken seriously, as, in the long-term, might Heinrich Brüning. Still, there were few rivals of Adenauer's generation. He was also aware that most of the possible contenders from the next generation had achieved their elevated positions only thanks to the chaotic conditions of the year 1945, and lacked many of the necessary qualities for overall leadership. This fact, it is only fair to point out, was noted by others as well as by himself. Overall, Adenauer's remarkable rise can thus be attributed to two major factors, first to his own realisation that he was better equipped than any rival to deal with the tasks facing the party, and second to the recognition among the more perceptive Christian Democrats that a leader of his stature was absolutely essential.

A form of national meeting of the party was held between 14 and 16 December 1945 in Bad Godesberg. It was attended by approximately two hundred Christian Democrats from the British, U.S. and Soviet Zones and from Berlin.[29] Events at this meeting revealed that the Rhineland and Westphalian party lacked an outstanding leader in the absence of Adenauer. The most important speech was given by Andreas Hermes, but this had to be read out on his behalf after he was refused permission to travel from Berlin. A few days later, Hermes was forced to resign as chairman of the CDU East when he declared his opposition to the land reform. A second much-admired speech was given by Maria Sevenich, a native of Cologne whose erratic political odyssey from the Communists to the Social Democrats had temporarily taken her to the Christian Democrats. Sevenich was active in the Hesse CDU, where the socialist wing was strong, before moving to Lower Saxony in 1947.

Adenauer, who had not been asked to make a keynote speech because of the ban on his political activity, observed the conference for a short time before leaving to take a walk with Paul Franken. The Godesberg *Reichstagung* clearly showed the popular appeal of the socialist programme. Among the key phrases in the resolution passed were references to 'economic control', 'nationalisation', 'involvement of the workforce in controlling the economy on the basis of equality', and 'socialism based on Christian responsibility'. However, the meeting also demonstrated that the Berlin 'national leadership' associated with Hermes and Kaiser was beginning to exert a strong ideological and organisational influence over the Western Zones. The Berlin party name – Christian Democratic Union of Germany, or CDU – was jubilantly adopted: 'This name is now valid for the entire German Reich.'[30]

The only consolation for Adenauer was that not a single representative of the Rhenish CDUD had managed to make a significant impact. This was greatly to his advantage in the long term; eventually, the desire for a capable chairman was to prove stronger than ideological reservations about a politician who was obviously on the right of his party. Behind the scenes, Pferdmenges began to work to move Adenauer into a better position. Yet the direct initiative came from Karl Arnold and his group, which stood clearly on the CDU's left.

It is impossible to reconstruct every detail of the contacts made in December 1945. On 28 December, however, Consul-General von Weiss reported to his government that Adenauer would probably be entrusted with the leadership of the CDU in the entire British Zone.[31] As in August, this step was initiated by the Düsseldorf group.

The crucial discussion took place on Adenauer's seventieth birthday, ten years after his sixtieth birthday spent in Maria Laach with Ildefons Herwegen and his family, when he had doubted whether he would live to see his seventieth. Adenauer invited to his home those members of the Rhenish Land executive who had signalled that they wanted him as the future chairman of the Zone. The meeting was attended by several people who soon advanced within the Rhenish CDU, including Karl Arnold, Johannes Albers, Christine Teusch and Baron Max von Gumppenberg. Most were Christian Democrats from the left of the party. Adenauer now realised that significant and influential figures in the CDU wanted him as Land chairman of the Rhenish Christian Democrats.

On the day after this important meeting, Adenauer wrote a letter to the participants which revealed that he was already considering issues outside of the Rhineland and even the British Zone.[32] He again assured them that he was ready to accept the chairmanship in the Zone executive, and outlined 'the great tasks which have to be solved now and in the near future, e.g.

a) unity with the Centre Party
b) establishment of close links with the Union in Bavaria and the French Zone … [he was apparently less interested in close relations with the left-wing Christian Democrats in Frankfurt!]
c) organisation of the state in the British and other Zones, foreign policy questions
d) press
e) economic future.

Adenauer added that, 'if it is insisted upon', he was also willing to accept the chairmanship of the Land party. In that case, however, he would need a plenipotentiary, 'who has the necessary qualities, has my full confidence and will make his best efforts available'. He had already had such a person in mind: his former and current head of department in the Cologne city administration, Ernst Schwering. Between 1926 and 1933, as Adenauer's deputy, Schwering had risen from the ranks, only to be dismissed along with Adenauer after the Nazi seizure of power. As a lawyer, he had performed capably during the difficult negotiations to obtain the financial compensation from the city of Cologne for the dismissed mayor Adenauer. After the war, Schwering returned to a key role as deputy in the Cologne city administration. In 1949/50, and again from 1951 to 1956, he was mayor of the city. There was only one obstacle to his appointment as Adenauer's representative: he was the younger brother of Leo Schwering, who was about to be removed from power and replaced by Adenauer. The proposal thus put him in an untenable position, forcing him to decline.

There has been some controversy about whether Adenauer planned his rise to the top position in his party from the outset, or whether he was persuaded to accept it by an influential group within the CDU. In fact, the issue is more complicated than this. As with all political events of this nature, the situation developed more as a result of the constant discussions and contacts of the major figures than as a consequence of Machiavellian planning.

On 8 January 1946, the Land executive of the Rhenish CDU met to produce its list of candidates for the Zonal Advisory Council. After a heated discussion, a preliminary decision was taken which gives an insight into the relative strengths of the two groups fighting for the leadership. The proposals included Adenauer, Arnold, Pferdmenges and three more participants at the Rhöndorf meeting. Leo Schwering, by contrast, was named only as a deputy.

During the weeks that followed, the groups continued their manoeuvres as Schwering fought with increasing desperation for his office. Adenauer managed to strengthen his own position by forming a coalition with the Wuppertal group, whose chairman was tempted by the office of deputy chairman on the Zone executive. At the same time, however, Andreas Hermes, who had lost his post in Berlin and moved to Bad Godesberg, was endeavouring to join the leadership of the CDU in the British Zone. To that end he conducted negotiations with the Cologne and Westphalian groups. In fact, he was a few days too late: the delegate elections to the Zone committee had already taken place. Hans Schlange-Schöningen in Schleswig-Holstein was also showing an interest; Leo Schwering was now prepared to accept the Protestant Schlange-Schöningen as Zone chairman if this meant saving his own party chairmanship in the Rhineland against Adenauer.

Schwering's endeavours were supported by another rising star of the Christian Democrats, the mayor of Herford, Friedrich Holzapfel. Like Schlange-Schöningen, Holzapfel's roots lay in the more moderate wing of the German National People's Party (DNVP). He was establishing a power base in Westphalia, and hoped to establish a favourable climate for his efforts by inviting the twenty-six delegates of the Zone committee to Herford during a period of acute food supply problems. If Schlange-Schöningen's efforts were unsuccessful, Holzapfel intended to make an attempt on his own behalf.

Many of the participants have provided accounts of the meeting in the Herford town hall[33] at which Adenauer was chosen as provisional chairman of the Zone CDU. Though these accounts are not identical on all points, there seems little doubt that Adenauer, as president by virtue of seniority, was in control from the outset.

The scene has frequently been described: 'The chair reserved for the president of the meeting was still empty. Suddenly Dr Adenauer appeared on the podium, sat in the chair and said: "I was born in 1876 so I am probably the oldest person here. If no-one contradicts, I will regard myself as president by seniority." Everyone fell silent in amazement.'[34] Holzapfel, who as host might have expected to take charge of the meeting, was thus outmanoeuvred.

Also excluded, even before the discussions began, was Andreas Hermes. Together with party colleagues from Berlin, including the executive member Heinrich Vockel, general secretary of the Centre Party before 1933, he had arrived in Herford as a guest. Adenauer maintained that the visitors from Berlin were not members of the CDU in the British Zone and therefore, by order of the Military Government, could not take part in meetings of the Zone committee. Since the representative of the Military Government, Lieutenant-Colonel Donner, had just delivered greetings to the meeting, it was impossible to dismiss the issue as a technicality. The guests were to be consulted only as the day progressed. Hermes, who was still taking lunch with Holzapfel, was irritated to learn that the meeting had decided to postpone the election to the executive, and left early with Vockel. In this he was mistaken. The election was held, though the results were theoretically provisional until the next meeting. The voting was unanimous: Adenauer as first chairman, Holzapfel as second, and Baron von Gumppenberg of Düsseldorf as secretary. Events subsequently proved the truth of the old assertion that there is nothing so permanent as a temporary arrangement: Adenauer and Holzapfel kept their posts until the disbanding of the Zone committee in autumn 1950.

Schlange-Schöningen was further handicapped by procedural problems. Carl Schröter of the Schleswig-Holstein Land association had declared that the situation there would not be clarified until a meeting of 4 February; as a result, he and the other representatives had to be regarded as observers only.

In the aftermath of the Herford meeting, Adenauer wrote a long and frank letter to the conservative Schlange-Schöningen explaining the reservations he had about his colleague's policies. At the same time, the letter reveals Adenauer's own ideas for the future development of the party.

The immediate occasion of his criticism concerned a number of letters Schlange-Schöningen had sent to party colleagues in northern Germany, one of which had advocated '*rallying* all those to the right of Social Democracy ...' Adenauer argued that the CDU should not be used as a *Sammlungspartei*, a kind of omnibus party, because the term '*Sammlung*' (rally) was not forward-looking. He also doubted whether it was wise to describe the Union as a 'party of the right' as Schlange-Schöningen had done. Not only would this provoke 'very sharp dissent from very broad circles of the CDU', but it was also rejected by Adenauer himself for complex reasons: '"Party of the right" and "party of the left" are relative terms which I think it inadvisable to apply to any party until a firm structure of several parties has been created. However, we do not know what parties will be established in Germany, nor where they will stand ...' If earlier descriptions were to be used at all, then the word "centre" would be best for the CDU'.[35]

In Herford, Schlange-Schöningen had already been made aware of the opposition he faced. Moreover, he was under pressure to make a decision about his future. A short time previously, the British had offered to make him head of the Central Office for Food Supply and Agriculture, a task for which he was well qualified but which could not be combined with the chairmanship of the CDU. He accepted the job immediately after the Herford meeting.

The notion of the CDU as a 'party of the right' was not a new one. To Adenauer's frustration, he had been accused of turning the CDU into a 'party of the right' by Josef Kannengiesser, the secretary of the Land association of Westphalia. The allegation was made when Christian Blank of Hanover nominated Adenauer, Holzapfel and von Gumppenberg at the Herford meeting. Kannengiesser called out that such an executive would create the impression of a right-wing party: 'That was not what people have worked and fought for ...' The executive of this 'new, great Christian people's party' ought to contain workers, women and young people as well. In addition, he argued, Adenauer was an 'outspoken Rhenish Catholic' and as such was ill-fitted to win the Protestant vote. This was followed by the allegation of separatism which continued to haunt Adenauer. It was this last argument that Adenauer was most vehement in rejecting: 'Not even the Nazis accused me of that.' For a short time after the Herford meeting, Kannengiesser was convinced that his insistence on the *temporary* election of Adenauer had 'averted the danger of a false start to the right by the new party'.[36]

In addition to the provisional election to the executive, the meeting produced two further important decisions. According to the minutes, the assembly of delegates in Herford agreed 'that the Zone committee, with its executive to be elected, is the actual party executive for the whole Zone and must have authority over the individual Land leaderships'.[37]

Moreover, Adenauer now produced the draft of his own party programme, and the committee appointed a programme and editorial committee. The new chairman was determined to have a programme for the whole Zone passed at the next meeting. On 7 February he wrote to Mayor Scharnagl in Munich: 'At the moment I am trying to draw up a programme and to get it accepted. I take the view that, as a new party, we must have a programme as soon as possible so that people can see what we want.' He enclosed his draft programme, asking Scharnagl whether it might prove acceptable to Bavaria.[38]

Adenauer was now certain that the 'Rhöndorf programme' would replace the previous drafts worked out in the Rhineland and Westphalia. He wrote to Schlange-Schöningen: 'A new party such as ours only develops funda-

mental ideas into firm and clearly outlined programme clauses over time. I
hope we will arrive at this conclusion of our development at the meeting of
the Zone committee at the end of February. Then, many of the submissions
which were made when our party was being formed will appear to be no
longer appropriate or as having being overtaken by events.'[39]

Still, Adenauer was aware that his success in Herford had not finally
resolved the issue. Strong reservations remained, especially in Westphalia.
The Westphalian secretary, Josef Kannengiesser, who had failed to win
appointment as general secretary, produced a memorandum arguing that it
was a mistake 'to give prominence to such a controversial personality as
Adenauer as first chairman … in my opinion he is not a political leader of
stature'. He also felt that Adenauer's treatment of the Berliners had been
'quite impossible'. Kannengiesser wrote to Hermes to tell him that
Johannes Gronowski 'takes the view that Herr A. has apparently mistaken
the Zone committee for the Cologne city council'. The Westphalians
agreed that an Adenauer 'party dictatorship' would be unacceptable.[40]

While Adenauer was gaining control over the Zone committee in
Herford, the disputes in the Rhineland Land association reached a climax. At a meeting on 21 January 1946,[41] which Adenauer did not attend,
Schwering proposed that the Land leadership should now be elected,
with himself as chairman. The Adenauer group, headed by Karl Arnold,
opposed him. When critical references were made to Adenauer's past
history, Michael Rott, who had recently visited Rhöndorf, read out a letter from Maria Laach 'that justified Adenauer'. It was eventually agreed
that a Land leadership, including Adenauer, should be elected. The election of a chairman was postponed until the next meeting.

The position of chairman was finally resolved in Krefeld-Uerdingen
on 5 February.[42] In the days before this meeting, Adenauer had done
some political horse-trading with Otto Schmidt, a Protestant from
Wuppertal, who had previously been a vigorous opponent of Adenauer
and who was to clash often with him in future. According to this deal,
Adenauer would be first chairman of the Rhineland Land association and
Schmidt one of his two deputies. Former supporters of Schwering in
Cologne now deserted him in favour of Adenauer, who was clearly moving towards victory. Adenauer was elected chairman by a substantial
majority, winning by twenty-four votes to five against Schwering. The
executive meeting ended with a furious argument in which Schwering's
supporters attacked Otto Schmidt for his *völkisch* (nationalist) past.
Schwering resigned from all of his party offices. On the following day he
wrote to Johannes Albers: 'Yesterday was a black day for the Christian
working people and a victory for reaction all down the line.' He complained bitterly that the left-wing of the CDU had abandoned him.[43]

Adenauer was not troubled by the anger of his defeated rivals. Wilhelm Warsch, who had written to him on 6 February, received a chilly

and pedantic reply of the kind Adenauer often produced when people quarrelled with him. He rejected all criticism of his conduct and added scornfully: 'I believe that the result of the vote has created complete clarity.'[44] In 1962, recalling the Uerdingen meeting, Schwering maintained that 'on 5 February 1946 Adenauer's "seizure of power" took place.'

Adenauer's victory was completed at the second meeting of the Zone Committee. On 1 March 1946, the delegates in Neheim-Hüsten finally confirmed his election as Zone chairman. With the power struggle in the Rhineland resolved, this was little more than a formality. However, the meeting was also significant because the CDU in the British Zone declared its acceptance of Adenauer's 'Rhöndorf programme', with some modifications, as the party programme.

The CDU now had its Neheim-Hüsten programme ready for use in elections, thereby granting the town its place in the history of the CDU. The local convent had been chosen as the meeting place on the grounds that the delegates would at least have some prospect of reasonable nourishment and accommodation, and the discussions took place in the refectory. Adenauer adopted the same procedure he had used as mayor of Cologne, allowing every speaker to present his case before summing up himself. On this occasion he spent the night in his room giving the programme a final polish.

During these discussions there were no clashes over the issue which would occupy centre stage in future – that of nationalisation.[45] Adenauer had accurately assessed the strength of the socialist wing in the party and, from his new position of power, was prepared for a compromise that left controversial issues open: 'The vital question of the nationalisation of parts of the economy is not practicable at the current time, as the German economy is not free. When the matter is settled later, economic and political approaches, and above all the general good, will be decisive.' On the other hand: 'Coal is the vital product for the entire German national economy. We demand the nationalisation of the mines.'[46]

Adenauer was prepared to accept this formula, since the claim that 'nationalisation … is not practicable at the current time' was in clear contrast to the demands of the socialist wing in the CDU. Moreover, there was a logical inconsistency between the readiness to postpone the issue to the distant future and the simultaneous demand for nationalisation of the mines. Nevertheless, the party's left-wing was satisfied for the moment; it hoped to recover the ground lost with the help of the '*Reichs-CDU*' of Jakob Kaiser in Berlin.

Even during the prelude to these discussions, the status of 'Christian' in the programme had appeared to pose far greater problems. On this subject, Adenauer clashed with his deputy chairman, Otto Schmidt of the Wuppertal group. As a representative of the Protestant camp and a member of the Confessing Church during the Nazi years, Schmidt had already been responsible for the adoption of a detailed clause in the programme discussions of autumn 1945: 'God is the lord of history and of all peoples, Christ the strength and law of our life ... Salvation and resurrection depend on the effectiveness of the forces of Christian life in the people. For that reason we declare our support for the democratic state that is Christian, German and social.'[47]

Schmidt now wrote to Adenauer to complain that the new draft, unlike the basic principles from Rhineland-Westphalia, was lacking in 'Christian substance'.[48] Adenauer's answer was cool; the question would be decided by the Zone committee – of which Otto Schmidt was not even a member.[49]

Adenauer did not intend to make the party programme into an avowal of Christian faith. His immediate strategic objective was to encourage fusion with the FDP and the Lower Saxony *Landespartei* which were currently being established. In the FDP, Wilhelm Heile was the foremost advocate of the creation of a non-socialist bourgeois mass party. Like his lifelong rival Theodor Heuss, Heile had been associated with the group around Friedrich Naumann, and had for a time been a Reichstag member of the German Democratic Party; after Germany's defeat in 1945 he became head of the administration in the Hoya region of Lower Saxony and was elected chairman of the FDP in the British Zone at the beginning of 1946. Heile was a stubborn and committed individual – a landowner, temporary editor of *Hilfe*, a passionate European, a Hanoverian Guelph and a convinced federalist. Despite the pressure from his FDP rivals Franz Blücher and Friedrich Middelhauwe, Adenauer believed that he had the support of the FDP.

Following his election as Zone chairman, Heile visited Adenauer to offer negotiations for a possible merger. Adenauer's response was immediate, and considerable progress was made by letter, at a meeting in Rhöndorf which also involved Middelhauve, and during further discussions on the occasion of the Zone Advisory Council meeting in Hamburg. During Schwering's ascendancy in the Rhenish CDU, the programme clause relating to the 'unity of the Reich' had been an obstacle to progress. This was now removed. Adenauer's phrase in the Rhöndorf programme: 'The unity of the Reich must be preserved', was sufficient for Heile. The two sides also moved more closely together on the issue of the schools. However, the party name remained a matter of dispute. Though Heile insisted on the abandonment of the word 'Christian', Adenauer could not agree.[50] Negotiations were finally broken off in April.

Adenauer knew that any strengthening of the Christian element in the programme, as desired by Schmidt, would have created new obstacles to talks with the FDP, which at the time appeared to have good prospects of success. He regarded the whole British Zone as a single unit and was aware that the FDP and NLP (Niedersächsische Landespartei) were not yet firmly established. Equally, he was convinced that these organisations and groups, and their sympathisers in the electorate, could only be won over by a programme which, while committing itself to the principles of Christianity, did not alienate them by making too many religious references. Moreover, the CDU was still uncertain of its own organisation in northern Germany. Just as the FDP and NLP, later the *Deutsche Partei* (German Party), were drawn into the orbit of the CDU elsewhere, in certain regions the CDU itself was strongly influenced by these liberal and conservative forces.

In Herford Adenauer therefore insisted on restraint. He was convinced that the CDU could only be made electable if the stress on its Christian nature was moderate rather than excessive. More than that, he thought, would 'not sell'.

When Schmidt's arguments were ignored, his response was impassioned.[51] In a letter dealing with basics, he criticised the inadequacy of the discussions and the fact that the Neheim-Hüsten programme had not been developed from below. He was also critical of Adenauer's style of leadership. After the experiences of the last fifteen years, Schmidt was not prepared to accept purely nominal responsibility: 'If I am to take responsibility, then I also ask that my voice be listened to.'[52]

In future, Adenauer's deputy chairmen were often to make similar complaints about their party leader. However, the willingness to express complaints openly declined, along with the importance of the Rhenish Land executive in the CDU leadership. Leo Schwering summarised this development later: 'From meeting to meeting, the Zone committee visibly strengthened its authority over the Land associations.'[53] Otto Schmidt, in retrospect, conceded that Adenauer had proved to be a perceptive and clever politician; accordingly, he believed that in Krefeld-Uerdingen he had been confronted by 'Adenauer the power-seeker'.[54]

Adenauer was thus able to establish firm control over the party. All of his colleagues, even those who had helped him to power, came to feel the strength of this grip. Only a few weeks later, he rebuked the *Oberpräsident* of Rhine Province, Robert Lehr, for failing to give him the opportunity to state his own position before the nomination of CDU members to the newly appointed Provincial Council, which was a stepping-stone to an elected parliament. There were important issues involved – not only the CDU quota, but also its composition. This dispute continued throughout 1946 and involved other issues, but it clearly showed that, as party chairman, Adenauer also claimed political leadership over party colleagues in public posts.

Later, other senior Christian Democrat politicians also felt the pressure. Among them were Karl Arnold, in his role as minister-president of North Rhine- Westphalia, and Friedrich Holzapfel in his capacity as chairman of the CDU *caucus* in the Bi-zonal Economic Council. Adenauer's interventions again revealed the remarkable mastery of the documents, and the fussiness over formal details, which had always aston-ished his subordinates in other fields.

Directly after taking office, Adenauer had begun to tighten the struc-ture of the Rhineland Land association in order to create an efficient organisation for the Zone chairman. His main lieutenant was Josef Löns. Adenauer had discovered the effectiveness of Löns, who was then thirty-five years old, when he had worked in the Cologne city administration. He was not worried by the fact that Löns was initially sympathetic to the left-wing of the CDU. Most younger members of the party were then influenced to some degree by socialist ideas, and Adenauer was appar-ently confident that Löns would change his views once the two men worked closely together.

Löns succeeded in building up an effective party machine. Though he returned to Cologne as councillor in 1948, Adenauer always remembered and rewarded people who had proved reliable and effective in his service. From 1953, as leader of the personnel department in the Foreign Min-istry, Löns laid the foundations for long-term dominance of the Foreign Ministry by CDU personnel, which did not begin to be broken until after 1966. Löns himself later became German ambassador in The Hague. In 1947, largely because of his work, the CDU in the British Zone ranked alongside the SPD as the most powerful party organisation in the west of Germany, and remained so until the start of the Adenauer era in summer 1949. 'The only office that functions is the Zone committee of the CDU', remarked deputy chairman Holzapfel with pride in June 1949: 'At the moment we are the backbone of our Union.'[55]

Adenauer's first major speech to a large audience was in front of a crowd of four thousand in the main hall of the damaged University of Cologne.[56] He devoted considerable attention to his speech, which con-tained all of the basic arguments he was to present throughout the coun-try in the years to come. His audience recognised that Adenauer was attempting to re-appraise the history of an entire century and suggest a path to recovery. It was one of the most effective and passionate perfor-mances of his life.

He began with a glance at the events of 1932 in the city. Nowhere else had the Nazi vote been as low as in Cologne at the last free elections of November 1932: 'But catastrophe, the unleashing of elemental, demonic forces, affects the innocent as much as the guilty.' Nevertheless, his fel-low-citizens should take courage from the fact that they had survived hard times before, between 1914 and 1924.

After this discreet references to his own achievements as mayor, Adenauer proceeded to ask some painful questions: 'How was it possible that the German Republic we established in 1918 only lasted for fifteen years? How was it possible that the Bismarckian Reich, founded in 1871 and soon the most powerful state in the world, a Reich that seemed stronger and firmer than almost every other European country of the time, how was it that this Reich collapsed in 1918 after only forty-seven years?' How was the incomparably wicked Third Reich possible? Why had Germany again resorted to a war 'which, despite dazzling early triumphs, was inevitably lost?'

The manner in which Adenauer asked these questions revealed his deep understanding of the state of mind of his fellow Germans. Thus, while he condemned National Socialism, he also acknowledged the 'miracle of courage and devotion to duty' exhibited by the German people during the war. Yet this praise did not prevent him from admitting that the same people had committed 'crime after crime of the most horrendous proportions'. At this stage he could offer only a tentative reappraisal of German history. In particular, he made an open appeal to the pride of his audience: 'Since 1933 I have often been ashamed to be a German, ashamed in my innermost soul, perhaps I knew more than most about the disgraceful deeds that were being committed ... Yet now, now I am proud to be a German again. I am more proud than ever before, more than before 1933 and before 1914.' His reason for this startling assertion of pride, apparently, was 'the great courage' with which the Germans had accepted their fate.

Nevertheless, he urged his audience to ask why these things had happened. How had National Socialism come to power? 'I am not demanding an admission of guilt ... But in our own interest we must examine our consciences so that we can find the right path to recovery.'

Of course, he told his audience, a full measure of blame must be borne by 'the bigwigs, the high military and the big industrialists'. Nevertheless, Hitler would never have come to power without being able to appeal to a widespread attitude of mind among broad sections of the population. In his view, the great failing was that the German people had 'made an idol of the state and raised it to the altar. It had sacrificed the individual, its dignity and value, to this idol.'

German history had taken several wrong turnings. After outlining the development of the 'omnipotent state', Adenauer turned to the theme of 'materialism', with which he linked urbanisation, militarism and the 'Prussian view of the state'. These topics led him to the idea of class struggle. A bare three sentences later, he had managed to link racism, National Socialism and Marxism: 'Nationalism found the strongest intellectual resistance among those Catholic and Protestant parts of Germany which had fallen least under the spell of the teachings of Karl Marx, of Socialism!!! That is absolutely certain!'

These assertions were followed by a positive message. The CDU, according to Adenauer, wanted to re-establish the principles of Christian natural justice. The vital clause in the CDU programme – his programme – emphasised the unique dignity of the individual, the irreplaceable value

of every human being. This was the foundation for the principles underlying democracy and economic life.

As befitted an increasingly clever party speaker, Adenauer then concentrated his attack on Kurt Schumacher and the SPD. If the Social
Democrats were not exactly 'anti-Christianity', they were certainly not
'pro-Christianity'. Moreover, Schumacher's propaganda methods were
intolerable and the declarations of the SPD manifested 'the old Prussian
spirit'. Then came another more general assault: 'Germany is one of the
most irreligious and un-Christian peoples of Europe. It was so even
before 1914. Though the Berliners have many valuable characteristics,
even at that stage I always felt that in Berlin I was in a heathen city.'

His speech was complex and intellectually demanding, short on platitudes but containing a clever mixture of analysis, polemic and appeals
for support. He claimed that the guilty must be punished, but those who
went along with Nazism and soldiers should not be rejected, though they
should show restraint in their conduct. People should speak calmly with
those who had been misled, rather than descending to agitation.

Adenauer followed these remarks with a warning: 'Despite the misdeeds of National Socialism, the German people have a claim not to be
judged solely by this epoch in their history.' Nonetheless, the occupying
power also deserved understanding. He ended with a reference to the policy of reconciliation he had supported for decades: '… In the 1920s I advocated an organic integration of the French, Belgian and German economies
to secure a lasting peace, because co-ordinated economic interests, running
parallel to each other, are and will always remain the most sound and
longest lasting foundation for good relations between peoples.' This was
followed by the key phrases, spoken six months before Winston Churchill's
speech in Zürich and drawing upon ideas which had already been developed in the European resistance movements for a number of years:

> A United States of Europe including Germany … The United States of Europe
> offers the best, most secure and lasting security for Germany's western neigh-
> bours. Until the foundation of the United States of Europe, wholly satisfactory
> security can be provided for these neighbours without dismembering Ger-
> many: no more Reich under Prussian leadership, no centralised Reich. Mili-
> tarism is dead, economic pacification and reassurance of Germany, support for
> the principle of democracy and international understanding in Germany, inte-
> gration of the economic interests of Germany and its western neighbours,
> including those of Britain.

Adenauer ended his speech with a return to parochial politics. After
his panoramic surveys of the last two hours his conclusion had a farcical
quality, but was nevertheless sincere. The people of Cologne, he urged,
'should not under any circumstances allow the central station to stay
where it is, since otherwise the city would be crippled for ever.'

This was typical of the man. He had just set out a programme for Germany and Europe containing ideas of major importance – but did not forget

the railway station in Cologne. In fact, over the next twenty years it was to prove easier to integrate a desperate people into Europe, and to bring peace to the continent, than to move the station away from Cologne cathedral.

Adenauer's speech in the University of Cologne marked the start of a campaign across the British Zone. It was undertaken at the same exhausting pace he had adopted as mayor of his home city. Adenauer travelled constantly in his old Horch car, to election appearances, party committee meetings, party rallies, negotiations with other parties and the British, meetings of the Zone Advisory Council and the Landtag of North Rhine-Westphalia. A flood of correspondence poured out of Cologne, and at weekends from Rhöndorf, to contacts throughout Germany.

His accumulation of official positions, so dear to him in the years from 1919 to 1933, too, provided Adenauer with insight into all aspects of west German politics, and the chance to intervene in many areas. In addition to his party posts in the British Zone, he became a member of the Zone Advisory Council in Hamburg, a member of the Rhine Province Provincial Committee, chairman of the CDU *Fraktion* in the Landtag of North Rhine-Westphalia from spring 1947, and member of the executive of the inter-zonal *Arbeitsgemeinschaft* of the CDU/CSU.

In these committees he was in constant touch with most of the important politicians and heads of administration in contemporary Germany. Adenauer also had links with the senior officers in the occupation administration and with their liaison officers, who played a significant role until 1949. He already had a wide circle of acquaintances from his years as mayor, and was now getting to know the personalities who had come to prominence since the collapse of 1945. As he took their measure, he became increasingly convinced of his own superiority. This was also recognised by outside observers. One of these was William Strang, political adviser to the British Military Governor in Berlin. Strang met Adenauer on 15 July 1946, when Adenauer flew to Berlin to join Kurt Schumacher and Jakob Kaiser and receive news of the establishment of the Land of North Rhine-Westphalia. Despite his strong political reservations about Adenauer, Strang cabled to London: 'Nevertheless, he is a powerful political personality in this region and possibly the most capable politician among the three.'[57]

The Party Leader

Adenauer possessed a number of qualities that allowed him to triumph over his rivals as party leader. Some have already been mentioned: his age, still an important factor in the early post-war years; his reputation from the period before 1933; his persecution by the Nazis; his mental and physical resilience; a considerable talent for organisation; and, not least, a remarkable faith in the rightness of his own beliefs.

Yet there were other factors involved in his success. Adenauer possessed a highly developed capacity to understand the overall political situation. Analysis of his confidential reports to the CDU Zone committee, for example, reveals his instinctive grasp of the conflicts between the four occupying powers. He was alert to the links between international conditions and the economic situation; equally, he understood the complexities of the infant German party system and the aims and limitations of its chief protagonists. Adenauer had clear ideas about the likely course of developments and, on the occasions when he misjudged the situation, he remained prepared to make rapid adjustments in response to convincing arguments. Though suitably sceptical in his approach during the early post-war years, he remained sufficiently optimistic to work for desirable changes. Unlike most other party politicians, Adenauer did not act mainly on the basis of temporary tactical considerations, but recognised the value of maintaining long-term strategies based on his view of likely or desirable developments.

Though he did not state it explicitly, Adenauer's ideas in the early post-war years were based on the primacy of foreign policy. Thus he acted on the understanding that overall developments would be determined almost exclusively by the victorious powers. Even in the summer of 1945, he had a clear idea of what to expect. In his opinion, Soviet Russia was the great danger. Europe and Germany were being divided into East and West, but the main problem was that the Western Powers had not yet fully adjusted to the new situation. They were not alone: the leaders of the non-Communist parties, including his own, had either misjudged the situation or were too weak to draw the appropriate hard conclusions.

Undeterred by the need for constant repetition of his views, Adenauer began to force his party colleagues, and from summer 1947 the general public, to take note of his political outlook. He never tired of emphasising that decisions in party politics were dependent mainly upon foreign-policy conditions. Since the main danger came from the Soviet Union, their own actions must be guided by the need to oppose Soviet influence.

Until the summer of 1946, Adenauer believed that Moscow was endeavouring 'to get the leadership in Germany with the help of the KPD and parts of the SPD'.[1] This belief also explained many of his efforts to forge an anti-socialist bloc of German parties. Through discussions and letters, he urged Scharnagl in Munich, Petersen in Hamburg, Heile of the FDP, and others to unite in opposition to the KPD, which he regarded as power-hungry and supported by the Soviet Union, and the SPD, which he considered too sympathetic to the Communists. The party system that was emerging after mid-1945 was becoming polarised. On 1 September 1945, he wrote to Petersen, the mayor of Hamburg, to explain his views: 'I think it not impossible that developments will ultimately result in the materialistic parties, the SPD and KPD, standing on one side and the Christian Democratic Party on the other.'[2] The SPD, he thought, was moving towards the KPD. Adenauer purported to see signs of this development in Cologne, where his old enemy Robert Görlinger was particularly active. On the other hand, he also foresaw that 'people on the right wing of Social Democracy' – he was thinking particularly of Carl Severing – 'will come over to the Christian Democratic Party in the course of developments'.[3]

In fact, the months of February and March 1946 did see the amalgamation of the KPD and SPD in the Eastern Zone and in East Berlin. Despite clear evidence of a forced merger, the development was accepted voluntarily by leading Social Democrats and many rank-and-file members. However, in the first six months of that year, Adenauer came to recognise that his views had been mistaken in two respects. First, in association with the London executive-in-exile, Kurt Schumacher had insisted upon and achieved a complete separation of his party from the Communists, thereby fulfilling a major demand of the Christian Democratic negotiators in discussions with their Social Democrat counterparts in the summer and autumn of 1945. Second, the Christian Democrats had not succeeded in establishing themselves as the only anti-socialist force. Despite promising early signs, attempts to merge the non-socialist groups came to a standstill in winter 1945/46. The FDP, the NLP and even the CSU in Bavaria all chose to continue their separate existences. Nothing more than a loose grouping of anti-socialist parties could be achieved. Moreover, in the Western Zones as well as Berlin, the CDU itself was far from united, even in its assessment of the Soviet danger and in its attitude towards socialism. Party headquarters in Berlin were producing additional ideas which were diametrically opposed to Adenauer's own views.

At the Paris Foreign Ministers' Conference in summer 1946, it became increasingly apparent that the Soviet Union was prepared to play the national card in the struggle for the soul of the German people. In consequence, the Berlin CDU of Jakob Kaiser, with its pronounced commitment to working for national unity, became more dangerous.

Adenauer was well aware of the complexities of the situation. His capacity to assimilate and understand political developments greatly impressed his colleagues on the Zone committee of the CDU. He was also becoming more knowledgeable in foreign policy. Moreover, Adenauer was determined to base his party's tactics on the great issues of international politics. The Soviet Union, he thought, now wanted 'to raise the national flag for Germany because it knows that the Germans will be quick to agree with the national thesis ... This policy of Russia is quite unmistakable. Russia clearly aims to win over the German people for its policy, for the policy of a unified Germany with Berlin as its capital city, about which the Russians are specific, and in brackets we can all say: under Russian leadership.'[4]

In his view, fear of such a development also lay behind the surprising British decision to establish the Land of North Rhine-Westphalia. He therefore welcomed the decision, while Kurt Schumacher was unequivocally hostile.[5] Though Adenauer regarded the re-establishment of German economic unity as the best solution, it was now necessary 'to demand as the second-best solution the establishment of unified economic life as soon as possible in the three Zones not occupied by the Russians'. In that case, the British, Americans and French must be prepared to permit the development of economic life in the three Western Zones.

Many of the foreign-policy manoeuvres of the victorious powers remained a source of mystery to the Germans until well into 1948. During this period, while the Soviet Union welcomed rapid changes in tactics and the British and Americans considered various political alternatives, the French became fixed in a negative role. Though he was committed in principle to the West, Adenauer was not yet convinced that the Western Powers were sufficiently committed to a fair policy to make cooperation with them feasible. He continued to advocate his own concept of reasonable cooperation, but shared Kurt Schumacher's view that the Germans were alone: they could not follow either the British or the French without reservations, while the course of U.S. policy was impossible to predict.

It is inaccurate to claim that Adenauer's policy was already directed mainly towards France. Since autumn 1945 his letters and internal discussions had contained strongly worded complaints about the short-sightedness of a French policy which was dictated both by its security trauma and by hard economic interests. Adenauer had no desire for a Europe in which France was the sole dominant power. On 8 April 1946 he wrote to a colleague in the party, Professor Ulrich Noack, who was later an advocate of a neutral Germany:

> I do not think it right that you describe France alone as the leading power in Europe. France is not strong enough biologically and economically for this role. I take the view that Europe must be led by Britain and France, and that an integration of the economic interests of France and Britain and Germany is necessary for that reason. Just like the British themselves, it is very much in our interests for Britain to regard itself as a European power. If one describes France as the only leading power in Europe, one eliminates Britain. I do not think that is right.[6]

For the moment, however, neither the British nor the French were ready to adopt a policy acceptable to the Germans. Adenauer thus explained his position to Friedrich Manstetten, a solicitor in Cologne who had offered him legal assistance during the emergencies of 1933-1937: '... I am neither francophile nor francophobe, neither anglophile nor anglophobe, but germanophile.'[7] Although this remark was made in order to refute the allegation of separatism, it also reflected the basic outlook underlying Adenauer's tentative European deliberations, even in the early days.

Adenauer's mental map of Europe was already divided into two, although the future organisation of the West remained wholly undecided. He believed that it was essential to prevent the Berlin CDU leadership from extending its authority to the Western Zones; whether the Berlin leaders admitted it or not, they were under the influence of the Soviet Union. In the current political climate, all – whether they supported him or not – must ensure that the 'Reich CDU' of Andreas Hermes and, since the end of 1945, of Kaiser and Lemmer, did not move beyond Berlin and the Eastern Zone.

Although the tactical situation changed repeatedly between the beginnings of summer in 1945, when Adenauer first began to establish contacts outside the Cologne region, and the spring of 1948, the underlying conditions remained unaltered. From 1945 to 1948 the Berlin party leadership, sometimes openly and sometimes more discreetly, laid claim to the leadership of the CDU throughout Germany. By contrast, Adenauer attempted to bring together an inner-party coalition against it in the Western Zones.

If Adenauer had been asked to list what he found most irritating about Berliners, he would not know where to start and where to end. First was their annoying claim to leadership, which was unacceptable for a number of reasons, including the fact that it would make the party leadership in the Western Zones appear to be under Soviet influence. Second, Adenauer was convinced that the CDU organisation in the West, especially the British Zone, would be a powerful political force when general elections were called. Why should leadership be granted to the CDU in the East, which had a much smaller area of operations than, for instance, the CDU in the British Zone? Furthermore, if the CDU chose Kaiser and Lemmer as its leaders, it would be appointing men who were desperate to maintain national unity at almost any price. In Adenauer's view, German unity had already been destroyed for the immediate future. In consequence, the proclamation of this objective could only strengthen Soviet influence throughout Germany even if this was not the aim. Adenauer was deeply suspicious of Kaiser's argument that, in foreign and economic policy, Germany must regard itself as a 'bridge between East and West'. He considered such attitudes as both arrogant and rash.

Adenauer was equally dismissive of the programme of 'Christian Socialism'. As chairman of the party in the British Zone, he was already engaged in attempting to control – and perhaps eventually to outmanoeuvre – the socialist wing of his organisation. He was therefore displeased by the arrival of documents and emissaries from Jakob Kaiser, attempting to strengthen the socialist group from outside and encouraging it to form a party within a party.

The British had an important role to play in this affair. Adenauer quickly perceived that Kaiser's group in Berlin was favoured by the political department of the British Military Government. This, he was convinced, had secretly encouraged Kaiser to oppose him as the party leader in the British Zone on certain issues, and even to remove him with the help of the socialist wing of the party.

The British were not acting solely for reasons of ideological sympathy, though this was understandable from civil servants and officers responsible to a Labour government. Their goodwill towards the Berlin CDU leadership was also based on considerations of policy towards Germany. After the SPD in the Eastern Zone had been eliminated in spring 1946, the only remaining non-Communist force of any significance was the CDU East. Rather than abandon all hope of achieving the unification of East and West Germany, the British thought it wise for the CDU leadership in every Zone to be in the hands of people who, though anti-Communist, might still prove acceptable to the Soviets. In principle, a CDU under Kaiser could also have worked with Schumacher's SPD. This would have established two potentially powerful parties advocating democratic socialism and given them a good chance of success against the SED and KPD.

A further factor was Adenauer's contempt for the leadership abilities of Kaiser and Lemmer. He was well aware that the supposed intellectual inadequacies of the two men might be an advantage in his struggles against them within the party. Nevertheless, he was affronted by the bid for leadership from Kaiser, who had been no more than Land secretary of the Christian trade unions during the Weimar Republic. Moreover, his deputy Ernst Lemmer, general secretary of the 'Gewerkschaftsring deutscher Arbeiter- und Angestelltenverbände', a union of white and blue collar employees before 1933, had consented to the Enabling Act *(Ermächtigungsgesetz)* in 1933.

Adenauer saw an attack being launched from the headquarters of the party in Berlin, with its epicentre in the Eastern Zone. Since the summer of 1945, emissaries had been sent to the Western Zones to persuade the founding groups to look to Berlin for leadership. One of these emissaries was a Berlin lawyer, Otto Lenz. Like Hermes and Kaiser, Lenz had been involved with the 20 July 1944 plot and had barely escaped with his life. Seven years later, Adenauer was to bring him into the Federal Chancellor's office as a state secretary and entrust him with the task of building up a propaganda machine to win the landslide election victory of 1953. Another of the Berlin *Reichsleitung* (Reich leadership) to win Adenauer's favour in later years was Heinrich Krone, who was to become an ardent supporter of the Chancellor's policies.

The national meeting *(Reichstreffen)* in Bad Godesberg was a major attempt to establish the Berlin party leader, Andreas Hermes, as the dom-

inant personality in the party. This was prevented by the clumsy intervention of the Soviet occupying power. After Hermes was replaced in
Berlin, Adenauer had some justification for suspecting the Berlin leadership of trying to manoeuvre Hermes into the chairmanship of the CDU in
the British Zone. The attempt failed, however, and Adenauer was elected.

Subsequently, Jakob Kaiser made an ambitious journey to the British
and U.S. Zones in an attempt to win the support of the various groups in
the CDU which subscribed to a socialist policy and accepted the claims
of Berlin to lead the party. At the same time, Andreas Hermes was planning a new *Reichstagung* in Heidelberg for March 1946.

Kaiser could rely with relative confidence on the trade union wing of the
party in Westphalia and the Rhineland, where he had been secretary before
1933. When the Berlin CDU chairman visited the British Zone in March, he
was given an enthusiastic welcome by the party's *Sozialausschüsse* (Social
Issues Committees) in Düsseldorf and Essen, Duisburg and Dortmund.
Meanwhile, his general secretary Georg Dertinger, another lawyer with considerable organisational talents, sought access to the address lists of the
Land and Kreis associations in the British Zone. Adenauer was alarmed at
these developments. He sensed the establishment of a faction within the
party, with Kaiser in the background, which would restrict his own freedom
of manoeuvre. Moreover, Kaiser had been flown in by a British aircraft, and
the British Military Government took considerable interest in the progress
of his efforts to protect the socialist line of the CDU in the British Zone.[8]

Adenauer's response came swiftly. The alliance he had sought with the
south Germans, especially the Bavarians, was now finalised. On 3 April,
in Stuttgart, Adenauer and the Oberpräsident of Schleswig-Holstein,
Theodor Steltzer, met leading CDU and CSU politicians from the U.S.
Zone. The CSU was represented by its Land chairman, Josef Müller, and
by Baron Prittwitz and Gaffron, Ambassador German envoy in Washington before 1933; the CDU in North Baden was represented by the deputy
minister-president, Heinrich Köhler; ministers André and Ersing came
from the CDU in Württemberg. Though we do not know who called the
meeting, the agreements reached were little short of sensational, and of
great significance for the development of the party system in Germany.
Since no minutes were taken, our knowledge of the discussions is based
on a note sent after the meeting by Adenauer to the participants, together
with his report on a meeting with Kaiser which occurred soon afterwards.[9]

The representatives in Stuttgart agreed to unite the CDU associations
into a party which would be called the 'Christian Union'. An application
to that end was to be made to the U.S. and British military governments.
In his note, Adenauer wrote innocently: 'All those present agreed that
everything should also be done to facilitate the amalgamation of the CDU
of Berlin and the Russian Zone with the parties of the other Zones, but
the site of the future party leadership should not be Berlin or a place in

the Russian Zone.' He was well aware that this last condition was not acceptable to the Berliners.

The meeting had also decided that Berlin could not be the seat of the party leadership even if the city were not occupied by the Russians: 'It was also agreed that an attempt must be made to make a place near the Main line into the seat of the party leadership ...' This was a concession to the Hesse group, which maintained strong reservations about Berlin and all things Prussian despite its sympathy for Kaiser's advocacy of the 'socialist order'. Such views were held even by Walter Dirks and Eugen Kogon, who were soon to become known in the *Frankfurter Hefte* as advocates of Christian Socialism and champions of the radical democratic wing of the European Movement.[10]

The implication of these assertions was that the party was committed to the creation of a supra-regional party, but with its focus and headquarters in the West, and with the Berlin CDU and CDU East as no more than an appendage.

Even the basic ideas of Kaiser's programme were rejected, such as his calls for 'a synthesis between East and West on German soil' and his assertions that 'the bourgeois epoch is over' and 'the Communist manifesto is a great achievement'. The meeting was unanimously of the opinion that references to 'Christian Socialism', and assertions that 'we are social', were out of place. These would only create confusion and discontent, especially in the CSU, even though it was agreed that a sociopolitical programme must be worked out in the near future. Kaiser's plan for a party assembly was also dismissed as undesirable.

Adenauer took a certain personal satisfaction in being deputed by the Stuttgart meeting to inform Kaiser of its decisions. He thus became the unofficial spokesman of the Western CDU organisations, enabling him to oppose Kaiser's bid to extend his influence in Adenauer's heartland. A few days later, when Kaiser called on him in Rhöndorf, Adenauer handed him his memorandum. This became the subject of a long discussion, at which Karl Arnold was also present, the following day.

This was the second important meeting between Adenauer and Kaiser in Rhöndorf – the first had been held in 1936 to discuss opposition to the National Socialists – and was almost as unproductive as the first. Nevertheless, Kaiser was able to make a few points, probably with the assistance of Karl Arnold as a representative of the left wing of the CDU. Adenauer was forced to concede that the idea of calling the party the 'Christian Union' would meet with determined resistance, both from the Land associations and from the Allies, whose permission would be required. If the word 'democratic' were removed from the party name, Kaiser argued, it would give the party's political opponents valuable election ammunition in their attempts to defame the party as a collection of reactionaries. The work of the CDU in Berlin would then become even more difficult. Adenauer not only retreated on the issue, but also promised to persuade the CDU chairmen in the U.S. Zone to accept Kaiser's arguments. He then made another concession: in principle, he could have no objection if the CDU and CSU in the U.S. Zone united into a single organisation, comparable to the CDU in the British Zone.

Adenauer also dropped his objections to Kaiser's plans for a *Reichstreffen* once the proposed name change had been effected. However, Kaiser was forced to accept that only a limited number of guests from the Western Zones would be able to attend, and that these would have to abstain from voting on the various resolutions. Meanwhile, Adenauer had discovered that one reason for U.S. and British support for Jakob Kaiser was his hard line against the Soviets and the Poles on the issue of the German territories in the east. He therefore urged his party colleagues in southern Germany to bolster the reputation of the CDU in Berlin and the Soviet Zone as much as possible. On the issue of Berlin as the capital, however, he would not budge: 'For the west and for the south of Germany, it is quite out of the question for the political headquarters of the new Germany to be sited in Berlin after the re-establishment of Germany. It would not matter whether and by whom Berlin and the east were occupied.'[11]

Apart from the concession over the party name, which was little more than the necessary correction to a snap decision, Adenauer had rejected Kaiser's arguments on all the relevant points. However, he could not be accused of having betrayed the interests of the Eastern Zone in the process. It is difficult to know whether the refusal to accept the claim of Berlin as capital originated with Adenauer, or whether it also reflected the uncompromising demands of the conservative wing of the CSU. Kaiser was left feeling that the western Land associations regarded the Berlin organisation as peripheral rather than central. However, this did not prevent him from continuing to work for changes in his favour until the end of 1947.

On his return to Berlin, Kaiser complained to the British about the reactionaries in the west. He also told them of Adenauer's belief that the Western Powers would not remain in Berlin and would accept the division of Germany into the Eastern Zone and the Western Zones.[12] Kaiser regarded this as a pretext. However, we know that Adenauer had been convinced since the summer of 1945 that Germany was, to all intents and purposes, divided. There is no need for far-fetched theories of an anti-Berlin effect, or of a lifelong antipathy towards Prussia, to explain a position that was actually rooted in a realistic appraisal of the political situation.

Detailed descriptions of the moves and counter-moves in the party over the following months are superfluous here. Adenauer's victory was not yet completely secure. Until spring 1947, an agreement between the four victorious powers still seemed possible – and that would have resulted in Kaiser rather than Adenauer becoming leader of the CDU.

Furthermore, Adenauer's own support in the Western Zones was far from solid. In the Bavarian CSU, a bitter power-struggle was being waged between arch-conservative federalists and the party chairman, Josef Müller, a supporter of Jakob Kaiser. Adenauer was aware that Kaiser also had many supporters in the British Zone, including the socialist sympathisers associated with Johannes Albers and Karl Arnold. Even Adenauer's deputy in the party executive, Friedrich Holzapfel, from the pre-Nazi conservative-national DNVP, had made a number of visits to Berlin. Though several truces were declared between Cologne and Berlin, all of them were broken. During this period, however, Adenauer managed to build a strong organisation within his own Zone association. His position was temporarily secured in September 1946 when his vigorous campaigning achieved major successes at the first municipal elections. At its first attempt, the infant CDU won 49.1 per cent of the votes cast, thereby inflicting a decisive defeat on the SPD, which won 30.2 per cent. As in any democratic society, this election victory was the best argument Adenauer could offer in support of his leadership. Adenauer had proved that majorities could be won by a party that 'is social, not socialist'. Even before the victory, Johannes Albers had written to his friend Kaiser describing the mood among the CDU rank-and-file: 'They virtually worship Adenauer.'[13] Albers, a leading figure on the left of the party, thereafter began to make cautious changes to his own position to bring it more into line with that of his successful leader.

During almost two years of disputes with the party in Berlin, Adenauer had never made the differences public knowledge. He was aware that an outward show of unity was essential, at least before elections. He was therefore prepared to make compromises, even on fundamental questions, on the condition that he could be sure of keeping personal control over developments.

With an eye on the Moscow Council of Foreign Ministers, which was to meet in March and April 1947, the CDU in Berlin pressed for the amalgamation of the CDU Land associations to guarantee that the party spoke with one voice. All the signs were that the Moscow conference would offer one last opportunity to stop the Eastern and Western Zones from drifting apart, and perhaps to make a breakthrough to the establishment of a national government.

The vital meeting of the Land chairmen took place in Königstein on 5 and 6 February. Here Kaiser advocated the creation of a CDU/CSU *Arbeitsgemeinschaft* (Working Association of the CDU/CSU) in the hope of being appointed as its spokesman on foreign policy. However, all the participants recognised that this would amount to a preliminary decision about the course of foreign policy, and even about the party leadership itself. Kaiser hoped for the support of Hesse and the CSU, which contained some sympathisers with his 'Christian Socialism' and others who believed that Adenauer was becoming too powerful. The Königstein meeting included all the leading figures in the Union.

Adenauer, the chairman of the CDU in the British Zone, arrived late for the meeting. By that time five committees had already been appointed, including one to consider foreign policy. Kaiser had openly declared that in summer 1945 the intention had been to establish the party 'throughout Reich'. Moreover, he argued, the national capital was not part of any occupation Zone, but was the site of the Control Council and had a supra-zonal function.[14]

When the issue of the chairmanship was raised in the foreign policy committee, a furious row broke out. The Bavarian side proposed Baron von Prittwitz und Gaffron, German ambassador to Washington between 1927 and 1933, for the post; Ernst Lemmer proposed Jakob Kaiser. When a member of the Adenauer faction applied for a postponement of the decision, von Prittwitz withdrew his candidacy. Ernst Lemmer then forced the issue by demanding an explanation of the party's reluctance to give the post to Kaiser, which had deeply offended the Berliners. This produced a list of the incidents that had aroused hostility to the activities of the Berliners in the Western Zones. Finally Adenauer himself entered the fray. By praising the expertise of von Prittwitz, he managed to question the competence of Jakob Kaiser in foreign affairs. Moreover, he signalled his belief that it would be unwise to appoint as spokesman a Berliner who might at any time be subjected to 'more or less pressure from the Allies'. Though Adenauer did not say so explicitly, his main concern was with the two different approaches to foreign policy – commitment to the West versus 'settlement and bridge building between East and West'. Finally, Adenauer criticised certain members of the Berlin CDU for 'talking drivel about the raising of a Black Reichswehr', a secret army.

In the ensuing storm, *Geheimrat* Katzenberger of the Kaiser group demanded that the executive of the Working Association be summoned. There the row continued. With typical pathos, Kaiser now declared that he had been 'placed by Fate in this position'.[15] Erich Köhler of the Hesse CDU, who had already discussed with Adenauer whether to grant Kaiser the chairmanship, put a direct question to Kaiser and Lemmer: Was the underlying reason for the claim the fact that Kaiser was demanding the leadership of the entire party? Kaiser and Lemmer both confirmed this. Kaiser, whose quick temper was notorious, flew into a rage and declared that the refusal to recognise his claim was incredible. Declaring that further discussion was superfluous, Adenauer left the room. No functioning foreign policy committee was established, though von Prittwitz and a number of others were asked to collate relevant material. An attempt by the Berliners to mend fences the following day yielded no results.

Kaiser's claim to leadership had been rejected. His initiative for the establishment of an above-party 'national representation' of all the parties also failed. Since Schumacher was not prepared to sit at a table with the leaders of the SED, Adenauer could afford to wait until the Moscow Council of Foreign Ministers had broken up without result.

From then on, Adenauer's star was in the ascendant and Kaiser's in decline. Eventually, Kaiser was permitted to speak at the Zone rally in Recklinghausen in August 1947, by which time the situation was calmer and Adenauer the undisputed leader in the British Zone. In one sense, history itself was to be the judge of the different foreign and economic policy programmes of the two men. When the victorious powers again failed to agree at the London Conference in December 1947, it was clear that Adenauer's sceptical assessment of the situation had been accurate and that Kaiser had over-estimated the possibilities for agreement between East and West. At the end of 1947, the Soviet Military Administration removed him from his power base as chairman of the CDU East. Thereafter, Kaiser had to content himself with such posts as Adenauer was prepared to offer him.

From the autumn of 1946, other issues came to the fore within the party. These included relations with the Social Democrats, the nationalisation of the mining industry in the Rhine and Ruhr as advocated by the British, and the coalition question in North Rhine-Westphalia. These three themes were inextricably linked. The conflict they aroused ultimately threatened the unity of the party in the British Zone. At the same time, the parties and leading politicians adopted positions which were decisive for the course of domestic politics in the Federal Republic for a number of years.

After Kurt Schumacher's SPD had distanced itself from the Communists, a short period of cautious contacts between the CDU and SPD began. The two party leaders met at the constituent meeting of the *Zonenbeirat* (Zonal Advisory Council) in Hamburg. The British had based this council of representatives of the various parties on the colonial model of advisory gatherings of native representatives. It was entitled to deliberate on matters which the occupying power thought suitable for discussion. The Germans also had the right to file petitions, although the occupying power alone would decide whether to accept them. Numerous important decisions continued to be taken without reference to the Advisory Council.

Directly after his confirmation as party leader in the British Zone, Adenauer arrived in Hamburg for the ceremonial opening of the *Zonenbeirat*. That evening a dinner was held in Hamburg city hall. Through the mediation of Minister-President Kopf of Lower Saxony, who was eager to forge a united German front against the occupying powers, Adenauer and Schumacher held their first discussions there.

At this stage Schumacher was still the preferred choice of the British. The SPD leader had been seriously wounded in the First World War (he had lost an arm) and was a resistance hero who had been held in a concentration camp for much of the Third Reich. A brilliant orator, he was also a courageous man who remained willing to confront the occupying powers whenever necessary. Schumacher was already famous for his caustic criticism of the Catholic Church and the CDU and FDP as 'defenders of private property', as well as for his relatively non-doctrinaire but enthusiastic commitment to state socialism.

The discussion revealed significant unanimity between the two men on the two issues which both regarded as urgent: the duty of the victors to improve the food supply, and opposition to industrial dismantling. However, any prospects for a united front were ended when Schumacher claimed that co-operation would depend on Adenauer's recognition of the SPD's claim to leadership. Adenauer coldly disagreed, suggesting that the decision should be left to the voters in the coming elections.[16] He then left the banquet and returned to his rooms in Hotel Perm, where it was so cold that he slept in his suit and coat.[17]

Nothing is as delightful and amusing for participants and observers of the political scene to watch as the encounter of two prominent party leaders who are united in amicable antipathy. One would often have this pleasure in the six years up to Kurt Schumacher's death. This was also recognised by British representatives. One of them, Noel Annan, has given a vivid description of one meeting between them in the summer of 1946. 'Kit' Steel had invited the chairmen of the CDU and SPD in the British Zone to Berlin for the official announcement of the establishment of the Land of North Rhine-Westphalia. Annan accompanied them:

> So one windy afternoon I found myself on an airfied near Lübbecke. Beside me was Adenauer, impassive, in formal dress, overcoat and homburg hat, as always dignified and calm. I never failed to be struck by the intelligence and by the mischievous delight with which in an elegant turn of phrase he would allude to some example, as he saw it, of British stupidity, his eyes shining in that expressionless oriental face. On the other side of me stood Schumacher, his thin hair blowing in the wind, hugging, as he often did, left shoulder with his right hand, his body twisted by torture in the concentration camp, each gesture revealing his demonic energy and sardonic, impatient disposition ... I watched the two men to see how they would greet one another. In Britain the leaders of the two opposing parties would quite probably not have liked each other, but they would have exchanged civilities. Throughout the journey, whether in the aircraft and the car, neither spoke a word to the other.[18]

The age difference between the two men may have played some part in their antipathy. Anyone who knew Adenauer was aware that it would go against the grain for him to accept the leadership claims of a man over twenty years younger than himself. He gave his real answer in his speech on 24 March 1946. Adenauer devoted just two sentences to the assurance that all parties must 'be prepared for honourable co-operation ... in the interests of the German people',[19] but spent a good thirty minutes detailing his differences with the SPD and disputing Schumacher's 'claim to leadership'. Schumacher's response was rapid, and helped set the tone of public polemic for the next six years: he described the CDU as the 'melting-pot of reaction' and Adenauer as the 'reactionary of all reactionaries'.[20]

Adenauer's attack on the Social Democrats intensified during the municipal election campaign in September. Here he made particularly effective use of a double-edged assault. Across the region, Adenauer proclaimed that the SPD was being granted many 'advantages' by the British and was really 'the governing party'. This enabled him to identify the success of the Social Democrats, some of whom were influential in the central offices of the British Zone, with the prevailing misery. If the British were unpopular, so was 'their' party. The argument was both simple and effective.

This successful election campaign also increased the hostility many important British representatives felt towards Adenauer. It did not concern him in the least. In fact, in the Bundestag elections of 1949 he was to repeat his claim that the SPD was receiving support from the British. The allegation was quickly followed by another. According to Adenauer, the British wanted to force socialism on Germany not only for ideological reasons, but also to prevent German competition in world markets. It is reasonable to assume that Adenauer believed both of these charges. Whatever the truth of the matter, his willingness to raise controversial issues and to pursue them with relentless conviction was an important contributing factor in all of his election victories.

The British were determined not to accept these attacks without protest. That spring, the atmosphere between Adenauer and the occupying power had already deteriorated to such an extent that the British seriously contemplated banning him from political activity for a month.[21] However, the authorities in London refused to give their consent. Experiences in the colonies had already shown that individuals 'excommunicated' by the authorities only became more popular among the population and emerged with their reputations not only intact, but actually enhanced.

Adenauer knew that the British had dealings with the Social Democrats and, on occasion, with his opponents within the party. For a time it seemed doubtful that he would remain undisputed leader of the CDU in North Rhine-Westphalia. The British, the SPD and the Centre Party would have been glad to see disputes within the CDU lead to a split in the party. The most controversial issue was that of nationalisation. After some hesitation, the Cabinet took a decision of principle to nationalise the mining industry of the Rhine and Ruhr, though only after the clarification of certain points. On the German side, responsibility for the appropriate legal regulations lay with the Land of North Rhine-Westphalia, naturally subject to the approval and implementation of all resolutions by the Military Government.

The SPD, KPD and the left wing of the CDU now saw the prospect of a fundamental reorganisation of the key industries in North Rhine-Westphalia. In the summer of 1946, a government had been formed with Rudolf Amelunxen, whose links with Adenauer went back to their schooldays and subsequently to the years of persecution by the National Socialists. Amelunxen had been associated with the Catholic social reformer, Carl Sonnenschein; at one stage during the Weimar Republic he had also been private secretary to the Social Democrat minister-president of Prussia, Otto Braun; and he was on good terms with the Prussian Minister of the Interior Carl Severing, and his son-in-law Walter Menzel.

Though Amelunxen was not attached to any party, it was no surprise to find him more sympathetic to the Social Democrats and the Centre Party than to Adenauer's CDU. At the outset the CDU – largely owing to Social Democratic influence – had been kept out of the government altogether. The SPD, KPD and Centre Party refused to allow the party to control the Ministry of the Interior. Adenauer's old enemy Robert Görlinger argued that 'genuine democratisation and denazification' would not be possible under a CDU Minister of the Interior, because far too many members of former right-wing parties had found a refuge within the party.[22] Offended by this attack, the CDU stayed out of the government, a fact which actually contributed to its success at the municipal elections of September 1946.

Subsequently, however, the British distributed the seats in the Landtag of North Rhine-Westphalia to reflect the strength of the parties in the election. As a result, CDU participation in the government became inevitable. Nevertheless, the left continued to have great influence in the Amelunxen government. Karl Arnold, mayor of Düsseldorf and deputy minister-president from December 1946, was becoming increasingly prominent as a supporter of a course of reformist cooperation with the SPD and Centre Party. Behind the scenes, he was receiving encouragement from the British and from Jakob Kaiser. Nevertheless, Arnold's relations with his party chairman remained relatively untroubled at this stage. Arnold took care not to irritate Adenauer, especially after Adenauer became chairman of the CDU *Fraktion* in the Landtag of North Rhine-Westphalia. Nevertheless, both men knew that a new situation would be created after the Landtag elections of May 1947, of which the CDU had great – and not entirely justified – expectations.

In view of the emerging tensions in the CDU of North Rhine-Westphalia, the programme discussions were particularly significant. An Economic and Social Issues Committee of the party had been at work since spring 1946. Adenauer took the view that this committee must make the attempt to reconcile the various different approaches. The committee had two chairmen: Johannes Albers, the representative of the trade union wing, and Robert Pferdmenges of the business wing, who was also the leading Protestant lay member and as such was likely to be supported by the Protestant camp. Adenauer and Pferdmenges continued to meet regularly to discuss the tactics to be adopted. During these months, Adenauer made a number of concessions to the party left in his speeches and in the various party committees. His aim was clearly to resolve the disputed issues of economic and social policy through integration rather than confrontation. Moreover, every day he was faced with the genuine distress of the population and the need for the administration of scarcity. Though the market economy could only be established in the long term, he remained convinced that it alone could create prosperity and that a state-controlled economy would act as a brake on economic activity. The temporary catastrophe confronting his country did not change his basic convictions on this subject.

Nevertheless, he believed that a cautious approach was both worthwhile and necessary. After the meeting of the Zone committee in Lippstadt in December 1946, Adenauer wanted to draw up a number of definite proposals. Quick action was essential to prepare the party for the imminent discussions of nationalisation in the Landtag, for the election campaign in North Rhine-Westphalia in February 1947, and for the continued disputes with the Berlin CDU and their pro-socialist allies in Hesse, Bavaria, and even North Rhine-Westphalia itself. He therefore wanted further discussions in smaller groups, then in the Zone executive. The vital decisions had to be made by the middle of January 'to give us two months ... to present our ideas to the electorate as a whole and to the world public'.[23]

Adenauer's authority had been significantly strengthened by the results of the municipal elections, leading him to expound his own views with some confidence. He opposed the nationalisation of the major firms. First, this would place 'greater power' in the hands of the central government 'than the National Socialist state had in the first years of its existence'. Second, industrial concentration into giant corporations had taken the German economy down the wrong path for several decades; nationalisation would only create 'much bigger mammoth structures'. For Adenauer, the great ideological debate could be reduced to the choice between freedom and socialism – and socialism, in his view, would 'lead with absolute certainty to the totalitarian state'.[24] He was convinced of the need to encourage the largest possible number of medium-sized and small businesses. These were more competitive, more resilient in times of economic crisis, and made it easier for workers to establish a personal relationship with their companies.

In effect, this was the Adenauer of the 'Rhöndorf Programme'. However, he was now more prepared to compromise and openly supported the concept of the 'mixed-economy firm'. Here he was contemplating mixed ownership by the municipality and private interests along the lines adopted in Bochum and Dortmund. However, he continued to regard private capital as the essential factor. This alone could offer any prospect of obtaining capital 'from the only country that is really in a position to provide it, namely from the United States of North America'.[25] Foreign loans were essential for the reconstruction of the German economy. For that reason, a united front must be established against British plans for nationalisation.

Adenauer knew that there was little enthusiasm for his ideas on the left wing of the party. Yet he remained surprisingly hopeful that differences of opinion could be reduced to a minimum. With typical self-confidence, he added: 'If one looks at things impartially, it is hardly possible to reach a different solution than the one I have indicated.'

The product of these brief discussions was the Ahlen Programme. Subsequently, it was to be the subject of more debate than almost any other programme in the history of the CDU. The general public was almost completely unaware that Adenauer was the father of the programme and that it would have been more accurate to refer to it as the 'Adenauer Programme'. He was responsible for the five-page draft of January 1947 which linked cooperative and libertarian principles, and for a second draft which may also have included suggestions from the Wuppertal district.[26] It was also Adenauer who made peace with Johannes Albers, thereby persuading one of the leading figures on the party left of the need for an agreement. The two vital meetings of the Economic and Social Issues Committee took place in the bank run by Robert Pferdmenges in Cologne. Ironically, the most famous of the leftist CDU programmes in 1947 was basically an Adenauer programme drawn up in a bank.

The key figures in the process of hammering out a compromise were Adenauer, Albers and Pferdmenges himself. Albers was prepared to abandon the references to socialism and nationalisation in favour of the term 'cooperative economic order' *(gemeinwirtschaftliche Ordnung)*. In return, some of the Walberberg demands were incorporated into the programme. Liberal principles were thus placed alongside ideas based on Christian Socialism even though the word socialism was never mentioned.

Adenauer took pains to emphasise that the programme would be vital during the coming conflict over the nationalisation plans of the SPD and KPD. A number of demands were therefore made: the break-up of the large companies – where these were not essential for technical, social or economic reasons – according to the 'distributive principle' or, as it was called in the Ahlen programme, 'the principle of the distribution of power' *(machtverteilendes Prinzip);* anti-cartel legislation against businesses with a monopoly character; public ownership of the mines and iron-producing heavy industry; 'right of co-determination' *(Mitbestimmungsrecht)* for workers on the fundamental issues of economic planning and social structure; economic chambers to be responsible for tasks of planning and management, taking account of current difficulties.

There is no doubt that, in this programme, Adenauer did much to accommodate the trade-union wing of his party. However, he also acted to frustrate the more ambitious nationalisation plans of Karl Arnold and to give his party a programme which was decisively different to the plans of the British and the SPD.

The decisions taken in the small mining town of Ahlen served largely to ratify the compromises agreed in Cologne between the bourgeois wing of the party and its trade-union element. By general agreement, state socialism was identified as the main enemy; it was to be opposed by a progressive solidarity, the aim of which was to stimulate rather than obstruct development.

Adenauer's achievement was two-fold. First, he had committed his party to a common platform after a period when it had threatened to fall apart over vital issues of economic and social policy. Second, a distinctive CDU policy had been formulated for use in Adenauer's offensive during parliamentary debates and the Landtag elections.

The Berlin group associated with Jakob Kaiser had missed the opportunity to cause problems for Adenauer within his own party. Adenauer was now in complete control, at least for the moment. As chairman of the CDU caucus in the Landtag of North Rhine-Westphalia, he could even influence the translation of these programme clauses into legislative initiatives.

The political battleground now moved to the Düsseldorf Landtag. The SPD demanded a referendum, to be held at the same time as the Landtag elections in April and phrased as follows: 'Should the mining industry, iron and steel-producing heavy industry and the big chemical trusts be taken into public ownership?' In response Adenauer persuaded the CDU delegation to submit six inter-related propositions: on the re-organisation of the raw-materials industry and the chemical industry; on the re-organisation of relations between employers and workers; and on the requirement to lay open share-holding structures in companies. Since the SPD and KPD could not impose their will on the current Landtag, the result of the new election would be crucial.

In the event, the Landtag election of April 1947 did not give a majority to any party. Though the CDU was unable to repeat its success in the municipal elections, it won 92 of the 216 seats to become the largest party, followed by the SPD with 64 members and the KPD with 28. The Centre Party won 20 seats and the FDP 12.

The economic debate thereafter became linked with the issue of the minister-presidency. As a result, the previously tolerable relationship between Adenauer and Arnold fell apart. Adenauer was aware that Arnold wanted to accommodate the socialist ideas of the British, the SPD, and the left wing of the Centre Party associated with Carl Spiecker. Arnold was also able to evade the control of chairman Adenauer as a result of the relative strength of the parties, which made a coalition between the SPD and the Centre Party appear the obvious solution. Adenauer attempted to advance the claims of Josef Gockeln, the chairman of the association of Catholic trade unions and an opponent of Christian Socialism, as minister-president. However, Arnold was not to be defeated. He was unanimously elected as minister-president and held the post for the following nine years.

Adenauer was now forced to watch Arnold conduct protracted negotiations which eventually led to a cabinet consisting largely of politicians from the left. During this process, a number of figures who were to play an important role in the 'Adenauer era' established themselves on the political scene. These included Gustav Heinemann, the Krupp company lawyer and prominent Protestant, as Minister of Justice, and Heinrich Lübke as Minister for Food, Agriculture and Forestry. Only the Finance Minister, Heinrich Weitz, was firmly on Adenauer's side. The SPD continued to hold a key post in the administration in the shape of the lawyer Walter Menzel, who became Minister of the Interior. In later years, Menzel and Adenauer were to clash repeatedly in the Parliamentary Council and subsequently the Bundestag. The Minister for Economic Affairs was the Social Democrat Ernst Nölting, who was destined to shadow Ludwig Erhard in the Bundestag in years to come. Rudolf Amelunxen, who had now joined the Centre Party, strengthened the influence of the left in the cabinet. Christine Teusch became Minister of Culture in December. (Adenauer, who quickly came to regard this stern woman as a thorn in his side, took his revenge by referring to her as Tristine Keusch, a play with the German words for 'triste' and 'chaste'.)[27] Though the composition of the cabinet pleased the British, it was light years away from the views of Adenauer, the chairman of the CDU caucus in the Landtag.

Over the following year, Adenauer's hostility to Karl Arnold increased and he made repeated efforts to thwart Arnold's work as minister-president. Despite the support of the party at large and most of the CDU delegation, Adenauer was largely unsuccessful. With the backing of the British, and with the assistance of the Social Democrats and Centre Party in addition to a minority of the CDU delegation, Arnold was able to approach the nationalisation issue in the manner he preferred. After much debate, a law on nationalisation was finally passed in August 1948. The CDU abstained. For the moment, however, the decision was purely symbolic. Since August 1947 it had been clear that the Americans were opposed to any nationalisation. The official argument was that such a measure would prevent the decision being taken by the German people at a later date. General Clay also objected on the grounds that nationalisation would have disastrous consequences for prospects of economic recovery.

Nevertheless, Karl Arnold had given a signal to the future Federal Republic, the outlines of which were beginning to emerge in August 1948. Future federal legislators would clearly have more chance of implementing the nationalisation plans which had been obstructed in North Rhine-Westphalia by the intervention of the Americans. Equally, the left could hope that co-operation between the SPD and parts of the CDU in Düsseldorf might serve as a model for the first federal government.

On the other hand, Adenauer worked hard to promote his own ideas and an alternative model for a coalition. During the period when Karl Arnold wanted to go further than the Ahlen Programme on the nationalisation issue, Adenauer made an enthusiastic defence of its principles for CDU economic policy in the British Zone. However, he was perfectly happy to let the compromise Ahlen Programme sink into oblivion later, when the opportunity arose to implement Ludwig Erhard's plans for a market economy in the Frankfurt Economic Council.

As far as the coalition was concerned, Adenauer did everything in his power to prise the CDU away from the SPD. With the support of the Westphalians and after a bitter dispute, he forced Arnold to accept Artur Sträter, an Adenauer supporter, as Minister of Justice, thereby ensuring more potential friction in the cabinet. The decision meant that Gustav Heinemann lost his post and did little to improve relations between Heinemann and Adenauer. In addition, Adenauer began to court the right wing of the Centre Party associated with Johannes Brockmann in the hope of building a CDU-Centre Party coalition. Though such a solution was mathematically possible, it did not come about.

Adenauer likewise began to cultivate relations with the FDP of North Rhine-Westphalia, which was still a party of the far right. He thus exchanged 'cordial' New Year greetings with the FDP chairman in the British Zone, Franz Blücher: 'You are quite right, our ways may be different here and there, but basically in our objectives we are of the same mind ... It is always a pleasure for me to meet you in person.'[28] In the hard parliamentary battles of North Rhine-Westphalia, contacts and alliances were being forged which would subsequently influence developments in the Parliamentary Council and the early Federal Republic.

Observers of Adenauer's skilful tactics during these years may find it easy to forget the political background against which these manoeuvres were taking place. Political apathy was widespread among the population. Of course, membership of the political parties was high until the currency reform, while the various party committees included representatives of the war generation as well as hundreds of former members of the Weimar parties. However, there were more prosaic reasons than democratic commitment for membership of all the parties, including the CDU: the attempt to achieve political rehabilitation by work in a democratic party; the hope of obtaining or keeping a post in the public service; and political ambition.

When elections were called, the voters went to the polls with their customary discipline. With the exception of the Communists, only democratic parties were allowed to stand, ensuring that these obtained overwhelming majorities. However, millions of Germans during these troubled years had little interest in democratic politics. The sobering fact remained that a new leadership élite was being created under Allied control in the first years of occupation. Amid bitter fighting between rival cliques, this élite became deeply embedded and ready to assume whatever political responsibility the Allies decided to endow it with.

During a period of German political impotence, powerful positions were thus being carved out, programmes developed and dropped, and coalitions formed and then abandoned. The full effect of this process was perceived only after 1948, when the Western Allies extended German freedom of action and decided on the foundation of a West German state. Those politicians who had reached a position of influence were likely to remain at the top for decades, even if the wider public had scarcely been aware of their rise. Relatively few spectators had observed their race for political power – and the most successful of these athletes was Konrad Adenauer. The discussions on programmes, inner-party leadership battles, and manoeuvres in the Landtag of North Rhine-Westphalia all played an important part in this race. Without his success in establishing himself as party leader, Adenauer could never have become Chancellor.

The process by which Adenauer transformed himself from a city mayor into a resilient and capable party leader remains a psychological and political mystery. He understood intuitively that the post-war German political system must be built up by the parties themselves rather than by the parliaments or the governments. Though previously he had mainly held municipal offices, he resisted every attempt to persuade him to accept ministerial office prematurely. If he had entered the cabinet in North Rhine-Westphalia – which he had every right to do – his freedom of manoeuvre in the British Zone would have been drastically reduced. He also avoided taking a leading role in the Bi-zonal Economic Council from 1948, allowing his deputy Friedrich Holzapfel to do the job instead. Adenauer instinctively understood the importance of working on the party programme in the early days of a new political organisation.

Most surprising of all, Adenauer revealed himself to be a formidable election campaigner. Formerly an elected official who had never run an election campaign, he knew that a party leader stood or fell by his success in elections. Such success could not be achieved by dogged persistence alone. It was also essential to court publicity and seek controversy – through vicious polemic, cruel jokes, and clear presentation of his party's policy. Adenauer was perfectly prepared, on occasion, to resort to wild attacks on his opponents, in a manner guaranteed to rouse them to fury and achieve the maximum publicity. Though the city councillors in Cologne knew that Adenauer had always possessed these abilities, his role as mayor had forced him to act with a degree of restraint. In post-war Germany, his supporters discovered that Adenauer was a natural campaigner and a master of all political tricks, dirty ones not excluded. Adenauer's triumph over

CDU rivals such as Jakob Kaiser, Karl Arnold, Hans Schlange-Schöningen, Werner Hilpert and Friedrich Holzapfel was due, at least in part, to his superior political temperament during election campaigns.

Equally remarkable was Adenauer's physical resilience. By spring of 1946 he had shared with most leading German politicians the experience of war and a further fall in living standards in the early months of occupation. As his correspondence during these years reveals, the food supply in Rhöndorf was little better than elsewhere in Germany. Occasional packages reached the family from Switzerland – from Marc Pont in Chandolin and Paul Silverberg in Lugano – but otherwise Adenauer shared the deprivations of his fellow citizens.

As a result, his discussions with Wilhelm Hamacher of the Centre Party were practical as well as political. For example, he sent his thanks to the 'head of the firm Elbs and Hamacher' for 'the prompt settlement of the boiler affair'.[29] Shortly before Christmas 1947, his old friend and later president of the German Soccer League Peco Bauwens received a note from Adenauer: 'The coal has not come! Please ensure that it comes soon or we will be cold this Christmas.'[30] Hermann Siemer, nephew of the head of the Dominicans in Oldenburg, was a farmer who later became a CDU Bundestag deputy; from time to time he stowed apples and eggs into Adenauer's car, causing great pleasure in Rhöndorf 'since it is quite impossible to get eggs here despite the coupons, and my wife needs them so desperately'.[31] Adenauer himself suffered hunger oedema as a result of protein deficiency during 1946-1947 and regarded cheese as unobtainable.[32] This was everyday life in post-war Germany, for the Adenauers as for millions of their fellow citizens.

During this period he found the continuous car journeys particularly exhausting. The car was unreliable and often broke down; the slovenly hotel rooms were usually freezing cold; the food was almost always poor. In photographs dating from this period, Adenauer looks as hollow-cheeked and emaciated as his contemporaries. Moreover, in 1946 he had entered his eighth decade, though with the temperament and robust health of a man still in his early sixties. Only to close friends did he occasionally complain that he had 'more work, and physically exhausting work through the constant travelling, than I have ever had before'.[33]

Nevertheless, he could always return to his quiet home in Rhöndorf. All of his children and grandchildren had survived the war and the occupation unscathed and were living either at home or close by. His oldest son Konrad was a member of the executive of the Rhenish-Westphalian Electricity Works; Max Adenauer worked for KHD and, in 1948, followed in his father's footsteps by becoming a deputy mayor in Cologne; Paul Adenauer was a student of theology in Bonn and spent much of his time at home; his younger daughters were also students, and his youngest son Georg was at school in Bad Godesberg.

Gussie Adenauer's condition, however, continued to deteriorate. During her imprisonment at the end of the war she had contracted a blood disorder which required repeated stays in hospital. The use of penicillin, acquired by von Weiss in Switzerland, brought only a temporary improvement. In June 1947 the couple travelled once more to Chandolin and Zermatt for their first stay abroad since July 1939. In the conditions of 1947 this was a great privilege, which they had applied for three months previously and the British had granted because of Gussie's poor health. Adenauer's message to Ria and Walter Reiners clearly reveals his feeling of liberation: 'Since 28 June we have been in our beloved Chandolin. It is almost completely unchanged and astoundingly beautiful in the wonderful weather ... Wonderful Switzerland. Everything is available, albeit expensive ... It is so beautiful here that my dearest wish would be to invite all the children, children-in-law and grandchildren here for a month.'[34] His wife, who spent the last contented month of her life in Chandolin, added: 'It is like a dream! Despite the excellent impression in the towns and the love that is shown us, one's mind always returns to the poor homeland. Despite all the pleasures there is always a "lump" in the throat ... Here in Chandolin the world has stood still.'

After their return home Gussie Adenauer soon returned to the clinic. Whilst his tasks in the various committees and his vast correspondence (some 6,100 letters between 1945 and 1949) claimed all of Adenauer's energy, his personal tragedy was played out in Rhöndorf and the Johannes Hospital in Bonn. The events of 1916 were repeated. Once again Adenauer spent all of his free moments with his dying wife, though this time his children were grown and able to support him. Paul Adenauer, who had intended to enter the monastery at Maria Laach as a Benedictine novice, abandoned the plan in order to stay near his mother in Bonn. Gussie Adenauer died there on 3 March 1948, surrounded by her husband and children.

As was his custom when he was deeply distressed, Adenauer withdrew to his study and avoided all condolences. Gussie Adenauer had been greatly loved, and her burial service at the forest cemetery in Rhöndorf was attended by large numbers of mourners. Even then, the discord of politics was felt. A month later, Adenauer wrote a bitter letter to Johannes Albers: 'It has been reported to me as a fact that at the burial of my wife you made the following remark to Herr Keller of Düsseldorf: "The people are all coming here now because they expect something of Adenauer. In six weeks he will be finished."' It was signed with a curt 'Hochachtungsvoll' (Yours faithfully).[35]

By the time Adenauer wrote this letter, he had thrown himself back into his work. He did not even communicate his feelings to close friends. It was three months before he explained to Paul Silverberg: 'In fact I feel extraordinarily tired and over-strained. At my age, with the cares of last winter and spring and with the whole serious situation in Germany, this is no surprise.'[36] Former Chancellor Brüning, who visited him at this time, regarded Adenauer as 'a lonely man'. Adenauer told him that his wife's death had been an 'amputation' and that 'he had really no more roots in this world'.[37]

This was 1948 – a decisive year in the history of post-war Germany. As in 1917/1918, Adenauer was forced to deal with the complex and rapid developments of the following months when burdened by great personal grief. The Berlin crisis was moving towards a climax, and possibly towards a third world war. The movement for European unification was under way, though it was far from certain that the Western Zones of Germany would be permitted to return to the community of Western nations on acceptable conditions. At every turn Adenauer was faced by uncertainty and problems.

Apart from the constant support of his family, it was the pressure of this work that helped him to bear his loss. He wrote to the wife of his old colleague Mönnig, who was going blind: 'The next months will bring a great deal of work, and in many respects that is fortunate. So long as one endures, one will try to do one's work conscientiously.'[38]

Nevertheless, as Adenauer became the central figure on the West German political stage, the oxygen of power began to take its effect. After the summer of 1948, instead of appearing tired and dispirited, he gave an impression of remarkable vitality and intelligence. Indeed, he even appeared to be enjoying the task of guiding his party and 'the German people' (or, more precisely, the West German people) through the troubled times ahead.

Towards the Federal Republic of Germany

In 1946 and 1947, East-West relations developed as Adenauer had predicted. Consul-General von Weiss, who continued to take coffee with his friend on Saturday afternoons, provided a version of Adenauer's ideas on foreign policy on 10 July 1946:

> At the moment Germany is basically falling apart into two regions: into the Russian Zone including Berlin, on one hand, and into the British, French and American Zone, on the other. With alarming speed these two parts are moving further away from each other in their economic and political structures. However Russian policy develops, even now it is safe to assume that eastern Germany will have to be cultivated anew from western Germany, both economically and spiritually, as it was seven-hundred years ago and before.[1]

Adenauer saw only two alternatives. At the beginning of August 1946, he argued that the first and best solution would be the removal of the

Notes for this section begin on page 719.

Zones and the establishment of a united administration for Germany through a Control Council containing representatives of the four powers. Only this solution could save Germany in its old form. 'If it does not occur, the two halves of Germany will continue their inevitable drift apart.' If unity could not be restored, however, the 'second-best' solution would be to amalgamate the Western Zones and integrate them into Western Europe.[2] Though these were the alternatives, it was impossible to predict exactly what would happen.

Whichever alternative came about – a reunited Germany or amalgamation of the Western Zones – Adenauer wanted the same structures to be established to deal with constitutional and foreign affairs. Consul-General von Weiss sent an outline of Adenauer's views on this subject to his government in the form of a memorandum. This document is so informative, and gives such a concise version of the views expressed by Adenauer to several interlocutors at the time, that it deserves to be quoted at length:

III Desired Solutions

1. Germany to suffer only minor border adjustments, especially in the East. Reason: its over-population, which compels expansion of an economic or political kind, inability of Russia and Poland to make use of the land they occupy.
2. The division into Zones to be removed. For as long as necessary, a Control Council for the whole of Germany to be appointed.
3. Germany to become a federal state which is as decentralised as possible. The central authority to be granted only as much power as is absolutely necessary for its cohesion. The seat of the control authorities must be moved to the west or south-west.
4. The political and economic focal point of Germany must be western Germany. A West German federal state must therefore be established, to include: the entire Rhineland, Westphalia, possibly Osnabrück, Rhine-Hesse, Rhineland Palatinate, at least part of Hesse-Nassau.
5. For the status of this state, the following points are important:

   a) two-chamber system.
   b) since the Ruhr is in this state, foreign countries must maintain economic representation with appropriate authority. This inevitably produces reciprocity with appropriate political effects.
   c) If Germany's western neighbours believe they cannot do without special control of this state, the duration and extent of such control should be limited. Attention should be given to the possibility of replacing this control, after a certain transition period, by the sending of representatives from the states involved to the first chamber.
   d) The duration of the occupation must be limited.

6. Mutual economic integration between Germany, or at least West Germany, and Holland, Luxembourg, France, Britain is the sole and lasting basis for a constructive solution which would bring a lasting pacification of Europe. The question of establishing common economic chambers is to be examined.

IV If the solutions outlined under III are not possible owing to the attitude of Russia, the measures cited under III must be taken for the three Western Zones. The comments under III 2-6 are then valid for this part of Germany.[3]

There were thus two possible ways to implement the entire plan – either in a united Germany with a federal constitution, or in a West German federal state. Adenauer would have preferred the former, but considered a solution involving the Western Zones alone to be more likely, at least for the time being.

For a short period towards the end of 1946, Adenauer thought that East and West might be on the verge of an agreement. In discussions within the CDU Zonal Committee, he even speculated that a secret agreement might already have been reached at the New York Conference of the Council of Foreign Ministers. Adenauer envisaged a possible deal along these lines: Poland would get the German eastern territories with the agreement of the Western Powers; in return, Soviet Union would release its Zone 'into the economic association' of the remaining Zones. The situation remained uncertain, however. He thought it possible that France would oppose such a decision at the Moscow Conference in spring 1947, thereby playing exactly the part intended for it by the Soviets. In the same breath, however, Adenauer declared that a decision to 'move back the Iron Curtain by several hundred kilometres' would be 'impossible and intolerable for every German'[4] if it meant recognising Polish and Soviet claims on the rest of Germany beyond the new Iron Curtain. Adenauer had personal knowledge of the provinces involved. He had visited Breslau in 1922 and hiked in the Riesengebirge, and he had travelled to Königsberg and Danzig in the summer of the same year. His children could remember his enthusiastic response to the experience. In the years of occupation, Adenauer thus responded like most other Germans to the loss of the eastern territories – by dismissing the idea out of hand.

For the first and only time in his life, the possibility of an agreement by the victorious powers led Adenauer to consider whether it would be wise for Germany to accept neutral status. At this stage he had no great hopes of the Western Powers. These sentiments were reflected in his letter to Wilhelm Sollmann in the distant Quaker College of Pendle Hill: 'The liberation is a terrible and hard disappointment. Unless a miracle happens, the German people will go down, slowly but surely!'[5]

It was in this frame of mind that Adenauer contributed a profoundly pessimistic New Year commentary to the *Rheinische Post* on 30 December 1946. In it he argued that the increasing misery and distress of Germany were not due to administrative incompetence on the part of the victorious powers, nor to the inevitable consequences of war devastation, but were the result of deliberate policy. For example, the country was being 'intellectually gutted' by the removal of patents and leading scientists. He regarded this as an attempt to destroy Germany as an industrial nation: 'They see us as the people that has unleashed two wars, the second of which brought the world to the edge of the abyss. They want to end that once and for all, that is the basic idea and leitmotiv of the victorious powers.'[6]

In view of the survival of the Morgenthau spirit advocating the de-indus-trialisation of Germany, Adenauer felt compelled to consider the feasibility of permanent neutrality on the Swiss model: 'We agree that we should be completely disarmed, that our pure war industry be destroyed, and that we should be subject to long-term control in both directions. Yes, we will go even further: I believe that the majority of the German people would agree if we were neutralised under international law, like Switzerland.'

Coming from a politician who, until the end of his life, was to oppose every proposal for a neutral Germany as paving the road to hell, this was a remarkable suggestion. He provided more detail in a letter of 17 Feb-ruary 1947, in response to a request from Dr Elsaesser of the Europa-Verlag (Europa Publishers) in Freiburg.[7] Here he maintained that it was 'still not completely clear' whether it was 'right to broach the topic of the neutralisation of Germany'. He had already mentioned the idea in a speech some months before, but had not met with any positive response.

> It should not be forgotten that a neutral state must defend its own neutrality, possibly by force of arms. If its neutrality is guaranteed only by other states, if it is unable to stand up for its own neutrality, then this is not a genuine neu-trality. But I do not believe that the idea of giving Germany the power to defend its neutrality has any prospect of success with the Allies. That I can understand. The Allies would fear that Germany had failed to provide suffi-cient proof of a real love of peace and would be reluctant to concede the inde-pendence that lies in neutrality. I would absolutely welcome complete neutralisation as the aim of German policy. Even if the aim is not immediately obtainable it should not be abandoned, and the meaning and content of such neutralisation should be explained to the German people.

At the same time, Adenauer stressed that he saw no contradiction between these ideas and his old scheme of a 'United States of Europe'.[8]

Adenauer was nevertheless reluctant to urge the rapid conclusion of a peace treaty at the potentially decisive Moscow Conference of the Coun-cil of Foreign Ministers. He told his party executive that time was on the side of Germany even though the current situation was illegitimate and unacceptable. They only had to consider what a peace treaty signed a year ago would have looked like to realise the truth of this assertion.[9] When Father Hubert Becher of the Aloisius College in Bad Godesberg warned against the sending of German experts to Moscow on the grounds that the peace would be little more than a diktat, Adenauer telephoned to assure him that he took the same view.

Adenauer was increasingly suspicious of the aims of Soviet policy. The Soviet Union, he thought, had forced twelve or thirteen million peo-ple into the over-populated territories of the West 'so that they will form the seeds and masses of discontent and further decline'. He regarded this as one part of a comprehensive Soviet plan 'to throw the whole of Europe into extreme unrest and economic depression, thus enabling it to extend its sphere of power over Germany, France and the small countries as far as the Channel coast and then to Britain'. In December 1946 he told senior officials of the CDU that the policy of the Bolsheviks was in some respects worse than the unscrupulous policy of National Socialism and Hitler: on one hand, the Soviet Union had guaranteed Poland its new western border; but on the other hand, 'a political Russian colonel' had told some CDU members that the Soviet Union wanted a strong Germany and was ready to abandon Poland.[10] Adenauer's conclusion was that Soviet promises were lies.[11]

Despite his negative assessment, Adenauer remained cautious. He did not advocate a premature appeal for open partnership with the Western Powers. As far as possible, he thought, Germany should keep out of the conflicts between the Soviets on the one side and the British and Americans on the other. However, it must 'not lean towards Russia under any circumstances'.[12]

In his view, the situation was desperate because the Western democracies were not prepared to revise their disastrous policies towards Germany. Though he had detected some positive signs in the United States since the speech by Secretary of State Byrnes in Stuttgart in September 1946, nothing was certain. He continued to regard the two West European victors with some cynicism. Adenauer was convinced that British industry was 'out of date and no longer competitive with German and American' industry. Equally, he considered France to be 'tired from a biological point of view', under-populated, economically backward and idle.[13] This view had been shaped during the war.

Adenauer believed that Britain's negative policy towards Germany was determined by a desire to eliminate a powerful economic rival by limiting its production, dismantling its industries, and imposing ruinous projects of nationalisation. (It is quite possible that his opinions on this particular subject were influenced by the after-effects of German anglophobia in the First World War.) He was also convinced that the French wanted to divide Germany and obtain lasting control over the western parts of the country. For that reason, be believed, French politicians were ruthlessly exploiting their Zone and making use of the coal supplies of the Ruhr.

Meanwhile, distress in Germany was growing. In discussions with foreign representatives or in letters, Adenauer repeatedly emphasised his pessimistic view of developments: 'Germany is utterly ruined economically, politically and morally …'[14] The economy was rotting; the population was sinking into hopelessness and indifference. He described the situation in a letter to the social democratic journalist Efferoth, who was now living in Bolivia: 'It remains impossible to predict what will become of it all. But I believe that many millions more will die in Germany. People are mostly apathetic and hopeless, the youth wild and depraved. The conditions of 1918 cannot remotely be compared with the conditions of today.'[15] His gloom deepened during the bitter winter of 1946-1947 and continued throughout 1947.

Closer analysis nevertheless reveals that there was, as so often occurred later, an element of ambivalence in his arguments. Adenauer honestly regarded the Germans as weak. He rarely omitted to warn foreign observers that continued misery would inevitably encourage the spread of a mixture of nationalist and Communist sentiment. To reinforce his arguments, he drew attention to the disquieting strength of the KPD in the large factories and trade unions of the Ruhr, Hamburg and Bremen. In the long term, right-wing nationalism might also be revived. At the end of 1947, during a discussion at Castle Röttgen, he told the British minister for Germany, Lord Pakenham, that there was a strongly nationalist atmosphere in the country – stronger than in 1918-1919. The parties which co-operated with the Allies were in danger of being branded as collaborators.[16] But though these comments revealed a genuine anxiety, they were also deliberately designed to persuade Pakenham, and high-ranking foreign officials like him, to change the thrust of occupation policy.

At the same time, Adenauer was proud of the fortitude displayed by the Germans in their distress. In December 1946 he wrote to Paul Silverberg in Lugano:

> It says much for the good qualities that survive in the German people that, even after twelve years of National Socialism, war, and all the misery that has come upon the German people since the collapse, the majority of the people have not turned to radical parties. I am convinced that, if we are lucky enough to survive the depths in which we find ourselves (hunger, sickness, cold, want of housing, shortage of clothing and footwear), the German people will emerge purified and strengthened from this test and have a just claim to a voice in Europe and the world again.[17]

Such arguments were an attempt to lift his own spirits as well as convince others.

Lord Pakenham received the same message when he visited Düsseldorf with Adenauer in autumn 1947. This Labour politician, a convert to Catholicism, was struck by Adenauer's conviction 'that an economic revival of Germany was possible, even certain. He had no doubt at all of the elementary physical strength of the Germans.'[18] In fact, Adenauer's assessment of national strengths and weaknesses – German as well as French – was profoundly biological. He was convinced that the German psyche had been unstable for decades, and that this weakness would continue to be a problem for years to come. Whether the bad qualities would gain the upper hand, or be overcome by the good, would depend largely on external conditions. However, it was also essential to set goals and give hope to millions of people who were sinking into nihilism.

Adenauer's objective was clear – the inclusion of Germany in a community of free West European democracies. This, he thought, would ultimately solve the problems facing the post-war generation: the question of security, the economic reconstruction of Europe, and the re-establishment of a stable system of values.

As his tentative contacts with Gaullist officers in the summer and autumn of 1945 had revealed, Adenauer was willing to explore every possible means of gaining support for his views, to find like-minded individuals and to re-establish his prewar contacts. Thus, for example, he wrote to Dannie N. Heineman and Lord Clive as well as to his small circle of emigré acquaintances. These personal contacts, however, were limited in scope.

Once he became party chairman, Adenauer was able to make use of other connections from spring 1946 onwards. He was now in a position to explain his views to the high-ranking officials and generals of the Military Government, to London politicians who visited the British Zone, to West European Christian Democrats (from 1947), and also to influential members of the U.S. Military Government.

One of his most important contacts in summer 1946 was Duncan Sandys. The son-in-law of Winston Churchill, Sandys was making arrangements for Churchill's visit to Europe in September 1946.[19] It was in Zürich that Churchill made his famous call for the creation of 'a kind of United States of Europe', thereby giving a powerful stimulus to the post-war European movement and presenting himself as the advocate of Franco-German partnership.[20]

Information about the meeting between Sandys and Adenauer was provided in the reports of Consul-General von Weiss, though the precise date that it took place remains unknown. According to his own testimony, Adenauer told Sandys that a Franco-German partnership was essential for the reconstruction of Europe. If one reads Churchill's speech in Zürich in the light of Adenauer's comments at Cologne University and the reports written by von Weiss, it seems clear that Churchill's speech was influenced by the meeting between Adenauer and Sandys. At roughly the time of this meeting, von Weiss made a note of Adenauer's European ideas: 'The aim of all work in Europe must be: to establish the United States of Europe or a similar structure. It is open to consideration whether it would be advisable to begin by bringing together one part of Europe, perhaps in the economic sphere alone – a customs union.'[21] Adenauer therefore welcomed Churchill's ideas in principle, though rejecting his proposal for a confederation of states as the future of Germany.[22] He also had the impression that the Tories were more inclined towards a positive settlement of the German problem than the ruling Labour Party.

In general, Adenauer's assessment of Britain and France was marked by the same mixture of hope and anxiety he displayed towards his own people. Whatever his hopes for the future, however, the present was clouded by misjudgements and confusion. Though for understandable reasons, British and French policy remained unacceptably negative; Adenauer therefore joined Kurt Schumacher in taking a public stand against it. At the same time, he continued to hope for, and to encourage, the emergence of politicians committed to reconciliation.

Adenauer was therefore eager to make use of the opportunities offered by the infant European Movement. However, it is important to note that he was interested almost exclusively in the European Movement outside of Germany. Wilhelm Heile, the expelled chairman of the FDP, was turned down when he tried to win Adenauer's support for the German 'Europa-Union' at the end of January 1947.[23]

On the other hand, Adenauer welcomed every opportunity for direct contact with leading foreign politicians in the European Movement. It was a preoccupation he shared with other CDU leaders. Under current conditions, German contacts with the outside world were routed through the bureaucracy of the Military Government; it was therefore vital for German politicians to obtain direct links with the West.

The chances for such contacts began to emerge from the summer of 1947 onwards. The first meeting of West European Christian Democrats, in which Adenauer took part, was staged by the 'Nouvelles Equipes Internationales' (NEI) in Luxembourg at the end of January 1948. Among others, Adenauer met Maurice Schumann of the French MRP and Josef Escher, president of the Conservative People's Party in Switzerland. For the first time since the war, he was able to discuss matters with a group of foreign politicians. Adenauer told von Weiss that 'the reception given the Germans was extraordinarily good. The German question, which was the sole subject of the day', had been 'treated more objectively and in a European sense'.[24] Adenauer used this platform to put forward his old ideas for West European and Franco-German cooperation. The attending representatives from the Benelux countries expressed great interest in independent trade relations with Germany. Adenauer took responsibility for establishing a German section of NEI, but with little success.

More significant was another discussion group that brought a number of leading Christian Democrat politicians to Geneva. The driving force behind the 'Geneva conversations' was Jakob Kindt-Kiefer, a Saar German of independent means, who had lived in Switzerland since 1935. During and after the war, Kindt-Kiefer acted as a mediator between various groups interested in German and European renewal on a Christian and cooperative basis. In the working group 'Democratic Germany', he was in contact with former Chancellor Joseph Wirth, with the veteran minister-president of Prussia, Otto Braun, and with Wilhelm Hoegner, who was soon to be appointed minister-president of Bavaria.

Adenauer was not impressed by this association with Wirth. However, he did not hesitate when the general secretary of the CDU/CSU Working Group, Bruno Dörpinghaus, informed him of the Geneva initiative in summer 1947. Later, Dörpinghaus recalled a typical conversation he had held with Adenauer in July 1946, in the Cologne office of the Zone secretariat on Herwarthstraße 17. Adenauer had begun the discussion by asking what Dörpinghaus thought of Jakob Kaiser's bridge theory. Dörpinghaus gave the desired answer: 'Nothing at all. The Soviet Union is living under a dictatorship. It can only be opposed by an uncompromising policy of toughness and resolution.' 'That', said Adenauer, 'means we must win political friends in the West.'[25]

A meeting was finally arranged at the end of March 1948. When Adenauer arrived by car at the Hotel Zum Storchen in Zürich, the Communist coup had just taken place in Prague. The U.S. press was filled with rumours that war was imminent. During an interview with journalists, Adenauer was asked about the possibility of establishing a German contingent within the framework of a European defence system. Adenauer gave his opinion that it would be simple for Soviet tanks to move through Lübeck and Hamburg as far as the French Atlantic coast. When asked how many divisions Germany must be allowed in order to prevent it, he replied: 'At least eighty'. One of the journalists promptly noted the implications of Adenauer's remarks: 'Then we could no longer do what we want with Germany'.[26] His unguarded comments could easily have provoked a furious political row – and would have made an unpleasant start to his meeting with influential West European Christian Democrats.

In 1948 and 1949, several senior CDU/CSU politicians took part in the confidential 'Geneva conversations'. In addition to Adenauer, they included Jakob Kaiser, Josef Müller and his party rival Fritz Schäffer, Heinrich von Brentano of the Hesse CDU, and Otto Lenz from Berlin. The most prominent French participant was Georges Bidault, president and co-founder of the MRP. Bidault and Adenauer did not meet until autumn 1948, after Bidault had given up the post of French Foreign Minister. Following their contacts, Adenauer wrote to the new French Foreign Minister, Robert Schuman, to prevent any misunderstanding: 'He gave a long talk about the European situation and also spoke at length of the Franco-German relationship. I found the talk good. Furthermore, one could only agree with his comments about France and Germany. However, neither he nor I discussed the details of this relationship and how it should be shaped. I deliberately avoided that, because I wanted to be cautious during this first meeting ...'[27]

The first and subsequent meetings were attended by senior representatives from France, Germany and the Benelux countries. Adenauer was particularly keen to involve the former mayor of Antwerp, Cauwelaert again, who was now president of the Belgian Chamber of Deputies and a minister.[28] He was well aware of the advantages of conducting the Franco-German dialogue within a circle that included representatives of the Benelux states, Italy, Switzerland and Austria. All these countries had a genuine economic interest in German reconstruction. To a certain extent, they could be relied upon to help if the French security trauma began to dominate proceedings. In addition, the Second World War had done enormous damage to the German relationship with the Christian Democrats of Belgium and Holland, which Adenauer hoped to repair.

Adenauer's participation in The Hague Congress of the European Movement from 7-10 May 1948 was more spectacular, but not immediately as productive. Only fifty out of over eight hundred delegates came from Germany, and these included a number of relative unknowns. It was at this meeting that Adenauer renewed his acquaintance with Edouard Herriot. He was also favourably impressed by Winston Churchill, who took pains to greet the German delegation warmly. However, Adenauer also recalled Churchill's earlier remark that 'the German is either at your throat or at your feet'. His private opinion of the great man therefore remained cautious. In a letter to Silverberg he made no more than a brief revision of his opinion of Churchill, which had been unfavourable at the end of the war: 'Of Churchill I gained a good impression. But he is already very old.'[29]

However, he was impressed by the congress at The Hague. Shortly afterwards, Adenauer reported to his party executive that the Germans could agree with point 7 of the resolution which had been carried unanimously.[30] The Congress had expressed its conviction that the only definitive solution to Germany's economic and political problems lay in the inclusion of the country in a European confederation.[31] He also supported the call for a parliamentary conference in Interlaken in September, and himself took part. He told his party colleagues: 'The idea of a European federation cannot be taken too seriously and the significance cannot be underestimated [sic]. Such a European federation would provide a feeling of security, including for the western neighbours of Germany, the French, Dutch, Belgians and Luxembourgers who are still very afraid of the Germans. It is correct to fear that if West Germany were to become Russia's [bridge]head, it would be all up with Western Europe.' His sketch of the future was optimistic. A union of Western Europe, he thought, would be able to make use of the 'colonial resources of Africa, Indonesia, Dutch East Indies etc.' This would create 'a third power' in the world which, though not equal to the USA and Soviet Russia, would be able 'to resolve tensions and to mediate between these very great powers, which currently regard themselves as the only factors of power with all the dangers that involves.' He therefore hoped for the rapid progress of the unification movement: 'Truthfully, in it lies the salvation of Europe and the salvation of Germany.'[32]

In autumn 1948 Adenauer also met Robert Schuman, the most important protagonist of the European Movement for Adenauer and for Germany. In the 1950s, much was made of the fact that the three great protagonists of European union – Adenauer, Schuman and de Gasperi – all came from border regions of their own countries and were thus particularly inclined to favour partnership with their neighbours. However, a border background can just as easily produce excessive nationalism – the German-Austrian Hitler is the obvious example, and Poincaré of Lorraine another. In many ways Robert Schuman spanned these worlds. An industrial lawyer from Lorraine with a perpetually anxious demeanour, Schuman had grown up in the German Reich and studied in Metz, Munich and Bonn, there having been a member of the KV Unitas-Salia fraternity. He was to remain deeply influenced by his German education and background and by the German language. The exact nature of Schuman's work on the German side during the First World War was the subject of constant disputes in the French Chamber of Deputies in later years. In particular after his involvement in putting down strikes during his period as premier in autumn 1947, Schuman's greatest enemies were the Communists. It was Communist deputies who accused him of acting as a German military judge during the First World War. Certainly he had been a reserve officer in the German army before becoming a deputy in the French chamber for the Moselle department in 1919. Later, during the Third Reich, the Gestapo had apparently suspected him of having links with Adenauer, but this was incorrect: the two men met for the first time in October 1948, in Bassenheim on the Mosel. Hettier de Boislambert, the arrogant French Governor of Rhineland Palatinate, had taken up residence there in the castle owned by Baron Oppenheim.

The meeting between the French Foreign Minister and Adenauer, then head of the CDU in the British Zone and President of the Parliamentary Council, was top secret. Schuman made his first-ever flight to the military airport of Niederming,[33] while Adenauer, wrapped up in a large travelling blanket, arrived in a Mercedes. The two men talked for two and a half hours. On the following day they were joined by Adolf Süsterhenn and Minister-President Altmeier. Süsterhenn was then head of the Ministry of Justice and Culture in Mainz and, until a serious car accident in Spring 1949, seemed on the verge of a career in high office.

In Schuman, Adenauer finally established links with an influential Frenchmen who – literally as well as metaphorically – spoke his language. Both of them had lived through the upheavals of Franco-German history over the last fifty years; both were fully aware of the economic conditions necessary for the 'organic integration' Adenauer had long sought. Some weeks later, he wrote to Schuman to emphasise the point again: 'I spoke to you about economic integration as the most secure basis for good neighbourly co-operation.'[34] On 24 November 1948, when he first met the U.S. ambassador Robert Murphy in Berlin, Adenauer outlined the main points of the discussion: the hereditary enmity between Germany and France must cease; French fears over security were understandable, but if joint efforts were made they could be shown to be unfounded; the mentality of the population in West Germany was more suited to such policies than that in many parts of East Germany, where Marxism and nationalism had a greater hold on the people, possibly as a result of a different religious development there.[35]

At the simplest level, Adenauer and Schuman discovered that the main outlines of their political approach were in agreement. However, they also discussed more specific and detailed issues. As Adenauer noted in his memoirs, Schuman had reassured him about French policy towards the Saar: the region might still be returned to Germany as long as French economic interests were protected.[36] The French Foreign Minister also conceded that France had been wrong to tamper with the education system in the French Zone, and promised to change the policy. Schuman also gave Adenauer his 'personal' theory about the German question: he would like to see Germany divided into three great parts, which he called 'Rhine state', 'Ruhr state' and 'Elbe state'. It was not clear whether he wanted these three states to be united in a federal state or to remain in a loose confederation.

On both sides there was much that remained unclear. Adenauer's own restless scepticism was perceptible in his comments to Robert Murphy. Both Adenauer and Schuman were cautious, and neither was prepared to abandon the interests of his own country or his own domestic political position out of sheer exuberant idealism. Nevertheless, the discussions established a basis of trust on which it was possible to build.

Adenauer's early involvement with the European Movement was deeply significant. His own European stance would have been useless had this movement not rapidly won support throughout the western continent and had its aims not coincided so closely with his own ideas. He remained suspicious of the policy towards Germany which was being pursued by Paris and London. However, in the crucial months of 1948 and 1949 he knew that the advocates of an intransigent French security policy were losing ground, and that the influence of politicians of reconciliation was increasing.

Of all the leading CDU politicians, Adenauer had the most awareness of the great European moment. Others had made appropriate contacts, but none was able to develop a new concept of foreign policy to match his own. This was also true of Kurt Schumacher's SPD, which had failed to send a Social Democrat delegation to the Congress in The Hague. Though Carlo Schmid and his associates quickly corrected this omission, they had given Adenauer's CDU the opportunity to present itself as the party of Europe. Not surprisingly, this course remained controversial within the CDU itself, and many influential CDU politicians discovered the possibilities of the European Movement only during the course of 1949.

All these developments gained real momentum in 1948. Before that year, it was impossible to predict whether the European ideal would amount to anything more than the activities of enthusiastic and well-meaning intellectuals. The year 1947 was dominated by an atmosphere of stagnation, misery and uncertainty over the German question.

Alongside the European Movement, however, a new policy was taking shape which was to transform conditions in Germany and Western Europe. This was the re-orientation of U.S. policy towards Europe which found its expression in the Marshall Plan.

Adenauer's attitude towards the United States in many ways resembled his approach to the West Europeans. Though he had always known that U.S. decisions would be crucial for all future developments, even in 1947 he had no real idea of what they would do. Several courses of action still seemed possible then: an agreement with the Soviets at the expense of Germany; withdrawal from Europe following the example set in 1919-1920; or a wise long-term policy of the kind he had been urging on his contacts in the United States. In March 1946 he had written to Wilhelm Sollmann: 'Help to spread the conviction in the U.S. that the salvation of Europe can only be achieved with their help and that the salvation of Europe is also essential for the U.S.'[37]

Adenauer tended to regard the community of Western democracies, including the United States, as an ideological unity: 'Occident, Christian Occident is not a geographical term', he explained to the CDU delegates at the party rally in Recklinghausen in August 1947, 'it is an intellectual and historical term that also includes America. We want to help save this Christian Occident.'[38]

Unlike the minister-presidents and party leaders in the U.S. Zone, Adenauer had no early contacts with influential U.S. officers or civil servants. Not even the most senior Germans in the U.S. Zone had any real insight into the details of American policy towards German and Europe. This policy was, moreover, subject to constant fluctuations during these months. Nevertheless, frequent contacts did provide information which was not available to the party leaders in the British Zone. By contrast, Adenauer depended mainly on newspaper reports for his information. Early in 1948 he contacted a certain Captain Schweizer, known to him since spring 1945, but not in the least an important figure in the American military apparatus, in an attempt to spread his own ideas and to increase his knowledge.[39]

This situation quickly began to change. After the establishment of Bizonia, the CDU chairman in the British Zone frequently travelled to Frankfurt. Once the Parliamentary Council was summoned early in summer 1948, Adenauer was in regular contact with General Clay's advisers and, from September 1948, with liaison officers based at the Parliamentary Council. Thereafter the Americans sought him out to discover his opinions.[40]

It was at this stage that Adenauer began his conversations with U.S. journalists based in Bonn, and others who were making brief visits to

Germany. In December 1948 he met General Clay for the first time. Until summer 1948, Adenauer had had only very informal contacts with U.S. headquarters. Nevertheless, he had long recognised that the Americans were increasingly sharing the responsibility for decisions in the British Zone. In September 1946, for example, he had reassured the party executive in the British Zone: 'The Americans, there is no doubt about it, want to get the German economy moving ... I believe that in the long term the Americans will take over the leadership in all these things ...'[41] The desire for U.S. private capital was another reason for his resolute opposition to the nationalisation of the mining industry.

Adenauer was thus aware of no more than the basic outlines of the proposals for a German inclusion in the Marshall Plan. In common with every non-Communist German politician, he welcomed the initiative. On this question, however, the Economic Directors of the Bi-zone in Frankfurt were much better informed.

Only during the course of 1948 did Adenauer obtain a clear idea of U.S. policy. In May of that year, Herbert Blankenhorn, a professional diplomat, was established as his closest adviser. Blankenhorn's role was crucial in the development of Adenauer's approach. He had personal knowledge of the United States and, as an 'Old Washingtonian', easily established good relations with the U.S. liaison officers. His role in the shaping of Adenauer's foreign policy can scarcely be overstated. Of course, the basic outlines of this policy had been fixed since summer 1945 and were rooted in Adenauer's own experiences in Cologne. But it was one thing to recognise the proper course in foreign policy and lay down the main guidelines, and quite another to maintain these priorities in the confusion of day-to-day politics. Adenauer was both a strategic thinker and a man famous for his ability to master practical details. Nevertheless, the operational details of diplomacy were a closed book to him, and he had no contact with the German experts available to pursue them.

Similarly, Adenauer was largely ignorant of personalities and practices at the vital working levels of the occupation administration, where plans for the future of Germany were proposed and worked out. Despite his growing contact with the most senior levels of the administration in his capacity as party leader, Adenauer could not afford to neglect these lower levels. He needed a day-to-day knowledge of the thinking, plans and intrigues there. Only then would he be fully prepared for his discussions with senior officials.

Under normal conditions, this task would have been undertaken by the diplomatic service or by specialist civil servants in the office of the head of government. Between 1945 and 1949, however, no such foreign service existed. After 1946, the West German Länder had recognised this lack and attempted to build up a bi-zonal Deutsches Büro für Friedensfragen (German Bureau for Peace Questions); here, it was hoped, experienced and politically untainted diplomats would be able to observe long-term developments, produce reports and propose ideas on operational issues. However, the development of this bureau had been halted by General Clay in 1947, and then restricted to the U.S. Zone. At the same time, the minister-presidents had established departments in their own state chancelleries to advise them on foreign affairs. This solution was unsatisfactory in terms of organisation and became an additional source of dispute between the parties, the Länder and the individual occupation Zones.

From Adenauer's point of view, the worst failing of this infant foreign service in the Western Zones lay in the fact that it worked almost exclusively for the minister-presidents. Adenauer himself – like Kurt Schumacher of the SPD – claimed to have a right to give political instructions to the minister-presidents and senior civil servants of his own party. However, he had no mechanism to do so, and until 1948 there was not even a professional diplomat on his own staff to give him sound advice on urgent questions of foreign policy.

It was here that Blankenhorn was so valuable. Between May 1948 and September 1949, he filled the place of the missing foreign service. Adenauer appointed him general secretary of the CDU in the British Zone, gave him the role of private secretary to the President of the Parliamentary Council and, in this capacity, entrusted him with the vital task of maintaining close links with the Allied liaison staffs.

For those with political insight, the appointment of Blankenhorn as successor to Josef Löns was a sign that, after the establishment of the CDU organisation, Adenauer was devoting increasing attention to issues of foreign policy. It can also be seen as an indication that Adenauer would no longer be content with the role of party leader. He wanted to become Chancellor of the state which was beginning to emerge in the Western Zones. No party leader could hope to exert more than a temporary influence on foreign policy; in the long term, foreign policy could only be made from a high government office.

In 1948 Blankenhorn was forty-four years old. By the time he decided to link his career with that of Adenauer, he was already a man of some standing. His origins lay in the well-to-do middle class. On his father's side his ancestors had been successful farmers and wine-dealers in Müllheim. His paternal grandfather, Professor Adolph Blankenhorn, had contributed to the fight against phylloxera by developing new varieties of grape, and had used scientific methods to improve the simple table wine of Baden. As president of the German Winegrowing Association he had also been able to put his theories into practice. Blankenhorn's father was a cavalry officer who had served on the General Staff during the First World War and helped to build up the Baden police during the Weimar Republic. In 1933 he was dismissed by the National Socialists and, like Adenauer, was abandoned by many former friends before withdrawing to Badenweiler.

Blankenhorn's links with the diplomatic service came through his mother, the daughter of the last German Regierungspräsident of Upper Alsace. At the end of 1937, his uncle Hans Dieckhoff had become German ambassador in Washington, replacing former Chancellor Hans Luther. Blankenhorn himself worked in the embassy there between 1935 and 1939. After studying in Heidelberg and London, he had joined the Foreign Ministry in 1929 at the age of twenty-five; despite his youth, he was accepted for training as an attaché thanks to the advocacy of his school-friend, Wolfgang Stresemann. Blankenhorn's support for the rapprochement policy of his friend's father, Foreign Minister Gustav Stresemann, was genuine and lasting.

The Nazi seizure of power and the treatment of his father had infuriated the liberal Blankenhorn and left him with few illusions about the régime. During his foreign postings in Athens and Washington, in Helsinki during the Winter War of 1939, and later in Berne, he had recognised that National Socialist policies would lead to war and to isolation in foreign affairs. Like many others, however, he had chosen to remain within the protective shell of the diplomatic service. Unfit for military service following a bout of rheumatic fever, Blankenhorn spent the last years of the Third Reich in the Foreign Ministry.

During this period he had spoken frankly about the régime to those he trusted. Eugen Gerstenmaier recalled a conversation with the young diplomat in Berne in 1942, when Blankenhorn had explained how Hitler 'could best be bumped off'.[42] Blankenhorn had also made contact with the British and Americans in Berne. After the war, these links helped him to establish himself in political life, and he became secretary general of the Zonenbeirat in Hamburg. By the winter of 1947/48 he realised that the Council was reaching the end of its existence and decided to accept Adenauer's call to Cologne. Not without a measure of condescension, his British and German acquaintances expressed regret that such an intelligent man had chosen to link his future with an old reactionary like Adenauer.

Adenauer and Blankenhorn established a positive relationship from the outset. In the months following the death of his wife, Adenauer had immersed himself in his work and was a demanding and sometimes difficult boss. Nevertheless, he was quick to appreciate Blankenhorn's engaging personality and intelligent use of his skills. Chief among these was a remarkable ability to keep track of developments – to 'hear the grass grow'. Blankenhorn maintained good relations with the Allied liaison officers and journalists, was skilful at presenting his master in the best possible light on the international stage and, as CDU general secretary in the British Zone, kept a close watch on political developments.

His roots in the Upper Rhine region provided Blankenhorn with links to the Baden border lands as well as to Alsace and France. On this basis he encouraged Adenauer's determination to shift the focus of German political life to the West, where there was greater understanding of Germany's neighbours and the need for a policy of reconciliation than in the Prussian heartland. Blankenhorn was convinced that Stresemann's policy of reconciliation must be revived, even in the difficult conditions prevailing after 1945. At the same time, he had a sound understanding of the somewhat inscrutable Americans. In his view such an understanding was essential, since one of the main tasks of future foreign policy would be to reconcile West European and U.S. attitudes.

Throughout this period Blankenhorn remained an anglophile. He believed that the British example had much to teach the Germans, particularly in finding ways to protect the interests of their own country in a manner that combined pragmatism and courtesy as well as determination. His approach was never one-sided. In fact, it was already clear in 1948 that the return of the West Germans to the community of civilised nations would demand an instinctive ability to exploit differences of opinion among the Western victors. These could and must be exploited, even though they were at the same time a cause of why the situation continued to be so precarious.

After the failure of the victorious powers to reach agreement at the Moscow Conference, Adenauer expected the process of economic, and then political, consolidation in the Western Zones to begin at last. Progress, however, was slow. The U.S. and the British began by establishing Bi-zonal central departments in Franfurt, buttressed by a quasi-parliamentary Economic Council in which the parties were represented according to their strength in the Länder. The interests of the various Länder were represented in a Länderrat (Council of States). In essence, this was a preliminary form of the two-chamber parliamentary system established later. For as long as possible, however, the Western Allies avoided giving the appearance that they were establishing the core of a 'Western state'.

Alongside the Zone CDU, the supra-zonal CDU, the Land of North Rhine-Westphalia and the British Zonal Advisory Council, a new political system was therefore being developed in Frankfurt. It became essential for Adenauer to exert an influence within this system. He therefore began to spend more of his time in Frankfurt, where he attempted to guide the CDU/CSU delegation in the Economic Council and to influence decisions on personnel and policy at senior level.

From the summer of 1947, Adenauer also saw an opportunity to move closer to his objective of establishing a 'bourgeois bloc' of the political parties. In the Bi-zonal Economic Council, the SPD and the CDU/CSU had been allocated twenty seats each and the Liberals four. There were three Communists on the left, but these were relatively isolated as a result of the deep rift between the KPD and the Social Democrats. In addition, there were two delegates from the Centre Party and one from the Bavarian Wiederaufbau-Vereinigung (WAV).

The Economic Council was responsible for the election of the Directorate in which the directors of the central offices worked together. Previously, six of the eight directors had belonged to the SPD. As was to be the case two years later during the formation of the first federal government, the CDU side on the Economic Council contained both advocates of a 'bourgeois bloc' and supporters of a Grand Coalition. In the cabinets of southern Germany in particular, there was considerable sympathy for cooperation with the Social Democrats. However, the system of indirect election through the Landtage resulted in the victory within the CDU of the 'bourgeois' groups, representing industry, the middle class and farming; of the twenty CDU/CSU members of the Economic Council, only three belonged to the trade-union wing. An alliance with the FDP and German Party (DP) was therefore possible in the Economic Council.

Adenauer's manoeuvres were aimed towards this objective. At the outset, the CDU announced that it wanted the office of Director of Economics but was prepared to tolerate Social Democratic candidates for other positions. When the SPD refused, Adenauer indicated his willingness to let the SPD have the post of Director of Economics, but only on condition that the CDU was permitted to have the Ministry of Economics in at least three Länder. Previously, all the economic departments in the Länder had been held by the SPD. As expected, the SPD refused – and Adenauer had reached the situation he had probably wanted from the start. After a great deal of confusion and dispute, the SPD delegation lost its nerve and abstained on the crucial vote. The way was thus left clear for a directorate composed solely of CDU and CSU directors.

Adenauer had not sought a post in Frankfurt for himself. His deputy Friedrich Holzapfel became chairman of the CDU/CSU caucus, though he had the duty – and the inclination – to take account of the wishes of the party chairman. Hans Schlange-Schöningen became Director for Food Supply, Agriculture and Forestry.

There was one further parallel with the formation of a government two years later, in 1949. As he was to be in the future, Kurt Schumacher unwillingly became Adenauer's best ally. Like Adenauer, Schumacher preferred a course of confrontation and therefore blocked every attempt to form a Grand Coalition on the basis of pragmatic compromise. After the election of the directors on 24 July 1947, Schumacher claimed that the CDU had 'abandoned socialism and indeed the social line'; it was now manifestly an 'employers' party'.[43] The argument of the information service of the CDU Zonal Executive made a stark contrast: 'Coup d'État failed in Frankfurt ... Democracy in Frankfurt saved by the resolute attitude of the CDU and the other non-Marxist parties.'[44]

However, Adenauer was sensible enought not to adopt an exposed public position on this issue. At subsequent rally in Recklinghausen he made only a brief reference to the incident. The reason was obvious.

Since nobody knew how the economy and the food supply would develop during the coming winter, a party that was burdened with sole responsibility for the misery could be greatly damaged, as the SPD had discovered to its cost in North Rhine-Westphalia. The CDU might be on the verge of making the same discovery on a much larger scale in the Bizone. In presenting his version of events in Frankfurt, Holzapfel was therefore careful to portray the CDU's bid for the central offices in Frankfurt as being not of its own making, but as a decision which need not be final given goodwill on all sides.[45]

Nevertheless, Adenauer remained committed to the 'bourgeois bloc' even when the U.S. and Britain changed the organisation of the Bi-zone. He did not actually need to take much action on the issue, since the SPD declared of its own accord that it would remain in opposition. However, another individual choice became necessary after the Allies abruptly dismissed the Director of Economics, Johannes Semler, at the beginning of January following a critical speech. A new Director of Economics had to be appointed, along with a candidate for the newly-created post of *Oberdirektor* (Chairman of the Directorate).

After various candidates for this position had been proposed and rejected, a preliminary decision was taken in Cologne. At an afternoon tea, Adenauer and Robert Pferdmenges persuaded the politically colourless mayor, Hermann Pünder, to accept the post. Adenauer and Pünder had been on friendly terms since the 1920s, when Pünder had spent some years as state secretary in the Reich Chancellery. In consequence, Adenauer had every reason to expect a smooth working relationship between them. Moreover, since Pünder had not played an important role in the CDU, he could not be expected to display great independence of mind in his new role. He would therefore be much more acceptable to Adenauer as *Oberdirektor* than one of the politicians under consideration, such the Bavarian minister-president, Ehard, or the finance minister from Hesse, Hilpert. Adenauer dismissed the objections to Pünder with the observation that he was the only candidate with 'the necessary stature for this, currently the highest and undoubtedly the most difficult office in Germany'. A few days later, the chairman of the CDU delegation, Holzapfel, told a public meeting of the Economic Council that Pünder was being presented mainly as a co-ordinator of the administration and leader of negotiations with the Allies rather than as a strong politician. Pünder was annoyed by this assessment; he recalled Adenauer's praise during their discussions over tea with Robert Pferdmenges.

When Pünder had asked why Adenauer did not take this important post for himself, Adenauer had answered that he was too old 'to take such an unpleasant post under current conditions'.[46] On 29 February 1948, when this conversation took place, Gussie Adenauer was dying in Bonn. During these weeks Adenauer was moving heaven and earth to obtain effective medicines, such as streptomycin, from abroad and was spending as much time as possible at his wife's bedside. 'Under current conditions' his refusal to accept the post was therefore no surprise. When Ludwig Erhard was appointed Director of Economics on 1 March, Adenauer apparently played no part in the decision and Erhard was nominated by the FDP. However, Adenauer was far from disturbed by this development. In his view, the crucial factor was that the unstable 'bourgeois bloc' had remained intact.

On the vital issue of whether, and when, the Western Zones should strike out on their own, Adenauer now opposed further delay. He welcomed the decision by Jakob Kaiser to take a stand against the Soviet Military Administration in December 1947, though he would have been happier if the subsequent discussions between CDU leaders from the East and West had been held in Cologne.[47] Adenauer was strongly opposed to Kaiser's candidacy for the Frankfurt Economic Council; he continued to fear that Kaiser would assume the leadership of the CDU's left wing in the Western Zones.[48]

In the first months of 1948 Adenauer continued to regard conditions, especially the food supply, as desperate. A good example of this attitude is provided by his letter to Simon Vogel in New York late in January 1948. The system of compulsory rationing at the level of 1550 calories had collapsed as expected: 'In my opinion the entire Marshall Plan for Europe will fail unless considerable quantities of food are brought very quickly into the British and American Zones by America. Europe can only be saved by the U.S. if at all.'[49]

Adenauer, moreover, had long argued that the Western Zones should proceed alone if necessary. He might thus have been expected to welcome the London recommendations early in June 1948, when the Western governments gave the green light to the foundation of a state in the Western Zones. His hostile response therefore came as a great surprise. The final communiqué in London, agreed after months of negotiations, laid down the procedure for summoning a Constituent Assembly and envisaged a referendum in the Länder to ratify the constitution it produced.

At the same time, however, plans were produced for the announcement of an occupation statute and the establishment of an International Authority for the Ruhr. The latter was to be composed of representatives of the U.S., Britain, France, the Benelux states and Germany, and to take all the important decisions regarding the production and distribution of coal and steel. Decisions would be based on a majority vote, thus creating the alarming prospect of foreign control of Germany's key industries for the foreseeable future.

Adenauer was appalled. His objections were stated immediately in an article for the *Kölnische Rundschau*. In the London protocol, he argued, all the talk had been 'of controls, controls, controls'.[50] Genuine security against Germany, however, could be achieved only through the voluntary cooperation of the Germans themselves. The decisions taken in London were incompatible with the ideas of a European federation. During a debate on the Allied documents in the Landtag of North Rhine-Westphalia, he cited Oswald Spengler's prediction of an age of economic annexations and claimed that this was the first case in history when 'a great, industrious people is being annexed'. In his view, the agreements made in London violated both international and natural law.[51]

Shortly afterwards, Adenauer observed that the Marshall Plan would be devalued by the Ruhr Statute. On 5 July, he wrote to the Dutch Social Democrat Alfred Mozer to complain that 'the Versailles treaty is a bed of roses by comparison'.[52]

Adenauer was so alarmed that he took the highly uncharacteristic step of visiting the Social Democrat headquarters in the hope of forging a united front among the German political parties. Owing to the illness of Schumacher, he had to hold these discussions with Erich Ollenhauer, Fritz Heine and Fritz Henssler. Despite significant areas of agreement – the SPD also had serious reservations – the Social Democrats were not prepared to make a joint declaration by the German parties.

For a time Adenauer hesitated between outright rejection of the proposals and acceptance under protest. At one moment, he claimed to see 'the day approaching when all the Germans can do is to save their honour before history by refusing their co-operation'.[53] At another, he indicated a willingness to compromise: 'We are forced to work on the ground and within the framework of these London recommendations. We are forced to do so to protect our people from ruin ...'[54]

Nor did the London recommendations for the preparation of a constitution tally with Adenauer's own ideas on the subject. In May 1948 he still argued that a constitution could only be discussed by an elected parliament. However, he had left one loophole: a committee elected directly by the Landtage might be permitted to work out a preliminary proposal before the parties debated the issue in the actual constituent assembly. Adenauer had already rejected the election of a national assembly before 1 September 1948 on the grounds that it might have given an advantage to the radical parties. Over the following months, this argument was to be repeated by a number of German politicians.[55]

Closer analysis of Adenauer's objections reveals that they were not identical with those presented by the minister-presidents between 8 and 10 July. The hesitation of the minister-presidents was largely the product of a deep malaise in German political life. They knew that the Allies had quarrelled over the German question for years and were now asking the West Germans themselves to bear the responsibility for the division of Germany by giving active cooperation in the establishment of a separate state. On these grounds, the minister-presidents wanted to postpone the drafting of a German constitution 'until the preconditions for an all-German settlement is reached and German sovereignty is restored to a satisfactory degree'.[56]

In the spring and early summer of 1948, Adenauer's own approach to the founding of a state was not entirely consistent. Earlier, in October 1947, he had produced an internal memorandum which envisaged 'the most rapid possible unification of the three Western Zones in the event of the failure of the London Conference'.[57] Indeed, he has gone down in history as the prime advocate of such a move. The division of Germany, he observed in April 1948, was not a danger but a fact: 'The need is to overcome the division of Germany into East and West, which has been completed by the East, by the re-establishment of German unity from the West.'[58] This was to be the approach he took for decades – and was one to which he was personally committed.

Elsewhere, however, he had sounded a more cautious note. At the end of April 1948, for example, he clashed with Eugen Kogon during the Ellwangen constitutional discussions. When Kogon advocated the foundation of a West German federal state as quickly as possible, Adenauer argued that no German federal constitution could be drafted without representatives from the Eastern Zone.[59] Were these no more than tactical manoeuvres on his part?

Clearly, the decisive factor for Adenauer were the conditions of political reconstruction set by the West. Temporarily he may have become too optimistic, and his hopes for the inclusion of West Germany in the Western community of nations may have been ahead of actual developments. On the other hand, he may have been aware that equal rights could only be the long-term goal and that, in practice, the Germans could only work for a slow and gradual withdrawal of the occupation. Whatever his reasoning, he felt bound to protest against the proposed procedures for founding a West German state.

Adenauer's anxieties were expressed in a number of letters and papers written during these weeks. When Erich Köhler, president of the Economic Council, told him that there had been some criticism of his negative attitude, he replied: 'At some stage I can explain to you the considerations that have persuaded me to take such a resolute stand against the "London recommendations". Today I will merely say that I lived through the signing of the Versailles Treaty and learned from it.'[60] He continued to worry about a revival of a radical German nationalism if hopes for Germany's inclusion as an equal member of the Western community of nations were obscured by sterile controls.

However, Adenauer was forced to concede that he had gone too far. The East-West conflict had begun to develop with alarming speed. On 7 June 1948 the London recommendations were published and were received with varying degrees of criticism throughout the Western Zones of Germany. The long-awaited currency reform was implemented on 20 June. Though this created the essential foundation for economic reconstruction in the Western Zones, it also removed one of the last ties between the Eastern Zone and the Western Zones. The Soviet Military Administration responded with the introduction of its own currency in the Eastern Zone and declared the Four-Power Administration of Berlin to be 'practically at an end'. A total blockade of Berlin was imposed. From 26 June, the United States and Britain organised the famous airlift to supply West Berlin. A mood of crippling fear was widespread in the Western Zones. Europe was approaching high summer – the traditional period of crisis and war. On 1 July 1948, in an atmosphere of confrontation and uncertainty, the three Western Military Governors presented the minister-presidents of the West German Länder with the recommendations worked out in London, in the form of the 'Frankfurt Documents'.

Between 8 and 10 July, in the Hotel Rittersturz in Koblenz, the minister-presidents worked out their response. The choice of Koblenz as the site of the conference offered final proof that the French Zone would be permitted to join the other Western Zones. In January of that year, Adenauer had told von Weiss of the prevailing 'fear that a three-fold division of Germany is being prepared: the East Zone, the Bi-zone, and the West Zone under French influence'.[61] This danger appeared to be over. However, the delaying action which was agreed upon by the minister-presidents infuriated General Clay, who felt that he had been left alone in his confrontation with the Soviets. Only after renewed negotiations with the Military Governors in Frankfurt, and another conference at the Niederwald hunting lodge in Rüdesheim, was the decision taken to summon a 'Parliamentary Council' on 1 September. This Council would have the task of producing a 'Basic Law' to be validated by the Landtage rather than through a referendum.

The situation remained unstable. Between 10 and 23 August, a constitutional convention of experts met at the picturesque Herreninsel in the Chiemsee to produce a draft for the Parliamentary Council. At the same time, however, discussions were taking place in Moscow between the Soviet government and the Western ambassadors. It became clear that Stalin was prepared to lift the blockade if the establishment of a state in the Western Zones was abandoned. Washington had not yet taken a final decision. Even after the failure of the Moscow discussions and the first meeting of the Parliamentary Council, the U.S. State Department continued to contemplate the re-establishment of the Four-Power Administration and a halt to preparations for a West German state. The main protagonist of this line, which was discussed until the spring of 1949, was the head of the State Department Planning Staff, George Kennan. Nor had French resistance been overcome by spring 1949. Overshadowing all these discussions and plans was the prospect of a third world war triggered by the confrontation in Berlin.

As always when the situation became critical, Adenauer abandoned his tendency to manoeuvre cautiously and called for clear and unequivocal decisions. One of the incidents that led him to revise his assessment was a long discussion with Professor Carl Joachim Friedrich, an influential adviser on Clay's staff.[62] Friedrich, along with other Americans, was giving detailed briefings on U.S. policy in the hope of persuading German politicians to change their negative approach. From Adenauer's point of view, the situation was complicated by General Clay's refusal to discuss his views in person with the party leaders, and his concentration on the minister-presidents and the officials in the Bi-zone. On the British side, General Robertson was prepared to let developments take their course.

Adenauer now took a more balanced view. He recognised the unstable mood in Washington and had a better understanding of British and U.S. tactics towards the French. On 10 July he told the CDU Zonal committee that in Paris 'there are two tendencies: Bidault is the sharper opponent of Germany; Premier Schuman is the milder ...'[63] In addition, the views of the Gaullist 'Rassemblement du Peuple Français' remained uncertain. He argued that the manoeuvres of French politicians should not prevent the Germans from giving a clear statement of opinion on the London agreement. In Paris, indecision over the German question, which continued to irritate Adenauer until the mid-1950s, was now apparent.

During these weeks Adenauer was infuriated by the deliberate attempts of the minister-presidents to escape his influence. Their response to pressure from the party leader was to defend their own autonomy as best they could. In view of the development of Adenauer's relationship with Karl Arnold, this was no surprise. Adenauer's relationship with the Bavarian minister-president, Hans Ehard, was also cool, though the two were united by a common aversion to Josef Müller, the chairman of the CSU. Of course, Adenauer had no control at all over the Social Democrat minister-presidents.

Adenauer was particularly annoyed that the Rittersturz conference had been attended by Erich Ollenhauer, as the representative of Kurt Schumacher, and by Josef Müller of the CSU, even though the minister-presidents had stressed the importance of holding their own independent discussions. Adenauer himself was asked to attend only on the afternoon of the second day. When this request was passed to him by Adolf Süsterhenn on behalf of Minister-President Altmeier, Adenauer's response was caustic: 'Have these wrens *(Zaunkönige)* not yet finished their business?'[64] By the time he arrived, the discussions had been completed.

At the meeting it became clear, however, that Adenauer had decided to set aside his objections and give virtually unconditional support to the line taken by Clay and Robertson. In consequence, he asked the participants 'at least to soften their expressions and to remove a passage categorically rejecting the creation of a state, because the course of events would most probably compel them to disavow their declarations in the not-too-distant future'.[65] Later, in comments before the CDU/CSU delegation to the Parliamentary Council, he made fun the SPD minister-presidents for their obedience to their party headquarters. Personally, he added, he had always regarded the resolution adopted by the first conference as a complete mistake.

Adenauer's attitude after June 1948 was certainly affected by his awareness that war was possible. After a confidential discussion with Robertson, he told his party colleagues in the middle of August that he did not believe there would be war. However, at these talks he had also warned Robertson that a line of retreat must be kept open. Yet his subsequent discussions in Switzerland, which also involved a visit to the 'Moral Rearmament' Movement at Caux, disturbed him greatly.

On 15 September, Adenauer appeared in the guise of a great strategist before the CDU/CSU delegation at the Parliamentary Council. The minute of his remarks reads as follows: 'The international situation is as follows: the Russians want to strike out, the Americans still want to delay. A decision will have to be made in 1950 at the latest. An ultimatum will be given to the Russians to evacuate not only Germany, but also Poland, Hungary and the whole of the satellite states. The view is that the Russians will now exert their main pressure in East Asia, and Berlin will enter into a period of calm. There can be no doubt, if the Russians do not strike out earlier, they will be forced back within a limited time ...'[66]

This, frankly, was the politics of the public bar. Adenauer's willingness to believe it was the result of his ignorance of the decision-making processes of the Western Allies. Otto Schumacher-Hellmold recalled him making similar arguments seven months later, as the constitutional discussions of the Parliamentary Council drew to a close.[67] The Soviet Union, Adenauer thought, would not make peace. If a conflict was inevitable, it would be best to fight now. At the end of November, when he spoke again to the CDU/CSU delegation, Adenauer was very despondent: 'Very calm and reasonable people reckon that we will have war in the spring at the latest. I believe that the situation must be judged exactly in that way.'[68]

Adenauer's early ideas for a German defence contribution were a result of his fears that war was imminent. In spring 1948, shortly after the Communists seized power in Prague, he was contemplating a contribution of eighty-odd German divisions. After all, at the end of the war only three years before, there had been no fewer than two hundred divisions in the Wehrmacht.[69] By the time Rudolf Augstein visited him in Rhöndorf in autumn 1948, however, Adenauer had scaled down his proposal to thirty German divisions.[70]

In December 1948, concern over the international situation persuaded Adenauer to invite General Speidel for discussions. Contact between the two men was brought about by Rolf Pauls, a colleague of Blankenhorn who had served as ADC to Speidel during the war. In summer 1948, Speidel had already written a memorandum on the future of the German armed forces for Minister-President Hans Ehard. Adenauer, who had a low opinion of generals, opened the conversation with some patronising remarks about soldiers. Speidel responded coldly that Adenauer himself had been neither a soldier nor a member of the resistance. As was often the case, Adenauer respected men with the courage to stand up to him. He asked Speidel for a memorandum, which the general wrote with Blankenhorn there and then. They argued that not even the Rhine line would be secure in the event of war. Speidel added some perceptive remarks: 'If a German contribution is held to be desirable within the framework af an overall European concept, it cannot be achieved through the incorporation of small German units into the national contingents of the other European states. Instead it seems appropriate to establish unified German security formations within the framework of a European army ...'[71] Adenauer accepted the document without revealing his own intentions.

At the beginning of 1949 he discussed the problem with Hans Simons, leader of the U.S. liaison staff. Despite its brevity, the report produced by Simons for the U.S. headquarters clearly reveals the intelligent approach adopted by Adenauer in dealing with this sensitive issue.[72] More and more people, Adenauer was careful to note, were anxious about rearmament; everywhere people were saying that the Allies wanted to organise and arm twenty-five divisions in the Western Zones. Various quarters had argued that he had a personal responsibility in the matter, which should be not left as the subject of irresponsible talk. Adenauer had therefore conducted a number of discussions, including a long conversation with General Speidel, who was apparently also in consultation with French agencies. These talks had convinced him that German security was under serious threat. Personally, he was convinced that the issue of West German security demanded close attention.

Adenauer was not alone in this concern. General Clay's staff, based in the former IG Farben headquarters in Frankfurt, discovered that the issue had also been discussed by Carlo Schmid, the leading Social Democrat on the Parliamentary Council.

The report about Adenauer's talk with Simon caused deep unease among the officers close to Clay. Lieutenant-Colonel Campbell asked that the President of the Parliamentary Council be informed that it was illegal to discuss the establishment of any form of German fighting force with General Speidel. If these events were repeated, disciplinary measures should be taken against him. General Hall wrote on the report: 'Dr Litchfield – No one of our people should permit such a conversation to continue. Dr Adenauer should be advised firmly and clearly that the U.S. has no intention of permitting any German rearming.'[73] There, for the moment, the matter rested.

The situation in 1948 contained all the features that were to mark the first years of Adenauer's chancellorship. Though the Germans stood at the beginning of a path that might lead to political autonomy for a German 'core state', no final decisions had been taken. The U.S. and Britain were pressing for progress, but continued to ponder the wisdom of seeking agreement with the Soviet Union – at the cost of the 'West state' – instead of confrontation in Germany. The French still did their best to delay the proceedings and to make difficulties wherever possible, but remained dependent on the British and Americans. Meanwhile, in Paris an influential group of politicians of reconciliation had emerged to support the idea of West Germany as a partner in a European union. The European Movement was the great hope, but it was impossible to predict how successful it would be. Reconstruction had begun; Ludwig Erhard's social market economy was already seen by many Germans as an attractive alternative to a socialist planned economy. Even here, however, it was not clear whether the concept could be sustained politically.

The Marshall Plan was still in its early stages. As a result, dismantling, limitations on German production and unfavourable Allied industrial controls made a greater political impact than U.S. capital assistance. In all of their plans for the future, the issue of Berlin was a millstone round the necks of the Western Powers and the Germans alike. Behind the scenes, the concept of a German defence contribution had begun to play a part. Above everything, however, there hung like a storm-front the threat of a third world war.

The President of the Parliamentary Council

Though he could not know his exact destination, by September 1948 Adenauer had reached the last stage before the chancellorship itself. The political situation remained unstable and changed from month to month. A day before the first meeting of the Parliamentary Council, he wrote to Paul Silverberg: 'We do not know what will become of this council. Still, though everything is in the balance, the overall improvement in the situation is unmistakable.'[1]

Adenauer was not directly involved in the choice of Bonn as the seat of the Parliamentary Council. The driving force behind the decision was State Secretary Hermann Wandersleb, head of Karl Arnold's state chancellery in Düsseldorf. The decision was reached over the telephone on 13 August, less than three weeks before the assembly was due to meet.

Notes for this section begin on page 721.

Adenauer himself had suggested a location in the French Zone – Bad Ems or Koblenz. However, he quickly accepted that there were major practical and political advantages in choosing Bonn.

Though Adenauer's previous work had taken him on an exhausting series of journeys through the Western Zones, his tasks in the Parliamentary Council in Bonn were to prove much less exhausting. Later, the minister-president of Stuttgart, Reinhold Maier, was to note that 'the town had no facilities whatsoever'.[2] Almost all of the founding fathers of the constitution were men without significant means who were forced to seek accommodation in a variety of private rooms, guest-houses and hotels. Adenauer himself, however, was able to return home to Rhöndorf every night and benefit from the 'extra sources of health and vitality' it provided, in the words of Kurt Georg Kiesinger.[3] This situation eased the strain on Adenauer, while his robust health served to improve his reputation among his backbenchers. Of course, living on the right bank of the Rhine was not without its problems. With the Rhine bridge still in ruins, Adenauer was dependent on the ferry service; not only did this stop when night fell, but it failed to run at all in thick fog or whenever there was a danger of flooding.

Despite its drawbacks, the arrangement proved a success. Adenauer explained his feelings to Wandersleb at the end of September: 'It's going splendidly. The people feel so well here that they don't want to leave. Now we could set about suggesting that Bonn becomes the provisional federal capital.'[4]

Two memoranda came to a positive conclusion about the suitability of Bonn as the capital. On 27 October, Adenauer persuaded the Ältestenrat (council of elders) to consider the issue. Minister-President Karl Arnold, who shared Adenauer's assessment, joined his state secretary, Wandersleb, in praising the merits of Bonn. The supporters of Frankfurt, who had been pressing the claims of that city for some time, now found themselves engaged in a contest for support. The administrators in North Rhine-Westphalia acted quickly: building work was being carried out on the north and south wings of the Pedagogic Academy by the middle of February, even before the Parliamentary Council had reached its decision. Wandersleb later related how the building work had delighted Adenauer, who normally hated loud noise: 'For me the most beautiful sound in the whole business is the hammering and pounding involved in the construction of the debating chamber.'[5]

Psychology often plays an important role in grand politics. This was particularly true of Adenauer, who was always moved by powerful inner feelings. The rebuilding of the state in this visible way increased his determination to bring the constitutional deliberations to a successful conclusion. Nevertheless, his advocacy of Bonn as federal capital was politically motivated. It was supported by a series of arguments that had been familiar in western and southern Germany since spring 1946, when they had encouraged the transfer of the seat of government to the west.

One main problem faced by the supporters of Bonn was the need to persuade the Belgian occupying troops to vacate the exclusive residential area and leave the town. On 8 October 1948 Adenauer wrote to his old Flemish colleague, Frans van Cauwelaert, who was now president of the Chamber in Brussels. He made a number of political arguments in his letter. Though Adenauer conceded that 'Frankfurt is campaigning hard for it', so were North Rhine-Westphalia and the town of Bonn: 'I am personally of the opinion that, from the standpoint of the Western Powers as well, Bonn is preferable to Frankfurt, because the old traditional ties between the Rhenish west and Germany's western neighbours are stronger than the relations between Frankfurt and the western neighbours. I also take the view that it is better for the work of the future federal parliament and the federal government if its is based in a relatively small town, which Bonn is, rather than in noisy Frankfurt.'[6]

The Parliamentary Council had barely begun its work when its president – discreetly at first – began to canvass in favour of Bonn. His conduct also reveals how hard he was now pressing for the founding of the new state. When the Parliamentary Council began its work, Bonn was far from being an ideal seat of government. Conditions for the opening ceremony in the Alexander Koenig museum on Koblenzerstraße had a surreal quality: though most of the stuffed animals had been removed or covered with sheets, the giraffes had been left towering over the gathering of minister-presidents, members of the Parliamentary Council and representatives of the occupying powers. A year later, Adenauer was to set up his federal chancellor's office there for a few weeks.

The beauty of the surroundings were regarded as compensation for many hardships, though the founding fathers had to tolerate long autumn and winter months before they were able to appreciate them. Even the cramped conditions brought some benefits. The delegates, out of necessity, came to know each other better, striking up friendships that crossed the party lines. An early discussion between Adenauer and Carlo Schmid was less than productive. Schmid began it with a reference to Adenauer's reputation of occasionally taking thruthfulness with a pinch of salt: 'I have been warned about you.' At the end of the conversation, Adenauer is reported to have told Schmid: 'What sets us apart is not just age, but something else: you believe in human beings, I do not believe in human beings and have never believed in them.'[7] Whether or not these were Adenauer's actual words, Schmid wasted no time in spreading news of them. Adenauer's contempt for his fellow men became a favourite topic of conversation in the taverns and clubs where delegates and journalists met for a drink in the evenings.

It is not clear what position Adenauer had in mind for himself when he came to the Parliamentary Council. As CDU Zonal chairman and chairman of the Landtag delegation of North Rhine-Westphalia, he was fully entitled to include himself on the list of nominations for the Parliamentary Council. Karl Arnold actually encouraged him to do so, quite possibly in the hope of getting him out of his hair for a few months. After his election as president of the Council, Adenauer wrote to a party colleague: 'Originally I had decided not to accept the leadership of the Parliamentary Council under any circumstances.' However, he had changed his mind after pressure from 'important party members …'[8] This may or may not be the case. In any event, Adenauer was the obvious choice.

The CDU/CSU delegation met on 31 August in a classroom at the Pedagogic Academy. There were few prominent politicians in its ranks. Though Jakob Kaiser was a member of the Berlin delegation, this group had only an advisory role and in any case, Kaiser had lost his power base in the party. From North Rhine-Westphalia, alongside Adenauer, the only influential figure was Robert Lehr. Adolf Süsterhenn, the Minister of Justice and Culture in Rhineland-palatinate, also had political weight, and Adenauer was eager for his support. Another was Heinrich von Brentano, chairman of the CDU delegation in the Hesse Landtag. One of the dominant figures, however, was the Bavarian minister Anton Pfeiffer of the CSU.

Pfeiffer, a secondary-school teacher and general secretary of the Bavarian People's Party before 1933, belonged to the strictly Catholic and markedly federalist wing of the CSU which was in conflict with the Land chairman, Josef Müller. In 1947 he had formed the 'Ellwangen Circle' of pro-federalist Union politicians, had played a leading role in the constitutional convention at Herrenchiemsee, and had come to Bonn hoping to defend the federalist cause. To some extent, Pfeiffer was preoccupied with the bitter civil war within the Bavarian CSU, and also between the CSU and the Bayernpartei (Bavaria Party), which had been followed with astonishment and anxiety by Union politicians outside Bavaria because of its debilitating effect on the Union camp as a whole. Finally, state secretary Walter Strauss was another of the CDU politicians to be taken into account. As an old civil servant he remained largely in the background, but exerted a considerable influence.

Adenauer was clearly the most powerful political figure within the twenty-seven-strong delegation. At seventy-two, he was also the oldest member of the Council, making it almost inevitable that the Union delegation would propose him as president. Adenauer wanted immediate links with the five Liberals and two DP delegates in order to prevent the election of a Social Democratic president; the SPD also had twenty-seven delegates and could rely on the support of two Centre Party delegates and two Communists.

Adenauer was infuriated to learn that, in the prelude to the Council session, an arrangement had been made between the CDU and the SPD.

Gebhard Müller, the state president of Süd-Württemberg-Hohenzollern, had proposed that one of the CDU seats should be conceded to the professor of law, Carlo Schmid, with the Hamburg SPD giving up one of its own seats in return. This agreement had apparently been reached through the mediation of Gebhard Müller and Josef Müller, on the grounds that the Parliamentary Council needed an accomplished delegate from the moderate wing of the SPD in order to achieve a constitutional compromise. To Adenauer's irritation, the SPD had acquired a delegate who was both an effective speaker and something of an expert in constitutional affairs. Moreover, Adenauer also suspected a plot to forge a Grand Coalition against his own wishes.

By the time the Parliamentary Council held its first meeting, it was clear that the Liberals (FDP) would be able tip the balance. Their delegation included the party's dominant figures – Theodor Heuss, Thomas Dehler and Hermann Höpker-Aschoff. The Deutsche Partei (DP) had also sent one of its leading personalities in the person of Hans-Christoph Seebohm. Another DP delegate was Wilhelm Heile, an old acquaintance of Adenauer's whose political wanderings had temporarily taken him from the FDP to the Guelph (i.e., Hanoverian) wing of the DP. From Adenauer's point of view, the fact that the bourgeois parties had sent prominent political figures to the Parliamentary Council, while his own CDU/CSU delegation contained none of his main rivals, offered significant advantages. He was the undisputed leader of the Union side and had important opportunities to encourage relations with the FDP and DP.

There was a price to be paid. In the case of the CDU/CSU delegation, there was controversy from the very first meeting. Adenauer had advocated the election of Adolf Süsterhenn as chairman of the delegation,[9] but the delegation promptly voted for Anton Pfeiffer. Adenauer's view that the Parliamentary Council should not come under the control of the Länder governments was thus ignored. His proposal to delay the Parliamentary Council for fourteen days, by which time the fate of Berlin might be decided at the East-West discussions in Moscow, met with no response. On this issue Adenauer had made the mistake of relying on information from the KPD delegate, Max Reimann, who had assured him that an agreement was imminent. There was a genuine reason for this hesitation, however out of tune with Adenauer's fundamental approach it may appear. If an agreement had been reached, the Allies would have interrupted the work of the Parliamentary Council; public opinion would then have turned against the politicians involved, not least Adenauer himself as a president of a constitutional assembly that was not permitted to complete its job. Finally, Adenauer's efforts to unite with the DP delegation came to nought. It was to be another twelve years before Seebohm joined the CDU.

Adenauer was more successful in his bid for the presidency itself. To his amazement, the SPD declared its willingness to vote for him as president, on condition that the CDU would accept Carlo Schmid as chairman of the Hauptausschuss (main committee). Schmid later described the SPD decision as a 'decisive mistake'.[10] The Military Governors were obliged to negotiate with the Parliamentary Council and its legitimate representatives. Adenauer, dissatisfied with a merely representative role, had exploited his high standing in order to obtain a key political position. Now he was both an autonomous party leader and the president of a vital German body representing the parties which had been given legitimacy by the Landtag elections. Since the population was more impressed by an office of state than a party office, his election also enhanced his reputation among the public and made him widely known outside of the British Zone for the first time.

After his election Adenauer made a brief speech which served to make his views clear.[11] Though the Parliamentary Council had been 'called into being by an act of the Military Governors', it was now 'completely independent in respect of the tasks placed before it'. The future remained uncertain, 'and Germany itself is politically powerless'. In contrast to the wording that was to be used in the more comprehensive preamble to the Basic Law, Adenauer noted that the Council members 'represent forty-six million Germans' – that is, only the Western Zones and West Berlin. Their task was to give the German people, which had been torn apart politically, 'a new political structure' even if only part of Germany would benefit at first: 'For, ladies and gentlemen, a start must be made, and an end must be put to the eternal muddle and drift.' Nevertheless, they would set about their work with the aim of 'achieving the unity of the whole of Germany once again'. The outcome would depend on factors outside of the control of the Parliamentary Council. Still, they faced '… an historic hour and an historic task', which they should tackle 'under God's protection' and with a 'sense of duty'.

None of the Military Governors put in an appearance on 1 September. Whether this was a good or a bad omen was not clear. The Military Governors were said to be conducting negotiations in Berlin over the lifting of the blockade, which might be a positive sign. The Military Government may also have realised that German constitutional discussions would be more credible if there were as few U.S., British and French uniforms to be seen as possible. On the other hand, the absence of Generals Clay, Robertson and Koenig could also mean that the work of the Parliamentary Council would be halted if an agreement was reached with the Soviet Union. Some representatives of the Military Government were, of course, present. Among them, Lieutenant-Colonel Pabsch, Lieutenant-Colonel Chaput de Saintonge and the French diplomat Jean Laloy soon became familiar to every member of the Parliamentary Council. The liaison staffs of the Western Allies, however, generally remained discreetly in the background.

It was at this stage that first-generation German-Americans emerged to play a prominent role on the U.S. side. One of General Clay's closest advisors, and a man in contact with Adenauer, was Professor Carl Joachim Friedrich, who had chosen to make his academic career as a political scientist at Harvard even before the Nazis came to power. Adenauer also valued his discussions with Hans Simons of the U.S. liaison staff. Then fifty-six years old and a dean at the New School for Social Research, Simons had been a German officer during the First World War. He had spent some years as a professor at the German Hochschule für Politik in Berlin and, as a Prussian civil servant until 1933, had also been Social Democratic Oberpräsident of Lower Silesia in Liegnitz.

Adenauer took up his new office with dignity, drawing on his experience at the head of Cologne city council and the Prussian State Council. In May 1949, Walter Henkels provided a portrait of Adenauer which revealed his effect on the journalists who had observed him in action. As a speaker he was 'honest and warm', though occasionally he could be 'sarcastic, sometimes cynical'. Adenauer was a man of great persuasive power and political ingenuity: 'His opponents, of whom he has not a few, call his basic conservative outlook stubbornness, and they call the political threads he spins slyness, inscrutability. However, very few living German politicians even approach his stature.'[12]

In fact, it was only in these months that German journalists really discovered Adenauer and began their attempts to shape his public image with varying degrees of goodwill, detachment or hostility. Members of the foreign press corps also began to notice him. One of these was the American Theodore H. White, who was already well known for his best-selling book *Thunder Out of China*. When White visited the U.S. liaison staff, his chief contact was Anton F. Pabsch, director of the Onondaga Freight Company in Syracuse. Despite his German descent, Pabsch was a typical American rather than a transplanted political scientist like his colleagues Hans Simons, Edward H.Litchfield and Carl Joachim Friedrich. He had used his innate political instinct to influence politicians in Albany, and he brought the same skills to Bonn: 'We observe them, then we cocktail them, dine them, and lunch with them.'[13] Pabsch also explained the details of the political situation to White: Adenauer was 'our' man, Schumacher was Britain's man, the French were closest to Carlo Schmid, and the Soviets' man, Walter Ulbricht, was far away in Berlin. Though this was a gross over-simplification, there was a core of truth in it. In fact, White added in retrospect, Adenauer was Germany's man.

The CDU leader struck White, who had spent the years between 1938 and 1945 in China, as a somewhat oriental politician: 'very grey, clean, immaculate, ageing, starched, detachable collar.' He offered no jokes or cosy observations, but gave White a dry lecture on current issues of constitutional dispute. White was impressed, but noted that Adenauer looked like a wrinkled mummy with a disconcerting capacity for bursting into speech. The American gave him one or two years at most, if he ever reached the top.

During these months in the Parliamentary Council, Adenauer recognised that he needed to become better known abroad. Journalists such as White were useful in this respect as were Europe's Christian Democrat politicians, whom he was now able to meet on a regular basis. To the dismay of many members of his delegation, Adenauer took to disappearing from Bonn at intervals, only to re-emerge in Interlaken, Caux, Geneva or Luxembourg for confidential discussions. He returned to his relatively provincial CDU/CSU delegation in the Parliamentary Council much better informed about the real intentions of the Western Allies in general, and the French in particular. By autumn 1948 Adenauer was already personally acquainted with Georges Bidault and Robert Schuman and had been introduced to Winston Churchill.

He would have appreciated an invitation to visit Britain in the footsteps of Kurt Schumacher. Through the good auspices of Michael Thomas, Blankenhorn sought to bring this about.[14] Various Britons with whom Adenauer had good relations – including Lord Pakenham and General Robertson – hoped that such a visit might change his anti-British attitude, though Robertson added that Adenauer would always be a 'difficult customer'.[15] However, whenever a plan to visit London looked like becoming a reality, Adenauer gave a speech criticising the Labour government, thereby making it easy for the German desk at the Foreign Office to designate him as a 'dangerous man' and keep him at a distance.[16]

Adenauer's chief opponent remained the SPD. He would not change his view that the British government was sympathetic towards the Social Democrats. To his hostility towards the economic and social policy of the SPD was now added an increasing disquiet over Schumacher's approach to foreign policy. At the end of 1948 he wrote to Heinrich Brüning to complain that 'the SPD under Schumacher's leadership is developing into an absolutely nationalist party'.[17]

In the early days of the Parliamentary Council, Adenauer was alarmed to discover that the Social Democrats' calculations concerning the distribution of leading posts had apparently been correct. Carlo Schmid rapidly exerted his authority over the main committee, while the CDU/CSU delegation was vexed by frequent disputes, forcing Adenauer to issue constant calls for solidarity and to insist on the deciding role of the CDU in the British Zone.

At first, his conduct was restrained in public. Thus he wrote to a party colleague in Hamburg at the end of September: 'I regard it … as my duty to keep out of the party political discussion in the Parliamentary Council as much as possible and, at a suitable moment, to attempt to bring about the unity of all the delegations with the exception of the Communists.'[18] Although this was impressive on the surface, it did not entirely square with the facts.

Within his delegation, Adenauer made stubborn efforts to enforce his own views on the important points – not always successfully. Furthermore, despite his assertions, until the final phase of the constitutional discussions it was open to doubt whether he really wanted a compromise with the Social Democrats. In March 1949, after the SPD's rejection of clauses providing for an all too decentralised structure of finance and taxation had produced a crisis in the Parliamentary Council, he abandoned his earlier calls for compromise: 'If the SPD rejects the Basic Law, we must do it with the small parties alone …'[19] Although Adenauer was ready to make an effort to win over the Social Democrats, he was perfectly prepared to move without them if necessary. In the event, following discussions with Carlo Schmid, he was able to establish a broad majority for a compromise solution on this issue.

Adenauer had strong personal views on the disputed constitutional questions. For some time he fought a vain battle against the Bavarians and in favour of a second chamber based on the model of the U.S. Senate. His qualms about the Bundesrat model, that envisaged a second chamber composed of Länder government representatives, were twofold: first as a party leader objecting to the power of the minister-presidents in general, and secondly to those of the SPD. He told his delegation that if each Land government were given two votes in the Bundesrat and Berlin was added, the SPD majority in that chamber would be 'absolutely secured'. If a Social Democrat federal government was then elected in the Bundestag, the SPD – 'our most dangerous enemy' – would be able to shape the Federal Republic as it saw fit.[20] Whatever principles it introduced could not then be altered. Nevertheless, Adenauer finally agreed to the Bundesrat solution when some of his objections were met by a procedure to weight the votes. On this issue the SPD and CSU had outflanked him by reaching a rapid agreement which, after a furious row, Adenauer was forced to accept.

On the issue of parental rights he was inclined towards compromise from the outset. The CDU/CSU, he believed, must not allow itself to be isolated on this issue, and must avoid driving the FDP over to the side of the SPD on cultural matters. Though he was pleased to hear that Cardinal Frings had joined the CDU at the start of the constitutional discussions,[21] he was aware that there might be a price to pay.

Adenauer and his delegation were compelled to adopt a convoluted approach to the issue. It supported the demand for parental rights to be enshrined in the Basic Law but avoided a complete break with the FDP and SPD over this during the final phases of the drafting process. This is why he dispatched the following letter to Cardinal Frings:

> Though I find the position of the FDP and SPD intolerant, I believe that nobody could take responsibility for voting against the Basic Law in the version agreed. The political consolidation of West Germany is an absolute

necessity domestically and in foreign policy, from the standpoint of Germany and Western Europe alike ... In my view, anyone who demanded a vote against the Basic Law because not all their demands on the issue of parental rights had been met – parental rights are neither affirmed nor denied – would be open to the criticism that they had acted against the interests of the German people in its hour of need ... There would be no telling the damage to the Catholic Church. For the CDU/CSU such a position would be of catastrophic significance. It would be equally intolerable for it to demand a vote for the Basic Law against the vote of the bishops, or to follow the vote of the bishops and vote against it.[22]

The subsequent Bishops' conference at Fulda chose not to take the extreme route proposed by Bishop Michael Keller of Münster. Nevertheless, the dispute was a serious test for the party and its relations with the Catholic Church.

All the delegations to the Parliamentary Council handled the issue of nationalisation with surprising restraint. The SPD was aware that it no longer had a majority on the Parliamentary Council. For his part, Adenauer was happy that the issue had virtually been set aside by the skilful wording of Articles 14 and 15 of the Basic Law, since otherwise there would have been even more discord in his already divided delegation. All the participants knew that the issue of nationalisation would be resolved by the outcome of the first elections to the Bundestag.

Throughout, the most complex question concerned the precise form of federal state to be created. This problem was inevitably linked with the relationship between the three Western Allies and the Parliamentary Council. For General Clay and his advisers, strong Länder were an essential aspect of the constitutional deliberations. The French were even more federalist, while the British were the least doctrinaire on this issue. The federal issue was thus the focus for all those who were not fully reconciled to the founding of the state, including certain groups in Paris and in the French Military Government in Baden-Baden. It was also true to some extent of Kurt Schumacher. In April 1949, Adenauer was convinced that Schumacher did not want the Basic Law to be passed.[23]

These disputes have often been described and documented elsewhere. In this context, it is enough to give a detailed account of one incident. Since the publication of the London recommendations in June 1948, the Germans had suspected that the Allied governments had agreed to far more detailed guidelines for a German constitution than they had revealed. This view had been confirmed by all subsequent discussions. All the participating parties, and indeed the Parliamentary Council as a whole, therefore faced something of a dilemma. If they made too many efforts to discover the ideas of the Western Allies in order to prevent the rejection of the Basic Law, they would be accepting a dependent status that no-one could regard as desirable. The impression on German public opinion, moreover, would be disastrous. However, if the Parliamentary

Council failed to have sufficient regard for Allied opinion, the proposed constitution might even be rejected by the Allies. Such a situation would be equally serious.

The issue was also heavily loaded with party politics. Since the ideas of the various German parties were roughly similar to those of one or the other of the occupying powers, there was a great temptation for each of the Allies, and for the individual delegations in the Parliamentary Council, to act discreetly together to promote their own constitutional objectives. The temptation was greatest for the members of the CDU/CSU group, who were aware of possible common ground between their federalist ideas and those of the Americans and even the French. Adenauer was a natural master of the game of intrigue that now began. Blankenhorn and his colleagues ensured a daily flow of accurate information and took care to send discreet signals regarding their own intentions. For the SPD, Carlo Schmid, Walter Menzel, Erich Ollenhauer and Ernst Reuter were committed and intelligent men, but they could not match the experience of Adenauer, who was also helped by his position as president of the Parliamentary Council. As the most influential party leader in the non-socialist camp, moreover, he was less dependent on others.

By contrast, the SPD delegation laboured under one major handicap: it had a strong leader, but this leader was far away due to his illness. Kurt Schumacher had been seriously wounded in the First World War, when he had lost an arm, and had spent more than ten years in the prisons and concentration camps of the Third Reich. His health had been shattered. Between early 1948 and the spring of 1949 he was desperately ill and his left leg had to be amputated. In consequence, he led the delegation from his sickbed. Schumacher was thus forced to rely on third parties for his information, and was unable to develop any instinct for the relationships that had developed between the Bonn delegations despite their political differences. He was also deprived of the opportunity to discover the views of the Western Allies through direct contact with their representatives. Schumacher was angered by the activities of the mayor of Berlin, Ernst Reuter, who exerted some influence over the Americans, urged the rapid establishment of a West German state, and helped to outflank Schumacher's own wish to keep the situation open. Most important of all, however, in a period in which the attention of ordinary Germans was fixed on Bonn, Schumacher was somewhat forgotten politically. In 1946 he had been easily the best known of West German politicians; by 1949 he was one of several.

The first major clash between Adenauer and the SPD and FDP occurred in December. Adenauer had proposed holding discussions with the Military Governors before the third reading of the Basic Law. He was worried that, if the Allies objected to specific clauses of the completed law, their wishes would have to be taken into account. This might have serious consequences for the reputation of the democratic parties.

The discussion with the Military Governors took place in Frankfurt on 16 December. Afterwards, Adenauer was criticised by the SPD and FDP delegates for ignoring a prior agreement with them. His question on the controversial issue of the Länder chambers had, they claimed, established the Western Allies as 'referees' in the dispute within the Parliamentary Council over the Basic Law. Adenauer defended himself by making full and precise reference to the facts, in a manner reminiscent of his struggles in the Cologne city council. However, he regarded the SPD attack as an indication that the SPD did not want the Basic Law at all and was looking for an excuse to start a conflict.

This was also the view taken by General Clay in his assessment of the 'Adenauer crisis'. Amid a storm in the press, the SPD delegation issued a carefully-worded statement to the effect that Adenauer no longer enjoyed the confidence of the Social Democrats as spokesman of the delegation. Though the Communists demanded his removal as president of the Parliamentary Council, the Social Democrats did not support them. The Americans, who had their own sources of information, suspected that the entire incident had been provoked from Hannover, and were relieved when the Bonn SPD delegation let the matter drop during the Christmas recess. However, Carlo Schmid had cause to recall the warnings against Adenauer. In his memoirs, he noted that the SPD's profound subsequent distrust of the Chancellor had one of its roots in this incident.[24]

The great crisis of the Parliamentary Council, in March and April 1949, again turned on the relationship between the federal authority and the Länder. Once again, the danger of failure was increased because of a renewed prospect that the Western Powers might reach agreement with the Soviets over Berlin. This would have had far-reaching consequences for developments throughout Germany.

At the beginning of March, the Military Governors signalled that the agreement reached so laboriously between the delegations was not in accordance with the guidelines laid down by the Western Allies. This was particularly true of the financial arrangements. The confrontation continued until the end of April. Though the Military Governors made public an amended – and more reasonable – Occupation Statute, they did not change their position on the financial constitution. Schumacher ordered his party to give a resounding 'no' in response, thereby presenting himself as the guardian of German autonomy vis-à-vis the occupying powers. The Allies eventually gave way. Shortly afterwards, however, Adenauer heard that the British had informed the SPD of a possible willingness to compromise even before the Social Democrat 'no'. This information he saved until the coming election campaign. During these weeks, he used his influence to bring the constitutional deliberations to a rapid conclusion. In November 1948 he had calculated that federal elections to the Bundestag could be held between March and May 1949.[25]

In this final phase of the Parliamentary Council, Adenauer's tactical line was comparatively simple: to reach agreement with the Social Democrats wherever possible. Carlo Schmid – a 'valuable man for us' – was now seen as an ally in achieving this objective. Nevertheless, Adenauer was still prepared to see the Basic Law passed by the Union delegation in alliance with the FDP and DP alone, if necessary.[26] One of the obstacles to discussions was the fact that the proposed constitution was not sufficiently federalist for a majority of the CDU delegates. After some of the disagreements with the SPD finally been settled, there remained a danger that the Basic Law would be rejected by the Bavarian Landtag – with highly damaging repercussions for the election campaign of the Union parties. Adenauer urged his own delegation to make a deal quickly. General Clay, he warned them on 5 May, would be Military Governor for only five more days and naturally wanted to crown his period of office with a success. On the other hand, the Allies were apparently 'contemplating the idea of giving in to the Soviets ... In any case, it is clear that if a halt is called before we have finished, we will have had it as far as our parties are concerned and in the whole of Germany.'[27]

At the same time as urging the rapid completion of the discussions, Adenauer attempted to make essential compromises on all sides. The Basic Law was passed by fifty-three votes to six from the CSU plus two each from the Centre Party, the DP and the Communists. Adenauer began his speech on the successful final resolution with the words: 'In truth, this is probably the first happy day since 1933 for us Germans.'[28]

Adenauer was also pleased by the vote on the provisional seat of the federal government. For some months, this debate had been deeply political, since the SPD supported Frankfurt while Adenauer's supporters favoured Bonn. One major argument in favour of Bonn was the fact that, unlike Frankfurt, it was some distance from the U.S. Military Government. Adenauer also attempted to persuade Carlo Schmid that the cumbersome machinery of the former Economic Council in Frankfurt would prevent a clear view of the political problems. In Bonn, on the other hand, there would be little bureaucracy and no mass demonstrations![29]

Adenauer's main problem was to persuade his own delegation to vote *en bloc* for Bonn. The CDU delegates from Hesse were naturally sympathetic to Frankfurt, and the CSU again proved awkward. Adenauer finally persuaded his own team to support him by reading out a 'confidential' report on Kurt Schumacher's remark that 'the choice of Frankfurt as federal capital means a defeat for the CDU/CSU'.[30] As Lothar Rühl noted in *Der Spiegel,* this news was enough to turn 'enthusiastic Frankfurt supporters into cheerful Bonn supporters'.[31] In addition to Adenauer, this ploy also involved a number of Bonn journalists, including Otto Schumacher-Hellmold, who was then mayor of Bonn, Heinrich Böx and Franz Hange then correspondent of DENA.[32] The vote was 33 to 29 in favour of a town that had not even been in the race a year earlier.

Minister-President Karl Arnold, who had strongly supported Bonn, received a warm – and surprising – letter of thanks from Adenauer for his efforts.[33] Cardinal Frings was also given the good news in a letter, 'because I know the interest you also take in this matter'.[34] Adolf Süsterhenn, who had been ruled out of the final stages of the Council by a traffic accident, received an enthusiastic telegram: 'All has ended well.'[35]

Setting the Course

From the vantage point of Adenauer's fourteen-year tenure as Chancellor, his journey from the presidency of the Parliamentary Council to the office of Federal Chancellor seems almost inevitable. Yet that was not how it appeared to the leading politicians and the press at the time, nor to Adenauer himself. Adenauer's aim, however, was clear from the outset: the formation of a government of non-socialist parties as quickly as possible. At the end of November 1948, he thought that this objective could be achieved in late April or early May 1949. The assessment was too optimistic, owing to differences between the Germans and the Western Allies during the constitutional deliberations and to developments on the international scene. Once the governments of the Western Allies had put the Basic Law into force, however, there could be no return to Four-Power Administration. In early February 1949 Edward Litchfield had written to Robert Murphy to discuss what could be done if the idea of a West German state had to be abandoned; anything more than damage limitation, thought Litchfield, would probably be impossible. The Western powers would be discrediting precisely those West German politicians on whom they could rely in the event of a clash with the SED in a reunited Germany: 'We have no others'.[1]

During these months Adenauer held the same view. Shortly after the passing of the Basic Law, and immediately before it came into force, he was given the opportunity to explain his opinions to the British Foreign Minister, Ernest Bevin. During a brief visit to Berlin, Bevin met Adenauer, Arnold and Schumacher on 9 May 1949 for separate discussions at Ostenwalde near Melle. Adenauer gave his views on the subject of the new conference of the Council of Foreign Ministers which was due to be held in Paris two weeks later.[2]

As always, Adenauer was deeply suspicious of Soviet intentions. In his view, no sincere offer of free elections and political openness throughout Germany could be expected from them. Adenauer wanted German unity, but only on the basis of democratic freedom and economic progress within the framework of a European community. This, in fact, was the approach to which he was to commit himself over the coming years. On this occasion, he also doubted whether the Americans had judged the situation correctly. Adenauer's great nightmare was of an agreement between East and West and the withdrawal of all the occupying forces, thus delivering the Western Zones into the hands of the People's Police and the Communists before a democratic state could be organised. He was greatly relieved by Bevin's assurance that the West understood this danger, and that the Western Allies would insist on the democratic principle in their dealings with the Soviets in Paris.

In the years to come, Adenauer was frequently troubled by similar anxieties whenever conferences were held on the German question. The memory of Yalta and Potsdam continued to alarm him. He never ruled out the possibility of compromises by the Western Allies at the expense of Germany, which would also discredit a foreign policy that was so closely associated with the West.

By the middle of June Adenauer recognised that the Western Powers had held firm. He wrote to Dannie Heineman on 12 June that 'the Paris conference will, in all probability, end either wholly or largely negatively. That is a good thing. Any link between West Germany and East Germany, so long as East Germany remains just a satellite of Soviet Russia, would increase the power of the Soviets in Germany.'[3]

No further disturbances in foreign policy were to be expected during the formation of the federal government and the coming election campaign. There were, however, more than enough uncertainties in domestic politics. Adenauer continued to regard the SPD as the main enemy: 'Everything will depend on preventing the socialist party from being able to form a majority with the Communist Party which can then elect a Social Democratic Federal Chancellor. This danger exists!'[4] On this issue, he was less concerned with the strength of the SPD than with the lack of unity in the CDU and CSU over the coalition question. If this problem could not be resolved, a Social Democratic election victory remained a possibility.

On the basis of the relative strength of the parties in the Parliamentary Council, the SPD and KPD could effectively be isolated as long as the CDU and CSU were persuaded to form a coalition with the other bourgeois parties. However, it was possible that the distribution of seats in the Parliamentary Council gave a false sense of security to the parties, as the situation had changed since the last Landtag elections in 1947. The outcome would also depend on whether Landtag elections alone were held, or whether federal elections were held throughout West Germany first.

Nevertheless, it was possible to build on the positive results obtained by the bourgeois coalition in the Frankfurt Economic Council. This had brought about a decisive shift of opinion within the CDU. Before the currency reform, it had taken all Adenauer's skill to keep the socialist wing of the party in check. Moreover, he and his opponents within the party, especially Karl Arnold and Werner Hilpert, knew that the amalgamation of the Western Zones would create an entirely new situation with everything to play for.

It was at this moment that Ludwig Erhard arrived on the scene. Adenauer first came into contact with Erhard during the latter's service as Director of Economics of the Bi-zone. Adenauer observed the experiment of the currency reform with interest and anxiety, and its success led him to commit himself to the economic policy laid down in Frankfurt. At the end of August 1948, he gave Erhard a major platform at the CDU rally in Recklinghausen, where Erhard's advocacy of the market economy was received with great enthusiasm.

Adenauer remained sceptical until Erhard's policy had withstood its first test. Then, however, he confessed to the Zonal committee of his party: 'When Professor Erhard spoke in Recklinghausen six months ago and told us so firmly that things were going to change, I – I admit it quite frankly – said, excellent speech, let's hope it comes true. When we look back, we must admit that it has come true, though not in every detail since there has not been enough time. Today one thing is certain: the principles that Herr Erhard presented to us, and on the basis of which he works and acts, are really good principles.'[5]

Erhard had many outstanding talents. He was a powerful speaker, and was by all means the best PR-man that could be imagined for the concept of the market economy. In addition he had good operational skills. Until then, the pro-market wing of the CDU had lacked an outstanding leader. Robert Pferdmenges and other representatives of the business community had, of course, worked tirelessly in the background and laid much of the foundation for Adenauer's successes in his conflict with the socialist wing of the party before 1948. In Ludwig Erhard, however, he had found the ideal ally.

Erhard was a Franconian, a trained economist who had been Bavarian Minister for Economic Affairs until 1947 and following the currency reform of 1948 had become an important personality in his own right. Driven by a genuine sense of mission, he remained an independent figure rather than a party man. In consequence, the relationship that developed between Adenauer and Erhard between the summer of 1948 and the summer of 1949 was an alliance. Adenauer put the support of his party behind the Frankfurt Director of Economics; Erhard, for his part, was intelligent enough to recognise the importance of support from the strongest non-socialist party and its leader. Both gained from the arrangement. Adenauer now had his great election theme, as well as a figurehead whose popularity was increasing rapidly. As chairman of the franchise committee, he took care to give prominence to Erhard as the CDU's most important campaign speaker. Rarely, if ever again, did the two men work so well and smoothly together as during the Bundestag elections of 1949. After the formation of the federal government, the relationship between them changed. Erhard now occupied more of a subordinate role – though never to the extent of other ministers. He remained an autonomous figure in his own right, a fact which Adenauer recognised despite his character-istic reluctance to concede it.

The cause of the CDU was particularly helped by the fact that Erhard was also held in high esteem by the FDP. He had, for example, made speeches in support of his economic policy at FDP as well as at CDU meetings. FDP politicians took care to point out that they, the liberals, had actually nominated him as Director of Economics. In the end, Erhard allowed himself to be nominated as the leading candidate of the CDU in Württemberg-Baden, and campaigned in the constituency of Ulm/Hei-denheim. However, his relations with the FDP continued to be good and he reached a personal 'fairness agreement' with Theodor Heuss. More-over, Erhard firmly advocated an alliance in support of the market econ-omy by all parties to the right of the SPD.

New programme discussions within the CDU of the British Zone were held from February 1948 and were given added impetus by the decision in Frankfurt to promote a market economy in Frankfurt. In April 1948, the Hamburg banker Hugo Scharnberg and the Duisburg corporate lawyer Franz Etzel began work on behalf of the Zonal Committee to pro-duce guidelines on the new economic order. When the first detailed papers were produced, however, the re-orientation was blocked by Johannes Albers. At first Adenauer adopted a cautious approach; but when Erhard's policy proved successful he pulled out the draft pro-gramme statements from the lower-level committees and persuaded the convention of the Zonal CDU to pass a resolution giving unconditional support to the economic policy of Frankfurt. Erhard's speech to the party had prepared the ground for this decision. The convention gave 'unani-mous' and 'emphatic' support to a call for the 'rejection of the failed state-directed planned and controlled economy ... The party assembly demands that the path taken by the CDU in the Economic Council be continued consistently'.[6]

The left wing of the party had been outmanoeuvred. In October 1948 Adenauer established a supra-zonal committee under the leadership of Franz Etzel responsible for an economic programme. This committee, which also contained members of the CSU, was instructed to co-ordinate its work with the Frankfurt Economic Council.

The socialist wing of the party was finally defeated at the meeting of the Zonal executive at Königswinter in February 1949. Once again Erhard made an impressive speech. Adenauer praised the Director of Economics for finding 'the secret of success' in his speech, by stating his ideas on 'the simplest possible level and in the clearest possible terms. That is what we will want to do when we launch our election propaganda.'[7] He quickly suggested a committee to put together useful basic principles from Erhard's speech. Friedrich Holzapfel, leader of the CDU delegation in the Economic Council, had prepared a list of committee members.

Resistance to Adenauer's bold coup was remarkably moderate.[8] Jakob Kaiser, for example, signalled a clear change of course when he noted that, though Erhard was reputed 'to be a liberal, the ideas he presented please me very well'. The only man to offer stiff resistance at this stage was Johannes Albers. Quite correctly, he noted that 'Professor Erhard's speech reverses the Ahlen Programme in its basic structure'. Adenauer then demonstrated his ability to build bridges to a defeated opponent: 'Now we have to make disctinctions in these two things. I have just said, Herr Albers, all these programmes and programme clauses have no eternal value, but are concerned with the things that are vital now. In the coming election campaign the vital question will be: planned economy or market economy. That is what we are dealing with here. Herr Albers, that has nothing to do with the Ahlen Programme, which I stand by entirely.' Albers responded by calling out: 'Then we are agreed'. Adenauer also held out the prospect of a social programme which would be developed later.

It was also significant that in these days Adenauer placed remarkably little emphasis on the artificial notion of the 'social market economy'. From his point of view, the real choice was between a market economy and a planned economy. When Albers interrupted him with a shout of 'social', Adenauer added, to general amusement: 'or let us say: bureaucratic planned economy or social market economy'.

It was the events at this meeting that committed the CDU to becoming the party of the social market economy. Most of what followed was the work of putting the decision into words. Adenauer was anxious to ensure that the economic principles developed under the overall control of Franz Etzel had the full agreement of Erhard. The CDU was to enter the election campaign as the party of the market economy; what Adenauer wanted was a short election manifesto that people would actually read, not a detailed tract which would have no effect. He was no longer concerned about the grumbles of the party's left wing, who realised perfectly well what was happening. Adenauer persuaded the Zonal committee to accept the principles of the 'social market economy' and offered reassurance to the other CDU Land associations. Finally, at a major press conference in Düsseldorf on 15 July, he presented the economic programme together with the principles of social policy, housing policy and agriculture. Once again the main speaker was Ludwig Erhard, who spoke immediately after Adenauer and launched a furious attack on the 'socialist heresy'.

With Adenauer as the guiding force, the CDU had thus abandoned four years of socialist discussion and careful programme compromises. At their core, the sixteen points of the Düsseldorf Principles were nothing more than a description of the liberal economic policy of Ludwig Erhard. The social element that was added to the market economy programme was much more difficult to grasp. Parts of it appealed to the German tradition of the welfare state; other parts would require legislation to give them form – for example in the controversial areas of financial compensation for losses in the Second World War, co-determination in industry and social insurance. The new element in the history of the CDU was the crucial switch to economic liberalism. It would not have been adopted so decisively without the alliance between Adenauer and Erhard.

However, the road to a coalition in support of the market economy involved more than the struggle against socialist sympathisers within the CDU. A more difficult problem was that of overcoming the sympathy felt by the minister-presidents for a Grand Coalition of the CDU and SPD. Adenauer was convinced that he would be unable to keep the socialist wing of his own party in check if such a coalition were formed. Two years of bitter, and in his view less than successful, disputes with the government of Karl Arnold had increased his fear that in any coalition of Social Democrats and Christian Democrats, the social and economic ideas of the SPD would dominate.

The West German minister-presidents took a different view. Most of them were deeply concerned over the almost insuperable problems of reconstruction and the restoration of German sovereignty. In their eyes, the scale of the problem was a decisive argument in favour of a Grand Coalition of the CDU and SPD.

Furthermore, the SPD and CDU, or the SPD and Liberals, were working together with considerable success in most of the Länder governments. Karl Arnold in North Rhine-Westphalia, Peter Altmeier in Rhineland-palatinate and Gebhard Müller in Süd-Württemberg-Hohenzollern were all CDU minister-presidents who had established good relations with the Social Democratic ministers in their cabinets. Similarly, the Social Democrat minister-presidents Hinrich Kopf in Lower Saxony, Christian Stock in Hesse and Ernst Reuter in Berlin all led coalitions which included the CDU.

Elsewhere, coalitions with a different composition were in operation. In Hamburg (under Max Brauer) and Bremen (under Wilhelm Kaisen) the SPD was in coalition with the FDP. In Württemberg-Baden, the Liberal Reinhold Maier had headed a successful all-party coalition for a rather longer period. 'One-colour' Land governments were to be found only in Bavaria, with Hans Ehard and a CSU cabinet, and in Baden, where Leo Wohleb and his CDU government were attempting to ward off the demands of the DVP and SPD for a south-western state, the so-called *Südweststaat*.

Once it became clear what powers the Bundesrat would wield under the Basic Law, the coalitions in the various Länder inevitably acquired enormous political significance at the federal level. Each minister-president at the head of a CDU-SPD coalition knew that his government would be placed under enormous strain if a 'small coalition' at national level ever forced the Bundesrat to reach a decision on controversial legislation. If, on the other hand, a Grand Coalition was formed most of the minister-presidents would find life much easier at home. Moreover, politicians in the Länder generally regarded their own Social Democrats and Christian Democrats as being by some margin more moderate than their belligerent party leaders, Schumacher and Adenauer. Was it not possible to reach a peaceful and amicable agreement in Bonn?

Relations were especially complicated in the south-west, where the usual internal disputes were complicated by the *Südweststaat* question. Here the SPD, the Liberals and a majority of the CDU Land associations of North Baden, North Württemberg and Württemberg-Hohenzollern were pressing for the establishment of what was to become Baden-Württemberg. This move was bitterly opposed by the CDU of South Baden, headed by the Freiburg state president Leo Wohleb and with the less than discreet support of the French occupying power. Supporters of a *Südweststaat* were convinced that all-party coalitions offered the best means of achieving their objective. On the other hand, Adenauer was concerned about the implications for the majority in the Bundesrat that might follow the creation of a large south-west federal Land ruled by an uncertain coalition.

It was not only in the south-west that political life was a law unto itself. The regional power-brokers of the CDU, SPD, FDP/DVP and DP all opposed outside attempts to restrict their freedom to build coalitions of their choosing. The party chairman of the CDU in the British Zone was not even strong enough to direct the coalition politics of North Rhine-Westphalia (where he was chairman of the CDU *Fraktion* in the Landtag) and Lower Saxony. Moreover, despite his influence on the self-confident CDU Land associations in the American and French Zones, Adenauer had no prospect of intervening in coalition politics there, let alone of influencing the divided CSU in Bavaria.

Among the minister-presidents a significant part was also played by personal rivalries. While General Clay determined policy in the American Zone, the minister-presidents remained the decisive figures on the German side. In consequence, the party chairmen remained relatively powerless. Similar conditions prevailed in the French Zone. Only in the British Zone did the SPD minister-presidents and Karl Arnold of the CDU labour under the yoke imposed by their respective party chairmen, Schumacher and Adenauer. During the critical months when the West German state was being founded, the minister-presidents in every Zone had a key role to play. Wherever possible, they were eager to evade the interference by their party leaders. To their annoyance, however, his role as president of the Parliamentary Council enabled Adenauer to establish a strong position as the legitimate spokesman of the Germans in discussions with the Western Allies. The structural resistance of the Länder to a 'small coalition' in Bonn thus became linked with less easily perceptible personal hostility.

In the case of the CDU, this was true not only of Karl Arnold but also, to a certain extent, of the Bavarian minister-president, Hans Ehard. On many issues he and Adenauer were allies; in calmer moments they were aware of the depth of agreement between them. Ehard, who was sixty-three years old in 1949, had spent his career in the administration of justice in Bavaria, where he had become minister-president in December 1946. His role in bringing the conference of German minister-presidents to Munich in summer 1947 had demonstrated the extent of his personal ambition, or at least his desire to play an active political role outside the confines of his native Bavaria. Ehard saw himself as a major protagonist in the federalist re-organisation of Germany. His federalism was more moderate than that of many other CSU politicians, not to mention the Bayernpartei. However, he was the most radical federalist among the minister-presidents, and also influenced the constitutional discussions in a federal direction.

Ehard's attempts to play a mediating role in Bavaria remained controversial. This, indeed, was one of the reasons why he was not considered for a senior post in the federal government in 1949. Moreover, Ehard was fully occupied with his attempts to deal with the conflicts within his own CSU. Even in 1946, Germans outside Bavaria had been bewildered by events within it. At the end of 1946, Adenauer had raised the topic with his Zone committee: 'Conditions in Bavaria are completely incomprehensible to non-Bavarians, or at any rate to me. The people there keep bashing one another's heads in, the heads heal up and then they get bashed in again.'[9]

In the spring of 1949, the conflicts within the CSU reached a new peak. The conservative wing associated with the Minister of Culture, Alois Hundhammer ('The Black Shadow over Bavaria') was determined to overthrow the party general secretary, Josef Müller. Müller had many faults in the eyes of the conservatives: he was not sufficiently federalist, not Catholic enough, too casual and too much of a party manager. Adenauer shared much of this distaste for Müller, telling the American ambassador, Robert Murphy, in November 1948 that Müller was an 'adventurer' with no future in the party.[10]

Differences within the CSU were intensified by the fact that it now had an adversary in the form of the arch-federalist Bayernpartei, which was appealing to the same middle-class electorate. At least in part, it was

concern for the Bayernpartei which led a majority in the Bavarian Landtag to reject the Basic Law on the night of 19/20 May 1949.

In this difficult situation, Adenauer's main concern was to prevent the
CSU from disintegrating. As he saw it, the Union had two main pillars:
the CDU in the British Zone and the CSU in Bavaria. If Bavaria, where
the Catholics were in a majority, broke away, this would reduce the
chances of the Union becoming the strongest party throughout the Federal Republic of Germany. If the SPD were to become the largest party
because of Union losses in Bavaria, calls for a Grand Coalition would be
much harder to resist.

Not long before, Adenauer had clashed with Ehard over the latter's
strongly federalist views. However, Adenauer now worked successfully
behind the scenes to have Ehard elected chairman of the CSU, on the
grounds that it was at least possible to reach agreement with him. Subsequently, Müller accused Adenauer of engineering his fall from power in
Straubing at the end of May 1949,[11] and presented himself as a victim of
Adenauer's Machiavellian political instincts. In truth, this was an over-esti-
mation of Adenauer's influence in Bavaria. Yet it is also true that Adenauer
preferred to deal with Ehard, who was deeply conservative and relatively
predictable despite his consciousness of his own rank and prestige.

Although there were many problems to be overcome, Adenauer succeeded in bringing together a relatively united Union bloc in the crucial
election months. During this period, the crucial instrument of his leadership was the Conference of Land Chairmen. When this group appointed
him chairman of the *Wahlrechtsausschuss* (franchise committee), he
sought to develop it into a central co-ordinating office. He was also happy
to lean on the Frankfurt General Secretariat of the CDU/CSU Arbeitsgemeinschaft under Bruno Dörpinghaus, which collected a considerable
sum of money from business interests. The money was used to provide
election funds and to organise a centrally planned nationwide poster campaign as well as other election publicity.

The first major rally of the CDU/CSU was held to celebrate the unity
of all the groups within the Union. On 21 July 1949, Adenauer, Ehard and
Heinemann followed one another to the rostrum in front of the flag-
bedecked Heidelberg Castle to speak to an assembled audience of 5,000
supporters. Every effort had been made to strike a chord in the German
soul: the politicians appeared to the strains of *Tannhäuser;* during the
interval there was music from *Aida;* the evening ended with the singing
of the Dutch thanksgiving hymn 'To the God of the Righteous'.[12]

In his speech, Adenauer laid out the basic themes of his election
campaign: 'The main enemy in the entire campaign will be Social
Democracy … But we will ensure that 14 August does not under any
circumstances signal the birth of a socialist economy. We want to prevent
it, and that is the supreme goal of our campaign.'[13]

In March 1949, in a major speech to the Swiss group of the Inter-Parliamentary Union in Berne, Adenauer had launched a vigorous attack on British dismantling policy. Supporting his arguments with examples, he had claimed that the British were motivated by a sinister commercial jealousy of German industry.[14] This attack had so infuriated the British that Adenauer's planned visit to London was cancelled.[15]

The incident did not worry him in the slightest. He had quietly prepared another onslaught which, though having the SPD as its main target, also appealed to anti-British sentiments throughout the British Zone. Adenauer now told the Heidelberg rally that Schumacher's famous rejection of the Military Government's proposal to alter the Basic Law had been mere histrionics. The SPD had known that the Military Governors had already prepared a fall-back position: 'An absolute put-up job, ladies and gentlemen, between the British government and the German Social Democrats, in order to allow the German Social Democrats to appear as the national party par excellence.'[16]

This was not a deliberate lie. Adenauer was convinced that this had indeed been the intention. At this stage, he saw the British government as his number one election enemy alongside the Social Democrats. He thus wrote an astonishingly frank letter to Dannie N. Heineman in Brussels giving his view of occupation conditions. Adenauer was well aware of Heineman's many links with the American establishment and sought to persuade him to act against the British government.[17] The results of the Bundestag elections of 14 August, he wrote, would be

> of the greatest international significance. If they result in a success for Social Democracy, a socialist German government will be dependent on the socialist British government. Both together will give the new Europe a socialist face. According to reliable sources, the Labour Party is providing large sums of money to support German Social Democracy. The British government has placed the media in the British Zone, which covers more than half of the three Zones, almost completely in the hands of the Social Democrats. That is true of the radio as well as of the news agencies and the newspapers. If you think so too, please remind important American circles that the CDU, my party, is democratic, progressive and social, but not socialist, and that the American offices must counteract the support given to Social Democracy by the British.

However, the best aide to the CDU election campaign was Kurt Schumacher himself. Adenauer knew how to appear statesmanlike even when his attacks were poisonous; Schumacher, however, was less skilful. Not only did his attacks appear excessive, but he made the mistake of using the election for a direct attack on the Catholic Church. By describing the Church as a 'fifth occupying power', he drove even semi-detached Catholics into the electoral arms of the CDU. For Catholic voters, the issue of religious schools was a major theme of the election. Later, the publisher of *Die Zeit,* Gerd Bucerius, looked back at the first Bundestag election campaign and drew attention to the significance of the schools issue. Bucerius had been a member of the CDU's liberal wing in the Economic Council and was himself often irritated by the clericals in his own party. He noted with some irony that 'the Liberals got a shock when they were told that they owed the market economy to religious schools'.[18]

Adenauer was aware that his work was not finished simply because the heterogeneous Land associations of the Union were relatively united. Equally important, in his view, was the need to encourage alliances or pacts in the weeks before a government was formed. This issue began with the question of the franchise, which had preoccupied the Parliamentary Council more than almost every other issue. Though the Union contained influential advocates of the first-past-the-post system, the idea naturally appalled the smaller middle-class parties which might face extinction under it. In the CDU/CSU franchise committee, Adenauer managed to win support for the view that doctrinaire solutions should be avoided: where party lists seemed appropriate in individual Länder, these should be permitted. Furthermore, when left-wing CDU members – Kaiser and Hilpert – argued that a threshhold clause should be included to remove small rivals, Adenauer supported regulations which allowed his indispensable allies to send sufficient deputies to the German Bundestag.

After much debate, the franchise question was settled largely as Adenauer had wanted. Thereafter, he used all his energies – with mixed success – to achieve election pacts. Here he had to cope with different conditions among each of the smaller parties. The FDP, which was known in parts of Germany as the Democratic People's Party (Demokratische Volkspartei, DVP) had voters in the middle-class Protestant areas of Württemberg, in North Baden, North Hesse, Siegerland, in some constituencies of Lower Saxony, and in Hamburg. Only in Hamburg, however, was a genuine electoral pact made. In Hesse, the left-wing CDU members who continued to dominate the party executive were understandably opposed to an agreement with the extremely conservative local FDP. In North Rhine-Westphalia, Adenauer engaged in negotiations with the FDP chairman Franz Blücher in an attempt to agree on joint candidates in vulnerable constituencies at least. Again he was unsuccessful, on this occasion because of the hostility of Catholic priests and CDU activists on the spot.

Particularly in North Rhine-Westphalia, the issue of election pacts was closely connected with the rivalry between the CDU and the Centre Party. Adenauer's original stategy of taking over the Centre Party 'bit by bit'[19] had not been completely successful. In the run-up to the Bundestag elections he therefore made new attempts to forge an election pact to ensure that the CDU and the Centre Party did not clash head-on – 'a fair Christian election', as it was called. Prelate Böhler, the representative of the Fulda Bishops' conference at the Parliamentary Council, offered his services as mediator. However, the endeavour to reach agreement eventually failed owing to the demand of the Centre Party to be recognised as 'equal'.[20] Adenauer, who was determined to swallow the Centre Party altogether, would not accept it.

Equally unproductive were Adenauer's hopes of concluding an election agreement with the DP in Lower Saxony. Here he was opposed by Günther Gereke, CDU leader in Hannover and deputy minister-president in the cabinet of the Social Democrat Hinrich Kopf. Adenauer's efforts therefore produced few concrete results. However, they had proved to the FDP, the DP and the Centre Party conservatives around Johannes Brockmann that Adenauer wanted an accommodation. The goodwill he invested in the prelude to the election was to reap rich dividends over the following months.

As the election approached, Adenauer became convinced that the result would be favourable as long as the Union parties could mobilise all their sympathisers. On 4 August he wrote to Ada Deichmann, an acquaintance from the early years of the century who was returning to Cologne from South Africa and was currently staying in Englefield Green, Surrey: 'I will be glad when you come back. Please, remember that the election is on 14 August and that every vote counts.'[21]

Adenauer spent election night with his family, some of whose younger members had just returned from a 'Moral Rearmament' meeting in Caux. He was in an optimistic mood, writing a cheerful letter to the organisers of the Caux meeting, the Peyers. As usual, he could not resist a touch of mockery: 'They all came back improved. If the improvement lasts I will be very content.' Gisela Adenauer added: 'The election die is cast, but how???'[22]

It would still be many years before election nights featured exit polls and television predictions almost as soon as the polling stations closed. Adenauer was able to go to bed in peace and wait for morning. The results confirmed that he had achieved much of his objective. The election which, in fact, was a plebiscite on the economic structure of the new Federal Republic of Germany had been won, though not as decisively as he had hoped. In comparison with the Economic Council and the Parliamentary Council, where the Union bloc and the SPD had been on an equal footing, the Social Democrats had been pushed into second place. The CDU/CSU emerged from the election as the strongest party, with 139 seats compared to 131 for the SPD. A few days later, at the 'Rhöndorf Conference', Adenauer admitted that the election had not produced a clear majority for his party. The decisive factor, however, was the overall strength of the parties favouring the market economy. In addition to 139 seats for the CDU/CSU, the FDP had won 52, and the DP and Bayernpartei 17 each. Whatever the nature of the final coalition, the result of the plebiscite on the market economy was clear. In this situation, the 15 seats and 5.7 per cent of the vote won by the Communists were irrelevant.

Adenauer then made his first comment on the election result: 'The election result clearly shows that the overwhelming majority of the German people wants nothing to do with socialism of any shade. The elections represent a clear rejection of socialism.'[23] With an eye on foreign countries, he went on: 'The task now is to ensure that the Bundestag and the new federal government do good work for the German people on the tasks they have been set by the voters.' This task, in his opinion, was to establish a coalition of the parties which supported the market economy. The only possible Federal Chancellor to lead such a coalition, however, was the man who had devoted all his energies to bringing it about.

VI

FIRST YEARS AS CHANCELLOR
1949–1950

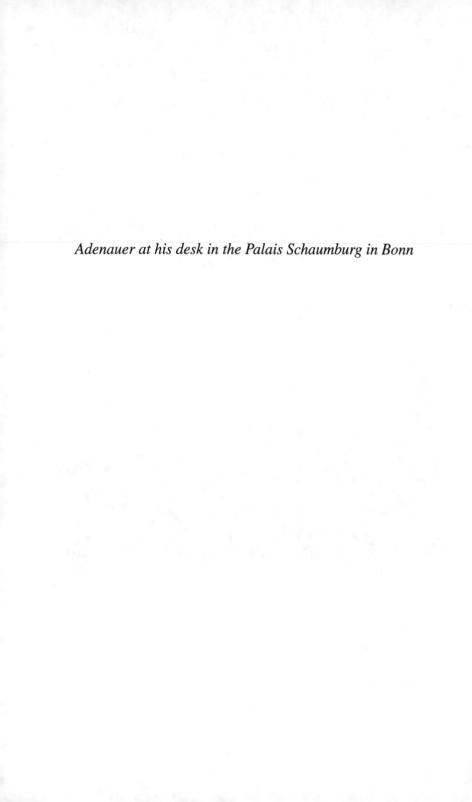

Adenauer at his desk in the Palais Schaumburg in Bonn

Forming a Government in 1949

It is virtually impossible to be sure exactly when Adenauer decided to set his sights on the chancellorship. The earliest evidence comes from Cardinal Frings, who recalled a conversation with Adenauer shortly before the Parliamentary Council completed its work. When the two men met at the celebration of the engagement between Adenauer's daughter Libet and Hermann-Josef Werhahn, Frings told Adenauer that he expected him to become president of the new federal state. Adenauer answered: 'No, I'd choose something else. I would like to be Federal Chancellor, you can make better use of your abilities there.'[1]

Once the appropriate articles of the Basic Law had been laid down, however, it seems safe to assume that Adenauer was determined to seek the office of Chancellor. After the FDP delegates Thomas Dehler and Max Becker had failed to gain support for their proposal for a presidential system based on that of the United States, the chancellorship was the obvious route to power. Leading politicians in the CDU and CSU knew Adenauer well enough to be sure that he had his eye on the most powerful office. Influential figures in the FDP were equally aware of it. On election day, Hermann Höpker-Aschoff, who had been able to assess the situation in the Parliamentary Council, wrote to Theodor Heuss, already being canvassed as the future federal president: 'If we were to obtain a coalition of the CDU and FDP after the elections, Adenauer must become Chancellor at all costs. Pünder is a zero and must be kicked upstairs to a higher court.'[2]

Höpker-Aschoff had mentioned Pünder, the former *Oberdirektor* in Frankfurt, as an alternative candidate. However, a Pünder candidacy was never a practical proposition, as he had no support in the CDU party organisation. Although Pünder had been directly elected to the Bundestag by the voters of Cologne, he recognised that he had no prospect of competing successfully against Adenauer. Pünder decided that the wisest course would be to support him. He probably hoped to be rewarded with the task of establishing a Ministerium für zwischenstaatliche Beziehungen, code-name for a new German Foreign Office, on the foundations he had already created in Frankfurt.

However, Pünder quickly discovered that Adenauer intended to concentrate all responsibility for issues of foreign policy in the Federal Chancellor's office, at least for the time being. When the process of forming a cabinet was complete, Pünder wrote a letter expressing his disappointment to Hans Luther, the former Reich Chancellor. Luther had noted the public expression of gratitude by President Heuss for all Pünder's work as Director-in-Chief and had asked him 'Is that all?'[3] Pünder replied: 'With some justice you ask "Is that all?" Personally, however, I feel extraordinarily relieved; speaking quite frankly – I would really not like to belong to this circle of fourteen auxiliary saints.'[4]

This was a case of sour grapes. In fact, relations between Adenauer and Pünder had already deteriorated during the eighteen months Pünder had spent as *Oberdirektor* of the Economic Council. There had been a number of quarrels, and Pünder may also have felt that he had been left isolated in Frankfurt. At any rate, he had written a sceptical letter to Luther early in March 1949: 'We must wait and see whether the new federation that is to be born in Bonn will grant us much improvement.'

Pünder was not the only one of the Frankfurt grandees to be left out in the cold. Another was Hans Schlange-Schöningen, previously Director for Food Supply and Agriculture in Frankfurt. He could have had few hopes of an exalted position. Adenauer was increasingly critical of him over agricultural policy in Frankfurt, which he had often regarded as unsatisfactory. To make things worse, he now saw Schlange-Schöningen as one of the main advocates of a Grand Coalition with the SPD.[5] Adenauer was also suspicious of Schlange-Schöningen's desire to give the highest priority to the restoration of national unity, and was aware of his good relations with Günther Gereke, chairman of the CDU in Lower Saxony, who held similar views.[6] These links dated from the Weimar Republic, when both men had been members of the national conservative DNVP – Gereke as the head of a Prussian administrative district, later as a member of the Reichstag, and finally as Reich Commissioner for Job Creation in the cabinets of Schleicher and Hitler.

Schlange-Schöningen had been elected to the Bundestag. His ambitions were slightly more modest than Adenauer's, since he wanted to be federal president. However, he was aware that this would disturb Adenauer's own carefully laid plans. He was therefore prepared, as second best, to accept the post of Minister of Agriculture. Schlange-Schöningen had considerable support from the Protestant CDU Land associations of northern Germany, a fact which forced Adenauer to take his ambitions much more seriously than those of Pünder, but which also increased his determination to shut Schlange-Schöningen out. And so the major distribution of posts in the first weeks after the Bundestag elections left Schlange-Schöningen empty-handed. He was eventually appointed consul-general in London. Adenauer had thus removed from the scene another potential source of discontent in the CDU/CSU *Fraktion*.

Most serious of all for Adenauer were the ambitions of Friedrich Holzapfel, who was admired for his work as chairman of the CDU delegation in the Economic Council. Gerd Bucerius, who had also taken a prominent role there, reported later that Holzapfel had even entertained hopes of becoming Chancellor himself.[7] Adenauer regarded him with the suspicion he reserved for all those who had their own power base within the CDU. Holzapfel had originally been prominent in the Bielefeld Chamber of Commerce, and had been co-owner of a broom and brush factory in Herford during the Third Reich. As a former member of the DNVP, he had good relations with Schlange-Schöningen, and can be regarded as a representative of the Protestant wing of the CDU. Liberal in economic matters, patriotic in foreign policy, he had previously been completely loyal to Adenauer.

On the surface Adenauer could have few criticisms of Holzapfel who, like himself, was a firm advocate of a 'small coalition'. However, after the first meetings of the CDU Bundestag caucus Adenauer became convinced that Holzapfel had decided to block his path to the Chancellorship. Holzapfel demanded that the party should provide both the federal president and the Chancellor, and firmly opposed the appointment of the FDP's Theodor Heuss as president. It seemed possible that he was trying to push Adenauer into the office of president, perhaps with the aim of eventually becoming Chancellor himself. Adenauer clashed with him on several occasions during these decisive weeks, and concluded that Holzapfel, like Schlange-Schöningen, must be kept out of the most important posts. In the end Holzapfel had to be satisfied with the post of deputy chairman.

Adenauer was aware that the greatest dissatisfaction was likely to come from men who had held high office in Frankfurt and therefore had strong claims on playing leading roles in Bonn. He was determined to make room only for those politicians on the Economic Council who offered unconditional support for his own ideas – Ludwig Erhard, Walter Strauss, the leader of the Bi-zonal Justice Department, and Anton Storch, who had been a reasonably competent Director of the Department for Labour.

At the same time, Adenauer regarded the numerous advocates of a Grand Coalition as much more dangerous opponents than the discontented members of the Economic Council. Fortunately for him, the most powerful among them were the minister-presidents of the Länder, who were not members of the Bundestag *Fraktion*. He did not hesitate to act against the threat from this faction, beginning in Bavaria. Adenauer sent a flattering letter to Minister-President Hans Ehard, a key figure in the internal struggle within the Union: 'It has been a very good thing that in this critical time the leadership of the CSU has been in your strong hands.'[8] The two men agreed to meet in Frankfurt on 20 August. Adenauer then invited selected leaders of the Union parties to a meeting at his home in Rhöndorf the following day, Sunday 21 August.

As a result of Rudolf Morsey's research, we know that the discussions between Adenauer and Ehard in Frankfurt were just as important as the 'Rhöndorf conference' next day. Both men were in favour of a small coalition with the FDP. On this occasion, Adenauer was polite and respectful towards Ehard. He claimed that, in his view, Ehard would have been the most suitable candidate as Chancellor, but that such a decision was impossible because the CSU had voted against the Basic Law. Though this had been a tactical vote by most CSU delegates, Ehard was forced to concede that it was a compelling argument against his candidacy. He therefore declared his willingness to support Adenauer as Chancellor. Both men were opposed to the prospect of Karl Arnold in the post. In return, Adenauer promised to support Ehard's candidacy as president of the upper chamber, the Bundesrat.

The two men also proposed to make Theodor Heuss federal president, thereby turning the office of federal president into a political bargaining counter. As they had foreseen, the offer proved to be a tempting bait for the FDP in the negotiations for a coalition. On the other hand, the decision in favour of Heuss quickly became a bone of contention among Union politicians, Protestant as well as Catholic.

Adenauer and Ehard proposed the name of Erich Köhler as president of the lower chamber, the Bundestag. This was a means of driving a wedge into the ranks of the CDU in Hesse, most of whose members supported a Grand Coalition. Adenauer had no high opinion of Köhler, but knew that he could be removed if necessary. After a year in office, Köhler was indeed dismissed; to add insult to injury, the Chancellor then proposed to send him off as consul-general to Australia.[9] Federal President Heuss regarded this as an unchivalrous gesture, and hoped to offer Köhler the more prestigious position of consul-general in Iran. Both schemes came to nothing: Köhler served as a backbencher in the Bundestag until 1957. In August 1949, however, he was also a former Frankfurt grandee and still a major figure in Adenauer's calculations.

From beginning to end, Adenauer's discussion with Ehard was a negotiation for a coalition between the CDU and CSU, without the need – for the moment – to take account of party negotiating committees. Both accepted that Ludwig Erhard would become federal Minister for Economic Affairs. Other important decisions were also anticipated. Jakob Kaiser, they decided, would become Minister for the Eastern Territories and for Refugee Questions, though in the course of coalition negotiations this was reduced to the Ministerium für Gesamtdeutsche Fragen (Ministry for All-German Affairs). Kaiser had taken Adenauer's side during the election campaign and no longer showed any inclination to join Karl Arnold and Werner Hilpert in pressing for a Grand Coalition, partly because he had been infuriated by the Schumacher's attacks during the election campaign.

Rather surprisingly, Adenauer made it clear even at this summit meeting in Frankfurt that he wanted to concentrate foreign policy matters in the Federal Chancellor's office; a state secretary under his direct supervision would be responsible for foreign affairs. This meant defeat for Hermann Pünder despite all his diligent preparations in Frankfurt. On the other hand, the outlines of a clash over the Ministry of Finance, which was claimed simultaneously by the Bavarian CSU and by the FDP, were already apparent. The idea of appointing Franz Blücher as Vice-Chancellor and Minister for Reconstruction was already under consideration. Blücher, it was thought, was likely to become federal chairman of the FDP after Heuss's election as federal president.

Only a few days later Ehard had cause to regret the rapidity with which he had committed himself to the concept of a coalition between the CDU/CSU and the FDP in the Frankfurt discussions. In so doing, he had destroyed the united front of the south German minister-presidents, who would have preferred to see a Grand Coalition. Ehard's aim had been to promote the influence of the CSU in Bonn as quickly as possible. One of his most important confidants, Anton Pfeiffer, former chairman of the CSU delegation in the Parliamentary Council, had not even been elected to the Bundestag owing to the poor showing of the CSU. Ehard had no real confidence in Fritz Schäffer, who had been elected, for Schäffer had a reputation of being obstinate, curt and devious. Furthermore, the new general secretary of the CSU, the young Franz Josef Strauss, was known within the party as a supporter of Josef Müller. Therefore, on 20 August, there had been many reasons for Ehard to reach an agreement with Adenauer. Characteristically, Adenauer was quick to exploit this opportunity to the full in forming his coalition. Two days later, when Ehard would have preferred to regain his distance, it was too late.

On the day after the meeting between Adenauer and Ehard, the famous 'Rhöndorf conference' was held. It has often been described as a tactical master-stroke on the part of Adenauer. The meeting took place in his sitting room, around a big coffee table, thus placing Adenauer in the position of host and chairman combined. He had personally drawn up the guest list, which contained twenty-six names. It included two minister-presidents, Peter Altmeier of Rhineland-palatinate and Gebhard Müller of Tübingen; Hermann Pünder and Ludwig Erhard represented the directorate of the Frankfurt Economic Council; CDU delegates from the Economic Council included Robert Pferdmenges, Erich Köhler and Theodor Blank; there were several Land chairmen of the CDU; Bavaria was represented by

Anton Pfeiffer, the president of the Bavarian Landtag, Horlacher, and Franz Josef Strauss. As was their custom, Herbert Blankenhorn and Josef Löns acted as additional eyes and ears for their chief. Subsequently, critics were to claim that the only supporters of a Grand Coalition present were relatively weak political figures. However, only the absence of Karl Arnold provides any evidence in support of such a Machiavellian interpretation. The advocates of a Grand Coalition were in fact well represented by the minister-presidents Altmeier and Müller, as well as by Werner Hilpert, Günther Gereke and Anton Dichtel from south Baden.

Adenauer began by stating his familiar arguments in favour of a minority government of the CDU/CSU and FDP. He pointed out that Kurt Schumacher himself was opposed to an SPD coalition with the CDU/CSU. Adenauer also announced that minister-president Ehard supported his preferred solution, particularly because of the agitation of the Bayernpartei in Bavaria. When the advocates of a Grand Coalition criticised the FDP because it contained right-wing radical elements, Adenauer turned the argument on its head and argued for the 'start of an attempt' to make common cause with the DP as well; its leaders Hellwege and Seebohm, he claimed, were 'honourable and decent' men.[10]

At this point it is useful to look more closely at the group which supported Adenauer. As expected, the transfer of the Frankfurt coalition to Bonn was supported by Ludwig Erhard, the Hamburg banker Scharnberg, and Robert Pferdmenges. Much more surprising was the resolute support for this approach from trade unionists such as Theodor Blank and Jakob Kaiser. In this matter Blank proved himself an enthusiastic supporter of Erhard's plan to facilitate 'reasonable social policy by pursuing proper economic policy'. For his part, Kaiser was now bitterly opposed to the SPD, describing Schumacher as 'a misfortune for Germany'. He wanted the CDU to mount direct opposition to the SPD, though not on a minority basis: he wanted to see an attempt to win over the Centre Party.

Perhaps most remarkable of all was the strong support given to Adenauer by Hermann Pünder and Erich Köhler. Help also came from the conservative Carl Schröter from Schleswig-Holstein. Like Franz Josef Strauss, Schröter pleaded for the inclusion of the DP in the coalition.[11] Otherwise – according to Strauss – the CSU would be forced to consider whether it was in fact ready to form a joint *Fraktion* with the CDU.[12]

The chief significance of the discussion was that it forced the supporters of a grand coalition to review their position. If they had not known it before, they now recognised that Adenauer had created a broadly-based group, in both regional and ideological terms, to support him. It consisted of the business wing of the party, trade unionists, Catholics and Protestants, south Germans and politicians from the south west as well as CDU members in the British Zone. Adenauer repeatedly intervened in the discussions in a manner reminiscent of his days as a lawyer in Cologne; his words fell on the participants 'like a steady rain that gently and persistently soaked all opposing arguments' and washed resistance away.

Towards the end of the discussions, the participants discussed the highest offices of state. Gebhard Müller made notes of the various contributions, which have the ring of authenticity. According to Adenauer,

> Herr Finck gave a completely naughty speech in Landau to the effect that I will be federal president. The most important person is the Federal Chancellor. Someone else should be president, I want to be Chancellor. I am seventy-three years old. But I would accept the office of Chancellor, because 1. the Federal President has to leave party life but the Chancellor does not. I have authority in the British Zone. Our party is not yet so well established that we could fulfil the great long-term tasks that were set before us last Sunday if I left. Good concentration is necessary in the long term. 2. I have certain experience in affairs of state and in the administration. 3. I have stronger elbows than I had previously thought.

He then suggested to the gathering that Theodor Heuss should be president.[13]

No decisions were taken. In fact, they could not be taken by a meeting which was not an official committee according to the rules. Nevertheless, the outcome was regarded as public confirmation of the fact that Adenauer would get his way in his party. A coalition of the CDU/CSU, FDP and, if possible, the DP now seemed the most likely solution.

As he had been during the election campaign, Schumacher remained Adenauer's most reliable helper. Despite the opposition of the SPD minister-presidents and Social Democratic politicians such as Carlo Schmid and Fritz Henssler of North Rhine-Westphalia, Schumacher committed his party to the role of opposition. He argued that if the SPD had no responsibility for economic policy at the centre of the new federal system, it could not participate in the government. Behind this concept of uncompromising opposition was Schumacher's conviction that the bourgeois government would quickly fail; after this the way might be open to form a Grand Coalition on terms laid down by the SPD. His approach, however, made it virtually impossible for those CDU politicians who wanted a Grand Coalition to make a convincing case.

Adenauer thus came to the first meeting of the CDU's parliamentary caucus with his authority strengthened. By the time it met, there was no viable alternative to the choice of Adenauer as chairman of the *Fraktion;* as well as being the oldest man on the committee, he was the former president of the Parliamentary Council and chairman of the CDU in the British Zone. His position enabled him to present himself as the leader of the negotiations in this crucial phase. Though he was not immune to criticism, there was every possibility that his wishes would be accepted.

Within the CDU and SPD alike, the advocates of a Grand Coalition now recognised that they could approach their objective only by an indirect route. Their party leaders were resolved on confrontation and were currently unwilling to compromise. However, it might still be possible for the supporters of a Grand Coalition to undermine the negotiations for a small coalition, and in particular to arouse suspicion and reluctance among the Free Democrats. At the end of August and the beginning of September, it was clear that much of the opposition to the choice of Heuss as federal president was coming from politicians who had reservations about the small coalition and Adenauer's claims on the chancellorship.

There were in fact a number of arguments against a Heuss presidency. One of these was that the office of president, committed to a supra-party role, ought not to be given to a party chairman. Furthermore, some politicians argued that it was wrong to link the coalition negotiations with the election of a federal president. During a confidential discussion with Blankenhorn, Carlo Schmid described the procedure as 'virtually a breach of the constitution'.[14] A similar objection, though in rather more muted language, was made by state president Gebhard Müller.[15] Finally, there was the issue of Theodor Heuss himself. As an arch-liberal, he had created very serious problems for the CDU/CSU delegation in the Parliamentary Council on cultural issues. Others found his economic liberalism equally difficult to swallow. During a stormy debate within the CDU caucus, Aloys Lenz, a member of the party's trade union wing, called Heuss a 'Manchester man' and urged the election of the chairman of the DGB (the German Trade Union Federation), Hans Böckler, instead.[16] However, negotiations between the CDU and FDP made it clear that a Heuss presidency was the *sine qua non* for the FDP's acceptance of a coalition with the CDU/CSU.

In response to the opposition within his own ranks, Adenauer also pointed to the links with the election of the President of the Bundesrat, the second chamber. If the CDU and CSU wanted to obtain the FDP's votes for Hans Ehard, then their own representatives in the federal assembly (Bundesversammlung) must be willing to vote for Theodor Heuss in return. In fact this manoeuvre went badly wrong. With the co-operation of the SPD and the CDU minister-presidents in the French Zone, Karl Arnold arranged his own election as President of the Bundesrat instead of Ehard. The incident cost Adenauer much prestige and Ehard felt betrayed. The CSU now clung even more stubbornly to its demand for the Finance Ministry, which was also being claimed by the FDP as the price of its support.

In this critical situation, the ubiquitous Blankenhorn informed Adenauer that there was considerable sympathy in the SPD for a Schlange-Schöningen presidency. At the same time, Hans Ehard indicated his own willingness to stand for the office of federal president; he apparently hoped to gain majority support from the CDU/CSU, FDP, DP and Bayernpartei. Adenauer, however, remained loyal to Heuss. He was supported in this decision by a majority of his caucus, though a minority opposed him.[17] Alongside these arguments over the highest office of state, the parties were also haggling over the Finance Ministry, the Ministry of Justice and the Ministry of Housing.

Circumstances were now changing from day to day. Schlange-Schöningen eventually made it clear that he would accept election as federal president even against the declared wishes of the leaders of the party and the CDU caucus. His decision caused a bitter clash with Adenauer. The situation was further complicated by the re-emergence of the denominational issue.

Once again it was Kurt Schumacher who inadvertently came to Adenauer's rescue by insisting on his own candidacy. His reasons were clear enough: Schumacher had no desire to see the emergence of a supra-party candidate for the office of Federal President if it might lead to the creation of a grand coalition. His decision forced a large majority of CDU and CSU delegates to vote for Heuss. Though Heuss fell short of a majority in the first round of voting, he was elected in the second round despite the failure of seventeen CDU/CSU delegates to vote for him.

Adenauer now had some reason for alarm over his own candidacy for the chancellorship. Initially his candidacy had been supported unanimously by the *Fraktion*, with Jakob Kaiser offering strong support for his victorious rival. However, over the following days many deputies had time to contemplate Adenauer's remark to them immediately after his nomination when, only half jokingly, he had observed: 'I thank you very much and I also warn you. It will not be very easy with me. You've seen nothing yet.'[18] The comment had been made on 1 September; since then much blood had been spilled.

Two weeks later, the day before the election of the Federal Chancellor, the mood within the party had deteriorated. Brentano and Holzapfel had raised a number of objections, most of which revolved around the issue of whether the federal president was entitled to reject specific names in the Chancellor's proposed cabinet. Beneath the surface, influential members of the CDU caucus were also irritated that they had been given no real insight into the details of forming a cabinet. Brentano in particular emerged as a staunch guardian of the interests of the *Fraktion* thereby qualifying himself for the post of its chairman after Adenauer became Chancellor. Already, however, the unspoken reproach was that Adenauer was treating the deputies of his party like a dictator. Despite his attempts to defuse the situation with humour, the deputies were well aware that they would be electing a hard taskmaster.

On 14 September, the day before the election of the Chancellor, Adenauer was forced to abandon negotiations with the other coalition parties and submit himself to a question and answer session before his own caucus. Discussion of the appointment of a Minister of the Interior could no longer be avoided. Several politicians, including Eugen Gerstenmeier, Gerd Bucerius, Oberkirchenrat Hermann Ehlers and Gerhard Schröder, who had won a notable personal election victory in Düsseldorf, had already pressed him to appoint Gustav Heinemann. This, they argued, would send a strong and positive signal to the Protestant camp in the CDU.[19]

Adenauer himself would have much preferred either of his former colleagues, Heinrich Weitz and Robert Lehr. He managed to avoid the issue temporarily by demanding that Heinemann could only be appointed Minister of the Interior on condition that he 'give up all his other offices'. However, he was then forced to concede that the position of the CDU might be damaged if Heinemann gave up the important post of president of the Evangelische Kirche in Deutschland (EKD). The question of a successor would have to be clarified. Thereafter, the coalition discussions became stalled on various points. The most important issues remained open, but Adenauer demanded that the vote must take place next day even without complete agreement on personnel issues, the organisation of offices and a government programme.

Provisional contacts had already been established with the Bayernpartei in case of difficulty with the vote. It emerged that the Bavaria Party intended to abstain on the first round of voting; subsequently, however, it might be prepared to formulate its terms for electing Adenauer in the second round. The DP, meanwhile, had managed to wrest written concessions from Adenauer in return for its own promise of support.[20]

The election of the Federal Chancellor was set for 11 am on 15 September. Shortly before the vote, according to Blankenhorn, the FDP deputy August-Martin Euler launched 'yet another brief blackmail attempt by trying to make the election dependent on the giving of the Finance Ministry to the FDP. Adenauer claims to be unavailable and does not receive him.'[21] The CDU/CSU delegation met at 9.30 am for further discussions concerning the Ministry of the Interior. When Blankenhorn called up the names of the deputies, three members were found to be absent. Adenauer argued for more efforts to win over the deputies from Schleswig and the Bayernpartei, but was vigorously opposed by Horlacher of the CSU.

The meeting broke up at 10.59 am, only a minute before the voting was due to begin. Adenauer received 202 votes, the absolute minimum he needed in order to become Chancellor. During the voting, Adenauer (who had voted for himself) sat with his old friend Robert Pferdmenges. When the result was known, he commented in his strong Cologne accent that things had 'always still turned out well'. Two members of the FDP had been absent for good reasons. Five members of his own party, it appeared, had either voted against him or abstained – and if anything, it was surprising that there were not more. The CSU was convinced that the crucial vote had been cast by Johann Wartner of the Bayernpartei.

After taking the oath of office, Adenauer celebrated briefly with his family in the Bundestag restaurant before hurrying back to a meeting of his caucus. At 3 pm that same day he had an unsatisfactory discussion with Heinemann, followed by further broad negotiations with the party. This process continued until nightfall before he returned with Blankenhorn to his home in Rhöndorf. During this period Adenauer was fulsome in his praise for his aide-de-camp Blankenhorn and insisted that he could never have become Chancellor without him. Yet Blankenhorn's work, Adenauer claimed, had only just begun: by relieving Adenauer of all inessential work and ensuring that he was properly looked after, he could keep the Chancellor fit for his job. On his return to Rhöndorf, Adenauer was welcomed by a torchlight procession before the arrival of Heinz Lubbers at 10 pm with important press matters for him to consider.

This hectic pace was maintained over the following weeks in the Museum Koenig, where the office of Federal Chancellor was set up on a temporary basis. The stuffed animals in the museum – some behind glass, others behind curtains – were a source of light relief to Adenauer and his team. However, the 'comédie humaine' in Bonn provided even better entertainment. In an atmosphere of political ambition, rumour, rancour and resentment, large numbers of deputies, civil servants, diplomats and corporate representatives were jockeying outside the offices of the Chancellor and his closest colleagues. Blankenhorn noted the fact in his diary: 'Numerous visits from people who want to be ministers and those who cannot be.'[22] The most important decisions, which would influence political developments for years to come, were still in the balance.

The struggle for the Ministry of Finance was finally won by Fritz Schäffer, a native of Munich who was now sixty-one years old. Though not a protégé of the Chancellor, he was a man after Adenauer's own heart. Schäffer was a political professional who had entered the Bavarian Landtag in 1920, had been chairman of the Bavarian People's Party between 1929 and 1933 and Bavarian Minister of Finance from 1931 to 1933. Like Adenauer, he had been swept up by the wave of arrests in Germany after 20 July 1944. In 1945 the Americans had appointed him minister-president in Bavaria, but removed him when the left-wing liberal press complained about the profound conservatism of his political outlook. Schäffer had been a co-founder of the CSU, but had left the party for a time following disagreements with Josef Müller. He had returned to the fold at precisely the right moment, in spring 1949, and now represented the constituency of Passau. Adenauer was convinced that Schäffer had helped to keep the restive CSU deputies within the CDU/CSU delegation following the election of Karl Arnold as president of the Bundesrat.

Adenauer had acquired a colleague with real political weight. Though Schäffer remained controversial even within his own party, he proved tenacious and effective in warding off various claims on the federal budget. Still, he was not always unthinkingly parsimonious and proved capable of recognising other obligations. Nahum Goldmann remembered Schäffer's key role in arranging restitution payments to Israel and the Jewish community as being difficult, but basically positive. Adenauer regarded Schäffer as a valuable buffer against all kinds of unwelcome spending claims, and thus as a man who could keep a check on the socially-committed wing of the CDU. Furthermore, his presence anchored the CSU in the cabinet. It was entirely characteristic of Adenauer that, whenever Schäffer opposed his own (always indispensable) projects, he would temporarily forget this high regard and describe his colleague as a mean-minded skinflint.

Apart from this success, the last stages of forming a government did not proceed as the new Chancellor had wished. Following his discussion with Heinemann, Adenauer was determined to appoint Robert Lehr as his Minister of the Interior. He had no desire to take Heinemann, a man from the Arnold wing of the party, into his cabinet. His doubts were actually increased by the strong support given to Heinemann from the party's Protestant wing, which he continued to find difficult to understand. The Protestant members of the parliamentary party were unanimously in favour of Heinemann and had begun to campaign actively in his support. In his attempts to ward off their pressure, Adenauer even called Robert Pferdmenges to Bonn to confirm that Heinemann had dubbed Adenauer a 'scoundrel' some six months before.[23] Such a man, he argued, must not be accepted into the cabinet.

Another discussion was arranged between Heinemann and Adenauer at which the former explained himself satisfactorily. Heinemann was appointed Minister of the Interior after all. According to Blankenhorn, Lehr was forced to 'retire from the fray disappointed'. Over the following months, Adenauer became convinced that his instinct about Heinemann had been correct, but not until autumn 1950 did he feel strong enough to dismiss a minister who had been forced on him by his party. Robert Lehr was then finally given the post he had coveted. Adenauer was well aware of his old colleague's strengths and weaknesses, but Lehr was at least predictable and had the added advantage of a much smaller personal power base in the party. Moreover, as the sardonic Otto Lenz noted, in cabinet Lehr could usually be relied upon to blow the Chancellor's trumpet.

Adenauer was similarly dissatisfied with the new Minister of Labour. He believed that the Christian trade unionist Anton Storch had, during his period as Director of Labour in Frankfurt, been too sympathetic to the idea of a unified national insurance system for workers and employees and the plans for a fundamental overhaul of the existing system, as demanded by the Social Democrats and trade unions. Adenauer had not forgotten this. Nor indeed had the FDP: on the evening of 19 September, the day before the submission of the 'statement of government policy', the FDP had even tried to make its participation in the coalition dependent on the omission of Storch.[24]

Adenauer would have preferred to take the energetic Theodor Blank into his cabinet. Blank had worked hard in Frankfurt to obtain the support of the trade-union wing of the CDU for Erhard's market economy. He was also a confident and assertive figure, telling Blankenhorn on 18 August that he was a better bet than the rest of the Christian trade unionists. In the end Adenauer decided to avoid a clash with the party's *Sozialausschüsse*. He appointed Storch, and contented himself with placing a watch-dog into the department in the person of State Secretary Maximilian Sauerborn of the CSU. Sauerborn was believed to have the 'necessary general confidence'[25] for the role and, unlike Storch, supported the retention of the existing system of national insurance. In the event, Storch did not distinguish himself in cabinet. However, he retained his post until 1957 owing to the lack of a convincing alternative from the trade-union camp.

Adenauer's third defeat came over the appointment of a Minister of Agriculture. His candidate was Karl Müller, an agriculture expert and former member of the Centre Party who had first met Adenauer when he was a city councillor in Cologne in 1919. The two men had also worked together after 1945. Müller had been a long-serving director of the Rhineland Chamber of Agriculture and, between 1947 and 1950, was Adenauer's deputy as chairman of the Düsseldorf Landtag *Fraktion*. Adenauer had already made several unsuccessful attempts to manoeuvre his old colleague into various posts. Now he informed his caucus that he wanted Müller in the cabinet.

Resistance to the appointment was led by the German Farmers' Association under its president, Andreas Hermes, though it is not clear whether Hermes was continuing to nurse political ambitions of his own. In the early stages of cabinet-building, the farmers' organisations tried to force Adenauer to accept Heinrich Lübke. Adenauer suspected that they had been encouraged by the SPD to take this step, since Lübke was regarded as sympathetic to the left. He refused to accept Lübke, particularly because of his controversial plans for agrarian reform.[26] In the final phase of building a government, he even contemplated offering the post to Andreas Hermes. However, Blankenhorn quickly informed him that Hermes should be ruled out because of his involvement with a group in Bad Godesberg which was too closely associated with Ambassador Nadolny, who was believed to be attempting to extend Soviet influence in the West.[27] As a result, Adenauer finally decided to approve the appointment of Wilhelm Niklas of the CSU, previously the deputy director of Agriculture in Frankfurt.

At this stage, he also fought hard to defeat attempts by Minister-President Ehard to place Anton Pfeiffer in the Federal Chancellor's office as State Secretary for International Affairs.[28]

By the time the cabinet posts were filled, Adenauer had very little time to work on the 'statement of government policy' which was to be made on 20 September. On 18 September he cheerfully told Blankenhorn that he would not complete it until the last minute, since ideas only came to him when he was under pressure of time.[29] He and his staff began to work seriously on the statement only at 3 pm on 19 September. After interruptions by further negotiations, he finished the draft that night. On the morning of 20 September some revisions were made, the list of cabinet ministers was typed out and approved by the Federal President at 10.30 am and, at noon, the first meeting of the new cabinet approved the main points of the declaration. Seven secretaries were drafted in to transform the twenty-five page draft into fair copy. The final pages were completed at 2.10 pm, when Adenauer had already begun to read the government statement in the Bundestag.

Even under the pressure of time, Adenauer had come up with little of note. Blankenhorn's subsequent assessment of the statement is valid: 'The statement was not a great success, it lacked any rhetorical brilliance. It was the speech of a man soberly listing the problems and tasks facing the newly constituted federal government.'[30] There were a few key phrases: the Federal Republic was the 'core German state'; its freedoms and responsibilities were to be extended 'step by step' in agreement with the Allied High Commission; 'for us there is no doubt that by our origins and ways of thinking we belong to the West European world!' Finally, Adenauer pleaded for an end to the centuries-old hostility between France and Germany and made some positive remarks about Britain and the United States.[31]

The speech was received with warm applause from his own ranks and polite clapping from the Opposition. Though none of his listeners could know that a long 'Adenauer era' had begun, all were aware that the new Federal Chancellor was a powerful and dominant personality. Assessments of him already differed widely. Even before Adenauer received hundreds of congratulatory letters following his election, he had heard from his old friend Dannie N. Heineman: 'You will surely do it. The very best of luck! Your age is not important; I am five years older than you. Do you still remember our conversation in the Berlin Kaiserhof, when you were offered the chancellorship and turned it down?'[32]

Immediately after Adenauer's election as Chancellor, Blankenhorn had noted: 'A great day in the life of a man who has twice already been cast down by fate from the height of power.'[33]

Yet already his friends were outnumbered by enemies, jealous rivals and politicians suffering from wounded pride. Among them was Hermann Pünder, who kept among his papers a diary entry made by an acquaintance in 1948: 'Yesterday dinner at Streng's. Great palaver about Adenauer. I don't know what so many people have got against Adenauer.

I have probably known him longest and best. He is more unreliable than a Frenchman, more mendacious than an Englishman and more devious than a Russian – making him the obvious statesman for our beaten and maltreated people!'[34]

The Political Tableau during Bonn's Early Days

Contemporaries and historians have generally agreed that the first four years of Adenauer's chancellorship were the most important of his time in government. Phrases such as 'laying the foundations', 'setting the course' and 'founding years of the republic' have frequently been used to describe these early years. Though at the time it was generally recognised that the situation facing him was complex and fraught with difficulties, this fact is often forgotten in retrospect. Adenauer's fourteen-year chancellorship remains a source of considerable fascination, also for historians. One consequence has been a tendency to exaggerate Adenauer's prospects for success in 1949 and to underestimate the problems he faced. In fact, in autumn 1949 failure seemed rather more likely than success.

Adenauer's age itself led many observers to assume that he would be no more than a transitional figure. In the early days this fact helped him. During the formation of his government, opponents and rivals were able to console themselves with the thought that time would soon eliminate an old man who had been under stress for years and was now on an exhausting political treadmill.

His success in creating an anti-socialist coalition clearly gave Adenauer an opportunity to consolidate his position. Nevertheless, even at the best of times, political leaders must sail in uncharted waters and remain vulnerable to sudden storms; this was even more true of the Chancellor of a new republic at a time of international instability and an uncertain domestic scene.

The parliamentary opposition facing Adenauer should not be underestimated. Adenauer had wanted the SPD to become the official Opposition. Though this reflected his own political convictions, his constitutional justification was rational and considered: 'In the delicate conditions that prevail in Germany, it is much better if the opposition is clearly present in parliament rather than gaining ground in an uncontrollable manner outside parliament if a grand coalition had made significant opposition

Notes for this section begin on page 723.

within parliament impossible.'[1] He got this opposition in full measure from the SPD under the determined leadership of Kurt Schumacher. The Social Democrat leader understood the political climate in which Adenauer had to operate. In its efforts to get the country back on its feet, the federal government would be forced to make highly unpopular decisions. Any economic setback might bring about its downfall; even if recovery was sustained, conditions for large sections of the population would remain so appalling that the Opposition would be bound to prosper.

Furthermore, the Chancellor was in a difficult position as regards his relations with the Western Powers. Though they had replaced their Military Governors with High Commissioners based in a large hotel mansion atop the nearby Petersberg, none of the Western Powers – neither the British nor the Americans, and certainly not the French – was prepared to allow the federal government too much autonomy. The Chancellor was thus placed in an extremely awkward situation in which mistakes were virtually inevitable. If he proved too accommodating to the wishes of the Allies and thereby avoided a risky policy of confrontation, it would be easy for the Opposition to dismiss him as the puppet of the High Commissioners. There was thus a particular force behind Schumacher's criticism of Adenauer during the heat of parliamentary battle: 'The Federal Chancellor of the Allies'.

On the other hand, if Adenauer were to mount an effective and public campaign against the Western Powers, as he had often done against the British in the British Zone, then the occupiers would soon cease to support him. It was no secret that the Americans were fickle and unreliable even though they were currently providing him with strong support.

Bevin, the British Foreign Minister, was currently following the U.S. lead, but only because British interests coincided with those of the U.S. It was common knowledge that the Labour government took a sceptical view of the market economy experiment in the Federal Republic. As far as the French were concerned, it was unlikely that Paris would sit tight if the West German government took a stand against the negative aspects of French policy.

Adenauer was well aware of this dilemma. At the same time, however, he was pleased to note that Schumacher's relations with the Western Allies had deteriorated significantly. Though the Allies might be dissatisfied with the Chancellor to varying degrees, none – not even the British – wanted to see him replaced by Schumacher. The French regarded Schumacher as an extreme Prussian nationalist, and Adenauer himself took every opportunity to denigrate his rival during discussions with the Allies. The U.S. Secretary of State, Dean Acheson, was astounded by the assertiveness of Schumacher's criticisms during Acheson's visit to Bonn in November 1949. Sure, the Western Allies still continued to feel a strong degree of personal respect for Schumacher's personal courage and his record of persecution during the Third Reich. He was also a very sick man. When the Bundestag met for the first time, he had to be carried into the assembly hall. Blankenhorn noted in his diary: 'Stood out, for me, because of his nervous tension. Seriously ill man who will probably not live much longer.' [2] In fact, Schumacher recovered from this crisis. As time passed, he also developed a more suitable tone in his dealings with the Allies and the Chancellor. His reputation as an incorrigible nationalist, however, continued to be a political burden to him.

Once again Schumacher's personality prevented Adenauer's opponents from developing a concrete alternative to his rule. By being simultaneously excessively nationalist, frighteningly socialist and annoyingly anti-Catholic, he repelled all those groups in the government coalition which resented Adenauer's authority. Karl Arnold and his supporters would have been glad to form a coalition with the Social Democrats at the first opportunity, but it was impossible for them, as devout Catholics, to make common cause with a man who constantly disparaged their church. Moreover, Arnold was a passionate supporter of the European Movement and had a healthy distrust of nationalism. On this point, too, there was a wide gap between him and Schumacher.

In the eyes of others, the major obstacle to any alliance was Schumacher's socialism. The north-German wing of the CDU, the FDP and the DP all contained a number of politicians who thought that Adenauer's committed European policy was going too far; several of them doubted whether the Chancellor was really serious about reunification. As a result, they had some sympathy for Schumacher's criticism of Adenauer on the subject. Economically and socially, however, the nationalist-conservative groups within the government coalition were to the right of Adenauer, whose position as coalition leader forced him to steer a moderate course irrespective of his own convictions. For them, Schumacher's socialism stood in the way of cooperation with the Social Democrats on the national question. Though moderate Social Democrats privately maintained that Schumacher's anti-capitalist rhetoric was largely for effect, no-one could be certain this was true. As long as Schumacher remained leader of the Opposition, there could be no prospect of a grand coalition – unless Adenauer himself decided in favour of it. In the great debates of the first Bundestag, Schumacher repeatedly drove the half-hearted and discontented members of the coalition back to the Adenauer camp. The Social Democrats would have been much more attractive to them with Ernst Reuter or Carlo Schmid as leader. As things stood, Adenauer's position could be threatened only by a change of Opposition leader or the decision of the coalition to unite behind another Chancellor from within its own ranks.

In fact, Adenauer never allowed a rebellion to develop within the CDU. Nor was there any convincing leader to lead one. Discontent within the CDU never progressed beyond conspiratorial conversations – and without those, Bonn would not have been Bonn. These discussions frequently centred on the former Reich Chancellor, Heinrich Brüning. In the crucial years, he was away from the centre of events at Harvard University's Lowell House. In summer 1948 Brüning spent a few weeks in the Western Zones, and returned for thee months in spring 1950. From early 1952, however, he spent three years as professor of Political Science at Cologne University. During this period his attitude towards Adenauer changed from positive expectation to disappointed rejection.

In 1948 Günther Gereke had already approached Brüning to urge him to place himself at the head of a group within the party that would oppose Adenauer. The two men had been associated since Gereke's days as a Reichstag deputy for the Christian-National Farmers' and Country People's Party. Brüning refused to take the bait, as he did when Gottfried Treviranus made a similar appeal shortly afterwards.[3] Adenauer – Gereke knew – could only be brought down by a powerful and determined opponent.

In fact, Brüning was at first sympathetic to Adenauer's approach. Even in November 1949 he wrote to Hermann Pünder, who had already recovered from his own political disappointment:

> I regard Adenauer as best suited for the post he has, because of his temperament, his gift for handling people and tactical skill – also because he can rule and he can put up with a great deal of hype for himself by his apparatus. (The journalists here report that people in Germany see him as equal to Bismarck and as the man who is completing the work that defeated Stresemann.) Today, especially in their effect here, such strong words are necessary to awaken interest in a man if he can withstand it. But that does not last. What is important then is that he does not lose the measure of things ...[4]

To his sister he wrote at the same time:

> Adenauer is the only man who is up to the situation, in so far as anything can be achieved at all.[5]

However, after the summer of 1949 his correspondence with various German observers reveals that he was developing a number of reservations. Adenauer's policy towards France and Europe seemed to be moving too quickly for Brüning, who was also unsettled by the Chancellor's reference, in August 1949, to the possibility of a 'lasting division' of Germany.[6] In June 1950 the two men met in Rhöndorf, but the meeting only served to reveal deep suspicions on both sides and to mark the beginning of the rift between them. Adenauer was annoyed by Brüning's travels throughout the country in the spring of that year and by his contacts with senior CDU politicians, and wanted to know whether Brüning was planning to return to active politics. After a few sharp comments about two CDU politicians, he asked Brüning directly when he would be leaving the country.[7]

From then on, Brüning wrote a flood of letters criticising virtually everything Adenauer did – his handling of the Schuman Plan, German policy towards the Saar, his insistence on the rearmament issue, the unwillingness to contemplate a long-term agreement with the Soviet Union. He shared his doubts and reservations with a number of CDU members, including Friedrich Holzapfel, Hermann Pünder, Jakob Kaiser, his state secretary Thedieck in the Ministry for All-German Affairs, Heinrich Krone, Gerd Bucerius and Heinrich Vockel. Brüning also contacted President Heuss and Paul Sethe of the *Frankfurter Allgemeine Zeitung*. His negative assessments became more frequent: 'I have slowly become accustomed to the knowledge that Bonn misses no opportunity for committing a stupidity ... The Chancellor lacks any world-political and military perspective ...'[8] ; 'The Chancellor is living in a world of illusion – even worse than Stresemann did.'[9] Brüning now claimed to see him as no more than a 'nimble day-to-day tactician'.

Closer examination of Brüning's long letters criticising Adenauer's foreign policy reveals that wounded pride had affected his judgement. Adenauer refused to accept his advice. He was quick to recognise that Brüning was stirring up trouble behind the scenes. After 1951, and especially following his return to Germany in 1952, Brüning played the same role in the discussions of discontented CDU politicians that he had in 1948 when Gereke approached him: perhaps he might provide a credible alternative to Adenauer as Chancellor.

However, the objections to Brüning also remained as strong as before. He had no aptitude for political in-fighting; he was physically far from robust; and he had lost touch with political developments both at home and abroad. Realistically, he was never more than a theoretical alternative. In order to become a serious candidate he would have needed to oppose Adenauer openly, get himself elected to the Bundestag, and forge his own power-base within the CDU. Instead he chose to give academic lectures in Cologne on the Weimar Republic, and to wait for others to provide him with an opportunity. This approach was no threat to a man like Adenauer.

Friedrich Holzapfel was another possible leader of the disaffected groups within the party. However, Adenauer had already ensured that he could not become leader of the parliamentary party in the Bundestag. He was also, like Schlange-Schöningen, a Protestant and a former member of the right-wing DNVP, which was a great handicap to his position with the CDU rank-and-file, the majority of whom were Catholics.

Another potential leader of opposition to Adenauer, Jakob Kaiser, was recognised by politicians and journalists alike as a much less credible Chancellor. Moreover, Kaiser believed in cabinet discipline and the avoidance of open dissent, and was never a real alternative. Nor would he have been acceptable to the FDP and DP, whose support would be essential for the success of any conspiracy.

The same was true of Karl Arnold, who did not even have a seat in the Bundestag. Heinrich von Brentano, the chairman of the CDU/CSU caucus in the Bundestag, might have been a man around whom the divergent groups could unite, but he too was regarded as much less capable than Adenauer. Even if he had been willing to lead an open rebellion – which he was not – he was not a credible Chancellor.

Adenauer was well aware of the identity of the would-be conspirators. He had not forgotten events during the formation of the government in 1949. In autumn 1950, he gave Holzapfel another chance to join the cabinet as Minister of the Interior. At that point Adenauer felt politically weak; he wanted to bring a potentially dangerous rival into the cabinet, where Holzapfel would be bound by the principles of cabinet discipline. But Holzapfel refused. Thereafter, Adenauer could argue that Holzapfel had been insufficiently confident of his abilities to accept the post of Minister of the Interior, let alone be a potential alternative Chancellor. In 1952 this potential rival was pushed to the sidelines as ambassador to Switzerland.

Hans Schlange-Schöningen had already been appointed General-Consul in London at the end of 1950 and had resigned from the Bundestag. Andreas Hermes, who was dissatisfied with Adenauer's political approach to the national question and certainly had the strength of character necessary for resistance, had found a more rewarding task rebuilding German and European agricultural organisations. He was also excluded from consideration because he was not even a member of the Bundestag. Werner Hilpert had resigned from the Bundestag in autumn 1949 when he recognised that he could not achieve his objectives. In summer 1950, after the Landtag election in North Rhine-Westphalia, Adenauer also made an unsuccessful attempt to increase pressure on Karl Arnold. He did have the satisfaction of having the failed conspirator Günther Gereke expelled from the CDU in summer 1950 because he had begun to flirt with East German politicians.

In reality, Adenauer's position in the CDU was never so precarious that the discussion of alternatives was likely to produce concrete results. Even politicians who chafed under the personal and political control of the Chancellor were forced to recognise that all rebellions would be unsuccessful as long as Adenauer remained healthy and avoided political disasters.

The other coalition partners were also aware of this fact. No major unrest was to be expected from the CSU. Despite its poor showing in the federal election, the party had been given two vital ministries in the shape of the Finance Ministry and the Ministry of Agriculture, in addition to the Federal Post Ministry. Furthermore, continuing turmoil in Bavarian politics ensured that the CSU remained preoccupied with its own affairs.

The FDP was in a different position. During Adenauer's first four years as Chancellor, the party had to accept a number of unpalatable decisions. These included the right of co-determination for workers in the coal and steel industry; the General Treaty with the Western Allies; Adenauer's European policy, about which many FDP politicians remained sceptical; a general failure to take account of its wishes; and inadequate information about the Chancellor's most important plans in foreign policy. However, the party had no real alternative to supporting Adenauer. On sober reflection, its leaders believed that bourgeois interests would be best served by an alliance with him. There was nobody in the CDU and CSU who would dare join it in toppling the Chancellor. The only man who might have been prepared to act was Karl Arnold – and he, as a supporter of cooperation with the SPD, was unacceptable to the FDP. Moreover, the dominant figure in the FDP, Theodor Heuss, admired Adenauer despite the official distance between President and Chancellor. Like the CSU, the FDP was preoccupied with internal affairs. Its struggles included liberals against national-liberals, nationalists and former National Socialists, south Germans against north Germans, pro-Adenauer groups against those hostile to the Chancellor. These heterogeneous elements were incapable of creating a force which could attract disaffected members of the CDU.

The chairman of the FDP, Franz Blücher, played a vital role in this situation. Blücher had hoped to move eventually from his post as Vice-Chancellor and Minister for the Marshall Plan into the key Foreign Ministry. When it became clear that he could not succeed, he was so greatly weakened within his own party that he was forced to cling to Adenauer in order to protect his position as chairman of the FDP. Prospects for rebellion were thus further diminished.

Particularly during the first three years of his chancellorship, Adenauer was forced to take account of all these currents in the party system. His life was complicated by political opponents, critical colleagues within his own party, and perennially dissatisfied coalition partners. At the same time, however, he could rely on support from other, equally powerful, groups and individuals. Moreover, Adenauer was at the centre of events, able and willing to use every available means – including the various powers of government – to achieve his objectives.

Support for Adenauer was provided by four main camps. The first group included the early Christian Democrats, whose aim was the renewal of the country on the basis of what they regarded as the spirit of the Occident; second there were the supporters of the market economy as the engine of recovery; the third group included the advocates of European union; the fourth and final group was composed of the many forces motivated by hatred and fear of the Soviets; their great objective was to force the Soviet Union and Poland out of the Eastern Zone and the lost territories in the East.

Some of Adenauer's greatest opponents and critics have accused him of being little more than the Machiavellian representative of the West German bourgeoisie. However, this view is certainly based on an underestimation of the strength of the Christian-democratic movement in his politics. The movement was always heterogeneous. It contained socialist, conservative and liberal groups, Catholics and Protestants, devout church-going Christians and others with only a general commitment to Christian-humanist values. It is equally true that the Christian-democratic core was at its strongest in the early years of the CDU. Nevertheless, the strength of Christian forces remained a crucial factor in Adenauer's chancellorship until well into the 1950s.

Adenauer himself represented the strong Catholic element in the new federal government. However, he omitted to place a highly visible conservative Protestant presence in his cabinet at an early stage, and regarded Gustav Heinemann, who was eventually forced on him by the CDU/CSU caucus, as a pernicious influence. The significance of this potential political weakness among Protestants was reduced by the support of a key group of parliamentary deputies, who bound the Protestant camp to Adenauer despite their lack in influence on his foreign policy. Public support for Adenauer's policies in Protestant circles was provided by Hermann Ehlers, Eugen Gerstenmeier, Robert Tillmanns, Gerhard Schröder and numerous backbenchers. He could also count on the discreet but important assistance of Lutherans in the regional Protestant churches. Not least among them was Bishop Dibelius, a member of the CDU who, along with Bishop Hans Lilje, had for a while been considered as a potential federal president by the CDU/CSU caucus.

In the early days, the convinced 'Europeans' among Adenauer's supporters were also poorly represented in the cabinet and in the CDU/CSU caucus as a whole. When Adenauer briefly became chairman of this group after the Bundestag election, he still had no reliable team to support him in disputes within this body. This situation quickly changed, partly because of the arrival of a number of younger deputies who were enthusiastic about the European idea.

The highest-ranking of these enthusiasts was Heinrich von Brentano, who had been a lawyer in Hesse and had risen to prominence in the main committee of the Parliamentary Council. Initially he kept a certain distance from Adenauer, possibly for tactical reasons. Indeed, his resolute stand towards the powerful older man so pleased the CDU/CSU *Fraktion* that it elected him chairman following Adenauer's election to the Chancellorship. Brentano was still infected with the 'Hessian virus' and was careful to take account of the political background from which he came. However, his family origins – von Brentano di Tremezzo – led him to regard himself as a European; in 1950 he joined the Assembly of the Council of Europe and returned from its gatherings an ardent European federalist. His efforts to influence European politics in Strasbourg meant that he was often absent from the Bundestag. The party whip, Heinrich Krone, was forced to take temporary responsibility for much of the chairman's work.

Meanwhile, Brentano's contacts with European politicians produced a lasting change in his approach to Adenauer's policy. Despite several occasions when he rebelled against the Chancellor, especially when Adenauer ignored him and his long letters, he was to become a loyal supporter of Adenauer. This positive relationship was maintained until the formation of a new government in 1961, when Brentano was disappointed by what he regarded as Adenauer's lack of resolve in negotiations with the other parties over the Foreign Ministry.

Within the party, Eugen Gerstenmeier occupied a position similar to Brentano. His background was one of the most interesting of all the younger CDU politicians (Gerstenmeier was still only forty-three years old in 1949). Coming from humble background in Swabia, he had qualified as a Protestant theologian in Rostock in 1937 but had been refused permission to teach by the Nazis. Even at this stage he was already renowned for his remarkable obstinacy and his boundless energy. The first of these aroused particular displeasure in the Third Reich, and was later to be a continuing source of exasperation to Adenauer. With the consent of the Foreign Ministry, Gerstenmeier had undertaken various missions abroad on behalf of his church before the war, and had established contacts with influential Protestants in other countries. His fascination with foreign policy, his many links abroad and his language skills all dated from this period.

Gerstenmeier was a member of the opposition 'Kreisau Circle' from 1942. After the failure of the 20 July 1944 plot he had been arrested and sentenced to seven years imprisonment, but was liberated by the Americans at the end of the war. He immediately devoted his energies to building up the Evangelisches Hilfswerk (Evangelical Relief Organisation) and acted as its leader until 1951. In 1949, when he campaigned for election to the Bundestag in the constituency of Backnang-Schwäbisch Hall, the Hilfswerk was already a vast organisation with many contacts in other Western countries.

Gerstenmeier quickly became involved in European politics. In summer 1950 he was a member of the first parliamentary group to attend the Council of Europe in Strasbourg, where he stirred up as much commotion as in Bonn. From Adenauer's point of view, Gerstenmeier was very useful: first as a thoroughly conservative Protestant who was respected both at home and abroad, and second as an enthusiastic European capable of undertaking a range of missions, including confidential ones. At the same time, Gerstenmeier came to prominence within the CDU/CSU *Fraktion* as an expert in foreign affairs. Adenauer's esteem was further enhanced by Gerstenmeier's co-ownership of the weekly paper *Christ und Welt,* which was influential in Protestant circles.

Adenauer, Gerstenmeier was convinced, sought to use him primarily because of his 'political usefulness'. Their personal relationship remained cautious and detached. Years after their first meeting, Gerstenmeier believed, 'he had not realised that I am an ordained minister. He regarded me as a church functionary in a significant position, as a manager who made life more difficult by being an intellectual as well. My past in the resistance – that was my lasting impression – counted little or nothing with him.'[10] His roots in the resistance ensured that Gerstenmeier had much in common both with Jakob Kaiser and with many Social Democrats. Politically he was very difficult to classify. Equally, as Adenauer soon became aware, he was never afraid to speak his mind. Gerstenmeier's attitude towards Adenauer was respectful but self-confident, akin to that of a respected priest in conversation with an influential member of his parish. Nevertheless, until he became president of the Bundestag after the death of Hermann Ehlers in 1954, Gerstenmeier was one of the most effective parliamentary supporters of Adenauer's European policy.

The same can also be said of Kurt Georg Kiesinger, a forty-five year-old lawyer and honorary CDU secretary of Württemberg-Hohenzollern. Immediately upon arrival as a Bundestag deputy, he had clashed with Adenauer at the first meeting of the parliamentary party. He was annoyed when Adenauer tried to cut his speech short, made a biting remark about Heuss – 'a lovable relic of the nineteenth century'[11] – which Adenauer took personally, and claimed to be baffled by the CDU's failure to engage in exploratory discussions with the SPD over the presidency. Kiesinger was careful to nurse his own links with the SPD, especially with his fellow Swabian Carlo Schmid and with Fritz Erler. His background, like that of Adenauer himself, was in the Catholic student fraternities, in his case in KV Askania. In 1929, his association had held a dinner at which Adenauer had been guest of honour in his capacity as President of the Prussian State Council.[12]

Kiesinger came to the Bundestag with the reputation of being an excellent lawyer. During the Third Reich, 'the master' was regarded as the best private tutor of law students preparing for their examinations in Berlin. He had spent the war years in the Foreign Ministry, working mainly on foreign propaganda. Though his membership of the NSDAP proved to be a significant handicap in post-war politics, especially after 1950, he made steady progress within the CDU/CSU *Fraktion*. Adenauer did not hold their early quarrel against him and regarded him as one of the party's rising talents. During this period, the Chancellor revealed an ability to tame younger, sometimes unruly talents by giving them tasks which achieved political results whilst simultaneously enhancing their own political ambitions. Gerhard Schröder and Franz Josef Strauss were two more politicians to follow this path.

When the federal CDU was founded in Goslar in 1950, Adenauer hoped to make Kiesinger general secretary and a member of the managing executive. Kiesinger had by now achieved prominence because his brilliant speeches in the Bundestag and his passionate support of the European ideal in the Strasbourg Assembly. However, he was attacked by the Berlin CDU on the grounds of his past membership of the NSDAP. The results of the election in the party committee were so poor that Kiesinger withdrew. Despite many disappointments and occasional disputes between the two men, he remained a committed supporter of Adenauer. His gift of oration and his European connections made him, like Gerstenmeier, an important representative of his Chancellor among European Christian Democrats and an influential supporter in domestic politics.

In the early years of Adenauer's chancellorship, another committed supporter of Adenauer's European policy was Franz Josef Strauss, whose importance was increased by his power-base in Bavaria as general secretary of the CSU. Thanks to his position in the CSU, Strauss remained more independent of the Chancellor than Gerstenmeier, Kiesinger or Schröder. Adenauer admired his talents, but made it clear to his political intimates that this respect was tinged with fear. Still, Strauss did not dispute the description of him as an Adenauer man.

Gerstenmeier, Kiesinger, Strauss – their importance in supporting the Chancellor's approach in the Bundestag, among the general public and abroad, was considerable. They and their less influential colleagues – including Hermann Pünder – shared Adenauer's conviction that the European idea was the key to most of the apparently insuperable problems of German foreign policy. They helped to push the entire CDU towards a pro-European stance; with their assistance Adenauer was able to make the CDU into the great party of Europe. Moreover, with the help of the European Union and European journalism, the party's approach over the years became the policy of the Federal Republic.

Europe was the great hope of the 1950s – and hope is a most powerful driving-force in politics. The word 'Europe' stood for partnership with the West European democracies, for equal rights, for new security in the international community, for a peaceful future and, not least, for a modern foreign policy. The concept of modernity was also useful in convincing voters, ensuring victory and immunising the coalition and the Chancellor against sterile criticism.

The economic liberals were another group to provide reliable support for Adenauer's chancellorship. Unlike the Europeans, whose power became fully apparent only after 1950, this group had played a vital role during Adenauer's political breakthrough. The federal election of 1949 was an Erhard election. During the political ups and downs of the years 1949-1953, moreover, Adenauer could always rely on this pillar of his anti-socialist coalition.

This was the group that contained the business wing of the CDU associated with Ludwig Erhard, Robert Pferdmenges, Günter Henle, Fritz Hellwig and Gerd Bucerius. Moreover, the idea of the market economy was also the powerful cement in the coalition between the CDU and FDP. Both parties' election campaigns were funded to a large extent by private business, with Robert Pferdmenges playing a key role. The BDI (League of German Industry) under Fritz Berg, the German Chamber of Industry and Commerce, companies and banks – despite occasional criticisms – all of them recognised that Adenauer was their man.

Adenauer himself was content to be associated with this camp. However, he was always keen to make essential compromises with those who advocated improved social welfare and the wishes of the German Trade Union Federation. As far as private business was concerned, he insisted on the primacy of politics. Sectional interests and individual desires, he constantly emphasised, must be subordinated to the requirements of overall social and economic policy. Adenauer was no doctrinaire laissez-faire liberal, but just as within four years he succeeded in transforming the CDU into the party of Europe, he also managed to infuse first it, and then the country as a whole, with the spirit of the market economy.

The market-economy wing of the CDU was blessed with an outstanding political figure – Ludwig Erhard – and a number of *éminences grises* who operated away from the spotlight to great effect. These included Robert Pferdmenges, Hermann Josef Abs, and a group of parliamentarians with claims to expertise in various sectors of the economy.

However, Adenauer was somewhat disconcerted to find that industry initially turned predominantly to the FDP, or chose to make its demands without showing genuine interest in his party. Shortly before the federal election of 1949 he wrote to Franz Etzel: 'It is clear that the industrialists have turned themselves to the CDU too late. Herr Henle and you … have been accepted straight away because your activity in the party is widely known.'[13] Henle was indeed an influential supporter of Adenauer to rank with Pferdmenges, Etzel and Abs.

Günter Henle, head of the Klöckner trust, was a member of the inner circle of industry on the Rhine and Ruhr whose father-in-law, Peter Klöckner, belonged to the famous Ruhrlade group of the Weimar days. Adenauer had many contacts with the Klöckner trust dating from the period when Peter Klöckner was one of the most powerful supporters of the industrial wing of the Rhenish Centre Party. Originally a diplomat, Henle had taken over as head of the Klöckner concern when his father-in-law died early in the war, only to be dismissed a little later by Gauleiter Josef Terboven. In the end, this was to be very much to his advantage: after the war, he was one of the first Ruhr industrialists to be allowed to resume work. Henle had been involved with the CDU *Fraktion* on the Frankfurt Economic Council before being elected to the first German Bundestag. In the difficult negotiations over decartelisation, the founding of the European Coal and Steel Community, and the co-determination issue with the trade unions he was indispensable to Adenauer.

His influence in industry, as well as his reputation abroad and in the CDU itself, ensured him considerable influence. Like Franz Etzel, Henle was also able to provide effective representation for the CDU in the organisations of the Coal and Steel Community.

Another parliamentarian who was then part of the Adenauer wing of the CDU was Gerhard Schröder. An industrial lawyer, Schröder had been legal adviser, since 1947, to the trustees appointed by the Allies to reorganise the coal and steel industry. Like Franz Josef Strauss and Theodor Blank, he was a member of the war generation, and was also a committed representative of the Protestant wing of the party. Adenauer had known him since his rise to prominence in North Rhine-Westphalia after the war.

The elegant Schröder was a man after Adenauer's own heart: a skilful tactician, always well briefed, and a determined supporter of the anti-socialist coalition. He also proved to be a headstrong individual who refused to toady to his party leader. As long as such conduct remained within acceptable limits and did not threaten his own position, Adenauer was quite prepared to tolerate it. Most rising politicians, however, found it very difficult to find a happy medium in their dealings with Adenauer. The Chancellor tended to despise men who did not dare contradict him and prove they had minds of their own, and refused them high office. Others, whose opposition was deemed to be too strong, suffered precisely the same fate. By 1951, however, Schröder had already joined the executive of the *Fraktion,* where he joined Franz Josef Strauss and Johannes Albers in the inner circle of the Adenauer coalition.

One of the most articulate advocates of the market economy in Adenauer's camp was Gerd Bucerius of Hamburg, who had already earned Adenauer's respect for his work as a delegate to the Frankfurt Economic Council. Bucerius was also useful because of his experience abroad. In spring 1950, when the Saar question was causing controversy as far away as the United States, Bucerius provided detailed and informative reports and also showed himself to be extremely well-briefed about opinion in London.

However, in Adenauer's view the most important role played by Bucerius was as a publisher who could provide him with media support. In these early years, *Die Zeit* gave almost unqualified support for Adenauer's Western policy and for the CDU/CSU-FDP coalition. From time to time, critical articles by Richard Tüngel aroused indignation in the French High Commission, while a nationalist tone (which later intensified) became apparent at an early date over the Saar question. Nevertheless, a paper like *Die Zeit* could write things that the Chancellor and his office only dared to think. Adenauer considered it a great advantage that *Die Zeit,* through Bucerius, and *Christ und Welt,* through Gerstenmeier, were indirectly linked to his government.

His relationship with Bucerius also revealed that Adenauer took a remarkably old-fashioned view of the press. During a row over an article by Paul Bourdin in spring 1953, for example, Adenauer clearly worked on the principle that a paper had to write whatever its publisher wanted. Since the publisher was a prominent member of the CDU/CSU *Fraktion* he was convinced that *Die Zeit* ought to support his own policy. He was extremely reluctant to accept the idea that a publisher could exert, at best, only a general control. Towards the end of the Adenauer era, this continuing conflict between the role of Bucerius as a publisher and his work as a CDU parliamentarian led to a rift between the two men. During the early years, however, Bucerius was one of the most reliable parliamentary supporters of Adenauer's policy.

Adenauer's adherents in the Bundestag did not consist entirely of supporters of the market economy. The position of Johannes Albers in the inner executive of the CDU/CSU *Fraktion,* for example, revealed that the left wing of the CDU was still a factor to be reckoned with. At this stage, the dispute was no longer about the fundamental nature of the economic order, but only about the complex issue of how far the market economy should be cushioned and made more acceptable through social policies. The problem led to several differences of opinion: on co-determination, the shape of the social-security system, and on the issues of import liberalisation and housing construction. However, fundamental dissension within the CDU, of the kind seen between 1945 and 1947 over the question of the best economic order, no longer existed.

Even the labour wing within the CDU now contained influential supporters of the market economy, led by Theodor Blank. From the outset, Blank was seen as a loyal supporter of Adenauer in the CDU/CSU *Fraktion.* The Chancellor had a high regard for Blank, who was a trade unionist from the executive of IG Bergbau. In many ways, his was a typical working-class success story of the period. Blank was the son of a worker and had risen to the position of secretary of his union; he had completed his secondary-school examination only at the age of thirty before becoming a student of engineering, and had spent six years with the Wehrmacht. In economic and social affairs, the assertive Blank was a committed supporter of the market economy, pro-European in foreign policy, and a resolute anti-Communist – a combination of qualities which made him particularly useful to Adenauer. Though the Chancellor was unable to appoint Blank as his Minister of Labour and Social Affairs as he had wished, he finally made him Defence Commissioner in October 1950.

In the early period of his chancellorship, Adenauer's support was least secure among those groups whose main objective was the reunification of Germany and the restoration of the lost territories in the east. The Berlin CDU members associated with Jakob Kaiser had temporarily made their peace with him and were prepared to offer loyal support, but only on condition that Adenauer supported their hard line on the 'German question'. This involved a constant demand for reunification and a revisionist policy towards Poland. The leading figures of the north-German CDU also doubted the strength of Adenauer's commitment to the national unity. However, they too promised to support him on condition that he accepted the objective of restoring the German Reich. Much the same approach was adopted by the largely national-liberal FDP and by the right-wing DP groups associated with Hans-Christoph Seebohm. Though these groups soon began to doubt whether Adenauer's reunification policy was as resolute as they had hoped, they did not break ranks.

There has been lasting, and sometimes bitter, controversy over the strength of Adenauer's commitment to reunification. In this context, however, it should be noted that even the groups who advocated a less patient and more risky approach than the Chancellor eventually decided to support and legitimise his policy. This was true of most of the expellees' associations and of the organisation of refugees from the Soviet Zone. In the disputes over rearmament it was also the approach adopted by the e-Servicemen's associations, which accepted that the existing government was the most reliable defender of their interests. The anti-Communist and revisionist forces were persuaded to toe the line by a combination of financial support and political education through such organisations as the Arbeitsgemeinschaft Demokratischer Kreise (Working Group of Democratic Circles). There could be no real doubt about the strength of Adenauer's own anti-Communism. His determination to force the Soviets out of the Eastern Zone, with the support of the Western Powers, was convincing. Ultimately he always managed to convince the sceptics that the dispute over reunification was not about the goal, but only about the timing and methods to be adopted. At crucial moments – during Bundestag debates and at elections – the strongly patriotic elements in the bourgeois camp and at least part of the expellees came out in support of Adenauer.

Unlike most CDU politicians after 1945, Adenauer always recognised that his policies could succeed only if he managed to forge an alliance of very disparate forces. This was the reason for his courtship of the liberal and nationalist groups in North Rhine-Westphalia and northern Germany. It was also the cause of his constant willingness to make written and public demands for the return of the expellees to their former homelands. Adenauer fully shared the sense of injustice felt by the Germans driven from the east; he did not have to be convinced that Breslau and Königsberg were German cities. Only over the course of time did he come to accept the need for compromise on the territorial question.

Adenauer's patriotic sentiments were not unbridled. He knew that of all the groups around him, the nationalists were the most dangerous. An alliance with them was like riding on the back of a tiger, but he regarded the ride as both possible and necessary. It was significant that most of the Adenauer team which fought for his foreign policy in the first Bundestag were pro-Europeans and supporters of the market economy. However,

Jakob Kaiser, Ernst Lemmer and Linus Kather also played their part, as did the backbenchers from the expellees camp. Though they did not decide the overall direction of policy, they were sometimes able to force modifications. Of equal importance, these groups protected the government against attacks from the SPD, from Communist forces who were attempting to exploit nationalist slogans, and from the right-wing radicals.

Adenauer's Political Machine

Adenauer could not have held together the diverse elements in his coalition without his mastery of the government machine. In the new Federal Chancellor's office, the former mayor was once again in his element. He knew that he could not treat his ministers as he had treated his deputies in Cologne during the Weimar years. Nevertheless, a survey of his ministerial correspondence and the cabinet minutes of 1949 reveals that same remarkable combination of strategic thinking and attention to administrative detail, the same insatiable interest in documents and dispatches, for which he had been famous in Cologne.

His interest in personal politics never flagged. No state secretary was appointed without Adenauer taking part in the discussion and making the final decision. The only appointment which was made over his unsuccessful opposition was that of Franz Thedieck as state secretary in the Ministry for All-German Affairs. Adenauer feared that Thedieck, who was well known to him from his involvement in revisionist agitation for a return of German territories lost to Belgium in 1919, might damage his Saar policy and arouse distrust in the West.

In general, the smaller parties obtained very little influence at state-secretary level. Seven of the thirteen state secretaries in office in 1950 belonged to the CDU/CSU and only one to the DP; the others were not members of any party. In the departments where Adenauer had been unable to appoint ministers of his own choice, he placed state secretaries who could be relied upon to oppose their chiefs where necessary. Among them were Ritter von Lex, appointed to keep watch over Heinemann in the Ministry of the Interior, and Sauberborn, who performed the same function with Storch in the Ministry of Labour. In the same way, the liberal Thomas Dehler in the Ministry of Justice was 'supervised' by Walter Strauss, whose influence he never managed to shake off. In spring 1951, a state secretary – Ludger Westrick – was also appointed to Ludwig Erhard's department with the brief of improving relations with the Federal Chancellor's office and bringing administrative order to the Ministry for Economic Affairs.

However, most of the CDU state secretaries were experienced administrators rather than mere party bureaucrats. Many of them had valuable experience in the ministries to which they were appointed. Although Walter Strauss, who had been a member of the Parliamentary Council, was first and foremost a politician, even he had spent some time in the judiciary; after several clashes with Dehler, Strauss eventually came to terms with his role as a servant of the state.

Adenauer's interest was not restricted to the most senior posts. To his great irritation, many of the important positions at the senior civil-service level in the Frankfurt administration had been occupied by Social Democrats. This was one of the reasons behind his reluctance to transfer the Frankfurt administration to the federal ministries; he regarded the Frankfurt administrators as both ineffective and too left wing. A cabinet commission strongly influenced by the Ministry of the Interior was appointed to produce guidelines for the future development of organisation and personnel. The ministers agreed that all appointments and promotions from *Ministerialrat* upwards, as well as all first-time appointments from *Oberregierungsrat* upwards, should be approved by the cabinet at the suggestion of the minister concerned. This would give the Federal Chancellor's office the opportunity to influence a wide range of appointments. Large numbers of senior Frankfurt civil servants who belonged to the SPD were ruthlessly weeded out, and CDU members or sympathisers placed in many important positions.

Most of Adenauer's attention was devoted to the key ministries. The Federal Chancellor's office worked to place additional, politically 'reliable' civil servants in ministries which were under the control of members of his own party of whom Adenauer did not approve, such as Heinemann and Storch. Adenauer also managed to put trusted civil servants in the ERP (European Recovery Program) Ministry under Vice-Chancellor Blücher, which administered U.S. economic assistance and the Marshall Plan. His protracted disputes with Blücher over this issue caused the first strains in relations between the two men.

These developments were directed, in close association with Adenauer, mainly by *Ministerialdirektor* Hans Globke. By the time he was finally promoted state secretary on the formation of a new government in 1953, Globke had managed to shape many of the ministries according to his master's will. In fact, Globke was one of the key figures in Adenauer's chancellorship, and his role reflected the basic personal and political convictions by which Adenauer operated. Ever since the winter of 1949/50, Adenauer and Blankenhorn had discussed the principles and personnel on which the new federal government would be based. In the Frankfurt central authorities, it had been a matter of principle not to employ any former

Reich civil servants who had also been members of the NSDAP. This had inevitably created a shortage of skilled candidates. In consequence, applicants had been drawn from the liberal professions, a move which had also made it easier for party-political appointments to be made. This had been one of the reasons for the notorious inefficiency of the Frankfurt administration. Adenauer was determined to restore a professional civil service which could assist the work of the federal government. During these months, his great worry was that the SPD might win an election victory. If this occurred, he was even prepared to consider a coalition with the SPD to prevent the federal bureaucracy from being filled with Social Democrats. For Adenauer, the issue was a major priority.

One great problem he faced was that almost all of the experienced civil servants had belonged to the Nazi Party. In such a situation, it was essential to conduct investigations to discover whether such membership had been active – which would disqualify candidates in future – or purely formal, which in principle made them eligible. Otherwise, like Kurt Schumacher for the Social Democrats, Adenauer was determined to appoint political sympathisers to the federal ministries. Since the civil service was traditionally conservative, he could expect political sympathies and specialist qualifications often to coincide. For senior posts, however, Adenauer deliberately sought out those relatively rare civil servants who were highly qualified, had not been members of the NSDAP, were not Social Democrats, and were either members of, or sympathetic to, the CDU. If the candidate was also a Catholic, so much the better, since Protestants had traditionally dominated the civil service at Reich Ministry level and it seemed reasonable to redress the balance.

Shortly before the foundation of the Federal Republic, Adenauer met Globke for the first time at the suggestion of Erich Kessler of the Bi-zone Audit Office, who was advising Adenauer on his personnel plans. Globke was then city treasurer in his native Aachen, but was eager to return to the national administration. Then in his early fifties, Globke came from a well-to-do middle-class family – his father had been a cloth wholesaler. He had worked in the Prussian Interior Ministry since 1929 and was then transferred to the Reich Ministry of the Interior, where he worked until 1945. Globke was a devout Catholic, a member of a Catholic CV fraternity and, between 1922 and 1933, had been a member of the Centre Party. During the Third Reich he had remained in his post at the request of his church. After the war, he was able to produce a host of affidavits to the effect that he had provided the church with a constant stream of important and confidential information. He had also been associated with the Catholic resistance in Berlin. After the war he had joined the new CDU.

Globke had never been a member of the NSDAP. Nevertheless, his reputation was tarnished in one absolutely crucial area: he had been largely responsible for writing the official commentary on the Nuremberg

Laws, the notorious race laws, of 1935. Globke's associates were convinced that he had worked to produce the least harsh interpretation for those affected by the laws, and he had also been able to offer his personal assistance to many partners in mixed marriages. The stain on his reputation, however, was permanent. The commentary had played a role in 1948, when Globke's appointment as head of personnel in the Düsseldorf Interior Ministry was postponed.

Globke had been investigated on various occasions after 1945. One of these investigations had been conducted by Robert Kempner, who showed no mercy in his judgements even of former colleagues. All of these analyses had produced results that were largely positive. Adenauer was well aware that all those who had been involved in the administration of a totalitarian state were tainted to some degree unless they had got out at the beginning. As a result, he did not believe that Globke's role in producing the commentary to the Nuremberg Laws should disbar him from public office.

Adenauer's detractors subsequently argued that he had appointed and protected Globke simply because it suited him to have a key subordinate who was entirely dependent on him for protection from the consequences of his past deeds. Though Adenauer was perfectly capable of devious conduct of this kind, in the case of Globke the argument is not convincing. Many civil servants in senior positions are likely to want to keep their posts, even at the price of unconditional loyalty to their superior. In this sense Globke's position was little different from that of other civil servants.

Globke himself advised a cautious approach. As a result, Adenauer postponed his appointment as state secretary, apparently out of concern for the possible repercussions of such a decision outside Germany. In December 1949 he wrote to Jakob Kaiser: 'I may further remind you that I have refrained from appointing vice-president Hans Globke as state secretary, refrained very reluctantly, because, though not a party member, he worked on the notorious commentary; in appointing state secretaries we must take great care not to provide material for any kind of attack.'[1] After some deliberation, he decided to let Globke do the work of a state secretary in the Ministry of the Interior though with the official rank of *Ministrialdirektor*. After 1950 the post state secretary was officially occupied by Otto Lenz. However, Lenz was happy to allow Globke, whom he had long known and admired, to continue to do most of the practical work.

Globke's understanding of people and situations, his discretion and diligence soon made him indispensable. 'Talk to Herr Globke ...' became Adenauer's stock response to requests and problems that were placed before him. From an early stage, Globke wielded influence in every federal ministry and even in the chancelleries of the various Länder. Despite the existence of a Bundesrat Ministry under Heinrich Hellwege,

Adenauer preferred to rely on Globke whenever he needed confidential handling of problems in his relations with Länder governments. These happened, in particular, when the coalition interests of regional CDU associations came into conflict with federal politics. As Richelieu had his Père Joseph, so Adenauer had his Globke – a man who kept in the background but knew everything and had a solution to every problem. Globke visited the Chancellor in his office two or three times each day, spoke with him frequently on a direct telephone line, and often went to Rhöndorf for discussions. Adenauer came to rely on the afternoon stroll the two men took in the park of Palais Schaumburg after he had awoken refreshed from his afternoon nap. Globke also attended many of Adenauer's discussions with his visitors, often as a silent witness.

Observers agreed that there was no question of friendship in the customary sense between the two men. Globke respected the barriers created by his official position and the age difference. The future state secretary Karl Gumbel, who had studied the two at close hand, noted: 'For his part Adenauer did nothing to meet him half-way. Both of them were wrapped up in their work.'[2]

By autumn 1949 it was clear that Globke could not be appointed state secretary, at least for the present. The resulting search for an individual to head the Federal Chancellor's office was not a simple one. Moreover, the choice always fell on men who were closely associated with Globke. Between October 1949 and February 1950 the job was taken, more or less on a trial basis, by the Bundestag delegate from Rhineland-palatinate, Franz-Josef Wuermeling, who had been friendly with Globke since the time they had worked together in the Prussian Interior Ministry. However, Wuermeling chose to return to his parliamentary responsibilities. The search for a head of the Chancellor's office continued until autumn 1950. The staff was still small, containing only nineteen officials in the senior service. Even in 1963, when Adenauer left office, there were only thirty-five, compared with 120 in 1978.

After a long search, Adenauer finally decided on Otto Lenz. After the departure of Lenz two-and-a-half years later, Globke was responsible to the Chancellor alone. In choosing Lenz, Adenauer drew into his inner circle a man from the opposing wing of the party. Otto Lenz had left the Reich Ministry of Justice in 1938. Subsequently, he had built up a private practice as a lawyer and had been a member of the resistance group associated with Carl Goerdeler and Jakob Kaiser. Like Gerstenmeier and Hermes, he had been sentenced to several years' imprisonment by the National Socialists and had been freed by the Soviets. Between 1945 and 1948 he had a legal practice in Berlin and became politically active there before moving to Munich in 1948 and working for Josef Müller's law firm. From Adenauer's standpoint, therefore, he was connected with two hostile camps – Jakob Kaiser's CDU and Müller's group in Munich.

Adenauer, who was in a difficult position in 1950, had good reasons for bringing Lenz to his side despite his political reservations. He needed more than a quiet and skilful administrator like Globke. Equally essential was a dynamic personality with ideas and the ability to translate them into action. Lenz was willing to fight every opponent of Adenauer's plans if that proved necessary, but he would also drink through the night with them in an attempt to change their minds.

The new state secretary played an important role in the negotiations over co-determination in the coal and steel industry, which enabled Adenauer to appease the unions for a time. He also worked to improve the neglected area of government publicity, built up the federal press and information office, established and financed organisations in the pre-political arena, channelled funds to the editors of pro-government weeklies, and intervened in the politics of various Länder. Tough, active and tenacious, Lenz also became involved on the international stage, in Paris, London and Washington. Adenauer soon trusted him to settle complex and difficult problems.

Lenz had been suggested for the role of state secretary by Globke. Both men had belonged to the 'Thursday Society' in Berlin during the Third Reich, a group of opposition-minded individuals from the Centre Party. As both were aware, they complemented each other. Without the need for any formalities, Globke dealt with much of the administrative work of a state secretary, leaving Lenz free to concentrate on grand policy.

One further member of the 'Thursday Society' was to appear at the centre of power and to obtain a growing influence over Adenauer. This was Heinrich Krone, a former deputy general secretary of the Centre Party and a leading figure in the pro-Republican paramilitary association, Reichsbanner Schwarz-Rot-Gold in the Weimar years. Krone had also had a hard time during the Third Reich, was one of the founder-members of the CDU in Berlin and had established influential political contacts in Bonn. While Brentano remained chairman of the CDU/CSU *Fraktion,* Krone played the role of the chief whip. Krone, Globke and Lenz developed a strong relationship of personal trust; to an increasing extent, Krone rather than Brentano acted as a channel for the transmission of information between the Federal Chancellor's office and the parliamentary party in the Bundestag.

In these early years, foreign policy continued to take up most of Adenauer's attention. As a result, Herbert Blankenhorn remained the most influential man in the Federal Chancellor's office. He was head of the central liaison office to the High Commission of the three occupying powers. In this office, which was established in September 1949, the major operations in foreign policy were prepared. Other departments concerned with foreign affairs were established alongside it. In Frankfurt, *Oberdirektor* Pünder had pressed in vain for the establishment of a 'Ministry of Inter-State Relations' immediately after the Federal Republic had been founded. Adenauer had opposed such an office because he suspected that Pünder would then lay claim to its leadership and expect to bring his own staff from Frankfurt to man it. He was therefore relieved by the proposal of the minister-presidents, supported by the SPD party executive, that foreign affairs should initially be concentrated in the Federal Chancellor's office.

By May 1950 enough groundwork had been completed for the various offices to be amalgamated into an 'Office for Foreign Affairs'. Blankenhorn was made *Ministerialdirektor* and charged with the task of co-ordination, but he was not appointed as head of the Office. One reason for this was that, despite his respect for Blankenhorn, Adenauer was reluctant to appoint a diplomat from the old Wilhelmstraße (the former site of the German Foreign Ministry in Berlin) to head the new department. He was suspicious of the cameraderie which linked its members, and had noted the critical reaction in the press and among the Opposition to the fact that the first men he had appointed had been members of the NSDAP. Like the vast majority of men in the Wilhelmstraße, Blankenhorn had been a member of the Nazi Party. If he had been made state secretary in 1950, it would have set an undesirable precedent and made an unfavourable impression.

The way was thus open for Walter Hallstein, who was not a member of any political party. Hallstein was a law professor in Frankfurt and, from 1946 to 1948 rector, then visiting professor at Georgetown University in Washington. He had been proposed by Professor Röpke in Geneva as a suitable head for the German Schuman Plan delegation and had won respect for his abilities in that role. Hallstein was appointed state secretary of the Office in August 1950.

In most of the fundamental issues of foreign policy, however, Adenauer continued to rely predominantly on Blankenhorn. Hallstein was forced to devote almost a year to his work in Paris, leading the complicated negotiations first on the Schuman Plan and then on the Pleven Plan which formed the basis of the abortive European Defence Community. Department 2 – the old liaison office to the High Commission – also remained firmly under the control of Blankenhorn. Adenauer's calendar reveals that, between 1950 and 1952, he continued to consult Blankenhorn much more frequently than Hallstein on major issues of foreign policy. Reports of a decline in Blankenhorn's influence in 1950 can therefore be dismissed as journalistic flights of fancy.

The question is important partly because there were some differences between Hallstein and Blankenhorn on issues of foreign policy. Of course, they had much in common. Both of them shared Adenauer's conviction that Germany's only prospect of a successful future lay in close integration with Western Europe. Moreover, by 'Germany' both meant either the

German core state in the West or a reunited Germany. However, Blanken-horn was more pragmatic; he enjoyed finding solutions to complicated issues without being committed to any fixed concepts. Hallstein's approach was more formal and influenced by concepts of contract law and constitutional law. In short, where Blankenhorn saw force fields, Hallstein saw institutions and paragraphs. Blankenhorn's approach was undoubt-edly closer to that of Adenauer. Nevertheless, the lawyer's contribution was indispensable for the successful negotiation of a whole series of treaties between 1950 and 1957. Since these would determine Germany's future for decades, Hallstein knew that precise formulations were essen-tial if Germany was to regain its sovereignty and minimise the inevitable weakness in its relations with the Western Powers. For these reasons, it was better to enshrine as many decisions as possible in treaty form, thereby removing them from the reach of arbitrary political decisions.

Adenauer needed both men. Indeed, he recognised the benefits of hav-ing close collaborators whose temperament and ways of thinking were very different from his own. Though tensions were natural, they could be productive and could even help him to understand the full implications of complex issues. On practical matters, there was a division of labour between Hallstein and Blankenhorn. After 15 March 1951 Adenauer was Foreign Minister as well as Chancellor, but had much less time than a normal minister to resolve the teething problems of the infant foreign ser-vice. This became Hallstein's responsibility; he was *de facto* foreign min-ister, but without being responsible to the Bundestag. As in Imperial Germany, and to the regret of many Bundestag deputies, the Foreign Ministry was run by a civil servant for four years.

Adenauer was interested mainly in the great questions of political organisation and re-organisation. Here, alongside Blankenhorn, he relied on Hallstein, on Otto Lenz, sometimes on individual members of the Bundestag, and also on the advice of outsiders. Among the latter was the banker Hermann Josef Abs, whom he had hoped to appoint as state sec-retary in the Foreign Ministry before the arrival of Hallstein. In June 1950, Adenauer told Blankenhorn that Abs was one of the few truly 'international' Germans that he knew;[3] the quality, he thought, was par-ticularly rare in a people so dominated by mediocrities. However, the French were stubbornly opposed to the elevation of Abs to a senior offi-cial position and made vague references to the unfavourable public reac-tion it would produce. Abs therefore remained within the banking world, though he did undertake an important special mission for Adenauer when he negotiated the London Debt agreement on Germany's foreign debts.

During these years, the Federal Chancellor's office also contained the core of the future Federal Ministry of Defence. Where foreign relations were concerned, the Allies had not objected to the establishment of departments by the West German government. Issues of military security, however, continued to be forbidden territory to the Germans, making a cautious approach essential. Not until 24 May 1950 did Adenauer appoint the former tank general Count Gerhard von Schwerin as 'Adviser to the Federal Chancellor on Security Questions', after Michael Thomas had apparently worked behind the scenes to persuade the British government to accept it. General von Schwerin, who had served with 1st Infantry Regiment in Königsberg before the war, had been suggested as a potential candidate by Marion Countess Dönhoff, a journalist with *Die Zeit*. As we have already seen, Adenauer had a poor opinion of German generals but very little personal knowledge of them, making him dependent on recommendations from third parties. Many candidates were considered – including generals Speidel, Wenck, Gehlen, Baron Geyr zu Schweppenburg. Adenauer's reasons for selecting Schwerin are not clear, though it was rumoured that he had been recommended by the British High Commissioner, Robertson. Certainly, Schwerin's political reputation from the Nazi era was impeccable. His democratic credentials, which Adenauer regarded as vital, were beyond doubt. The Chancellor was also pleased by the fact that Schwerin's bearing was not intimidatingly military; Walter Henkel reported a remark made by the Chancellor after the first long discussion between the two men: 'That's not a soldier, that's a normal human being ...'[4]

In July 1950 the 'Büro Schwerin' was turned into a working staff bearing the cover name Zentrale für Heimatdienst (Central Office for Home Service). When Theodor Blank took responsibility for further planning in October 1950, the department – which had never been an official organisation – was dissolved. Schwerin was dismissed, along with a number of officers who had worked for him. The new Dienststelle Blank remained under the control of the Chancellor. In 1950 it contained some twenty employees, rising to seven hundred by January 1953. Blank had considerably more room for manoeuvre than Hallstein in the Foreign Ministry. Nevertheless, Adenauer kept all developments in the defence sphere under his own overall control for some years.

Like the CDU/CSU caucus and the FDP, the Chancellor was well aware of the significance of his decision to exercise personal control over the future Ministry of Defence. It enabled him to retain final responsibility for all questions connected with a West German defence contribution until May 1955, without the danger that the coalition would make trouble over his choice of Blank. Adenauer was not the defence minister – and could not be, given the restrictions imposed by the Allies. Nevertheless, whichever CDU politician he appointed had to follow Adenauer's instructions on major issues if he hoped to become minister in the full sense once the protracted period of planning and negotiation was complete.

From Adenauer's point of view, there was one further advantage in having the Dienststelle Blank headed by a CDU politician whom he trusted. When the time finally came to turn the office into a fully-fledged ministry, the FDP would have no real opportunity to claim Blank's post for itself. There was in fact a compelling argument in favour of single overall control of the Federal Chancellor's office, the Foreign Ministry and the Dienststelle Blank. It seemed to offer the best way of maintaining the integral links between the shaping of relations with the Western Allies, the preparation of an integrated defence contribution, and getting support for the desired solution in domestic politics. Of course, the decision strengthened the position of the Chancellor himself.

Adenauer also obtained direct control over other instruments of influence and power. All his associates have testified to his great sensitivity to public opinion. His determination to exploit the possibilities of information policy, to the very limits of what was acceptable in a democracy, was equally marked. At the outset, however, he made several poor personal choices which, as a number of historians have noted, led to difficulties in his relations with the press. In the beginning, Adenauer's knowledge of press affairs was as limited as his knowledge of diplomacy and defence.

No matter who was chosen for the difficult role of federal press chief, Adenauer was determined to anchor the post in the Federal Chancellor's office. When Otto Lenz was state secretary, Department 2 – the Federal Press and Information Service – became more of an autonomous authority. Not until February 1952 and the appointment of Felix von Eckardt, which ended the experimental phase of Adenauer's information policy, did the Chancellor finally find a successful press chief. Nevertheless, the Bundespresse- und Informationsamt was not officially separated from the Federal Chancellor's office until 1958, and even then its state secretary remained under the Chancellor's control.

With an entirely characteristic combination of insatiable curiosity and deep suspicion, Adenauer also turned his attention to the secret service. He ordered an information and intelligence service to be established under the Büro Schwerin. Alongside it, Globke developed working contacts with General Reinhard Gehlen, whose 'Organisation' – though still financed and set up by the Americans – also provided analyses for the Federal Chancellor.

The picture that developed in the first year was clear. As soon as Adenauer became Chancellor, he began like an octopus to expand his influence in every direction. This process occurred more or less irrespective of the legal foundations, which were in any case far from precise in the early years. For Adenauer, the crucial fact was that the Allies left him a relatively free hand. Moreover, the threat of war seemed to justify many actions that would have been unthinkable later.

Throughout this period, Adenauer was never so preoccupied by his chancellorship that he lost his grip on his own party. The CDU in the British Zone continued to exist, with Adenauer as chairman, until the

Christlich-Demokratische Union Deutschlands was formed in Goslar in autumn 1950. He also remained chairman of the Rhineland CDU. In 1950 the CDU regional organisations outside the Eastern Zone merged into one party, naturally under his chairmanship. At the same time, he continued his efforts to keep his deputies Jakob Kaiser and Friedrich Holzapfel in check. With Kaiser now subjected to cabinet discipline and Holzapfel's opportunity to influence the CDU/CSU caucus temporarily reduced, both men were forced to proceed with caution. Adenauer's attempt to install his own man – Kurt Georg Kiesinger – as general secretary of the party failed, owing to the resistance of the Berlin CDU. For a time, Adenauer postponed making important decisions on issues of organisation because he feared that his power might be impaired by the appointment of a secretary general to run the CDU headquarters.

Only with the approach of the 1953 federal election did Adenauer accept the need for change. Kiesinger now proposed his fellow Swabian, Bruno Heck, for the post of *Bundesgeschäftsführer*. A doctor of classical philology who had carved out a short, but successful career in local politics, Heck was currently a senior civil servant in the Ministry of Culture in Südwürttemberg-Hohenzollern. He had no real desire to move to Bonn in order to assume responsibility for the development of a party organisation and the planning of an election campaign. This reluctance was initially shared by Adenauer, but the party executive persuaded him to appoint Heck. Despite these early reservations, Adenauer quickly recognised that Heck was both efficient in organising Bundestag elections and personally loyal to him.

Before 1949 Adenauer had regarded the party organisation as crucial. Once he became Chancellor, however, he came to depend mainly on this position as the basis of his power. The Land associations of the CDU had extensive autonomy; Adenauer was careful to prevent the party's national executive from becoming too strong, since this would have given too much power to his rivals. As long as the CDU Chancellor was successful, the office of state would reinforce his relatively weak formal powers as party chairman. During election campaigns he was indispensable, as main speaker, as the leadership figure, and as the man who – either directly or indirectly – obtained money for the campaign.

The longer the Adenauer era continued, the more the general public and even political scientists tended to forget that Adenauer had reached the top as a tenacious party leader. It became easy to misjudge the CDU as a machine for electing the Chancellor, and the party as little more than the tool of a democratic monarch ruling from the Palais Schaumburg. In fact, such a view overlooks the CDU's inborn and continued stubbornness. It is also based on a misinterpretation of Adenauer's own approach: he continued to regard himself as the leader of a political fighting force which he had led to success and from which he drew strength. The Chancellor himself began as a party man and was to remain one, even though he relied increasingly on his office in order to impose his will on the cabinet, the CDU/CSU *Fraktion,* and the CDU party organisation.

Strenuous Beginnings of *Westpolitik*

> In the area of foreign policy our line is fixed. In the first instance it is aimed at a close relationship with our neighbouring states in the Western world and, especially, with the United States. We will devote all our energy to ensuring that Germany is accepted as quickly as possible as a member of the European federation with equal rights and equal obligations. In carrying out these intentions we will cooperate particularly closely with the other Christian Democratic forces that are growing in strength among the West European peoples.[1]

Such concepts of foreign policy were easy to express, in this case in a letter to Helene Wessel on 27 August 1949. With hindsight, it is equally easy to assume that the success of the approach was assured.

In reality, the Federal Republic of Germany was still a virtual protectorate of the Western Allies. It remained to be seen whether the new Adenauer government would suffer the same fate as the late and unlamented Quisling regimes which had been established throughout German-occupied Europe between 1940 and 1944. Immediately after he had delivered his 'statement of government policy', Adenauer was expected to present himself and his cabinet to the High Commissioners on the Petersberg. The High Commissioners had originally planned to hand over the Occupation Statute with full ceremony on this occasion, and were only dissuaded from doing so with great difficulty. Adenauer thought it bad enough that the actions of his government could be obstructed by Allied discretionary powers, opportunities for objection and Control authorities; there was, he felt, no need to draw attention to these unpalatable facts.

Supreme authority continued to lie with the Allies. The areas reserved for them were much more significant than those left in the hands of the federal government. Foreign affairs, security and the upkeep of the occupation, disarmament and demilitarisation, reparations, foreign trade and foreign exchange controls, Ruhr controls, the breaking up of big companies and banks – there was no area of any importance in which the High Commission was not either totally responsible or at least involved in regulating and approving developments. Even areas which clearly involved domestic policy, such as taxation, regulations governing industrial relations and industrial tribunals, continued to be covered by its supervision until the passing of appropriate German legislation. Furthermore, the High Commissioners continued to have the right of veto even in non-reserved areas.

The super-bureaucracies of the Western Powers were involved in almost every aspect of activity at both federal and regional level. The British Control Commission alone had over 10,000 civilian employees in September 1949. It is scarcely an exaggeration to claim that the occupation was draining the country dry. The occupying forces themselves consisted of no more than 100,000 men belonging to the Allied armed forces and civilian employees. However, they were accompanied by 250,000 family members and they employed over 445,000 Germans. The occupation thus claimed no less than thirty-six per cent of the entire federal budget. Adenauer knew that this situation must be ended or its effects at least mitigated, as soon as possible, partly because of the repercussions on public opinion. Otherwise, he feared, the new German democracy would be vulnerable to the same anti-Western sentiments that had poisoned political life during the Weimar Republic. He was also convinced that the connections which had been built up in Frankfurt between the German administration and the Americans must be cut back. In the early weeks, he informed his cabinet several times that contact with the Allies must stop. In future, the only negotiations to be permitted would be between the High Commission and the federal government.[2]

Adenauer was especially displeased by the way in which the High Commissioners threw their weight about. As Chancellor, he was ultimately responsible to the Bundestag. Until April 1951, however, this did not prevent the High Commissioners from summoning him regularly to the top of the Petersberg, where they had established their headquarters. According to rumour, the Hotel Petersberg had been chosen as the residence because it was there that the British Prime Minister, Neville Chamberlain, had stayed before his humiliating talks with Hitler at the Hotel Dreesen during the Sudeten crisis of 1938. Adenauer always resented these trips to the conquerors, who had established their residence on the heights of his beloved Siebengebirge. As a gesture of conciliation, the High Commissioners occasionally called on the Chancellor for informal and individual talks at his home in Rhöndorf.

General Robertson was the High Commissioner whom Adenauer knew best. However, two people can know each other well without trusting or liking each other. Admittedly, Robertson was virtually bound to be an improvement on the first Military Governor, Sir Sholto Douglas, who had been deeply hostile to the Germans. Yet there remained difficulties to be overcome with his successor. The British minister for Germany, Lord Pakenham, admitted in the 1970s that Robertson had found it difficult to establish reasonable relations with the Germans. Pakenham portrayed the Military Governor and subsequent High Commissioner as 'strong, cool, highly intelligent, occasionally sharp-tongued', and thought that he 'kept his pronounced personal feelings under iron control'. In Pakenham's view, there was no great liking between Robertson and the CDU chairman in the British Zone: 'During my time relations between Adenauer and Brian Robertson were cool, to put it mildly.'[3]

Robertson was the British High Commissioner at a time when the Foreign Secretary, Ernest Bevin, was also hostile to Germany. Later Robertson himself noted that Adenauer had been 'extraordinarily reasonable, highly intelligent and nimble in conducting negotiations'; 'he was not a man whom everyone liked at once, and who sometimes took offence. But in the end I did like him.'[4] As time passed, Adenauer also grew to respect Robertson. Years later, in September 1961, Robertson visited the Chancellor at the height of the Berlin crisis, bringing a gift of biscuits baked by his wife. On this occasion Adenauer greeted him like an old friend and reminisced that the situation had been easier and happier when Robertson was High Commissioner.[5] The passage of time had made both men take a more benevolent view of the past. Between 1948 and 1950, however, they were always wary of one another. Though their relationship was correct and was occasionally improved by the cynical sense of humour they shared, there was no real trust between them.

Robertson at least had the virtue of adopting an objective approach and was prepared to take a background role. In Adenauer's eyes, the French High Commissioner François-Poncet was a much greater problem. The Chancellor had nothing but contempt for the foreign diplomats who had flattered Hitler and the other senior Nazis between 1933 and 1939. François-Poncet, French ambassador in Berlin from 1933 to 1938, had been one of them and, if anything, had been more optimistic than most in his view of the possibilities for peaceful cooperation with the Third Reich. As a result, he now felt obliged to maintain strict control over post-war Germany.

François-Poncet was a Germanist with a deep knowledge of the country's language and culture. Among the three High Commissioners, he had the best claim to knowledge of Germany. However, his arrogance and vanity were proverbial, and he was known to believe that he knew the Germans better than they knew themselves. He continued to maintain, as he had during the Third Reich, that the goal of Franco-German cooperation was his life's work.[6] Nevertheless, Adenauer did not trust him an inch – and François-Poncet returned these feelings. Even more problematic, the High Commissioner with the greatest pretensions and ambitions was also the weakest in political terms. As a result, his relations with Adenauer were characterised by a regular exchange of vitriol, disguised on both sides by witty repartee and double-edged jokes.

Some years later, when Adenauer was recognised as a great statesman, François-Poncet was full of praise for him. The Chancellor himself then felt compelled to look more favourably on the earlier relationship between them. In the early days of the Federal Republic, however, Adenauer's hostility to the Frenchman was far more apparent than his occasional sympathy. At least the appointment of this veteran diplomat proved that the French were taking the infant Federal Republic seriously. In French eyes, indeed, the core state based on the Rhine was simply 'Germany'.

The leading political figure among the High Commissioners was the American, John McCloy. At the outset, he was also the man with the least understanding of Germany. During the war he had been Assistant Secretary of War under Henry Stimson, where his successful campaign against the Morgenthau Plan had at least broadened his knowledge of the country. Nevertheless, McCloy was a Wall Street lawyer who had been President of the World Bank before he came to Germany, and his main area of expertise lay in the politics of international finance. To a certain degree, his appointment as High Commissioner was a signal of intent from the United States about the main focus of their policy towards Germany. He was given his great opportunity to use these talents in the negotiations over the Schuman Plan.

It was Adenauer's good fortune that McCloy was influential in Washington. This was vital, since in the early days all German-American relations were conducted with the High Commissioner as the sole channel. McCloy and Secretary of State Dean Acheson were both alumni of the Harvard Law School and had come to admire each other's work during the war – McCloy in the Department of War, Acheson in a comparable position within the Department of Commerce.

At first, Adenauer's relations with McCloy too were strained. McCloy was far from uncritical of the Germans; until the very end of his time in Germany he continued to doubt whether democracy could take permanent root in a society he found difficult to understand. He was constantly worried by German inclinations towards authoritarian thinking, German power politics and German nationalism. He was also aware that it would be folly to rely completely on a Chancellor who had not yet proved his trustworthiness.

In the early days, the fact that McCloy was not fully briefed about the problems facing him ensured that he would be vague in negotiations and remain dependent on his staff. Among them, however, were advocates of several different approaches all jockeying for position: Keynesians and free traders, advocates of a Grand Coalition and anti-socialists, opponents of trusts, sympathisers with the European idea, left-wing liberals and conservative protagonists of a German military contribution. It was therefore essential for the Germans to pay close attention to McCloy's advisers.

Though McCloy was impressed by Adenauer's quiet dignity, he was repeatedly warned about the Chancellor's cunning. Immediately after his appointment, Adenauer made a point of informing McCloy through various channels that the American was a distant relative of his late wife

Gussie Zinsser.[7] Despite a show of polite interest, however,[8] McCloy actually regarded this family link as a reason to keep his distance. In wartime and the early post-war United States, very few Americans liked to be reminded of family ties with Germans. This situation too was to change. As Adenauer's star rose, McCloy took pleasure in recalling that he had been one of the 'Three Wise Men' who had attended the birth of his chancellorship.

Adenauer nevertheless had some advantages in his relations with the High Commissioners, and he did not hesitate to use them. He was by some margin the oldest, a fact which he combined with an impressive dignity of bearing. This was shown to the full on his official visit to the Petersberg to present his cabinet on 21 September 1949. The three High Commissioners had expected Adenauer to remain in front of the carpet on which they were standing in order to introduce his cabinet. Instead, Adenauer stepped quickly onto the carpet, deliberately establishing a form of equality with the High Commissioners. He was a head of government responsible to an elected parliament. From 1951 he was also Foreign Minister, thus becoming the direct equivalent of their own chiefs, to whom he was also officially superior in his role as head of government. Such factors soon worked in his favour, helping to obscure the fact that the High Commissioners represented the victorious powers and Adenauer the defeated Germans.

Still, these early days remained difficult. They would have been more difficult but for the fact that Kurt Schumacher remained an unacceptable alternative to Adenauer in the eyes of all three High Commissioners. During these first months Adenauer had no real opportunity to influence the course of events in any significant way. Instead, he was preoccupied with the burdens imposed on the new state from outside. Three main issues confronted him: the exchange rate question; Berlin; and the Allied programme of industrial dismantling.

Adenauer was still in the early days of his chancellorship when the High Commissioners compelled him to devalue the Deutsche Mark in response to the sterling crisis. After much discussion, the federal government had proposed a higher exchange rate, but was forced to change its policy. Reaction in the Bundestag and the German press was correspondingly critical. Adenauer was convinced that the Allies – and especially the French – were exploiting their powers in order to secure economic advantage. He was also infuriated by the callous way in which the High Commissioners had undermined his own position before the German public.

He was equally displeased that the Western Allies had acted so ruthlessly in support of their own economic interests at the very time when the Soviet Union was engaged in establishing the German Democratic Republic. While the West Germans dared not even think about a foreign policy of their own, an East German Foreign Minister was appointed in Berlin – not even a Communist, but the former general secretary of the CDU East, Georg Dertinger. Though the GDR's was a purely sham sovereignty, Adenauer was well aware of the power of make-believe in politics.

He believed that it was essential for the Federal Republic to improve its position as soon as possible in its dealings with the Western Allies. At the same time, he also considered it necessary to dissociate the government from the undemocratic state which had been established in the East. On this issue there was complete agreement not only in the cabinet, but also between government and Opposition. All the West German parties with the exception of the Communists regarded the Cold War against 'Soviet Prussia' (in the words of Herbert Wehner in the Bundestag[9]) as a sacred duty.

On the other hand, there were differences first between Adenauer and his cabinet concerning the Berlin question. After the lifting of the blockade, the mood in the Western sectors of the city soon deteriorated. The economic situation was desperate and the GDR government chose Berlin as the seat of government. The West Berliners thereupon pressed for the free sector to be declared the twelfth Land of the Federal Republic. The Berlin Senate and the SPD in Bonn argued that, following the violation of Four Power status by the East, the Western Powers had a unique opportunity to answer the Soviet *fait accompli* with one of their own. Carlo Schmid, who was still chairman of the foreign relations committee of the Bundestag, told the French deputy Bérard that the SPD would uphold its plan of declaring West Berlin as the twelfth Land even if it meant war against the Soviet Union. On this issue, the unity of the High Commissioners was breached. For a time Acheson was prepared to integrate Berlin into the Federal Republic, but met with stubborn resistance from the British and, even more so, of the French.

During this period Adenauer made what appears in retrospect to have been a major error: he strongly opposed the move to integrate West Berlin. He had three main reasons for doing so, two of which he declared openly and one which he kept secret. The incorporation of Berlin as the twelfth Land, he told the High Commissioners, would create the danger of Soviet reprisals and would thus not improve the security of West Berlin. Second, he argued that it would not be desirable for the Soviet Union to make claims on any part of a country as weak as the Federal Republic. How, in that case, could they be opposed?[10] The Western Powers, he maintained in cabinet, ought not to be released from their responsibility for Berlin.[11] The third reason was well known to both government and Opposition, but was not openly discussed: the Social Democrats would probably be the largest party in the Berlin Senate, thereby reducing the government's majority in the federal second chamber, the Bundesrat.

In these considerations of sober *raison d'état* and political opportunism, Adenauer does not seem to have been greatly influenced by anti-

Berlin prejudices, although the SPD – and Rudolf Augstein in *Der Spiegel* – constantly maintained that he was. Since the blockade, his respect for the qualities of the Berliners had been restored after a period of considerable antipathy during the last years of the Weimar Republic and the early years of the Third Reich. In cabinet discussions he was a determined advocate of sustained economic assistance for Berlin, partly for reasons of fighting Communism: Berlin, he argued, was 'the most important bulwark against the East',[12] but it could only be sustained if it was rehabilitated economically.

The return of his positive attitude towards Berlin was certainly helped by the presence of several trusted faces among the negotiating delegation. Along them was Ernst Reuter, a veteran Social Democrat (and also, as Adenauer never forgot, a former Communist), but a man who had been a fellow mayor in better days. Reuter wisely brought with him to the negotiations in Bonn the chairman of the board of AEG, Friedrich Spennrath, who had known Adenauer in Cologne and had been one of the few men he had trusted completely during his sufferings in the Third Reich. Spennrath explained to the Chancellor that Berlin was in desperate need of help. Adenauer agreed that financial contributions and generous economic assistance must be provided, but opposed suggestions from Jakob Kaiser for the transfer of various federal government offices to the former capital. Berlin was close to his heart, it appeared, but only so long as no claims were made based on its old position as Reich capital. Adenauer regarded any suggestion of transferring important federal authorities to the city as the height of folly.

Assistance to Berlin was thus increased. However, the High Commissioners could not be persuaded to grant it the status of twelfth federal Land. It is difficult to be sure what part Adenauer's rejection of the proposal played, but the Allies obviously had to take the Federal Chancellor's view into account when reaching their decision. At any rate, Adenauer succeeded in persuading the SPD leaders to remove the Berlin question from the political agenda as a source of confrontation between government and Opposition.

Political conflict flared up again over the third great theme of Adenauer's early chancellorship: the dismantling programme. No other problem had greater domestic or foreign-policy resonance in the early months. In fact, Allied industrial plans had frequently been revised since 1946. The list of 744 firms which were to be dismantled or destroyed was, to some extent, part payment of the abandoned plan to obtain security against Germany by making drastic cuts in German industrial capacity. In 1949, it was not only the Germans who realised that the dismantling programme was out of step with the overall direction of Western policy. How could a new democracy be constructed with nine per cent unemployment if the establishment of the new state was accompanied by a wholesale destruction of jobs? How could the bewildered population be given confidence in the goodwill of the Western Powers? Were the objectives of the Marshall Plan really compatible with the destruction of German industrial potential?

However, Adenauer was old enough to know that absurdities and conflicts over objectives were the rule rather than the exception in international relations in the twentieth century. He was convinced that the main motive for the dismantling list, at least as far as the British were concerned, was the desire to weaken the Germans as competitors in the world market. Though he believed that similar motives also played a part with the French, he was more prepared to accept the validity of their security concerns.

The dismantling issue was closely connected with developments in German domestic politics. In fact, the federal government, the unions, the employers and parts of the SPD would have welcomed the establishment of an all-party consensus on this issue at least. There were indeed signs that such a consensus was emerging. The government had agreed to accept the Social Democrat Carlo Schmid as chairman of the foreign relations committee in the Bundestag, thus providing the institutional conditions for discreet cooperation. Adenauer himself did not oppose fairly regular evening discussions between Herbert Blankenhorn and Schmid on the prospects for a 'bipartisan policy'. Schmid, however, could not convince his own party leader. As a result, the dismantling issue turned into the first bitter foreign-policy controversy between Adenauer and Schumacher.

On 12 November, shortly before the dispute reached a peak, Blankenhorn contemplated the discussions which had begun well but ended in failure:

> Two-hour discussion with Carlo Schmid, who gives an impression of utter exhaustion. With a swollen, pale, tired face, he sits opposite me and has the posture of a despairing, depressed and disappointed man. Most disappointed at his own party people and at Schumacher, whom he calls introverted, and whose touchiness is the reason for the powerful attacks on Adenauer's policy. I explain emphatically to Schmid that I regard the efforts to reach a joint approach with the Opposition in the area of foreign policy as being in serious danger. Schumacher's interview has let the dogs loose in the streets and it will take great deal of effort and patience to get joint discussions going again. I looked forward with serious concern to the debate on Tuesday. Carlo Schmid largely shared this view. He accused the Chancellor of being insufficiently informed about the essential problems of the Ruhr and of European Union ...

The two men then discussed the problems of personal politics and Schmid took leave of Adenauer's envoy with the words: 'It is good to know one is not alone.'[13]

Nevertheless, this did not prevent Schmid from accusing Adenauer of a *dolus eventualis* during the heat of parliamentary debate on foreign policy on 15 November. (He subsequently claimed that this was the result of a mental block during his speech and that he had meant to say *reservatio mentalis*.)

It was tempting for Adenauer to use Blankenhorn in an attempt to win over one of the most powerful members of the SPD *Fraktion*. He also sought personal discussions with the SPD leader. Schumacher, however, was convinced that he could drive Adenauer into a corner over the dismantling question. The Western Allies were demanding that, in return for a halt being called to the dismantling of vital plants, the federal government should finally fill the seat in the Ruhr Authority which it had been given. Adenauer had delayed taking this step until now, but on 25 October he admitted in cabinet that refusal to cooperate with the Ruhr Statute would be regarded abroad as obstruction, while participation would be seen as a positive sign. It was essential to improve the international atmosphere, or no U.S. loans would be made available to the Ruhr. The cabinet as a whole agreed with this approach, with only the Minister of the Interior, Heinemann, expressing reservations.[14]

Schumacher promptly launched his attack. He maintained that Adenauer was absolutely wrong to agree to the control of Ruhr industry by foreign states for an indefinite period. This was, he claimed, a dereliction of duty on the part of the Chancellor.

Privately, Adenauer knew that it was dangerous for him to appear in public as an advocate of a policy of fulfilment; he had not forgotten the tragic fate of Erzberger and Rathenau, who had been murdered by nationalist extremists after the First World War. Since summer 1949 he had considered whether it would be possible to prevent the dismantling of large steelworks and chemical concerns by re-introducing his old ideas on 'organic integration'. Controls would then be a European virtue rather than a one-sided attack on German interests. On 26 July, even before the federal election, he had therefore written a beseeching letter to the French Foreign Minister, Robert Schuman. Adenauer had just returned from election engagements in the countryside and had seen at first hand the catastrophic mood of the population. Would it not be better, he suggested, to contemplate joint control by the three Western Allies rather than dismantling?[15] Schuman, however, did not respond; he believed that Adenauer was seeking a foreign-policy success solely to aid his election campaign.

In the emergency situation of autumn 1949, Adenauer revived the ideas that had been favoured by Hugo Stinnes in 1922 and 1923 for French ownership of certain parts of Ruhr industry. Such ideas were also being discussed elsewhere: an outline proposal had already been prepared by Vereinigte Stahlwerke (United Steelworks), on 5 November 1949, and an SPD negotiating committee under Kurt Schumacher actually sent a proposal to McCloy for the internationalisation of the ownership of the August-Thyssen-Hütte.[16]

Adenauer first explained his famous European concept for the solution of the dismantling issue at a meeting with the High Commissioners on 14 October.[17] He pointed out that the Ruhr Statute could not provide a lasting solution for the organisation of peaceful Franco-German relations. Instead, reciprocal economic interests must be used as the basis for political co-operation. Here Adenauer recalled his own support for a Franco-German customs union in the mid-1920s, and mentioned his discussions with Emile Mayrisch, the president of ARBED (United Metal Works Burbach-Eich-Düdelingen) in Luxembourg. When none of the High Commissioners responded, Adenauer made more specific proposals. German industry, he argued, needed capital for reconstruction. France wanted to control this industry because of its need for security, but it had insufficient capital to do so. Might it not be possible for the United States to provide the French with capital for the purchase of shares in German companies? The British could also involve themselves in an ambitious plan of this kind.

Again the High Commissioners failed to respond. Adenauer, however, was emphatic: 'When two neighbouring peoples have fought each other for centuries, only two possibilities are left. Either one kills the other, or they become friends. As we have seen, though, it is rather difficult for one to kill the other.' François-Poncet chaffed him by saying: 'I am still alive', but Adenauer answered seriously: 'I was speaking about us.'

Somewhat undiplomatically, Adenauer then chose to reproach François-Poncet for the French failure to take the opportunity of becoming a good neighbour to Germany in 1918. Instead, he maintained, the French had chosen to support separatism in Germany. In those days he had been a private individual, but now he could use his official role as Chancellor to advocate a policy of reconciliation. Adenauer closed his remarks by noting that he was deeply disappointed that Robert Schuman had recently dismissed German criticisms of the Western dismantling plan.

His comments were followed by some sharp comments from François-Poncet, and the French High Commissioner had complained bitterly about a number of nationalist speeches that had been made in the Bundestag. Some of the deputies there had exploited the dismantling issue and other delicate matters and used the opportunity to make demands, complaints and attacks. Adenauer merely observed that the responsibility for German disillusionment did not lie with the federal government. He himself had intervened to rebuke some of the speakers in the Bundestag, and he felt that their remarks should not be taken too seriously.

Adenauer had hoped that this informal meeting would lead to a breakthrough, but it ended very frostily.[18] And yet, Adenauer continued to claim, in cabinet[19] and to the press, that 'cooperation with France' was the main objective of the West German government. Such an approach was also essential in order to evoke a positive response from U.S. public opinion. If the West Germans wanted good American-German relations, then relations with France would have to be improved. He was aware of how difficult it would be for any French government to change course. At the beginning of November, Adenauer gave an interview to Ernst Friedländer of *Die Zeit* which created considerable interest in Paris.[20] However, there was no shift in policy as yet.

Future developments now depended on a hastily summoned conference of the three Western foreign ministers in Paris. Even before it took place, Adenauer instructed Blankenhorn to send an aide-mémoire to the French High Commission, containing a brief summary of his ideas. He enclosed a proposal from Vereinigte Stahlwerke for the re-organisation of industrial joint-stock companies through the incorporation of foreign capital.[21] On the following day, he followed it up with an interview with a correspondent of the *Baltimore Sun,*[22] having heard that President Truman was a regular reader of this minor newspaper. Here he even put a figure – forty per cent – on possible French participation in German industry. When this led to criticism at home, however, he claimed that the journalist in question had made a mistake.[23]

The Western foreign ministers met in Paris on 9 and 10 November 1949. It quickly became apparent that the time for a reorganisation in a genuinely European spirit had not yet arrived. Nevertheless, the first moves were made towards the inclusion of the Federal Republic as a partner. The ministers authorised the High Commissioners to conduct negotiations over the dismantling list and modifications to the Ruhr Statute. In return, however, West Germany would have to cooperate in the Ruhr Authority and accept economic controls through the Military Security Office.

At this stage, Adenauer became aware of the significance of another political figure: the U.S. Secretary of State, Dean Acheson. Adenauer had been told by his diplomats that at first Acheson had been no friend of Germany. He was a member of the group associated with Felix Frankfurter, continued to have many friends among left-wing liberals and – according to those who knew him well – was 'too good a lawyer not to be a tactician and opportunist'.[24] At the beginning of 1949 it was widely feared that General Marshall's successor might return to a course of appeasement of the Soviet Union. In reality, Acheson chose to go down in history as the founder of NATO. In that respect he was at one with public opinion in the United States, which in autumn 1949 was still as anti-Communist as it had been during the Berlin blockade.

The meeting in Paris on 9 and 10 November at last offered Adenauer's Westpolitik some prospect of progress. Acheson approached the German question with one simple basic conviction: the United States and Western Europe could not hope to check the Soviet Union while continuing to suppress their former enemies, Germany and Japan. The Americans must therefore make every effort – though with the necessary caution – to turn former foes into willing supporters.[25] At the end of October he noted with relief that the British had finally softened their stance on the dismantling issue. They knew that the main pressure of German public opinion was directed against them; moreover, Bevin was aware of doubts within the House of Commons about the wisdom of his hard line.

The situation that had developed since spring 1948 thus continued: the U.S. tried to move forward; the British followed, though with less than good grace; the French, however, went on blocking progress. In the end the key factor was not the agreement between the three governments, but the subsequent approval of the recommendations by the French cabinet. As far as the dismantling issue was concerned, this meant that four-hundred factories producing synthetic petroleum and rubber products, in addition to all the works in Berlin and the August-Thyssen-Hütte in Hamborn, were removed from the dismantling list. The Hermann-Göring-Werke in Salzgitter and the Krupp factory in Essen remained on the list. As Schuman observed during the negotiations, it would cost him his political career if these were spared as well. In addition, the Federal Republic would be entitled to join the various organisations of the Western world, in particular the OEEC (Organisation for European Economic Co-operation) and GATT (General Agreement on Tariffs and Trade). There would be no objection to West German participation as an associate member in the Council of Europe.

In the prelude to the conference in Paris, McCloy had urged his Secretary of State to visit Berlin and Bonn afterwards. Acheson arrived on 11 November for his first meeting with Adenauer. He was favourably impressed by the Chancellor's explanation of his European programme. These views were confirmed by a subsequent meeting with Schumacher, who hardly allowed the Secretary of State to open his mouth before launching a furious argument. From then on, Acheson made it clear that Washington preferred Adenauer as a partner, although the SPD without Schumacher also seemed acceptable. The Chancellor was thus able to begin his rise in Germany and Europe with the clear backing of the United States.

The concessions made by the Western Allies during the subsequent negotiations on Petersberg were actually less significant that the German public believed. Important works remained on the dismantling list; Adenauer's appeals for a revision of the Ruhr Statute went unheeded; and the Germans were forced to accept the Allied regulations on decartelisation. Adenauer was also aware that the issue of West German entry to the Council of Europe would probably be very controversial both in Bonn and in Paris. Schumacher would do his utmost to prevent German membership in case the government of the Saar was admitted separately at the same time. Conversely, it was likely that the hardliners in Paris would insist that the Federal Republic could only join the Council of Europe if the Saar was granted membership.

Nevertheless, much of the German public felt that a genuine breakthrough had been achieved. This was due largely to a heated debate in the Bundestag in which Adenauer used his cool tactical skills to provoke Schumacher. The leader of the Opposition had launched a two-pronged attack. On one hand, he wanted to show that the acceptance of the Ruhr Statute was an unacceptable gamble with the future of Germany. On the other hand, he also attacked it as a wicked act of international capitalism which was 'putting an Allied gendarme in Germany in front of the safe of large-scale property'.[26] His party colleague Adolf Arndt supported him with a constitutional argument to the effect that Adenauer had negotiated the Petersberg agreement as a government agreement without the participation of the Bundestag: 'We believed we were on the way to a parliamentary democracy and we find ourselves on the way to a monarchy without a constitution.'[27]

This did not deflect Adenauer from his aim, which was to convince German and foreign opinion that Schumacher was an extreme nationalist. In fact, Schumacher fell into the trap when he called Adenauer the 'Federal Chancellor of the Allies'. On 17 November Adenauer reported to the High Commissioners after the first great Bundestag debates. He now argued that, in comparison with the 1920s, the political roles had been reversed – now 'the nationalists were sitting on the left of the house while the right was reasonable ...'[28] At the same time, he hoped to prove that his own method of gradually breaking down negative Allied policies, had a better chance of success than the SPD's approach.

In this respect, the support of the trade unions was a priceless asset. At the height of the debate, he received information to the effect that the DGB (German Trade Union Federation), despite some reservations, approved of the government line. This support was guaranteed by Hans Böckler, a key figure on the German political scene until his death in February 1951. Böckler, the chairman of the DGB, was a year older than the Chancellor and had won Adenauer's respect as a trade-union secretary on Cologne city council. Like his party colleagues Haas and Meerfeld, Böckler was a union leader Adenauer could admire: hard working, reasonable, moderate and willing to compromise. After the defeat of Germany in 1945, Adenauer and Böckler had travelled to meetings of the Zonal Advisory Council in Hamburg in the same car. With Böckler on his left flank and Pferdmenges on his right, Adenauer was well equipped to withstand the stormy domestic scene in the first months of his chancellorship.

On 1 January 1950, Blankenhorn assessed the overall situation in his diary. In general he was convinced that the federal government had made a positive beginning between September and December 1949. There were, however, two major worries. The first of these was the danger of 'a new appeasement policy on the part of the Americans … at the expense of central Europe, i.e., Germany'. The second involved relations with France: he had heard disturbing news about French policy towards the Saar. Nevertheless, Blankenhorn wrote that the New Year 'begins with favourable conditions for foreign and domestic issues'.[29] In fact, this optimistic assessment was premature. The year 1950 was to be one of the most critical Adenauer had ever faced.

'The Most Disappointed Man in Europe'

Only a week after Blankenhorn's diary entry, Adenauer was forced to recognise that his European policy had reached an impasse. Franco-German relations were strained and, as usual, both sides had good reasons for their resentment. There were two great themes which dominated Franco-German relations over the following months and even years. One of these, expressed in a variety of ways and perceptible at every level, was the French security trauma. The other was the Saar.

Without doubt, the more important motive for all the difficulties created by the French was the fear of a revival of German power. At every opportunity, publicly and in private, Adenauer acknowledged that recent history gave the French good reasons for their almost unquenchable thirst for security against Germany. He was convinced that, on this subject, he could make a real and progressive contribution to a solution in the form of his concept for European integration, though he was aware that there would be many practical problems in the way of its implementation.

However, every tentative step towards a long-term understanding was vulnerable to the pitfalls of the Saar question. The Saar was a side-issue of Franco-German relations which had a disastrous tendency to appear as the main problem. The dispute began in the early months of 1950 and continued, with interruptions, until a definitive solution was reached in the middle of the decade. At the beginning of the 1950s there seemed to be no solution which might leave both sides even partly satisfied.

In January 1950, François-Poncet had made it clear to Blankenhorn that France wanted the Saar to become a second Luxembourg.[1] In theory, that would mean autonomy for the Saar under international law and close economic ties with France. However, the reality was that the French intended the Saarland to have an inferior status to that enjoyed by Luxembourg, which was a fully sovereign, though economically dependent country. The Saar, under the French-supported government of Johannes Hoffmann, was to remain a protectorate.

Now that a potentially strong German state had been re-established, the French were anxious to anchor the special status of the Saar in international law. The region, later enlarged by 109 municipalities from the Rhineland Palatinate, was separated from the French Zone of occupation from the outset. The Saar government was composed mainly of Germans who had emigrated to France and would, in varying degrees, be receptive to the wishes of the French government. Many of these Germans had undoubtedly become involved with the aim of finding the best solution available for the Saar. In 1947 and 1948, none of them could predict what would happen to Germany, and close association with France had much to recommend it. When the position began to change in 1949 and 1950, the pro-French forces in the Saar were too deeply committed for withdrawal to be possible.

A monetary and customs union with France was intoduced in 1947. The sequestered coal mines and the Röchling works, under forced administration, were included in French economic planning. Britain and the United States had agreed to support French wishes concerning the Saar during peace negotiations, leaving Bonn unaware of the extent of this agreement and its specific details.

At the beginning of January 1950 it emerged that the French Foreign Ministry was preparing three conventions between France and the Saar. These were designed to cement the position of the region as a virtual protectorate. The draft conventions stipulated that foreign policy representation and the defence of the 'autonomous' Saar would be the responsibility of France. On every question that the French regarded as significant, a representative of the French Republic would have an absolute or limited right of veto. The Saar coal mines would be run by France for fifty years, irrespective both of the settlement of the property question and of a peace treaty with Germany. France also obtained extensive rights over the railways in the area. By deciding to couple Germany's entry to the Council of Europe with the simultaneous entry of the Saar, the French were also attempting to obtain the indirect recognition of the West German government for its measures.

At the root of French policy towards the Saar lay a mixture of economic and political motives. From an economic point of view, control over the Saar mines and steelworks would help to reduce the traditional inferiority of French mining *vis-à-vis* the German coal and steel industry. In political terms, the protectorate status of the Saar would be a consolation prize for the French after the abandonment of plans to set up, on its eastern border from the Upper Rhine to Siegerland, a *glacis* of autonomous or semi-autonomous German satellite states, separated either fully or partly from the rest of Germany. By 1950, only the Saar remained of this concept, which had originally been espoused by General de Gaulle and the Quai d'Orsay.

What was Adenauer's approach to this French policy towards the Saar? The question is significant because his Saar policy was one of the most controversial aspects of Adenauer's *Westpolitik* in the early 1950s. In terms of substance, Adenauer's attitude did not differ from that of other West German party leaders. When the British Foreign Minister Bevin announced the separation of the Saar in October 1946, Adenauer made a strong protest in an interview with correspondents of *Die Welt*.[2] His arguments were clearly based on the right of peoples to self-determination and the lack of a peace treaty with Germany which alone could legalise cession.[3]

Adenauer was already aware that the Saar issue was political dynamite. The problem took up a substantial part of his first meeting with Robert Schuman in Bassenheim in October 1948. Schuman, Adenauer recalled later, had assured him that he regarded the return of the Saar to Germany as within the realms of possibility: 'France merely wanted to secure her economic interests.'[4]

During the first months of his chancellorship, Adenauer continued to adopt a restrained approach while Kurt Schumacher made vehement attacks on French policy towards the Saar. The potential for domestic political damage was obvious. The Opposition had no need to feel hesitant about playing the national card in what it regarded as a just cause. Moreover, the crisis also affected the ranks of the coalition, since the FDP and DP both contained strong and vociferous nationalist elements. Vice Chancellor Blücher and President Heuss both made several references to the problem. Thomas Dehler, an FDP minister, used such strong language that the Chancellor was forced to make excuses for his Minister of Justice in a letter which promptly found its way into the press.[5]

The national-minded wing of the CDU was also roused to fury. In the middle of January 1950, Jakob Kaiser, ex officio responsible for All-German Affairs, sent the press a supposedly confidential 'Saar Memorandum' he had initialled. His desire for publicity was in fact fulfilled, but led to a public controversy between the minister and his head of government and to a bitter exchange of letters. Adenauer was angered both by the frank language used by Kaiser, and by the criticism of himself in the memorandum.[6]

A scapegoat had to be found. It came in the shape of the press chief, Paul Bourdin, who was accused of taking insufficient care to conceal differences within the cabinet from public notice. He resigned, thus becoming the second federal press chief Adenauer had lost within four months. Almost inevitably, press coverage of the Saar issue was less than tactful. François-Poncet was even moved to remark that official press guidance reminded him of unfortunate instances in the recent past.[7]

The German indignation of January 1950 gradually subsided. Nevertheless, Adenauer continued to fear that the Saar issue might damage his coalition, if not to destroy it altogether. This was the reason for his comparatively restrained response to the anti-French invective of Dehler's speech in Hamburg, though Blankenhorn had advised the Chancellor to dismiss Dehler from his cabinet at once. He also contented himself with sending a firm letter to Kaiser. In Adenauer's view, the greatest potential danger of the Saar issue was the possibility that it might destroy the domestic political basis of his entire policy towards the West.

In foreign affairs, Bonn was already in a weak position in its relations with France. Adenauer had a natural interest in joining the Council of Europe as soon as possible. He also knew that French willingness to be reasonable over issues of dismantling, the Ruhr control, the revision of the Occupation Statute and basic questions of European integration was more important than specific aspects relating to the status of the Saar, especially as these could in any case not be changed for a number of years. Realistically, he did not expect that the United States and Britain, both of which had many difficulties with the French, would be prepared for a major dispute with Paris over the Saar. They were unlikely to be interested in minor Franco-German quarrels when there were many more vital issues at stake.

Adenauer was therefore inclined to accept many setbacks – under protest – if he could be sure that the reservation 'pending the peace treaty with Germany' was undamaged and that democratic principles were not flouted too openly in the Saar. The great need was to gain time and prevent a final, unfavourable settlement. He calculated that the growing economic, political and moral authority of the Federal Republic would begin to make an impression in due course.

Between January and March 1950, Adenauer adopted tactics which were to be typical of his conduct over the following years. Phase One consisted in a firm rejection of French policy along with an attempt to gain time; Phase Two included an endeavour behind the scenes to induce modifications in the French approach, in order to limit the domestic and foreign policy damage; Phase Three involved a deviation from his original hard line, justified on the grounds of favourable developments in the interim, which enabled the retreat to be overlooked or even hailed as a victory.

Phase One of Adenauer's approach coincided with the first visit to Bonn by the French Foreign Minister, Robert Schuman. On 2 January 1950, Adenauer was notified that the visit would take place from the 13th to the 15th of that month. At the outset, the event seemed to be planned largely as a gesture – perhaps to match the U.S. Secretary of State, Dean Acheson, who had been to Bonn and Berlin two months before. This is the most likely explanation of Schuman's strange plan to pay a visit to the Federal President but not the Chancellor. After some negotiation, it was agreed that Schuman's train would go to Bonn after all, where, like Acheson, he could be welcomed by Adenauer at the station.

As soon as Schuman's itinary was announced, Adenauer ordered the Palais Schaumburg – which was still full of craftsmen – to be finished within six days. He also asked his son-in-law, Willi Suth, *Oberstadtdirektor* of Cologne, to provide furniture, paintings and silver from the city's treasures. The silver, which arrived at the last minute, gave Adenauer the opportunity to quarrel with the architect Hans Schwippert, who considered Cologne's silver tableware in poor taste.[8]

When details of the French plans for the Saar emerged, the German assessment of the visit changed. Adenauer suspected that Schuman was hoping to create a good atmosphere during his visit, without touching on any issues of substance, in an attempt to make it difficult for the Germans to put forward harsh criticisms of French policy towards the Saar. In the days before Schuman's arrival, Adenauer worked diligently to build a united front against the Saar conventions. He dispatched Blankenhorn to assure Carlo Schmid that the federal government would not accept them, and to suggest a renewed opportunity for a 'bipartisan policy'. The chairmen of the Bundestag caucuses were also informed and agreed that, if France completed the Saar conventions, their delegations would oppose German entry into the Council of Europe.

By comparison with their first meeting in Bassenheim over a year earlier, the prospects for an understanding between Schuman and Adenauer could scarcely have been worse. Schuman, who was also under political pressure at home, was annoyed by the preoccupation of the German press with the single theme of the Saar. For his part, Adenauer was angry with Schuman for failing to keep the promises he had made in Bassenheim. He did not hesitate to make his displeasure known.

The mood at this first great state visit to the Palais Schaumburg was far from good. Thirty-eight guests were invited to the lunch, including Cardinal Frings and Kurt Schumacher, who could scarcely climb the steps to the first floor and had to be carried from room to room. Schuman adopted a conciliatory tone and gave a speech in German. However, Adenauer, normally a witty speaker on informal occasions, chose to read from a prepared text. The mood was no better that evening at Castle Ernich, where Adenauer and Schuman talked over dinner; Schuman's chef de cabinet, the Comte de Bourbon-Busset, told Blankenhorn that the Germans had no right to interfere in the Saar.[9]

On the following morning, Adenauer instructed Blankenhorn to recall Baron von Maltzan from Paris for talks. The signing of the Franco-German commercial treaty, planned for 16 January 1950, was to be postponed.[10] Adenauer discussed strategy with Blankenhorn in Rhöndorf on Sunday morning; the Chancellor was now convinced that Schuman's visit was designed to create a favourable atmosphere and thereby ease the passage of the treaties with the Saar government, which were planned for 8 and 9 February.

Georges Bidault, the French premier and an old enemy of Schuman, used Viktor Koutzine in Geneva to inform Adenauer that he personally stood by the agreements he had made with the Chancellor in Geneva. According to these agreements, there were to be no important changes in the status of the Saar. The message also claimed that Schuman was untruthful and not to be trusted. Not without a degree of Schadenfreude, Adenauer recognised that Schuman's domestic political position was being undermined. This meant that he could return to the discussions that afternoon with more confidence.

Adenauer and Schuman talked for two hours. The details are known to us only from Adenauer's own report, since the two men spoke alone and without translators. Adenauer infuriated François-Poncet by deliberately keeping him out of the room; after holding forth about the servility of the Germans, François-Poncet announced that he would wait an hour before entering the room with dustpan and brush to interrupt the discussion and sweep up the pieces of broken china.

Two details of the discussion are of particular interest. The first was Adenauer's suggestion of a three-cornered discussion of all Saar issues between France, Germany and the Saarland. Not surprisingly, Schuman refused to be drawn. Schuman then mentioned his party colleague, Bidault: if he became Foreign Minister, French policy towards the Saar would become much more negative. Adenauer once again entreated Schuman to leave the Saar problem alone for the present, and Schuman returned to Paris with the Chancellor's warning that developments in the region could jeopardise German entry to the Council of Europe. It would be better to wait with the signing of the conventions, at least until the Federal Republic had joined the Council of Europe.

When Adenauer returned to Bonn with Blankenhorn, he remarked that the talks had not produced a positive result. Schuman had been astonished by the German obsession with the Saar. Nor did he produce plans that might lead to closer cooperation between France and Germany. Blankenhorn noted that the parting between the two men at Bonn station had been cool, 'rather meaningless'. For his own part, Schuman was as dissatisfied as Adenauer. French journalists were told only that: 'We have no reason to despair' and, resignedly: 'We are not magicians.'[11]

During these unsuccessful talks, neither Adenauer nor Schuman was blinded by pro-European sentiment. Both were prisoners of their respective domestic politics; both proved to be tough champions of their differing national interests.

On the following day, Adenauer held a press conference at which he made public his legal reservations about French policy towards the Saar and repeated his warnings to France. He also asked McCloy and

Robertson, in separate discussions, to encourage French moderation. A speech by Thomas Dehler then led to a further deterioration in relations. The French let it be known that, if the commercial treaty were not initialled within two days, negotiations for it would be broken off. Adenauer was forced to give way. And again he had to recognise that his freedom to manoeuvre in foreign policy was extremely limited.

Adenauer now considered various ways in which the Saar question might be defused without loss of face on either side. Soon after Schuman left, the Chancellor held bilateral talks with McCloy to consider the idea of placing the Saar economy under an international regime similar to that of the Ruhr. McCloy either did not understand, or acted as if he did not, so as to avoid having to give an answer.[12]

In March 1950 Adenauer was willing to consider the idea of a separate economic status for the Saar. In his view, the region should be re-attached to the French Zone in legal terms, thus establishing that it continued to be part of Germany in international law. However, it might be possible to concede the Saar some economic autonomy, such as a special customs union in its relations with southern Germany and Lorraine. However, any special arrangement would have to be subject to a referendum in the Saar, like that of 1935. There were the proposals discussed in the Saar White Book, which Adenauer had approved in March 1950.[13]

By the beginning of that month, however, events had already outstripped such plans. The Saar conventions were signed in the French Foreign Ministry on 3 March. Adenauer was informed of this event only the day before, at the end of a routine discussion with the High Commissioners. He was now forced to perform a difficult balancing act. For the time being, he had no choice but to repudiate the Saar conventions just as firmly as the other party leaders in West Germany. In fact, he did so in the most damaging way conceivable, observing at a special press conference that the French action towards the Saar that day was reminiscent of National Socialism: 'The name "Protectorate" would perhaps be too mild. Rather one might speak of a "colony" – though of course I would not do so.'[14] The federal government, he claimed, had been abandoned, if not betrayed; West Germany had lost much of its faith in the West. Once again he raised doubts about Germany's entry to the Council of Europe, though without explicitly stating that it would refuse to join. Adenauer was particularly bitter because of the possible effect of these conventions on the issue of the eastern territories: '… if that happens and is tolerated or sanctioned in the West, how in the world can one say anything to Poland over the Oder-Neisse line?'[15]

His performance at the press conference was vigorous and determined. Journalists who witnessed it were therefore astonished to read, three days later, of an interview he had given on 7 March 1950 to Kingsbury-Smith, an American journalist.[16] Since Kingsbury-Smith was head of the European section of the International News Service in Paris, the interview was assured of wide coverage in the press. Adenauer's comments contained nothing less than a proposal for complete union between France and Germany with a single parliament.

Almost in passing, Adenauer also stated his view that entry to such a 'United Parliament' should also be open to Britain, the Benelux states and Italy. In an attempt to demonstrate his goodwill, he stated that, although West Germany had 25 million more inhabitants than France, both countries should have the same number of deputies. There was one condition: first, of all, the Saar must be returned to Germany. Nevertheless, this did not affect his basic concept of Franco-German union as the core from which a united Europe could develop.

The response in diplomatic circles was not encouraging. It was widely considered that the interview was not serious and had been designed solely to create a favourable impression in the United States. It was also thought to be in doubtful taste for the German Chancellor to make the proposal for complete union with France; in so doing he was repeating a proposal made by Winston Churchill during the campaign against France in June 1940 – except that had been for union between Britain and France against the armed might of Germany.

Oddly enough, the only positive response came from General de Gaulle. The general, the leader of the 'Rassemblement du Peuple Français', was strongly opposed to the ruling parties in France, and was still continuing his anti-Communist crusade in the country. At a press conference, de Gaulle responded positively to the call for a link between France and Germany, recalling the comradeship-in-arms of Gauls, Germans and Romans against Attila, and also the great empire of Charlemagne. Like Adenauer, he thought that such a move might offer a solution to the problem of the Saar. Until then, however, the region must remain in French hands.[17]

The sceptical overall response prompted Adenauer to give a second interview to Kingsbury-Smith on 21 March.[18] Here his arguments were somewhat more realistic. Moreover, observers with some knowledge of his thinking could see that Adenauer was scaling back the Utopian plan for a European Union until it closely resembled his own long-standing ideas for closer integration.

First – perhaps encouraged by de Gaulle's response – he took the idea of Franco-German union as the core of a United States of Europe and placed it within the political framework of the East-West conflict. If Western Europe were to show signs of new political life, he argued, the Soviet Union would be deterred from attempting to conquer the continent. Second, he recalled the model of the German *Zollverein* (Customs Union) of 1834 and pointed out that a customs parliament and customs union had provided the first moves towards the unification of Germany in the nineteenth century. Adenauer now claimed that he had been thinking of a similar procedure in his proposal for a union between France and Germany. The interview included a number of significant phrases: the call for a gradual 'fusion of the two countries with regard to customs and economy'; the proposal for a 'common economic parliament' formed from the legislatures of the two countries; and the suggestion that the governments should appoint an 'organ' responsible to the economic parliament. The tasks of the economic parliament and of this authority could be extended over the course of time and eventually bring about the unification of the two countries 'step by step'.

In Adenauer's view, this political approach could be expected to have positive political effects. French demands for security would be satisfied and the revival of German nationalism prevented. This, then, was an economic union with a predominantly political objective. To illustrate his case, Adenauer referred to the current efforts to achieve union between the Benelux states and in Scandinavia, and to the negotiations for a customs union between France and Italy. All these moves, he believed, would also give fresh boost to the Marshall Plan.

During his second interview with Kingsbury-Smith on the following day, it became even more apparent that Adenauer was reviving his own long-held ideas for European integration. In an attempt to arouse the interest of François-Poncet and his fellow High Commissioners for the idea, he referred specifically to his plans of 1925 for a customs union with France.

Adenauer's move should not be dismissed as a transparent attempt to obscure his inevitable capitulation over the issue of entry to the Council of Europe behind glowing references to the future of Europe. It cannot be denied that short-term tactical motives did play a role. Nevertheless, Adenauer was more than ever convinced that the almost insuperable divisions between France and Germany could be overcome only if their peoples and governments were inspired by an idea that was fundamentally different to that of the nation state. Even if national interests would continue to be asserted in the European context, it would at least be possible to modify and control them.

The international response remained cool.[19] The French Minister of Information, Teitgen, dismissed the proposal as mere improvisation; France, he argued, must refrain from throwing itself into the arms of Germany. The official British response was equally cool. Adenauer found little consolation in the positive reaction of the British Leader of the Opposition, Winston Churchill, who viewed some aspects of a Franco-German union in a favourable light. Adenauer's ideas were also subjected to considerable criticism in the Bundestag. Gerhard Lütkens, the SPD spokesman on foreign affairs, compared Adenauer's interviews with the unpredictable personal regime of Kaiser Wilhelm II.

It appeared that Adenauer's initiative had failed. During these weeks the Chancellor felt isolated[20] and snubbed by Paris and London. It was not clear whether the movement for European union had any future at all. With McCloy absent from Bonn for weeks at a time, Adenauer relied on the press for virtually all of his information about the plans of the West European governments and the Truman administration on security matters. He perceived that international politics were in a state of flux, but that the governments involved did not know precisely where it was leading. Was a revived entente between Britain and France likely, as the Bidault government seemed to hope? Would the Council of Europe and the various plans for a customs union between specific European states yield any practical results? What would become of NATO, which had not yet progressed beyond the level of staff planning? How would the East-West conflict develop? The situation in Germany had again deteriorated, but Adenauer had also heard from Washington that Acheson wanted an agreement with Communist China. Was a new period of appeasement more likely, or a critical intensification of the Cold War?

Part of the responsibility for the inadequate intelligence available to Adenauer lay in his failure to progress towards the establishment of an effective foreign service. No satisfactory state secretary had yet been found. Hermann Josef Abs, chosen by Adenauer in October 1949, was unpopular with both the Americans and the French and was himself reluctant because he believed that on the important issues, German foreign policy should be supported by both government and opposition.[21] However, Adenauer was unwilling to make a second choice. In particular, he wanted to avoid the appointment of diplomats from the old German Foreign Ministry on the Wilhelmstrasße to senior posts in the Federal Foreign Ministry and the important missions abroad. He also delayed the nomination of German consul-generals to Paris, London and New York because he was annoyed that the High Commissioners would not permit a German diplomatic presence in other countries.

Three men, none of whom from the old Wilhelmstraße organisation, were finally appointed as consul-generals. Heinz Krekeler, an FDP deputy from North Rhine-Westphalia, became consul-general in New York; Schlange-Schöningen went to London; for Paris, Adenauer was persuaded by his neighbour Frau Schlüter-Hermkes to appoint rather an unpolitical art-historian, Wilhelm Hausenstein. The actual work in Paris was done by the second man, Gebhard von Walther, a typical product of the old Wilhelmstraße.

Entry to the Council of Europe, at first with associate member status only, was now unavoidable. Attempts to link this issue with the Saar conventions had proved unproductive, although the Social Democrats continued to urge this course. Nevertheless, relations between Adenauer and Schumacher remained relatively cordial during these weeks. Adenauer now started a detailed correspondence with the High Commissioners in an attempt to minimise the possible domestic and foreign-policy damage that would be caused by West Germany's entry to the Council of Europe. He had a number of points to make. First, Germany should not request to be accepted, instead the country should be invited to join. Second, if the Saar was admitted at the same time, this should not be interpreted as a tacit German recognition of the autonomy of that region. Third, West Germany's provisional status as an associate member should be turned into full membership as soon as possible. Adenauer also attempted to convince the High Commissioners that the Bundestag would provide majority support only if the Allies made another positive 'gesture'.[22] This would distract attention from the negative atmosphere created by the Saar conventions.

Adenauer's approach was intensely irritating both to the French and to the British Foreign Minister Ernest Bevin, who remained hostile to the Germans. As soon as they began to accept the Germans into the gathering of civilised European nations, they believed, the Germans responded by making demands and conditions of acceptance. François-Poncet was blunt in expressing his disapproval: 'Every time we try to do you a service we get our ears boxed.'[23]

When the Western Allies demanded West German entry to the Council of Europe virtually without conditions, Adenauer resorted to another argument: the repercussions of such a move on the Soviet Union.[24] On Easter Monday he told Lord Layton, a British Liberal and proprietor of the *Economist* and the *News Chronicle,* that a German entry to the Council of Europe would mean not only an unequivocal commitment to Western Europe, but also deepen the division of Germany.[25]

These hesitations should not be regarded as evidence that unsympathetic treatment by the Western Powers had caused Adenauer harbour doubts about Germany's ties with the West. This was far from being the case. In fact, his claims were designed mainly to elicit specific promises from the Western Allies. As he told Lord Layton, he was thinking both of greater responsibility in European affairs and, even more important, of a security guarantee for West Germany and shared information on defence.

McCloy held a five-hour discussion with the Chancellor three days later at his home in Bad Homburg. Adenauer's message was the same. A decision in favour of the Council of Europe would, he claimed, be an enormous risk for the Federal Republic and must therefore bring rights as well as duties. Moreover, Western Europe was shattered, disunited, unprepared and weakened by Communist parties at home. Resignation was already widespread in West Germany, even in industry. In the longer term, the arguments for seeking reinsurance in the East might become overwhelming. Stabilisation in Europe thus required a major effort from the Americans as well as the West Europeans. At the end of this argument Adenauer let the cat out of the bag: he was convinced that the situation demanded the completion of rearmament and the stationing of the necessary troops in Western Europe.[26]

McCloy responded rather nervously, even irritated. He claimed that if West Germany continued to delay its entry to the Council of Europe, and if Britain and France continued to take such a negative approach to the issue of European union, then the United States might lose interest in Western Europe altogether. Some groups in the United States already wanted to draw the 'defense perimeter' more closely to the American continent. In this context McCloy mentioned an article by Walter Lippmann, who had long been an advocate of the neutralisation of Germany and had little confidence in NATO. Since the High Commissioner had visited Washington shortly before the discussion, Adenauer regarded his comments as a clear and authoritative warning.

The meeting also showed that the U.S. occupation authorities were still tempted to intervene in German legislative matters. McCloy thus expressed very great reservations about Ludwig Erhard's plans to reduce income tax in order to stimulate investment and purchasing power. He was equally critical of the reluctance of the majority parties in the Bundestag to accept U.S. ideas for the reform of the professional civil service. Furthermore, Adenauer had discovered at a recent meeting that the High Commissioners were continuing to press for the decartelisation of major industrial concerns.

If Adenauer had recently spoken of the Saar as a protectorate or even a colony, his discussions with the High Commissioners convinced him that the position of West Germany itself was not a great deal better. The Chancellor's reaction to this apparent crisis of his Western policy was complex. Sympathisers will point to his constant avowals of commitment to Western Europe – particularly in his interviews with Kingsbury-Smith – as evidence that he remained a convinced European. However, his stubborn haggling over the details of German entry to the Council of Europe reveals a different Adenauer – a man who was determined to maintain both German rights and his own power base. On this issue, he seemed more like a cunning lawyer than a far-sighted statesman. Moreover, during these weeks he showed another side of his character, acting as a proud German who gave cautious but determined voice to the patriotic sentiments he shared with the mass of the population. He was, and continued to be, a mixture of all three: a far-sighted statesman, a tenacious tactician, and a German with strong feelings of national pride.

Since the federal election, Adenauer had spent almost all of his time in Bonn. He had made a number of brief excursions outside the federal capital, for example to the August-Thyssen-Hütte in Hamborn, where the workers had welcomed him as their saviour from Allied dismantling. Now – in the first half of April 1950 – Adenauer travelled the country in an attempt to demonstrate to the Allied governments that they were dealing with the spokesman of a great and powerful nation. Two official visits, to Munich and to Berlin, served as a platform.

On both occasions, Adenauer took the opportunity to criticise the conduct of the Western Allies. He addressed the Wirtschaftstag of the CSU in Munich, pointing out that the Allies should reduce occupation costs, which were eating up half of the tax income of the Federal Government. It was also time to agree on a reciprocal liberalisation of trade and, in particular, to increase the German steel quota. West Germany must, at the very least, be granted status as an observer in the ministerial council of the Council of Europe; mere membership of the advisory assembly was 'not worthy of us'.

His most bitter attacks were reserved for the British Foreign Minister. During a debate with Winston Churchill in the House of Commons on 28 March, Bevin – now very ill – had declared that the Germans still had a National Socialist character with roots in the Bismarckian era.[27] To loud applause from his audience, Adenauer gave his answer: 'Look anywhere in the world for a people that has shown such excellent qualities as the German one in this time of need, in such a situation of collapse.'

However, it was in Berlin that he beat the patriotic drums most loudly. Adenauer took with him other influential politicians, among them Ludwig Erhard, Thomas Dehler and Jakob Kaiser, though the thrifty Fritz Schäffer remained in Bonn. The Chancellor spent three days in the city, where reconstruction still lagged far behind West Germany and where the inhabitants were desperate for encouragement and hope. The visit was acclaimed as a great success. From that time on, Adenauer made a point of offering the city his personal protection and ensuring the constant flow of aid. During this first visit he also opened the residence of the federal representative and proclaimed on numerous occasions that Berlin was part of the Federal Republic. Cordial relations were established between Adenauer and the mayor of Berlin, Ernst Reuter of the SPD. He also made his personal peace with the Berliners, being greeted by enormous and jubilant crowds wherever he appeared. It was a more enthusiastic welcome than he had received anywhere else.

The high point of his visit was a speech in the Titania Palace,[28] where he spoke to some 1,800 invited guests who included the members of the Berlin Senate and the Western Allied city commandants. The room was decorated with the flags of all the German Länder; those from Länder in the Eastern Zone bore black ribbons. Blankenhorn had presented him with a carefully drafted speech, the main points of which he outlined in his diary: 'The Chancellor's object was to show in Berlin that the German federal government was independent of the Allies and had an autonomous approach which, first and foremost, took account of German interests, and the interests of West and East Germany at the same time. Hence the critical remarks addressed to the Western Powers with regard to their policies towards Europe, hence the unequivocal rejection of Soviet Russia and hence, at the same time, an avowal of faith in European union.'[29] On this occasion, Adenauer appealed publicly for the admission of West Germany into the Western European Union on equal terms. He even indicated that he wanted to join the Council of Europe, but only after changes were made to the Occupation Statute.

His demonstration of robust patriotism, however, was reserved for the conclusion of the speech. Adenauer urged his audience to stand and sing the third verse of the national anthem, the 'Deutschlandlied'. Naturally enough, hardly anybody knew the words. Most of them sang the traditional and controversial first verse, 'Deutschland, Deutschland über alles ...' The city commandants, who were furious, remained in their seats; Franz Neumann, leader of the left wing of the SPD in Berlin, left the platform with some of his comrades.

The reponse was powerful, not least in the Eastern Zone. Adenauer was convinced that the move had been correct. When rebuked by the High Commissioners, he told them: 'I see one of my most important tasks within the federal government as being, in contrast to the republic after 1919, not to give anything away to the nationalist tendencies in order to ensure that patriotic sentiments are channeled in the right direction.' His speech had been aimed mainly at the Germans in East Berlin. He also spoke of the national anthem: 'The first verse is so antiquated and so old-fashioned that no halfway reasonable person can sing it any more. The second verse is slightly silly. However, the third verse contains a truth that is still valid today.'[30]

Few events in the early years of Adenauer's chancellorship show his intentions as regards the national idea and patriotic feelings so clearly. His aim was to adopt and remodel these sentiments. First, he wanted to adopt them so that neither the SPD on the left, nor the extremists on the right would be able to exploit nationalist slogans against him. Second, he aimed to remodel such sentiments by emphasising those elements in the third verse of the national anthem which were compatible with the democratic state: unity, justice and freedom.

Adenauer's dispute with the government of the Eastern Zone was thus founded on the conviction that unity could be restored only in the context of freedom and democracy. The West German population had to be persuaded that links with the West were not incompatible with the quest for national identity; that it was possible to be nationally minded and to join the community of Western democracies for that very reason. At the same time, he was signalling to the Western Powers that he was not a push-over. Adenauer saw himself as the representative of all Germans and their national traditions; he had the power to guide patriotic emotions in the direction of reasonable *Westpolitik* or towards an uneasy search for lost unity.

Immediately afterwards, the German public was convinced that the Western Allies were putting Adenauer in his place when they used their power to veto the government's income-tax law. Though their disagreement on this issue had been known for some time, this was the first time that the High Commissioners had used their veto, and its proximity to Adenauer's speech in Berlin can hardly have been coincidence. Though the veto was withdrawn at the end of April, the negative public mood remained. On the other hand, Adenauer had succeeded in making himself the spokesman of the discontented, and thus gained support from nationalist groups who actually viewed his European ideas with considerable scepticism. National Liberals like Paul Sethe, editor of the *Frankfurter Allgemeine Zeitung,* were convinced that the Chancellor was moving in their direction. In an editorial, Sethe wrote that Adenauer was 'the most disappointed man in Europe'.[31] The previous autumn, he had been ready to accept sacrifices in order to take Germany into the Western community, as long as the West showed itself prepared to regard West Germany as an equal. Today he doubted the sincerity of the Western Powers. In barely a year, argued Sethe, the West had managed to turn 'a devout believer in Western ideas into a stiff and embittered sceptic'.

Adenauer continued to be particularly alarmed by his exclusion from the great decisions taken by Western cabinets. In late April and early May, there were detailed discussions in London and Paris over Western defence planning, including Germany and the role of the Federal Republic. Once again, the West Germans themselves were not consulted.

At the same time, the Western Allies increased their pressure on West Germany to join the Council of Europe. During a visit to London in late April 1950, Blankenhorn met Sir Ivone Kirkpatrick, then still head of the German desk in the Foreign Office but already General Robertson's designated successor as High Commissioner. Deep down Kirkpatrick was among those who believed that Germany should be prevented from recovering too quickly and making use of its great potential. That is why he wanted the Federal Republic to join the Council of Europe. Blankenhorn was told that further hesitation on the matter of entry might be regarded as evidence that Germany, as in Hitler's time, was contemplating foreign-policy 'surprises'. On the other hand, if West Germany made a clear decision to join the Council of Europe, Western concessions could be expected. The Federal Republic would then have more freedom to shape its foreign policy, though Kirkpatrick was cautious not to be more specific.

Kirkpatrick gave little encouragement to Blankenhorn on the security issue. The British themselves, he argued, would not be secure if the Russians advanced westwards. More important than the reinforcement of the British troops in Germany was the fact that powerful bomber formations, equipped with the atom bomb, were stationed in North Africa; in the event of war they would be able to carry out a devastating attack against the heart of Soviet industry in Rostov and Baku. So long as the Soviet Union feared this response, it would not march into central Europe.

Churchill also made an appeal to Adenauer to join the Council of Europe without delay. Its assembly was due to meet in July. He would personally advocate that only nations with equal rights could be members.

Adenauer concluded that the decision to join must be made, even at the cost of a bitter dispute with Kurt Schumacher and the SPD. Opinions in his own ranks were also divided. He already knew that Jakob Kaiser and Gustav Heinemann would express strong reservations in cabinet. However, on 11 May the spring conference of the Atlantic Council would begin in London. The situation had to be resolved by then.

The Schuman Plan

There now began the week which was quickly recognised by the public as a turning-point in the history of post-war Europe. On the morning of 8 May 1950, exactly five years after the unconditional surrender of the Wehrmacht, Adenauer approved, with some amendments, a draft memorandum on West German entry to the Council of Europe. It was published immediately.

At noon that Monday, Robert Jean Mischlich, a representative of the French Foreign Ministry, handed Blankenhorn a personal letter from Robert Schuman to Adenauer. Mischlich stressed that his mission must be treated in the strictest confidence. No-one must know the content of the letter; not even the French High Commission in Bad Godesberg had been told of his visit, and he had been instructed not to make contact for the present.[1]

Schuman's two-page letter was dated 7 May and was signed by hand – 'with my most cordial regards, Schuman'.[2] It began as follows: 'As I am about to propose to the French government the taking of an important decision for the future of Franco-German relations, of Europe and of peace, I would like to explain to you the declaration that I will ask my government to accept and to publish. I would also like to make clear to you the spirit in which I have written this declaration.'

The following sentences were taken from the famous memorandum by Jean Monnet, who was soon to be recognised by Adenauer as the creator of the Schuman Plan: 'World peace cannot be guaranteed without creative efforts proportional to the dangers that threaten it. The contribu-

Notes for this section begin on page 725.

tion which an organised and living Europe can make to civilisation is indispensable for the maintenance of peaceful relations.'

The subsequent remarks can also be attributed to Monnet. Adenauer could detect in them an echo of his own ideas for step-by-step progress, and see them as entirely compatible with his preference for starting with economic relations and allowing Europe to grow from a Franco-German core: 'Europe will not develop at a stroke, nor as a common construction. It will develop when concrete achievements create a first tangible solidarity. The gathering together of the European nations demands first of all the elimination of the centuries-old opposition between France and Germany.' A subsequent section convinced Adenauer that his interviews with Kingsbury-Smith had, after all, made an impression: 'You yourself have emphasised, in public statements and in the conversations we have had together, your full agreement with such an intention. Above all, you have proposed the establishment of an economic union between our two countries.'

In the view of the French government, the time was ripe to adopt this course. It therefore wished to take the initiative in a limited but vital area: 'The French government proposes that the entire Franco-German coal and steel production be placed under the control of a joint high authority within the framework of an organisation which the other European countries can join.'

Schuman appeared to have in mind a governmental agreement to be worked out with the help of an arbitrator accepted by all participants. The issue of ownership of the businesses involved would not be affected by the decision to establish a high authority. Furthermore, the responsibilities of the Ruhr authority, along with other obligations imposed on West Germany, would have to be taken into account 'in so far as these will continue to exist'.

The most crucial points in the letter were the calls for 'peaceful cooperation' and for the establishment of the 'foundations of a European economic organism'. Schuman was confident of success at home, even though the French Council of Ministers had not yet been involved: 'I stress once again that this declaration will undoubtedly be published by the French government on Thursday evening.' Until then, the greatest discretion was required.

Adenauer discussed the French proposal with Blankenhorn that afternoon. He was convinced that the French initiative would create an entirely new situation in Europe, and that it was entirely in keeping with the ideas he had supported for decades. He wrote immediately to signal his agreement. The need for detailed negotiations ensured that the risks were tolerable, especially in comparison with the enormous opportunities that would open up. Not least, the French proposal provided the kind of backing Adenauer needed to secure acceptance of West German entry to the Council of Europe.

Two letters of reply were drafted, one official and one personal. The official letter contained a declaration of sympathy with the idea, but also revealed Adenauer's innate caution:

> I welcome the ideas developed in this letter as a vital step towards a close association between Germany and France and thus to a new order in Europe built on the basis of peaceful cooperation. Of course the federal government will give thorough consideration to the French plan as soon as its details are known. However, even now I can declare Germany's readiness to take part in the scrutiny of the plan and in preparing the organisational measures that will be needed in future.'[3]

In his personal letter to Schuman, Adenauer freely expressed his pleasure 'that this plan of the French government has given the relations between our two countries, which threatened to be paralysed by mistrust and reserve, a fresh impetus towards constructive cooperation.' At the same time he told Schuman that the cabinet would shortly decide to join the Council of Europe; he added the warning that the SPD would probably oppose the decision. In the final sentence he used a term that Schuman, despite his positive tone, had not employed – the idea of 'equality': 'The plan of the French government, which you have outlined for me in broad terms, will find a strong response in German public opinion because, for the first time since the catastrophe of 1945, Germany and France are to work with equal rights on a common task'.[4]

That evening at 6.50 pm, Mischlich was invited to the Foreign Ministry and given the two letters. Adenauer promised that he would speak about the proposal in public only after Schuman had made his announcement at a press conference. It was not until later that he discovered how much weight Schuman had attached to his response. The French Council of Ministers met on Thursday morning. Monnet and Schuman had taken great care to inform only the key figures in cabinet, but now hoped for rapid agreement in order to provide something for Robert Schuman to take to the London conference the next day, where he would be confronted by a demand for French agreement to an increase in the German steel quota. That Sunday, Dean Acheson was also informed. As a dyed-in-the-wool anti-truster from the school of Felix Frankfurter, his first reaction was unenthusiastic; Acheson suspected that the Europeans were about to re-establish another of those cartels that he and his liberal friends so despised.

At the same time that the French Council of Ministers was meeting, the federal cabinet gathered in Bonn to decide on German entry to the Council of Europe. Two brief accounts by participants – Seebohm's[5] and Blankenhorn's[6] – have survived. These reveal that Adenauer made the case for entry as he had done before, on the basis of his analysis of the international situation. Only if Europe became the 'third force' between the two world powers, he argued, would it be able both to assert itself and to secure peace. For that to take place, Germany was needed. If it refused, the Council of Europe would also fail.

Jakob Kaiser and Gustav Heinemann disagreed with the Chancellor's analysis. Kaiser feared that a German entry might have negative consequences for the Eastern Zone, to which Adenauer replied that the Eastern Zone could only be saved by economic and political moves to strengthen the West. On the other hand, Heinemann and Kaiser argued that a decision to join the Council of Europe would increase the danger of war. In Kaiser's view, the Council of Europe was the first step towards an Atlantic pact and meant the incorporation of Germany into the defence system of the Western Powers. In effect, this was the first round of the major dispute which was to lead to Heinemann's departure from the cabinet in October 1950. Both Adenauer and Heinemann had already settled on the arguments they were to use throughout. The Chancellor claimed that Germany could not remain in no-man's land: it must decide. If the country wanted neutrality, it must be able to defend itself by force of arms – and this was inconceivable as things stood. Soviet Union would not hesitate to overrun a neutral Germany and make use of the country for its own purposes.

Heinemann and Kaiser were isolated in the cabinet. However, the disagreements were so fierce that the CDU members of the government withdrew for a separate discussion; only thereafter did the two ministers give way and permit a unanimous decision in favour of entry to the Council of Europe.

The reason given for this decision reveals that an attempt had been made to deal sympathetically with the reservations of the dissenting ministers, at least in the form of words used: 'The coming together of Europe with the inclusion of the Federal Republic of Germany is a necessary route to the maintenance of peace and to the restoration of German unity. With the intention of serving these objectives, the federal government recommends the acceptance of the invitation sent to the Federal Republic for entry into the Council of Europe.'

Blankenhorn quickly telephoned to Paris to report the positive outcome of the cabinet meeting. Adenauer discovered that the Schuman Plan had also been accepted.

Both governments were now anxious to present the good news to their respective populations in the most effective manner possible. The French deputy High Commissioner, who had intended to announce the Schuman Plan at a press conference in Bonn, thus cancelled it so that the Chancellor himself could break the news. At six o'clock that evening, Schuman met representatives of the world press at the Quai d'Orsay in order to make his own announcement. He made such an effort to avoid giving precise details that one journalist was moved to remark: 'So it's a leap into the unknown, then?' 'That is exactly what it is', Schuman replied calmly, 'a leap into the unknown'.[7]

At 8 pm another major press conference was held for three-hundred journalists in the Bundesrat assembly room in Bonn. Here Adenauer, accompanied by most of his ministers, gave news of the cabinet decision that morning and responded to the Schuman Plan.[8] He emphasised the points he had used against his critics in the cabinet. A 'federal Europe', a 'third force' would be 'an eminently peaceful factor in the world'. It was very far from 'a decision in favour of the re-militarisation of Germany', because the Council of Europe and the Atlantic pact were pursuing quite different goals. As regards the possible negative consequences for the Eastern Zone, he reminded his listeners that the same arguments had been made when the Parliamentary Council was summoned: had people not feared that it would strengthen the Iron Curtain and lead to the abandonment of Berlin? Adenauer countered such arguments with his own theory: 'The stronger the Federal Republic of Germany becomes, economically and politically, and politically also includes from an international point of view ... the better it will be for Berlin and the German east ...'

He then passed on the information he had received from Kirkpatrick: measures would soon be introduced to moderate the occupation regime; political developments had moved very quickly 'in the last eight days'. For France and for Schuman personally, he had nothing but praise: 'Magnanimous', 'of the greatest conceivable significance', 'I have had this goal in mind for more than twenty-five years'.

Kurt Schumacher was much more sceptical in his approach, though he did not reject the plan outright. The SPD, he argued, also saw Europe as the solution, but not Europe in the shape of a joint-stock company.[9] Where was nationalisation in the French plan, where was co-determination by the workers? In the following months, this was to be the focus of his criticism, even though he recognised that there was little political mileage to be gained from opposing entry to the Council of Europe.

At least for the moment, Adenauer had emerged triumphant. This was also the view taken by the press. The *Neue Zürcher Zeitung,* for example, wrote that over the preceding months he had looked to his fellow-countrymen like an 'unrealistic idealist', but that the events of the past days had opened up an entirely new political perspective.

Over the following days it became apparent how much the situation had changed. The Americans offered the initiative their enthusiastic support; the Italian Foreign Minister gave his approval. Only Bevin, who felt upstaged by the French and the Americans, was furious. The British had two major fears: the loss of their previous influence on the Ruhr coal industry, and possible exclusion from the emerging coal and steel union on the Continent. At this stage, Britain continued to be preoccupied with the Commonwealth. Nor would it have been possible to continue Labour's industrial policy under the High Authority envisaged by Jean Monnet.

From the available sources, it is difficult to be sure exactly when Adenauer realised that the Schuman Plan would also have far-reaching implications for Franco-British relations. Certainly he had understood it by the time Jean Monnet informed him about the state of the negotiations with Britain.

In the days after the announcement of the plan, it emerged that the real architect was not Robert Schuman but Jean Monnet. The discovery was bound to awaken some reservations in Adenauer. Throughout the First World War, Monnet had been a key figure in the organisation of naval transport for the Entente. In 1917, from London, he had initiated a transport pool for Allied supplies – the Allied Marine Transport Executive (AMTE) – where he had learned to motivate international teams, to bypass the inertia of national bureaucracies, and to achieve impressive results by the skilful organisation of a key area. After the war he had also served as deputy Secretary General of the League of Nations. From 1923 until the Second World War he had worked in international finance, turning up for example in Poland, the Balkans, San Francisco and on the Yangtze.

In autumn 1938, with another war imminent, the French government had sent Monnet to Washington to purchase 1,700 aircraft. At the outbreak of war, the French and British governments immediately entrusted him with the task of re-establishing the supply pool that had been so effective in 1918. It was Monnet, moreover, who had been behind Churchill's remarkable plan to delay the collapse of France in June 1940 by creating a Franco-British union.

On Churchill's behalf, Monnet then became a member of the British 'Supply Council' and continued to work in the United States which, though still neutral, regarded itself as the 'arsenal of democracy'. He was active behind the scenes in Washington before transferring to North Africa in 1943, where he joined de Gaulle and, as before, shipped masses of military equipment across the Atlantic to supply the Free French armed forces. When the war ended Monnet was fifty-seven years old. Subsequently he was appointed 'Commissaire au Plan' by the French government, with the task of supervising the modernisation of French industry. In this context, Monnet also played a key role in the deliberate expansion of the steel industry. The development had created considerable over-capacities; now, with the German steel industry regaining its strength, the moment of truth for his ambitious modernisation programme had come.

Monnet had always kept out of party politics and never sought elected office. However, in 1950 acute political observers regarded him as a key figure behind the scenes: a committed advocate of modernisation, supported by selected groups of like-minded individuals, and with an unparalleled ability to define French needs at an international level. Monnet knew everyone of significance in the political and economic spheres of France, the United States and Britain. In these countries at least, he was enormously respected.

Germany, however, was an alien landscape to him. Moreover, if any single figure can be said to have embodied the co-operation of the western democracies against Germany in two world wars, it was Monnet. He was a powerful man and, as Adenauer quickly recognised, a potentially dangerous one; as 'Commissaire au Plan', his reputation would be damaged if the German coal and steel industry could not be controlled and directed according to French requirements. Could he really be trusted? Was it possible that the leaders of the former Entente and the Allies of the Second World War had decided, with the aid of the capable and cunning Monnet, to retard the development of Germany's key industries over the long term?

This was certainly Brüning's fear, who, during a long conversation in June 1950, brought the background of the Schuman Plan to Adenauer's attention.[10] On the other hand, Monnet seemed a curiously familiar figure to the Chancellor. In some ways he resembled Dannie N. Heineman, though Monnet was a much more political figure. Monnet apparently possessed the same ability to grasp the global connections of international politics and economics; he had the same extraordinary knowledge of leading figures on both sides of the Atlantic; he had – it was to be hoped – the same visionary qualities as Heineman. Perhaps he sincerely recognised that the peoples on both sides of the Atlantic could only survive and prosper if they chose close integration based on genuine partnership. Only time would tell whether Monnet was an enlightened realist or simply a cunning representative of the policy of French self-interest.

At the beginning of June, after Monnet's first visit to Bonn, Adenauer discussed the Frenchman with Hans Schäffer, who had been state secretary in the Reich Finance Ministry under Brüning. He was encouraged by what he heard. Schäffer, who had known Monnet for twenty-five years, assured him that Monnet had always wanted an understanding with Germany and had frequently offered good advice on the subject.[11]

And yet, Adenauer would have been greatly concerned if he had been aware of the *note de réflexion* written by Monnet on 3 May in order to persuade Bidault's cabinet of the merits of his plan.[12] The United States, he claimed, would insist on granting Germany a place in the Western camp, partly because they could see no other solution and partly because they doubted French stability and dynamism. Within a short time France would be exposed to the full competitive force of German industry.

At a time when French steel production stood at 9 million tons, Germany was already demanding an increase in its quota from 11 million to 14 million tons. The French would oppose the increase, but the Americans would insist on granting it. As a result, French steel production would stagnate or even decline; Germany would flood the world market at knock-down prices, French industry would respond with a demand for protective tariffs, and the old pre-war cartels would be revived. Monnet thought that Germany might then turn to the markets of the East as a prelude to political agreements. France, on the other hand, would again fall into the rut of restricted production that was protected from the competition of the world market.

It is true that Monnet also referred to a dynamic and constructive new concept, a major advantage of which was that it was being proposed by France. However, he made it clear that the creation of a pool for coal and steel was designed to counter a threatening German preponderance. His formula was for joint expansion in mutual competition, but without either side predominating. French industry should thus be brought to the same level as German; it should be given the opportunity to expand without fear of dumping by German industry, and without being forced to join any form of cartel. German industrial comeback was taking place against the background of the Cold War. Ultimately, France would not be strong enough to prevent German rearmament. This, he thought, was the last chance for a genuine French initiative to prevent a disastrous future that was already appearing on the horizon.

It was still possible to direct German energies towards Europe and thereby change the course of developments. Monnet's planned High Authority with supra-national powers would work for a balanced relationship, and would be based on a treaty which could be negotiated with Germany while the country was still weak. He saw the alternative in stark terms: the United States would dominate, pulling the British along in its wake; the Americans would set Germany more or less free, in order to gain an ally in the Cold War; and France would be left behind.

Monnet, it appears, thus wanted to achieve a long-term control of Germany. However, this aim was to be facilitated through an entirely modern concept designed to lead to partnership and – so his sketch even then – in the longer term to a European federation.

When Adenauer subjected the Schuman Plan to critical scrutiny, he was forced to recognise that Monnet and Schuman were not the only important personalities in Paris. He was aware that representatives of a more old-fashioned and distinctly anti-German security policy continued to be influential among the civil servants in the Quai d'Orsay. These included Alexandre Parodi, the general secretary of the Quai d'Orsay, Maurice Couve de Murville and Henri Alphand, the leaders of the political and economic departments, and François Seydoux, then responsible for European affairs. This group hoped to reinforce in a lasting manner the control elements in the Schuman Plan. It was a policy that would not be short of support among the political parties in the National Assembly.

German industry was still persuaded to welcome the Schuman Plan in principle because it hoped to be released from Allied controls of the Ruhr. Closer analysis – such as a memorandum written for Adenauer by Günter Henle on 10 June 1950 – nevertheless revealed that the plan to create a

High Authority for coal and steel enabled Paris to pursue precisely the objectives that had been set out in Monnet's internal memorandum.

The French wanted to obtain a larger market area through the fusion of markets while retaining their current lead. The development of the German steel industry was to be geared to French needs. Equally, the French wanted to share German coal resources on favourable terms, having failed in the attempt to make their own coal mines competitive by means of increased investment. In the short term, the fusion was bound to lead to a reduction in German coal and steel prices and thus to adjustment difficulties for the German coal and steel industry. From the German point of view, it could be argued that Monnet's failure with his ambitious modernisation plans had persuaded him to attempt an eleventh-hour 'flight forwards', undertaken in an attempt to disguise the bad investment policies over which he had presided.

Adenauer himself wavered between hope and scepticism. He was eager to encourage France to take a revolutionary new approach to Franco-German relations and was tempted to see Monnet's plans as such a move. At the same time, his sceptical realism told him that he might be in danger of walking into a trap.

There remained many arguments in favour of taking the risk. Success would be of immense value to Germany, for a variety of reasons: Germany's return on equal terms to a modern organised community of free European peoples; the dismantling of the Ruhr controls; the elimination of Franco-German rivalry; security against the Soviet Union within a bloc of West European democracies. Between January and May 1950, Adenauer had recognised the price he would have to pay for the stagnation of his Western policy.

Although he felt a sense of relief about the Schuman Plan, Adenauer approached his first meeting with Monnet on 23 May 1950 with some concern. Monnet, who was an acute observer, recalled later: 'That was not a confident man but one who was curious about what I had to say and who found it difficult to free himself of a certain mistrust. Apparently he could not believe that we were really offering him equal rights, and the years of difficult negotiations and wounded pride still marked his attitude.'[13]

A few days later, however, the Chancellor told Hans Schäffer that he had been favourably impressed by Monnet. He had been warned that, unlike Schuman, Monnet was not influenced by religious motives, being an agnostic liberal with an anti-clerical streak. In the end this did not prejudice Adenauer's judgement. Adenauer saw Monnet as 'very clever, very well-meaning, very well-informed, calm, free of vanity', and as a man who genuinely wanted to bring about a political understanding between their two peoples.[14]

Monnet had come to him from London, where he had begun to realise quite clearly that the British would not take part, at least for the time being. Before meeting Adenauer he had visited the High Commission, which was still responsible for West German foreign policy. The crucial question to be decided was whether West Germany and France were to be allowed to negotiate with each other directly. Monnet insisted that this must be accepted, even if the High Commissioners had to be represented at the negotiating table in some form. McCloy and Monnet had been acquainted since the Frenchman's sojourn in Washington and had established a good working relationship; the Schuman Plan negotiations, moreover, were to reveal that Washington had chosen its representative well. The British, however, were aware that the surprise French initiative was likely to force them out of the Ruhr control mechanism, and insisted at first on a High Commission presence at the negotiations. Eventually they backed down: Monnet was authorised to begin negotiations with Adenauer after a promise to keep the High Commissioners informed of developments. That afternoon he was able to tell Adenauer the good news that the High Commission had dropped the demand to send an observer to the negotiations.

Adenauer and Monnet spoke together for two hours in the presence of the deputy French High Commissioner Bérard, Bernard Clappier, Schuman's *chef de cabinet,* and Herbert Blankenhorn. The talks decided the future progress of the project, and with it the fate of Adenauer's foreign policy.[15]

Monnet described the project in convincing terms, even though it was clear that he would not only be the team captain but would also decide both the rules and the identity of the players. He began with an overall survey of the state of negotiations. The United States was strongly in favour, the High Commissioners had signalled their acceptance, and the Benelux countries would probably want to join. He thought that the British were hesitating, but that they would probably join as well after a period of observation. Once again Monnet described his great vision: the organisation of heavy industry– previously the basis of war industries – and the elimination of Franco-German enmity to achieve peaceful cooperation and the renewal of Europe's major role in the world.

The Frenchman then turned to procedural questions. Technical-economic aspects, he thought, would have to take a back seat at first. In the early stages, a group of delegates equipped with special powers – here Clappier made it clear that Monnet would be chairman – must work on equal terms for a general treaty. Only thereafter would 'the technicians' be involved. The enterprise itself, however, was political; specific problems could be solved as long as they were approached with the great idea in mind.

This was precisely what Adenauer wanted to hear. It was exactly the approach he had taken to his own projects throughout his long life – first the big idea and then a complex negotiating process which gave full rein to his tactical skills. Of course, there was much that had to be taken on trust. Monnet would be the key figure, so much in control of the process that he might well emerge at the head of the new High Authority. Once the rules of the game were fixed, the West Germans would be forced to accept Monnet's decisions on the major economic issues of production quotas, prices and markets.

Yet Adenauer wanted to believe, and was therefore prepared to accept Monnet's method. He himself was not a technician, he claimed, nor even one-hundred per cent a politician. His view was similar to that of Monnet: the project was primarily of a moral nature, although technical aspects could not be ignored. He agreed that it would be wrong to cling to details; he was eager to confirm that the German federal government had no desire to achieve a new German supremacy.

Thus these two experienced practitioners took their first steps towards the great venture of European reconciliation. Once agreement had been reached on general philosophy and procedures, Adenauer was prepared to discuss potential members of the German delegation with Monnet. This was a very rare concession from Adenauer, particularly since he and Monnet were meeting for the first time.

Monnet proposed that the negotiating delegation should be placed directly under the control of the Federal Chancellor. In France, Robert Schuman alone was responsible, the technical ministries having been excluded for the time being. When Monnet broached the subject of the leader of the German negotiating team, Adenauer put forward the names of Walter H. Merton, Hermann Josef Abs and Hans Schäffer.

Though Adenauer did not make this clear, his preferred choice was Abs, who was then deputy chairman of the board of directors of the Bank for Reconstruction in Frankfurt. It was apparent that the regulations of the Schuman Plan would be worked out by a small group under the chairmanship of the capable Monnet, who would also be personally involved in the subject matter. In this situation, Adenauer was keen for German interests to be represented by an equally capable expert; he was convinced that Monnet had an acute understanding of the coal and steel problem which the German representation should match. Monnet's reaction revealed that he did not want an economist as the leader of the German delegation and hoped to dominate the proceedings alone. The Germans, he believed, should send an academic instead. Moreover, he pointed out – though in vague terms – that French public opinion had responded badly to a visit by Abs to the United States because of his role as representative of German interests during the occupation of France. Not for the first time, Adenauer discovered that Abs was persona non grata for the French.

When Adenauer mentioned Hans Schäffer, who was greatly respected for his work as financial adviser to the Wallenberg group during his exile in Sweden, Monnet nodded in approval. The Chancellor also mentioned Karl Bernard, president of the Zentralbankrat of the Bank deutscher Länder. Monnet, however, explained his belief that it was better not to appoint a banker since the leader of the negotiations must be completely independent. This was the case with Bernard, in Adenauer's view, but he decided it was time to end the discussions.

Before the two men parted, Monnet again emphasised how crucial it was for the delegation leader to have an understanding of the general interest. Adenauer said good-bye with the following words: 'Monsieur Monnet, I regard the French proposal as the most important task before me. Should I succeed in handling it well, I believe, I will not have lived in vain.'[16]

Adenauer did not reveal his attitude towards the participation of Britain. He contented himself with observing to Monnet that, as a people, the British had to be given time. In reality, he would have preferred Germany and France to reach agreement first before asking other countries to participate. When Monnet described this approach as impossible, Adenauer did not insist.

Nevertheless, as to the British, Adenauer continued to suspect them of following the principle of 'divide and rule': they feared a union between France and Germany because the two states would then achieve supremacy. Though he did not say so to Monnet, Adenauer was convinced that the British saw their own power slipping away everywhere. When he discussed the situation with Hans Schäffer shortly afterwards, he made his views on the subject perfectly clear.[17]

Adenauer was therefore pleased to agree to a press communique which provided Monnet, who was equally disappointed with the British, with a powerful diplomatic weapon: 'Herr Jean Monnet and the Federal Chancellor have established complete agreement in their views, especially as regards their interest in a rapid realisation of the proposal.'[18]

In his memoirs Monnet hints that the outcome of the negotiations with Britain was virtually decided at the outset. Adenauer had accepted both the concept of a coal and steel pool and Monnet's idea that the decisions of an independent High Authority must be binding for all participants. London appeared to have little room for manoeuvre. When negotiations between Britain and France broke down at the beginning of June, Adenauer had achieved a situation he had hardly dared to dream about only a month before: a visible Franco-German rapprochement at the expense of an equally obvious deterioration in relations between France and Britain. He had not worked for this, but it would have been naive not to make the most of the opportunity.

The following weeks were taken up with an intensive search for a leader of the German delegation. Despite strong warnings from Heinrich Brüning, Adenauer was eager to appoint Hans Schäffer, but his Swedish citizenship eventually proved to be an insuperable obstacle. Nevertheless,

Schäffer was happy to work in the background as an expert and to advise Adenauer on his choice of members for the delegation. Like Adenauer, he would have preferred to see Abs in the leading role. Adenauer pointed out that the French had expressed reservations but, after a discussion with Abs, authorised Schäffer to broach the issue with Monnet.[19]

Adenauer also held detailed discussions with Professor Röpke of Geneva, who had considerable reservations about Monnet's planning optimism. He regarded a merger of coal and steel production as desirable in order to solve the security problem, but warned against plans to extend the concept of integration into other branches of the economy. Like Schäffer, he was also prepared to work for the conference as an expert authority. It was Röpke who proposed Walter Hallstein as leader or deputy leader of the delegation.

Time was running out. On 20 June the negotiating committee was due to assemble in Paris under the chairmanship of Monnet. Adenauer offered Blankenhorn the post of leader of the delegation on 15 June, but Blankenhorn provided a number of convincing reasons why he could not be appointed, and instead joined the delegation simply as Adenauer's personal representative. Adenauer told Monnet that the two men could contact each other directly through Blankenhorn whenever it proved necessary. That afternoon Hallstein met Adenauer for the first time and made an excellent impression. Adenauer thereupon appointed him leader of the German delegation.

Adenauer was determined to establish personal control over the delegation, which also included a trade-union representative, Hans vom Hoff. Meanwhile, the various authorities in the federal government had begun to take notice. At the urgent request of Vice Chancellor Blücher, Adenauer held a meeting in Rhöndorf for Blücher, Ludwig Erhard and Fritz Schäffer. They agreed on the establishment of a ministerial committee to supervise the delegation, consisting of Adenauer and the three ministers, plus the cabinet's own nominee, Anton Storch. Erhard had already set up two working staffs – one legal and one economic.[20]

In the Ministry for Economic Affairs and the Ministry for the Marshall Plan, there was some dissatisfaction at the way Adenauer had taken control of negotiations on this vital issue. Yet there was no serious opposition when the negotiating team left for Paris. On 20 June the German delegation arrived at the Quai d'Orsay – the first time since the Second World War that German representatives appeared on equal terms in the international arena. Adenauer felt that he had taken his country's first step back towards full membership of the international community. His position had also been strengthened by the vote on entry to the Council of Europe, which had been passed by the Bundestag five days before. In view of the unsatisfactory position concerning the Saar, a very small majority had been expected, but in the event he obtained a comfortable majority of sixty-eight. More than anything else, this was testimony to the power and appeal of the Schuman Plan within West Germany.

In the short period between 9 May and 20 June, the danger of stagnation in Adenauer's Western policy had disappeared. No sooner had this occurred, however, than his foreign policy was shaken once more. Five days after the beginning of the negotiations on the Schuman Plan, North Korean troops invaded South Korea. The security question now returned to the centre of the political stage. Over the preceding months, West German entry to the Council of Europe and the Schuman Plan could be – and had been – presented as great acts of peace. As far as the Western democracies were concerned, this was precisely what they were. It could even be argued that the policy was also undertaken with the aim of guaranteeing peace with the Communist powers.

However, the security debate which began in June 1950 was of a very different nature. It fed off the gnawing fear of an attack from the east, either immediately or in the near future. The Korean War did no more than act as the trigger for the debate. In reality, the willingness to establish West German forces in some form dated from the months prior to the North Korean aggression – both in the Pentagon, in the British general staff, and from Adenauer himself.

'That Bully Adenauer'

Even contemporaries regarded Adenauer's offer of a German defence contribution, in whatever form, as the riskiest of his many risky decisions. In retrospect, that is exactly what it was. Though the history books record that the attack by North Korea against South Korea was the reason for his offer, new sources have become available which make it necessary to revise this view. On 6, 7 and 8 June – two weeks before the North Korean invasion – Adenauer had proposed to all three High Commissioners that discreet moves should be made to establish German contingents. If the details had become public knowledge at the time, the resulting outcry might have driven him from office.

Another popular theory is that Adenauer regarded the offer of German soldiers mainly as a political instrument to regain German sovereignty, rather than as a military force to be used in the event of war. This view, too, requires correction. There is no disputing that, during the long negotiations over the European Defence Community, the political function of a West German defence contribution came increasingly to the fore. In spring and early summer 1950, however, this was not the case.

Notes for this section begin on page 725.

At that time Adenauer believed that an attack from the East would almost certainly be launched in the short or medium term, and therefore pressed with great vigour for the creation of a German force as soon as possible. His approach to the explosive issue of a military contribution was thus relatively straightforward. Fearing an attack by the enemy, he believed that it was essential to re-arm as quickly as possible in the hope that this would deter the attacker. If deterrence failed, then at least the defenders would be prepared for the struggle ahead.

During the domestic political conflict over the defence contribution, Adenauer's pacifist critics on the Protestant and Catholic left saw the problem largely in moral terms: should a people such as the Germans, with the Second World War on their conscience, ever bear to arms again? Adenauer appears to have been either unable or unwilling to understand such thinking, let alone allow himself to be influenced by it. In his view, armed self-defence was one of the natural rights of every people. A military contribution would only become a moral issue if the West or the Federal Republic were to plan an unprovoked war of aggression. This was never a possibility for Adenauer, for whom an armed force had an exclusively defensive function.

The issues which concerned him were predominantly political. What kind of effective defence contribution could best be realised at international level? How could the German people, many of whom had adopted profoundly anti-militarist attitudes, be convinced of the need for a German military contribution? Was it necessary to seek an agreement with the SPD for this change, and at what price? Could he risk the hostility of the Social Democrats instead of seeking agreement? How could he ensure that the officer corps remained under strict political control?

In Adenauer's view, German soldiers or armed police units could not solve the security problem on their own. Of equal, if not more, importance was an immediate reinforcement of the inadequate Allied forces in Germany, plus a formal Western security guarantee. In all his references to the security problem in the two years between the start of the Berlin blockade and the outbreak of the Korean War, whether in confidential discussions or in risky press interviews, this was always his main emphasis.

In this context Adenauer was aware of two dangers, which were connected but could be countered in different ways. The most disturbing in the short term appeared to be the rapid expansion of the garrisoned Volkspolizei ('people's police') in the Eastern Zone. In the longer term, however, he was convinced that the West must correct the imbalance of forces in central Europe between the powerful Red Army and the relatively weak and unco-ordinated armies of the Western Powers.

The Volkspolizei of the German Democratic Republic comprised some 70,000 men in summer 1950, though it was expected to develop into a force of 150,000 men in the near future. For the time being, it was not an impressive strike-force. However, the Federal Republic had nothing at all to match it. Though the Allied divisions had at their disposal some 80,000 Germans in the service units, these were not combat troops and could not have been sent into action independently. Nor would the Allied troops stationed in West Germany have been able to mount effective resistance to the occupation of large areas by the Volkspolizei, a fact which would have enormous psychological repercussions across the entire Federal Republic. Still, Adenauer was convinced that determined action could bring about the establishment of a defence force in West Germany capable of dealing with the Volkspolizei.

If East German forces alone were regarded as the potential enemy, then the establishment of a garrisoned federal police force was the appropriate answer. As a result of the long border and the ability of the Volkspolizei to choose the place of an armed incursions, such a West German force had to be numerically superior.

Adenauer had another reason for wishing to establish a counter-weight to the Volkspolizei. In the early days of the Federal Republic, it was always possible that the Western Powers would agree to withdraw the occupying troops to specific bridgeheads, leaving the Federal Republic utterly unprepared for limited advances by well-equipped East German units. In theory, the problem of providing a counterweight to the Volkspolizei could have been solved technically, and perhaps even militarily, without any fundamental decision about the establishment of West German divisions.

In the event, this latter issue could not, after all, be avoided. It was brought to the fore by the fear that the Soviet Union might employ its armoured divisions and air force in an attempt to conquer Western Europe, as Hitler had done in May 1940. In 1950, many of the Western general staffs, and a good number of the politicians, had come to see this as a possible, and even likely, development. It could only be resisted if the Federal Republic itself made an important defence contribution. Such a contribution, however, was possible only within the framework of an extensive rearmament programme.

Following the founding of NATO, the Western general staffs had been working towards that end. Since the onset of deep East-West tensions in spring 1948, the balance of forces between the Red Army and the West had become so uneven that only a defence at the Pyrenees appeared to have any chance of success. Plans for a defence effort along the Rhine, of the kind that emerged in general staff discussions, were little more than placebos for politicians without the strength or the foresight to begin a major programme of rearmament. In spring 1950, the situation appeared so critical that NATO members discussed detailed planning papers and took their first decisions at two major conferences in Paris and London.

The general staffs of the Western states were fully aware that such decisions were indispensable. In November 1948, the Joint Chiefs of Staff

in Washington approved a war plan for Operation 'Offtackle'. The underlying assumptions of this plan, which remained in force until 1952, were
so depressing that the U.S. planners were never prepared to incorporate it
in the general staff planning of NATO.

In their deliberations the Joint Chiefs of Staff envisaged four phases of
war. According to their assessment, the first phase would see the European continent occupied by the Red Army as far as Britain and Portugal.
North Africa would remain in the hands of the Western Powers, and it
might also prove possible for them to hold Spain. In a second phase, the
main effort would have to be devoted to the defence of Britain, as well as
Spain, North Africa and Egypt. Without these bridgeheads, no re-con-
quest of Europe was likely to be possible. Given the experiences of the
Second World War, it was not certain that strategic air raids on the Soviet
Union would be effective in this phase. Nevertheless, as in the years
1942-1943, the United States could hope to build up its forces for a re-
occupation of Europe and to create initial bridgeheads in Italy.

At the end of the second phase, and during the third, the invasion of
1944 was to be repeated. The first spearhead would be directed at the area
between Cherbourg and the German Bight, the second in southern
France. As many Soviet divisions as possible would be enveloped and
destroyed in a vast pincer movement. This would lead to a fourth phase
ending with the capitulation of the Soviet Union.

Such was the planning for 'Offtackle'. The sober reality was that continental Europe would become the helpless victim of the Soviet Union if
the latter decided to attack. The best that could be offered was the hope
of liberation in the distant future.

Naturally enough, there were no plans to share this assessment with
Adenauer. Only the British chiefs of staff were informed of the 'Offtackle'
scenario in autumn 1949. Not surprisingly, they were appalled by it.

However, in winter 1948/49 Adenauer had read an aide-mémoire by
General Speidel, based partly on data from the Gehlen Organisation.
Speidel also assumed that the Soviet Union would be able to break through
to the Pyrenees, although the Western general staffs regarded the Rhine as
a 'possible and secure' defensive line. With the current balance of forces,
almost all of Germany would be occupied even in the best case scenario.[1]

The situation did not change in 1949. From that time onwards, however, the plans of the Western Allies revealed a characteristic tendency on
the part of the Europeans to fool themselves. In the staff discussions of the
Western Allies and NATO, it became customary to plan for the defence of
the Rhine line, Italy and parts of Scandinavia. In view of their own lack of
forces, West European planners expected a massive injection of U.S. land
forces and tactical air forces which the Americans, until spring 1951, were
neither willing nor able to supply. By contrast, the United States assumed
that it was mainly the task of the Europeans to prevent themselves from

being overrun by the Soviets by building up their own forces. Owing to the fact that East-West tensions declined for a time in 1949, nothing concrete was done. However, all the leading military and political figures knew that Dean Acheson was correct when, at the London Conference of May 1950, he described NATO as standing naked.[2]

In this situation, the general staffs in Washington, London and Paris reached identical conclusions. If there was to be any prospect of a successful defence even of the countries and regions west of the Rhine, German fighting forces would be indispensable. The Pentagon would have preferred to include the demand for German contingents in the NATO plans of May 1950, but the State Department refused out of regard for public opinion in France and Britain. However, British-American discussions in May 1950 revealed that the British too believed that the arming of Germany could not be avoided. Bevin and Acheson secretly agreed to accept West Germany into NATO if necessary.

Still, the decisive factor in this respect would be the future development of the Federal Republic in the fields of domestic and foreign policy.[3] General Speidel had been informed by French generals that the need for German contingents was not in dispute, at least among influential military experts in the French capital. But in Paris, as in Washington and London, measures that were agreed to be appropriate were not necessarily politically feasible.

Adenauer himself was almost completely excluded from the decision-making process. He had to be content with such information as the High Commissioners and their senior officials were prepared to give him and Blankenhorn. Otherwise, he and his staff were forced to rely on the newspapers for their information. Only from mid-1950 did the German consulate-general under Hans Schlange-Schöningen begin its work in London as the first consular representation of the Federal Republic abroad; it was quickly followed by offices of equal standing in Paris and New York under consuls-general Hausenstein and Krekeler. Official business with the Western capitals, however, continued to be routed through the High Commission until spring 1951.

During these months, Blankenhorn was a key figure and a tireless worker. His task was to gather individual pieces of information on the 'grand policy' of the Western Powers, obtained through his frequent discussions with officials in the High Commission, and to use the pieces to complete the jigsaw puzzle. Not until April 1950 was the Chancellor's alter ego able to participate in discussions in London.

Since the beginning of the negotiations on the Schuman Plan in May, Blankenhorn had also travelled frequently to Paris. Gradually, a stream of information began to reach Bonn from the German negotiating team led by Hallstein. A few weeks previously, in the middle of April, General von Schwerin had been invited to London for a briefing by the British, who saw him as their military contact in the Chancellor's office. At the same time, the German newspapers were beginning to establish a network of foreign correspondents with wider access to information than before.

The information upon which vital decisions were based was therefore fragmentary and uncertain. In reality, owing largely to its early links with General Gehlen, the government was much better informed about the military threat from the East than about the military and political projects of the Western Powers.

It remained uncertain whether, and to what extent, the Western Powers possessed the will to beef up the appalling security situation. Clearly, the prospects of the Federal Republic were worst of all, since France, Britain and Belgium could at least take comfort in the illusion of successful defence along the Rhine. As long as no specific crisis arose, this appeared to satisfy them. On the other hand, the federal government could scarcely afford to take comfort in illusion if its own assessment of the situation was correct.

There is a natural temptation for politicians in democracies to avoid difficult decisions for reasons of convenience. In the West German case this temptation was particularly great. Adenauer would have had many good reasons to suppress news of the gravity of the situation: moral reluctance, genuine considerations of foreign policy, and domestic political factors. The effort required to win acceptance of a German defence contribution would be so enormous that there was an obvious inclination not to make a serious attempt at solving the problem until the tanks from the East were already on the move.

Adenauer's preoccupation with the military situation, long before he was encouraged or forced into it by the Western Allies, is one aspect of his character that is not easy to explain. Obviously, his ability to perceive the danger is less of a surprise; ever since he was mayor of Cologne he had taken account of the possibility of crisis and war in designing his long-term policy. More surprising is the intensity of his determination to master strategic and technical military issues, irrespective of the fact that he was a civilian known to be critical of the generals. However, it should not be forgotten that, for members of his generation, an interest in military matters was almost as normal as a concern for economic and social processes. Adenauer remembered the strategy discussions that had taken place before 1914; he had lived through the First World War; he could recall the military preparations of the later 1930s and the experiences of the Second World War. Even as a layman in military affairs, he knew from personal experience that security questions had to be taken seriously.

Even so, there was an argument for ignoring or postponing difficult issues until the Western Allies finally approached the Federal Republic in their own self-interest. This was the line advocated by Heinrich Brüning, for example in a letter to Helene Weber on 5 April 1950: 'We should not commit ourselves. In the long run everything is working in our favour, without us Europe cannot be held. For that reason, if we wait and seize the right moment we can demand a great deal.'[4]

Adenauer did not wait. Some historians have tried to explain his constant ventures into the security question as an attempt to use the offer of German forces as a diplomatic instrument to free himself from the Occupation Statute. Others have argued that, in summer and autumn 1950, he persistently exaggerated the dangers of the situation in order to obtain domestic political advantages. This is certainly not correct for the years 1948 and 1949, nor for the months before the outbreak of the Korean War. Until the United States began to press for a German military contribution – and it did not do so until June 1950 – all German proposals were counter-productive to both domestic and foreign policy. There was no benefit to be gained. In fact, Adenauer was reprimanded on several occasions when he raised the issue of the defence of Germany, initially by the Americans in January 1949.

As a result, when the U.S. Secretary of State visited Bonn on 13 November 1949, Adenauer thought it wise to assure him that West Germany had no wish to make a defence contribution for two reasons: the losses of the Second World War, and the threat to the Federal Republic that this would involve.[5] He noticed that the U.S. Secretary of State did not contradict him. Two days before, however, in an interview with Paul Baar of *L'Est Républicain* in Nancy, Adenauer had asserted that if a joint high command were established, the Federal Republic would be prepared 'to integrate itself into the European defence system' at an appropriate date. Possible participation of German contingents in a European force was affirmed.[6]

This interview produced little in the way of public response. On 3 December, however, the Chancellor gave another, to the European correspondent of the *Cleveland Plain Dealer,* John Leacacos. This time the effect was dramatic. Adenauer made it plain that he was deeply concerned by the establishment of the Volkspolizei as a military force. He stressed that he was opposed to the service of German mercenaries in Western armies and to the creation of a West German Wehrmacht. However, he would be prepared to consider providing a German contingent within the framework of a European army.

Unlike the situation in January 1949, when Adenauer had been privately reprimanded by the United States, he was now attacked publicly by the German and foreign press. He was quick to amend his remarks: German participation in the defence of Western Europe could only occur if the situation became desperate. Moreover, the High Commissioners decided not to issue a public rebuke. At a private meeting on 9 December 1949, they issued a relatively mild request for the Chancellor to show restraint in his public declarations. Controversy was nevertheless inevitable. In the Bundestag he was subjected to bitter criticism from various pacifist groups and from other quarters.

Von Brentano, the chairman of the CDU/CSU *Fraktion,* thus argued that the German people themselves had no thought of rearmament. The SPD delegation refused 'even to consider German rearmament. The responsibility for safeguarding federal territory rests with the occupying powers'. The nationalist right attacked the 'outrageous idea' that a defence contribution might be demanded of the Germans in view of the war-crimes trials and the continued imprisonment of hundreds of thousands of German soldiers. On all sides, fears were expressed that a revived German militarism might endanger the new democracy. The Social Democrats, in particular, argued that a strong democracy and an attractive economic and social order would be sufficient to neutralise Soviet military power. Finally, and almost inevitably, some members of parliament argued that military rearmament would only deepen the division of Germany.

All these arguments were made during the security debate of 16 December 1949. Nevertheless, Adenauer did not change the views he had expressed in his interview with Leacacos. If his only concern had been to improve his position *vis-à-vis* the Western Powers, he could easily have made the grand gesture and used the negative response in the Bundestag as an excuse to drop the matter. This incident demonstrated that he could not make progress towards the revision of the Occupation Statute by trying to accommodate the Allies on the issue of a German military contingent. It would be equally wrong to believe that Adenauer saw the defence contribution mainly as an instrument of diplomacy.

In reality, there was one major reason for Adenauer's preoccupation with the themes of security and German defence forces. During the course of his life he had seen how one totalitarian dictatorship, in his own country, had used military force to eradicate its enemies. Now, in either the short or medium term, he believed that once again there would be war in Europe – either as the result of attacks by the Volkspolizei on West Berlin or the regions near the demarcation line, or because the Soviet Union had decided to occupy Europe. The balance of power seemed not to have changed since autumn 1948, when he had first predicted that war was imminent. Like Western public opinion as a whole, Adenauer was unaware that the United States, in the meantime, had strengthened its atomic-weapon capability, and was no longer as dependent on bluff as it had been during the Berlin crisis. But atomic weapons did not appear to provide a secure defence against a conventional attack from the east either.

Adenauer's pessimism was not a pretence. After all, what might such a demonstration have been good for in domestic or foreign policy? The fear of incursions from the East, and even major aggression, was genuine. Given that this was his main motive, it was surely sensible for the

Chancellor to advocate precautions to deal with the worst-case scenario. Obviously Adenauer hoped that the Soviet Union would be deterred from military adventures by a closing of the armaments gap, but he also believed that the Soviet Union was probably prepared to attain expansion through war.

It is true that, in 1950, Adenauer publicly stated on several occasions that there was no acute danger of war. He argued that the main threat came not from the Red Army, but from the 'fifth column' of Communist parties in France, in Italy, and to some extent from industrial centres in West Germany. In part these statements can be explained by his desire to prevent panic among the general public and even to strengthen his own resolve. Nevertheless, all the indications are that in 1948, 1949 and 1950, Adenauer was privately convinced that the East was bent on aggression. His constant broaching of the rearmament issue would simply be incomprehensible otherwise. These initiatives were not a response to suggestions from the Western Allies, but were intended to convince the Western Powers that the Federal Republic needed military defence – provided not only by the Western Powers, but also by its own troops, whether these were police units or regular divisions.

In the first three months of 1950 – internally and in interviews – Adenauer concentrated on his request for formal security guarantees from the Western Powers. Against the background of recent news about 'Offtackle', this was a somewhat futile exercise. The Soviets were aware in any case that incursions or a major attack would lead to incalculable counter-measures by the United States. At the London conference in May 1950, a declaration was issued that the NATO Treaty extended to the territory of the Federal Republic. It sounded like the most natural thing in the world: as major powers, Britain and the United States could scarcely allow themselves to be thrown out of West Germany without a struggle, particularly not by the Volkspolizei – military units composed of Germans who had been beaten as recently as 1945. Adenauer's insistence on security guarantees was designed to make the Western Powers commit themselves publicly to the principle of protecting the Federal Republic. Once this was accepted, the demand for a rapid reinforcement of Allied forces could be made much more effectively.

Adenauer was convinced that West German defence measures were essential. It was therefore an obvious step to try and achieve these in the form of a federal police. Since attempts by the GDR to stir up civil war-like troubles posed one of the most likely threats, border troops and forces to protect the Ruhr and Bonn would be necessary. Another possibility was mobile police formations in the Länder, which would need to take co-ordinated action in an emergency. This solution, not surprisingly, was strongly favoured by the Länder themselves. In current circumstances, however, a federal police force seemed likely to prove much more effective. In

Adenauer's view, it would have the advantage of greater efficiency and could also form the core of a concealed rearmament, though only to the extent that the Western Allies would allow. Since the Occupation Statute left the ultimate authority in Allied hands, the Federal Chancellor's office was aware that a simple decree would suffice to implement such a solution. The establishment of a garrisoned federal police force suitable for military operations, would merely be reproducing a development that had been under way in the Eastern Zone since 1948.

The Chancellor supported such a policy until September 1950. Opposition to it was not the sole prerogative of the Länder. The Minister of the Interior, Heinemann, was clearly reluctant to build up a federal police, and Adenauer became convinced that his minister hoped to sabotage the whole process. He maintained angrily that Heinemann accepted that the idea of a federal police was correct, but only 'with the emphasis on both words'.[7] Heinemann had no desire for the federal police units to be disguised military formations.

This, however, was exactly what Adenauer had in mind. Aware of Heinemann's opposition, he therefore decided to have the Büro Schwerin handle the issue of internal as well as external security. In February 1950 an application was made to the High Commission, through the Minister of the Interior, for permission to establish a garrisoned federal border protection force, organised in groups of one hundred. The High Commissioners refused the application. Subsequently, in a memorandum of 28 April, Heinemann requested the use of paragraph 2 of Article 91 of the Basic Law, which would allow the centralised use of a federal police or respectively of Land police forces. He also proposed the establishment of a 25,000 man mobile border-protection service, mechanised and organised on a military basis. Such a force, equipped with automatic weapons, could be operated centrally by the federal government on the authority of the Minister of the Interior.[8] Adenauer's request was discussed at the London conference. The British, in particular, took the view that such a federal police force would be a suitable springboard to a German military contribution. In their response to Adenauer, however, the High Commissioners prevaricated.[9]

During these weeks the security question became even more urgent. For some time the Socialist Unity Party had been preparing a massive Whitsuntide meeting which would bring half a million young people to East Berlin. In the West, it was feared that this would be the prelude to a surprise attack on West Berlin; during the Whitsuntide holiday at the end of May, Adenauer put the Federal Chancellor's office on increased alert.[10]

Four days before, on 24 May, he held his first personal discussion with General von Schwerin. (Previously matters had been dealt with by Blankenhorn and Globke.) Without the knowledge of the U.S. and French High Commissioners, von Schwerin had recently visited Britain, where he had discussed security issues with British officers and with Kirkpatrick, the head of the German desk at the Foreign Office. During his stay, von Schwerin had been given some idea of how far the British might be prepared to go in an emergency. Adenauer explained to the general that he had two main worries: the threat to internal security as a result of infiltration from the GDR, and open aggression by the Red Army which would unleash a flood of refugees to the West. The problems of managing and supplying large numbers of refugees, he thought, required a mobile federal police which must be built up quietly. Von Schwerin was given the task of reporting on these two issues.

In short, even before the first example of a war by proxy arose in Korea, Adenauer was aware of the danger. His actions during these weeks were guided to a considerable extent by fear that the East Germans might instigate a civil war situation in Germany.

Von Schwerin and his small staff had already been working on planning papers for some time. He now moved quickly and on 29 May 1950 submitted a memorandum entitled 'Contribution of Ideas for the Construction of a Mobile Federal Gendarmerie'.[11] There is no doubt that it was strongly influenced by ideas then under consideration by the British general staff, and that certain groups in London were willing to encourage cautious West German advances on the security question.

In May 1950, for the first time since becoming Chancellor, Adenauer fell ill and was forced to stay in bed at Rhöndorf. Blankenhorn kept him informed of developments. It was a characteristic of Adenauer that, whenever he had time to reflect – on feast days, on holidays, or while recuperating from illness – he emerged with an important decision. His intimates were well aware of the Chancellor's alarming tendency to produce key documents, launch major initiatives and reach abrupt decisions on issues he had not touched for months on end. It was during this illness, moreover, that von Schwerin's memorandum lay before him.

Von Schwerin calculated that, in the event of an attack using all the means available to them, the major Soviet formations could reach the Rhine within days. At best the Rhine would be the first line of resistance for the West. Such an attack would probably be accompanied by attempts to stage Communist uprisings inside the Federal Republic. In these circumstances, the former tank general considered an effective defence to be impossible. Between eight and ten million refugees would take to the roads; there would probably be mass liquidations and deportations to the Soviet interior; the terror that had been unleashed on the German East in 1944 and 1945 would be repeated in the Federal Republic. All that the government could do was to limit the catastrophe, to try to keep control of developments and to prevent the worst consequences.

The general had also completed a second memorandum for the Chancellor entitled: 'Outline of Practical Possibilities for the Establishment of

German Cadre Units within the Framework of United West European Combat Forces'. Here von Schwerin discussed two possible forms of German contribution to the defence of the Federal Republic: first, the establishment of German contingents in a European force; and second, the transformation of the Länder border police into a 'mobile federal gendarmerie'. The Allied service groups also had some potential, but Schwerin regarded these as 'corrupted'. Moreover, their enlistment would convince the public that the Germans would play only a mercenary role, akin to the Russian 'auxiliaries' with the German army during the Second World War. Schwerin believed that the clearest solution, and probably the one most acceptable to the population, would be the establishment of German contingents within a European framework.

At the beginning of June, the American press published reports of a note from the Federal Chancellor demanding a 25,000 strong mobile police force.[12] Adenauer had been urged by McCloy and Robertson to observe complete discretion. He was therefore furious, though not surprised, at the speed with which explosive state secrets had found their way into the American press.

Adenauer was now so alarmed that he decided to act. On 6, 7 and 8 June he asked for a series of separate discussions on the security question with Robertson, McCloy and François-Poncet in Rhöndorf.[13] These discussions, separate but linked, were of the greatest significance. It was here, and not in the famous security memorandum at the end of August, that German forces were 'offered' for the first time. The move was made before the outbreak of the Korean War, but at a time of dangerous tension within Germany.

Adenauer did not conceal the depths of his anxiety. Drawing on Schwerin's memorandum, he outlined his view of the security situation and the possible consequences of a Soviet invasion. It was possible, he claimed, that an initial wave of between eight and ten million refugees would stream towards and across the Rhine, crippling the transport system and obstructing the operations of Allied troops. If the Soviets moved to deport those Germans in the occupied territory who were able to work, for example to Siberia and the uranium mines, a second wave of refugees would set in. As Federal Chancellor, he would be forced to deal with the situation; it was therefore his responsibility to ask the representatives of the Allies for their response.

His information from von Schwerin, he continued, had persuaded him that defence against a Soviet invasion would have a chance of success only if West Germany was permitted a certain degree of rearmament. Schwerin had calculated that between ten and twelve German armoured divisions would have to be established between the Rhine and the Elbe in order to contain the first Soviet onslaught and make it more difficult for Soviet forces to plan an attack on the Western Allies. He had no doubt that the time for German rearmament had not yet come. But could they not consider the establishment of an 'international legion' in France in order to train German volunteers, both officers and men?

The advantage of an 'international legion', he thought, lay in the fact that it could be established inconspicuously. Here Adenauer was apparently thinking of the Foreign Legion, to which hundreds of young Germans were recruited each year and which could provide a cover. This was also the reason for his choice of the term 'international legion'; it sufficed to conceal what was in fact happening while making it clear that it did not involve the Foreign Legion. Adenauer told McCloy that the French could hardly complain, since these forces would protect their own security and, at the same time, could be controlled by France.

In response to the fact that the French had expressed the greatest reservations in London about a strong federal police force, the Chancellor took pains to ask his last interlocutor, François-Poncet, for his views on a federal police and an 'international legion'.

Adenauer's initiative was genuinely sensational. Moreover, the answers he received were highly instructive. It was clear that his alarm about the prospect of a Soviet attack in the near future was shared by the Western Powers. Among the High Commissioners, the man with the greatest understanding of military issues was General Robertson, who was also aware that the British general staff was pressing for a German defence contribution. His remarks thus carried great weight with Adenauer. McCloy and François-Poncet were naturally less well-informed about military matters – 'as clueless as any backwoodsman in Hether Backwash', to use the disrespectful words of Kirkpatrick in an internal discussion paper of December. On this occasion, Robertson told Adenauer that the Soviet Union was not yet ready economically for a third world war, partly because its development of atomic weapons was only just beginning. He was convinced that there was no danger for one or two years. After that, however, he considered that a Soviet invasion was likely and that Western preparations must be completed in good time. For the moment, British intelligence was keeping a constant watch on events in the East; so far, there had been no sign that an attack was imminent.

In his discussions with the Chancellor, McCloy conceded that Allied forces in Western Europe were totally inadequate, particularly those of the French. Scarcely any progress was being made, save in the field of armour-piercing weapons. As things stood, it was likely that the Soviets would overrun Western Europe in the event of war, provided that they were prepared to accept the destruction of their cities by atom bombs in retaliation. McCloy had been made very uneasy by the recent Communist youth rally in East Berlin, when the Communists had succeeded in mobilising half-a-million young people. Nothing like that had ever happened in the West. McCloy therefore suggested that the federal government should become more active among young people, and made it clear that he was prepared to provide money for youth associations of all kinds, including scouts and church groups, if Adenauer could offer suitable suggestions. On this issue Adenauer's response was cautious. In fact, the federal government had done very little for young Germans; the Chancellor accepted that it would be sensible to support youth organisations and youth hostels in future, as well as attempting to inspire the young with enthusiasm for the European idea. He reserved the right to send suggestions and proposals to McCloy.

François-Poncet shared Adenauer's general view of the military situation and provided some figures to support his case. Currently, the French army had over 500,000 men at its disposal, but 150,000 of them were in North Africa and another 120,000 in Indochina. Only 80,000 – far too few – were in Europe. He agreed that the West had between one and two years in which to act and that the time must be used well. For precisely this reason, however, it was sensible not to irritate the Soviets unnecessarily. This, thought François-Poncet, was something the Americans tended to forget.

Adenauer received relatively precise answers to the questions he put to the High Commissioners. Robertson went furthest, expressing his agreement with von Schwerin's basic assumptions. He believed that no reasonable person in Britain, the United States or France doubted the need for German rearmament, but none was prepared to take appropriate steps for fear of the public's reaction. At the same time, Robertson, like François-Poncet later, had one major reservation – he feared that German rearmament might hasten the very development it was designed to stop. Robertson saw a danger that the Soviets would march in order to nip West German rearmament in the bud.

As far as the British were concerned, the modernisation of the French army took priority. Without it, neither France nor the other countries would be prepared to receive German formations. The only way forward was therefore to increase military preparedness in Germany 'little step by little step'. Adolf Hitler, noted Robertson ironically, had provided a perfect example of how this was done. One such 'little step' would be the establishment of a federal gendarmerie, though the publication of this German idea in the American press had been a dreadful mistake. Nevertheless, a federal police force was sure to come; only its size was open to dispute. On this point, the French were creating difficulties.

In addition, the 80,000 men in German service groups could gradually be trained, armed, and organised in military formations. Robertson was impressed by the idea of an 'international legion' and promised to discuss it with leading figures on the British general staff. In general, then, the British High Commissioner supported the trend towards pragmatic – and largely covert – action.

McCloy, on the other hand, was unimpressed by the proposals for an 'international legion', though it was supported by several leading British and French representatives. His reason was that French efforts at rearmament might be damaged by the establishment of large German contingents on French soil. Strangely, in these discussions no account was taken of the negative response that might be expected from German public opinion ('a new foreign legion!'), nor of the outcry it would produce in France.

Unlike Robertson, McCloy was interested in the prospects for a European army, to which Adenauer had referred on several previous occasions. First of all, however, the national armies of West Europe would have to be strengthened; then, as European integration progressed, the idea of an international army with German contingents could be considered. McCloy was also convinced that the most important issue now was to gain time.

Even François-Poncet refrained from adopting a purely negative stance. He did, however, complain about U.S. indiscretion over Adenauer's application for the establishment of a federal police, and admitted that France did not want the force to be so large that it could serve as the core of a new German army. He believed that it should be no larger than 11,000 men for border protection and 5,000 to protect the federal capital. Certainly a gendarmerie of over 25,000 men could not be accepted at the moment. However, François-Poncet stressed that France also saw European integration as the only way forward to end the problem of a German defence contribution. First the economic basis had to be laid, then – he hoped – political and military union would follow within a short time. That would be the moment when Germany could send a significant contingent to a future European army. The French High Commissioner claimed also to understand the dissatisfaction among former officers and men of the Wehrmacht. The only way to help them now was through the payment of adequate pensions to those who were too disabled to work.

At the outset, Adenauer gave no details of these top secret exchanges to his ministers, let alone the parties in the Bundestag. Once Communist aggression in Korea had made the Western democracies aware of the inadequacies of their defences, the Chancellor believed that he was adequately informed about the thinking of the Western Allies. The most important result of these exploratory discussions was the discovery that all the High Commissioners accepted the need for a German defence contribution. None of them, however, could suggest a way to convince the public. The form of a military contribution was equally uncertain – as regards both hidden rearmament and the open establishment of German formations within the framework of an international army. However, there was no time to lose. Adenauer was convinced that the covert phase had to be initiated immediately, with the aim of providing contingents strong enough to have a deterrent effect within two years.

The North Korean aggression effected a dramatic change in public opinion. To this extent, the Communists had done those Western politicians and general staffs who were pressing for rearmament an enormous favour. Yet, the plans which were produced up to September continued to be plagued by indecision: should one take immediate measures against a Soviet invasion to be expected within months, or was there still time to plan ahead for 1952 or even 1953, at the time seen by many as the most likely date for the start of a third world war?

In all the Western capitals, it was widely believed that the aggression in Korea was part of a comprehensive 'general plan'. In July, the British in particular perceived a 'real danger' of action by the Volkspolizei against Berlin or West Germany; they were also alarmed at the prospect of a Communist 'fifth column' in the Federal Republic. According to Blankenhorn, François-Poncet feared a Soviet attack in July, August or September.[14] His argument was that Stalin might be provoked into striking before U.S. rearmament, now underway, changed the balance of forces in a fundamental way. If the Soviet Union did attack, there were no preparations that would suffice to stop it. Even the German service groups would be relatively impotent because of a shortage of weapons. François-Poncet then repeated his previous warning: German rearmament would only hasten the Soviet invasion.

Blankenhorn, who had just returned from Paris, confirmed to Adenauer that the prevailing mood in France was one of hopelessness. The officer corps was lethargic because U.S. weapons deliveries had failed to arrive; the government was unstable; there was also a real fear of unrest in Algeria.[15] Adenauer was even more deeply influenced by the scepticism of his closest aide than by the somber scenarios provided by von Schwerin.

It was difficult for the Germans to judge how far French alarmism was genuine. The French High Commissioner was aware that recent developments had given the Americans and British – and even Adenauer himself – an ideal opportunity to bring about an irreversible move towards a German defence contribution. Was he trying to delay this development by arguing that it was futile anyway?

Whatever his reasons, François-Poncet also turned to the question of where the federal government could take refuge during an invasion from the East. During a Sunday motor-boat trip with Blankenhorn on 16 July 1950, he claimed that the federal government would have to follow the High Commission. When Blankenhorn asked what alternatives were being considered, the French High Commissioner remarked that Canada was a possibility. Blankenhorn protested that if the federal government were forced to move to Canada, it would lose all contact with events. In the event of an invasion, it would surely be better to move to south-west Germany at first; then, if the Soviets pushed further, Spain or North Africa could be considered. Adenauer, however, maintained that he would not leave Bonn and preferred to wait for the Soviets to arrive at his desk.[16]

Shortly afterwards, François-Poncet told General Speidel that the French anticipated Communist uprisings in France and Italy in the event of war and would be unable to accept any German refugees. The French High Commissioner expected Berlin to fall into the hands of the East in September. Even in mid-August, he was predicting an invasion by the Volkspolizei 'with some certainty'.

During these weeks of high tension, Adenauer and his colleagues maintained contact with the United States through the deputy High Commissioner, General Hays. The discussions took place at his home, with the Germans entering through the back door in order to maintain strict secrecy. Though Hays regarded the situation as serious, he did not believe that the danger was acute.[17] There were no indications of an imminent attack from the east; the situation would not become critical for a year or eighteen months, when the Soviet Union would be at its strongest. All Western preparations should be made with that period in mind. It was therefore sensible to exploit the favourable psychological situation that had been created, a view with which the British concurred.

Notwithstanding this assessment, both Hays and Kirkpatrick were also eager to discuss immediate emergency measures. Would the Germans be prepared to work with Allied formations in the event of a Soviet attack? This was doubted by Blankenhorn and von Schwerin, who discussed the issue with the two men on 10 July 1950 in the company of General Gehlen, who was still working for the Americans. They warned that the German public might well take the view that the German soldiers were being treated as cannon-fodder. The response would be different if, in the event of a Soviet attack, the federal government could appeal for a common defence by Germany and the Western Allies with whatever weapons were available.

These discussions also demonstrated how great the political difficulties of a German defence contribution continued to be. It was made clear that the French were still taking a negative line. In the opinion of General Hays there were only three possibilities: first, the immediate creation of German volunteer formations, with these units being attached to the U.S. formations in the event of a Soviet invasion; second, the expansion of the service groups, although this was a political decision yet to be taken; and third, the reinforcement of the Länder police forces, which could be placed at the disposal of the federal government in an emergency.

Adenauer decided that the time had come for detailed discussions with the leader of the Opposition. The meeting with Kurt Schumacher took place on the day after the talks with Hays. The Chancellor spoke more frankly with Schumacher than with the leading figures in his own coalition. The outcome was a remarkable degree of agreement about the general situation and the measures necessary to deal with it. Both men believed that the reinforcement of the U.S. troops was essential. They also talked vaguely of a German police force of 100,000 men. The Chancellor stated that he intended to present his views to the U.S. President in an appropriate form. Adenauer and Schumacher agreed to maintain close contact and to exchange views regularly in future. It now seemed possible for Adenauer to broach the domestically awkward subject of German rearmament in agreement with the SPD.[18]

Meanwhile, von Schwerin had made further plans. At the beginning of July he produced a memorandum for the event of a 'national emergency'. The document contained two separate aspects, a 'semi-military' immediate programme and a 'long-term plan' for the establishment of twelve mechanised and armoured German divisions. By mid-July, separate German and Allied deliberations had reached a stage that detailed discussions could begin between the Federal Chancellor's office and representatives of the High Commissioners on the basis of a detailed memorandum from von Schwerin. Adenauer was sufficiently satisfied with the progress achieved to grant himself a month's holiday in Switzerland between 13 July and 14 August. Before he left, he told Kirkpatrick frankly that 'we are living on a volcano'. Kirkpatrick, who had just taken over as High Commissioner, was reluctant to go down in history as the first victim of German rearmament. He therefore insisted that Adenauer must be extremely discreet and cautious, and refrain from public comments.

McCloy also spoke with Adenauer shortly before his holiday. He found the Chancellor still relatively weak – mentally, physically and spiritually. The Chancellor argued that no German army could be considered at least until France had substantial combat forces. Nevertheless, he remained alarmed by the possibility of an attack by the Volkspolizei. It was essential to take some action so as to enable the Germans to participate in an emergency.

Adenauer had obviously earned a few quiet weeks in the Palace Hotel on the Bürgenstock above Lake Lucerne. In summer 1949 there had been no time for a rest. Since his last holiday in Switzerland with his wife in summer 1947, he had been under constant strain. The tension did not cease during the holiday, since the Schuman Plan negotiations and the security situation demanded constant attention. Furthermore, one domestic political problem – the formation of a government in North Rhine-Westphalia – continued to concern him. Blankenhorn travelled frequently between Bonn, Paris and Switzerland to keep the various proceedings under control. Meanwhile, von Schwerin moved ahead with his preparations.

By now the road to be taken was comparatively clear: rapid expansion of a strong federal police, which Adenauer believed would also have to be used against unrest in the Ruhr, plus development of the service groups as cadres for future German forces. There was no further mention of the unrealistic scheme to build up an 'international legion' in France. Moreover, the aim of establishing German formations only within the framework of a European army was being overtaken by the need for improvised measures. In his hotel at the end of July, Adenauer learned that the High Commissioners had rejected the application for the establishment of a mobile federal police force. The Länder alone were to be permitted to set up garrisoned police units up to an overall strength of 10,000 men. Yet this was not necessarily the last word; von Schwerin continued with his plans.

In fact, the Korean War had produced major repercussions in the United States. Adenauer was apparently unaware about the direction which discussions within the U.S. High Commission and in Washington itself were taking, though he suspected that since the outbreak of the Korean War McCloy had become an energetic advocate of a massive German defence contribution.

In the middle of July, McCloy gave Secretary of State Acheson a clear warning: politically and militarily the West would lose Germany – with no hope of regaining it – unless a way was found for the country to defend itself in an emergency.[19] It is difficult to judge to what extent this position was influenced by McCloy's staff, or by opinion in Washington, and how much by Adenauer's own arguments. It must also be remembered that, during these weeks, Schumacher was likewise encouraging McCloy to move towards German rearmament. He could be in no doubt that the strongest political figures in Bonn were among the hawks on the issue of rearmament. Whatever the reason, over the next few weeks McCloy himself was one of the driving forces behind a German defence contribution.

Certainly Adenauer had no idea that between early July and 1 September opinion in Washington was moving with remarkable speed towards support for an immediate and open German defence contribution. The Pentagon urged the adoption of the following package: an agreement to station U.S. troops in Europe and to establish an integrated defence force under a U.S. commander-in-chief, but on the basis of strong German participation. The transfer of between four and six U.S. divisions to the Continent to be tied to the immediate establishment of between two and four German infantry divisions, with the longer term objective of creating between ten and fifteen. However, there would be no German air force, no German general staff, and no significant German armament industry.

After some hesitation, the State Department accepted this case in principle. However, it laid great emphasis on the maximum integration into a 'European Defense Force' under a commander-in-chief with full powers of command. Such a force, it considered, should include all the Allied forces stationed on the Continent within the framework of NATO. Withdrawal of formations by any participant would only be permitted with the agreement of all involved. This and other measures would, in the view of Washington's Foggy Bottom, provide adequate precautions against the possibility of a German withdrawal.

By the beginning of September, President Truman was ready to accept the 'single-package' plan. The European Allies, and France in particular, were to be confronted with a virtual ultimatum at the negotiations in New York between 12 and 26 September. Without an immediate agreement to German rearmament, there would be no U.S. divisions and no delivery of modern armaments. In view of these developments, Adenauer's schemes had apparently been overtaken by events.

The process of rethinking had also proceeded rapidly in London, partly because Bevin took his own lead from the Americans, and partly because the Foreign Office and the British general staff were convinced that a third world war was imminent. Nevertheless, Bevin approached the New York discussions with the concept of a mobile federal police force, which could serve as a counterweight to the Volkspolizei while also forming the core for a military defence contribution. Bevin was contemplating a force of some 100,000 men. This was the start of a genuine British initiative, also supported by von Schwerin with his links in London, and by Adenauer.

However, the British general staff had now begun to propose almost bizarre figures. As well as a 100,000 men federal police force, it also wanted the Germans to provide twenty regular and ten reserve divisions, a tactical air force with 1,100 aircraft to intervene in land fighting and another 1,000 fighters for air defence, plus naval forces for tasks of coastal defence. The New York negotiations were to reveal that the British commitment to a federal police force alone was far from final. After a number of vehement discussions, Bevin accepted the U.S. line.

Initially the French were opposed to all proposals by the British and Americans: no federal police, no expansion of the service groups and certainly no German divisions in an integrated defence force. Robert Schuman arrived in New York with nothing to offer.

The available sources leave no doubt that the breathtaking speed of developments had scarcely included Adenauer. However, it is not true to say that the Americans were forcing him to accept their solutions. Independently of the opinion-forming process in Washington and London, he had reached his own conclusions and tried to persuade the High Commissioners to accept them. Of course, he did acquire fragmentary information about the course of events; he and his advisers were aware that the various Allies had their own plans and were hoping to persuade the Germans to accept them. It appears that the British were most successful with von Schwerin and Blankenhorn, the Americans with Heusinger and Gehlen, and thus – indirectly – with Speidel.

In general, however, throughout August and September the Chancellor had little idea of what was happening or of the course the Western Allies would choose to adopt. The sensible approach was therefore for him to signal, at every opportunity, that he regarded an immediate improvement in the security situation as essential and was prepared to provide German security forces in whatever form was required. That aside, Adenauer concentrated his pressure in the area he thought most effective and in need of the most rapid attention: the establishment of a federal police force as a counterweight to the Volkspolizei.

Adenauer's assessment of the situation appears to have been influenced to a degree by the course of the Korean War. When the North Korean forces drove the South Korean army, and then the U.S. strike forces, back as far as Pusan in the south of the peninsula, there was increasing fear that the Soviet Union might unleash the expanded East German Volkspolizei army and even overrun the Western Allies.

During this period, Blankenhorn had the task of keeping Adenauer informed of developments. He was therefore extremely well-briefed about the Chancellor's concerns and plans. On 9 August, Blankenhorn met Jean Monnet in the offices of the Commissariat du Plan in Paris to explain the views of the federal government.[20] Rather than invasion by Soviet troops, the German government was afraid of intervention by the Volkspolizei coupled with the activities of a 'fifth column' operating under the slogan 'Unity of Germany'. Walter Ulbricht had just announced that the government in Bonn would sooner or later be swept away by the will of the people, and that Adenauer, Pferdmenges and Ernst Reuter would be taken before a 'people's court'.[21]

Even in the Western Zones, both officers and men were currently being recruited for the Volkspolizei. The badly-equipped forces of the Western Allies – two-and-a-half American and two British divisions, along with a few French divisions of doubtful military value – could not hope to stop this East German army of between 200,000 and 300,000 men equipped with modern weapons. Panic among the West German population in the face of such aggression would further assist the East. Repeatedly, but without success, the federal government had made the request for between ten and twelve U.S. and British armoured divisions to be stationed along the Elbe as a deterrent. Without the protection of such a force, claimed Blankenhorn, Western Europe would not be able to undertake even the limited rearmament that had been planned. Preventive measures by the Soviet Union could not then be ruled out. During this discussion of 9 August, Blankenhorn noted that 'we are already at war' – or, at least, in the preliminary stages. It was essential for the Allies to create a unified command which could also exert political authority.

Monnet later explained that until this meeting he had not fully understood the dangers of the situation. He went at once to his premier, Pleven, who was then involved in discussions with McCloy, and briefed him about the meeting. They agreed to urge the U.S. and British governments to reinforce their troops along the Elbe frontier.

Following Adenauer's return to Bonn, two important events contributed to the production of the famous security memorandum at the end of August. The first was Churchill's speech in Strasbourg on 11 August, made in connection with the security resolution of the Assembly of the Council of Europe. The second was a memorandum written by generals Hans Speidel, Adolf Heusinger and Hermann Foertsch on 7 August.

The leading West European parliamentarians had been gathered in Strasbourg since 3 August, as members of the Consultative Assembly of the Council of Europe. They included Winston Churchill, Harold Macmillan and Hugh Dalton from Britain, Robert Schuman, Paul Reynaud, Guy Mollet and André Philipp of France, and Paul-Henri Spaak of Belgium. On 11 August Churchill demanded the immediate establishment of a European army with German participation, stressing that an army of this kind would counter the objections that had been raised to German participation. A resolution on the subject was accepted by a large majority: all the French parliamentarians voted for it, along with all the German delegates except for the Social Democrats.

As far as Adenauer was concerned, the Strasbourg discussions were very valuable. They gave legitimacy to his preoccupation with a German defence contribution and focussed attention on the prospect of a European army, which he supported. Of equal importance, for the CDU delegates who were attending for the first time, the discussions revealed the mood of the most influential parliamentarians in Europe. For the first time also German delegates – von Brentano, Gerstenmaier, Kiesinger and Carlo Schmid – were able to take part in the meetings.

Three days after the North Korean aggression, the powerful CDU politicians had been shocked when McCloy raised the issue of a German defence contribution.[22] Furthermore, Gerstenmaier had been well briefed by Blankenhorn before he gave the first speech in German in Strasbourg and offered cautious support for the concept of a common defence of Europe. However, Adenauer had not informed his cabinet nor the CDU/CSU *Fraktion* of his discussions on the subject. As a result, the discovery by German delegates that there was widespread support in the West for German rearmament was of crucial importance for the future. Von Brentano, who had previously adopted a cautious approach to this issue, now began to revise his opinion.[23] It was the Strasbourg assembly that did much of the work of persuasion that the Chancellor had previously neglected – or been forced to neglect – in his own party.

An additional stimulus was provided by a detailed memorandum from generals Speidel, Heusinger and Foertsch, with the assistance of the journalist Klaus Mehnert and the Chicago University professor Arnold

Bergstraesser. This group had not previously been involved in the official planning process. Hans Speidel was known to the German public as a leading military expert, particularly for his book *Invasion 1944*. As a result of his involvement with the 20 July 1944 plot, as Rommel's chief of staff, his political reputation was beyond reproach. Between 1933 and 1935 Speidel had been German military attaché in Paris and had retained links with the French military establishment. After the end of the Second World War he worked successfully to restore these connections and, in the summer of 1950, he had an unrivalled understanding of thinking in the French capital. Adenauer had known Speidel since January 1949 and was aware of the general's conviction that the only desirable German defence contribution would come within a European framework.

If Speidel was close to the French, then Adolf Heusinger's closest links were with the Americans. In the Third Reich deputy to the chief of the General Staff, Franz Halder, Heusinger had participated in the work for the 'Operational History' of the Second World War undertaken by the Historical Division of the US armed forces. Since 1948 he had worked for the Gehlen Organisation as an analyst.

Speidel, Heusinger and the officers associated with them had become convinced at an early stage of the need for German rearmament in the European-Atlantic theatre. Since the winter of 1949/50 they had pressed for the establishment of an advisory group to the federal government. Their main political contact was the Free Democrat housing minister, Wildermuth, who had been commander of the German defence of Le Havre during the war. In the longer term, Wildermuth had set his sights on the defence ministry for himself and his party; he was the only minister with whom, from time to time, Adenauer was willing to discuss military issues. This fact, however, encouraged him to claim the right to participate in the opinion-forming process.

During his holiday in Switzerland, the Chancellor was displeased by the outbreak of a conflict over responsibilities between Blankenhorn and von Schwerin, on one side, and Wildermuth and the generals, on the other. Adenauer was eager to retain personal control of security policy and was constantly worried that his own discreet efforts might be discredited by an excess of military zeal. These sentiments led him to restrain the activities of Wildermuth, whom he regarded as too military-minded in any case. The security issue, he informed his minister through Blankenhorn, involved so many domestic and foreign-policy problems that it could not be dealt with at ministerial level.

The Chancellor now felt that he was crossing a political minefield. He was also aware that von Schwerin had the goodwill of the British, that Heusinger and Gehlen were close to the Americans, and that Speidel had links with the French. Furthermore, the various military discussion groups in West Germany were at loggerheads with each other. In the longer term a civilian representative would be essential – and one who would keep the generals in check. For the time being, however, Wildermuth continued to take an active interest. He encouraged his military associates among the generals to work on a security memorandum, which he presented to the Chancellor immediately after his return on 14 August. Speidel had also sent a copy of the document to Colonel Truman Smith in Washington, where it was brought to the attention of the White House.

The Speidel-Heusinger memorandum of 7 August, to which Gehlen and others had also contributed,[24] had much in common with the thinking of the Americans, probably because this group was more aware of the ideas then current in the Pentagon than anyone else in the German government machine. Adenauer was greatly influenced by its contents. Though it was not immediately clear from the outside, Speidel began to play a more important role. Where von Schwerin's planning papers were dominated by immediate emergency measures, Speidel had outlined a long-term and twin-track concept, which brought together situation reports, analyses of the international and domestic situations, and proposals for organisational implementation. Adenauer was impressed by this method of approaching the problem. At the same time, however, he realised the dangers that the involvement of military representatives might bring. Though he recognised Speidel's sincerity and knew that he and his colleagues were an essential part of the planning for a German defence contribution, Adenauer was aware of the need to ensure that the generals were never in a position to dominate.

The Speidel memorandum confirmed the pessimistic view of the security situation and supported the prevailing opinion in the Chancellor's circle, which was that planning must be directed mainly towards 1952, when aggression from the East would be most likely.

Speidel and his group argued against half-measures. The creation of a federal police force was accepted as one of several approaches, but mainly for reasons of camouflage. The expansion of the Allied service groups was explicitly rejected on the grounds of unsatisfactory attitudes among the men involved and the danger of Communist infiltration: 'The direct route to the establishment of army and tactical air force formations is relatively also the quickest way to achieve the objective.' Since the year 1952 was apparently the date to be worried about, speed was essential.

Adenauer saw confirmation of his own views in another assertion by the authors: 'The reconstruction of a German armed force can only occur as a contingent in the European-Atlantic defence framework'. However, the sentence continued – and this was astonishingly bold in summer 1950 – 'involving German army units with modern equipment up to corps formation and with its own tactical air force, without which modern co-operation between land forces and air forces is not possible'. Certainly this was no system of stopgaps; it was very far from the 'little-step by little-step' route advocated by General Robertson in his discussions with Adenauer in June. Instead, the Speidel group was calling for something which von Schwerin had described as a 'long-term programme'. The memorandum gave the figure of fifteen modern peace-time divisions, for which the West Germans could provide sufficient trained 'human material'. The establishment of such a force should be begun at once in order to ensure that the necessary forces would be ready for action in 1952.

As a logical step, the authors paid particular attention to the political background to the German defence contribution. This was an issue that had scarcely been taken into account since the emergency discussions began in June. The memorandum thus ran as follows: 'The German Federal Republic has not been given a peace treaty. It is not sovereign. It is not incorporated into the European community and the Atlantic pact ...' West German commitment to the Western community 'is not matched by a readiness on the part of the Western world to incorporate West Germany on equal terms ... The security guarantee demanded on several occasions has not yet been given. In their strength and equipment the occupation troops are not in a position to guarantee our security.'

Adenauer was aware of all these points, and had even addressed them in some form. However, he was now convinced that the time had come for them to be taken fully into account in whatever emergency plans were made. Clearly, some of the basic ideas in the Speidel memorandum were included in Adenauer's security memorandum, and thus introduced into the deliberations of the Western Allies at the end of August. His main objective continued to be to deter an attack by the Volkspolizei by means of two specific measures: a significant reinforcement of Allied military power, and the establishment of a federal police force.

A long conversation between Adenauer and the High Comissioners on 17 August played an important role in the drafting of the security memorandum.[25] Adenauer conducted it in the belief that a breakthrough was now possible on the question of the federal police. In his capacity as a civilian strategist, and armed with the Speidel document, he gave the High Commissioners full details of the alarming security situation facing the Federal Republic and the strength of the Eastern bloc. The core of his assessment was that the Soviet Union would probably hold back until it possessed sufficient atomic weapons. Once that was achieved, however, the experiences of the Second World War might be repeated. If both sides refrained from using their most terrible weapons for fear of being destroyed, then the superior Soviet land armies and air force would take control. He feared that Stalin would deliberately distance himself politically from the East German government over the coming months, thereby enabling a superficially independent Volkspolizei to march in and 'liberate' West Germany on the model of events in Korea. He believed that 1952 would be the critical year for the development of the Volkspolizei.

The Chancellor was determined to make two main points to the Allied representatives. First, the West German population needed to be fortified psychologically. He was therefore anxious for the Western Powers to make a show of their military strength, not only to deter the Soviets but also to encourage the Germans. Recalling his own feelings and those of his countrymen between 1942 and 1945, he suggested in all seriousness that huge air squadrons should be ordered to circle above the Federal Republic. The droning of Allied aircraft engines would demonstrate Allied willingness to defend West Germany far better than anything else.

His second point was that the Federal Republic should be allowed to establish a force to repel troops from the Eastern Zone. By spring 1951 this force should be strong enough to act as an effective counterweight to the Volkspolizei. It would, he thought, require volunteer formations up to an overall strength of 150,000 men. In his security memorandum of 29 August, Adenauer was to give no such figures. However, he did include another remark made to the High Commissioners on this occasion: that Article 3 of the Occupation Statute gave the High Commissioners the right to authorise the federal government to take appropriate measures.

Even at this stage, Adenauer was thinking ahead to the conference in New York which was to begin on 12 September. In the course of the discussion with the High Commissioners, he stressed his hope that the planned volunteer formations would remove any need for the rearmament of Germany; he still hoped for an agreement between the Soviet Union and the United States. But if this was not forthcoming, then the idea of an agreement with France would, with the assistance of the United States, offer the prospect of a new development. As before, Adenauer continued to call for the adoption of immediate measures, with the possibility of turning them into a 'long-term programme' if required.

McCloy, whose adviser Robert Bowie was a leading advocate of a European army, then asked the Chancellor for his opinion of Churchill's idea for a European army. Adenauer answered that, if a German contingent proved to be necessary, he would be ready to make a contribution to such a force. Yet he felt it only reasonable to ask: 'When will we get it?' These were the points he was to make in his security memorandum shortly afterwards.

These discussions convinced Adenauer that the time was right for him to take action. Immediately afterwards, he provided information for Kurt Schumacher, since he had assured the High Commissioners that he wanted the support of the Opposition before beginning the establishment of a 150,000 man federal police force. His previous discussions with Schumacher had left him with considerable respect for the Social Democrat's judgement. However, Adenauer's hope for agreement from the SPD was misplaced. McCloy seemed to suspect that this would be the case: he asked the Chancellor on several occasions whether he would establish the volunteer force against resistance from the Social Democrats, should the need arise. Like other Chancellors after him, Adenauer was trying to win over the Opposition by means of detailed discussions but without making any political concessions. As the later Chancellors were also to discover the prospects of success in such an approach were limited.

Events were now unfolding with great speed. In reality, Adenauer had not even waited until his discussion with the High Commissioners before launching a public call for a German defence contribution. The interview with Jack Raymond of the *New York Times,* which caused an immense stir both in Bonn and abroad when it was published on 19 August, was actually given on 16 August. Blankenhorn, who had been present during the interview, had made some revisions on the morning of 17 August. That same afternoon he had begun to draft the security memorandum on behalf of the Chancellor.[26]

The *New York Times* interview reiterated much of Adenauer's discussion with the High Commissioners: his fear of attack by the military-style Volkspolizei; the demand for a strong German 'defence force' to ward off aggression on the North Korean model; a distress call for the United States to send two or three divisions to Europe over the next three months; references to Soviet offensive capabilities; and the argument that there would shortly be an alarming equality between the superpowers with regard to atomic weapons.

The response from the German public was vigorous and largely negative, with the strongest reaction from Kurt Schumacher. On 22 August the two men met to discuss the issue for more than two hours. The meeting was apparently stormy, though no records of it have survived. Schumacher's public repudiation of Adenauer's proposal arouses the suspicion that he was trying to outflank the government on the right. With some justification, Schumacher disputed the Korean analogy. He pointed out that, on German soil, an invading Volkspolizei force would be confronted by the troops of the three greatest military powers. In these circumstances the East German forces would not move alone, but only in tandem with the Red Army – and such a force could not be stopped with an 'anti-people's police' of the kind advocated by Adenauer. For the Federal Republic to have any chance of defending itself against Soviet attack, the defensive concept would have to be rejected. If the Western Powers feared an invasion by the Red Army, they must be prepared to concentrate their military forces in West Germany; the military forces of the democracies would have to be strong enough 'to wage the defensive by offensive means'. Schumacher did not merely 'want to prevent West Germany from becoming the forefield in the battle for Europe; instead the Eastern Zone and Berlin must be liberated in one rapid blow'.[27] Seldom in the history of West Germany has a more challenging roll-back programme been outlined than in these words.

Furthermore, the leader of the Opposition accused the Chancellor of serious psychological and foreign-policy errors. German troops were surely the 'trump card' which could be used to obtain major political concessions from the Western Allies. In that case, the West German position was surely weakened by Adenauer's offer in the interview with Jack Raymond. On the same day, Adenauer himself gave a press conference at which he modified his position and sought to emphasise the differences between 'internal security' and 'external security', which he took to include a threat by the Volkspolizei. External protection, he now stressed, must be guaranteed by the Western Powers; in his interview he had been concerned with issues of internal security.

By now the cabinet ministers and government parties in the Bundestag were also becoming alarmed. Adenauer, characteristically, did not discuss the matter with the leaders of the coalition parties in the Bundestag until 22 August. He then outlined the threat described in the analysis by von Schwerin and provided additional information from the security services. The Chancellor then asked Blankenhorn to read out the draft security memorandum, which was accepted by all those present. Adenauer was thus able to enter the cabinet discussions with the support of the coalition parties in the Bundestag.

Von Brentano, the chairman of the CDU/CSU *Fraktion* in the Bundestag, had actually favoured more gradual action and, in an emergency, would have preferred German contingents in a European army to the police force solution. However, he was under pressure from events in Strasbourg and chose not to make further problems for the Chancellor. Despite this approach, Brentano unwittingly made it more difficult for Adenauer to conceal his real intentions for the time being by using the harmless-sounding title 'protective police'. In front of representatives of the press, the chairman of the parliamentary party remarked that this police force would undertake military and not police tasks.[28] Otherwise Brentano accepted Adenauer's chosen line, as did the FDP and DP, which were in any case less cautious on military questions.

It is not clear why this explosive issue was not raised by ministers at the cabinet meeting of 23 August, which was convened to discuss the Schuman Plan. This gave Adenauer the opportunity to calm an enfuriated McCloy the following day. In a telephone conversation with Blankenhorn on 22 August, McCloy had complained bitterly about Adenauer's interview with Jack Raymond:[29] how could secret negotiations be conducted with a Chancellor who was prepared to broadcast the entire contents in an interview with the *New York Times*?

Neither Adenauer nor Blankenhorn suspected the main reason for McCloy's irritation. The U.S. High Commissioner knew that opinion in Washington had already begun to shift in favour of regular German military contingents, but that the issue had yet to be settled between the Western

Allies. Probably without realising the full implications, Adenauer had thus intervened in support of the model of rearmament favoured by the British. In a conversation with Wildermuth two days later, Adenauer assured him that the 'police solution' was the only one the British would accept.

During his discussion with McCloy on 24 August, Adenauer was alarmed to discover that the Americans were opposed to the establishment of a federal police force.[30] He left the meeting in a dejected mood.[31] However, on the following morning McCloy called to assure Adenauer that he personally supported the 'police solution'. The Chancellor was apparently unaware of the real reason for McCloy's hesitation: the battle among the Washington bureaucracies, locked in negotiations over a full-sized defence contribution.

A discussion in cabinet could now no longer be avoided. It was already possible to predict the critical questions that would be asked by the Minister of the Interior, Heinemann. His previous handling of the issue of a federal police force had demonstrated that Heinemann wished its duties to be limited to internal disturbances – a force that could provide no counterweight to the Volkspolizei, not to speak of the core of a West German military contribution.

Since the issue of a federal police force was the responsibility of the Minister of the Interior, Heinemann could not easily be bypassed. Adenauer had already drawn up appropriate plans in the Federal Chancellor's office and had previously tried to maintain links at preparatory level between the Ministry of the Interior and the planners in the Federal Chancellor's office. However, in the long term the situation was untenable since Heinemann was clearly the responsible minister. Any official removal of the federal police force from the control of the Ministry of the Interior would make it apparent that the 'police solution' was primarily associated with military tasks.

As yet no detailed record of the cabinet discussions on the morning of 25 August has emerged. Three shorter reports are available: various notes and descriptions by Heinemann;[32] a diary entry by Blankenhorn, who was present at the cabinet meeting; and accounts of the previous cabinet discussions given by Adenauer, Heinemann and Kaiser at a later cabinet meeting on 10 October. The precise content of the discussion is of interest for two reasons. First, both before and after his dismissal Heinemann emphasised the institutional aspect as the cause of his conflict with the Chancellor; he criticised Adenauer for giving the security memorandum to the High Commissioners before a final discussion and decision in cabinet. Second, the issue is significant because it permits us to draw some conclusions about Adenauer's relations with the cabinet.

The course of events appears to have been as follows. On the morning of 25 August, Adenauer gave a long report – which has not survived – on the situation. He was already aware that McCloy had been persuaded to accept the 'police solution'. However, he appears to have assured his ministers that no concrete application had been made to the High Commissioners, though these would have to be made by 5 September because Bevin was leaving for New York on that day.

This was, it should be noted, still the more leisurely age when foreign ministers travelled to New York by boat. The era of 'shuttle diplomacy', though at hand, had not yet begun. Had Adenauer himself been overtaken by the speed of developments, as he was soon to claim? Heinemann asserted later that no mutually agreed decision had been made. However, Blankenhorn made a diary record of a telephone conversation with McCloy shortly before the cabinet meeting, in which the U.S. High Commissioner asked for 'the security memorandum to be completed as soon as possible so that he can take it before his departure for New York scheduled for the next few days'. There was no mention of an exact date. Adenauer remarked later in cabinet that he learned only on 30 August that McCloy had to fly out immediately. In reality, urgent work was still being done on both memoranda on 29 August. According to Blankenhorn, the two documents were given to the High Commissioners shortly after 11 am on 30 August.[33]

Adenauer had now decided that the issue of the revision of the Occupation Statute should be linked with the security memorandum. His attention had been drawn to this point by Speidel's memorandum, by Schumacher, and by Vice Chancellor Blücher. Parts of the second memorandum were based on the ideas of Georg Vogel, a diplomat in the ministry of Blücher, in discussions with Blankenhorn.[34] Only at this late stage, apparently, was the security memorandum coupled with the 'memorandum on the question of reorganising relations with the occupying powers'.

The fact that the two issues were not brought together until the last minute was important evidence that, between June and August, Adenauer was concerned primarily with the immediate security threat. Throughout this period he regarded the establishment of a 'defence force' as vital in its own right. The assertion that he offered a German defence contribution mainly in an effort to release the Federal Republic from the Occupation Statute is not supported by an analysis of the decision-making process.

Adenauer had frequently demanded the revision of the Occupation Statute and was generally prepared to take every opportunity to diminish Allied sovereignty over West Germany. After some consideration, he therefore decided that it was appropriate for him to link the two issues. The main points in the second memorandum were as follows: the state of war between Germany and the Allied Powers should be ended; the aim of the occupation in future should be understood as the provision of security against a threat from outside; most important of all, 'the relations between the occupying powers and the Federal Republic will progressively be regulated by a system of contractual agreements'.[35]

Outside observers could be forgiven for taking a different view of developments. The simultaneous presentation of the security memorandum and the memorandum on the reorganisation of relations made a strong impression on many Allied diplomats. In particular, it led them to assume that Adenauer had always intended to use the 'offer' of German troops as a means of progressing towards his long-term goal of the sovereignty of the Federal Republic.

The exact wording of the security memorandum itself did not become known until 1977.[36] It contained a detailed description of the alarming security situation, of the kind Adenauer had frequently given to the High Commissioners. Once again Adenauer devoted particular attention to the Volkspolizei. It appears that he still favoured the 'police solution'. As before, the Chancellor continued to make a somewhat confusing distinction between 'external' and 'internal' security. The defence of West Germany against outside forces – he meant the Red Army, but did not name it – was a matter for the Allies. He repeated 'in the most urgent form' his appeal for the reinforcement of the occupying forces. He also used his well-known argument that 'the defence measures currently getting under way in Western Europe can only be carried out behind the protection of an adequate number of well-equipped Allied divisions'. This was followed by a key section: 'Moreover, the Federal Chancellor has repeatedly declared his willingness to make a contribution in the form of a German contingent in the event of the creation of an international West European army. This is a clear expression of the fact that the Federal Chancellor rejects a re-militarisation of Germany through the creation of its own national military power.'

On this specific issue, then, the cabinet position had been reflected entirely accurately. Adenauer made it clear that this offer of German contingents – and this was the subject, despite subsequent denials – had previously been made 'repeatedly' by himself alone.

Adenauer's proposal for the establishment of a federal police force was obviously a greater problem with regard to the rights of the cabinet. In the memorandum, he observed that 'the federal government' was proposing the immediate creation of a 'protective police' force at federal level. If the reports of the meeting of 25 August are correct, Adenauer was thus using the name of the cabinet to support a request on which his ministerial colleagues had yet to reach a decision. The very fact that he forced a decision on 31 August makes it clear that none had existed before.

The terms of the security memorandum do not outline with any clarity the tasks of the 'protective police'. The phrase 'internal security' was used to include every eventuality connected with the provision of security against the German Communists. It was argued that the Federal Republic was threatened by the activities of the fifth column and attacks from the Volkspolizei and East German Communist youth movement.

Should the Allies be unwilling 'for any reason' to commit their forces if the Volkspolizei 'begins open or camouflaged actions against West German territory', then it would be essential to have a protective police force strong enough to intervene. The police concept could only be justified by the presentation of this danger as an 'internal' threat.

In answer to persistent questions at a meeting with the High Commissioners on 31 August, Adenauer was forced to concede that the draft of the memorandum contained some inconsistencies. Nevertheless, he emphasised that the federal police force must be large enough to mount effective resistance to the Volkspolizei if necessary. During these talks, the Chancellor looked to George Hays to be rather depressed.[37]

At a cabinet meeting on 29 August, Adenauer had apparently given his colleagues some idea of the contents of the security memorandum, which had not yet been completed. This, at any rate, was what he maintained without contradiction at a later meeting of 17 October. The cabinet met again on 31 August. In their morning newspapers the ministers had read that the Chancellor had given the High Commissioners a written statement of his position. Our knowledge of this meeting depends on the same sources as before; its course cannot be reconstructed with certainty.

At this meeting, Heinemann demanded that Adenauer account for his actions. The Chancellor explained that there had been no time to inform them of the content of the document because McCloy's departure had been brought forward. When the Minister of the Interior asked for the details of the document, Adenauer read out parts of it and gave details of the second memorandum. Heinemann, however, was not satisfied. He asked to be allowed to examine the document directly. The Chancellor agreed, whereupon Heinemann left the meeting in order to examine the document in the Federal Chancellor's office.

It is not entirely clear whether a decision was actually reached in Heinemann's absence. In any case, Blankenhorn noted in his diary: 'The cabinet puts itself solidly behind the Chancellor and declares itself unanimously in favour of the establishment of a federal uniformed police force.'[38] Only Fritz Schäffer raised constitutional objections to the use of the term 'police' to describe the planned force. Adenauer took note of his objection; a few days later he proposed to the High Commissioners that the term 'federal defence force' should be used instead.

When reading the memorandum, Heinemann quickly spotted the sentences in which 'the Federal Chancellor' states his willingness to provide a German contingent for an international European army. He returned to the meeting in great excitement and accused Adenauer of unacceptable conduct: he had not told the cabinet that he was offering German divisions. According to Heinemann, he added: 'I am leaving the federal government.'[39] It remained unclear whether this was an announcement or a threat.

Blankenhorn described the scene as follows: 'Incident with Minister Heinemann, who complains about inadequate information from the Chancellor and asks to be relieved of his responsibilities. The Chancellor responds with strong criticism of the inadequate conduct of business by the Minister of the Interior, criticisms which in my view are fully justified, since nothing of note has been achieved in either the area of protecting the constitution or the area of police.' Heinemann, who had not left the meeting, informed his colleagues that he had personally read Adenauer's offer of German divisions in the security memorandum. Not until 17 October that year, when Heinemann finally left the cabinet, did Adenauer respond to Kaiser's pressure and read the relevant passages to the cabinet. When Kaiser asked politely whether it would not be possible to give the ministers a transcript, Adenauer replied with his customary bravado: 'I myself do not have a transcript. There is only one copy and that is in Herr Blankenhorn's safe.'

By the end of August both Heinemann and Adenauer were aware that this dispute, ostensibly about procedural issues, was really about the military contribution itself. Throughout September, the crisis revolved around Heinemann and his relations with the Chancellor. The two men watched each other warily, with neither being willing to make the dangerous first move.

Adenauer was aware that Jakob Kaiser was also unhappy. Nor could he be entirely confident of the support of the chairman of the CDU/CSU caucus, Heinrich von Brentano. The leaders of the party caucuses had been informed about the memorandum after the cabinet meeting of 31 August and had offered their support. Still, Brentano was making veiled criticisms of the Chancellor in speeches across the country, by asserting that foreign policy should not be over-emphasised and that it would be better to concentrate on domestic reforms carried out in a Christian spirit.[40]

Adenauer's critics were aware that his initiative on security policy had left him exposed. Furthermore, the handing over of the two security memoranda was not his last intervention in the issue. Immediately after the cabinet meeting and his talk with the delegation chairmen on 31 August, Adenauer went to the High Commissioners on Petersberg in order to urge them once again to establish a strong federal police force. He also wanted to reiterate an old argument – that his second memorandum was designed to achieve a gradual evolution rather than a sudden upheaval in relations between West Germany and the Western Allies. Once again he requested an Allied declaration that an attack on the territory of the Federal Republic would immediately lead to war.

Further documents were produced at the end of August and during September. One of them outlined detailed plans for the defence police, specifying 60,000 men in a second phase with further reinforcements available if the situation required. Adenauer also sent a letter to the U.S.

government in which – as Kurt Schumacher had done – he demanded the transfer of twelve Western Allied armoured divisions to the eastern border of the Federal Republic as a pre-condition for the inclusion of West Germany in the defence of Western Europe. In a formal document, he again asked for an Allied security guarantee. In addition, Count von Schwerin sent a memorandum to General Hays relating to the establishment of 'squads' of front-line soldiers as a preliminary move towards the establishment of the core of a German contingent for the European army.[41] On the night before the security memorandum was handed over, Blankenhorn had confidently predicted to Charles W. Thayer of the U.S. High Commission that 'we will have the divisions ready in six months'.[42]

The Federal Chancellor's office had certainly given sufficient signals of Adenauer's willingness to co-operate with whatever solution proved necessary. The question was now put before the Foreign Ministers in New York. They chose to block Adenauer's path, although he was not fully aware of what had happened until some time later. In fact, it was not Adenauer alone whose will was thwarted: the United States, despite its status as a world power, had been unable to impose its own preferred policy on its opponents.

After this summit conference, Adenauer had to wait more than four years before the Paris Treaties finally came into effect on 5 May 1955. We can only speculate on what might have happened in both international and German domestic politics if Dean Acheson had refused to yield to the stubborn resistance of the French and had insisted upon the integration of West German divisions into NATO, which Bevin and the other NATO ministers were prepared to accept. Would the Soviet Union really have responded with a preventive war? Even if the development had been peaceful there would probably have been many passionate protests in the Federal Republic itself, to say nothing of France.

However, it is also conceivable that the adoption of a policy of strength in Germany five years earlier might have made it more difficult for the Eastern bloc to consolidate its position; it might even have led to some form of Soviet withdrawal. A different decision in New York would also have spared Adenauer the bitter struggle over the European Defence Community (EDC). This issue was to burden the movement for European union with the security issue at too early a stage, and eventually end in the failure of plans to create a European army. Yet even an unequivocal decision at the New York conference might not have guaranteed rapid progress towards a German defence contribution, given the tactical skill with which the French managed to delay the German military contribution for five years.

Once again, the course of the Korean War had produced clear psychological repercussions. Until the middle of September, Europeans and Americans alike had feared that the North Koreans might succeed in throwing the U.S. expeditionary force into the sea at Pusan. On 12 September, a series of conferences began in New York with the United States apparently determined to force rapid agreement to German rearmament. On 15 September, however, UN forces under the command of General MacArthur achieved a surprise amphibious landing at Inchon. Once the North Korean offensive began to falter, there was less urgency among the U.S. politicians and generals over the European theater of operations. The controversial issue of the German defence contribution was therefore relegated to subordinate negotiating committees. Adenauer's central demand for the establishment of a strong federal police force was rejected. For many months, the question was stuck in the slow-moving foreign-policy bureaucracy of the Western Allies. Still, the taboo surrounding a West German defence contribution had been broken; the 'long-term programme' was already under negotiation; the Western governments had abandoned their previous plans for a preparatory phase. The issue was now a topic for negotiation between governments and for vehement dispute at home in both West Germany and France. The great leap forward had been achieved. However, instead of rapid decisions, there was to be an apparently endless series of conferences and discussions.

The effects of this change on West German domestic politics were not long delayed. As had been the case before May 1950 when the Schuman Plan was launched, from November 1950 onwards, Adenauer found himself in another critical phase of his policy. And it was only a year later that he was gradually able to extricate himself from it, beginning in autumn 1951.

By the middle of September 1950, largely owing to his acute sensitivity to emerging difficulties, Adenauer had realised the need for caution. On 17 September, during the conference in New York, General Hays called to ask him for the federal government's views on the issue of a German contingent within a European army. The Chancellor was aware that his cabinet had not yet formed an opinion, largely because he had taken care to concentrate its attention on the police solution alone. Furthermore, he had no idea of the struggles among the delegations in New York.

Adenauer therefore replied cautiously that the Allied foreign ministers might send a formal enquiry to the federal government on the issue. This alone would enable the various responsible German authorities, especially the Bundestag, to discuss the matter and reach a decision.[43] The Chancellor, in effect, was providing himself with an alibi: in future he could tell the party leaders, the Bundestag, and the cabinet – and even assert in a letter to Gustav Heinemann – 'that an offer [of German Troops] is absolutely excluded, also by me'.

However, he added: 'In the foreseeable future – it might be some weeks, but it might come very soon – the official question will be put to the federal government and Germany as to whether it will place its human reserves and its material reserves for the protection of Western freedom at the disposal of an international army, which under some circumstances will have the task of repelling a Soviet Russian attack.'[44] He left no doubt that in such a case he would answer an enquiry in the affirmative.

Meanwhile, the theme of rearmament had become the central issue of domestic politics, for the SPD as well as the CDU. Schumacher could no longer maintain his pro-military stance – or, at least, he regarded it as tactically inopportune to do so. Carlo Schmid, who had always been regarded as on the right-wing of the SPD, had also begun to make pacifist speeches: 'We would prefer undamaged people in undamaged houses coming under Bolshevik rule to cripples living in earth holes.'[45] Schumacher himself recognised that the German pacifist movement, known as *Ohnemich* ('count me out') was offering a great opportunity to the Opposition. He therefore opposed the Chancellor's plans. Nevertheless, an unwillingness to be tied down on the issue led Schumacher to demand fresh elections on the grounds that the Bundestag elected in 1949 had no mandate to decide such a novel issue.

In the FDP many different opinions were expressed – from emphatic approval of a German military contribution from Thomas Dehler and Eberhard Wildermuth, to rejection on grounds of national conscience. However, most of the party leadership was on Adenauer's side.

The German trade-union federation under Hans Böckler adopted a restrained approach. It has often been argued – though not on the basis of concrete evidence – that Böckler and the Chancellor had made a bargain, according to which the trade-union federation would hold back on the question of a military contribution in return for Adenauer's support of the union demand for co-determination in industry.

The Catholic Church was a relatively reliable supporter of Adenauer. However, the Protestants were completely divided on the issue of rearmament. Though the Union parties were not threatened with collapse on the subject, the outcome remained uncertain.

Adenauer therefore decided to start by preparing the way in cabinet before the CDU/CSU *Fraktion* itself became infected by doubts. He was now convinced that he had made a mistake in waiting so long. When Franz-Josef Wuermeling offered a mild reproach for the 'way he discussed the Heinemann case in the caucus executive',[46] Adenauer's answer was brief and to the point: 'There was no point in dithering any longer.'[47]

Heinemann's objections, which continued to take shape over these weeks, were based on several fears. For example, he took seriously the threat of a Soviet preventive war in the event of rearmament. Though Adenauer himself did not dismiss the possibility out of hand, he had been convinced by Speidel and Hays that the Soviet Union was not yet sufficiently well-armed, particularly in the nuclear sector, for it to launch an attack. Like Schumacher, Heinemann also believed that it was primarily the task of the Western Allies to defend the Federal Republic, and that it was in their own best interests to do so. He could not accept the counter-argument – that self-defence was also in the best interests of the Federal Republic itself.

One further objection involved the issue of the division of Germany. This had already played a role in Heinemann's reservations about entry to the Council of Europe and now acquired additional significance. Confessional politics also influenced thinking on the matter. At this time the Protestant Church saw itself as the last remaining, politically significant link between the Germans in the East and West. Heinemann was the president of the All-German Synod of the Protestant Church of Germany and was well aware of its fears, which he shared.

Heinemann clearly felt closer to his doubtful or critical fellow Protestants than to the Chancellor and his cabinet, who were ready for military self-assertion. In this context, Heinemann's links with the famous anti-Nazi pastor Martin Niemöller were highly significant. From the outset Niemöller had been one of the Chancellor's sternest critics, from motives rooted both in foreign-policy assessment and anti-Catholicism. Once the rearmament discussion was under way, Niemöller publicly reproached Adenauer and the Allies for allowing former officers in the Wehrmacht to set up staffs.

Adenauer responded angrily to such criticisms – somewhat against his better judgement.[48] He was well aware that all kinds of preparations were indeed being made – all of them in the belief that a third world war was imminent. To that extent he was sincere in his belief that Niemöller was committing 'naked treason'.[49] If the government and the Allies were making the necessary preparations against attack, then any publication of specific details was highly questionable. Heinemann's unwillingness to distance himself from Niemöller, whom Adenauer regarded as 'an enemy of this state to which he denies the right to exist', eventually became the issue which led to the break.

The affair was linked with an assessment by the Minister of the Interior which annoyed Adenauer intensely because it expressed Protestant convictions which caused him great displeasure. At a discussion with the Chancellor on 4 September 1950, Heinemann argued that 'God has twice taken the weapons from our hand, we may not take them into our hands a third time but must wait patiently'.[50]

Adenauer was profoundly irritated by such arguments. In the first version of a letter of 23 September to Heinemann, which was not sent, he gave his own views:

> While you take the view that one must hold back and wait, even in the face of the threat from Soviet Russia, in the hope that God will guide everything towards peace, I take the view that it is precisely as Christians that we are also obliged to use our strengths in order to defend and save the peace. I take the view that a passive attitude towards Soviet Russia from our side will virtually encourage Soviet Russia not to keep the peace. From the experiences we have had with totalitarian National Socialism, I think it must be clear that a totali-

tarian state is never persuaded to refrain from its goals of conquest by patient waiting, but only by the establishment of forces which show it that it can only achieve its goals of conquest by endangering its own existence.[51]

His experience of the policy of expansion pursued by the Third Reich was one of the main factors shaping Adenauer's policy towards the Soviet Union. Stalin's Politburo, he was convinced, was driven by the same motives as Adolf Hitler, from whom humanity had been liberated in the spring of 1945. It was therefore essential to confront the Soviet dictator with a very different policy to that which had been adopted by the Western Powers during the period of appeasement between 1936 and 1938. The totalitarians understood only one language – 'the language of power!'

The Chancellor had little difficulty in winning the cabinet over to his side. Apart from Heinemann, only Jakob Kaiser frankly expressed his unease – and Adenauer already knew that occasional rebellions by this minister were of little consequence. The participants realised that on this issue, which took 'absolute priority' for Adenauer, there existed only the alternatives of outright rebellion or agreement. Most, moreover, found it easy enough to agree.

During the final cabinet discussions of 17 October, Anton Storch described Heinemann as 'a foreign body in the cabinet'. Thomas Dehler continued the attack: 'The entire approach of Herr Heinemann is one of combat and corresponds to the vicious attitude of Niemöller, it is the mobilisation of the Protestant Church against the Catholic Chancellor.'

Heinemann and Adenauer made some attempt to part with dignity, but without complete success. In a letter of 9 October which was designed to bring the matter to a close, Adenauer left it open as to whether Heinemann's departure was a dismissal or the result of a request to the President to dismiss him; he also included some words of thanks for Heinemann's work.[52] On the same day, however, he sent Heinemann a bitter letter which referred to a press release the minister had issued concerning a conversation with the Chancellor. Adenauer now adopted his most formal and officious tone: 'I draw your attention to the fact that you are still in office and ask you to refrain from further comments with regard to the official secrecy which you are obliged to maintain.'[53]

Adenauer had thus ejected a minister he had never wanted and whom his party had forced him to accept. Both men were convinced of the justice of their cause – and of the other's reprehensible character. In future Heinemann and his supporters did not hesitate to describe the Chancellor in very unflattering terms: he was depicted as authoritarian, fundamentally undemocratic, devious and generally insensitive to the ethical problems of rearmament. In addition, it was insinuated that Adenauer was making personal and lonely decisions which could easily lead the country to the abyss of a third world war. This view was summarised by a Swabian supporter of Heinemann during a conversation with Eugen

Gerstenmaier: Heinemann, he claimed, was 'a man of peace who, unlike that bully Adenauer and you, conducts politics under the eyes of God'.[54]

Adenauer as a 'bully' – it is a remark which illustrates the vast moral indignation, often coupled with a sense of moral superiority, which the Chancellor now faced from the pacifist camp. Since the beginning of the rearmament debate his image had changed for the worse. Previously, the only personal reproach he had faced had been the lingering charge of separatism, with all the resulting suspicions regarding his policy towards the German question. Now another accusation had been added: that Adenauer was a war-monger and an exponent of disastrous power politics.

In the Depths of Unpopularity

Adenauer's government was not particularly popular even at the outset. In a sample poll in spring 1950,[1] only 28 per cent of respondents – less than a third – declared that they agreed 'on the whole' with Adenauer's policies. Another 26 per cent were 'not in agreement', while by far the biggest proportion – 46 per cent – were undecided or expressed no opinion. In effect, the population was still waiting for the federal government to prove its worth. Subsequently, in June 1950, the Chancellor's approval rating temporarily rose to 31 per cent after the announcement of the Schuman Plan.

General scepticism about the government included an element of hostility towards democracy itself. A poll undertaken by the Institute for Demoscopy in Allensbach revealed that despite twelve years of Nazi rule, a full 25 per cent of all respondents still believed that one-party government would be best for the country; another 22 per cent were undecided, while only just over half regarded the multi-party system embodied in the Basic Law as the best system of government. In January 1950, 10 per cent of people felt that Adolf Hitler had done more for Germany than any other German statesman.[2]

The limited degree of approval for the Adenauer government declined still further with the onset of the rearmament controversy. Between August 1950 and autumn 1951 it lay between 23 and 24 per cent. The proportion of hostile respondents rose to 36 per cent in November 1950 and to 39 per cent in May 1951, while the 'don't knows' remained roughly the same at around 40 per cent. On 20 April 1951 Adenauer returned triumphant from Paris, where he had just signed the Schuman Plan. He remarked to Otto Lenz that the population would surely see this as a success, but Lenz pointed out that he was supported by a relatively

Notes for this section begin on page 727

small proportion of German voters. According to the latest opinion polls, his approval rating had fallen to 20 per cent.[3]

A similarly depressing picture was provided by the regional elections in West Germany. Adenauer was fortunate that the Landtag election in North Rhine-Westphalia took place a week before the outbreak of the Korean War. The CDU and SPD share of the vote there did not change, but the FDP vote increased from 6 per cent to 12 per cent while the Communist Party share fell from 14.5 per cent to 5.5 per cent. Between June and August 1950, despite many other claims on his attention, Adenauer was preoccupied with the attempt to force minister-president Karl Arnold out of office in Düsseldorf. To his chagrin he did not succeed, although the creation of a CDU-Centre coalition ensured that the federal government could still count on the votes of North Rhine-Westphalia in the second chamber. Adenauer would have preferred a CDU-FDP government to strengthen the national coalition. Thereafter, however, the government sustained a number of serious setbacks in the regional elections.

Shortly after the damaging departure of Heinemann from the cabinet in October 1950, regional elections were held in Hesse and Württemberg-Baden, followed by others in Bavaria a week later. Everywhere the Union did badly. In Hesse the CDU share fell below 20 per cent – a loss of 12 per cent of the vote compared with its showing in the Landtag election of 1946. Adenauer regarded this setback as bearable; he had never liked the relatively left-wing CDU regional association there and the SPD was already the sole governing party. He hastened to inform von Brentano of the Hesse CDU that the appalling result was due to internal feuds within the party 'more than anything else'.[4] This was the old Adenauer, responding to problems by launching an immediate attack on someone else.

The result in Württemberg-Baden was much worse. In North Baden and North Württemberg, where Protestant voters were in the majority, the CDU did particularly badly and its share of the vote fell from 38.4 per cent to 26.3 per cent. The Bavarian election was the final straw: the vote share of the CDU's sister-party, the CSU, collapsed from 52.3 per cent to 27.4 per cent. Not surprisingly, Kurt Schumacher began to call for fresh national elections to the Bundestag even though such a move would not have been in accordance with the Basic Law (which laid down fixed-term legislative periods).

If the regional elections were a true barometer of the national mood, then most of the damage had been sustained not by the government as a whole, but mainly by the CDU – and, above all, by Adenauer. On the other hand, the FDP, with its blend of national-liberal and national-conservative policies, had made significant advances: it doubled its vote in North Rhine-Westphalia and even made gains in Bavaria. The FDP's share of the vote also increased in Württemberg-Baden, though this was already its main stronghold where it had the support of some 20 per cent of the voters.

Part of the reason for the CDU's poor performance was the spread of 'count me out' or pacifist sentiments in West Germany. However, the election landslide also had regional causes, in addition to demonstrating that the refugee problem had not been solved. In Bavaria, the election defeat could be attributed to the civil war between the CSU and the Bayernpartei, which obtained 17.9 per cent of the votes. Across the Federal Republic there was a clear trend in favour of the expellees party BHE (Association of Expellees and Disenfranchised): 12.3 per cent in Bavaria, 14.7 per cent in Württemberg-Baden and a startling 23.4 per cent in Schleswig-Holstein, which had the largest proportion of refugees and the worst levels of unemployment.

It was small consolation for Adenauer that none of these changes had directly benefitted the SPD and that its vote had tended to stagnate. However, not until the election for the Berlin chamber of deputies at the end of a catastrophic series of autumn election results was there any evidence that the tide was turning in Adenauer's favour. In Berlin the SPD lost 20 per cent of its vote, with the gains being shared by the CDU and FDP.

The election results had painful consequences for the CDU with regard to the formation of regional governments. In Stuttgart, for example, Reinhold Maier formed a government of the DVP/FDP and SPD – and excluded the CDU. Adenauer reserved his most intense dislike for this model, which enabled Liberals and Social Democrats to make common cause against Catholic schools policy. Adenauer and Reinhold Maier had established a relationship of mutual distrust from the outset. Their first clash had come over the election of Bonn as federal capital, when Maier had allied himself with the deputy minister-president of Hesse, Hilpert, to support the claims of Frankfurt. At one stage in the negotiations, Adenauer (who was still President of the Parliamentary Council) had sneered as Maier began to speak: 'Now Dr Maier will say what Dr Hilpert has just whispered to him.'

During the Landtag elections of 1950, Maier travelled the region telling his audiences that Adenauer was a man who had achieved the 'impossible': 'a Basic Law which allowed him to be elected Chancellor with a majority of one vote; and he has even managed to set up the seat of government six kilometres from his home'. Adenauer was furious. Though he enjoyed making jokes at the expense of others, he regarded it as intolerably disrespectful when he was paid back in his own coin.

Maier caustically described Bonn as the 'federal theatre'.[5] He and Adenauer were also at odds over issues of substance, since Maier had been part of the plot to elect Karl Arnold – a fellow Swabian – as president of the Bundesrat. Yet from Adenauer's point of view, the real issue was Maier's determination to establish a large new Land in the south west. The Chancellor was convinced that it could only damage the position of the CDU in the Bundesrat. If the Land were established, the CDU would lose the two predominantly Catholic regions of Württemberg-Hohenzollern and Baden, in which it had a safe majority. He was also angry that the arguments on the subject were leaving the CDU hopelessly divided in these areas, to the benefit of the DVP/FDP. Adenauer suspected that this problem would not be solved if the *Südweststaat* came into being: in that case, Maier might be tempted to form a government on the basis of support for the south-west state rather than national issues, to say nothing of his general sympathy for an alliance with the SPD.

Throughout the 1950s Adenauer was forced to co-exist with Maier. The Swabian, a cunning and shrewd politician, fought him on many issues, though usually for purely local reasons; he was never prepared to expand his horizons beyond the national-liberal convictions to which he had always been committed. For the moment, Adenauer was forced to accept that Maier was more firmly in control than ever.

The CSU had also been weakened in the regional elections. Though Hans Ehard remained in power in the Bavarian state chancellery, he was forced to take the SPD and BHE into his government.

Only in Schleswig-Holstein did the CDU prove that it was possible to lose the elections and still form a government. Its coalition with the BHE, FDP and DP was welcomed by Adenauer, partly because he was aware that the BHE was now a force to be reckoned with for good or ill. He was therefore glad to see it being led towards the government camp in Bonn.

Overall, Adenauer had suffered an enormous setback. He was quickly made aware that the self-confidence of the FDP had been given a powerful boost. Only days after the elections in Hesse and Württemberg-Baden, Adenauer received a critical seven-page letter from the FDP chairman Blücher, and the deputy chairman of the FDP parliamentary party, Hans Wellhausen.[6] It was clear that the party intended to take a tough stand: 'The alienation of the federal government from the people, the ignorance of fundamental questions of foreign policy, the inadequate information about the political events of the day – these points are made time after time ...' The real criticism was that Adenauer was engaging in too much secret diplomacy – secret not only from the population, but also from the FDP Vice-Chancellor and his Free Democrat cabinet colleagues.

The document contained a long list of complaints and demands. It argued that Adenauer should appoint an official to the Foreign Service who would be responsible to parliament; he should also make appointments to the consulates-general as soon as possible; he should install parliamentary state secretaries to facilitate better control by the coalition partners; he should appoint an FDP politician as second state secretary in the Federal Ministry of the Interior; he should act vigorously against signs of corruption and re-organise the Bundespresseamt (federal press office). The high-minded Blücher did not wish to press demands on his own behalf, and left it to Wellhausen to push for the development of the

ERP Ministry into a genuine foreign-trade ministry, and the establishment of a Foreign Ministry.

Adenauer was aware that Blücher wanted one of these posts for himself (in fact he would certainly have preferred to be Foreign Minister). The Chancellor at once penned a five-page letter, an unmistakable sign that he was taking the problem seriously. Although he ended by making a few minor concession to the FDP, he insisted that these issues must be handled within the coalition as a whole.[7]

On the question of the Foreign Ministry, Adenauer persuaded Federal President Heuss that the time was not ripe for the appointment of a foreign minister. Heuss, who was not convinced that Blücher could do a better job than the Chancellor, undertook to explain the situation to his party colleagues. In the case of the Foreign Trade Ministry, Adenauer encouraged a dispute between Blücher and Erhard. The Chancellor was no longer satisfied with Erhard after the balance-of-payments crisis which had been looming since autumn 1950. If Erhard now found himself having to ward off the demands of Blücher, this internal dispute might also take the pressure off the Chancellor. The climate within the coalition had clearly deteriorated after the various disputes of the summer.

One other FDP minister, Eberhard Wildermuth, was growing dissatisfied with the Chancellor's personnel policy. Adenauer had apparently led him to believe that he was responsible for defence issues – and that he would eventually be appointed Minister of Defence. Instead, Adenauer eventually preferred Theodor Blank when the time came, and – according to the memoirs of Erich Mende – 'without the slightest consultation with the federal ministers of the FDP and DP'.[8] The FDP now suspected that all the crucial ministries would be kept in the hands of the Union. The unexpected appointment of Blank was particularly irritating for the Free Democrats because the FDP had for some time been cultivating ex-Servicemen in general and the professional soldiers in particular. For Adenauer, this fact was one more good reason to deny them the post. It was no consolation to Wildermuth and his friends in the FDP to discover that President Heuss supported the Chancellor on this issue as well. Heuss was persuaded by Adenauer's argument that Blank was best placed to win the support of the trade unions for a German defence contribution.

Even within the Union itself, there was significant unrest. As yet there has been little research into the central sources which might illuminate the friction in relations between Adenauer and the CDU/CSU Bundestag *Fraktion* between 1950 and 1953. Nearly all records of the caucus meetings have been lost. Those documents which are available do provide some indications of the personal and political manoeuvres, concealed threats and barely-suppressed complaints of the period. For example, why did Adenauer want the caucus's deputy chairman, Friedrich Holzapfel, to take over as Minister of the Interior after the departure of

Heinemann?[9] Was he hoping to muzzle an obvious malcontent by subjecting him to the discipline of cabinet responsibility? However, Holzapfel was by no means sure that he could do the job. At the suggestion of the caucus, the position was therefore offered to Robert Lehr, who had first wanted it in 1949.

Adenauer knew that Lehr, a former DNVP politician of with a track-record of toughness in the Ruhr struggle against France in 1923, would not protest at the establishment of a border defence force. Yet he was not always so accommodating. At the first cabinet meeting he attended as a minister, Lehr opposed the choice of Blank to chair a committee of state secretaries which would deal 'with questions relating to a change of Allied troops', and offered to take on the co-ordinating task himself. Mercifully Adenauer could rely on Thomas Dehler, who intervened to argue that it would not be right for the Minister of the Interior, who was responsible for the protection of the constitution, to be given responsibility for questions of constitutional law as well. These should come under the control of the Chancellor instead.[10]

The appointment of Blank and the change at the Ministry of the Interior inevitably caused much comment. Adenauer himself was not sure that Blank was the right man for the job. As he remarked during the crucial discussions in cabinet, he would have preferred to appoint Otto Gessler, the former *Reichswehrminister* during the Weimar period. But Gessler was too old. Above all Adenauer wanted a man who would show the outside world that the old traditions were not being slavishly upheld.

Blank's abruptness of manner was already well known. Yet it might even have had some advantages, since Adenauer believed that the generals would tolerate strong language from a man they respected. By now he was losing his confidence in von Schwerin. On the other hand, if the self-confident Speidel and Heusinger were given key roles, it would be very important for the senior civilian to supervise them carefully. Blank was hard-working, a civilian, and a trade unionist, as well as a younger man whose loyalty was assured. All these were important factors. In addition, Blank was a CDU man who would not lay too much emphasis on the need for non-partisan security policies as did Adenauer's generals von Schwerin and Speidel – the latter maintaining close links with his fellow Swabian Carlo Schmid in the SPD.

Adenauer was thus able to maintain the balance in the cabinet: a shift to the right with the appointment of Robert Lehr, but with a counter-weight offered to the unions in the person of Blank. Nevertheless, Jakob Kaiser noted with disquiet that it was the right wing of the unions that Blank represented; he was a committed admirer of Ludwig Erhard with little sympathy for the *Sozialausschüsse*.

The minor cabinet re-shuffle of October 1950 did not solve the problem of the CDU's relationship with the Protestant church, but an ingenious solution to this problem quickly presented itself. Adenauer proposed that the president of the Bundestag, Erich Köhler, who by general agreement was not up to the job, should be given a post in the foreign service instead. Adenauer had first suggested Australia and then, when President Heuss protested that this was too much of a humiliation, a more prestigious position in Iran.[11] The removal of Köhler opened up a place for a prominent Protestant.

On 19 October 1950, therefore, just as Heinemann was leaving the cabinet, Hermann Ehlers was elected president of the Bundestag. Ehlers had been active in the anti-Nazi Confessing Church before taking up a leading position in the High Consistory of the Protestant Church in Oldenburg in 1945. He was also well respected in the EKD, the national organisation of the German Protestants. Adenauer was aware that Ehlers belonged to the conservative wing of the CDU and that he was determined to encourage contacts between East and West Germany. However, this approach was commonly adopted by most prominent Protestants at the time. If the CDU seriously wanted to integrate such personalities into the party, and to use them in order to gain the support of Protestant voters, then they had to be allowed to do what they could to maintain links with fellow Protestants in the Eastern zone.

The appointment of Otto Lenz as state secretary in the Federal Chancellor's office was another attempt to escape from the depths of unpopularity. The proposal almost certainly came from Globke. Adenauer's precise personal objectives in engaging Lenz are difficult to ascertain, partly because of the difficulty in defining the political views of this versatile man. When his appointment was under consideration, Lenz was highly praised by Jakob Kaiser.[12] Clearly, Kaiser hoped that the appointment of Lenz, who had been an active anti-Nazi and also had links with the leaders of the Berlin CDU, would strengthen his own position. Subsequently Lenz had worked with Josef Müller in a lawyer's society in Munich, but had since abandoned a connection which would have made him unacceptable to Adenauer.

The Kaiser group was quickly disappointed to learn that Lenz had become one of the strongest advocates of Adenauer's policy towards the West. In the cabinet discussions Schäffer had criticised the appointment of Lenz: 'Yes, I know him, but only as an opponent. As such he did his job well.'[13] Schäffer felt instinctively that the new man would cause trouble – for him personally, but also for Blücher, Erhard, Kaiser, Seebohm, Lukaschek, Niklas and the rest. If Lenz was to play the role of a troubleshooter in the Federal Chancellor's office, no minister was likely to escape his scrutiny.

What Adenauer sought, and found in Lenz, was a man who could get things moving, who could motivate ministers, experienced state secretaries in the government, diplomats, and professors. Furthermore – or so

Adenauer hoped in the early days of the relationship – Lenz would tell him the unvarnished truth. This new key personality in Adenauer's entourage was a man of independent means who did not mince his words, even with the Chancellor. Lenz was bold enough to insist on a trial period of two months, and had to be asked repeatedly if he would accept a permanent post as state secretary in the Federal Chancellor's office. In the end Adenauer placed the letter of appointment into his hand and declared that the matter was settled.[14]

Adenauer always valued new brooms as long as they swept clean. Throughout 1951 and into 1952 Lenz had the ear of the Chancellor and was given a relatively free rein. However, like all those who were closely associated with Adenauer, he also aroused mistrust and hostility. His powerful position and his willingness to cause offence ensured that there was no shortage of people ready to criticise him in front of the Chancellor. In August 1952 the relationship between the two men deteriorated when Lenz joined forces with von Brentano and Franz Josef Strauss to urge Adenauer – while he was on holiday – to undertake a cabinet re-shuffle after which Brentano would be made Foreign Minister.[15] Adenauer rejected this as a conspiracy and an act of disloyalty which he judged as intolerable, coming from one of his closest collaborators. Even before this incident there had been serious disagreements between the two men; after August 1952 Adenauer no longer trusted his tireless state secretary. He made no protest when Lenz decided to abandon the chancellery and to take a seat in the Bundestag in 1953.

In the critical year of 1951, meanwhile, Lenz produced a number of initiatives to overcome the stagnation which threatened Adenauer and his divided cabinet. At the first discussion, the Chancellor had 'proposed the production of persuasive propaganda as the most urgent task'.[16] Lenz turned enthusiastically to the task; he created a 'brains trust' in the federal press office, ensnared or threatened various editors, radio directors, and correspondents; he founded organisations and raised money; he even contacted Americans and Frenchmen for his purposes where necessary. After a year-long search, Lenz at last found a talented press chief in the person of Felix von Eckardt, the former editor-in-chief of *Weserkurier*. Gradually, he improved the grey and plodding image of the federal government from the spring of 1952 onwards. However, the establishment of a federal media machine was only one of his many activities. Shortly after he began work in January 1951, Lenz became involved in the major battle over co-determination in the coal and steel industry.

Co-determination in coal and steel on the basis of equal representation between 'capital' and 'labour' was a legacy of the early period of occupation. It had originally been initiated by the British, with the support of the Trade Union Federation of the British Zone. The weakened employers had no choice but to accept the new system. The unions, the SPD, and even the union wing of the CDU in Bonn had always pressed for co-determination to be formally put on the Federal statute book. The complex industrial issues of these years all played a part in the debate: the Allied deconcentration policies and ban on cartels, the demand for nationalisation which was still supported by the Social Democrats and the German Trade Union Federation (DGB), and the Schuman Plan negotiations. The unions saw a regulation on co-determination in the coal and steel industry as a step towards a comprehensive co-determination law for all sectors of big industry. Its opponents, on the other hand, regarded it as the objectionable core of a development that should be stopped. To them co-determination had originated in the ideas of the Labour government in London, aided and abetted by the SPD, DGB, and the left-wing CDU in the Rhine and Ruhr regions.

This was also Adenauer's own view. One of his successors as Chancellor, Helmut Schmidt, attempted to portray him as a supporter of the idea of co-determination when the controversy re-emerged during the mid-1970s: 'Historically it was the great service of Konrad Adenauer to have recognised the signs of the times and advocated the implementation of co-determination in the firms of the coal and steel industry.'[17] The facts, however, tell a rather different story.

As CDU chairman in the British Zone, Adenauer had seen some positive aspects in a certain measure of co-determination by the workers. He was, however, opposed to the idea of the parity of capital and labour in the running of companies. His correspondence with Günter Henle of the Klöckner firm at the beginning of 1947 leaves no room for doubt on this point: 'We do not want the unions to be the leaders among those involved in management. We also want that part of the votes at the annual shareholders' meeting and on the supervisory board that does not represent shares in private hands to be distributed among as many owners as possible – Land, city, district, co-operative societies and trade unions etc. We want this because we do not wish to see concentrations of power, which we have recognised as damaging in the past, being re-constituted in another form and another place.'[18] At that stage he was considering supervisory boards to have a ratio of 55:45 of private to public representatives. Adenauer was hence opposed to more radical proposals that were being formulated at the time by the hard-pressed and desperate employers themselves. In 1950 he continued to be convinced that some people were 'bent on establishing a new dictatorship through the trade unions.'[19] Nevertheless, Adenauer was aware that circumstances had changed. There now seemed to be a real opportunity to separate the moderate wing of the trade unions – first under the DGB chairman Hans Böckler, then under Christian Fette – from the SPD. Adenauer never forgot the unrest in the Ruhr in the years following the 1918 revolution. Even in autumn 1959, when the Federal Republic had a long record of political stability, he warned the CDU/CSU Bundestag deputies: 'If you let your thoughts go back, then you will know that in the Weimar Republic unrest in the industrial regions always spread into other parts of Germany and provoked unrest there.'[20]

With civil war apparently threatening between the two halves of Germany during the early stages of the Korean War, Adenauer believed that unrest was a real possibility. Certainly the Communists continued to hold a strong position in the works' councils of large firms on the Rhine and Ruhr. In confidential discussions, leading unionists themselves admitted that they were worried about the activities of the radical wing of IG-Metall. Moreover, in the event of unrest the German police would be unable to deal either with acts of sabotage orchestrated from the East, or with other forms of violence. As long as the moderates remained in command, therefore, Adenauer believed that the unions ought to be strengthened in their role as a force of order. The international situation also had to be taken into account. Once the SPD had turned against the Schuman Plan, it was vital for him to persuade the unions to tolerate this core of his foreign policy. The same was true of the conflicts over a German military contribution. There were thus good reasons for the government to try and accommodate the DGB on the issue of co-determination in coal and steel. Furthermore, the CDU in the Bundestag was itself so split on this question that some form of compromise was desirable.

Adenauer certainly knew that any attempt to accommodate the DGB over co-determination would provoke serious tensions within the coalition. Both right-wing parties, the FDP and DP, were on the side of industry. The FDP, moreover, was concerned about the financing of its election campaigns and the support of its middle-class voters.

Throughout 1950 Adenauer had avoided the issue, but in January 1951 the question of co-determination could no longer be ignored. A political strike had been called for 1 February 1951 in all the firms of the coal and steel sector in order to support the union demand for co-determination on the basis of parity between capital and labour. This would be a disastrous development for a Chancellor and a government already reeling from the regional electoral setbacks the previous autumn. Adenauer asserted that any attempt to blackmail the hand of the legislators through a massive strike would be undemocratic, but he showed a willingness to act as mediator in summit talks between employers and workers' representatives under his chairmanship. Once again he was supported by Robert Pferdemenges. Adenauer also had the assistance of the tenacious Lenz, who shared his largely non-ideological approach. The state secretary's willingness to exert pressure on ministers, employers and unions alike was particularly useful at a time when Adenauer himself wanted to adopt the role of conciliator.

The negotiations in the Federal Chancellor's office led to the famous 'parity' solution, which did not actually grant parity to the trade unions but at least helped them to save face. It stipulated that next to five representatives of the share-holders and another five of the employees an eleventh supervisory board member was to be appointed; ideally, this person was to be nominated by agreement between the two sides, but the candidate would have to be elected by the annual meeting of share-holders. Nevertheless, the employers grumbled, and secretly hoped that the small parties in the coalition would block the measure. Blücher, Wildermuth and other ministers did indeed threaten Lenz with their resignation before the crucial cabinet meeting on 26 January. However, threats of resignation were commonplace in the first Adenauer government – the record was held by Fritz Schäffer – and by the afternoon tempers had cooled. The DP then thanked the Chancellor for his successful mediation and attacked the FDP for its indecision. According to notes made by Lenz, Blücher now heartily agreed with this assessment.[21]

The solution had been found. Adenauer was able to present himself as a peacemaker, while the claims of the Minister of Labour, of Karl Arnold, and of the CDU/CSU caucus were forgotten. However, the dispute in the coalition dragged on for months. The third reading of the bill in April also witnessed one of the more bizarre events of the early Adenauer era, when the CDU and SPD jointly voted down the opposing FDP and DP *Fraktionen*.

Following the vote on the controversial paragraph 8 of the bill which regulated the election of the eleventh supervisory board member, there was a noisy debate about the rules of procedure. Ehlers interrupted the debate and Adenauer – again assisted by Pferdemenges – once more stepped into the breach. Direct negotiations followed between the leaderships of CDU/CSU and SPD. When the SPD asserted that it had inadvertently accepted the CDU/CSU's version, Adenauer intervened to repair the damage.[22] Over the protests of the FDP and DP, the CDU introduced a new version of paragraph 8 which was then pushed through. In the final vote the measure was passed with a broad majority and some fifty votes against, mainly from the FDP and DP.

The decision on co-determination had several political consequences. Adenauer described the most important of these to the party executive of the CDU: 'I take the view that co-determination in coal and iron was politically a smart move; for we have separated the DGB from the SPD. The DGB could never have been won over to the Schuman Plan if it had been defeated over co-determination.' At the same time, he made it clear that the accord was not to be taken as a step towards an expansion of co-determination to all industries: 'I am not in favour of this being a model law for the whole economy. Coal and steel are a special case and, as before, I take responsibility for this law. In the treatment of co-determination in general, however, the CDU must remain firm and not give way.'[23] Despite these words, relations with the FDP were now worse than before.

In West Germany as a whole, the decision on co-determination did not increase the popularity of the CDU, since the voters had more pressing concerns than the extent of the influence of IG-Metall over the coal and steel industry. For the unions and the forces associated with them, however, and for the CDU *Sozialausschüsse,* the decision had a great symbolic value; for decades they chose to regard it as a milestone in domestic politics. Adenauer himself, it is fair to say, regarded the issue as of secondary importance. He was much more concerned to ensure that the DGB did not achieve its objective of parity in the *Betriebsverfassungsgesetz* (Works' Constitution Act) the following year.

Scarcely had the threat of a strike been overcome when a balance-of-payments crisis developed. This was accompanied by a sudden and apparently dramatic gap in the imports of bread, cereals and sugar and came before the cabinet just after a precarious armistice had been forged on the issue of co-determination. Adenauer could now vent his fury on Erhard and Nikas, two ministers from his own party, and thus disguise the extent of his disagreement with the FDP.

The Chancellor was particularly indignant at the admission of Niklas, the Minister for Food, that the supply was no longer secured. Adenauer now faced the embarrassing prospect of having to ask McCloy to direct grain shipments to Germany as quickly as possible – and just when the High Commissioner was stepping up the pressure over the deconcentration of German industry. Bread rationing, he would have to admit to the High Commissioners, would be a severe political setback which the East would exploit to the full. Adenauer was well aware that, for him personally, it could be the step leading from stagnation to his steep fall. An appeal to the High Commissioner for help was also embarrassing because Adenauer had to admit openly that the Federal Republic was still utterly dependent on the Allies.

On Adenauer's behalf, Lenz went to Andreas Hermes, the president of the German Farmers' Association, in order to discuss possible successors to Niklas.[24] Hermes suggested the names of two very different experts, Heinrich Lübke and Alois Hundhammer. He had no desire to take the post himself, especially since Adenauer had not wanted him during the formation of the government in 1949. However, Lenz had given him a broad hint when he asked Hermes about his political views on the East. Adenauer had never really trusted Hermes on this subject, but in the spring of 1951 he was in such deep trouble that he might even have been willing to accept Hermes, whatever his views, if it meant acquiring an experienced agrarian expert. In the event, the problem of food supply was resolved without a major public crisis. Niklas remained in office until 1953.

During these months even Erhard was in danger. Since the formation of the government in 1949, the previously harmonious relationship between Adenauer and his Minister of Economics had deteriorated. Like

all the other heads of departments, Erhard came in for stinging criticism
from the Chancellor whenever there were problems in his area of responsibility. Twice – in spring 1950 and winter 1951/52 – the number of
unemployed rose to almost two million. Erhard's position became especially critical after January 1951, when West Germany went into the red,
with the European Payments Union. The effects of the Korean War,
which had produced a sharp rise in raw-material prices and freight rates,
were primarily to blame for this situation. Adenauer criticised Erhard for
his ecessive zeal to liberalise foreign trade, which he regarded as largely
to blame for the EPU deficit since trade with Western Europe was already
60 per cent liberalised. Thenceforth hardly a cabinet meeting went by
without Adenauer criticising his Economics Minister.

A main reason for Adenauer's difficulties was the way in which economic matters were organised. In autumn 1949 he had been prepared, for
reasons of pure coalition politics, to cobble together a Marshall Plan
Ministry for Blücher. This decision left two ministers responsible for
negotiating, without adequate coordination, with the High Commission
on economic matters. A further problem was created by the relatively
high demand for imported foodstuffs, which comprised 44 per cent of
West German imports in 1950. In these circumstances, the Ministry of
Agriculture was another key economic department which appeared in
urgent need of coordination. Adenauer attempted to gain control of the
problem in several ways. The first of these involved Erhard's ministry.
Erhard's opponents had persuaded the Chancellor that Erhard was incapable of leading a ministry effectively; they pointed out that, when
Erhard was Minister of Economics in Bavaria, his ministry had been
nicknamed Villa Kunterbunt (Villa Helter-Skelter).

Behind the back of his minister, Adenauer thus spent several months
negotiating with potential state secretaries to replace Eduard Schalfejew
in the Ministry for Economic Affairs. Such an appointment, he hoped,
would enable him to bring order to Erhard's department and to ensure
better coordination with the other ministries. However, his first contact,
Friedrich Ernst, formerly *Ministerialdirektor* in the Prussian Ministry for
Trade and Industry, refused the position – on the revealing grounds that
there was no prospect of 'orderly work as state secretary given the particular nature and disposition of Herr Erhard'.[25] Contact was also made
with Karl Blessing, director of the Unilever corporation and subsequently
President of the Deutsche Bundesbank. Finally Adenauer persuaded
Ludger Westrick, finance director in the German coal mining association,
to accept the post at least on a temporary basis.

At the same time, Adenauer began to concentrate authority for the coordination of economic policy in the Federal Chancellor's office. Early in
March a ministerial committee was created, with the Chancellor as chairman, to oversee issues of raw material distribution, prices and wages,

food supply, and import-export matters – most of which were already the responsibility of the Minister of Economics. Adenauer then offered the chair to Friedrich Ernst, whom he wanted to appoint as his 'commissioner' with special powers. A serious decline in the influence of Erhard appeared to be imminent.

The situation became more serious following an intervention by McCloy. On 6 March 1951, in his capacity as representative of the U.S. Marshall Plan administration, McCloy called for a change in German foreign economic policy.[26] Pointing to the West German deficit with the European Payments Union, which was $60 million in February alone, he demanded the immediate abandonment of liberalisation. The demand for state intervention to manage the economy, for controls on prices and foreign exchange, was linked with a threat to stop dollar aid and vital imports of raw materials. A main motive for this drastic intervention was the American desire for a German economic contribution to the defence effort of the West. At the same time, at the instigation of the French, the Americans were pressing for the elimination of the Central German Coal Sales Agency, and for progress in the deconcentration of certain companies, to enable the Schuman Plan negotiations to be completed speedily. In March and April, therefore, economic affairs in general were in a state of flux.

Erhard, however, refused to be driven into a corner. By means of a major speech in the Bundestag, he managed to swing the coalition parties behind himself and his policies. At the same time Erhard blocked McCloy's intervention by persuading leading representatives of the German business community to introduce the necessary measures of direction without outside interference. He appointed Otto A. Friedrich, director general of Phoenix AG in Hamburg and industry's liaison-man to act as the government's raw materials adviser. Adenauer's resistance proved futile. Erhard was determined to mobilise public opinion, which continued to be favourable towards him. Several newspapers – *Industriekurier, Welt am Morgen,* and *Volkswirt* – published articles which had clearly been inspired by the Economics Ministry, and which attacked the 'economic shadow government' in the Federal Chancellor's office as well as Schäffer and Blücher.

Adenauer responded with a highly critical letter to Erhard: 'Your whole conduct is impossible. I must express to you my serious displeasure. You completely misunderstand the nature of a federal government. No federal minister has the right to pursue policy on vital questions on his own initiative and to turn to political parties over and against the decisions of the cabinet or the guidelines of the Chancellor ...' After listing some of Erhard's failings, he came to his main point: 'You personally bear a great deal of the blame for current conditions in the economic sphere. For some time you have evidently failed to appreciate economic developments properly … By your exaggeratedly optimistic speeches you have deceived yourself and others about the seriousness of our economic situation.' This was followed by stern criticisms of the administrative incompetence of his ministry. At the end, Adenauer adopted a more conciliatory tone and paid credit to Erhard's past achievements: 'But that cannot and must not prevent me from making these serious criticism given the threatening situation in which we now find ourselves.'[27]

The milder comments towards the end of the letter had been suggested by Lenz, although he was sure that the criticisms would leave Erhard with no alternative but to resign.[28] Adenauer, who knew Erhard better, doubted that this would happen. The Chancellor may well have been aware that it would have been folly to drive from his cabinet a man who was both a symbol of hope and the cement of the coalition agreement with the FDP. During a cabinet meeting two days later, he invited Erhard, Schäffer, von Brentano and Abs to a separate discussion. Erhard defended himself against an attack by Lenz and assured Schäffer of his loyalty, but refused to resign. The cabinet finally agreed to a series of measures which incorporated proposals from Erhard, Schäffer and Abs.

During these disputes behind closed doors, Adenauer discovered that the appointment of an economic commissioner in the Federal Chancellor's office, in the person of Friedrich Ernst, had only increased solidarity among his ministers. As a result, Ernst's function was described in future as that of a secretary of the co-ordinating committee.

Erhard was fortunate in several respects. The balance-of-payments deficit vanished as quickly as it had appeared; from May 1951, the investment boom triggered by the Korean War ensured growing export surpluses for the West German economy. By December 1951 the Federal Republic had net foreign exchange reserves of 1.5 billion marks. The rise in domestic prices also slowed down, and unemployment fell. In autumn 1951 both Friedrich Ernst and Otto A. Friedrich left their posts. The crisis was over. By the beginning of 1952, when import restrictions were removed, Erhard once more enjoyed massive popular approval. Once again he had been proved right – whatever the views of the Opposition, the High Commissioners, and the Chancellor himself.

Fortunately for Adenauer, Erhard's thick skin had prevented the Chancellor from losing his Economics Minister during March and April 1951. Though his neo-liberal ideas on how to shape the Republic's economic system continued to irritate Adenauer also in the future, Erhard was obviously blessed with either good luck or good judgement, or both. And this is what counted in politics and also with Adenauer. When the fortunes of the government finally began to revive after spring 1952, the causes lay partly in the field of foreign policy but also – and most of all – in the economic miracle that now began. Both in West Germany and abroad, its successes now appeared dazzling. Just as the voters had previously blamed Adenauer's government for economic and political setbacks, so they now gave it credit for growing economic success.

In 1951, however, the government remained profoundly unpopular. This was due partly to difficult circumstances, but also to the fact that Adenauer never managed to make his first cabinet function as a team. It would be true to say that he could not do it – but also that he did not wish to do so. Adenauer frequently acted on the belief that his ministers – with the possible exception of Schäffer – lacked political understanding. He was constantly troubled by the suspicion that ministers would pursue their own policies, at the expense of cabinet responsibility, unless they were kept on a tight rein. It would be an exaggeration to claim that Adenauer's leadership style consisted of setting his ministers loose against each other. Still, whether through accident or design, he often failed to define their areas of responsibility clearly; restless ministers were kept in check by the rival claims and ambitions of their colleagues. In the final analysis Adenauer was convinced that he was in a class by himself; and he let his ministers know it. This belief was vividly illustrated by a remark he made to Otto Lenz at the height of the balance-of-payments crisis: 'What am I supposed to do with this cabinet? The only man I can rely on is the foreign minister.'[29]

With a combination of luck and judgement, Adenauer steered his government through its crisis period and kept it on course. In so doing, whether intentionally or not, he strengthened his own position. Yet there was a price to be paid: problems were always blamed mainly on the Chancellor himself, while his authoritarian style burdened him with a massive extra workload.

During these years most Germans, if they were interested in affairs in Bonn at all, did not genuinely love or revere this argumentative, authoritarian and unbending Chancellor. He began to gain their respect only after two or three years, when it became clear that, although often insufferable, he was also successful, both in economic affairs and in his dealing with the occupying powers. Out of respect grew popular trust, out of trust veneration, and even – particularly among those who watched from a distance – affection. Yet that was far from being the case in the depths of his unpopularity in 1951.

Adenauer's Daily Life

In an objective sense, the first years of Adenauer's chancellorship were the hardest. Though he often complained later on that times had never been so bad, his problems then could not really be compared with those he had faced in the early days. During his first years as Chancellor, Adenauer did not have the benefit of the aura which surrounded him later and made him almost immune from criticism. This aura did not begin to develop until 1952, when the economic miracle began to take shape. In foreign policy, Germany – as the Federal Republic deliberately styled itself – gradually returned to the European concert of nations after the signing of the General Treaty. Though Adenauer's contribution to economic success consisted largely of letting Erhard have his own way, progress in foreign policy was his own achievement. At the 1953 federal elections, the voters gave him credit for both. Only now, when negotiating abroad, did he have the benefit of an almost impregnable position at home.

Subjectively, things looked different, even after the resurgence of 1952 and 1953. At no time in his entire chancellorship did Adenauer regard his own position, or that of the state itself, as being entirely secure. He was often to share his gloomy view of the future with his cabinet, with the CDU executive, and with members of his closest circle: 'The situation has never been so serious ...' He constantly felt under pressure and under attack.

Even when the uncertainties of 1951 were past, ratification of the General Treaty in May 1952 brought no more than a brief respite. Adenauer continued to struggle – for ratification in the Bundestag, the Bundesrat, and the Constitutional Court, and then for victory in the federal election of 1953. His election triumph was followed by suspense over the fate of the European Defence Community in Paris. Even in May 1955, when sovereignty was restored and Germany's inclusion in the Western community was achieved, the problems of the Military Service Law and the raising of German armed forces had yet to be solved. The situation in the Middle East began to deteriorate, while the East-West conflict constantly threatened the position of the Federal Republic.

Not even in summer 1957, when Adenauer won an absolute majority for the CDU/CSU in the federal election, did the pressures upon him disappear. He was confronted by the Berlin crisis, the crisis in France caused by the Algerian war, and the manoeuvres between Kennedy, de Gaulle, and Macmillan. In addition, the Chancellor continued to be plagued by fears of an unsuitable successor whose failings might undo all his careful work. Until 1963 he regarded himself as an ageing pilot, whose task it was to steer the new ship of state through dangerous rapids and around submerged obstacles. When his own party finally forced him to resign, his outlook became even more pessimistic.

Adenauer's success in overcoming these problems remained something of a mystery even to those who knew him well. He was never by nature an optimistic statesman who could bear the burdens of office lightly. Unlike Bismarck, who had often been prepared to leave Berlin for months on end, cultivating a *Junker's* devil-may-care attitude, Adenauer was the conscientious son of a petty-bourgeois civil servant, constantly aware of his responsibilities as leader of his state and its people.

It would be true to say that, as Chancellor, Adenauer never enjoyed a single day that was completely free from politics. Even at weekends, in Rhöndorf, he was close to Bonn, while his 'so-called holidays'[1] involved frequent contact with his closest associates and were never without of work.

Given the hours he worked from week to week, it would be easy to characterise Adenauer as an obsessive who devoted his entire life to politics. On closer examination, however, it becomes clear that he made a deliberate effort not to become a complete slave to work. His sons and daughters, and a few close friends, were aware that he cherished his free moments. Occasionally this neglected side of his life was reflected in his letters. For instance, he wrote to Dannie N. Heineman during a holiday in the early spring 1958 near Vence, 500 metres above sea level on the Mediterranean: 'I am striving to gain some distance from Bonn and politics. But unfortunately, when one bears the responsibility, this is not entirely possible. It moves in on you from the outside and even your inner self is, however reluctantly, constantly preoccupied with it. It is the curse of our time.'[2] Politics as the curse of our time – this was an unexpected admission from a man who seemed to be driven by politics. In fact, Adenauer's self-discipline did enable him to preserve a personal core that was untouched by the pressures of work. The ability to detach himself was probably one of the secrets behind his remarkable fitness and intellectual presence during these years.

Since his youth in Cologne Adenauer had been aware that his resilience and political success depended on establishing a steady and productive routine. The rhythms of his life hardly varied at all over the years. He maintained his daily routine with remarkable strictness. At night he rarely slept for more than six hours. Adenauer usually needed sleeping tablets to help him to sleep, and not even these always had the desired effect; his family doctor, Frau Bebber-Buch, was forced to change his medication at regular intervals in order to ensure that it remained at least partly effective. Like many older people he woke early, usually at 5 am, and would then bathe his legs in a tub of cold water in order to get his circulation going. In the first years of his chancellorship, when his reserves of physical energy appeared inexhaustible, he would often walk in his garden, weather permitting.

Here the old man was alone in his kingdom. Down in the valley was the village of Rhöndorf, with Bonn lying to its right. Further to the right lay the towering walls of the Drachenfels, and behind them – probably still in the morning clouds – his home city of Cologne that seemed more and more distant. To his left were the hills he loved on the left bank of the Rhine, with the romantic Rolandsbogen where he had got engaged half a century before. Past the blue line of the Eifel was Maria Laach, where he had sought refuge during the Nazi era, and beyond that the lands of the West, with which he hoped to link Germany's future.

Adenauer no longer had the time to do his own gardening, but in the early morning hours and at weekends he would examine and supervise the work of the gardener. He knew every flower and shrub – and was baffled and irritated by the failure of modern state schools to teach their pupils the Latin and German names of plants. These quiet morning hours were a highlight of Adenauer's day. 'In the morning, immediately after waking,' he assured Anneliese Poppinga, 'one's mind is at its best.'

After strolling in the garden, the Chancellor would take his place at the desk in his study. Until 1960 this desk was a solid piece of working furniture, but made of myrtle and manufactured to Adenauer's own design. He then replaced it with a smaller but equally beautiful antique desk from the Italian dealer Frau Colombo, which was as old-fashioned and awkward as the old man himself. Before beginning his perusal of his papers and the early editions of the newspapers, he would take his first cup of coffee from a thermos flask.

During the early 1950s Adenauer would often call Blankenhorn at 7 am. Blankenhorn, who lived in Honnef, took care to read the papers beforehand in order to prepare himself for a call from the chief. Around this time the house in Rhöndorf would come to life. The first messenger would arrive between 6 and 7 am, bringing diplomatic post, the news digest from the national press office, and the latest reports. These were handed to Adenauer at 7 am. Between 7 and 8 am his private secretary Fräulein Hohmann (after marrying she became Frau Köster), who had worked for Adenauer since 1946, would arrive. A native of Cologne, she had been reluctant to put her name forward when Adenauer had looked for assistance with his correspondence during his time as chairman of the CDU in the British Zone; the former mayor was reputed to be a tough and fussy man. Frau Adenauer had reassured her. By 1951 she was a familiar figure in the Rhöndorf household, dealing with important correspondence and memoranda until 8.30 or 9 am and coming in at the weekend if required. Adenauer drank his breakfast coffee some time between 7 and 8.30 am, when he would be accompanied by whichever members of his family were present – his daughter Lotte, who stayed at home until her marriage in 1954, the theologian Paul, or his youngest son Georg.

At 8.30 am, sometimes earlier, Adenauer would leave for Bonn. At first the only security precaution adopted was the dispatch of a single car with security men to travel in front of the Chancellor's Mercedes. In 1951, however, the security services in Bonn became nervous. That spring six explosive devices were found in Adenauer's coal cellar and, in September, the Federal Chancellor's office was informed that a killer squad from the Czech secret service was planning to attack him on the road between Rhöndorf and Bonn.[3] After a lone motor cyclist attempted to attach an explosive device to Adenauer's car, a motor cavalcade was established. As long as Adenauer remained Chancellor, it was a familiar sight on the right bank of the Rhine: at the front two security men in an open Porsche, then Adenauer's Mercedes 300, followed by another Mercedes equipped with radio. The Dollendorf ferry was instructed to set off as soon as the Chancellor was on board.

In the Palais Schaumburg the discussions and meetings would begin at 9 am. These followed a rough schedule that was drafted four weeks in advance, though detailed plans of each day's events were generally arranged in the middle of the preceding week for the sake of flexibility. Unless a diplomatic breakfast had been arranged, Adenauer took lunch at 1 pm, eating alone to give himself time to collect his thoughts. He continued to eat sparingly – soup, meat, vegetables; in this as in other matters, Adenauer followed the path of moderation. Lunch was followed by a midday nap. Like the elderly Churchill, he would retire to bed in a proper bedroom which, along with a small living room, had been set up behind the small cabinet room in the Palais Schaumburg. These were private rooms for which, since they were not 'official' rooms in the strict sense, Adenauer paid rent.

The older he grew, the longer his nap lasted. Whenever he felt slightly unwell after his sleep, he would remain in his shirt-sleeves on a couch in the dining room behind his study for a few minutes, listening to music or talking to one or other of his closest colleagues.

Adenauer continued to appreciate the fresh air. He developed the habit of taking a walk after his nap, along the paths that had been laid out according to his instructions in the palace grounds – and which were reserved for his use. These walks usually began at 3.30 pm and were used as an opportunity to resume his discussions, with Globke, Blankenhorn, or Hallstein. Adenauer returned to his office after half an hour to continue business there.

The Chancellor continued to set great store by punctuality, in himself and in others. The High Commissioners became particularly aware of this aspect of his personality after 1951, when they began to call on him rather than making him travel all the way up to the Petersberg, which he had always resented. Adenauer, a fanatical lover of routine and order, was also a lover of grandfather clocks with beautiful chimes, and kept various examples in the Palais Schaumburg as well as in his Rhöndorf home. When he left the government, his farewell gift to the cabinet was a table clock with faces on all four sides, so that 'all speakers in discussions will remain aware of the time that cannot be regained'.

Adenauer made frequent telephone calls during his working day. The telephones on his desks in the Palais Schaumburg and at home had nine direct lines to enable him to contact his closest associates without going through the switchboard. Globke was one of these individuals, along with

Blankenhorn, Hallstein, the chief of the federal press office, Foreign Minister Brentano (after 1955), and Heinrich Krone. Erhard, who from 1957 was Vice Chancellor as well as Economics Minister, had line number two.

In the evening, Adenauer generally worked on his documents and held further discussions with his colleagues. If he had no speech to give, he would return to Rhöndorf at about 8 pm, often with a stack of letters and documents to study. Adenauer no longer had any interest in a private social life. He had never been fond of drinking and even now could take wine only in moderation – only in exceptional circumstances did he drink more than one glass.

Adenauer preferred not to be disturbed at home if at all possible. Only a few colleagues were allowed to telephone him there: Globke, Krone from the mid-1950s onwards, and other holders of a direct line. At home he would eat a light dinner and catch up on family and local news. He tried to avoid politics if possible, and only on rare occasions did his colleagues travel to Rhöndorf for further discussions in the evening. His favourite way of relaxing was to listen to tapes of classical music, especially Haydn, Mozart, Schubert and Beethoven.

Sometimes Adenauer would sit in front of one of his pictures and contemplate its composition and use of colour. To prepare himself for sleep, he would read a detective story or leaf through the newspapers. However, as a true son of the German middle class, he usually had a volume of poetry at his bedside – old-fashioned poetry of the kind he had learned by heart at grammar school: Eichendorff, Schiller, Uhland, Heine. He told Felix von Eckardt that he never put out his light without reading a poem first.[4]

Adenauer's life had a weekly as well as a daily rhythm. At the beginning of his chancellorship this weekly routine was marked by a clear distinction between working days and Sundays. Like the rest of the country, the Federal Chancellor's office was organised according to the biblical commandment to rest on the seventh day. On Saturdays, Adenauer would occasionally remain in Rhöndorf in order to hold important discussions, perhaps with one of the High Commissioners, with Blankenhorn or Hallstein. He would then sit down to work on matters which he did not want interrupted: reading position papers for international conferences, or writing drafts for detailed memoranda and letters. His papers contain numerous drafts of important speeches, usually written over the weekend in his upright script.

Weekends in Rhöndorf always included attendance at church, but were otherwise dominated by the home and family. It was at weekends that Adenauer also studied and answered his private correspondence. Often he would be visited by those of his children who lived further away. His son Konrad was now a director of Rheinbraun in Cologne, while Max Adenauer was following in his father's footsteps, becoming a councillor in the city in 1948 and its *Oberstadtdirektor* in 1953. Adenauer's eldest daughter and her husband were living in Mönchengladbach; Libet Werhahn was in Neuss. On the other hand, the younger children were usually at home during the first years of his chancellorship, at least during term time when they were studying in Bonn. Not until the mid-1950s did they leave home: Lotte Adenauer married an architect, Heribert Multhaupt, in 1954; a year later the youngest boy, Georg, married a Swedish woman, Ulla-Britta Jeansson, and subsequently realised his father's boyhood ambition of becoming a notary in the country. Paul Adenauer remained with his father in Rhöndorf for as long as his theological studies allowed. For ten years the household was run by Elsbeth Noelle, who lived with her mother in the house at Zennigsweg 8a. After she married, Adenauer employed a housekeeper for a while but found her excessively formal. From 1960 the house was run by Frau Schlief, a Rhinelander from Unkel with the kind of temperament Adenauer liked – energetic and confident, efficient and quick-witted.

This was the world to which Adenauer withdrew, at least at the weekend. It was this contact with his children, and then with his grandchildren, which helped him retain his lively mind and relative youthfulness until well into his seventies. On Monday Adenauer would return dutifully to work, though with the same reluctance as countless others. On Monday mornings he was frequently in a bad mood, quick to take offence and eager to escape irksome tasks.[5]

Despite frequent interruptions, this was the steady rhythm of Adenauer's life as Chancellor. The most arduous days were past. He no longer had to travel through the region in a battered old car with his sandwiches and a thermos flask, as he had been forced to do during his time as CDU chairman in the British Zone. Now the people he wanted to see came to visit him in Bonn. The exhausting travels of the first years after 1945, which had so disrupted his lifestyle, were reduced. His weekly routine was more ordered.

However, Adenauer resumed his travels whenever regional elections were held, though with the creature comforts to which his post entitled him. Longer journeys were made by train or, as time passed, by aeroplane. Adenauer always remained a lover of powerful cars, preferably driven at great speed by his driver. Though the regional elections tired him, he also enjoyed them; they presented him with a slice of real life and were thus a valuable corrective to the isolated world of Bonn politics. Often, in meetings and conversations, he would refer to issues seen in a fresh light during these excursions.

From 1951 Adenauer also made a series of state visits abroad, usually by aeroplane, to Paris, London, Rome, Brussels, Luxembourg, Strasbourg. In 1951 and 1952 he made twelve trips abroad, taking into account his holidays in Switzerland; between 1951 and 1963 there were 71 in total.

During his first visits to Paris, Adenauer allowed the younger men of his entourage to persuade him to ignore his strict habits of diet and rest.

Von Eckardt, who with Blankenhorn was the leading bon viveur in his circle, even boasted of having persuaded Adenauer to order oysters and champagne to his room.[6] However, the Chancellor quickly realised that he could not sit and drink with his colleagues or embassy officials and still do himself justice at meetings next day. After arriving in a foreign capital, therefore, he adopted the custom of attending the inevitable dinner only to soak up the atmosphere, returning to his room before 11 pm to look through his papers.[7]

Once he had become used to certain hotels, Adenauer did not like changing them. Just as during his time as mayor, when he had preferred to have his usual suite in the Kaiserhof, he now became used to the Hotel Bristol in Paris, Claridge's in London, and later, the Waldorf Astoria in New York. Once West Germany had established embassies abroad, he also stayed in the residences of the various ambassadors.

Adenauer's daily and weekly routines were part of an annual schedule which changed little. During his first years as Chancellor, the two great events were Christmas and New Year, on one hand, and the summer holiday, on the other. Later, on the advice of his doctors, he took an extra vacation in a warmer and healthier climate: on the hills of Baden-Baden, on the Riviera, and from 1959 by Lake Como.

In November Adenauer was often stricken with influenza or attacks of bronchitis. These attacks were not life-threatening, but they imposed an additional strain on an already over-stretched head of government because they put him out of action for two weeks. During these attacks he was confined to his bed in Rhöndorf and was forced to ask his colleagues to visit him or to deal with issues by telephone. His doctors were unanimous in their opinion that he always returned to work without giving himself sufficient time to recuperate.

Christmas remained the high-point of Adenauer's year, as it was for most Germans of his generation. Each year a detailed Nativity scene would be built in the living room at Rhöndorf and the whole family would gather to celebrate the festive season – sons and daughters, sons-in-law and daughter-in-law, and grandchildren. Adenauer always worked hard on his Christmas message, which was broadcast over the radio on Christmas Day each year. He was aware that this speech would be listened to with particular care. As his intimates were aware, he was often melancholic over the Christmas period and used it to attend to personal matters such as his correspondence. As he began his personal new year with his birthday on 5 January, political life also began again in Bonn.

Adenauer came from a devoutly Catholic family in which name-days were treated as seriously as birthdays, if not more so. He always took care to congratulate his children on their name-days and expected them not to forget Konrad's day on 26 November. However, it was his birthday rather than his name-day that came to be celebrated as a major event in the federal capital after January 1950. At major milestones – his 75th, 80th, and 85th birthdays – these celebration came to resemble a festival in honour of a reigning monarch rather than a republican Chancellor.

Adenauer's first birthday as Chancellor was observed in relatively restrained fashion. Even so, a substantial number of gifts were presented by the various regions. Adenauer also received the congratulations of his cabinet, his party, messages from Bonn and Cologne, and – for the first and last time, thankfully – from three girls dressed in costumes, each representing one of the occupation zones.

The following year, the Chancellor's 75th birthday was celebrated in some style. Adenauer was well aware that a lavish ceremony might help to improve his image, which had been damaged by the struggle over the defence contribution, and did not order restraint. The day's events began in somewhat startling fashion at 9 am, with green-clad huntsmen blowing a salute and bringing game from all the regions of West Germany to lay on the grass of Palais Schaumburg. The official ceremonies began at 9.30 am, when President Heuss congratulated Adenauer 'in the name of the German people' and gave him a rare collection of pre-Gregorian chants. From the cabinet he received a beautiful Madonna dating from 1490, which was granted pride of place in his study; the Chancellor was sufficiently touched to make the unusual gesture of addressing his cabinet as 'my friends'. Other presents followed: from the Bundestag a carved oak trunk containing valuable wines; Nymphenburg porcelain from the Bundesrat; a gift from every Land, handed over by the minister-presidents or deputies; 75 exquisite tea-roses as a handsome gesture from Kurt Schumacher and the SPD; gifts from Hans Böckler and the DGB, assuring him of the respect of five million trade unionists (and with parity co-determination on their minds); a painting from the German industrialists, presented by Fritz Berg, president of the BDI. So it went on. At 4 pm Adenauer received the good wishes of the outside world. The diplomatic corps – sixteen countries were now accredited – sent its salutations, then the High Commissioners arrived with their own gifts. Not without a certain irony, the federal press corps sent him two plump 'canards'. Finally, a reception was held for Adenauer in Bonn, attended by the cabinet, at which he was given the freedom of the city. The ceremony took place in the baroque town hall, where he had reached his settlement with the National Socialist mayor of Cologne fourteen years previously. In the market square, 2,000 inhabitants of Bonn had gathered to greet the Chancellor, including numbers of young people with torches and the flags of their youth clubs. Adenauer made a short speech from the balcony: 'We will devote all our efforts to restoring the unity of our country. For that we need the assistance of the German youth.' At the end of the ten-hour celebrations, a confused small girl was ushered forward to offer her tribute: 'Congratulations, uncle president.'

The significance of these celebrations should not be under-estimated. They also provide some idea of the flavour of the times. With a certain personal pleasure, but also with an awareness of the effect, Adenauer permitted himself to be feted like a king each year. As the event became a fixture (and annoyed the Federal President by overshadowing his New Year reception), it helped to convince millions of voters that an elected monarch had taken control in Palais Schaumburg – and that he ought to rule for as long as possible.

In January 1951 Adenauer's popularity was at its lowest point. The fact that his birthday was still celebrated in such a fashion demonstrates that, even then, he had acquired enormous prestige. It was reasonable to wonder how exuberant the celebrations would become if succeeded in winning a stunning election victory.

The major break in Adenauer's working routine during these years came in summer. Even where his holidays were concerned, Adenauer was a creature of habit: the holiday must last a full four weeks, preferably longer, and it could only be truly relaxing in the Swiss mountains. However, the days when his luggage was carried to Chandolin on a donkey were over; the conditions there were insufficiently imposing, and possibly rather too spartan, for an elderly Chancellor. Instead Adenauer chose the Bürgenstock. In summer 1950, the flags of three nations – Switzerland, West Germany, and Israel – were flying outide the Palace Hotel:[8] the Israeli President Chaim Weizmann was a guest at the same time as Adenauer, though the two men kept out of one another's way. Adenauer enjoyed the breathtaking view over Lake Lucerne, but was less fond of the hustle and bustle; in his view the atmosphere was not Alpine enough and there were too many journalists. Between 1953 and 1956 he spent his holidays at the Bühlerhöhe in the Black Forest. In 1955 he also took rooms high above the Lauterbrunn valley in Mürren to observe the Geneva Conference from there. Family holidays of the kind he had enjoyed in the 1920s were no longer possible, of course, but he always had one of his sons or daughters with him to try to stop him working. Occasionally his children would take turns. To him, the presence of his daughters and sons was always a delight; he remained very much a family man.

Adenauer was still a remarkably vigorous walker. Wilhelm G. Grewe, who was a frequent visitor to Mürren during the 1955 Geneva Conference, reported that the old man took him on one of his walks along with von Brentano and Hallstein: 'Instead of "walk" I should say "march", since Adenauer went marching for hours over steep and boulder-strewn paths and it was not easy to keep up with him.'[9]

The Chancellor's Bürgenstock holidays in 1951 and 1952 are vaguely reminiscent of the summer breaks taken by eastern potentates during the nineteenth and early twentieth centuries, which were punctuated by regular arrivals of ministers, messengers and generals. So it was with Adenauer. In summer 1950, during the Korea crisis, Heuss paid Adenauer a private visit in the company of his son, Ludwig. During those tense weeks, when the German defence contribution was being considered and the Schuman Plan negotiated, Blankenhorn was in almost perpetual motion between Bonn, Paris and the Bürgenstock.

Even then Adenauer was not content to concentrate on the major outlines of policy. Far too often for some people's taste, he also intervened in the details. Despite the threat of a third world war, he was also preoccupied with the formation of a government in North Rhine-Westphalia, where to his great annoyance he failed to oust Karl Arnold. Franz Blücher had hoped that, in the absence of the Chancellor, he would be able to make something of the office of Vice-Chancellor. However, before Adenauer left he sent Blücher a detailed letter which restricted his responsibilities: 'In view of the extraordinarily tense situation, I do not, unfortunately, feel able to withdraw entirely from government business during this period, as I would have liked to do. I will therefore take a small office to the Bürgenstock with Herr *Ministerialrat* Dr Rust and *Oberregierungsrat* Ostermann. I would be grateful if you would take charge of regular business here on my behalf. I know that if necessary you will make contact with me on significant issues.'[10]

Since the situation was also to be 'extraordinarily tense' in subsequent years, this became standard practice. Routine business was looked after by the Vice-Chancellor, supported and carefully supervised by Hans Globke, Herbert Blankenhorn, Otto Lenz and Walter Hallstein. Adenauer, however, continued to deal with everything that he regarded as significant.

In the following summer the stream of visitors to the Bürgenstock increased. By now it had become a matter of prestige to be invited to the Chancellor's summer residence. A delegation from the DGB arrived for talks, as did the heads of the CDU/CSU parliamentary party. Vice Chancellor Blücher, however, was insulted at being passed over.

There was no possibility of a complete break from official business of the kind Adenauer had enjoyed as mayor of Cologne, when Hans Wolfgarten had taken charge on his behalf. Nevertheless, those around him agreed that these weeks of walking in the mountains did much to regenerate him physically and mentally. His physical constitution in the early and mid-1950s was particularly good – better than it had been during his years in Cologne. He continued to suffer from insomnia, which he attributed to the strains of his arrest in 1944. His headaches had not disappeared either, but he had learned to live with these. In old age Adenauer was reaping the benefits of looking well after his health for many years.

His medical treatment in Bonn was supervised by Paul Martini, who had been professor of medicine at the Friedrich-Wilhelms University since 1932 and was also a CDU town-councillor in the town. The results of his examinations were usually highly satisfactory for a man of Adenauer's age. 'He has the heart of a logger from Adenau', Martini told the former mayor of Bonn, Schumacher-Hellmold. Physically Adenauer had three weaknesses, the most troublesome of which was his old chronic bronchitis, aggravated by the humid climate of Bonn. He also suffered from associated skin allergies, and from the onset of age-related diabetes. Exercise in the fresh air, more frequent holidays in the south or in the mountains, and a specific diet were the best treatment for these conditions. As ever, his doctors complained that Adenauer never gave himself enough time to recover from influenza or bronchitis before returning to work. He did, however, take an entirely characteristic pride in remembering to take his various medicines punctually.

Adenauer's day-to-day medical care was in the hands of his family doctor in Rhöndorf, Frau Ella Bebber-Buch, partly under the guidance of Martini. She played an important part in keeping him physically fit and was always on hand when he fell ill. Between 1953 and 1956 Adenauer also visited Professor Strooman in the sanatorium at Bühlerhöhe. There was no shortage of competent doctors, though they were dealing with a remarkably healthy patient. The contrast with former Chancellors – with the ailing Stresemann, and Bismarck with his almost suicidally unhealthy lifestyle – was striking.

Adenauer maintained moderate habits in order to conserve his energy, which was enhanced by frequent exercises and regular holidays. He was quite prepared to supplement this regime by taking Pervitin or Revitalin for extra energy in critical periods. There were frequent rumours that he paid secret visits to Zürich to see Professor Niehans, the creator of 'Niehans therapy' or fresh-cell therapy, but this was strongly denied by Frau Bebber-Buch.[11]

In general Adenauer led a thoroughly orderly private life, regrettably (for a biographer) free of excesses, major mood swings or hidden vices. Restraint and self-control had become second nature to him. His life, almost pedantic in its routine, was saved from boredom by the burdens of his work and the inner tensions of his temperament.

His nature did harbour an undercurrent of strong feeling and a desire for self-assertion and occasional emotional outbursts, which were self-controlled and occurred mostly in the presence of his closest associates and his family. Adenauer also had a sense of humour, which was usually expressed at the expense of others but also helped to mask a profound pessimism of outlook. Until very old age he retained in private a mischievous, almost boyish streak and an enjoyment of boisterous pranks while on his holiday. His close circle regarded him as a complicated man with a number of contradictory characteristics. Adenauer was unsentimental and generally without compassion in everyday political life, but combined this with an instinctive and often warm-hearted sympathy for others. Cold and impulsive; self-controlled and excitable; sometimes extremely open, at other times calculating and incalculable; thick-skinned and sensitive; rational but prey to strong emotions – in all of these respects Adenauer was a man of contradictions.

Despite these features, his was a life of bourgeois normality in everything except his elevated position. In the early years of the Federal Republic, when economic need was widespread, his lifestyle appeared upper class. However, this label was recognised as misplaced by those who, like Adenauer, remembered the lifestyle enjoyed by the upper class of the inter-war years. In fact he led a bourgeois existence, no more and no less. Certainly his house contained some valuable furniture and a number of late medieval and sixteenth- or seventeenth-century works of art. But his paintings – either from Emma Weyer or bought by Adenauer himself – were his only real luxury. Otherwise his home comforts were relatively modest; his bathroom, bedroom and study were plain and simple. The director generals, bankers and wealthy businessmen of the 1950s and 1960s lived more expensively than the Chancellor who dominated the political life of his country.

His sufferings in the first years of the Third Reich appear to have persuaded Adenauer that the expensive lifestyle of his years in Cologne had been a mistake – at least for a man of his origins and outlook. In small matters he had always been thrifty, but now he was careful in large ones as well. A disinclination to spend large amounts of money was particularly obvious in his wardrobe – though this may have been no more than the indifference to fashion of the very old.

Adenauer participated in the return to normality in personal life which was the experience of most West Germans in the 1950s. In his case, however, normality meant the kind of private life that would have been enjoyed by a respectable citizen of reasonable means 40 or 50 years previously. He continued to give absolute priority to the conscientious carrying out of his job, to value a harmonious and decent family life, and to devote his few hours of leisure to artistic contemplation, simple evening pastimes, and moderate food and drink. To all those who know only the fragmentation of the modern century this may look like a suspect dream world. For Adenauer, however, it seemed totally natural, part of a code of behaviour to which he remained personally committed.

This quiet lifestyle also included the careful nursing of those few friendships that had stood the test of time. For as long as he worked in Brussels, and sometimes afterwards, Dannie N. Heineman came to visit Adenauer in Bonn. Whenever Adenauer travelled to New York, he would spend an evening with Heineman at Deer Park, perhaps listening to Rudolf Serkin at the piano or examining Heineman's priceless collection of Goethe first editions and his superb material on Napoleon.

Robert Pferdemenges was an even closer friend. Politically and personally, the two were inseparable. Adenauer continued to celebrate birthdays and spend holidays with the Pferdemenges family even after he had more or less abandoned any social life outside of his immediate family. He also remained close to Friedrich Spennrath, another man who had proved his loyalty between 1933 and 1945.

Adenauer no longer made new friends. His disillusioning experiences after the Nazi seizure of power had destroyed whatever spontaneity he had left after his period as mayor. Aware that the people he met usually wanted something from him, he kept them at arm's length.

There remained, of course, the family. Alongside politics, it was his life. Adenauer's personal life and his public duties now became intermingled, at least to an extent; his adult daughters, in particular, were indispensable to him during state visits by foreign statesmen and his own trips abroad. Until her marriage in 1954, his daughter Lotte often took the part of 'first lady'. However, the family appears to have kept its distance from leading politicians and Adenauer's close colleagues; its members understood that they could best support their father by refusing to become too closely involved in political decisions. The events surrounding Adenauer's decision to seek the Federal Presidency in 1959 – and then to abandon the attempt – were an exception to this rule. In general, relations between Adenauer's family and his assistants remained easy and cordial, partly because Blankenhorn, Hallstein, and Globke prudently maintained distance.

The most important influence of the family during these years lay in providing the old man with emotional stability. Without the shelter and solace he found with his children and their own families, Adenauer would have been emotionally barren in his last years. Regular contact with his lively children, who were always respectful but were also willing to offer benevolent criticism, brought him as near to complete relaxation as he ever came. The private side of Adenauer is revealed at its most attractive in his many letters to his children during his years as Chancellor. He wrote the letters of any busy father to his grown children, sympathising with them on personal matters, providing snippets of information about his travels and his more pressing tasks, offering critical or contented remarks about the weather and the state of his garden, and – occasionally – making ironic or serious remarks about political issues.

For example, on 25 March 1958, two days after her name-day, Adenauer wrote to his daughter Ria Reiners. He penned the letter from the government benches, in the middle of a long debate in the Bundestag:

> Only now am I writing to wish you happiness because I have simply been unable to do so for the last few days. Today is the fourth and last day of the awful Bundestag debate, and a good speech made in a relatively calm house gives me the opportunity to write you this letter … It was really beautiful in Vence and I think back to it with pleasure. But how far away it is already! On 5 March I returned, today is the 25th, such a lot has happened in these 20 days! You will have lovely, sunny weather and, I hope, will continue to

improve. Slowly, very slowly, spring seems to be arriving here. I hope it will be here by Easter. To you, dear child, and to Walter, I send most cordial greetings. As always your father.[12]

With his children, at least, Adenauer was an ordinary elderly man who found the Bundestag debates as dire as everybody else and thought wistfully of his holiday with his daughter in the Maritime Alpes; he often complained about the wet weather in the Rhine valley and never forgot name-days.

The picture of Adenauer's personal life is clear: an upright German citizen of a remarkably old-fashioned kind. His home and love of gardening, his enjoyment of music and holidays at the same resort, his social and family life – it was a lifestyle that was solidly middle class, unintellectual, and very little affected by the pace of modern life.

The only luxury Adenauer allowed himself was his art collection. He had already, as he related proudly, made a few 'little catches' when he was mayor of Cologne, but it was in his years as Chancellor that he was able to extend his collection with the help of the shrewd Rhenish art dealer Heinz Kisters, to whom he had been introduced by Pferdemenges. Adenauer's taste was for late-Gothic painting, as well as for sixteenth-century Italian art and El Greco. He was especially interested in altarpieces, biblical scenes, and portraits. Kisters reported[13] that opposite the desk in his study in Rhöndorf was a crucifixion scene, painted by an Italian master of the thirteenth century. Near it was the lamentation of Christ by Jan Joest van Kalkar, a late-mediaeval image of the crucified Christ supported by Mary and John, with Golgatha and its three crosses in the background. On the same wall was a painting by a Bruges master of Mary adoring the Christ child.

Adenauer was particularly fond of the painting on the wall to his right, Titian's portrait of a dignified and inscrutable statesman, the Doge Francesco Donà. Next to it was another Titian, Saint Hieronymus as an anchorite, accompanied by the lion that had stayed with him after he removed the thorn from its paw. The last portrait on the wall was a noblewoman, painted by Vincenzo Tamagni of the school of Raphael. On the fourth wall, above Adenauer's sofa, hung another Madonna with Child, this time by Joos van Cleve, next to a death of Mary painted by a Bohemian master.

These were the surroundings in which the German Chancellor of the 1950s worked, dealt with his correspondence, and drafted his speeches and papers. From time to time he would sit in his armchair, a woollen blanket over his knees, lost in contemplation of his pictures.

The rooms on the ground floor were also full of pictures. Adenauer was most proud of a portrait of Pope Paul III which, he was convinced, had been painted by El Greco. He was equally fascinated by the Joest van Kalkar painting of Christ's arrest, especially by the base faces of the heavily armed soldiers and the repulsive softness of the face of Judas. Such paintings, showing human beings in extreme situations or in the grip of religious feeling, had a profound impact upon Adenauer.

His collection was constantly changing. Adenauer sought to enlarge it through exchange, frequently had pictures brought for him to examine, and was prepared to lend out items from his own collection. The negotiations between Kisters and the Chancellor were conducted with patience and cunning on both sides. They did business together until the end of Adenauer's life, though each would complain to others that he had been cheated. Once, on his way home from a holiday, Adenauer would even drop in on Kisters at his home in Meersburg in order to reassure himself that a beautiful painting was not being withheld from him. When he wanted a work of art, he was as tenacious and cunning in pursuing it as during his diplomatic negotiations. He would listen carefully to advice, but only to a certain extent. His judgement was not easily influenced, and his taste hardly at all.

Adenauer was most fascinated by works of art from an epoch far removed from his own. The paintings clearly touched the heart of a man who was deeply old fashioned. Yet one should remember that his lifestyle was less uncommon in the 1950s and early 1960s than it would be today: large families were still regarded as being the centre of private life; everyday life was more naturally permeated by religious belief; conscientious work was given clear priority over leisure and relaxation. This was still a dominant social reality in West Germany during the twenty years after the Second World War.

It would therefore be incorrect to dismiss Adenauer's personal life as of the 'nineteenth century'. Nevertheless, it is true to say that, even in the 1950s, his behaviour and routines were regarded as profoundly conservative and traditional – as indeed they were. As a politician Adenauer had always been more modern than his lifestyle, both before 1933 and after the Second World War.

In the political field he repudiated many of the ideas and beliefs held by large sections of the German middle classes even after 1945. Adenauer was always a faithful Catholic, and had not been brought up to believe in the desirability of partnership and cooperation with the Protestants. And yet, in domestic politics he was a prime mover behind the establishment of the Christian Democratic Union, and thereby helped to make a long overdue break with established tradition of mutual mistrust between Catholics and Protestants. Equally, in foreign policy he recognised much earlier than most of his countrymen that the old map of Europe had been changed beyond recognition in 1945. He was also aware that all the states of Europe had lost the ability to act as autonomous great powers after the Second World War. Many conservative Germans regarded his departure from the principles of the sovereign nation state as a betrayal of traditions which they continued to value even after the experiences of the Third Reich.

This assessment holds true in many areas. In his politics Adenauer was more progressive than many members of the German middle classes – a reformer and very far from a traditionalist. This is not to deny that he continued to think in traditional terms in many of his political ideas. It was a point which was constantly made against him by the Opposition, and one he did not dispute. Like most successful conservatives, Adenauer embodied an irritating combination of traditionalism and modernity. The resulting mixture of the old-fashioned and the modern, of views from a world that had vanished and values of the later twentieth century, was not always consistent. In political practice it produced a number of contradictions which he either could not recognise or would not admit. Yet Adenauer was aware that progress in the world was full of inconsistencies, and did not worry about resolving them.

In his personal life the conservative element was always dominant. In all probability he would have been unable to deal with the chaos of the post-war years, the uncertainties of his early chancellorship, and the breathtaking pace of international change throughout his term of office, without the constant renewal of his strength and self-confidence through the traditional lifestyle with which he was comfortable. In this sense, the non-political aspects of his life had a profound effect on the achievements of a man who was obsessed by politics. His private interests never took up enough of his time to lead to laziness – which he regarded, along with incompetence, as a cardinal sin for any elected official. Politics was, and always would be, his destiny. Nevertheless, his home and garden, nature and art, family and church occupied a large enough place in his life to make his destiny tolerable.

VII

EUROPEAN STATESMAN
1950–1952

Adenauer signs the German Treaty (26 May 1952)

'I Too Have My Nightmare: Its Name is Potsdam'

Adenauer was constantly troubled by his ignorance of the hidden intentions of the Western Allies with regard to Germany. In April 1950 he complained bitterly about the situation during a confidential conversation with McCloy. He was expected to make a decision that was vital for his country – here he was referring to entry to the Council of Europe – even though, without representation abroad, he could not know what was going on in the world.[1]

This 'impossible situation'[2] lasted for the whole of that year and improved only gradually during 1951 and 1952. For endless weeks in the autumn of 1950, Adenauer had no clear idea of the agreements being made behind the closed doors of the Foreign Ministers' Conference in New York. Even the official information was contradictory. As regards a German defence contribution, the communiqué was highly ambiguous. On 27 September 1950, General Hays informed Blankenhorn and von Schwerin that they could count on the establishment of six German divisions from the mobile police force of 30,000 men. On the other hand, only minor reinforcements of the Länder police had actually been approved. In a private exchange of views, François-Poncet told the Chancellor that French public opinion must be given time to adjust to the idea of a German defence contribution. Adenauer answered sarcastically that precisely the same situation existed with regard to German public opinion, but concluded that the French had not in fact agreed to a German defence contribution at all. This view was largely confirmed by McCloy.[3]

Instead of making decisions on the issue of German 'protective forces', the New York Conference of Foreign Ministers had demanded that the Federal Republic must recognise German foreign debts. Even this looked suspiciously like a delaying tactic. Adenauer was nevertheless prepared for it; with the Marshall Plan due to run out in 1952, West Germany would need fresh foreign loans, and would only get them if the old debt burden was recognised. Moreover, the West Germans were now claiming to be the legitimate legal successor of the Reich, a step which was necessary and useful in several respects but was bound to cost money. Adenauer, however, was incorrect in his assumption that the Bundestag would be ready to give the Western Allies what amounted to a blank cheque.

From the end of September 1950, Adenauer nevertheless maintained his offer of a German defence contribution, for which he was strongly attacked by the Opposition and the Protestant left. How would his opponents have responded had they known that he had been making official moves even *before* the outbreak of the Korean War? The Social Democratic Opposition fluctuated between defeatist slogans along the general lines of 'better red than dead', and Kurt Schumacher's utopian demand that, before the establishment of German forces, the Western Allies should move an army with offensive capabilities to the Elbe, strong enough to defend Western Europe in the event of a Soviet attack east of the Oder or Vistula.

Defeatism became even more widespread in West Germany in November 1950, when Chinese troops intervened in the Korean War and inflicted serious casualties on the UN forces, mainly the American expeditionary corps. Not until spring 1951 did it become clear that the front in Korea had stabilised. In these critical weeks the Western Powers ignored Adenauer's outstretched hand.

Meanwhile Adenauer was vexed by the suspicion that the British had 'taken him for a ride'. In fact, London had been the first of the Western Allies to take action on the rearmament issue. We now know that a visit by General von Schwerin to London in April 1950 had not been coordinated with the U.S. And when Adenauer's defence initiative of early June 1950 became known in Washington, President Truman was extremely irritated. Moreover, Secretary of State Acheson at once suspected that the British were behind it.[4] After all, London had invited Count von Schwerin to secret talks in April, and it seemed possible that Adenauer's initiative concerning the federal police force had been inspired, or even partly formulated, by the British.

In fact, it was significant that Bevin had introduced the concept of a federal police force at the New York conference at the beginning of September 1950. As a 'first step', London envisaged the establishment of no more than a 100,000-men force. However, an important role in the memorandum sent to Acheson by Bevin the argument played an important role that the Germans themselves were now ready for a defence contribution: 'Federal Chancellor Adenauer has strongly supported the establishment of a volunteer force of 150,000 men in order to have a counter-weight to the 'stand-bys' in the Eastern zone. He promised that he could secure the agreement of the Opposition to this and also believed he could levy 150,000 reliable volunteers. Here he may have been inappropriately optimistic, but he has always been a determined man of well-known political cleverness. In any case the initiative had come from the German side.'[5] When the French strongly opposed the move in Washington, however, Bevin dropped the British plan for a West German federal police force.

It is not certain exactly when Adenauer first became suspicious of the British on this point. When he dismissed von Schwerin, he not only argued that the generals had to be taught a lesson, but also indicated in cabinet that von Schwerin had been recommended to him by Robertson and was being used by the British.[6] His removal was designed to signal to London that Adenauer had seen through their plans and, in future, was determined to rely on generals such as Heusinger and Speidel who supported the concept of rearmament associated with the Pentagon.

Over the following weeks it became clear not only that Paris was opposed to a German defence contribution, but also that the British had reversed their policy on the issue. The Labour government was facing growing political problems at home; with an election in the offing, it seemed necessary to close ranks with the left of the party on the controversial issue of a German military contribution. Bevin was no longer well enough to withstand the strains of his job as Foreign Minister, and was losing influence even before his resignation in March 1951.

Within Germany, the election setbacks sustained by the CDU in autumn 1950 were also related with the sudden silence of the Western Allies on the rearmament question. Even before the elections, Adenauer had come under fire from his own parliamentary party whose leader, von Brentano, had been particularly critical of the timing and manner of Heinemann's dismissal.[7]

In October 1950 the situation was further complicated by two new factors: Jean Monnet's plan for a European army, and clever propaganda initiatives from the east for an alternative to the military contribution.

The genesis of the European Defence Community concept was rooted in the same considerations concerning the European situation as the Schuman Plan. Once again Monnet hoped to make the control of Germany into a European virtue. The proposals which he developed in mid-October drew on Adenauer's declarations that he was prepared to cooperate within a European army, should the need arise. In a memorandum on the subject, Monnet expressed his main ideas as follows: 'that the solution of the military aspect of the German problem is to be sought in the same spirit and according to the same methods that guided the coal and steel pool: creating a European army which, in its command, its organisation, its equipment and its financing, will be unified and subordinated to the leadership of a supra-national high command (the integration of German formations into this original core is to proceed progressively).' Monnet also emphasised one vital pre-condition: the solution was only to be implemented after the signing of the Schuman Plan. This condition clearly reveals the element of control inherent in the plan. Monnet thought – understandably – that if Germany was again to be allowed the prospect of its own soldiers, and eventually sovereignty, then it might be reluctant to limit its industrial power by accepting supranational economic ties.[8]

Monnet was contemplating something very different from the concept of a European coalition army which dominated U.S. thinking and was also at the basis of Adenauer's own earlier ideas. The European coalition army was to be a NATO army, including the U.S. forces in Europe, and being led by an American general – probably General Eisenhower, who was currently president of Columbia University in New York. German contingents would be incorporated into a European-American army of this kind much as the South Korean army was being incorporated into the UN forces on its territory. The U.S. generals considered that control would flow naturally from the fact that the United States would have to provide the equipment, supplies, and air cover, while the German forces would have no general staff and would be fully integrated into the coalition army at division and corps level.

Monnet had put forward a very different idea. His European defence force included only West European contingents. From the outset, German troops would be established merely as part of an integrated European army: '... the first soldier who is recruited in Germany is a European soldier'.[9] It was true that the armies of the other states stationed in Europe would also be fused into the European army. On the other hand, the German demand for equal status was to be thwarted. In terms of organisation, this meant 'a complete unification of men and material'; politically, it meant a European defence minister, a Council of Ministers, a joint assembly and a common budget.

The proposal went before the French Council of Ministers under minister-president René Pleven. However, the 'Pleven Plan' that emerged on 24 October was, from the point of view of the Germans, much more problematic. The French cabinet had decided that the contingents supplied by the participating states 'should be incorporated into the European army at the level of the biggest possible units'. The words 'in the same uniform', found in Monnet's draft, had been removed. It was also noted that the contingents of the French overseas army were not to be integrated.[10]

Adenauer's private reaction, as Blankenhorn noted that same day, was 'completely negative. Reasons: first the close linking of the armament preparations with the Schuman Plan, second the discrimination against the German contingents, third, instead of immediate action, the postponement of the whole idea as a result of difficult international negotiations which were to begin after the signing of the Schuman Plan'.[11] On 25 October, when the details of the Plan became known, Adenauer had hosted a dinner at the Palais Schaumburg in honour of General Clay. McCloy, General Hays and Ivone Kirkpatrick had also been present. Their unanimous view was that the idea was 'completely out of the question.'

Blankenhorn added: 'The sharpest in their rejection are the Americans. Kirkpatrick only slightly milder.' At a separate discussion later, Kirkpatrick offered the opinion that the only alternative was the 'big solution' which had been discussed in New York: 53 divisions in Western Europe, including six German divisions of front-line troops and four reserve divisions. The SPD would eventually agree, as it had voted for war credits in 1914, if the U.S. and Britain applied enough pressure. Apart from that, much to Adenauer's satisfaction, Bevin wanted to visit Bonn in November in order to discuss the Franco-German relationship with Adenauer who very much welcomed the prospect.

In his discussions with Hallstein and Blankenhorn, Adenauer decided to refrain from comment on the French plan, either official or unofficial. However, Hallstein was instructed to inform Schuman of 'the great concerns and the disappointment of the Chancellor'.

The French now began to make every effort to overcome German objections. As part of this process, Monnet invited McCloy – with Pleven and Schuman – to his home at Houjarray in order to win his support. François-Poncet also attempted to make the plan acceptable to Adenauer.[12] However, the Chancellor remained convinced that French intentions were less than honourable. At this critical stage the French were not alone in using well-conceived delaying-tactics: the Soviet Union also intervened with its own proposals.

At the end of October, the Eastern bloc, at a meeting in Prague, published a declaration which provided the framework for all subsequent discussions. It was followed by a letter from the East German minister-president, Grotewohl, to President Heuss. Finally, on 3 November 1950, a note arrived from the Soviet government to the Western Powers proposing an immediate conference of the foreign ministers of the Four Powers on Germany. The main points were as follows: a return to the Potsdam agreement; the demilitarisation of Germany; the creation of a provisional all-German government; the conclusion of a peace treaty with Germany; and the withdrawal of the occupying troops within a year of the peace treaty being signed. To prepare the establishment of an all-German provisional government, there should be an 'All-German Constituent Council with parity composition of representatives from East and West Germany', eventually to be legitimised by plebiscite.

Adenauer was greatly alarmed by this development. At the outset, he was particularly worried that the French and British might be tempted by the deliberations of a Four Power Conference. Such a gathering would obviously delay the development of Western defences with West German participation and make it more difficult to ease the restrictions of the

Occupation Statute. He did not trust the Western Powers an inch, not even the Americans, on this issue. Quite apart from the delaying effect, Adenauer suspected that new negotiations on Germany might lead to a fundamental change in Western policy.

Two-and-a-half years later, in a frank moment during an interview with Ernst Friedlander, Adenauer revealed the thinking that had underpinned his actions during these months: 'Bismarck spoke of his nightmare of coalitions against Germany. I have my nightmare too: its name is Potsdam. The danger of a common policy by the great powers at the expense of Germany has existed since 1945 and has continued to exist since the founding of the Federal Republic. The foreign policy of the Federal Republic was always directed towards getting out of this danger zone. Germany must not come between the millstones or it is lost.'[13]

Adenauer had long been convinced that, Robert Schuman notwithstanding, the Quai d'Orsay was dominated by men who preferred to solve the problem of security towards Germany in cooperation with the Soviet Union. His youthful memories of the visit by the French fleet to Kronstadt, with all its implications, remained strong, and this obsession had been intensified by the German experience of a war on two fronts in both world wars and by the Franco-Soviet treaty of 1944. Like the majority of his fellow countrymen, Adenauer's great foreign-policy trauma was 'encirclement'. He therefore doubted whether the new line of French policy towards Germany, as embodied by Schuman and Monnet, would survive the arduous process of Four Power negotiations. Consequently, he feared that the course of German history was in danger of reverting to its position as 'the country in the middle', which had led to catastrophe twice in the twentieth century.

Moreover, it was precisely during these weeks that the United States seemed in danger of succumbing to the temptations of isolationism once again. Adenauer had long feared such a development, which, for the Americans, would have been little more than a return to normality. He still remembered how the U.S. expeditionary force had been withdrawn from western Germany after the First World War, with the consequent loss of a restraining U.S. influence on French policy. That had been in 1922, and the United States had occupied only a small area of territory around Koblenz, but the effects of its withdrawal had been catastrophic. There was, he felt, an even greater danger that the situation in central and western Europe would get out of hand if the Americans again cut themselves off from Europe.

The Chancellor was horrified by a letter sent to him by Consul-General Krekeler in New York. Former President Herbert Hoover, himself a friend of the Germans, had made a speech on 20 December 1950 in which he advocated a U.S. withdrawal from Europe in favour of peripheral defence. The influential publicist Walter Lippmann had been supporting such an approach for some time. Hoover had been disappointed by the West Europeans' delay in building up a credible defence, but in December 1950 he also feared that the Russians might launch a preventive war if 60 Western divisions were placed on West German soil.

It was easy to imagine what the effect of a U.S. withdrawal on French policy would be. Inevitably, the temptation for France to make an arrangement with the Soviet Union would be intensified. Moreover, the near-disaster suffered by the U.S. expeditionary force in Korea in the Winter of 1950/51 was hardly likely to increase confidence in U.S. support.

From Adenauer's point of view, then, the likely result of Four Power negotiations appeared to be an agreement to neutralise Germany along with the simultaneous withdrawal of the occupying troops. This would leave the Americans uninvolved in Europe or engaged with minimal forces, while the Soviet Union retained powerful forces behind the Oder. The Volkspolizei might then begin to play a crucial role. At the same time, the withdrawal of the Americans would increase the confidence of the Communists in France and Italy. In late 1950 and early 1951, Adenauer viewed the future with grim foreboding.

Inevitably the situation had its effects on West Germany. Adenauer believed that public opinion was already being influenced by a trend which, if it continued, would lead to Soviet hegemony over continental Europe. As in France, the opponents of a defence contribution in the Federal Republic saw the Four Power negotiations as an excellent means of postponing a solution to the problem. The idea of neutrality also had a genuine appeal. Considerable numbers of Germans saw it as a way of escaping from the confrontation between the superpowers, and even as a means of returning to the international system of the pre-war years and restoring German freedom of manoeuvre. Such a course was advocated by Rudolf Nadolny, former German ambassador in Moscow, and by the Nauheim circle associated with Professor Ulrich Noack. They received open, rather than discreet, support from Soviet representatives in East Germany.

It was true that the East German regime had fallen into disrepute as a result of the sham elections of 15 October 1950. Repression in the Eastern Zone had increased, and no self-respecting West German politician was likely to be attracted by the proposal for an all-German Council with parity representation for democratically elected West German representatives, on one hand, and representatives of the East German dictatorship, on the other. However, the East German slogan of 'Germans at one table' was not without effect. There was no support in West Germany for a general recognition of the East German government – but negotiations between East German and West German representatives under the auspices of the occupying powers might be a different matter. Secretly, many members of Adenauer's coalition wondered whether a neutral Germany might not offer a solution to the German problem. They doubted whether the democratic parties in the Federal Republic need have any fears of the popular appeal of the Communists in the East if all the occupying forces – including the Soviets – withdrew. Was it really necessary to keep staring at the Communist menace like a rabbit mesmerised by the proverbial snake?

Occasionally these issues were openly discussed in the CDU. At the beginning of February 1951, for example, vehement discussions took place in its Bundesausschuß, when Robert Tillmanns of the Berlin CDU maintained that some form of neutrality might be looked on favourably even by the German themselves. Adenauer made no bones about his disagreement.[14] However, there was some doubt about how much longer he could keep the party in line.

At the same time, certain elements in West German society began to modify their position in an attempt to insure against any possible outcome. Even among the industrialists, Adenauer knew, there were signs of weakening. In summer 1951, when the government had urged the establishment of factory-based security services to defend companies against sabotage attempts directed from the East, several representatives of these firms had justified their inactivity by commenting that 'you can't be sure that the Soviets won't be ruling Germany in six months time'.[15]

At this critical stage of his policy towards the West, Adenauer decided on what may be called a 'flight forward'. With regard to the Western Powers, he decided to undertake several measures as quickly as possible: the completion of the negotiations on the Schuman Plan; the rapid disposition of U.S. and British divisions on the border with East Germany; the beginning of a German defence contribution, in whatever form; and the replacement of the occupation statute by treaty agreements. Adenauer never tired of pointing out that he should at least be consulted on the issue of East-West negotiations. In fact, of course, he wanted much more – firm treaty commitments and an assurance that there would be no settlement of the German question with the Soviet Union against the will of Bonn.

His fears related to this issue rose steadily. In October 1951 these fears had led him to put forward and idea from which emerged the controversial Article VII,3 of the General Treaty. At home, however, he had warned ceaselessly against what he saw as the four great errors: nationalism, pacifism, neutralism, and U.S. isolationism.

As things stood, he regarded the United States as the crucial factor. The myth of the relationship between the 'great Europeans', Adenauer and Schuman, has given rise to the belief that Adenauer's foreign policy was chiefly directed, even at this early stage, towards Franco-German co-operation. Of course, both men did seek this long-term objective, but diplomatic practice was very different. The French continued to create problems for German foreign policy, and even Robert Schuman – for understandable reasons – did not seek an equitable solution of Franco-German problems between equal partners. Progress was possible only because Adenauer directed most of his attention towards the United States – and the United States exerted pressure on a reluctant French cabinet.

Time and time again, to his intimates or to the cabinet, Adenauer explained his priorities amid the complexities and difficulties of his European policy. Otto Lenz, for example, made the following note on Adenauer's comments at the cabinet meeting of 21 February 1951: 'The Federal Chancellor gave a detailed survey of his attitude towards the Eastern Zone and the need to make an absolutely clear policy which does not give the impression, especially in the U.S., that Germany is vacillating between the East and the West. He pointed out that both French and British policy are extraordinarily unfavourable for us at the moment and that we must therefore attempt to hold on to the Americans.'[16]

A month before, on the subject of the strike threat over co-determination, he had said the same thing to the delegation chairman. The strike, he claimed, must be prevented because the U.S. isolationists would see it as an argument to withdraw from Europe: 'The French are for the neutralisation and non-armament of West Germany anyway.'[17] In the same vein, he gave extensive details of the main lines of his policy to the Protestant bishops at the beginning of February. In the presence of Hermann Ehlers, he told them 'that a vacillating attitude on the part of the Federal Republic would immediately have negative repercussions in the U.S.'.[18] In 1951, all of Adenauer's energies were devoted to America: the United States must keep the Russians away from West Germany's throat, and persuade the French, maybe also the British, to change their dangerous course.

During this period the Chancellor was convinced that Washington was considering the option of peripheral defence and the abandonment of Europe, perhaps in association with the destruction of German industrial centres in order to prevent the Soviet Union from reaping any benefit from their capture. He felt that the United States would be prepared to abandon this option – which was highly tempting given the course of U.S. history – if the Western Europeans, including the West Germans, adopted an unequivocally pro-American line. U.S. isolationism would be enormously strengthened by uncertainty, by German longings for another Rapallo, by unwise attempts to respond to Soviet overtures.

It was in the light of this thinking that, in November 1950, Adenauer intensified his appeal to the Western Allies to pursue a policy of *faits accomplis*. As he had done during the Rhineland occupation after the First World War (an eternity had passed since these days), he turned to his old friend Dannie Heineman. Aware that Heineman was travelling from Brussels to the United States in the middle of November, he sent his friend a five-page personal letter by courier.[19] This letter – in effect a cry for help – contained another summary of his most important demands:

1. The discussions among the Atlantic pact powers, which have continued since September, must at last be brought to a reasonable conclusion so that the

German people can see the Atlantic pact powers are united. 2. It is most urgent that American troops are transferred here in considerable strength as quickly as possible, so that the German people once again believe in the will of the United States to resist in Europe. Two divisions, which are here now, could be withdrawn in an emergency, an army could not be withdrawn.

There was one further point which Kurt Schumacher impressed on Adenauer at every opportunity. It was essential, he argued, to recognise that a high standard of living in Germany was essential for bolstering the weak German will to resist the Soviets; the Federal Republic must not be burdened with excessive defence spending. Then he returned to his perpetual theme of removing the Occupation Statute: 'Certainly that would not be possible all at once, but there must be very significant progress for all to see.' Finally, Adenauer stressed the need to oppose the agitation of the SPD, which – so he claimed – was based on selfish motives of party politics.

Heineman, as ever, proved a reliable ally. At the beginning of December the businessman met General Eisenhower and handed him a copy of the letter. Eisenhower was impressed and promised to inform Secretary of State Marshall at once. By the middle of December, Adenauer's letter was on the desks of the leading members of the administration in Washington. Its great value was that it described Adenauer's view of the situation openly and directly, in a manner possible only in a letter to a trusted friend.[20]

At the end of March 1951[21] Heineman also wrote to McCloy and outlined Adenauer's political and psychological programme. According to Heineman, the Chancellor's strongest feature was his 'Germanism (in a good sense)'. Heineman had personally seen how much Adenauer had suffered from the moral and physical misery that had afflicted his country. If he was unable to realise what enormous progress had been made since 1945, that sense was probably the reason. He continued: 'Adenauer's intense Germanism is coupled with a limited personal knowledge of foreign countries. For that reason it is perhaps difficult for him, from time to time, to recognise that people west of the Rhine are not so easily convinced of the good intentions of the Germans, irrespective of which government is in office.'

Heineman then praised Adenauer's courage and creativity, which he had demonstrated during his time as mayor of Cologne. He did not deny the Chancellor's dictatorial tendencies, which sometimes alienated people and ensured that he had not always been loved. However, it was essential to recall the courage and moral strength with which he had withstood the Nazi tide, and the personal distress he had suffered.

McCloy, by now, did not need to be convinced. He had decided to stake everything on the Adenauer card. This was crucial. Between the outbreak of the Korean War and the signing of the General Treaty in May 1952, the U.S. High Commissioner was the most important figure in the struggle for the re-orientation of West German foreign policy, which entered its decisive phase in autumn 1950. McCloy's own views had now crystallised. The U.S. High Commissioner still regarded German democracy as precarious; the OMGUS opinion polls painted a depressing picture. This was the reason for his constant pressure for certain internal reforms – in the civil service law, in the decartelisation of big industries – which had often led to clashes with Adenauer. On these issues, McCloy was influenced by a typical liberal view of German history.

However, Adenauer and McCloy were united in their view of the danger of a nationalist resurgence that was calling for reunification at all costs. Both men expected that Moscow and the Communists in East Germany would play the nationalist card in order to prevent the Federal Republic's integration in the West. McCloy, like Adenauer, regarded close links with the West as the best way to stabilise the new West German democracy and to shield its citizens from nationalist temptations which – even unwittingly – might lead to Soviet hegemony in Germany. In winter 1950/51, he considered that it would be better if democracy in West Germany had put down some roots before the process of reunification got under way. In any case, integration with the West should proceed as far as possible, while they were dealing with the Adenauer government.

McCloy therefore used his full political weight to bring the negotiations over the Schuman Plan to a successful conclusion, and to offer a helping hand over the Saar. His contacts with David Bruce, the U.S. ambassador in Paris, and also with Jean Monnet, were extremely close. As a result of French influence, on the issue of a German defence contribution McCloy moved increasingly towards a solution within the framework of the Pleven Plan. He had now grasped that Adenauer was the great – and perhaps the last – chance for a successful U.S. policy towards Germany. He therefore considered it necessary to support the Chancellor in his ceaseless pressure for a revision – and in the medium term the removal – of the Occupation Statute, on condition that the process of anchoring West Germany in Western Europe continued alongside it.

It would be an exaggeration to claim that McCloy was moving from the role of advocate of U.S. interests to becoming Adenauer's ambassador to his own government. The situation was never as simple as that, and the two men continued to clash on various issues. Nevertheless, there was a distinct shift in the balance between 1950 and 1952. Within the Western decision-making process, the U.S. High Commissioner offered increasing support for Adenauer's foreign policy.

Some U.S. observers were deeply critical of McCloy's approach. The chief of the *New York Times* overseas bureau, Cyrus L.Sulzberger, held various conversations with Adenauer and McCloy during these years, and, from his base in Paris, had serious reservations about the relationship. Sulzberger later looked back over McCloy's period as High Commissioner: 'All in all I gained the impression of Adenauer as a clever, patient, resolute, autocratic and arrogant man ... Of course he skilfully pulled the wool over McCloy's eyes, but that was not too difficult. McCloy is not as clever as he thinks he is.'[22]

Adenauer was now operating systematically on two separate levels. Currently, the most important was his dialogue with McCloy, who could influence his colleagues in the High Commission and bring Washington into play. Parallel to this were Adenauer's formal talks with the High Commission.

In the middle of November, the Chancellor sent the High Commissioners an aide mémoire which he had not discussed beforehand with either the cabinet or the Foreign Affairs Committee of the Bundestag. Once again, he urged with great vigour the revision of the Occupation Statute: without it, the defeatist mood in Germany could not be overcome. If there was no prospect of freedom, no-one would be prepared to make sacrifices for freedom! Adenauer also raised the perennial problems of the German-Allied relationship: occupation costs, the dismantling of machinery, the fate of former Wehrmacht soldiers who had been sentenced for war crimes.[23]

On the defence issue, Adenauer went so far as to declare his agreement to the integration of German contingents at brigade level – though with the transparent reservation that technical and not political considerations should be paramount.[24]

The French, however, made it clear that they advocated German combat teams in the strength of 5,000 – 6,000 men for political and not military reasons. Paris even demanded that the German contingent should not make up more than 20 per cent of the entire Western force – which would have meant 150,000 men. One again, Kingsbury-Smith was called to Bonn in order to inform the Western public of the Chancellor's misgivings. His concern was centred on one main issue: the German units must have weapons as modern as the other contingents; they must not be treated as cannon-fodder. Germany should also be represented in the Allied High Command. These were demands of principle, but they were made with a certain detachment. McCloy informed Adenauer that no major progress towards his ideas was to be expected at the next meeting of Foreign Ministers in Brussels, as a result of which the Chancellor decided not to make this the occasion of his first appearance among the foreign ministers of the Western Allies.[25]

In terms of procedure, Adenauer demanded that the Western governments should produce appropriate proposals and discuss them with him, at first in confidence and then openly. This should apply to all the outstanding issues – the defence contribution, the removal of the Occupation Statute, the debt agreement. He refused to discuss the issue of the defence contribution in the Bundestag at this stage and left the High Commissioners in no doubt as to his reasons: there was a real danger that the Bundestag would fail to agree. He reminded on the High Commissioners of the importance of not making any requests of the West Germans that would be turned down. The message for the foreign ministers was clear: first there should be negotiations with appropriate concession to the Germans; only then would German agreement be possible.[26] The Western Allies had been thinking in precisely the reverse terms and so, for the time being, no progress was possible.

On one issue alone, Adenauer took up an unequivocal position: the question of Four Power negotiations on Germany. If the West Germans were faced with the choice between a rapid restoration of unity with the prospect of Soviet rule, or freedom in the Western camp, there could be only one answer: 'Better to be free, even if the unity of Germany could not be restored immediately.' In a long personal conversation with McCloy, he again stressed his main argument – it was better to delay reunification than to have a united Germany under Bolshevik control.

The constant traffic between Washington, London and Paris eventually resolved itself into a complex process. On the Petersberg, there were technical discussions on a German defence contribution, with the German wishes being represented by Blank, Speidel and Heusinger. In Paris, on the other hand, a commission began to discuss the arrangements for a European army on the basis of the Pleven Plan. Adenauer dispatched Hallstein to attend these talks. Later, when the negotiations had made little progress, the Federal Republic was represented by a middle-ranking diplomat and by a former Wehrmacht officer, Lieutenant-Colonel Ulrich de Maizière. Minor revisions to the Occupation Statute were now proposed by the Western Allies and introduced in March 1951. They did not, however, amount to the reshaping of treaty relations that Adenauer had expected.

The most important development during these months, Adenauer suspected, was not the German-Allied dialogue but the Four Power negotiations which got under way in March 1951. It was clear that the Americans were playing for time, only agreeing to a preliminary conference in the Palais Marbre Rose in Paris to work out a schedule. This conference broke up without success on 22 June 1951. However, as long as there was any prospect of a Foreign Ministers' Conference on Germany, discussions about a German defence contribution stagnated. The sources that have become accessible in the meantime show that both Paris and London were working towards such a conference. Adenauer had good grounds for his suspicion that influential forces in both capitals were pressing for a fundamental change of policy on Germany. It was only firm and tactically superior U.S. diplomacy, in addition to the clumsiness of Soviet conduct, which prevented a meeting of the Foreign Ministers' Conference which Adenauer had dreaded.

As before, the Chancellor tried to relieve his positions on foreign and domestic policy by stepping up his dialogue with Schumacher. Adenauer sent the Social Democrat leader a long letter at the end of January 1951, in which he openly admitted his anxieties, and in particular his fear of the 'latent tendency' towards isolationism in the United States. The decision of whether to station an army in Europe would, he thought, be made in the first quarter of 1951. The Four Power Conference would 'in all probability take place ... At this conference Soviet Russia will propose in a package deal the restoration of the unity of Germany, its neutralisation and demilitarisation and evacuation ... I see the greatest danger for the German people and for Europe in such a proposal by Soviet Russia at the conference'.[27]

Adenauer drew what he considered to be the essential conclusions: 'The danger of the departure of the United States from Europe, and thus its abandonment to the Soviet sphere of power that is inherent in the Four Power conference, can only, or at any rate more surely, be averted by the prompt clarification of the attitude of the Federal Republic on the question of a defence contribution.' Adenauer largely accepted Schumacher's conditions: forward defence, financial support to bear the extraordinary financial burden, replacement of the principle of occupation by the treaty principle, inclusion of Bonn in the common determination of Western policy towards the East, and equal rights in the military arena. Adenauer hoped for a great deal as a result: 'We would become a sovereign state again. We then have the prospect of achieving the unity of Germany in freedom again in the course of developments.'[28]

Schumacher answered with a detailed memorandum a week later.[29] Unlike Adenauer, he regarded the threat of an U.S. withdrawal as dangerous propaganda. Senator Taft's isolationism notwithstanding, he thought it inconceivable that the United States would abandon Europe. Schumacher insisted that the Western Allies must create the genuine conditions for a West German military contribution before binding German declarations could be made. The Opposition leader also questioned Adenauer's panicky fear of a Four Power Conference: such a conference might actually clarify the situation, and the Anglo-Saxon powers would never be willing to leave Germany to the Soviets. Schumacher's most important demand of a Four Power Conference was that it should 'create the preconditions for free elections as the foundation of German unity'.[30] A Bundestag resolution to that effect was passed almost unanimously on 9 March 1951.

It was clear that Schumacher wanted to prevent his hands being tied. And yet, never before or after did the Chancellor and Opposition leader again have such a constructive exchange of views. For the first time, the CDU party executive heard Adenauer say that Schumacher's intentions were honourable: 'Dr Schumacher is a very curious man. Perhaps he wants the best, but his decisions in foreign policy questions are very often affected by domestic political considerations and by a hunger for power!'[31] At a meeting between Adenauer and Schumacher at the end of February, the two men reached broad agreement over the basic policy line towards the East, as the Chancellor subsequently reported to Otto Lenz. However, Lenz maintained that 'Schumacher reckoned on a neutralisation of Germany at the Four Power Conference.'[32]

It is open to debate whether Adenauer would have accepted neutralisation if this had been agreed at a Four Power Conference. To date only one, not wholly reliable, remark has been found which might be taken to indicate a willingness to respond flexibly. During a discussion with McCloy in January 1951, Adenauer is reputed to have remarked that it would be possible to envisage leaving the structure of both parts of Germany unchanged for the time being, setting up a German Council above them, and organising a complete demilitarisation and the withdrawal of all occupying troops.

However, such moments of resignation were rare. Adenauer's basic line remained constant: pressure for continued progress towards Western integration and opposition to any East-West dialogue over his head. If the desire was for delay, however, the Western Allies could point to a factor which was re-emerging in West Germany at this time. Since the regional elections in Lower Saxony on 5 May 1951, there was once more a significant extreme right-wing party in German politics: the Sozialistische Reichspartei (SRP), which immediately achieved 11 per cent of the votes cast. Clearly there was a fear that this might be the first ripple of a major neo-Nazi wave.

Though Adenauer had predicted this turn of events for some years, the misfortune came at the worst possible moment. Of course he attempted to make political capital for himself out of this disquieting development, and the most obvious course was to blame it on his political opponents. Three days after the Lower Saxony election, Adenauer told the High Commissioners that the Social Democratic government in Hanover could not escape responsibility:[33] it had passed an electoral law which gave opportunities to splinter groups and had failed to mobilise the police adequately in order protect meetings of democratic parties. Moreover, the Basic Law forbade any repressive measures against a political party even though the anti-democratic impulses of the SRP were glaringly obvious. In a broader sense, he claimed, it was the SPD which was to blame for the revival of National Socialism in Germany. It was an issue which Adenauer was to raise frequently in future, for example, during a visit to Bonn at the end of May by Herbert Morrison, Bevin's successor as British Foreign Secretary.

Adenauer sought to use Morrison, like other Western statesmen, against the SPD leader Kurt Schumacher.[34] The Chancellor asked the British politician, who was personally on the right wing of the Labour

Party, to use his influence on the leader of the German Opposition. Schumacher's strategy of using the SPD to absorb latent German nationalism, he explained on this occasion, was fundamentally misconceived: 'If nationalism – and it is pronounced nationalism which he demonstrates – begins anywhere at all, then it always gravitates to the extreme and goes to a radical right-wing nationalist party.'

There is no doubt that Adenauer believed what he said, here and elsewhere, about Schumacher. However, it must also be noted that he never missed an opportunity to abuse the Social Democrat leader. Though most politicians are able to turn current developments to party-political ends, Adenauer was a master of the art.

Adenauer was well aware that right-wing radicalism was an expression of deep-seated errors in German attitudes, which were difficult to eradicate. In the short term, he was prepared to rely on the old methods: the police, repression through legal means, intimidation, government propaganda. However, he also believed that the younger generation could only be won for democracy if democracy itself had something positive to offer. As the Chancellor explained his views to Morrison – and repeated them often, before and after this meeting: 'The federation, the federal government, is without power and without lustre ...', an 'amorphous structure under foreign rule ... We have no sign of an effective state authority. The young, and especially the Germans, need such signs if they are to turn to something.'

In his complaints about the lack of authority, Adenauer was not thinking solely about the supreme powers of the High Commission. For some time, he had been much more disturbed about the 'delusions of grandeur of the Länder'. Worst of all were the new Länder that had been established, and North Rhine-Westphalia was the classic example. These new Länder, he told Morrison, were 'like the new rich'. The conversation then took a startling turn, with Adenauer wondering how the situation would develop if much of the Occupation Statute were rescinded. The Chancellor, admitting that he was about to express ideas that could be dangerous for him, requested absolute discretion, at least for the time being. After this attempt to safeguard his position, he sought to discover whether the British would support a transfer of political authority from the Länder to the central government.

Adenauer did not argue that the occupiers should make changes to the Basic Law on the strength of their legal position. Such a step would be intolerable for the Germans and impossible for the High Commission. However, he did wonder whether the High Commission could transfer to the central government some of their remaining powers for a period of three or five years, always with the proviso that they could recall these powers at any time. In three or five years, general pacification would have taken place in Europe and the world, making new regulations necessary. If such a step were taken, the federal system would be strengthened externally. In addition, it would appear to the volatile Germans themselves as a genuine state, worthy of respect.

Morrison refused to be drawn, and the idea came to nothing. Nevertheless, the incident reveals that Adenauer was aware, even at this early stage, that the great difficulties for his policy lay not only in the Social Democrat Opposition, but also in the federalism of the Basic Law. This fact had been apparent before, during the long disputes over the Länder police and riot police, and had re-emerged over the issue of right-wing radicalism.

The Chancellor could not, and did not, contemplate a breach of the constitution. However, his respect for the untried Basic Law was not absolute; he was prepared to consider using the Occupation Statute, at least in the short term, to overcome his difficulties. When in doubt, then as later, Adenauer tended to resort to *raison d'état*. If he had been reproached with undermining the Basic Law, he would certainly have protested. He did not wish to violate it directly, but was certainly prepared somehow to evade it, if necessary, by resorting to the Occupation Statute.

The discussion with Morrison was interesting in one further respect. It provides an insight into Adenauer's evolving view of the European state system. In these early years, it is clear, Adenauer's European policy was not obsessed with the primacy of Franco-German relations. Rather like Bismarck before him, Adenauer carried the map of Europe constantly in his head, and his long observation of the international scene had given him an acute awareness of the political geography of Europe. The new British Foreign Secretary thus received a panoramic survey of Adenauer's views in foreign policy. The Chancellor liked to offer these assessments when he first met senior representatives of foreign governments. They were designed to persuade his discussion partners – in case they did not know it already – that Adenauer was an old and wise statesman, a keen observer of international relations since the 1890s, and a man who drew on a long experience to frame his day-to-day tactics.

Morrison was reminded of Winston Churchill (with whom he had sat in cabinet) when Adenauer argued that the European structure had been knocked out of balance by the dismemberment of Austria-Hungary. However, the Chancellor made the point of adding: 'and of Germany'. Twice in the twentieth century a power vacuum had been created on the Continent – in 1918/19 and again in 1944/45. He believed that Europe's democracies – Germany, France, Italy and the Benelux states – no longer had the strength to offer firm long-term resistance to Soviet pressure. Britain must become involved as well, in order to re-establish and strengthen the structure of Europe. However, Adenauer was sufficiently aware of the peculiarities of British policy towards Europe not to propose a concentration on the Continent as a first priority. He contented himself with observing to Morrison that Britain must stand on two legs – the Commonwealth and Western Europe.

In return, Morrison gave him an amicable description of British psychology in foreign policy. God had made Britain an island, and the British must make the best of it. In addition, the British revered the principle of parliamentary sovereignty, which made it impossible for them to submit themselves to supra-national organisations. Morrison summarised the basic British attitude to Europe as 'trial and error', pragmatic co-operation, and faith in gradual evolution. When the Conservatives under Churchill and Eden came to power in October 1951, Adenauer found that the two main parties were generally in agreement on this central issue.

In this first detailed discussion with a British Foreign Minister, Adenauer paid more attention to the Russian threat than to British European policy. Here, too, he outlined his objectives with a broad brush. He tried to alarm Morrison by recalling the links between the Prussian court and the tsars, and the close relations between the Red Army and the German military during the Weimar Republic: 'Just when the Rhineland was occupied by French troops, the anniversary of the Red Revolution in Berlin was celebrated in the Russian ambassador's residence by an intimate group, the heads of the Red Army who had come over for this purpose, and the heads of the German army.'[35]

Why did Adenauer choose to tell this story? It seems that he was trying to show Morrison that the Soviets had always wanted to draw Germany over to their side because of its industrial potential, its people, and its military potential. How would the Soviet Union try to reach these aims in current circumstances? Following the stabilisation of the situation in Korea, Adenauer was largely convinced that war would not be in the Soviet interest. Moscow was more likely to approach its objectives by means of the neutralisation of Germany. If that occurred, he thought, then Soviet influence would become dominant in Germany within a very short time – and there would be corresponding repercussions for the rest of the Continent. There was only one way to combat this problem, as well as the threat of a 'fifth column' (which Adenauer continued to take seriously): the integration of the Federal Republic into Western Europe, with rearmament as part of the integration process.

This was the Chancellor's argument in all his contacts, German and non-German visitors alike, during 1951. His motives to argue for a rapid German defence contribution had changed markedly since 1950, when he had feared an armed intervention by the Volkspolizei and even a major Soviet invasion. Though he remained convinced that totalitarian power politics could be countered only by the military strength of the free democracies, other political priorities had begun to play a part in his thinking.

Adenauer summarised his motives in one of a number of talks with selected German journalists. If '12 German divisions are in the Atlantic army, and as many American, British and French divisions as is necessary are in West Germany', he told them, then the neutralisation of Germany would be out of the question. It was for that reason, and not from fear of a mere 250,000 German troops, that 'the Russian' was working to prevent a German defence contribution.[36]

Today we know that the Quai d'Orsay and the British Foreign Office tried to bring the Four Power Conference on Germany into being at almost any cost. The attempt failed only because of Soviet determination to put the issues of the U.S. bases and NATO at the centre of the agenda. It was President Truman who put his face against this development.[37]

In all of Adenauer's 14 years as Chancellor, these months were the hardest on his nerves. He faced not only complete stagnation in his foreign policies, but also disputes within the coalition and deep unpopularity at home. When Otto Lenz accepted his appointment as state secretary by remarking that he did not feel able to deal with the difficulties of the situation, Adenauer's answer was blunt: 'No-one is up to dealing with the difficulties of the situation, and that includes me.'[38]

It is difficult to say whether domestic policy or foreign policy was more urgent for Adenauer during this period. Occasionally the strain led him to lose his temper. At the beginning of June 1951 – the preliminary conference at the Marbre Rose Palace was under way – the parliamentary spokesmen for the agricultural 'green front' among the coalition parties threatened to vote against an increased sales tax unless agricultural interests received certain tax breaks. Adenauer thereupon lost his temper, shouting that it was impossible to pursue a reasonable policy in these circumstances and that he might as well let the SPD take charge, or hand over the government to the Communists. Needless to say, the deputies withdrew in confusion. However, the outburst of rage had not been calculated. That afternoon, in conversation with Lenz, Adenauer again complained about the indiscipline of the cabinet and claimed that he was sick of trying to govern under these conditions.[39]

These complaints ceased when the threat of the Four Power Conference had receded. Adenauer then became determined to press for a definitive settlement of the defence contribution and the re-organisation of relations with the Western Powers. However, as he constantly told his ministers and German journalists, success could be achieved only if there was calm on the domestic front and West Germany could adopt a self-confident approach to the outside world. A divided Federal Republic, he asserted, was no use as an ally. As Adenauer became more closely involved in the effort to lead Germany back into the Western community of nations, his tendency to stress the primacy of foreign policy became more and more pronounced.

Europe

Amid the setbacks and humiliations Adenauer had to face between autumn 1950 and autumn 1951, he was able to claim a single success in foreign policy: the founding of the European Coal and Steel Community in Paris on 18 April 1951. He welcomed this development as a great 'foundation stone for the building of a European federation',[1] an assessment which was to be justified by the subsequent course of events. But during the slow negotiations over the treaty and even its signing, his confidence appeared less well-founded. There seemed a danger that the Chancellor was pursuing a mirage, and even abandoning most valuable German industries to foreign competition in the process.

This, at least, was the view adopted by the Social Democratic Opposition. After the signing, Schumacher noted caustically that the European Coal and Steel treaty would extend the Occupation Statute by 50 years. The way would be paved for French 'right of disposal over the Germans'.[2] Not surprisingly, East German propaganda was even more hostile, with some support from sympathisers in the West German Bundestag. Yet even in economic circles, Jean Monnet's plans were frequently regarded with scepticism. This cynical view was given clear expression in the *Deutsche Zeitung und Wirtschafts-Zeitung:*[3]

> The Germans have made their heavy industry very productive through a century of diligent work and clear organisation. For love of peace and in order to promote the unity of Europe, they are now giving these advantages up, down to a modest remnant. How far they will be allowed to use this remnant for themselves, the High Authority is to decide. In order to push through this core, M.Monnet has negotiated with great skill according to the theme: 'to the Americans in the background, pure dogmatism, to the Germans in the foreground, constitutional European ideology, and to ourselves on the main stage, the traditional French routine of cartel politics. Monnet's success in sailing a hyper-cartel in front of the Americans under the flag of a ban on cartels will be listed as a masterpiece of French negotiating skills in the annals of international cartel history.

Adenauer was well aware that such anxieties and views were widely held in the sectors of industry affected. Officially, however, West German industry gave the proceedings its blessing. The reason was significant, but had little to do with any enthusiasm for Europe: it seemed the only way to get rid of the Ruhr Statute and the intolerable burdens associated with it. Meanwhile the firms, industrial associations and unions exerted pressure from all sides to keep the anticipated damage as slight as possible.

As had been the case over co-determination, there was also opposition from the FDP and the industrial wing of the CDU. Pferdemenges and Henle had great difficulty in keeping their friends in the business camp

Notes for this section begin on page 729.

loyal to the Chancellor's line, while also explaining to Adenauer and his chief negotiator Walter Hallstein where they had to stand firm.

Originally, Adenauer would have been glad to see the coal and steel community negotiated by France and Germany alone at the outset. In the course of negotiations, however, he quickly realised the advantages of involving the Benelux states and Italy. These states demanded the strengthening of the Council of Ministers, a parliamentary assembly and a Court to keep the power of the High Authority in check – and all this at a time when Jean Monnet was doggedly insisting on its central role.

Adenauer was fully aware of the problems associated with the concept, especially when the French and Americans linked their demands with the Schuman Plan in the course of negotiations. Jean Monnet pressed for the treaty to be completed before further steps were taken on the issues of the German defence contribution and the dismantling of the Occupation Statute. For a time, in autumn 1950, it even seemed that the control of the Ruhr might not completely disappear once the coal and steel community had come into being. Adenauer opposed this possibility with great vigour and eventual success.

Other demands were not long in emerging. The French were anxious to disband the German Coal Sales Association in order to weaken West Germany's position in the common coal and steel market. The U.S. High Commission also regarded it as the last chance to force through the desired anti-trust legislation, which was one of the reasons for McCloy's vigorous intervention in the treaty negotiations. So great was his involvement, in fact, that Adenauer teased him at the end of the negotiations by asking whether he would ever want to make a Schuman Plan again. By now McCloy had learned that it was best to stand up to the Old Man; he replied that he would not, any more than he would ever again wish to be High Commissioner in Germany.[4]

Shortly before the final round of ministerial negotiations in Paris, Monnet visited Adenauer to demand that France and Germany should have the same voting rights within the coal and steel community. Bonn would have preferred to couple voting strength with the coal and steel production of the member states (which would have given greater weight to the German side). However, Adenauer agreed to this demand with remarkable calmness.[5] He knew that the French would refuse to become involved in a system of integration in which Germany was the stronger partner from the outset. Without his willingness to concede, Michel Debré – that most loyal of Gaullists – would have had further justification for his denunciation of Monnet's scheme during the ratification debate in the National Assembly: 'It is only an illusion, it is a puppet theatre, behind which the strongest, the most resolute players are hiding and forcing their conceptions upon us.'[6]

In the eyes of the Gaullists, even Walter Hallstein was suspect. When de Gaulle later described Hallstein in the first volume of his *Mémoirs d'espoir,* he noted: 'Within the framework of Europe as he wanted it, his country would be able, without payment in return, to recover the reputation and equality that had been lost to it by Hitler's rages and defeat, then to obtain the preponderance that its economy would undoubtedly bring, and finally to get a powerful unified nation to adopt the struggle for borders and unity according to the doctrine to which he gave his name as State Secretary for Foreign Affairs.'[7] In reality, during these first negotiations with Monnet Hallstein became a convinced federalist. In the future his federalism would be far more rigorous than that of Adenauer, whose approach was more pragmatic. Yet one could always count on Hallstein's stubborn determination to commit the Chancellor to the strengthening of genuinely supra-national European institutions.

It is difficult to be sure how Adenauer estimated the possibilities and limits of European federalist policy. He had the pleasing ability not to waste energy on contemplating the incompatibility of the objectives he was pursuing; he was able to regard conflicts of goals as a challenge to his inexhaustible capacity for tactical compromise. Adenauer was thus able to pursue several seemingly very different goals: to regain German freedom of action at the same time as building a European federation; to pursue integration with the West at the same time as German reunification. Hugh Gaitskell described this indispensable talent of the born politician: 'A man who can't ride two bloody horses at once has no right to a job in the bloody circus.'[8] What appears to the analytical observer as lack of principle or Machiavellian cunning was actually an instinctive survival technique in the face of otherwise insoluble contradictions in the international arena and at home.

On closer examination, however, the European constructions of these years were designed to solve genuine German problems. Like Monnet and the other 'Europeans' of that decade, Adenauer was convinced that European solutions – whatever their individual form – would suit German interests as much as the national interests of the other Europeans. In effect, he was giving a specific European slant to a fundamental desire for reconciliation and cooperation between the free democracies.

Adenauer did not abandon the convictions with which he had grown up and which he had held throughout his life. For him, the peoples of Europe were distinct entities whose unique characteristics seemed more real than those sociologists who stressed the common traits of modern societies were prepared to admit. On this subject his views were shaped by a mixture of biological determinism and socio-psychological stereotypes. Adenauer often stressed that the Germans were a people of great vitality, but were politically unstable as a result of the terrible course of twentieth-century history. In rare moments of frankness, he admitted that he perceived biological weakness in the French, and was inclined to blame at least part of the annoying instability of the Fourth republic on this fact.

The Chancellor also told the British Foreign Secretary, Herbert Morrison, that he recognised 'a powerful element of stubbornness'[9] in the British national character. However, he did not explain that he meant this description as a euphemism for ponderousness, a reluctance to adopt up-to-date views, and an inability to master international and economic change. In his caustic moments he was wont to compare Britain with an impoverished landowner who had failed to recognise that he was bankrupt.[10]

Adenauer clearly had strong views about the character of the European nations. He believed that their virtues, weaknesses and abnormalities of outlook would alter with circumstances, but that this would be a very gradual process. At any rate, he did not expect the national characteristics of the peoples to disappear in a united Europe. There was no alternative, in his view, to a Europe in which the individual nations would bring their unique features.

Nor did Adenauer believe that the states themselves belonged to the past. Admittedly, his speeches contained many references to the fact that the era of nation states in Europe was at an end – or, more accurately, must be at an end if the Europeans wanted to maintain their position in their relations with the superpowers and keep the peace among themselves. Yet, despite his rejection of narrow nationalism, Adenauer's rejection of the nation state was not as absolute as it appeared at first sight. He believed that the state, so long as it was not given god-like status, had an indispensable function and a unique value as the political form of a people. Anyone who accepted the state as indispensable must also accept its established reality in the form of the European nation states. Moreover, in Western Europe the existing nation states were democracies. Even politicians with supra-national objectives must take seriously the fact that their position was given legitimacy by the citizens of their own states. Every head of government, first and foremost, must represent his own people.

Since the Federal Republic had no sovereignty, it was comparatively easy for West Germans to accept the idea of restrictions on sovereignty. However, even in the early 1950s Adenauer saw the issue as one of principle and of long-term significance. He was always in favour of bold first steps towards a European federation, but he maintained a sense of proportion and a preference for proceeding through the application of sound common sense. Moving beyond the Europe of nation states would take time and could only occur by a process of evolution. After all, the nation states themselves were the result of historical developments over a long period.

It is essential to remember that, in the 1950s, Adenauer's European ideas had many facets. For example, he was thoroughly familiar with the original constitution of united Germany in 1871. From school textbooks and from personal experience, he knew that the individual German states had developed into a united nation that was vital and vigorous without being homogeneous. He could still recall that Bavaria, the federal structure of Germany notwithstanding, had maintained its troops under the command of the king of Bavaria in peacetime – until the outbreak of the First World War. Similarly, the Austro-Hungarian monarchy had survived for decades as a multi-national state and dual monarchy, held together by the Crown, the German civil service and a coalition of feudal German and Hungarian aristocrats.

With these memories of recent European history, Adenauer had no objections to experiments such as a coal and steel community or a European army. He believed that force of circumstances, allied to the ingenuity of able politicians, could achieve much that was difficult to reconcile with traditional constitutional theory. His always startling willingness to experiment in Europe was largely the result of specifically German constraints, but it also expressed the fact that he was a statesman with a command of broad historical perspectives.

In his constant advocacy of the European idea, Adenauer was not thinking purely of specific projects of integration. The concept itself was important if the reorientation of German thinking was to succeed. 'The people must be given a new ideology', he remarked in cabinet during a discussion on the coal and steel community, 'it can only be a European one'.[11]

Adenauer had few illusions about the coal and steel community itself. Of course, it was first and foremost an instrument of French control. Yet even if the European hopes associated with it remained unfulfilled, the organisation had to be accepted. Without it, French control over the Ruhr could not be removed; without some control over the German steel industry, the French cabinet would not be willing to make concessions in the much riskier areas of a German defence contribution and the Saar. Besides, overall developments depended on the creation of a genuine understanding between Germany and France, which had still not yet been reached in early 1952.

During the early stages of Adenauer's foreign policy, there is no doubt that the Franco-German relationship played a central role in his thinking. However, he was neither obsessed with France nor any kind of 'little Europe'. Adenauer was fully aware of the importance of Britain for West European developments. He had few hopes of the Labour Party and, as might have been expected, hoped for more from the Conservatives. In October 1951 Churchill entered Downing Street for a second time. Might he have greater sympathy for the process of integration?

Throughout 1951 the French remained cool. If, at the eleventh hour, the British had been willing to place themselves at the forefront of the European movement, then Adenauer – who had not forgotten his positive experiences in Cologne between 1919 and 1926 – would not have found it difficult to concentrate his European policy on Britain. It is nonsense to suggest that his dismissal in 1946 would have prevented him from adopting this policy. The real obstacle was British caution, the reasons for which were sketched out for him on a place card by Churchill in spring 1953, during his second visit to London. Britain, Churchill explained, was in the intersection of three circles: the Commonwealth, the United States, by virtue of the famous 'special relationship', and 'United Europe'. It could not be part of Europe alone.[12]

In addition to the British and French, Adenauer also met the Italians, and Belgians, Dutch and Luxembourgers on the European stage. The Chancellor quickly learned that German foreign policy could not operate between Washington, London and Paris alone. As yet we cannot be precise about Adenauer's different responses to the participation of the Netherlands, Belgium and Luxembourg in the work of European unification. For decades he had been aware of the importance of Belgium and Luxembourg for the European steel industry; his time as mayor of Cologne had made him something of an expert on economic links between Germany and these two neighbours in the West. By contrast, he had few ties with the Netherlands, and seventeenth-century Dutch masters always moved him more profoundly than current Dutch policy towards Europe, which demonstrated an unfortunate mixture of trade calculations, aversion to French or German hegemony, openness to British influence, and deep concern about the prospect of being absorbed into larger units. Adenauer was well aware that, particularly in the case of the Dutch, there were powerful anti-German sentiments which had their roots in the years of occupation between 1940 and 1944.

Adenauer's flair for European affairs was seen at its height during the negotiations over the founding of the European Coal and Steel Community, which were to be completed with a foreign ministers' conference of the six founder-members. Previously the Federal Chancellor had avoided official visits abroad. After the minor revision of the Occupation Statute, however, the federal government was permitted to set up a regular foreign service. On 15 March 1951 Theodor Heuss handed the Chancellor the notification of his appointment as foreign minister. This enabled him, in future, to take part in the increasingly important multilateral conferences without losing face in terms of protocol. The way was clear for West Germany's entry to the diplomatic concert. Adenauer was pleased that the first western capital he visited was to be Paris.

Previous visits to Paris by German chancellors had always been difficult. Bismarck had been the first, in circumstances which no Frenchman was likely to recall with pleasure. On 1 March 1871 Bismarck had reviewed the Prussian and Bavarian regiments on the race-course at Longchamps in the Bois de Boulogne,[13] following the Prussian victory over France in the Franco-Prussian war. The Chancellor had been 'forced into his uniform, the breast curved, the shoulders broad, bursting with strength'. Demonstrations had been feared, just as they were feared 80 years later during Adenauer's visit. Count Beust recalled how a blue-clad Frenchman had accosted Bismarck with the words: 'T'es une fameuse canaille'. 'I could have had him arrested', said Bismarck, 'but I was pleased by the courage of the man'.[14] On his ride to Paris he was said to have ridden up to a particularly grim-looking bystander and asked him for a light for his cigar.[15]

Sixty years passed before a German Chancellor visited Paris for a second time. Once again it was a man the French viewed with reserve – Heinrich Brüning, and in circumstances which were almost equally dramatic and unpleasant: the international financial system was on the verge of collapse, Germany was forced to ask France for a loan, and when Brüning arrived he was greeted by an ugly demonstration from the radical right wing Action Française.[16]

The third visit had been Hitler's clandestine *tour de ville* after the fall of France. On 23 June 1940, the day after the armistice was signed in Marshal Foch's railway carriage at Compiègne, the Führer and Reich Chancellor landed at Le Bourget airport and toured the empty suburbs in the company of Albert Speer and the sculptor Arno Breker. At the entrance to the Grande Opéra, Colonel Speidel waited to show him the Arc de Triomphe, Trocadéro, the Eiffel Tower, Les Invalides, Sacré-Coeur. When a women at the market caught sight of Hitler, she screamed as if she had seen the devil himself. This sightseeing trip, the most notorious visit by a German Chancellor, had lasted only three hours.[17]

Since then a world had fallen in flames. Paris, however, had survived relatively unscathed, thanks partly to the reasonable conduct of General von Choltitz. Eleven years after Hitler's visit, Adenauer arrived at Orly, breaking the tradition according to which German Chancellors visited Paris only at times of international crisis or crushing military victory.

The unedifying history of relations between France and Germany, of which Adenauer was painfully aware, explains the failure of the French government to greet the seventy-five-year-old Chancellor with due ceremony even though he was known to be sincere in his commitment to reconciliation. Only Jean Monnet was at the airport to greet him. In his memoirs, one cool sentence reveals how much Adenauer had been angered by this deliberate slight: 'My reception at Orly airport was not very ceremonious. I was the first member of the German federal government to visit Paris since the end of the war.'[18]

On this occasion, Adenauer – usually so touchy on questions of etiquette – overlooked the provocation. His overriding objective was to ensure Germany's return to the circle of West European democracies. Given the fact that the last German Chancellor to visit Paris had been Adolf Hitler, he knew that there was a price to be paid.

Besides, Adenauer was determined not to let the incident spoil his good mood. He had to be 75 years old before having the opportunity to become acquainted with Paris. His lightning visit to Versailles in June 1919 could not be regarded as a genuine encounter with the city. Though he had broken his journey to buy a few rubber balls for his children, he had been given no time to admire the city. In 1951, therefore, he left plenty of time for the tourist side of his visit. Now he was happy to have the art historian Wilhelm Hausenstein, German consul-general in Paris, as his guide to Notre Dame, Sainte Chapelle and the Louvre. François-Poncet acted as his tourist guide in the Bois de Boulogne, along the Champs Elysées, and to the Arc de Triomphe.

François-Poncet and Herbert Blankenhorn also introduced Adenauer to the gourmet delights of Paris. One anecdote from Blankenhorn, about Adenauer's first visit to Lucas-Carton in the Place Madeleine, speaks volumes about the man and his attitudes: 'When we entered the restaurant, Poncet asked the head waiter "Have you something for us to eat?" Answer: "Monsieur l'Ambassadeur, vous aurez un déjeuner, simple mais correct", thereby giving notice of the quality and abundance of the food prepared. When the Chancellor heard it he nudged me and said: "Simple but correct, wouldn't that be an inscription for our Foreign Ministry?"'[19]

In reality, the company of François-Poncet was not merely a gesture of politeness. It seems fair to conclude that the Chancellor was unable to move in Paris without the discreet presence of the French High Commissioner, who still exercised supreme authority in the Federal Republic. Six months later Adenauer's experiences in London were very similar, except that it was Sir Ivone Kirkpatrick rather than François-Poncet who acted as a human reminder of the Occupation Statute.

Adenauer's walks through Paris brought him a pleasure greater than that of a tourist. He noted with relief that Parisian passers-by took notice of him with calm indifference, and sometimes with friendly curiosity. There was no hatred, though he had been expecting unpleasant demonstrations following the Communist agitation of recent weeks. On the last day of his stay, he was overwhelmed when a young woman student sent a gift to his suite at the Hotel Crillon: the 'Croix de Guerre' won by her late father in the First World War, accompanied by a moving letter. Adenauer kept the souvenir in his desk in Rhöndorf for the rest of his life.[20]

The day after his arrival, official Paris remembered its customary international good manners. President Auriol, a noted opponent of Germany, received him at an official breakfast and was cordial. Robert Schuman showed his most committed European face, and also promised the Chancellor – to Adenauer's relief – that there was no intention of permitting the neutralisation of Germany.[21] Less pleasingly, he also raised the Saar issue and obtained a reluctant concession from Adenauer. The Chancellor was forced to agree that, if necessary, a treaty comparable to the peace treaty might finally regulate the status of the Saar. There were clearly likely to be further pressures in future. The Germans had to accept the unpalatable fact of French representation of the Saar in the Coal and Steel Community, in the same way that it represented Monaco and Andorra.

The ambience of the Elysée Palace and the Quai d'Orsay made a powerful impression on the Chancellor. Even as mayor of Cologne he had come to respect the importance of physical surroundings in creating a suitable atmosphere for diplomacy. During the negotiations of the Six in the Beauvais Salon of the Quai d'Orsay, with its expensive wall hangings, Adenauer noted the ability of Germany's neighbours to put on an impressive show. Here, as in Rome or in London, the state revealed its dignity and grandeur. By contrast, he regretted the ponderous homeliness which was all Bonn could muster. If he gave a large dinner in the Palais Schaumburg – one which required both ground floor salons – then there was nowhere for the guests to drink their aperitif. State guests had often to be taken to the inhospitable Königshof. From there – in these early days of the federal republic – the Chancellory also had to borrow plates and cutlery. Even the paintings and carpets in the Palais Schaumburg were on loan, while the food had to be transported from the Königshof because of inadequate kitchen facilities. (These facts did not prevent the anti-government press from attacking the luxury of Bonn).[22]

Though these appeared to be peripheral issues, Adenauer told his associates that the new democracy was lacking in dignity, brilliance and style. Such qualities, he felt, would not only impress foreign visitors, but would also help to convince the Germans themselves that democracy was worthy of their respect. During his trips abroad, Adenauer grew in polish and confidence. Acheson, who had a sharp eye, noted at their second meeting at the end of 1951 that the Chancellor's self-confidence had increased in those two years. He had become a genuinely impressive figure.[23]

As the foreign ministers' negotiations for the foundation of the European Coal and Steel Community got under way, Germany re-entered the community of West European nations on an equal basis, at least in terms of protocol. From the outset, Adenauer relied on his air of personal dignity and authority. He was careful not to pander to the established members of the club by offering servile confessions of guilt or striking attitudes of excessive humility. Of course the Chancellor was wise enough, then and later, to suppress signs of his natural arrogance, but he negotiated in the knowledge that his country would sooner or later return to its position among the 'great powers' of Europe.

A few months later, Adenauer gave selected German journalists an insight into his personal views on the subject: 'If I want to be a great power again – and that is what we Germans must be – I must begin to behave as a great power behaves.'[24] This remark was made in annoyance about press criticism of extravagant spending on West Germany's foreign representation, and should not be regarded as the announcement of a revived German power politics. Nevertheless, the term 'great power' was guaranteed to arouse public concern.

It is very doubtful that, over thirty-five years later, any Federal Chancellor would choose to use this term about his country. Yet Adenauer used it only six years after 1945, when the Second World War and the atrocities of the SS were fresh in the memory of the world. In his view, past events would not prevent Germany from striving for that place in the international community to which, in his view, it had a rightful claim. Germany hegemony was out of the question – and Adenauer would have rejected any suggestion of it. His ambition was not for German dominance, but rather for a brilliant role in a co-ordinated concert of Europe.

The effect of Adenauer's long negotiations within the Six on the development of his European ideas can scarcely be exaggerated. Among the founder members of the community of Six, and then in the Council of Ministers of the Coal and Steel Community, the German Chancellor became acquainted with the important representatives of Western European foreign policy and the interests of their states. Between 1951 and 1955 he was both Foreign Minister and Chancellor, which enabled him to work with the heads of government and the foreign ministers of the Six.

By 1951 he already knew Robert Schumann well, and had some knowlegde of Dirk Stikker. It was at this time that he also met other important actors: Foreign Minister Count Sforza and Minister-President Alcide de Gasperi of Italy, the Belgian Foreign Minister van Zeeland, and the Foreign Minister of Luxembourg, Bech. Though there were changes of personnel from time to time, on the whole Adenauer had to deal with a relatively stable group of West European statesmen during these years. Despite many differences of opinion they worked well together, and quickly accepted Adenauer as an equal. Indeed, after only a short time he became the doyen of the group.

Adenauer developed a keen sense of what was, and was not, possible in Europe. This did not always save him from making serious misjudgements, for example over the EDC; but the frequent meetings with leading Europeans provided him with sources of information which no other German politician could match. There were some echoes of his days as mayor of Cologne, when he had regularly left the city to work in the numerous committees in Prussia and the Reich, with the aim of safeguarding the interests of his city and keeping abreast of developments. Now, as Chancellor, he often left the provincial Bonn scene in order to involve himself in European affairs in Paris, Strasbourg, Luxembourg, Brussels or Rome.

Inevitably, his relationship with the High Commissioners changed. Adenauer was now able to discuss important issues directly with the French foreign minister. The influence of François-Poncet declined, slowly but surely, until it resembled that of an ambassador. Nor could the U.S. and British High Commissioners treat the Chancellor as a subordinate now that he was negotiating on equal terms with the West European foreign ministers and heads of government. Once the Chancellor had established a respected position among the Six, the Western occupying powers found it necessary to treat him as the head of government and foreign minister of a European democracy.

This development did not happen all at once. However, in was perceptible in August 1951 and had become an accepted fact a year later. In 1950 and even in early 1951, Adenauer had claimed to be the representative of a protectorate of the three Western occupying powers; by 1952 he had become a West European statesman. Blankenhorn, who accompanied the Chancellor to most conferences, in January 1952 gave Carlo Schmid – with whom he was on good terms – an admiring description 'of how, for example, particularly at the last Paris Conference at the end of December 1951, the leadership had inevitably passed from the imprecise and confused view of the Italian Foreign Minister de Gasperi, and the excessively yielding and soft French Foreign Minister Schuman, to the Federal Chancellor, whose clear will and resolution impressed all the conference participants. The Chancellor is today, beyond dispute, the leading European statesman.'[25]

This development had a major effect on West German public opinion. The Adenauer of 1949 was a party man; the Adenauer of 1950 had been a highly controversial figure; by 1952, however, the Chancellor was a figure of European stature, wearing the mantle of a statesman. The contrast was especially striking, and Adenauer's reputation even further enhanced, because West German foreign policy had begun literally from nothing. Many Germans had found the contemptuous treatment of themselves and their country difficult to bear, but even they were consoled by the rise of a Chancellor who was given a respectful hearing in the European concert. Moreover, he was seen as representing the Federal Republic with self-assured dignity, and bringing it from its pariah status to membership of the community of democratic states.

In April 1951, of course, the transformation of Adenauer had only just begun. At that stage, the foreign ministers' conference of the Six was still seeking a solution to the unresolved problems of coal and steel union. One main difficulty was the allocation of political power to the member states within the High Authority; another concerned the site of the headquarters. At a preliminary discussion in Bonn, as we have seen, Adenauer had accepted Monnet's proposal for France and West Germany to be given the same weight in the organisations of the Community. This agreement was based on the expectation that the two countries, which together produced 70 per cent of the community's raw steel, would also make joint use of their decisive influence. For the first, but not the last time in Western Europe, it became obvious that there could be problems for the smaller states if France and Germany moved too close together. The consequence was a rebellion by the Benelux states and Italy, whereupon the two larger states were forced to make concessions and agree to complex voting regulations. Nevertheless, the resolutions were carried unanimously in the end, allowing the signing to take place as planned.

A few months later there was a less edifying dispute between the heads of government and foreign ministers over the site of the headquarters of the community. France, supported by Italy, proposed Strasbourg, the Dutch wanted The Hague and the Belgians Liège. During the course of negotiations, Robert Schuman made the surprising suggestion that the community should be based in Saarbrücken, which would prepare the way for a 'Europeanisation' of the Saar question. Adenauer was unwilling to move, but aware that it was wise to keep this option open. For this, among other reasons, the ministers decided – after a marathon sitting lasting 18 hours – to select Luxembourg as the 'provisional' headquarters. When Adenauer left the negotiations temporarily, after midnight, in order to fortify himself with coffee, the German officials in the anteroom heard him sigh 'Poor Europe!' When he returned, no progress had been made. In all this horse-trading, there was precious little sign of the much-vaunted European spirit.[26]

However, there were also positive signs on the European scene. In June 1951, for example, Adenauer went to Rome to meet Alcide de Gasperi, the true advocate of federal European policy. Why was Adenauer's first official state visit made to Italy? The answer is simple, and slightly depressing: it was only in Italy that he was absolutely welcome. De Gasperi had invited the Chancellor earlier, in October 1950. Another invitation had since come from London, but on that score Adenauer preferred to wait and see whether Attlee would be replaced as Prime Minister by Churchill.

De Gasperi, who had already been minister-president for five years, was regarded as the prototype of a European federalist. Like Robert Schuman, he came from the border regions where two distinct nationalisms had come into collision in the past. De Gasperi was born in 1881 near Trente, as an Austrian citizen, completed his schooling in the city, and took his doctorate in Vienna in 1905.[27] He was very much a man of two worlds, who spoke Adenauer's language and brought his experiences under the Austro-Hungarian empire to bear on the European politics of the 1940s and 1950s.

As a student, de Gasperi had joined a group which aimed to improve the material and intellectual position of Italian workers in imperial Vienna. Unlike Hitler, who was already soaking up the poison of nationalist and racist resentments, unlike Trotsky, whose Marxist convictions were reinforced by the crass class conflicts of Vienna, and also unlike the culturally dominant German bourgeoisie, de Gasperi was convinced that the Christian-social movement offered the most humane principles for overcoming the crisis of modernity. His views were rooted in a rock-like religious conviction, which led him to accept the papal encyclical 'Rerum

novarum'. Following his return home, de Gasperi joined the Trente People's Party, which represented the socially declassé and culturally
oppressed Italian population, and eventually became a member of the
Reichsrat. In 1919, after the break-up of the Austro-Hungarian Empire,
he joined the Italian People's Party of Don Luigi Sturzo. De Gasperi was
a man of the Christian-democratic left, always much more critical than
Adenauer of economic liberalism, but also more of an integralist in cultural and political matters and more responsive to the clergy. Yet both
men were within the mainstream of Christian-democratic thinking; both
regarded communism and even socialism as dangerous to democratic
and humanitarian developments; both recognised – de Gasperi long
before Adenauer – the destructive power of modern nationalism.

Since 1900, as both a journalist and a parliamentarian, de Gasperi had
been deeply concerned with the nationalist question which was tearing
the Austro-Hungarian Empire apart. He advocated a federalist solution,
based on mutual acceptance and reason. Until 1918 the aggressive pan-
Germans were his chief opponents, but after the incorporation of South
Tyrol into Italy he also argued against Italian nationalism. De Gasperi's
federalist convictions were powerfully expressed, based on constitutional
experience, and more carefully nuanced than Adenauer's own ideas about
Europe, both in the 1920s and after the Second World War.

The two men had met briefly, in 1921, when an Italian group headed
by Don Luigi Sturzo had been received by the mayor of Cologne. At that
time Adenauer was already a leading figure of Catholic Germany, while
de Gasperi was a young deputy in the Palazzo Montecitorio. As chairman
of the parliamentary Partiko Popolare Italiano he clashed with the Fascists and was sent to prison for 16 months, before spending the years
between 1929 and 1943 in virtual hiding as a librarian in the Vatican
library. In 1945 he became a central figure of Italian politics.

Italy had left the Axis in good time in 1943. Though often criticised for
its conduct under Mussolini, especially by the French, the country was still
among the founder members of NATO and the Council of Europe. There
was an understandable temptation for every post-war Italian government to
copy the approach of the Communists and Nenni Socialists, and to adopt
an anti-German stance which would draw attention away from the fact that
during the 1930s and early 1940s Germany and Italy had both pursued
aggressive and imperialist policies. However, de Gasperi and Sforza
opposed this temptation. They regarded it as a main task of democratic
Italy to lead the new Germany back into the community of civilised European peoples, and to work to overcome Franco-German hostility. Both
worked within NATO and the Council of Europe for the integration of
West Germany on equal terms, and for a German defence contribution.

Adenauer was well aware of the situation. Nevertheless, when he was
received in Rome with full ceremony and with a cordiality he had never

previously encountered abroad, he was overwhelmed. Despite his political imagination and insight, Adenauer was a man who needed to see things with his own eyes before he could fully understand them. In Rome he encountered a Christian-democratic movement leading an independent republic – not a Western Allied protectorate with its 'provisional' capital in a small town. He noted with some envy that the Italians still had a proper state: the carabinieri in their parade uniforms, the national anthem, the tomb of the unknown soldier on which Adenauer laid a wreath trimmed with red, black and gold. The minister-president spoke German, was committed to the same values as Adenauer, had also suffered under dictatorship, and was ready to support him diplomatically. Of course Italian self-interest played a role, but the solidarity of Christian-democratic Europe was equally important. Though Robert Schuman, Georges Bidault and Henri Teitgen were Christian democrats, too, they were also representatives of the occupying power, which made Adenauer unable to feel the same sense of solidarity he received from his conversations with de Gasperi and Count Sforza.

In addition, he was overwhelmed by Rome itself. Since his travels in upper Italy Adenauer, like many other middle-class Germans, had felt drawn to the country. His humanist education at school had prepared him for the greatness and charm of the city, and for the emotional response of his first visit to the 'Eternal City'. On the first evening he was accompanied by his daughter Lotte on the Pincio before walking among the evening crowds. When they went to the Piazza del Popolo – which Goethe had called the most beautiful square in the world – Adenauer apparently said that it was 'the loveliest moment of my life'.[28] He was guided through the Forum Romanum and the Colosseum by the archaeologist Ludwig Curtius. At a reception in the Capitol, he saw the cupola of St Peter's and the Pantheon glinting in the evening sun.

Adenauer had an audience with Pius XX, with whom he was already acquainted from the 1920s, when Pacelli was papal nuncio in Germany. There were difficult matters to discuss: the religious denomination of the German ambassador to the Vatican, the Concordat. Adenauer was aware that suspicious Protestants were watching this part of his visit to Rome with particular attention. Years later, he told Nahum Goldmann that he had been advised in Bonn not to kneel before the Pope because he was there as German Chancellor. But 'when the double doors opened and the Holy Father stood before me in all his glory, I was on my knees before I even knew where I was'.[29] He dined with prelate Kaas, now head of archaeological research at St Peter's, and was able to discuss with him their experiences since the spring of 1933.

Both Adenauer and de Gasperi were aware of the problems of too close a cooperation between Italy and Germany. The memory of the Axis between Hitler and Mussolini had not been forgotten in the rest of Europe.

The last German Foreign Minister to visit Rome and to stay at the Grand Hotel had been Joachim von Ribbentrop. Some officials in Bonn feared that the Italians wanted specific agreements that were bound to arouse distrust in Paris and London.[30] Fortunately, the official visit stayed at the level of cementing the ties of friendship between the two countries.

Adenauer had good reason to return home content. He had been strengthened in his determination to extricate the Federal Republic from its isolation and outside control by means of further developing the European idea.

Negotiations over the German defence contribution, on the Petersberg and in Paris, now took an unexpected turn. Prospects for a European army, with U.S. participation and General Eisenhower as Commander-in-Chief, began to vanish. In the interests of West German equality, as well as practical reasons of defence policy, Adenauer would have preferred full West German membership of NATO. Without his participation, however, the favoured concept was now the European Defence Community (EDC), which the French had supported from the outset. In this context, a decisive development had been the conversion of Eisenhower, then Supreme Commander of the Allied Forces in Europe, to the idea of the EDC.

The NATO Commander-in-Chief had visited West Germany in January 1951 for discussions with Adenauer, and had given Speidel and Heusinger an *amende honorable* for the German soldiers. Adenauer had gladly accepted Eisenhower's assurance that a German defence contribution must be voluntary and that there would be no second-class soldiers under his command. The Chancellor, possibly unwisely, noted that the political status of Germany would have to change if there was to be a defence contribution.[31] This suggestion irritated Eisenhower, the military conqueror of Germany in 1945. In the report he made to Truman's cabinet after his return home, he did not mince his words.[32] He would certainly like to have German soldiers under his command, since there was every likelihood that they would be good fighters once more, but he would only accept them if they were offered without terms and conditions. He had made this point clear to all the German politicians. He had also told them that he could not care less about German disputes with France, which were a matter for the two countries to resolve between themselves; in any case, the West Germans must not use the defence contribution in an attempt to improve their political status.

Eisenhower's comments reveal very little understanding of the psychological situation facing the Germans, and even Adenauer himself. Instead, they demonstrate the continued strength of anti-German sentiments, which had their roots in recent history and were not confined to Eisenhower alone.

In consequence, Eisenhower had no need to be convinced of the justice of French security fears. McCloy, David Bruce, the U.S. ambassador to France, Jean Monnet – all made it clear to him that the quickest and safest way to German divisions was through a modified Pleven Plan. When Eisenhower declared in Washington that the EDC was practicable from a military point of view, the matter was well on the way to being resolved. In order to make the decision easier for his government, Eisenhower even declared in August 1951 that he was prepared to accept the role of European defence minister for a limited period.[33] However, a much more tempting opportunity was shortly to offer itself – the office of the President of the United States.

Eisenhower had also given his consent more readily because the socialists, including Jules Moch, the most bitter opponent of a German defence contribution, had left the French government. Paris now declared its willingess to accept 'small divisions' as the largest German units.

In July, the framework of U.S. policy towards Germany and Europe took shape in Washington; it was to last until the failure of the EDC to pass the French National Assembly on 30 August 1954. The United States was prepared to incorporate the German defence contribution into the complex framework of a European Defence Community, and to envisage full German membership of NATO. The Occupation Statute would disappear, to be replaced by freely negotiated treaty arrangements. In barely a year since the handing over of the two memoranda at the end of August 1950, Adenauer had achieved remarkable success with his argument that the Bundestag would not accept German defence legislation unless German-Allied relations were placed on a treaty basis at the same time.

Nevertheless, the Western Powers intended to retain supreme authority in four areas: the right to station troops in Germany, including the right to guarantee their safety; Berlin; the reunification of Germany and the subsequent conclusion of a peace treaty; and territorial questions. On 5 July, sensibly if somewhat prematurely, Adenauer had told McCloy of his realisation that the Occupation Statute could not be fully rescinded with respect to these points. He also mentioned the problem of internal unrest, which might eventually become acute. The issues that became the subject of heated debate over the following months had, in principle, been conceded before the Allied position papers had actually been completed.

On 30 July President Truman gave his approval for this solution. At the end of August, Adenauer sent a cautious but positive memorandum to the Petersberg, accepting the concept of a European Defence Community as the basis for further negotiations. However, he proposed that an agreement should be made before the negotiations – which would probably proceed quickly – to allow at least a start to be made on the complex legal and military measures. He still feared, not without cause, that Paris wanted to delay the EDC negotiations, and thus the elimination of the Occupation Statute.

In the event, France did succeed in removing the issue of German membership of NATO from the negotiations. We now know, from a letter sent by Robert Schuman to Dean Acheson on 25 August 1951, that the French Foreign Minister had been opposed to the idea from the outset.[34]

Adenauer, like the Americans, held to the concept of the EDC for three years, though he believed at this stage that the matter could be brought to a conclusion by spring 1952. Once Washington had suggested this course, Adenauer saw no prospect of following any other. Nor was it difficult for him, since he had always advocated the inclusion of German forces in a European army without giving specific details of what he had in mind. From now on, his entire political approach was to present the EDC as the only sensible solution.

The Chancellor continued to have misgivings about the sincerity of the French in taking this course. However, he consoled himself with the conviction that the United States would not keep its military forces in Europe in the long term; it would then be necessary to rely on the EDC, which would have been brought into being in the intervening period. His scepticism was also mitigated by the progress of the movement for a united Europe, which was then in full swing. At a conference in Lugano in April 1951, the successful European associations had demanded the setting up of a 'constituent European federal assembly'. Prospective or developing European authorities should 'be extended and coordinated under the leadership and control of a federal government and a federal parliament'. Adenauer knew from his talks with de Gasperi and Count Sforza that Italy wanted to press for the establishment of political institutions.[35] Since he was aware of the hesitation in France and the Benelux countries, he had some doubts as to whether these objectives would be achieved. Nevertheless, in 1951 the European movement was still being driven forward by powerful sentiments. Altiero Spinelli, who formulated the crucial position papers for de Gasperi, firmly believed that Europe was in a pre-federal phase. There were frequent attempts to make the analogy with the establishment of the U.S. federal constitution in the 1780s.

Adenauer's main aim was to bring about rapid *faits accomplis* on the issue of the defence contribution and the restoration of sovereignty. After a reduction in East-West tensions, he was also less obsessed with the prospect of Soviet aggression in 1952, and more concerned with certain other dates: the U.S. presidential election in November 1952, which would exert an increasing influence on U.S. foreign policy from the beginning of the year, and the Bundestag elections in summer 1953. In June 1951, the elections to the Chamber in France had seen a shift to the right, and the establishment of a government which appeared more likely to make concessions than the previous one had been. 'God provide that Schuman is Foreign Minister again!'[36] Adenauer had remarked to German journalists shortly before the French elections. God had answered the prayer, but no-one knew for how long. In London, Labour had faced economic failure; the October election brought the Tories to power and returned Churchill as Prime Minister. Even though the British premier could not be expected to announce participation in the EDC, benevolent support seemed likely.

There was only a short period for the treaties to be negotiated and ratified. If a start was made in the autumn, Adenauer considered, then the ratification process would begin in December 1951. Much would depend on the U.S. Congress ratifying the measure before the summer recess in 1952. On closer observation, even greater speed was necessary, for it seemed likely that the Republicans would win the November election and that Senator Taft would emerge as the spokesman of a group which gave priority to Asia and was neo-isolationist in sentiment. Whether he was successful would be decided, in Europe too, in winter 1951/52 and spring 1952.

In these circumstances, Adenauer was not deeply concerned whether a more or a less federalist solution was adopted for the EDC. The crucial point was that things progressed swiftly; everything else would sort itself out in time. This was the standpoint from which he gave his views at the important foreign ministers' conferences, and according to which he directed the work of the West German EDC delegation, which carried out negotiations in Paris, under the leadership of Theodor Blank, from early October 1951 to 9 May 1952.

The organisation of the European Defence Community was to be established on the model of the Coal and Steel Community: a High Authority, called the Commission, also with nine members and complex voting arrangements; a Council of Ministers; a parliamentary assembly, identical to that of the Coal and Steel Community; and a Court. However, no-one yet knew whether Monnet's Coal and Steel Community would be a success. It did not begin its work until 10 August 1952. In these circumstances, it was surely open to doubt whether the much more complex regulations of the EDC were likely to lead to a form of supra-national defence community, which was ostensibly the objective. The treaty which was eventually negotiated aroused fears of a possible obstruction of the decision-making process, if the treaty was ratified at all. Only time would tell. In Adenauer's view, the vital point was that the establishment of German divisions was beginning at last, and the Occupation Statute would shortly become part of German political history.

At the crucial meeting of the Council of Ministers in Strasbourg on 11 December 1951,[37] de Gasperi rightly argued that the entire project would achieve little unless it was immediately underpinned by a federal system. This, he continued logically, would be shown by the creation of the EDC budget. Besides, such a new organisation could only be ratified by the parliaments if it was seen as the preliminary stage of the imminent creation of a political community.

The reaction of the other ministers demonstrated that there were many ulterior motives involved with the project. At first the Benelux states firmly opposed the inclusion of any such intention in the treaty. Their fear of losing their identity in a community of the great West European states was tangible. Robert Schuman also offered every conceivable objection, though emphasising that he was in agreement with de Gasperi's basic ideas.

The debate was so passionate that the participants stopped waiting for the translation and conducted the negotiations in German, which all of them knew. Adenauer's own intervention was crucial. It took the form of an elegant procedural device – a favourite tactic of his – which postponed the solution to the future (though not too distant a future, since the problem had to be settled) and enabled the treaty itself to be completed.

Agreement was thus reached on the essentials of the famous 'de Gasperi Article 38' of the EDC Treaty, according to which the Parliamentary Assembly would investigate, within six months of beginning its work: a) the creation of an assembly of the European Defence Community by election on a democratic basis; b) the powers that would be transferred to such an assembly; c) the changes which might have to be made to the provisions of this treaty through the other organs of the community, especially in order to secure appropriate representation of the states.

It continued – and this was the objective that both de Gasperi and Adenauer regarded as vital: 'The definitive organisation, which takes the place of the current provisional one, must possess a federative form and especially an assembly with two chambers and an executive body.'[38] The cooperation of existing organisations with those which had yet to be established was also to be considered, and the issue was to be passed to the EDC Council, which would convene a conference to examine the proposals.

Here the federalist hopes were expressed which, in the view of the Italians, would bring the EDC through the difficulties of the ratification debate. De Gasperi himself modified his own proposal in the face of powerful opposition, which was then withdrawn: he was surprised that any objections at all had been raised 'in view of such a weak text'. Adenauer returned from the Strasbourg meeting of foreign ministers convinced 'that the Pleven Plan would be achievable at the beginning of 1952'.[39]

In the event, the real difficulties in the negotiations over the EDC did not relate to its federalist or confederalist objectives, but to the issue of equal rights for the Federal Republic and the associated question of West German entry into NATO. None of the participants could shake off the view that the EDC might prove to be an artificial offshoot of conference diplomacy, and that attention might again switch to the NATO solution. The Benelux states were hostile to the EDC until the end of 1951; NATO fulfilled their needs perfectly. Their resistance would have to be overcome by the great powers. Despite his own participation, Adenauer was forced to recognise that he was helping to destroy West German prospects of being accepted into NATO.

When the French argued that West Germany could not be a member of the EDC and of NATO at the same time, Adenauer initially adopted a tough negotiating stance. Hallstein was instructed to declare that any regulation that excluded Germany completely from NATO would be unacceptable. In order to resolve these difficulties, Adenauer proposed corporate membership of the EDC in NATO in January 1952.[40] He received little response, since all the other participants except France would have preferred full German membership of NATO, if necessary. Adenauer then dispatched Blankenhorn for a 'private' visit to London. There he called on Frank Roberts at the Foreign Office and, after much beating about the bush, informed him that 'corporate membership' might simply mean appropriate representation of the EDC on NATO committees.[41] For the time being, Adenauer had to rest content with the communiqué of the Paris Conference of 28 January 1952, which included a claim made by Hallstein, 'that the inclusion of Germany in the Defence Community which is currently in the process of creation may not be interpreted as renunciation by Germany of a later association with the North Atlantic Pact'.[42]

The EDC was, and remained, acceptable as an emergency solution. From now on Adenauer devoted all his energies to bringing this European organisation into being. However, he did not for a moment forget his aim of achieving West German membership of the Atlantic alliance on equal terms once the EDC had become a reality.

Western Treaties and Soviet Initiatives

Few events during Adenauer's chancellorship were as controversial as his decisions on foreign policy in the months between September 1951 and May 1952. The negotiations over the rescinding of the Occupation Statute and the EDC were now in full swing. These were being encouraged by the United States, but were not given the sustained support of the British and were persistently made more difficult by the French. Nevertheless, the long lull of 1951 had come to an end; developments were moving in the desired direction.

From the outset, however, a strong trend in the opposite direction was also perceptible. Before the negotiations between Adenauer and the High Commissioners on Petersberg and the meetings of the EDC delegations in Paris had even begun, the East German parliament, the Volkskammer, held long discussions with the Soviet embassy in East Berlin before directing an appeal to the West German Bundestag. Its proposal for joint consultations between East and West Germany, and hence for the acceleration of moves towards a peace treaty, was not new. There was, however, a sensational new aspect, since one of the themes of joint discussions was to be 'The holding of free all-German elections with the aim of building a united, democratic and peace-loving Germany'.[1] A representative from minister-president Grotewohl provided the president of the Bundestag, Hermann Ehlers, with supplementary information. East Berlin also made it publicly clear that the GDR would be prepared to accept the Reichstag electoral law of the Weimar Republic.[2]

Adenauer suspected that this was only the beginning. The period of immobility in Soviet policy towards the West, which had still been apparent during the preliminary conference at the Marbre Rose Palace, had come to an end. In future, negotiations with the West would be undertaken against the background of a wide-ranging initiative from Moscow.

Fissures now began to appear in the united front of the democratic parties in the Bundestag. In a move which had not been agreed with Adenauer beforehand, Ernst Reuter persuaded the Berlin chamber of deputies to greet the East German move by proposing free elections in the whole of Berlin as a first step. Privately the Chancellor was alarmed that the East might actually accept this demand, thereby making enormous psychological impression on West German public opinion.[3] In the event, the Soviet side was not yet prepared to play for such high stakes, and chose to let the opportunity pass.

Ernst Reuter was a man with few illusions about the nature of the Soviet threat. Nevertheless, he told McCloy that, if the Germans faced a serious choice between immediate integration into the West or reunification in freedom but with neutral status, they would be sorely tempted to opt for reunification.[4] Even more important, Schumacher and the SPD caucus did not accept Adenauer's own assertion on radio that the East German proposal was was no more than a propaganda initiative.

In cabinet, too, disputes broke out afresh. On 25 September 1951, Jakob Kaiser mentioned the changed approach of the Social Democrats and argued that it would eventually be necessary to negotiate seriously with the Soviets. He took the view that Bonn must openly declare its willingness to hold all-German elections. Franz Josef Strauss, who took part on behalf of the parliamentary party, also warned against sending Grotewohl a curt rejection.

On the other hand, on this occasion Adenauer was supported by the entire FDP. Blücher stated bluntly that there should be no change in German policy on the basis of the Soviet initiative. Von Brentano urged that the negotiations with the Western Allies must be concluded with all dispatch. Adenauer held fast to his line: it was essential to negotiate with the

Western Allies as rapidly as possible and reach a satisfactory conclusion; then the West Germans could adopt a genuine all-German policy and even look forward to the elections without fear.[5]

The issue of all-German elections now had to be taken seriously. The Western powers were less than delighted when Adenauer responded to the East German initiative by demanding in the Bundestag that the conditions for free elections in Germany should be investigated by a neutral international commission under the supervision of the United Nations. Despite their fear that their sole control over events in West Germany would then be lost, however, the Western Powers eventually gave their consent. At the same time, the Bundestag was to draw up election regulations for free all-German elections. Once again a joint approach with the SPD had been established, but this united front quickly collapsed when the Social Democrats rejected the draft electoral law produced by the majority parties.

The East Germans then stepped up the mixture of inducements and threats. At the end of October Ernst Lemmer informed the Chancellor of a new move, this time emanating from his old colleague, the East German Foreign Minister, Dertinger.[6] Until the end of 1947, Lemmer had been the chairman of the Eastern CDU and Dertinger its general secretary. A meeting had been arranged between the two by a mutual acquaintance, though without Lemmer knowing whom he was about to meet. Dertinger claimed that his message was brought with the knowledge of Semyonov and Grotewohl, and that the offer was serious because it had been initiated from Moscow. The SED, he told Dertinger, was furious. The East German Foreign Minister claimed that agreement was possible on every issue, including voting procedures and the supervision of the all-German elections. The Soviets were well aware that the Communist-led National Front would have very few supporters in a fair election, but were prepared to accept the idea because Moscow wanted German reunification. However, there was one vital condition: a reunited Germany would have to guarantee not to let its policy be determined by Washington. Both parts of a reunited Germany must move away from their respective occupying powers. The Soviets would be prepared to pay a high price for a neutral Germany, Dertinger claimed, and might even accept its integration into Europe and the Schuman Plan.

When Lemmer expressed doubts, Dertinger resorted to threats. The West, he argued, was heading for a catastrophe. The Soviets now had the atom bomb as well and were ready to make any sacrifice necessary. In the event of a Western attack using the atomic bomb, the Soviets would respond in kind and target New York, Chicago and Washington. Semyonov had authorised him to say that the Soviet Union would not tolerate German rearmament.

The war of nerves had begun. However, Adenauer hoped for a rapid conclusion of the negotiations with the Western Allies before the Soviet counter-offensive could take full effect. Before the start of negotiations between himself and the High Commissioners, both Adenauer and the Americans believed that all the outstanding issues could be settled quickly. The State Department schedule of August 1951[7] envisaged that the foreign ministers would take the final decisions on the EDC and a network of treaties with the Federal Republic by 15 November 1951. The treaties could then be put to the Bundestag on 15 December. McCloy, however, was more cautious; he maintained that the Americans must be prepared to wait longer or else the Germans would make unreasonably high demands. On this point his assessment of Adenauer was correct. The Chancellor was hoping for a treaty similar to that being worked out in San Francisco, where the Japanese were negotiating an acceptable peace treaty which was signed on 8 September 1951.

On the Bürgenstock, where Adenauer took his second summer holiday in 1951, a major war council was held.[8] It was 1 August, a Swiss national holiday, and bonfires were being lit on all the hills overlooking Lake Lucerne. Present at these talks were Theodor Blank and his adviser Lieutenant-Colonel Count Kielmannsegg, Hallstein, Blankenhorn, Globke and Rust. Also present, for the first time, was Wilhelm G.Grewe, Professor of International Law at Freiburg, who had been in charge of the negotiations for the removal of the Occupation Statute since May 1951.

Adenauer was inclined to adopt a risky course of action. He hoped to negotiate a 'security treaty' similar to that between Japan and the U.S., which would include his most important wishes: sovereignty; the integration of German contingents into a European Defence Community on an equal footing; West German entry into NATO; and a security guarantee by the Western Powers which would include their right and duty to station troops in the Federal Republic. He was also determined to add a consultation clause, which would enable the West Germans to prevent, or at least obstruct, any Western attempts to make an arrangement with the Soviet Union at the expense of Germany. At the same time, Adenauer wanted the Western Powers to accept the goal of reunification. Moreover, since the Marshall Plan was due to come to an end in 1952 before the economic future of the Federal Republic was fully assured, Adenauer also wanted a binding promise from the Western Powers 'to continue the previous economic support of the Federal Republic, in order to preclude economic chaos and unemployment and the resulting danger of totalitarian systems'.[9] On the basis of the known objections of the Allies, some specific rights were to be conceded to them: with regard to Berlin, for a peace treaty with Germany, and in the case of an external threat or internal unrest, for the protection of Allied troops.

These deliberations led to a draft which was discussed with the deputy U.S. High Commissioner, General Hays, on 11 August.[10] This was a delicate issue, because the British and French High Commission were excluded from the German-American discussion. Hays proposed a number of changes, and on 30 August the High Commissioners were handed the two-page German draft treaty, which contained ten articles. Adenauer hoped that the negotiations could be completed by November on this basis.

The communiqué of the Foreign Ministers' Conference in Washington, which met in the middle of September, also seemed to promise much, despite evidence that the French were still attempting to delay the process. For these reasons, the start of the negotiations was a sobering experience for Adenauer.

On 24 September the negotiations were opened at Castle Ernich high above the Rhine valley, now the residence of the French High Commissioner François-Poncet. In some ways the choice of venue was an ominous one, since almost exactly 15 years previously it had played a part in Adenauer's unhappy experiences during the Third Reich. However, the situation had been reversed since 1936. The French, whose troops Adenauer had hoped to see when Hitler re-occupied the demilitarised Rhineland, were now firmly established as occupiers. He himself was no longer disgraced but, as head of government, faced the task of transforming the burden of occupation into an alliance.

The early signs were extremely unfavourable. All the reports of the participants – McCloy's telegrams to Washington, Adenauer's detailed description of the negotiations in his memoirs[11] – tell the same story. At the exact moment when the counter-offensive from the Eastern bloc had begun to have a psychological effect, the Western Powers chose to demonstrate a profound indifference to Adenauer's domestic political difficulties.

During a pause in the negotiations, when he had the chance to examine the proposal of the Western Allies with Hallstein and Blankenhorn, Adenauer was appalled. The fond hopes of the 'Bürgenstock draft' had been shattered. It now seemed likely that he would be offered nothing more than another revision of the Occupation Statute. There was no mention of sovereignty, but only of far-reaching, though ill-defined, reserved and emergency powers for the Western Allies; the High Commissioners were to continue to exist as a Council of Ambassadors; there was no assurance of equal treatment in the defence contribution; there was no mention of strong support for the reunification policy of the Federal Republic.

Adenauer was extremely alarmed. He felt, in short, that the rug was being pulled from under his feet. German public opinion was watching the negotiations, which had been announced amid great publicity, with high expectations, but he had been handed a document that would seriously compromise both himself and the policies he stood for if he should present it either to the Cabinet or to the Bundestag Foreign Affairs Committee. Proudly, he told the High Commissioners that a treaty of the kind laid out in the proposal would never be put by the West German government to the Bundestag for ratification. However, he was also told by McCloy that none of the Allied governments would be able to sign the German draft.

The meeting was adjourned for a week. Adenauer was so angry after this first clash that he decided to let the negotiations fail if the form and substance remained as unsatisfactory as in this first meeting.[12] He was particularly furious with McCloy, since he had taken care to discuss the position of the two countries with the Americans in the prelude to the negotiations. McCloy's criticism, both in its content and its form, was thus deeply offensive to him.

He did not know, or could only suspect, that McCloy was currently among those Americans who advocated keeping the Germans under firm control for the time being. There were a number of reasons for his attitude, including alarm at the successes of the SRP and outrage at threats which had been made against his family. Moreover, the irritating activities of the German ex-Servicemen's associations during recent months also persuaded him that caution was the best policy. Other U.S. diplomats and military figures, including General George P. Hays, Henry A. Byroade, director of the German Section in the State Department, and Martin J. Hillenbrand, later ambassador to the Federal Republic, feared that McCloy's rigid negotiating style was playing into the hands of Adenauer's opponents – and thus the opponents of U.S. policy.

Adenauer was especially annoyed to discover that Schumacher and Ollenhauer, whom he intended to inform of events next day, were already aware of the Allied negotiating papers. He complained bitterly about this fact during his next meeting with the High Commissioners. What would the French government say if he had intimate discussions with de Gaulle, as various people were recommending him to do?[13] It was obvious that Schumacher would not be converted to Adenauer's *Westpolitik* on the basis of the Allies' negotiating strategy.

On the German side, opinions varied. Hallstein, who generally adopted a very tough negotiating stance, argued in Cabinet that the maximum position should not be abandoned. Moreover, the Federal Republic had to achieve the status of a NATO country. Adenauer was more cautious, claiming that this could not be demanded without the ground being prepared.[14] However, he did not inform the Cabinet about the full extent of the difficulties, and obtained a promise from McCloy to adopt a more restrained information policy in future.[15]

Even more so than before, Adenauer committed himself to progress through secret diplomacy. There were several good reasons for this. At this stage he had nothing positive to show for his efforts and could only hope to improve the situation through tenacious negotiation. Even if his success was limited, as he already feared would be the case, discretion would be equally essential. Otherwise the coalition parties, of whom he took more notice than he did of his cabinet, would try to commit him to positions which were non-negotiable and which might lead to the collapse of the negotiations as a whole. By contrast, he felt confident that, once negotiations were concluded, he would be able to overcome all resistance in his well-tried manner, as long as there was only a short period between the publication of the text and the final signing to prevent the formation of a broad parliamentary opposition. His need for secrecy was equally urgent in view of the propaganda of the Eastern bloc, which was particularly intense in these critical months.

Absolute discretion was not difficult for Adenauer. All his life he had been convinced that parliamentary bodies should be given only as much information as was absolutely necessary, in order to avoid the difficulties that often accompanied the revelation of the whole truth. Thus, in October, he informed the sub-committee of the Foreign Affairs Committee that the Western Allies did not want to abandon their hold on sovereignty. Even Schumacher realised this. In conversation with McCloy, the SPD leader had already criticised Adenauer's announcement that the Federal Republic would soon become fully sovereign. Of course, he was well aware that the Berlin problem and the unique issue of relations with the Soviet Union would not allow it. In the final analysis, however, the Opposition could not demand anything less than the head of government himself.[16]

The information Adenauer gave to the Cabinet and coalition parties was selective, usually late, and imprecise. The Chancellor was particularly anxious to avoid letting them have copies of any relevant texts. This was not without its problems. When the full extent of the treaties and their undesirable limitations became public knowledge in May 1952 – and that against the background of the exchange of Notes initiated by Stalin – the ministers and parliamentary parties were somewhat unprepared, or were at least able to behave as though they were.

As the Western Allies insisted on negotiating all the complicated supplementary treaties together with the main treaties, the issues under negotiation unravelled into a multiplicity of detailed problems which even included such issues as the hunting rights of the occupying forces. During the EDC negotiations, questions of finance were inevitably particularly controversial, with Finance Minister Schäffer making an early appearance on the international stage with all the charm of the hatchetman.

Thanks to his dual role as Federal Chancellor and Foreign Minister, Adenauer managed to centralise the complex negotiating process and to achieve tactical mastery of its direction. Within the government the negotiations on the re-organisation of German-Allied relations were structured on three levels. At the base, various working groups of experts were in charge under the leadership of Wilhelm Grewe. Their work was led and co-ordinated in daily meetings by an Instruction Committee led by Hallstein. Adenauer's chief advisers were Hallstein and Blankenhorn, and later also Grewe.

The negotiating strand in Paris was similarly complex. Here, a one-hundred-strong delegation was working with Theodor Blank at its head and with Hans Speidel as chief military delegate.

These two strands came together in the person of Walter Hallstein, who chaired the inter-ministerial planning group and, during this period, became Adenauer's most important assistant alongside Herbert Blankenhorn. Then and later, Hallstein rightly came to be regarded as a genuine 'European'. However, in his temperament, style of work, and toughness of approach, this native of Rhine Hesse was more of a Prussian. Like the rest of the group associated with Adenauer, he was totally committed to the aim of raising Germany from the depths. No-one in the leading group which was negotiating and implementing the links with the West had any doubt that the core state of the Federal Republic was the only true Germany – a Piedmont in the West which, by means of calm and skilful use of the international situation, must aim eventually to absorb the Irredenta in the East Zone.

The main negotiations were conducted by Adenauer himself. He was personally involved in 30 long meetings – Grewe recalled that the last meeting alone, with the High Commissioners on 17 May 1952, lasted for seventeen hours.[17]

The negotiations on the General Treaty always turned on the question of sovereignty and on the associated issue of Allied emergency rights. Adenauer was far from achieving his objectives. If the General Treaty, which he eventually christened the 'Germany Treaty', had actually been ratified in 1952, it would have imposed a heavy burden on the Federal Republic. In this sense Adenauer was fortunate: the failure of the EDC changed the situation, and in autumn 1954 the General Treaty was modified along the lines of Adenauer's original objectives in the 'Bürgenstock draft'.

An equally vexed issue was the West German desire for direct membership of NATO. Despite numerous approaches, Adenauer was not overcome French objections. The great aim of German equality could not be achieved in this respect. It must remain an open question whether the problem would have been solved 'on its own' after ratification, as Adenauer boldly maintained in the Bundestag on 7 February.[18] The only concession he obtained was a commitment from the treaty partners that there must be a joint meeting of the NATO Council and the council of the EDC whenever the territorial integrity, political independence or security of a member state was threatened.

Equally discriminatory were the regulations on armaments production. Neither military nor civilian aircraft, neither warships nor atomic and chemical weapons, could be manufactured by the Federal Republic. After great effort Adenauer did manage to obtain agreement for West German gunpowder production, the development of certain anti-aircraft missiles, and limited participation in peaceful atomic research.

He was also unable to make significant progress on the central issues of organisational equality within the EDC. The Federal Republic was forced to accept the French refusal to subordinate its colonial army together with support formations, and even part of the occupying forces themselves, to the EDC. At the same time the German side was forced to follow literally Monnet's famous comment that the first German soldier called up by Bonn must be a European soldier.

The goal of partnership on equal terms, pursued with such persistence by Adenauer, was not achieved in any area. When the Opposition in the Bundestag used this as a stick with which to beat him, the Chancellor could only take refuge in the argument that once the process was under way it would create its own logical momentum. When he was attacked in the Cabinet and by the CDU parliamentary party, his response was typically caustic: he simply asked his colleagues who had lost the war – the Germans or the Allies? Among his closest advisers, however, he conceded that he was prepared to set aside his objection for one reason only – and that was the nagging fear that a Four Power Conference might be held before the treaties were complete.

His attempt to commit the Western Allies through a binding clause grew directly out of a fear of a restoration of Four Power authority in some form. The situation in Austria offered an unattractive example to all the participants: though that country had a legitimate democratic Grand Coalition government, it was also occupied by the Four Powers, and the Soviet Union was constantly finding new excuses to postpone the conclusion of a peace treaty. An obligation to consult in the event of Four Power negotiations, which the Western Allies originally resisted, would not in Adenauer's view offer any protection in the final analysis. Above all, there was still a risk that an all-German government might be forced to accept a greatly inferior status than the Federal Republic hoped to achieve in the treaties now being negotiated.

At the instigation of the Chancellor, Hallstein therefore proposed to the Advisory Committee that a regulation be adopted in the article of the General Treaty dealing with the peace treaty in Germany and with reunification, according to which a reunited Germany should not be granted fewer rights than were conceded to the Federal Republic in the treaty currently being negotiated. The negotiators of the Western Allies, under the central direction of Robert Bowie, then formulated a counter-proposal. If a united Germany wanted to claim the rights in the treaty, it would also have to accept the obligations therein – in the form of integration into the EDC.

On 2 November 1951, the first discussions were held at the highest level. Here Adenauer admitted that a quid pro quo was justified, but no decision was reached on the wording.[19] On 14 November the problem was discussed once again. The Allies had suggested a vague declaration of intent, but Adenauer insisted on an obligation which would be binding on both sides.[20] The formula which was eventually found ran as follows: 'The Three Powers and the Federal Republic agree that a unified Germany shall be bound by the obligations of the Federal Republic under this Convention and the related Conventions and the Treaties for the formation of an integrated European Community, as adjusted according to their terms or by agreement of the parties thereto, and shall likewise be entitled to the rights of the Federal Republic under these Conventions and Treaties.'[21] Thus a consensus between Adenauer and the High Commissioners had been achieved on this point.

The question of mutual ties played no part in the following discussions at the Foreign Ministers' Conference, probably because all the participants knew that, on such a highly political issue, treaty words could not provide any reliable support if the Western Powers wanted to evade their obligations. However, the Federal Republic had at least assured itself of a veto right in the treaty – its agreement would be necessary if another status was envisaged for a united Germany, but would not be prevented from accepting a different status if it seemed appropriate at the time. In this sense, the Federal Republic might conceivably see an alternative between links with the West and reunification. On the other hand, the Western Powers would have been free – without a binding clause – to agree to a peace treaty with Eastern and Western Germany only if this also belonged to the EDC. They therefore had no need of a binding clause in order to impose on both Bonn and Moscow their desire to keep the Federal Republic in the EDC.

The decisive factor was that West Germany would enter the EDC of its own free will – and that this decision would bind it. If, during reunification negotiations, it wanted to leave, it would be unable to do so against the will of the Western Powers. On the other hand, if the Germans wanted to see a reunited Germany in the EDC, that too could only be achieved if the Western Powers were willing to permit it as negotiations progressed.

In other words, the nature of the problem was highly theoretical. Nevertheless, it enabled Adenauer to make clear his desire for a reunited Germany to be closely allied with the Western democracies in every conceivable area.

Two months later it was clear that this regulation, which was by no means central to the overall context of negotiations, was the key to the political debate over the treaties. The basic issue revolved around the consequences of the Western treaties for reunification – consequences which would arise with or without a binding clause. During the negotiations, however, the problem of reunification caused controversy between Adenauer and the Allies in a different context, i.e., in regard to the German territories east of the Oder-Neisse Line.

Adenauer had been extremely tenacious in urging the Western Allies to accept reunification as a main objective of the treaty. But which Germany was to be reunited? On this issue there was a bitter debate on 14 November,[22] with the foreign ministers also subsequently becoming involved. Adenauer insisted that the 'common goal' of German reunification must also extend to the territories beyond the Oder and Neisse. He warned that a Western policy which planned to use these territories for future negotiations with the Soviet Union would be 'opportunistic', especially as the Allies had previously based their thinking on the German borders of 1937.

By contrast, Kirkpatrick made the classic argument to accept of the claims of the new rulers, which was that the Poles and Czechs must not be driven into the arms of the Soviets. In response, Adenauer argued that opinion in West Germany should also be taken into account. Eventually Kirkpatrick asked sharply: 'Are we by any chance obliged to give you back the Polish Corridor?'[23]

McCloy, too, stated that a Western commitment on the issue of the borders in the east was not possible. Despite initial attempts at mediation by François-Poncet, Adenauer was stubborn: why could a common policy not be pursued with regard to the territories east of the Oder and Neisse? The issue was of the utmost importance, and might produce the failure of the Schuman Plan and the collapse of the entire European idea. After more debate, François-Poncet remarked that, judging by today's declarations, the French public would think that the main aim of the joint approach was to restore the German eastern territories through force of arms. Was that really the meaning of European integration?

Coolly and even arrogantly, Adenauer continued to demand that the Western Allies must be prepared to remove the Polish administration in the German eastern territories. His arguments were both legalistic and political. Neither the Bundestag nor the German public was ready to accept a distinction between the lands west and east of the Oder-Neisse Line. If such an approach were attempted, millions of expellees would press for the rejection of the treaties with the West. There would then be an alliance of socialist and neo-Nazi forces against the treaties, with a neutralised Germany as a possible consequence.

For the time being Adenauer was not prepared to drop the issue. Shortly before his departure to Paris for the final negotiations, he handed McCloy a draft which stated that the settlement of the border question must be 'in the spirit of the Atlantic Charter', that is, on the basis of the right to national self-determination.[24] At the following negotiations in Paris, the border issue was one of the two problems which had remained unresolved.[25]

The news of Adenauer's declarations produced considerable agitation in Western cabinets. There was much debate about why the Chancellor had chosen to raise this explosive issue at such a critical moment. McCloy believed that Adenauer simply wanted to see how far he could go. Perhaps he also had a domestic political objective in mind: if he were criticised on this issue later, he would be able to shift the blame onto the Western Allies. Acheson, Eden and Schuman agreed that support for German territorial claims was impossible, but that it was a different matter if the demand came from the Germans themselves. After much debate, a formula was adopted in Article VII, Paragraph 1, stipulating that, in line with the Potsdam agreement of August 1945, the final settlement of the border issue was reserved for the eventual peace treaty with Germany.

We still cannot be sure why Adenauer was so adamant on this issue. Certainly, the argument itself was no more than the reiteration of views he had held since 1946 and which were then shared by all non-Communist parties. McCloy was probably right to suspect domestic political motives as well. However, there is another possible interpretation. Adenauer was well aware that neither the Soviet Union nor East Germany were prepared to negotiate over the issue of the Oder-Neisse Line. Consequently, he may well have thought it sensible to prepare this bone of contention in good time. Then, if he was ever put under pressure to agree either to East-West negotiations on Germany or to a dialogue between the two Germanys at an inconvenient time, the issue was perfectly designed to obstruct them. Or did he really believe that it would be possible to force the Soviet Union to retreat? If so, he may genuinely have been staking out Germany's claim to the recovery of the lost provinces. During these weeks he made his demand public, exclaiming in Berlin: 'Let me say very clearly, for us the land on the other side of the Oder-Neisse Line is part of Germany.'[26]

Many U.S. and French citizens remembered these demands for a very long time. Such remarks fed the suspicion that Adenauer, despite his apparent role as an entirely reasonable Western statesman, was really an ice-cold revisionist, who was only waiting for the right moment to force the Soviet Union and the Poles out of German territory with the support of the West. As far as the Western Allies were concerned, his tone offered another good reason to keep the West Germans on a short leash for the time being. If Adenauer himself – Western orientated and moderate – was so determined to press home his revisionist demands, then what would his successors as Chancellor be like?

Despite these reservations, all the Western governments had by now concluded that Adenauer was indeed the most moderate of all conceivable West German politicians. As a result, they were resolved to reach an agreement with him as quickly as possible. There was also a rapid rise in Western willingness to grant public recognition of his significance by treating him on equal terms, at least where protocol was concerned.

On 22 November 1951 the General Treaty was initialled in Paris. For the first time, Adenauer was invited to negotiate with the foreign ministers of the three Western great powers. It had taken over two years since he became Chancellor for this step to be achieved. In a telegram to his

President, Dean Acheson noted that, in Europe, the fact that the four foreign ministers had met as equals was more important than the agreements they had reached.[27] Equality of status itself, however, was far from
being achieved. The three foreign ministers had discussed their positions
beforehand in some detail. There had been some discussion of Adenauer's systematic attempts to sow divisions between the High Commissioners by means of bilateral discussions. Moreover, it was agreed that
the initialled treaty should be kept under lock and key until all the other
treaties – and especially that on the EDC – were also initialled. The package was not to be unwrapped.

At this meeting in November 1951, Adenauer's primary objective
was to obtain assurances that the Western Powers would not reach an
agreement with the Soviet Union on the issue of reunification at the
expense of Germany. He told Acheson that on this issue he was chiefly
concerned about Britain and France. And what was the state of U.S.
public opinion? In a year's time there would be elections in the United
States.[28] Acheson pacified him, pointing out that hostility towards the
Soviet Union and China was much stronger in the U.S. than in France
and Britain. Adenauer was very relieved by this assurance, particularly
as it was followed by similar statements from the other foreign ministers. Following his return to Bonn, he was able to affirm a background
briefing: 'This is the most important result of the Paris conference, the
fact that no decisions can be made about Germany in future without the
Federal Republic being asked about them beforehand.'[29]

Scarcely had Adenauer made his first appearance among the Western
foreign ministers than he was invited to London. At this stage, the British
loomed large in the Chancellor's thinking. Though he relied mainly on
the United States, the British were second in line. He regarded the French
as the least reliable and most difficult of the Western Powers, although he
was well aware that his entire European policy would stand and fall on
the issue of Franco-German reconciliation. The question of the Saar was
again arousing unrest, despite the expressions of European sentiment
uttered by both Adenauer and Schuman.

At this stage the British did not hesitate to draw closer to the Federal
Chancellor. Since he had never been treated as a genuine state visitor during his trips to Paris, his visit to Britain between 3 and 7 December was
his first official visit at the invitation of one of the three victorious powers. Adenauer was received with all the ceremony that a statesman was
entitled to expect, if not more. He returned to Bonn with the feeling that
his welcome 'had been a truly cordial one'.[30] He had been given an audience with King George VI, even before the king had fully recovered from
a serious illness. In February 1952 Adenauer was to return to London –
this time for the funeral of the King. By that time he was virtually a
member of the club of Western heads of government.

During his state visit Adenauer had long discussions with Churchill and Eden, and gave an address at Chatham House. Official London spared nothing in its efforts to signal that, under his leadership, West Germany was well advanced on its road from an occupied country to an ally. In Oxford, to which he had been attracted all his life, he visited half a dozen of colleges. Here he saw with his own eyes, in case he should ever have forgotten, further evidence that Britain was as much part of the 'community of western Christian culture' as the Catholic states on the continent.[31] Nevertheless, he did not change his fundamental view of the British: 'They are just different from us'[32] – perhaps because, unlike their counterparts in Europe, the leading British politicians did not speak German!

His discussion with Churchill was respectful but far from easy. The British statesman was visibly eager to treat his German guest according to the maxim described in his memoirs: 'In victory magnanimity.' However, old age was taking its toll on Churchill. As Blankenhorn noted: 'His way of speaking is jerky, sometimes stuttering, hesitating, indecisive, until suddenly four, five sentences emerge which are reminiscent of the big stones of an enormous building.'[33] From time to time he made utterly undiplomatic comments. Of course, there is always the possibility that his remarks, once Adenauer had brought up the subject of Europe, were in fact deliberate: 'Britain must keep the balance. Germany is stronger than France. In France there is great fear of an attack by Germany. In such a case we would place ourselves at the side of France. I do not, however, accept that this case will occur'.

A dismayed Adenauer replied: 'These ideas should not even be voiced. I ask that Germany be trusted. It is sometimes hard to judge Germany correctly. The German is inclined to extremes. He is often too theoretical. But we have learned the hard way …'[34] He then made discreet reference to the fact that in two years' time there would be elections in West Germany. The alliance between France and Germany must 'be completed in the next two years. Germany is a mass which is still to be formed. The issue is whether it will be by good or bad hands.'

Churchill's answer was politically desirable, if not entirely logical: 'I look forward to the time when German and French soldiers march together and the one sing the Marseillaise and the others "The Watch on the Rhine".'[35] Adenauer informed the Prime Minister, in 'strictest confidence', that he regarded European integration as the pre-condition of reunification. Without integration there could be no reunification. However, he could not say so openly, or his opponents would take it as proof that he was opposed to reunification.

The Chancellor also raised, with some subtlety, the issue of the Soviet Union and the East-West negotiations. He eventually received the assurance he had sought from Churchill and Eden: 'We will not betray you. We will not abandon the Federal Republic in order to achieve a peace with the Soviet Union. An agreement with the Soviet Union will only happen with your consent.' With a view to the negotiations in Bonn, Churchill warned against raising the issue of the Oder-Neisse Line. Eden made the point again: 'If Germany terrifies its neighbours, it is playing into the hands of the Soviet Union.' Adenauer hastened to offer the assurance that he was eager for good relations with the Poles. In return, he received further promises: 'You can have complete confidence in England, we will not make deals behind your back.' Yet in the next sentence but one there was another unsettling remark: 'One must keep the doors open to an agreement with the Soviet Union ...'

From time to time, the ghosts of the past flitted through Churchill's mind, which had begun to lose its former clarity: 'Are you a Prussian? The Prussians are rascals. I am afraid of them.' Adenauer was able – credibly, if not with entire historical accuracy – to say that no, he was no Prussian. But Churchill's thoughts had already moved on: 'But the Prussians have a good fighting spirit.' At the end he asserted melodramatically: 'We will all be destroyed if we do not reach an understanding ... If we should go under nevertheless, then at least it will not be our fault.' Adenauer answered with a statement of his faith in the policy of strength: 'If we become stronger, we will not be destroyed.'

At the close of the discussion there was a discreet exchange about the release of Field Marshal Manstein and other Wehrmacht soldiers sentenced for war crimes – there were still 200 of them – from Werl prison. Churchill explained that he had joined in paying for Manstein's lawyer and agreed to set the prisoners free. However, it should not appear that this had been a result of the visit.

All in all, it had been a successful, though irritating, discussion. Churchill was obviously not the man he had once been; when it came to difficult questions it would be necessary to go through Eden.

'The Wings of World History'

The most important meeting of Adenauer's stay in London took place neither at 10 Downing Street nor in the Foreign Office, but in Adenauer's suite at Claridge's. His visitor – who used the back stairs of the hotel in order to preserve essential secrecy – was the Chairman of the World Jewish Congress, Nahum Goldmann. On this occasion, however, Goldmann was acting in his capacity as President of the Conference on Jewish Material Claims against Germany. Goldmann wrote in his memoirs: 'Of all the important conversations I have ever held, this was the most difficult emotionally and perhaps the most significant politically.' Adenauer too was in a state of deep emotion on 6 December 1951. During the meeting, he told Goldmann that he 'felt the wings of world history in this room.'[1]

What was at stake was restitution to the Jews, an issue to which Adenauer was deeply committed. Long before the Holocaust, during his time in Cologne, he had been recognized as a true friend of the Jewish community: he had supported the Orthodox community in all its variety and unique identity; he had admired assimilated Jews such as Louis Hagen, whom he recognised as one of his most important supporters; he had appreciated the contributions of Jewish academic professors; he had enjoyed performances by Jewish musicians; and he had been sympathetic to the Zionists. In 1933, he had also been touched by Jewish generosity, when Dannie N. Heineman, who had never made an issue of his own Jewishness, had been one of the few people to stand by him in his hour of need. Even before 1933 Adenauer had been utterly opposed to Nazi anti-Semitism, which he regarded as barbaric and primitive.

How did he see the issue of restitution after 1945? Discrimination against and persecution of German Jews between 1933 and 1939 had – or so it appeared – been only one of the many injustices meted by the regime to opponents and selected groups. Later, Adenauer was frequently to use the relatively restrained term 'injustice' to describe such conduct – in the sense of offence against the legal order, as well as sin in the Christian sense. As regards Nazi harassment during the years 1933-1939, his position was unequivocal: the victims of state-sponsored injustice had the right to 'restitution'. In each individual case personal rights had been violated and specific injury incurred, and the 'restitution' would be fixed according to the injury sustained. Guilt in the legal and moral sense attached to those who ordered the 'injustice' or took a direct part in it, and such individuals must be punished.

Adenauer generally used the word 'crime' to describe the genocide of the European Jews during the war years. He did not refer to it often, since he regarded it as a crime almost beyond the bounds of human understanding. After his return from imprisonment in Brauweiler, however, he had stated simply: 'I have recognised that evil is a power'. Adenauer was well aware of the metaphysical dimension of the atrocity. Though he believed that the perpetrators would surely be brought to judgement before Almighty God, he was determined that they should also stand trial before judges in this life. Once again, guilt attached only to the perpetrators of specific acts. Responsibility, on the other hand, was to be applied more widely.

Adenauer was convinced that the consequences of genocide could not be dealt with by legal means alone. On the one hand, there were the survivors of the concentration camps, many of whom had made their home

in Israel: to these human beings, too, there was a legal duty to make restitution. On the other hand, the German state – and thus the Federal Republic as the legal successor to the German Reich – had a duty to accept
responsibility for the crimes committed by the German government. This
responsibility was of a moral and legal nature.

From a moral stand-point, the government of the new Germany could
not be expected to feel personal guilt. Firstly, politicians such as Adenauer, who were now responsible for the government, had themselves
been persecuted. Secondly, the German people as a whole were not guilty
of the atrocities of the regime, because the concept of guilt must always
be applied to the specific individuals who had perpetrated the crimes.
Nevertheless, the outrages committed by the Nazi government, and the
conduct of the many Germans who had stood idly by, had brought disgrace upon the country. For the state itself, restitution for the horrors suffered by the Jews was thus a question of honour. The central significance
of the concept of 'honour' in Adenauer's consideration of the issue of
reparation is striking. During this first crucial meeting, he told Nahum
Goldmann that restitution was 'an obligation of honour for the German
people'.[2] Disgrace and honour – the link was umbilical. Hitler had dis-
honoured the German people; by offering restitution to the victims, the
new Germany could begin the work of restoring the country's reputation.

In this context, Adenauer also made frequent use of the term 'moral':
'My intention to make restitution is sincere. I regard it as a great moral
problem ...' Of course, the term 'moral' tends to be used widely and
loosely in political rhetoric, but Adenauer used it deliberately and with
intent. In his view, restitution was a 'moral problem' because the atrocities committed against the Jews had violated the moral order. Active
repentance was also an attempt to restore and strengthen moral values –
both in Europe and in the souls of the Germans themselves.

Such were the considerations which moved Adenauer to regard restitution to the Jews as one of the greatest tasks of German post-war politics. The precision of the approach was remarkable. Rather than vague
avowals of guilt, there were to be clear categories: the responsibility of
the individual, the responsibility of a people and a state, disgrace and
honour, the claims of the victims and the obligation of the government to
make a symbolic restitution of the moral law.

Of course, Adenauer would not have been Adenauer without an
awareness of the practical political dimension – the Realpolitik – of the
issue. In view of the influence of the Jewish community in the United
States everything he did in this area could also be seen as a necessary act
of wise statesmanship. The massive sum of 1.5 billion U.S. dollars for
material restitution would also pay political dividends.

The analogy with Reich debts, which were also to be negotiated in
1951 and 1952, was obvious. If the Federal Republic laid claim to legal

succession to the German Reich, it would also have to accept Reich debts and the debts of the occupation period. Otherwise, no restoration of German credit would be possible. The same was true of Germany's moral responsibility, particularly for the persecution and murder of the Jews. A gradual restoration of moral credit thus required the recognition of an obligation of honour to make restitution.

Adenauer's meeting with Goldmann had been preceded by difficult preparations. Among Jewish organisations and in Israel, raged a passionate debate about whether it was right to accept a single Deutschmark from the murderers of the Jews. Reparations, however, would be a different matter. Yet the Western Allies had cautiously postponed consideration of the reparations problem, largely because of the threatening shadows of the past. The U.S. and the British hoped to prevent the world economic order and the establishment of a peaceful post-war order from being destroyed by a misguided reparations policy of the kind which had blighted the years between 1919 and 1932. Moreover, if German reparations were to be paid, then they would go mainly to the countries it had damaged rather than to Israel, which had not even existed during the Nazi era.

In March 1951, in a note to the Allied governments, Israel had demanded a billion U.S. dollars in reparations from West Germany and half a million from East Germany. However, the Western response had been indeterminate, while the Soviet Union had failed to reply. As a result, if the impoverished Jewish state hoped for significant amounts of money from Germany, it could only be obtained on the basis of a voluntary contribution from the Federal Republic.

Eventually, in Israel, the argument was won by the advocates of *raison d'état*. Nevertheless, Nahum Goldmann, who was appointed Chairman of the Conference on Jewish Material Claims against Germany in 1951 (the body which also represented the demands of Israel), had to be protected by a bodyguard for several months because his life was threatened by Jewish extremists. Adenauer himself was threatened, and in March 1952 an amateurish plot to kill him with a parcel bomb was foiled.

The question of restitution was also linked with the debt negotiations. To the Chancellor's great irritation, the New York Foreign Ministers' Conference, which had examined his two memoranda in September 1950, had announced that further positive development of German-Allied relations would depend on the settlement of Reich and post-war debts. Preliminary negotiations had been going on for some time. The actual debts conference, at which West Germany was represented by the banker Hermann J. Abs, began in London in February 1952 and lasted a full year. It was no surprise that Abs – who was still being considered as West German foreign minister by Adenauer in the spring of 1952[3] – was one of the most bitter opponents of a restitution agreement, especially when he discovered the size of the sum to which Adenauer had committed

West Germany. The German negotiating strategy at the London debt conference was, naturally, to make a credible case to the effect that West Germany was able to take on no more than part of the debt, and even that only in the form of a long-term repayment plan. The overall debt which was finally agreed upon was some 13 milliard Deutschmarks – not quite twice the amount of the Jewish restitution demand.

Adenauer was thus confronted by an almost impossible conflict of goals. The voluntary acceptance of huge financial obligations towards Israel and world Jewish organisations would clearly endanger the strategy being pursued in the negotiations on the debt agreement and the ability of the Federal Republic to pay. In 1950, West Germany had a foreign exchange deficit of 61 million Deutschmarks, and in 1951 there was only a meagre surplus of 186 million Deutschmarks.

Looked at coldly, a recognition of Jewish demands to the tune of 7.5 milliard marks was impossible. Adenauer was well aware of this fact, which was one of the reasons for his initial hesitation. Through Herbert Blankenhorn, he made cautious contacts with the Jewish side.[4] In April 1950, for the first time, Blankenhorn met a colleague of Noah Barou, and met Barou himself in London shortly afterwards. In this preliminary phase, Nahum Goldmann, one of the leading figures in the Zionist movement since the 1920s, also became involved.

Goldmann was born during the last decade of the nineteenth century, the son of a rabbi in a Jewish *shtetl* in old Russia. After the pogroms of the period, his parents had moved to Frankfurt and, between 1900 and 1933, Nahum Goldmann had lived in Germany. Here this highly intelligent and cultivated man developed a lifelong admiration for German science and literature as well as becoming involved in the Zionist movement at an early stage. During the First World War, he spent three years working on Jewish affairs at the German Foreign Ministry. After completing his doctorate in law at the liberal University of Heidelberg, Goldmann worked as a journalist, as a speaker for Zionist organisations and as an organiser. He lived for part of the time in Murnau, Upper Bavaria, and for part of the time in Berlin, where he edited the *Encyclopedia Judaica* until the Nazis came to power. During this period he had never come into contact with Konrad Adenauer. After 1933 the main focus of his activities was the United States, where he took on a leading role in the worldwide Jewish support organisations and established a complex network of valuable ties with political and financial circles. Goldmann played an important part in the foundation of the state of Israel and, by the early 1950s, was recognised as a towering figure in the Jewish and international community.

His initial attitude towards Adenauer was cautious and restrained. When Adenauer held court at the Park Hotel on the Bürgenstock in summer 1951, Goldmann was by chance staying at the same hotel only one-hundred yards away. Despite Blankenhorn's mediation, Goldmann refused to meet the Chancellor until a declaration on the question of restitution had been agreed in advance and presented by Adenauer in the Bundestag. Adenauer was ready to do this. In a government declaration of 27 September 1951, which was unanimously accepted, he stated that he wished to resolve the problem of restitution with representatives of the Jewish world organisations and the state of Israel, in order 'to smooth the way for a spiritual easing of boundless suffering'.[5] This gave him a form of *carte blanche* for negotiations.

However, one vital issue had still to be resolved: whether the Jewish demand of 1.5 billion dollars was accepted as the basis for negotiations. It was an enormous sum, more than half of the 2.7 milliard dollars that West Germany had received from the Marshall Plan between April 1948 and June 1952. This was the issue to be settled at the meeting at Claridge's on 6 December 1951.

After a discussion which lasted an hour, and without having been authorised by the Cabinet, Adenauer took one of the biggest solitary decisions of his chancellorship. At the end of the meeting he asked Goldmann to go into the adjoining room and dictate to his secretary the draft of a letter which Adenauer then sent to Goldmann that afternoon through Noah Barou. The vital sentence ran as follows: 'The federal government is prepared, in these negotiations, to accept, as the basis for the discussions, the claims made by the government of the state of Israel in its note of 13 March 1951.'[6]

Most Cabinet members reacted with incredulity when they heard what Adenauer had done. The Finance Minister, Schäffer, was particularly furious and made some ferocious criticisms of Adenauer. Abs felt that the rug had been pulled out from under him in the negotiations over the debt agreement, and made some vain attempts to reduce the amount.

Adenauer stubbornly resisted the pressures placed upon him in Germany. In addition to one billion U.S. dollars for Israel, he also agreed to 500 million U.S. dollars as the basis of claims from Jewish organisations. The vital talks ran parallel to the final negotiations on the Germany Treaty and the EDC, though the Western Allies did not make a specific connection. Both men revealed their determination and strength of personality in these talks of 10 June 1952, Goldmann for his sheer boldness in obtaining this half a billion dollars, and Adenauer for his courage and dignity in accepting it almost without argument.

Goldmann's description of this scene in his memoirs provides one of the most striking of all anecdotes about Adenauer: When the Chancellor asked about my arguments, I answered that I would explain my position through a joke: one Israeli asks another why Israel has asked for exactly a billion dollars from the Federal Republic for the settlement of those victims of the Nazis who have emigrated to Israel: 'How did they assess the cost of doing this? It might cost hundreds of millions more, or hundreds of millions less.' The other Israeli answers him:

'In my *shtetl* there was a grocer who stammered. Once a customer came to him and asked the price of a pound of potatoes. The man said: "Twenty kopecks." She asked how much half a pound of butter would cost, and he said: "Twenty kopecks." Whatever she asked, the answer was "Twenty kopecks". The woman wondered why everything should cost twenty kopecks, and the shopkeeper replied: "It's easier to say."' I added: 'What impression would it make if, after months of negotiations, I were to go to the Claims Conference and the 25 organisations represented there with an offer of 300 or 350 millions? 500 million is a round sum and is easier to say.' The Chancellor laughed and decided that 500 million was how it would stay ...[7]

Deep in his heart, however, Adenauer knew that this was no matter for jokes. For years the Germans had followed the Austrian monster Hitler; some had taken part in the persecution of the Jews, while many more had stood by and allowed it to happen. The least they could do now was to pay without protest, as well as to punish the guilty. There is no doubt that, through a generosity which was motivated by moral sentiment, Adenauer gained the trust of the international Jewish community – in part for West Germany, but even more so for himself. This trust was to be of incalculable value. From now on, in the United States and everywhere where opinion-formers in the Jewish community gathered together, Goldmann praised Adenauer and defended him against attack. In numerous later meetings, he also was able to communicate valuable information to Adenauer, unacceptable from others.

In 1952, however, Adenauer's promises had placed him in difficulties reminiscent in many ways of his days as mayor of Cologne. As before, the obligations he had accepted for the coming years represented an enormous burden. The extent of the demands made on the Federal Republic is difficult to comprehend. In the budget of 1952/53, 13 billion Deutschmarks were to be set aside for rearmament within the framework of the EDC and for Allied troops in West Germany. That was some 10 per cent of the German gross national product and almost 60 per cent of the federal budget, which was approximately 23 billion marks in 1953.[8]

The Western Powers stubbornly insisted on a massive contribution. With great difficulty, the Germans finally managed to reduce it to 10 billion marks – still a heavy burden.[9] In addition there were the annual payments of interest and repayment of Germany's foreign debts. Though Abs successfully negotiated an annual servicing of the debt of 567 million marks for the first five years, even that was a great strain on the federal budget.

At the same time, the Bundestag passed an expensive Equalization of Burdens bill for the expellees. As well as answering the dictates of solidarity, this was essential from a political point of view in order to prevent the radicalisation of some 13 millions expellees and refugees. The means were to be obtained through a special property tax. Once again, however, there would be increasing costs over the coming years. On top of that, there was now the promise of restitution payments.

This was the financial aspect of Adenauer's foreign and domestic policy. Just as during his period in Cologne, every single obligation could be justified on political and moral grounds as well as on the merits of the case. However, it would only be possible to meet future financial burdens in exceptionally favourable circumstances.

On this occasion Adenauer was lucky – in contrast to the years in Cologne between 1929 and 1933. The economic miracle, the extent of which was still inconceivable at the beginning of the 1950s, solved every problem. Moreover, it proved to be a blessing that the German defence contribution – wholly against the Chancellor's intentions – did not begin fully until 1956, and so the economy and the public purse were both given some breathing-space. There must be some doubt about whether the economic miracle could have developed so strongly if the defence contribution had begun in 1952.

In 1952, however, the Cabinet members were desperately anxious. Once again Adenauer had gained the reputation that had dogged him since his time in Cologne. According to critics in the Ministry of Finance, and also in the coalition supporting him, he was an appalling profligate with a diabolical gift for creating situations which left his government with no choice but to accept his decision and impose heavy burdens on the country. It was small consolation that the full force of these decisions would not be felt until after the federal elections of 1953. Though the Chancellor's office took the view that time would bring an answer, there was an obvious danger that Adenauer's policies would end in disaster. If so, there would be no proud Adenauer era, but only a relatively short-lived government ending in a morass of inflation, high taxes, social misery and insolvency.

These fears help to explain the rebellion within the FDP, DP and CSU against the restitution law. Schäffer, Blücher and Franz Josef Strauss all regarded the extent of the contributions as utterly irresponsible and were appalled by the Chancellor's conduct of the negotiations. Representatives of industry, especially those with an interest in trade with Arab states, were also hostile; the Arab countries were already beginning to exert well-orchestrated pressure on West German policy towards Israel. In spite of all this, in March 1953 Adenauer's agreement with Israel won a parliamentary majority of 239 votes, including all of the Social Democrats. However 86 members of the coalition abstained, with a few dozen failing even to attend the vote. Adenauer was particularly annoyed by Schäffer's decision to vote against the agreement, but was powerless to act in view of the fact that his Minister of Finance had the full support of the CSU.[10]

Small majorities had never worried Adenauer, however, and he was indifferent to resistance. With the restitution agreement enormously enhancing his international reputation, he was able to make his first visit to the United States in spring 1953. Nine months previously, on 17 June 1952, after the Cabinet had approved to the agreement, he had attended a dinner for the minister-presidents of the Länder and told them that the accord with the world Jewish community was no less important than the restoration of German sovereignty. The minister-presidents had risen from their seats to applaud him.

Warding off the Moscow Note Offensive

There was still no great haste to restore German sovereignty in the spring of 1952. The negotiations on the European Defence Community entered a critical phase in February of that year. In addition, the re-organisation of German-Allied relations came to a halt amid fierce debate over the supplementary treaties.

Both before and after this date, when difficulties arose over the treaties with the West, Adenauer was forced to recognise that Franco-German reconciliation was an intention and an idea rather than a reality. The opponents of a German defence contribution in the Quai d'Orsay and the National Assembly played their cards skilfully. At the end of January 1952 Adenauer was surprised by the news that the French Foreign Minister had appointed Gilbert Grandval as ambassador to the Saar government. Previously, as French High Commissioner, he had ruled the region like a proconsul. His appointment had to be regarded as a clear expression of French determination to continue its previous uncompromising course. Adenauer was placed in a difficult position.

In Paris, the government was tottering once again. There were rumours that Robert Schuman was in severe political difficulties and was being forced to make increasingly high demands for the EDC. The European rhetoric in Bonn and Paris sounded increasingly shallow. Adenauer too was under pressure. In view of opinion within the coalition, he correctly assumed that the question of German entry into NATO would cause public disputes. At the EDC conference in Paris, Hallstein made it clear that Germany would postpone its request for membership for a short time only. Adenauer gave himself some room for manoeuvre within the coalition at the beginning of February, when he made it clear that agreement to the EDC would depend on an acceptable settlement of the Saar question and West Germany's links with NATO. Tensions grew following a report from the dpa, the German press agency. Though an official denial was issued, observers were convinced that Adenauer had decided to answer rudeness with rudeness.

At the same time, Adenauer was eager to reduce the effects of the conflict with Paris. During a major debate in the French Chamber, it looked as if the fate of the government was at stake. In a cabinet meeting in Bonn, where, as often, the heads of the parliamentary parties were also present, Adenauer therefor attempted to delay the impending Bundestag debate on the Saar. He was unable to prevail over his own party and the FDP and DP ministers. Some Cabinet ministers, including Jakob Kaiser and Thomas Dehler, still hoped that the SPD could be won over to the idea of a defence contribution. Jakob Kaiser argued that it was essential to build bridges to the Opposition, whose leader Schumacher was again seriously ill.

During these passionate exchanges, Adenauer observed that U.S. public opinion was currently more important to him than German. He hoped to persuade the Americans to put pressure on the French. However, he was also aware that Washington was perfectly prepared to play down the Saar question, since the U.S. regarded the sham autonomy of the Saar as a form of consolation prize for France. Still, the State Department had begun to work for a European solution to the Saar question. It was not long before the French High Commission also made tentative inquiries regarding Bonn's willingness to accept the 'Europeanisation' of the issue. In the West German cabinet itself, there was some sympathy for the idea of making Saarbrücken a European territory and the headquarters of the High Authority of the Coal and Steel Community.

In the Bundestag debate on 7 and 8 February, which Adenauer attended with a fever and in poor health,[1] he insisted that one day, sooner or later, Germany should become a full member of NATO. Abroad, there was an almost universal sense in these weeks that Germany had begun to state its demands strongly and without the former restraint. This attitude was reflected in a Bundestag resolution, which demanded 'sovereignty for the Federal Republic', though with certain limitations. Yet in the end, only 48 votes were cast for this resolution of the coalition parties. The mood in the government camp was poor and depressed.

In the French National Assembly the opponents of the EDC had been marshalling their forces and passed a resolution which tied the hands of the government: there was to be no German membership of NATO. As NATO was a purely defensive alliance, it was argued, no members who made territorial claims against other countries could be accepted. German recruits for the European army could only be accepted after the ratification of the treaties, and there should be no more than gradual progress in the build-up of military units.

On this occasion, Robert Schuman seemed resigned to the course of developments. Almost all the French parties were affected by fears of Germany, and the European impulse was scarcely perceptible. The EDC appeared primarily as an elaborate organisation to muzzle German soldiers. In many places, in fact, there was a widespread view that the EDC was a dead letter even before the treaties were signed.

At the height of the crisis in the EDC negotiations came the death of George VI. Washington and London recognised an opportunity for a final push before the NATO Conference in Lisbon, whose failure was already being predicted. The British informed Adenauer that his attendance at the funeral would be welcome, but the Chancellor travelled to London without knowing whether he would be invited to the discussions among the foreign ministers of the Western Great Powers. In a preliminary meeting, Schuman had to be converted by Acheson. Only after the Allies had struggled to find a common approach to the controversial issues did Adenauer become involved.

In retrospect, both Adenauer and Acheson accepted that this improvised conference was vital to further progress. Acheson described it as the most important Foreign Ministers' Conference in the West since the discussions in New York in September 1950,[2] while Adenauer felt that it had been one of the most tense conferences he had ever attended. Before he left Germany, he was still feverish and unwell.[3] In London, however, he quickly recovered and, with Acheson, managed to get the stalled negotiations moving again.

At last, Adenauer saw the emergence of a constellation he had long desired: German-American cooperation on behalf of the EDC project, which was half-European but should also be half-Atlantic. Most of his demands were supported by Acheson, whose respect for the German Chancellor was growing. After some resistance, Eden also supported most of their ideas. Schuman, under concerted pressure from all sides, was forced to give way on important points.

Nor did Adenauer escape unscathed. West German NATO membership was again deferred, the financial defence contribution was set alarmingly high, and many restrictions on German armaments production remained in force. On the Saar question, all that was achieved by his personal talks with the French Foreign Minister was an agreement to shelve it. While Schuman aimed at a European solution and made certain promises to Adenauer, it seemed that his days in office were numbered.

When Adenauer returned from the negotiations, which had been relatively successful, he was confronted by demands that he should give up the Foreign Ministry. The chairman of the parliamentary party, von Brentano, now laid his own claim to the job, but was told that the Defence Ministry was much more important. Adenauer had also promised Abs that he would appoint him Foreign Minister at the next opportunity, and he intended to keep to this plan.[4] After the London conference, it appeared that, once the treaties with the West came into effect, Adenauer would be able to give up the foreign ministry. In fact, it was almost three years before he did so. For the moment, however, he assumed that the negotiations would be complete in two to three months' time and that ratification would follow soon after. On 9 March 1952, at a public meeting, he mentioned summer 1953 as the time when between 40,000 and 60,000 German volunteers would provide the first divisions of the West German defence contingent.[5]

Into this situation the Soviet Note of 10 March 1952 burst like a bombshell. In it, Moscow invited the Western Allies to an immediate Four Power Conference to discuss a German peace treaty. A draft of the basic principles was enclosed. This draft made various proposals for the solution of the German question, some known and some sensationally new. New was the idea that a reunited Germany should have its own national armed forces and the right to manufacture armaments. Relatively new, too, was the emphasis given to a neutralisation of a reunited Germany. The Note also provided a starting-point for a return to the old Western demand for free elections under correct conditions.

Adenauer's first reaction – as far as we know – came during the Cabinet meeting of 11 March. Otto Lenz noted in his diary:

> Jakob Kaiser thinks that the note is certainly aimed at the Western governments, but we must adopt a positive attitude at all costs. Federal Chancellor thinks it is directed primarily at France, in order to bring it back to its old, traditional policy with Russia. Under no circumstances must we arouse suspicion that we are wavering in our policy. He also thinks it necessary to have an agreed terminology for dealing with the press. Rather vehement debate between Jakob Kaiser and the Federal Chancellor. Jakob Kaiser takes the view that a national German army would be more valuable than a European one. Federal Chancellor points out that the European states alone would not be in a position to defend themselves.[6]

Felix von Eckardt and Theodor Blank were given the task of producing a statement for the federal press conference which highlighted the negative aspects and pointed out that the Note was no surprise. 'The basic aim of Soviet tactics is always the same: to prevent European integration ... The Kremlin wants the entire German area to be in a vacuum in which the Soviet Union, thanks to its geographical proximity and its instruments of power, could exert the decisive influence.'[7] Second, it was emphasised that the Soviet Union was demanding abrogation of the German territories east of the Oder and Neisse. Finally, it was argued that Germany alone would not have the financial or the technical means to defend herself. Accepting Soviet wishes 'would mean nothing other than Germany sinking back to a wholly unsatisfactory status like the country which is its neighbour in the east'. The position paper for the press was also critical of the fact that the Note made no reference to free elections. This was said to be in line with the Kremlin's refusal to permit the entry of the UN Commission to investigate whether the conditions for free elections actually existed in the Eastern Zone.

This approach should be regarded as typical. Obviously, Adenauer did not spend much time considering whether the Soviet Note could set the process of reunification in motion. He appears to have accepted this as a fact and based his opposition solely on the status of the reunited Germany that would emerge. The Chancellor had spent three years crying wolf whenever he feared the emergence of Soviet proposals for the neutralisation of Germany. Now the wolf was at the door – and it looked exactly as he had always thought it would. Small wonder, then, that he was completely opposed to the idea.

On the day of the cabinet meeting Adenauer met with the High Commissioners for discussions summarised in a report by Sir Ivone Kirkpatrick.[8] The British representative sent a cable to London with news of Adenauer's assurance that the Soviet Note would not influence the policy of the federal government. The Cabinet had discussed it and agreed on guidelines for the press because uninformed observers might otherwise be attracted to certain points in the Note. Its main aim, the neutralisation of Germany, was to be made palatable by the proposal for German national armed forces. However, the federal government did not want a national army; in addition, Germany did not have the means to establish one. In the Chancellor's view, one further striking feature of the Note lay in its compliments to the Nazis and the German militarists. Adenauer had asked for a rapid response from the Western governments to prevent the possibility of serious confusion in German public opinion. He had expressed his opinion that the Western Allies would not accept a Four Power Conference. Kirkpatrick's message thus reveals Adenauer's absolute rejection of the Soviet proposals, but also demonstrates that he took very seriously its potential effect on public opinion.

Two days later another British report was made, this time on a conversation held on 12 March between Adenauer and some 20 journalists sympathetic to the government.[9] During this briefing, Adenauer had upheld the approach he had taken with the High Commissioners, i.e., that it would be a great mistake for the Western powers to agree to discussions with the Soviets. William Strang reported that 15 of the 20 pro-CDU or FDP journalists had expressed the view that, given the current state of public opinion in West Germany, such an approach would be disastrous. It was absolutely essential for the Western reply to be conciliatory; it must not be interpreted as an attempt to avoid discussions with the Soviets.

Adenauer's next known comment on the Note came on 14 March,10 when the cabinet discussed the matter once more.[10] At this meeting there was much criticism of Jakob Kaiser for statements he had made on the radio regarding the Note. According to Otto Lenz: 'Federal Chancellor states that negotiations on the treaties were largely complete. Main attempt at disruption was the Russian Note, which was aimed at exploiting the weakness of the French government. Supreme duty now was to keep quiet. To his regret he had to say that Hallstein had talked too much in the USA … He then also criticised the comment by Jakob Kaiser on the Soviet Note.'

Kaiser defended himself by arguing that he had been forced to speak out because the comments of the federal press office had been inadequate. Interestingly, he then remarked – without being corrected by the Chancellor – McCloy and François-Poncet had also expressed their agreement. Given that the entire situation could still change, it was essential to talk rather than to remain silent. Adenauer stressed that the cabinet had agreed not to adopt a specific position, and that Kaiser had behaved unacceptably in breaking this agreement. It would have been better to let the Allies do the talking, since they would obviously prefer the Germans to speak first.

At this meeting Adenauer's tactics became clear. He himself was to have the right to comment on the Note – through the federal press office, in countless speeches and interviews, in background briefings with journalists, and not least in confidential discussions with the High Commissioners. His ministers, on the other hand, were to keep quiet.

During this period, however, the Chancellor discovered that his outright rejection of the Soviet initiative was not achieving the desired effect on the West German public or on the Western Allies. He therefore changed his tactics.

This slight change first appeared in a forceful speech to the founding assembly of the CDU's Evangelischer Arbeitskreis (Evangelical Working Group) that met on 16 March in Siegen. The CDU had no Catholic Working Group, but needed a Protestant one for obvious reasons, and Adenauer had agreed after some resistance that one should be established. In this speech he boldly sketched out the more flexible tactical approach which he was to adopt in future: fundamental rejection of neutralisation, using the arguments that were already well known; support for steadily progress in working out the treaties with the West, but accompanied by an attempt to reach a peaceful understanding with the East. Adenauer also set out his support for the policy of strength, of the kind long advocated by Acheson: 'If we continue in this way, if the West including the United States is as strong as it must be, if it is stronger than the Soviet government, that will be the time when the Soviet Union starts to listen.'[11]

On the following day he expressed similar sentiments to the High Commissioners. Although Adenauer also mentioned this conversation in his memoirs,[12] the telegrams sent by the High Commissioners give a much more precise account of what was said.[13] As before, Adenauer rejected outright the idea of a Four Power Conference on the grounds that it would lead to endless delays and slow both the process of integration and the founding of the EDC. However, public reaction in France and Germany would have to be taken carefully into account. He now favoured a policy of asking the Soviet Union some detailed questions. First, how would an all-German government be created? Through free elections? Would the UN Commission be allowed into the Eastern Zone?

Second, what was meant by a ban on alliances? Was it directed against the Schuman Plan, the EDC and other first steps towards the peaceful union of Europe?

According to a telegram from General Hays to the State Department,[14] Adenauer had specifically opposed broaching the issue of the Oder-Neisse Line in the answering Note. This problem, he felt, must be left to later agreements with a free Poland. When Kirkpatrick objected, however, Adenauer conceded that a reference might be useful, since the Potsdam agreement did not contain any definitive regulation on the Oder-Neisse Line or an agreement about Königsberg. In conclusion, the Chancellor remarked that work on the treaties must not be delayed by the exchange of Notes – in fact it should be accelerated.

Adenauer had thus adopted the approach to which the Western Allies had also decided to commit themselves. A discussion with the three foreign ministers in Paris on 21 March revealed the extent of agreement between them.[15] As the British Foreign Office had suggested, the West's reply placed great emphasis on the theme of 'free elections' and the conditions for them, but also indicated the fundamental differences of opinion about the status of Germany, including the border question.

The Chancellor returned to Bonn very contented. To the parliamentary party he stressed how important it was that the federal government had been consulted before the reply was dispatched. The government had also been allowed to offer its views on the draft versions. The crucial factor, however, was that all the Western Powers had adhered to the concept of European integration and had opposed the neutralisation of a reunited Germany. In particular, they had refused to accept a German national army.

Significantly, the Social Democrats were in full agreement with the government in rejecting the idea of neutralisation. They did, however, call for negotiations to examine whether the Soviet offer was serious.

This phase saw Adenauer begin to give particular prominence to an argument which was increasingly to dominate public discussion of the German question over the following years – the connection between the problem of Germany and a 're-organisation' of the satellite states in the Soviet sphere of influence. Was it really likely that the Soviet Union would release the Eastern Zone, in disregard of the probable repercussions within the entire Eastern block?[16] This was the thinking behind Adenauer's interview with Ernst Friedländer in *Die Zeit,* a newspaper much favoured by the Chancellor as a means of conveying his views to the general public.[17]

His views were best expressed, however, in a background conversation with the editor of the London newspaper *The Times* on 3 June 1952: 'If we were to accept that the Soviet Union would set free the Soviet Zone, restore the unity of Germany by means of free, secret elections, and abandon the idea of creating a sphere of influence in this newly-created Germany, then they would also have to abandon their policy in the satellite states. Such conduct would kindle the spirit of resistance and the hope of liberation among the many opponents of Bolshevism in Poland, Czechoslovakia and Hungary, and would be bound to produce a complete change in Soviet policy which would run counter to developments since 1945 and bring the Soviet Union no tangible return.'[18] The only conceivable way-out, therefore, was an overall solution. But Moscow would be prepared to accept this only if the West was stronger and its own internal difficulties much more urgent. One of his British guests asked, mockingly, whether this would happen in 25 years or 100. Adenauer answered calmly: 'In my view in five to ten years'.

If Adenauer's assessment was correct, it would be right to reject the Soviet offers because they could not have been serious. However, it must also be recognised that, even if they had been seriously meant, Adenauer would still have rejected them because he believed that a neutralised Germany would be hopelessly insecure. In any event, he always had sufficient reasons for opposing the proposals.

During this weeks, there were many – including Jakob Kaiser, but also journalists such as Paul Sethe of the *Frankfurter Allgemeine* Zeitung, Rudolf Augstein from *Der Spiegel* and Hans Zehrer, editor of *Die Welt* – who were infuriated by Adenauer's refusal to negotiate. All were particularly displeased by the linkage of the German question with the reorganisation of eastern Europe. If the argument was correct, then reunification of Germany would be impossible in the foreseeable future. Yet Adenauer had chosen to highlight this difficult aspect during the debate following the Soviet Note. The conclusion is inescapable: he regarded all negotiations as futile at the current time and was contemptuous of those who regarded Stalin's Note as a historic opportunity.

In his detailed survey of the episode in the second volume of his memoirs, Adenauer himself later described the incident as though it had offered a unique opportunity: 'In politics one may well never find ideal conditions; if these ever appear, they are great moments in history. But then the question arises – do the statesmen exist who will recognise these conditions, and will their peoples follow them?'[19]

These sentences are reminiscent of Bismarck's famous comments regarding the 'mantle of God'. However, the context of his remarks makes obvious what Adenauer saw as the great opportunity of spring 1952. He did not mean the 'lost opportunity' for reunification, but rather his policy towards the West, of which he was always proud. The 'great moment' which might have been missed was to bring about West Germany's 'firm attachment to the free peoples of the West' by means of the Western treaties. Furthermore, the statesman who had recognized this opportunity and carried a hesitant people with him, was – of course – himself! A year before his death, this was Adenauer's last word on the theme of 'lost opportunities'.

Within the coalition Adenauer was able to assert his negative view of the March Note. Only Kaiser's radio address of 12 March had publicly revealed differences in the government. How deep these were, and the extent and intensity of the arguments within the coalition, remains unclear even today. On this point as others, the disappearance of the CDU/CSU caucus records for the years 1950-1953 is a serious loss to researchers.

Even the U.S. High Commission resorted to speculation. McCloy, who had discussed the Note with both Adenauer and Jakob Kaiser, remarked in a cable on 15 May that the basic difference of opinion between the two was that Kaiser thought there was a ten per cent chance that the Note was sincere, while Adenauer denied the possibility altogether. McCloy also suspected, quite correctly, that Kaiser would not take his opposition to Adenauer too far.[20]

A sharper picture is provided by McCloy's telegram of 29 March,[21] in which he stated that Adenauer rejected the Note outright. Some Kremlin-watchers among his associates were convinced that the Soviets were seriously attempting to turn Germany eastwards, initially in a way more like Finland or even Sweden than Czechoslovakia. They saw parallels between the current situation and that of summer 1939, when the endeavours of the Western Powers to prevent an alliance between Hitler and Stalin had failed and Stalin's overtures led to the signing of the Nazi-Soviet pact. Adenauer was aware of this challenge.

The Chancellor, so the report continued, had to take pains not to appear more American than the Americans. There were some elements in the cabinet who were more fearful on this point, or more receptive to nationalist slogans. This group recommended that the tempo of negotiations over the Western treaties should be slowed and the new possibilities explored. The group was not very strong; it included only a few 'soft-headed nationalists' such as Vice-Chancellor Blücher, and some representatives on the left wing of the CDU, including Jakob Kaiser and von Brentano. At the end of March McCloy was unable to predict whether Schumacher wanted to make common cause with those politicians within the coalition who wanted to play for time.

Overall, McCloy had the impression that there were certainly internal differences of opinion, but not of a sufficient number to pose any real threat.

The critical moment for Adenauer's policy of links with the West came with the arrival of the second Soviet Note on 9 April 1952. In it, Moscow recognised the need for free German elections as the precondition for establishing an all-German government. Though the UN Commission continued to be refused entry into the GDR, the Soviet government stressed that this issue could be cleared up by the four occupying powers. As regards the status of a reunited Germany, Moscow reiterated the position laid out on 10 March. Further clarification and, if necessary, modification of Soviet intentions could only be expected through Four Power negotiations.

The rapid reply and the courteous tone of the Note left no doubt that the Soviet Union wanted to enter into discussions without delay. How long these talks would last, once progress towards the Western treaties had been delayed or even brought to a standstill, was another matter.

Once again Adenauer was determined to oppose any delay in the negotiations which, he calculated, ought to lead to the signing of the Western treaties in May. At home he felt strengthened by the results of the election to the Landtag of the newly created Land of Baden-Württemberg. Even though the formation of a government did not proceed as he would have wished, eventually leading to a coalition of the FDP/DVP, SPD and BHE under Minister-President Reinhold Maier, the CDU had emerged as the strongest party with almost 36 per cent of the votes.

The Social Democrats had conducted the election campaign on national issues and been beaten. Otto Lenz had also presented the Chancellor with opinion poll findings from the Allensbach Institute, showing that the federal government was at last beginning to regain popularity.[22] Throughout the critical weeks of April and May, Adenauer used these figures against those who wavered in their support of his foreign policy, including Hans Baumgarten, the critical editor of the *Frankfurter Allgemeine Zeitung*. He was also certain that, under the resolute direction of Acheson, the Americans were now making every effort to ensure that the Western treaties were signed and ratified in the first half of 1952.

The second Soviet Note had scarcely arrived when Acheson made an urgent appeal to the West European foreign ministers to conclude the treaty negotiations by 9 May.[23] He left no doubt about the possible consequences of further delay. Congress would have to decide on the military aid programme by the middle of May at the latest. If the West Europeans – this was clearly implied although not stated outright – failed to commit themselves to the EDC, then the fate of the military aid, of which France in particular was in urgent need, would hang in the balance. In addition, after 9 May there would be only a few weeks for the vital ratification of the treaties with Germany by Congress, which was due to go into recess on 3 July. The British Foreign Secretary, Anthony Eden, was also pressing for a rapid conclusion of the negotiations.[24]

Adenauer was aware that the French would be happy to use the new Note as an excuse to play for time. When he requested a meeting with the High Commission on 12 April, François-Poncet refused to discuss the Note with the Chancellor.[25] Kirkpatrick did not state his own views with clarity, but Adenauer's own approach was direct and straightforward. Since the Soviet Note – in Adenauer's view not a particularly skilful manoeuvre – was aimed primarily at German public opinion, the Chancellor argued that the answer must also be framed so as to achieve the desired propaganda effect. However, the federal government would not yet express its views in public. This is why he had asked his ministers to avoid the temptation to make headlines on the matter.

The Chancellor then set out his own provisional assessment. First and foremost, out of regard for German public opinion, the Western Powers must confirm their intention to achieve reunification. It was equally important for them to confirm their basic willingness to take part in a Four Power conference. However, it was essential to explain that such a conference, as had been shown by the negotiations over the treaty with Austria and the armistice in Korea, would serve no useful purpose unless a degree of agreement had been reached on important points beforehand.

In Adenauer's opinion, the important points were: the full future sovereignty of Germany, including the right to enter alliances as it saw fit; the possibility of German defence forces integrated into Europe and the borders of Germany. The new Soviet Note contained no sign that successful negotiation was possible on any of these questions.

The Chancellor considered that the issue of all-German elections and the UN Commission, despite their importance, should be placed at the end of the reply out of concern for German public opinion. He still took the view that the UN Commission was essential, since Four Power control of free elections would be little more than a farce and everyone knew what the Soviets meant by free elections. However, it was essential to separate the issue of the status of a reunited Germany from the issue of free elections. Otherwise there was a great danger that the two would become intertwined.

In other words, Adenauer was urging the Western Powers to incorporate in their reply all those points – including the UN Commission – which the Soviet Union was extremely unlikely to accept. On the other hand, he knew that he would find himself in difficulties during the internal debate with the SPD and his adversaries within the coalition if the exchange of Notes was to turn in future solely upon the issue of free elections. A propaganda battle with regard to the Western treaties – this was the name of the game underlying the exchange of Notes.

On this occasion Adenauer had no reason to address the interesting question of whether there was a logical inconsistency between his demand for full freedom of manoeuvre for an all-German government and his readiness to accept Article VII, 3 of the General Treaty. Strictly speaking, there was not: Article VII, 3 left an all-German government free to dispense with its obligations as laid out in the treaties, provided that it was also prepared to dispense with the corresponding rights. It was theoretically free to choose neutralisation, links with the West or links with the East, while the Soviets were demanding that an all-German government must be committed to neutrality.

A second discussion, this time with all three High Commissioners, took place on 16 April.[26] The representatives of the Western Allies showed caution in their own answers. Adenauer continued to hold the views he had expressed four days previously. McCloy informed the Chancellor that, when the Western answering Note had been handed over, the Soviet Foreign Minister Wyzhinski had declared that NATO membership would be out of the question for a reunited Germany.

François-Poncet was clearly irritated at having to discuss the Note with the Chancellor at all, and took little part in the talks. However, he did make one illuminating remark: If the Western Powers hastened to complete the Western treaties without having demonstrated the insincerity of the Soviet proposals beforehand, then the Social Democrats would be able to accuse them of burning their bridges behind them. The last Soviet Note came very close to Schumacher's position. What did Adenauer think? McCloy confirmed that the SPD was now advocating a revival of Four Power negotiations.

Adenauer replied by regretting that the SPD's position was close to the line taken by Moscow; the same, he argued, was true of the Labour Party in Britain and the Socialists in France. As regards burning their bridges prematurely, he made a powerful case for continued and rapid progress. However, in order to avoid criticism that they were pressing on with the Western treaties while neglecting the Soviet Note, the Western Powers should reply quickly, perhaps by 26 April, in order to maintain the rhythm of the exchange.

This time the cabinet remained calm when, on 22 April, Adenauer stated that he had urged the High Commissioners to answer the Note in a friendly fashion, but to continue their insistence on the UN Commission. In this context he also discussed Acheson's urgent telegram. He concluded that the Soviet Note had made a significant impression in Washington. Moreover, McCloy had told him that the SPD wanted negotiations to discover whether or not the Soviets were serious.[27]

That same day, Schumacher also wrote to the Chancellor to explain the new line taken by the Social Democrats. His letter was beseeching, but also courteous: 'The Soviet Note of 9 April offers the possibility of ascertaining in Four Power negotiations whether an agreement of the four Powers can be achieved to guarantee the preconditions for free elections in the four Zones and Berlin ... In my view it is necessary to put it to the governments of the three Western Powers as the common German standpoint that no stone should be left unturned to determine whether the Soviet Note offers an opportunity to bring about the reunification of Germany in freedom. In order to determine this, Four Power negotiations should take place as soon as possible.' It was impossible to know 'whether there will be another chance for peaceful and democratic reunification' in the foreseeable future.[28]

The West German government and Opposition had now taken up their battle positions. Decades after the events discussed here, these positions are still a source of debate and historical controversy.

At precisely this moment, however, there was a crucial volte-face in American policy. At the beginning of May, Acheson, who had previously been inclined to dismiss the Soviet Note as a transparent piece of trouble-making, produced an outline for an answering Note in which the State Department took up the Soviet proposal for representatives of the High Commissioners to meet in Berlin as soon as possible in order to clarify the issue of free all-German elections.[29] The demand for the UN Commission was dropped, though the United States wanted the holding of free elections to be based upon the categorical 14 Point Resolution passed by the German Bundestag on 27 September 1951. It must be said that, for the U.S., this suggestion was made more in something of a self-confident poker game mood and did not reflect any real desire to seek a compromise with the Soviets. In addition, the U.S. was anxious to call the Soviet bluff well before the ratification debates over the West treaties.

Adenauer reacted with confusion. When McCloy first showed him the U.S. draft, the Chancellor said that such a meeting might actually help to convince the German people that the Western Allies were serious in their desire to obtain reunification on acceptable terms. However, such a meeting must be limited solely to discussing the conditions for free elections, as well as their supervision by a non-party international commission. The reference to the Bundestag proposals for an all-German electoral law might have a particularly positive effect on German opinion. Nevertheless, it was essential to avoid the impression that Four Power Control was being revived, and the High Commissioners themselves ought not to participate in such a meeting for that reason.[30]

In the light of his previous attitude, Adenauer's conditional approval was as astonishing as the change in the U.S. position. Scarcely had he adopted this attitude than he began to have reservations about it. His conversation with McCloy took place on 2 May. On 3 May, a Saturday, he was due to be visited by George F. Kennan, the recently appointed U.S. ambassador to Moscow, a man in whom Adenauer had an instinctive confidence because of his mastery of the German language and his lively interest in German culture. The days when the two men were to clash were still in the distant future. McCloy was also due to attend the diplomatic breakfast for Kennan, so that the problem could be discussed for a second time.

As was often the case when he faced a difficult issue, Adenauer slept badly and spend half the night brooding over the problem. In the morning he then had a meeting with Blankenhorn and von Eckardt, to discuss McCloy's suggestion that a conference be held between the Western High Commissioners and the Soviet High Commissioner, Chuikov. Both his advisers had reservations. As Blankenhorn recalled, von Eckardt 'rightly indicated that such a division of the Soviet Note into the problem of free elections and other problems involves great dangers. If the Soviets make concessions regarding free elections at such a conference, then there is the danger that German public opinion will see this problem alone and demand that all the other questions raised in the Russian Note should be put aside. Also the danger that public opinion and parliament might demand postponement of the signing of the General Treaty and supplementary treaties like the EDC. In this case European integration would be greatly threatened.'[31] On this decisive point Adenauer's watchful advisers thus drew him back to his standard line. He instructed Blankenhorn to discuss the new objections with the American deputy High Commissioner without delay.

In the High Commission itself, however, the British had already made these same objections the day before. On the other hand, both the British and French were considering whether the revival of Four Power discussions in Berlin might not provide a useful warning to the procrastinating Germans. It could be made clear to them that the Western Powers had the alternative of returning to Four Power Control if Bonn continued to cause problems over the EDC and other treaties.[32]

After the official breakfast, Adenauer held an hour-long conversation with Kennan. The American was about to travel to Moscow with his family to take over the post of ambassador. However, his wife remained behind in Bonn, where she gave birth to a child five days after her husband left for the Soviet Union.[33]

Kennan had a great deal of knowledge about the Soviet Union, but – at that stage – no information about what was actually happening in Moscow. Adenauer was unaware that, before his departure, Kennan had met Dean Acheson and his senior advisers for talks. It had been made crystal clear to him that Washington currently had no desire for an East-West agreement over Germany, nor for any discussions which might help to bring it about. The treaties with Bonn and the EDC had to be concluded before discussions with the Soviets could be resumed, since such talks could only complicate the entire issue. When Kennan disagreed, Acheson told him that U.S. policy towards Europe would suffer a severe setback unless the treaties were signed within six weeks. Nothing should be said or done to direct attention away from these projects.[34]

Between 1944 and 1948 Kennan had been one of the advocates of a hard-line policy against the Soviet Union. Yet in spring 1952, he was increasingly critical of the prevailing spirit in Washington. In contrast to the period between 1949 and 1950, he believed, the Americans were now strong and even superior. The hydrogen bomb was in production and was to be successfully tested on 1 November 1952, immediately before the Presidential election. As a consequence of the Korean shock, the United States had also restored its military strength. The economy was booming. Kennan sensed a mood akin to that of the last years of the Second World War, when the U.S. had demanded unconditional surrender from their enemies. This was U.S. omnipotence, with no sign of any willingness to reach a compromise with the country's opponents.[35]

The Ambassador made a powerful impression on Adenauer as he mentioned a few days later in cabinet.[36] He strengthened his own view that there would be no war, and told the Chancellor that Soviet policy, too, was dictated partly by fear. At a suitable moment, therefore, it would be necessary to remove that fear and negotiate with the Soviets. Of course, East-West relations must be seen as a single whole. Nevertheless, Kennan believed that negotiations were possible and explained that it was his task not to let the moment pass. It was not flattery, but rather reflected Kennan's genuine opinion, when he assured Adenauer that there were only two embassies in the Soviet Union before the war which had made the effort to understand: that of the U.S. and that of Germany. Adenauer, who was always gratified to hear praise of Germany, was not likely to ignore such a remark.

Subsequently, Adenauer and McCloy discussed the Allied reply yo the Soviet Note yet again.[37] The Chancellor explained that he had considered the issue for a day and night and concluded that the U.S. proposal for a meeting of the High Commissioners in Berlin would be a mistake at the moment. If the suggestion was made now, he doubted whether the cabinet would authorise him to put his signature to the treaties until it was discovered whether the Soviets were sincere in their offer of free elections.

It was to be expected not only that the Opposition would make this demand, but also that certain cabinet members would be sympathetic to such an suggestion. Adenauer then explained to McCloy the objection that had been raised by von Eckardt: to focus the negotiations exclusively on the demand for free elections, in which the Soviets might conceivably make concessions, might distract public attention from the unacceptable structural aspects of the Soviet peace initiative. Once German public opinion became obsessed with the idea that free elections were within reach, it would be impossible to conclude the negotiations over the Western treaties.

Adenauer therefore made a tactical proposal that the High Commissioners should immediately remind their Soviet colleague Chuikov, in writing, of an earlier letter on the subject of free elections which had not been answered. If Chuikov answered promptly, then the Allies could react appropriately; if – as seemed likely – he did not, this too could be mentioned in the reply. However, it was essential for the West to focus attention on the question of whether an all-German government would be allowed to take part in the Coal and Steel Community, the EDC, and other moves towards European integration.

Before McCloy's cable arrived in Washington on 3 May, the steering group in London had decided – on the basis of British and French objections – to drop the call for a meeting of the High Commissioners in Berlin.

When the Western reply was finally sent on 13 May, Adenauer was satisfied both with the content and the nature of his own participation. He was to record later in his memoirs that 'The Note had my full approval'.[38] Lenz, on the other hand, recalled a more graphic remark of the Chancellor: the Western Powers had managed the Note very well. He himself would not have succeeded in that way.[39]

Meanwhile, the attention of the German public had turned once again to the negotiations over the Western treaties, which were now entering their final phase.

The Breakthrough:
The Signing of the Western Treaties

Seldom in the course of Adenauer's life was there such a fine line between success and failure as in the weeks before the signing of the Western treaties on 26 and 27 May 1952. On no other occasion, moreover, were his skill in negotiations and his toughness more convincingly displayed.

Since the middle of April all the West European governments had been aware of Dean Acheson's deadline – his demand that the treaties must be completed by the middle of May at the latest. And yet, Adenauer's constant negotiations with the High Commissioners on the General Treaty and the supplementary agreements continued until the foreign ministers conference which had been planned for the second half of May. a number of important points had to be resolved at the summit negotiations themselves.

The agreement on the EDC was initialled on 9 May, but even then the negotiations for this complex treaty were not complete, ensuring that a crisis at the conference was inevitable. The greatest difficulties were made by the Dutch, who intended to withdraw from the EDC should the NATO treaty be terminated at some unforeseen future date. Moreover, it remained uncertain to the last whether the Pinay government in France would sign at all without some guarantees from the British and Americans to cover the possibility of a withdrawal of the German contingents from the EDC.

During these crucial weeks in international politics, the coalition in West Germany also showed signs of instability. Previously Adenauer had been successful in his brazen determination to keep the cabinet and the coalition parties out of the hairy treaty negotiations. Constitutionally he had done so with a clear conscience: treaty negotiations were clearly the responsibility of the federal government, and specifically of the Foreign Minister and the Federal Chancellor, who was also responsible for the actions of Theodor Blank.

From the outset Adenauer had been unhappy with the manner in which the Opposition had attempted to make the Foreign Affairs Committee of the Bundestag, under the chairmanship of Carlo Schmid, into a foreign-policy alternative government. He was also aware that certain influential members of the CDU/CSU, led by von Brentano but also including Eugen Gerstenmaier and Kurt Georg Kiesinger, were dissatisfied with the failure to involve them in most decisions. Even fifteen years later in his memoirs, Adenauer did not hide his opinion of the Foreign Affairs Committee and the sub-committee established to deal with the Western treaties: 'The Bundestag was a very young parliament, and many of its members tried to get involved everywhere in the executive, where they had no business. In our view the federal government had to take great care that the executive and legislative branches remained separate. That was particularly true of all matters affecting relations with the High Commission and the Allied powers.'[1]

In view of the struggle waged against the treaties by the SPD, this can be seen as simple good sense; subsequent West German governments were to behave in the same way when engaged in highly controversial treaty negotiations. However, this determination to avoid giving the Opposition any ammunition to use against the treaties before it was necessary also meant that influential frontbenchers in the coalition parties were kept in the dark. Not even the cabinet was fully informed about the progress of negotiations.

This was certainly deliberate, even though Adenauer knew that he would face difficulties as soon as he revealed the explosive contents of the treaty. However, he believed that his policy would be destroyed if he kept his own side fully informed. Too many of his coalition had reservations about either all or part of it, and might easily wreck everything if they were given the opportunity. Adenauer was aware of the profound objections of the 'all-German' wing of his party; he also knew that deputies with an interest in the budget were anxious that he might accept heavy financial burdens in the interests of his foreign-policy objectives. Fritz Schäffer, though a firm advocate of ties with the West, did not trust the Allies or Adenauer where the budget was concerned, and was determined to limit the damage as much as possible.

Adenauer was particularly alarmed by the internal tensions and divisions within the FDP. Some of its Land associations had plans to transform the FDP into the great party of the right in time for the federal election of 1953; by contrast, the south-west German liberals, under the influence of Reinhold Maier in Stuttgart, were engaged in forming a coalition with the SPD. Though the right wing of the FDP was a vital pillar of the federal government, there was inevitably opposition to Adenauer's approach on the issues of reunification, the Saar, and various points in the treaties. Equally, the DP – which would be competing with the CDU and the FDP for the same voters in 1953 – could not afford to stand back on these issues.

The Chancellor was also aware of the relevance of the situation in France. There the foreign affairs committee of the National Assembly possessed the same extensive powers *vis-à-vis* the executive that Carlo Schmid – with the discreet support of some coalition members – hoped to obtain for the Foreign Affairs Committee in Bonn. The consequences of this situation in Paris were serious, since the French government was repeatedly bound by resolutions which had won simple majorities in the plenum of the National Assembly. This was one of the reasons why Robert Schuman, in in terms of his political influence in 1952, was little more than a shadow of his former self.

By contrast, one of the reasons for the Chancellor's influence in his dealings with Britain and the United States, at least, was the fact that he could demonstrate firm control of his coalition. Negotiations with the German Chancellor were therefore free of the perennial difficulties which for years had bedevilled discussions with French governments. It was this factor, above all others, that stemmed Western fears of uncontrollable fluctuations in the foreign policy of the infant Federal Republic. Western governments were certainly well aware of Adenauer's readiness to resort to a battery of annoying tactical expedients. However, in the final analysis his course was largely predictable, and the outside world came to regard his ability to control the centrifugal forces in the Bundestag as a factor for stability.

Now that the treaties were to be placed before the Bundestag for approval, such a policy of secrecy could no longer be sustained. Von Brentano put himself at the head of a mutiny by the parliamentary CDU/CSU and demanded to see the text of the treaty in its current form. Adenauer, who had actually hoped to avoid revealing the text until after the signing ceremony, was now forced to abandon this plan.

Von Brentano was also irritated by Adenauer's failure to welcome his wish to become West German Foreign Minister. When he saw the first summary of the General Treaty and the annexe treaties, he was appalled – or at least behaved as if he was.[2] The unrest within the parliamentary CDU/CSU coincided with similar turmoil in the FDP. With Blücher refusing to stand aside from this turmoil, a special committee of ministers and deputies belonging to the coalition parties was formed under his chairmanship. The genie had been let out of the bottle, with consequences that were impossible to predict.

Von Brentano received the first detailed information during the weekend of 19/20 April. On 25 April, in the company of Pferdmenges, he informed Adenauer that the treaties in their current form would not obtain a majority in the Bundestag. With some justice, he also pointed out that the parliamentary calender would already be fully stretched during May.

The legislation on the *Lastenausgleich* (Equalization of Burdens) was about to be passed, threatening a major row with the dissatisfied expellees within the party. A rally was being planned by the expellee associations to bring 60,000 of their members to Bonn – a huge number in current circumstances. Moreover, there was cause for concern about the result of the federal election if the troublesome CDU expellee politician Linus Kather actually carried out his threat to leave the party. In that case, the unstable expellee party, the BHE, might hold the balance of power after the election.

As if that were not enough, the trade unions were protesting against the government's draft legislation governing industrial relations. The coalition was no longer prepared – as it had been in the law on co-determination in heavy industry – to keep the peace by expanding the 1951 coal and steel model of co-determination throughout large-scale industry, as the DGB demanded. As a consequence of the token strike that followed, no newspapers appeared during the prestigious foreign ministers conference in Bonn.

Von Brentano was insistent in his argument that the treaties should not be initialled within the next two weeks. If Adenauer were to initial them without being aware of opinion within the coalition, and if the Bundestag were then to vote them down, 'that would be the end of our policy.[3]

In a long letter of 25 April, which Adenauer was now certain to study closely, von Brentano listed the criticisms which lay at the heart of the debate: Article VII, 3 of the Germany Treaty, the emergency clause, the annexe treaties, and – not least – the financial burdens associated with them. In addition, the failure to make progress in granting pardons to Germans sentenced for war crimes was also giving rise to discontent. The CDU politician did not hide his own views: 'But I have the impression – and I cannot remain silent – that the negotiations may not have been conducted as they ought to have been conducted.'[4]

Three days before the EDC treaty system was initialled on 9 May, von Brentano still had not received a copy of the text. His reaction was bitter. It was, he argued, an impossible state of affairs 'when not even the chairman of the biggest party in the Bundestag, and the party which also bears the vital responsibility in the mind of the German people, is informed about the contents'.[5]

Von Brentano's comments to Theodor Blank in Paris were less restrained: 'Over the course of the last months I have detected such a misjudgement of the tasks and also the rights of parliament that I must fight against it resolutely. If we want to return to the secret policy of the bureaucracy, then we must have the courage to say so openly, and each of us must draw the conclusions he thinks are right.'[6] He was about to send this letter on 7 May when Lieutenant-Colonel de Maizière arrived from Paris with the text of the treaties.

On 25 April, the day on which von Brentano attacked Adenauer's secret policy with the unanimous support of the leadership of the parliamentary party, minister-president Maier in Stuttgart was forming a government of the FDP/DVP, SPD and BHE. Adenauer was appalled. He was well aware of the implications for the ratification of the treaties in the German upper house, the Bundesrat – the possibility of a majority against the treaties. The consequences at federal level were immediately apparent. On 9 May, together with the SPD-governed Länder, the government of Baden-Württemberg rejected government legislation designed to raise the federal share of income and corporation tax from 27 per cent to 40 per cent.

Adenauer's response was swift. Three days after the formation of a government in Baden-Württemberg, he asked the High Commissioners to remove from the supplementary treaties all those regulations which required approval by the Bundesrat. On 8 May he repeated his warnings – with some justification, it soon became clear – and asked the High Commissioners to recognise the seriousness of the situation. His entire policy was under threat, and the issue was the most important to emerge to date. He also threatened to leave it to his cabinet to decide whether to risk rejection in the Bundestag. Specifically at stake was the controversial subject of reimbursement for confiscated German assets. The High Commissioners, however, insisted on the agreed texts and rejected Adenauer's suggestion that the provisions in question should be lifted from the treaties and be put – unchanged – to the vote in the Bundestag as simple federal laws.

McCloy responded by pointing out that the one per cent of provisions which required the assent of the Bundesrat and which Adenauer hoped to remove from the treaties, were precisely the issues which the Germans found least palatable. The implication, though unspoken, was clear: Adenauer was trying to remove a number of irksome conditions from the treaties and submit them to a separate vote. Then, should the legislation be rejected, he would be able to appear before the High Commissioners with clean hands and blame its failure on the ill-will of the majority in the Bundestag. At the same time, however, the federal government would have endorsed the advantageous provisions of the General Treaty. As a result of these objections, the treaties remained in their original form, a fact which led to considerable difficulties in the Bundesrat in the spring of 1953.

In fact, Adenauer himself had encouraged the suspicions of the High Commissioners at the end of April when, under pressure from within the coalition, he had asked for further examination of the annexe treaties. The deputies, he argued, would be unable to master them in their current form, and the treaties would be greatly improved if part of the regulations of an administrative nature were removed. Clearly these last-minute objections had aroused suspicion that the Chancellor was hoping to eliminate or soften many of the provisions he found unpalatable. This attempt to improve certain aspects of the texts produced no significant results.

Further critical points related to the financing of the defence contribution, which had not yet been fully clarified, and the winding down of occupation costs. In addition to the German defence contribution, the Western Allies wanted a major contribution to the cost of stationing Allied troops, and were also eager to use the treaty in order to shift the costs for the restitution of German assets onto the Germans themselves. Once again Fritz Schäffer offered his resignation. Adenauer told Otto Lenz that such a move was completely incomprehensible at this time; Schäffer had antagonized the Allies with his petty-minded negotiating style and had 'certainly cost us millions'.[7] At the cabinet meeing of 11 May, where financial issues were discussed, Schäffer repeated his criticism of excessive Allied demands. Though he was no longer talking of resignation, he announced that, in future, all payments of over 500 million marks for occupation costs must be authorized by him personally. If this did not suit the Allies, they would have to demand his resignation from the Chancellor.

Adenauer was greatly concerned that his Vice Chancellor, Blücher, had joined the ranks of his critics during these crucial weeks, though it was not clear how far his political associates would risk destroying the coalition. Nor was it clear whether Adenauer knew that, at the beginning of May, the FDP executive committee had decided to leave the coalition if the treaties were not improved.[8] The letter Adenauer received from Blücher on 9 May[9] revealed that the crisis in the coalition might even topple the government, because elements of the CDU/CSU and the DP were among the rebels.

Blücher demanded a whole series of amendments to the General Treaty. For example, he saw the Emergency Article V as 'unacceptable in this form as a gross violation of equal rights'. However, the FDP was most opposed to Article VII, 3, which it deemed to be 'unacceptable'. Blücher's justification of the rejection of the binding clause was somewhat tortuous: 'It opens up the possibility for the Eastern Zone to conclude a treaty with the Russians in which the Eastern Zone assures the Russians of the binding nature of the obligations undertaken for the reunited Germany. Paragraph 3 in its current form would also justify the Soviet thesis, which will certainly be advanced, that any possibility of negotiations over reunification is being closed.'

The accompaniment to this warning shot was provided by the FDP deputy Ernst Mayer, who described the General Treaty as a 'treaty of subjugation'. Similarly, Hans Mühlenfeld, chairman of the DP parliamentary party, declared that his party would not vote for 'a second Versailles' – though he was to deny it later.[10] Even young Franz Josef Strauss from the CSU, in an interview with *Die Welt*, expressed 'serious reservations' and demanded the opening of new negotiations.[11]

Adenauer sent Blücher a long letter by return of post, and gave him a severe dressing-down.[12] As always when he felt himself to be under siege, he began by attacking the conduct of his critics as foolish or improper. He was particularly angry that the FDP had decided to assemble its party executive along with the parliamentary party executive and representatives of the FDP's Foreign Affairs Committee for an initial discussion of the General Treaty: 'If I were to imagine the CDU/CSU and DP parliamentary parties behaving in the same way, then by my reckoning the result would be four separate committees, with around one hundred people in total here in Germany, all making suggestions about changes. Imagine, please, the same thing being done in France, in England, in the United States ...'

There was no need to explain how ludicrous such a situation would be. Adenauer did, however, take care to stress that such conduct would also be 'extraordinarily damaging', because the secrecy which was an indispensable part of foreign-policy negotiations would – intentionally or not – be endangered. He ended with another barb, reminding Blücher that the FDP parliamentary party had already discussed the General Treaty in some detail – which included reading out some of the provisions – before the February defence debate. Moreover, every cabinet member had received a copy of the text of the General Treaty.

Adenauer's letter included several bitter reproaches which were barely offset by occasional courtesies. Such conduct, he wrote, was 'completely against any agreement and brings the entire matter into terrible confusion'. He saw Blücher's letter as threatening 'the collapse of any foreign policy', warned of the domestic political consequences, and thundered: 'The foreign policy future of Germany is thus called completely in question. It is my impression that many of our gentlemen, by taking pleasure in tinkering with the wording of the treaties, are failing to have due regard for the facts and the dangerous situation in which we are living.'

This was the prelude to the virtually continuous cabinet meetings of 10, 11, 12, 13, 14, 16, 20 and 23 May, in which the ministers and chairmen of the parliamentary parties were involved in bitter debate. Throughout this period, Adenauer and his representatives were also continuing to negotiate with the High Commissioners.

The great round of cabinet meetings was preceded by a fraught meeting of the CDU/CSU parliamentary executive,[13] at which a crotchety von Brentano outlined the objections of the parliamentary party and claimed that the party could not commit itself because it was still inadequately informed. He was well aware of the consequences of a failure of the negotiations, he stated ominously – they would bring about the fall of the government.

Adenauer listened to the attack white-faced and with both hands bandaged because of an eczema. Still, he remained calm and adopted a placatory tone with his colleagues. McCloy was aware, he told them, that the Chancellor would not know whether he was in a position to sign until after his discussions with the cabinet and the parliamentary party.

On 10 May, when the series of crucial cabinet meetings began, Adenauer remained in poor physical health[14] and continued to wear bandages on his hands. Yet even with the fate of his entire policy in the balance, he left the cabinet meeting for several hours in order to visit his brother August, who was celebrating his 80th birthday and was to be presented with the Great Federal Service Cross by the President.

Before the deliberations began, the Minister for the Postal Service, Schuberth, announced that the room had been thoroughly searched and that it was technically almost impossible to introduce a listening device undetected. He was not, however, completely certain that this was the case.

Adenauer began by endeavouring to place the discussions in their overall context. To that end, he mentioned a conversation he had conducted with the High Commissioners the day before, when he had asked whether it was true that there would be no possibility of new negotiations if the Bundestag voted down the treaties. The three High Commissioners, he informed the cabinet, had looked at him in astonishment before confirming unanimously that there would be no further negotiations. If the Bundestag rejected the treaties, that would be the end.

The Chancellor then spoke of the motives of the Allies during the negotiations, which had lasted well over a year. These negotiations had not been conducted out of love for the Germans, but solely because of the Soviet threat. Sentiments towards the Germans remained very negative abroad, except among the Americans. Not only were the misdeeds of the Nazis still fresh in the memory, but the rapid economic recovery had aroused fears of German competitive strength. Adenauer then adopted an approach which was later taken up by subsequent Chancellors when they faced the task of explaining unsuccessful negotiations to the cabinet and coalition: he stressed that the Germans were facing the consequences of a war Germany had lost. If his colleagues thought that positive political and economic developments since 1949 had already brought the country back to the ranks of equal and free peoples, they were mistaken. If the Bundestag failed to ratify the treaties, the Occupation Statute would be re-imposed in full. Of course the Western Allies had loosened their controls on the defeated Germans to a certain degree, and he had not been called to the Petersberg since April of the preceding year – but he could be summoned back at any time.

Adenauer described what he saw as the disastrous consequences of non-ratification before continuing with his favourite ploy – a panoramic survey of the international political situation. If Germany were not included in the defence of the West, then the NATO defensive concept could not be sustained. Germany would be the battleground if war broke out. In such circumstances the Soviets would make sure that industrial plants in Germany were destroyed, while the Americans and British would dynamite everything that might help the Soviets.

However, he believed that current tensions would pass without war, a view which was also held by Eisenhower and Kennan. Adenauer was also convinced that both the United States and Britain wanted German unification, without which there could be no peace in Europe. Even in France, where this view was far from universal, it was shared in influential circles. However, an agreement with the Soviet Union could only come to pass in the context of an overall settlement. Clearly there would be enormous repercussions if the Eastern Zone was released from its position as a Soviet satellite. The German question could not be isolated from worldwide and European East-West tensions. Two-thirds of the treaty system under negotiation was in the nature of a peace treaty and its positive aspects had to be understood; his colleagues must consider what would happen if Germany were not a member of the Western alliance. We are, he told them, a defeated people.

A major element in his plea for the acceptance of the treaties involved the effect of German decisions on U.S. public opinion. Two weeks previously,[15] in cabinet, he had bemoaned the American people's susceptibility to mass psychoses and and their well-known instability. Profound shifts in U.S. opinion within 24 hours could not be ruled out. If Senator Taft became President, or so one U.S. Senator had told Hallstein, he would reverse policy on the spot and withdraw from Europe. The result would be catastrophic.

On this occasion, then, Adenauer laid more stress on the consequences of non-ratification than on his visions of a positive European future. However, he also emphasised that European federation was the only alternative to the defeat of Occidental culture.

The Chancellor's views were then supported by Hallstein, who pointed out that – in contrast to the Versailles Treaty of 1919 – the current treaties had been negotiated. In this process the federal government had managed to secure more than 130 changes to improve the Allied drafts.

During this cabinet meeting, the emergency article was the source of numerous objections. When it was attacked by von Brentano, Adenauer calmly maintained that, once German troops were established, the right to declare a state of emergency under Article V could no longer be exerted without the participation of the federal government.

From the beginning, however, the discussion focussed primarily on Article VII, 3. As Hallstein outlined the prelude to this article, it became clear that the crucial role had been played by Robert Bowie. Since the original intention had been to bind the Allies, it would be dangerous to drop Article VII, 3 because that would also ensure that the Western Allies were no longer committed. This was also the argument used by Adenauer to dismiss a version proposed by the DP deputy von Merkatz. The Chancellor noted dryly that his colleagues must decide whether they wanted to bind the Western Powers or – out of regard to the Soviets – refuse any ties on behalf of a new government. He pointed out that the Germans had not been offered the transfer of rights and that his negotiators had been forced to fight for it. When the deputy Wellhausen remarked that it would be hard to convince the German people that the Article would bind the unreliable French, Adenauer stated: 'We will manage it though!'

Adenauer gladly took up a suggstion from the FDP that the link between the implementation of the EDC and the General Treaty should be dropped. This particular argument was to be taken up at the foreign ministers conference.

The Chancellor remained remarkably calm during the day-long meeting, although the strains led one of his minister, Niklas, to suffer a fainting fit. At one stage Lenz showed Adenauer a newspaper extract which argued that the Chancellor was resorting to a threat to resign in the attempt to force the treaty through. Lenz noted: 'He pushed it aside with a smile, as if to say that was the last thing to happen.'

The following day was devoted to financial questions. Once again Adenauer collected arguments for the final negotiations.

In the cabinet meeting of 12 May,[16] Adenauer began by complaining that the pro-CDU newspaper *Kölnische Rundschau* had published a number of indiscreet comments which could only have come from participants at the cabinet meetings. Theodor Blank then introduced the EDC Treaty. When the ban on chemical weapons was discussed, Blank noted: 'It is a good thing that we won't be able to produce this filth.' The subsequent report by General Heusinger was designed to convince the cabinet members – as well as the representatives of the parliamentary parties, who were equally, if not more important – that Germany could not be defended without German divisions.

Minister Hellwege of the DP then raised the question of Germans imprisoned for alleged war crimes, and argued that the German people could not be expected to fight as long as officers such as von Manstein remained in prison. Adenauer, however, refused outright to make a link between ratification and the granting of pardons and showed signs of agitation when he discussed the Nazi era. The Chancellor also emphasised that he had taken every opportunity to declare that this matter would have to be settled.

Of particular interest to the participants was an intervention by Adenauer when the subject returned to the financing of armaments. He maintained that West Germany must pay for its heavy weapons, but that he himself would not recruit a single man unless the Germans received the same weapons as the others.

Adenauer had now concluded that he would not be able to gain acceptance for the binding clause in its current form. Further negotiations would probably also be required over the emergency clause. On the morning of 13 May[17] the cabinet discussed proposed amendments to both the issues under dispute. The crucial point, to which Adenauer held firm throughout with all his old obstinacy, was that the Western Powers must be bound by treaty. Any form of agreement with the Soviets at the expense of the Germans had to be avoided.

This he linked with another line of argument. It was essential to proceed with a certain caution in demanding changes to Article VII, 3 because of the need to avoid arousing suspicion in the West that the Federal Republic would try to wriggle out of the treaties after reunification. In this context he mentioned an impending conversation with an American journalist, who would be asking him whether an SPD government would keep the treaties. He intended to answer by wagering that there would be no SPD government in 1953.

This somewhat confused discussion in cabinet of prospective alterations was followed that same day by seven hours of negotiations with the High Commissioners. Subject to the agreement of the government, a significant new version of Article VII was agreed upon. Paragraph 1 was to remain unchanged, but Paragraphs 2 and 3 were rewritten:

> (2) Pending the peace settlement, the three powers and the FedRep will cooperate to achieve, by peaceful means, their common aim of a unified Ger enjoying a liberal-democratic constitution, like that of the FedRep, and integrated within the Eur community.

> (3) The three powers and the FedRep agree that a unified Ger shall be entitled to the rights and be bound by the obligations of the FedRep under the present convention and the related conventions and the treaties for the formation of an integrated Eur community, as adjusted according to their terms or by agmt of the parties thereto.[18]

The meeting at which the differences were to be settled ended in general exhaustion at 10 pm. Adopting his usual jocular manner on such occasions, François-Poncet suggested a new version of the German national anthem 'Thoroughness, justice and freedom' (instead of 'unity, justice and freedom').

On the following day,[19] Adenauer reported to the cabinet that concessions would be granted over Article VII. If necessary, some formal changes could be made to the emergency clause. The arguments over Article VII, 3 now broke out anew. Adenauer commented that the achievement of this formula was worth more than all the idle talk about the new version. Jakob Kaiser, however, argued that in reality France wanted the current version because it prevented the reunification of Germany. Adenauer reproached him for adopting the position of the SPD, to the effect that all-German elections must be held before the treaties could be signed. Dehler then observed, quite correctly, that the discussion of Article VII was really about whether the entire basis of previous policy had been correct.

The lines of conflict were clearly drawn. In the final analysis Jakob Kaiser was opposed to any definitive ties to the Western Powers. Adenauer, on the other hand, was using all the means at his disposal to prevent these issues remaining open in the event of reunification.

Under the direction of Grewe, the German side continued to negotiate throughout this period, with particular attention being devoted to the transitional treaty. The negotiations on 15 May, for example, ended only at 5 am the following day. Neither side, Adenauer declared in the cabinet meeting of 16 May, was now sure exactly what had been decided. It was essential to pause and take stock. This also meant that the Foreign Affairs Committee ought not to be informed of the proceedings immediately.

After a discussion of critical points in the treaty with Israel, the cabinet met at 8.30 pm to continue its interminable discussions of Article VII. Hallstein reported that the negotiations with the Western Allies were reverting to the old formula. Once again Hallstein urged his colleagues to adopt his approach, which was to see the question as a whole. He maintained that the only reason the SPD was opposed to ties was because of their desire to accommodate the Soviets, which could not be done. One aspects in these discussions was the Western reply to the Soviet Note on 13 May, which had been based on the idea of a German government with freedom of action. Adenauer listened to further attacks by Blücher on Article VII, 3, before returning home in irritation.

According to notes taken by Lenz, the Article was then attacked both by Thomas Dehler and by the representative of the parliamentary parties, von Brentano of the CDU, Franz Josef Strauss of the CSU, and Hermann Schäffer of the FDP. On the other hand, Fritz Schäffer and von Merkatz of the DP were in favour.

On this issue, then, the opposition to Adenauer came from the FDP and influential members of the CDU/CSU caucus. Schäffer summarised the results of the discussion by proposing that the Chancellor be urged to drop Article VII, 3 if this was possible.

The issue continued to create instability within the coalition. On the afternoon of 20 May, with the preparations for the signing programme already under way, Adenauer finally decided to give in to the pressue from the parliamentary parties. Lenz, who on the previous day had tried to provide palatable versions of the Article for the cabinet, himself now pleaded for it to be dropped. The mood in the Bundestag was such that ratification of the General Treaty with Article VII, 3 in its current form appeared unlikely. Lenz now wanted a common sense approach: if an all-German government took Adenauer's view, it would be committed to the Article anyway; if it did not, then not even Article VII, 3 would bind it. During the discussion between Adenauer, Lenz and Globke, though Globke continued to urge that the Article should be retained, Adenauer finally accepted the assessment of Lenz.[20]

At the beginning of the cabinet meeting of 20 May[21] Adenauer asked about the current position of Article VII, 3 before consenting to submit to the will of the majority. His ministers should decide as they wished; his only desire was to make their responsibility clear to them. Blücher declared that the majority in the cabinet was convinced that the Article should be dropped. This was followed by lengthy and familiar remarks from Jakob Kaiser concerning the need to work for the unity of Germany. However, the meeting then switched abruptly to a renewed debate on the fundamentals.

Retention of Article VII, 3 was urged by Ludwig Erhard, Robert Lehr, Hans-Christoph Seebohm, and Fritz Schäffer. Of the FDP ministers, Blücher and Dehler wanted to drop it because they regarded it as superfluous, while opposition from CDU members came not only from Kaiser and Robert Tillmans, but also from Anton Storch, the latter stressing the tactical point that otherwise there would be no majority for ratification.

For Adenauer the position held by the representatives of the parliamentary parties was decisive, since it indicated that the opposition of the FDP ministers was shared by only part of the party. The 17 DP deputies were also divided. Although von Merkatz supported retention of the Article, Adenauer read out a letter from the chairman of the parliamentary DP, Mühlenfeld, arguing that it should be dropped. The CDU/CSU parliamentary party continued to be split. Von Brentano declared that a majority of the party was against the Article and pleaded for it to be dropped in order to achieve ratification. He also attacked von Merkatz, who had accused the parliamentary CDU/CSU of instability. The CDU's Gerstenmaier then launched an attack on the chairman of his own parliamentary party, pointing out that he had spoken with two working groups and found that eight members of both had supported Article VII while two had opposed it. He personally favoured retention and believed that the attitude of the parliamentary party was far from clear.

Finally Adenauer called for a formal vote in which only three ministers – Blücher, Dehler and Jakob Kaiser – voted for the Article to be dropped. However, with the SPD resolved to vote against, it was clear that there would be no majority in the Bundestag, and Adenauer declared that he was prepared to drop the Article.

On the morning before the Western foreign ministers met in Bonn, a new cabinet meeting took place on 23 May. Adenauer informed his colleagues that the High Commissioners had refused to drop the Article. Such a fuss had been made of Article VII, 3 by the German press that its abandonment would be interpreted as a Soviet victory. The Allies, argued the Chancellor, were now deeply suspicious and he wondered whether the issue should be discussed among the foreign ministers yet again. In the meantime, a remark by Schumacher – that the man who signed these treaties would cease to be a German – had caused enormous ill-feeling.

Shortly before the first discussion with Dean Acheson, Adenauer again discussed the disputed Article with his closest advisers, Lenz,

Blankenhorn and Globke. He was particularly concerned by the opposition of the chairmen of the parliamentary parties and instructed Lenz to ask them for a written insistence on the abolition of Article VII, 3.[22]

On the morning of 25 May a crucial discussion took place between a number of deputies, led by von Brentano, and the American Secretary of State Dean Acheson. It is not certain whether Adenauer had given his reluctant consent to this meeting beforehand. Acheson, who combined a lawyer's expertise with a common-sense approach, argued that the Germans were exaggerating the significance of a purely theoretical question.[23] Could any third party – the Three Powers or the Federal Republic – really conclude a treaty that would be binding for a reunited Germany, which had not participated in the decision? Clearly they could not; they had power solely to limit their own freedom of action.

The assumption must be that only the Federal Republic and the Western Powers, and not a reunited Germany, would be bound by such agreement. However, these parties could of course be released from their obligations by mutual consent. He thus proposed a formula prepared by Philipp Jessup, which was accepted by the deputies and then by the other foreign ministers:

> In the event of the unification of Germany the Three Powers will, subject to such adjustments as may be agreed, extend to a unified Germany the rights which the Federal Republic has under the present Convention and the related Conventions and will for their part agree that the rights under the Treaties for the formation of an integrated European community should be similarly extended, upon the assumption by such a unified Germany of the obligations of the Federal Republic toward the Three Powers or to any of them under those Conventions and Treaties. Except by common consent of all the Signatory States the Federal Republic will not conclude any agreement or enter into any arrangement which would impair the rights of the Three Powers under those Conventions and Treaties or lessen the obligations of the Federal Republic thereunder.[24]

Individuals who had opposed the original formula so bitterly now accepted the new version as the solution to all their problems. Yet it is a mystery why these clear restrictions on the Federal Republic should be regarded as politically more acceptable than the anticipated – and legally impossible – ones on a reunited Germany. In the event of conflict, even without Article VII, 3, any of the Western governments could oppose the Federal Republic joining a reunited Germany unless that country was prepared to accept the obligations in the treaties.

In this version, the Western Allies themselves were bound only with regard to the status rights of the Federal Republic, which in any case did not extend to full sovereignty. After ratification of the treaties the West German government would have a right of veto over any deterioration in its status as long as it adhered to the EDC. The obligations of the Western Allies, however, remained somewhat unclear. The whole arrangement was too ambiguous, would immediately lead to differences of opinion in an emergency, and did not in any case provide complete security against a Western breach of faith. Yet what treaty guarantees by great powers have ever been wholly reliable?

It has been said that Adenauer bore a grudge against the participants for months after their intervention with Acheson. Whether or not this is true, on 29 May, after the signing of the Western treaties, von Brentano felt moved to assure the Chancellor of the 'special esteem and admiration' of the parliamentary CDU/CSU and to send him a bouquet of 'wonderful roses'.[25]

It would have been entirely uncharacteristic for Adenauer to accept the new version without comment during the final negotiations with the Western foreign ministers. When Acheson proposed the formula hammered out with the parliamentarians as the basis for an agreement, the Chancellor declared that he would agree to it only on condition that the Three Powers accepted the same obligations. Eden protested immediately, though he pointed out that an exchange of letters was being added to the treaty system as Appendix VI, in which the Western Allies undertook not to interpret their rights in regard to Article VII, Paragraph 1c in such a way 'that it permitted the Three Powers to deviate from the obligations which they have undertaken towards the Federal Republic in the treaty signed today'. Adenauer pointed out with some force, this solution was not satisfying. Since the Federal Republic was about to proclaim its loyalty to the treaty according to Article VII, 3, Sentence 2, he requested the same commitment from the Three Powers. However, he made no progress on this issue. Acheson declared authoritatively that this was the meaning of the letter in Appendix VI. Despite further objections from Hallstein, Adenauer was aware that he could not afford to push too hard and decided to let the matter drop.[26]

Later, in his memoirs, Acheson briefly outlined the great dispute over Article VII, 3 and dismissed it as a purely theoretical problem. Since there was no progress towards reunification during these years, his judgement is, in retrospect, correct. It was thus logical for the controversial Article VII, 3 to be dropped from the new version of the Germany Treaty in autumn 1954. By that stage, in Adenauer's view, it had fulfilled its purpose of providing preventive cover against a Western breach of faith and could safely be eliminated. In spring 1952, however, the international situation looked very different.

The unresolved and insoluble issues of policy towards Germany also appeared in another context. As regards the re-organization of German-Allied relations, the Western powers referred to 'contractual agreements', while the term General Treaty, with its unfortunate associations, had come into use on the German side. When Adenauer expressed the desire for another description, Lenz proposed the name Deutschlandvertrag

(Germany Treaty). This pleased the Chancellor, who sought to gain support for it during the final phase of negotiations with the High Commissioners. He argued that the official title 'Germany Treaty' should be adopted, at least in brackets, partly because it would make the task of public relations easier. Though McCloy preferred to refer the problem to foreign-minister level, François-Poncet made his own reservations clear. As the French High Commissioner pointed out, the General Treaty, far from being a 'Germany Treaty', was a treaty about 'West Germany', a 'partial piece', a 'prelude' to a German peace treaty! For good or ill Adenauer was forced to give way, remarking that he had no objections to the term 'partial piece'.[27]

This skirmish illustrated the continuing underlying uncertainties connected with the system of treaties. The Federal Republic deliberately called itself 'Germany', and for the Western Allied governments and their peoples Adenauer did indeed represent the 'German' government. Nevertheless, to a considerable degree the debates turned on an 'all-Germany' which existed only as a subject in international law. Though the Federal Republic claimed to be the legal successor to the German Reich, and indeed to be identical to it, not even the Americans were willing to concede so much.

And what would this 'all-Germany' or 'reunified Germany' eventually be? Would it simply be the Federal Republic of the Basic Law, enlarged by the Eastern Zone and, as the majority of Germans still hoped, as much as possible of the lost eastern territories? Article VII, 3 was basically in alignment with this view, since it stipulated that the links between the Federal Republic and the West would also extend to a reunited Germany.

On the other hand, would a reunited Germany be a completely new state, produced by all-German elections and probably equipped with its own constitution? This was apparently the view taken not only by the SPD, but also by Jakob Kaiser and the 'all-German' wing of the coalition, and was also the logic underlying the remarks made by François-Poncet at the High Commissioners' meeting with Adenauer. According to this view, the Federal Republic would be no more than an ephemeral phenomenon. Any attempt to determine the nature of a reunited Germany beforehand would, accordingly, be highly questionable from both a legal and a political point of view.

At this stage there was no serious consideration, either in the Federal Republic or among the Western Allies, of the possibility that two German states – a liberal democracy in the West and a Communist state in the East – could claim a legitimate right to existence. To the extent that a clear view was possible at all, the only alternatives seemed to be a Federal Republic extended to all-Germany, or a new creation which would absorb the structures established by the occupying powers.

Adenauer himself was unwilling to draw the line too sharply. Nevertheless, he clearly felt that Germany had already found the best constitutional form, and the best foreign policy orientation, in the Federal Republic. There was a clear logical analogy with Italy in the years of the *Risorgimento.* Just as modern Italy had gradually developed from the core state of Piedmont, so a reunited Germany would only take shape over a period of time. In this sense the Federal Republic was the German Piedmont, the Eastern Zone and the Saar were the *Irredenta* – and the issue of the borders in the east remained open.

In Adenauer's view, this development was well under way. He therefore disagreed fundamentally with those among his countrymen who regarded the events since the end of the war as a temporary phenomenon and wanted to restore the German Reich which had fallen under the sovereignty of the victorious powers with the unilateral proclamation of 5 June 1945. Adenauer believed that the Federal Republic of Germany, as the legal successor to the German Reich, was an established and permanent structure, not as a German part-state alongside the GDR but as the core state which would be the basis for reunification.

In this sense his foreign policy, despite its peaceful intent, was fundamentally revisionist. The same was also true of his approach to the eastern territories. Of course, Adenauer's stubborn revisionism during the negotiations over the eastern border contained strong tactical elements, not only domestically where he was aware of the sensitivities and the political weight of 13 million expellees, but also in foreign policy. By raising the border question in 1951, he was deliberately placing obstacles across the path towards a possible Western acceptance of the Soviet position on the German question. Yet his approach was by no means purely Machiavellian: in 1951 and 1952 Adenauer was a genuine revisionist in *Ostpolitik,* along with every other influential politician in the Federal Republic at the time.

Like many other Frenchman, Robert Schuman had been appalled by Adenauer's comments regarding the Oder-Neisse Line in autumn 1951. Shortly afterwards, however, Adenauer assured him that he was aware of the need to achieve a peaceful settlement with Poland.[28] The Chancellor said the same thing to Acheson, and was probably sincere. Though he was personally convinced that the utmost that could be achieved for the eastern territories was a complicated status under UN supervision which also took account of Polish claims, it remains true that, in the early 1950s, he was less resigned to the inevitable than he was to become by the middle of the decade.

All these issues and more were involved in the apparently trivial question of the name of the treaty, which remained open to the last. Eventually, at the final negotiations, Acheson proposed a compromise which Adenauer was content to accept: the General Treaty would not be given any official supplementary title, leaving each signatory free to give it the title it saw fit. Acheson considered that a generally accepted supplementary title would emerge naturally as time passed.

While the cabinet discussions were in full swing, the information came through that Bonn was likely to be chosen as the location of the foreign ministers conference and the signing of the General Treaty. Adenauer had made this proposal at a relatively early stage, but had been convinced that The Hague would be preferred. Now, however, it had been decided that the treaty system would be signed in two places – the Germany Treaty and the supplementary treaties in Bonn, the EDC Treaty in Paris.

For the purposes of gaining acceptance of the treaties within West Germany, the choice of Bonn as location for the conference was a great success. Nothing could demonstrate the change in the status of the Federal Republic more vividly than Adenauer's appearance there, alongside the foreign ministers of the three Western Great Powers. The Chancellor was also determined to use every instrument of mass persuasion in order to stress that the signing of the treaty would inaugurate a new era in German history. President Heuss was at last persuaded to consent to the restoration of the third stanza of the *Deutschlandlied* as the national anthem. Subsequently, Otto Lenz requested that the anthem should be played for the first time by the German radio stations after the signing. However, the Social Democrat director of the Nordwestdeutscher Rundfunk, Adolf Grimme, refused to cooperate; the national anthem was therefore broadcast on 6 May, the day of the President's announcement.

Other attempts by the Chancellor's office to obtain the maximum positive publicity from the signing met with opposition from the Social Democrat-controlled Länder. The proposal for a school holiday on the day of the ceremony was blocked. Adenauer was also unable to persuade all the minister-presidents to come to Bonn for the signing when the heads of government of the SPD-ruled Länder refused the invitation. Even the plan for a great torchlight parade through Bonn came to nothing; the treaties were so controversial at home that the coalition parties themselves were reluctant to celebrate too enthusiastically.

In the prelude to the signing ceremony, the most bitter criticism again came from Kurt Schumacher. The planned ceremony was 'a quite blatant victory celebration on the part of the Allied-clerical coalition over the German people ... Whoever assents to this General Treaty ceases to be a good German!'[29] Even his fellow Social Democrats were uneasy at the vehemence of his attacks. Some senior SPD politicians, aware that Schumacher was a dying man, hinted that his remarks should not be taken too seriously. Shortly before the treaties were signed, Jakob Kaiser had told Seebohm, the way to a Grand Coalition would be clear after the ceremony.[30]

As the conference drew near, Adenauer became increasingly worried that his original desire to have the treaties signed in Bonn and used as the focus for a great celebration had been a serious mistake. Until the end it remained possible that a grave crisis within the coalition might erupt over Article VII, 3. Even more dangerous, however, were developments at international level. A few days before the foreign ministers conference was due to begin, it suddenly seemed that the schedule could not be met. The Dutch were refusing to cooperate over early withdrawal from the EDC in the event of a termination of the NATO Treaty. Only after great effort did Acheson and Eden manage to overcome the Dutch opposition by the day of the conference.

Acheson's departure for Europe was thus delayed until 22 May. Despite an urgent telegram from Eden, Acheson feared that the Bonn conference might end in a fiasco and became extremely cautious. It was only after talking over the arguments for and against participation that he was persuaded by President Truman to make the attempt. If the conference ended in disaster, the President himself would bear the responsibility and Acheson would probably escape unscathed. For Adenauer, however, the failure of the Bonn conference would in all likelihood mean political disaster.

Meanwhile all participants in Washington, London and Bonn had realised that the French cabinet no longer had any real desire to sign the EDC Treaty so quickly.[31] During the great debate in the National Assembly, a joint British-American guarantee against a West German withdrawal had become a major issue. Yet political circles in Paris were fully aware that assurances given by a President during his final year in office were almost worthless; no reliable contractual promises could be expected from a departing U.S. administration. If the Democrats tried to bequeath such a treaty to the Congress that was due to be elected in November, they would be handing the Republicans free ammunition for the election campaign.

The only possible conclusion was that the French knew exactly what they were doing when they issued a virtual ultimatum for guarantees: they were hoping to delay, or even put a stop to further progress. Robert Schuman, now under severe political pressure, could do little to prevent this development. The leading figure in the background was President Auriol, a bitter opponent of German rearmament.

In order to block it, the government in Paris had only two choices. Either it could refuse to sign the treaty, as the Pinay government threatened to do during the Bonn conference; or it could delay and eventually refuse ratification – the slow death of the EDC between the signing of the treaty and the final debâcle on 30 August 1954.

However, the French were dependent on the United States, for example, because of their inability to wage the war in Indochina without U.S.

support. Moreover, the collapse of the treaties with the inevitable political repercussions in the U.S. might endanger the hard-won progress towards stability in the European states system. Such an outcome would be a nightmare for non-Communists in France as much as elsewhere. Yet politicians do not always act rationally; the foreign ministers continued their negotiations over the weekend in Bonn while the Council of Ministers was in almost permanent session in Paris.

Though outwardly Adenauer seemed unmoved, in fact he was deeply troubled. From a domestic political perspective he was desperate to avoid the failure of the foreign ministers' conference in Bonn, which was due to be followed by the ceremonial signing of the treaties. Federal press chief Felix von Eckardt, who stayed close by Adenauer throughout the weekend of 24 and 25 May, later looked back on what was probably the most critical situation during Adenauer's early chancellorship: 'On that weekend the success of his whole previous policy was at stake. If the treaties could not be signed he had lost his political game, since anyone with any experience in this area knew that a catastrophe of that kind, occurring for all the world to see, would be almost impossible to repair. In domestic politics also, literally everything was at stake. If the treaties failed, the Social Democrats would have won and would undoubtedly have emerged victorious at the elections in the coming year.'[32]

The conference began on the evening of Friday 23 May with a meeting between Acheson and Schuman. It became apparent that the situation in Paris was extremely serious. Schuman, exhausted, nervous and depressed, was not receiving adequate support either from the cabinet or from the Quai d'Orsay.[33] Despite worries of his own, Adenauer remarked to Acheson: 'Can't you give some encouragement to our poor friend?'[34]

The most critical day was Sunday. The final foreign ministers' conference had been planned for Sunday morning, with the aim of settling the remaining issues in negotiations between the Western Allies and Adenauer. However, the Chancellor was informed, first, that the meeting was being postponed until after lunch, and then that there would have to be another delay until 4 pm. Time was running out, as the treaties were due to be signed at 10 am on Monday morning before all four delegations flew to Paris to sign the EDC treaty system.

The final meeting eventually began on Sunday afternoon. Adenauer now took charge of the discussions on the German side, thereby managing to keep control over Hallstein, who had some – justified – legal reservations. Thanks to the collaboration between Acheson and Adenauer, the agenda was successfully negotiated in time for the gala dinner in the Palais Schaumburg that evening.

In view of the gloomy prospects for ratification in the French National Assembly, Adenauer's last-minute attempt to sever the link between the General Treaty and the EDC should come as no surprise. Schuman, who feared further complications in the French Council of Ministers, refused to accept. However, he did agree to a written assurance by the Three Powers. In this, the Western Allies promised 'in the event of an unacceptable delay on the part of other powers in the ratification for the establishment of a treaty on the European Defence Community, to meet with the federal government at a conference in order to examine the situation and to decide whether precautions could be taken in order to put into force certain of the provisions contained in the treaties before the actual treaties come into operation'. Not surprisingly, Adenauer insisted on clarification of the meaning of 'unacceptable delay', but managed to achieve nothing more than the replacement of the vague word 'precautions' with the more precise 'provisions'.

Schuman – now largely under the direction of the French Council of Ministers and the Quai d'Orsay – revived the reparations issue which had long been regarded as settled. As far as a German peace treaty was concerned, he declared, France could not in principle abandon its claim to reparations, though it was prepared to abandon claims to future reparations from current production. Adenauer replied that this argument would jeopardise the ratification process in Bonn. He began by summarising his old approach. The GDR had already been cannibalised for reparations. How could Soviet demands for reparations at peace negotiations be opposed if the French insisted on the possibility of making the same claims as a matter of principle? Besides, the British had already made it clear that, as far as the British government was concerned, the reparations issue had been settled by the dismantling programme and the confiscation of German overseas assets. Schuman then insisted – and this is a stock-in-trade argument in such cases – that his sole concern was to overcome opposition to ratification in France. Adenauer retorted that he, too, had to take domestic concerns into account: Schumacher was up in arms against the treaties and had openly claimed that the Chancellor would cease to be a good German if he signed. The French claim would make his own position much worse. In order to solve the problem, however, he declared his willingness to accommodate Schuman's wishes regarding the troop treaty for forces of states belonging to the EDC.

At 6.30 pm, with the time for the gala dinner fast approaching, the meeting was adjourned on this issue. Acheson now came to Adenauer's assistance by proposing that the article in question, Article I, 1, Sentence 2, should remain in the form decided, but that the French position should be published in a separate protocol. Schuman was prepared to agree on condition that Adenauer would agree to concessions on the financial question. The experts were instructed to draft a proposal within the hour.

Eventually the meeting adjourned for the celebration dinner in the Palais Schaumburg. Even then it was not certain whether the French cabinet committee that controlled Schuman, would actually give their consent for the ceremony to go ahead. Adenauer, despite the knowledge that the conference might still collapse, managed his role as host with some aplomb. Dean Acheson, who always thrived on the stress of responsibility and high office, was fascinated by the drama and recalled it in his memoirs.[35] He had been told – or had understood – that the Palais Schaumburg had once been the residence of the Archbishop of Cologne and subsequently the home of the Kaiser's sister. When the guests moved to the great outdoor staircase after the meal, the scene was highly romantic: the Rhine shining in the moonlight, a male-voice choir singing traditional songs. For the heads of the delegations, the evening was given an extra *frisson* because of the possibility that disastrous news might come from Paris. By late evening the conference had apparently been saved, but some possibility of French intervention persisted until the signing ceremony. Certainly it was obvious that Schuman's great years as foreign minister were over. In January 1953 he was replaced by his rival Georges Bidault.

Acheson and Eden had met the French desire for a guarantee by making a solemn declaration. This, however, was little more than a gesture – 'du blabla', as Vincent Auriol accurately suggested.[36] Even after the signing, of course, the opponents of the treaties would still have the chance to postpone ratification and even to prevent it altogether.

On 11 May Acheson had received a telegram from his ambassador in Paris, claiming that the prospects for ratification were extremely poor. Maurice Schumann and Hervé Alphand of the Foreign Ministry had indicated that there was no longer a majority for the treaties in the National Assembly. As things stood, they would not be put to parliament before October, and no decision would be taken until after the U.S. presidential election. Similar pessimistic assessments were available to Adenauer. At the EDC signing ceremony in the Quai d'Orsay, for example, Felix von Eckardt found himself standing next to a French deputy with whom he was on friendly terms. The Frenchman remarked thoughtfully: 'Pity about the treaty, it will never be ratified in France!'[37]

With the outcome of the conference on Sunday uncertain, Adenauer had ordered that no festivities should be prepared for 26 May. However, the old mayor was well aware of the importance of dignified ceremonial and had issued appropriate instructions. The delegations met in the Bundesrat chamber, where the Basic Law had been announced under the presidency of Adenauer on 23 May 1949. The German people were to be given evidence of the progress their country had made in the intervening three years.

A platform had been erected in front of the great windows so that the invited guests would be able to see the four delegations, whose members sat behind a long table covered in a silver-grey cloth. On behalf of his colleagues, Robert Schuman welcomed Germany as a member of the free states of the West, in a tone that was echoed by the subsequent press conference. Though such ceremonies are almost always hailed as events of historical significance, in this case the claims, for once, were true.

The documents themselves were signed at a smaller table. Adenauer, who was the last to sign, gave a short speech before taking up his pen in which he outlined the goals of peace and freedom and assured the Germans in the Eastern Zone 'that with this treaty we have taken the first step to reunification'.[38] Then, his face immobile, he added his signature to the various copies.

The event was soon over. After a cold buffet Adenauer travelled to Wahn airport, where a large crowd was waiting, and from there to Paris to sign the EDC Treaty.

On the following morning, at the signing ceremony in the Clock Room of the Quai d'Orsay, the French made it perfectly clear how reluctantly they had accepted the inevitable. The proceedings passed off without dignity or decorum in an ill-organised scramble surrounded by hordes of photographers. Two days later, Adenauer was still sufficiently annoyed to grumble in the cabinet about the inadequacies of the French organization.[39] German protocol had been much better, he told his ministers. He was also dismayed that the Big Three had subsequently met separately to discuss trilateral issues and to exchange their views on another Soviet Note which had arrived on 24 May during the hectic events in Bonn. It was obvious that the concept of equal rights was a long way from being realised.

The first draft of the Western reply to the Soviet Note, which reached Adenauer at the end of June, revived his deep mistrust with regard to the Allied prerogatives.[40] There was no sign of the proclaimed 'common policy' towards the Soviet Union. At an emotional meeting with the High Commissioners,[41] he complained that the Western Powers apparently planned to negotiate a German peace treaty with the Soviets and only then to present it to the federal government. Rather than being the 'common policy' which had been agreed upon , such conduct reminded him of the peace-making at Versailles after the First World War. The ghosts that had haunted Adenauer for years were as powerful as ever. He pointed out to the High Commissioners that, as far as dealings with the Soviet Union were concerned, the signing of the treaties had fundamentally changed the relationship between the West German government and the Western Powers. This, however, was not what they wanted to hear.

Adenauer's report on the negotiations, delivered to the cabinet on 30 May, was bleak. He was particularly concerned, he told his colleagues, by the new version of Article VII, 3. This had now been amended to the benefit of the East and left a reunified Germany a completely free hand.

The uncertainties thus remained. It was no surprise that the Chancellor was anxious to force the treaties through the Bundestag, if not the upper chamber, before the summer recess. He continued to be plagued by fears of a Four Power Conference before the treaties came into force, particularly as nothing more than an interim stage had yet been achieved.

With hindsight it is possible to see that the great breakthrough to freedom of action in domestic and foreign policy occured in May 1952. However, at the time Adenauer could not be sure that the most critical stage was over. Two factors helped to calm him during these weeks. Among the German people, support for his policy was increasing significantly and the number of opponents declining. In June he was able to tell McCloy that, for the first time, 53 per cent of those questioned had expressed support for his policy; previously only 30per cent had done so.[42] Though such figures had to be interpreted with caution, there was no doubt that public opinion was moving in his favour.

One further ray of hope was provided by the attitude of Britain and the United States, especially after Franco-German relations had – as he noted in July – 'suffered an extraordinary deterioration'. Though he did not fully trust the British on the issue of Four-Power negotiations, he was greatly influenced by the indirect British link with the EDC. Shortly after the signing ceremony, he informed his cabinet that, for the first time for one hundred years, Germany was allied with Britain.[43] He had been favourably impressed by Eden during the negotiations, and he continued to place his hopes in Churchill's promise: 'We will not betray you'.[44]

During these months he could also be certain of the firm support – and perhaps even the admiration – of Dean Acheson. In fact Acheson was now determined, as long as he remained in office, to do everything within his power to secure Adenauer's election victory in 1953. During a discussion after the signing of the EDC Treaty, State President Vincent Auriol of France was bitterly critical of the U.S. Secretary of State for forcing Robert Schuman to conclude the treaty. Auriol was secretly dismayed to discover how much Acheson had come to rely on the German Chancellor: 'We must try to strengthen Adenauer's position and we must help him to win the Bundestag elections of 1953. But it is possible that Adenauer will be toppled before 1953 and that we will be faced with Schumacher. In view of this alternative we have, I believe, decided on the better solution.'[45] Even now, until released from his suffering by his death on 20 August 1952, the combative Schumacher proved to be Adenauer's greatest help.

Acheson's cable to President Truman on 26 May, reporting the successful conclusion of the treaty negotiations, speaks for itself: 'Adenauer, though a good and patriotic bargainer, has revealed himself once again to be a European statesman who knows when it is essential to compromise in order to save a possible great future from the threat of present difficulties of detail. I hope we have him with us for a long while.'[46]

AFTERWORD

A biographer hesitates before writing an afterword, since readers have had plenty of time to draw their own conclusions about the subject. Is it reasonable to add an explanation of what the author actually hoped to achieve and what he sees as the likely achievements and problems of his work? However, there are those readers who do ask for an element of reflection and self-explanation from the biographer. It is on their behalf that I am providing the following observations.

1. My study of the life and work of Adenauer consists of two volumes. This first volume describes the vicissitudes of his career until the great turning-point of May 1952, the date which saw the beginnings of a decisive change in public perceptions of him. The Chancellor who signed the Western treaties on 26 and 27 May still remained a highly controversial figure in the opinion of most observers; it was impossible to foretell whether his policies would meet with success or end in failure. Yet this ambivalent image on the part of the German public was about to change. By the time he returned to Hamburg from his triumphant visit to the United States in April 1953, an increasing number of people in Germany and abroad had come to regard him as a great statesman. From then on he ruled his country like a republican monarch. Though he remained a controversial figure, and continued to be sceptical about his own prospects of success, he was seen in a different light by the public at large. And this great shift in public opinion began in the spring of 1952.

The division of a major work of biography into two volumes inevitably brings problems. Even so, May 1952 can truly be said to have marked the end of a long and difficult journey through the desert. The Promised Land was at hand – and unlike Moses, the German Chancellor would be able to enter it. It is this perspective which explains the subtitles of the original German edition: 'On the Ascent, 1876-1952', and 'The Statesman: 1952-1967'.

Notes for this section begin on page 733.

2. Like the two volumes of my *Ära Adenauer* in the series *Geschichte der Bundesrepublik Deutschland,* this biography is a work of historiography. However, whereas in the *Ära Adenauer* study I sought to describe and analyse an entire period, the current work has as its focus the life and achievements of Adenauer himself. Readers familiar with the concluding section of Volume 3 in *Ära Adenauer* (pp.323-82) will be aware that I do not share the simplistic belief that 'men make history'. Even as important a figure as Adenauer during his years as Chancellor can only be understood in the context of the conditions, forces and ideas of the age.

On the other hand, it is equally true that he was the dominant figure in the history of the Federal Republic until the middle of the 1960s. The critical importance of the first Federal Chancellor is not disputed even by those historians whose assessment of his political aims and methods is tainted by animosity. A biographical approach can therefore be fruitful, on the condition that author and readers remain aware of its limitations.

More than a decade ago the historian Golo Mann made an observation which is also relevant for the study of Adenauer's long life: 'Abbreviation is the supreme law of the historical profession … It takes place through selection: with this the events, scenes, persons, evidence of personal or general life are moved into the spotlight for the sake of example or because they appear to have particularly serious consequences in a given context; the great mass of material remains in the shadows.'[1] I am very well aware that almost all of the events described here could have been documented and analysed in more detail. On a number of occasions such an approach might well have been useful – and indeed, has sometimes been adopted elsewhere. However, I decided in the interest of readability to be as concise as possible.

My efforts to base my description and personal interpretations on the widest possible range of source material, while also taking due account of relevant secondary works, does not require detailed explanation. The books and articles which have increased my understanding, as well as those whose opinions I do not share, are mentioned in the bibliography or the notes. In a departure from my usual custom I have kept my footnotes to a minimum. The expert reader will realise where I share the prevailing view and where I have departed from it. On this occasion at least, it has not been my intention to produce a work of positively Teutonic erudition.

I should also point out that the writing of biography – or, at least, the biography I hoped to produce – has its own laws which are quite independent of the general demands of historiographical accuracy. Though the aim is to bring to life an important figure, the main emphasis is on that figure as an historical actor whose personal and emotional life is not to be neglected.

One critical reviewer of the first volume of the *Ära Adenauer* complained that I ought to have mentioned, in my account of the negotiations between Adenauer and Khrushchev in the Kremlin, the fact that they actually raised their fists to each other at one point. In my view such details can have at most a peripheral place in the description of an entire era. However, such incidents clearly have a place in a biography, and I hope that readers with a taste for dramatic scenes will not be disappointed.

It may be that my account, by paying such attention to major confrontations and incidents, tends to overshadow analyses of the political background and context, though obviously these are not altogether absent. Though in recent years I have been somewhat alarmed by a perceptible tendency to portray Adenauer – who remained, despite his dignity and composure, an extremely lively and emotional man – as something akin to a human statue. I therefore thought it appropriate to recall the elements of movement and turbulence which marked his life.

3. One main problem faced by any biographer of Adenauer lies in the fact that he began his great post-war achievements at an age when most men are usually either retired or dead. This has the effect of making the first seventy years of his life appear as little more than a prelude to his career on the world stage between 1949 and 1963.

In these circumstances, two different perspectives are essential . The first comprehends Adenauer's long life before he became party leader in the spring of 1946 as the mould and preparation for 'the real thing'. Given this perspective, a number of important questions suggest themselves. How did Adenauer's views during his term as mayor – his attitude towards western Europe, to the German Reich, to the European great powers, the parties and the economy – come to influence his objectives and visions when he finally became Chancellor? What role did his experience in the Third Reich play in his subsequent assessment of nationalism, totalitarianism, or détente policy? How did his early observations and experiences with other public figures colour his attitudes towards them when they reappeared on the national stage after the collapse of Nazi Germany? If the first seventy years of Adenauer's life are indeed regarded as a mould and a time of preparation, this perspective will include an assessment of the abilities which he had developed with the municipal administration of Cologne, during his activities in Berlin, and in his dealings with society at large.

There is a second perspective which is equally indispensable in terms of methodology. No holders of public office can ever regard their 'previous history' as unimportant, as no more than preparation for the very highest offices. No individual can hope to succeed without regarding his or her current activity as crucial – irrespective of what the future might hold.

In the same way, the biographer's description of the early development of the subject must be based on an awareness that the future is always shrouded in mystery. It is essential for the historian to remain conscious of the sheer unpredictability which surrounds great moments in history.

Those who are not willing to concede this would be better advised to enter the legal profession and to act as public prosecutors, where specific actions can be investigated according to the criterion of whether they justify criminal proceedings and what punishment should be demanded. Readers of my account of Adenauer's Rhineland policy in 1918-1919, and again in 1923, will understand what I mean.

I have attempted to make equal – and, I hope, fruitful – use of these two perspectives. On the one hand, this implies a search for the deeper personal reasons behind certain important decisions and their justification, while on the other, it involves the attempt to understand and explain an important figure at each individual stage of his or her development.

4. In describing the life of a politician, artist or scientist, biographers are frequently inclined to concentrate on one overarching theme and present it as the dominant and continuous factor in the life of the subject. At first sight this approach has certain attractions, and may even be fruitful in the case of some individuals. In planning this book, I therefore considered a number of potential unifying themes.

For example, might the 'victory of the citizen and bourgeois' be regarded as the great theme of Adenauer's career as CDU party chairman and Chancellor? It might then be argued that, for the first time in German history, the country's future was shaped by a proud and vigorous representative of the self-confident urban bourgeoisie. Such an approach might provide thematic links between his tenure as mayor and his conduct as Chancellor. Adenauer could also be said to have followed in the tradition of great mayors of the past, such as Otto Guericke in Magdeburg and Johann Rudolf Wettstein in Basle, who tried to re-establish their cities in the concert of the European powers after the Thirty Years' War. He could be portrayed as a mayor and a bourgeois (*Bürgermeister und Bürger*) – imaginative but reasonable, solid but daring, tough but with the ability to convince his community that his decisions were in the public interest.[2]

There is another unifying theme. It has often been observed that Adenauer's career could best be explained by reference to his roots in Cologne and the Rhineland. The portrayal of Adenauer as a 'man of Cologne' had much to commend it at first sight. His foreign-policy ideas and domestic political convictions, it could be argued, were profoundly influenced by the interests and experience of the Rhineland in which he lived and worked all his life. On a previous occasion, before I was fully conscious of the need for academics to be cautious in their use of suggestive images, I had summarised this approach as a 'German and European policy with Cologne cathedral at the centre'.[3]

This overarching theme contains within it a number of different and tempting aspects: urban-democratic Germany versus agrarian-authoritarian Germany; Adenauer's sense of the need for 'organic' economic integration between the west of Germany and the liberal industrialised states of Western Europe; a value system strongly influenced by the Occidental tradition; the attempt to gear overall German foreign policy to give priority to the security and economic needs of the German West. Such an approach need not be combined with any exaggerated assertion of Adenauer's hostility to Prussia and Berlin – and certainly not with the claim that he had any desire, whether latent or manifest, to 'bail out' of the German Reich.

It would also be possible to examine Adenauer's work from a very different angle, and to choose as the great unifying theme his function as the great moderniser. Clearly modernisation had been a recurrent theme in his life ever since he witnessed the demolition of the city wall as a boy in the 1880s; it was to be one of the key themes of his tenure as mayor. Furthermore, the concept was again a major issue after 1946, in the form of modernisation of the German party system through the elimination of religious divisions, the modernisation of the state and society of the Federal Republic, and the modernization of the west European states system itself. Yet it must be recognised that his desire to modernise was not limitless – or, better, was not rootless. As mayor, for example, Adenauer planned a new Cologne, but was eager to conserve its lovely old buildings and trees. As West German Chancellor, too, he was determined to incorporate the virtues of the old Germany into the new.

Other great themes also suggest themselves, and all of them would be accurate up to a point. Yet they could only be pursued to a conclusion by omitting or distorting important aspects. Inaccurate descriptions of the life and work of politicians, it must be said, are often the result of an attempt to impose a single unifying theme. This is a particular danger in the case of Adenauer, who was forced to prove himself in a variety of conditions. His rise to mayor coincided with the occupation of Cologne between 1918 and 1926, with its rapid sequence of revolution, the threat of a resumption of hostilities, the danger posed by separatist groups, the Franco-Belgian occupation of the Ruhr. The subsequent years of consolidation were then followed by the worldwide economic depression and the fatal crisis of the Weimar Republic. Rapid change was also the hallmark of Adenauer's years of achievement in the post-war period: occupation, a form of protectorate status for the Federal Republic followed by limited sovereignty, then – in the second half of the 1950s – a leading role for Adenauer in Western Europe and new dangers in relations with the Soviet Union over Berlin.

In the final analysis, it is impossible to describe Adenauer's thinking and tactical approach to the solution of these many problems within the confines of a single overarching theme. Any attempt to do so inevitably produces the omission or manipulation of much of the evidence.

Moreover, every significant democratic politician – and Adenauer was no exception – requires a Protean capacity to change and avoid precise definition. The attempt to produce a sharp and unambiguous portrait is, whether deliberately or not, a falsification of the truth. Historical truth is not simple, but usually complex and frequently full of contradictions. Although the desire to reduce complicated circumstances to simple formulae appears to be an innate human characteristic, that is precisely why historians should refrain from the attempt to impose overarching biographical themes. Both German history in the twentieth century, and the personality of Adenauer himself, are too complicated to support it.

5. Though we should abstain from imposing a single unifying theme, it remains the main task of any biographer to delineate the main themes in the life of the subject. Development and various fields of activity, important changes of direction and controversial events, crises and triumphs – this is the stuff of any genuine biography. The value of such work is greatly increased, of course, by the use of the widest possible range of sources and the inclusion of previously unknown information and *'petits faits significatifs'*, as Hyppolyte Taine put it. The reader is thus presented not with an idealised image but with a living person who develops, learns, makes mistakes, has both attractive and unappealing traits and, despite inner consistency of thinking, is not always consistent in his actions.

Since Adenauer devoted his whole adult life to public affairs, the personal elements in the biography must be interwoven with a description both of the changing historical background and of the many people who played a significant part in his long life. German history in the late nineteenth and twentieth centuries – both splendid and horrific as it has been – provided more than the mere backdrop to his life; between 1933 and 1945 he was himself a victim, and in the post-war period he was to help shape the course of German history in a new and more positive direction.

Political biographers cannot afford to confine themselves to the writing of a purely personal history. This is especially true when the subject is Konrad Adenauer, whose influence on contemporary German history has been so profound. The biographer must also explain how, and how intensely, the subject both reflected and shaped the course of history. Two slightly different perspectives are essential to such an approach: the first concentrates on the great controversies which arose during his lifetime, and the second will attempt an assessment of his historical achievements.

Opinions about all major German Chancellors fluctuate, as in the case of Wallenstein, with the 'favour and hatred of the parties'. This was certainly the case with Konrad Adenauer. On the other hand, some of the great controversies which surrounded him during his lifetime are now obsolete. In domestic politics, for example, much of the most bitter dispute has abated. The fears of some political opponents to the effect that his authoritarian leadership style and his attempt to re-establish bourgeois society might present a danger to democracy, have been laid to rest by the course of history. Germans are now aware that other Chancellors have been ruthless too, in their handling of the opposition and equally capable of mounting demagogic election campaigns. Even social Democrats now have greater respect for Adenauer as a party leader than was once the case. German democracy has proved sufficiently robust to endure party-political disputes and the activities of strong Chancellors. The passage of time has provided space for a calmer assessment of the first Federal Chancellor and his legacy of economic and political success, greater social harmony and respect for the law and the constitutional state.

Nevertheless, the biographer must take account of the fact that *at the time* Adenauer's domestic policies, including his style of leadership, were highly controversial. This aspect of his chancellorship cannot be ignored. We may even consider whether his tough conduct, in the critical early years of democratic stabilisation in West Germany, might have been more effective than the milder rule of a Chancellor more intent on harmony. The biographer is inevitably tempted to compare Adenauer's style as mayor of Cologne with his first years as Federal Chancellor.

Though Adenauer's record in domestic politics has become less controversial over the years, his foreign policy and his approach to the 'German question' remain the subject of intense debate both among the public and in academic circles. There are two main reasons for this fact: firstly, the long division of Germany, which was for many years the great burden and legacy of the Federal Republic; and secondly, Adenauer's determination to bind West Germany to the community of Western liberal democracies.

Even today, crypto-nationalist historians are eager to condemn Adenauer for having shown a lack of patriotism, for being anti-Prussian, and for rejecting of opportunities to achieve reunification in 1952 and 1953. The issue of Adenauer and the 'German question' is one of the most important themes facing his biographer, and is as relevant to his time as mayor of Cologne, as it is to his tenure as Chancellor. A sober analysis of his policy towards the Rhenish Republic between 1918 and 1923, and of his thinking and policies in 1945 and thereafter is thus essential.

I have outlined my own judgement in the crucial chapters of this biography at such length that a summary would be superfluous. Furthermore, a more definitive account of Adenauer's reunification policy will be included at the end of the second volume. Until then I can only refer to my interpretation in the third volume of the *Geschichte der Bundesrepublik Deutschland:*

> Admittedly, even he did not escape the internal inconsistencies of the German point of view. A sober *Realpolitik* set the tone and led him to direct the foreign policy of Bonn towards irrevocable inclusion in the community of western democracies. Yet mixed with this sober *Realpolitik* was a strong element of outrage at the suffering of his fellow countrymen in the GDR, and the old Reich patriotism lived on in the recesses of his heart. When he dedicated his memoirs 'To My Fatherland' he did not mean the Federal Republic alone.[4]

Any assessment of Adenauer's life must be based not only on the controversies surrounding him at the time, but also on his historic achievements. He will, of course, continue to be remembered first and foremost as the founding Chancellor of the Federal Republic. We are therefore obliged to consider how his attitudes as Chancellor were influenced by his long years of activity before 1933 and his forced inactivity between 1933 and 1945. Clearly he did not enter the post-war world with the inclination to adjust his own beliefs for short-term opportunist reasons. Instead Adenauer revealed strong convictions which were the product both of experience and of a realistic assessment of actual conditions. These receive particular attention in this book and can be mentioned briefly here: his Christian beliefs, the rejection of a state-run bureaucratic economy, the deep anti-socialist thrust of his economic and social policy, his resolute anti-Communism and passionate rejection of a nationalist foreign policy. Throughout this volume I have endeavoured to indicate the roots of these convictions. But the reader may have noted that Adenauer's attitude towards social democracy was not a linear development; this will remain a major theme of the second volume. Another issue which deserves continued attention concerns the elimination from German party politics of religious divisions between Catholic and Protestant, which is rightly regarded as one of his most important achievements.

Equally, any biographer of Adenauer needs to discover whether his European ideas demonstrated a number of constant elements dating from the period following the First World War, and to examine the extent to which the changing international situation suggested a need for alterations in policy. His approach to relations with France and Britain must be subjected to a similar analysis.

In this and other areas I regard it as the task of the biographer not to simplify, but to explain and to make distinctions. The drawing of caricatures, I hope, I have left to others.

6. The biography of a great politician will necessarily include some, but not all, of the circumstances of his personal life. In this case, my criterion for deciding what to incorporate and what to omit is a simple one and relates to the effect of these personal matters on the public performance and overall development of the subject. Adenauer's place in European history does not rest on his role as an excellent father and husband, as an art collector or enthusiastic walker, or as a gardener or inventor, despite the fact that he was all of these things and took his private life as seriously as his public duties.

During my research, like any other biographer, I discovered a great deal of information about the private life of the subject. Only a fraction of it, however, needs to be incorporated into a biography which is primarily concerned with political affairs. I am well aware that some critics will think I have included too much, while others would have preferred to learn more about Adenauer as a private individual. In cases of doubt I have tended to use too little rather than too much – not because there is anything to hide, but to reflect my own belief that an individual's private life deserves to be treated with respect.

On one particular point, however, I did find it necessary to provide considerable detail: Adenauer's financial position as mayor and the speculation in American shares which so nearly brought about his ruin. Both were important because of the role they played in the controversy which surrounded him during his final years as mayor. They also explain why Adenauer's dismissal as mayor left him in desperate financial straits for some years.

Adenauer's personal relations with Dannie N. Heineman also deserve our attention. It has frequently been claimed by his detractors that – especially as an old man – Adenauer was incapable of friendship. His relations with Heineman, which will also play a part in the second volume, tell a very different story. At the same time – and here Adenauer was no different from many other politicians – personal friendships could also have implications for his role in public life. This is true of his contacts with Heineman as well as with Robert and Dora Pferdmenges.

Frequently during the writing of this book I found myself asking the perennial question of biographers everywhere. What kind of man was this? To lapse into the vernacular, what made him tick?

Adenauer's physical and mental reserves, even in old age, were nothing short of remarkable. His resilience, his patient determination to do his duty, his work-rate, his insatiable hunger for information and sheer intellectual power – all these attributes can still astonish, all the more since they continued unabated when he was well past the age of eighty. His character in personal relations, ranging from a capacity for amiability and charm through to an occasional tendency to indulge in violent and bitter outbursts, is also striking.

On various occasions throughout this volume I have tried to indicate possible keys to Adenauer's complex personality: a conscientiousness shaped by his religious faith; strong devotion to duty; real pleasure in constructive achievement; a desire to obtain and use power; a combative spirit. None of them, however, are sufficient to provide a full explanation of his motives. On occasion I have allowed Adenauer to speak for himself about his opinions and drives. Frequently I have repeated the opinions of third parties, which run the gamut from devotion to blind hatred. Adenauer was a man who could fascinate and repel in equal measure. I still do not know whether he remained a mystery even unto himself, but if my biography captures something of his force and vitality it will have achieved one of its objectives.

If I may be permitted a personal observation, I would say that I have been particularly impressed by several facets of Adenauer's personality. Among these I would number his creative will and his lifelong determination to withstand his opponents and overcome all resistance. In addition, he manifested a regality of bearing which he never entirely lost even *in extremis,* plus an unbroken pride which was most apparent after 1945, when he acted as the representative of a defeated and guilt-laden people in his dealings with the occupying powers. As I complete this first volume of biography, however, it is Adenauer the fighter who has made the deepest impression on me. Whatever my other reservations about him, for this aspect of his personality I have the utmost sympathy and respect. By the word 'fight' I do not mean sterile confrontation, but rather a tenacious determination to gain support for his attempts to overcome intractable problems, to mobilise a majority, to convince supporters and out-manoeuvre opponents. From his early days as mayor until the protests against the nuclear test-ban treaty in the months before his death, Adenauer's life was a drama and a perpetual struggle. He himself can properly be regarded as a creative force who was never content with the world as it was.

Throughout his life Adenauer's outlook was based on firm Christian principles. He was nevertheless a political sceptic rather than an enthusiast, was remarkably free of illusions, and maintained an acute awareness of the realities of a given situation. This solid realist, who once remarked ironically that he would like to see Goethe's *Faust* at the top of the Catholic Church's Index of proscribed books, was the antithesis of a political romantic. He loathed chaos and disorder but, having grown to manhood in an age of bourgeois security, was plunged between 1914 and 1967 into a world which was either out of control or threatened to become so. In a chaotic century, Adenauer attempted to establish or maintain at least a measure of order – in his native city, in Germany, and in Europe. It was a task he addressed with devotion, always pessimistic about the outcome but never abandoning the attempt: 'The wonder is he has endured so long.'

7. My aim was to provide an understanding critical biography. The real virtue of the biographer lies in the desire to understand. Dead men are equally unable to defend themselves against undeserved abuse or mindless veneration, but they have a right to something approaching fair treatment.

An understanding critical biography will regard its subject with a certain sympathy but will also maintain detachment – respectful where respect is due, ironical where irony is deserved, frankly critical of evident political or moral mistakes, and properly inquiring whenever the subject's motives and objectives are difficult to distinguish.

I must conclude by thanking at least some of the people and institutions whose kindness and assistance were so important in the writing of this book.

I had the opportunity of talking with many men and women who were linked with Adenauer in some way or were able to provide important information. Some of them asked not to be cited by name, while there is always a danger that others would by accident be omitted from any long list. I therefore ask for their understanding of my decision to offer instead my general and sincere thanks to all of them for their valuable assistance.

Some individuals, of course, must be mentioned by name. I owe a great debt of gratitude to Frau Ria Reiners, Dr Max Adenauer and Herr Konrad Adenauer, who allowed me access to a number of previously unknown letters and other material. I am grateful to former ambassador Herbert Blankenhorn for kindly permitting me to read his diary and for his patient and encouraging reading of parts of the manuscript. My stay in the Blankenhorn household is among my fondest memories of working on this volume. I am equally grateful to the Lenz family for granting me permission to quote from the diary of Otto Lenz, state secretary in the Federal Chancellor's office. My particular thanks are due to Herr Heinz Pferdmenges, who placed at my disposal a number of important and previously unknown letters from Adenauer for the purposes of this biography.

My work has been greatly assisted by my use of the archive of the Bundeskanzler-Adenauer-Haus Foundation in Rhöndorf. Dr Anneliese Poppinga, who has devoted her time and energy to this unique institution since its establishment, provided me with constant information and encouragement during the writing of the book. She has also been kind enough to read parts of the manuscript in progress and to make a number of relevant criticisms; her suggested amendments have improved the end result. I also offer my thanks for the assistance of Herr Engelbert Hommel, MA, Rhöndorf, in my search for documents and photographs.

Over the years my knowledge has been enriched by my discussions with Dr Hanns Jürgen Küsters and Dr Hans Peter Mensing of the Rhöndorf foundation. The help of Dr Küsters in the search for sources requires my special thanks. In their work on the *Rhöndorfer Ausgabe* the two located the reports of the Swiss consul-general Rudolph von Weiss, which are among the most informative sources for the period 1944-1948. They have edited this material in parallel to the appearance of this volume. Dr Küsters also read the first draft of the manuscript and proposed useful amendments.

Of similar significance to the Rhöndorf sources was the Archiv für Christlich-Demokratische Politik at the Konrad-Adenauer-Foundation in St Augustin. Dr Klaus Gotto and Dr Günter Buchstab were knowledgeable and helpful guides to the material there and have helped in a number of cases by obtaining the owners' permission to use the sources in the custody of the Foundation.

In addition, though without mentioning names, I would like to thank various colleagues at archives in Germany and abroad for their assistance in my search for material for this first volume of the biography and for the ensuing second volume which will be largely based on hitherto classified sources.

Ever since the late 1960s, researchers into the life and work of Konrad Adenauer must inevitably take into account the work of a small but important group of academics. I have obtained much valuable information from the books and articles written by its members, and have gained much from the exchange of information and ideas. Rudolf Morsey must be mentioned at the top of this list, which also includes Arnulf Baring, Konrad Repgen, Hugo Stehkämper, Karl Dietrich Erdmann, Hans-Günter Hockerts and Klaus Gotto. Moreover, Hans Peter Mensing and Hanns Jürgen Küsters have been working with Rudolf Morsey and myself on the *Rhöndorfer Ausgabe*.

My conversations with the above-mentioned scholars have frequently led me to subject my views to critical re-examination. With so influential and complex a man as Adenauer, of course, there is plenty of opportunity for different interpretations of specific events, as I have frequently had cause to remember. This, then, is the proper place for the time-honoured disclaimer. My biography of Adenauer was written by me alone; though I am grateful for the ideas and assistance of others, they bear no responsibility for my work and the interpretations I offer.

Within the framework of their duties at my academic home at Cologne University, a small team has provided much assistance in my checking of quotations and in making corrections. In particular I would like to thank my assistant Marc Defossé for his careful work. Equally valuable was the assistance of Frau Hildegard Maxrath, for whose patience, thoroughness and speed in producing various versions of a complicated manuscript I have the greatest admiration.

The volume could not have been completed without the provision by the Fritz Thyssen Foundation of a four-month academic grant. I am grateful for this essential assistance and would like to thank in particular its *Vorstand* Dr Rudolf Kerscher.

As on previous occasions, my contacts with my publishers have been so delightful that I would like to express to them my gratitude, in particular to Ulrich Volz. Herr Ulrich Frank-Planitz, managing director of the DVA and himself the author of a volume on Adenauer, provided a number of useful suggestions during the completion of the work.

This book is dedicated to my wife. Our discussions of Adenauer have now been going on now for over twenty-five years of our life together. Formerly I admit to having been a somewhat sceptical observer, distinguishing between Adenauer's policies – many of which won me over – and the man himself, with whom I was less impressed. My wife took a rather different view. She had less admiration for his policies but was fascinated by personality of the Old Man who was so unique in his regal pride, his remarkable vitality in old age, and in personal qualities, not forgetting the undoubted rough edges. For her, at least, Adenauer has always been just as remarkable as a human being as in his incarnation as an anti-totalitarian, pro-Western politician who has brought about the birth of modern West Germany, but also preserved some of the evening twilight of the old Germany, largely wrecked by the Nazis and further eroded during the 1960s. It was her conviction that Adenauer the man was worthy of study which persuaded me to embark on this work, and without her constant encouragement I would not have continued or completed it.

The biography of a great man, she has often reminded me, is both an academic and a literary challenge. During the writing she acted as the ideal reader – a reader who wanted to achieve a better understanding of Adenauer's policies as the first priority, but also hoped to gain some insight into the mind of a complex man and to be gripped by the story of an eventful and often dramatic life.

Whether this book will fulfil these expectations only time will tell, but I am proud to dedicate it to her as a token of our attachment.

Bad Godesberg   Hans-Peter Schwarz

NOTES

PROLOGUE: COLOGNE

1. V. Hugo, *Le Rhin* (Paris, 1842).
2. H. Borger, ed., *Der Kölner Dom im Jahrhundert seiner Vollendung*, 2 vols. (Cologne, 1980), p.36.
3. *Die Stadt Köln im ersten Jahrhundert unter preussischer Herrschaft 1815 bis 1915*, vol.1, part 1 (Cologne, 1916), p. 520f.
4. Memorial address for Wilhelm Becker by Mayor Adenauer, 20 January 1924, MS, Stiftung Bundeskanzler-Adenauer-Haus (henceforth: StBKAH), 1.04.
5. H. von Treitschke, *Deutsche Geschichte im Neunzehnten Jahrhundert*, part 1 (Leipzig, 1882, 1927), p.24.
6. B. von Bülow, *Denkwürdigkeiten*, vol.4 (Berlin, 1931), p.135f.
7. Neue Preußische Kreuzzeitung quoted in: H. Lademacher, *Rheinische Geschichte*, vol.2 (Düsseldorf, 1976), p.571.
8. Quoted in: *Köln 1850-1920*, with an introduction and commentaries by M.L. Schwering (Luzern/Frankfurt am Main, 1980).
9. Bundesarchiv Koblenz (henceforth: BA), Falk Papers, No.385, p.6.
10. Ibid., p.46.
11. Heineman to Adenauer, 28 February 1956, StBKAH, Heineman Papers, vol.3.

THE YOUNG MASTER ADENAUER

Early Beginnings

1. Copy in StBAKAH.
2. Ibid.
3. K. Wehmann, *Das Infanterie-Regiment Vogel von Falckenstein (7. Westfälisches) Nr.56 in den ersten 50 Jahren seines Bestehens* (Berlin, 1910), p. 12f.
4. P. Weymar, *Konrad Adenauer. Die autorisierte Biographie* (Munich, 1955), p. 17f.
5. Adenauer to his son Konrad, 2 April 1962 (in private posession).
6. Th. Fontane, *Der deutsche Krieg von 1866*, vol. 1 (Berlin, 1870), p. 490.
7. Wehmann, *Infanterie-Regiment 56*, pp. 57 and 96.
8. G. Wendt, *Sammlung deutscher Gedichte für Schule und Haus* (Karlsruhe, 1907), p. 86.
9. Historisches Archiv der Stadt Köln (henceforth: HAStK), 902/300/1.
10. Copy in StBKAH.
11. Ibid.
12. Weymar, *Adenauer*, p. 15.
13. BA, Falk Papers, No. 385, p. 47.
14. Weymar, *Adenauer*, pp. 16ff.
15. Diary entry by Adenauer, 31 December 1917, StBKAH.
16. Ibid.
17. 3 October 1932, HAStK, 902/233/1.
18. Adenauer to Heineman, 10 September 1960, StBKAH, Heineman Papers, vol. 4.

19. Quoted in: H. Borger and G. Zehnder, *Köln. Die Stadt als Kunstwerk. Stadtansichten vom 15. bis 20. Jahrhundert* (Cologne, 1982), p. 285.
20. A. Poppinga, *Meine Erinnerungen an Konrad Adenauer* (Stuttgart, 1970) p. 184.
21. Examples of a sense of sin and trust in God in D. Krein, *Konrad Adenauer und seine Familie* (Frieberg bei Augsburg, 1957), passim.
22. Information given to the author by Dr. Konrad Adenauer.
23. Weymar, *Adenauer*, pp. 22-8.
24. Poppinga, *Erinnerungen*, p. 184.
25. Ibid.
26. Information given to the author by Herr Wolf Jobst Siedler.
27. *Köln und seine Bauten. Festschrift zur VIII. Wanderversammlung des Verbandes deutscher Architekten- und Ingenieur-Vereine in Köln vom 12. bis 16. August 1888* (Cologne, 1888), p. 429.
28. Poppinga, *Erinnerungen*, p. 186.
29. Staatliches Apostelngymnasium Köln, Jahresbericht 1966/67, p. 18.
30. R. Amelunxen, *Ehrenmänner und Hexenmeister. Erlebnisse und Betrachtungen* (Munich, 1960), p. 17.
31. BA, Falk Papers, No. 385, p. 4f.
32. Amelunxen, *Ehrenmänner*, p. 19.
33. School certificate dated 6 March 1894 (with essay attached), in private possession.
34. Poppinga, *Erinnerungen*, p. 181.
35. F. von Eckardt, 'Konrad Adenauer – eine Charakterstudie', in: D. Blumenwitz et al. eds., *Konrad Adenauer und seine Zeit*, 2 vols. (Stuttgart, 1976), vol. I (henceforth: *KAZeit I*), pp. 137-48, 140. p. 140 (pp. 137-48).
36. Poppinga, *Erinnerungen*, p. 237.
37. Ibid., p. 188.
38. Memorandum on a conversation with Cyrus Leo Sulzberger, 6 August 1957, StBKAH.
39. Poppinga, *Erinnerungen*, p. 189.
40. H. Lehmann, *Ein grosser Jurist des Rheinlandes. Jugend und Beruf. Seine Lebenserinnerungen* (Cologne, 1976), pp. 27f.
41. Weymar, *Adenauer*, pp. 29-31.

Student Years in Freiburg, Munich and Bonn

1. Lehmann, *Lebenserinnerungen* (Cologne, 1976), pp. 36-8.
2. Weymar, *Adenauer*, pp. 32-6.
3. Pages from the diary of Emma Adenauer (in private possession).
4. Adenauer to Giesen, 4 October 1935; and in similar vein on 4 June 1936, StBKAH, VI-B 68.9.
5. Weymar, *Adenauer*, p. 32.
6. Poppinga, *Erinnerungen*, p. 190.
7. Lehmann, *Lebenserinnerungen*, pp. 41-6.
8. Poppinga, *Erinnerungen*, p. 190.
9. Weymar, *Adenauer*, p. 36f.; Krein, *Konrad Adenauer*, p. 22.
10. Information given to the author by Dr. Anneliese Poppinga.
11. M. Wallraf, *Aus einem rheinischen Leben* (Hamburg/Berlin, 1926), p. 25.
12. Information given to the author by Dr. Konrad Adenauer.
13. Lehmann, *Lebenserinnerungen*, pp. 50-6.

Justitia Coloniensis

1. Personal records on Adenauer of Cologne Royal District Court, Hauptstaatsarchiv Düsseldorf (henceforth: HStAD).
2. Poppinga, *Erinnerungen*, p. 247.

3. This and the following quotations and descriptions on his activity in the the legal service are taken from Adenauer's personal records, as cited in note 1 above.
4. Poppinga, *Erinnerungen*, p. 248.

'A Talent Takes Shape in Stillness'

1. In private possession.
2. Weymar, *Adenauer*, p. 37f.
3. F.W. Esser, *Meine Kölner Tenniserinnerungen* (Cologne, 1931). Published as a special issue of the club journal 'Rot-Weiss', Cologne, n.d.
4. Quotations from the obituary in *Vereinsblatt für Deutsches Versicherungswesen,* vol. 12, No. 9 (1884).
5. Quoted in: K.J. Bollenbeck, 'Der Kölner Stadtbaumeister Johann Peter Weyer', unpubl. PhD. thesis, Aachen University, 1969.
6. In: H. Vey, 'Johann Peter Weyer. Seine Gemäldesammlung und seine Kunstliebe', in: *Wallraf-Richartz-Jahrbuch,* vol. XXVIII (Cologne, 1966), pp. 159-224.
7. In: 'Geheimer Ober-Justiz-Rat Berghaus. Nekrolog', in: *Kölnische Blätter,* No. 243 (1869), p. 2.
8. Weymar, *Adenauer*, pp. 42-5.
9. Hugo Stehkämper, 'Eine Bewerbung Konrad Adenauers in Gelsenkirchen?', in: *Westfalen*, vol. 58 (1980), pp. 218-26.
10. Weymar, *Adenauer*, p. 41.
11. Ibid., p. 45f.; Poppinga, *Erinnerungen*, p. 247.

FIRST RAPID RISE 1906-1917

Adenauer's Lucky Streak – Rise in the Cologne Municipal Administration

1. CBS interview, 21 August 1962, StBKAH, 02.27.
2. Weymar, *Adenauer*, p. 46.
3. Häusermann in: *Bonner Rundschau*, 4 May 1973.
4. Weymar, *Adenauer*, p. 47.
5. H. Kisters, *Adenauer als Kunstsammler* (Munich, 1970), p. 18.
6. Copy of the draft in the author's possession.
7. Wallraf, *Aus einem rheinischen Leben*, p. 108f.
8. Written on 30 November 1909 for Tax Office I, HAStK 21, No.3, p. 19. See the account of the event by E. Kleinertz, 'Konrad Adenauer als Beigeordneter der Stadt Köln (1906-1917)', in: H. Stehkämper, ed., *Konrad Adenauer. Oberbürgermeister von Köln.* Festgabe der Stadt Köln zum 100. Geburtstag ihres Ehrenbürgers am 5. Januar 1976 (Cologne, 1976), pp. 51-53.
9. Meeting of the Liberal Caucus, 8 June 1909, Fraktionsakten 1908-1917. Niederschrift der Fraktionssitzung der Liberalen, HAStK, 1068 K 1.
10. Kölner Stadtverordnetenversammlung, 22 July 1909, p. 302.

The First World War

1. R. Strobel, *Adenauer und der Weg Deutschlands* (Lucerne/Frankfurt am Main, 1965), p. 31.
2. Conversation with Dulles, 1 May 1957.

3. H.-P. Schwarz, ed., *Konrad Adenauer. Reden 1917-1967. Eine Auswahl* (Stuttgart, 1975), p. 127.
4. Quoted in: *Europäische Gespräche*, vol.5, No. XII (1927), p. 611; see also HAStK, 902/278/1.
5. Adenauer – Ben Gurion, 14 March 1960, StBKAH III/58.
6. Adenauer – Couve de Murville, 6 January 1960, ibid.
7. Information provided to the author.
8. Certificate of 27 June 1898, StBKAH.
9. Ibid., VI-B 68.4.
10. Draft of 1 August 1902, ibid.
11. *Kölner Stadtverordetenversammlung*, 13 June 1906, p. 149.
12. 'Kölnisches. Zum Scheiden Wallrafs', in: *Rheinische Zeitung*, 4 August 1917.
13. Arnold Brecht, *Aus nächster Nähe. Lebenserinnerungen 1884-1927* (Stuttgart, 1966), p. 409.
14. Felix Hirsch, 'Wilhelm Sollmann. 1881-1915', in: B. Poll and W. Janssen, eds., *Rheinische Lebensbilder. Im Auftrag der Gesellschaft für Rheinische Geschichtskunde* (Cologne, 1961-1982), vol. VI, p. 267.
15. *Rheinische Zeitung*, 28 December 1920.
16. 'Die Wahl des Kölner Oberbürgermeisters', in: *Rheinische Zeitung*, 19 September 1917.
17. Adenauer to Sollmann, 16 March 1946, in: R. Morsey and H.-P. Schwarz, eds., *Adenauer. Briefe 1945-1947* (Rhöndorfer Ausgabe) (Berlin 1983), pp. 189-91.
18. Nachrichtenamt der Stadt Köln, ed., *Wilhelm Sollmann. Zum 100. Geburtstag am 1. April 1981*, vol. II (Cologne 1991), p. 57.
19. See Adenauer's appreciation of Rings in: *Kölner Stadtverordnetenversammlung*, 8 January 1925, pp. 5f.
20. *Der Mittag* (Düsseldorf), 9 October 1932, quoted by W.E. Mosse, 'Louis Hagen', in: J. Bohnke-Kollwitz et al., eds., *Köln und das rheinische Judentum. Festschrift Germania Judaica, 1959-1984* (Cologne, 1984), p. 331.

The Youngest Mayor in Prussia

1. Wallraf to Adenauer, 9 July 1916, StBKAH, 01.01; see the detailed account by Gertrud Wegener in: *Adenauer. Oberbürgermeister*, pp. 79-98.
2. Wallraf to Adenauer, 22 July 1916, StBKAH, 01.01.
3. Adenauer to Wallraf, 26 July 1916, ibid.
4. Wallraf to Freiherr von Rheinbaben, 15 May 1916, HAStK, 902/301/4.
5. 'Bulgarische Abgeordnete in Köln', in: *Kölner Lokal-Anzeiger*, 17 May 1916.
6. Draft of letter of 14 July 1916, StBKAH, 01.01.
7. Wallraf to Adenauer, 9 July 1916, ibid.
8. Adenauer to Wallraf, 14 July 1916, ibid.
9. Wallraf to Adenauer, 16 July 1916, ibid.
10. Adenauer to Wallraf, 24 July 1916, ibid.
11. Information given to the author by Frau Ria Reiners.
12. Adenauer's diary entry of 31 December 1917, StBKAH.
13. Ibid.
14. Louis Hagen to Adenauer, 11 August 1917, ibid., 01.01.
15. Weymar, *Adenauer*, p. 60.
16. Louis Hagen to Adenauer, 25 August 1917, StBKAH, 01.01.
17. BA, Falk Papers, No. 385, p. 48.
18. Ibid, p. 49.
19. *Kölner Stadt-Anzeiger*, 13 August 1917.
20. Rings to Adenauer, StBKAH, 01.02.
21. *Kölner Stadtverordnetenversammlung*, 18 October 1917, pp. 233-37.
22. A. Klein, *Köln im Dritten Reich. Stadtgeschichte der Jahre 1933-1945* (Cologne, 1983), p. 241.

THE MAYOR, 1917-1933

Revolution and Occupation

1. *Kölner Stadtverordnetenversammlung,* 10 January 1918, p. 2.
2. Ibid., 6 March 1918, p. 67f.
3. Ibid., p. 72.
4. Hamspohn to Adenauer, 21 October 1920, StBKAH, 01.19.
5. Adenauer to Hamspohn, 26 July 1921, HAStK, 902/302/1.
6. Hamspohn to Adenauer, 21 July 1921, ibid.
7. H. Fürstenberg, *Erinnerungen. Mein Weg als Bankier und Carl Fürstenbergs Altersjahre* (Wiesbaden, 1965), p. 264f.
8. Heineman to Adenauer, 8 June 1960, StBKAH, Heineman Papers, vol.4.
9. Heineman to Adenauer, 28 February 1956, ibid., vol.3.
10. Adenauer to Hamspohn, 11 December 1917, HAStK, 902/103/1.
11. *Kölner Stadtverordnetenversammlung,* 19 September 1918, p. 349; see also ibid., 2 January 1919, p. 16.
12. W. Sollmann, *Die Revolution in Köln. Ein Bericht über Tatsachen* (Cologne, 1918), p. 5.
13. Letter from Josef Thedieck to his family, 20 November 1918, HAStK, 902/252a.
14. Weymar, *Adenauer*, p. 64.
15. BA, Falk Papers, No. 385, p. 96.
16. Sollmann, *Revolution*, p. 11.
17. BA, Falk Papers, No. 385, p. 96.
18. Ibid., p. 97.
19. Letter from Josef Thedieck, 20 November 1918, as in note 13 above.
20. *Kölner Stadtverordnetenversammlung,* 21 November 1918, p. 400.
21. Ibid., 21 November 1918, p. 399.
22. Memorandum of General Staff Major Schwink, HAStK, 902/241/1.
23. Besatzungsangelegenheiten 1918-1927, ibid.
24. Einquartierungslasten, 1918/19 – 1 November 1925, ibid.
25. *Kölner Stadtverordnetenversammlung,* 27 December 1918, p. 420.
26. Chassaigne interview with Adenauer, 4 January 1919, HAStK, 902/241/1.
27. Adenauer – Fergusson, 30 December 1918, ibid.
28. Adenauer memorandum of 12 December 1918, ibid.
29. Adenauer to Fergusson, 10 January 1919; Fergusson to Adenauer, 13 January 1919, ibid.
30. Record of negotiation with Fergusson, 12 December 1918, ibid.
31. Adenauer – Fergusson, 21 December 1918, ibid.

The Rhineland Movement 1918/19

1. According to a report in *Der Mittag* (Düsseldorf), 23 December 1918.
2. H. Köhler, *Autonomiebewegung oder Separatismus? Die Politik der 'Kölnischen Volkszeitung' 1918/1919* (Berlin, 1974), pp. 18ff.
3. J.-C. Montant, 'Une tentative française d'infiltration dans la presse allemande: L'affaire de la "Kölnische Volkszeitung" (février-décembre 1918)', in: *Revue d'Histoire moderne et contemporaine*, vol. 27 (1980), pp. 658-85.
4. From R. Morsey, 'Karl Trimborn (1854-1921)', in: *Rheinische Lebensbilder*, vol. III, p. 243; Morsey, *Zentrumspartei*, p. 221. Sources in: HAStK, Abt. II, No. 253, vol. 2.
5. H. Stehkämper, ed., *Der Nachlass des Reichskanzlers Wilhelm Marx* (Cologne, 1968), vol.II, p. 84.
6. Memorandum from the Chamber of Commerce in Cologne to the Foreign Ministry, 1 March 1919, Politisches Archiv des Auswärtigen Amtes (henceforth: PAAA), Deutschland 182.

7. Adenauer's record of the events from 9 November 1918 to 17 March 1919 (HAStK, 902/253/6), in: K.D. Erdmann, *Adenauer in der Rheinlandpolitik nach dem Ersten Weltkrieg* (Stuttgart, 1966), pp. 238-53.
8. Düsseldorfer Zeitung, 23 December 1918.
9. BA, Falk Papers, No. 385, p. 48.
10. Memorandum by Captain Loog, 22 December 1918, PAAA, Deutschland 182.
11. *Kölnische Volkszeitung*, 10 December 1918.
12. Dorten, *Mein Verrat*, BA, Zsg. 105, p. 40.
13. Adenauer's record of the events from 9 November 1918 to 17 March 1919, as note 7 above, p. 245.
14. BA, Falk Papers, No. 385, p. 50.
15. Text of speech of 1 February 1919, in: Adenauer. Reden, pp. 25-38.
16. Meeting of the westdeutscher politische Ausschuss, 30 May 1919 (HAStK, 902/253/2), in: Erdmann, *Rheinlandpolitik*, p. 272.
17. *Georges Clemenceau: Grösse und Tragik eines Siegers* (1930), p. 153.
18. H. Köhler, *Adenauer und die rheinische Republik. Der erste Anlauf 1918-1924* (Opladen, 1986), pp. 95-104.
19. Meeting of the westdeutscher politische Ausschuss, 30 May 1919, as note 16 above, p. 256f.
20. Ibid., p. 266f.
21. Ibid., p. 278.
22. Weymar, *Adenauer*, p. 81.
23. PAAA, Brockdorff-Rantzau Papers, Versailles II.
24. Adenauer to von Buhl, 16 June 1919, HAStK, 902/253/3.
25. Von Buhl to Adenauer, 9 July 1919, ibid.

Pater Familias

1. Inaugural speech as President of the 62nd Meeting of German Catholics in Munich, 28 August 1922, *Adenauer. Reden*, p. 45.
2. Adenauer to the Provinzial-Schulkollegium, 23 June 1923, HAStK, 902/288/1.
3. Information given to the author by Frau Ria Reiners.

Modern Cologne

1. Weymar, *Adenauer*, p. 94.
2. Minutes of the administrative conference of 2 December 1918, HAStK, 902/239/1.
3. F. Schumacher, *Stufen des Lebens. Erinnerungen eines Baumeisters* (Stuttgart/Berlin, 1935), p. 345.
4. Ibid., p. 369.
5. Hamspohn's record, 8 November 1920, HAStK, 902/105/1, in: Erdmann, *Rheinland-politik*, p. 294.
6. Hamspohn to Adenauer, 26 July 1921, HAStK, 902/302/1.
7. *Kölner Stadt-Anzeiger*, 8 June 1920.
8. 'Konrad Adenauer's work in sport politics as mayor of Cologne 1917-1933' has been described in detail in a thesis by Petra Adenauer (Deutsche Sporthochschule Köln, 1985). See also a description of the bid to get the Olympic Games to Cologne, ibid., pp. 62-6.
9. Schumacher, *Erinnerungen*, p. 369.
10. Inaugural speech on 24 March 1946 in the University of Cologne, in: *Adenauer. Reden*, p. 105.
11. Speech by Mayor Konrad Adenauer at Cologne University, in: *Reden gehalten bei der Versammlung von Dozenten der Kölner Hochschulen und der Akademie für praktische Medizin am 17. Januar 1919 im Hansasaal des Rathauses* (Cologne, 1919), p. 4.
12. *Adenauer. Reden*, p. 39f.

Political Recognition at National Level

1. Herwegen to Adenauer, 22 January 1919, HAStK, 902/302/1.
2. Heineman to Adenauer, 24/28 August 1955, StBKAH, Heineman Papers, vol.3.
3. Adenauer to Hamspohn, 26 June 1922, HAStK, 902/302/1.
4. Opening speech as President of the 62nd Meeting of German Catholics in Munich, 28 August 1922, in: *Adenauer. Reden*, pp. 42-51.
5. Hamspohn to Adenauer, 25 February 1920, StBKAH, 01.19.
6. R. Morsey and K. Ruppert, eds., *Die Protokolle der Reichstagsfraktion der Deutschen Zentrumspartei, 1920-1925* (Mainz, 1981), p. 196:Vorstand, 10 May 1921 (henceforth: Zentrumsfraktion).
7. Ibid., pp. 197 and 199. Detailed account of these events by Stehkämper, *Konrad Adenauer. Oberbürgermeister*, pp. 405-12.
8. *Zentrumsfraktion*, p. 199.
9. *Kölner Stadtverordnetenversammlung*, 2 June 1921, pp. 395f., 419.
10. Sollmann to Adenauer, 22 October 1921, StBKAH, 01.03.
11. Opening speech on 28 August 1922, in: Adenauer. Reden, p. 42f.

1923 – Year of Crisis

1. Schumacher, *Erinnerungen*, p. 369.
2. H.T. Allen, *Mein Rheinland-Tagebuch* (Berlin, 1923), p. 336f.
3. Adenauer note of 14 February 1923, HAStK, 902/253/3.
4. K.-D. Erdmann and M. Vogt, eds., *Akten der Reichskanzlei, Die Kabinette Stresemann I und II* (Boppard, 1978), p. 711.
5. Cited in Erdmann, *Rheinlandpolitik*, p. 94. Along with the most important documents, Erdmann provides the most comprehensive account to date. Also important is M.-L. Recker in: *Konrad Adenauer. Oberbürgermeister*, pp. 113-20. Henning Köhler has attempted to revive the separatism theory (Köhler, *Rheinische Republik*).
6. Akten der Reichskanzlei, Stresemann I and II (as note 4 above), p. 765.
7. Ibid., p. 766f.
8. Ibid., pp. 769-82.
9. Ibid., pp. 782-86.
10. Adenauer to Hamspohn, 2 November 1923, HAStK, 902/253/7.
11. Weymar, *Adenauer*, p. 120f.
12. Quoted in: Erdmann, *Rheinlandpolitik*, p. 129.
13. Akten Reichskanzlei, Stresemann I and II, p. 1059.
14. Adenauer's record, 6 December 1923, HAStK, 902/253/4.
15. Principes sur lesquels pourrait être basée la constitution d'un État Rhénan, HAStK, 902/253/7.
16. Adenauer's counter-proposal to Tirard's 'Principes', 12 December 1923, ibid.
17. Arnaud to Adenauer, 13 December 1923, HAStK, 902/253/4.
18. Arnaud to Hamspohn, 14 December 1923, ibid.
19. K.-D. Erdmann and G. Abramowski, eds., *Akten der Reichskanzlei. Die Kabinette Marx I und II* (Boppard, 1973), pp. 211-15, 9 January 1924.
20. Information given to the author by K. Adenauer.
21. Stresemann to Marx, 16 January 1924, Marx Papers, HAStK, II, p. 99. Quoted in full in: Erdmann, *Rheinlandpolitik*, pp. 361-5.
22. G. Stresemann, *Vermächtnis. Der Nachlass in drei Bänden*, ed. H. Bernhard (Berlin, 1932), p. 300.
23. Marx to Lammers, 20 October 1933, NL Marx, HAStK, II, p. 118.
24. Declaration of Julian Piggott, 3 April 1934, StBKAH, 01.16; G. Sidney Clive to von Hoesch, 22 January 1935, in: R. Morsey and K. Repgen, eds., *Adenauer Studien* III (Mainz, 1974), p. 223.

'The Mayors of Contemporary Germany Are the Kings of Today'

1. J.H. Herz, *Vom Überleben. Wie ein Weltbild entstand. Autobiographie* (Düsseldorf, 1984), passim.
2. F. von der Leyen, *Leben und Freiheit der Hochschule. Erinnerungen* (Cologne, 1960), p. 179.
3. H. Mayer, *Ein Deutscher auf Widerruf. Erinnerungen,* vol. I (Frankfurt, 1982).
4. Adenauer's note to the Deputy Dr Wirsel, 15 May 1924, HAStK, 902/175/2.
5. Commemmorative address for Friedrich Ebert, 8 March 1925, in: *Adenauer. Reden,* p. 53.
6. Amelunxen, *Ehrenmänner,* p. 81.
7. *Kölner Stadtverordnetenversammlung,* 9 March 1928, p. 187.
8. Amelunxen, *Ehrenmänner,* p. 82.
9. Adenauer to Hamspohn, 1 April 1926, HAStK, 902/302/1.
10. Adenauer to Hamspohn, 12 April 1926, ibid.
11. In Licht und Leben. *Evangelisches Wochenblatt,* vol. 40, 14 August 1928, p. 535.
12. Herriot to Adenauer, 9 August 1928, HAStK, 902/288/4.
13. Heineman to Adenauer, 19 April 1929, StBKAH, Heineman Papers, vol. 1.
14. Adenauer's note of 14 November 1929, HAStK, 902/288/3.
15. Heineman to Adenauer, 6 January 1958, StBKAH, Heineman Papers, vol.4.
16. Adenauer to Heineman, 4 October 1930, ibid., vol. 1/1.
17. Henry Morgenthau to Adenauer, 30 August 1928, HAStK, 902/288/4.
18. Ulrich Frank-Planitz, *Gustav Stresemann. Eine Bildbiographie* (Stuttgart, 1978), p. 114; Stresemann, Vermächtnis, vol. 2, p. 300.
19. Adenauer to Heineman, 22 April 1930, StBKAH, Heineman Papers, vol. 1/1.
20. Jean de Pange, *Die Mühlen Gottes. Frankreich-Deutschland-Europa* (Heidelberg, 1954), p. 316f.
21. D.N. Heineman. Skizze eines neuen Europa. Vortrag gehalten in der Mitgliederversammlung des Vereins der Freunde und Förderer der Universität Köln im Hansasaal des Rathauses am 28. November 1930 (Cologne, 1931).
22. Heineman to Adenauer, 28 November 1961, StBKAH, Heineman Papers, vol. 4.
23. Adenauer to Heineman, 21 January 1931, ibid., vol. 1/1.
24. Heineman to Adenauer, 6 September 1949, ibid., vol. 3.
25. Heineman to Adenauer, 14 September 1954, ibid.
26. W. Stresemann, *Mein Vater Gustav Stresemann* (Munich/Berlin, 1979), p. 416.
27. Weymar, Adenauer, p. 132f. A nuanced account of the event is provided by Stehkämper, Konrad Adenauer. *Oberbürgermeister,* pp. 412-20.
28. Info Gespräch, 23 June 1958, Archiv für Christlich-Demokratische Politik (henceforth: ACDP), von Eckardt Papers, I-010-002/1.
29. *Vossische Zeitung,* 16 May 1926.
30. Zapf to Adenauer, 27 January 1927, HAStK, 902/233/1.
31. Albers to Adenauer, 6 April 1927, ibid.
32. Horion memorandum, 18 June 1923, HAStK, 902/302/1.
33. Kölner Stadtverordnetenversammlung, 12 January 1928, p. 4.
34. Görlinger to Adenauer, 14 December 1927, HAStK, 902/101/5.
35. Rings to Adenauer, 26 February 1928, HAStK, 902/101/4.
36. Adenauer to Centre Party Fraktion, 7 March 1928, ibid.
37. *Kölner Stadtverordnetenversammlung,* 3 March 1927, p. 69.
38. W. Stresemann, *Mein Vater,* p. 494.
39. Miller to Riesen, 27 April 1933 (see appendix with reference to Riesen to Schmidt, 20 March 1933), HAStK, 902/99/1.
40. *Rheinische Tageszeitung,* 17 December 1929.

In the Maelstrom of the World Economic Crisis

1. Adenauer to Heineman, 5 September 1933, including appendices, StBKAH, Heineman Papers, vol. 1.

2. Adenauer to Ahn, 31 July 1924, HAStK, 902/103/1.

3. HAStK 902/105/3.

4. Adenauer to Heineman, 10 October 1931, StBKAH, Heineman Papers, vol. 1.

5. Heineman to Adenauer, 22 December 1955, ibid., vol. 3.

6. Adenauer to Kaas, 1 April 1930, HAStK, 902/118/3.

7. Adenauer to Brüning, 9 July 1930, HAStK, 902/118/3.

8. H. Brüning, *Memoiren 1918-1934* (Stuttgart, 1970), p. 214.

9. Adenauer to Brüning, 22 December 1930, HAStK, 902/2/1.

10. Adenauer to Brüning, 28 September 1931, ibid.

11. Adenauer to Kaas, 19 March 1930, HAStK, 902/118/3.

12. Adenauer to Heineman, 17 September 1930, StBKAH, Heineman Papers, vol. 1.

13. Steiniger to Adenauer, 9 May 1932, HAStK, 902/41/1.

14. J. von Leers, *Juden sehen Dich an* (Berlin/Schöneberg, 1936).

15. Kaas to Adenauer, 20 December 1926, HAStK, 902/285/1.

16. CBS interview, 21-23 August 1962, StBKAH, 02.27, also for the following comments.

17. Speech on 24 March 1946, in: *Adenauer. Reden*, pp. 86-8.

18. CBS interview, 21-23 August 1962, StBKAH, 02.27.

19. Heineman to Adenauer, 29 September 1931, StBKAH, Heineman Papers, vol. 1.

20. Adenauer to Heineman, 23 October 1931, ibid.

21. Adenauer to Heineman, 26 January 1932, ibid.

22. Heineman to Adenauer, 18 January 1932, ibid.

23. Adenauer to Heineman, 30 May 1932, ibid.

24. Heineman to Adenauer, 31 February 1932, ibid.

25. Heineman to Adenauer, 23 February 1932, ibid.

26. Heineman to Adenauer, 9 March 1933, ibid.

27. *Vita and Harold. The Letters of Vita Sackville-West and Harold Nicolson 1910-1962* (Phoenix, 1992), p. 211-12.

28. Adenauer to Pacelli, 11 July 1929, HAStK, 902/263/3.

29. R. Strobel, *Adenauer und der Weg Deutschlands* (Lucerne-Frankfurt am Main, 1965), p. 29.

30. *Die Gegenwart*, 30 September 1947.

31. R. Morsey, 'Adenauer und der Nationalsozialismus', in: *Konrad Adenauer. Oberbürgermeister*, pp. 447-497, 455. Many documents on Adenauer under the Nazi dictatorship can be found in *Adenauer im Dritten Reich* (Berlin, 1991) (henceforth: AiDR).

32. Strobel, *Adenauer*, p. 28.

33. Adenauer to Countess Fürstenberg-Herdringen, 22 October 1946, *Adenauer. Briefe 1945-1947*, p. 350.

34. Adenauer's memorandum of 2 August 1932, quoted in: Morsey, 'Adenauer und der Nationalsozialismus', as note 31 above, p. 456.

35. Von Lersner to Bosch and Schmitz, 20 August 1932 (copy in the possession of Prof. Morsey, to whom I am grateful for informing me of this letter).

36. Adenauer to Kaas, 12 December 1932, HAStK, 902/11/1.

37. Maus to Adenauer, 6 March 1930, HAStK, 902/105/3.

38. Adenauer to Dora Pferdmenges, 4 May 1933 (in private possession).

IN THE THIRD REICH 1933-1945

Fall from Power

1. Minutes of the negotiation of 6 February 1933, HAStK, 902/11/1; AiDR, pp. 50-52.

2. Westdeutscher Beobachter, 21 February 1933.

3. Adenauer to von Papen, 1 March 1933, HAStK, 902/11/1; AiDR, pp. 71f.

4. *Westdeutscher Beobachter*, 7 March 1933.

5. Adenauer's note of 7 March 1933, HAStK, 902/105/4; AiDR, p. 73.

6. Hofmann, *Erinnerungen 1916-1947*, p. 74.

7. Outline of a speech on 10 March 1933, *Adenauer. Reden,* pp. 68-76.
8. Adenauer's declaration on oath, 2 May 1951, StBKAH, 01.06.
9. Riesen to Adenauer, 21 March 1933, facsimile in: *Konrad Adenauer. Oberbürgermeister,* illustration 63; AiDR, pp. 93f.
10. Adenauer's declaration on oath, 2 May 1951, StBKAH, 01.06.
11. Morsey, 'Adenauer und der Nationalsozialismus', in: *Konrad Adenauer. Oberbürgermeister,* p. 468.
12. Pünder to Adenauer, 21 March 1933, BA, Pünder Papers, No. 606, p. 130.
13. Adenauer to Pünder, 23 March 1933, ibid., Nr. 606, p. 131; facsimile in: *Konrad Adenauer. Oberbürgermeister,* illustration 64; AiDR, p. 95.
14. Heineman to Adenauer, 9 March 1933, StBKAH, Heineman Papers, vol.1.
15. Adenauer to Heineman, 11 April 1933, ibid.
16. Adenauer to Heineman, 12 April 1933, ibid.
17. K. Adenauer, *Erinnerungen 1953-1955* (Stuttgart, 1966), vol. I, p. 57.
18. Ibid., p. 158.
19. Adenauer to Herwegen, 17 April 1933, facsimile in: *Konrad Adenauer. Oberbürgermeister,* illustration 65; AiDR, p. 111.
20. Herwegen to Adenauer, 19 April 1933, StBKAH; AiDR, p. 123.

Struggle for Survival

1. Adenauer to Heineman, 14 October 1933, StBKAH, Heineman Papers, vol. 1; AiDR, p.129.
2. Adenauer to Dora Pferdmenges, 16 May 1934. (This and the following letters to Dora Pferdmenges are in private possession.)
3. Adenauer to Heineman, 31 December 1933, StBKAH, Heineman Papers, vol. 1.
4. Adenauer to Vollmar, 25 September 1949, *Adenauer. Briefe 1949-1951,* p. 114.
5. E. Matthias and R. Morsey, eds., *Das Ende der Parteien 1933. Darstellungen und Dokumente* (Königstein/Düsseldorf, 1979), p. 390.
6. Adenauer to Dora Pferdmenges, 27 July 1933.
7. Adenauer to Dora Pferdmenges, 4 May 1933.
8. Ibid.
9. Adenauer to Dora Pferdmenges, 6 May 1933.
10. Adenauer to Dora Pferdmenges, 29 June 1933.
11. Adenauer to Dora Pferdmenges, 5 July 1933.
12. Adenauer to Dora Pferdmenges, 29 June 1933.
13. Adenauer to Dora Pferdmenges, 5 July 1933.
14. Adenauer to Dora Pferdmenges, 6 May 1933.
15. Adenauer to Dora Pferdmenges, 16 May 1934.
16. Adenauer to Dora Pferdmenges, 5 July 1933.
17. Adenauer to Dora Pferdmenges, 29 June 1933.
18. Adenauer to Heineman, 2 May 1933, StBKAH, Heineman Papers, vol. 1; AiDR, p. 126.
19. Adenauer to Dora Pferdmenges, 4 March 1934.
20. Adenauer to Dora Pferdmenges, 4 May 1933.
21. Ibid.
22. Adenauer to Dora Pferdmenges, 6 May 1933.
23. Ibid.
24. Adenauer to Dora Pferdmenges, 16 May 1934.
25. Ibid.
26. Adenauer to Dora Pferdmenges, 29 June 1933.
27. Adenauer to Dora Pferdmenges, 5 July 1933.
28. Adenauer to Dora Pferdmenges, 27 July 1933.
29. Ibid.
30. Adenauer to Dora Pferdmenges, 29 June 1933.
31. Adenauer to Dora Pferdmenges, 27 July 1933.
32. Ibid.

33. Adenauer to Dora Pferdmenges, 29 August 1933.
34. Ibid.
35. F. Grimm, *Mit offenem Visier. Aus den Lebenserinnerungen eines deutschen Rechtsanwalts* (Leoni am Starnberger See, 1961), pp. 131-5.
36. Ibid., p. 134.
37. H. Giesler, *Ein anderer Hitler. Bericht seines Architekten Hermann Giesler. Erlebnisse-Gespräche-Reflexionen* (Leoni am Starnberger See, 1978), p. 122f.; A. Speer, *Spandauer Tagebücher* (Frankfurt am Main/Berlin/Vienna, 1975), entry of 24 October 1949, p. 212f.
38. Piggott to Adenauer, 3 April 1934, StBKAH, 01.16; AiDR, pp. 208f.
39. Clive to von Hoesch, 22 January 1935, quoted in: H.G. Lehmann in *Adenauer-Studien* III, p. 223; AiDR, pp. 240f.
40. Schulte to Adenauer, 9 June 1934, StBKAH, 01.03; AiDR, p.41.
41. Adenauer to Heineman, 18 June 1933, StBKAH, Heineman Papers, vol. 1.
42. Adenauer to Heineman, 26 July 1933, ibid.; AiDR, p. 159.
43. Heineman to Adenauer, 27 July 1933, StBKAH, Heineman Papers, vol. 1.
44. Adenauer to Heineman, 1 August 1933, ibid.
45. Heineman to Adenauer, 7 August 1933, ibid.
46. Five-page undated memorandum by Adenauer on his financial situation at the end of 1933, in: StBKAH, Heineman Papers, vol. 1. See also the ten-page appendix detailing Adenauer's claims on the Dedi. Accompanying letter from Adenauer to Heineman, 15 September 1933.
47. Adenauer to Heineman, 14 October 1933, ibid.; AiDR, p. 182.
48. Heineman to Adenauer, 24 October 1933 and 28 October 1933; Adenauer to Heineman, 28 October 1933; Heineman to Adenauer, 31 October 1933; Adenauer to Heineman, 2 November 1933; Heineman to Adenauer, 6 November 1933; Adenauer to Heineman, 7 November 1933, ibid., StBKAH, Heineman Papers, vol. 1.
49. Adenauer to Heineman, 16 December 1933, ibid.
50. Adenauer to Heineman, 31 December 1933, ibid.
51. Adenauer to Heineman, 17 January 1934, ibid.; AiDR, p. 197.
52. Heineman to Hermann Bücher, 1 February 1934; Adenauer to Heineman, 14 February 1934, ibid., StBKAH, Heineman Papers, vol. 1.
53. Adenauer to Heineman, 9 March 1934, ibid.
54. Adenauer to Heineman, 26 February 1934, ibid.; AiDR, p. 204.
55. Adenauer to Dora Pferdmenges, 4 March 1934.
56. Ibid.
57. Adenauer to Heineman, 28 March 1934; AiDR, p. 206.
58. Adenauer to Heineman, 21 April 1934; Heineman to Adenauer, 24 April 1934; Adenauer to Heineman, 29 April 1934, StBKAH, Heineman Papers, vol. 1.
59. Dorff to Heineman, 2 May 1934, ibid.
60. Herwegen to Adenauer, 10 May 1934, StBKAH, 01.03.
61. Pater Severin to Adenauer, 8 May 1934, StBKAH, 01.16.
62. E. Nebgen, *Jakob Kaiser. Der Widerstandskämpfer* (Stuttgart, 1970), p.60.
63. Adenauer to Heineman, 4 September 1934, AiDR, p. 225.
64. Adenauer to Heineman, 21 September 1934, StBKAH, Heineman Papers, vol. 2.
65. Amelunxen, *Ehrenmänner*, p. 135.
66. Weymar, *Adenauer*, p. 180. See also AiDR, pp. 234-36, 579-82.
67. Adenauer to Dora Pferdmenges, 17 April 1935.
68. Adenauer to Heineman, 30 May 1935, StBKAH, Heineman Papers, vol 2.
69. Adenauer to Dora Pferdmenges, 5 May 1935.
70. Adenauer to Heineman, 26 March 1936 and 1 October 1936, StBKAH, Heineman Papers, vol. 2.
71. NSDAP Kreisleiter in Siegburg to the Landrat in Siegburg, 23 July 1935, AiDR, p. 227.
72. Report of police sergeant Butt of 24 July 1935, sent that same day by the mayor of Honnef to the Landrat in Siegburg, ibid., p. 256.
73. Police record of interrogation of 29 and 30 July 1935, StBKAH.
74. Order of the district president of Cologne to Herr Dr. Konrad , Adenauer, Rhöndorf, 10 August 1935, AiDR, pp. 257f.

75. Memorandum (unsigned) of the discussion with Diels on 29 August 1935, ibid.
76. Poppinga, *Erinnerungen*, p. 239.
77. Memorandum of 26 October 1936, AiDR, pp. 299-301.
78. Ernst Jäckh to Adenauer, 1 May 1937, ibid., pp. 310f.
79. Undated memoranda, StBKAH, VI-B 68.9.
80. Rülf to Adenauer, 19 September 1935, ibid.
81. Adenauer to Spennrath, 1 June 1936, ibid.
82. Adenauer to Giesen, 24 May 1936, ibid.
83. Adenauer to Vieth, 10 July 1936, ibid.
84. Adenauer to Thiess, 27 February 1938, StBKAH.
85. P. Franken, '20 Jahre später', in: *Akademische Monatsblätter des KV*, vol. 68 (January, 1956), p. 94.
86. Adenauer to Heineman, 12 February 1936, AiDR, p. 285.
87. Adenauer to Heineman, 1 October 1936, StBKAH, Heineman Papers, vol. 2.

Pensioner in Rhöndorf

1. Amelunxen, *Ehrenmänner*, p. 132.
2. Nebgen, *Jakob Kaiser*, p. 60.
3. K. Dreher, *Der Weg zum Kanzler. Adenauers Griff nach der Macht* (Düsseldorf/Vienna, 1972), p. 72.
4. Ibid., p. 74.
5. G.N. Shuster, *In Amerika und Deutschland. Erinnerungen eines amerikanischen College-Präsidenten* (Frankfurt am Main, 1965), pp. 76, 165f. See also AiDR, pp. 331-37.
6. Conversation between Adenauer and Altschull, 30 December 1960, ACDP, von Eckardt Papers, I-010-002/2.
7. Dreher, *Adenauer*, p. 77; in similar vein: Franken, '20 Jahre später', p. 98.
8. F. Thedieck, 'Gespräche und Begegnungen mit Konrad Adenauer – Aus einem halben Jahrhundert deutscher Politik', in: *KAZeit* I, pp. 326-339, 330.
9. Conversation between Adenauer and Altschull, as note 6 above.
10. Adenauer to von Weiss, 14 July 1938, AiDR, p. 330.
11. Heineman to Adenauer, 8 August 1938; Adenauer to Heineman, 4 November 1938, StBKAH, Heineman Papers, vol. 2; AiDR, p. 349.
12. Weymar, *Adenauer*, p. 192.
13. Adenauer to Heineman, 30 July, also 13 and 15 August 1939, StBKAH, Heineman Papers, vol. 2.
14. Heineman to Adenauer, 19 August and 26 August 1939, ibid.
15. Tea with the Chancellor on 10 March 1959 (memorandum by a participant), in private possession.
16. Adenauer to Ria Reiners, 6 June 1940 (in private possession).
17. Adenauer to Dora Pferdmenges, 11 January 1941 (in private possession).
18. Adenauer to Paul Adenauer, 30 October 1941, 28 November 1941, 3 January 1942, in: *KAZeit* I, pp. 159-64.
19. These and the following letters and cards all in StBKAH.
20. Von der Leyen, *Erinnerungen*, p. 244.

'It Is a Miracle of God That I Have Survived!'

1. Adenauer to Ria and Walter Reiners, 27 July 1944, AiDR, pp. 407f.
2. Von Weiss, Bericht, 23 August 1944, StBKAH, Weiss Papers.
3. Adenauer to Ria and Walter Reiners, 9 September 1944, AiDR, pp. 417f.
4. Adenauer to Ria and Walter Reiners, 23 July 1944, AiDR, p. 408.
5. R. Cartier, *Der Zweite Weltkrieg*, (Munich, 1967), vol. 2, p. 896.
6. Adenauer to Manstetten, 7 October 1947, Adenauer. Briefe 1947-1949, p. 83f.

7. Weymar, *Adenauer*, p. 243.
8. Info-Gespräch, 23 June 1958, ACDP, von Eckardt Papers, I-010-002/1.
9. Max Adenauer to Adenauer, 5 March 1952 (in private possession).
10. Weymar, *Adenauer*, p. 247.
11. Adenauer to Max Adenauer, 29 November 1944, AiDR, pp. 427f..
12. Conversation between Adenauer and Altschull, 30 December 1960, ACDP, von Eckardt Papers, I-010-002/2.
13. Adenauer to Magda and Paul Hunold, 14 January 1945, *Adenauer. Briefe 1945-1947*, p. 33f.
14. CBS interview, 21-23 August 1962, StBKAH, 02.27.
15. Weymar, *Adenauer*, p. 259; Adenauer, *Erinnerungen* I, p. 18.
16. Von Weiss, Bericht, 11 March-17 March 1945, StBKAH, von Weiss Papers.

THE PARTY LEADER 1945-1949

Attempts at Reorientation amongst the Ruins

1. Conversation between Adenauer and Altschull, 30 December 1960, ACDP, von Eckardt Papers, I-010-002/2.
2. W. Bornheim, 'Der rheinische Phönix. Konrad Adenauer 1945 (I/II). Erinnerungen eines Weggefährten', in: *Die politische Meinung*, vol. 27 (1982), p. 46.
3. H.L. Wuermeling, *Die weisse Liste. Umbruch der politischen Kultur in Deutschland 1945* (Frankfurt/Vienna, 1981), p. 283.
4. *Adenauer. Briefe 1945-1947*, 13 May 1945, p. 37.
5. Adenauer to Rörig, 5 July 1945, ibid., p. 52.
6. Poppinga, *Erinnerungen*, p. 253.
7. Adenauer to Heineman, 6 July 1945, *Adenauer. Briefe 1945-1947*, p. 53.
8. Adenauer to Rörig, 5 July 1945, ibid., p. 52.
9. Adenauer to Efferoth, 16 April 1946, ibid., p. 223.
10. Ibid., p. 224.
11. Von Weiss Report, 24 March 1945, StBKAH, von Weiss Papers; *Berichte*, pp. 100f.
12. Bornheim, 'Phönix', p. 106.
13. Von Weiss Report, 9 April 1945, StBKAH, von Weiss Papers; *Berichte*, pp. 100f.
14. Von Weiss Report, 4 June 1945, StBKAH, von Weiss Papers.
15. Von Weiss Report, 22 May 1945, ibid.
16. R. Grosche, *Kölner Tagebuch 1944-1946*, ed. M. Steinhoff (Cologne/Olten, 1969), p. 137.
17. Adenauer, *Erinnerungen I*, p. 29.
18. Bornheim, 'Phönix', p. 53.
19. S. Spender, *European Witness* (London, 1946), pp. 49-53.
20. Adenauer to Patterson, 21 June 1950, *Adenauer. Briefe 1949-1951*, p. 237f.
21. Adenauer to Schweitzer, 16 February 1948, *Adenauer. Briefe 1947-1949*, p. 173.
22. Von Weiss Report, 18 May 1945, StBKAH, von Weiss Papers.
23. Information given by O. Schumacher-Hellmold; see also O. Schumacher-Hellmold, 'Konrad Adenauer – ein Porträt', in: *Demokraten Profile unserer Republik*, ed. C.H. Casdorff (Königstein, 1983), p. 13.
24. Adenauer to the Cologne Military Government, 5 June 1945, *Adenauer. Briefe 1945-1947*, pp. 42-6.
25. Von Weiss Report, 8 July 1945, StBKAH, von Weiss Papers.
26. Adenauer to Schweitzer, 5 October 1945, *Adenauer. Briefe 1945-1947*, p. 114.
27. Memorandum by Just Lunning on a conversation with Adenauer, 4 April 1945, 226, Records of the Office of Strategic Services, National Archives, Correspondence France (including 1945), Entry 75, p. 4f.; AiDR, pp. 440-42.
28. Schumacher-Hellmold, 'Konrad Adenauer', p. 13.
29. Memorandum by Just Lunning, as note 27 above.

30. Von Weiss Report, 26 June 1945, StBKAH, von Weiss Papers; *Berichte*, p. 173.
31. Von Weiss Report, 8 July 1945, ibid., p. 174.
32. Adenauer to Heineman, 6 July 1945, *Adenauer. Briefe 1945-1947*, p. 53f.
33. Adenauer to Rörig, 5 July 1945, ibid., p. 51.
34. Memorandum by Just Lunning, as note 27 above.
35. Bornheim , 'Phönix', p. 51.
36. Annan, N.G. (Lord), 'How Dr Adenauer Rose Resilient from the Ruins of Germany', Institute of Germanic Studies, University of London (London, 1983), p. 12.
37. 'Adenauers Vorschläge für Deutschlands Zukunft' in: *Kölnischer Kurier*, 10 July 1945.
38. Von Weiss Report, 1 August 1945, StBKAH, von Weiss Papers; *Berichte*, p. 180.
39. StBKAH, 07.03.
40. Entrevue du 1er Septembre 1945 du capitaine Goussault du cabinet du Général assisté du lt. Matter avec M. Adenauer, maire de Cologne, chez M. de Weiss, Consul Générale de la Suisse, Cabinet du Général No. 169/CAB, 13.9.1945, Très Secret, C.C.F.A. Cabinet Civil. Archives, Pol III G l b.- Le Lieutenant Colonel Gouraud, Délégué Supérieur pour le Gouvernement Militaire de Rhénanie-Hesse-Nassau à Monsieur l'Administrateur Général Adjoint pour le Gouvernement Militaire de la Zone Française d'Occupation, 6.10.1945, Très Secret.
41. Von Weiss, Report, 8 September 1945, StBKAH, von Weiss Papers; *Berichte*, p. 197.
42. Ibid., pp. 198f.; also the report by Goussault of 13 September 1945 (see note 40 above), on which the following account is based.
43. Von Weiss, Postscript of 11 September to the report of 8 September 1945, StBKAH, von Weiss Papers; *Berichte*, p. 204.
44. Von Weiss Report, 22 September 1945, Schweizer Bundesarchiv (henceforth: SBA), E 2300 Köln 9; *Berichte*, p. 206.
45. Von Weiss Report, 26 September 1945, StBKAH, von Weiss Papers; *Berichte*, pp. 207-220.
46. StBKAH 07.03. See also Report No. 45; *Berichte*, pp. 219f.
47. Von Weiss Report, 22 September 1945, StBKAH, von Weiss Papers.
48. Political Department in Berne to von Weiss, 5 October 1945, SBA, E 2300 Köln 9; *Berichte*, pp. 204-7.
49. Von Weiss Report, 27 October 1945, StBKAH, von Weiss Papers.
50. Adenauer's memorandum of 5 October 1945, Adenauer, *Erinnerungen* I, p. 34f.
51. Adenauer to Weitz, 31 October 1945, *Adenauer. Briefe 1945-1947*, p. 130f.
52. Adenauer to Sollmann, 16 March 1946, ibid., p. 191.
53. Adenauer to Weitz, 31 October 1945, ibid., p. 130f.

Dismissal by the Liberators

1. CBS interview, 23 August 1962, StBKAH, 02.07.
2. Adenauer to Weitz, 31 October 1945, *Adenauer. Briefe 1945-1947*, p. 129.
3. 'The dictatorial dismissal that made Dr Adenauer forever suspicious', in: *The Times*, 1 December 1980, p. 10.
4. *Kölner Stadtverordnetenversammlung*, 1 October 1945, p. 4f.
5. Ibid., p. 6f.
6. Adenauer, *Erinnerungen* I, p. 34; see also Annan, 'Adenauer', p. 2.
7. M. Thomas, *Deutschland-England über alles. Rückkehr als Besatzungsoffizier* (Berlin, 1984), p. 137f.
8. Adenauer, *Erinnerungen I*, p. 36f.; Annan, 'Adenauer', p. 9f.
9. Report of Lt.-Col. Gouraud, 6 October 1945 (see previous chapter, note 40).
10. Adenauer, *Erinnerungen I*, p.27f.; *Strang to Bevin*, 21 August 1945, Public Record Office (henceforth: PRO), FO, C 5032/4757/18, Political Summary No.2. I am grateful to Dr Heitzer of Cologne for this reference.
11. Von Weiss Report, 13 October 1945, StBKAH, von Weiss Papers; *Berichte*, p. 231; Report by Gouraud, 6 October 1945, ibid. (No. 9).
12. Adenauer, *Erinnerungen I*, p. 38.

13. Pferdmenges to Adenauer, 14 October 1945, StBKAH, 08.02, reproduced in part in *Adenauer. Briefe 1945-1947*, p. 119.
14. Adenauer to the Military Government of North Rhine Province, 8 October 1945, *Adenauer. Briefe 1945-1947*, pp. 121-3.
15. 'The dictatorial dismissal ...', as note 3 above.
16. Thomas, *Deutschland-England*, p. 137.
17. Adenauer to Clive, 14 October 1946, *Adenauer. Briefe 1945-1947*, p. 339.
18. Adenauer, *Erinnerungen* I, p. 38f.; Annan, 'Adenauer', p. 11f.
19. Dreher, *Adenauer*, p. 137.
20. Von Weiss Report, 28 December 1945, StBKAH, von Weiss Papers; *Berichte*, p. 244.

Adenauer's Seizure of Power

1. Memorandum by Just Lunning, 28 March 1945.
2. L. Schwering, *Frühgeschichte der Christlich-Demokratischen Union* (Recklinghausen/Gelsenkirchen, 1963), p. 15.
3. P.L. Siemer, *Aufzeichnungen und Briefe* (Frankfurt am Main, 1957), p. 157.
4. Schwering, *Frühgeschichte*, p. 92.
5. H. Pütz, ed., *Konrad Adenauer und die CDU in der britischen Besatzungszone 1946-1949. Dokumente zur Gründungsgeschichte der CDU Deutschlands* (Bonn, 1975) (henceforth: *Adenauer und die CDU der britischen Besatzungszone*), 26-28 June 1946, p. 149f.
6. Bornheim, 'Phönix', p. 52.
7. Grosche, *Kölner Tagebücher 1944-1946*, 12 April 1945, p. 136.
8. Bornheim, 'Phönix', p. 116.
9. Schumacher-Hellmold, 'Adenauer', p. 14.
10. Adenauer to Heile, 14 February 1946, *Adenauer. Briefe 1945-1947*, p. 160.
11. 6 August 1957, StBKAH.
12. Adenauer to Silverberg, 30 May 1947, *Adenauer. Briefe 1945-1947*, p. 508.
13. Conversation with the author.
14. Bornheim, 'Phönix', p. 50f.
15. Conversation with the author.
16. Adenauer to Scharnagl, 21 August 1945, *Adenauer. Briefe 1945-1947*, p. 77f.
17. Interview by Dr Heitzer with Otto Schmidt, 29 October 1981 (information from Dr Heitzer).
18. Adenauer to Petersen, 1 September 1945, *Adenauer. Briefe 1945-1947*, p.87.
19. Adenauer to Schwering, 1 September 1945, *Adenauer. Briefe 1945-1947*, p. 88.
20. Lehr to Adenauer, 30 August 1945, StBKAH, 07.01.
21. Minute of the Council of Chairmen, 4 October 1945, HStAD, RWV 26, No. 2363.
22. Schwering to Adenauer, 9 October 1945, StBKAH, 07.01.
23. Schreiber to Kannengiesser, 10 October 1945, ACDP, Kannengiesser Papers, I-182-008/3.
24. Adenauer to Schwering, 16 October 1945, Adenauer. *Briefe 1945-1947*, p. 127.
25. Thomas, *Deutschland-England*, p. 139.
26. Adenauer's programme for the Rhenish CDU, 'Rhöndorfer Programme', Part I, handwritten, StBKAH, 08.07, also in: *Adenauer. Briefe 1945- 1947*, p. 150f.
27. Severing to Schwering, 6 May 1946, HAStK, Schwering Papers, No. 271,2.
28. Adenauer to Sollmann, 16 March 1946, *Adenauer. Briefe 1945-1947*, p. 190.
29. Schwering, *Frühgeschichte*, pp. 150ff.
30. 1. Reichstagung der Rheinischen CDU in Bad Godesberg, Heft 5 der Schriftenreihe der CDU des Reinlandes, ed. K. Zimmermann, n.d. (1946).
31. Von Weiss Report, 28 December 1945, StBKAH, von Weiss Papers.
32. Adenauer to members of Land executive of the CDU Rhineland, 6 January 1946, *Adenauer. Briefe 1945-1947*, p. 141f.
33. Minutes of the first meeting of the Zonal Committee of the CDU on 22 and 23 January 1946 in Herford, BA, Schlange-Schöningen Papers, 71/21, fol. 1: also in: *Adenauer und die CDU in der britischen Besatzungszone*, pp. 113-15.
34. Weymar, *Adenauer*, p. 291.

35. Adenauer to Schlange-Schöningen, 29 January 1946, *Adenauer. Briefe 1945-1947*, p. 145f.
36. Short report of 23 January 1946, ACDP, Kannengiesser Papers, I-182- 010/3.
37. Minutes of the first meeting of the Zonal Committee of the CDU on 22 and 23 January 1946 in Herford. BA, Schlange-Schöningen Papers, 71/21, fol.1, p. 23; also in: *Adenauer und der CDU in der britischen Besatzungszone*, p. 113.
38. Adenauer to Scharnagl, 7 February 1946, Adenauer. *Briefe 1945-1947*, p. 152.
39. Adenauer to Schlange-Schöningen, 29 January 1946, ibid., p. 312.
40. Kannengiesser to Hermes, 26 January 1946, BA, Holzapfel Papers, No. 312; see also Report from Westphalia on the meeting of the Zonal Committee, HAStD, Schmidt Papers, RWN 119, No. 6, p. 54f.
41. Minutes of the Land executive of the CDU Rhineland, 21 January 1946, HAStD, RWV 26, No. 1018, p. 48f.
42. Minutes of the Land executive of the CDU Rhineland, 5 February 1946, ibid. p. 50f.
43. Schwering to Albers, 6 February 1946, HAStK, Schwering Papers, No. 99,1.
44. Adenauer to Warsch, 22 February 1946, *Adenauer. Briefe 1945-1947*, p. 171f.
45. Dreher, *Adenauer*, p. 157f.
46. Text in: Schwering, *Frühgeschichte*, p. 225 (pp. 223-7).
47. Principles of the Christian-Democratic Party in Rhineland and Westphalia, Cologne, Bochum, Düsseldorf, September 1945, in: Schwering, *Frühgeschichte*, p. 219 (pp. 219-22).
48. Schmidt to Adenauer, 20 December 1946, HAStD, Schmidt Papers, RWN 119, No. 1.
49. Adenauer to Schmidt, 23 February 1946, Adenauer. *Briefe 1945-1947*, p. 174f.
50. Adenauer to Schmidt, 18 April 1946, ibid., p. 226f.
51. Interview by Dr Heitzer with Otto Schmidt, 15 July 1981 (information from Dr Heitzer).
52. Schmidt to Adenauer, 6 March 1946, HAStD, Schmidt Papers, RWN 119, No. 1.
53. Schwering, *Frühgeschichte* , p. 182.
54. Interview by Dr Heitzer with Schmidt.
55. Minutes of the Zonal Committee in Königswinter, 2/3 June 1949, ACDP, Dörpinghaus Papers, I-009-004/1.
56. Adenauer. *Reden*, pp. 82-106.
57. Strang to Bevin, 17 July 1946, PRO/FO 371, C 8143/2/18. I am grateful to Dr Heitzer for this reference.

The Party Leader

1. Minutes of the Zonal Committee in Neuenkirchen, 1/2 August 1946, in: *Adenauer und die CDU in der britischen Besatzungszone*, p. 170f.
2. Adenauer to Petersen, 1 September 1945, Adenauer. *Briefe 1945-1947*, p. 86.
3. Ibid. Similar discussions took place a month later; see minutes of the Council of Chairmen, 4 October 1945, HStAD, RWV 26, No. 2363.
4. Minutes of the Zonal Committee in Neuenkirchen, 1/2 August 1946, as note 1 above, p. 171.
5. Annan, 'Adenauer', p. 19.
6. Adenauer to Noack, 8 April 1946, *Adenauer. Briefe 1945-1947*, pp.210f.
7. Adenauer to Manstetten, 29 November 1946, ibid., p. 135.
8. Intelligence Review, 8 April 1946, PRO/ FO 371, C 3805/143/18.
9. Adenauer's note of 6 April 1946 and letter to the participants at the meeting in Stuttgart on 8 April 1946, Adenauer. *Briefe 1945-1947*, pp. 202-9.
10. Lenz to Kaiser and Dertinger, 15 February 1946, BA, Kaiser Papers, No. 57.
11. Adenauer to the participants at the meeting in Stuttgart on 8 April 1946, *Adenauer. Briefe 1945-1947*, p. 205.
12. Strang to FO, 14 April 1946, PRO/FO 371, C 4198/2/18.
13. Albers to Kaiser, 15 August 1946, BA, Kaiser Papers, No. 164.
14. Gerigk memorandum on the meeting of the meeting of the CDU/CSU working group on 5/6 February, BA, Kaiser Papers, No. 58.

15. Adenauer note on the meeting on 5/6 February 1947, *Adenauer. Briefe 1945-1947*, p. 439 (pp. 437-40).
16. Weymar, *Adenauer*, p. 316f.
17. Adenauer, *Erinnerungen I*, p. 66.
18. Annan, 'Adenauer', p. 19.
19. Adenauer. *Reden*, 24 March 1946, p. 94f.
20. Zonaler Informationsdienst der CDU 2/46, n.d.: 'Demokratie in Theorie und Praxis'.
21. Steel to FO, 7 May 1947, PRO/FO 371/64272.
22. Adenauer's note of 19 August 1946, *Adenauer, Briefe 1945-1947*, p. 312.
23. Minutes of the Zonal Committee in Lippstadt, 20 December 1946, in: *Adenauer und die CDU in der britischen Besatzungszone*, p. 261.
24. Ibid., pp. 254, 257f.
25. Ibid., p. 259f.
26. Minutes of the Economy and Social Office in the Land party, 20 January 1947 and drafts of 7 January 1947 and 20 January 1947, HStAD, Ziersch Papers, RWN 116, No. 3, pp. 279f., 284-90, 293-7.
27. Bucerius, *Der Adenauer. Subjektive Beobachtungen eines unbequemen Weggenossen* (Hamburg, 1976), p. 19.
28. Adenauer to Blücher, 3 January 1948, *Adenauer. Briefe 1947-1949*, p. 134.
29. Adenauer to Hamacher, 14 January 1946, *Adenauer. Briefe 1945-1947*, p. 144.
30. Adenauer to Bauwens, 17 December 1947, *Adenauer. Briefe 1947-1949*, p. 125.
31. Adenauer to Siemer, 2 December 1946, *Adenauer. Briefe 1945-1947*, p. 373.
32. Adenauer to Silverberg, 25 January 1947, ibid., p. 427.
33. Adenauer to Heineman, 11 April 1947, ibid., p. 467.
34. Adenauer to Ria and Walter Reiners, 3 July 1947, ibid., p. 517f.
35. Adenauer to Albers, 4 April 1948, *Adenauer. Briefe 1947-1949*, p. 197.
36. Adenauer to Silverberg, 24 May 1948, ibid., p. 236.
37. Brüning to Hans von Raumer, 3 November 1948, in: C. Nix, ed., *H. Brüning, Briefe und Gespräche*, vol. II 1946-1960 (Stuttgart, 1974), p. 155.
38. Adenauer to Frau Mönnig, 3 January 1948, *Adenauer. Briefe 1947-1949*, p. 379f.

Towards the Federal Republic of Germany

1. Von Weiss Report, 10 July 1946, StBKAH, von Weiss Papers; also in: H. J. Küsters and H.-P. Mensing, 'Konrad Adenauer zur politischen Lage 1946-1949. Aus den Berichten des schweizerischen Generalkonsuls in Köln Franz-Rudolph von Weiss', in: VfZ, vol. 32 (1984), pp. 299f.
2. Adenauer's speech at the meeting in Neuenkirchen, 1/2 August 1946. Copy in possession of the author; see also *Adenauer und die CDU in der britischen Besatzungszone*, p. 171.
3. Von Weiss Report, 10 July 1946, StKAH, von Weiss Papers.
4. Minutes of the Zonal Committee, 17 December 1946 in Lippstadt (copy of the text of Adenauer's speech in the possession of the author).
5. Adenauer to Sollmann, 18 January 1947, *Adenauer. Briefe 1945-1947*, p. 419.
6. 'Mässigung, Vernunft und Recht', in: *Rheinische Post*, 30 December 1946.
7. Adenauer to Elsaesser, 17 February 1947, *Adenauer. Briefe 1945-1947*, p. 433f.
8. Adenauer to Elsaesser, 18 February 1947, ibid., p. 435.
9. Minutes of the Zonal Committee 17 December 1946 in Lippstadt, as note 4 above.
10. Ibid.
11. Minutes of the Zonal Committee 27/28 June 1946 in Neuenkirchen, StBKAH, 08.58.
12. Minutes of the Zonal Committee 17 December 1946 in Lippstadt, as note 4 above.
13. Von Weiss Report, 10 July 1946, as note 1 above, p. 298.
14. Ibid.
15. Adenauer to Efferoth, 16 April 1946, *Adenauer. Briefe 1945-1947*, p. 223.
16. Five-page memorandum by Adenauer on a conversation with Pakenham, 28 October 1947, StBKAH, 341.
17. Adenauer to Silverberg, 10 December 1946, *Adenauer. Briefe 1945-1947*, p. 387.
18. Pakenham in: Der Spiegel, 9 October 1963, p. 124.

19. Von Weiss Report, 10 July 1946, as note 1 above, pp. 295, 301-3.
20. Text of the speech in: R.S. Churchill, *The Sinews of Peace. Post-War Speeches by Winston S. Churchill* (Wellington, 1948), pp. 198ff. Extracts also in: *Europa. Dokumente zur Frage der europäischen Einigung*, vol. I, p. 113f.
21. Von Weiss Report, 10 July 1946, as note 1 above, p. 299.
22. Adenauer to Sonnenschein, 12 October 1946, *Adenauer. Briefe 1945-1947*, p. 337.
23. Adenauer to Heile, 17 February 1947, ibid., p. 436.
24. Von Weiss Report, 4 February 1948, as note 1 above, p. 313.
25. B. Dörpinghaus, 'Die Genfer Sitzungen – Erste Zusammenkünfte führender christlich-demokratischer Politiker im Nachkriegseuropa', in: *KAZeit I*, p. 540 (pp.538-65).
26. Ibid., p. 547.
27. Adenauer to Schuman, 4 November 1948, *Adenauer. Briefe 1947-1949*, p. 337.
28. Adenauer to Cauwelaert, 26 August 1948, ibid., p. 303.
29. Adenauer to Silverberg, 24 May 1948, ibid., p. 237.
30. *Europa. Dokumente zur Frage der europäischen Einigung*, vol. I, p. 152.
31. 19/20 May 1948 in Bad Meinberg, in: *Adenauer und die CDU in der britischen Besatzungszone*, p. 497.
32. Ibid., p. 499.
33. Claude Hettier de Boislambert, *Les fers de l'espoir* (Paris, 1978), p. 476f.
34. Adenauer to Schuman, 4 November 1948, *Adenauer. Briefe 1947-1949*, p. 339.
35. Murphy to Bohlen, 24 November 1948, BA, OMGUS POLAD, 461/16 (Murphy File).
36. Adenauer, *Erinnerungen I*, p. 296.
37. Adenauer to Sollmann, 16 March 1946, *Adenauer. Briefe 1945-1947*, p. 191.
38. 14 August 1947 in: *Adenauer und die CDU in der britischen Besatzungszone*, p. 351.
39. Adenauer to Schweizer, 16 February 1948, *Adenauer. Briefe 1947-1949*, p. 173f.
40. Adenauer to Murphy, 19 December 1948, ibid., p. 368f.
41. Minute of the Zonal Committee in Vechta, 26-28 September 1946, in: *Adenauer und die CDU in der britischen Besatzungszone*, p. 189.
42. R. Morsey, ed., *Rhöndorfer Gespräche*, vol. III: *Konrad Adenauer und die Gründung der Bundesrepublik Deutschland*, (Stuttgart, 1979), p. 41.
43. *Süddeutsche Zeitung*, 29 July 1947.
44. Informationsdienst-A des Zonenausschusses der Christlich- Demokratischen Union, No. 16, 7 August 1947.
45. First party gathering in Recklinghausen, 14/15 August 1947, in: *Adenauer und die CDU in der britischen Besatzungszone*, pp. 368-72.
46. H. Pünder, *Von Preussen nach Europa* (Stuttgart, 1968), p. 321f.
47. Adenauer's note, 21 December 1947, *Adenauer. Briefe 1947-1949*, p. 128.
48. Adenauer to Weitz, 23 January 1948, ibid., p. 153.
49. Adenauer to Vogel, 26 January 1948, ibid., p. 162.
50. Adenauer, 'Kontrollen und wahre Sicherheit', in: *Kölnische Rundschau*, 8 June 1948.
51. Landtag Nordrhein-Westfalen, 1. Wahlperiode, Stenographische Berichte (Düsseldorf, 1947-1950), Report on the 49th meeting on 14 July 1948, pp. 636-43.
52. Adenauer to Mozer, 5 July 1948, *Adenauer. Briefe 1947-1949*, p. 272.
53. Adenauer, 'Die Empfehlungen von London', *Die Welt*, 10 June 1948.
54. Adenauer to Mozer, 5 July 1948, *Adenauer. Briefe 1947-1949*, p. 272.
55. Speech in Düsseldorf, 22 May 1948, CDU Kreis rally, StBKAH, 02.04.
56. R. Salzmann, ed., *Die CDU/CSU im Parlamentarischen Rat. Sitzungsprotokolle der Unionsfraktion* (Stuttgart, 1981), p. 146.
57. Adenauer's note of 13 October 1947, SKtBKAH, 338; also in: *Konrad Adenauer. Seine Zeit – Sein Werk*, ed. *Historisches Archiv der Stadt Köln* (Cologne, 1976), pp. 170-2.
58. 'Deutsche Einheit vom Westen her', in: *Kölnische Rundschau*, 3 April 1948.
59. *Der Tagesspiegel*, 20 April 1948.
60. Adenauer to Köhler, 26 June 1948, *Adenauer. Briefe 1947-1949*, p. 270.
61. Von Weiss Report, 20 January 1948, as note 1 above, p. 309.
62. Information given to the author by Professor Friedrich.
63. Minutes of the Zonal Committee in Minden, 10 July 1948, in: *Adenauer und die CDU in der britischen Besatzungszone*, p. 521f.
64. *Rhöndorfer Gespräche III*, p. 25.

65. Adenauer to Reger, 23 August 1948, *Adenauer. Briefe 1947-1949*, p. 300.
66. CDU/CSU im Parlamentarischen Rat, 15 September 1948, p. 9f.
67. Conversation of Schumacher-Hellmold with the author.
68. CDU/CSU im Parlamentarischen Rat, 25 November 1948, p. 179.
69. C.H. Hermann, *Deutsche Militärgeschichte. Eine Einführung* (Frankfurt am Main, 1966), p. 545.
70. R. Augstein in: *Der Spiegel*, 9 October 1963, p. 66.
71. H. Speidel, *Aus unserer Zeit. Erinnerungen* (Berlin/Frankfurt am Main/Vienna, 1977), p. 254.
72. Memorandum Simons to Director CAD, 15 January 1949, BA, OMGUS CAD, 3/1 62-3/9.
73. General Hall to Litchfield, 20 January 1949, ibid.

The President of the Parliamentary Council

1. Adenauer to Silverberg, 30 August 1948, *Adenauer. Briefe 1947-1949*, p. 307.
2. R. Maier, *Erinnerungen 1948-1953* (Tübingen, 1966), p. 66.
3. K. Dreher, *Ein Kampf um Bonn* (Munich, 1979), p. 52.
4. Hermann Wandersleb, 'Erinnerungen an Konrad Adenauer', in: *Bonner Geschichtsblätter*, vol. 27 (1975), pp. 209-28, 212.
5. Ibid., p. 215.
6. Adenauer to Cauwelaert, 8 October 1948, *Adenauer. Briefe 1947-1949*, p. 318.
7. C. Schmid, *Erinnerungen* (Berne/Munich/Vienna, 1979), p. 358.
8. *Rhöndorfer Gespräche* III, p. 28; Adenauer to Fischer, 24 September 1948, *Adenauer. Briefe 1947-1949*, p. 311.
9. CDU/CSU im Parlamentarischen Rat, 31 August 1948, p. 5.
10. Schmid, *Erinnerungen*, p. 356.
11. *Adenauer. Reden*, 1 September 1948, p. 132f.
12. *Südkurier*, 12 May 1949.
13. T.H. White, *In Search of History. A Personal Adventure* (San Francisco/London, 1978), pp. 327ff.
14. Mr. Thomas: *Conversation with Herbert Blankenhorn*, n.d., Mil. Gov. to FO, 10 November 1948, PRO/FO 371, C9922/2/18.
15. Robertson to FO, 1 December 1948, PRO, CCG/BE, C9842/2/18.
16. P. Dean, Minute, 6 December 1948, PRO/FO 371, 70488.
17. Adenauer to Brüning, 30 December 1948, *Adenauer. Briefe 1947-1949*, p. 372.
18. Adenauer to Fischer, 24 September 1948, ibid., p. 311.
19. CDU/CSU im Parlamentarischen Rat, 17 March 1949, p. 433.
20. Ibid., 28 October 1948, pp. 95-8.
21. Adenauer to Frings, 10 November 1948, *Adenauer. Briefe 1947-1949*, p. 341.
22. Adenauer to Frings, 7 February 1949, ibid., p. 398.
23. CDU/CSU im Parlamentarischen Rat, 21 April 1949, p. 489.
24. Schmid, *Erinnerungen*, p. 381f.
25. Adenauer to Frings, 1 November 1948, *Adenauer. Briefe 1947-1949*, p. 334.
26. CDU/CSU im Parlamentarischen Rat, 21 April 1949, p. 495.
27. Ibid., 5 May 1949, p. 551.
28. *Adenauer. Reden*, 8 May 1949, pp. 133-6, 133.
29. Schmid, *Erinnerungen*, p. 399.
30. CDU/CSU im Parlamentarischen Rat, 10 May 1949, p. 563.
31. *Der Spiegel*, No. 21/1949, p. 11.
32. Dreher, *Ein Kampf um Bonn*, pp. 91-113.
33. Adenauer to Arnold, 11 May 1949, *Adenauer. Briefe 1947-1949*, p. 451.
34. Adenauer to Frings, 11 May 1949, ibid., p. 452.
35. Adenauer to Süsterhenn, 11 May 1949, ibid., p. 453.

Setting the Course

1. Litchfield to Murphy, 6 February 1949, BA, OMGUS CAD, 3/162-3/10.
2. Record of a Conversation between the Secretary of State and Dr. Adenauer at Ostenwalde, 9 May 1949, PRO/FO 371, C 4382/4/18.
3. Adenauer to Heineman, 12 June 1949, *Adenauer. Briefe 1949-1951*, p. 33.
4. Adenauer to Huth, 4 July 1949, ibid., p. 49f.
5. Minutes of the Zonal Committee in Königswinter, 24/25 February 1949, in: Adenauer und die CDU der britischen Besatzungszone, p. 854.
6. Resolution of 29 August 1948, ibid., p. 712.
7. Minutes of the Zonal Committee in Königswinter, 24/25 February 1949, as note 5 above, p. 854f.
8. Ibid., pp. 857ff.
9. Minutes of the Zonal Committee in Lippstadt, 17/18 December 1946, ibid., p. 251.
10. Murphy to Bohlen, 24 November 1948, BA, OMGUS, POLAD 461/16.
11. J. Müller, *Bis zur letzten Konsequenz. Ein Leben für Frieden und Freiheit* (Munich, 1975), p. 357.
12. See U. Wengst, 'Die CDU/CSU im Bundestagswahlkampf 1949', in: VfZ, vol. 34 (1986), pp. 1-52, esp. p. 43; see also Rally of the CDU, 21 July 1949, StBKAH, 02.05.
13. *Adenauer. Reden*, 21 July 1949, p. 146f. (pp. 137-49).
14. Speech in Berne, 23 March 1949, extracts in Adenauer, *Erinnerungen* I, pp. 182-92.
15. British Liaison Staff Bonn to CCG/BE, 31 March 1949, PRO/FO 371, C2741/14/18.
16. *Adenauer. Reden*, 21 July 1949, p. 144.
17. Adenauer to Heineman, 12 June 1949, *Adenauer. Briefe 1949-1951*, p. 33f.
18. Bucerius, *Der Adenauer*, p. 54.
19. Adenauer to Schulte, 3 December 1946, *Adenauer. Briefe 1945-1947*, p. 375.
20. See Adenauer to Hamacher, 23 July 1949, *Adenauer. Briefe 1949-1951*, p. 65f.; see also Documents No. 23, 24, 42, 47 and 53.
21. Adenauer to Frau Deichmann, 4 August 1949, *Adenauer. Briefe 1949-1951*, p. 75.
22. Adenauer to Peyer, 14 August 1949, ibid., p. 84.
23. Statement concerning the 'Results of the Elections to the 1st , Bundestag', ibid., p. 86f.

First Years as Chancellor in 1949-1950

Forming a Government in 1949

1. Josef Kardinal Frings, 'Erinnerungen an Konrad Adenauer', in: *KAZeit* I, pp. 149-55, 52.
2. Höpker-Aschoff to Heuss, 14 August 1949, in: U. Wengst, ed., *Auftakt der Ära Adenauer. Koalitionsverhandlungen und Regierungsbildung 1949* (Quellen zur Geschichte des Parlamentarismus und der politischen Parteien), 4th series, vol. 3 (Düsseldorf, 1985), p. 8 (henceforth: *Auftakt*).
3. Luther to Pünder, 26 September 1949, BA, Pünder Papers, No. 631, p. 3.
4. Pünder to Luther, 30 September 1949 and 4 March 1949, ibid.
5. Schlange-Schöningen to Adenauer, 29 August 1949, in: *Auftakt*, p. 79f.
6. G. Gereke, *Ich war königlich-preussischer Landrat* (East Berlin, 1970), p. 360f.
7. *Rhöndorfer Gespräche* III, p. 53.
8. Adenauer to Ehard, 16 August 1949, *Adenauer. Briefe 1949-1951*, p. 86.
9. Adenauer to Köhler, 18 November 1950, ibid., p. 309.
10. Notes by Gebhard Müller on the Rhöndorf conference of 21 August 1949, in: *Auftakt*, p. 33 (pp. 33-41).
11. Ibid., p. 39.
12. Adenauer's report at the meeting of leading CDU/CSU politicians on 31 August 1949, ibid., p. 96 (pp. 89-130).
13. Notes by Gebhard Müller, 21 August 1949, ibid., p. 40f.
14. Blankenhorn Diary, 9 September 1949, BA, Blankenhorn Papers, 1351/a.

15. Müller to Pfeiffer, 23 August 1949, in: *Auftakt*, p. 68.
16. Meeting of the CDU/CSU parliamentary party in the Bundestag, 1 September 1949, ibid., pp. 191, 195.
17. Meeting of the CDU/CSU parliamentary party in the Bundestag, 11 September 1949, ibid., 331-3.
18. Meeting of the CDU/CSU parliamentary party in the Bundestag, 1 September 1949, ibid., p. 191.
19. Blankenhorn Diary, 14 September 1949, BA Blankenhorn Papers, 1351/a.
20. Adenauer to Hellwege, 14 September 1949, *Adenauer. Briefe 1949-1951*, p. 107.
21. Blankenhorn Diary, 15 September 1949, BA, Blankenhorn Papers, 1351/a.
22. Ibid., 17 September 1949.
23. Ibid., 19 September 1949.
24. Ibid.
25. Adenauer to Blücher and Hellwege, 19 September 1949, *Adenauer. Briefe 1949-1951*, pp. 108, 111.
26. Blankenhorn Diary, 8 September 1949.
27. Ibid., 17 September 1949.
28. Ibid., 20 September 1949.
29. Ibid., 18 September 1949.
30. H. Blankenhorn, *Verständnis und Verständigung. Blätter eines politischen Tagebuchs 1949-1979* (Frankfurt/Berlin/Vienna, 1980), p. 61.
31. *Adenauer. Reden*, 20 September 1949, pp. 153-69.
32. Heineman to Adenauer, 6 September 1949, StBKAH, Heineman Papers, vol. 3.
33. Blankenhorn Diary, 15 September 1949, BA, Blankenhorn Papers, 1351/a.
34. BA, Pünder Papers, No. 606, p. 84.

The Political Tableau during Bonn's Early Days

1. Government declaration of 20 September 1949, *Adenauer. Reden*, p. 154.
2. Blankenhorn Diary, 7 September 1949.
3. Gereke, *Ich war königlich-preussischer Landrat*, p. 353.
4. Brüning to Pünder, 10 November 1949, BA, Pünder Papers, No. 613, p. 71.
5. Brüning to Maria Brüning, 5 November 1949, in: *Brüning. Briefe 1946-1960*, p. 198.
6. Brüning to Olef, 25 August 1949, ibid., p. 195.
7. Ibid., p. 230.
8. Brüning to Pünder, 10 June 1952, BA, Pünder Papers, No. 613, p. 35.
9. Brüning to Pünder, 6 August 1951, ibid., p. 44.
10. Gerstenmaier, *Lebensbericht*, p. 361.
11. Meeting of the CDU/CSU parliamentary party in the Bundestag, 6 September 1949, in: *Auftakt*, p. 255.
12. Kurt Georg Kiesinger, 'Erlebnisse mit Konrad Adenauer', in: *KAZeit* I, p. 59 (pp. 59-72).
13. Adenauer to Etzel, 6 August 1949, *Adenauer. Briefe 1949-1951*, p. 77.

Adenauer's Political Machine

1. Adenauer to Kaiser, 9 December 1949, *Adenauer. Briefe 1949-1951*, p. 144.
2. K. Gumbel, 'Hans Globke – Anfänge und erste Jahre im Bundeskanzleramt', in: K. Gotto, ed., *Der Staatssekretär Adenauers. Persönlichkeit und politisches Wirken Hans Globkes* (Stuttgart, 1980), p. 97 (pp. 73-98).
3. Blankenhorn Diary, 2 June 1950, BA, Blankenhorn Papers, 1351/4.
4. Walter Henkels: 'Gar nicht so pingelig, meine Damen und Herren ...', in: *Neue Adenauer-Anekdoten* (Düsseldorf/Vienna, 1965), p. 149.

Strenuous Beginnings of Westpolitik

1. Adenauer to Frau Wessel, 27 August 1949, *Adenauer. Briefe 1949-1951*, p. 97.
2. H. Booms, ed., *Die Kabinettsprotokolle der Bundesregierung*, vol. I, 1949 (Boppard, 1984), 21 October 1949, p. 143; 25 October 1949, p. 15.
3. Francis Pakenham, 'Erfahrungen mit Adenauer als Minister für die britische Besatzungszone', in: *KAZeit* I, p. 417f. (pp. 415-20).
4. T. Prittie, *Konrad Adenauer. Vier Epochen deutscher Geschichte* (Stuttgart, 1971), p. 164.
5. Robertson in: *Der Spiegel*, 9 October 1963, p. 123; Conversation 9 October 1963, p. 123; Conversation between Adenauer and Robertson, 12 September 1961, StBKAH, III/60.
6. Kabinettsprotokolle 1949, 21 October 1949, p. 144.
7. Adenauer to Ellen McCloy, 13 June 1949, *Adenauer. Briefe 1949-1951*, p. 34.
8. Heineman to Adenauer, 26 July 1949, StBKAH, Heineman Papers, vol. 3.
9. Verhandlungen des Deutschen Bundestages. Stenographische Berichte, 21 October 1949, p. 315 (pp. 314-19).
10. AHC with Adenauer, verbatims, 20 October 1949, PRO/FO, 1005/1628.
11. Kabinettsprotokolle 1949, 11 October 1949, p. 119.
12. Ibid., 18 October 1949, p. 130.
13. Blankenhorn Diary, 12 November 1949.
14. Kabinettsprotokolle 1949, 25 October 1949, p. 148f.
15. Adenauer to Schuman, 26 July 1949, *Adenauer. Briefe 1949-1951*, p. 67f.
16. Adenauer, Erinnerungen I, p. 256.
17. AHC with Adenauer, verbatims, 14 October 1949, AHK I, pp. 434-36.
18. Adenauer, *Erinnerungen* I, p. 251.
19. Kabinettsprotokolle 1949, 18 October 1949, p. 138.
20. Die Zeit, 3 November 1949.
21. Blankenhorn Diary, 7 November 1949, BA, Blankenhorn Papers, 1351/18.
22. Interview with *Baltimore Sun* on 7 November 1949, StBKAH, 02.05.
23. Kabinettsprotokolle 1949, 11 November 1949, p. 193f.
24. Blankenhorn Diary, 4 February 1950, BA, Blankenhorn Papers, 1351/4.
25. D. Acheson, *Present at the Creation. My Years in the State Department* (New York, 1969), p. 338.
26. Adenauer, *Erinnerungen* I, p. 259.
27. Ibid., p. 285.
28. AHC with Adenauer, verbatims, 17 November 1949, AHK I, p. 18.
29. Blankenhorn Diary, 1 January 1950, BA, Blankenhorn Papers, 1351/4.

'The Most Disappointed Man in Europe'

1. Blankenhorn Diary, 20 January 1950, BA, Blankenhorn Papers, 1351/4.
2. Adenauer's stance in: *Die Welt*, 26 October 1946.
3. Adenauer to Wolff, 13 January 1948, *Adenauer. Briefe 1947-1949*, p. 146.
4. Draft of a letter from Adenauer to Schuman, early January 1950, *Adenauer. Briefe 1949-1951*, pp. 155-7; Adenauer, *Erinnerungen* I, p. 296.
5. Adenauer to François-Poncet, 24 January 1950, *Adenauer. Briefe 1949-1951*, p. 166.
6. Adenauer to Kaiser, 30 January 1950, ibid., pp. 167-9.
7. Blankenhorn Diary, 20 January 1950, BA, Blankenhorn Papers, 1351/4.
8. Ibid., 13 January 1950.
9. Ibid.
10. Ibid., 15 January 1950.
11. *Neue Zürcher Zeitung*, 17 January 1950.
12. Blankenhorn Diary, 19 January 1950, BA, Blankenhorn Papers, 1351/4.
13. 'Denkschrift zur Saarfrage', Bonn, n.d. (1950).
14. Press conference of 4 March 1950, reported in: *Neue Zürcher Zeitung*, 6 March 1950.
15. Record of the speech, StBKAH, 02.06.

16. Adenauer, *Erinnerungen* I, pp. 311-16; see also *Die Neue Zeitung*, 8 March 1950.
17. Interview of 16 March 1950 in: C. de Gaulle, *Discours et Messages*, vol. II: *Dans l'attente*. Fév. 1946-Avr.1958 (Paris, 1970), pp. 348-50.
18. Interview with Kingsbury-Smith on 21 March 1950, StBKAH, 16.05.
19. Also the reports in *Neue Zürcher Zeitung* on 24 March, 1 April and 5 April 1950.
20. Thus Blankenhorn to Bérard, in: Blankenhorn Diary, 4 April 1950.
21. Ibid., 21 October and 11 October 1949.
22. Adenauer, *Erinnerungen* I, p. 321.
23. Ibid., p. 320.
24. In a conversation with Robertson and Blankenhorn, in: Blankenhorn Diary, 5 April 1950, BA, Blankenhorn Papers, 1351/4.
25. Ibid., 10 and 12 April 1950.
26. Ibid., 13 April 1950.
27. A. Bullock, *The Life and Times of Ernest Bevin*, vol. 3 (London, 1983), p. 764.
28. Speech of 18 April 1950, StBKAH, 12.41.
29. Blankenhorn Diary, 18 April 1950, BA, Blankenhorn Papers, 1351/4.
30. AHC with Adenauer, verbatims, 28 April 1950, AHK I, p. 200.
31. P. Sethe, 'Ob sie es selber wissen?' in: *Frankfurter Allgemeine Zeitung*, 24 April 1950.

The Schuman Plan

1. Blankenhorn Diary, 8 May 1950, BA, Blankenhorn Diary, 1351/4.
2. Schuman to Adenauer, 7 May 1950, Adenauer. Briefe 1949-1951, pp. 210f., 508-10.
3. Adenauer to Schuman, 8 May 1950, ibid., p. 208.
4. Adenauer to Schuman, 8 May 1950, ibid., p. 208f.
5. Kabinettsprotokolle 1950, 9 May 1950, p. 369f.
6. Blankenhorn Diary, 9 May 1950, BA, Blankenhorn Diary, 1351/4.
7. J. Monnet, *Erinnerungen eines Europäers* (Munich/Vienna, 1978), p. 388.
8. StBKAH, 16.05.
9. *Neue Zürcher Zeitung*, 11 May 1950.
10. Brüning, *Briefe 1946-1960*, p. 230.
11. Diary entry by Schäffer, 3 June 1950, in: E.. Wandel, 'Adenauer und der Schuman-Plan (Dokumentation)', in: VfZ, vol. 20 (1972), p. 199.
12. 'Note de réflexion' of 3 May 1950, translated from the German version in: G. Ziebura, *Die deutsch-französischen Beziehungen seit 1945. Mythen und Realitäten* (Pfullingen, 1970), pp. 195-200.
13. Monnet, *Erinnerungen*, p. 393.
14. Wandel, 'Schuman-Plan', p. 199.
15. The following account is based on the record of Jean Monnet (*Erinnerungen*, pp. 393-401), the report by Adenauer (Erinnerungen I, p. 336f.) and Blankenhorn Diary, 23 May 1950, BA, Blankenhorn Papers, 1351/4.
16. Monnet, *Erinnerungen*, p. 395.
17. Wandel, 'Schuman-Plan', p. 198.
18. Press communiqué of 23 May 1950, Fondation Jean Monnet, AMG, 2/1/3, 4 June 1950.
19. Blankenhorn Diary, 4 June 1950, BA, Blankenhorn Diary, 1351/5.
20. See Kabinettsprotokolle 1950, 12 June 1950, p. 453, and 16 June 1950, pp. 462-4.

'That Bully Adenauer'

1. Speidel, *Erinnerungen,* pp. 249f., 252-4, 454-67; see also C. Greiner, 'Die alliierten militärstrategischen Planungen zur Verteidigung Westeuropas 1947-1950', in: *Anfänge westdeutscher Sicherheitspolitik 1945-1956*. Bd.I: Von der Kapitulation bis zum Pleven-Plan, ed. by Militärgeschichtliches Forschungsamt (Munich/Vienna, 1982), pp. 171-79.
2. Acheson, *Creation*, p. 399.

3. FRUS 1950, III, pp. 1016f., 1021, 1026, 1062f.
4. Brüning, *Briefe 1946-1960,* p. 224.
5. Memorandum of conversation 13 November 1949, FRUS 1949, III, p. 311.
6. R.G. Foerster, 'Innenpolitische Aspekte der Sicherheit Westdeutschlands 1947-1950', in *Anfänge Sicherheitspolitik,* vol. I, pp. (403-575), 450.
7. D. Koch, *Heinemann und die Deutschlandfrage* (Munich, 1972), p. 170.
8. McCloy to Secretary of State, 4 May 1950, FRUS 1950, IV, p. 684f.
9. Wahnerheide to FO, No. 752, 17 May 1950, PRO/FO, 371/85085 74100.
10. Blankenhorn Diary, 28 May 1950, BA, Blankenhorn Papers, 1351/5.
11. Foerster, as note 6 above, p. 475f.
12. Wahnerheide to FO, No. 855, 6 June 1950, PRO/FO, 371/85085 74100.
13. Blankenhorn Diary, 6, 7 and 8 June 1950.
14. Ibid., 17 July 1950.
15. Ibid., 9 July 1950.
16. Ibid., 17 July 1950.
17. Kirkpatrick to Sir Gainer, FO, 12 July 1950, PRO/FO, 371/85049 74100; Blankenhorn Diary, 10 July 1950.
18. N. Wiggershaus, 'Die Entscheidung für einen westdeutschen Verteidigungsbeitrag 1950', in: *Anfänge Sicherheitspolitik,* vol. I, p. 364f.
19. McCloy to Secretary of State, 14 July 1950, FRUS 1950, IV, pp. 696-8.
20. Blankenhorn Diary, 9 August 1950, BA, Blankenhorn Papers, 1351/5.
21. *Neue Zürcher Zeitung,* 8 August 1950.
22. Gerstenmaier, *Lebensbericht,* p. 326.
23. Ibid., p. 324.
24. 'Gedanken über die Frage der äusseren Sicherheit der Deutschen Bundesrepublik', 7 August 1950, in: Speidel, *Erinnerungen,* pp. 477- 96.
25. McCloy to Secretary of State, 18 August 1950, FRUS 1950, IV, pp. 706-9; Adenauer, *Erinnerungen* I, p. 360; AHK I, pp. 222-30 (17 August 1950).
26. Blankenhorn Diary, 17 August 1950, BA, Blankenhorn Papers, 1351/5.
27. Press conference of 23 August 1950, reported in: *Neue Zürcher Zeitung,* 25 August 1950.
28. *Die Welt,* 23 August 1950.
29. Blankenhorn Diary, 22 August 1950, BA, Blankenhorn Papers, 1351/5.
30. Ibid., 24 August 1950; McCloy to Secretary of State, 25 August 1950, FRUS 1950, IV, pp. 710-12.
31. Blankenhorn Diary, 25 August 1950, BA, Blankenhorn Papers, 1351/5.
32. Kabinettsprotokolle 1950, 25 August 1950, n. 35 p. 639; Blankenhorn Diary, 25 August 1950, BA, Blankenhorn Papers, 1351/5.
33. Blankenhorn Diary, 30 August 1950, BA, Blankenhorn Papers, 1351/5.
34. G. Vogel, *Diplomat unter Hitler und Adenauer* (Düsseldorf/Vienna, 1969), p. 175f.
35. 'Memorandum des Bundeskanzlers Konrad Adenauer zur Frage der Neuordnung der Beziehungen der Bundesrepublik Deutschland zu den Besatzungsmächten', 29 August 1950, in: K. von Schubert, ed., *Sicherheitspolitik der Bundesrepublik Deutschland. Dokumentation 1945-1977,* Part I (Bonn, 1977), p. 84f.; Adenauer, *Erinnerungen I,* p. 358f.
36. 'Memorandum des Bundeskanzlers Konrad Adenauer über die Sicherung des Bundesgebiets nach innen und nach aussen', 29 August 1950, ibid., pp. 79-83.
37. Hays to Secretary of State, 1 September 1950, FRUS 1950, IV, pp. 714-716.
38. Blankenhorn Diary, 31 August 1950, BA, Blankenhorn Papers, 1351/5.
39. Koch, *Heinemann,* p. 169.
40. Adenauer to von Brentano, 27 September 1950, *Adenauer. Briefe 1949-1951,* p. 282; *Kölnische Rundschau,* 18 September 1950.
41. Wiggershaus, as note 18 above, p. 372f.
42. C. Thayer, *Die unruhigen Deutschen* (Berne/Stuttgart/Vienna, 1958), p. 241.
43. Blankenhorn Diary, 18 September 1950, BA, Blankenhorn Papers, 1351/5.
44. Adenauer to Heinemann, 28 September 1950, *Adenauer. Briefe 1949-1951,* p. 283.
45. AdG (1950), p. 2638 G.
46. Wuermeling to Adenauer, 14 October 1950, *Adenauer. Briefe 1949-1951,* p. 295.
47. Adenauer to Wuermeling, 16 October 1953, *Adenauer. Briefe, 1949- 1951,* p. 295.

48. Adenauer in Cabinet on 10 October 1950, StBKAH, III/115.
49. Adenauer in Cabinet on 17 October 1950, ibid.; see also Kabinettsprotokolle 1950, 17 October 1950, p. 748.
50. Adenauer, *Erinnerungen I,* p. 374.
51. Draft of a letter from Adenauer to Heinemann, 23 September 1950, *Adenauer. Briefe 1949-1951,* p. 546.
52. Adenauer to Heinemann, 9 October 1950, ibid., p. 289f.
53. Ibid.
54. Gerstenmaier, *Lebensbericht,* p. 330.

In the Depths of Unpopularity

1. H.P. Schwarz, *Die Ära Adenauer. Gründerjahre der Republik 1949-1957* (Geschichte der Bundesrepublik Deutschland, vol. II) (Stuttgart/Wiesbaden, 1981), p. 187.
2. Table 31 in: *KAZeit II,* p. 553.
3. *Lenz Diary,* 20 April 1951.
4. Adenauer to von Brentano, 9 December 1950, *Adenauer. Briefe 1949-1951,* p. 323; also Kabinettsprotokolle 1950, 21 November 1950, p. 839f.
5. Maier, *Erinnerungen. 1948-1953,* pp. 150, 251.
6. Blücher and Wellhausen to Adenauer, 17 November 1950, StBKAH, 12.32.
7. Adenauer to Blücher and Wellhausen, 23 November 1950, *Adenauer. Briefe 1949-1951,* pp. 311-15.
8. E. Mende, *Die neue Freiheit* (Munich/Berlin, 1984), p. 183.
9. Adenauer to Holzapfel, 11 October 1950, *Adenauer. Briefe 1949-1951,* p. 292.
10. Cabinet meeting on 17 October 1950, StBKAH, III/115.
11. Heuss to Adenauer, 20 October 1950, StBKAH III/47; Adenauer to Heuss, 23 October 1950, *Adenauer. Briefe 1949-1951,* pp. 298, 558.
12. *Lenz Diary,* 16-20 January 1951, p. 14.
13. Ibid., p. 15.
14. Ibid., 23 May 1951, pp. 85f.
15. Ibid., 18 and 19 August and 2 September 1952, pp. 410-14, 422f.
16. Ibid., 16-20 January 1951, p. 15.
17. H. Schmidt, 'Die Mitbestimmung der Arbeitnehmer – Von Adenauer als eine der grossen Aufgaben unserer Zeit verstanden', in: *KAZeit I,* p. 53 (pp. 45-58).
18. Adenauer to Henle, 25 January 1947, *Adenauer. Briefe 1945-1947,* p. 421f.
19. Adenauer to Henle, 9 February 1947, ibid., p. 430.
20. CDU/CSU Caucus, 14 September 1950. Sten. Protokolle, ACDP, VIII- 001-1008/2.
21. *Lenz Diary,* 26 January 1951, p. 19.
22. Ibid., 10 April 1951, p. 66.
23. Minutes of the federal executive meeting of 10 May 1951, in: G. Buchstab, ed., Adenauer: 'Es musste alles neu gemacht werden'. Die Protokolle des CDU-Bundesvorstandes 1950-1953 (Forschungen und Quellen zur Zeitgeschichte, vol. 8) (Stuttgart, 1986), p. 34.
24. *Lenz Diary,* 26 February 1951, pp. 45f.
25. Vockel to Adenauer, 5 February 1951, StBKAH, 10.05.
26. McCloy to Adenauer, 6 March 1950, in: W. Abelshauser, 'Ansätze "Korporativer Marktwirtschaft" in der Korea-Krise der frühen fünfziger Jahre. Ein Briefwechsel zwischen dem Hohen Kommissar John McCloy und Bundeskanzler Konrad Adenauer', in: VfZ, vol. 30 (1982), pp. 715- 57.
27. Adenauer to Erhard, 19 March 1951, in: Die Korea-Krise als ordnungspolitische Herausforderung der deutschen Wirtschaftspolitik. Texte und Dokumente. Symposium der Ludwig-Erhard-Stiftung (Stuttgart/New York, 1986), p. 341f.
28. *Lenz Diary,* 19 March 1951, p. 60.
29. Ibid.

Adenauer's Daily Routine

1. Adenauer to Ria Reiners, 10 April 1963 (in private possession).
2. Adenauer to Heineman, 24 February 1958, StBKAH, 10.14.
3. *Lenz Diary,* 22 September 1951, p. 136.
4. F. von Eckardt, 'Konrad Adenauer – eine Charakterstudie', in: *KAZeit I,* pp. 137-48, 140.
5. W. Hallstein, 'Mein Chef Adenauer', in: *KAZeit I,* pp. 132-6, 133.
6. Eckardt, 'Charakterstudie', as note 4 above, p. 141.
7. H. Osterheld, *Konrad Adenauer. Ein Charakterbild* (Bonn, 1974), p. 21.
8. *National-Zeitung,* Basle, 24 July 1950.
9. W.G. Grewe, *Rückblenden 1976-1951. Aufzeichnungen eines Augenzeugen deutscher Aussenpolitik von Adenauer bis Schmidt* (Frankfurt am Main/Berlin/Vienna, 1979), p. 230.
10. Adenauer to Blücher, 12 July 1950, *Adenauer. Briefe 1949-1951*, p. 247f.
11. *Der Spiegel,* 9 October 1963, p. 11; Osterheld, *Adenauer,* p. 115.
12. Adenauer to Ria Reiners, 25 March 1958 (in private possession).
13. Kisters, Adenauer als Kunstsammler, p. 17. Previously the most reliable information about Adenauer, the art collector, was provided by H.A. Peters, 'Der Kölsche Doge von Bonn und die alten Meister', in: *Der Rotarier,* vol. 33 (July 1983), pp. 495-8.

EUROPEAN STATESMAN 1950-1952

'I Have My Nightmare Too: Its Name Is Potsdam'

1. McCloy to Secretary of State, 14 April 1950, FRUS 1950, IV, p. 627.
2. Adenauer, *Erinnerungen* I, p. 387.
3. McCloy to Secretary of State, 25 September 1950, FRUS 1950, IV, p. 725; Adenauer, *Erinnerungen I,* p. 373.
4. Acheson to McCloy, 21 June 1950, ibid., p. 689.
5. Bevin to Acheson, 5 September 1950, ibid., p. 720.
6. Adenauer at the cabinet meeting of 17 October 1950, StBKAH, III/115.
7. Blankenhorn Diary, 11 October 1950, BA, Blankenhorn Papers, 1351/5.
8. Monnet, *Erinnerungen,* p. 437.
9. Ibid., p. 441.
10. Ibid., p. 440.
11. Blankenhorn Diary, 24 and 25 October 1950.
12. Ibid., 7 November 1950.
13. Interview with Friedlaender, 13 June 1953, in: *Bulletin des Bundespresseamts,* 13 June 1953, No. 109, p. 926.
14. Protokoll Bundesparteiausschuss, 12 February 1951, ACDP, VII-001- 019/3.
15. *Lenz Diary,* 27 July 1951, p. 114.
16. Ibid., 21 February 1951, p. 39.
17. Ibid., 16-20 January 1951, p. 16.
18. Ibid., 1 February 1951, p. 28.
19. Adenauer to Heineman, 15 November 1950, *Adenauer. Briefe 1949-1951,* pp. 305-8.
20. Heineman to Anna M. Rosenberg, 11 December 1950, StBKAH, Heineman Papers, vol. 3; Heineman to Messersmith, 14 December 1950, ibid.
21. Heineman to McCloy, 27 March 1951, ibid.
22. C. L. Sulzberger, *Auf schmalen Strassen durch die dunkle Nacht. Erinnerungen eines Augenzeugen der Weltgeschichte 1939-1945* (Vienna/Munich/Zürich, 1971), 17 August 1953, p. 512.
23. McCloy to Secretary of State, 17 November 1950, FRUS 1950, II, pp. 780-4.
24. Ibid., p. 782.
25. Adenauer, *Erinnerungen* I, p. 396.
26. Minutes, 19 December 1950, FRUS 1950, IV, pp. 803-11.

27. Adenauer to Schumacher, 31 January 1951, Adenauer, *Erinnerungen* I, p. 416.
28. Ibid., p. 419.
29. Schumacher to Adenauer, 6 February 1951, StBKAH, 06.08, printed in: K. von Schubert, ed., *Sicherheitspolitik der Bundesrepublik Deutschland. Dokumentation 1945-1977*, Part I (Cologne, 1978), pp. 114-17.
30. Ibid.
31. Protokoll Bundesparteiausschuss, 12 February 1951, ACDP, VII-001- 019/3.
32. *Lenz Diary*, 21 February 1951, p. 39.
33. AHC meeting with Adenauer, Minutes, 9 May 1951, PRO, FO, 1005/1124.
34. Part of the conversation in: Adenauer, *Erinnerungen* I, pp. 495-500.
35. Ibid., p. 496.
36. 14 May 1951, Adenauer, *Teegespräche 1950-1954*, p. 100.
37. Memorandum by Lucius D. Battle, 14 May 1951, FRUS 1951, III/1, p. 1139.
38. *Lenz Diary*, 23 May 1951, p. 86.
39. Ibid., 8 June 1951, p. 93.

Europe

1. *Die Welt*, 10 April 1951.
2. Verbatim record of Schumacher's press conference of 9 April 1951, StBKAH, 12.12.
3. *Deutsche Zeitung und Wirtschaftszeitung*, 4 April 1951.
4. *Lenz* Diary, 8 March 1951, p. 55.
5. Monnet, *Erinnerungen*, p. 447.
6. Ibid., p. 463.
7. C. de Gaulle, *Memoiren der Hoffnung. Die Wiedergeburt 1958-1962* (Vienna/Munich/Zürich, 1971), p. 228f.
8. B. Crick, *In Defence of Politics* (Harmondsworth, 1969), p. 138.
9. Adenauer, *Erinnerungen* I, pp. 495-500.
10. To de Gaulle on 3 July 1964, StBKAH, II/106; see also de Gaulle on 13 September 1958, Adenauer, *Erinnerungen* III, p. 428.
11. *Lenz Diary*, 4 February 1952, p. 30.
12. Adenauer, *Erinnerungen* I, p. 512.
13. M. Busch, *Graf Bismarck und seine Leute*, vol. 2 (Leipzig, 1878), p. 377f.
14. F.F. von Beust, *Aus drei Vierteljahrhunderten*, vol. 2 (Stuttgart, 1887), p. 478.
15. Busch, as note 13 above, p. 377f.
16. Brüning, *Memoiren*, pp. 324-7.
17. Speidel, *Erinnerungen*, pp. 98ff.; A. Speer, *Erinnerungen* (Berlin, 1969), p. 187.
18. Adenauer, *Erinnerungen* I, p. 427.
19. Blankenhorn, *Verständnis*, p. 120.
20. Adenauer, *Erinnerungen* I, p. 440f.
21. Ibid., p. 428f.
22. Von Eckardt, *Unordentliches Leben*, p. 187.
23. Acheson, *Creation*, p. 583.
24. 1 June 1951, Adenauer, *Teegespräche 1950-1954*, p. 93.
25. *Blankenhorn Diary*, 10 January 1952, BA, Blankenhorn Papers,1351/10.
26. D.U. Stikker, *Bausteine für eine neue Welt. Gedanken und Erinnerungen an schicksalhafte Nachkriegsjahre* (Vienna/Düsseldorf, 1966), p. 349f.; Monnet, *Erinnerungen*, p. 468f.
27. A. Kohler, *Alcide de Gasperi 1881-1954. Christ, Staatsmann, Europäer* (Bonn, 1979).
28. *Hamburger Abendblatt*, 16 June 1951.
29. N. Goldmann, *Mein Leben als deutscher Jude* (Munich/Vienna, 1980), p. 417f.
30. *Lenz Diary*, 25 June 1951, p. 103.
31. McCloy to Secretary of State, 24 January 1951, FRUS 1951, III/1, p. 445f.
32. Notes on Meeting at the White House, 31 January 1951, ibid., p. 453.
33. Holmes to Secretary of State, 10 August 1951, ibid., p. 852f.
34. Schuman to Acheson, 26 August 1951, ibid., p. 1190.

35. W. Lipgens, 'EVG und Politische Föderation', in: VfZ, vol. 32 (1984), pp. 637-88, 652f.
36. 1 June 1951, Adenauer, *Teegespräche 1950-1954*, p. 90.
37. Lipgens, 'EVG', as note 35 above, pp. 667-88.
38. Ibid., p. 679.
39. Blankenhorn Diary, 12 December 1951, BA, Blankenhorn Papers, 1351/ 8a.
40. Background Paper (January 1952), FRUS 1952-1954, V/1, p. 604.
41. Gifford to Department of State, 31 January 1952, ibid., p. 607f.
42. Communiqué of the Paris Conference on the European Defence Community of 28 January 1952, in: *Europa. Dokumente zur Frage der europäischen Einigung*, 3 vols., ed. under the auspices of the Auswärtiges Amtes (Bonn, 1962-1964), Part 2, p. 831f.

Western Treaties and Soviet Initiatives

1. *Europa-Archiv*, vol. 6 (1951), p. 4404.
2. *Neue Zürcher Zeitung*, 24 September 1951.
3. McCloy to Secretary of State, 25 September 1951, FRUS 1951, III/2, p. 1788.
4. McCloy to Secretary of State, 23 September 1953, ibid., p. 1786f.
5. *Lenz Diary*, 25 September 1951, pp. 136-38.
6. Lyon to Office HICOG, 29 October 1951, FRUS 1951, III/2, p. 1803.
7. McCloy to Secretary of State, 18 August 1951, ibid., p. 1178.
8. Grewe, *Rückblenden*, p. 138.
9. Ibid., p. 144.
10. McCloy to Secretary of State, 28 August 1951, FRUS 1951, III/1, p. 1517f.; AHK I, pp. 517-19.
11. Adenauer, *Erinnerungen* I, pp. 474-82; McCloy to Acheson, 25 September 1951, FRUS 1951, III/1, p. 1523; AHK I, pp. 381-87, 513-16.
12. *Lenz Diary*, 3 October 1951, p. 140.
13. Adenauer, *Erinnerungen* I, p. 483.
14. *Lenz Diary*, 25 September 1951, p 137.
15. McCloy to Secretary of State, 26 September 1951, FRUS 1951, III/2, p. 1534.
16. McCloy to Secretary of State, 26 August 1951, ibid., p. 1515f.
17. Grewe, *Rückblenden*, p. 147.
18. Bundestag, Sten. Berichte, 7 February 1952, p. 8103 C.
19. McCloy to Acting Secretary of State, 3 November 1951, FRUS 1951, III/1, pp. 1566-71; AHK I, pp. 419f. (2 November 1951).
20. McCloy to Acting Secretary of State, 15 November 1951, FRUS 1951, III/1, pp. 1579-82; AHK I, pp. 570-79 (14 November 1951).
21. FRUS 1951, III/1, pp. 1565f.
22. McCloy to Acting Secretary of State, 15 November 1951, FRUS 1951, III/1, pp. 1579-82; AHK I, pp. 570-79 (14 November 1951).
23. Ibid.
24. Minutes of the Tripartite Foreign Ministers Meeting, 23 November 1951, FRUS 1951, III/1, p. 1598.
25. McCloy to Acting Secretary of State, 15 November 1951, ibid., pp 1579- 82.
26. Speech in Berlin, 6 October 1951, StBKAH, 02.09.
27. Acheson to Truman, 23 November 1951, FRUS 1951, III/1, p. 1610.
28. Acheson, *Creation,* p. 584.
29. 29 November 1951, Adenauer. *Teegespräche 1950-1954*, p. 169.
30. 13 December 1951, ibid., p. 173.
31. Adenauer, *Erinnerungen* I, p. 511.
32. 13 December 1951, Adenauer. *Teegespräche 1950-1954*, p. 172.
33. Blankenhorn Diary, 4 December 1951, BA, Blankenhorn Papers, 1351/8a.
34. Conversation with Churchill, 4 December 1951, Adenauer, *Erinnerungen* I, pp. 505-12.
35. Quoted in: Blankenhorn, *Verständnis*, p. 130.

'The Wings of World History'

1. Goldmann, *Mein Leben*, pp. 382-87.
2. Adenauer, *Erinnerungen* II, p. 138.
3. *Lenz Diary*, 21 February 1952, p. 262.
4. Blankenhorn Diary, 4 April 1950, BA, Blankenhorn Papers, 1351/4; Goldmann, *Mein Leben*, p. 378.
5. Bundestag. Sten. Berichte, 27 September 1951, p. 6698B.
6. Adenauer, *Erinnerungen* II, p. 138f.
7. Goldmann, *Mein Leben*, p. 400.
8. Decision on German Financial Contribution to Defense, 27 November 1951, FRUS 1951, III/2, p. 1685; McCloy to Secretary of State, 22 December 1951, ibid., pp. 1695-9.
9. Acheson, *Creation*, p. 616.
10. *Lenz Diary*, 18 March 1953, pp. 591f.

Warding off the Moscow Note Offensive

1. *Lenz Diary*, 7 February 1952, p. 249; *Neue Zürcher Zeitung*, 12 February 1952.
2. Acheson, *Creation*, p. 615.
3. *Lenz Diary*, 13 February 1952, pp. 257.
4. Ibid., 21 and 22 February 1952, pp. 262f.
5. *Neue Zürcher Zeitung*, 11 March 1952.
6. *Lenz Diary*, 11 March 1952, p. 273.
7. *Neue Zürcher Zeitung*, 13 March 1952.
8. Kirkpatrick to Foreign Office, 12 March 1952, PRO, FO, 371/97877/C 1072/2, printed in: R. Steininger, *Eine Chance zur Wiedervereinigung? Die Stalin-Note vom 10. März 1952. Darstellung und Dokumentation auf der Grundlage unveröffentlichter britischer und amerikanischer Akten* (Bonn, 1985), p. 119f.
9. Note of William Strang, 13 March 1952, PRO, FO, 371/97877/C 1074/26.
10. *Lenz Diary*, 14 March 1952, pp. 276f.
11. Text in: *Siegener Zeitung*, 17 March 1952.
12. Discussion with the High Commissioners, 17 March 1952, Adenauer, *Erinnerungen* II, pp. 73-6; AHK II, pp. 27f.
13. Kirkpatrick to Foreign Office, 17 March 1952, PRO/FO, 371/97878/C 1074/20, printed in: Steininger, *Stalin-Note*, p. 151f.
14. Hays to Secretary of State, 17 March 1952, State Department 662.001/3-1752, ibid., p. 150f.
15. Adenauer, *Erinnerungen* II, p. 4f.
16. 2 April 1952, Adenauer. *Teegespräche 1950-1954*, p. 234f.
17. Friedlaender interview of 5 March 1952, in Bulletin des Bundespresseamts, No. 27, 6 March 1952, p. 261ff.
18. 3 June 1952, Adenauer. *Teegespräche 1950-1954*, p. 299f.
19. Adenauer, *Erinnerungen II*, p. 88.
20. McCloy to Secretary of State, 15 March 1952, State Department, 662.001/3-1552, printed in: Steininger, *Stalin-Note*, p. 146f.
21. McCloy to Secretary of State, 29 March 1952, State Department, 662.001/3-2952, ibid., p. 177f.
22. *Lenz Diary*, 2 April 1952, pp. 291f.
23. Acheson to Bruce, 11 April 1952, FRUS 1952-1954, V/1, pp. 639-42.
24. Adenauer in Cabinet, 22 April 1952, in: *Lenz Diary*, 22 April 1952, pp. 299-301.
25. McCloy to Secretary of State, 12 April 1952, State Department, 662.001/4-1252, printed in: Steininger, *Stalin-Note*, p. 196f.
26. Adenauer, *Erinnerungen* II, pp. 91-3; Kirkpatrick to Foreign Office, 17 April 1952, PRO/FO, 371/97881/C 1074/82; AHK II, pp. 79-80 (16 April 1952).
27. *Lenz Diary*, 22 April 1952, p. 300.

28. Schumacher to Adenauer, 22 April 1952, Adenauer, *Erinnerungen* II, pp. 84-6.
29. Acheson to McCloy, Entry 30 April 1952, State Department, CS/H 662.001/4-2852.
30. McCloy to Secretary of State, 2 May 1952, State Department, 662.001/5-252, printed in: Steininger, *Stalin-Note*, p. 239f.
31. Blankenhorn Diary, 3 May 1952, BA, Blankenhorn Papers, 1351/10.
32. McCloy to Secretary of State, 2 May 1952, as note 30 above, p. 240.
33. G.F. Kennan, *Memoirs 1950-1963* (London, 1972), p. 112.
34. Ibid., p. 109.
35. Ibid., p. 118f.
36. Adenauer's report in Cabinet, 10 May 1952, StBKAH, III/Bd.2.
37. McCloy to Secretary of State, 3 May 1952, State Department 662.001/5-352, printed in: Steininger, *Stalin-Note*, p. 241.
38. Adenauer, *Erinnerungen* II, p. 93.
39. *Lenz, Diary*, 9 May 1952.

The Breakthrough: The Signing of the Western Treaties

1. Adenauer, *Erinnerungen* I, p. 284.
2. Von Brentano to Adenauer, 25 April 1952, in: A. Baring, *'Sehr verehrter Herr Bundeskanzler!' Heinrich von Brentano im Briefwechsel mit Konrad Adenauer 1949-1964* (Hamburg, 1974), pp. 91-7.
3. Ibid., p. 93.
4. Ibid., p. 96.
5. Von Brentano to Adenauer, 6 May 1952, ibid., p. 97f.
6. Von Brentano to Blank, 7 May 1952, ibid., pp. 98-100.
7. *Lenz Diary*, 30 April 1952, p. 307.
8. Mende, *Die neue Freiheit*, p. 227.
9. Blücher to Adenauer, 6 May 1952, BA, Blücher Papers, No. 80.
10. *Lenz Diary*, 9 May 1952, p. 316; *Frankfurter Allgemeine Zeitung*, 3 May 1952.
11. *Die Welt*, 3 May 1952.
12. Adenauer to Blücher, 6 May 1952, in: Adenauer, *Erinnerungen* I, pp. 528-30.
13. *Lenz Diary*, 9 May 1952, pp. 314-16.
14. Ibid., 10 May 1952, p. 317; Adenauer's report in Cabinet on 10 May 1952, StBKAH, III/82.
15. Cabinet meeting on 25 March 1952, StBKAH, III/82.
16. *Lenz Diary*, 12 May 1952, pp. 325-28.
17. Ibid., 13 May 1952, pp. 328-30.
18. FRUS 1952-1954, VIII, p. 65.
19. *Lenz Diary*, 14 May 1952, pp. 330-33.
20. Ibid., 20 May 1952, p. 338.
21. Ibid., pp. 338-40.
22. Ibid., 23 May 1952, p. 344.
23. Acheson, *Creation*, p. 645f.
24. FRUS 1952-1954, VII/1, p. 116.
25. Von Brentano to Adenauer, 29 May 1952, Baring, *Brentano*, p. 105; Adenauer to Brentano, 29 May 1952, StBKAH, 11.04.
26. AHK II, pp. 351-56 (25 May 1952).
27. Ibid., pp. 221f., 231 (15 May 1952); ibid., pp. 250f. (19 May 1952); ibid., p. 340 (24 May 1952).
28. V. Auriol, *Journal du Septennat*, 7 vols. (Paris, 1970-1979), vol. VI, p. 307.
29. Schumacher interview with United Press, 22 May 1952, in: AdG, vol. 22 (1952), p. 3841Af.
30. *Lenz Diary*, 30 May 1952, p. 343.
31. Dunn to Department of State, 11 May 1952, FRUS 1952-1954, V/1, p. 656.
32. Von Eckardt, *Unordentliches Leben*, p. 188.
33. Auriol, *Journal*, vol. VI, p. 342.

34. Acheson, *Creation*, p. 644.
35. Ibid., p. 646.
36. Auriol, *Journal*, vol. VI, p. 360.
37. Von Eckardt, *Unordentliches Leben*, p. 189.
38. *Neue Zürcher Zeitung*, 27 May 1952.
39. *Lenz Diary*, 30 May 1952, p. 352.
40. Adenauer's note to the High Commissioners, 2 July 1952, Adenauer, *Erinnerungen II*, p. 114f.
41. Discussion with the High Commissioners, 3 July 1952, ibid., pp. 116-23.
42. Conversation with McCloy on 17 June 1952, ibid., p. 108.
43. *Lenz Diary*, 30 May 1952, p. 352.
44. Discussion with the High Commissioners on 25 June 1952, Adenauer, *Erinnerungen II*, p. 113.
45. Auriol, *Journal*, vol. VI, 28 May 1952, p. 366.
46. Acheson to Truman, 26 May 1952, FRUS 1952-1954, V/1, p. 683.

AFTERWORD

1. G. Mann, *Zwölf Versuche* (Frankfurt am Main, 1973), p. 20.
2. See my essay 'Konrad Adenauer, 1876-1967', in: L. Gall, ed., *Die grossen Deutschen unserer Epoche* (Berlin, 1985), pp. 156-72.
3. H.-P. Schwarz, *Vom Reich zur Bundesrepublik. Deutschland im Widerstreit der aussenpolitischen Konzeptionen in den Jahren der Besatzungsherrschaft 1945-1949* (Stuttgart, 1980), p. 432.
4. Schwarz, *Ära Adenauer 1957-1963*, p. 382.

ARCHIVAL SOURCES

Stiftung-Bundeskanzler-Adenauer-Haus, Rhöndorf (StBKAH)
- Konrad Adenauer Papers
- Dannie N. Heineman Papers
- Franz-Rudolph von Weiss Papers

Archiv für Christlich-Demokratische Politik, Sankt Augustin (ACDP)
- Bruno Dörpinghaus Papers
- Felix von Eckardt Papers
- Otto Lenz Diaries, 1951-1952
- Protokolle der Sitzungen der Arbeitsgemeinschaft der CDU/CSU
- Protokolle der Sitzungen des Bundesvorstandes der CDU
- Protokolle der Sitzungen des Bundesausschusses der CDU
- Protokolle der Sitzungen der CDU/CSU-Bundestagsfraktion

Bundesarchiv, Koblenz (BA)
- Herbert Blankenhorn Papers
- Franz Blücher Papers
- Ferdinand Friedensburg Papers
- Bernhard Falk Papers (Kleine Nachlässe 385)
- Walter Hallstein Papers
- Friedrich Holzapfel Papers
- Karl Jarres Papers
- Jakob Kaiser Papers
- Erich Koch-Weser Papers
- Hermann Pünder Papers
- Hans Schlange-Schöningen Papers
- Paul Silverberg Papers
- Rheinlandakten; therein, inter alia, Manuscript by H.A. Dorten, Mein Verrat. Das Rheinische Drama 1918-1924. 1937; Tirard Papers
- Files of the Office of Military Government for Germany, United States (OMGUS), microfilm copies

Hauptstaatsarchiv, Düsseldorf (HStAD)

- Otto Schmidt Papers
- Guido Ziersch Papers
- Files of the CDU-Landesverband Rheinland
- Adenauer's Personnel File, Königliches Landgerichts zu Köln (photocopy in StBKAH)

Historisches Archiv der Stadt Köln (HAStK)

- Konrad Adenauer Files
- Wilhelm Marx Papers
- Ernst Schwering Papers
- Kölner Stadtverordnetenversammlung, Party Caucus Files

Politisches Archiv des Auswärtigen Amtes, Bonn (PAAA)

- Rheinlandakten (Deutschland No. 182)
- Brockdorff-Rantzau Papers

Public Record Office, London (PRO)

- Council of Allied High Commission with Adenauer, Verbatims, 1949-1950 (AHC with Adenauer, Verbatims)
- Council of Allied High Commission with Adenauer, Minutes, 1950-1952 (AHC with Adenauer, Minutes)
- Foreign Office, London, General Political Correspondence, 1949-1952

Fondation Jean Monnet pour l'Europe, Lausanne

- Schuman Plan Materials

Also incorporated were individual documents from the State Department, held by the National Archives in Washington, the Swiss Federal Archives in Berne, and the Archives Politiques du Quai d'Orsay in Paris.

Finally the Adenauer and Pferdmenges families allowed me to see materials in their possession.

PICTORIAL SOURCES

Thanks are due to the Stiftung Bundeskanzler-Konrad-Adenauer-Hans, Rhöndorf for making available the photos on pp. 1, 33, 83, 113, 229, 289, 433, and to the Bundesbildstelle, Bonn, for the photo on p. 587.

PUBLISHED SOURCES AND SELECT BIBLIOGRAPHY

Acheson, Dean, *Present at the Creation. My Years in the State Department* (New York, 1969).

Adenauer. *Briefe 1945-1947.* (Berlin 1983); *Briefe 1947-1949.* (Berlin 1984); *Briefe 1949-1951* (Rhöndorfer Ausgabe), ed. by Rudolf Morsey and Hans-Peter Schwarz with Hans Peter Mensing (Berlin, 1985).

Adenauer im Dritten Reich (Rhöndorfer Ausgabe), ed. by Rudolf Morsey and Hans-Peter Schwarz with Hans Peter Mensing (Berlin, 1991) (=AiDR).

Adenauer und die Hohen Kommissare, 1949-1951 (Akten zur Auswärtigen Politik der Bundesrepublik Deutschland), ed. on behalf of the Auswärtiges Amt by Hans-Peter Schwarz, 2 vols. (Müchen, 1989; 1990) (=AHK I;II).

Konrad Adenauer und die CDU der britischen Besatzungszone 1946-1949. Dokumente zur Gründungsgeschichte der CDU Deutschlands, ed. by Helmuth Pütz (Bonn, 1975).

Adenauer, Konrad, *Erinnerungen 1949-1953* (Stuttgart, 1976); *Erinnerungen 1953-1955* (Stuttgart, 1966); *Erinnerungen 1955-1959* (Stuttgart, 1967); *Erinnerungen 1959-1963.* Fragmente (Stuttgart, 1968).

Konrad Adenauer. Oberbürgermeister von Köln. Festgabe der Stadt Köln zum 100. Geburtstag ihres Ehrenbürgers am 5. Januar 1976, ed. by Hugo Stehkämper (Köln, 1976). (= Adenauer, Oberbürgermeister)

Adenauer: 'Es mußte alles neu gemacht werden.' Die Protokolle des CDU-Bundesvorstandes. 1950-1953, ed. by Günter Buchstab. (Forschungen und Quellen zur Zeitgeschichte, Bd.8) (Stuttgart, 1986).

Konrad Adenauer. Reden 1917-1967. Eine Auswahl, ed. by Hans-Peter Schwarz (Stuttgart, 1975).

Adenauer-Studien I, ed. by Rudolf Morsey and Konrad Repgen (Mainz, 1971).

Adenauer-Studien III. Untersuchungen und Dokumente zur Ostpolitik und Biographie, ed. by Rudolf Morsey and Konrad Repgen (Mainz, 1974).

Adenauer. Teegespräche 1950-1954. (Rhöndorfer Ausgabe), ed. by Rudolf Morsey and Hans-Peter Schwarz with Hanns Jürgen Küsters (Berlin, 1985).

Konrad Adenauer und seine Zeit. Politik und Persönlichkeit des ersten Bundeskanzlers. Vol. l, Beiträge von Weg- und Zeitgenossen, ed. by Dieter Blumenwitz et al. (Stuttgart, 1976). (= KAZeit I)

Konrad Adenauer und seine Zeit. Politik und Persönlichkeit des ersten Bundeskanzlers. Vol. 2, Beiträge der Wissenschatt, ed. by Dieter Blumenwitz et al. (Stuttgart, 1976). (= KAZeit II)

Allen, Henry T., *Mein Rheinland-Tagebuch* (Berlin, 1923).

Amelunxen, Rudolf, *Ehrenmänner und Hexenmeister. Erlebnisse und Betrachtungen.* (München, 1960).

Anfänge westdeutscher Sicherheitspolitik 1945-1956. Vol. 1: Von der Kapitulation bis zum Pleven-Plan, ed. by Militärgeschichtliches Forschungsamt (München-Wien, 1982).

Annan, Noel, G., *How Dr Adenauer Rose Resilient from the Ruins of Germany* (London, 1983).

Auftakt der Ära Adenauer. Koalitionsverhandlungen und Regierungsbildung 1949 (Quellen zur Geschichte des Parlamentarismus und der politischen Parteien), 4th Series, Vol. 3, ed. by Udo Wengst (Düsseldorf, 1985). (=Auftakt)

Auriol, Vincent, *Journal du Septennat*, 7 vols. (Paris, 1970-1979).

Bariéty, Jacques, *Les relations franco-allemandes après la Première Guerre Mondiale. 10 november 1918-10 janvier 1925. De l'exécution à la négotiation* (Paris, 1977).

Bark, Dennis L. and David R. Gress, *A History of West Germany,* Vol. I: From Shadow to Substance, 1945-1963 (Oxford, 1989).

Baring, Arnulf, *Außenpolitik in Adenauers Kanzlerdemokratie. Bonns Beitrag zur Europäischen Verteidigungsgemeinschaft* (München-Wien, 1964).

Baring, Arnulf, *'Sehr verehrter Herr Bundeskanzler!' Heinrich von Brentano im Briefwechsel mit Konrad Adenauer 1949-1964,* (Hamburg, 1974).

Benz, Wolfgang, *Von der Besatzungsherrschaft zur Bundesrepublik. Stationen einer Staatsgründung 1946- 1949* (Frankfurt, 1984).

Bérard, Armand, *Un Ambassadeur se souvient.* Vol. 2: *Washington et Bonn, 1945-1955* (Paris, 1978).

Billotte, Pierre, *Le Temps des Armes* (Paris, 1972).

Bischof, Erwin, *Rheinischer Separatismus 1918-1924. Hans Adam Dortens Rheinstaatbestrebungen* (Bern, 1969).

Blankenhorn, Herbert, *Verständnis und Verständigung. Blätter eines politischen Tagebuchs 1949-1979* (Frankfurt-Berlin-Wien, 1980).

Bornheim, Werner gen. Schilling, 'Der rheinische Phönix. Konrad Adenauer 1945 (I/II) . Erinnerungen eines Weggefährten', in: *Die politische Meinung,* vol .27 (1982), pp.44-58; pp.104-119.

Bracher, Karl Dietrich, *Die deutsche Diktatur. Entstehung, Struktur, Folgen des Nationalsozialismus* (Frankfurt, 1979).

Brüggemann, Fritz, *Die rheinische Republik. Ein Beitrag zur Geschichte und Kritik der rheinischen Abfallbewegung während des Waffenstillstandes im Jahr 1918/19* (Bonn, 1919).

Brüning, Heinrich, *Briefe und Gespräche,* ed. by Claire Nix, Vol. 2: 1946-1960 (Stuttgart, 1974).

Brüning, Heinrich, *Memoiren 1918-1934* (Stuttgart, 1970).

Bucerius, Gerd, *Der Adenauer. Subjektive Beobachtungen eines unbequemen Weggenossen (*Hamburg, 1976).

Bullock, Allan, *The Life and Times of Ernest Bevin,* Vol. 3: *Foreign Secretary 1945-1951* (London, 1983).

Verhandlungen des Deutschen Bundestages. 1. Wahlperiode 1949. Stenographische Berichte (Bonn, 1950-1953).

Die CDU/CSU im Parlamentarischen Rat. Sitzungsprotokolle der Unionsfraktion (Forschungen und Quellen zur Zeitgeschichte, Vol. 2), ed. by Rainer Salzmann (Stuttgart, 1981).

Die Stadt Cöln im ersten Jahrhundert unter preußischer Herrschaft 1815 bis 1915. Vol. 1, Part 1: Verfassungs- und Wirtschaftsgeschichte der Stadt Cöln vom Untergange der Reichsfreiheit bis zur Errichtung des Deutschen Reiches. By Geheimer Hofrat Professor Dr Eberhard Gothein (Köln, 1916).

Die Stadt Cöln im ersten Jahrhundert unter preußischer Herrschaft. Vol. 1, Part 2: Die Entwicklung der Stadt Cöln von der Errichtung des Deutschen Reiches bis zum Weltkriege. Vom Direktor des Statistischen Amts der Stadt Cöln. By Dr Georg Neuhaus (Köln, 1916).

Die Stadt Cöln im ersten Jahrhundert preußischer Herrschaft 1815 bis 1915. Vol. 2: Die Verwaltung der Stadt Cöln seit der Reichsgründung in Einzeldarstellungen (Köln, 1915).

Conze, Werner, *Jakob Kaiser. Politiker zwischen Ost und West. 1945-1949* (Stuttgart-Berlin-Köln-Mainz 1969).

Der deutsch-französische Krieg 1870-1871, ed. by Kriegsgeschichtlichen Abteilung des Großen Generalstabes in 2 Parts, 5 vols. (Berlin, 1874-1880).

Dorten, Jean Adam, *La tragédie rhénane* (Paris, 1945).

Dreher, Klaus, *Ein Kampf um Bonn* (München, 1979).

Dreher, Klaus, *Der Weg zum Kanzler. Adenauers Griff nach der Macht* (Düsseldorf-Wien, 1972).

Duchene, François, *Jean Monnet. The First Statesman of Interdependence* (New York/London, 1994).

Eckardt, Felix von, *Ein unordentliches Leben. Lebenserinnerungen* (Düsseldorf-Wien, 1967).

Eckert, Christian, *Widerlegung von Anwürfen der Broschüre Ilges-Schmid, 'Hochverrat des Zentrums am Rhein'* (Köln, 1934).

Erdmann, Karl Dietrich, *Adenauer in der Rheinlandpolitik nach dem Ersten Weltkrieg* (Stuttgart, 1966).

Eschenburg, Theodor, *Jahre der Besatzung. 1945-1949* (Geschichte der Bundesrepublik Deutschland, Vol. l) (Stuttgart-Wiesbaden, 1983).

Europa. Dokumente zur Frage der europäischen Einigung. 3 vols., ed. under the auspices of the Auswärtiges Amt (Bonn, 1962-1964).

Foreign Relations of the United States 1949. Vol. III: Council of Foreign Ministers. Germany and Austria (Washington, 1974). (= FRUS)

Foreign Relations of the United States 1949. Vol. IV: Western Europe (Washington, 1975).

Foreign Relations of the United States 1950. Vol. III: Western Europe (Washington, 1977).

Foreign Relations of the United States 1950. Vol. IV: Central and Eastern Europe; The Soviet Union (Washington, 1980).

Foreign Relations of the United States 1951. Vol. III: European Security and the German Question. Parts 1 and 2 (Washington, 1981).

Foreign Relations of the United States 1952-1954. Vol. V: Western European Security. Parts 1 and 2 (Washington, 1983).

Frank-Planitz, Ulrich, *Konrad Adenauer. Eine Biographie in Bild und Wort* (Bergisch-Gladbach, 1975).

Franken, Paul, '20 Jahre später', in: *Akademische Monatsblätter des KV*, Vol. 68, Januar 1956, pp.94-100.

Frings, Josef Kardinal, *Für die Menschen bestellt. Erinnerungen des Alterzbischofs von Köln* (Köln, 1973).

Gelberg, Karl-Ulrich, *Hans Ehard, Die föderalistische Politik des bayerischen Ministerpräsidenten* (Düsseldorf, 1992).

Gereke, Günther, *Ich war königlich-preußischer Landrat* (Berlin-East, 1970).

Gerstenmaier, Eugen, *Streit und Friede hat seine Zeit. Ein Lebensbericht.* (Frankfurt-Berlin-Wien, 1981).

Goldmann, Nahum, *Mein Leben als deutscher Jude* (München-Wien, 1980).

Gotto, Klaus, ed., *Der Staatssekretär Adenauers. Persönlichkeit und politisches Wirken Hans Globkes* (Stuttgart, 1980).

Graml, Hermann, 'Die Legende von den verpaßten Gelegenheiten. Zur sowjetischen Notenkampagne 1952', in: *VfZ*, vol. 29 (1981), pp. 307-341.

Graml, Hermann, *Die Alliierten und die Teilung Deutschlands. Konflikte und Entscheidungen 1941- 1948* (Frankfurt, 1985).

Grewe, Wilhelm G., *Rückblenden 1976-1951. Aufzeichnungen eines Augenzeugen deutscher Außenpolitik von Adenauer bis Schmidt* (Frankfurt-Berlin-Wien, 1979).

Grimm, Friedrich, *Mit offenem Visier. Aus den Lebenserinnerungen eines deutschen Rechtsanwalts* (Leoni am Starnberger See, 1961).

Grosche, Robert, *Kölner Tagebuch 1944-1946.* Aus dem Nachlaß, ed. by Maria Steinhoff (Köln-Olten, 1969).

Heidenheimer, Arnold J., *Adenauer and the CDU. The Rise of the Leader and Integration of the Party* (Den Haag, 1960).

Heineman, Dannie N., Skizze eines neuen Europa. Vortrag gehalten in der Mitgliederversammlung des Vereins der Freunde und Förderer der Universität Köln im Hansasaal des Rathauses am 28. November 1930 (Köln, 1931).

Henkels, Walter, *Zeitgenossen. Fünfzig Bonner Köpfe* (Hamburg, 1954).

Henle, Günter, *Weggenosse desJahrhunderts. Als Diplomat, Industrieller. Politiker und Freund der Musik* (Stuttgart, 1968).

Hillgruber, Andreas, *Deutsche Geschichte 1945-1982* (Stuttgart, 1983).

Hilty, Carl, *Glück,* 3 vols. (Leipzig-Frauenfeld, 1899 and 1920-1922).

Hofmann, Wolfgang, *Zwischen Rathaus und Reichskanzlei. Die Oberbürger-meister in der Kommunal- und Staatspolitik des Deutschen Reiches von 1890-1933* (Stuttgart-Berlin-Köln-Mainz, 1974).

Huffmann, Helga, *Geschichte der rheinischen Rechtsanwaltschaft* (Köln-Wien, 1969).

Ilges, Walter F. and Schmid, Hermann, *Hochverrat des Zentrums am Rhein. Neue Urkunden über die wahren Führer der Separatisten* (Berlin-Charlottenburg, 1934).

Jahrbuch der öffentlichen Meinung 1947-1955, ed. by Elisabeth Noelle and Erich Peter Neumann (Allensbach, 1956).

Justitia Coloniensis. Landgericht und Amtsgericht Köln erzählen ihre Geschichte(n), ed. by Adolf Klein und Günter Rennen (Köln, 1981).

Die Kabinettsprotokolle der Bundesregierung. Vol. I, 1949, Vol. II, 1950. ed. by Hans Booms with Ulrich Enders and Konrad Reiser (Boppard, 1982 and 1984).

Die Kabinettsprotokolle der Bundesregierung, Vol. III, 1950, Vol. IV, 1951, Vol. V, 1952, ed. by Hans Booms with Ulrich Enders, Konrad Reiser, Ursula Hüllbüsch and Kai von Jena (Boppard, 1986; 1988; 1989) (=Kabinettsprotokolle, 1950, 1951, 1952).

Kisters, Heinz, *Adenauer als Kunstsammler* (München, 1970).

Klapheck, Richard, *Eine Kunstreise auf dem Rhein*. Vol. II: Niederrhein. (Düsseldorf, 1928, 1980).

Klein, Adolf, *Köln im Dritten Reich. Stadtgeschichte der Jahre 1933-1945* (Köln, 1983).

Klein, Peter, *Separatisten an Rhein und Ruhr. Die konterrevolutionäre separatistische Bewegung der deutschen Bourgeoisie in der Rheinprovinz und in Westfalen, November 1918 bis Juli 1919* (Berlin, 1961).

Koch, Diether, *Heinemann und die Deutschlandfrage* (München, 1972).

Koch, Peter, *Konrad Adenauer, Eine politische Biographie* (Hamburg, 1985).

Köhler, Henning, *Adenauer und die rheinische Republik. Der erste Anlauf 1918-1924* (Opladen, 1986).

Köhler, Henning, *Autonomiebewegung oder Separatismus. Die Politik der 'Kölnischen Volkszeitung', 1918/1919* (Berlin, 1974).

Köhler, Henning, *Adenauer. Eine politische Biographie* (Berlin, 1994).

Kohler, Adolf, *Alcide de Gasperi.1881-1954. Christ, Staatsmann, Europäer* (Bonn, 1979).

Köln und seine Bauten. Festschrift zur VIII. Wanderversammlung des Verbandes deutscher Architekten- und Ingenieur-Vereine in Köln vom 12. bis 16. August 1888 (Köln, 1888).

Der Kölner Dom im Jahrhundert seiner Vollendung. Vols. 1 and 2, ed. by Hugo Borger (1. Katalog zur Ausstellung der Historischen Museen in der Josef-Haubrich-Kunsthalle Köln, 16. Oktober 1980 bis 11. Januar 1981) (Köln, 1980).

Köln und das rheinische Judentum. Festschrift Germania Judaica, 1959-1984, ed. by Jutta Bohnke-Kollwitz et al. (Köln, 1984).

Sitzungsprotokolle der Kölner Stadtverordnetenversammlung 1917-1932 and 1945.

Widerstand und Verfolgung in Köln 1933-1945. Publ. by the Historisches Archiv der Stadt Köln zur Ausstellung vom 8. Februar bis 28. April 1974. Vol. 2: Zwei Jahrtausende Kölner Wirtschaft, ed. by Hermann Kellenbenz under the auspices of the Rheinisch-Westfälisches Wirtschaftsarchiv (Köln, 1975).

Kosthorst, Erich, *Jakob Kaiser. Bundesminister für gesamtdeutsche Fragen 1949-1957* (Stuttgart-Berlin-Köln-Mainz, 1972).

Krein, Daniela, *Konrad Adenauer und seine Familie* (Frieberg bei Augsburg, 1957).

Küsters, Hanns Jürgen and Mensing, Hans Peter, 'Konrad Adenauer zur politischen Lage 1946-1949. Aus den Berichten des schweizerischen Generalkonsuls in Köln Franz-Rudolph von Weiss (Dokumentation)', in: VfZ, Vol. 32 (1984) pp. 289-317.

Küsters, Hanns Jürgen and Mensing, Hans Peter, eds., *Kriegsende und*

Neuanfang am Rhein. Konrad Adenauer in den Berichten des Schweizer Generalkonsuls Franz-Rudolph von Weiss 1944-1945 (Biographische Quellen zur deutschen Geschichte nach 1945, Vol. 4) (München, 1986).

Kuske, Bruno, *Die Großstadt Köln als wirtschaftlicher und sozialer Körper* (Köln, 1928).

Landtag für Nordrhein-Westfalen. 1. Wahlperiode. Stenographische Berichte (Düsseldorf, 1947-1950).

Lehmann, Heinrich, *Ein großer Jurist des Rheinlandes. Jugend und Beruf. Seine Lebenserinnerungen,* ed. by Gerhard Kegel (Köln, 1976).

Lenz, Otto, *Im Zentrum der Macht. Das Tagebuch von Staatssekretär Lenz 1951-1953,* ed. by Klaus Gotto, Hans Günter Hockerts, Rudolf Morsey and Hans-Peter Schwarz with Klaus Gotto, Hans-Otto Kleinmann and Reinhard Schreiner under the auspices of the Konrad-Adenauer-Stiftung (Düsseldorf, 1989) (=Lenz, Diary).

Leyen, Friedrich von der, *Leben und Freiheit der Hochschule. Erinnerungen* (Köln, 1960).

Macmillan, Harold, *Tides of Fortune 1945-1955* (London-Melbourne-Toronto, 1969).

Maier, Reinhold, *Erinnerungen 1948-1953* (Tübingen, 1966).

Stehkämper, Hugo, ed., *Der Nachlaß des Reichskanzlers Wilhelm Marx,* vols. I-IV (Köln 1968).

Mayer, Hans, *Ein Deutscher auf Widerruf. Erinnerungen,* Vol. 1 (Frankfurt, 1982).

Mende, Erich, *Die neue Freiheit 1945-1961* (München-Berlin, 1984).

Monnet, Jean, *Erinnerungen eines Europäers,* (München-Wien, 1978).

Montanmitbestimmung. Das Gesetz über die Mitbestimmung der Arbeitnehmer in den Aufsichtsraten und Vorständen der Unternehmen des Bergbaus und der Eisen und Stahl erzeugenden Industrie vom 21. Mai 1951, ed. by Gabriele Müller-List (Quellen zur Geschichte des Parlamentarismus und der politischen Parteien, 4th Series, Vol. 1) (Düsseldorf, 1984).

Morsey, Rudolf, 'Adenauer und der Nationalsozialismus', in: Adenauer, *Oberbürgermeister,* pp.447-497.

Morsey, Rudolf et al., *Konrad Adenauer. Leben und Werk* (Bayerische Landeszentrale für politische Bildungsarbeit) (München, 1976).

Morsey, Rudolf, 'Der politische Aufstieg Adenauers 1945-1949', in: *Adenauer-Studien* I, pp.20-57.

Morsey, Rudolf, *Konrad Adenauer und die Gründung der Bundesrepublik Deutschland.* (Rhöndorfer Gespräche, Vol. 3) (Stuttgart-Zürich, 1979).

Morsey, Rudolf, 'Die Rhöndorfer Weichenstellung vom 21. August 1949. Neue Quellen zur Vorgeschichte der Koalitions- und Regierungsbildung nach der Wahl zum ersten Deutschen Bundestag', in: VfZ, Vol. 28 (1980), pp.508-542.

Morsey, Rudolf, *Die Bundesrepublik Deutschland. Entstehung und Entwicklung bis 1969 (Oldenbourg Grundriß der Geschiche),* (Müchen, 1995).

Müller, Josef. *Bis zur letzten Konsequenz. Ein Leben für Frieden und Freiheit* (München, 1975).

Nebgen, Elfriede, *Jakob Kaiser. Der Widerstandskämpfer* (Stuttgart, 1970).

Osterheld, Horst, *Konrad Adenauer. Ein Charakterbild* (Bonn, 1974).

Der Parlamentarische Rat 1948-1949. Akten und Protokolle, Vol. 1:

Vorgeschichte, ed. by Kurt Georg Wernicke and Hans Booms with Johannes Volker Wagner (Boppard, 1975).

Poidevin, Raymond, *Les relations économiques et financières entre la France et l'Allemagne de 1898 a 1914* (Paris, 1969).

Poppinga, Anneliese, *Meine Erinnerunen an Konrad Adenauer* (Stuttgart 1970).

Poppinga, Anneliese, *Konrad Adenauer. Geschichtsverständnis, Weltanschauung und politische Praxis* (Stuttgart, 1975).

Prittie, Terence, *Konrad Adenauer. Vier Epochen deutscher Geschichte* (Stuttgart, 1971).

Pünder, Hermann, *Von Preußen nach Europa* (Stuttgart, 1968). (= Pünder, *Lebenserinnerungen*)

Akten der Reichskanzlei. Weimarer Republik. Das Kabinett Cuno. 22. November 1922 bis 12. August 1923, ed. by Karl Dietrich Erdmann with Karl-Heinz Harbeck (Boppard, 1968).

Akten der Reichskanzlei. Weimarer Republik. Die Kabinette Stresemann I und II. 13. August bis 6. Oktober 1923; 6. Oktober bis 30. November 1923. Vols. 1 and 2, ed. by Karl Dietrich Erdmann with Martin Vogt (Boppard, 1978).

Akten der Reichskanzlei. Die Kabinette Marx I und II. 30. November 1923 bis 3. Juni 1924; 3. Juni 1924 bis 15. Januar 1925. Vols. 1 and 2, ed. by Karl Dietrich Erdmann with Günter Abramowski (Boppard, 1973).

Rheinische Geschichte in drei Bänden, ed. by Franz Petri and Georg Droege, vols. 2 and 3 (Düsseldorf, 1976 and 1979).

Rheinische Lebensbilder. Under the auspices of the Gesellschaft für Rheinische Geschichtskunde ed. by Bernhard Poll and Wilhelm Janssen, vols. 1-9 (Köln, 1961-1982).

Rhöndorfer Gespräche, Vol. III: Konrad Adenauer und die Gründung der Bundesrepublik Deutschland, ed. by Rudolf Morsey (Stuttgart, 1979).

Schmid, Carlo, *Erinnerungen* (Bern-München-Wien, 1979).

Schnitzler, Victor, *Erinnerungen aus meinem Leben* (Köln, 1921).

Schnütgen, Alexander, *Kölner Erinnerungen* (Köln, 1919).

Schumacher, Fritz, *Stufen des Lebens. Erinnerungen eines Baumeisters* (Stuttgart-Berlin, 1935).

Schumacher-Hellmold, Otto, 'Konrad Adenauer - ein Portrait', in: *Demokraten-Profile unserer Republik*, ed. by Claus Hinrich Casdorff (Königstein/Ts., 1983), pp. 11-25.

Schwartz, Thomas Alan, *America's Germany. John J. McCloy and the Federal Repbulic of Germany* (Cambridge, Mass., 1991).

Schwarz, Hans-Peter, *Die Ära Adenauer. Gründerjahre der Republik 1949-1957* (Geschichte der Bundesrepublik Deutschland, Vol. 2) (Stuttgart-Wiesbaden, 1981).

Schwarz, Hans-Peter, *Die Ära Adenauer. Epochenwechsel 1957-1963* (Geschichte der Bundesrepublik Deutschland, Vol. 3) (Stuttgart-Wiesbaden, 1983).

Schwarz, Hans-Peter, *Vom Reich zur Bundesrepublik. Deutschland im Widerstreit der außenpolitischen Konzeptionen in den Jahren der Besatzungsherrschaft 1945-1949* (Stuttgart, 1980).

Schwarz, Hans-Peter, *Adenauer. Der Staatsmann, 1952-1967* (Stuttgart, 1991).

Schwarz, Hans-Peter, "Adenauer as Political Innovator", in: Gabriel Sheffer, ed., *Innovative Deaders in International Politics* (New York, 1993), pp. 109-140.

Schwering, Leo, *Frühgeschichte der Christlich-Demokratischen Union* (Recklinghausen-Gelsenkirchen, 1963).

Shuster, George N., *In Amerika und Deutschland. Erinnerungen eines amerikanischen College-Präsidenten* (Frankfurt, 1965).

Siemer, P. Laurentius, *Aufzeichnungen und Briefe* (Frankfurt, 1957).

Sollmann, Wilhelm. 2 vols., ed. by Nachrichtenamt der Stadt Köln zum 100. Geburtstag am 1. April 1981 (Köln, 1981).

Sollmann, Wilhelm, *Die Revolution in Köln. Ein Bericht über Tatsachen* (Köln, 1918).

Speidel, Hans, *Aus unserer Zeit. Erinnerungen* (Berlin-Frankfurt-Wien, 1977).

Spierenburg, Dirk and Raymond Poidevin, *The History of the Authority of the European Coal and Steel Community. Supranationality in Operation* (London, 1994).

Steimel, Robert, *Mit Köln versippt,* Part I and II (Köln, 1955/56).

Steimel, Robert, *Kölner Köpfe* (Köln, 1958).

Steininger, Rolf, *Eine Chance zur Wiedervereinigung? Die Stalin-Note vom 10. März 1952. Darstellung und Dokumentation auf der Grundlage unveröffentlichter britischer und amerikanischer Akten* (Bonn, 1985).

Steltzer, Theodor, *Sechzig Jahre Zeitgenosse* (München, 1966).

Stikker, Dirk U., *Bausteine für eine neue Welt. Gedanken und Erinnerungen an schicksalhafte Nachkriegsjahre* (Wien-Düsseldorf, 1966).

Stresemann, Gustav, *Vermächtnis.* Der Nachlaß in drei Banden, ed. by Henry Bernhard (Berlin, 1932).

Stresemann, Wolfgang, *Mein Vater Gustav Stresemann* (München-Berlin, 1979).

Strobel, Robert, *Adenauer und der Weg Deutschlands* (Luzern-Frankfurt, 1965).

Stürmer, Michael, *Das ruhelose Reich. Deutschland 1866-1918* (Berlin, 1983).

Sulzberger, Cyrus Leo, *Auf schmalen Straßen durch die dunkle Nacht. Erinnerungen eines Augenzeugen der Weltgeschichte 1939-1945* (Wien-München-Zürich, 1971).

Thomas, Michael, *Deutschland, England über alles. Rückkehr als Besatzungsoffizier* (Berlin, 1984).

Wallraf, Max, *Aus einem rheinischen Leben* (Hamburg-Berlin, 1926). (= Wallraf, *Erinnerungen*)

Wandel, Eckard, 'Adenauer und der Schuman-Plan (Dokumentation)', in: VfZ Vol. 20 (1972), pp. 192-203.

Wehmann, Karl, *Das Infanterie-Regiment Vogel von Falckenstein (7. Westfälisches) Nr.56 in den ersten 50 Jahren seines Bestehens* (Berlin, 1910).

Weymar, Paul, *Konrad Adenauer. Die autorisierte Biographie* (München, 1955).

White, Theodore H., *In Search of History. A Personal Adventure* (San Francisco-London, 1978).

Wulf, Peter, *Hugo Stinnes. Wirtschaft und Politik 1918-1924* (Stuttgart, 1979).

Zeitgeschichte in Lebensbildern. Aus dem deutschen Katholizismus des 19. und 20.Jahrhunderts, ed. by Jürgen Aretz, Rudolf Morsey and Anton Rauscher, vols. 1-6 (Mainz, 1973-1984).

Die Protokolle der Reichstagsfraktion der Deutschen Zentrumspartei 1920-1925, ed. by Rudolf Morsey and Karsten Ruppert (Mainz, 1981). (=Zentrumsfraktion, Protokolle 1920-1925)

INDEX OF PERSONS